Encyclopedia
of the
Confederacy

Editorial Advisers

Encyclopedia of the Confederacy

RICHARD N. CURRENT, Editor in Chief
Emeritus, University of North Carolina, Greensboro

Editorial Board

PAUL D. ESCOTT
Wake Forest University

LAWRENCE N. POWELL
Tulane University

JAMES I. ROBERTSON, JR.
Virginia Polytechnic Institute and State University

EMORY M. THOMAS
University of Georgia

Volume 1

S I M O N & S C H U S T E R
A Paramount Communications Company

New York   London   Toronto   Sydney   Tokyo   Singapore

Simon & Schuster
Academic Reference Division
15 Columbus Circle
New York, New York 10023

Printed in the United States of America

printing number
1 2 3 4 5 6 7 8 9 10

Library of Congress Cataloging-in-Publication Data

Encyclopedia of the Confederacy

Richard N. Current, Editor in Chief; editorial board, Paul D.
Escott . . . [et al.].
p. cm..

Includes bibliographical reference and index (p.).
ISBN 0-13-275991-8 (set: alk. paper)
1. Confederate States of America—Encyclopedia.
I. Current, Richard Nelson.

E487.55 1993   973.7′13—dc20   93-4133 CIP

ISBN 0-13-275991-8 (set)
ISBN 0-13-276015-0 (v. 1)

*Acknowledgments of sources, copyrights, and
permissions to use previously printed materials
are made throughout the work.*

*The paper used in this publication meets the minimum requirements of
American National Standard for Information Sciences—Permanence
of Paper for Printed Library Materials ANSI Z39.48-1984.*

Editorial and Production Staff

Publisher
Charles E. Smith

Editorial Director
Paul Bernabeo

Project Editor
Robert M. Salkin

Manuscript Editor
Cecile Rhinehart Watters

Illustration Editor
Patricia Brecht

Proofreaders
Clifford H. Browder   Dorothy Bauhoff Kachouh   Michael Mark Madore

Editorial Assistants
Danielle Lewis   Steven P. Ninivaggi   John Roseman
Stefanie B. Siegmund   Sara E. Simon

Compositor
Graphic World, Inc.
St. Louis, Missouri

Cartographer
Applied Academic Services
Fort Worth, Texas

Indexer
AEIOU Inc.
Pleasantville, New York

Case Design
Mike McIver

Production Supervisor
Winston Sukhnanand

Preface

The Confederacy looms large in the American past. True, the Confederate States of America lasted only four years—the four years of the Civil War (1861–1865)—and never amounted to an independent country except in the minds of its own people. It failed to gain membership in the family of nations. Foreign governments, such as the British and the French, recognized its belligerency but not its independence when they declared their neutrality and thereby granted the Confederacy the rights of a nation at war. Yet, brief and tenuous though its existence was, the Confederacy has great significance for the history of the United States. In asserting their independence, the Confederates brought to a head two great issues that had long divided Americans and that continue to do so—slavery and the relation of the states to the federal government. The question of the relationship of people of color to the white majority continues to be an urgent issue, as does the question of state rights.

In losing their war for independence, the Confederates failed to establish either of the two principles on which they had based their nation-making effort. These twin principles were the right of states to secede from the Union and the right to hold black people as slaves. Yet the Confederates, in their devotion to what became the Lost Cause, left an impressive record of heroism and self-sacrifice. It is a record that continues to appeal to many in the North as well as in the South; Confederate general Robert E. Lee today is an American hero as well as a Southern hero. A growing interest in the Confederacy has accompanied the growing interest in the Civil War.

Those curious about the Confederacy have hitherto had no comprehensive reference work to which to turn as a convenient and reliable source of information on all aspects of the subject. *The Encyclopedia of the Confederacy* is intended to meet that need. The work is directed not only to professional historians and history students but to everyone who ever has occasion to answer a question about the South during the period of 1861 to 1865.

This encyclopedia is broad in scope. Included in it, of course, are accounts of the important campaigns and battles of the war, with emphasis on the role and the perspective of the Confederates. Also included are biographical sketches of political leaders, military and naval officers, and other significant men and women, with particular attention to the Confederate phase of their careers. But the coverage extends far beyond these obvious categories. There are articles tracing the origins of the Confederacy and describing the various features of its government and politics, its warmaking facilities, its economic system, and its conduct of foreign affairs. Many entries deal with nontraditional and often neglected topics, both social and cultural. Among these are the roles of Indians, African Americans (free as well as slave), other ethnic minorities, and women, in addition to the place of religion, education, literature, theater, and music in Confederate life.

In the preparation of the encyclopedia the first step was the selection of a board of editors who would themselves be recognized experts in Southern history and who would be widely acquainted with others in the field. The four historians selected for the board are associated with universities in North Carolina, Virginia, Georgia, and Louisiana, thus representing a wide geographical range from the upper to the lower South. Each of these historians is the author of numerous relevant studies reflecting the broad spectrum of approaches to understanding the Confederate era. Paul D. Escott, of Wake Forest University, has been the Reynolds Professor of History since 1990. He has published numerous articles and authored, coauthored, or coedited seven books, including *After Secession: Jefferson Davis and the Failure of Confederate Nationalism; Many Excellent People: Power and Privilege in North Carolina, 1850–1900; Major Problems in the History of the American South;* and *Race, Class, and Politics in Southern History.* Lawrence N. Powell, of Tulane University, is associate professor of history. He was associate editor of the *Frederick Douglass Papers* at Yale University, has published numerous articles, coedited *The Cotton Kingdom,* and authored *New Masters: Northern Planters during the Civil War and Reconstruction.* James I. Robertson, Jr., of Virginia Polytechnic Institute and State University, has been the Alumni Distinguished Professor since 1992. He was the C. P. Miles Professor of History at Virginia Polytechnic from 1976 to 1992 and was executive director (by White House appointment) of the U.S. Civil

War Centennial Commission. Dr. Robertson has written numerous articles and over two dozen books, including *Civil War Virginia: Battleground for a Nation, Soldiers Blue and Gray, The Stonewall Brigade,* and *General A. P. Hill: The Story of a Confederate Warrior.* Emory M. Thomas, of the University of Georgia, has been Regents Professor of History since 1987. He has published dozens of articles and authored six books, including *The Confederate Nation, 1861–1865; The Confederate State of Richmond: A Biography of the Capital; The Confederacy as Revolutionary Experience;* and *Travels to Hallowed Ground: A Historian's Journey to the American Civil War.*

After convening the board, the next step was for the editors to decide what topics to include and how much space to allot to each of them. It was agreed that no article should be a mere snippet; none should contain fewer than 250 words. This was the number that would be specified for such subjects as relatively inactive and obscure members of the Confederate Congress. At the other extreme, the entry on the Civil War would be allotted a total of 17,250 words, broken up into five separate articles treating subjects such as the causes of the war and strategy and tactics. To ensure adequate coverage of particular topics, specialists in various fields were called upon for suggestions and advice. W. David Baird, Catherine Clinton, Jean W. Friedman, Anne Firor Scott, and Edgar A. Toppin advised us on our coverage of racial, gender, and social issues; Russ A. Pritchard guided us concerning arms, weapons, and ammunition; and William N. Still, Jr., on naval matters. Once the list of articles was finalized, assignments for writing them were given to leading authorities throughout the country. Each contrib-
utor was given a description of the article's scope, and every article was reviewed by the editorial board.

In all this planning and development of the project, the directors of Simon & Schuster's Academic Reference Division played an indispensable part. The president of the division, Charles E. Smith, conceived the idea of the encyclopedia and took the initiative in bringing it to reality. The editorial director, Paul Bernabeo, supervised the actual launching of the enterprise. The in-house project editor, Robert M. Salkin, together with his staff, performed the essential day-to-day managerial and editorial labor. He and his staff were responsible for making contracts with contributors, providing a preliminary appraisal of the submitted drafts of articles, sending these to the editors for their evaluation with respect to fairness and accuracy, and finally copyediting the drafts for clarity and for uniformity of style. The staff at Simon & Schuster's Academic Reference Division also researched and collected all of the illustrations used in the encyclopedia and wrote the captions. The maps of battles were commissioned from Donald S. Frazier and his staff at Applied Academic Services.

From start to finish, this cooperative effort has taken all of four years. We the editors are proud of the result, and we wish to offer our sincere thanks to all who helped make it possible. We commend the encyclopedia to readers in the hope that it will be as useful for them as we have tried to make it.

Richard N. Current
Editor in Chief

Foreword

Work on the *Encyclopedia of the Confederacy* began in 1989 with an idea by Charles E. Smith, president of Simon & Schuster's Academic Reference Division, for a reference work treating the Confederate States of America as a nation unto itself. The encyclopedia was not to be just another Civil War book, but a social, cultural, and political overview of the South during the years of the Confederacy's existence. Mr. Smith's first task was to find an editor in chief respected by his peers and possessing a broad base of knowledge about the Confederacy and current trends in Confederate scholarship. After seeking advice from several historians, he wisely chose Richard N. Current. Dr. Current is Distinguished Professor, Emeritus, at the University of North Carolina at Greensboro and past president of the Southern Historical Association. He has written seventeen books, coauthored almost a dozen others, and published numerous articles. His books include *Lincoln's Loyalists: Union Soldiers from the Confederacy, Those Terrible Carpetbaggers, Daniel Webster and the Rise of National Conservatism,* and *Lincoln and the First Shot.*

Dr. Current and Mr. Smith then assembled an outstanding editorial board composed of Paul D. Escott, Lawrence N. Powell, James I. Robertson, Jr., and Emory M. Thomas, who developed the plan for the encyclopedia. The plan was also reviewed by a group of editorial advisers, composed of W. David Baird, Catherine Clinton, Jean E. Friedman, Russ A. Pritchard, Anne Firor Scott, William N. Still, Jr., and Edgar A. Toppin, each of whom examined a particular dimension of the plan reflecting a specific area of expertise. (See Dr. Current's preface for an elaboration of the contributions of particular board members and editorial advisers.) With the plans complete, Dr. Current, the editorial board, and the staff at the Academic Reference Division together collected and edited over 1,400 articles by more than 300 leading scholars.

The encyclopedia is intended both for the specialist and the general reader. As such, it was designed so that readers familiar with Confederate history could turn quickly to the information they desired, while readers new to the field could be led from topic to topic through a detailed system of cross-references and a comprehensive index. Entry terms are arranged in alphabetical order; identical terms are arranged by subject matter according to the rule people first, places second, and things third (e.g., biographies of persons named Jackson are followed by articles on the city of Jackson, Mississippi, which, in turn, are followed by an entry about the ship *Jackson*).

To further aid the reader and bring a greater degree of systemization to the work than would be possible under a completely alphabetical arrangement, articles treating similar subjects have been grouped together into composite entries (e.g., the three articles discussing antebellum slavery, slavery during the war, and slave life have been collected under the heading *slavery*). Editorial notes before the start of such composite entries explain their structure and point the reader to related topics. A synoptic outline, which appears at the end of the encyclopedia, was designed to provide an additional aid for the reader by grouping together all entries pertaining to a major subject area.

Entries have been titled and organized in a manner we hope readers will be most likely to consult first. Alternate titles appear within the work to point readers to the actual location of the article; cross-references also appear at the ends of articles and in the index. The spelling and choice of certain names and terms required editorial solutions specially tailored to this work. It was our policy to avoid overturning well-ingrained, common usage. On the other hand, we were eager to balance this service to familiarity with our concern for scholarship. Where it would not interfere with ease of reading, alternative forms of names are included within parentheses immediately following the preferred forms. Of special consideration are the names of Native Americans. Where possible, transliterations of Indian names were used in place of English names. Exceptions were made for persons who appear in modern scholarship predominantly by their English name (e.g., *Stand Watie* is preferred over *Da-ga-ta-ga*).

When referring to battles with different Confederate and Federal names, we have preferred Confederate nomenclature throughout. Exceptions were made in cases where the Confederate name has disappeared on both sides of the Mason-Dixon Line (e.g., the September 14, 1862, clash at South Mountain, Maryland, which was initially called the Battle of Boonsboro by Confederates). A table of battles with dual names appears within the entry "Battles, Naming of." For battles with more than two names, we have used the name found most frequently in modern scholarship (e.g., we use the name *Frayser's Farm* for the fighting on June 30, 1862, also known as *Charles City Cross Roads*, *Glendale*, *Nelson's Farm*, *New Market Road*, and *Willis Church*). I would like to thank Terry L. Jones, Charles M. Spearman, Warren Wilkinson, Brian S. Wills, and Terrence J. Winschel for their advice in selecting appropriate names for battles.

At the end of each article is a bibliography ranging from two to fifteen citations. These bibliographies are selective and meant to give the reader a short list of works to consult for further information on the topic. The entries "Diaries, Letters, and Memoirs" and "Bibliography and Historiography" contain extensive general bibliographies arranged by subject matter. Where possible, reprint editions currently in print have been listed along with older editions. Several standard eighteenth- and early-nineteenth-century–Civil War sources such as the U.S. War Department's *War of the Rebellion* and the magazine *Confederate Veteran* exist in several reprint editions.

The encyclopedia contains over six hundred illustrations. Acknowledgements of sources for illustrations can be found in captions. Because most of the photographs used are over one hundred years old, their quality will vary. Every effort has been made to improve the clarity of these reproductions.

Photographs were also commissioned especially for this project. Phil Kramer of Philadelphia photographed a great number of contemporary arms and accoutrements. We would like to thank John A. Cleveland, George J. Lincoln III, Benjamin P. Michel, Russ A. Pritchard, and the Civil War Library and Museum in Philadelphia for the use of items from their collections. We would also like to thank Gordon Bleuler for allowing us to photograph items from his collection, including all the stamps and currency reproduced in the encyclopedia.

The encyclopedia also reproduces a large number of contemporary etchings from three post–Civil War collections: Alfred H. Guernsey's and Henry M. Alden's *Harper's Pictorial History of the Great Rebellion*, 2 vols., Chicago, 1866 and 1868; Louis Shepheard Moat's *Frank Leslie's Illustrated Famous Leaders and Battle Scenes of the Civil War*, New York, 1896; and Paul F. Mottelay's and T. Campbell-Copeland's *The Soldier in Our Civil War: A Pictorial History of the Conflict, 1861–1865*, vol. 1, New York, 1890.

In order to enhance the description and understanding of Civil War battles, we commissioned sixty-seven maps from Applied Academic Services of Fort Worth, Texas. These maps were produced electronically and reviewed for historical accuracy by the contributors of the articles with which they appear. We would like to thank those contributors who assisted in the development of these maps and especially Donald S. Frazier, president of Applied Academic Services, and his assistant, Robert F. Pace, for their skill and care in preparing them.

In addition to the articles, photographs, etchings, and maps that appear in the encyclopedia, we have included in the appendix the complete texts of several key documents of Confederate history, ranging from South Carolina's ordinance of secession to the various surrender treaties signed by Confederate commanders. We would like to thank Guy Swanson at the Museum of the Confederacy in Richmond, Virginia, and Thomas E. Schott for their help in tracking down these documents.

Of course, thanks are also due the more than three hundred scholars who contributed articles to this encyclopedia. Each of them has played an important part in the creation of this work, and each is acknowledged within the work for the contribution of particular entries. We would especially like to thank the following people, without whose advice and patience this encyclopedia could not have been produced: Gordon Bleuler, for suggestions concerning numismatics and philately; Russ A. Pritchard and the staff at the Civil War Library and Museum, for advice concerning ordnance and a host of other questions about the Civil War; Corrine P. Hudgins at the Museum of the Confederacy for help with illustrations; Kenny A. Franks, Paul F. Lambert, and the staff at the History Research and Consulting Company of Oklahoma City, for work on our table of state governors; Tom Broadfoot and his staff at the Broadfoot Publishing Company, for advice concerning bibliographic matters; Roger L. Ransom and Orville Vernon Burton, for assistance with statistical and demographic questions; and finally Kevin J. Foster and A. Robert Holcombe, Jr., for advice concerning naval matters.

Finally, I would like to express my personal gratitude to Dr. Current, the editorial board, and the editorial advisers for the many hours they gave to this project. I would also like to thank the project's manuscript editor, Cecile Rhinehart Watters; the proofreaders, Clifford H. Browder, Dorothy Bauhoff Kachouh, and Michael Mark Madore; the illustration editor, Patricia Brecht; Cynthia Crippen and the indexers at AEIOU, Inc.; Kelly Hinch and the folks at Graphic World, Inc.; my editorial assistants, Danielle Lewis, John Roseman, and Stefanie B. Siegmund; and finally Charles E. Smith and the entire staff at the Academic Reference Division. I would especially like to thank our editorial director, Paul Bernabeo, who introduced me to reference publishing and never wanted in patience or assistance to ensure that this project would be a success.

Robert M. Salkin
Project Editor

Directory of Contributors

A

RICHARD H. ABBOTT
Eastern Michigan University
Sumner, Caning of

THOMAS G. ALEXANDER
Brigham Young University
Whig Party

TRACY L. ALEXANDER
Los Angeles, California
Whig Party

TYLER ANBINDER
University of Wyoming
Politics

MICHAEL J. ANDRUS
Richmond, Virginia
Dahlgren Papers
Johnson, Edward

STEPHEN V. ASH
Knoxville, Tennessee
Tennessee
Union Occupation

WILLIAM THOMAS AUMAN
*North Carolina A&T State
University*
Clark, Henry T.
Heroes of America
Johnson, John Lewis
Peace Movements
Tyson, Bryan

B

L. E. BABITS
East Carolina University
Archaeology
Balloon

ANNE J. BAILEY
Georgia Southern University
Blanchard, Albert Gallatin
Boggs, William Robertson
Cabell, William Lewis
Churchill, Thomas James
Clark, John B., Jr.
Cooper, Douglas Hancock
Elkhorn Tavern, Arkansas
Forney, John Horace
Gano, Richard Montgomery
Greer, Elkanah Brackin
Hays, Harry Thompson
Hébert, Louis
Hébert, Paul O.
Hindman, Thomas C.
Holmes, Theophilus H.
Liddell, St. John Richardson
McCulloch, Ben
McCulloch, Henry Eustace
McIntosh, James McQueen
McNair, Evander
Major, James Patrick
Nicholls, Francis
Pike, Albert
Prairie Grove, Arkansas
Preston, William
Preston, William Ballard
Roane, John Selden
Robertson, Jerome Bonaparte
Sabine Pass, Texas
Slack, William Yarnel
Smith, E. Kirby
Trans-Mississippi Department
Twiggs, David E.

Van Dorn, Earl
Walker, Lucius Marshall
Wharton, John Austin

FRED ARTHUR BAILEY
Abilene Christian University
Arkansas
Arkansas Campaign of 1864
Gillem, Alvan C.
Knoxville and Greeneville Conventions
Little Rock, Arkansas
Temple, Oliver Perry

W. DAVID BAIRD
Pepperdine University
Indians
Indian Territory
Quapaws
Senecas
Shawnees

DOUGLAS A. BALL
R. M. Smythe and Co., New York
Bonds
Currency
    An Overview
    Numismatics
Debt
Direct Tax Act
Inflation
Memminger, Christopher G.
New Plan
Public Finance
Treasury Department
Trenholm, George

MICHAEL B. BALLARD
*Archives, Mississippi State
University*
Pemberton, John C.

RICHARD BARDOLPH
*Emeritus, University of North Carolina
at Greensboro*
Avery, William Waighstill
Davis, George
Desertion
Dortch, William Theophilus
Lutheran Church
McLean, James Robert
Morehead, John Motley

WILLIAM L. BARNEY
*University of North Carolina at Chapel
Hill*
Baldwin, William Edwin
Bowen, John Stevens
Cosby, George Blake
Fire-eaters
Garrott, Isham Warren
Green, Martin Edwin
Hawes, J. M.
Rhett, Robert Barnwell, Sr.
Secession
Smith, Martin Luther
Smith, William Duncan
Vaughn, John Crawford
Yancey, William Lowndes

ALWYN BARR
Texas Tech University
Branch, Anthony Martin
Darden, Stephen Heard
Galveston, Texas
City of Galveston
Gregg, John
Murrah, Pendleton
Texas
Waul, Thomas Neville
Wright, William Bacon

JOHN G. BARRETT
*Emeritus, Virginia Military
Institute*
Carolinas Campaign of Sherman
Young, Pierce Manning Butler

ROBERT T. BARRETT
Clemson University
Butler, Matthew Calbraith
Fort Hill
Gary, Martin Witherspoon
Hammond, James H.
Hampton, Wade

EDWIN C. BEARSS
*National Park Service,
Washington, D.C.*
Forts and Fortifications
Field Fortifications and Trench
Warfare
Monuments and Memorials
Battlefields

SARA B. BEARSS
*Virginia Historical Society,
Richmond*
Hunter, Robert M. T.
Rives, William C.
Tyler, John

CARYN COSSÉ BELL
Tulane University
Free People of Color
Free Creoles of Color
Roudanez Brothers
Trévigne, Paul

MICHAEL LES BENEDICT
Ohio State University
Johnson, Andrew

RICHARD FRANKLIN BENSEL
New School for Social Research
Cabinet

ARTHUR W. BERGERON, JR.
*Louisiana Office of State Parks,
Baton Rouge*
Buchanan, Franklin
Mallory, Stephen R.

RICHARD E. BERINGER
University of North Dakota
Civil War
Strategy and Tactics
Election of 1863

WILLIAM ALAN BLAIR
Pennsylvania State University
Allen, Henry W.
Brandon, William Lindsay
Early, Jubal
Early's Washington Raid
Fisher's Hill, Virginia
Hill, D. H.
Ramseur, Dodson

Scurry, William R.
Winchester, Virginia

ARCH FREDRIC BLAKEY
University of Florida
Baker, James McNair
Dawkins, James Baird
Hilton, Robert B.
Martin, John Marshall
Maxwell, Augustus Emmett
Morton, Jackson
Owens, James B.
Rogers, Samuel St. George
Sanderson, John Pease
Ward, George Taliaferro
Winder, John H.

F. N. BONEY
University of Georgia
Brown, Joseph E.
Georgia
Letcher, John
Smith, William "Extra Billy"

PATRICIA DORA BONNIN
*University of Illinois,
Urbana-Champaign*
Cotton

CHARLES E. BRODINE, JR.
*Naval Historical Center,
Washington, D.C.*
Maury, Matthew Fontaine

KENT MASTERSON BROWN
Lexington, Kentucky
Benning, Henry L.
Engineer Bureau
Leadbetter, Danville

NORMAN D. BROWN
Univesity of Texas at Austin
Stanly, Edward

RICHARD H. BROWN
Newberry Library, Chicago
Missouri Compromise

ROBERT S. BROWNING III
*San Antonio Air Logistics Center,
San Antonio, Texas*
Albemarle
Cooke, James W.

Forrest, French
Gosport Navy Yard
James River Squadron
Loyall, Benjamin P.
Maury, William L.

DICKSON D. BRUCE, JR.
University of California,
Irvine
Dueling

CHARLES F. BRYAN, JR.
Virginia Historical Society,
Richmond
Chattanooga, Tennessee
City of Chattanooga
Harris, Isham G.
Hatton, Robert Hopkins

JOHN A. BURRISON
Georgia State University
Handicrafts

ORVILLE VERNON BURTON
University of Illinois,
Urbana-Champaign
Cotton
Family Life
Society
Tobacco

VICTORIA E. BYNUM
Southwest Texas State
University
Brock, Sallie A.
Cary, Hetty
Marriage and Divorce
Pember, Phoebe Yates

FRANK L. BYRNE
Kent State University
Andersonville Prison
Belle Isle Prison
Castle Thunder Prison
Fort Delaware Prison
Johnson's Island Prison
Libby Prison
Point Lookout Prison
Prisoners of War
Prisons
Salisbury Prison
Wirz, Henry

C

ROBERT M. CALHOON
University of North Carolina at
Greensboro
Presbyterian Church

CHRIS CALKINS
Petersburg National Battlefield Park,
Petersburg, Virginia
Appomattox Campaign
Bocock, Thomas S.
Brevard, Theodore Washington
Cook, Philip
Fort Stedman, Virginia
Girardey, Victor Jean Baptiste
Hagood, Johnson
Pegram, John
Thomas, Allen
Whiting, W. H. C.

EDWARD D. C. CAMPBELL, JR.
Virginia State Library and Archives,
Richmond
Education
    Primary and Secondary Schools
Film and Video
    Documentary Film and Video
    Fictional Presentations
Popular Culture
Textbooks
Theater

MARK LEA ("BEAU") CANTRELL
Oklahoma Heritage Association,
Oklahoma City
Davis, Nicholas

MARK T. CARLETON
Louisiana State University
Baton Rouge, Louisiana
Louisiana State Seminary and
    Military Academy

DAVID L. CARLTON
Vanderbilt University
Urbanization

PETER S. CARMICHAEL
Pennsylvania State University
Alexander, Edward Porter
Bee, Barnard E.

Brandy Station, Virginia
Cedar Creek, Virginia
Grimes, Bryan
Longstreet, James
Magruder, John B.
Rains, Gabriel J.
Wharton, Gabriel Colvin

JOAN E. CASHIN
Ohio State University
Davis, Varina Howell

WILLIAM LAMAR CAWTHON, JR.
University of Georgia
Petigru, James L.

MICHAEL B. CHESSON
University of Massachusetts-Boston
Bread Riots
Richmond, Virginia

PAUL A. CIMBALA
Fordham University
Confiscation
    Federal Confiscation Acts

JOHN F. CISSELL
Kennesaw Mountain National Battle-
field Park, Marietta, Georgia
Chickamauga Campaign
Deshler, James
Smith, Preston
Wilson, Claudius Charles
Wood, Sterling Alexander Martin
Wright, Marcus Joseph

BLUE CLARK
Oklahoma City University
Chickasaws

CATHERINE CLINTON
Harvard University
Courtship
Plantation
Plantation Mistress
Prostitution
Tubman, Harriet

PETER A. COCLANIS
University of North Carolina at
Chapel Hill
Rice

KENNETH COLEMAN
Emeritus, University of Georgia
Soldiers' Aid Societies

JAMES LEE CONRAD
*U.S. Air Force, Judge Advocate
General Department,
Washington, D.C.*
Georgia Military Institute

B. FRANKLIN COOLING
*U.S. Department of Energy,
Washington, D.C.*
Floyd, John B.
Henry and Donelson Campaign
Pillow, Gideon

ROBERT E. CORLEW
*Department of Conservation, Tennessee
Historical Commission, Nashville
(Retired)*
Caruthers, Robert Looney
Foote, Henry S.
Gentry, Meredith Poindexter
Henry, Gustavus Adolphus
Jones, Thomas McKissick
Murray, John Porry
Thomas, James Houston
Tibbs, William Henry

DUDLEY T. CORNISH
Emeritus, Pittsburg State University
African American Troops in the Union
Army

JAMES W. CORTADA
*IBM Consulting Group, Madison,
Wisconsin*
Cuba

JOHN M. COSKI
*Museum of the Confederacy, Richmond,
Virginia*
Curry, Jabez L. M.

MERLIN G. COX
Emeritus, University of Florida
Florida
Olustee, Florida
Perry, Madison S.

LYNDA LASSWELL CRIST
*Papers of Jefferson Davis, Rice
University*
Davis Bend

DANIEL W. CROFTS
Trenton State College
Baldwin, John B.
Gilmer, John A.
Graham, William A.

JOHN R. CRONIN
*London School of Oriental and African
Studies, England*
Rules of War

EDWARD RILEY CROWTHER
Adams State College
Baptist Church

CHARLES P. CULLOP
Emeritus, East Carolina University
Index
Propaganda

RICHARD N. CURRENT
*Emeritus, University of North Carolina
at Greensboro*
Battles, Naming of
Calhoun, John C.
Confederate States of America
Emancipation Proclamation
Fort Sumter, South Carolina
Horses and Mules
Star of the West
State Rights
Tories

D

W. HARRISON DANIEL
University of Richmond
Bible Societies
Sermons

STEPHEN DAVIS
*Blue and Gray Magazine, Atlanta,
Georgia*
Stevens, Clement Hoffman
Tyler, Robert Charles

WILLIAM C. DAVIS
Mechanicsburg, Pennsylvania
Army
   Confederate Army
Espionage
   Federal Secret Service
Hardeman, William Polk
Lewis, Joseph Horace
Military Training
Orphan Brigade
Photography
Saltville Massacre

MARY A. DECREDICO
U.S. Naval Academy
Confiscation
   Confederate Sequestration
Economy
Gregg, William
Impressment
Speculation
State Socialism
Substitutes
Tax-in-Kind
Textile Industry

CARL N. DEGLER
Stanford University
Unionism

NORMAN C. DELANEY
Del Mar College
Kell, John McIntosh
Privateers
Tuscaloosa

JACK L. DICKINSON
Huntington, West Virginia
Jenkins, Albert Gallatin

HARRIET E. AMOS DOSS
University of Alabama in Birmingham
Mobile, Alabama
   City of Mobile

ALAN C. DOWNS
Georgia Southern University
Arrington, Archibald Hunter
Carroll, William Henry
Craige, Francis Burton
Ector, Matthew Duncan

Jackson, William Hicks
Mercer, Hugh Weedon
Ramsay, James Graham
Vaughan, Alfred Jefferson, Jr.
Venable, Abraham Watkins
Vicksburg Campaign
Walker, W. H. T.
Walthall, Edward Cary
Young, William Hugh

RICHARD R. DUNCAN
Georgetown University
Baltimore Riot

RUSSELL DUNCAN
John Carroll University
Post Office Department
Southern Express Company
Taliaferro, William Booth

WALTER T. DURHAM
Tennessee Historical Society, Knoxville
Memphis, Tennessee
Nashville, Tennessee

WAYNE K. DURRILL
University of Cincinnati
Farming
Helper, Hinton Rowan

E

WALTER B. EDGAR
University of South Carolina
Barnwell, Robert W.
Boyce, W. W.
Keitt, Lawrence

BRUCE W. EELMAN
University of Maryland, College Park
Constitutional Union Party
Crittenden Compromise

RICHARD E. ELLIS
State University of New York at Buffalo
Nullification Controversy

JOHN R. ELTING
U.S. Army (Retired)
Artillery
An Overview

Infantry
Signal Corps

ROBERT FRANCIS ENGS
University of Pennsylvania
Slavery
Antebellum Slavery
Slavery during the Civil War
Slave Life

PAUL D. ESCOTT
Wake Forest University
Averasboro, North Carolina
Bragg, Thomas
Compromise of 1850
Fort Fisher, North Carolina
Judiciary
Kenan, Owen Rand
Keyes, Wade
Lander, William
Leach, James Madison
Leach, James T.
Logan, George Washington
Morale
North Carolina
Poor Relief
Poverty

DAVID EVANS
Athens, Georgia
Andrews Raid
Dockery, Thomas Pleasant
Hawthorn, Alexander Travis
McRae, Dandridge
Stoneman's Raids
Wheeler's Raids

ELI N. EVANS
Charles Revson Foundation, New York
Benjamin, Judah P.

F

MICHAEL FELLMAN
Simon Fraser University
Anderson, William
James Brothers
Quantrill, William Clarke
Todd, George
Younger Brothers

DALE FETZER, JR.
Historical Impressions, Inc., Wilmington, Delaware
Reenactments

PAUL FINKELMAN
Virginia Polytechnic Institute and State University
Constitution
Dred Scott Decision
Wilmot Proviso

BERNARD S. FINN
Smithsonian Institution, Washington, D.C.
Telegraph

MICHAEL W. FITZGERALD
St. Olaf College
Class Conflicts

TERRENCE W. FITZMORRIS
University College, Tulane University
Hahn, Michael
Kenner, Duncan F.

KEVIN S. FONTENOT
Tulane University
Conrad, Charles M.
de Clouet, Alexandre
Dupré, Lucien Jacques
Hodge, Benjamin Louis
Roman, André Bienvenu

GEORGE B. FORGIE
University of Texas at Austin
Austin, Texas
Brownsville, Texas
City of Brownsville

GAINES M. FOSTER
Louisiana State University
Lee Monument Association
Lost Cause
An Overview
Memorial Day
Monuments and Memorials
An Overview
Southern Historical Society

KEVIN J. FOSTER
*National Maritime Initiative, National
    Park Service, Washington, D.C.*
Atlanta
Banshee
Camilla
Chickamauga
Colonel Lamb
Commerce Raiders
Don
Georgia
Harriet Lane
H. L. Hunley
Hunley, Horace
Jefferson Davis
Laird Rams
Rams
Rappahannock
Read, Charles W.
Robert E. Lee
Savannah
Shenandoah
State Navies
Tallahassee
Tombs, James H.
Waddell, James

WILLIAM M. FOWLER, JR.
The New England Quarterly,
    Northeastern University
Navy
    Navy Departments

ELIZABETH FOX-GENOVESE
Emory University
Diaries, Letters, and Memoirs
Education
    Women's Education
Evans, Augusta Jane

JIMMIE LEWIS FRANKLIN
Vanderbilt University
Lynch, John Roy

KENNY A. FRANKS
*Oklahoma Heritage Association, Okla-
    homa City*
Clanton, James Holt
Clay, Clement C.
Duke, Basil C.
Ellet, Henry T.
Gibson, Randall Lee
Hanly, Thomas B.

Hart, Nancy
Jemison, Robert
Jomini, Henry
Lewis, David Peter
McRae, Colin J.
Maxey, Samuel Bell
Watie, Stand

WALTER J. FRASER, JR.
Georgia Southern University
Charleston, South Carolina
    City of Charleston
    Bombardment of Charleston
Free Markets
Ripley, Roswell Sabine
Savannah, Georgia
    Savannah Campaign
South Carolina

DONALD S. FRAZIER
*Applied Academic Services, Fort Worth,
    Texas*
Brownsville, Texas
    Battle of Brownsville
Civil War
    Losses and Numbers
Education
    Military Education
Galveston, Texas
    Battle of Galveston
Glorieta Pass, New Mexico
Harrison, Thomas
Hood's Texas Brigade
Kentucky Campaign of Bragg
Mill Springs, Kentucky
Oury, Granville H.
Perryville, Kentucky
Ross, Lawrence Sullivan
Wheeler, Joseph

WILLIAM W. FREEHLING
*State University of New York at
    Buffalo*
Expansionism in the Antebellum South
Fugitive Slave Law
Kansas-Nebraska Act

DENNIS E. FRYE
*Harpers Ferry National Historical
    Park, Harpers Ferry, West Virginia*
Ashby, Turner
Harpers Ferry, West Virginia
    Arsenal and Armory
    John Brown's Raid
    Battle of 1862
Imboden, John D.
Sharpsburg Campaign
Shenandoah Valley
    Shenandoah Valley Campaign of
        Sheridan
South Mountain, Maryland
Stuart's Raids
Walker, John George

G

JUDITH FENNER GENTRY
University of Southwestern Louisiana
Erlanger Loan

WILLIAM E. GIENAPP
Harvard University
American Party
Republican Party

E. STANLY GODBOLD
Mississippi State University
Thomas, William Holland

JAMES W. GOODRICH
*State Historical Society of Missouri,
    Columbia*
Bell, Caspar Wistar
Centralia Massacre
Clark, John B.
Conrow, Aaron H.
Cooke, William Mordecai
Freeman, Thomas W.
Harris, Thomas A.
Norton, Nimrod Lindsay
Peyton, Robert Ludwell Yates
Wilkes, Peter Singleton

THOMAS GOODRICH
Topeka, Kansas
Guerrilla Warfare

LESLEY JILL GORDON-BURR
University of Georgia
Beefsteak Raid
Cockrell, Francis Marion
Elzey, Arnold
Fort Pickens, Florida
Gaines' Mill, Virginia
Garland, Samuel, Jr.
Grayson, John Breckinridge
Higgins, Edward
Kilpatrick-Dahlgren Raid
Maury, D. H.
Mobile, Alabama
   Battle of Mobile Bay
   Mobile Campaign
Moore, John Creed
Peninsular Campaign
Smith, Gustavus W.
Taylor, Thomas Hart
Thomas, Bryan Morel
Villepigue, John B.

NORMAN A. GRAEBNER
Emeritus, University of Virginia
Canada
Diplomacy
France
Mann, A. Dudley
Russia
Spain
State Department

DONALD E. GREEN
Chadron State College
Creeks
Opothleyahola

W. TODD GROCE
East Tennessee Historical Society,
   Knoxville
Border States
Haynes, Landon Carter

BERT HAWTHORNE GROENE
Southeastern Louisiana University
Tallahassee, Florida

H
_____

JAMES O. HALL
U.S. Department of Labor (Retired)
Harrison, Henry Thomas

JUDITH LEE HALLOCK
Middle Country Schools, Centereach,
   New York
Bragg, Braxton
Mackall, William W.
Trapier, James H.

FRITZ P. HAMER
South Carolina State Museum,
   Columbia
Conner, James
Evans, Clement A.
Evans, Nathan "Shanks"

KEITH ANDERSON HARDISON
Beauvoir, The Jefferson Davis Shrine,
   Biloxi, Mississippi
Beauvoir

WILLIAM C. HARRIS
North Carolina State University
Holden, William W.
Pearson, Richmond
Walker, Leroy P.

LOWELL H. HARRISON
Emeritus, Western Kentucky University
Breckinridge, John C.
Breckinridge, Robert J.
Breckinridge, Robert J., Jr.
Johnson, George W.
Kentucky
Magoffin, Beriah

DALE F. HARTER
Virginia State Library and Archives,
   Richmond
Jones, J. R.

D. SCOTT HARTWIG
Gettysburg National Military Park,
   Gettysburg, Pennsylvania
Fort Wagner, South Carolina
Gettysburg Campaign

RICHARD W. HATCHER III
Fort Sumter National Monument,
   Sullivan's Island, South Carolina
Wilson's Creek Campaign

HERMAN HATTAWAY
University of Missouri at Kansas
   City
Beall, John Y.
Lee, Stephen D.

JOHN J. HENNESSY
National Park Service, Harpers Ferry,
   West Virginia
Jones, David Rumph "Neighbor"
Manassas, First
Manassas, Second

JANET SHARP HERMANN
Berkeley, California
Davis, Joseph E.
Montgomery, Benjamin

LAWRENCE L. HEWITT
Southeastern Louisiana University
Beall, William N. R.
Carter, Jonathan H.
Cottonclads
Duncan, Johnson K.
Eastport
Hollins, George N.
Lovell, Mansfield
Missouri
New Madrid and Island Number 10
New Orleans, Louisiana
   Capture of New Orleans
Port Hudson, Louisiana
Webb
Whittle, William C.

WALTER R. HIBBARD, JR.
Blacksburg, Virginia
Mining

DAMON D. HICKEY
Director of the Library, College of
   Wooster
Society of Friends

WILLIAM C. HINE
South Carolina State College
Rivers, Prince
Smalls, Robert

A. ROBERT HOLCOMBE, JR.
Confederate Naval Museum, Columbus,
    Georgia
Charlotte Navy Yard
Chattahoochee
Columbus Naval Iron Works
Edged Weapons
    Edged Weapons in the Navy
Elliott, Gilbert
Farrand, Ebenezer
Graves, William A.
Guthrie, John J.
Ironclads
Jackson
Naval Guns
    Naval Munitions
Naval Stations
Neuse
Pee Dee
Porter, John L.
Small Arms
    Naval Small Arms
Spar Torpedoes
Tennessee
Tift Brothers
Virginia
Williamson, William P.

KIM BERNARD HOLIEN
Heritage of Honor, Inc., Alexandria,
    Virginia
Ball's Bluff, Virginia
Special Units

MICHAEL E. HOLMES
Sons of Confederate Veterans, William
    E. Jones Camp #850
Salt

HAROLD HOLZER
The Metropolitan Museum of Art,
    New York
Burial of Latané
Lost Cause
    Iconography of the Lost Cause
Printmaking
Stamps
Volck, Adalbert
White House

JAMES J. HORGAN
Saint Leo College
Civil Service
Hotze, Henry
Rost, Pierre A.
Soulé, Pierre

REGINALD HORSMAN
University of Wisconsin-Milwaukee
Blockade
    An Overview

SAMUEL L. HORST
Eastern Mennonite College
Mennonites

THOMAS J. HOWE
Monona Grove High School, Monona,
    Wisconsin
Petersburg Campaign

C. A. HUEY
Lexington, South Carolina
Artillery
    Imported English Artillery
Small Arms
    Imported English Small Arms
    Imported English Long-Range
    Rifles

A. V. HUFF, JR.
Furman University
Ayer, Lewis Malone
Columbia, South Carolina
Farrow, James
McQueen, John
Magrath, Andrew G.
Miles, William Porcher
Orr, James L.
Pickens, Francis W.
Simpson, William Dunlap
Withers, Thomas
Witherspoon, James Hervey

NATHANIEL CHEAIRS HUGHES, JR.
Chattanooga, Tennessee
Hardee, William J.
Rains, James Edwards
Shoup, Francis

JAMES A. HUSTON
Emeritus, Lynchburg College
Roads
Transportation
Waterways

I

JOHN C. INSCOE
University of Georgia
Akin, Warren
Anderson, Clifford
Bartow, Francis S.
Bass, Nathan
Bell, Hiram Parks
Blandford, Mark Hardin
Clark, William W.
Clingman, Thomas Lanier
Crawford, Martin J.
Echols, Joseph Hubbard
Forman, Thomas Marsh
Hartridge, Julian
Hill, Benjamin H.
Holt, Hines
Ingram, Porter
Johnson, Herschel V.
Kenan, Augustus Holmes
Lester, George N.
Lewis, David W.
Lewis, John W.
Munnerlyn, Charles James
Nisbet, Eugenius Aristides
Shewmake, John Troupe
Smith, James Milton
Smith, William Ephraim
Strickland, Hardy
Trippe, Robert Pleasant
Wright, Augustus Romaldus

J

THOMAS E. JEFFREY
Thomas A. Edison Papers, Rutgers
    University
Ashe, Thomas S.
Bridgers, Robert R.
Cooperationists
Davidson, Allen Turner
Fuller, Thomas C.
Gaither, Burgess S.
McDowell, Thomas David Smith

Puryear, Richard C.
Reade, Edwin Godwin
Ruffin, Thomas
Smith, William N. H.
Turner, Josiah

LES JENSEN
U.S. Army Center for Military History,
Washington, D.C.
Medals and Decorations
Uniforms
    Army Uniforms
    Navy and Marines Uniforms

TERRY L. JONES
Northeast Lousiana University
Louisiana Tigers
Mansfield, Louisiana
Stafford, Leroy A.
Starke, William Edwin
York, Zebulon

ERVIN L. JORDAN, JR.
Alderman Library, University of Virginia
Free People of Color
    Free Blacks

K

RIC A. KABAT
Gainesville College
Black Belt
Selma, Alabama
    City of Selma

HENRY KAMERLING
University of Illinois,
Urbana-Champaign
Tobacco

DENNIS KELLY
Kennesaw Mountain National
Battlefield Park, Marietta,
Georgia
Benton, Samuel
Capers, Ellison
Cumming, Alfred
Fort Pulaski, Georgia
Kennesaw Mountain, Georgia

JAMES C. KELLY
Virginia Historical Society, Richmond
Brownlow, William G.

JOHN KENNINGTON, JR.
Tidewater Atlantic Research, Inc.,
Washington, North Carolina
Sailors

ROBERT C. KENZER
Brigham Young University
Community Life

ALVY L. KING
Texas Attorney General's Office,
Austin
Wigfall, Louis T.

JOSEPHINE S. KING
University of South Florida
Confederate Veteran

WILMA KING
Michigan State University
Childhood
    Slave Children

FRANK L. KLEMENT
Emeritus, Marquette University
Copperheads
Northwestern Conspiracy

JODI KOSTE
Tompkins McCaw Library, Richmond,
Virginia
Hospitals

MICHAEL KREYLING
Vanderbilt University
Lanier, Sydney

ROBERT E. L. KRICK
Fredericksburg, Virginia
Brockenbrough, John Mercer
Heth, Henry
Walker, Henry H.
Walker, Reuben Lindsay

ROBERT K. KRICK
Fredericksburg and Spotsylvania
County Battlefields Memorial
National Military Park,
Fredericksburg, Virginia
Anderson, George B.
Army of Northern Virginia
Barksdale, William
Barksdale's Mississippi Brigade

Battle, Cullen Andrews
Branch, Lawrence O'Bryan
Bryan, Goode
Cedar Mountain, Virginia
Chancellorsville Campaign
Chilton, Robert Hall
Cobb, Thomas R. R.
Cross Keys and Port Republic,
    Virginia
Dearing, James
Fredericskburg Campaign
Front Royal, Virginia
Gregg, Maxcy
Harris, Nathaniel Harrison
Hunton, Eppa
Jones, John M.
Loring, W. W.
McLaws, Lafayette
Pender, William Dorsey
Rodes, Robert
Rosser, Thomas Lafayette
Wilcox, Cadmus Marcellus
Wilderness Campaign

L

PAUL F. LAMBERT
Oklahoma Heritage Association,
Oklahoma City
Adams, John
Duke, Basil Wilson
Macwillie, Marcus H.
Pugh, James Lawrence
Quarles, William Andrew
Smith, Robert Hardy
Smith, William Russell
Stone, Kate
Watts, Thomas H.
Wiley, Calvin H.

NELSON D. LANKFORD
Virginia Historical Society, Richmond
Boteler, Alexander R.
Brockenbrough, John White
Caperton, Allen T.
Chambliss, John Randolph, Sr.
Collier, Charles Fenton
de Jarnette, Daniel C.
Funsten, David
Garnett, Muscoe Russell Hunter
Gholson, Thomas Saunders
Goode, John, Jr.

Holcombe, James P.
Holliday, Frederick William Mackey
Johnston, Robert
Lyons, James
MacFarland, William H.
McMullen, Fayette
Mason, James M.
Miller, Samuel Augustine
Montague, Robert Latane
Preston, Walter
Russell, Charles Welles
Scott, Robert Eden
Whitfield, Robert Henry

THOMAS J. LEGG
College of William and Mary
Bee, Hamilton P.
Gray, Henry
Green, Thomas
Harrison, James Edward
Mouton, Alfred
Polignac, Camille J.
Red River Campaigns
Steele, William
Waterhouse, Richard

JOHN A. LENT
Temple University
Magazines
　De Bow's Review
　Southern Illustrated News
　Southern Literary Messenger
　Northern Magazines in the
　　South

RICHARD I. LESTER
*Center for Professional Development,
Air University, Maxwell Air Force
Base, Alabama*
Anglo-Confederate Purchasing
　An Overview

RUDY LEVERETT
*Idaho State Department of Education,
Boise*
Jones County, Mississippi

JAMES M. LINDGREN
*State University of New York at
Plattsburgh*
Arlington House

CHRISTOPHER LOSSON
University of Mississippi
Cheatham, B. Franklin

LESLIE A. LOVETT
Houston, Texas
Marshall, Henry
Perkins, John, Jr.
Sparrow, Edward
Villeré, Charles Jacques

CHRISTINE A. LUNARDINI
New York, New York
Felton, Rebecca Latimer
Merrick, Caroline E.
Newsom, Ella King
Spencer, Cornelia Phillips

M

CHARLES MCARVER
Woodberry Forest, Virginia
Censorship
Forsyth, John
Newspapers
Russell, William H.
Stanley, Henry Morton
Turner, Joseph A.
War Correspondence

JOHN MCCARDELL
Middlebury College
Bluffton Movement
Georgia Platform

ROBERT H. MCKENZIE
*New College, University of Alabama in
Tuscaloosa*
African American Forgeworkers
Naval Ordnance Works
Selma, Alabama
　Selma Naval Ordnance Works
Shelby Iron Compnay

GORDON B. MCKINNEY
*National History Day at the University
of Maryland, College Park*
Vance, Zebulon

SALLY G. MCMILLEN
Davidson College
Clothing
Food

RICHARD M. MCMURRY
Decatur, Georgia
Anderson, Robert
Army of Tennessee
Bate, William Brimage
Brantly, William Felix
Brown, John Calvin
Browne, William M.
Bullock, Robert
Campbell, Alexander William
Carter, John Carpenter
Clayton, Henry DeLamar
Cleburne, Patrick
Cold Harbor, Virginia
Corinth, Mississippi
Davis, William George Mackey
Deas, Zachariah Cantey
Ferguson, Samuel Wragg
Finley, Jesse Johnson
Franklin and Nashville Campaign
French, Samuel G.
Gist, States Rights
Gordon, George Washington
Gracie, Archibald, Jr.
Granbury, Hiram Bronson
Helm, Benjamin Hardin
Hill, Benjamin Jefferson
Jackson, Henry Rootes
Johnston, George Doherty
Johnston, Joseph E.
Lowrey, Mark Perrin
Lowry, Robert
Maney, George Earl
Manigault, Arthur Middleton
New Market, Virginia
Palmer, Joseph Benjamin
Pettus, Edmund Winston
Polk, Leonidas
Polk, Lucius Eugene
Scott, Thomas
Shelley, Charles Miller
Smith, James Argyle
Smith, Thomas Benton
Stevenson, Carter
Stewart, Alexander P.
Stovall, Marcellus Augustus
Strahl, Otho French

W. K. MCNEIL
*Ozark Folk Center, Mountain View,
Arkansas*
Folk Narratives
Oral History

JAMES M. MCPHERSON
Princeton University
Civil War
    Causes of the War
    Causes of Defeat

HOWARD MICHAEL MADAUS
Buffalo Bill Historical Center, Cody, Wyoming
Arms, Weapons, and Ammunition
    Army Ordnance
Flags
    Confederate Flags
    Military Flags
    State Flags
Small Arms
    Alterations to U.S. Small Arms
    Imported English Small Arms
    Imported Austrian, Belgian, and French Small Arms

JACK P. MADDEX, JR.
University of Oregon
Pollard, Edward A.

MICHAEL G. MAHON
Benbrook, Texas
Cocke, Philip St. George
Danville, Virginia
Davidson, Henry Brevard
Gilmer, Jeremy Francis
Govan, Daniel Chevilette
Holtzclaw, James Thadeus
Kirkland, William Whedbee
Lilley, Robert Doak
Lynchburg, Virginia
McLean, Wilmer
Martin, William Thompson
Moore, Patrick Theodore
Morgan, John Tyler
Perrin, Abner Monroe
Scales, Alfred Moore
Shenandoah Valley
    An Overview
Simms, James Phillip
Toon, Thomas Fentress
Wayne, Henry Constantine

JOHN F. MARSZALEK
Mississippi State University
Jackson, Mississippi
    City of Jackson
March to the Sea, Sherman's

JAMES MARTEN
Marquette University
Childhood
    Free Children
Wells, James Madison

SAMUEL J. MARTIN
Hilton Head Island, South Carolina
Ewell, Richard S.

WILLIAM D. MATTER
U.S. Air Force (Retired)
Spotsylvania Campaign

GRACE RUSHING MAXWELL
Florida A&M University
Walls, Josiah

ROBERT E. MAY
Purdue University
Imperialism

P. NEAL MEIER
Ohio State University
Commissary Bureau
File Closers
Foraging
Galvanized Yankees
Lawton, Alexander R.
Myers, Abraham C.
Oath of Allegiance
Quartermaster Bureau

MAURICE K. MELTON
LaGrange, Georgia
Charleston Squadron
Glassell, William T.
Ingraham, Duncan N.
Mitchell, John K.
Powder Works
Shipyards

ANNE BLYTHE MERIWETHER
Columbia, South Carolina
McCord, Louisa Cheves

FRANK J. MERLI
Queens College of the City University of New York
Alexandra
Bulloch, James Dunwoody
Laird Rams

RANDALL M. MILLER
St. Joseph's University
Methodist Church
Slave Drivers

GARY B. MILLS
University of Alabama in Tuscaloosa
Miscegenation

REID MITCHELL
Princeton University
Nationalism

CLARENCE L. MOHR
Tulane University
Berry, Harrison
Dallas, Moses

CARL H. MONEYHON
University of Arkansas at Little Rock
Batson, Felix I.
Carroll, David W.
Garland, Rufus K.
Graham, Malcolm D.
Gray, Peter W.
Hemphill, John
Herbert, Caleb C.
Johnson, Robert W.
Lubbock, Francis R.
Mitchel, Charles Burton
Murphy, Isaac
Ochiltree, William B.
Oldham, Williamson S.
Reagan, John H.
Rector, Henry M.
Royston, Grandison D.
Rust, Albert
Sexton, Franklin B.
Thomason, Hugh French
Watkins, William W.
Wilcox, John A.

HORACE MONTGOMERY
Emeritus, University of Georgia
Cobb, Howell

RAYBURN S. MOORE
Emeritus, University of Georgia
Book Publishing
Literature
    Literature in the Confederacy
Timrod, Henry

WINFRED B. MOORE, JR.
The Citadel
Citadel, The

JAMES F. MORGAN
Green River Community College
Counterfeiting

MARK MORGAN
Steamtown National Historic Site,
  Scranton, Pennsylvania
Forts and Fortifications
  An Overview

DAN L. MORRILL
Charlotte Law Library, Charlotte, North
  Carolina
Charlotte and Mecklenburg County,
  North Carolina

WILLIAM MOSS
Wake Forest University
Broadsides
Clemens, Samuel Langhorne

ELISABETH MUHLENFELD
Florida State University
Chesnut, Mary Boykin

TERRENCE V. MURPHY
Mount Sterling Rebel, *Mount Sterling,*
  Kentucky
Hanson, Roger
Hood, John Bell
Virginia Military Institute
Williams, John S. "Cerro Gordo"

N

JOSEPH MILTON NANCE
Texas A&M University
Morgan, Simpson Harris

MARK E. NEELY, JR.
St. Louis University
Booth, John Wilkes
Election of 1860
Freedom of the Press
Habeas Corpus
Lincoln, Abraham
  Image of Lincoln in the Confederacy
  Assassination of Lincoln

LARRY E. NELSON
Francis Marion College
Thompson, Jacob

WILLIAM H. NULTY
Florida Historical Society,
  Tallahassee
Milton, John

O

JOHN O'BRIEN
Emeritus, University of Connecticut,
  Storrs
Campbell, John A.
Chapman, Conrad Wise
Cooper, Samuel
Jones, J. B.
Julio, E. B. D.
Seddon, James A.
War Department
Zollicoffer, Felix K.

JOHN E. OLSON
Mt. Airy, Maryland
Johnson, Bradley Tyler

TED OWNBY
University of Mississippi
Extortion
Fast Days
Leisure

FRANK L. OWSLEY
Auburn University
Florida
Maffitt, John N.
Mobile Squadron
Page, Richard L.

P

ROBERT F. PACE
Longwood College
Allen, William Wirt
Hodge, George Baird
Humes, William Young Conn
Iverson, Alfred
Marshall, Humphrey

SANDRA V. PARKER
Richmond Civil War Round Table,
  Virginia
Godwin, Archibald Campbell
Nursing
Tompkins, Sally L.

WILLIAM E. PARRISH
Mississippi State University
Allison, Abraham K.
Bonham, Milledge L.
Clark, Edward
Ellis, John W.
Flanagin, Harris
Fletcher, Thomas
Hawes, Richard
Jackson, Claiborne F.
Missouri
Reynolds, Thomas C.
Shorter, John G.

CHARLES V. PEERY
Charleston, South Carolina
Edged Weapons
  Edged Weapons in the Navy
North, James H.

THEDA PERDUE
University of Kentucky
Cherokees

PERCIVAL PERRY
Emeritus, Wake Forest University
Mason-Dixon Line

CHRISTOPHER PHILLIPS
Emporia State University
Frost, Daniel Marsh
Gardner, Franklin
Jackson, John King
McCown, John P.
Marmaduke, John Sappington
Miller, William
Price, Sterling
Price's Missouri Raid
Shelby, Joseph O.
Tracy, Edward Dorr

WILLIAM GARRETT PISTON
Southwest Missouri State University
Seven Pines, Virginia

LAWRENCE N. POWELL
Tulane University
Butler's Woman Order
Lousiana
Moore, Thomas O.
New Orleans, Louisiana
   City of New Orleans
Semmes, Thomas

WILLIAM S. POWELL
University of North Carolina at Chapel Hill
Moravian Church
Raleigh, North Carolina

J. TRACY POWER
South Carolina Department of Archives and History, Columbia
Anderson, George Thomas "Tige"
Baker, Laurence Simmons
DuBose, Dudley McIver
Forney, William Henry
Fry, Birkett Davenport
Gardner, W. M.
Goggin, James Monroe
Huger, Benjamin
Johnston, Robert Daniel
Law, Evander McIvor
Loring-Jackson Incident
O'Neal, Edward Asbury
Perry, William Flank
Pettigrew, J. Johnston
Posey, Carnot
Ransom, Matt Whitaker
Ransom, Robert, Jr.
Semmes, Paul J.
Starke, Peter Burwell

RUSS A. PRITCHARD
The Civil War Library and Museum, Philadelphia
Artillery
   Confederate Artillery
   Captured U.S. Artillery
de Lagnel, Julius Adolph
Edged Weapons
   Edged Weapons in the Army
Hand Grenades and Land Mines
Palmetto Armory
Small Arms
   Confederate Long Arms
   Confederate Handguns
   Captured and Purchased U.S.
      Small Arms

PAUL M. PRUITT, JR.
School of Law Library, University of Alabama in Tuscaloosa
Alabama

R

GEORGE C. RABLE
Anderson University
Refugeeing

KENNETH RADLEY
Canadian Armed Forces, Ontario
Military Justice
Provost Marshal

JAMES A. RAMAGE
Northern Kentucky University
Buckner, Simon Bolivar
Johnson, Adam Rankin "Stovepipe"
Kelly, John Herbert
Morgan, John Hunt
Morgan's Raids

ROGER L. RANSOM
University of California, Riverside
Army
   Manpower
Population

GEORGE A. REAVES III
Shiloh National Military Park, Shiloh, Tennessee
Gladden, Adley Hogan
Hogg, Joseph Lewis
Holly Springs, Mississippi
Iuka, Mississippi
Shiloh Campaign

KAREN G. REHM
Fredericksburg and Spotsylvania County Battlefields Memorial National Military Park, Fredericksburg, Virginia
Lee, Fitzhugh

LOWELL REIDENBAUGH
Brentwood, Missouri
Anderson, Richard Heron
Archer, James Jay
Barringer, Rufus
Barton, Seth Maxwell
Beale, Richard Lee Turberville

Bratton, John
Chambliss, John Randolph, Jr.
Colquitt, Alfred H.
Cox, William Ruffin
Doles, George Pierce
Drayton, Thomas F.
Featherston, Winfield Scott
Finegan, Joseph
Gordon, John
Hoke, Robert Frederick
Jenkins, Micah
Johnson, Bushrod Rust
Kennedy, John Doby
Kershaw, Joseph B.
Lane, James
Lee, Edwin Gray
Leventhorpe, Collett
McComb, William
McGowan, Samuel
MacRae, William
Mahone, William
Peck, William Raine
Pendleton, William N.
Roberts, William Paul
Slaughter, James Edwin
Sorrel, Gilbert Moxley
Stevens, Walter Husted
Thomas, Edward Lloyd
Wofford, William Tatum
Wright, Ambrose Ransom "Rans"

JOSEPH P. REIDY
Howard University
Contraband
Labor
   An Overview
   Skilled Labor

OTIS K. RICE
West Virginia Institute of Technology
West Virginia
West Virginia Operations
   Operations of 1862 and 1863

J. V. RIDGELY
Emeritus, Columbia University
Literature
   The Confederacy in Literature

JAMES L. ROARK
Emory University
Planters

CHARLES ROBERTS
*California State University,
Sacramento*
Choctaws

JAMES I. ROBERTSON, JR.
*Virginia Polytechnic and State
University*
Armistead, Lewis A.
Barry, John Decatur
Big Bethel, Virginia
Bristoe Station, Virginia
Brothers of War
Civil War
Names of the War
Cloyds Mountain, Virginia
Colston, Raleigh Edward
Cooke, John Rogers
Davis, Joseph Robert
Echols, John
Field, Charles W.
Funerals
Garnett, Richard Brooke
Hampton's Legion
Hill, A. P.
Jackson, Thomas J. "Stonewall"
Jackson, William Lowther
"Mudwall"
Jones, Samuel
Jones, William Edmondson
"Grumble"
Jordan, Thomas
Kemper, James Lawson
Lead
Lomax, Lunsford Lindsay
Long, Armistead Lindsay
Northrop, Lucius B.
Paxton, Elisha Franklin
Ruggles, Daniel
Shenandoah Valley
Shenandoah Valley Campaign of
Jackson
Soldiers
Steuart, George Hume
Stonewall Brigade
Terrill, James Barbour
Terry, William
Trimble, Isaac
Virginia
Walker, James Alexander
Winder, Charles S.

WILLIAM GLENN ROBERTSON
*Combat Studies Institute, U.S. Army
Command and General Staff Col-
lege, Fort Leavenworth, Kansas*
Army
Army Departments

W. STITT ROBINSON
University of Kansas
Bleeding Kansas

WILLIAM WARREN ROGERS
Florida State University
Chilton, William P.

WILLIAM WARREN ROGERS, JR.
*Gainesville College
Montgomery, Alabama*

CHARLES P. ROLAND
*Emeritus, University of Ken-
tucky*
Johnston, Albert Sidney

R. B. ROSENBURG
*The Andrew Johnson Project, Tennes-
see Presidents Center, Knoxville,
Tennessee*
Atkins, J. D. C.
Cluskey, M. W.
Colyar, A. S.
Currin, David M.
DeWitt, William H.
Gardenhire, E. L.
Heiskell, J. B.
House, John F.
Jones, George Washington
Keeble, Edwin A.
McCallum, James
Menees, Thomas
Soldiers' Homes
Swan, William G.
Wright, John V.

DAVID R. RUTH
*Richmond National Battlefield Park,
Richmond, Virginia*
Chesnut, James

S

RICHARD A. SATTLER
*D'Arcy McNickle Center, Newberry
Library, Chicago*
Seminoles

WILLIAM K. SCARBOROUGH
University of Southern Mississippi
Overseers
Ruffin, Edmund

HERBERT M. SCHILLER
Winston-Salem, North Carolina
Health and Medicine
Sickness and Disease
Battle Injuries
Medical Treatments
Medical Training
Medical Department

LOUIS E. SCHMIER
Valdosta State College
Jews

THOMAS SCHOONOVER
*University of Southwestern
Louisiana*
Mexico
Monroe Doctrine
Nicaragua
Pickett, John T.

THOMAS E. SCHOTT
Oklahoma City, Oklahoma
Cornerstone Speech
Hampton Roads Conference
Montgomery Convention
Stephens, Alexander H.
Stephens, Linton
Vice Presidency

GLENNA R. SCHROEDER-LEIN
*The Andrew Johnson Project,
Tennessee Presidents Center,
Knoxville, Tennessee*
Beers, Fannie
Jones, Joseph
Moore, Samuel Preston
Niter and Mining Bureau
St. John, Isaac M.
Saltpeter
Stout, Samuel Hollingsworth

FREDERICK SCHULT
New York University
Anderson, Joseph R.
Fagan, James F.
North, James H.
Tredegar Iron Works

MARVIN SCHULTZ
Texas Christian University
Adams, Daniel Weisiger
Robertson, Felix Huston
Tucker, William Feimster

LARRY SCHWEIKART
University of Dayton
Banking
Shinplasters

LOREN SCHWENINGER
*University of North Carolina at
Greensboro*
Thirteenth Amendment

ANNE FIROR SCOTT
Duke University
Women

J. L. SCOTT
Salem, Virginia
McCausland, John
Piedmont, Virginia

RICHARD SELCER
Northlake College
Pickett, George E.
Terry, William Richard

GEORGE GREEN SHACKELFORD
*Emeritus, Virginia Polytechnic Institute
and State University*
Bledsoe, Albert T.
Randolph, George Wythe

ROYCE SHINGLETON
Darton College
Wood, John Taylor

EDWARD M. SHOEMAKER
Emory University Police
Savannah, Georgia
City of Savannah

NINA SILBER
Boston University
Frietchie, Barbara

JOEL H. SILBEY
Cornell University
Democratic Party

JASON H. SILVERMAN
Winthrop College
Foreigners
Germans
Irish
Northerners

KOHAVA SIMHI
Temple University
Magazines
De Bow's Review
Southern Illustrated News
Southern Literary Messenger
Northern Magazines in the South

RALPH B. SINGER, JR.
Piedmont College
Atlanta, Georgia
City of Atlanta
Macon, Georgia

J. CARLYLE SITTERSON
*University of North Carolina at
Chapel Hill*
Sugar

RAY SKATES
*Air War College, Maxwell Air Force
Base, Alabama*
Alcorn, James L.
Barksdale, Ethelbert
Barry, William Taylor Sullivan
Bradford, Alexander Blackburn
Brooke, Walker
Brown, Albert Gallatin
Campbell, Josiah A. Patterson
Chambers, Henry Cousins
Clark, Charles
Clayton, Alexander M.
Davis, Reuben
Harris, Wiley Pope
Harrison, James Thomas
Holder, William Dunbar

Humphreys, Benjamin Grubb
Jackson, Mississippi
Battle of Jackson
Lamar, L. Q. C.
Lamkin, John Tillman
Leon, Edwin de
McRae, John Jones
Meridian Campaign
Mississippi
Orr, Jehu Amaziah
Pettus, J. J.
Phelan, James
Singleton, Otho Robards
Tupelo, Mississippi
Watson, John W. C.
Welch, Israel Victor
Wilson, William Sydney

JENNIFER LUND SMITH
University of Georgia
Anderson, Samuel Read
Bentonville, North Carolina
Cantey, James
Conscription
Dunovant, John
Fort Harrison, Virginia
Gordon, James Byron
Jackson, Alfred Eugene
Kelly's Ford, Virginia
Logan, Thomas Muldrup
Mine Run Campaign
Preston, John Smith
Reynolds, Daniel Harris
Yellow Tavern, Virginia

JOHN DAVID SMITH
North Carolina State University
Bradley, Benjamin Franklin
Bruce, Eli M.
Bruce, Horatio Washington
Burnett, Henry C.
Burnett, Theodore Legrand
Chrisman, James Stone
Crockett, John Watkins
Elliott, John Milton
Ewing, George Washington
Ford, Samuel Howard
Johnson, Thomas
Machen, Willis Benson
Monroe, Thomas Bell
Moore, James William

Read, Henry English
Simms, William E.
Thomas, John J.
Triplett, George Washington
White, Daniel Price

JAMES M. SORELLE
Baylor University
Juneteenth

CHARLES M. SPEARMAN
*Chickamauga and Chattanooga
   National Military Park, Lookout
   Mountain, Tennessee*
Crittenden, George B.
Donelson, Daniel Smith
Murfreesboro, Tennessee
Vance, Robert Brank
Withers, Jones Mitchell

WARREN F. SPENCER
Emeritus, University of Georgia
Laird Shipyards
Semmes, Raphael
Stonewall
Sumter

DONNA J. SPINDEL
Marshall University
Crime and Punishment

C. VAUGHAN STANLEY
*Jessie Ball duPont Memorial Library,
   Stratford Plantation, Stratford,
   Virginia*
Lee Memorial Association

ROY R. STEPHENSON
Galveston College
Armstrong, Frank Crawford
Bagby, Arthur P.
DeBray, Xavier B.
Gordon, B. Frank
Jackman, Sidney D.
King, William H.
Lane, Walter Paye
Lewis, Levin M.
Little, Lewis Henry
Maclay, Robert P.
Nelson, Allison
Parsons, Mosby Monroe
Randal, Horace
Reynolds, Alexander Welch

Sears, Claudius Wistar
Tappan, James Camp
Terrell, Alexander W.
Tilghman, Lloyd

JOSEPH M. STETAR
Seton Hall University
Education
   Higher Education

PETER C. STEWART
Old Dominion University
Norfolk, Virginia

KENNETH L. STILES
Centreville, Virginia
Buckland Mills, Virginia
Cavalry
Chambersburg, Pennsylvania
Martin, James Green
Payne, William Henry Fitzhugh
Robertson, Beverly Holcombe
Sanders, John Caldwell Calhoun
Walker, William
Wallace, William Henry
Wickham, Williams Carter

WILLIAM N. STILL, JR.
East Carolina University
Arkansas
Brown, Isaac Newton
Enchantress Affair
Jones, Catesby
Nashville
Navy
   Confederate Navy
Savannah Squadron
Tattnall, Josiah

ALEXANDER R. STOESEN
Guilford College
Greensboro, North Carolina

JOHN F. STOVER
Emeritus, Purdue University
Railroads

DAVID M. SULLIVAN
*Marine Corps Association, Quantico,
   Virginia*
Marine Corps

DANIEL E. SUTHERLAND
*University of Arkansas at
   Fayetteville*
Plain Folk

GUY R. SWANSON
*Museum of the Confederacy, Richmond,
   Virginia*
Museums and Archives

CRAIG L. SYMONDS
U.S. Naval Academy
Atlanta, Georgia
   Atlanta Campaign
Bummers
Parker, William

T

MICHAEL TADMAN
University of Liverpool, England
Slave Traders

DEAN S. THOMAS
*Thomas Publications, Gettysburg,
   Pennsylvania*
Small Arms
   Munitions

EMORY M. THOMAS
University of Georgia
Bibliography and Historiography
Lee, George Washington Custis
Lee, Robert E.
Lee, William Henry Fitzhugh
Patent Office
Stuart, J. E. B.
Toombs, Robert

JERRY BRUCE THOMAS
Shepherd College
Hotchkiss, Jedediah
Peirpoint, Francis H.

JERRY THOMPSON
Laredo State University
Baylor, John R.
Benavides, Santos
Sibley, Henry Hopkins

WILLIAM A. TIDWELL
   MITRE Corporation, Fairfax, Virginia
   Espionage
      Confederate Secret Service
      Confederate Military Spies

LARRY E. TISE
   Benjamin Franklin National Memorial,
      Philadelphia
   Antislavery
   Fitzhugh, George
   Proslavery

EDGAR A. TOPPIN
   Virginia State University
   African Americans in the Confederacy
   Rillieux, Norbert

BLAKE TOUCHSTONE
   Tulane University
   Civil Liberties
   Shepley, George F.

JOSEPH G. TREGLE, JR.
   Emeritus, University of New Orleans
   Beauregard, P. G. T.
   Creoles
   Slidell, John

SPENCER C. TUCKER
   Texas Christian University
   Arms, Weapons, and Ammunition
      Naval Ordnance
   Brooke, John M.
   Naval Guns
      Confederate Naval Guns
      Captured U.S. Naval Guns
      European Naval Guns

MAXINE TURNER
   Georgia Institute of Technology
   Davids
   Davidson, Hunter
   Gift, George W.
   Lynch, William F.
   Randolph, Victor M.
   River Defense Fleet
   Rousseau, Lawrence
   Scharf, John Thomas
   Submarines
   Torpedoes and Mines
   Warley, Alexander Frazier

LYON G. TYLER
   The Citadel
   Washington Peace Conference

V

DAVID L. VALUSKA
   Kutztown University
   Navy
      Manpower
      African Americans in the
         Confederate Navy

FRANK E. VANDIVER
   The Mosher Institute of Defense
      Studies, Texas A&M University
   Arsenals and Armories
   Davis, Jefferson
   Gorgas, Josiah
   Ordnance Bureau
   Presidency

ELIZABETH R. VARON
   Wellesley College
   Baxley, Catherine Virginia
   Boyd, Belle
   Ford, Antonia
   Greenhow, Rose O'Neal
   Moon Sisters
   Morris, Augusta Hewitt
   Slater, Sarah
   Van Lew, Elizabeth

W

JON L. WAKELYN
   Catholic University
   Chaplains
   Episcopal Church
   Religion
   Roman Catholic Church

LEE A. WALLACE, JR.
   Falls Church, Virginia
   Cooke, John Esten
   Corse, Montgomery Dent
   Pryor, Roger A.
   Weisiger, David Addison

PETER WALLENSTEIN
   Virginia Polytechnic Institute and State
      University
   Arizona
   Army
      African Americans in the Confederate Army
   New Mexico
   Produce Loan
   Staples, Waller R.
   Taxation

BEVERLY WATKINS
   National Archives, Great Lakes Region,
      Chicago
   Garland, Augustus Hill

GORDON WATTS
   East Carolina University
   Advance
   Alabama
   Alabama Claims
   Great Britain
   Trent Affair
   Wilkinson, John

ROSS A. WEBB
   Winthrop College
   Paducah, Kentucky

MARLI F. WEINER
   University of Maine at Orono
   Memorial Organizations

DAVID P. WERLICH
   Southern Illinois University
   Patrick Henry
   Tucker, John Randolph

JEFFRY D. WERT
   Centre Hall, Pennsylvania
   Mosby, John S.
   Mosby's Rangers

LEEANN WHITES
   University of Missouri at Columbia
   Clay-Clopton, Virginia

SARAH WOOLFOLK WIGGINS
   Southern Center for History and
      Culture, University of Alabama in
      Tuscaloosa
   Clopton, David
   Cruikshank, Marcus H.

Dargan, E. S.
Dickinson, James Shelton
Fearn, Thomas
Foster, Thomas J.
Hale, Stephen Fowler
Jones, Henry Cox
Lyon, Francis Strother
Moore, Andrew B.
Ralls, John Perkins
Robinson, Cornelius
Walker, Richard Wilde

WARREN WILKINSON
Acworth, Georgia
Anderson, James Patton
Chattanooga, Tennessee
   Chattanooga Campaign
Dalton, Georgia
Frazer, John Wesley
Garnett, Robert S.
Knoxville Campaign
Munfordville, Kentucky
West Virginia Operations
   Operations of 1861
Wise, Henry A.

BRIAN S. WILLS
Clinch Valley College
Adams, William Wirt
Bell, Tyree Harris
Brice's Cross Roads, Mississippi
Buford, Abraham
Burnside's Expedition to North
   Carolina
Chalmers, James Ronald
Dibrell, George Gibbs
Drewry's Bluff, Virginia
Forrest, Nathan Bedford
Forrest's Raids
Fort Pillow Massacre
Frayser's Farm, Virginia
Gatlin, Richard Caswell
Gholson, Samuel Jameson

Griffith, Richard
Joe Brown's Pikes
Lyon, Hylan Benton
Malvern Hill, Virginia
Mechanicsville, Virginia
Moody, Young Marshall
Perry, Edward Aylesworth
Port Royal, South Carolina
Richardson, Robert Vinkler
Roddey, Philip Dale
Selma, Alabama
   Wilson's Raid on Selma
Seven Days' Battles
Whitfield, John Wilkins
Williamsburg, Virginia
Yorktown, Virginia

CHARLES REAGAN WILSON
University of Mississippi
Death and Mourning

TERRY P. WILSON
University of California, Berkeley
Boudinot, Elias C.
Callahan, Samuel Benton
Jones, Robert McDonald
Osages

TERRENCE J. WINSCHEL
Vicksburg National Military Park,
   Vicksburg, Mississippi
Port Gibson, Mississippi

STEPHEN R. WISE
University of South Carolina
Anglo-Confederate Purchasing
   Anglo-Confederate Trading Company
Blockade
   Blockade Running
   Blockade Runners
Lamar, Gazaway B.
Wilmington, North Carolina
Wood, Fernando

CHARLES K. WOLFE
Middle Tennessee State University
Discography
Dixie
Music

JOHN R. WOODARD
Z. Smith Reynolds Library, Wake
   Forest University
Baker, Alpheus
Daniel, Junius
Elliot, Stephen, Jr.
Gartrell, Lucius Jeremiah
Lewis, William Gaston
Sharp, Jacob Hunter

STEVEN E. WOODWORTH
Toccoa Falls College
Belmont, Missouri
Johnson, Waldo
Snead, Thomas L.
Taylor, Richard
Vest, George G.

RALPH A. WOOSTER
Lamar University
Declaration of Immediate Causes

BERTRAM WYATT-BROWN
University of Florida
Dorsey, Sarah Anne
Honor

Y

W. BUCK YEARNS
Emeritus, Wake Forest University
Citizenship
Congress
Currency
   Congressional Money Bills
Governors

Alphabetical List of Entries

Abbreviations and Symbols Used in This Work

A.D. *anno Domini*, in the year of the (our) Lord
Adj. Gen. adjutant general
Adm. admiral
Ala. Alabama
A.M. *ante meridiem*, before noon
Ariz. Arizona
Ark. Arkansas
b. born; beam (interior measurement of width of a ship)
B.C. before Christ
brig. brigade
Brig. Gen. brigadier general
c. *circa*, about, approximately
Calif. California
Capt. captain
cf. *confer*, compare
chap. chapter (pl., chaps.)
cm centimeters
Col. colonel
Colo. Colorado
Comdr. commander
Como. commodore
Conn. Connecticut
Cpl. corporal
C.S. Confederate States
C.S.A. Confederate States of America, Confederate States Army
CSS Confederate States ship
cwt. hundredweight (equals 772 lbs.)
d. died
D.C. District of Columbia
Del. Delaware
diss. dissertation

div. division
dph. depth of hold
ed. editor (pl., eds.); edition; edited by
e.g. *exempli gratia*, for example
Eng. England
enl. enlarged
Ens. ensign
esp. especially
et al. *et alii*, and others
etc. *et cetera*, and so forth
exp. expanded
f. and following (pl., ff.)
1st Lt. first lieutenant
fl. *floruit*, flourished
Fla. Florida
frag. fragment
ft. feet
Ga. Georgia
Gen. general
Gov. governor
HMS Her Majesty's ship
ibid. *ibidem*, in the same place (as the one immediately preceding)
i.e. *id est*, that is
Ill. Illinois
Ind. Indiana
Kans. Kansas
km kilometers
Ky. Kentucky
l. length
La. Louisiana
lb. pound (pl., lbs.)
Lt. lieutenant
Lt. Col. lieutenant colonel

Lt. Comdr. lieutenant commander
Lt. Gen. lieutenant general
m meters
M.A. Master of Arts
Maj. Major
Maj. Gen. major general
Mass. Massachusetts
mi. miles
Mich. Michigan
Minn. Minnesota
Miss. Mississippi
Mo. Missouri
Mont. Montana
n. note
N.C. North Carolina
n.d. no date
N.Dak. North Dakota
Neb. Nebraska
Nev. Nevada
N.H. New Hampshire
N.J. New Jersey
N.Mex. New Mexico
no. number (pl., nos.)
n.p. no place
n.s. new series
N.Y. New York
Okla. Oklahoma
Oreg. Oregon
p. page (pl., pp.)
Pa. Pennsylvania
pdr. pounder (weight of projec tile in pounds; pl., pdrs.)
pl. plural, plate (pl., pls.)
P.M. *post meridiem*, after noon
Pres. president
pt. part (pl., pts.)

Pvt. private
r. reigned; ruled; river
Rear Adm. rear admiral
regt. regiment
Rep. representative
rev. revised
R.I. Rhode Island
S.C. South Carolina
S.Dak. South Dakota
sec. section (pl., secs.)
2d Lt. second lieutenant
Sen. senator
ser. series
Sgt. sergeant
sing. singular
sq. square
supp. supplement; supplementary
Tenn. Tennessee
Tex. Texas
trans. translator, translators; translated by; translation
U.S. United States
USS United States ship
Va. Virginia
var. variant; variation
vol. volume (pl., vols.)
Vt. Vermont
Wash. Washington
Wis. Wisconsin
W.Va. West Virginia
Wyo. Wyoming
° degrees
' feet; minutes
" inches; seconds
£ pounds
? uncertain; possibly; perhaps

Key to Map Symbols

Symbol	Description	Symbol	Description
	Troops, Confederate		Trees
	Troops, Union		Marsh
	Cavalry, Confederate		Elevation
	Cavalry, Union		River
	Tactical Movement, Confederate		Railroad
	Tactical Movement, Union		Unfinished Railroad
	Strategic Movement, Confedederate		Road
	Strategic Movement, Union		State Boundary
	Retreat		
	Engagement		Building
	Artillery		Church
	Encampment		Village
	Headquarters		Town, Strategic
	Fortifications		Town, Tactical
	Entrenchments		Pontoon Bridge
			Bridge
	Casemate Ironclad		
	Gunboat		
	Monitor		
	Warship		

Encyclopedia
of the
Confederacy

ADAMS, DANIEL WEISIGER (1821–1872), brigadier general. Born in May or June 1821, in Frankfort, Kentucky, Adams moved with his family to Mississippi in 1825. A brother of Gen. William Wirt Adams, he graduated from the University of Virginia and practiced law in Natchez. In 1843, he killed an editor in a duel over criticism of Adams's father. Adams served as state senator in 1852, but after one term he moved to New Orleans where, during the secession crisis, Governor Thomas O. Moore appointed him to a committee to prepare for war.

Adams volunteered as a lieutenant colonel in 1861, serving at Pensacola and Mobile. By April 1862, he commanded the First Louisiana Infantry, and at Shiloh, where he was blinded in his right eye, he assumed command of the First Brigade. Promoted to brigadier general on May 23, 1862, he led the Second Louisiana Brigade at Perryville. Adams fought with William J. Hardee's corps at Murfreesboro, where he suffered another wound. While serving as a brigade commander at Chickamauga, he was wounded again and captured by Union forces. After exchange, Adams led a cavalry brigade in northern Alabama and Mississippi, assuming command of the District of Central Alabama on September 24, 1864. In March, he took over all Confederate units in northern Alabama, leading troops at Selma on April 2 and at Montgomery on April 16. He was paroled at Meridian, Mississippi, on May 9, 1865.

Adams died in New Orleans on June 13, 1872, and was buried in Jackson, Mississippi.

BIBLIOGRAPHY

Connelly, Thomas L. *Army of the Heartland: The Army of Tennessee, 1861–1862*. Baton Rouge, La., 1967.
Connelly, Thomas L. *Autumn of Glory: The Army of Tennessee, 1862–1865*. Baton Rouge, La., 1971.
Spencer, James, comp. *Civil War Generals: Categorical Listings and a Biographical Directory*. New York, 1986.
Wakelyn, Jon L. *Biographical Dictionary of the Confederacy*. Edited by Frank E. Vandiver. Westport, Conn., 1977.
Warner, Ezra J. *Generals in Gray: Lives of the Confederate Commanders*. Baton Rouge, La., 1959.

MARVIN SCHULTZ

ADAMS, JOHN (1825–1864), brigadier general. Adams, born in Nashville, Tennessee, on July 1, 1825, was reared at Pulaski. Upon graduation from West Point in 1845 he was commissioned a second lieutenant of the First Dragoons, served in the Mexican War, and was brevetted for gallantry at the Battle of Santa Cruz de Rosales. Afterward he continued his service on the Indian frontier, rising to the rank of captain.

At the outbreak of the Civil War Adams was stationed at Fort Crook, California. Resigning his commission, he sailed for New York City, where he was ordered arrested. He escaped to Tennessee, however, and was appointed captain of cavalry in the Confederate army and given command of troops at Memphis, Tennessee. He was promoted to colonel on May 27, 1862, and acting brigadier general the same month; the rank became permanent on December 29. On May 16, 1863, he assumed command of Tilghman's brigade of six Mississippi infantry regiments and was assigned to the Army of Tennessee; he commanded the Fourth Military District, Department of Mississippi and East Louisiana.

Adams led his troops into action at Vicksburg; at Jackson, Mississippi; in opposition to William Tecumseh Sherman's Meridian campaign; in the Atlanta campaign; and in the invasion of middle Tennessee. After the Battle of Atlanta he served with John Bell Hood's army and took part in the

JOHN ADAMS.   LIBRARY OF CONGRESS

Battle of Franklin on November 30, 1864. Wounded early in the fighting, Adams continued to lead his troops in assaults against the Federal lines until he was killed. He is buried at Pulaski, Tennessee.

BIBLIOGRAPHY

Evans, Clement A., ed. *Confederate Military History*. 12 vols. Atlanta, 1899. Extended ed. in 19 vols. Wilmington, N.C., 1987–1989.

Johnson, Robert U., and C. C. Buel, eds. *Battles and Leaders of the Civil War*. 4 vols. New York, 1887–1888. Reprint, Secaucus, N.J., 1982.

Warner, Ezra J. *Generals in Gray: Lives of the Confederate Commanders*. Baton Rouge, La., 1959.

PAUL F. LAMBERT

ADAMS, WILLIAM WIRT (1819–1888), brigadier general. Adams was born in Frankfort, Kentucky, on March 22, 1819. His brother, Daniel Weisiger Adams, also became a Confederate general. Educated and reared in Kentucky, William left to join the army of the Republic of Texas in 1839. He became adjutant of his regiment and served against the Indians in Texas. Subsequently, Adams returned to become a planter and banker in Mississippi. He served as a member of the state legislature in 1858 and 1860.

Following the secession of Mississippi, Adams acted as commissioner from that state to Louisiana, successfully encouraging the latter's secession from the Union. With the formation of the government of the Confederate States of America, President Jefferson Davis offered him the office of postmaster general, but he declined, preferring to serve in the military.

Adams then raised the First Mississippi Cavalry and became the regiment's colonel. The unit saw primarily independent service as pickets and scouts for the first year of the war but served as the rear guard in Gen. Albert Sidney Johnston's retreat from Kentucky. It fought at Shiloh in April 1862 and at Iuka under Maj. Gen. Sterling Price. Subsequently, Adams's performance against Union Maj. Gen. William Tecumseh Sherman's forces in their advance on Jackson, Mississippi, following the surrender of Vicksburg, earned him a promotion to brigadier general to date from September 25, 1863. Toward the end of 1864, his brigade was attached to Maj. Gen. Nathan Bedford Forrest's cavalry command, with which it served until the end of the war. Adams surrendered his men on May 4, 1865, receiving his parole eight days later.

Following the war, Adams lived at Vicksburg and Jackson. He served as state revenue agent from 1880 to 1885, when he resigned to accept President Grover Cleveland's appointment as postmaster at Jackson. On May 1, 1888, he died in a street fight with a Jackson newspaper editor who had publicly criticized him.

BIBLIOGRAPHY

Henry, Robert Selph. *"First with the Most" Forrest*. Indianapolis, 1944.

Johnson, Allen, and Dumas Malone, eds. *Dictionary of American Biography*. New York, 1937–1964.

Warner, Ezra J. *Generals in Gray: Lives of the Confederate Commanders*. Baton Rouge, La., 1959.

Wyeth, John Allan. *Life of General Nathan Bedford Forrest*. New York, 1899. Reprint, Baton Rouge, La., 1989.

BRIAN S. WILLS

ADVANCE. Like many of the steam-powered blockade runners that maintained the Confederacy's foreign commerce, the *Advance,* had been designed and built for the British packet service. Both the steamer's hull and machinery had been constructed by the celebrated Glasgow shipbuilding firm of Caird and Company for the Dublin and Glasgow Sailing and Steam Packet Company. Constructed of iron, the hull was 236 feet in length and 26 feet in beam. Two oscillating steam cylinders of 63-inch bore and 78-inch stroke provided power for paddlewheels 30 feet in diameter. The vessel was launched as *Lord Clyde* on July 2, 1862, and after highly successful trial runs in October 1862 was placed in service between Dublin and Glasgow. Although quite

ADVANCE.

successful, *Lord Clyde* was sold after six months to John Key of County Kirkcaldy, Scotland, and immediately transferred discreetly to the state of North Carolina. John White, a special commissioner appointed by North Carolina Governor Zebulon B. Vance, paid $170,972 for the ship and such refitting as was necessary to accomplish a transatlantic passage and make the vessel serviceable as a blockade runner.

After departing from Great Britain with a cargo of military supplies purchased for the state of North Carolina by John White, *Advance* (or A. D. Vance, rechristened for a pun on the name of North Carolina's governor) coaled in Nassau and ran through the Union blockade into Wilmington. Between June 1863 and September 1864 *Advance* made seventeen successful runs through the blockade. On an inbound voyage in October 1863 the ship carried 1,700 heavy blankets, 2,000 pairs of shoes, 5,000 pairs of socks, 30,000 yards of flannel, 96 dozen wool and cotton cards, and bagging and cord for baling cotton. Other shipments included tools, weapons, and food. When finally captured by USS *Santiago de Cuba* on September 10, 1864, *Advance* was outbound from Wilmington with a typical cargo of cotton and turpentine.

After being taken to Boston, *Advance* was condemned by a U.S. prize court and its cargo auctioned. The vessel was sold for $120,000 to the U.S. Navy and dispatched to the North Atlantic Blockade Squadron. USS *Advance* arrived off the Southern coast too late in the war to play a significant role in enforcing the blockade, but the vessel remained in the U.S. Navy for almost two decades as USS *Frolic*. In 1883, J. P. Agnew of Alexandria, Virginia, purchased the ship for $11,500 and two years later resold it for service in South America.

BIBLIOGRAPHY

Bradlee, Francis B. *Blockade Running during the Civil War and the Effect of Land and Water Transportation on the Confederacy.* Philadelphia, Pa., 1974.

Cochran, Hamilton. *Blockade Runners of the Confederacy.* Westport, Conn., 1958.

Silverston, Paul H. *Warships of the Civil War Navies.* Annapolis, Md., 1989.

Wise, Stephen R. *Lifeline of the Confederacy: Blockade Running during the Civil War.* Columbia, S.C., 1988.

GORDON WATTS

AFRICAN AMERICAN FORGEWORKERS.

Critically important to the Confederate war effort, African Americans often comprised half or more of the labor force of a given foundry. Furnaces were located in Virginia, eastern Tennessee, central Alabama, and northern Georgia. Principal manufacturers were located in Norfolk, Richmond, Charlotte, Fayetteville, Charleston, Columbia, Macon, Atlanta, Columbus, Selma, New Orleans, and Memphis. Available records and research permit no comprehensive statements for all establishments, but known situations in a number of specific firms provide representative pictures.

When the Civil War began, the Tredegar Iron Works of Richmond, Virginia, the South's preeminent iron manufacturer, employed 900 workers, of whom about 100 were slaves. As Northern and immigrant laborers left and native white workers enlisted for military service, the number of slaves in the work force increased. By 1864, blacks held over half of all Tredegar's 2,500 jobs. Many were laborers in mines and charcoal pits, but many also held more skilled positions in the rolling mill and blacksmith shops.

The Shelby Iron Company in central Alabama employed 350 to 400 slaves throughout the war, some three-fourths of their total force. They performed service in all aspects of work, with 70 to 100 employed in skilled positions.

Near the end of the war, Secretary of the Navy Stephen R. Mallory reported to Jefferson Davis that he needed 677 black workers and 675 white workers in his ordnance and machinery works at Richmond, Augusta, Charlotte, and Selma. This ratio of black to white workers appears in the records of other firms as well.

BIBLIOGRAPHY

Dew, Charles B. *Iron Maker to the Confederacy: Joseph R. Anderson and the Tredegar Iron Works.* New Haven, 1966.
Starobin, Robert S. *Industrial Slavery in the Old South.* New York, 1970.

ROBERT H. McKENZIE

AFRICAN AMERICANS IN THE CONFEDERACY.

More than a third of the population of the Confederate States of America was African American. The 9.1 million people living in the eleven future Confederate states as of 1860 consisted of 5.5 million whites and 3.6 million blacks. Of the latter, approximately 3.5 million were slaves. During the Civil War, these blacks played an important role in keeping the Confederate war machine functioning. The Confederacy was dealt a heavy blow, therefore, when President Abraham Lincoln's Emancipation Proclamation impelled at least half a million and perhaps as many as a million of the Confederate blacks to flee their posts in order to follow or serve with the Union forces.

Following the firing on Fort Sumter and Lincoln's call to arms in April 1861, some Southern free blacks rallied to the cause of their region. Historian Emory Thomas has written that "during 1861 several groups of free black Southerners offered themselves as soldiers to the Confederate War Department, and although the War Office rejected each of these applications, some blacks did serve in the Southern armies." In Louisiana, some well-to-do African Americans from New Orleans were allowed to form regiments of free blacks who served as home guards. Their function was to protect their state against invaders. In the light of subsequent developments—emancipation and the antislavery crusade into which the war turned—it seems strange that some Southern blacks volunteered to aid the bastion of slavery. Most were caught up, however, in the general Southern view of Northerners as aggressively bent on imposing their materialistic way of life on the South. Moreover, the president, the U.S. Congress, and the Republican party declared vigorously at the beginning of the war that the North's sole aim was to preserve the Union and that there was no intention to disrupt slavery where it existed.

Although the Union had twice as many states and people as the South and far more naval, financial, and industrial resources, the Confederacy had better generals at the outset and was fighting a defensive war on home ground with soldiers accustomed to hunting, riding, and outdoor life. Alongside these strong points of the Confederacy should be placed the value of its black population, only 3 percent of which was free. (In contrast, in the five border slave states on the Union side—Delaware, Maryland, Kentucky, Missouri, and later West Virginia—the 150,000 free blacks constituted 25 percent of the black population of 591,000. Baltimore alone had nearly 26,000 free blacks, more than any other city North or South.) In the North, all 238,000 blacks listed in the 1860 census were free persons, since slavery had ceased north of the Mason-Dixon line and the Ohio River. Often overlooked is the importance to the Confederacy of having 3.4 million persons who could be forcibly mobilized for the war effort. They were used in two ways: first, as military laborers, freeing white males to fight, and second, as workers on the home front.

Blacks as Military Laborers. The Confederate armies were greatly aided by the use of blacks, especially slaves, as military laborers. The historian Bell I. Wiley has written that

> much of the hard work entailed by military activities of the Confederacy was performed by Negroes. The aversion of the white soldier to menial tasks was one reason for this, but it was not the only one. Conservation of white man-power for fighting purposes was an appreciable factor. Every [black] wielding a shovel released a [white] for the ranks.

Southern blacks loaded, transported, and unloaded supplies. They dug trenches, built roads, erected barricades, constructed fortifications, repaired and built railroads, bridges, trestles, and tunnels, and cooked and served food. Some troops raised money to hire black cooks, and in 1862 the Confederate Congress enacted a law authorizing four black cooks per company, to be paid fifteen dollars a month if free and used with their master's permission if slave. Blacks washed uniforms, shined boots, mended clothes and tents, moved ordnance, and generally did much of the drudgery for the armed forces. Wiley points to the use of blacks "as teamsters, many of whom were expert from prior plantation experience," and adds that "slaves and free Negroes were employed as hospital attendants, ambulance drivers, and stretcher bearers." In contrast, far more Union army soldiers were tied down in such tasks, since the Union did not have a large pool of free black labor to take over these noncombat duties.

SLAVE FAMILY.   Timothy O'Sullivan photographed the five generations of this family on J. J. Smith's plantation near Beaufort, South Carolina, in 1862. The plantation was part of the early Federal Reconstruction experiments at Port Royal and was occupied as a campsite by the First South Carolina Colored Volunteers, an African American unit led by Col. Thomas Wentworth Higginson. O'Sullivan's various depictions of slaves were included in a display of Civil War scenes at Alexander Gardner's gallery in Washington, D.C., in September 1863.

LIBRARY OF CONGRESS

Blacks' Work on the Home Front. African Americans in the Confederacy were also essential as workers throughout the economy. Plantations continued to function under the supervision of the mistress of the house when masters, sons, overseers, and neighbors enlisted. Even though overseers supervising twenty or more slaves were exempted from the draft in 1862, many plantations and smaller farms functioned without the presence of any white males to supervise the slaves' labor.

Blacks manned the factories of the Confederacy, too, such as the Tredegar Iron Works in Richmond, the South's leading manufacturer and a crucial cog in turning out Confederate war goods. Historian James H. Brewer says that this firm "at the peak of its productivity . . . employed over 1,200 Negroes, free and slave, and 1,200 whites. Negro

manpower enabled this plant to fulfill vital contracts with the various bureaus of the War Department." As the war continued, the plant became increasingly dependent on blacks, who were "engaged in highly skilled tasks previously performed almost exclusively by white technicians."

Slave-Master Relations. These wartime experiences affected the relationships of slaves and masters. When large numbers of slaves were pulled from plantations and urban households to work as military laborers or in arms production, subtle changes developed in how they viewed themselves. Their sense of self-esteem and relative freedom inevitably increased as they fulfilled important duties under new circumstances. Their newfound attitude of self-confidence did not escape the notice of whites, who worried about the consequences. According to historian Joseph

Reidy, slavemasters objected to slaves being employed in ways other than as field hands and house servants. To have them taken over by governmental and military authorities for other uses in the war effort tended, they thought, to undermine the institution of slavery.

Objections were made to use of slaves as mechanics in work outside of the plantation. The trouble, according to one observer, was that slaves were brought "into habitual contact with white men, beyond those to whom they owe obedience. It is at the hazard of themselves and of society when this occurs." Others nevertheless saw the need to utilize slaves in any fashion necessary to save the Confederacy, since President Lincoln seemed increasingly determined to free them and use them against the South.

The dislocations caused by the war also had an impact on slave-master relations. For example, the flight of coastal plantation owners inland with their entire plantations temporarily saved them from the invading Union armies, but the uprooting of the plantation made it almost impossible physically and psychologically to retain the traditional patterns. As historian Clarence Mohr has written, "the entire refugee process served to undermine the traditional authority structure of previously autonomous and self-contained plantation units."

Blacks as Soldiers. As in the Confederacy, free blacks in the Union volunteered to serve at the start of the war, hoping to strike a blow at slavery. But since the Lincoln administration had five border slave states on the Union's side (Virginia's western counties seceded from that state in 1861 and became West Virginia in 1863), it could not initially make the conflict an antislavery war, nor did it especially want to. Hence, free blacks were turned away. But pressures by abolitionists, Congress, and generals, coupled with Union losses in the East, caused Lincoln to conclude, as he later recalled, that "things had gone on from bad to worse, until I felt that we must change our tactics, or lose the game. I now determined upon the emancipation policy." In a preliminary proclamation on September 22, 1862, and the final proclamation in 1863, he declared slaves in areas still in rebellion on January 1, 1863, to be free. He also urged slaves to flee their masters and serve in the Union armies.

The first unit of free Southern blacks accepted by the Union was the First Louisiana Native Guards, which entered the army on September 27, 1862, five days after the preliminary proclamation. Confederate defenders had fled when Union forces seized New Orleans on April 26, 1862, but the home guard regiments that had been formed by free blacks remained. Union Gen. Benjamin Butler was puzzled as to why they were fighting for the Confederacy, and their leaders explained that they volunteered so they could serve on their own terms in a dignified role rather than being impressed as military laborers and that they hoped to improve the standing of blacks and increase their chances for equality by serving alongside whites. With Federal forces occupying the city, they were willing to switch to the side more likely to end slavery.

As soon as he received word of Lincoln's proclamation, Butler enrolled this unit officially. Two other regiments entered in October and November 1862 as the Second and Third Louisiana Native Guards. These men were the first of what would become a torrent of Southern blacks, mostly former slaves, joining the Union army. Nearly 200,000 soldiers and sailors of African descent served in all, about 140,000 of them former slaves and the rest free blacks, mostly from the North. The first regiment of former slaves to enlist was the First South Carolina Volunteers. This regiment had been organized in April 1862 by Union Gen. David Hunter. He had done so contrary to the policy at that time of the Lincoln administration. Hunter commanded the Port Royal and Sea Islands area of the South Carolina and Georgia coast, which had been taken by Union forces in November 1861. Lacking authority and funds to pay or provision this regiment, Hunter had had to disband it in August, keeping together only Company A (about one hundred men) as a nucleus around which to rebuild the regiment when policy changed and authorization was forthcoming. During November 1862, Company A participated in a coastal raid in which they freed 155 slaves and killed or captured a dozen Confederate defenders. With Company A as a nucleus, the First South Carolina Volunteer Regiment was rebuilt and taken into the Union army in January 1863. Also joining that month was the First Kansas Colored Volunteers, a regiment made up primarily of runaway slaves congregated in Kansas.

Emancipation Policy. President Lincoln became increasingly convinced that emancipation was the key to victory. In August 1864, he noted that emancipation was "inducing the colored people to come bodily over from the rebel side to ours." Answering a suggestion that the emancipation policy should be abandoned as soon as the Union was victorious, Lincoln replied that blacks would desert the Union ranks and return to the Confederate side in the face of such betrayal. He pointed out: "Drive back to the support of the rebellion the physical force which the colored people now give and promise us, and neither the present nor any coming administration can save the Union. Take from us and give to the enemy the hundred and thirty, forty, or fifty thousand colored persons now serving us as soldiers, seamen, and laborers, and we can not longer maintain the contest." He told Judge Joseph Mills of Wisconsin that "no human power can subdue this rebellion without using the Emancipation lever as I have done. Freedom has given us the control of 200,000 able bodied men, born and raised on southern soil. It will give us more yet. Just so much has it subtracted from the strength of our enemies." And in September 1864 he wrote in a letter of the physical force represented by the African American soldiers: "Keep it and you can save the Union. Throw it away and the Union goes with it."

Lincoln's enthusiasm was not shared universally in the North. Some Union commanders were very pleased with the African American troops, but others had less regard for them. Early in the war, before the Emancipation Proclamation was issued, some Union generals—such as William S. Harney in Missouri, Don Carlos Buell in Tennessee, and George B. McClellan in Virginia—had enforced the Fugitive Slave Law and restored to their owners those slaves who escaped and made their way to the Union lines.

A different stance was taken by Gen. Benjamin Butler. When three runaway slaves came to Fort Monroe, along Virginia's southeastern coast at Hampton, on May 23, 1861, Butler questioned them closely and learned that they were field hands who were being employed along with other slaves to build fortifications for the Confederates. When a Southern major came on behalf of Col. Charles Mallory to reclaim the three runaways, Butler labeled them "contrabands of war," saying they were being used by the Confederate States as part of the war effort. Hence, he confiscated them and claimed them as property of the United States.

In August 1861 the U.S. Congress, seeing the value of drawing black labor from the Confederates, passed a law confiscating any property, including slaves, used in the Confederate war effort. In July 1862 Congress enacted another law freeing the slaves of masters who were "disloyal or treasonous" or bore arms against the United States. Lincoln's Emancipation Proclamation, issued by the commander in chief, struck yet another blow at slavery. Finally, the Thirteenth Amendment ending slavery was proposed by Congress early in 1865 and ratified by the states in December.

Treatment of Black Soldiers. Confederate reaction initially caused much hardship for black soldiers in the Union army. Authorities announced two somewhat contradictory policies concerning Union soldiers of African descent: first, that none would be allowed to surrender, meaning they would be killed on the field of combat; and second, that any free blacks captured would be sold into slavery in the Deep South. Both policies were abandoned before long, however, because of the consequences. Black soldiers, with no chance to surrender, fought to the death, even in hopeless situations, adding to Confederate casualties. And the Lincoln administration pledged to impose "hard labor" on one Confederate prisoner of war for every Union soldier sold into slavery.

Black soldiers in the Union army suffered other discrimination, also. They were paid less than their white counterparts until Congress equalized their pay in 1864, and they did not receive the bonuses, pensions, and support for dependents other troops did. Moreover, black soldiers served in segregated units under white officers; only one hundred African Americans were officers, mostly in the Louisiana Native Guard regiments or as chaplains or physicians. Nonetheless, they fought valiantly. Some 37,000 died in combat, a mortality rate 40 percent higher than for white Union soldiers.

Desertions by Southern Blacks. Naval forces, Union and Confederate, had integrated crews (not until World War I did the U.S. Navy become segregated). In the famous encounter between USS *Monitor* and CSS *Virginia* in March 1862, about one-third of the *Monitor*'s crew was black. African Americans, usually slaves, served on Confederate ships, too, both merchant and naval. Robert Smalls and his fellow slave crewmates on the Confederate vessel *Planter* took that steamship out of Charleston Harbor early one morning in May 1862 when its three white officers were ashore. In a well-planned escape, the crew members were joined by seven women and children, including two wives, one sister, and four youngsters. They steamed past the Confederate guns with Smalls wearing the captain's hat and waving as if he were the captain. Then they hastily ran up a flag of truce to keep the Union blockading ships from firing on them. *Planter,* which was an armed steamer used for dispatch and transportation purposes, was taken over by the U.S. Navy, along with its six guns.

Smalls's escape was spectacular, but many other slaves abandoned their masters in less dramatic ways. Most were inspired by the Emancipation Proclamation, but some fled to the Union lines before the proclamation was issued. Partly they were driven by Confederate actions, state and national, to force slaves and free blacks to contribute to the South's war effort. In Virginia, for example, the state legislature passed laws, such as those in October 1862 and February 1863, that required slave owners to furnish their bondsmen for military labor with compensation to the owners and also required free blacks to pay, along with whites, a poll tax to support the war. The tax on free blacks was set at sixty cents in February 1863 and then was increased to two dollars two months later, with slave owners required to pay ninety cents for every slave twelve years of age and older. Many free blacks resented having to pay a tax to support a war intended to keep their people in slavery.

Fears of slave uprisings and conspiracies permeated the South's white population, although later, it became a staple of Southern belief that the slaves had been loyal. True, most remained at their stations and worked as before, and there were only a few isolated cases of slaves attacking their masters. But about a million deserted to the Union side at the first opportune moment, usually when Northern troops reached their vicinity. This steady erosion, which began

UNION HOSPITAL AT NASHVILLE, TENNESSEE.   NATIONAL ARCHIVES

before the Emancipation Proclamation and swelled there-after, played a large role in weakening the Confederate side. The twin impact of drawing African Americans away from the Confederate side and of adding nearly 180,000 fresh troops to the war-weary Union ranks during the last two and a half years of the war helped tip the scales. At one point there were more black soldiers on the Union side than the total number of men able to engage actively in combat on the Confederate side. In addition, the emancipation policy persuaded England, France, and other European nations not to come to the aid of the Confederacy. This turn of events caused the Confederates to consider enlisting black soldiers and inaugurating a diplomatic approach based on ending slavery.

Arming Slaves as Soldiers in the South. As early as the summer of 1863, a council of Confederate officers had considered the question of arming slaves and enlisting them in the military but rejected the idea. During 1864, more talk of developing black soldiers to fight in the Confederate

ranks was heard. President Jefferson Davis opposed the plan in November 1864, but by March of the next year, he was converted to the proposal. While still believing that slavery was the best way for the two races to coexist in the South, Gen. Robert E. Lee said in January that if military necessity made it imperative to use black soldiers he would do so, though on the basis that any such troops would be set free and that slavery in time would have to be abandoned. Writing on February 18, Lee indicated his support of a bill in the Confederate House to arm and free 200,000 slaves: "I think the measure not only expedient but necessary. The enemy will certainly use them against us if he can get possession of them. . . . I think those who are employed should be freed. It would be neither just nor wise, in my opinion, to require them to serve as slaves."

Opposition to enlisting the slaves was strong. Gen. Howell Cobb, an ardent secessionist from Georgia, said that the proposal to make soldiers of our slaves is the most pernicious idea that has been suggested since the war began. . . . Use all the Negroes you can get for all purposes for which you need them but don't arm them. The day you make soldiers of them is the beginning of the end of the revolution. If slaves make good soldiers, our whole theory of slavery is wrong.

The Confederate Congress, after considerable debate, enacted a modified law on March 13, 1865, permitting the arming of 300,000 slaves as soldiers. The measure came too late. Lee surrendered to Ulysses S. Grant less than a month later at Appomattox on April 9. Meanwhile, a number of black units were formed and began drilling, but the war ended before they could be mustered in.

The decision to arm slaves virtually sounded the Southern death knell for slavery. The Confederate States had been founded on the idea that the institution was to be preserved forever, as Vice President Alexander H. Stephens had asserted at his inauguration. Now the Confederacy in 1865 was moving to abandon the practice. Confederate envoys James Mason and John Slidell made approaches to the British and French governments, respectively, in early 1865 indicating the South's readiness to abandon slavery in exchange for help. The Confederacy's last desperate moves—arming the bondsmen and offering to end slavery—are indicative of the importance of blacks in the Southern nation.

[See also African American Forgeworkers; African American Troops in the Union Army; Army, article on African Americans in the Confederate Army; Contraband; Emancipation Proclamation; Free People of Color; Labor; Miscegenation; Navy, article on African Americans in the Confederate Navy; Slavery.]

BIBLIOGRAPHY

Brewer, James H. The Confederate Negro: Virginia's Craftsmen and Military Laborers, 1861–1865. Durham, N.C., 1969.

Mohr, Clarence L. On the Threshold of Freedom: Masters and Slaves in Civil War Georgia. Athens, Ga., 1986.

Quarles, Benjamin. The Negro in the Civil War. Boston, 1953.

Reidy, Joseph. From Slavery to Agrarian Capitalism in the Cotton Plantation South: Central Georgia, 1800–1880. Chapel Hill, N.C., 1992.

Spraggins, Tinsley Lee. "Mobilization of Negro Labor for the Department of Virginia and North Carolina, 1861–1865." North Carolina Historical Review 24 (April 1947): 160–197.

Stephenson, Nathaniel W. "The Question of Arming the Slaves." American Historical Review 18 (January 1913): 295–308.

Thomas, Emory M. The Confederate Nation, 1861–1865. New York, 1979.

Toppin, Edgar. The Black American in United States History. Boston, 1973.

Wesley, Charles H. "The Employment of Negroes as Soldiers in the Confederate Army." Journal of Negro History 4 (July 1919): 239–253.

Wiley, Bell I. Southern Negroes, 1861–1865. New Haven, 1938.

Wish, Harvey. "Slave Disloyalty under the Confederacy." Journal of Negro History 23 (October 1938): 435–450.

EDGAR A. TOPPIN

AFRICAN AMERICAN TROOPS IN THE UNION ARMY.

Jefferson Davis condemned Abraham Lincoln's Emancipation Proclamation as "the most execrable measure recorded in the history of guilty man." In that proclamation Lincoln had finally authorized the use of black soldiers by the Union. This, "the enlistment of black soldiers to fight and kill their former masters," concludes historian James M. McPherson, "was by far the most revolutionary dimension of the emancipation policy." That revolution had been a long time coming.

Lincoln's primary war aim was the preservation of the Union; his War Department had consistently rejected black offers of military service, and commanders of the first blue columns marching south in 1861 were careful to offer civil authorities aid in putting down slave insurrections "with an iron hand" and in returning fugitive slaves to their masters. This stirred Northern indignation with the result that the U.S. Congress, in March 1862, enacted a new article of war prohibiting the return of fugitives by army officers. Increasingly antislavery in disposition, the Congress in April provided compensated emancipation for slaves in the District of Columbia and in May prohibited slavery in all U.S. territories. Two months later, on July 17, the Second Confiscation Act authorized the president to enlist black men. Lincoln, still wedded to colonization and compensated emancipation, was not yet persuaded of the necessity for that move, although some subordinates pressed forward, with or without War Department approval or authority. Gradually, inevitably, the conflict slipped from political to social revolution.

The spring and summer of 1862 saw unprecedented activity in three widely separated sections of the country: South Carolina, Louisiana, and Kansas. These shared common characteristics: military manpower shortages, safe distances from War Department interference, and ambitious, imaginative, and radical leadership. In all three locations, experimental organizations of black troops attracted national attention and stirred spirited discussion, North and South.

Maj. Gen. David Hunter, commanding the Department of the South, began recruiting among the thousands of former slaves on the Sea Islands along the Atlantic coast. Privates in the first company of what was to become the First South Carolina Colored Volunteer Infantry were enlisted on May 8, 1862. The War Department declined to support the experiment beyond forwarding a supply of red Zouave trousers. Hunter could secure neither pay for his troops nor

TWENTY-SIXTH COLORED VOLUNTEER INFANTRY.

commissions for their officers. He did, however, set one precedent that lasted throughout the war: he chose officers for his black companies from among experienced noncommissioned officers in the white regiments around him. Sgt. Charles Trowbridge, First New York Engineers, became the captain commanding Company A; the end of war found him a lieutenant colonel commanding the regiment.

Bitterly disappointed by lack of War Department support, Hunter disbanded his "red-trowsered" regiment on August 10—but two weeks later, the same War Department authorized Brig. Gen. Rufus Saxton to raise five thousand black troops. Saxton invited Thomas Wentworth Higginson of Massachusetts to command the regiment. The result was a unique combination of Boston Brahmin and Sea Island ex-slaves. Their story, as Higginson told it in his classic *Army Life in a Black Regiment,* is a monument to both officer and men, as well as a sensitive and revealing eyewitness account of a revolutionary experiment, social as well as military.

Meanwhile, Maj. Gen. Benjamin F. Butler of Massachusetts found himself commanding the Department of the Gulf after the U.S. Navy had captured New Orleans in late April. Butler needed men, but the demands of George B. McClellan's Peninsular campaign took precedence over all else. Then Butler discovered a military bonanza—thousands of "free men of color," many of

whom had earlier belonged to Confederate militia units. Applying his authority to enroll former Confederate personnel (after they had taken a loyalty oath), Butler mustered into Federal service the First, Second, and Third Louisiana Native Guards in September, October, and November 1862. Eventually Louisiana furnished 24,000 black troops for the Union, more than any other state.

Out in the Trans-Mississippi West, on the Kansas-Missouri border, other Union leaders were also in dire need of troops. Kansas had joined the Union in January 1861, only three months before the firing on Fort Sumter. The new state faced twin challenges: organizing itself politically and defending itself militarily. Among the political giants of the time none stood taller than Senator (and erstwhile general) James Henry Lane, a genuine, charismatic radical with a brutally practical turn of mind. He began to enroll fugitives from Missouri in early August 1862, just as Hunter was disbanding his South Carolina levies. For officers, Lane turned to abolitionists who had learned border warfare in the bitter struggles between Kansas jayhawkers and Missouri bushwhackers. Capt. James Williams began the work in Leavenworth, eventually becoming the commanding colonel. Lane encouraged enlistments with such blandishments as "We have been saying that you would fight, and if you won't we will make you." By whatever means—and ignoring War Department orders—Lane and Williams had raised a battalion by early October and started it down the border to augment the garrison of Fort Scott, pivotal Union post in southeastern Kansas.

En route the new troops ran into a sizable force of bushwhackers at Island Mound, Missouri, thus earning the plaudits of the Northern press and the distinction of seeing action in the first recorded engagement between Confederate forces and Union blacks. Continuing to Fort Scott, the battalion was mustered into Federal service on January 13, 1863. The First Kansas Colored was the first black regiment raised by a Northern state, although by virtue of the Trowbridge company's record of unbroken service from May 8, 1862, Higginson's First South Carolina Colored Volunteer Infantry deserves the distinction of being the very first black regiment in the Union army.

President Davis's denunciation of Lincoln's proclamation was hardly surprising, nor was his promise to hand over captured officers of black units to state governments for punishment as "criminals engaged in servile insurrection." Generals Butler and Hunter had already been outlawed for their activities. By the end of May 1863, Confederate policy set by Davis and Congress had been refined to these points: former slaves "taken in arms" were to be delivered to state authorities for trial; their officers were to be tried and punished by military courts. "Wartime atrocities against the USCT [black troops]," writes historian Joseph Glatthaar, "were commonplace." Hardly surprising. As historian Bell I. Wiley explains it: "if the wishes of the private soldiers who fought them [black troops] had prevailed, no quarter would have been granted." One private soldier from Mississippi wrote his mother, "I hope I may never see a Negro Soldier or I cannot be . . . a Christian soldier."

The effects on black soldiers of these grimmer realities of combat seem to have run counter to Confederate anticipation. After the Fort Pillow massacre of April 12, 1864, Union blacks went into action shouting "Remember Fort Pillow." West of the Mississippi, a similar result followed the massacre of a foraging party of the First Kansas Colored near Camden, Arkansas. Its sister regiment, the Second Kansas Colored (recruited from Missouri and Arkansas ex-slaves) vowed to take no prisoners and thereafter sprang into action shouting "Remember Poison Spring." The men of the Second Kansas forgot themselves in combat and brought in a prisoner. Col. Samuel J. Crawford sent him back to Confederate lines under a flag of truce with a warning note pinned to his chest. Retaliation as a Union countermove to Confederate practices worked in limited circumstances only, serving in the main to magnify the horrors of war. Col. James Williams won no discernible military advantage by ordering the execution of a member of Maj. T. R. Livingston's guerrilla band in southwest Missouri because Livingston had killed a captured private of

the First Kansas Colored. Whatever the actions of field commanders, whether in Arkansas, Missouri, Tennessee, or Virginia, the official positions of North and South on the treatment of black troops created an insoluble deadlock, one result of which was a breakdown in the cartel for prisoner exchange. In evident frustration, Gen. Ethan Allen Hitchcock, Federal commissioner for prisoner exchange, concluded in August 1863 that a solution could "only be effectually reached by a successful prosecution of the war." Lincoln, after hearing about Fort Pillow, put it this way: "The difficulty is not in stating the principle, but in practically applying it."

Thus, when Lincoln authorized black recruitment on January 1, 1863, between three and four thousand blacks were already in uniform in those first five regiments, all raised on a catch-as-catch-can basis with little or no control from Washington. In the first weeks of 1863 the same pattern, or lack thereof, continued: on January 13, the day the First Kansas Colored was mustered in at Fort Scott, the War Department authorized Col. Daniel Ullman of New York to recruit an officer cadre and lead it to Louisiana to raise a brigade there. On the same day, the department ordered Col. James Montgomery, an old Kansas colleague of abolitionist John Brown, to South Carolina to recruit the Second South Carolina Colored Volunteer Infantry. On January 26, 1863, Secretary of War Edwin Stanton gave Governor John Andrew authority to raise a regiment in Massachusetts. Here was the inception of that most famous of all black regiments, the Fifty-fourth Massachusetts Infantry.

Obviously, piecemeal organization by individuals and states was hardly the way to build an effective army, and Stanton's War Department moved, quickly and effectively, to bring the enterprise under centralized control. The result was the Bureau for Colored Troops established in May. The first major stride forward, however, had come a few weeks earlier when Stanton had ordered Adj. Gen. Lorenzo Thomas out to the Mississippi Valley to announce the new

African American Units in the Union Army

Troops	Regiments
United States Colored Troops	
Infantry[1]	139
Cavalry	7
Artillery	14

[1]Includes one independent artillery battery.

Source: Compiled by Robert Francis Engs and Dudley T. Cornish from data in Frederick F. Dwyer, *A Compendium of the War of the Rebellion,* vol. 3, New York, 1908; U.S. War Department, *Official Army Register of the Volunteer Forces of the United States Army for the Years of 1861, '62, '63, '64, and '65,* vol. 8, Washington, D.C., 1865; and U.S. War Department, *War of the Rebellion: A Compilation of the Official Records of the Union and Confederate Armies,* 70 vols. in 128 parts, Washington, D.C., 1880–1901.

policy and stimulate the organization of new regiments. By the end of the year Thomas had initiated organization of twenty regiments in the valley; by the end of the war he could take credit for having started fifty.

While the adjutant general labored in the field, drawing on the great numbers of fugitive slaves engulfing every Union post, the Bureau for Colored Troops in Washington developed an effective office to advise, direct, and supervise. It encouraged recruitment in Northern cities as well as the occupied sections of the South and established a fairly efficient mechanism for selecting officers for the new regiments. The bureau meticulously supervised examining boards for officer candidates in Northern cities and in Union army divisions in the field. The result was a selection of generally better officers than those in the white volunteer regiments. The vast majority of white officers serving in black regiments had been junior or noncommissioned officers in white regiments, with invaluable troop and combat experience. Over one hundred black officers also served, the majority in Butler's Louisiana regiments.

Another important decision by the bureau was to federalize all black regiments by designating them United States Colored Troops. Higginson's First South Carolina became the Thirty-third USCT, for example; Butler's Native Guards became the Seventy-third, Seventy-fourth, and Seventy-fifth, and the First Kansas Colored served out the war as the new Seventy-ninth USCT. This put the black regiments in a national army rather than in state units. The symbolism was good, and the Federal umbrella covered all black regiments—aside from a handful permitted to retain their initial state designations, like the Fifty-fourth and Fifty-fifth Massachusetts and the Twenty-ninth Connecticut.

Organizing, recruiting, selecting officers, and training the troops went ahead steadily through 1863; at least 50,000 blacks were in the Union army by the end of that year. During 1864 the number tripled. Altogether, black troops in the Federal army numbered 180,000. Of these approximately 37,000 were listed as fatalities. Some 2,800 were killed in action or died of wounds; most of the others were victims of disease. It is impossible to give precise figures on the sick and wounded who survived. Possibly the worst case was that of the Fifty-Sixth USCT. They served for two years, chiefly on post and garrison duty around Helena, Arkansas, and participated in three minor engagements with combat losses of 4 officers and 21 enlisted men. But the regiment lost 6 officers and 647 men from disease. Substandard medical facilities and personnel and inadequate diet contributed largely to that sorry record. Here was one problem the Bureau for Colored Troops found insoluble. Another was the continuing, nagging struggle for equality of pay, solved finally in the spring of 1865 by which time thousands of black soldiers had given their lives for the Union at cut-rate prices: seven dollars per month plus a three-dollar clothing allowance (retained by the company) for the black soldier, whatever his rank, against thirteen dollars for white privates (including the clothing allowance in cash).

Although it was expected at first that blacks would serve largely in garrison duty, thus releasing white men for active service, by mid-1863 several engagements involving blacks had attracted startled and favorable attention. These first important tests of black fighting qualities came in May, June, and July, at Port Hudson and Milliken's Bend in Louisiana and Fort Wagner guarding Charleston, where the Fifty-fourth Massachusetts fought its way to permanent glory. In addition, the First Kansas Colored won praise for two engagements in June and July, at Cabin Creek and Honey Springs in present-day Oklahoma. A Wisconsin cavalry officer exclaimed after Cabin Creek: "I was never much for niggers, but, be Jasus, they are hell for fighting."

Black regiments served in every theater of war from Virginia to Texas. They fought in 449 engagements, 38 of them major, from Florida to Tennessee and well beyond the Big River in Nathaniel P. Banks's Red River campaign and Frederick Steele's equally ill-fated Camden expedition. What did these 160-plus underpaid and overworked black regiments do? Everything their white commanders asked or permitted them to do, from garrison duty up and down the Mississippi to escort duty for miles of wagon trains, from excessive fatigue duty (always and forever) to guarding confiscated plantations—and prisoners—as well as actual combat from the Petersburg Crater to Nashville, to Hatcher's Run, to Palmetto Ranch on the Rio Grande.

And what rewards did they win for this service to a republic that cheated them of half their wages? Slow, grudging acceptance in the white army around them—and fourteen Medals of Honor. But far more important was their active participation in a prodigious revolution. They had been more than spectators. Whether drafted in the North as substitutes for white men, free volunteers, or impressed fugitives, African Americans had won the right to fight. In so doing they gave emphatic affirmation of Howell Cobb's presentiment. Arguing against arming slaves to fight for the Confederacy, Cobb wrote in January 1865: "The day you make soldiers of them is the beginning of the end of the revolution. If slaves will make good soldiers, our whole theory of slavery is wrong."

Lt. Col. Charles F. Adams, Jr., commenting on the Petersburg Crater, said of the black troops caught in that fiasco: "They seem to have behaved just as well and as badly as the rest and to have suffered more severely." That cool judgment applies as well to the record of all African American troops in the Union army.

[*See also* Emancipation; Emancipation Proclamation; Fort Pillow Massacre; Fort Wagner, South Carolina; Petersburg Campaign; Port Hudson, Louisiana; Prisoners of War; Red River Campaigns; Saltville Massacre.]

BIBLIOGRAPHY

Cornish, Dudley Taylor. *The Sable Arm: Black Troops in the Union Army, 1861–1865.* New York, 1956. Reprint, Lawrence, Kans., 1987.

Durden, Robert F. *The Gray and the Black: The Confederate Debate on Emancipation.* Baton Rouge, La., 1972.

Glatthaar, Joseph T. *Forged in Battle: The Civil War Alliance of Black Soldiers and White Officers.* New York, 1990.

Gooding, James Henry. *On the Altar of Freedom: A Black Soldier's Civil War Letters from the Front.* Edited by Virginia Matzke Adams. Amherst, Mass., 1991.

Higginson, Thomas Wentworth. *Army Life in a Black Regiment.* Boston, 1870. Reprint, New York, 1984.

McPherson, James M. *Abraham Lincoln and the Second American Revolution.* New York, 1990.

Thomas, Emory M. *The Confederate Nation, 1861–1865.* New York, 1979.

DUDLEY T. CORNISH

AGENT, NAVAL. *For discussion of naval purchasing agents, see* Anglo-Confederate Purchasing; Navy, *articles on* Confederate Navy *and* Navy Department.

AKIN, WARREN (1811–1877), congressman from Georgia. Akin was born in Elbert County, Georgia, on October 11, 1811. With only a single term of formal schooling, Akin nevertheless formed an early ambition to be a lawyer. While working as a clerk in a Monroe, Georgia, store, the eighteen-year-old youth heard of the discovery of gold in the North Georgia mountains and joined the rush that converged in and around Dahlonega in the early 1830s. Though he had only limited success in finding gold, he spent his years in Dahlonega studying law and was admitted to the bar in Cherokee County in 1836. He moved to Cassville (in present-day Bartow County) where he acquired a small plantation and several slaves and opened a law practice with A. R. Wright. As a colonel in the Georgia militia, he was involved in the enforcement of Cherokee removal from North Georgia in 1838 and 1839.

Once settled, Akin became actively involved in state and local politics. In 1840 he served as a Whig presidential elector and ten years later attended the Nashville Convention, where he actively supported the Georgia Platform that urged compromise. He remained a leader in the state Whig party until its demise and was a gubernatorial candidate for its successor, the Opposition, in 1859, when he was soundly defeated by over twenty thousand votes by Democratic candidate Joseph E. Brown.

Akin was also an ordained Methodist minister, and though he never held a regular pastorate, he often preached at a local Methodist church, where he was known for the volume and projection of his voice. On occasion, while serving in the Confederate Congress in Richmond, he delivered sermons to Georgia troops camped nearby, some of whom reported that though there might be better preachers, none was louder. He served as a trustee of Emory College.

Sources vary as to the degree of Akin's opposition to secession as that crisis developed; at most he appears to have been no more than a conditional Unionist. But once Georgia left the Union, he shifted his allegiance to the new Confederacy. He served in the state legislature from 1861 to 1863, during which period he served as its Speaker of the House. In the fall of 1863, Akin was elected to the Confederate Congress but spent much of the period before moving to Richmond the following spring in relocating his family (which included thirteen children, though only six lived to adulthood). Following the Chattanooga campaign in November, he feared that Cassville would be in the path of a Union drive toward Atlanta and that his status as congressman would make him a prime target. He moved his family to Oxford, thirty miles southeast of Atlanta, and only narrowly escaped capture. In May 1864, Union troops burned his law office and home in Cassville. He was soon forced to move his family again, as Oxford proved to be in the path of Sherman's March to the Sea, and Akin again only narrowly avoided capture. His family then relocated in Elberton, his birthplace, where they spent the remainder of the war.

As representative of Georgia's Tenth District in the Confederate House of Representatives from May 1864 until the end of the war, Akin took an active role despite his preoccupation with his family's safety in Georgia. He served as a member of the House Committee on Claims, where his involvement never extended beyond rather routine business. He demonstrated sympathy for the common people, a reflection of his district's makeup, on a number of issues, including support of pay increases for enlisted men, their inclusion in the election of field-grade officers, and the elimination of slaveholder exemptions for military service. Like many of his colleagues, he supported only reluctantly the recruitment of slaves into Confederate military service, but he argued that they should be furnished not by a draft but on the basis of President Jefferson Davis's requisition to the states.

Akin became a close friend and loyal supporter of Davis during the latter days of the war when the president was losing much of his congressional support (though he was by no means alone among Georgia congressmen who sided with Davis over Governor Joseph E. Brown). Akin was most vocal in opposing a move in January 1865 to appoint a general in chief, which would have challenged Davis's powers as commander in chief. But his amendment specifying that such a position not interfere with presidential authority was soundly defeated. After a visit with Davis on January 9, Akin wrote to his wife that

> he has been greatly wronged. . . . He is a patriot and a good man, I think. He will have to do something more than anything he has done before I can denounce him. He is the best man in the Government for his place. Many want him out of office. Were he removed today we should be ruined in a few months, and I fear we shall be any way.

Akin left Richmond and returned to Georgia in late February 1865, nearly a month before Congress adjourned, either out of concern for his family or resignation that the Confederacy's end was near. He moved his family back to Bartow County where he resumed his law practice in the new county seat of Cartersville. He took an active part in Democratic party politics, but never again sought elective office. Though ill and close to death in 1877, he submitted proposals in writing to the state constitutional convention that met that summer, a number of which were incorporated into the new constitution. He died on December 17, 1877.

BIBLIOGRAPHY

Avery, I. W. *History of the State of Georgia from 1850 to 1881.* New York, 1881.

Bell, Hiram P. *Men and Things: Being Reminiscent, Biographical, and Historical.* Atlanta, 1907.

Coleman, Kenneth, and Charles Stephen Gurr, eds. *Dictionary of Georgia Biography.* Vol. 1. Athens, Ga., 1983.

Cunyus, Lucy J. *History of Bartow County.* Cartersville, Ga., 1933.

Wiley, Bell Irvin, ed. *Letters of Warren Akin, Confederate Congressman.* Athens, Ga., 1959.

JOHN C. INSCOE

ALABAMA. In the presidential election of 1860, Southern Democrat John C. Breckinridge carried Alabama, receiving support in all regions of the state: northern Alabama and the Tennessee valley, the black belt in southern Alabama, and the southeastern Wiregrass. Alabama seceded from the Union on January 11, 1861. Less than a month later, the Confederate States of America was launched at a convention in Montgomery, the state capital. Alabama's population consisted of 437,930 black people (of whom 2,850 were free) and 526,271 whites. Of the latter, approximately 75,000 served in the Confederate army, while about 3,000 joined the Union forces; in addition, 10,000 black Alabamians would fight for the Union.

Secession and Early Confederate Politics

By the late 1850s, slavery and other sectional issues had long been important in Alabama politics, but it was possible to make a case that Alabama was secure in the Union. In 1857, moderate Democrat Andrew Barry Moore was nominated for governor and elected without opposition. Two years later he was reelected, defeating his opponent, a fire-eater, by a huge margin. Most Democrats still looked to the national Democratic party for protection of the Southern way of life. Yet a series of events drove Alabamians toward the radical Southern rights stance of William Lowndes Yancey.

John Brown's raid in Virginia in October 1859 touched off a wave of fear and anger in the state. With Governor Moore's blessing the legislature authorized the formation of volunteer units, appropriated $200,000 for defense, and took steps to establish direct trade with Europe. On February 24, 1860, the legislature called for a state convention in the event of a Republican presidential victory.

Within a year the dynamics of presidential politics had made secession a certainty. Alabama delegates walked out of the Democratic National Convention at Charleston when supporters of Illinois senator Stephen A. Douglas would not approve a platform protecting slavery in the territories. A subsequent convention at Baltimore produced similar results. Breakaway Southerners nominated Kentuckian John C. Breckinridge for president.

Yancey campaigned for Breckinridge, who captured the state with 48,000 votes. Union-minded Democrats supported Douglas, who received 13,000 votes. Whigs cast 27,000 votes for Constitutional Union candidate John Bell of Tennessee. For backers of Douglas and Bell, the election had been one last chance to prove that political compromise could save the Union.

With no support in the state, Abraham Lincoln had been only a frightening abstraction during the campaign. After his election, Governor Moore—now a thoroughgoing secessionist—called for election of delegates to a January 7, 1861, state convention. Anticipating the arguments of "cooperationists" (who favored pan-Southern action), Moore sent commissioners to other slave states to arrange for coordinated action. Early in January he used Alabama troops to seize the Federal forts guarding Mobile Bay and the arsenal at Mount Vernon.

Moore had a firm grasp of sentiment in Alabama. Debates prior to the delegate elections had concerned only the method of secession. The voters elected a clear majority of "immediate secessionists" (fifty-four) over cooperationists (forty-six). Even some of the state's leading Whigs, including such previous moderates as Thomas Hill Watts, had gone over to the secessionist side. The cooperationists, for their part, were largely from northern Alabama—vulnerable to invasion in event of war and the closest thing the state had to a center of Unionist sentiment.

At the state convention, secession leaders claimed simply that Alabama, as a sovereign state, had the right to secede.

ALABAMA DELEGATION TO THE U.S. CONGRESS.   This group attended the Thirty-sixth Session of the U.S. Congress, from March 4, 1859, to March 3, 1861. They left on January 11, 1861, when Alabama passed its ordinance of secession. Pictured in the top row, from left to right, are Rep. Sydenham Moore, Rep. Williamson R. W. Cobb, and Rep. James L. Pugh. In the middle row are Sen. Clement C. Clay, Sen. Benjamin Fitzpatrick, and Rep. Jabez L. M. Curry. In the bottom row are Rep. James A. Stallworth, Rep. David Clopton, and Rep. George S. Houston.

HARPER'S PICTORIAL HISTORY OF THE GREAT REBELLION

The cooperationists were divided, though some favored using a Southern convention to demand constitutional amendments. Yancey, Watts, and other secessionist leaders allowed four days for debate; then on January 11, amid scenes of wild rejoicing, they voted Alabama out of the Union and issued a call inviting other Southern states to send delegates to a February 4 convention in Montgomery.

For all the firing of cannon and unfurling of flags, the convention was far from unified. The vote on the secession ordinance was sixty-nine to thirty-one. Subsequently, thirty-three cooperationists refused to sign the official copy, though most of them recognized secession as legal and binding. Before and after the January 11 vote, cooperationists urged submission of the ordinance to the people. The majority refused to comply, and cooperationist bitterness probably contributed to a movement to deny Yancey and other fire-eaters seats in the Confederate convention. In this the cooperationists were successful, and the delegation was of a markedly Whiggish cast.

Yet secession was apparently popular, and the high tide of Confederate political support in Alabama came with the state elections of 1861. The Democrats were the dominant party, but there was a feeling that patriotism demanded a suspension of partisanship. Gubernatorial candidates were nominated by newspapers and as a rule did not campaign. By August 8, election day, only two candidates remained: John Gill Shorter, a black belt fire-eater who was a member of the Provisional Congress, and Watts, the Whig secessionist leader.

Despite the avoidance of politics as usual, voting seemed to follow traditional lines. Shorter won 37,000 to 28,000, carrying northern Alabama and the southeastern Wiregrass counties like any good Democrat. The legislature also was staunchly secessionist, and it was in an atmosphere of hopeful determination that Shorter turned to the task of governing a state at war.

Military Affairs

In the meantime, preparations for war had been ongoing. Numerous volunteer regiments were raised in 1861, most of which were mustered into Confederate service. After the first year of war, enlistments tapered off; however, the passage of the Conscription Act of 1862 stimulated another wave of volunteering. Alabamians served in sixty-three infantry regiments, eleven cavalry regiments, and a number of artillery and naval units.

State officials worked hard to arm and equip many of Alabama's units, but arms procurement was an intractable problem. Governor Moore had sent agents out to scour the nation for weapons. Governor Shorter promoted local weapons production, contracting with small shops in Mobile, Selma, Talladega, and other towns and giving $250,000 in subsidies to the Alabama Arms Manufacturing Company in Montgomery. None of these ventures produced the hoped-for results, and the state was sometimes reduced to giving its fighters pikes or bowie knives.

As to military operations, Shorter gave much of his attention in 1862 to the defense of the Gulf coast. He understood the importance of Pensacola (where Moore had already sent state troops) and was instrumental in delaying evacuation of that city until May, thus saving guns and stores for the defense of Mobile. When that city was threatened by Federal forces in the spring of 1862, he arranged for recently formed regiments to be sent there and armed them with militia weapons.

At the same time a more pressing situation was developing in northern Alabama. The Shorter administration had helped commanders in Tennessee and Kentucky obtain troops and had impressed slaves to work on fortifications. Nonetheless, after the fall of Forts Henry and Donelson (February 1862), northern Alabama was open to invasion. By April the mixed plantation and hill lands of the Tennessee valley were occupied by Union forces under Gen. O. M. Mitchell. In the course of occupation, towns like

MONTGOMERY, ALABAMA, 1861.

HARPER'S PICTORIAL HISTORY OF THE GREAT REBELLION

Huntsville, Florence, Decatur, and especially Athens suffered violence and property damage. Shorter arranged for the continued defense of the area by securing Confederate cavalry under John Tyler Morgan and authorizing volunteer cavalry to serve under Philip Dale Roddy—but in fact the governor had few options. Except for brief intervals, the Tennessee valley and large areas of hill country to the south would be in Union hands for the duration.

Occupation brought disastrous consequences for northern Alabamians, aside from deaths and damage inflicted by Northern troops. Violent feuds broke out between Unionists and Confederate sympathizers. By the latter stages of the war the woods throughout the state were full of "Mossbacks" who sought to avoid Confederate service, deserters who sometimes traveled together to resist capture, and bands of outlaws. These groups often stole food and supplies, as did Federal and Confederate cavalry—though the soldiers used such terms as *foraging* or *impressment* to cover their depredations. Since large numbers of men were away in service, there was little protection for isolated farm families, and food was increasingly scarce.

Citizens might have been more secure had the state possessed a usable militia. At the time of secession the militia existed mostly on the statute books. Late in 1862, when the need for a state defense and peacekeeping force had become all too apparent to Governor Shorter, the legislature refused to cooperate. Evidently they reasoned that military affairs were the responsibility of the central government. Besides, they supposed that any troops raised by the state would be absorbed into the Confederate army, as had been the case with the Alabama volunteers of 1861. The state government appeared indifferent, and public opinion was increasingly skeptical.

After the fall of Vicksburg in July 1863, deserters and paroled soldiers flooded into the state. Called into special session, a new legislature finally revised the militia law, but in so doing they created a cumbersome two-class system. One class consisted of sixteen-year-olds and men aged forty-five to sixty, who by law could not be used outside their home counties. The system never really worked. Moreover the efforts of Shorter's successor, Thomas H. Watts, to obtain an effective militia met with failure in the legislature, which had become a refractory and virtually anti-Confederate body.

Thus it was that northern Alabama and the north-central border counties were left to the protection of cavalry commanders such as Morgan, Roddy, and Nathan Bedford Forrest. These were resourceful men, but their main purpose was to harass the Federals, not defend the local population. Skirmishes and small battles were common in 1863 and 1864, though there were no decisive fights. The most celebrated Confederate victory of this period came in May 1863, when Forrest pursued a Union raiding force commanded by Col. A. D. Streight. Sweeping through several northern Alabama counties with about 1,500 men, Streight intended to cut Chattanooga-to-Atlanta railroad lines and to destroy supplies stored in Rome, Georgia. Forrest pursued with a much smaller force, and after a chase of more than one hundred miles, Streight turned at bay. Some of his men were too tired to fight; and Forrest's placement of his 600 troops convinced the exhausted Federals that the Confederates had superior numbers. Persuaded by his officers, Streight surrendered.

Until the summer of 1864, central and southern Alabama had been spared the worst rigors of war. In July 1864, however, Gen. Lovell H. Rousseau launched a raid with some 2,300 men from Decatur in northern Alabama to Opelika in the southeast. His object was to destroy the railroad depots, track, and equipment of the Montgomery and West Point Railroad, thereby cutting off an important source of supplies for Confederate forces before Atlanta. Rousseau burned and wrecked as he went, accomplishing his mission without effective opposition and spreading insecurity among people in the interior of the state.

Residents of Mobile, on the other hand, had often felt insecure. Yet even the outer defenses of the city were not truly tested until August 1864—when Adm. David Farragut attacked Fort Gaines, Fort Morgan, and other posts that defended the entrances to Mobile Bay with 1,500 infantry, artillery, and a fleet of more than eighteen vessels. After a fierce naval battle on August 5 in which the Union warship *Tecumseh* was sunk by a mine and the Confederate ironclad *Tennessee* was captured after a heroic resistance, Farragut besieged the forts. Though Fort Morgan held out through a terrific bombardment, the outlying positions had been surrendered by August 23. For the time being the city itself—its fortifications built up by the labor of thousands of impressed slaves—was left to wither. Its downfall was delayed for eight months until more than 40,000 Federal troops converged upon a much smaller Confederate force. After prolonged fighting, Confederate Gen. D. H. Maury evacuated the town from April 10 through 12, 1865.

By the time Mobile fell, Gen. J. H. Wilson's brigade of 13,500 cavalry had carried its own brand of hell from northwestern Alabama into the black belt. Wilson's chief target was Selma, where important arms manufactories, powderworks, and a naval yard had been assembled at the behest of Confederate Quartermaster General Josiah Gorgas. Traveling in three columns through a countryside already stripped bare of foodstuffs, Wilson's men reached Elyton (near present-day Birmingham) on March 29 and burned the ironworks there. Wilson then detached a portion of his command under Gen. John Croxton to Tuscaloosa, where—after a brief fight with university cadets—they burned the University of Alabama and other facilities.

Nine thousand strong, Wilson's main force arrived at

Selma on April 2 and soon defeated Forrest's force of five thousand. Over the course of several days the Union troops proceeded to destroy the legitimate prizes of their conquest. But the blue-coated soldiers also carried out one of the most complete devastations of a town during the war. When Wilson left Selma on April 10, the town was a smoking ruin, its streets filled with the carcasses of the hundreds of mules and horses that he had ordered shot. Terrified by Selma's fate, Montgomery surrendered without resistance on April 12 upon the approach of Union troops. After burning and confiscation of a more restrained sort, Wilson took his command farther east, into Georgia, taking the war with him.

Civil and Political Affairs

For decades before the war, Alabama Whigs and Democrats had debated the merits of state support for banks, schools, prisons, and business enterprises. Democratic leaders who had been reluctant to turn government to economic purposes reversed themselves after 1861. Their use of economic power began at the most basic levels, even before fighting broke out. In the winter of 1860–1861, the state persuaded banks to suspend specie payments. Subsequently these banks purchased quotas of state bonds with specie, thereby giving the state control of the supply of hard money. In 1861, the legislature gave Governor Moore power to issue paper money, a power that became the single most important means of state funding. The amount of state issues (some $7.5 million) was small in comparison to the massive Confederate output, but it contributed to inflation.

State taxes remained comparatively low for at least a year. Prewar property taxes were largely retained; apparently many citizens were exempt from these. By December 1862, however, the legislature needed money and was in a mood to raise it from persons who were too prosperous or who flaunted wealth. At that time, in addition to a poll tax, the state imposed taxes on luxury goods, "vices" (packs of cards, billiard tables), and some occupations. A more revolutionary tax passed at that session levied 5 percent of "legacies, profits and sales, [and] incomes."

A year later the state's needs were more pressing still, and the legislature taxed speculators in Confederate bonds while increasing taxes on profits. In December 1864, with inflation running away and government on the point of collapse, all taxes were increased by one-third. Radical as it seems, this measure was mild compared to the Confederate taxes-in-kind of 1863 and 1864. Since the latter often took food from families already in danger of starvation, the legislature asked the Confederate government to exempt white yeoman families from the tax-in-kind—evidently to little purpose.

State officials often subordinated their own goals to Confederate war aims; yet they did carry out sweeping policies aimed at helping ordinary citizens. By 1862, for example, the price of salt had risen by more than 2,000 percent. Determined to protect the people from speculators and to ensure an adequate supply of this vital substance, Governor Shorter bought salt from abroad and leased state salt reservation lands to private companies. Soon the state began to produce its own salt; and in the summer of 1862, Shorter opened other reservation lands to all Alabamians. Eventually he contracted with Virginia salt producers to obtain yet more. Much of the state-controlled salt was to be distributed to indigent families.

The state likewise tried to cope with the larger issues of hunger and deprivation raised by the war. Enlistments and conscription drained manpower from the whole state, but especially from the small-farm districts of northern Alabama and the Wiregrass. In 1861 legislators had set aside tax moneys for poor relief. In 1862, at Shorter's urging, they set aside $2 million for indigent families, adding $4 million the following year for soldiers' families.

Even so, food supplies dwindled in the troubled areas. Surveys by probate judges indicated that in 1863 three families out of ten needed help. "Corn women" from northern Alabama, who walked for days begging for food with sacks on their backs, were commonly seen in the black belt by 1863. The problem was not confined to rural areas: Mobile was troubled by shortages, food riots, and marching women in the same year.

As the story of the corn women indicates, not every part of the state was destitute. The black belt especially produced a surplus of food, which state officials sometimes tried to purchase directly for distribution to the poor. Yet the state's wretched (or nonexistent) roads and the Confederate control of rail transport frustrated most of their efforts. The food problem was accompanied by a shortage of medicines caused by the blockade of Mobile and by the scarcity of wool cards used in the home manufacture of cloth. These and other hardships could not be kept secret from soldiers in the field, and many men deserted to look after their families. Of course, such deserters were likely to have trouble with the authorities, thus increasing the cycle of violence in the state. Add to the above the resentment over increasingly demanding taxes and regulations and fears touched off by the likelihood of Union invasions, and it is easy to see why many Alabamians came to lose their enthusiasm for the Confederacy and for secessionist politicians.

In the state elections of 1863, Governor Shorter and his allies were caught in a wave of popular anger. Shorter hoped to be reelected but did not campaign. He was opposed once again by Watts, who had served as attorney general of the Confederacy since 1862. Watts was a committed Confederate; yet his Whiggish past history and his own refusal to campaign misled the people, thousands of whom thought that he would favor peace. The elections of 1863 were marked by the activities of a shadowy peace party whose activities were centered in (though not confined to) northern Alabama. In the event, Watts defeated Shorter by a vote to 28,000 to 9,000, winning all but four persistently Democratic northern Alabama counties. The state legislators chosen in 1863 included many little-known men whose sentiment may be gauged by their election of cooperationists Robert Jemmison and Richard Wilde Walker to the Confederate Senate. Likewise, the electorate sent several antiadministration politicians to the Confederate House of Representatives. Jabez L. M. Curry, one of the state's ablest young secessionists, was defeated for reelection.

During his term of office, Watts struggled with impossible conditions. The state continued to appropriate millions of dollars for poor relief and attempted to supply salt, wool cards, and other goods to its citizens. Despite his loyalty to the Confederacy, Watts quarreled so frequently with national officials over impressment and conscription policies that he is remembered as a state rights governor. On the other hand, in September 1864, Watts opposed peace resolutions introduced in the legislature by Lewis Parsons (future provisional governor). These resolutions were defeated by a vote of forty-five to thirty-two, which may indicate how strong the peace party had become. Indeed, peace party men expected to carry the state in 1865, and some scholars think they would have if the Confederacy had endured.

As it was, though, Watts with many others fled Montgomery in April 1865 at the approach of Wilson's raiders. After staying briefly in Eufaula on the Georgia border he returned to Montgomery. There was little for him to do, so he joined other Confederates who were assembling at the nearby town of Union Springs. He was captured by Union forces on May 1. The rebellion in Alabama—in reality an attempted revolution—was over.

[*For further discussion of battles fought in Alabama, see* Mobile Bay, Alabama, *articles on* Battle of Mobile Bay *and* Mobile Campaign; Selma, Alabama, *article on* Wilson's Raid on Selma; Shiloh Campaign. *For further discussion of Alabama cities, see* Mobile, Alabama, *article on* City of Mobile; Montgomery, Alabama; Selma, Alabama, *article on* City of Selma. *See also biographies of numerous figures mentioned herein.*]

BIBLIOGRAPHY

Barney, William L. *The Secessionist Impulse: Alabama and Mississippi in 1860.* Princeton, 1974.

Bergeron, Arthur W., Jr. *Confederate Mobile.* Jackson, Miss., 1991.

Brewer, Willis. *Alabama: Her History, Resources, War Record, and Public Men.* Montgomery, Ala., 1872. Reprint, Spartanburg, S.C., 1975.

Fleming, Walter L. *Civil War and Reconstruction in Alabama.* New York, 1905. Reprint, Spartanburg, S.C., 1978.

Jones, James Pickett. *Yankee Blitzkrieg: Wilson's Raid through Alabama and Georgia.* Athens, Ga., 1976.

McMillan, Malcolm C. *The Alabama Confederate Reader.* University, Ala., 1963. Reprint with intro. by C. Peter Ripley. Tuscaloosa, Ala. 1992.

McMillan, Malcolm C. *The Disintegration of a Confederate State: Three Governors and Alabama's Wartime Home Front, 1861–1865.* Macon, Ga., 1986.

Rogers, William Warren. "Alabama." In *The Encyclopedia of Southern History.* Edited by David C. Roller and Robert Twyman. Baton Rouge, La., 1979.

Smith, William R. *The History and Debates of the Convention of the People of Alabama, Begun and Held in the City of Montgomery, on the Seventh Day of January, 1861.* Montgomery, Ala., 1861. Reprint, Spartanburg, S.C., 1975.

Thornton, J. Mills. *Politics and Power in a Slave Society: Alabama, 1800–1860.* Baton Rouge, La., 1978.

Wheeler, Joseph. *Alabama.* Vol. 7 of *Confederate Military History.* Edited by Clement A. Evans. Atlanta, 1899. Vol. 8 of extended ed. Wilmington, N.C., 1987.

PAUL M. PRUITT, JR.

ALABAMA. In June 1861, Comdr. James Dunwoody Bulloch of the Confederate navy arrived in England to purchase ships, guns, and ammunition for the Navy Department. The following month Bulloch contracted with Laird's Shipyard in Birkenhead, across the Mersey from Liverpool, for a wooden barkentine. According to the contract for vessel number *290*, the ship was to be 220 feet in length and 32 feet in beam and have a 15-foot draft. Although designed and built along the lines of a fast merchant ship, the *290* was to be unusually well equipped for extended cruising. In addition to being rigged for sail, the ship was equipped with a 300-horsepower steam engine that powered a patented screw propeller system. To reduce drag under sail, the propeller could be raised into a specially designed well in the stern.

In spite of protests by Charles Francis Adams, American minister to London, British authorities determined that the *290* did not violate Queen Victoria's May 1861 proclamation of neutrality, which prevented the sale of warships to either the United States or the Confederacy. After the *290* had been launched and christened *Enrica*, Bulloch took the ship down the Mersey on a trial and never returned. Later in the Azores *Enrica* rendezvoused with the bark *Agrippina* and transferred ordnance, ammunition, provisions, and coal that Bulloch had previously purchased in England. Four days later the vessel had been fitted out for war and, under the command of Raphael Semmes, *Enrica* was rechristened CSS *Alabama*. Captain Semmes assembled the crew and informed them of his orders from President Jefferson Davis to use the ship against the U.S. Merchant Marine.

Semmes initiated an unparalleled campaign with an

CSS *ALABAMA*.   Wash drawing by Clary Ray, November 1894.   NAVAL HISTORICAL CENTER, WASHINGTON, D.C.

attack on U.S. whaling ships in the vicinity of the Azores and merchant vessels off Newfoundland. After moving operations into the Gulf of Mexico *Alabama* encountered and sank in only thirteen minutes USS *Hatteras* off Galveston, Texas. After putting the rescued crew of *Hatteras* ashore at Port Royal, Jamaica, Semmes took the Confederate warship south to the coast of Brazil. With supplies from more than a dozen captured vessels, Semmes headed *Alabama* across the South Atlantic. En route to the Cape of Good Hope, Semmes captured the bark *Conrad.* Instead of destroying it, Semmes armed the vessel, put a small crew aboard, rechristened it CSS *Tuscaloosa,* and sent that vessel commerce raiding as well. Following a visit to Cape Town and a moderately successful cruise across the Indian Ocean, *Alabama* returned to Cape Town before recrossing the South Atlantic. It was apparent to Semmes that the ship was badly in need of repairs after nineteen months at sea, and he headed the raider for Cherbourg, France.

At Cherbourg USS *Kearsarge,* one of more than a dozen U.S. warships in pursuit of the Confederate raider, finally caught up with Captain Semmes. He considered his vessel a close match for *Kearsarge* and informed its captain, John A. Winslow, of his intention to fight. On June 19, 1864, *Alabama* steamed out of the French port and opened fire on *Kearsarge* at 10:57 A.M. Although one of *Alabama*'s initial shots lodged in the sternpost of *Kearsarge,* the shell failed to explode. As the engagement intensified, shots from *Kearsarge* began to take effect, while those of *Alabama* hit the Union warship only twenty-eight times. In seventy minutes *Alabama* began sinking, and Semmes struck his colors to avoid continued loss of life. The U.S. Navy had destroyed *Alabama,* but Semmes and forty members of the crew escaped capture when the British yacht *Deerhound* came to their rescue.

In 1984 the wreck of the Confederate ship was discovered by a French navy mine hunter. Expeditions to the site carried out by divers and archaeologists of the CSS *Alabama* Association have documented the wreck and uncovered a unique collection of artifacts that illuminate life aboard the commerce raider.

During *Alabama*'s cruise Semmes had captured and burned fifty-five Union merchant vessels valued at more than $4.5 million. Ten other vessels were bonded at $562,000 and released. The impact of commerce raiding by *Alabama* and other Confederate warships was disastrous for the U.S. Merchant Marine. In what has been described as an unparalleled "flight from the flag," hundreds of U.S. vessels were sold or shifted to foreign registration in an effort to avoid capture and destruction. That impact on the Merchant Marine was felt until the end of the century.

[*See also* Alabama Claims.]

BIBLIOGRAPHY

Adams, Ephram Douglass. *Great Britain and the Civil War.* 2 vols. New York, 1958.

Merli, Frank J. *Great Britain and the Confederate Navy, 1861–1865.* Bloomington, Ind., 1970.

Merli, Frank J., ed. *Special Commemorative Naval Issue: CSS* Alabama, *1864–1989.* Vol. 4 of *Journal of Confederate History.* Brentwood, Tenn., 1989.

Scharf, J. Thomas. *History of the Confederate States Navy.* New York, 1887. Reprint, New York, 1977.

Semmes, Raphael. *Service Afloat; or, the Remarkable Career of the Confederate Cruisers* Sumter *and* Alabama *during the War between the States.* New York, 1869.

Summersell, Charles G. *The C.S.S.* Alabama: *Builder, Captain, and Plans.* University, Ala., 1985.

GORDON WATTS

***ALABAMA* CLAIMS.** During the Civil War commerce raiders fitted out by the Confederate navy carried out a series of successful campaigns against the U.S. Merchant Marine. Vessels like *Alabama, Georgia, Florida,* and *Shenandoah* cruised the routes of Union commerce and captured, destroyed, or released on bond millions of dollars worth of ships and cargoes. *Alabama* alone was credited with losses totaling $5 million. The success of Confederate commerce raiders caused a "flight from the flag" that forced 750 U.S. merchant ship owners to sell or shift their vessels to foreign registration in an effort to avoid capture or destruction. Whereas 65 percent of New York's maritime commerce was carried in American bottoms in 1860, U.S. ships carried only 25 percent three years later. Although the decline of U.S. maritime commerce was not entirely the result of Confederate attacks, they were a major factor.

Because many of the Confederacy's most effective commerce raiders were built in Great Britain, the United States maintained that Britain should be held responsible for their destructive activities. The U.S. government asserted that Great Britain had violated its May 1861 neutrality proclamation by permitting Confederate agents to obtain vessels for purposes of war with virtual impunity. When the Confederacy collapsed in 1865, the United States moved to press its claims against Great Britain. Both countries prepared arguments to support their position, and Charles F. Adams, U.S. minister to Great Britain, relayed that "nothing remains but arbitration." But in spite of Adams's optimism, the issue of reparations was far from arbitration or resolution.

Neither Great Britain nor the United States was willing to make significant concessions. The United States expected Britain to recognize the validity of U.S. claims before any negotiations could begin. Britain, to the contrary, refused to admit culpability for the commerce raiders' actions and adamantly refused to have a third power involved in deciding if it had been right or wrong in the matter. Negotiations reached an impasse and were suspended. When Lord Russell's government collapsed in June 1866, William H. Seward ordered Adams to reopen the issue. Though the attitude of both nations was more conciliatory and each informally offered to make concessions, both Seward and Lord Stanley, Lord Russell's successor, refused to compromise on the issue of British violation of the neutrality proclamation. Again the negotiations collapsed.

In 1868 the status of the negotiations was complicated by Adams's resignation and the need to resolve other issues that arose, but in November, President Andrew Johnson redirected attention to the *Alabama* claims. By January 1869 he and British Foreign Secretary George W. F. Clarendon had developed an agreement that both parties signed concerning the method of resolving the dispute.

A commission of two Britons and two Americans would hear the claims and decide on resolution. Wherever they could not come to an agreement, an arbitrator would be mutually approved and those matters submitted to his consideration. In the event that the commission could not agree on an arbitrator, two would be selected and lots cast to determine which would rule on the matter at hand. Heads of state could be selected as arbitrators by any two members of the commission. The agreement was anything but satisfactory, and the U.S. Senate voted against it in April 1869.

After the vote Senator Charles Sumner of Massachusetts voiced such vehement opposition to the agreement that it created a wave of renewed public resentment against Great Britain. In his speech Sumner reiterated U.S. grievances and condemned the Johnson-Clarendon agreement because there was no admission of British responsibility, no provisions for future policy on the matter, and no reparations for the United States. Sumner also claimed that Great Britain's violation of Queen Victoria's neutrality proclamation had prolonged the war by several years and resulted in over $100 million in damages to the American Merchant Marine. His accusations not only increased public antagonism against Britain but raised expectations for reparations to unrealistic levels. In Congress Michigan Senator Zachariah Chandler demanded that Canada be ceded to the United States to compensate for fully half of the expense of the Civil War.

The atmosphere made resolution of the issue seem unlikely, but when President Ulysses S. Grant came into office in 1869, his secretary of state, Hamilton Fish, moved to reopen negotiations. Although Great Britain and the United States appeared as polarized as ever, Grant was receptive to compromise within the bounds of political expediency, and the British appeared to be similarly disposed. After a year of delicate negotiations that were complicated by peripheral issues of British dominion in Canada, Canadian-American fishing and trading agreements, and the San Juan Island water boundary, both countries agreed on the formation of a joint high commission to resolve all issues between the United States, Great Britain, and Canada. The commission met in Washington, D.C., in March, and after considerable deliberation a treaty was drafted that included the *Alabama* claims articles. The United States and Great Britain signed the Treaty of Washington on May 8, 1871, and on May 24 Congress ratified it over last-minute objections. Parliament followed suit several weeks later, and ratifications were exchanged on June 17, 1871.

In addition to addressing the matter of future responsibilities of neutral governments toward the fitting out, arming, and equipping of vessels by belligerents, the articles of the treaty included an agreement to settle direct claims by arbitration. Accordingly an international commission of jurists was assembled in Geneva in December 1871. After the United States and Great Britain presented their arguments, the process of arbitration almost collapsed owing to the intensity of disagreement over the issue of indirect claims. After heated exchanges the tribunal was charged with consideration of the direct claims and retired to reach a decision. On July 22 the members voted to dismiss outright the claims associated with CSS *Georgia,* but Britain was held responsible for damage done by CSS *Florida,* CSS *Alabama,* and CSS *Shenandoah* after that vessel was permitted to refit and resupply in Melbourne, Australia. A total of $15.5 million was determined to be the amount of damages for which Britain was responsible to the United States. Although the decision met with some dissatisfaction, both sides decided it was acceptable. The precedent set by two nations settling their differences by arbitration rather than war was lost in the power politics of the twentieth century, but the exercise contributed to a strengthening of Anglo-American relations that helped shape world history.

[*See also entries on the ships* Alabama; Florida; Georgia; Shenandoah.]

BIBLIOGRAPHY

Adams, Ephram Douglass. *Great Britain and the Civil War.* 2 vols. New York, 1958.

Beaman, Charles C., Jr. *The National and Private "Alabama Claims" and Their "Final and Amicable Settlement."* Washington, D.C., 1871.

Callahan, James Morton. *Diplomatic History of the Southern Confederacy.* Baltimore, 1901. Reprint, New York, 1964.

Cook, Adrian. *The* Alabama *Claims: American Politics and Anglo-American Relations, 1865–1872.* Ithaca, N.Y., 1975.

Lambert, C. S. "The CSS *Alabama* Lost and Found." *American History Illustrated* 23 (October 1988).

GORDON WATTS

ALBEMARLE. Constructed in a cornfield along the Roanoke River at Edward's Ferry, North Carolina, between January 1863 and March 1864, the ironclad ram *Albemarle* was designed by John L. Porter, the Confederacy's chief naval engineer, who had helped rebuild USS *Merrimack* into CSS *Virginia.* He designed *Albemarle* as a similar casemated, ironclad ram. Built with a flat bottom to ease navigation in shallow coastal areas, *Albemarle* was 152 feet long overall and 45 feet in the beam, with a freeboard of about two feet. The central casemate was 60 feet long and protected by two layers of two-inch-thick iron plate bolted to a wooden backing. The ram was solid oak sheathed in iron. *Albemarle* carried two 8-inch Brooke rifled guns. Power came from a pair of two-hundred-horsepower steam engines.

The initial impetus for the construction of *Albemarle* came from Gilbert Elliott, a grandson of North Carolina shipbuilder Charles Grice, who knew both ship construction and mechanics. Elliott and his partner, Col. William F. Martin, won the contract to build the ironclad in January 1863.

Construction of the vessel was hampered by the fact that Edward's Ferry was not served by a railroad, by shortages of crucial materials, especially iron, and by inefficient labor practices. Skilled shipwrights were in short supply. In January 1864, Navy Secretary Stephen R. Mallory ordered Comdr. James W. Cooke to take charge of construction. A thirty-three-year veteran of the U.S. Navy, Cooke was aggressive and hardworking, and by March 16, he had *Albemarle* on its way downstream to support Confederate troops trying to recapture Plymouth, North Carolina.

Around 3:00 A.M. on March 19, *Albemarle* encountered a pair of Federal steamers under Commdr. Charles W. Flusser. Steering *Albemarle* along the south shore, Cooke suddenly swung toward the Federal steamers, struck Flusser's flagship, *Miami,* a glancing blow and smashed open the side of *Southfield.* Narrowly escaping being dragged under when its ram stuck in *Southfield, Albemarle* proved impervious to the fire of *Miami.* A ricocheting shell killed Flusser, and *Miami* fled. Confederate forces retook Plymouth on March 20.

On May 5, *Albemarle* steamed south to assist in an attack on New Bern, but seven Federal ships in Albemarle Sound forced the vessel into a two-hour engagement. *Albemarle* suffered damage and had to return to Plymouth. During the summer, Cooke periodically steamed downriver to raise alarm in the Federal flotilla, but had not fought another engagement when he became ill and was relieved by Capt. John N. Maffitt. Unhappy with the assignment, Maffitt requested another in September 1864 and was replaced by Lt. Alexander F. Warley.

In the early morning of October 28, 1864, *Albemarle* was sunk at anchor in an attack led by Union Lt. William B. Cushing. Using a small steam launch, Cushing and his crew rammed partway through a log boom surrounding the ironclad and detonated a spar torpedo against its hull. Of the Federal attackers, only Cushing and one other man survived. In April 1865 *Albemarle* was raised and towed to Norfolk where it was sold for scrap in 1867.

BIBLIOGRAPHY

Gibbons, Tony. *Warships and Naval Battles of the Civil War.* New York, 1989.

Johnson, Robert U., and C. C. Buel, eds. *Battles and Leaders of the*

CSS *ALBEMARLE*.   Photographed at the Norfolk Navy Yard after being salvaged, c. 1865.   NAVAL HISTORICAL CENTER, WASHINGTON, D.C.

Civil War. 4 vols. New York, 1887–1888. Reprint, Secaucus, N.J., 1982.

Jones, Virgil Carrington. *The Civil War at Sea.* 3 vols. New York, 1962. Reprint, Wilmington, N.C., 1990.

Still, William N., Jr. *Iron Afloat: The Story of the Confederate Armorclads.* Nashville, Tenn., 1971.

ROBERT S. BROWNING III

ALCORN, JAMES L.

(1816–1894), Mississippi State legislator, postwar governor, and U.S. senator. James Lusk Alcorn, born in Illinois, was reared and educated in Kentucky. As a young man, he moved to Friar's Point, Coahoma County, Mississippi, to practice law. He served in the Mississippi legislature as a representative in 1846 and 1856 and as a senator in 1852 and 1854. In 1857 he refused the Whig nomination for governor in order to run against L. Q. C. Lamar for a seat in Congress. His opposition to secession contributed to his losing the race. In 1861 as a delegate to the Mississippi secession convention, he proposed a doomed amendment that would postpone Mississippi's secession until at least four other Southern states had seceded. The ordinance to secede passed, and Alcorn reluctantly signed it.

Alcorn turned down a seat in the Confederate Congress to accept a commission as a brigadier general of the Mississippi militia, and during the summer of 1861, he oversaw the enlistment of state troops. Although he sought a commission in the Confederate army, he never received one; his lack of military training, his Whig background, and his ambivalence toward the war were too well known. In the fall of 1861, he took some Mississippi troops to Hopkinsville, Kentucky, but when he failed to get a Confederate commission, he asked to be relieved from service and returned to Mississippi. A month later, he again went to Kentucky with Mississippi troops, again was refused a commission, and again returned home, this time to sit out the rest of the war.

Alcorn's bitterness with the Confederacy intensified. He labeled Jefferson Davis a "corrupt tyrant" and regretted Mississippi's secession, yet throughout the war he refused to take the oath of allegiance to the Union. Alcorn was clearly torn between his loyalty to Southern traditions and his distaste for the Confederate government. In 1862, although twice arrested and briefly detained, Alcorn developed friendly relations among Federal officers. In 1863 Federal troops wrecked his plantation, but spared his house and family any harm. Despite his disillusionment with the war, he reported information about Federal movements to Confederate scouts.

In 1863 Alcorn was elected to the Mississippi legislature and, while serving there in 1863 and 1864, was friendly with Union officers. Nonetheless, he still refused to take an oath of allegiance to the Union and, at the request of Governor Charles Clark, even served briefly as a colonel of state troops to prevent desertion from Confederate ranks. Unlike most slaveholders, however, he began to sympathize with the freedmen and favored granting them civil and legal rights. Alcorn's inconsistencies were later summarized by a contemporary, "Gen. Alcorn was a Whig up to '59, a Union man in '60, a secessionist in '61, a fire-eater in '62, a reconstructionist in '66, a scalawag in '67, a radical in '68, and a bitter-ender in '69."

During Reconstruction, Alcorn affiliated with the Republican party and became Mississippi's first Republican governor in 1869 with the support of the carpetbagger military governor Adelbert Ames. Alcorn resigned the governorship in 1871 to take a seat in the U.S. Senate, where he served until 1877. During this period, Alcorn's moderate Republican position conflicted with Ames's radical views, and the Democrats returned to power. After retirement, Alcorn returned to politics only briefly—to serve in the Mississippi constitutional convention of 1890.

BIBLIOGRAPHY

Pereyra, Lillian A. *James Lusk Alcorn: Persistent Whig.* Baton Rouge, La., 1966.
Rowland, Dunbar. *History of Mississippi.* Chicago, 1925.

RAY SKATES

ALEXANDER, EDWARD PORTER (1835–1910), brigadier general.

Born on May 26, 1835, in Washington, Georgia, Alexander graduated from West Point in 1857, standing third out of thirty-eight cadets. He received a brevet second lieutenant's commission in the Engineer Corps and remained at the academy as an instructor. Expeditions to Utah and the Washington Territory interrupted his teaching routine. Promotion came slow for Alexander, but on October 10, 1858, he became a full second lieutenant. With his native state out of the Union, followed by Abraham Lincoln's call for troops, Alexander reluctantly tendered his resignation on May 1, 1861. "My people are going to war," he wrote. "If I don't come and bear my part, they will believe me to be a coward."

A captain's commission, dated March 16, 1861, waited for Alexander when he arrived in Richmond the following month. Jefferson Davis placed the Georgian in charge of the Signal Corps in Richmond, and on June 29, he was instructed to perform the same service with the Confederate army at Manassas. From an observation tower that

EDWARD PORTER ALEXANDER.   NATIONAL ARCHIVES

Alexander constructed near the Van Pelt house, he alerted officers to a Federal flanking movement on July 21. In the aftermath of the victory at Manassas, Gen. P. G. T. Beauregard complimented Alexander and his Signal Corps.

Alexander's superiors quickly recognized his wide talents. He consequently shouldered a number of diverse assignments. Not only was he chief of ordnance for Beauregard after Manassas, but he also handled similar duties for Gen. Joseph E. Johnston that fall; William N. Pendleton remained in control of Johnston's Ordnance Department but in name only. Besides his engineering and reconnoitering responsibilities, Alexander found time to create a more efficient supply system and experimented with new weapons ranging from rockets to flaming spears. For his efforts, he received a major's commission on April 18, 1862. After Robert E. Lee took command in May 1862, he instructed Alexander to oversee the operation of an observation balloon during the Seven Days' campaign (June 25–July 1). Alexander earned the confidence of his new superior who promoted him to lieutenant colonel on July 17, to date from December 31, 1861.

After the Army of the Potomac had been repelled outside

Richmond, Alexander maintained his varied duties, plus the new chore of training the reserve artillery batteries. Pendleton had proved woefully inadequate as chief of artillery, but Lee could not find a delicate way of dismissing him. Alexander, as a result, consistently handled many of Pendleton's assignments throughout the war. While the fighting raged at Second Manassas (August 29–30) and Sharpsburg (September 17), Alexander busied himself behind the lines with the Ordnance Department. Supported by Lee's recommendation, Alexander received command of Stephen D. Lee's famous artillery battalion on November 7, although he did not relinquish control of the Ordnance Department until December 4. At Fredericksburg on December 13, Alexander insisted that Confederate batteries unlimber on the brow of Marye's Heights so that the guns could blast the infantry, a decision that sealed the fate of the attacking Union soldiers. On March 3, 1863, he was boosted in rank to full colonel.

Alexander constantly strove to enhance the artillery's effectiveness on the battlefield. During the winter of 1862–1863, he helped implement a battalion system that took tactical control of the artillery away from infantry commanders and restored it to ordnance officers. It also corralled batteries into groups of sixteen guns, which made it possible for Lee's artillery to concentrate its firepower. Alexander revealed the potency of this new system at Chancellorsville on May 3, when he massed over thirty guns at Hazel Grove. His skillful direction of Confederate artillery broke the Union defense at Fairview.

After the reorganization of the army following Thomas J. ("Stonewall") Jackson's death, Gen. James Longstreet and Lee wanted Alexander as chief of artillery of the First Corps. Because they did not wish to offend the senior officer, Col. James B. Walton, Longstreet decided on an awkward arrangement that allowed Walton to maintain his post while Alexander directed the tactical operations of the battalions. At Gettysburg on July 3, Alexander not only organized the massive cannonade that preceded Pickett's Charge but was also given the responsibility of determining when the infantry should advance toward Cemetery Ridge. "It was no longer Gen. Lee's inspiration" that would decide the battle, Alexander recalled, "but my cold judgment." Though his missiles proved indecisive, Alexander overall expertly managed the logistical problems that plagued his command during the entire Gettysburg campaign.

Alexander accompanied Longstreet's corps to the West in the fall of 1863 but arrived too late to participate in the fighting at Chickamauga (September 19–20). From October to December, Alexander's battalion saw limited action during the Chattanooga and Knoxville campaigns. The following winter, Johnston asked for Alexander's promotion to brigadier general and his transfer to the Army of Tennessee as chief of artillery. Jefferson Davis refused Johnston's application, confiding to a friend that Alexander was "one of a very few whom Gen Lee wd [sic] not give to anybody." Davis, however, promised Alexander a brigadier generalship, which he received on February 26, 1864. With the promotion—one of three such commissions awarded to a Confederate artillery officer during the war—came official control of artillery in the First Corps.

The spring of 1864 found Alexander and the rest of Longstreet's troops reunited with the Army of Northern Virginia. When the overland campaign opened in the Wilderness on May 5, Alexander had ninety-one guns under his command. He had little opportunity to use them until June 3 at Cold Harbor where the disposition of his ordnance produced a withering cross fire that doomed the Federal assault. During the siege of Petersburg, Alexander commanded the guns that guarded a twenty-four-mile line between the Appomattox and Chickahominy rivers. Because of Alexander's engineering expertise, Lee relied on him to perfect the mazelike fortifications of the Richmond defenses.

When Lee surrendered at Appomattox on April 9, Alexander had established himself as the army's most prominent artillerist. He recounted his war experiences in *Military Memoirs of a Confederate* (1907). A more revealing look at the Army of Northern Virginia is contained in Alexander's personal recollections, *Fighting for the Confederacy* (1989). This work stands as one of the richest firsthand accounts of Confederate operations in Virginia. Alexander also enjoyed a distinguished postwar career as a railroad president and professor of engineering while serving in a number of appointed government positions. He died on April 28, 1910.

BIBLIOGRAPHY

Alexander, Edward P. *Fighting for the Confederacy: The Personal Recollections of General Edward Porter Alexander.* Edited by Gary W. Gallagher. Chapel Hill, N.C., 1989.

Alexander, Edward P. *Military Memoirs of a Confederate: A Critical Narrative.* New York, 1907. Reprint, Dayton, Ohio, 1977.

Klein, Maury. *Edward Porter Alexander.* Athens, Ga., 1971.

PETER S. CARMICHAEL

ALEXANDRA. Built by William C. Miller and Sons of Liverpool in 1862 through 1863, *Alexandra* displaced 286 tons, measured 145 feet by 20 feet by 10.6 feet, and was expected to have a speed of 10 knots. Rumors of special construction features not usually found in commercial vessels and reports that it might be destined for the Confederacy brought it to the attention of British authorities, who seized it on the eve of its launching.

Though the ship never sailed for the South, it has a special place in the history of the Confederate navy. *Alexandra* served as a test case of the British response to the American Civil War and to the efforts of Southern agents to buy or build naval craft in the neutral domain of the United Kingdom. In April 1863 Her Majesty's government tried to determine the legal limits of the Foreign Enlistment Act of 1819, the antiquated statute that set out the rules of proper neutral conduct, and sought to determine the responsibilities of British citizens to the war in America. In the summer of 1863 the British Court of Exchequer examined those complex questions and concluded that the law did not prohibit the construction of ships for the South—provided that those ships were not equipped in the United Kingdom. The curious case of *Alexandra* seemed to mean that the South might purchase any sort of ship, regardless of its warlike potential, send it to a rendezvous beyond the crown's jurisdiction, and then, in a separate package, forward that vessel's armament to the same meeting place. "If the jury were convinced that the contract was *to equip* the vessel within Her Majesty's dominions, that was a matter 'justifying conviction,' but if they believed 'the object really was to build a ship in obedience to an order [and] in compliance with a contract'... then it appears... that the Foreign Enlistment Act has not been broken." In such circumstances—and operating under a charge from one of the preeminent legal experts in England—the jury "without hesitating for more than half a minute" returned a verdict against the crown.

Though superficially a Southern victory, this case, in reality, set in motion the forces that eventually doomed Confederate efforts to acquire naval craft in Great Britain. The British foreign secretary had made what he thought was a sincere effort to show the North that "a kind of neutral hostility should not be allowed to go on [in the UK] without some attempt to stop it." That attempt failed. Instead, the *Alexandra* trial demonstrated beyond all reasonable doubt that the Foreign Enlistment Act could not cope with the sophisticated challenge that James D. Bulloch had launched on the legal limits of neutrality during the Civil War.

The rigidly legalistic framework embodied in the *Alexandra* decision set off currents of reconsideration about the proper British response to the war in America. It soon became clear to Lord John Russell (himself a staunch advocate of free trade and constitutional guarantees of property rights) that if he wished to resolve the issues of the American war, he would have to go "above and beyond" the law to preserve peace between the United States and the United Kingdom. He was willing to take that step.

BIBLIOGRAPHY

Bulloch, James Dunwoody. *The Secret Service of the Confederate States in Europe: Or How the Confederate Cruisers Were Equipped.* 2 vols. New York, 1884. Reprint, New York, 1959.

Merli, Frank J. "The Confederate Navy." In *In Peace and War: Interpretations of American Naval History, 1775–1984.* Edited by Kenneth J. Hagan. 2d ed. Westport, Conn., 1984.

Merli, Frank J. *Great Britain and the Confederate Navy, 1861–1865.* Bloomington, Ind., 1970.

Parkes, Oscar. *British Battleships, 1860–1950: A History of Design, Construction, and Armament.* Hamden, Conn., 1971.

Spencer, Warren. *The Confederate Navy in Europe.* University, Ala., 1983.

FRANK J. MERLI

ALLEN, HENRY W. (1820–1866), brigadier general and governor of Confederate Louisiana. Allen's energy and initiative kept resources available to fuel the war effort after the Union army severed the Trans-Mississippi from the Confederacy. Historian E. Merton Coulter judged that "it was Henry W. Allen who showed the rest of the Confederate governors how good a Confederate a state governor could be."

Born April 29, 1820, in Farmville, Virginia, Allen moved with his family to Missouri when he was thirteen. He attended Marion College and left for Grand Gulf, Mississippi, where he worked as a tutor and set up his own law practice in 1841. On a six-month tour in Texas in 1842, he saw minor action with the militia against the Mexicans. Allen became a prosperous sugar planter in West Baton Rouge, Louisiana, attended law classes at Harvard, and showed promise as a politician.

As a soldier, Allen demonstrated considerable bravery under fire—a trait that also cut short his military career. Late in July 1861, he assumed command of the Fourth Louisiana, which was ordered to Tennessee to serve with the Second Corps of the Army of the Mississippi under Braxton Bragg. At Shiloh (April 6–7, 1862) the recently commissioned colonel led his men in a number of assaults on what became known as the Hornet's Nest. Despite wounds in both cheeks, Allen would not leave the field and even assisted in rallying stragglers to resist the successful Federal counterattack of April 7. At Baton Rouge on August 5, 1862, he sustained a crippling wound to his right leg while charging a Federal battery. Allen refused amputation, but the shattered leg caused great pain and prevented his return to active duty. Jefferson Davis recognized his contribution by promoting Allen to brigadier general on August 19, 1863.

The war hero returned home to Louisiana and on November 21, 1863, was elected governor of the Confederate government sitting at Shreveport. Rejecting any talk of peace, he vigorously pursued the Confederate cause, instituting a number of progressive actions to sustain the war effort. Allen placed a priority on regulating currency to reduce rampaging inflation, traded cotton with Mexico to secure supplies and medicines, instituted programs for relief of disabled veterans and their families, and imposed governmental direction on mining and manufacturing. Though he collided now and then with the Davis government over irregularities in impressment procedures, Allen time and again favored continued resistance: he called for arming slaves to fight and at first supported Gen. E. Kirby Smith's desire to battle on after the Army of Northern Virginia surrendered in April 1865. Only in the next month—when he realized the war was lost—did Allen meet with other governors to discuss acceptable terms for peace.

Fearing for his safety, Allen with a number of other Confederates fled to Mexico where he began publishing an English-language newspaper, *Mexican Times*. His wounds, however, continued to plague him, contributing to a general breakdown in his health. The former governor died in Mexico on April 22, 1866.

BIBLIOGRAPHY

Cassidy, Vincent H., and Amos E. Simpson. *Henry Watkins Allen of Louisiana.* Baton Rouge, La., 1964.

Dorsey, Sarah A. *Recollections of Henry Watkins Allen, Brigadier-General, Confederate States Army, Ex-Governor of Louisiana.* New York, 1866.

Kerby, Robert L. *Kirby Smith's Confederacy: The Trans-Mississippi South, 1863–1865.* New York, 1972.

WILLIAM ALAN BLAIR

WILLIAM WIRT ALLEN.   LIBRARY OF CONGRESS

ALLEN, WILLIAM WIRT (1835–1894), brigadier general. Born in New York City, Allen moved to Montgomery, Alabama, as a child. After graduating from the College of New Jersey (now Princeton) in 1854, he studied law but left that profession in 1861 to farm in Alabama. Although unenthusiastic about the war, Allen entered the Confederate army as first lieutenant in the Montgomery Mounted Rifles. On March 18, 1862, he was elected major of the First Alabama Cavalry.

After his first serious action at Shiloh, Allen was promoted to colonel, leading his regiment in Gen. Braxton Bragg's invasion of Kentucky. He gained distinction at Bear Wallow, Horse Cave, and Green River and was wounded at Perryville. Allen commanded Brig. Gen. Joseph Wheeler's brigade during Wheeler's tenure as Bragg's chief of cavalry. He led this brigade on a raid near Murfreesboro, Tennessee, on November 27, 1862, earning praise from Bragg and Wheeler. Allen lost part of his right hand to a gunshot wound at Overall's Creek on December 31.

After recovering, Allen was commissioned brigadier general as of February 26, 1864, and commanded the only remaining full-strength cavalry brigade in the Army of Tennessee, stationed at Dalton, Georgia. He probed Maj. Gen. William Tecumseh Sherman's front and guarded against movements toward Atlanta. After the Army of

Tennessee retreated into Georgia, Allen commanded an all-Alabama brigade during the Atlanta campaign. On a raid through Tennessee in August 1864, he succeeded Maj. Gen. William Thompson Martin as commander of the division containing his own and Col. Charles C. Crew's brigades. Allen further distinguished himself at Cassville, Pickett's Mill, and Decatur, and in the July 29 capture of Maj. Gen. George Stoneman's raiding column near Macon.

Allen's original brigade, now commanded by Brig. Gen. Robert Anderson, was added to his division in late 1864. When Allen fought at Waynesboro, Georgia, he remained on the field even though he was wounded and had two horses shot from under him. He then entered South Carolina, continually harassing Sherman's March to the Sea. His division prevented the enemy occupation of Aiken, drawing praise from Governor Andrew G. Magrath. The ladies of Aiken gave Allen a silk flag with the inscription: "Your valor cheers our hearts."

On March 4, 1865, Allen was appointed temporary major general, the last such promotion made by President Jefferson Davis. The Confederate Senate, however, failed to confirm the promotion before its final adjournment on March 18. Allen surrendered at Salisbury, North Carolina, on May 3, 1865, and was paroled as a brigadier general before the end of the year. He had a distinguished war record, suffering three wounds and having ten horses shot from under him.

After the war, Allen returned to his plantation and became involved in the railroad business. He served as federal marshal during President Grover Cleveland's first term. Allen died in Sheffield, Alabama, on November 21, 1894.

BIBLIOGRAPHY

Barrett, John G. *Sherman's March through the Carolinas.* Chapel Hill, N.C., 1956.
Derry, Joseph T. *Georgia.* Vol. 6 of *Confederate Military History.* Edited by Clement A. Evans. Atlanta, 1899. Vol. 7 of extended ed. Wilmington, N.C., 1987.
Wheeler, Joseph. *Alabama.* Vol. 7 of *Confederate Military History.* Edited by Clement A. Evans. Atlanta, 1899. Vol. 8 of extended ed. Wilmington, N.C., 1987.

ROBERT F. PACE

ALLISON, ABRAHAM K. (1810–1893), governor
of Florida. Born in Jones County, Georgia, Abraham Kurkindolle Allison spent his early career as an Indian trader, settling in Apalachicola, Florida, around 1830. He saw service in the Seminole War and thereafter began the practice of law, serving almost continually in the Florida legislature from 1845 to 1865. He participated in the secession convention of 1861 where he attempted unsuccessfully to make Florida's secession dependent upon that of Georgia and Alabama. Allison later saw military service in Georgia and Florida. He was also active in the distribution of relief supplies to the needy families of Florida's soldiers under a program initiated by Governor John Milton in 1863.

He was serving as president of the Florida senate when Governor Milton took his own life on April 1, 1865. Allison became acting governor and sent reassurances to Jefferson Davis that he would continue Milton's policies. Union forces arrived in Tallahassee on May 10. Hoping to achieve a quick reconciliation, Allison on May 12 appointed a commission to confer with authorities in Washington on the restoration of Florida's relationship with the Union. He also called a special session of the legislature for June 5 and ordered a gubernatorial election for June 7. These plans were nullified by orders from Washington. Martial law was declared, and Allison, with others, was arrested and imprisoned at Fort Pulaski, Georgia, until January 1866. After his release he returned to his law practice in Quincy, remaining active in politics. In 1871 he was convicted of voter intimidation in a local election and served a six-month prison sentence.

BIBLIOGRAPHY

Johns, John E. *Florida during the Civil War.* Gainesville, Fla., 1963.

Tebeau, Charlton W. *A History of Florida.* Coral Gables, Fla., 1971.

WILLIAM E. PARRISH

AMERICAN PARTY. The American party was a
secret nativist organization that enjoyed momentary success in the South in the mid-1850s. Growing out of the Secret Order of the Star-Spangled Banner, the party capitalized on hostility to immigrants and Catholics and quickly became a power in the border states and Louisiana where there were significant immigrant populations. Throughout the South, it also attracted a number of ex-Whigs looking for a national conservative alternative to the Democratic party. When questioned, members pretended to know nothing about the party; hence, they became known as Know-Nothings.

A number of prominent Southern political leaders, including John J. Crittenden of Kentucky, Kenneth Rayner of North Carolina, John Bell of Tennessee, and Sam Houston of Texas, joined the party, and by 1855 it was the major rival to the Democrats in the South. The party's defeat that year in the Virginia gubernatorial election, however, coupled with deepening sectional divisions in the national organization over the slavery issue, severely weakened it in the region. In 1856 the Southern-controlled national convention nominated Millard Fillmore for president. Running as a Union candidate, Fillmore made a strong race in the South, polling almost 45 percent of the popular vote; he carried Maryland and only narrowly lost several other Southern states. But Northern desertions left Fillmore a distant third nationally and sealed the fate of the party.

The American party retained a separate organization in some parts of the South until 1860 (New Orleans elected a Know-Nothing mayor that year), but ultimately the bulk of its southern members joined various opposition coalitions and voted for Bell in 1860. The significance of Southern Know-Nothingism lay in its role in opposition to the Democratic party and in sectionalism before the war.

BIBLIOGRAPHY

Holt, Michael F. *The Political Crisis of the 1850s.* New York, 1978.
Overdyke, W. Darrell. *The Know-Nothing Party in the South.* Baton Rouge, La., 1950.

WILLIAM E. GIENAPP

ANDERSON, CLIFFORD (1833–1899), captain
and congressman from Georgia. Anderson was born in Nottoway County, Virginia, a member of one of the Shenandoah Valley's wealthiest and most politically prominent families. But the family fortune dissolved a few years later, and he was orphaned at the age of twelve. In 1848, he moved to Macon, Georgia, to work in the law office of an

older brother and live with his sister, the mother of poet Sidney Lanier. Admitted to the Georgia bar at age nineteen, Anderson practiced law with his brother-in-law, Robert S. Lanier, in a partnership that lasted until 1893. Anderson served as a judge of the Macon city court from 1856 to 1858 and was elected to a term in the legislature (1859–1860).

Though initially an avid Unionist and member of the Constitutional Union party, he was converted after Abraham Lincoln's election and quickly became a strong advocate of Georgia's secession in speeches before Macon citizens. When war broke out, he entered military service as a private in Floyd's Rifles. He distinguished himself in Virginia and rose to the position of brigadier inspector on the staff of Gen. Ambrose Ransom Wright. His heroism at Gettysburg earned him a captain's commission, but by that time he had been elected to the Confederate House of Representatives, and he resigned his military position to serve in Richmond. Like several other Georgia congressmen, Anderson fully supported President Jefferson Davis and, in doing so, opposed the obstructionist tactics of Georgia's governor Joseph E. Brown. Anderson spoke out on several occasions on behalf of relief efforts for Confederate soldiers' families and other civilians.

Though disbarred after the war, he received a pardon from President Andrew Johnson and resumed his law practice. After Reconstruction, Anderson became active in Democratic politics and served as the state attorney general from 1880 to 1890. When Mercer University moved to Macon, Anderson joined the faculty of its new law school. From 1893 to 1895, he helped revise Georgia's law code, which he considered his most significant accomplishment.

BIBLIOGRAPHY

Candler, Allen D., and Clement A. Evans, eds. *Cyclopedia of Georgia.* Vol. 1. Atlanta, 1906.

Coleman, Kenneth, and Charles Stephen Gurr, eds. *Dictionary of Georgia Biography.* Vol. 1. Athens, Ga., 1983.

Northen, William W. *Men of Mark in Georgia.* Vol. 3. Atlanta, 1908. Reprint, Spartanburg, S.C., 1974.

JOHN C. INSCOE

ANDERSON, GEORGE B. (1831–1862), brigadier general.

A native of North Carolina, George Burgwyn Anderson was born April 12, 1831 (thirty years to the day before the firing on Fort Sumter). He attended West Point and performed so brilliantly a contemporary called him "the *very superior* mind" in the class of 1852. But nine years later, when he left the U.S. Army, he had advanced only to the rank of first lieutenant.

Anderson was commissioned commanding colonel of the Fourth North Carolina Infantry on May 16, 1861. He impressed his troops as "a splendid specimen." The regiment arrived at Manassas in July just after the battle

GEORGE B. ANDERSON.   LIBRARY OF CONGRESS

there. Colonel Anderson served for months as post commandant at Manassas Junction. He led the Fourth during the Confederate retreat in March 1862 and on to the peninsula in April. Anderson and the Fourth fought their first battle at Seven Pines, where the colonel commanded Featherston's Brigade in the absence of its brigadier. In bitter fighting, the brigade lost nearly half of its strength.

Anderson won promotion to brigadier general soon after Seven Pines. His brigade included his old Fourth North Carolina and three other regiments from the state. He led his new command with real distinction during the Seven Days' fighting and was wounded in the hand at Malvern Hill. The brigade missed the Battle of Second Manassas, but played an important role at South Mountain. At Sharpsburg on September 17, 1862, Anderson posted his brigade in a sunken lane that his men immortalized as the Bloody Lane. A bullet wound in the ankle knocked the general out of the fight. Although the injury appeared to be more painful than serious, infection forced amputation of the limb and Anderson died of complications on October 16. His intellect, training, and early war performance all suggest that Anderson's premature death halted a career that might well have been spectacular.

BIBLIOGRAPHY

Gales, Seaton. "Gen. George Burgwyn Anderson." *Land We Love* 3 (1867): 93–100.

Waddell, A. M. "General George Burgwyn Anderson." *Southern Historical Society Papers* 14 (1890): 387–397.

ROBERT K. KRICK

GEORGE THOMAS ("TIGE") ANDERSON.   NATIONAL ARCHIVES

ANDERSON, GEORGE THOMAS "TIGE"

(1824–1901), brigadier general. George Thomas Anderson, more often called "Tige" by his soldiers, was one of eight colonels promoted to brigadier general in the Army of Northern Virginia on November 1, 1862. Of those eight, four—including Anderson—commanded their brigades, except when absent due to wounds, until the surrender at Appomattox in April 1865. They were among the most efficient brigadiers in the Confederate army.

Anderson was born in Covington, Georgia, on February 3, 1824, and left his studies at Emory College to enlist as a cavalryman in the Mexican War. He was later commissioned in the regular army and served as a captain in the First U.S. Cavalry from 1855 to 1858.

When the Eleventh Georgia Infantry was organized in July 1861, Anderson became its first colonel. He commanded his regiment until the summer of 1862, after the Seven Days' campaign, when he succeeded to brigade command. Anderson, though still a colonel, led the brigade through the Second Manassas and Sharpsburg campaigns and won the praise of his superiors.

Anderson's first battle as a brigadier general was in December 1862 at Fredericksburg. For the rest of the war his brigade of Georgians served in James Longstreet's First Corps in the division commanded by John Bell Hood and later by Charles W. Field. Anderson's brigade, with almost all of Longstreet's corps, did not participate in the Chan-

cellorsville campaign. It rejoined Robert E. Lee for the Gettysburg campaign, however, and engaged in the fierce fighting in the Wheatfield on July 2, 1863, where Anderson was severely wounded in the thigh. He recovered in time to lead his brigade in the Knoxville campaign of November 1863 and later commanded it in the final campaigns from the Wilderness to Appomattox, from May 1864 to April 1865.

Though not truly a brilliant officer in the mold of Robert Rodes, John B. Gordon, or William Mahone, Anderson was an able administrator, a fine combat leader, and one of the most dependable brigadiers under Lee. "Brave Old Tige, how his boys loved him!" a veteran who served in Anderson's brigade remembered years later. "With such officers as we had in the Army of Northern Virginia, how could the boys help fighting as we did?"

After the war Anderson lived in Georgia and Alabama and held several local government positions, most notably as a chief of police. He died in Anniston, Alabama, on April 4, 1901.

BIBLIOGRAPHY

Compiled Military Service Records. George T. Anderson. Microcopy M331, Roll 6. Record Group 109. National Archives, Washington, D.C.

Derry, Joseph T. *Georgia*. Vol. 6 of *Confederate Military History*. Edited by Clement A. Evans. Atlanta, 1899. Vol. 7 of extended ed. Wilmington, N.C., 1987.

J. TRACY POWER

ANDERSON, JAMES PATTON (1822–1872),

congressman from Florida and major general. Born on February 16, 1822, in Winchester, Franklin County, Tennessee, James Patton Anderson was raised on the family farm, known as Craggy Hope, until after his father, William Preston Anderson, a former U.S. Army officer and Federal district attorney, died in April 1831. Following his father's death, Anderson's mother, Margaret Adair Anderson, took him and his five siblings to live at her parents' home in Mercer County, Kentucky. There he received his early education in country schools and from private tutors. In October 1836, Anderson was enrolled at Jefferson College in Cannonsburg, Pennsylvania, but because of family financial misfortunes, his education there was curtailed after one year. Moving to Hernando, DeSoto County, Mississippi, Anderson, known to his friends as Patton, spent part of the years 1838 and 1839 working with his mother's new husband, Dr. J. N. Bybee, in constructing a new family home. There, he also began the study and practice of medicine, presumably under Dr. Bybee's tutelage. Resuming his studies at Jefferson College early in 1839, Anderson was graduated from that school in the fall of 1840.

mustered out of service at Vicksburg, Mississippi, and he arrived back in DeSoto County on July 4, 1848.

Anderson continued his law practice after returning home, until the fall of 1849, when he was elected to the Mississippi legislature. During his term of office, Anderson closely supported the views of U.S. Senator Jefferson Davis and Governor John Quitman—both of Mississippi— regarding the Compromise of 1850, which they opposed. As a result of this stance, he lost his bid for reelection in 1851.

Once more reentering the field of law, Anderson remained in that profession until he left for Washington in 1853 in an attempt to secure a commission in a new regular infantry regiment. But when the bill responsible for creating the regiment failed to become law, Anderson instead accepted the position of U.S. marshal for the Territory of Washington. In obtaining this position in the administration of President Franklin Pierce, he was indebted to Jefferson Davis, then serving as secretary of state.

Before leaving for the Pacific coast, Anderson traveled to Memphis, Tennessee, where he married his cousin, Henrietta Buford Adair, on April 30, 1853, and within an hour of the ceremony he and his new bride were en route by steamer to Washington Territory. Traveling via New Orleans through Nicaragua and San Francisco, they finally reached Astoria, Oregon, in late June. Leaving his wife with relatives in Astoria, Anderson traveled overland to Olympia, Washington Territory, arriving on July 4. The next day, he began a months-long foot and canoe journey through the territory taking the census.

Upon completion of the census, Patton and Henrietta Anderson set out in a canoe up the Cowlitz River and then on foot overland to settle in Olympia. There the Andersons soon bought a house in which they lived for the rest of their stay in Washington Territory. During that time Anderson discharged his duties as marshal and practiced law when time and circumstances allowed.

Running as a Democrat, Anderson was elected in June 1855 as a delegate from the Territory to the Thirty-fourth U.S. Congress. In October of that year, he and his wife left for the District of Columbia, reaching the city several days before the first session of Congress began in December. Also in 1855, the Andersons spent the Christmas holidays with their aunt, Ellen Adair Beatty, at her plantation, Casa Bianca, in Monticello, Jefferson County, Florida, a few miles east of Tallahassee. During that time he agreed to manage his aunt's quite extensive holdings, which, among other property, consisted of at least 130 slaves.

When his term in Congress expired on March 4, 1857, Anderson was offered the position of governor and superintendant of Indian affairs of Washington Territory by newly elected President James Buchanan. Fearing the dissolution of the Union, however, he declined to leave the South. Wanting to be on hand for any eventuality, he then

JAMES PATTON ANDERSON.   LIBRARY OF CONGRESS

After graduation, Patton Anderson returned to DeSoto County and studied the practice of law with the firm of Buckner and Delafield, and in 1843 he was admitted to the bar. But, finding the legal profession overcrowded in that section of Mississippi, Anderson accepted a position as deputy sheriff of DeSoto County offered by his brother-in-law, the sheriff there. He held the position until 1846. During the years 1844 and 1845, Anderson spent his summers furthering his law studies at Montrose in Frankfort, Kentucky. Following his term as deputy sheriff, he formed a law partnership and began practicing law full-time.

Complying with a request of the governor of Mississippi, in October 1847, Anderson organized a company of volunteer troops from a local militia regiment and was quickly elected its captain. With the addition of four more companies, the First Battalion of Mississippi Rifles was formed, and, after being supplied in New Orleans, the battalion was sent to Tampico, Mexico, in January 1848. There the battalion performed garrison duty during the Mexican War, and on February 22 Anderson was elected lieutenant colonel of the unit at the age of twenty-six. Contracting malaria in Mexico, he suffered from the disease for the rest of his life. When the war ended, Anderson and his men were returned to manage Casa Bianca as his sole occupation.

In December 1860, nearly four years later, Anderson was elected as a delegate from Jefferson County to the Florida secession convention, which convened in Tallahassee on January 1, 1861. There he endorsed wholeheartedly the state's ordinance of secession, which was passed on January 10. While this convention was still in session, it chose Anderson and three others as delegates to the Provisional Congress in Montgomery, Alabama. There he served on the committees of Public Affairs and Public Lands and offered the unusual proposal that slaves serve the Confederate military as nurses, cooks, pioneers, and teamsters. After adopting the Provisional Constitution and electing Jefferson Davis provisional president, Congress adjourned, and Patton Anderson returned to Casa Bianca.

Late in March 1861, at the request of Florida Governor Madison S. Perry, Anderson organized a company of infantry (the Jefferson Rifles), which he took to the Chattahoochee Arsenal to become part of the First Florida Infantry (the Magnolia Regiment). While at Chattahoochee, Anderson was elected the regiment's colonel on April 5, and later that night the command left for Pensacola to join Confederate Gen. Braxton Bragg's army. Arriving at Pensacola on April 11—the day before the Civil War began— Anderson and his troops spent the next eight months in that vicinity drilling and organizing. During much of that time, Anderson served as a brigade commander, but the only action seen was a small but apparently successful amphibious raid on October 8 and 9, 1861, against Union defenders—the Sixth New York Infantry—on Santa Rosa Island, a mile and a half offshore.

On February 10, 1862, Anderson was commissioned brigadier general, and from March 29 until June 1862, he commanded the Second Brigade in Gen. Daniel Ruggle's First Division, Bragg's Second Corps, of Gen. Albert Sidney Johnston's Army of the Mississippi. On the first day of the Battle of Shiloh, April 6, 1862, he led his brigade of green troops credibly, helping to capture a Federal battery and overrunning the camps belonging to the Union troops of Gen. William Tecumseh Sherman's division. Later that day Anderson and his men battled successfully in the horror known as the "Hornet's Nest," where the brigade suffered heavy casualties. The next day, his troops covered the Confederate retreat after Gen. Ulysses S. Grant secured a decisive Union victory.

Following Shiloh, Anderson took divisional command in June without being formally promoted. At Perryville, Kentucky, on October 8, 1862, during Bragg's ill-fated Kentucky campaign, Anderson led his division satisfactorily, although as a result of the drawn battle, Bragg withdrew his army to Chattanooga, Tennessee, thereby signaling the failure of the campaign.

On November 20, 1862, Anderson was put in command of a division in Gen. William J. Hardee's First Corps, Army of Tennessee, until December 27, when he was assigned command of the Third Brigade in Gen. Jones M. Withers's Second Division of Gen. Leonidas Polk's Corps. From December 31, 1862, until January 2, 1863, at the Battle of Murfreesboro, Tennessee, Anderson gained in his military prominence by leading this brigade bravely. On the morning of the first day of the battle, in a series of bloody charges made against Gen. James S. Negley's division of the Federal Fourteenth Corps, Anderson's Mississippi and Alabama infantrymen were cut to pieces but eventually routed the Northerners and captured nine artillery pieces and many prisoners. Nevertheless, the result of this battle on January 2 was the resounding defeat of Bragg's army by Gen. William Rosecrans's Union forces.

From that point until the second day of the Battle of Chickamauga (September 19–20, 1863), Anderson, for the most part, continued commanding at brigade level. But when Gen. Thomas C. Hindman, who had replaced Withers, was wounded during the battle, Anderson again rose to division-level command when he replaced Hindman late on the night of September 20. During the Confederate breakthrough earlier that day, Anderson's men had helped defeat the Federal army's right, taking eight fieldpieces, a number of flags, and many prisoners. Sent to another part of the battlefield later, Anderson's brigade continued its efficient service, helping to secure the Confederacy's greatest victory in the western theater.

Remaining in command of Hindman's division after the battle, he led it all through the siege of Chattanooga in October and November 1863. On November 25, however, Anderson's men were routed at the Battle of Missionary Ridge. This disaster was Anderson's greatest humiliation of the war.

On February 17, 1864, Patton Anderson finally was appointed to the rank of major general in the Confederate army, a rank more in keeping with his military position. But with this promotion came his transfer from the Army of Tennessee on March 4 to the command of the relatively small District of Florida, where he held sway over some twelve thousand soldiers. His sojourn in Florida provided no great battles, and his duties there were comparatively pedestrian.

After Sherman began his campaign for Atlanta in May 1864, Anderson was recalled in July to again take over Hindman's division in the Army of Tennessee, now commanded by Gen. Joseph E. Johnston, who had succeeded Bragg after that general's defeat at Chattanooga. The division, at that time, belonged to Gen. Stephen D. Lee's corps, and Anderson took command on July 30, just after the Battle of Ezra Church near Atlanta.

During the Battle of Jonesboro, south of Atlanta, on August 31, 1864, Anderson was in charge of Lee's right division. The Confederate plan of attack against the Federal forces that day was to be a coordinated assault by Lee and Gen. William J. Hardee's corps, under the command of Gen. Patrick Cleburne, which was to begin at 3:00 in the afternoon. Lee, for some reason, advanced too early, however, stepping his men off at 2:20 against Union Gen. John Logan's Fifteenth Corps. Anderson pushed his troops hard over open ground until he reached a spot about eighty yards from Logan's entrenched Federals, who then rose to give the Southerners a brutal, killing fire that mowed them down in rows. With his soldiers pinned to the ground and waiting for reinforcements that never came, Anderson bravely rode along his line, trying desperately to rally his men to continue the charge. But, during this attempt, he received a wound which tore through the lower part of his face, fracturing his jawbone on both sides and slicing his tongue. So serious was the injury that he was nearly mustered out of service by military doctors for disability. After about an hour Lee withdrew his corps from the field and early the next morning marched off to the north. The Confederates lost the Battle of Jonesboro later that day after continued Federal pressure forced them to retreat to Lovejoy's Station.

While recuperating in Monticello, Anderson followed, as well as he could, the continuing defeat of the Confederate armies. Finally, feeling obliged for patriotic reasons to rejoin the Southern cause in the field—and against the better judgment of his physicians—he took command, on April 9, 1865—the day that Gen. Robert E. Lee surrendered his Army of Northern Virginia to Gen. Ulysses S. Grant—of a division of Georgia and South Carolina troops formerly under the command of Gen. William B. Taliaferro, Gen. Alexander P. Stewart's corps, Army of Tennessee. Fighting through some of the last battles of the Civil War in the Carolinas, James Patton Anderson finally surrendered with General Johnston and the Army of Tennessee at Durham Station, North Carolina, on April 26, 1865, thereby ending the Civil War in the East. Anderson and his men were paroled—under the same terms given General Lee at Appomattox—at Greensboro, North Carolina, shortly after the surrender.

With the war over, Anderson moved his family to Memphis, Tennessee, but his wound received at Jonesboro was too debilitating for a physically active occupation. To support himself, he served as a tax official, sold insurance, and edited a small journal devoted to agricultural topics until he died on September 20, 1872.

As a soldier, Anderson was considered to be quite capable and brave, although he certainly is not one of the Confederacy's better-known general officers. While serving under Braxton Bragg, who was extremely unpopular with his lieutenants because of his abrasive, erratic personality and his overall military incompetence, Anderson is said never to

have participated in the verbal attacks and undermining tactics engaged in by those other officers. Later, though still ill from the effects of his gunshot wound, he felt it his duty to return to field command. He obviously was a man of high principals, abilities, and loyalties.

BIBLIOGRAPHY

Anderson, General James Patton. "Autobiography of General James Patton Anderson." *Southern Historical Society Papers* 24 (1896): 52–72. Reprint, Wilmington, N.C., 1991.

Bailey, Ronald H. *Battles for Atlanta: Sherman Moves East.* Alexandria, Va., 1985.

Cozzens, Peter. *No Better Place to Die: The Battle of Stones River.* Urbana, Ill., 1990.

Davis, William C., ed. *The Confederate General.* Vol. 1. Harrisburg, Pa., 1991.

McMurry, Richard M. "Patton Anderson: Major General, C.S.A." *Blue and Gray Magazine,* 1, no. 2, October–November, 1983.

U.S. War Department. *War of the Rebellion: A Compilation of the Official Records of the Union and Confederate Armies.* Washington, D.C., 1880–1901. Ser. 1: Vol. 10, pts. 1–2; vol. 16, pts. 1–2; vol. 20, pts. 1–2; vol. 30, pts. 1–4; vol. 38, pts. 1–5; vol. 47, pts. 1–3.

WARREN WILKINSON

ANDERSON, JOSEPH R.

ANDERSON, JOSEPH R. (1813–1892), industrialist and prime developer of the Tredegar Iron Works. Born in the Shenandoah Valley of Virginia on February 16, 1813, on the family farm, Anderson was the youngest child of William and Anna Thomas Anderson. After some education at an academy in Fincastle, Anderson entered West Point and graduated fourth in his class in 1836. On active duty he served in the engineering corps at Fort Monroe, Norfolk, Virginia, where he met and married the post surgeon's daughter, Sally Archer, in 1837.

Soon after marriage, Anderson's broader concerns with transportation and internal improvements and their influence on the commercial advancement of Virginia led him to leave military life and take up a post as a state engineer in charge of turnpike development in the valley. These interests involved him as a delegate to periodic state commercial conventions and identified him with the emerging Whig party in the late 1830s. At one of these commercial conventions in November 1838 he met business associates of the newly chartered Tredegar Iron Company (Works) in Richmond. Anderson became the company's commercial agent in March 1841, charged with overcoming Tredegar's persistent troubles with sales and indebtedness. Renewed investments and contracts soon bolstered Tredegar operations, although its indebtedness persisted. In November 1843, seeking more control of the company's operation, Anderson became a leaseholder of the entire plant, and in 1848 he purchased the company outright from its stock-

JOSEPH R. ANDERSON.   LIBRARY OF CONGRESS

holders for $125,000. By this time he and his family had moved to Richmond, becoming prominent citizens as his fame as an industrialist increased.

The 1850s brought competitive challenges to Anderson's company from larger Northern ironworks and from lower-cost British rail and iron products. Anderson strongly advocated a protective tariff to diminish foreign imports, and he kept the Tredegar Works competitive through several stratagems: he sought Northern sources of raw materials to supplement the pig iron he and his brothers were extracting in the valley for Tredegar's use; he maintained high-quality productivity to ensure the continuance of U.S. government contracts for iron plate and ordnance; he promoted the increased use of slave labor for highly skilled jobs over the protests of white workers; and he offset the advantages of Northern manufacturing by urging Southern railroads and other customers to "buy Southern."

In 1859, after a period in which Anderson had formed varied partnerships to run Tredegar's several operations, he attempted to maximize expertise and improve management by buying off some old partners, merging a separate adjacent munitions operation run by his father-in-law, and consolidating remaining partners as Joseph R. Anderson and Company. In this way, as the nation's sectional crisis intensified, Anderson achieved the formation of the Tredegar Iron Works as the largest industrial complex in the South; it stood ready to become the industrial backbone of Southern independence.

Success with Tredegar's growth brought Anderson prominence in Richmond's civic and Whig political life. He won his first elective office as a Richmond city councilman in 1847. His Whiggish interests in commerce and transportation also gained him a seat in the Virginia General Assembly in the 1850s. With the disintegration of the national Whig party in 1854, Anderson shifted his support to the Democrats.

When the secession crisis erupted in December 1860 and the Confederacy was formed, Anderson and his partners stood with the South. Tredegar's operations remained intact as the last orders from the U.S. government were filled and successive seceding states placed new orders for big guns and munitions. Tredegar quickly supplied ordnance to Charleston, South Carolina, prior to the bombardment of Fort Sumter on April 12, 1861. Anderson then organized civic support in the state capital for the Confederacy and participated as a delegate in the convention that affirmed Virginia's secession on April 17. Anderson offered Tredegar for lease or purchase to the Confederate government, but officials turned it down, anticipating only a short war with no need for interruption of Southern private industry.

Tredegar maintained its status as the South's leading industry during the first two years of warfare, its most profitable period. Orders from individual states soon gave way to orders from a more centrally coordinated Confederate government. Agencies of the Navy and War departments, such as the Ordnance Bureau led by Josiah Gorgas, contracted with Tredegar for cannons, iron plate, munitions, and other essential iron products. At the same time the government promised adequate supplies of raw pig iron and coal, a promise that became increasingly difficult to fulfill. The Confederacy achieved a remarkable expansion of industrial facilities with other private and government works. But in the long run, there were severe limitations on the government's ability to exempt skilled workers from military duty and to provide loans to Anderson so that he could find his own sources of raw materials and fuel. Because of the shortage of supplies, Anderson's company, even as it expanded, operated at only one-third its capacity throughout the war.

In order to encourage exemptions for skilled labor, Anderson organized a volunteer company militia, the Tredegar Battalion, soon after the war started, with himself as major. This group proved vitally important as a supplementary guard for the works and as a fire-fighting unit on occasion. Anderson also sought a field command early in the war, leaving his partners to take care of Tredegar affairs but reserving the right to return when needed. He became a brigadier general assigned to coastal defenses in North Carolina on September 3, 1861. By the next spring Anderson had seen action in the Peninsular campaign and was wounded in a battle at Frayser's Farm on June 30, but soon recovered. Commended for his service, he resigned to return to the Tredegar Works, where problems regarding labor, raw materials, finances, and provisions were mounting.

The later years of the war took a heavy toll on Tredegar's effective war production. By 1863 its work force numbered two thousand men, nearly half of whom were slaves. But acquiring provisions to feed and clothe the labor force became steadily more difficult, and Union incursions in the valley shut down the operations of blast furnaces. The competition for food supplies with the military increased. Anderson attempted blockade running to exchange cotton for tools and supplies abroad. What came back provided salable consumer goods, affording Anderson some profits with which to maintain a sterling account in London to hedge against losses and collapse at home. Adding to these difficulties and worsening Tredegar's crippled productivity was the government's inability to keep up with payments for what Tredegar supplied.

The Confederacy's collapse came in April 1865. Although Tredegar's operations had been sharply curtailed, its plant for the most part was spared any damage. Anderson, fearing confiscation, immediately sought to restore Tredegar, his partners, and himself to the United States; the men soon received personal pardons from President Andrew Johnson by September. Tredegar was reorganized in 1867 with Joseph Anderson continuing as its president. The London account plus new investments, including some from Northern financiers, got the company's operations underway again. Peacetime work for the renewal of Southern commerce and industry now occupied Anderson and his partners.

Some financial distress was experienced in the 1870s as a consequence of failed railroad investments during the panic of 1873, which the Tredegar Works survived with Anderson still at the helm. The iron industry, however, was fast giving way to steel production, and Tredegar financially could not make the shift. Joseph Anderson remained as head of a more locally oriented company until his death on September 7, 1892.

[See also Tredegar Iron Works.]

BIBLIOGRAPHY

Anderson Family. Papers. University of Virginia Library, Charlottesville, Virginia.

Bruce, Kathleen. *Virginia Iron Manufacture in the Slave Era.* New York, 1931.

Dew, Charles B. *Ironmaker to the Confederacy: Joseph R. Anderson and the Tredegar Iron Works.* New Haven, Conn., 1966.

FREDERICK SCHULT

ANDERSON, RICHARD HERON (1821–1879),

lieutenant general. The grandson of Col. Richard Anderson, who commanded the Maryland Line in the Revolutionary War, was born on October 7, 1821, near Statesburg, Sumter County, South Carolina. Following his education at Edge Hill Academy, Anderson entered the United States Military Academy. He graduated in 1842, ranking fortieth of fifty-five in a class that also included future Confederate generals James Longstreet, Lafayette McLaws, and D. H. Hill. As brevet second lieutenant of Dragoons, Anderson saw extensive service on the western frontier and was with the troops occupying Texas in 1845 and 1846. During the war with Mexico, Anderson accompanied Gen. Winfield Scott's expedition from Vera Cruz and was breveted first lieutenant for gallant and meritorious conduct in the engagement at San Augustín. Ten years after the war the young officer was presented a sword by his native state inscribed: "South Carolina to Capt. Richard Heron Anderson, a memorial of gallant conduct in service at Vera Cruz, Cherubusco, Molino del Rey, Mexico."

On the secession of South Carolina in December 1860, Anderson resigned his commission and became colonel of the First South Carolina Infantry Regiment. He was present at the firing on Fort Sumter, and when P. G. T. Beauregard went north to take charge of forces in Virginia, Anderson was placed in command of the defenses of Charleston. He was promoted to brigadier general on July 18, 1861, and a month later was ordered to Pensacola as the top assistant to Gen. Braxton Bragg. In this capacity, Anderson directed the only engagement in the territory, a night attack against the Wilson Zouaves of New York.

Increased activity in Virginia caused the removal of Anderson to that state in early 1862. There he was given command of a brigade in the division of his old West Point classmate, James Longstreet. Anderson's conduct in the Battle of Williamsburg elicited high praise from Longstreet, who reported that the attack "of the two brigades under Gen. R. H. Anderson . . . was made with such spirit and regularity as to have driven back the most determined foe. This decided the day in our favor."

On July 14, following the repulse of the Federals in the Seven Days' Battles around Richmond, Anderson was promoted to major general and given command of a division formerly led by Benjamin Huger. When Longstreet's other units moved northward to combat a new Northern army under John Pope, Anderson remained behind to cover

Richmond until it could be determined that the capital was safe from further attack. He rejoined the Army of Northern Virginia in time to participate in the final day's action at the Battle of Second Manassas. In the ensuing Maryland campaign, Anderson's division reinforced D. H. Hill at the Bloody Lane in the Battle of Sharpsburg. Anderson suffered a thigh wound early in the fighting but remained on the field until the victory was no longer in doubt; then, according to a contemporary, he "fell fainting from loss of blood."

Anderson returned to duty before the Battle of Fredericksburg in December. He saw little action in that contest, however, as his division held the left of the Confederate position and was not attacked in the Federals' assault on Robert E. Lee's lines.

In the Battle of Chancellorsville in May 1863, the divisions of Anderson and McLaws held the Federals in check while Thomas J. ("Stonewall") Jackson made his famous flank march and attack on the right of the Union line. Later Anderson and McLaws rushed to the assistance of Jubal Early, whose division was under attack by the Union Sixth Corps. Their vigorous action forced the enemy back across the Rappahannock River and closed another Northern "On to Richmond" campaign. For his conduct in this action, Anderson was cited by Lee: "Maj. Gen. R. H. Anderson was also distinguished for the promptness, courage, and skill with which he and his division executed every order."

When Lee reorganized the army in the wake of Jackson's death, Richard S. Ewell and A. P. Hill joined Longstreet as corps commanders. That Anderson was considered for such a post was implied in Lee's message to President Jefferson Davis that "R. H. Anderson and J. B. Hood are also capital officers. They are improving too and will make good corps commanders if necessary."

Anderson's division, one of three in Hill's corps, was at the rear of the column on the first day of the Battle of Gettysburg and saw no action. The next day, in conjunction with two of Longstreet's divisions, Anderson's troops participated in the attack on the Union left. In this maneuver one of Anderson's brigades reached enemy batteries on Cemetery Ridge before they were surrounded and forced back. On July 3 Anderson supported Pickett's ill-starred attack on the Union center.

When Longstreet was wounded seriously in the Battle of the Wilderness, Anderson was placed in charge of the First Corps until "Old Pete" returned. Anderson's most notable achievement during his chief's absence occurred on the night of May 7–8, 1864. Ordered by Lee to begin his march to Spotsylvania Court House at 3:00 A.M. on the second day, Anderson left four hours earlier. Marching through smoke and searing heat caused by burning woodlands on both sides of the road, Anderson attained the strategic road junction ahead of the Federals. Had he failed in his objective, and

enemy forces arrived there first, the Federals would have interposed between Lee and Richmond and enjoyed a shorter route to the capital. Commissioned a lieutenant general on May 31, 1864, Anderson led the corps creditably until Longstreet returned in October, at which time the South Carolinian was given command of the divisions of Robert Hoke and Bushrod Johnson.

On the retreat from Petersburg, Anderson's and Ewell's commands were routed at Sayler's Creek on April 6, 1865. Anderson's shattered divisions were subsequently divided between Longstreet and John B. Gordon. As a general without a command appropriate to his rank, Anderson was authorized to return home. His name, therefore, does not appear on the surrender rolls of Appomattox.

Trained in the profession of arms, Anderson found no demand for his talents in the postwar era. He tried to make a livelihood as a planter and failed. Ultimately, he went to Charleston and became a day laborer in the yards of the South Carolina Railroad. When his plight was called to the attention of authorities, Anderson was appointed state inspector of phosphates, a position he held until June 26, 1879, when he died of apoplexy in Beaufort, South Carolina. He was buried there in St. Helena's graveyard.

BIBLIOGRAPHY

Elliott, Joseph C. *Lieutenant General Richard Heron Anderson: Lee's Noble Soldier.* Dayton, Ohio, 1985.

Thurston, Edmund M. "Memoir of Richard H. Anderson." *Southern Historical Society Papers* 39 (1914): 146. Reprint, Wilmington, N.C., 1991.

Walker, C. Irvine. *The Life of Lieutenant General Richard Heron Anderson.* Charleston, S.C., 1917.

Warner, Ezra J. *Generals in Gray: Lives of the Confederate Commanders.* Baton Rouge, La., 1959.

LOWELL REIDENBAUGH

ANDERSON, ROBERT (1835–1888), brigadier general. Born in Savannah, Georgia, October 1, 1835, Robert Houston Anderson graduated from the U.S. Military Academy in 1857, thirty-fifth in a thirty-eight-man class. For four years he was a lieutenant in the U.S. Army. He resigned on May 17, 1861, to join the Confederacy.

Commissioned a lieutenant in the Confederate army, Anderson served first as a staff officer in Georgia and Florida. In July 1862 he was appointed major in the First Battalion of Georgia Sharpshooters, and in January 1863 he became colonel of the Fifth Georgia Cavalry.

In early 1864 coastal garrisons were stripped to furnish reinforcements to the major armies. Anderson and his regiment joined the Cavalry Corps of the Army of Tennessee and were placed in the brigade of Brig. Gen. William Wirt Allen. When Allen took over the division, Anderson

ROBERT ANDERSON.   LIBRARY OF CONGRESS

assumed command of the brigade. On July 26, Anderson was promoted to brigadier general. He commanded his brigade in the Atlanta campaign and during the March to the Sea. In early 1865 he was with Confederate forces in the Carolinas campaign. He was paroled in Hillsboro, North Carolina, May 3, 1865.

In 1867 Anderson became Savannah's chief of police, a post he held until his death on February 8, 1888. He is buried in Bonaventure Cemetery in Savannah.

His superiors valued Anderson's abilities. On July 15, 1864, Maj. Gen. Joseph Wheeler called him "a good disciplinarian and an efficient officer . . . . [who] has exhibited coolness and gallantry in all engagements in which he has been present."

BIBLIOGRAPHY

Bailey, Anne. "Robert Houston Anderson." In *The Confederate Generals*. Edited by William C. Davis. Harrisburg, Pa., 1991. 1:30–33.

Warner, Ezra J. *Generals in Grey: Lives of the Confederate Commanders*. Baton Rouge, La., 1959.

RICHARD M. MCMURRY

ANDERSON, SAMUEL READ (1804–1883),
brigadier general and Conscription Bureau officer. A native of Bedford County, Virginia, Anderson was living in Tennessee in 1861. Because he had fought in the Mexican War,

Governor Harris appointed this former bank cashier and postmaster of Nashville as major general of the Tennessee state troops. Later in the year, when the Provisional Army was organized, he received a commission as brigadier general.

Owing to a combination of bad luck, poor timing, and ill health, Anderson failed to distinguish himself in Confederate service. In August 1861, troops in western Virginia, Anderson's brigade among them, eagerly awaited the appearance of Robert E. Lee, who planned to drill and prepare them for battle. But when he arrived, bad weather hampered the maneuvers. The heavy downpours also bred disease, and a third of the soldiers died. Later, Anderson's brigade took part in an unsuccessful attack on a Federal fort on Cheat Mountain. During the winter of 1861–1862 Anderson and his men joined Thomas J. ("Stonewall") Jackson in the campaigns near Winchester, but the brigade most often found itself assigned to picket duty and marching. In the spring of 1862 Anderson resigned his commission, pleading ill health.

Two years later, President Jefferson Davis recalled Anderson to work in the Bureau of Conscription, recommissioning him as a brigadier general. In November 1864, he took charge of the Bureau of Conscription in Tennessee, headquartered at Selma, Alabama. Despite his efforts, Anderson once again failed to make a name for himself; the

SAMUEL READ ANDERSON.   LIBRARY OF CONGRESS

Confederacy abolished the bureau four months later, in March 1865.

Following the war, Anderson returned to Nashville where he established a mercantile business.

BIBLIOGRAPHY

Porter, James D. *Tennessee.* Vol. 8 of *Confederate Military History.* Edited by Clement A. Evans. Atlanta, 1899. Vol. 10 of extended ed. Wilmington, N.C., 1987.

Warner, Ezra J. *Generals in Gray: Lives of the Confederate Commanders.* Baton Rouge, La., 1959.

JENNIFER LUND

ANDERSON, WILLIAM

ANDERSON, WILLIAM (1842?–1864), Missouri guerrilla. Tall, dark-haired, blue-eyed, and handsome, William Anderson, known to later generations as "Bloody Bill," proved to be one of the most brutal of the Confederate guerrillas who terrorized rural Missouri throughout the war. After his father was killed in Kansas by Union militiamen early in the war, Anderson joined the guerrilla band led by William Clarke Quantrill. On August 14, 1863, Anderson's sister, Josephine, was among the female kin of noted guerrillas killed in the collapse of the Kansas City Union Jail, where they were being held. In revenge, on October 21, Anderson was one of the 450 guerrillas who ravaged Unionist Lawrence, Kansas, killing about 150 unarmed men and boys.

While vacationing in Texas the following winter, Anderson led about fifty guerrillas who broke with Quantrill to carry on independently back home—burning, looting, slaughtering, and scalping along both banks of the Missouri River in the center of the state. Anderson's 1864 summer activities climaxed on September 27 at Centralia, when his band killed and mutilated about 150 Union soldiers, including 25 unarmed men who were pulled off a train and executed by the trackside.

Anderson's guerrillas served as scouts for regular Confederate Generals Sterling Price and Joseph O. Shelby during the unsuccessful Southern raid of October 1864. Isolated in northern Missouri, Anderson's band was caught in a Union ambush on October 24. While his men dashed on horseback into the woods, Anderson charged the Union line alone, pistols blazing. The day after he was shot down, his body was exhibited and photographed, giving his enemies a parting pleasure.

BIBLIOGRAPHY

Brownlee, Richard S. *Gray Ghosts of the Confederacy: Guerrilla Warfare in the West, 1861–1865.* Baton Rouge, La., 1958.

Castel, Albert. *William Clarke Quantrill: His Life and Times.* New York, 1962.

Connelley, William Elsey. *Quantrill and the Border Wars.* Cedar Rapids, Iowa, 1909. Reprint, New York, 1956.

Fellman, Michael. *Inside War: The Guerrilla Conflict in Missouri during the American Civil War.* New York, 1989.

MICHAEL FELLMAN

ANDERSONVILLE PRISON. In November 1863, the Confederate War Department ordered Capt. William Sidney Winder, son of Gen. John H. Winder (the most prominent official in charge of prisons), to locate a site for a new prison in southern Georgia. The Confederates wanted to reduce the problems caused by the accumulation of prisoners of war at Richmond. The younger Winder chose land close to the railroad station at Andersonville, which gave its name to what its creators formally called Camp Sumter (after the county in which it was then located).

The supervisor of the prison's construction was Winder's cousin, Capt. Richard B. Winder, a quartermaster. From the beginning, local opposition and shortage of materials slowed the work. Nonetheless, in January 1864, Richard Winder put impressed slaves and free blacks to work cutting pine trees and trimming the trunks into twenty-foot posts. The laborers buried the butts of these in a trench and thus formed a stockade surrounding about sixteen and a half acres. There were two gates with enclosures outside. Sentry boxes were spotted along the stockade's top.

Deficient planning paved the way for disaster. On February 18, 1864, before the prison was ready, the Confederates at Richmond shipped the first trainload of prisoners who arrived seven days later at a stockade whose unfinished end was closed only by threatening cannon. Far from providing shelter, the jailors had not even laid out streets or any other organization to facilitate the future cleansing of a camp intended to hold ten thousand men. While the Confederates finished the stockade, the prisoners used bits of scrap wood and pieces of cloth to cover burrows in the ground that served as shelter.

The Confederates at first issued uncooked rations to prisoners who often lacked utensils. By May the bakery and cookhouse were providing a below-standard version of army rations. Meat was often lacking in quantity and quality, and the cornmeal contained so much husk it caused bowel problems. Richard Winder exacerbated the problems by locating the cooking facilities upstream on the brook running through the stockade, so that the waste together with that of the latrines of the guards' camps polluted the already inadequate water supply. Prisoners dug wells from which to drink, but lacking soap in any case they were unable to keep themselves clean. Since from the start no discipline had been enforced in the disposal of human waste, a sewage-filled swamp along the stream rapidly expanded.

On March 27, 1864, Captain Henry Wirz was ordered to Andersonville to take charge of the prison's interior.

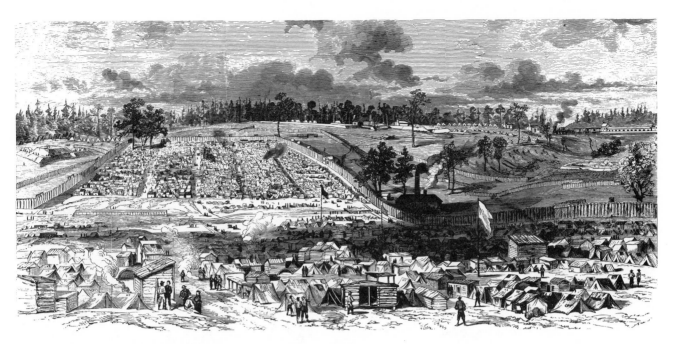

THE GREAT PRISON PEN AT ANDERSONVILLE.   From a drawing by R. Sneden.

Frank Leslie's Illustrated Famous Leaders and Battle Scenes of the Civil War

Although he made efforts to impose some order, he had only limited authority over the quartermaster, commissary, and guard forces. The latter, who at first were line units of the Confederate army, were soon replaced by Georgia reserve troops composed of youths and older men whose inefficiency concerned everyone except their own commanders. Nonetheless, they manned the guard posts, called the roll within the stockade, and supervised the paroled prisoners who did an increasing amount of the work outside the walls. In the eyes of the inmates, Wirz was seen as responsible for whatever the others did and for all the deteriorating conditions; he became an object of hatred. One of his few popular actions was his support of a prisoner attempt to stop the robbing and murder of fellow captives by so-called raiders and his facilitating the hanging of six of them on July 11, 1864.

The ultimate responsibility for the executions as well as for all else at Andersonville by then lay with General Winder, who had taken command of the post on June 17, 1864. As in other aspects of his service with prisoners, Winder devoted his primary attention to matters of security. He repeatedly expressed concern about inmates' attempts to tunnel out or otherwise escape, and his warnings to the guards to be more vigilant may well have encouraged some to shoot prisoners who crossed the "deadline," which paralleled the stockade about fifteen feet inside, reducing the land available for prisoners.

Under Winder's command the Confederates enlarged the stockade on the north end in late June to take in an additional ten acres. To forestall Union raids on the prison, Winder recruited slaves to build earthworks and surround the enlarged stockade with a second wall and part of a third. He used this work force to repair the damage done to the stockade by an August flood, which also opened a new source of drinking water that prisoners dubbed the "Providence Spring." The spring's name represented an appeal to God—one of the prisoners' responses to the growing horror of conditions at Andersonville.

By July 1, Richmond authorities had sent 26,367 captives to a prison intended for 10,000. With rare exceptions these were enlisted men, and the bulk lived within the enlarged stockade where—even counting the uninhabitable swamp—they had only a bit more than four square yards per man. About 1,355 were in a hospital consisting of a few tents covering five acres. There they received scant treatment for diarrhea, dysentery, and scurvy (the leading killers) and such conditions as typhoid fever, smallpox, and gangrene. The dead were buried in trenches in which locations were marked for 12,912 bodies during the prison's existence.

The prison's population reached a maximum in August 1864 of some 33,000 men. A month later the Confederates began to remove prisoners to camps at Millen, Georgia, and elsewhere. At about the same time, responding to complaints about conditions at Andersonville, the Confederates erected sheds called "barracks." These later were used by the sick as the site became more a hospital than a prison.

MASS GRAVE AT ANDERSONVILLE.   Photograph by A. J. Riddle, August 17, 1864.

When Union invading armies penetrated deeper into the Confederacy, many of the prisoners originally moved from Andersonville were returned, and the prison continued in use until the Confederacy's collapse. Captain Wirz was there paroling prisoners until May 1865, when Union troops arrested him.

After the war, the United States designated the Andersonville graveyard a national cemetery. Union veterans' groups also purchased and preserved the site of the prison yard, where several states erected monuments to their dead. Meanwhile Andersonville's sheer size, high mortality rate, and terrible conditions made it notorious as one of the Civil War's unique atrocities. It became a leading feature in attacks on the memory of the Confederacy, to which Southerners responded defensively. In the twentieth century, Andersonville became a national historic site whose interpreters point out its significance as a memorial to all American prisoners of war.

[*See also* Wirz, Henry.]

BIBLIOGRAPHY

Blakey, Arch Fredric. *General John H. Winder, C.S.A.* Gainesville, Fla., 1990.

Futch, Ovid. *History of Andersonville Prison.* Gainesville, Fla., 1968.

Hesseltine, William B. *Civil War Prisons: A Study in War Psychology.* Columbus, Ohio, 1930. Reprint, New York, 1964.

FRANK L. BYRNE

ANDREWS RAID. On April 12, 1862, the General, a northbound locomotive on the Western and Atlantic Railroad, pulled into Big Shanty, Georgia (present-day Kennesaw), twenty-five miles north of Atlanta. The crew and most of the passengers ambled to the nearby Lacy House for breakfast, but James J. Andrews lingered near the cars.

Andrews, another civilian, and twenty-two Union volunteers had left Shelbyville, Tennessee, on April 7 with orders from Brig. Gen. Ormsby M. Mitchel to steal a train and burn the bridges south of Chattanooga while Mitchel moved against Huntsville, Alabama. After rendezvousing in Marietta, Georgia, Andrews and nineteen of his men were aboard the train when it stopped at Big Shanty. While a dazed Confederate sentry looked on, they uncoupled the General, its tender, and three boxcars and sped northward.

Conductor William A. Fuller, engineer Jeff Cain, and shop foreman Anthony Murphy immediately gave chase on foot. Two miles north of Big Shanty, the winded trio borrowed a handcar and, with the help of some section hands, poled northward until the speeding car was derailed by a break Andrews's men had made in the tracks. Righting the car, the railroad men continued to Etowah, where they found the engine Yonah sitting on a siding.

Andrews had stopped several times to cut the telegraph wires, but for fear of arousing suspicion he had failed to disable the Yonah. Keeping to the railroad's timetable, he sidetracked the General upon reaching Kingston to allow a southbound freight to pass. But a second train followed, and a third. Claiming he had imperative orders to deliver a trainload of gunpowder to Confederate Gen. P. G. T. Beauregard, Andrews demanded an explanation for the delay and learned the increased traffic resulted from Mitchel's capture of Huntsville. Sixty-five minutes passed before the General left Kingston.

Five minutes later, the pursuing Yonah encountered the three southbound trains parked on the main line. Abandoning the little engine, Fuller, Murphy, and Cain sprinted to a junction two miles north of Kingston and commandeered the William L. Smith. A broken rail soon stopped the Smith, but Fuller and Murphy, setting out on foot again, flagged down the Texas just after it left the siding at Adairsville. Engineer Peter J. Bracken promptly backed his cars into the station and took up the chase, still in reverse.

Hampered by a lack of tools that made it difficult to pry up rails, the raiders cut loose two boxcars and dropped crossties across the tracks, desperately trying to gain enough time to burn the rain-soaked bridges north of Adairsville. The Texas pushed both cars onto the nearest siding and, avoiding all obstacles, pursued the fleeing General at speeds exceeding sixty miles per hour. Unable to stop for wood or water, the General ran out of steam two miles north of Ringgold.

The relentless Confederate pursuit, bad weather, and just plain bad luck prevented the raiders from doing any lasting damage to the railroad. Captured and tried, Andrews and seven of his men were hanged. Eight others, including two who had missed the train when it left Marietta, later escaped from an Atlanta jail. The six remaining raiders, exchanged as prisoners of war, were the first recipients of the U.S. Medal of Honor.

BIBLIOGRAPHY

"The Battle of the Locomotives." *Atlanta Journal Magazine*, September 29, 1935.

Grose, Parlee C. *The Case of Private Smith and the Remaining Mysteries of the Andrews Raid.* McComb, Ohio, 1963.

McBryde, Randell W. *The Historic "General": A Thrilling Episode of the Civil War.* Chattanooga, [1904].

O'Neill, Charles. *Wild Train: The Story of the Andrews' Raiders.* New York, 1956.

Pittenger, William. *The Great Locomotive Chase: A History of the Andrews Railroad Raid into Georgia in 1862.* New York, [1893].

DAVID EVANS

ANGLO-CONFEDERATE PURCHASING.

[*This entry is composed of two articles that discuss Confederate trade and purchasing with Great Britain during the Civil War:* An Overview *and* Anglo-Confederate Trading Company. *See also* Alabama Claims; Enchantress Affair; Erlanger Loan; Laird Rams; New Plan.]

An Overview

In 1861, the wealth of the South consisted chiefly of land and slaves. An agricultural society, it was poor in industrial and manufacturing resources, and its means of transportation were far behind those of the North. Its cities, with the exception of Charleston, Richmond, and New Orleans, were of little importance as trade centers. The states against which the Confederates waged war held roughly two-thirds of the country's population, and their financial and industrial resources were far superior to those of the South.

Despite these circumstances, however, the Confederacy was able to sustain a war lasting four years, largely because of the energetic activities of its commercial agents in Great Britain, who labored steadily to supply the needs of the Southern military forces. Confederate troops were valiant fighters and, in the main, were well led. But they could not fight without arms or supplies, and Southern arsenals and manufacturers could not possibly meet all their needs. The Confederate government, rapidly organized, was quick to appreciate the situation, and very early in the war, before the North had been thoroughly aroused, it dispatched its financial agents and purchasing emissaries to Great Britain.

From the outset, the Confederates were faced with a delicate commercial task. Great Britain, then the leading industrial power in the world, was obviously the most likely source of supplies and finance, and it was also the champion of free trade. But the majority of English people were opposed to slavery, so it was necessary to avoid discussions on the slavery issue and to concentrate on free trade. Of all the European powers, the Confederates looked to Great Britain first for sympathy and assistance. Thus, the primary need was to establish good relations between Great Britain and the Confederate States. In this the South succeeded, quickly laying the foundations of an entente, which, although subject to fluctuations, served admirably as a basis for four years of trade and financial cooperation.

The Confederate government, however, committed an error by using its available sterling exchange and coin at the outset of the war for procurement purposes. As later events showed, these valuable assets should have been held in reserve and cotton sent to Britain to purchase essential war supplies. The weakness of Confederate purchasing in Great Britain was its reliance on fiat money and its futile funding operation by means of unsecured bonds. These errors of policy eventually destroyed Confederate finance abroad and weakened its purchasing power.

The Civil War stimulated the shipbuilding industry in Great Britain. Altogether about four hundred steamers, many of them iron, and eight hundred sailing vessels were sold to the South, including the cruisers *Alabama, Florida,* and *Shenandoah.* English lawyers advised Confederate agents that ships might be built for the South in British yards, providing three conditions were observed: the Confederate government concealed its ownership; the ship's destination was concealed; and the South adhered to a prohibition against the shipping of war equipment and the enlisting of a crew in British waters. Capt. James D. Bulloch, C.S.N., who expertly planned, coordinated, and controlled Confederate naval activity in Britain, consistently observed these requirements. He always tried to dispatch ships as ordinary sailing vessels.

The difficulties encountered by Confederate officials in Great Britain, however, revealed that the U.S. consular agents had a well-organized and highly developed espionage system, the function of which was to prevent the shipment of goods and materials to the Confederacy. It says a great deal for the tact, diplomacy, and energies of Bulloch and the other agents that so many ships got away and so much equipment and materials were shipped. Although Confederate ships bought and constructed in Great Britain were too few in number to act with effective aggressive power against the U.S. Navy, the commanders of the Confederate ships were able to inflict great injuries upon the merchant vessels of the North and thus drive up insurance rates to a prohibitive degree.

Although the Confederate Congress appropriated large sums for the navy (to be spent in Great Britain), the rate of exchange in the money market always worked against the Confederates, and the Southern navy was always smaller than Congress might have hoped. Jefferson Davis was fairly consistent in his naval policy and clearly understood and strongly supported the need for ship construction in Great Britain.

In the area of ordnance, the Confederate government was never able to equip its forces adequately. The original stock of arms consisted almost wholly of smoothbore muskets, altered from flint to percussion. These disappeared almost entirely during the first two years of the war and were replaced by English rifled and percussion arms of high quality. No official account was kept of the value of the Confederate government's purchases in Great Britain, and records are discouragingly fragmentary. Some statistical data has been collected in an attempt to record the quantity and value of articles that passed through the blockade, but it is difficult, in some instances, to give more than a reasoned estimate. About 1,350,000 bales of cotton were sent to Great Britain during the war, and approximately 600,000 items of equipment were shipped to the Confederacy through the blockade (the majority of blockade runners were English vessels). These included small arms, cannons, munitions of all kinds, clothing, hospital stores, manufactured goods, and some luxuries. Goods entering the Confederate States from British ports can be valued at almost $200 million. Agents of the Southern War Department alone spent more than $12,250,000 in Great Britain. Throughout the war, munitions and supplies of all kinds also poured into the North from Europe. In comparison, the South was isolated and had great difficulty equipping and supplying its armed forces. Without these essential imports, the Civil War could have ended possibly in eighteen months.

A careful analysis of the Confederate purchasing agents and their mission in Great Britain reveals that they did nothing that was not justified by the rule of fair and honorable warfare, nothing contrary to English law as construed by English jurists and confirmed by the judgment of English courts. These agents—poorly organized and badly instructed by their superiors (especially during the first thirty months of the war), inexperienced, sometimes guilty of serious errors of judgment, prone to disputes caused by vague orders from senior officers who knew little of the circumstances under which they were working, almost always short of funds, harried by Federal spies, and working for a government unrecognized by Great Britain—made it possible in spite of all their handicaps for the Confederates to sustain a war lasting over four years. Given the crippling difficulties, it is a tribute to their initiative, skill, and energy that they accomplished so much with so little.

BIBLIOGRAPHY

Bulloch, James D. *The Secret Service of the Confederate States in Europe.* 2 vols. New York, 1883.
Lester, Richard I. *Confederate Finance and Purchasing in Great Britain.* Charlottesville, Va., 1975.
Owsley, Frank L. *King Cotton Diplomacy.* 2d ed. Revised by Harriet Chappel Owsley. Chicago, 1959.

RICHARD I. LESTER

Anglo-Confederate Trading Company

The Anglo-Confederate Trading Company was a British shareholding blockade-running venture that was formed in early 1862 in Liverpool by members of the shipping firm Edward Lawrence and Company. The supercargo for the company was Thomas E. Taylor, whose zeal and attention to detail was instrumental in establishing a highly successful line of blockade runners that operated primarily between Nassau and Wilmington, North Carolina.

The company also took the lead in the technical development of blockade runners by constructing the steel-hulled sidewheeler *Banshee.* This was the first vessel built from the keel up as a blockade runner. In April 1863, she became the first steel-hulled vessel to cross the Atlantic. *Banshee* and her following consorts were hired by the Confederacy to carry in munitions. The contracts were so lucrative that a successful round trip paid the construction cost of a blockade runner and the salary of the crew. Besides the inbound cargo, the company also carried out over ten thousand bales of cotton.

The Anglo-Confederate Trading Company was one of the war's most successful blockade-running firms. Although its total fleet numbered only nine vessels, with no more than four operating at one time, its ships completed forty-nine runs out of fifty-eight attempts. Unlike its competitors, the company did not invest heavily in Confederate bonds and additional steamers. Instead, profits were returned to shareholders. In the fall of 1864, the firm paid dividends that amounted to 2,500 percent over the original cost of a share of stock. Even though at the war's end the company sold off its blockade runners at a substantial loss, these transactions were more than covered by the firm's profits.

BIBLIOGRAPHY

Bradlee, Francis B. C. *Blockade Running during the Civil War and the Effect of Land and Water Transportation on the Confederacy.* Salem, Mass., 1925.
Taylor, Thomas E. *Running the Blockade.* London, 1897.
Wise, Stephen R. *Lifeline of the Confederacy: Blockade Running during the Civil War.* Columbia, S.C., 1988.

STEPHEN R. WISE

ANTIETAM CAMPAIGN. *See* Sharpsburg Campaign.

ANTISLAVERY. Opposition to the practice of slavery was a long-range movement that began in colonial America. To understand the broad and complicated parameters of antislavery, however, one must distinguish between and among a variety of impulses causing Americans and others in the Western world to oppose the institution of slavery.

Among the first to do so were those who objected to the practice on religious grounds. The Society of Friends, or Quakers, in both England and America began to grieve the practice during the eighteenth century, especially in and around the Quaker-owned colony of Pennsylvania. By the time of the American Revolution, Anthony Benezet, a Philadelphia Quaker, was issuing strenuous condemnations of slaveholding and urging Quakers to set an example by ridding themselves of their slaves in works like *A Serious Address to the Rulers of America, on the Inconsistency of Their Conduct Respecting Slavery* (1783).

WILLIAM LLOYD GARRISON.   NATIONAL ARCHIVES

Close on the heels of Quaker antislavery testimony came the libertarian influences of the American Revolution and other subsequent democratic revolutions in France, Haiti, and eventually Latin America. As each of these focused on the rights of man and produced various declarations concerning "inalienable" rights to life, liberty, and property, the practice of slaveholding was sharply questioned. In each of these areas and in England there arose an antislavery tide that led first to the abolition of the African slave trade in 1808 in both Britain and America, and then to the emancipation of slaves in Northern American states and in 1833 in the British West Indies.

Religious and political scruples about slaveholding had its effect as well in Southern states. Prior to the 1830s thousands of slaveholders ranging from George Washington to ultraconservative John Randolph of Roanoke voluntarily manumitted their slaves. Viewing slavery as morally wrong or inconsistent with American republicanism, or at best as a "necessary evil," these Southerners were impelled to end slavery—usually through their last wills and testaments.

Southern qualms about slavery and frequently also about the role of African Americans in American society led after the War of 1812 to a spate of efforts to rid the nation both of slavery and of its African population. Manumission societies were formed throughout much of the South, especially in North Carolina and Tennessee, beginning in 1816. By 1827 forty-one organizations devoted to the ending of slavery existed in North Carolina alone. The American Colonization Society, founded in 1817 and headed by such men as James Madison, James Monroe, and John Marshall, also generated antislavery interest throughout the South as it sought to eliminate both slaveholding and Africans from the United States.

With the rise of radical abolitionism in the 1830s, however, the moderate antislavery position of many Southerners became untenable, at least publicly. Indeed, the emergence of American abolitionism, usually identified with William Lloyd Garrison and the founding of his Boston newspaper, the *Liberator,* on January 1, 1831, tended to undermine many moderate antislavery positions in the North and South. Given the view of abolitionists that slavery was a moral evil and that it should be abolished immediately without compensation for slaveholders, abolitionism attacked virtually every other antislavery position. Northern opponents of abolitionist radicalism were quickly labeled "anti-abolitionists," and Southerners found it increasingly difficult to maintain any witness against slavery. Quakers throughout the South grew quiet on the subject, and manumission societies disappeared. Colonization efforts, largely discredited by abolitionists, continued until the Civil War but at a less significant pace. Laws regulating the manumission of slaves were enacted in the South. Other laws forbidding the migration of blacks into Northern states virtually halted voluntary acts of emancipation. The rise of a militant and sophisticated defense of slavery on religious, philosophical, ethical, scientific, and economic grounds during the 1830s and 1840s eliminated public expressions of antislavery opinion.

Southerners who had strong qualms about slavery found it expedient to move to the North. James Birney moved from Alabama to Kentucky and finally Ohio as he changed from slaveholder to abolitionist. William Henry Brisbane of South Carolina followed the same route until he settled in Wisconsin. North Carolina Quakers such as Levi Coffin followed suit and later helped establish the famous Underground Railroad that aided runaway slaves. Sarah and Angelina Grimke, sisters from a distinguished Charleston family, played key roles in propelling abolitionism in the North after 1835. Angelina's *Appeal to the Christian Women of the South* (1836) and Sarah's *Epistle to the Clergy of the Southern States* (1836) placed them at the forefront of abolitionism and in defining a reformist role for women.

By 1850 abolitionists from the North were no longer welcome or safe to proclaim their message in the South. Two Wesleyan Methodists sent from New York, Adam Crooks and Jesse McBride, were arrested and convicted that year of distributing "incendiary literature" in western North Carolina. Before their appeal could be heard, they were hounded out of the state by a mob. A decade later not even a native Southerner could operate openly as an abolitionist. In 1859 Daniel Worth, former Quaker from Guilford County, North Carolina, and kinsman of governor Jonathan Worth, was arrested and convicted of the same crime as Crooks and McBride.

Interestingly, however, Worth was convicted of distributing a book written by another North Carolinian containing yet another antislavery position. Hinton Rowan Helper, in his sensational *Impending Crisis of the South* (1857), held that slavery was a curse on the South that hampered its economic development. Indeed, he argued, the costs of sustaining slavery had to be borne directly by nonslaveholding whites throughout the South. Though Helper's book was held publicly to be incendiary and was banned in much of the South, it is clear that many Southerners shared his views. Calvin Wiley, North Carolina's first public school administrator, said as much in a pamphlet he titled *A Sober View of the Slavery Question* in 1849. Frederick Law Olmsted encountered the same viewpoint as he traveled throughout the South in the 1850s.

A similar refrain appeared in the extensive writings of Daniel Reaves Goodloe, a native North Carolinian who published the moderate antislavery newspaper *National Era* in Washington, D.C. The title of his 1846 tract reveals his perspective: *Inquiry into the Causes Which Have Retarded the Accumulation of Wealth and Increase of*

Population in the Southern States: In Which the Question of Slavery is Considered in a Politico-Economical Point of View. A similar economic comparison of South and North appeared a year later in *Address to the People of West Virginia,* written by Henry Ruffner, clergyman and president of Washington College (present-day Washington and Lee). Such strenuous arguments that were both antislavery and anti-Negro gave a new boost to large-scale colonization schemes in the 1850s.

With the publication of Harriet Beecher Stowe's *Uncle Tom's Cabin* in 1852 and of Helper's *Impending Crisis* in 1857, and with John Brown's raid on Harpers Ferry in 1859, the South became so embattled on the subject of slavery that it was no longer possible for strong antislavery views to be expressed publicly. Nevertheless, private doubts persisted. When the Civil War began, concerns about fighting a war to maintain slavery were expressed in a variety of ways. Antislavery opinion must have been part of the strong antisecessionist vote taken in North Carolina on February 28, 1861, even after seven other states had left the Union. It was probably also a factor in the decision of a hundred thousand men from Confederate states to join and fight in the Union army during the Civil War.

Incipient antislavery opinion loomed in discussions about making use of slaves as Confederate soldiers. In 1864 various proposals were floated by Confederate generals to arm part of the slave population, and in November of that year the matter came before the Confederate Congress. By January of 1865 even Gen. Robert E. Lee was proposing that the Confederacy should consider abolishing slavery. Finally, in March 1865, the policy of arming slaves and giving them emancipation for their service became the law of the Confederacy. By that time, of course, the Confederacy was already doomed, and the question of the fate of antislavery and abolitionism was settled.

[See also Harpers Ferry, West Virginia, *article on* John Brown's Raid; Helper, Hinton Rowan; Tubman, Harriet; Wiley, Calvin H.]

BIBLIOGRAPHY

Degler, Carl N. *The Other South: Southern Dissenters in the Nineteenth Century.* New York, 1974.

Dillon, Merton L. *Slavery Attacked: Southern Slaves and Their Allies.* Baton Rouge, La., 1990.

Dumond, Dwight L. *Antislavery: The Crusade for Freedom in America.* Ann Arbor, Mich., 1961. Reprint, New York, 1966.

Filler, Louis. *Crusade against Slavery: Friends, Foes, and Reforms, 1820–1860.* New York, 1960. Rev. ed., Algonac, Mich., 1986.

Kraditor, Aileen S. *Means and Ends in American Abolitionism: Garrison and His Critics on Strategy and Tactics, 1834–1850.* New York, 1969.

Perry, Lewis, and Michael Fellman, eds. *Antislavery Reconsidered: New Perspectives on the Abolitionists.* Baton Rouge, La., 1979.

Stewart, James Brewer. *Holy Warriors: The Abolitionists and American Slavery.* New York, 1976.

Walters, Ronald G. *American Reformers, 1815–1860.* New York, 1978.

LARRY E. TISE

APPOMATTOX CAMPAIGN.

Beginning on March 29, 1865, and lasting until April 9, this campaign in the concluding days of the Civil War is commonly referred to as Lee's Retreat. Lasting only twelve days, it culminated in the surrender of the largest and most powerful Confederate army.

The movement began on the twenty-ninth when Gen. Ulysses S. Grant sent a force of about 50,000 troops—the Second Corps under Gen. Andrew A. Humphreys, the Fifth Corps under Gen. Gouverneur K. Warren, and cavalry commanded by Gen. Philip Sheridan—to move around the Confederate right flank west of Petersburg and gain the South Side Railroad. This was Gen. Robert E. Lee's last major supply line into the city, and if captured, he would be forced to withdraw from the defenses of both Richmond, the Confederate capital, and Petersburg.

Lee, realizing the importance of protecting the railroad, dispatched a force under Gen. George E. Pickett to hold a strategic crossroads known as Five Forks. A preliminary series of battles (Quaker Road, March 29; White Oak Road and Dinwiddie Courthouse, March 31) allowed the Union army to maneuver into position to attack Pickett on April 1. Pickett, whose force numbered about 10,000 infantry and cavalry, confronted a similar force of 22,000 men led by General Sheridan at Five Forks. Pickett was defeated with the loss of over 2,000 prisoners, assuring the capture of the South Side Railroad. Federal casualties amounted to 633.

At dawn on the second, Grant issued orders for numerous assaults on the Petersburg lines, and the Sixth Corps under Gen. Horatio G. Wright broke through at one point. There was more fighting at Confederate Forts Mahone and Gregg and at Sutherland Station where the railroad was seized. Confederate Gen. A. P. Hill was killed in these battles. That night Lee issued orders for his troops to withdraw from both Petersburg and Richmond.

When General Lee left the two cities, his intention was for the scattered contingents of the Army of Northern Virginia, numbering about 58,000 men, to rendezvous at Amelia Court House, located on the Richmond and Danville Railroad. At this point he could replenish his army with needed supplies. The army would then continue into North Carolina and join with Gen. Joseph E. Johnston's force. Successfully bringing his army together at this county seat, Lee found to his dismay that, because of a mix-up in communications, no supplies had been sent. Deciding to remain in the area while his army foraged, Lee allowed

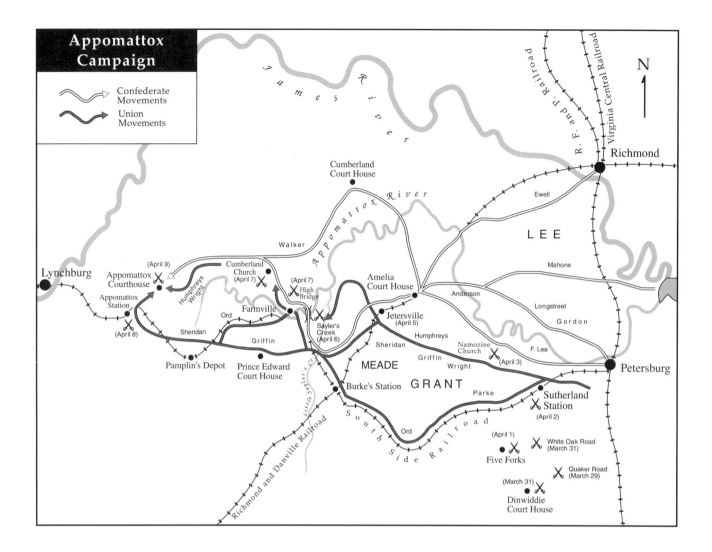

General Grant with his force of about 76,000 men (the Army of the Potomac and Army of the James) to begin a pursuit that eliminated the one-day lead Lee held. Consequently, hard riding by Sheridan's cavalry, along with an occasional skirmish such as one at Namozine Church on April 3, enabled the Federals to move around and in front of the Confederate army. They then cut the path of Lee's retreat along the railroad at the next station, Jetersville.

The following day, the fifth, when the Southerners pulled out of Amelia Court House, they found not only Federal cavalry blocking their way but fast-marching Union infantry arriving in support. Lee, deciding not to engage in battle at this point, changed his plans and ordered a night march around the entrenched enemy left flank. His destination was the town of Farmville, where he could find rations for his men at the South Side Railroad station.

The Confederate army was able to carry out this plan until dawn on the sixth. Then the Federals spotted the rear of their column near Amelia Springs, north of Jetersville, and immediately gave chase. Traveling along roads parallel to the one Lee's column was moving on, Sheridan's cavalry intercepted his line of march near Sayler's Creek. With the Second and Sixth Corps also close behind, the Confederates had to make a stand to save themselves. In three separate engagements, at the Hillsman farm, Lockett's farm, and Marshall's crossroads (or Harper's farm), the Federal infantry and cavalry put 7,700 men, almost a quarter of Lee's army, out of combat, mainly as prisoners. Those who survived continued on another night march to Farmville, situated on the southern bank of the Appomattox River.

It was also on this day that General E. O. C. Ord, commander of the Army of the James, sent a body of infantry and cavalry to destroy High Bridge so the Confederates could not use it in their retreat. High Bridge was a large trestle by which the South Side Railroad crossed the Appomattox River. Confederate cavalry learned of the raid and overtook the enemy force near the bridge. In the fight that ensued, most of the Federals were either killed or captured. Union Gen. Theodore Read and Confederate Gen. James Dearing were also mortally wounded.

When Lee's men arrived at Farmville at daylight on the seventh, they found some 40,000 rations of bread and 80,000 of meal in trains at the depot. As allotments were being issued to the troops, word came that Federal cavalrymen were coming into the town from the east. Lee had no alternative but to send the trains off toward Lynchburg. (These were captured the next day at Pamplin's Depot.)

Realizing that the Federals were also moving south of Farmville through Prince Edward Court House to cut off that avenue of escape, the Confederate commander decided to move his army to the north bank of the generally unfordable Appomattox River. If he could get his army safely over and burn all the bridge crossings behind him, including High Bridge to the east, he might delay Grant's men in their relentless chase. Unfortunately for Lee, the plan failed. One of the four bridges spanning the river (the wagon bridge under High Bridge) was not destroyed in time, which allowed the Union Second Corps to cross.

Lee then entrenched his army around Cumberland Church, about three miles north of Farmville, to protect his wagon train. Federal attempts to break the Confederate defense line that afternoon were unsuccessful but held a good portion of the Southern army at bay until darkness

fell. The Confederates once again had to make a night march. That evening Grant sent the first of a series of dispatches to Lee requesting the surrender of his army.

The next point along the South Side Railroad where Lee could hope to obtain supplies was Appomattox Station, about three miles west of Appomattox Courthouse. To reach that point, the Confederates would have to march thirty-eight miles. A thirty-mile route was available south of the river, but this route, which generally followed the railroad, was open to Grant and his troops.

Lee's army was relatively unmolested on the eighth, the final day of the campaign, although two Federal corps, the Second and Sixth, pursued him north of the river. To the south, with Sheridan's cavalry leading, the Fifth Corps and the Army of the James were taking advantage of the situation. Arriving at Appomattox Station before the van of Lee's column, the cavalry captured the supply trains and, later that evening, a portion of the Confederate artillery and wagon train in the Battle of Appomattox Station. This put a segment of the Union forces directly in front of Lee's force now gathering around Appomattox Courthouse. With the Federals in his rear and cavalry across his line of march, Lee decided to attempt a breakthrough early the next morning.

At daybreak on the ninth, assuming that only Federal horsemen were confronting him, Lee pushed his combined force of infantry and cavalry under Gen. John B. Gordon

WILMER MCLEAN'S HOUSE.   Site of Robert E. Lee's surrender to Ulysses S. Grant, April 9, 1865.

HARPER'S PICTORIAL HISTORY OF THE GREAT REBELLION

against the enemy position, forcing them to give ground. But as they fell back, the Army of the James began arriving on the field in support, and it became apparent to Lee that he was about to be surrounded, especially when the Fifth Corps appeared on his flank. The Southerners sent out white flags of truce to suspend hostilities. That afternoon Lee met with Grant at Appomattox Courthouse in the home of Wilmer McLean to discuss terms of surrender. After four years of bloodshed, the fighting in Virginia was over.

The casualties for the Appomattox campaign totaled approximately 9,000 for the Federal army and 28,000, including desertions, for the Confederates. Lee surrendered close to 30,000 men at Appomattox. All were paroled and allowed to go home.

BIBLIOGRAPHY

Calkins, Christopher. *Thirty-Six Hours before Appomattox, April 6–7, 1865.* Farmville, Va., 1980.

Calkins, Christopher. *The Battles of Appomattox.* Lynchburg, Va., 1987.

Calkins, Christopher. *The Final Bivouac.* Lynchburg, Va., 1988.

Davis, Burke. *To Appomattox: Nine April Days.* New York, 1959.

Newhall, Colonel F. C. *With General Sheridan in Lee's Last Campaign.* Philadelphia, 1866.

Schaff, Morris. *The Sunset of the Confederacy.* Boston, 1912.

The Shenandoah Campaigns of 1862 and 1864, and the Appomattox Campaign. Papers of the Military Historical Society of Massachusetts, no. 6. Boston, 1906. Reprint, Wilmington, N.C., 1989.

Tremain, Henry Edwin. *Last Hours of Sheridan's Cavalry.* New York, 1904.

CHRIS CALKINS

ARCHAEOLOGY.

Archaeology is the study of past societies through the material remains that have been left behind. A form of archaeological investigation of the Confederacy began immediately after the war, as people collected souvenirs and materials from veterans and battlefields. Veterans' groups and the Daughters of the Confederacy, in particular, tried to preserve items of the Lost Cause.

In the twentieth century, the initial excavation of most Confederate sites was conducted by relic hunters searching for salable or collectible items. The most common excavators today are still relic hunters using sophisticated electronic and research techniques to identify sites and then exploit them. For most sites undergoing this type of disturbance, little written documentation about what was found and its context exists.

Since about 1950, professional archaeologists have tried to discover patterns of material remains related to the Confederacy. Initially, their excavations focused on sites associated with important people and events. More recently, professional archaeology in the South has been funded by government agencies or by developers wishing to obtain government permits. Such permits require archaeologists to explore nontraditional sites like small farms and minor industrial sites as well as the better known locations. This work has opened the wide expanse of unwritten Confederate history to public view. The newly recovered materials encouraged a reevaluation of public and private documents to interpret atypical sites located during the surveys.

Battlefield archaeology originally tended to concentrate on studying people within forts, investigating extant structures on the battlefield, or trying to determine where houses once stood. This approach changed as archaeologists grew more sophisticated in developing research questions about battlefields. Important federal work has been done on battlefields such as Chancellorsville, Vicksburg, Shiloh, and Petersburg in conjunction with restoring the sites to their original ground conditions. More innovative work has tried to trace battle lines by examining artifact distributions, especially along now-buried trench lines.

Only within the last decade have archaeologists studied the major Confederate fortification type—the earthwork—as an artifact. Most earthwork research has been funded through government-mandated permit requirements on inland battlefields in Georgia and Tennessee, defense systems like those around Harpers Ferry, and coastal cities such as Wilmington, Savannah, Charleston, and Mobile. In Savannah and Wilmington, massive sand mounds have been found to contain enough remnants of the wooden frames and walls to allow schematic reconstructions of the interior chambers. Underwater obstructions and related defenses have been studied in Mobile Bay and the Cape Fear and Savannah rivers, revealing distinct differences between contemporary drawings and the actual barriers.

A growing number of excavations are concerned with the home front, especially urban and plantation life, including the slaves who made up more than a third of the Confederacy's population. Plantation archaeology originally concentrated on the "big house" because the occupants were famous, but more recent work has examined the slave rows and overseer cabins as well. Urban archaeology is common, but small farms have been receiving attention owing to highway, power, and pipe line surveys since the early 1970s. One unusual pattern relating to slave cabins on the southeastern coast is the large number of weapons found there. In one cabin in McIntosh County, Georgia, at least four weapons—a flintlock and a percussion pistol, a musket, and a shotgun—were represented by artifacts recovered during excavations in 1987 and 1988.

Industrial sites such as the Harpers Ferry and Fayetteville arsenals and Tredegar Iron Works have long been known, but archaeologists have done little work on these sites. Amateurs have reported on the lesser known sites such as the Mendenhall, Jones, and Gardner Machine Shop in North Carolina. Grapeshot recovered from the Savannah defenses was stacked in two tiers, rather than the more usual three and five tiers, indicating iron shortages late in the war. A 24-pounder flank howitzer recovered from CSS *Georgia* was not bored straight, nor were the molding seams removed.

Mundane operations such as salt extraction are even less well known, although some documentation does exist and abandoned sites have been encountered during coastal surveys in Georgia and Florida. Train yards have not been investigated in the South to the same extent as in the North, although Chattanooga and Savannah have been examined.

Along coastal and inland river systems, underwater archaeology has provided a wealth of information about the Confederacy. Sunken vessels are time capsules containing materials representative of those who sailed them. Among these vessels are the ironclads CSS *Neuse* and CSS *Georgia*, and the Richmond flotilla. Artillerymen in Fort Branch on the Roanoke River threw their entire complement of artillery into the river, and divers recovered it in the 1970s. The Fort Branch artillery revealed that iron field carriages were used for Blakely rifled cannon rather than Whitworths, and that Blakely cannon shipped to the Confederacy apparently had serial numbers that were separated by one number from other guns in the series. A cannon from *Georgia* had been marked on the barrel band to indicate elevation of the tube without recourse to sighting implements. This same gun was disabled by breaking off the

CSS *Neuse*. Bow view of the ship's hull on display at Kingston, North Carolina, c. 1964.   Naval Historical Center, Washington, D.C.

sights and putting a live, percussion-fused shell down the barrel backwards as a booby trap.

Blockade runners such as *Modern Greece, Georgiana,* and *Minho* have yielded substantial information about Confederate imports ranging from cannons to straight pins. What has been found tends to confirm speculation about nonessential Confederate imports in many cases as well as attempts to obtain the latest ordnance such as Whitworth and Blakely rifled artillery. Confederate newspaper editorials often railed against blockade runners bringing luxury goods at the expense of war matériel. Finding both military goods (rifles, cannons, bowie knives, canteens, lead, tin) and civilian luxury goods (whiskey, fine china, pins) in wrecked vessels tends to confirm newspaper allegations. Outside the Confederacy, the ruptured hulk of CSS *Alabama* was recently found off the coast of France.

Although archaeology of the Confederacy as a separate field of endeavor does not exist, excavations have provided information about previously unsuspected aspects of Confederate life or have confirmed well-known facts such as the shortage of iron. No consolidation of Confederate-related material culture has been attempted from an archaeological standpoint. Such an effort would prove useful in confirming patterns of material culture already noted by collectors of items such as Confederate uniform coats, the botonée cross pins worn by Maryland Confederates, and frame buckles. Additional recovery and analysis of artifacts might show projectile, sword, and leather goods' affiliations with certain arsenals and time periods.

Archaeological publications relating to the Confederacy are not numerous or readily available. But military sites owned by state and federal governments usually have research material regarding the particular site on hand, and the reports required by government agencies for construction projects on private sites are filed with the historic preservation officer of the state. The long interest in Confederate material culture that spawned relic hunting also resulted in artifact documentation.

[*See also* Museums and Archives.]

BIBLIOGRAPHY

Camp Chase Gazette. Lancaster, Ohio, 1979–.

Crouch, Daniel R. *Relic Hunter.* Falls Church, Va., 1978. Privately printed.

Lord, Francis. *The Civil War Collector's Encyclopedia.* Secaucus, N.J., 1982.

Military Collector and Historian, Journal of the Company of Military Historians. Westbrook, Conn., 1949–.

North-South Trader. Orange, Va., 1973–.

L. E. BABITS

ARCHER, JAMES JAY (1817–1864), brigadier general. A native of Bel Air, Maryland, where he was born

JAMES JAY ARCHER.   LIBRARY OF CONGRESS

December 19, 1817, Archer graduated from Princeton in 1835 and studied law at the University of Maryland. At the outbreak of the war with Mexico in 1846, Archer raised a company of infantry and served as its captain. When United States troops stormed Chapultepec, a strongly defended fortress, on September 13, 1847, Archer led his company on a diversionary attack on a battery. His gallantry in this action earned him a promotion to the brevet rank of major. Mustered out of the army on August 31, 1848, he resumed his legal career, but returned to the army in 1855 as a captain in the Ninth Infantry.

Archer resigned his commission in June 1861 while stationed at Fort Walla Walla, Washington Territory, to join the Confederacy and was appointed colonel of the Fifth Texas. In the spring of 1862 Archer was placed in command of the Texas Brigade. He was promoted to brigadier general on June 3 and given command of the Tennessee Brigade in A. P. Hill's division, succeeding Robert Hopkins Hatton, who had been killed in the Battle of Seven Pines.

At the Battle of Mechanicsville, June 26, 1862, Archer's horse was shot from under him. The next day, in the Battle of Gaines' Mill, the brigade "moved out in regular line of battle toward the enemy's impregnable lines of breastworks. Our general was in front leading the charge," wrote M. T. Lebetter of the Fifth Alabama. When "the boys began to waver" under furious enemy fire, "Archer waved his sword over his head and gave the command 'Follow me!' "

Archer's Brigade performed conspicuously in the Battle of Chancellorsville, May 3, 1863, clearing Hazel Grove of enemy resistance and enabling Confederate artillery to be placed on that eminence, thereby hastening the rout of the Army of the Potomac. In the reorganization of the Army of Northern Virginia during the weeks that followed, Archer's Brigade was placed in the division of Henry Heth, A. P. Hill's corps.

On the first day of the Battle of Gettysburg, July 1, 1863, Archer was warned by fellow officer James J. Pettigrew of strong enemy forces on McPherson's Ridge west of the town. Archer, according to Captain Louis G. Young, "listened, believed not, marched on unprepared." As a consequence the general and most of his brigade were captured. Archer thus became the first general officer to be captured after Robert E. Lee took command of the army thirteen months earlier. Many men in Archer's column, including the general, "fainted and fell by the wayside" as they were marched to the rear, according to Thomas Herndon of the Fourteenth Tennessee. Southerners' treatment at the hands of their captors was "cruel, tyrannical and inhuman." A lieutenant ordered "the guards to use their bayonets freely on the weak, fainting and exhausted members." For two days the captives were denied food.

Initially, Archer was imprisoned at Fort McHenry. Later he was transferred to Fort Delaware and finally to Johnson's Island in Lake Erie where temperatures during the winter of 1863–1864 plunged to as much as thirty degrees below zero. Archer was exchanged on August 3, 1864, and returned to duty on August 19. His health already shattered by exposure to the elements on Johnson's Island, the general was weakened further by pneumonia, contracted after exposure to an all-day "pelting cold rain." He died in Richmond on October 24, 1864, and was buried in Hollywood Cemetery.

William McComb, who succeeded Archer as brigade commander, extolled his former leader as "one of the bravest officers in the army—one competent to fill any position in the corps. He could see, decide and act with as much alacrity as any officer I ever knew."

BIBLIOGRAPHY

"Brigadier General James T. Archer." *Confederate Veteran* 8, no. 2 (1900): 65–67. Reprint, Wilmington, N.C., 1985.
Coddington, Edwin B. *The Gettysburg Campaign.* New York, 1968.
Herndon, Thomas. *Reminiscences of the Civil War, 1861–1865.* Oklahoma City, Okla., n.d.
Hollyday, Lamar. "Maryland Troops in the Confederate Service." *Southern Historical Society Papers* 3 (1877): 136. Reprint, Wilmington, N.C., 1990.
Ledbetter, M. T. "With Archer's Brigade before Richmond: Battle of Gaines' Mill and Mechanicsville." *Atlanta Journal,* August 31, 1901.

LOWELL REIDENBAUGH

ARCHIVES. *See* Museums and Archives.

ARIZONA. The southwestern state of Arizona traces its origins as a separate jurisdiction to the Civil War. At the start of the war, the area was only sparsely settled, and it had yet to be broken off from New Mexico Territory. Conventions in the southern half of the territory, at Mesilla and Tucson in March 1861, called for separating it from the northern half of New Mexico and joining the Confederacy. The withdrawal of Federal troops from Forts Buchanan and Breckenridge left the Tucson area unprotected from either Confederate forces or Apache raids.

In August 1861, Lt. Col. John R. Baylor proclaimed a Confederate territory of Arizona, the region south of the thirty-fourth parallel from Texas all the way to California. He named Mesilla the capital and himself the governor, and in January 1862 the Confederate Congress established Arizona Territory. But on April 15, 1862, in the westernmost engagement of the war, Union troops from California defeated a small force of Texas Confederates northwest of Tucson at Picacho Pass. Confederate influence waned, and the California Column pushed east to the Rio Grande.

In February 1863, the U.S. Congress passed and President Abraham Lincoln signed a bill establishing Arizona as a territory comprising the western half of New Mexico Territory. Early in 1864, the first territorial governor, John N. Goodwin, established its first capital near Prescott. A census that spring counted 4,187 white residents, far fewer than the estimated 30,000 Indians there. Most of these white residents were Spanish-speaking people born in the territory. As late as 1870, the census enumerated only 9,658 non-Indian residents.

As elsewhere in the West, Indians in Arizona sought to take advantage of the war to bolster their own position, but in 1864 a force led by Kit Carson defeated the Navahos in the largest confrontation between Union forces and Indians during the Civil War.

BIBLIOGRAPHY

Colton, Ray C. *The Civil War in the Western Territories: Arizona, Colorado, New Mexico, and Utah.* Norman, Okla., 1959.
Lamar, Howard Roberts. *The Far Southwest, 1846–1912: A Territorial History.* New Haven, 1966.

PETER WALLENSTEIN

ARKANSAS. On the eve of the Civil War, Arkansas was a microcosm of the American South, its people immersed in

SEVEN GENERALS WHO ENLISTED FROM PHILLIPS COUNTY, ARKANSAS.
NATIONAL ARCHIVES

a stratified society characterized by class and race. Their ways of life varied widely: a few resided on comfortable plantations, most subsisted on piney-woods or mountain plots, and many labored on other people's land as white tenants or black slaves. The vast majority of its 324,191 whites and 111,269 blacks lived in the countryside, though a lesser number dwelt in the small, but important towns of Little Rock, Fort Smith, Camden, Pine Bluff, and Helena. Foreign-born whites constituted just over 1 percent of the population, and the free inhabitants included only 144 blacks.

The state's geographic features shaped its antebellum culture and its political and military dynamics in the Confederate era. Poised on the western fringe of Southern civilization, Arkansas encompassed a diverse landscape sculpted into low mountains, fertile alluvial plains, and mosquito-infested swamps. Mountains dominated Arkansas's northwestern half, and river bottoms, swamps, and bayous marked its eastern and southern regions. Although frequently inundated by floods, the latter sector had fecund soils suitable for plantation agriculture. The rivers that traversed the state had only marginal commercial worth, for in dry seasons shallows hindered steamboat traffic.

A plantation culture dominated the area southeast of an

imaginary line drawn from the Missouri boot heel to the Texas boundary. Committed to cotton and slavery, that region's aristocrats campaigned for internal improvements: levees to prevent floods and railroads to tap markets at Memphis and New Orleans. Political bickering and difficult topography delayed the construction of the latter so that by 1860 the state's major project, a rail line from Memphis to Little Rock, was only two-thirds completed. Mountain citizens with little investment in slavery found themselves politically at odds with their aristocratic neighbors to the southeast.

Although disheartened by Abraham Lincoln's election in November 1860, few Arkansans advocated the Union's immediate demise. South Carolina's secession on December 20, however, galvanized powerful political voices. Recently inaugurated Governor Henry M. Rector pledged that should "any of the Southern states . . . deem it necessary to declare independence" Arkansas must give its "active support." Even though Senator Robert Ward Johnson, Congressman Thomas C. Hindman, and Little Rock attorney Albert Pike added their endorsements, the state legislature demurred until mid-January before authorizing an election for convention delegates on February 18.

This crisis highlighted Arkansas's sectional dichotomy. Fearing domination by the slavocracy, Arkansas mountaineers firmly supported the Union, and emboldened by Tennessee's rejection of secession, they sent a solid pro-Union majority to the convention. At the same time, the cotton counties overwhelmingly backed secession. The convention assembled in Little Rock (March 3–18), fended off proposals for immediate dissolution, and in the end submitted the issue to a statewide plebiscite scheduled for August.

While politicians bickered, pro-Confederates in the southeast finessed Arkansas out of the Union. In February, Helena militia units marched on Little Rock, besieging its Federal arsenal and forcing its surrender; a Pine Bluff mob seized military supplies destined for Fort Smith; and regional leaders threatened to secede from the state should Arkansas fail in its duty to the South. Following the bombardment of Fort Sumter and Lincoln's subsequent call for volunteers, momentum shifted to the secessionists. Rector ordered Fort Smith seized on April 23, and the convention reconvened in Little Rock's volatile atmosphere. Cowed by secessionist mobs, even the mountain delegates, with one exception, declared for the Confederacy on May 6. Even though threatened by a lynch party, Isaac Murphy cast the dissenting vote. In 1864, he became the state's Union governor.

As the Civil War developed, crises in the Virginia and Trans-Appalachian theaters overwhelmed Jefferson Davis and his advisers, and they largely ignored Arkansas, forcing its leaders to plan their own campaigns. In the summer of

1861, they focused upon their own borders—the Indian Territory to the west and Missouri to the north. Commissioned to negotiate treaties with the Indians, Albert Pike bound several tribes—especially the Cherokees—to the Confederacy and thus ensured Arkansas's safety from that quarter. Missouri proved more troublesome. In July, Arkansas troops commanded by Gen. Ben McCulloch rushed to the aid of Gen. Sterling Price encamped near Springfield. Together they defeated Nathaniel Lyon at Oak Hills (August 10, 1861), but unfortunately for the Southern cause, personal conflicts led McCulloch to withdraw, leaving Price a force inadequate to hold Missouri.

Arkansas's Confederate leaders also faced difficult internal problems. Although the cotton counties enthusiastically fulfilled their quota of soldiers, mountain districts rarely supplied more than one-third of their allotments. Throughout the regions north and west of Little Rock, citizens fled Confederate recruiters, formed peace societies, and volunteered for the Union army. As civilian government collapsed, the military only partially replaced its functions. Threatened by Union forces in September 1863, Governor Harris Flanagin, Rector's successor, fled Little Rock and established a new capital in the southwestern village of Washington, but he exercised little control over the state's weal. In this atmosphere of anarchy, Confederate guerrillas, Union partisans, and common bandits wreaked havoc upon the civilian population.

Cursed with inept and uncongenial military leaders, Arkansas's Confederate cause faltered. Arkansans Thomas C. Hindman and Albert Pike played major roles along with the North Carolinian Theophilus H. Holmes and the Missourian Sterling Price. The initial Trans-Mississippi commander, Hindman, proved incompetent as both an administrator and a strategist. Relieved of theater command in October 1862, he marched to defeat at the Battle of Prairie Grove (December 7) and thereafter transferred to the Army of Tennessee. Hindman's replacement, Holmes, was considered "a splendid example of a North Carolina patriot and gentleman," but he too floundered until March 1863 when E. Kirby Smith superseded him and moved the theater command to Louisiana. Holmes remained in Arkansas as an ineffectual field general. Pike and Price also commanded troops. Following his successful Indian negotiations, Pike assumed command of Indian soldiers, led them in the Battle of Elkhorn Tavern (March 7–8, 1862), and then resigned his commission in a jurisdictional dispute with Hindman. Price proved a competent leader, but his quarrels with Arkansas authorities diminished his effectiveness. Late in the war he executed a spectacular, but strategically inconsequential, cavalry raid thrusting out of Arkansas to strike across half of Missouri.

Under this flaccid command structure, Arkansas's martial course developed in three phases: the shoring up of Federal control north of the Arkansas River; actions associated with the siege of Vicksburg; and operations in conjunction with the Red River campaign of 1864. The Confederate defeat at Elkhorn Tavern in 1862 allowed Federal forces to consolidate their hold on pro-Union mountain counties. Only the national government's more pressing commitments to the east and difficulties of campaigning in Arkansas's swamps prevented greater Union advances. Hindman's check at Prairie Grove ended the one Confederate effort at regaining its lost territory.

As Gen. Ulysses S. Grant marched on Vicksburg, he exposed his western flank to attack. To remedy this he sent a flotilla up the Arkansas River to invest the Confederate citadel at Arkansas Post; it fell after a brief siege (January 8–11, 1863). Although numbers of Confederate troops ranged across Arkansas, command incompetence prevented serious threats to Grant before Holmes and Price attacked Helena on July 4. Repulsed in a sharp engagement, their defeat opened the state to further Federal incursions. But the Arkansas River's low water slowed the Union advance, and not until September 10 did Little Rock fall to Frederick Steele's Federals; the city thereafter served as the headquarters for Union military activities in the state.

The Red River campaign drew Steele south in March 1864. His command of thirteen thousand effectives, including two black regiments, trooped out of Little Rock intent on joining forces with Nathaniel Banks's army moving up the Red River to Shreveport. But Banks's defeats at Mansfield and Pleasant Hill, Louisiana (April 8, 9, 1864), stranded Steele deep in Arkansas's Confederate territory. Following an initial reverse at Okolona (April 2), he suffered further defeats at Poison Springs (April 17), Mark Mills (April 25), and Jenkins's Ferry (April 28). Harassed by Confederate cavalry, Steele abandoned his wounded and nonessential supplies; and his black troops suffered severe casualties. The Confederate commander at Poison Springs attacked a Union force he estimated at 1,500 blacks and 1,000 whites. Refusing to accept the surrender of African Americans, he boasted that his men killed 430 blacks and only 30 whites. The First Kansas Colored Volunteers' colonel raged that his men were "murdered on the spot." Having lost the confidence of Arkansas's Union leaders and the Lincoln government, Steele left his command in December 1864, effectively ending Union military movement in the state.

In the fall of 1863, Arkansas's Confederate government exercised suzerainty over little more than the state's southwestern third, a region roughly bounded by the Saline River to the east and the Ouachita River to the north. By necessity the military eclipsed civil authority, rendering the governor and his bureaucracy virtually impotent. Civilians—small farmers and planters alike—despaired of their personal fortunes. Typical of the South as a whole, antebellum Arkansans had depended upon small farmers for corn, pigs, and other foodstuffs, and they had allowed planters to concentrate upon the profitable production of cotton. With husbands and older sons marching in the Confederate army, small farmsteads declined in their output, fields became fallow, and hungry families consumed seed corn, draft animals, and breeding stock. Impoverished, many non-slave owners sold their land and other property to wealthy neighbors. As a result, by 1865 Arkansas experienced a net decline in noncommercial farms. Planters confronted their own difficulties. Burdened by antebellum debts, they resisted government orders to switch from cotton to less remunerative grain crops, and whenever possible they smuggled their cotton bales to Mexican and Northern speculators.

Confederate and Union armies further exasperated civilian problems. Southern commanders impounded draft animals, purchased foodstuffs with inflated Confederate currency, and conscripted slaves to labor as construction workers, teamsters, and hospital stewards. In the summer of 1864, Gen. E. Kirby Smith ordered the drafting of one-fifth of all male slaves aged 18 to 45—a move that enraged planters, many of whom had rushed their human chattel away from Union dominated areas. Federal General Steele's campaign through southwest Arkansas in the spring of 1864 strained a population already desperate for life's necessities.

In vain, Lincoln hoped that Arkansas would prove a model for the restoration of Federal rule. Appointed provisional governor, Isaac Murphy organized Union sympathizers who elected him to a four-year term in April 1864, but his administration could not control the countryside. Unionist citizens suffered attacks by Confederate sympathizers, robbery by bandits, and persecution by Federal soldiers who made no distinction between loyal and disloyal Arkansans. Along with former slaves, desperate Unionists fled to Little Rock and other Federal-controlled towns. Overwhelmed by resulting social problems, Union commanders transported some of them to the North and settled others on agricultural colonies established on land confiscated from Confederate supporters.

Murphy and his allies appealed to class hostilities in their attempt to construct a viable postwar Republican party. President Andrew Johnson unwittingly undermined the Republican cause with his liberal pardon policy, which enabled the former elites quickly to reestablish their control over local governments and then to engage in a campaign of anti-Republican violence—often under the rubric of the Ku Klux Klan. In 1874, the Republican party acknowledged defeat when it failed to nominate candidates for state office and thus conceded the government to prewar leaders.

Ironically, Arkansas's elites emerged from the Civil War in better financial shape than its other citizens. Although their affluence had been considerably diminished by the loss of slave property and the decline of real estate values, they retained a larger percentage of wealth than other Arkansans. By the century's end, many of the state's less affluent inhabitants—white as well as black—found themselves trapped in peonage, toiling as sharecroppers in debt to a comfortable few. As late as the civil rights movement of the 1960s, Arkansas retained social values and economic practices rooted in the antebellum epoch.

[*For further discussion of battles fought in Arkansas, see* Arkansas Campaign of 1864; Elkhorn Tavern, Arkansas; Prairie Grove, Arkansas. *For further discussion of Arkansas cities, see* Little Rock, Arkansas. *See also* Price's Missouri Raid; Red River Campaigns; Wilson's Creek Campaign; *and biographies of numerous figures mentioned herein.*]

BIBLIOGRAPHY

Dougan, Michael Bruce. "Confederate Arkansas: The People and Politics of a Frontier State in Wartime." Ph.D. diss., Emory University, 1970.

Ellenburg, Martha A. "Reconstruction in Arkansas." Ph.D. diss., University of Missouri, 1967.

Moneyhon, Carl H. *The Impact of the Civil War and Reconstruction in Arkansas, 1850–1874.* Baton Rouge, La., forthcoming.

Staples, Thomas S. *Reconstruction in Arkansas, 1862–1874.* New York, 1923.

Thomas, David Y. *Arkansas in War and Reconstruction, 1861–1874.* Little Rock, Ark., 1926.

Thompson, George H. *Arkansas and Reconstruction: The Influence of Geography, Economics, and Personality.* Port Washington, N.Y., 1976.

Woods, James M. *Rebellion and Realignment: Arkansas's Road to Secession.* Fayetteville, Ark., 1987.

Worley, Ted R. "The Arkansas Peace Society of 1861: A Study of Mountain Unionism." *Southern Historical Quarterly* 24 (1958): 445–456.

FRED ARTHUR BAILEY

ARKANSAS. CSS *Arkansas* was laid down at Memphis, Tennessee, in October 1861, built by John Shirley. Before she could be completed, Memphis was threatened by Union forces descending the Mississippi River. The incomplete ironclad was towed down the Mississippi and up the Yazoo River. At Yazoo City, Mississippi, she was completed and commissioned in July 1862.

Arkansas was a twin-screw-propeller ram, 165 feet in length, 35 feet in width, with a draft of 11 to 12 feet. In contrast to the other Confederate armored vessels, the sides of her casemate were perpendicular, although the two ends were slanted. The casemate was covered with railway T-rails. The ship carried a crew of approximately two hundred officers and men and a battery of ten guns: two

CSS *ARKANSAS*. Sepia wash drawing by R. G. Skerrett, 1904.

NAVAL HISTORICAL CENTER, WASHINGTON, D.C.

9-inch smoothbores, two 9-inch shell guns, two 64-pounders, two 6-inch rifles, and two 32-pounder smoothbores.

On July 15, 1862, as the ironclad descended the Yazoo River, she encountered three Union vessels—*Carondelet, Tyler,* and *Queen of the West.* In the engagement that followed, *Carondelet* was disabled and the other two Union vessels retired downstream with *Arkansas* in pursuit. The chase continued into the Mississippi River where the Confederate ironclad found at anchor the combined naval forces of flag officers Charles Davis and David Farragut, some thirty warships in all. *Arkansas* steamed slowly through the Union force, hit repeatedly by shot and shell. Several of the Union vessels were hit by *Arkansas*'s guns, but only *Lancaster* was seriously damaged.

Arkansas reached Vicksburg and that night came under attack a second time by Farragut's vessels as they ran the Confederate batteries and headed back downstream. The Confederate ironclad, already damaged from the early morning engagement, was hit several times again.

On August 3, *Arkansas,* repairs completed, left Vicksburg to cooperate in an attack on Baton Rouge, Louisiana. Twenty-four hours after leaving Vicksburg, the ironclad's engines began giving trouble, and the ship was anchored while engineers worked on them. The crew got the ship underway again the following morning, but when she was within sight of Baton Rouge, the engines broke down completely. With a Union naval force led by the ironclad *Essex* approaching, the Confederates abandoned *Arkansas* after setting her on fire. She drifted downstream before sinking.

BIBLIOGRAPHY

Milligan, John D. *Gunboats down the Mississippi.* Annapolis, Md., 1965.
Still, William N., Jr. *Iron Afloat: The Story of the Confederate Armorclads.* Columbia, S.C., 1986.

WILLIAM N. STILL, JR.

ARKANSAS CAMPAIGN OF 1864. Also designated the Camden Expedition, the Arkansas campaign of March 23 to May 3, 1864, was a Union thrust into southwestern Arkansas designed to divert the Confederate forces under Maj. Gen. Sterling Price away from Union Maj. Gen. Nathaniel P. Banks's army heading up the Red River from New Orleans. Headquartered at Little Rock, Maj. Gen. Frederick Steele's Federal troops were commissioned to defeat Price, unite with Banks, and invade Texas.

Motivated by domestic and international considerations,

President Abraham Lincoln overrode Lt. Gen. Ulysses S. Grant's objections to the Red River and Arkansas campaigns. Lincoln not only intended to establish a Union government in Texas but also desired to intimidate the French-imposed puppet regime in Mexico. Union defeats in both Louisiana and Arkansas frustrated his goals.

For Trans-Mississippi Confederates the Arkansas campaign was a moment of tactical success in a largely humiliating war. By spring 1864, Confederate control of Arkansas had been compressed into its southwestern third roughly bounded by the Saline River to the east and the Ouachita River to the north. Union troops occupied an extensive line along the Arkansas and Mississippi rivers with the region between the two enemies abandoned to ranging cavalry, guerrillas, and bandits.

Neither the Union nor the Confederate armies were prepared for a protracted campaign. Charged with the occupation of northern Arkansas, Steele had spread his thin forces along the Arkansas River with concentrations of 5,000 men under Brig. Gen. John M. Thayer at Fort Smith, 8,400 under his personal command at Little Rock, and 2,400 under Col. Powell Clayton at Pine Bluff. Severely handicapped by logistical problems—wretched roads, inadequate rail lines, and Arkansas River shallows—Steele not only had failed to stockpile rations for his men but also lacked sufficient fodder for his horses and mules. While half his cavalry was dismounted, the remainder rode steeds incapable of extensive field operations; his pack animals were undernourished and unable to manage his baggage and supply trains. Ordered to strike deep into Confederate territory, Steele faced difficult terrain—mountains to his west and bayous or swamps to his east. He marched into a region denuded of forage by hungry Confederates and depended for supplies upon barely passable roads vulnerable to inclement weather and enemy cavalry. Having assessed these conditions, Steele recommended his army create little more than a feint, but his superiors demanded a more vigorous crusade.

Confederates under Price were no more ready for the campaign than their Union counterparts. During the winter of 1863–1864, Price assembled his forces at Camden—the state's second largest city—constructing extensive earthworks. Deeming Banks the greater threat to the Trans-Mississippi Department, theater commander E. Kirby Smith shifted two infantry divisions from Price, leaving him with 7,000 cavalry and 1,500 infantry—a force insufficient to man the works at Camden or to challenge Steele's army in open combat. Alerted to Union movements, Price employed his cavalry to advantage, ordering it to vex his opponent with hit-and-run attacks.

Steele planned a diversionary push toward Arkansas's Confederate capital at the village of Washington and then a shift eastward to Camden, his real objective. Once there he hoped to establish a secure line of supply either by road to Pine Bluff or by water on the Ouachita River, which was navigable as far as the city. If successful, he could then defeat Price and link with Banks.

On March 23, Steele trooped out of Little Rock, ordering Thayer to join him at Arkadelphia and directing Clayton to scout the region below Pine Bluff in order to clear a potential supply route to Camden. The ensuing martial drama played out in three acts: Steele's push to Camden (March 23–April 15), his occupation of the city (April 15–26), and his retreat to Little Rock (April 26–May 3).

As Steele and Thayer edged toward Arkadelphia, Clayton struck south of Pine Bluff with a mixed force of 1,200 infantry and cavalry and achieved the Union's initial success. On March 28, he defeated a small Confederate contingent at Mt. Elba, entrenched his infantry there, and the following day spurred his cavalry forty miles due south to Long View on the Saline River. He surprised and captured a Confederate supply train, taking thirty-five wagons loaded with war matériel, 260 prisoners, and an undetermined number of freed slaves; in addition he destroyed his enemy's pontoon bridge. Returning to Mt. Elba, he discovered that his infantry had fended off a determined counterattack, forcing a Confederate retreat westward. By the evening of March 30, he had neutralized Confederate forces along the Saline River, opening the supply route to Camden.

Steele's caution more than neutralized Clayton's boldness. Hampered by poor roads and rain-swollen creeks, Steele required six days to negotiate fifty miles along the west bank of the Ouachita River to Arkadelphia. Arriving on March 29, he camped, waiting in vain for Thayer who struggled along tortuous mountain paths. With his supplies dwindling, Steele departed Arkadelphia on April 1, placed his men on half rations, and continued his chary advance toward Washington. Meanwhile Price posted Brig. Gen. Joseph O. Shelby's cavalry brigade to Princeton, thirty miles east of Arkadelphia. Learning Steele's location, Shelby darted toward Arkadelphia, missing the Union army by scant hours. The following day, he fell on Steele's rear guard at Okolona, scrimmaging in a driving rain for two days. Having killed or captured 160 Federal soldiers, he broke off the harassing attacks and skirted westward past Steele to join Brig. Gen. John S. Marmaduke's defense of Washington.

Commanding a force inferior to Steele's 13,000 men (Thayer finally arrived on April 9), Marmaduke resorted to guile to delay the Union's progress. At Prairie de Anne, the Confederates threw up imposing log and earthworks, but lacked sufficient numbers to adequately hold them. Nonetheless, the works' existence induced further caution in Steele, who spent three days probing Confederate lines without bringing on a full confrontation. At the same time,

Price moved the balance of his forces to Washington, and on April 12 he ordered Marmaduke to fall back to a more defendable position. Even though Steele gained the disputed ground, the delay further exacerbated his supply crisis. As Marmaduke boasted, the ruse served its "purpose forcing [Steele] to waste his time and keep his army starving in a barren country."

Steele then sprung his own surprise on Price who wrongly assumed that the Union general planned an attack upon Washington. Instead Steele rushed east to Camden, occupied the lightly defended Confederate works, and settled to assess his strategic situation. Having lost contact with the Union advance up the Red River, he was unaware that Banks had suffered defeat below Shreveport a week earlier. Although reinforced by troops no longer needed in Louisiana, Price hesitated to challenge Camden's strong defenses. Nonetheless, he now possessed the military advantage, comforted by the intelligence that Steele's army courted starvation. As Union troops stumbled into Camden, they swarmed into kitchens, smokehouses, storage rooms, and slave cabins desperate for sustenance.

Unsure of his next move, Steele dispatched couriers to search for Banks, directed Clayton to transport supplies from Pine Bluff, and sent out foraging parties to glean food and fodder from the countryside. The latter proved disastrous. Learning that five thousand bushels of corn could be taken sixteen miles west of Camden, Steele ordered 1,170 men—including 438 from the First Kansas Colored Infantry—to secure the prize. On the morning of April 18, they blundered into a Confederate ambush at Poison Springs and within forty-five minutes the Union lost 200 heavily ladened wagons along with 204 men killed and missing. Over half the dead (117) were African Americans. "Many wounded men belonging to the First Kansas Colored Infantry," raged their colonel, "fell to the enemy and . . . were murdered on the spot," a claim substantiated by exaggerated Confederate reports of 300 black and 75 white Federal dead. The Confederates suffered 252 casualties, 34 of whom were killed.

Two days later 150 wagons reached Steele from Pine Bluff. Much appreciated, it only partially met the army's needs. On April 24, the wagon train commenced a return journey across bayous created by the Moro and Saline rivers. Judging Federal control of Camden tenuous at best, a multitude of fearful Unionists attached themselves to the column: 500 dismounted Iowa cavalry whose enlistments had expired, 300 newly emancipated slaves anxious for more secure freedom, several merchants who had rashly pledged loyalty to the Federal government, and a number of sutlers and cotton speculators. Unknown to them, 4,000 Confederate cavalry commanded by Brig. Gen. James F. Fagan had departed El Dorado with instructions to close Steele's communications. He pounced on the hapless

convoy at Mark Mills (April 25) and in a spirited five-hour engagement killed 500 Federals, took 1,300 prisoners, and confiscated the Union wagons along with an equal number of civilian vehicles.

This galvanized Steele. Finally cognizant of Banks's retreat in Louisiana and having little faith that Union gunboats would paddle up the Ouachita, he evacuated Camden on the night of April 26, his only avenue of escape being the road north to Little Rock by way of Princeton. Lacking fit horses, he abandoned many of his wagons in Camden, and in their hasty march, his soldiers marked their trail by shedding garments, haversacks, and plunder stolen during the expedition.

With Price in spirited pursuit, the Federal retreat stalled at Jenkins' Ferry twenty-two miles north of Princeton. There the Saline River bottom stretched for two miles on either side of its flooded banks. Forced onto the narrow high ground of a single road, Union troops, horses, and wagons intermingled as they struggled to cross Steele's rickety pontoon bridge. On the morning of April 30, exhausted Confederates charged the tired, desperate Federals, both sides enduring a heavy downpour. Fighting across swamps and dense woods, neither yielded until Steele had transported his artillery and ammunition wagons to the Saline's north bank. Taking advantage of a lull in the battle, he abandoned his dead and wounded, destroyed nonessential supplies (tents and medical stores), and cut loose his pontoons. Unable to cross the Saline, Price concluded his chase, allowing Steele to limp back to Little Rock without further molestation. Following the Battle of Jenkins' Ferry, Price reported losses of 86 killed and 356 wounded; Steele listed 63 killed, 413 wounded, and 45 missing.

Delighted with Confederate successes in Louisiana and Arkansas, E. Kirby Smith congratulated the soldiers of the Trans-Mississippi Department, proclaiming they had killed or wounded 8,000 Union troops and captured 6,000 prisoners, thirty-four artillery pieces, 1,200 wagons, one gunboat, and three river transports. Steele's expedition to Camden virtually ended serious campaigning in Arkansas. Returning to his line along the Arkansas River, he and his forces lapsed into lethargy. When in late August, Price led 12,000 cavalry on a spectacular raid across half of Missouri, Steele made little effort to block his exit out of Arkansas or to intercept him on his return in the fall. Infuriated, Lincoln removed Steele from command in December, replaced him with Maj. Gen. Joseph Reynolds, and then allowed Arkansas to languish while he and Grant concentrated on the more critical contests in Virginia and the Carolinas.

BIBLIOGRAPHY

Dougan, Michael Bruce. "Confederate Arkansas: The People and Policies of a Frontier State in Wartime." Ph.D. diss., Emory University, 1970.

Edwards, John N. *Shelby and His Men: The War in the West.* Cincinnati, 1867.

Moneyhon, Carl H. *The Impact of the Civil War and Reconstruction on Arkansas, 1850–1874.* Baton Rouge, La., forthcoming.

Parks, Joseph H. *General Edmund Kirby Smith, C.S.A.* Baton Rouge, La., 1954.

Ross, Margaret. "Chronicles of Arkansas: The Years of the Civil War." *Arkansas Gazette,* March 22–May 8, 1964.

FRED ARTHUR BAILEY

ARLINGTON HOUSE. Situated on a knoll overlooking the Potomac River and the city of Washington, Arlington was the Virginia home of Robert E. Lee. The mansion now lies in the heart of Arlington National Cemetery. Composed of a two-story center with flanking one-story wings, Arlington was set on an eleven-hundred-acre tract of land, most of which was wooded. Construction began in 1803 on the north wing, but the entire house was not completed until about 1817 or 1818. It was planned and built by George Washington Parke Custis, step-grandson of George Washington. George Hadfield, second architect of the U.S. Capitol, designed Arlington's portico, which is fronted by six massive Doric columns and modeled on the Greek temple at Paestum. The building is constructed of brick, but its exterior is stuccoed and patterned to simulate cut stone. It is considered one of the finest and earliest examples of the Greek Revival style in the United States.

Lt. Robert E. Lee married Mary Ann Randolph Custis at Arlington in 1831, and there the family raised seven children. With the outbreak of war in 1861, Lee left Arlington, never to return. The estate was occupied by Federal troops, and it became a training camp. The army felled the forests and ransacked or impounded the family's Washington memorabilia. In 1862 Congress levied a direct tax on all properties in insurrectionary territory and required that the owners personally appear to make payment. The Lees proved unable to cross Federal lines to pay the $92.07 tax. Pursuant to an amendment of the direct tax in 1863, the government purchased the plantation at a public auction.

In May 1864 Secretary of War Edwin Stanton ordered that a national cemetery be created on two hundred acres of the grounds at Arlington. The first burials began that year, and Quartermaster General Montgomery Meigs directed that the lawn and gardens be ringed with burial sites. Shattered by the loss of her family home, Mary Lee mourned that those officials had desecrated Arlington. More than seventeen thousand casualties or veterans of the Civil War were eventually buried there. Emancipated slaves also established Freedman's Village on the grounds. Over a twenty-year period, some two thousand residents lived in the settlement.

Remorseful over losing his wife's estate, Lee attempted to regain Arlington after the war, but failed. President Andrew Johnson proposed returning the Washington relics to the Lee family, but Congress balked. After Lee's death in 1870, his son George Washington Custis Lee pursued the matter, and the Supreme Court finally ruled in 1882 that the government had acted illegally in seizing the house. The Lee family settled the case with the government for $150,000. Arlington still served as headquarters for the cemetery until the late 1920s.

The fate of the mansion changed considerably with the cultural politics of the Southern Renaissance. Thousands of visitors annually paid homage to Lee at Arlington, and proposals were aired to restore the mansion to its earlier appearance. In 1921 author Frances Parkinson Keyes urged the formation of a private preservation society to shepherd the project, but Republican Congressman Louis C. Cramton of Michigan proposed instead that the government establish a national shrine at Arlington. In 1925 Congress unanimously passed legislation that directed the secretary of war to restore the building as "Arlington House, The Robert E. Lee Memorial." Arlington was transferred to the National Park Service in 1933. Today Arlington House displays the history of the Custis-Lee family, as well as upper-class Virginia life.

BIBLIOGRAPHY

Connelly, Thomas L. *The Marble Man: Robert E. Lee and His Image in American Society.* New York, 1977.

Lindgren, James M. *Preserving the Old Dominion: Historic Preservation and Virginia Traditionalism.* Charlottesville, Va., 1993.

Nelligan, Murray H. *"Old Arlington": The Story of the Lee Mansion National Memorial.* Washington, D.C., 1953.

U.S. National Park Service. *Arlington House: A Guide to Arlington House, The Robert E. Lee Memorial, Virginia.* Washington, D.C., 1985.

JAMES M. LINDGREN

ARMISTEAD, LEWIS A. (1817–1863), brigadier general. Son of an army general, Lewis Addison Armistead was born February 18, 1817, in Newbern, North Carolina. He entered West Point in 1834 but left the academy two years later following an altercation with Cadet Jubal Early of Virginia. In 1839 Armistead joined the army as a lieutenant in the Sixth Infantry. Following active service in the Seminole War, Armistead fought in the Mexican War and received brevet promotion to major for heroism at Chapultepec. He spent the next fourteen years on frontier duty. One of his closest friends was fellow officer Winfield Scott Hancock of Pennsylvania.

With the advent of the Civil War, Armistead resigned his

LEWIS A. ARMISTEAD.   LIBRARY OF CONGRESS

army commission and rushed from Texas to Virginia to offer his sword to the Confederacy. Older than most of his compatriots and thoroughly imbued with army ways, Armistead served the first year of the war as colonel of the Fifty-seventh Virginia. On April 1, 1862, he was promoted to brigadier general. His new command (Ninth, Fourteenth, Thirty-eighth, Fifty-third, and Fifty-seventh Virginia) became one of the most celebrated and battle-hardened brigades in the Army of Northern Virginia. One reason for its success was Armistead's leadership. He regarded obedience to duty, a superior noted, "as the first qualification of a soldier. For straggling on the march or neglect of duty on the part of his men, he held the officer in immediate command strictly responsible. The private must answer to the officer, but the officer to him."

From Seven Pines through Second Manassas, a colleague observed, Armistead increased his reputation—"displaying everywhere conspicuous gallantry, and winning by his coolness under fire, by his stern perseverance and his indomitable pluck, the applause of his superiors and the entire confidence of his men."

Armistead served as provost marshal for Robert E. Lee's army during the Sharpsburg campaign. His brigade then became part of Gen. George E. Pickett's division. Armistead played only a minor role at Fredericksburg and was with James Longstreet's command at Suffolk during the Chan-

cellorsville campaign. He gained immortality at Gettysburg, however.

On July 3, 1863, his brigade was part of the climactic Pickett-Pettigrew assault against the Union center. Armistead received the order to advance and then turned to his drawn-up columns and shouted: "Men! Remember what you are fighting for—your homes, your friends, and your sweethearts! Follow me!"

With his hat on the point of his sword, Armistead led his men forward. Barely 150 of them were left when they reached the Federal lines. Armistead jumped over the enemy obstruction on Cemetery Ridge and fell mortally wounded among the Federal cannon. He died July 5 in a Federal hospital, after requesting that his watch and other valuables be given to his old friend, Winfield Hancock—whose troops, unknown to Armistead, were the ones who had repulsed the Virginians.

The general is buried in the family plot at St. Paul's Church, Baltimore. Of Armistead and three other brigadiers slain at Gettysburg, Lee wrote that they "died as they had lived, discharging the highest duty of patriots with devotion that never faltered and courage that shrank from no danger."

BIBLIOGRAPHY

Dowdey, Clifford. *The Seven Days.* Boston, 1964.
Poindexter, James E. "Address on the Life and Services of Gen. Lewis A. Armistead." *Southern Historical Society Papers* 37 (1909): 144–151. Reprint, Wilmington, N.C., 1991.
Stewart, George R. *Pickett's Charge.* Boston, 1959.

JAMES I. ROBERTSON, JR.

ARMORIES. *See* Arsenals and Armories.

ARMS, WEAPONS, AND AMMUNITION.

[This entry is composed of two articles, Army Ordnance *and* Naval Ordnance, *which serve as an introduction to the discussion of ordnance used by the Confederacy. For more detailed discussions of weaponry used during the Civil War, see* Artillery; Edged Weapons; Hand Grenades and Land Mines; Naval Guns; Small Arms; Torpedoes and Mines. *For discussion of the production and acquisition of ordnance by the Confederacy, see* Arsenals and Armories; Niter and Mining Bureau; Ordnance Bureau; Powder Works. *For discussion of the changes in military tactics brought about by developments in weaponry, see* Civil War, *article on* Strategy and Tactics.]*

Army Ordnance

The small arms of the Confederate soldier were of diverse type, quality, and source. The primary weapons of infantry and mounted soldiers were long arms, which fell into four basic categories. Muskets and rifle-muskets were arms with long, thin barrels, the former smoothbore, the latter rifled, both of which ranged in length from 37 to 42 inches. Rifles were arms with rifled, thick-walled, 33-to-34-inch barrels. Musketoons were generally muzzle-loading smoothbore arms with 24-to-30-inch barrels, favored by cavalry and mounted artillery for their ease of loading and use on horseback. Finally, there were carbines, similar to musketoons but generally breech-loading and often rifled, with 21-to-24-inch barrels, favored by cavalry. Of more limited value were handguns — revolvers and obsolete single-shot pistols — carried by officers and by cavalry for close mounted combat.

Many soldiers, especially officers and cavalrymen, also carried edged weapons. Sabers were used by cavalry and mounted artillery for hand-to-hand combat. Bayonets, used by infantry, inflicted very few documentable casualties. They were of two types: socket bayonets, which slid over the muzzle of muskets and rifle-musket, and saber bayonets, which locked to a lug on the side of a barrel. Long swords were carried by officers as a symbol of their rank. Short swords were carried by siege or garrison artillery to defend their artillery pieces at close quarters. At the beginning of the war, many Confederate enlisted men also brought crudely wrought bowie knives in anticipation of fighting at close quarters; they were soon discarded.

Prior to 1862, the majority of small arms had been secured through purchase in the North or through the seizure of Northern-made arms from Federal arsenals in the South. Early in the war, Confederates also attempted to increase the quantity, if not the quality, of their store of small arms by altering to a percussion ignition system those obsolete flintlock arms stored in Southern state arsenals (either as a result of earlier attempts at state production or from receipts of Northern-made arms allotted under the 1808 Militia Act).

This initial supply of arms would be supplemented through mid-1862 with the captured and repaired arms gleaned from the battlefields controlled by the dominant Army of Northern Virginia. At the same time, nascent Southern domestic production began contributing to the arms pool available to the Confederate Ordnance Bureau. Plagued by inadequate resources in machinery, skilled mechanics, and eventually raw materials, this home production would, however, never prove a significant factor in equipping the Confederacy. Providently, in early 1861 both the Confederate government and the state governors had realized the probable inadequacy of domestic production and had sent agents abroad to secure arms. As a result, by mid-1862, importations of European (primarily English) weapons formed the backbone of the Confederate ordnance effort, stymied only by the lack of ready funds and the

relatively ineffectual Union blockade. As a result of the massive importations, the Confederate armies were able to re-equip those army units that had received inferior arms in 1861 with the more technologically advanced rifled arms then available. Logistical problems, however, prevented the completion of this effort until the winter of 1863–1864.

The diverse nature of Confederate small arms would have a subtle impact on Southern tactics. The vast majority of the arms initially secured from the North or seized in Southern arsenals, with a few exceptions, were smoothbore, muzzle-loading, single-shot muskets. The maximum effective range of these arms was essentially one hundred yards, and only the employment of massed volley fire could compensate for their lack of accuracy. The smoothbore musket had been supplanted technologically in 1855 by the rifle-musket. This arm, though still muzzle-loading and single-shot, was rifled. Rifling itself was not new, but the muzzle-loading procedure of rifled weapons prior to 1855 had been a slow and tedious process. With the adoption of a hollow-base, conical projectile (known as the "minié ball") developed by the French Ordnance Bureau, however, the rifle-musket could be loaded and fired as fast as the old smoothbore musket. The new projectile in conjunction with the rifle-musket was theoretically capable of accurate fire up to nine hundred yards. The high trajectory of the rifle-musket and its minié ball projectile, however, in combination with the inability of most field commanders to accurately judge the distance to an opposing force, reduced the practical range of the new weapon to three hundred yards.

Had the Northern forces been fully armed with this weapon at the outset of the conflict, the South would have been at a severe tactical disadvantage. But the production of the rifle-musket had been so limited that the North was forced to rely on the same inferior smoothbore arms as the South until mid-1862. In the interim, the doctrine of tactical offensive with massed volley fire still ruled the battlefield, an advantage the Southern armies, with their superior leadership and élan, exploited throughout 1862 (though often with dreadful consequences in terms of casualties). Additions of improved arms, either through import, capture, or limited domestic production, kept Southern forces at a par with their Northern counterparts through 1862 and 1863, so that neither side possessed a tactical advantage based solely upon weaponry. The tactical defensive advantage evolved in 1864, when the superior range of the rifle-musket was combined with defensive earthworks that severely reduced the ability of an attacker to inflict casualties on his opponent. Having finally completed the re-equipping of its forces with the rifle-musket during the winter of 1863–1864, the South was fully able to exploit this combination during the spring campaigns of 1864, probably adding an extra year to the short life of the Confederate States of America.

The same problems that the South encountered in equipping its military forces with small arms also applied to artillery. Like the small arms, the artillery of the Confederacy came from diverse sources: pre–Civil War acquisition of light artillery under the 1808 Militia Act, seizure of heavy ordnance at seacoast fortifications, capture of Union light artillery on the battlefield, importation, and domestic manufacture.

The light artillery in the South at the commencement of hostilities consisted of Mexican War–vintage guns. Prior to 1857, the standard six-gun field (also called "light") battery had consisted of four 6-pound guns and two 12-pound howitzers, both of whose tubes (barrels) were cast in bronze. The prime difference between a gun and a howitzer was the interior of the bore. Howitzers had a chamber of lesser diameter than the actual bore of the gun and so accepted a small amount of propellant charge; the small charge caused the projectile to travel in a relatively high arc to its target. Guns, on the other hand, had a chamber that was the same diameter as the bore; this permitted the projectile to travel a relatively low arc to its target. Until the introduction of rifled guns, light or field artillery was designated in terms of the weight of a solid round shot: 6-pound solid shot was 3.67 inches in diameter; 12-pound solid shot was 4.62 inches in diameter. Only the larger guns and mortars were designated by the true diameter of their bores.

The 6-pound gun, model 1841, formed the backbone of Confederate field artillery in 1861. Many were rifled during the early months of the conflict for increased accuracy and range (the latter increased from 1,523 to 1,700 yards). Rifling made the 6-pounder equivalent in range and striking power to the 12-pound smoothbore light gun introduced in 1857 and commonly known as the "Napoleon" (after Napoleon III of France, whose army pioneered its development). The "Napoleon" was the standard smoothbore gun of the U.S. Army in 1861 and continued in service throughout the war. At 1,227 pounds its tube was 530 pounds less than the old model 1841 12-pound gun, making it much more maneuverable on the field of battle. In addition to capturing Union Napoleons, the Confederacy widely copied the gun in its cannon foundries, and by 1863 many of the older 6-pound guns and 12-pound howitzers had been turned over to Ordnance Bureau authorities to be recast into the Napoleons.

At the beginning of the conflict, rifled muzzle-loading cannon were just beginning to be widely accepted by artillery tacticians. Two rifled field guns predominated in the Confederacy: the Parrott rifle with its shrunken band of reinforcing steel at its breech, and the light, sleek, evenly tapered "Ordnance" rifle. Both were made of iron. Although Virginia had acquired a few Parrott rifles just before secession, nearly all of the rifled iron guns in the Confed-

eracy had been captured in combat. The Ordnance rifle was generally manufactured with a 3-inch diameter rifled bore that threw a 9.5-pound elongated projectile up to 1,830 yards. The Parrott came in three field grades: the 10-pound, 3-inch (actually 2.9-inch) Parrott threw a solid shot of 9.5 pounds 1,900 yards; the 20-pound, 3.67-inch threw a solid shot of 20 pounds the same distance; and the 30-pound, 4.5-inch threw a solid shot of 30 pounds 1,670 yards. (The last was usually considered a siege rather than a field gun, but numerous guns of this size were used by the Union and a few were captured by Confederate forces and pressed into service.)

The weight of the projectile that designated the type of gun was for a solid elongated shot, also called a "bolt." Such projectiles were primarily used for battering fortifications or for firing at long range at relatively fast-moving targets. When the target was not moving fast, the artillerist's preference was for shrapnel or case shot. These projectiles consisted of a sphere or bolt with a hollow cavity. The cavity was filled with a bursting charge and a number of musket balls. A fuze plugged or screwed into a hole in the nose of the projectile was supposed to catch fire upon the explosion of the propellent charge and spray the target with fragments. Shell, a similar projectile but lacking the musket balls, was intended primarily to burn structures. The standard fuze for the U.S. Army prior to the Civil War was the Bormann fuze, consisting of a zinc cylinder and a circular powder train within, all of which screwed into the nose of a projectile. Its exterior was marked at intervals with explosion times; a cut across the mark exposed the proper timed detonation. The Confederacy attempted to copy this fuze at its laboratories, but its failure was so common that Southern gunners resorted to the old prewar wooden tapered fuze, a portion of which was cut off for timed explosions before being pounded into the hole at the nose of the projectile.

Because fuzes so often failed to ignite (the expanding bases of rifled projectiles often prevented the hot gasses of the cartridge's explosion from reaching the fuze at the nose of the projectile), percussion fuzes that detonated on impact were experimented with by both sides. But because these fuzes often buried into the ground before detonating or failed to detonate at all due to the low angle of the trajectory, they were not generally favored for field use.

The final antipersonnel projectile used during the war was called "canister." Sometimes erroneously referred to as "grape," the canister projectile gained its name from the shape of its exterior, a sheet-iron cylinder. The cylinder was filled with sawdust intermingled with small iron balls. Upon leaving the bore of a gun or howitzer, the momentum of the iron balls burst the cylinder, showering the area within three hundred yards of the muzzle with a shotgun-like blast of iron balls that was particularly destructive against advancing infantry or cavalry. At close range (one hundred yards or less), double and sometimes even triple loads of canister were used against oncoming forces.

All of these same type of projectiles were available not only to field batteries but also to the larger cannons for the defense of coastal or river fortifications. For the most part, these larger guns were captured or seized at Federal fortifications or naval stations in the South. The most common types captured consisted of 24-, 32-, and 42-pound iron guns. Many of these were subsequently rifled and fired elongated projectiles weighing respectively 48, 64, and 84 pounds. Smoothbore guns with diameters of 8 and 10 inches, throwing a ball of 68 and 128 pounds, respectively, were also captured and used by the Confederacy. By shifting these guns to vulnerable coastal and river defenses, the Confederacy was able to stall invasions at several critical places, though at the forts below New Orleans and at Forts Donelson and Henry they would not prove effective against superior Union naval power.

BIBLIOGRAPHY

Coates, Earl J. *Arms and Equipment of the Confederacy.* Vol. 2 of *Echoes of Glory.* Alexandria, Va., 1991.

Coggins, Jack. *Arms and Equipment of the Civil War.* New York, 1962.

Hazlett, James E., Edwin Olmstead, and Hume M. Parks. *Field Artillery Weapons of the Civil War.* Newark, N.J., 1983.

Ripley, Warren. *Artillery and Ammunition of the Civil War.* New York, 1970.

Todd, Frederick P. *American Military Equipage, 1851–1872.* Providence, R.I., 1974.

HOWARD MICHAEL MADAUS

Naval Ordnance

The beginning of the Civil War found the world's navies in a period of transition. In ordnance, there had been little change in the centuries-old smoothbore muzzle-loading guns firing solid shot. Extensive experiments were being conducted, however, with rifled breech-loading guns. Explosive shell had found favor at sea, and shell guns (as opposed to the old shot guns) were designed specifically for their use. Although rifled guns came into their own during the war, breechloaders continued to be plagued with problems; as a result, virtually all heavy pieces aboard ships during the Civil War were muzzleloaders. Cast iron had no serious rivals as a material for heavy ordnance, but there were numerous experiments with heavy wrought-iron guns despite the disastrous 1844 "Peacemaker" explosion aboard USS *Princeton.* Some guns were even being made of steel.

In composition of ship batteries, broadside batteries made up of many smaller guns were giving way to fewer guns of larger caliber and longer range mounted in pivot on the spar

deck. This was particularly true aboard the new steamers. Civil War ironclad vessels were generally armed with a few heavy guns, usually a mix of rifled and smoothbore pieces. The largest gun in common broadside use during the war was the 9-inch shell gun. Pivot-mounted guns might be of any size, but were generally up to 11-inch.

Explosive shell fired at low velocity rendered wooden vessels extremely vulnerable. Ironically, shells proved largely ineffective against the new ironclad vessels during the war, and it was shot fired with higher charges of powder that did the most damage.

The U.S. Navy conducted important gunnery experiments in 1839, but the first experimental ordnance vessel was *Plymouth*, launched in 1857. The 1850s also saw the beginnings of scientific application to casting techniques (the Rodman process) and the design of guns (the Dahlgren design, which put the weight of metal at the breech, the point of greatest strain).

Improvements in gunpowder had led to reductions in the weight of charges. The Civil War saw continued improvements in cannon powder and the introduction of larger-grained powder.

Some new gun carriages had been introduced. The most prominent of these was the Marsilly, or two-truck (wheel) wooden carriage, which was much easier to train (aim) than the old four-truck carriage. It was adopted for the new 11-inch shell guns in broadside mounts.

The Confederacy secured a substantial quantity of cannons in the seizure of the Norfolk (Gosport) Navy Yard in April 1861 and also purchased some abroad. A limited number of guns were manufactured at home.

Confederate naval ordnance, including small arms and ammunition, was remarkably similar to that of the U.S. Navy, and ordnance practices were the same. This may be seen in a comparison of the U.S. Navy and Confederate States Navy ordnance manuals.

The Confederacy obtained small arms, too, by capture, purchase from abroad, and local manufacture. Most Federal arsenals within Confederate territory yielded many smoothbore muskets and some rifles, virtually all of which went to arm land forces. But the Confederacy failed to secure a substantial quantity of small arms from the Norfolk Navy Yard. The 1,329 carbines, 274 rifle-muskets, 950 naval pistols, and 337 Colt revolvers in the yard were either carried off in the frigate *Cumberland* or broken and thrown overboard by the Federals. Works were also established throughout the Confederacy for the manufacture of small arms and powder. Nonstandardization in small arms remained the rule in the South during the Civil War, and this applied to the navy.

Besides standard U.S. .58-caliber Springfield rifled muskets and local production of similar arms, Confederate agents purchased a variety of British carbines and muskets ranging from .44- to .75-caliber, Austrian .54-caliber rifles, and French .42-caliber carbines and Le Mat revolvers. Some may have found their way to the navy. The 1864 *Ordnance Instructions of the Confederate Navy* makes specific reference to Colt revolvers. The Model 1851 Navy .36-caliber pistol, weighing 2 pounds 10 ounces, was very popular in the South and the prototype of virtually all Southern-made revolvers.

Small arms were utilized by seamen and Confederate Marines. Afloat, Marines either augmented sailor crews or acted as sharpshooters and formed boarding parties. Their maximum number was only 540 officers and men, with many of these not available for service afloat. Their place was often taken by volunteers from cavalry and infantry units. As a result, Enfield .577-caliber rifles and shotguns were popular small arms on Confederate vessels. Boarding parties found shotguns particularly useful, as in the capture of USS *Harriet Lane* at Galveston, January 1, 1863.

The *Ordnance Instructions* called for regular exercise with the musket, carbine, pistol, and sword, and target practice with small arms. Captains of vessels determined when they were to be distributed and loaded and were also responsible for seeing that they were properly cleaned and stored. Small arms were to be inspected regularly and stored in unlined chests, if no proper armory was available.

Men armed with muskets afloat or on shore duty were to wear musket cartridge boxes, fitted with shoulder belt, and frog and scabbard for bayonet on their waist belt. Those armed with carbines on shore duty were to wear cartridge boxes with shoulder belts. For boat duty, or when armed with pistols and swords, they were to wear a waist belt with proper frog and boxes.

Allowance tables of the 1864 *Ordnance Instructions* specified quantities of small arms authorized for each class of ship. These included edged weapons such as battle axes, pikes, cutlasses, and swords, and muskets, carbines, revolvers, and pistols. The tables also provided ammunition allowances for each class of vessel.

BIBLIOGRAPHY

Albaugh, William A., III, and Edward N. Simmons. *Confederate Arms*. Harrisburg, Pa., 1957.
Ordnance Instructions for the Confederate States Navy. London, 1864.
Scharf, J. Thomas. *History of the Confederate States Navy*. New York, 1887. Reprint, New York, 1977.
Tucker, Spencer C. *Arming the Fleet: U.S. Navy Ordnance in the Muzzle-Loading Era*. Annapolis, Md., 1989.

SPENCER C. TUCKER

ARMSTRONG, FRANK CRAWFORD (1835–1907), brigadier general and U.S. assistant commissioner of Indian affairs. Armstrong was born November 22, 1835, on the Choctaw Agency, Indian Territory. His father, an army officer, died early in Armstrong's life, and his mother married Gen. Persifor Smith, who took the boy on at least one military expedition. Armstrong attended Holy Cross Academy and after graduation was commissioned directly into the regular army. As captain, Second U.S. Cavalry, he participated in the Battle of First Manassas on the Union side, but resigned his commission on August 13, 1861, one of the highest ranking soldiers to switch sides during the Civil War.

Sent west, Armstrong served on the staff of Gen. Benjamin McCulloch and during the Battle of Elkhorn Tavern was not more than a few feet from McCulloch when the latter was killed. Afterward Armstrong was elected colonel of the Third Louisiana Infantry, a promotion quickly followed by his selection to command the cavalry of Sterling Price. He was promoted to brigadier general on January 20, 1862, to reflect his command. Armstrong subsequently served under most of the cavalry commanders in the West such as Joseph Wheeler, James Ronald Chalmers, Stephen D. Lee, and Nathan Bedford Forrest. His last engagement was fought near Selma, Alabama, where he surrendered with Forrest's corps.

After the war Armstrong became a U.S. Indian inspector and rose to the position of assistant commissioner of Indian affairs in 1893. He died on September 8, 1907, at Bar Harbor, Maine.

Armstrong was an aggressive commander regarded by his superiors as efficient, brave, and demanding. Assigning him a cavalry unit in Mississippi, which already had several cavalry commanders, was a mark of praise.

BIBLIOGRAPHY

Booth, Andrew B., comp. *Records of Louisiana Confederate Soldiers and Louisiana Confederate Commands*. New Orleans, 1920.
Jordan, Gen. Thomas, and J. P. Pryor. *The Campaigns of N. B. Forrest*. New Orleans, 1868.
Oates, Stephen B. *Confederate Cavalry West of the River*. Austin, Tex., 1961.

ROY R. STEPHENSON

ARMY. [*This entry is composed of four articles:* Confederate Army, *which overviews the organization of the Confederate army and profiles several of its more prominent departments and special units;* Manpower, *which discusses the demographic makeup of the Confederate army;* Army Departments, *which discusses the location, command, and organization of the army departments; and* African Americans in the Confederate Army, *which examines the role of African Americans in the defense of the Confederacy. For further discussion of the organization and leadership of the cabinet-level department overseeing the Confederate war effort, see* War Department.]

Confederate Army

At the commencement of the secession crisis, hundreds of volunteer companies flocked to Montgomery, and then Richmond, to muster into the Confederate service. Specific field armies did not emerge at first, as companies were simply sent where needed without reference to organization. Jefferson Davis determined to pattern his new nation's forces after the armed forces of the old Union during the Mexican War of 1846 through 1848. He would have a small standing Regular Army, a cadre of professional soldiers, envisioned as lasting long after the conclusion of a peace and, presumably, the establishment of Confederate independence. But for meeting the urgent manpower needs of the current crisis, there would also be a Provisional Army of the Confederate States, comprising these volunteer outfits enlisted for specific terms of service, whether ninety days, twelve months, or eventually three years or the duration of the war.

The Regular Army

The Confederate Regular Army never really got off the ground. Authorized by Congress on March 6, 1861, it was to contain a corps of engineers, a corps of artillery, one cavalry regiment, and six infantry. But Regular enlistments were not attractive to would-be soldiers, since volunteers would do most of the fighting and win most of the glory and promotion. Moreover, volunteers would muster out as soon as the conflict was finished; Regulars were indentured for full terms of service regardless of when the war ceased. Thus, even though the enabling legislation called for 15,003 Regulars—roughly the size of the U.S. Regular service in 1860—only about 1,000 enlisted men and 750 officers and cadets eventually took their oaths. Not a single regiment was raised, and the few companies that did enlist were parceled out among other volunteer commands. Most of the officers took commands in the Provisional forces, achieving substantially higher rank there than their Regular commissions. Later in the war, a number of so-called Confederate regiments did appear, but they were not actually Regulars. Depleted companies from volunteer regiments from several states were consolidated to form full-strength units. Unable to decide what state designation to give such polyglot units, the War Department finally just called such outfits—twelve regiments and battalions of cavalry, nine regiments and battalions of infantry, five regiments and battalions of artillery—Confederate.

Most of the Regular companies served in the western theater of the war, but their histories—as distinct from the volunteers with whom they were grouped—are shadowy and difficult to extract. Indeed, even the War Department did not always keep track of them, and in 1864 Adjutant and Inspector General Samuel Cooper (the senior officer in the

Regular service) seems to have forgotten that they even existed, telling a would-be appointee that "there have been no appointments in the regular army for several years, there being no regular army." In fact, recruiting stations for the Regular service had been closed as early as July 1861, never to open again.

The Regulars were hampered from the outset by the fact that the Confederacy needed men quickly. Accepting locally and privately raised companies and regiments furnished by the governors of the states met those needs much more rapidly and at less expense than recruiting Regulars. In the early days of the war, the volunteers arrived often already uniformed and armed and sometimes even trained, especially those companies that had existed as local home guard and privately maintained drill units before the war. With the ever-present strains on the Confederate Treasury, the government naturally had to channel all of its resources toward maintaining and equipping this instant army, leaving little or nothing for the fledgling Regulars. Thus, though it may have had much potential, the Regular Army died aborning, all but forgotten even by the men who served it.

The Provisional Army

Symbolic of the negligible role destined for the Regulars, Congress created them a week after addressing the immediate manpower needs by authorizing, on February 28, 1861, the Provisional Army of the Confederate States (PACS). Two days previously it had created the several staff departments of the new army, and the same day that it created the Regulars, Congress authorized the president to raise up to 100,000 volunteers for periods of no more than twelve months' service. In subsequent months, more recruitment bills were passed as manpower needs quickly expanded following the secession of Virginia. In May Congress authorized an additional 400,000, this time for three years' service or the duration of the war. These issues of numbers of men and terms of service were continuing vexations for Davis, as some state governors persisted in dangling regiments before him, but for less than the mandated terms of service.

Recruitment and Organization. In return for being furnished the roughly 1,000 men in ten companies that formed an ideal regiment, the government agreed to feed, clothe, train, arm, and equip the men, and pay them on a regular basis the eleven dollars per month mandated for private soldiers, with higher rankings receiving more. But before the war was very old, payment became a haphazard thing at best, its chronic absence hardly ameliorated by a subsequent increase in the soldiers' monthly allowance.

Eventually, somewhere between 650,000 and 750,000 Southern men enlisted in the PACS (authorities differ on the exact number). Virtually all of the men, exclusive of

JEFFERSON DAVIS AND HIS GENERALS.   Davis is seated at left. Behind him, from left to right, are James Longstreet, John Bell Hood, J. E. B. Stuart, Thomas J. ("Stonewall") Jackson, Robert E. Lee, A. P. Hill, Joseph E. Johnston, and P. G. T. Beauregard.   NAVAL HISTORICAL CENTER, WASHINGTON, D.C.

Regulars and militia and home guardsmen, served in PACS units, whose numbers have been estimated at from 750 to 1,009. As with so many other Confederate statistics, the numbers of regiments, battalions, companies, and batteries are disputed, thanks to incomplete records and duplication of the same unit at times under more than one designation. In 1861, for instance, two Fifth Kentucky Infantries were raised. One later became the Ninth Kentucky, yet it often shows up as separate from the original Fifth.

The PACS units were to consist of ten companies of from 64 to 100 men for infantry regiments, and up to twelve companies of no fewer than 64 men for the cavalry and no fewer than 70 men in an artillery battery. In actual practice, companies averaged between 81 and 93 men in 1862, but they rapidly dwindled thereafter as casualties, disease, and desertions took their toll. By 1865, some regiments could muster fewer than 200, and many even smaller remnants were consolidated in 1864 and 1865 in order to create new regiments by combining those no longer large enough to perform effectively as battlefield units.

The dispersal of these volunteer regiments to the growing field armies of the Confederacy lay entirely with Davis and the War Department. From the outset efforts were made to combine units—from 3 to 5—from the same state into brigades, to serve under a brigadier from that state appointed by Davis; although there were many departures from this policy as the war ground on, it was honored more often than not. Further, the government did attempt to put such brigades into service more or less in their native region. Thus the major field army of the East, the Army of Northern Virginia, was composed chiefly of Virginia, North Carolina, South Carolina, Georgia, and Florida units, all of them raised east of the Appalachians. There were only smatterings of western regiments in Lee's army, just one regiment from Arkansas, and none at all from Kentucky and Missouri. The principal field army west of the mountains, the Army of Tennessee, was composed in its entirety of western units and those from the Deep South, with but a single brigade of Virginians and North Carolinians. Far to the west, across the Mississippi, E. Kirby Smith's Army of the Trans-Mississippi was similarly composed. It was a sound policy on the part of the War Department, for men could be expected to maintain their morale and élan more if they felt they were fighting for their own hearths. Moreover, it made recruiting to fill gaps, and the granting of occasional furloughs to visit home, that much more practicable. Some of the greatest discontent in the Southern forces arose when regiments were sent too far from their native states, often resulting in a commensurate rise in desertion.

Almost from the outset, the manpower available to the PACS lagged far behind needs. Only at the very outset did Davis have at his disposal more troops than he could arm and equip, forcing him reluctantly to turn away some proffered regiments that years later he would sorely miss. The largest field army, Robert E. Lee's in Virginia, never mustered more than about 85,000 men at its highest, while the Federal army opposing it rose at times as high as 130,000. The Army of Tennessee consistently hovered between 40,000 and 70,000, its numbers far less stable thanks to the much larger territory it had to defend and Richmond's frequent tampering with its organization.

At the beginning of the war, Congress authorized no organization larger than the brigade. Soon divisions composed of two or more brigades appeared, and then in 1862 Lee divided his army into "wings" that were finally formalized as corps in September. In the Army of Tennessee they began as "Grand Divisions" and were also called corps in the Shiloh campaign, but not until November 1862 did official corps organization appear.

Theoretically, at least, the military forces of the Confederacy assigned within a military department and commanded by the department officer in charge constituted its "army." By this definition, the Confederacy fielded at least forty "armies," though the number could be far higher thanks to departments changing names, being split or consolidated with others, and the commands themselves adopting designations other than those of the departments they served. (Ordinarily an army took its name from its department.) Most such armies were that in name only, being too small to merit the appellation. In 1864 the Army of Southwest Virginia was barely of brigade strength, for instance.

Army of Northern Virginia. The largest of the field armies of the Confederacy was also its best known and most storied, the Army of Northern Virginia, commanded by General Lee. It began, in fact, as the Army of the Potomac, and its origins lay in the first volunteers sent to the Department of Alexandria in April and May 1861. In June they were organized as the Army of the Potomac by Gen. P. G. T. Beauregard and fought as such at First Manassas. Even when forces from the Departments of Norfolk and the Peninsula were subsequently added, the combined organization continued to be the Army of the Potomac until June 1, 1862, when Lee assumed command. Informally he had taken to calling it the Army of Northern Virginia as far back as March. Now he made the change in fact, and the government quickly followed suit.

Certainly Lee and the government both took that designation literally to heart, for no other major field army of the Confederacy would operate through its entire career in so restricted an area. Although major portions of the First Corps did go to eastern Tennessee in the fall of 1863, and much of the Second Corps joined with other forces to form the Army of the (Shenandoah) Valley for a summer 1864 raid into Maryland, the Army of Northern Virginia as a whole set foot outside its department only three times. In September 1862 it crossed the Potomac into Maryland for the Sharpsburg campaign. In June and July 1863 it did so again, moving into Pennsylvania to Gettysburg. And in the summer of 1864 it withdrew to the defenses of Richmond and Petersburg, later to race toward Appomattox. With these exceptions, virtually all of its operations were conducted in an area sixty miles long, north of Richmond, and about sixty miles wide, from the Rappahannock River to Gordonsville.

As with all the field armies of the Confederacy, manpower for the Army of Northern Virginia always lagged behind needs. At its largest, Lee's command numbered about 85,000, first when he took command just prior to the Seven Days' Battles of June and July 1862, and again at Gettysburg in July 1863. Thus Lee was consistently outnumbered on virtually every battlefield of the war—by a minimum of about 10,000 at Gettysburg and by as much as 70,000 during the Chancellorsville campaign two months earlier. Of all the Confederate field armies, it was the one hardest hit by a heavy attrition of battlefield losses among senior commanders at corps, division, and brigade levels. Gettysburg almost crippled its high command, which never recovered thereafter. Men who started the war as captains could finish it as major generals commanding a corps, as did John B. Gordon.

Strategically the army operated with the freest rein of any major field command, chiefly because of the excellent relationship between Lee and President Davis. Moreover, it remained almost untroubled by the command squabbles that so crippled the Army of Tennessee and others. This was chiefly due to the pacific influence of Lee, and the fact that for much of its career it was a winning army, with outstanding morale. Although unsteadily and somewhat timorously led by Joseph E. Johnston from First Manassas through Seven Pines, it enjoyed answering to the premier field commander of the war when Lee took charge, and he in turn was able, before the carnage of Gettysburg, to build an infrastructure of subordinates at every level whom he knew and understood, and with whom he could mold victories. After Gettysburg, the army, its officers, and Lee himself were simply too worn down to attempt ever again a major offensive.

Army of Tennessee. "The Confederacy, its government, its territory, its every thing is concentrated in these two armies," a Union officer said in March 1865. One was the Army of Northern Virginia; the other was the Army of Tennessee, a command as troubled and ill-starred as its counterpart was favored by fortune.

It had its origins in Department No. 2, created by Davis in July 1861 with Leonidas Polk in command, soon to be superseded by Albert Sidney Johnston. On March 5, 1862, the troops of the department were redesignated the Army of Mississippi, though the department did not change its name, and as such Johnston led them at Shiloh. After Johnston's death, P. G. T. Beauregard took command, and he was in turn replaced by Gen. Braxton Bragg on June 27. Five months later the Army of Tennessee was joined with the small Army of Kentucky, and on November 20, 1862, Bragg assumed command of the whole under the new designation Army of Tennessee, the name it would bear to the end.

Unlike Lee's army, this western command ranged in its career over the entire length of Tennessee, northern Mississippi, and Alabama, and across Georgia and both of the Carolinas; it also launched a major offensive into Kentucky almost to the Ohio River. In all, the army campaigned over a vastness of nearly 200,000 square miles. Its manpower also ran consistently lower than Lee's. In most of its battles—Shiloh, Murfreesboro, Chickamauga—it numbered between 40,000 and 60,000. At its largest, commencing the Atlanta campaign in May 1864, it counted perhaps as many as 60,000 to 65,000 men.

Also unlike Lee's army, it was cursed with a command chaos almost from the start. The Virginia army benefited from a substantial percentage of professionally trained graduates of West Point and private military academies; the Army of Tennessee had far more amateurs in positions of responsibility. And again unlike Lee, Bragg and his successors from the start faced more able enemies in the likes of Ulysses S. Grant and William Tecumseh Sherman. Bragg himself was the most discordant element of all. Hesitating and indecisive, he blamed his defeats on his subordinates, engaging in blatant scapegoatism, and thereby fomented virtual rebellion among his corps and division commanders. From November 1862 on, the high command fought among themselves. When Bragg was replaced by Joseph E. Johnston on December 27, 1863, the squabbling did not cease but did abate somewhat, only to return with renewed vigor when John Bell Hood—one of the anti-Bragg faction—replaced Johnston on July 18, 1864. Following Hood's disasters at Franklin and Nashville in the fall, Richard Taylor succeeded him briefly on January 23, 1865, only to be himself replaced by Johnston once more on February 25. Twice during the war President Davis had to visit the army headquarters to try to put down the infighting, but to no avail. Consistently outnumbered by its foes, sometimes by two to one, and crippled by an inept commander in 1863 and by internal strife throughout, it was an ill-starred command from the outset. Except for the one shining moment at Chickamauga, when almost by chance it inflicted one of the most demoralizing losses ever suffered by a Union army, its whole career was one long tale of sacrifice and defeat.

Army of Vicksburg. Substantially smaller, though still important, secondary field armies operated east of the

Mississippi. Best known is the one surrendered by Gen. John C. Pemberton at Vicksburg, Mississippi, July 4, 1863. Officially the army of the Department of Mississippi and East Louisiana, it was more generally referred to as the Army of Vicksburg. Constituted almost exclusively for the defense of that river city, it never saw open field campaigning except for the May 1863 operations east and south of the city when futile attempts were made to impede the approach of Grant's Federal army. Its manpower was always woefully inadequate, made worse by Richmond's failure to appreciate the magnitude of Grant's threat and the foot dragging of Joseph E. Johnston when ordered to come to its relief with additional forces. Commencing the campaign with about 30,000 to 35,000 men, Pemberton at last had to surrender about 29,000, the only instance in the war of a complete field army yielding prior to the 1865 collapse.

Army of Alabama, Mississippi, and East Louisiana. Richard Taylor, briefly the commander of the Army of Tennessee, also led another major field command, the Army of East Louisiana, Mississippi, and Alabama—later redesignated the Army of Alabama, Mississippi, and East Louisiana. This was the last army east of the Mississippi to surrender, accepting terms on May 4, 1865, and paroling some 12,000 men, mute testimony to the pitiable manpower available to army commanders at war's end. This army saw action in 1864 in cooperation with Johnston's forces during the Atlanta campaign, but otherwise spent its entire career in Alabama resisting Federal thrusts at Mobile and Selma.

Army of the Trans-Mississippi. The last major Confederate army to surrender was also the only principal force west of the great river, the Army of the Trans-Mississippi. It began as the Army of the West, organized in the winter of 1861–1862 by Gen. Earl Van Dorn as a subcommand of Department No. 2. It served briefly in Arkansas, including the defeat at Elkhorn Tavern in March, and was then reconstituted as the Army of the Trans-Mississippi in May under Gen. Thomas C. Hindman and shortly thereafter under Gen. Theophilus H. Holmes. Then in February 1863 this subdistrict was incorporated into a larger command including virtually all of Texas, Arkansas, and Louisiana west of the river. The new Trans-Mississippi Department and army were commanded thereafter by Gen. E. Kirby Smith until the close of the war.

Its activities were widespread, at least geographically, for the army had the task of defending fully one-third of all the territory of the Confederacy. Consequently, Smith's army was usually dispersed in detachments covering posts in Arkansas, chiefly along rivers and overlooking the Mississippi during the Vicksburg campaign, and along the Rio Grande and the Texas Gulf to repel Federal seaborne raids. The army saw major action in only two campaigns: the Red River campaign of March to May 1864, and the raid into Missouri led by Gen. Sterling Price in September and October of the same year.

Unlike the armies east of the river, the Trans-Mississippi—given its large territory and the ways of life of the men who filled its ranks—showed a heavy imbalance in favor of cavalry. Indeed, Price's raid was made by an army of cavalry, at least 12,000 of them, and their subsequent defeat at Westport, Missouri, involved the largest number of cavalry in any battle of the war. Nearly a third of the men, however, were poorly armed or lacking arms entirely, a condition common to the Trans-Mississippi. In 1863 and 1864 Smith's whole command numbered in the low 30,000s, though at times it rose higher, but so many were unarmed and so many were cavalry that were costly and troublesome to maintain that Smith actually tried to reduce his ranks occasionally in the name of improving efficiency. When he finally surrendered on May 26, 1865, there were over 40,000 men on his rolls, though it is doubtful that they could all have been mustered for battle in any one spot. Like the Army of Tennessee, the Trans-Mississippi also had its command problems, for the War Department made a habit of banishing inept or disgraced commanders to the region. Smith himself was alternately ambitious and timid, and operated in an imperious manner that alienated many subordinates, including Richard Taylor before that officer got his own army. Several of the cavalry generals were high-strung, one killing another in a quarrel, and another killing a fellow general in a duel. It was fortunate for the department that major Federal efforts at penetration were so few, for concert of action and cooperation were nearly impossible to achieve among such officers. The repulse of the Red River thrust owed as much to Federal ineptitude as it did to Confederate performance.

Guerrilla Units and Home Guards

Besides the Regular Army and the PACS, the Confederacy had a third organized force in its several state militia. In addition, there was an army of sorts in the less formally organized and maintained county and local home guards scattered about the country, and in those irregular and guerrilla commands that abounded in the less accessible mountain reaches and west of the Mississippi in Missouri, Arkansas, and Texas. Few records exist for such units because their members were often never formally enrolled or sworn in, nor were their officers officially commissioned. Instead, men often just appeared from their homes when a call went out, engaged in an operation, and then melted back into the shadows or returned to homes and hideouts until needed again. Their officers were little more than natural leaders informally selected because of community standing or their ability to maintain order over irregulars.

Most famous of all, probably, was William Clarke Quantrill and the band of raiders that he led in Missouri and the West. Rarely numbering more than 30 to 100 at a time, his raiders preyed on outposts, trains, and civilians, and obeyed

Confederate army orders only as it suited them, making them eventually anathema to Southern as well as Northern military authorities. Moreover, such commands were often composed of several lesser bands, with their own leaders who might, at any time, challenge an overall commander to seize his power, as happened with Quantrill. Estimates of the number of such organizations are haphazard at best, and as to their strengths one can only guess. During the whole course of the war, perhaps 5,000 or more men served intermittently.

The home guards and local citizenry militia—as distinct from the organized state militia—present a similar conundrum for historians, and for much the same reasons. They appeared when Northern raiders or armies threatened their locality, and they rarely if ever set foot outside their home county. Occasionally they were appended to a major army and acted under military orders, but as soon as the emergency was past or the army moved on, they returned to their civilian pursuits. Most of those so engaged were under eighteen or over forty-five, the legal ages for conscription and enlistment. Estimates of home guardsmen have ranged as high as 98,720, but this is certainly an exaggeration. Moreover, they were frequently incorporated later into PACS regiments, especially as manpower needs became more critical in 1864 and after. Especially in the Trans-Mississippi they emerged—often at the same time as the irregulars—as well as in the Deep South.

Although the irregulars—as distinct from *enlisted* home guards—were almost to a man mounted, the reserves served almost exclusively as foot soldiers, their chief service being the provision of information about local roads, bridges, and landscape. As for the numbers engaged in this army throughout the Confederacy, again only guesswork can suggest an answer. Perhaps as many as 300,000 were eligible for such service. Probably no more than 100,000 actually considered themselves members of such organizations, and barely 20,000 likely ever saw more than momentary service.

All of the myriad forms of organizations, whether Regulars, PACS, militia, home guards, or irregulars, faced the same insurmountable problem. Their task was to try to do too much with too little, over too large a territory. Complicating their task immeasurably was the nature and diversity of their several organizations. Command divisions were indistinct, authority clouded or overlapped, and vital manpower and attention were wasted on duplicated efforts. The Regulars were unnecessary; most of the home guards and militia were needed in the field armies; the irregulars were so ill-controlled and disorganized as to be sometimes as dangerous to friend as to foe. That these various components of the Confederate service achieved so much is testimony to the commitment of the men in the ranks to their cause.

[*For further discussion of the various branches of the army, see* Artillery, *overview article;* Cavalry; Engineer Bureau; Infantry; Medical Department; Signal Corps. *For further discussion of particular armies and special units, see* Army of Northern Virginia; Army of Tennessee; Special Units; Trans-Mississippi Department. *See also* Conscription; Desertion; File Closers; Morale; *and entries on particular battles and biographies of numerous figures mentioned herein.*]

BIBLIOGRAPHY

Connelly, Thomas L. *Army of the Heartland: The Army of Tennessee, 1861–1862.* Baton Rouge, La., 1967.
Connelly, Thomas L. *Autumn of Glory: The Army of Tennessee, 1862–1865.* Baton Rouge, La., 1971.
Davis, William C. *Jefferson Davis: The Man and His Hour.* New York, 1991.
Freeman, Douglas S. *Lee's Lieutenants: A Study in Command.* 3 vols. New York, 1942–1944. Reprint, New York, 1986.
Kerby, Robert L. *Kirby Smith's Confederacy: The Trans-Mississippi South, 1863–1865.* New York, 1972.
Livermore, Thomas. *Numbers and Losses of the Civil War in America.* Boston, 1901.
McMurry, Richard M. *Two Great Rebel Armies.* Chapel Hill, N.C., 1989.
Weinert, Richard P. "The Confederate Regular Army." *Military Affairs* 25 (1962): 97–107.
Weinert, Richard P. *The Confederate Regular Army.* Shippensburg, Pa., 1991.

WILLIAM C. DAVIS

Manpower

Most of the men who fought in the armies of the Confederacy came from the eleven states that had seceded from the Union in 1861. At the outbreak of the war, the population of the Confederate States of America totaled just over 9 million people. Of these, 1.8 million were young men aged fifteen to thirty-nine—the likely age of men serving in the armed forces. About 700,000 of these, however, were black slaves, rejected by the South as prospective soldiers. This means that the Confederacy had just over 1 million young men of fighting age for service in its army. Allowing for the facts that some men over the age of forty might serve in the military and that additional youths would become old enough to fight during the course of the war, a reasonable estimate of the pool of available soldiers from within the Confederacy itself would be about 1.75 million men.

Some additional manpower was available from the slaveholding border states (Delaware, Maryland, Kentucky, and Missouri). A reasonable guess would be that perhaps one-third of the half million young men (or about 185,000) in the border states would choose to serve in the South rather than remain loyal to the Union. (The fraction would be somewhat higher in the western states such as Kentucky and Missouri, somewhat lower in Delaware and Maryland.)

Thus, a generous estimate of the total manpower upon which the Confederacy could draw for soldiers would be somewhere in the neighborhood of 2 million men.

In contrast, the North, with a population of 18.9 million people, had a far larger pool of young men from which to obtain soldiers. If we construct an estimate of the number of men available to fight for the Union comparable to that just presented for the South it would be more than 6 million men. To this we must add a final source of manpower: freed blacks who left the South to fight for the Union. Although we do not have an accurate estimate of the number of freed slaves who served in the Union forces, we do know that as many as 200,000 blacks served in the Union army and navy during the Civil War.

If we look, then, simply at the number of *potential* soldiers, the South was at a disadvantage of at least three or four to one in terms of military manpower. Fortunately for the Confederates, this disadvantage was partially offset by the fact that the South was relatively more successful in actually getting men to serve in its army than the Union was. Over the course of the war, the Confederate armies enlisted a total of just under 900,000 men, while the Union, with more than three times as many young men, managed to get about 2.1 million in its armed forces. Because they recruited a higher fraction of young men into the army, the Confederate commanders faced a disadvantage of about 2.3 to 1 in favor of the North.

The success in mobilizing men for its armed forces left the Confederacy with fewer men to fill the needs of production on the home front. Some of this work could be done by the slaves who stayed behind on the farms and plantations of the South. And slaves could perform such military tasks as transporting goods to the front, ditching, and constructing fortifications, and a variety of other tasks behind the lines. In many instances their efforts were a crucial element in the Confederate military effort. A few slaves even accompanied their owners to the front lines.

But the contribution of slaves to both the Confederate military effort and production for the home front was limited by several factors. One was the problem posed by the presence of a population whose loyalty to the Southern cause was obviously questionable. White Southerners were understandably reluctant to use slaves as soldiers in the front lines. Not until February 1865, when the Southern cause was lost, did the Confederate Congress finally approve the enlistment of black slaves as soldiers. Another factor was that even when military tasks could be entrusted to slaves, many of their owners were reluctant to lease them to the army, where mistreatment by their overseers or capture by the Federals was all too likely. Moreover, throughout the war, there was a steady flow of blacks fleeing to the Union lines and offering their services to the South's enemy. At the time of Robert E. Lee's surrender, approxi-

mately 110,000 blacks were serving in the Union armed forces, many of them ex-slaves who had fled with their families to the protection of Union lines. Their presence in the enemy's army served as a constant reminder to Southerners of the danger inherent in an excessive reliance on slave labor. Of even greater concern to many whites was the threat of slave uprisings. Responding to this fear, state governments in the Confederacy sought to keep troops within their own borders despite pleas for more men from the government in Richmond. Fears of black rebellion spurred the Confederate Congress to pass an act exempting all whites who owned twenty or more slaves from military duty. In addition to reducing the number of men available for service in the army, this act had a very negative effect on the morale of nonslaveholders who were called up. All in all, it could be argued that the *Northern* military effort had been served as well by the labor of the former slaves who fled the Confederacy as were the interests of the South by those slaves who stayed behind.

The armies that campaigned in 1861 and early 1862 were manned by volunteers answering either Abraham Lincoln's or Jefferson Davis's call for soldiers at the outbreak of hostilities. By 1862, however, it had become clear that reliance on volunteers alone would not provide the manpower necessary to win the war. On March 29, 1862, the Confederate Congress enacted a Conscription Law that made every white male aged eighteen to thirty-five liable for service in the army and extended the length of service of those already in the army to the duration of the war. A subsequent act in 1864 set the age range at seventeen to fifty years. The Union also passed a draft law in March 1862, calling for all able-bodied males between the ages of twenty and forty to register for military service. Because of generous exemptions, however, neither draft law produced huge numbers of men for military service. About 82,000 were actually drafted into the Confederate army. Over 200,000 men were called up for service in the Union army, but only about half of them either served or purchased a substitute. It should be noted that these numbers do not reflect the full effect of the conscription laws. In both the North and the South, the threat of being drafted was often sufficient reason for young men to accept the bonuses offered by state governments to induce men to volunteer for military service.

The total number of men serving in Southern armies reached a peak at about the time of the Battle of Gettysburg; thereafter it declined steadily. The reasons for this were clear enough. First was the enormous casualties sustained by the Confederates during four years of heavy fighting. Over 250,000 Confederate soldiers died, and another 200,000 men were listed as wounded in the course of the war. As the fighting dragged on and morale deteriorated both at the front and at home, desertions increased steadily.

At least 100,000 Southern men abandoned their units during the course of the war, and desertions reached epic proportions in the final year. The effect can be seen by the fact that at the end of the war, the Confederate army rolls listed 359,000 soldiers, but only 160,000 were on active duty and only 126,000 were actually present on the front lines. In the North, by contrast, mobilization efforts produced an ever-increasing flow of men that was able to offset the even higher numbers of Northern soldiers who deserted or were killed or wounded. At the time of Appomattox, there were nearly a million men in the U.S. armed forces.

[*See also* African American Troops in the Union Army; Civil War, *article on* Losses and Numbers; Conscription; Contraband.]

BIBLIOGRAPHY

Livermore, Thomas L. *Numbers and Losses in the Civil War in America, 1861–1865.* Boston and New York, 1901.

McPherson, James M. *Battle Cry of Freedom: The Civil War Era.* New York, 1988.

Mohr, Clarence. *On the Threshold of Freedom: Masters and Slaves in Civil War Georgia.* Athens, Ga., 1986.

Ransom, Roger L. *Conflict and Compromise: The Political Economy of Slavery, Emancipation, and the American Civil War.* Cambridge, Mass., 1989.

ROGER L. RANSOM

Army Departments

To defend the borders of a new nation whose land area approximated that of western Europe, President Jefferson Davis in 1861 organized the Confederacy's territory and military resources into administrative entities called departments. Occasionally, specific tasks within departments were assigned to smaller entities called districts, but these districts were normally subordinate to their respective departments. Before the war ended in 1865 at least forty-six named departments and independent districts had been created, although not all existed at any one time.

Under Davis's scheme a general officer commanded each department, with responsibility for both defensive and offensive movements within its confines. Normally the department commander controlled all forces within his department, which, in the larger departments, were usually named armies. Well aware of the vastness of the South and the vagaries of communication, Davis generally allowed department commanders wide latitude in the conduct of business within their respective commands. In addition, the opinions of department commanders carried great weight whenever questions arose about the transfer of assets between departments.

Criticized by historians as indicative of Davis's rigidity of mind, this departmental system initially seemed to be a useful mechanism to control military activity over such a large area. In theory several advantages were apparent. Militarily, a department commander would be much more responsive to local conditions and enemy threats than would the central government, positioned on the edge of the Confederacy in Richmond, Virginia. Logistically, department commanders could both defend resource centers more effectively and organize distribution more efficiently than the bureaus in the War Department. Politically, the department system guaranteed that every section of the Confederacy had a military structure devoted to its specific protection. Diplomatically, organization of the new nation's territory into a coherent structure for military defense projected abroad an air of stability without being aggressive. Thus Davis's departmental system seemed at first to be an intelligent response to military problems of immense proportions.

Major geographical features divided the eleven states of the Confederacy into three large regions. In the East, a flat coastal strip gave way initially to rolling hills and then to the first great barrier, the Appalachian Mountains. In this region was the Confederacy's capital and much of its population. Beyond the Appalachians lay a rich agricultural domain of plains and hills stretching all the way to the Mississippi River. West of the river an even vaster region began in the Mississippi's flooded lowlands and ended somewhere in the arid high plains of Texas.

Davis paid little heed to these large regions when he established the first series of military departments. Virginia alone was divided into at least seven commands. Similarly, three departments covered Alabama. As 1861 ended, however, a gradual consolidation of small departments had begun to take place. In Virginia, departments north of Richmond merged into the Department of Northern Virginia, creating a unified command from the Shenandoah Valley to Chesapeake Bay. West of the Appalachians, an even greater consolidation formed the massive Department No. 2. This department stretched from Cumberland Gap to the Mississippi River and beyond into Arkansas and Missouri.

In theory Department No. 2, commanded by Gen. Albert Sidney Johnston, exemplified the principle of unity of command in the face of the multiple Union departments facing it. In practice, however, Johnston's resources permitted him to do no more than create a weak cordon defense along the northern boundary of his department. When that cordon was pierced at Forts Henry and Donelson in February 1862, Johnston withdrew precipitately, losing Nashville and central Tennessee in the process. Confederate fortunes were only partially retrieved by the first great concentration of military units from adjacent departments into Department No. 2. Orchestrated by Gen. P. G. T. Beauregard, this concentration gathered troops from all parts of Johnston's command as well as from Department No. 1 (the lower Mississippi) and the Department of Alabama and West Florida. Although the offensive mounted by Johnston's enlarged army came to grief at Shiloh in April 1862, the principle of interdepartmental transfers was established. Meanwhile, in the East, the Department of Northern Virginia continued to expand at the expense of smaller departments as a large Federal army menaced Richmond from the southeast.

Federal threats from both the east and the west caused a reorganization of Davis's departmental system by the summer of 1862. The earlier consolidation of several small departments within the Department of Northern Virginia became permanent, giving that department primary responsibility for defending Virginia from the north. The territory below Richmond fell under a new Department of North Carolina and Southern Virginia, which faced Federal enclaves around Norfolk and the North Carolina sounds. Farther south still, the defense of the Confederacy's remaining Atlantic coast was entrusted to an expanded Department of South Carolina, Georgia, and Florida.

West of the Appalachians Davis acted even more vigorously. In late May he removed the vast area beyond the Mississippi River from Department No. 2 and gave it independent existence as the Trans-Mississippi Department. This new superdepartment now included Texas, Indian Territory, Arkansas, Missouri, and western Louisiana. Not long afterward, Department No. 2 was expanded to include the territory formerly belonging to Department No. 1 and the Department of Alabama and West Florida, both of which passed out of existence. Department No. 2 and its Army of Tennessee thus joined the Department of Northern Virginia and its army as the Confederacy's primary defenders.

For the next few months the departmental structure in the East remained intact as Gen. Robert E. Lee either defeated Federal thrusts toward Richmond or raided into Northern territory. Affairs in Department No. 2 were in flux, however, because of Gen. Braxton Bragg's decision to strike northward into Kentucky. Leaving a relatively small force in northern Mississippi, Bragg transferred the bulk of his army to Chattanooga, Tennessee, for an advance northward. Chattanooga lay within the boundaries of the Department of East Tennessee, one of two minor departments that provided a physical link between Bragg's and Lee's forces. Commanded by Maj. Gen. E. Kirby Smith, this department now became the host for Bragg's Army of Tennessee. The ensuing invasion of Kentucky was thus conducted by two semi-independent armies whose attempts at cooperation failed miserably. After the invasion ended in defeat, the two departments merged briefly, but this seemingly logical step was revoked by the end of 1862. Meanwhile, the forces Bragg had left behind in Mississippi

had come under threat from Federal troops operating in the Mississippi River valley.

The deteriorating situation in Mississippi led Jefferson Davis in October 1862 to create a new department from within Department No. 2. Commanded by Lt. Gen. John C. Pemberton, the new Department of Mississippi and East Louisiana focused almost entirely upon the defense of the Mississippi River around Vicksburg, Mississippi. As the Federal threat to Vicksburg grew and Bragg's invasion of Kentucky receded, Davis recognized that coordination would be required between Bragg's and Pemberton's departments. In response he created the Department of the West in November 1862 and assigned Gen. Joseph E. Johnston to its command.

Envisioned by Davis as another superdepartment, Johnston's actual command was ill defined at best. Although Johnston apparently had supreme powers within his domain, Bragg and Pemberton continued to exercise the prerogatives of department commanders, including the right to correspond directly with the Confederate War Department. If nothing else, Johnston's position should have enabled him to see the area between the Appalachians and the Mississippi River as a whole. In turn, this unified vision should have permitted the allocation of scarce resources to counter the most dangerous of several Federal threats. Unfortunately, Johnston did little to produce such a vision.

The year 1863 saw little change in the Virginia and coastal theaters, where the enemy was easily contained. West of the Appalachians, Federal forces in central Tennessee remained quiescent for six months, permitting Bragg to reinforce Johnston's weak attempt to lift the siege of Vicksburg. In July reverses struck all major Confederate field armies as Pemberton surrendered Vicksburg, Johnston withdrew to eastern Mississippi, Bragg evacuated central Tennessee, and Lee's invasion of the North was repulsed at Gettysburg. In response to these disasters, Davis again reorganized some of his western departments. Renamed the Department of Tennessee, Bragg's command by the end of the summer had absorbed the Department of East Tennessee once more. Johnston nominally retained both his title and his coordinating function, but in reality he commanded only the forces in eastern Mississippi. Aided by an infusion of units from the Department of Northern Virginia, Bragg won a Pyrrhic victory at Chickamauga in September but was driven into northern Georgia after his resounding defeat at Missionary Ridge in November.

The disastrous events of the second half of 1863 in the western Confederacy caused still another change in departmental boundaries. Now severed from the remainder of the Confederacy, the Trans-Mississippi Department became virtually independent of central government control. Upon Bragg's removal from the Department of Tennessee in

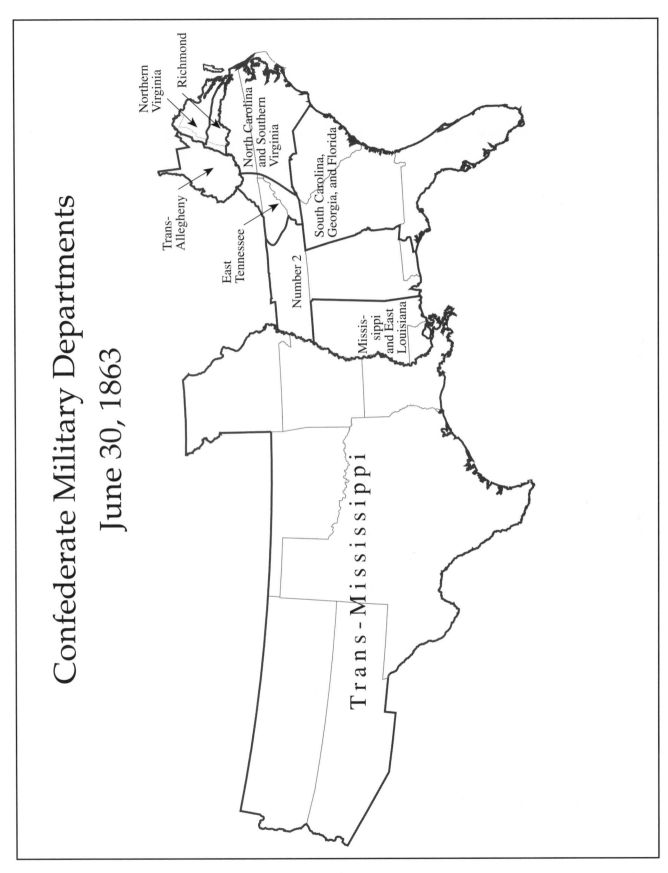

Confederate Military Departments
June 30, 1863

Northern Virginia

Richmond

North Carolina and Southern Virginia

Trans-Allegheny

East Tennessee

Number 2

South Carolina, Georgia, and Florida

Mississippi and East Louisiana

Trans-Mississippi

December 1863, Johnston assumed command in his stead. Johnston's Department of the West was abolished and the Department of Tennessee expanded to include eastern Alabama and part of western Florida. The remnants of Pemberton's old Department of Mississippi and East Louisiana in early 1864 became first the Department of the Southwest and then the Department of Alabama, Mississippi, and East Louisiana. Elsewhere, the Virginia and coastal fronts remained stable as the Department of Northern Virginia, the Department of North Carolina and Southern Virginia, and the Department of South Carolina, Georgia, and Florida.

The year 1864 brought further Confederate reverses in both the East and the West. By midsummer, Lee's army was pinned to its fortifications around Petersburg, which straddled the boundary between the Department of Northern Virginia and the Department of North Carolina and Southern Virginia. In Georgia, Johnston gradually retreated to Atlanta's defenses, where Davis replaced him with Gen. John Bell Hood. After several bloody battles Hood was forced to relinquish the city. In September, he began an advance that would eventually take him into central Tennessee and would at the same time call forth the last major reorganization of Davis's departmental system. On October 17, 1864, Hood's Department of Tennessee became the Department of Tennessee and Georgia. Unlike the old, the new department excluded Alabama but in a bit of wishful thinking included western Tennessee. At the same time Johnston's old superdepartment, the Department of the West, reappeared as the Military Division of the West. Commanded by General Beauregard, the new organization was created to coordinate activity in both Hood's department and Lt. Gen. Richard Taylor's Department of Alabama, Mississippi, and East Louisiana.

The destruction of Hood's army at Nashville at the end of 1864 signaled the approaching end of the Confederacy and its departmental system. With the heartland either under Federal occupation or devastated, only the departments on the Confederacy's periphery continued to hold out. First to go was Lee's Department of Northern Virginia in April 1865. Next to collapse were the forces collected from the Department of Tennessee and Georgia; the Department of South Carolina, Georgia, and Florida; and the Department of North Carolina and Southern Virginia, all of which surrendered under Beauregard, Johnston, and Bragg in North Carolina later that same month. Taylor's Department of Alabama, Mississippi, and East Louisiana followed the others into oblivion in early May, and on May 26, 1865, Smith's Trans-Mississippi Department negotiated the capitulation of the final remnant of Confederate territory.

Created in 1861 to meet a variety of valid needs, Jefferson Davis's departmental system served to the end as a necessary administrative mechanism to command and control the Confederacy's scarce military assets. Where a brilliant commander like Lee was present or a major Federal threat was absent, as in the coastal departments and the Trans-Mississippi, the departmental system worked well. Where both brilliant commanders and resources were lacking and the Federal threat was great, as in Department No. 2 and its successors, no organizational system could have produced success. As events proved, neither fragmentation nor consolidation could succeed without adequate resources in the vast heartland of the Confederacy, and it was there that the war was lost.

BIBLIOGRAPHY

Connelly, Thomas L. *Army of the Heartland: The Army of Tennessee, 1861–1862.* Baton Rouge, La., 1967.

Connelly, Thomas L. *Autumn of Glory: The Army of Tennessee, 1862–1865.* Baton Rouge, La., 1971.

Connelly, Thomas Lawrence, and Archer Jones. *The Politics of Command: Factions and Ideas in Confederate Strategy.* Baton Rouge, La., 1973.

Jones, Archer. *Confederate Strategy from Shiloh to Vicksburg.* Baton Rouge, La., 1961.

Kerby, Robert L. *Kirby Smith's Confederacy: The Trans-Mississippi South, 1863–1865.* New York, 1972.

Vandiver, Frank E. *Rebel Brass: The Confederate Command System.* Baton Rouge, La., 1956. Reprint, Westport, Conn., 1971.

Woodworth, Steven E. *Jefferson Davis and His Generals: The Failure of Confederate Command in the West.* Lawrence, Kans., 1990.

WILLIAM GLENN ROBERTSON

African Americans in the Confederate Army

African American Southerners played a wide range of roles in support of the Confederate war effort. The war brought all kinds of new tasks at the same time that it gave new significance to customary work. On the home front, slaves grew the corn that fed Confederate soldiers, and they produced the cotton that clothed them. Emphasizing the battlefront, historian Bell Wiley employed a military metaphor: "Together they worked, white and black, . . . an army of soldiers and an army of laborers." Even in microcosm the metaphor worked, as, especially in the summer of 1861, slave men accompanied many masters to war and carried out various camp chores.

Throughout the Confederacy and the war, by the tens of thousands, black men, free and slave alike, contributed directly to the Confederate war effort. They worked in war industries—for example, at Tredegar Iron Works in Richmond, Virginia. They manufactured salt, vital to the preservation of meat. Supporting the South's transportation system, they worked on railroads, repaired bridges, and manufactured and replaced or moved rails. As teamsters

THE SLAVE MARLBORO. Ambrotype of Marlboro wearing a Confederate frock coat and a variety of battlefield souvenirs. Many Confederate soldiers took their slaves to the front, where their duties included looking after the camp, cleaning equipment, helping to bring in the wounded, and burying the dead. Marlboro accompanied his owner, Maj. Raleigh S. Camp of Georgia. Reproduction by Katherine Wetzel.   ELEANOR S. BROCKENBROUGH LIBRARY, THE MUSEUM OF THE CONFEDERACY, RICHMOND, VIRGINIA

and stevedores, they moved Confederate supplies. As cooks, they prepared soldiers' meals, and as medical attendants, they bore stretchers, drove ambulances, and worked in hospitals. In each of their tasks, black workers released white men for combat duty.

Still more closely associated with the battlefront, black Confederates dug ditches, obstructed rivers, and erected batteries. A general impressment law, enacted in March 1863, followed the example of many states and made impressment universal. It authorized the secretary of war to impress free black men and, when their numbers proved insufficient, as many as twenty thousand male slaves between the ages of eighteen and forty-five. Impressment produced too few workers, however, and in late 1864, President Jefferson Davis proposed that the government purchase forty thousand slaves as military laborers. The winter of 1864–1865 brought urgent requests from Gen. Robert E. Lee for thousands of black laborers to support his efforts at Richmond and Petersburg.

By the autumn of 1864, white Confederates were widely discussing plans to go beyond black Confederates' combat support roles and arm slaves as part of the South's combat forces. As early as 1861, some state leaders had displayed a readiness to accept free black men into state service; the Tennessee legislature authorized the recruitment of free black men, either as volunteers or as conscripts, and a regiment of free men of color in Louisiana, the "Native Guards," entered state service. Meanwhile, the Confederate army proved unprepared to recruit free blacks; recruiting slaves had even less support. Howell Cobb, politician and general from Georgia, objected as late as January 1865 that "if slaves make good soldiers our whole theory of slavery is wrong." Yet such plans gained increasing acceptance. By the winter of 1864–1865, tens of thousands of black Unionists were fighting against the Confederacy and demonstrating that black men could indeed make good soldiers. Confederate Secretary of State Judah P. Benjamin was one who asked, in December 1864, "Is it better for the negro to fight for us or against us?" Proponents of the plan argued that it would provide manpower for the Confederacy's depleted army, counter nonslaveholding whites' jibes about "a poor man's fight," and attract diplomatic support in Europe. Those proponents differed, however, over significant details regarding the emancipation of black soldiers and their families.

By February 1865, General Lee's support for enrolling black troops became public knowledge. Still the Confederate Congress hesitated to adopt any version of such a plan. Only on March 13, 1865, did a Confederate measure to recruit black soldiers become law. Rather than promise anyone emancipation, the act barred freedom "except by consent of the owners and of the States" where slave soldiers resided. Lee then asked Virginia Governor William Smith for one-fourth of the able-bodied slave men of military age in that state. Davis, having come to support the policy, still sought to avoid conscription and rely on owners' volunteering their slaves. In any case, the law came too late for companies of black soldiers to fight in large numbers for the Confederacy. But the image of slaves and free blacks drilling together in Richmond gave evidence that both slavery and the Confederacy were unraveling.

Having grown the corn to feed white soldiers, black Confederates worked on the railroads and drove the wagons that carried that food to the soldiers, and then cooked and served it to them. Moreover, they constructed Confederate defensive works. By the closing weeks of the war, they were forming companies to join forces with the white soldiers whom their labor had done so much to support.

BIBLIOGRAPHY

Berlin, Ira, Barbara J. Fields, Steven Miller, Joseph P. Reidy, and Leslie S. Rowland, eds. *Free at Last: A Documentary History of Slavery, Freedom, and the Civil War.* New York, 1992.

Brewer, James H. *The Confederate Negro: Virginia's Craftsmen and Military Laborers, 1861–1865.* Durham, N.C., 1969.

Durden, Robert F. *The Gray and the Black: The Confederate Debate on Emancipation.* Baton Rouge, La., 1972.

Mohr, Clarence L. *On the Threshold of Freedom: Masters and Slaves in Civil War Georgia.* Athens, Ga., 1986.

Wesley, Charles H. *The Collapse of the Confederacy.* Washington, D.C., 1937. Reprint, New York, 1968.

Wiley, Bell Irvin. *Southern Negroes, 1861–1865.* New Haven, Conn., 1938.

PETER WALLENSTEIN

ARMY OF NORTHERN VIRGINIA.

The principal eastern army (1862–1865) of the Confederate States fought under the direction of Gen. Robert E. Lee with steady and sometimes spectacular success against the Federal Army of the Potomac. With a strength ranging between 35,000 and 85,000 men, the army opened its career by driving away an early threat to Richmond and then defending the capital across a broad arc of northern Virginia through the middle years of the Civil War. In 1864 and 1865 the Army of Northern Virginia was obliged to assume a limited defensive posture in siege lines surrounding Richmond and Petersburg. It surrendered at Appomattox Courthouse on April 9, 1865.

Early Operations in Virginia. During the war's first year Confederate detachments positioned around Virginia's northern perimeter resisted Federal threats on several fronts. The largest of these Confederate forces fought the First Battle of Manassas (or Bull Run) on July 21, 1861, when Gen. Joseph E. Johnston's command hurried eastward from the Shenandoah Valley to join with troops under Gen. P. G. T. Beauregard in repulsing an enemy advance southward from Washington, D.C. The unified Southern force, commanded by Johnston, became known as the Confederate Army of the Potomac—a label fraught with confusion because the premier eastern army of the Union became famous under precisely that name.

While Johnston maintained a line near Manassas and along the Potomac below Washington during 1861 and early 1862, Confederate forces concentrated at three other points on the state's military frontier. Gen. John B. Magruder commanded a modest army on Virginia's peninsula; a smaller detachment defended the important naval facilities around Norfolk; and Gen. Thomas J. ("Stonewall") Jackson led a small but aggressive command in the Shenandoah Valley. Pressure from Union forces brought action on all four fronts by the spring of 1862. Johnston felt obliged to abandon northern Virginia—and huge quantities of ordnance and other war matériel—in an awkward movement during March. A mighty Federal army under Gen. George B. McClellan successfully completed a waterborne movement to the peninsula opposite Magruder. Confederates near Norfolk witnessed the revolutionary first duel between ironclad warships as Northern strength became manifest in that area. In the Shenandoah Valley, Jackson launched in March the remarkable campaign that would win him lasting fame.

During the three months beginning with the dramatic events of March 1862, the components of what would become the Army of Northern Virginia played out their roles in the defense of Richmond. Most of Johnston's command moved east of Richmond to the peninsula, where it absorbed Magruder's men into a unified force facing McClellan's slow but massive advance. Johnston fought McClellan on May 5 at Williamsburg and then fell steadily back to the outskirts of the Southern capital. Confederates south of the James River who had been centered on Norfolk eventually moved toward Richmond and by June had augmented the strength of the main army directly defending the capital. Stonewall Jackson retained his independent command as a diversionary force in the Shenandoah Valley and exploited every opportunity he found there to attract the attention of Northern leaders away from the main prize at Richmond. From March 23 to June 9 Jackson fought six battles and marched hundreds of miles, occupying many times his own numbers in fruitless reaction to his daring thrusts.

While Jackson bedazzled a succession of foes in the Valley, Johnston committed his combined forces to battle under promising circumstances on May 31 and June 1, 1862, at Seven Pines (or Fair Oaks). Poor planning and an almost unbelievable degree of confusion among his ranking subordinates, particularly Gen. James Longstreet, dissipated Johnston's golden opportunity. Johnston also lost command of the army when he fell wounded late on May 31. The next day President Jefferson Davis designated Robert E. Lee as Johnston's replacement. Lee never relinquished command, to the intense disgust of Johnston and Longstreet but of almost no one else in the Confederate States.

Lee at once began to sculpt the army into his image of an effective field force. Although the Department of Northern Virginia had existed formally for months, Johnston had continued to call his command the Army of the Potomac. From his post as a nearly powerless military adviser in Richmond, Lee had referred to Johnston's force in March as the Army in Northern Virginia. By the end of that month he had begun, evidently on his own volition, to call the army he soon would make famous "The Army of Northern Virginia."

With Federals in great strength at the very gates of Richmond, Lee had little leisure in which to organize and prepare for the contest that he knew must come almost at once. The general did his best to organize the disparate elements that made up his new command, but his first priority was to entrench the lines it held in order to

ROBERT E. LEE AND STAFF. Clockwise, from the top, are Brig. Gen. Walter Husted Stevens, chief engineer; Lt. Col. Charles Marshall, aide-de-camp; Lt. Col. J. L. Corley, chief quartermaster; Lt. Col. B. G. Baldwin, chief of ordnance; Surgeon L. Guild, medical director; Maj. H. E. Young, judge advocate general; Brig. Gen. William N. Pendleton, chief of artillery; Lt. Col. H. E. Peyton, inspector general; Maj. D. B. Bridgeford, provost marshal; Lt. Col. W. H. Taylor, assistant adjutant general; Lt. Col. R. G. Cole, chief of commissary stores; and Lt. Col. C. S. Venable, aide-de-camp. Robert E. Lee is at center. Photograph by Vannerson and Jones, from original negatives, Richmond, Virginia.   LIBRARY OF CONGRESS neutralize to some degree his enemy's preponderance in numbers. Southern soldiers still afflicted with naive notions of chivalry grumbled bitterly about wielding shovels instead of weapons. This stodgy new commander, they muttered, deserved the derisive title "King of Spades," and he might well blunt their offensive élan by turning them into laborers rather than warriors.

The Seven Days' Battles. A key element in Lee's planned combination was the triumphant army of Stonewall Jackson in the Shenandoah Valley. Jackson's men rested in the upper valley after dual victories at Cross Keys and Port Republic on June 8 and 9, 1862, and then moved eastward across the Blue Ridge toward Richmond. Confederate cavalry under the daring young Gen. J. E. B. Stuart had ridden all the way around McClellan's ponderous army during mid-June, so Lee knew that the Federal right flank north of Richmond dangled precariously. Jackson's men would approach from that direction and might be able to fall on that point with deadly effect. Lee's new fortifications dramatically increased his ability to secure the approaches to Richmond south of the Chickahominy. He concentrated his strength north of that river and during the last week of June hurled the Army of Northern Virginia against the Federals there.

The opening battles of the new army came to be known as the Seven Days' Battles because they covered a full week from June 25 to July 1, 1862. Stonewall Jackson repeatedly failed during the week in his important role as both the threat to the Federals' flank and the bludgeon to be applied there when necessary. At Mechanicsville on June 26, Gen. A. P. Hill launched a premature attack when Jackson's column arrived tardily and behaved without the wonted aggression once it reached the vicinity. The next day Jackson again failed to perform well as the army's maneuver element, and the result was a ghastly, grinding frontal assault at Gaines' Mill. Despite savage losses, Lee's infantry supplied him with his first major victory when they surged over the enemy line near sunset.

Pursuit of the beaten foe proceeded sluggishly and awkwardly on June 28 to 30, with missed opportunities at White Oak Swamp and another poorly coordinated bloodbath at Frayser's Farm. The week's crowning tactical disaster came at Malvern Hill on July 1, after which McClellan pulled his Federals back under shelter of Northern naval might well downstream from Richmond. Lee had struggled to apply his army to its opportunities and had been failed egregiously by many of his high-ranking subordinates as they all came to grips with the new organization. In the process of its tactical groping, however, the new army had won a great strategic victory by driving McClellan from the edge of Richmond. Jackson never again disappointed Lee and the lessons of the Seven Days' Battles served the army commander well as he prepared to

reorganize and move forward. On the basis of his observations during the Seven Days', Lee sent away officers who had displayed incapacity and promoted promising candidates to fill their places.

Through July and into early August, McClellan's Federals continued to menace Richmond from the new base to which Lee had driven them. Meanwhile another Northern force moved into northern Virginia under the leadership of Gen. John Pope. To counter Pope's threat Lee divided his army and sent Stonewall Jackson toward Gordonsville and Culpeper with a sizable detachment of Confederate troops. A series of draconian anticivilian orders issued by Pope made him a particularly urgent target. With uncharacteristic choler Lee ordered Jackson "to suppress" this belligerent enemy, whom he called "the miscreant Pope." Jackson did just that in a campaign climaxed by a victory at Cedar Mountain on August 9. Soon thereafter Lee began moving the rest of the Army of Northern Virginia away from Richmond, where McClellan's threat had lapsed, to join Jackson.

Second Manassas. The campaign that ensued represented the first great battlefield collaboration between Lee and Jackson. Although Confederate law did not provide for any military organization larger than a division, nor for any rank higher than major general, Lee readily grasped the truth that his army must have direction at that higher level. Accordingly he assigned Jackson and Longstreet to the leadership of two wings into which the army's infantry was distributed. Stuart commanded all the cavalry and reported directly to Lee. Jackson's wing had been facing Pope for some time when Lee arrived with the vanguard of the remainder of the army. The rest of Longstreet's men reached the front in northern Virginia only in piecemeal fashion during the campaign; some arrived too late to participate in the Battle of Second Manassas. Because his wing was on the scene intact—and because it must have been already apparent that he was infinitely more aggressive than Longstreet—Jackson executed the bold initiatives that marked Lee's late August operations.

After failing to trap Pope between the Rapidan and Rappahannock rivers, Lee slipped Jackson up the right bank of the latter stream looking for an opening. On August 25 and 26 Jackson dashed far behind the Federal army on a march that covered more than fifty miles. Jackson's tattered "Foot Cavalry," as his hard-marching infantry came to be called, captured a vast Federal supply base at Manassas Junction and reveled in the unaccustomed bounty they found there. Jackson's march made Pope's line on the Rappahannock untenable and forced the Federals to fall back hurriedly. When Pope retired toward Manassas, Jackson grappled with him near Groveton on August 28 and then held tenaciously to a position behind an unfinished railroad until Lee and Longstreet arrived in support on August 29.

The Second Battle of Manassas reached its climax on August 30 when Jackson blunted renewed enemy attacks and Longstreet unleashed his wing of the army onto Pope's vulnerable left flank. The resultant rout swept the Federals from the field. Two days later Jackson tangled with an enemy force north of Manassas at Ox Hill (or Chantilly) in a blinding thunderstorm, killing two capable Union generals and compelling Pope's complete withdrawal into the defenses of Washington.

Maryland Campaign. In barely more than one month from its first battle, the Army of Northern Virginia had reoriented the war from the outskirts of the Confederate capital to the vicinity of the Union's capital. Lee eagerly pressed his advantage by ordering his divisions across the Potomac and into Maryland. He was riding the crest of a military tide of impressive proportions and of his own making. Any other strategic decision in the circumstances would have been utterly foolish. Circumstances conspired against Lee once he reached Maryland, however, and he eventually chose to offer battle when his chances had become so slender as to suggest that a return to Virginia without fighting was the only prudent alternative.

By September 10 the Army of Northern Virginia was centered on Frederick, Maryland, well situated to threaten Washington and other points to the north and east; but more than 12,000 Federals menaced the army's flank and rear from their bypassed positions around Harpers Ferry. Lee determined to remove that irritant by capturing the Federals and the bonanza of supplies, armaments, and equipment they held. Jackson's confident veterans received the mission and set out on another of the long marches designed to expend their sweat but not their blood. The operation worked reasonably well, if not as rapidly as Lee had hoped. Jackson captured Harpers Ferry and its garrison with its rich stores on September 15.

Unfortunately for Lee, a copy of his detailed operational order (Special Orders No. 191) fell into enemy hands. General McClellan, who had assumed command of his old army augmented by the troops of the disgraced Pope, knew how thoroughly Lee had dispersed the elements of his army. The eternally cautious Union general frittered away much of the dazzling advantage presented to him, however. Even so, he was able to penetrate westward through the gaps of Maryland's South Mountain, pushing aside the Confederate rear guard and forcing Lee back toward the Potomac.

Late on September 15 Lee took up a position near the village of Sharpsburg, behind Antietam Creek, with the Potomac River at his back. Resisting McClellan there, with an army shrunken by straggling and other causes to the smallest size it would ever number until the end of the war, offered Lee no prospect for a great success and posed the real danger of disaster. Lee nevertheless stayed to fight. The Army of Northern Virginia staged one of its most

impressive performances on the banks of Antietam Creek on September 17, 1862, when it contrived to win a costly draw. Federal dispersion and irresolution served Lee's army well, but even so the Confederates repeatedly stood at the brink of catastrophe. Lee had infected his army with his own sturdy spirit, and the men redeemed their general's poor strategic decision with their personal valor. The army returned to Virginia on the night of September 18, having stood through the day after the battle on its hard-won line.

A Renewed Army. In the aftermath of the Maryland campaign, Lee found time to rebuild carefully the army he had inherited at a moment of crisis. The army enjoyed a halcyon period in the beautiful and bountiful Shenandoah Valley that fall while its commander planned and organized. More than a dozen general officers had fought with the army in Maryland for the last time. In addition to replacing those men with the best available talent, Lee finally was able to formalize his wing system when the Confederate Congress authorized corps units and created the rank of lieutenant general. Jackson and Longstreet received promotions to the new rank that were confirmed on October 11. The new lieutenant generals took command of the Second Corps and the First Corps, which contained all of the army's infantry.

Lee also streamlined the army's support functions that fall as part of perfecting its organization. The acute straggling and near-starvation that had bedeviled the 1862 Maryland campaign never again plagued Lee until the Confederacy verged on collapse late in the war. When the army moved through the same territory during the succeeding summer, en route to Gettysburg, the severe problems that had marked its 1862 operations did not recur.

In mid-November 1862, the Federal Army of the Potomac, now commanded by Gen. Ambrose E. Burnside, moved southeastward toward Fredericksburg, in the process drawing the Army of Northern Virginia away from the Shenandoah Valley and Piedmont Virginia. For three weeks beginning November 20, the Confederates concentrated near Fredericksburg as Burnside's army gathered across the Rappahannock from the city. On the morning of December 11 the Federals opened the Battle of Fredericksburg by bombarding the city and building pontoon bridges across the river against stiff resistance.

Two days later the Northerners marched steadily westward from town against imposing positions held by the Army of Northern Virginia. The result was the easiest major victory won by Lee's army during the war. Confederate riflemen slaughtered enemy infantry, and Confederate artillery found ample targets from elevated positions rising above a shelterless plain. Federal casualties mounted all out of proportion to Southern losses, but Lee was unable to reap any substantial additional fruits of his victory.

The Army of Northern Virginia went into winter camps

secure in the knowledge that it had achieved enormous success during its first six months of existence. Within sixty days the army had, almost unaided, relocated the war from its own capital to the environs of the enemy's capital. It had won a startling succession of victories for a nation that had known few. The brilliantly creative collaboration of Lee and Jackson at the army's head, augmented by Longstreet's stalwart defensive aptitude, boded well for the future of the army and of the country it recently had saved. For nearly five months the army sprawled across central Virginia from northwest at Germanna Ford to southeast around Carmel Church, with the Rappahannock and Rapidan as a front-line moat. Stuart's cavalrymen rode daring and exciting raids behind enemy lines, building élan and providing grist for campfire talk if not actually accomplishing much substantive good.

During the winter Lee approved an important reorganization of the army's artillery. Conventional dogma had assigned most batteries to infantry brigades, often turning the artillary, Lee's "long arm," into little more than larger-caliber infantry weapons. Henceforth batteries would be grouped into battalions of sixteen or more guns and directed by artillery officers with enough rank to determine the appropriate employment of their powerful weapons. As campaigning weather approached in the spring of 1863, the Army of Northern Virginia stood at the height of its power and potential.

Chancellorsville. Gen. Joseph Hooker commanded the army's familiar foe as it advanced across the Rappahannock and Rapidan west of Fredericksburg in late April 1863. Hooker skillfully stole a march on Lee and concentrated behind the Confederates on April 30 at a country crossroads called Chancellorsville. Lee and Jackson hurried to meet this serious threat (Longstreet was away on a feckless mission in southern Virginia). On May 1 the two leaders blunted Hooker's drive near the edge of a seventy-square-mile body of densely thicketed woodland known as the Wilderness of Spotsylvania. Scrubby undergrowth in the region made maneuver, movement, and fighting difficult except in the clearings and along the roads. That negated much of Hooker's enormous advantage in numbers. Facing a disadvantage of more than two-to-one, Lee fought against the heaviest odds he encountered until the wars' closing weeks. On May 2 Lee and Jackson collaborated on their boldest and most successful—and last—tactical initiative. Lee calmly faced Hooker's legions with a handful of troops while Jackson carefully and secretly led nearly 30,000 men across the front of the Northern army. When Stonewall's troops thundered out of the Wilderness behind Hooker's right, screaming the Rebel yell and driving everything before them, the Army of Northern Virginia stood at its highest tide.

Jackson's mighty flank attack did much to win the battle,

THOMAS J. ("STONEWALL") JACKSON AND STAFF. Clockwise, from top left, are Maj. W. J. Hawks, chief of commissary stores; Maj. R. L. Dabney, assistant adjutant general; Lt. Col. W. Allan, chief of ordnance; Lt. Col. A. S. Pendleton, assistant adjutant general; Capt. J. G. Morrison, aide-de-camp; Maj. D. B. Bridgeford, provost marshal; Maj. H. K. Douglas; Capt. J. P. Smith, aide-de-camp; Maj. Hunter McGuire, medical director; and Capt. Jedediah Hotchkiss, topographical engineer. General Jackson is at center. Photograph by Vannerson and Jones, from original negatives, Richmond, Virginia.   LIBRARY OF CONGRESS

but its aftermath cost the Confederacy one of its few absolutely irreplaceable military commodities. Mistaken fire from the muskets of North Carolinians in Gen. James H. Lane's brigade struck Jackson down, mortally wounding him in the darkness of that confused night. When he died eight days later at Guiney Station, Jackson took with him much of the army's and the Confederacy's best hope for success. Back at Chancellorsville the Army of Northern Virginia had put the seal on Jackson's masterful movement by fighting its way stubbornly through the Wilderness on May 3 to sweep the field.

Lee considered the victory at Chancellorsville a springboard for his army to use in taking the war back into enemy country. Before he could use the army in an advance, however, the general faced the necessity of reorganizing it extensively in the absence of Stonewall Jackson. Lee had already considered splitting his infantry into three corps as a means of controlling it more effectively. In the weeks after Chancellorsville he followed that premise when he established a new corps and gave command of it to Gen. A. P. Hill. For Jackson's old Second Corps, somewhat truncated by the creation of the new corps, Lee selected Gen. Richard S. Ewell. Neither officer would begin to fill the enormous gap left by Jackson's death, nor would either of them satisfy even the reduced expectations that their commanding general had for them.

Gettysburg and its Aftermath. The army shifted northwestward from the vicinity of Fredericksburg in early June 1863. Stuart's cavalry won a stern test at Brandy Station on the ninth, but for the first time their mounted foe had fought on approximately equal terms. That boded ill for a Confederate future that would be affected by declining horseflesh and armaments. Ewell accomplished as much as Jackson could have done around Winchester on June 14 and 15, clearing the way for an advance into Pennsylvania and raising hopes that the Second Corps might continue its invincible record.

The meeting engagement that developed on July 1 through 3 at Gettysburg, however, revealed shortcomings in the high command as well as in the new organization. Stuart led his cavalry on another daring adventure en route to Pennsylvania, but this time it left Lee without the screening and reconnaissance support that he badly needed. Ewell equivocated when Lee gave him typically discretionary orders. Longstreet sulked, to the detriment of tactical arrangements on the field, when Lee disregarded his advice. The army commander himself was driven to a desperate and ill-advised attack when better opportunities had evaporated. Stout defense by the old adversary the Army of the Potomac, now led by the eminently competent Gen. George G. Meade, also must be credited in generous measure for the outcome.

The Army of Northern Virginia actually won a signal victory on July 1 north and west of Gettysburg and then swept into town on the heels of two routed Federal corps, gathering prisoners by the thousands. Bitter fighting on July 2 led to the brink of success, but never beyond. The dramatic and dreadful assault on July 3 directed by Gens. George E. Pickett and J. Johnston Pettigrew is one of the most famous episodes in all of American military history under the familiar—if unfair to Pettigrew—name of Pickett's Charge. The defeated army fell back through Pennsylvania and Maryland to the Potomac in a muddy, bloody, and painful retreat.

Once back in Virginia the Confederates regrouped and soon were ready for further action, but they simply could not replace the skilled officers and brave men buried in Pennsylvania. Lee realigned his cavalry command during this interval, leaving Stuart at its head but for the first time authorizing subordinate divisions under that general's control. Before fighting began anew against Meade's Federals, Longstreet had taken the First Corps to the western

theater, where it remained in Georgia and Tennessee until the following spring.

The two remaining corps of the Army of Northern Virginia fought intermittently against Meade's army through the late summer and fall of 1863 in the Piedmont region of northern Virginia. Lee maneuvered the army northward in October and forced the enemy back with considerable success before a grotesque tactical fiasco under A. P. Hill's direction at Bristoe Station blunted the movement. The embarrassment at Bristoe was compounded on November 7 when a Federal storming party captured Lee's fortified bridgehead at Rappahannock Station.

At the end of November Meade crossed the Rapidan west of the Wilderness and attempted to find a means to close with the Army of Northern Virginia. For several days the armies jousted near Mine Run before Meade recognized that he faced checkmate. The Northern general fell back without launching a major assault because he recognized that it would fail, thus earning the gratitude of his troops but calumny from the Unionist press.

Grant's Offensives. The Army of Northern Virginia wintered in 1863–1864 in Orange County and prepared for the stern test that it knew spring would bring. Gen. Ulysses S. Grant, of western theater prominence, assumed command of all Federal armies in March 1864 and made his headquarters with Meade's Army of the Potomac opposite Lee. At the beginning of May, Grant and Meade put their troops across the Rapidan River into the same Wilderness that had foiled Hooker precisely one year earlier. As the Federal column attempted to slice through the thickets in the direction of Richmond, the Army of Northern Virginia surged into its flanks from the west on two parallel roads about two miles apart. The confusing woods fighting that resulted on May 5 and 6 inflicted enormous casualties on the Federal army but also pushed Lee's army to the verge of destruction. Longstreet's First Corps arrived on May 6 to fight with the army for the first time since Gettysburg, too late to prevent a major Federal success but just in time to avoid complete disaster. In the crisis Lee attempted to lead the famous shock troops of the Texas Brigade in a desperate assault. The men turned Lee back and hurled themselves into the breach, suffering terrible losses in the process.

Although his army had suffered appreciably more than had Hooker's in May 1863 and had hurt Lee appreciably less, Grant calmly pushed south from the Wilderness to continue with a war of bloody attrition. His route took him to Spotsylvania Court House—or nearly there, for the Army of Northern Virginia managed to block the Federals' path outside the village with moments to spare. For fourteen days the armies locked in incessant combat, often fighting over imposing lines of breastworks in a first precursor of the trench warfare of later conflicts.

Three more times Lee attempted to lead men personally

as his army faced crisis after crisis. On May 10 a Federal frontal assault broke temporarily into the entrenched projection in the Confederate line known as the Mule Shoe Salient because of its shape. Two days later an enormous Northern assault crushed the nose of the salient and came close to breaking the Army of Northern Virginia in half. Lee crafted a new line near the base of the bulge as two brigades of his army sacrificed themselves in hand-to-hand fighting in a delaying action that lasted twenty hours. Their blood christened the curving line of earthworks where they fought as the Bloody Angle. Grant hammered brutally against other earthworks without success, one major attack on May 18 being repulsed by the Confederates so easily that most contemporary writers did not even mention it.

Meanwhile the Army of Northern Virginia suffered a tremendous loss on May 12 when its cavalry chief, J. E. B. Stuart, died in Richmond, victim of a wound suffered in resisting a passing raid on the capital. For the rest of the war, Wade Hampton and Fitzhugh Lee would try to fill Stuart's place.

When the Federal army side-slipped to the southeast again on May 21, leaving the vicinity of Spotsylvania Court House, the history of the Army of Northern Virginia entered a new phase. For nearly eleven months the army would remain locked in steady contact with its foe in a war featuring fortification and attrition rather than the meeting engagements and maneuver at which Lee had excelled since assuming command. The contending forces wrestled their way steadily across Virginia from May 21 to June 10, fighting regularly and sometimes fiercely. The Army of Northern Virginia missed a golden opportunity on the North Anna River May 23 through 27 because all three corps commanders were absent and Lee was ill. The troops next fought with their accustomed tenacity and skill at Totopotomoy Creek and Bethesda Church and then almost effortlessly butchered a mindless frontal assault ordered by Grant at Cold Harbor on June 3. The deterioration in command by this time was affecting the army almost as much as shortages of manpower and matériel. Longstreet had been hit hard in the Wilderness and would not return for five months; Ewell had collapsed and been removed from his corps command, replaced by Jubal Early; and A. P. Hill remained so regularly incapacitated by sickness as to require frequent relief.

With the army high command in disarray, Lee faced alone the tremendous burden of protecting Richmond. Operations in Virginia took a new and ominous turn when the Federal army succeeded in crossing the James River and attacking Petersburg before Lee had divined their intention. Fortunately for the Confederates, Grant had left the heart and brains of his army dead or bleeding in central Virginia when he destroyed its midlevel command in frontal assaults during May and early June. The Army of Northern Virginia managed to lunge across the James and into the

Federals' path just outside Petersburg. Barred from Richmond and foiled at Petersburg, Grant settled into the siege operations that were the next logical extension of the intense but mobile trench war of May.

Lee's Army at Low Tide. The final chapters in the life of the Army of Northern Virginia were written in ten months of often colorless and always deadly trench warfare. Lee endeavored to inject maneuver back into the military equation by sending Jubal Early with the veteran Second Corps back into the Valley where it had won so many laurels in past years. Early used his fragment of the army to good effect in a campaign that swept the Valley from Lynchburg to Harpers Ferry and beyond, reaching in July to the suburbs of Washington, D.C. After a surprising series of successes, however, Early finally fell victim to Federals in overwhelming force during September and October.

Lee's other attempts at movement and fresh initiatives covered less ground and usually met with less dramatic results. Soon after Grant reached the doorsteps of Richmond and Petersburg two immutable strategic verities became apparent: the Confederates could not protect both cities against concentrated forces, so Grant repeatedly sought to concentrate on one or the other; and the railroad lifelines of the Army of Northern Virginia that approached from the south and southwest were vulnerable. In response to the first of those unavoidable issues, Lee deftly moved his dwindling resources back and forth between the two fronts on either side of the James River during the last half of 1864. Bitter battles at such places as Fort Harrison, Fort Gilmer, Darbytown Road, and Deep Bottom captured occasional small tracts of ground for the Federals; more than that, they killed and wounded irreplaceable Southern soldiers. Fighting over the railroads flared at Weldon Railroad, Globe Tavern, and Reams's Station.

None of these affairs accumulated casualties on the scale of the army's great meeting engagements from 1862 through the spring of 1864, but each further enervated the army. The most famous of the battles around Petersburg erupted on July 30 when some soldiers from Pennsylvania mining country blew up several tons of black powder in a tunnel under the Confederate lines. The Battle of the Crater resulted in no change in the military situation—just more casualties.

Lee commanded the Army of Northern Virginia in these closing scenes with the assistance of a new generation of young generals. Some five dozen of the general officers who played a role in the closing months were either new to their ranks or new to the army. Men like John B. Gordon and William Mahone proved to be capable replacements for the famous officers who had fallen, but others could not accomplish what was required of them for lack of ability or lack of experience. Using the dwindling resources in men and officers and supplies available to him, Lee directed the army's operations in early 1865 across a steadily expanding front. The deep reservoir of manpower in the Army of the Potomac allowed Grant to extend around Lee to the southwest and then press westward toward the last roads and railroads. Fighting at Hatcher's Run in February killed Confederate Gen. John Pegram and brought the end closer.

The last offensive gasp of the Army of Northern Virginia came on March 25, 1865, against Fort Stedman near Petersburg. Gen. John B. Gordon led the forlorn hope whose initial success soon disappeared in the face of a horde of Northern reinforcements. A week later the army's tautly stretched lines finally snapped. Federals swarmed into Petersburg and Richmond, and Confederates hurried westward seeking refuge in the direction of Lynchburg, or junction with friendly troops coming up from North Carolina, or at least food near Farmville. All of those goals proved chimerical. Battered and fragmented at Five Forks and Sayler's Creek, and then hemmed in near Appomattox Courthouse on Palm Sunday, the Army of Northern Virginia ceased to exist when Robert E. Lee put on his best uniform and went to see Ulysses S. Grant in the village about terms of surrender.

Lee wrote a famous epitaph for the army in his General Orders No. 9, reviewing in moving terms the soldiers' "four years of arduous service marked by unsurpassed courage and fortitude," and expressing his "unceasing admiration of your constancy and devotion to your Country." William Swinton, a dedicated foe of the army and the early chronicler of the opposing Army of the Potomac, delivered an equally fitting tribute from across the lines:

Who that ever looked upon it can forget that body of tattered uniforms and bright muskets—that body of incomparable infantry which for four years carried the revolt on its bayonets . . . which, receiving terrible blows, did not fail to give the like; and which, vital in all its parts, died only with its annihilation?

[See also Appomattox Campaign; Beefsteak Raid; Bristoe Station, Virginia; Buckland Mills, Virginia; Cedar Mountain, Virginia; Chancellorsville Campaign; Cloyds Mountain, Virginia; Cold Harbor, Virginia; Early's Washington Raid; Fredericksburg Campaign; Gettysburg Campaign; Kelly's Ford, Virginia; Lynchburg, Virginia; Manassas, First; Manassas, Second; Mine Run Campaign; Peninsular Campaign; Petersburg Campaign; Piedmont, Virginia; Seven Days' Battles; Sharpsburg Campaign; Shenandoah Valley; Spotsylvania Campaign; Stuart's Raids; West Virginia Operations; Wilderness Campaign; and biographies of numerous figures mentioned herein.]

BIBLIOGRAPHY

Alexander, Edward Porter. Military Memoirs of a Confederate. New York, 1907. Reprint, Dayton, Ohio, 1977.
Allan, William. The Army of Northern Virginia in 1862. Boston, 1892. Reprint, Dayton, Ohio, 1984.
Dowdey, Clifford. Lee's Last Campaign. Boston, 1960. Reprint, Wilmington, N.C., 1988.
Evans, Clement A., ed. Confederate Military History. 12 vols. Atlanta, 1899. Extended ed. in 19 vols. Wilmington, N.C., 1987–1989.
Freeman, Douglas S. Lee's Lieutenants: A Study in Command. 3 vols. New York, 1942–1944. Reprint, New York, 1986.
Freeman, Douglas S. R. E. Lee. 4 vols. New York, 1934–1935.
McClelland, Henry B. The Life and Campaigns of Maj-Gen. J. E. B. Stuart. Richmond, Va., 1885.
Wise, Jennings Cropper. The Long Arm of Lee. 2 vols. Lynchburg, Va., 1915. Reprint, Richmond, Va., 1988.

ROBERT K. KRICK

ARMY OF TENNESSEE. This army was the major Confederate military force in the area between the Appalachian Mountains and the Mississippi River—a vast region known in the 1860s as the West. The Army of Tennessee was one of some two dozen independent field armies organized by the Confederates. It and the Army of Northern Virginia were the largest and longest-lived of those armies. In a very real sense, they were the Confederacy. They embodied its hope for national independence.

Although the Army of Tennessee was not formally so named until November 1862, its history dates from the first days of the Confederacy when its predecessor units came into being. Upon leaving the Union, each seceding state created its own army, and eventually these state-organized military forces were absorbed into Confederate service. The Army of Tennessee evolved from the forces of the western states of the Confederacy.

Organized by Governor Isham G. Harris in the spring and summer of 1861, the state army of Tennessee—although not the first predecessor unit—was the nucleus of what became the Confederate Army of Tennessee. Harris inadvertently created several problems that haunted the Army of Tennessee throughout the conflict. He overcommitted his force to protect the Mississippi River, for example, which left the northern border of Tennessee relatively vulnerable. Harris also appointed to positions of command several officers who displayed pettiness and questionable competence. Maj. Gen. Gideon Pillow, commander of the state army, was disgruntled at being commissioned only a brigadier general in the Confederate army, and he became a thorn in the side of the officers assigned to command him. He displayed incompetence and moral cowardice at Fort Donelson in early 1862 when he fled, leaving his men to be captured. He also exhibited physical cowardice at Murfreesboro almost a year later when he hid behind a tree rather than go into battle with his troops.

Formation under Albert Sidney Johnston

By late summer 1861 there were important concentrations of Confederate troops in northern Arkansas and southern Missouri, south central and southeastern Kentucky, western Tennessee, and at Columbus, Kentucky, New Orleans, Mobile, and Pensacola. Realizing the need for centralized control in the West, President Jefferson Davis sent Gen. Albert Sidney Johnston to command all Confederate forces between the Appalachian Mountains on the east and the Ozark Mountains on the west except the troops on the Gulf coast.

Johnston's assignment was the first of three attempts Davis made to establish a centralized military structure in the West. All three efforts failed because the president could never find a general willing or able to exercise such a command. In Johnston's case, the failure came when he established himself at Bowling Green, Kentucky, where he became so bogged down in local matters that he largely neglected other parts of his far-flung command.

To be sure, Johnston's task was difficult. He had far too few men—about forty thousand—to hold the extended frontier line for which he was responsible. Many of his soldiers were untrained and poorly armed and equipped. Johnston was also hampered because his line was pierced by three great rivers—the Mississippi, the Tennessee, and the Cumberland—that provided avenues of invasion for Northern armies. To complicate matters, local political pressure to defend the Mississippi River was so great that nothing could be done about Harris's overcommitment of forces to western Tennessee. Worst of all, Maj. Gen. Leonidas Polk, commanding Southern forces on the Mississippi River, had violated the neutrality of Kentucky by occupying Columbus. Polk's action helped drive the Bluegrass State into the arms of the Federal government and enormously complicated the Confederates' military problems in the West.

In early 1862 Johnston's forces were scattered unevenly along a thin east-west line roughly matching the southern borders of Kentucky and Missouri. The line was vulnerable, and it was menaced by Federal armies at several points. The position lacked both naturally defensible terrain and good means for the east-west movement of troops. Despite its manifest drawbacks, Johnston's line had to be held. To abandon it and fall back to a better, more defensible position to the south would have given up much of the more valuable, most productive parts of Tennessee as well as all practical hope of having Kentucky and Missouri adhere to the Confederacy.

In January Johnston's line began to unravel. On the nineteenth at Mill Springs in southeastern Kentucky, a Federal force smashed the right of his line, and the Confederates fled back into Tennessee. In the following month Union forces pushed the Confederates out of Missouri and then on March 7 and 8 at Elkhorn Tavern, Arkansas, defeated the Southerners' effort to regain their old position. Meanwhile, another Federal column began the conquest of Tennessee itself by thrusting up the Tennessee

and Cumberland rivers to capture Forts Henry and Donelson near the points where those streams crossed the Tennessee-Kentucky border. Possession of the river forts opened those waterways to the Union navy, enabled the Federals to outflank the massive Confederate fortifications in western Tennessee, and put the Northerners in position to cut off Johnston's force at Bowling Green.

Realizing the magnitude of these defeats, Johnston evacuated Bowling Green, abandoned Nashville and most of western Tennessee, and retreated to Corinth, Mississippi. There he brought together fragments of his command and united them with reinforcements rushed from New Orleans, Mobile, Pensacola, and other points. The force that resulted from this Corinth concentration was known at its March birth as the Army of Mississippi (sometimes the Army of the Mississippi).

Gen. P. G. T. Beauregard was second in command of Johnston's new army, which was organized into four corps. The commanders of these units were men who played leading roles in the war in the West. Polk commanded the First Corps; Maj. Gen. Braxton Bragg, fresh from the Gulf coast, the Second; Maj. Gen. William J. Hardee, who had been with Johnston at Bowling Green, the Third; and Brig. Gen. John C. Breckinridge, a former vice president of the United States, the Reserve Corps. (Although called "corps," these units were, in fact, large "grand divisions.")

The army that Johnston assembled at Corinth was—and would remain—overwhelmingly a western army. Most of its troops hailed from Alabama, Georgia, Mississippi, and Tennessee. Almost all the others were from Texas, Louisiana, Arkansas, Kentucky, and Missouri. Unfortunately for this army, the great majority of Southerners with prewar military education and training came from the eastern states. Virginia, for example, had 104 living graduates of the U.S. Military Academy in 1860; the other ten Confederate states together had only 184. By one 1860 count, more than 70 percent of the U.S. Army officers who came from the soon-to-secede states were from the eastern Confederacy. To make matters worse, the few trained, experienced men available in the West usually joined the first units their states organized in 1861, and most of those units were rushed to Virginia early in the war. The western army usually got the later-organized regiments—those raised after most of the state's trained personnel had gone.

Owing in large part to this maldistribution of militarily knowledgeable Confederates, the Army of Tennessee never had the strength of command that the Army of Northern Virginia enjoyed. The western officers were brave and intelligent enough, but they lacked—especially at the beginning of their service—the familiarity with military weapons and equipment and the knowledge of small-unit drill, tactics, and administration possessed by many of their counterparts in the East.

In early April 1862 Johnston moved his newly organized army out from Corinth to strike a Federal force that had advanced up the Tennessee River to Pittsburgh Landing just north of the Mississippi-Tennessee border. Johnston hoped to destroy that army and regain much of what he had lost in the preceding three months. He had about forty thousand men, and he was hopeful that the Confederate force that had fought at Elkhorn Tavern a month earlier and was now on the way east would join him before the battle.

On April 6 Johnston caught the Federals by surprise. His men overran their camps near Shiloh Church and drove them back to the Tennessee River. That afternoon, however, Johnston was killed. Beauregard, taking command, halted the attack, hoping to regroup and finish the victory on the seventh. That night thirty-five thousand Northern reinforcements arrived, and on the following day the combined Union forces drove Beauregard's men away. The Confederates pulled back to Corinth where they were joined by the men from the Trans-Mississippi. The Federals followed slowly, and at the end of May Beauregard was forced out of Corinth and back to Tupelo, some fifty miles to the south. The Confederate counteroffensive had failed.

The Army under Braxton Bragg

Soon after reaching Tupelo, Beauregard went on sick leave. Davis, who had been displeased by his behavior in Virginia in 1861 as well as by his conduct at Shiloh and his evacuation of Corinth, removed him from command and promoted Bragg to full general to replace him. Davis also reorganized the western command structure, separating eastern Tennessee and the area west of the Mississippi from Bragg's authority. Internally, too, the army was reorganized. Bragg created two wings of two divisions each. One wing was commanded by Polk; the other by Hardee.

Hoping to strike before the Federals in northern Mississippi could resume their advance, Bragg left about thirty thousand men and swung the rest of his army around to Chattanooga. (Most of the men remaining in Mississippi were the New Orleans garrison and the Trans-Mississippi troops who reached the army after Shiloh.) From Chattanooga, the Confederates moved into Kentucky to reestablish their claim to that state. Confident that thousands of Kentuckians would flock to their ranks, the Southerners advanced in two columns, one consisting of Bragg's army, the other the eastern Tennessee forces under Maj. Gen. E. Kirby Smith.

This second Confederate counteroffensive quickly ran into three major problems. For one thing, Davis—as was his habit—had not created clear lines of command. Assuming that officers of goodwill would cheerfully cooperate, Davis did not give Bragg authority over Smith until such time as their columns were united, when Bragg's higher grade would automatically put him in command of the combined force. Smith wanted to retain independent command, however, and refused to cooperate with Bragg. A second problem arose when the Southerners discovered that very few Kentuckians were sympathetic to the Confederacy or wished to join its army. Most pro-secession Kentuckians had long since left the state. The final problem developed because the two chief subordinates in the army—Polk and Hardee—personally disliked Bragg, resented his authority, often disobeyed his orders, and began what became a campaign to undermine his position and bring about his removal from command. For his part Bragg realized that several of his high-ranking generals—especially Polk—were major liabilities whose presence blocked the promotion of more able men. He urged that he be permitted to rid the army of its "deadwood."

After some early successes—which came mostly from the hard marching and fighting of his troops—Bragg found his campaign dissolving into confusion. Smith was off on his own in eastern Kentucky, and when Bragg left to attend the inauguration of the Confederate governor of Kentucky, Polk, who assumed command, disregarded Bragg's orders to attack the Federals and move on to Harrodsburg.

In the midst of this confusion, the Confederates blundered into the Federals at Perryville on October 8. The outnumbered Southerners won a tactical victory in the battle, but Bragg realized he could not remain in the state without more popular support than he had. He therefore fell back into middle Tennessee and took up a position at Murfreesboro. Bragg's counteroffensive had failed in its major objective, but it did transfer the Confederates' main western operations from Mississippi to Tennessee.

During the lull after Perryville the army acquired its new name—the Army of Tennessee—and was formally divided into two infantry corps. Polk and Hardee were promoted to the newly created grade of lieutenant general and assigned to command them. Smith, also named a lieutenant general, was transferred to the Trans-Mississippi. The army's cavalry, which had previously operated in small units, was consolidated under Brig. Gen. Joseph Wheeler.

Strains caused by the unsuccessful Perryville campaign brought into the open the rift in the army's high command. Bragg, bitter at the failure in Kentucky, sought scapegoats and blamed Polk for most of the army's troubles. Polk and Hardee—joined by Smith—renewed and intensified their campaign against Bragg. They sent criticisms of their commander to the president and to members of Congress. Hardee, who had great influence within the army, managed to turn many subordinate officers against Bragg and to undermine his support. Polk urged his old friend President Davis to get rid of Bragg. The army soon divided into pro-Bragg and anti-Bragg factions. Much of Bragg's support came from the Pensacola-Mobile units he had brought north to the Corinth concentration. The Polk-Hardee bloc found its strongest adherents among the Tennessee-Kentucky officers. In one form or another this civil war within the army raged until Bragg left in December 1863, and vestiges of it lingered to the end of the war.

Two other post-Perryville developments affected the army. In November Davis again attempted to provide coordination for military efforts in the West, appointing Gen. Joseph E. Johnston to oversee Confederate activities in the area. Davis expected Johnston to provide guidance for both Bragg's army and the Southern forces in Mississippi. Specifically, Johnston was to transfer troops between the two areas to meet a threat to either. This second attempt at coordinated western command eventually failed because of intelligence, logistical, and transportation problems and because Johnston, lacking faith in the scheme, proved unwilling to assume responsibility for deciding when troops should be sent from one area to the other.

Bragg's army also received a visit from Davis himself. The president was pleased with the condition and morale of the troops when he visited their camps in December, but he was unable to curtail the bitter feuding among the generals. He ordered a division of nine thousand men transferred from the army to Mississippi, in effect taking over the command he had assigned to Johnston.

Not long after Davis departed, the Federals ventured out from their base at Nashville against Bragg at Murfreesboro. The two armies met along Stones River on December 31. Bragg attacked and, despite bungling by several of his subordinates, drove back the Federals. The Southerners, however, were too weak to complete the victory, and both armies settled down for the night. New Year's Day was quiet, but on January 2 Bragg launched a foolish attack that was repulsed with great loss of lives. On January 3 and 4, Bragg fell back to Tullahoma. Once again the Confederate troops had fought well and had won a tactical success. The army lacked the strength to complete the victory, however, and the generals were unable to provide the leadership their men deserved.

The army rested at Tullahoma for more than five months. Meanwhile, the Federals were threatening Vicksburg, Mississippi, and the Confederate government urged Johnston to coordinate an effort to save the town. When Johnston proved unwilling to do so, Davis ordered him to take personal command of the forces in Mississippi. Believing that this order ended his responsibility as overall commander in the West, Johnston ceased even to go through the motions of that office. Davis's second attempt at a western command structure had evaporated.

While the Army of Tennessee was at Tullahoma, the sniping between Bragg and the Polk-Hardee coterie intensified. Murfreesboro joined Perryville as a subject of controversy. Bragg proved especially clumsy in the interne-

cine squabbling, exposing himself first to one criticism and then to another. Davis, in fact, seems to have lost confidence in Bragg and desired to replace him with Johnston. The president, however, was unwilling to give a direct order on the subject, and his subtle maneuverings to that end were frustrated by Johnston's refusal to act on presidential hints. In May Johnston went to Mississippi, and the army faced its next crisis with its high command even more weakened than it had been earlier.

The Federal troops did not strike again at the Army of Tennessee until mid-June. When they did, Bragg's position quickly collapsed. Advancing in five columns, the Union forces deceived Bragg and outflanked his position. By the end of the month Bragg realized his predicament and retreated to the south side of the Tennessee River near Chattanooga.

While the army was being maneuvered out of middle Tennessee, it underwent another reorganization. Hardee, sent off to Mississippi, was replaced by Lt. Gen. D. H. Hill. Substitution of Hill for Hardee, however, did nothing to cool the anti-Bragg furor in the army's high echelons. The East Tennessee Department was reunited with Bragg's command, and the troops there under Maj. Gen. Simon Bolivar Buckner were designated a third corps in the Army of Tennessee.

In August and September the Federals crossed the Tennessee River below Chattanooga. By so doing, they threatened Bragg's supply line and forced him back into North Georgia. Meanwhile, an alarmed Confederate government rushed reinforcements to Bragg from Mississippi and Virginia. The troops from Mississippi arrived first, and their presence led Bragg to create another corps. Thus, in early September the army consisted of four corps, each of two divisions, under Polk, Hill, Buckner, and Maj. Gen. W. H. T. Walker.

After some confused maneuvering in North Georgia during which several of Bragg's subordinates refused to obey his orders, the Army of Tennessee met the Federals along Chickamauga Creek late on September 18. Heavy but indecisive fighting went on all the following day. That night reinforcements from Virginia under Lt. Gen. James Longstreet reached the field, and Bragg reorganized his army yet again. He now created two wings—the left under Longstreet; the right under Polk. Longstreet's wing contained some of the troops of Polk's old corps, Buckner's Corps, and the troops from Virginia. Polk's wing contained part of his old corps, Hill's Corps, and Walker's Corps.

On September 20 the Confederates were lucky enough to attack at a time and place where a misunderstanding had created a gap in the Northerners' line. The Southerners broke through and chased about half of the Federals from the field. The remaining Union forces held on until dark and then withdrew to Chattanooga. Bragg followed and occupied the heights east and southwest of the town. He hoped to cut the routes by which food reached Chattanooga and force his enemy to surrender or abandon the area.

Once the army settled down to besiege Chattanooga, the generals renewed their squabbling. Bragg sought to discover why his orders had not been obeyed on so many recent occasions. Polk, Longstreet, Hill, and Buckner all emerged as anti-Bragg critics, joined by several of their subordinates. Bragg sought to deal with the trouble by relieving Polk from command and sending him away to await orders. Far from quieting matters, however, his action only intensified the clamor of his critics who circulated a petition denouncing their commander.

President Davis himself traveled west to intervene in the dispute. At an incredible meeting, Davis and Bragg listened as, one by one, the senior generals of the army declared that Bragg should be removed from command. Davis decided to sustain Bragg, but he made several changes in the army's organization. Polk was sent to Mississippi to replace Hardee who returned to the army to command Polk's Corps. Hill was simply sent away to await orders. Buckner was given command of a division. Many of the units commanded by anti-Bragg generals were broken up and scattered through the army. Bragg also acted to get rid of Longstreet by sending him off to eastern Tennessee to operate against Knoxville. Unfortunately for Bragg, he also sent Longstreet's troops off with him. As a result of these changes, the army now consisted of Hardee's Corps and what had been Hill's Corps under the command of its senior officer, Maj. Gen. John C. Breckinridge.

This turmoil helped to destroy the unity of the army and demoralize the troops. All through October and November they sat on the hills around Chattanooga, watching the North pour reinforcements and supplies into the city. At the Battle of Missionary Ridge, November 23 through 25, the Federals attacked Bragg's army. When the Confederates' position collapsed, they fled south to Dalton, Georgia. Bragg asked to be relieved from command, and Davis granted his request.

The Command of Joseph E. Johnston

The Confederate government now faced the daunting task of rebuilding its main western army. The first problem—selecting a new commander—presented a dilemma. Davis had only one army commander of demonstrated ability—Robert E. Lee—and he commanded the main army in Virginia. The Army of Tennessee's new commander had to be selected from the Confederacy's other high-ranking generals, all of whom were political enemies of Davis, or of limited ability, or both. Finally Davis resurrected Joseph E. Johnston as the least undesirable choice and ordered him to Dalton. Lt. Gen. John Bell Hood came to take command of the second corps.

Over the next four months Johnston did a creditable job restoring the army's morale and preparing it for the next campaign. As was his wont, however, he also spent a great deal of time bickering with the government and explaining why he would not be able to accomplish very much. He and the government authorities were unable to reach any agreement about what strategy they should adopt, and when the 1864 campaign opened, the Confederates were working at cross purposes. The government wanted Johnston to launch an offensive; Johnston believed that he was too weak for aggressive action and that he should fall back into Georgia, hoping the Federals would make a mistake that would give the Southerners a chance to strike.

When the Federals advanced in May 1864, the Southern government rushed reinforcements, building Johnston's strength up to about seventy-five thousand men. The largest single element of these reinforcements came from Mississippi and was commanded by Polk. Although technically a separate army operating with Johnston, Polk's command evolved into a third corps in the Army of Tennessee. Thus, in the Atlanta campaign, the army consisted of infantry corps under Hardee, Hood, and Polk and a cavalry corps under Wheeler. When Polk was killed on June 14, Alexander P. Stewart, a division commander, was promoted to lieutenant general to replace him.

All through May and June, Johnston sought a position in which he could block the Federal advance into Georgia. Unable to find one and constantly outmaneuvered by his adversary, he fell back toward Atlanta, abandoning valuable territory, exposing the heartland of the Confederacy, and demoralizing many soldiers and civilians. By mid-July Johnston had retreated to the outskirts of Atlanta and had lost some twenty-two thousand men.

The Final Offensive under Hood. Johnston's retreat created great alarm in both Georgia and Richmond, but when queried about his plans, Johnston gave only vague replies. Faced with these facts, Davis decided to replace Johnston with Hood who, on July 17, was promoted to the temporary grade of full general and named the Army of Tennessee's fifth commander. Lt. Gen. Stephen D. Lee was ordered from Mississippi to command what had been Hood's Corps.

Hood soon launched three attacks around Atlanta (Peachtree Creek, July 20; Atlanta, July 22; and Ezra Church, July 28). In all three the Confederates suffered tactical defeats, but they managed temporarily to check the Federals' progress. For a while, it seemed, Hood had thwarted the Federal advance and would hold the city.

In early August Hood tried to force the Northerners out of Georgia by cutting their railroad supply line from Chattanooga. He sent Wheeler with much of the army's cavalry north to wreck the railroad. Wheeler made a few half-hearted attempts to rip up the track. He soon abandoned efforts to wreck the railroad and rode off into northeastern Tennessee where, for several weeks, he was effectively out of the war.

With Wheeler gone, Hood was without his best means of gathering intelligence. In late August the Federals swung around southwest of Atlanta and cut the Confederates' rail line. Hood sent Hardee with two corps to drive them away. In a two-day battle at Jonesboro (August 31 and September 1) the Confederates failed to force back the Northerners. With his supply line cut, Hood had to surrender Atlanta. He evacuated the city and shifted to Palmetto. Both armies were exhausted, and both rested for several weeks.

Once again President Davis came west to visit the army. He removed Hardee from command of his corps and sent him to the south Atlantic coast. Maj. Gen. B. Franklin Cheatham, a division commander, took Hardee's place. Davis and Hood agreed that Hood should move the army into North Georgia and threaten the Union line of supply. Such a maneuver, they hoped, would force the Federals to leave Atlanta in order to preserve their connection with the North. The president also created a new command structure in the West, appointing Beauregard to oversee both Hood's army and the Confederates in Mississippi.

The new effort began auspiciously, with Hood slashing at the rail line as he moved north. The Federals followed and even pursued Hood into northern Alabama. Soon, however, they sent part of their army to defend Tennessee while the remainder abandoned its connection with the North and marched off across Georgia to the sea.

This development convinced Hood that he should move into Tennessee—a decision he reached without consulting either Davis or Beauregard. Indeed, Hood had come to resent Beauregard, and he ignored him as much as possible. Beauregard, for his part, decided not to do more than try to keep Hood's army supplied. Hood wandered west along the south bank of the Tennessee River to Tuscumbia. There he was delayed for about three weeks by high water in the river and by his preparations for the Tennessee campaign.

In late November Hood marched north to the Duck River where he found the Federals near Columbia. On November 29 he sent most of his army around to the east, crossed the river, and marched for Spring Hill. If he reached the road there, he would be north of the Federals and in position either to dash on to Nashville or to try to destroy them as they attempted to escape northward.

In one last fiasco, the Army of Tennessee approached Spring Hill and then halted. All night the Southerners sat around their campfires while a few yards to the west the Federals raced past. There have been allegations that some of the Confederate generals were drunk, or using drugs, or spending time with ladies in the area. Certainly, Hood was exhausted from a long day in the saddle and went to bed, leaving no orders to block the road. This collapse of command has never been satisfactorily explained.

The next morning the Confederates followed the Federals north to Franklin. There, Hood threw the army into a headlong assault against a very strong position. In a battle that lasted long into the darkness, the army lost some five thousand men. During the night, the Northerners pulled back to Nashville.

On December 1 Hood followed the Federals northward. For two weeks he kept the army sitting near Nashville while the Unionists brought in reinforcements and built up a mighty force. When the Federals struck (December 15–16) Hood's army collapsed and fled south to Corinth, Mississippi—where it had been born almost three years before—and then on to Tupelo. There, on January 23, Hood turned the battered Army of Tennessee (now only eighteen thousand officers and men) over to Lt. Gen. Richard Taylor.

Taylor soon sent parts of the army to other areas. Some went to Mobile to help defend that city. Others left to join the meager force being assembled in North Carolina in an effort to block the Federals who had crossed Georgia and turned north toward Virginia. Still others remained in Mississippi. Many units were en route to one of these points when the end came in April and May 1865.

Throughout its existence, then, the Army of Tennessee struggled with numerous handicaps. It was defending an area where geography aided the enemy. It did not share equitably in the Confederacy's supply of trained officers. Often the army was neglected by its government, receiving short shrift with regard to supplies and weapons. It was hampered by internal feuds among its generals—by what historian Steven Woodworth has called "the ugly world of Army of Tennessee politics." Its greatest handicap, however, was the absence of a strong, confident, stable hand at the helm. Because of these weaknesses, the Army of Tennessee, in the end, could not hold the West.

[*See also* Atlanta, Georgia; Chattanooga, Tennessee; Corinth, Mississippi; Elkhorn Tavern, Arkansas; Franklin and Nashville Campaign; Henry and Donelson Campaign; Kentucky Campaign of Bragg; Mill Springs, Kentucky; Murfreesboro, Tennessee; Shiloh Campaign; *and biographies of numerous figures mentioned herein.*]

BIBLIOGRAPHY

Connelly, Thomas L. *Army of the Heartland: The Army of Tennessee, 1861–1862.* Baton Rouge, La., 1967.

Connelly, Thomas L. *Autumn of Glory: The Army of Tennessee, 1862–1865.* Baton Rouge, La., 1971.

Connelly, Thomas L., and Archer Jones. *The Politics of Command: Factions and Ideas in Confederate Strategy.* Baton Rouge, La., 1973.

Daniel, Larry J. *Cannoneers in Gray: The Field Artillery of the Army of Tennessee, 1861–1865.* Tuscaloosa, Ala., 1984.

Daniel, Larry J. *Soldiering in the Army of Tennessee: A Portrait of Life in a Confederate Army.* Chapel Hill, N.C., 1991.

Horn, Stanley F. *The Army of Tennessee: A Military History.* Indianapolis, 1941.

McMurry, Richard M. *Two Great Rebel Armies: An Essay in Confederate Military History.* Chapel Hill, N.C., 1989.

Woodworth, Steven E. *Jefferson Davis and His Generals: The Failure of Confederate Command in the West.* Lawrence, Kans., 1990.

RICHARD M. MCMURRY

ARRINGTON, ARCHIBALD HUNTER (1809–1872), congressman from North Carolina.

Born in Hilliardston in Nash County, North Carolina, Arrington attended local schools and Louisburg Academy before pursuing an interest in law. With the death of his father in 1830, much of his time and attention focused upon managing the family's extensive wealth and property. As a large landowner and lawyer, Arrington naturally gravitated toward the world of politics and ran successfully for Congress in 1840. He served two terms in the House of Representatives before losing his bid for reelection in 1844.

An outspoken advocate of state rights, Arrington was elected to North Carolina's secession convention in May 1861. The following November, he defeated the former Unionist Josiah Turner in a bid for election to the First Confederate Congress. Arrington took his seat in the House of Representatives on February 20, 1862, and, five days later, was appointed to the Committee on Indian Affairs.

While in Congress, Arrington proved to be a friend of the common soldier. He offered resolutions to inquire into the provisions made for the shelter and subsistence of troops passing through the Confederate capital. He also moved to increase their pay to thirty dollars a month. On more controversial matters, he voted against the tax-in-kind bill, arguing that the "government's portion, when collected together in large quantities, would be too liable to waste."

His support for exemptions from military service and specifically the Twenty-Slave Law vacillated. Arguing first that it was necessary "that the most vigilant and efficient police should be kept over the slaves," Arrington voted for its passage. Later, possibly sensing the bill's unpopularity with his less well-to-do constituents, he changed his mind and voted for its repeal. Arrington ran unsuccessfully in 1863 for election to the Second Congress, losing to his earlier political rival, Josiah Turner.

After the war, the former congressman managed his still-extensive property and held local office, including that of county commissioner for Nash County. He died at his home in Hilliardston.

BIBLIOGRAPHY

Alexander, Thomas B., and Richard E. Beringer. *The Anatomy of the Confederate Congress: A Study of the Influences of Member Characteristics on Legislative Voting Behavior, 1861–1865.* Nashville, Tenn., 1972.

Journal of the Congress of the Confederate States of America, 1861–1865. 7 vols. Washington, D.C., 1904–1905.

Powell, William S. *Dictionary of North Carolina Biography.* 4 vols. to date. Chapel Hill, N.C., 1979–.

Warner, Ezra J., and W. Buck Yearns. *Biographical Register of the Confederate Congress.* Baton Rouge, La., 1975.

ALAN C. DOWNS

ARSENALS AND ARMORIES.

The terms *arsenal* and *armory* were used interchangeably in both the Union and the Confederacy, although the former usually referred to a manufacturing establishment and the latter to a storage facility. Most Southern states at the beginning of the Civil War had armories, but arsenals were fewer and of

ARMORY AT HOLLY SPRINGS, MISSISSIPPI.

HARPER'S PICTORIAL HISTORY OF THE GREAT REBELLION

Production Limits for Ammunition and Lead in 1863

	SMALL ARMS AMMUNITION (ROUNDS PER DAY)	FIELD AMMUNITION (ROUNDS PER DAY)	LEAD (POUNDS PER MONTH)
Atlanta	25,000	125 to 150	20,000
Augusta	30,000	125 to 150	30,000
Charleston	10,000	100 to 125	9,000
Columbus, Ga.	10,000	75 to 100	10,000
Columbus, Miss.	15,000	125 to 150	10,000
Macon	10,000	100 to 125	8,000
Richmond	60,000	300 to 500	60,000
Selma	10,000	50 to 75	8,000
Total	170,000	1,000 to 1,375	155,000

limited capacity, as were ordnance manufacturing plants of almost all other kinds.

A quick survey of Confederate small arms at the start of the war showed only 159,010 housed in arsenals and armories across the South. Gen. Josiah Gorgas, the Confederacy's able chief of ordnance, concentrated on expanding and improving existing establishments and building new ones. At the beginning of the war, before Virginia joined the Confederacy, the South had arsenals at Baton Rouge, Louisiana; Mount Vernon, Alabama; Charleston, South Carolina; Augusta, Georgia; Little Rock, Arkansas; and Fayetteville, North Carolina. All were short on manufacturing machinery, however, and those that did have production capacity were inhibited by a powder shortage. New Orleans and a few other places had limited powder-making facilities.

When he became secretary of war in late 1861, Judah P. Benjamin asked for a report on the Ordnance Bureau. He noted that Virginia's admission to the Confederacy brought the famous Harpers Ferry arsenal and armory, along with Richmond's arsenal and armory, to the Confederate inventory, and that there were smaller depots (Memphis and Nashville, Tennessee, and Savannah, Georgia, were operational and others were under construction), laboratories, foundries, shops, and ironworks scattered across the Confederacy that added to production.

When planning a centralized program, Gorgas sought to concentrate production in Augusta and Macon, Georgia, and those cities did become ordnance centers, with arsenals, armories, and, in Augusta, a major powder works, and in Macon, the Confederate States Central Laboratories. Arsenals were built in Atlanta and Columbus, Georgia, Selma, Alabama, and Tyler, Texas.

A severe lead shortage restricted production at the end of 1862 and hampered operations throughout the remainder of the war. Desperate efforts to find lead through the Niter and Mining Bureau and the navy produced too little. John William Mallet, superintendent of laboratories, bombarded Richmond with warnings of impending shortages and advocated offering sporting percussion caps for private

donations of lead as well as earmarking space for lead on blockade runners. The chief of ordnance had done these things and had also requisitioned window weights from Charleston and unused water mains from Mobile to make up a third of the needed total. In November 1863, he reported to the secretary of war that from September 1862 to September 1863 monthly cartridge output averaged above three million, with daily production of about 150,000 throughout the Confederacy. Blockade runners brought in critical amounts of lead to sustain the war effort.

The chief of ordnance worried about shortages and issued a memorandum in November 1863 limiting daily ammunition production at the main arsenals, but the maximums were nonetheless generous.

Arsenals and armories continued production through makeshift substitutes (whisky stills were raided for copper in the Carolina hills) and talented commanders. Mallet, in the sensitive position of supervising standardization and laboratory production, had solid scientific credentials (he belonged to Britain's Royal Society), and George W. Rains, who built a world-class powder works in Augusta, Georgia, shared impressive scientific repute. James H. Burton, builder of the Macon Armory, came with a set of plans to make copies of Britain's famed Enfield Rifle and with important connections to English arms manufacturers. Julius A. de Lagnel first commanded the Fayetteville, North Carolina, arsenal and finally took charge of all arsenal, armory, and depot affairs. General Gorgas had an uncanny knack for picking able ordnance officers.

Justifiably proud, Gorgas wrote in his diary on April 8, 1864:

Large arsenals have been organized at Richmond, Fayetteville, Augusta, Charleston, Columbus, Macon, Atlanta and Selma, and smaller ones at Danville, Lynchburgh, and Montgomery, besides other establishments. . . . Armories here [Richmond, Virginia] and at Fayetteville. . . . Where three years ago we were not making a gun, a pistol nor a sabre, no shot nor shell (except at the Tredegar Works)—a pound of powder—we now make all these in quantities to meet the demands of our large armies.

By the end of the Civil War, the Confederacy had become a small but significant industrial nation. The arsenals and armories were the bases for that development.

[*See also* Atlanta, Georgia; Baton Rouge, Louisiana; Charleston, South Carolina; Columbus Naval Iron Works; Harpers Ferry, West Virginia; Lead; Little Rock, Arkansas; Macon, Georgia; Niter and Mining Bureau; Palmetto Armory; Powder Works; Selma, Alabama; and Tredegar Iron Works.]

BIBLIOGRAPHY

Coulter, E. Merton. *The Confederate States of America, 1861–1865.* Baton Rouge, La., 1950.

Thomas, Emory M. *The Confederate Nation.* New York, 1979.

Vandiver, Frank E., ed. *The Civil War Diary of General Josiah Gorgas.* University, Ala., 1947.

Vandiver, Frank E. *Ploughshares into Swords: Josiah Gorgas and Confederate Ordnance.* Austin, Tex., 1952.

FRANK E. VANDIVER

ARTILLERY. [*This entry is composed of four articles: An Overview, which discusses the organization and role of artillery in the Confederate Army; Confederate Artillery, which discusses artillery produced within the Confederacy; Captured U.S. Artillery, which discusses U.S.-made artillery used in the Confederate Army; and Imported English Artillery, which discusses English-made artillery produced for or used by the Confederates. See also Naval Guns.*]

An Overview

The Confederate artillery was created around a number of militia companies formed in the years before the war by men who had a serious interest in military matters, inspired by Napoleon's campaigns and the exploits of the U.S. artillery in the Mexican War. Most of their officers and men were well educated and of considerable social standing. In 1861 these elite units attracted a better than usual type of volunteer and were able to organize and train additional companies. Organizations such as the Richmond Howitzers, the Rockbridge Artillery, and the Washington and Palmetto battalions were noted all through the war for their efficiency and morale.

Major weaknesses were the shortage of trained officers and the total lack of veteran noncommissioned officers to match the regular army artillerymen of the Federal armies. Though continued service gave the South excellent company and battalion officers and some competent corps artillery commanders, none of its army chiefs of artillery was really capable.

Another major weakness in 1861 was the almost total lack of modern field guns. Captures, imports, and domes-

tic manufacture gradually provided enough weapons, but none of these sources was reliable, and the Confederate gunners were never as well armed as their opponents. For all their courage and increasing skill, Confederate artillerymen were continually overmatched—their successes at Second Manassas and Fredericksburg canceled by their losses in the "artillery hell" of Sharpsburg and their failure at Gettysburg.

Organization

Artillery of this period was classified as field, horse, pack, or heavy. Of these, field (sometimes called "light") artillery was the most common, being armed and equipped for service with infantry. In theory, during marches and maneuvers its cannoneers were mounted on their battery's caissons and limbers; in vulgar practice they walked—or when necessary, ran—beside their guns. Horse artillery (also called "flying artillery") served with the cavalry; its cannoneers all had individual mounts. Pack (or "jackass") artillery was used only briefly and unsuccessfully by the Confederates. Heavy artillery (also called "foot artillery") handled siege, seacoast, and fortress guns; they were usually armed and equipped as infantry.

The basic artillery unit was the company. (The modern term *battery*—which previously had meant only an indefinite number of guns emplaced together in the same position—came into general use during this war.) An ideal Confederate company consisted of a captain; four lieutenants (three serving as section chiefs, one in charge of the caissons); eight sergeants, including an orderly (first) sergeant and a quartermaster (supply) sergeant; twelve corporals; two artificers (blacksmith and saddler); two buglers; a guidon bearer; and approximately ninety drivers and cannoneers. (Confederate regulations set the number of privates at 64 to 125.) Horse artillery needed two extra privates per section to serve as horse holders while their company was in action.

This company would have four guns and two howitzers, each with its accompanying caisson, loaded with ammunition. Gun and caisson together formed a platoon, commanded by a sergeant "chief-of-piece" assisted by two corporals—one the gunner, the other in charge of the limbers and caisson. Two platoons made up a section. In addition, the company was to have a battery wagon for supplies, spare parts, and tools and a traveling forge, which was a mobile blacksmith's shop. (Artillery theory held that each 12-pounder or heavier gun should have two caissons, but this seems to have been followed only rarely in the Federal forces and very rarely, if ever, in the Confederate.) Officers, sergeants, buglers, and guidon bearers were to have individual mounts, and there would be seven to a dozen spare horses to replace casualties.

In fact, however, the existing Confederate artillery

CONFEDERATE ARTILLERY.   The Palmetto Battery near Charleston, South Carolina.   LIBRARY OF CONGRESS

companies very seldom attained such a state of perfection and those that did could not long maintain it. The average company had four cannon (often of different types and caliber) and sometimes only two or three. It frequently was hampered by a shortage of horses and a lack of proper feed for those it had. Competent soldier-mechanics were scarce throughout the South. By late 1864, satisfactory recruits were increasingly hard to procure, most of the replacements furnished by the now-omnivorous Confederate conscription being too young, too old, or men who had been evading service for years and still had no appetite for soldiering.

During the 1862 campaigns most Confederate artillery companies were attached to infantry brigades; any remaining (and those companies still completing their organization) were lumped into temporary battalions as part of a haphazardly managed artillery reserve. This made it practically impossible to mass artillery at a critical point, with the result (as at Malvern Hill) that individual Confederate batteries were hurried into action against larger numbers of Federal guns and so were smashed piecemeal.

Consequently, during late 1862 and early 1863, the Army of Northern Virginia reorganized its artillery into battalions of four to six companies. Normally one of these was attached to each infantry division, and two additional ones to each

corps, under the direct control of a corps chief of artillery. This flexible system never achieved its full possibilities because of the deficiencies of Confederate weapons, ammunition, and training. Nevertheless, for a time, Confederate artillery organization above company level was considerably superior to that of the Federals. Its effectiveness forced the Army of the Potomac to institute similar improvements in its artillery organization during 1863.

Other Confederate armies also initially attached artillery companies to infantry brigades. At Chickamauga in September 1863 the Army of Tennessee still had part of its artillery assigned in this fashion, but several divisions had grouped their artillery under division control, and there was a five-company army reserve. By the following November, however, it had adopted the Army of Northern Virginia's system.

In addition to the artillery serving with its field armies, the Confederacy had a large number of independent artillery companies assigned to seacoast and river defenses.

Clothing and Equipment

The uniforms of the Confederate artillery were practically identical with those of the infantry, with the exception that collars, cuffs, braid, and caps might be scarlet, that being the artillery's distinctive color. Exact patterns varied from company to company; generally they became plainer as the war went on. Some "dandy" organizations, such as the Washington Artillery, began the war in smart blue-and-scarlet uniforms, with short white gaiters. As in the infantry, there was considerable use of captured Union light blue trousers and overcoats. Final clothing issues included dark blue trousers and brown coats with black collars as the Confederate quartermasters used whatever materials they could get. Most companies must have made a variegated appearance by 1865, especially as many of the last replacements were not issued uniforms on enlistment and so arrived wearing citizens' clothes.

An artilleryman's individual equipment also resembled the infantryman's. By 1863 it seems usually to have consisted of a horseshoe blanket roll, haversack, and canteen, though—being able to pack some of their belongings on their limbers and caissons—the cannoneers seem to have been more inclined to keep their overcoats.

Weapons

Initially, enlisted men of the field and horse artillery were armed with sabers and revolvers when such weapons were available. The first quickly proved a nuisance and were either "lost" or turned in. Proving both a source of accidental shootings and too handy in personal quarrels, the pistols soon were collected, only officers being permitted to retain them. Consequently, when a battery was overrun by enemy troops, the cannoneers were defenseless except for their rammer staffs and handspikes. During the last months of the siege of Petersburg, field artillery units serving entrenched batteries were issued muskets so that those men not actually manning the guns might help the overextended infantry. Heavy artillery, as previously noted, was normally armed as infantry, often with older models of muskets.

The artillery's real weapon was its cannon, and here the Confederates remained at a disadvantage throughout the war. At first many companies had the old bronze (usually termed "brass") 6- and 12-pounder guns and 12-pounder howitzers. Even some of the light 12-pounder mountain howitzers were used for lack of better ones. The Virginia Rockbridge company had to improvise its caissons from the running gear of farm wagons and homemade ammunition chests; undoubtedly a good many other companies had the same experience.

Howitzers were shorter and more lightly built than guns. They had shorter ranges, but higher trajectories that were useful in shelling an enemy partially sheltered behind buildings or rough terrain. Since they weighed less, a 24-pounder howitzer could be mounted on a 12-pounder gun's carriage. This mix of weapons gave the battery commander greater flexibility in dealing with different targets; also the howitzers were very effective firing

canister. But the need for two different calibers of ammunition and different types of equipment was always a problem; both armies came to favor only one type and caliber of cannon in each company.

The cannon that became the Confederate field artillery's major weapons were the smoothbore 12-pounder bronze gun-howitzer (the Napoleon gun), the wrought-iron 3-inch Ordnance rifled gun, and the 10-pounder Parrott rifle, made of cast iron with a distinctive wrought-iron reinforcing tube around its breech. A few James, Brooke (a Southern invention resembling the Parrott), and Blakely (a short, light English import with a vicious recoil) rifles also were in service. Some four-gun Confederate companies had three different types of cannon, each requiring its own particular ammunition. Heavier guns included the 20-pounder and 30-pounder Parrotts, the latter being much disliked because of its tendency to blow up while in action. (The Confederates had two at Fredericksburg; both exploded, one showering fragments around Robert E. Lee and James Longstreet.)

All of these cannon were muzzle-loaders. The rifled guns had a longer range and were more accurate, but the Napoleon had a higher rate of fire and was much more effective for short-range fighting since its smooth bore gave its canister a wider spread than rifled guns produced—the effect being like that of a 4.6-inch shotgun, making it an excellent infantry-killer.

The Confederates also imported newly developed breech-loading guns such as the Armstrong and Whitworth. The latter had a hexagonal bore and was extremely accurate, with a range of almost six miles, but its projectiles were too light to do appreciable damage. Also it took longer to load from the breech than the Napoleon did from the muzzle. (Federal artillerymen tested it, but found it too heavy, long, and cumbersome for active campaigning.)

Artillery ammunition consisted of solid shot, explosive shell, shrapnel (usually called "case"), and canister. Solid shot was effective against buildings and masses of troops; explosive shell against field fortifications, buildings (it had an incendiary effect), and hostile batteries; shrapnel against troops at over 400 yards range. Canister was for close-range fighting at 350 yards or less; as the range shortened, artillery would use double canister (two cans of shot with a single propelling charge), producing a blast of some fifty-four 7-ounce balls. The effectiveness of explosive shell and shrapnel was limited by the low power of their black-powder bursting charge and the unreliability of their fuzes; a round might explode anywhere between the muzzle of the gun and the target, to the hurt and anger of any friendly infantry in front of the battery. The Confederates were especially unfortunate in this respect, their fuzes being so unreliable that a high percentage of their shells and shrapnel rounds would not explode and so were no more effective than solid shot. Also many of these projectiles were so poorly made that they tumbled in flight, landing anywhere but near the target. After damning the ammunition regularly issued to them, those artillery units of the Army of Northern Virginia that were sent west with Longstreet in late 1863 found the Army of Tennessee's munitions were even more unreliable. Finally, the Confederate-manufactured versions of the Ordnance rifle and the Napoleon were inferior to the Federal originals in accuracy and general serviceability.

Taken as a whole, these matériel deficiencies not only put Confederate cannoneers at a serious disadvantage in their duels with Federal artillery but greatly complicated the problem of supporting their own infantry. Because of the tendency of their shrapnel and shell to explode short of the target, it was unwise for them to attempt to fire over their infantry. On more than one occasion Southern soldiers suffering from such friendly fire reportedly threatened to call the war off while they went back and cleaned out the offending batteries!

During the trench warfare around Petersburg in 1864 and 1865, some batteries were rearmed with 12-pounder iron mortars, newly manufactured by the Confederate Ordnance Department. These were supplemented by 12- or 24-pounder howitzers mounted on inclined skids and fired with reduced charges to give their shells the higher trajectory needed to drop them into the Federal earthworks.

As for seacoast and fortress artillery, the Confederacy had secured large numbers of excellent heavy guns by its seizure of lightly guarded U.S. coastal fortifications and naval bases during the first days of hostilities. The Norfolk naval yard alone provided over one thousand cannon, including some three hundred of the new Dahlgren 9- and 11-inch guns. These were soon distributed throughout the Confederacy, where they were used largely as fortress artillery. They were supplemented by a small number of British-made Armstrong guns (both breech- and muzzleloaders) and Blakely rifles. Seacoast batteries might employ grapeshot, a heavier form of canister, for short-range action against warships and attacking infantry. (Despite frequent mention, grapeshot apparently never actually was used by field artillery simply because the greater number of balls in a canister round provided a more effective spread of shot.)

Confederate artillerymen also experimented with rocket batteries and various novel types of ordnance, including double-barreled cannon; revolving cannon, which were described as looking like a huge revolver on wheels; and steam-guns, which were to employ compressed steam as a propellant. None was successful.

Tactics

Artillery employment during the Civil War tended to be clumsy. To begin with, few generals on either side—even veterans of the Mexican War—had much experience with combined infantry-artillery tactics. Though artillery had contributed substantially to the American victories in Mexico, it had usually fought as individual companies, driving recklessly forward, often in advance of their own infantry, into canister range of the Mexicans. The latter, being armed with often-indifferent smoothbore muskets, could not reply effectively to their devastating fire. Also, these had been small-scale battles; the largest American army, including a half-dozen companies of artillery, had numbered less than fifteen thousand, little more than half the strength of a single Confederate corps at Gettysburg.

This dashing use of artillery became too costly once the majority of the infantry were armed with rifle-muskets, accurate at roughly twice canister's range. Field artillery therefore was increasingly relegated to a supporting mission, especially during attacks, firing from commanding positions behind its infantry. In this role its effectiveness was sharply limited, especially at long range, by the unreliability of its ammunition and limited explosive power of its shells. Though it could destroy buildings, it could not significantly damage earthworks or cause serious casualties among dug-in troops. Similarly, in a defensive situation shrapnel and explosive shell were usually too inaccurate to stop a determined charge. If the enemy were advancing through a wooded area, solid shot could inflict heavy casualties at long range, ricocheting through the timber and bringing down branches and whole trees on the troops. At short range, however, the artillery would shift to canister, taking the same deadly part that machine guns play in modern defensive fighting.

These weaknesses were intensified by the general topography of the United States during the mid-nineteenth century—a rugged country of few roads (and those often bad) and extensive forests. Few battlefields offered large areas of open ground— as at Antietam and Gettysburg— where guns could be emplaced and employed in mass. And even under such favorable conditions, inexperienced generals and artillery officers alike might fail to take full advantage of their opportunity. (An excellent example is the third day of Gettysburg, where the Confederate preparatory bombardment before Pickett's charge was poorly planned, failing both to enfilade the Federal "fishhook" position from the north and to properly concentrate its fire against the Confederate objective on Cemetery Ridge.) Elsewhere, the artillery usually faced short-range engagements in terrain where maneuvering was difficult and only companies or battalions could get into position. Later, the increasing use of field fortifications sharply reduced the effectiveness of artillery fire, making it mostly a defensive arm against enemy attacks and counterattacks.

Whenever possible artillery commanders looked for positions from which they could deliver enfilade fire against the flank of attacking enemy troops or enemy defensive positions, thus sweeping the length of their lines. If the ground were hard, ricochet fire could be used—solid shot or

CONFEDERATE QUAKER GUNS. At Centreville, Virginia, March 1862. Photograph by George N. Barnard and James F. Gibson. Named for the pacifist tenets of the Society of Friends, Quaker guns were nothing more than logs or tree trunks placed in artillery embrasures to deceive the enemy into thinking a position was manned and armed. One of the most successful examples of their use occurred on July 18, 1862, when Confederate Gen. Adam Rankin ("Stovepipe") Johnson used a charred log and a stovepipe to trick Federals into surrendering their arsenal at Newburg, Indiana.   NATIONAL ARCHIVES

explosive shell fired so as to strike the ground at a shallow angle just short of the enemy and then go bouncing and rolling through their lines. Such rounds retained a killing velocity even when apparently barely moving; only a fool or a greenhorn got in their way.

Throughout the war in sudden emergencies—an enemy breakthrough of the front, an unexpected flank attack— artillery might still drive forward in the old style through their broken infantry into canister range of the advancing enemy for a stand-up fight in the open. This usually meant heavy losses in men and horses, if not the sacrifice of the units involved, but the application—even if casualties made it brief—of artillery's superior fire power often was successful in checking or even stopping the enemy. In the same spirit, batteries in position might continue firing until overrun by hostile infantry, their last point-blank blasts of double canister being the most destructive, to give their infantry time to rally.

Horse artillery had a particular reputation for dash and daring. Confederate officers like Lt. Col. John Pelham of J. E. B. Stuart's horse artillery soon became legends in both armies and mostly died young. Their guns were pushed recklessly forward into the cavalry skirmish lines; some companies had the reputation of joining in cavalry charges, employing the superior weight of their formation to shatter the Federal cavalry formations.

In spite of its handicaps, the Confederate artillery achieved an honorable reputation. Even through the war's disastrous last months in 1865, while desertion was gutting the Army of Northern Virginia's famous infantry regiments, few artillerymen "went over the hill." In part, this can be attributed to the good quality of the original artillery personnel. In greater part it probably was due to the fact that the artillery had very seldom suffered casualties comparable to those the infantry took in action after action; consequently it still had many of its first volunteers, both officers and men. At Appomattox, a much higher proportion of artillerymen than infantry remained with Lee's dwindling army, standing by their guns, ready for another battle they knew they could not win.

BIBLIOGRAPHY

Alexander, Edward P. *Fighting for the Confederacy.* Chapel Hill, N.C., 1989.

Coggins, Jack. *Arms and Equipment of the Civil War.* Garden City, N.Y., 1962.

Department of Military Art and Engineering, U.S. Military Academy. *Supplemental Material: Weapons of the Civil War and Organization and Tactics.* West Point, N.Y., 1959–1960.

Elting, John R., and Michael J. McAfee. *Long Endure: The Civil War Period.* Vol. 2 of *Military Uniforms in America.* Novato, Calif., 1982.

Freeman, Douglas S. *Lee's Lieutenants.* 3 vols. New York, 1942–1944. Reprint, New York, 1986.

Krick, Robert K. *Parker's Virginia Battery, C.S.A.* Berryville, Va., 1975.

Todd, Frederick P., ed. *American Military Equipage.* Vol. 3. Providence, R.I., 1977.

Wise, Jennings C. *The Long Arm of Lee.* Richmond, Va., 1915.

JOHN R. ELTING

Confederate Artillery

The seizure of Federal installations in the South provided the Confederacy with sufficient heavy artillery to arm coastal and inland fortifications. The need for field artillery for the armies was partially filled by cannons received under the Militia Act of 1808, initial seizures, and early battlefield captures, but there remained a considerable deficiency. What little industry existed in the South set about to fill this need.

The Tredegar Iron Works in Richmond, operated by Joseph R. Anderson, had been casting cannons since 1842. Anderson, a West Point graduate, was the driving force at Tredegar and greatly expanded the capacity of the foundry in the two decades before the war. On the eve of conflict Tredegar was fully operational with proven leadership.

Most of the production at Tredegar in the prewar years had been large cannons. Anderson had to realign production to meet the requirement for field artillery. From April through December 1861 Tredegar delivered at least 33 field guns including 5 brass 12-pound howitzers in December, the first such guns from the foundry, and 8 iron Parrott rifles of current pattern. At least 98 were heavy guns of 8-, 9-, and 10-inch bore. In all, 214 guns of all types were delivered during 1861.

The next year proved to be the most productive at Tredegar with delivery of 351 guns of various calibers. Only about 85 were heavy guns. Of these, 11 were 6.4-inch (32-pound) Brooke rifles and 14 were 7-inch Brooke rifles, all of an advanced design by John M. Brooke, head of the Naval Ordnance and Hydrography Department. The Brooke gun, like the Federal Parrott, was cast iron with a wrought-iron reinforcing band or bands around the breech of the gun. Tredegar furnished two 6.4-inch and two 7-inch Brooke rifles as well as the armor plate for CSS *Virginia.* The bulk of production was made up of brass 12-pounders and iron 3-inch Parrott rifles together with 6-pounders and 24-pound howitzers.

In 1863, production of 12-pound Napoleons became the priority, with at least 111 delivered out of a total production of 286 guns. Only some 22 were heavy 6.4-inch, 7-inch, and 10-inch Brooke pieces. Output again declined in 1864 to 213 guns, the primary problem being the lack of high-grade iron. Bursting guns had become a major problem. Production centered on Napoleons and 10-, 20-, and 30-pound Parrott rifles with 104 of the former and 36 of the latter being delivered. At least another eighteen 6.4-inch, 7-inch, and 8-inch Brooke rifles were also furnished.

Cannon production continued to be hampered by lack of raw materials. Loss of the Cloverdale furnace in Botetourt County, Virginia, to Federal units was a major blow, for Cloverdale was the primary source of high-grade iron in the South. Skilled labor at the foundry also decreased as more workmen were called into the army and replaced by slave labor. Only thirty-five guns were fabricated before production ceased about March 1, 1865. Twenty of these were Napoleons and five were heavy pieces.

During the course of the war Tredegar cast guns as small as the Williams breech-loading iron rifle and the 2.25-inch bronze mountain rifle, and as large as an 11-inch naval smoothbore, for a total of 1,099 guns of all types, over half the guns made in the Confederacy. Only one other foundry, that of R. P. Parrott, Cold Spring, New York, boasted higher production.

The Bellona Foundry, thirteen miles above Richmond on the James River, had also been involved in the manufacture of cannons since the 1840s. The operation was run by Dr. Junius L. Archer. Providentially, Bellona was casting guns for the Federal government under an 1857 contract when the war began. The state of Virginia confiscated the twenty-three completed guns of various calibers and reimbursed the Federal government.

Tredegar expansion plans included the leasing of Bellona in 1861, but this was soon given up in favor of enlarging the facility in Richmond. The two foundries cooperated, however. Large guns cast at Bellona were floated downriver to Tredegar for finishing, sighting, and testing. Bellona manufactured only 8-inch, 9-inch, and 10-inch guns, of which an estimated 135 were produced.

The central government tried to manufacture cannons also at arsenals in Augusta, Columbus, and Macon, Georgia; Charleston, South Carolina; and Selma, Alabama. The importance of this effort was magnified by the loss, owing to Federal occupation of parts of Louisiana and Tennessee, of small private manufactories that had furnished cannons early in the war.

The Federal arsenal at Augusta was seized by the South at the beginning of the war, and cannon production began there late in 1862. A circular issued by the Ordnance Department in November stipulated that production be restricted to 12-pound Napoleons and Parrott rifles. This arsenal turned out about 130 guns, probably all Napoleons.

Columbus became the site of an arsenal when the Confederates moved a facility at Baton Rouge to a safer location after the Federal occupation of New Orleans. Authorities acquired the Columbus Iron Works and set about making cannons, with deliveries beginning in March 1863. Production at this facility, destined for western armies, was limited to the 4.62-inch, 12-pound Napoleon, although a small number of brass 9-pounders were also cast, raising total production to about eighty pieces.

The Macon arsenal began in April 1862 with the purchase of the Findlay Iron Works. Production here was restricted to Napoleons and Parrott rifles in accordance with the Ordnance Department circular of November 1862. Fifty-six Napoleons and eighteen Parrotts, 10- and 20-pounders, were cast at Macon.

Charleston arsenal produced a considerable amount of artillery and small arms ammunition. Production of guns was quite small, about twenty to thirty at best, and only Napoleons are known to have been made there.

The Selma foundry was a different matter. The facility began as a private enterprise and was taken over by army and navy authorities on a joint basis. Initial construction proved problematic, and the Navy Department took control on June 1, 1863. Casting of cannons finally began that summer. The name of the installation was changed to the Selma Naval Gun Foundry, but no guns had been accepted

by the fall of 1863, all having been condemned. January 1864 found the facility nearly complete and 7-inch Brooke rifles being finished for armament of the ironclad CSS *Tennessee*. In early 1864 a number of 6.4-inch and 7-inch Brooke rifles were finished, but bursting guns proved troublesome. Production at the factory was continually hampered by poor materials and a lack of skilled labor. Of the 450 men employed, at least 300 were unskilled slaves. Nevertheless, the factory managed to produce some guns before the place was captured April 2, 1865. It would appear that at least 102 Brooke guns (6.4-inch, 7-inch, 10-inch, and 11-inch), twelve 30-pound Parrott rifles, nineteen mortars, and twenty experimental 6-pounders were made during the fifteen months of operation. At least a third of the Brooke guns were for the navy.

Private gun makers contributed to cannon production during the early months of the war. Most were small foundries with limited skills and facilities. Federal occupation terminated much of this production.

During 1861 and until the occupation of New Orleans by Federal troops on April 26, 1862, much ordnance activity took place in that city. The firms of Bennett and Lurges, Bujac and Bennett, John Clark & Company, Leeds and Company, and S. Wolff & Company produced some types of artillery. Bennett and Lurges, also known as the New Orleans Foundry and Ornamental Works, manufactured

CONFEDERATE NAPOLEON GUNS.   These bronze, smoothbore, 12-pound field guns were captured by Federals at Missionary Ridge, Tennessee. Stenciled on the trail of the nearest and the third gun is "Macon Arsenal 1863."

NATIONAL ARCHIVES

twelve or thirteen guns, five 8-inch Columbiads, and eight 6-pound guns before the city fell. Bujac and Bennett products were known for their poor quality, with the twenty Parrott rifles and six 32-pounders the firm turned out being prone to burst. Clark was very active the summer of 1861, manufacturing brass 6-pounders and 12-pound howitzers of excellent quality. The company had delivered over one hundred guns by March 1862.

Leeds was the largest foundry in New Orleans. The company delivered forty-nine guns, variously 6-pounders, 6-pound rifles, 12-pounders, and 12-pound Napoleons. Wolff set up his foundry at a personal cost of $100,000. The foundry never really got started and finished only six fieldpieces and one 10-inch mortar. The estimated output of all the New Orleans makers was about two hundred guns at best, and none was of the latest pattern. These early guns had been replaced by Napoleons and Parrott rifles by late 1863.

The firm of T. M. Brennan & Company of Nashville, Tennessee, was an active source of ordnance until that city was occupied by Federal troops February 25, 1862. Also known as the Claiborne Machine Works, the firm manufactured iron guns of excellent quality. A total of seventy-one 6- and 12-pounders were delivered to western armies.

Quinby & Robinson of Memphis, Tennessee, produced some of the best guns made in the western Confederacy. A total of seventy-seven were delivered before Federal troops occupied this city June 6, 1862. During the preceding weeks, the firm had sent much of its material down to Columbus, Mississippi, but production was never resumed. Quinby & Robinson products were primarily 6-pounders, 12-pound Napoleons, 12- and 24-pound howitzers, and some 24-pound iron guns. Also in Memphis was the foundry of Street, Hungerford & Company. Its guns were of poor quality, and many burst during use. Some 32- and 64-pound heavy guns were made along with ten small Hughes breech-loading 1-pound guns. Three Parrott rifles of unknown caliber were also delivered. Production was limited to about twenty guns in all.

Noble Brothers & Company of Rome, Georgia, produced fifty-eight fieldpieces and six 8-inch siege howitzers before problems with ordnance inspectors and the Union sympathies of one of the principals impelled the government to confiscate the plant and move most of the machinery to Augusta. From April 1861 until October 1862 the company delivered a variety of iron ordnance including 3-inch rifles, 6-pound rifles, and 12-pound howitzers.

A. B. Reading & Brother of Vicksburg, Mississippi, delivered forty-five brass guns between December 1861 and April 1862. Most were 6-pounders and 3-inch bronze rifles. It appears that production terminated over a year before Federal troops took the town. The firm of J. R. Young & Company of Huntsville, Alabama, also produced some

guns before that city fell to Northern troops on April 11, 1862. Total production may have reached ten pieces. Examples of guns made at the Briarfield Arsenal, Cameron & Company, the Congaree Foundry, A. T. Patterson Company, A. M. Paxton Company, and Skates & Company exist, but production was very limited.

Combined production of the smaller private foundries may have approached 300 guns of all types, and government arsenals fabricated about 475 pieces. Add to these figures the output of Tredegar and Bellona, and Confederate production of artillery totals about 2,100 pieces. By comparison, Federal production was over 6,000 guns, which were consistently superior in quality. Lack of materials and a shortage of skilled labor were the major hampering circumstances in the South.

Ammunition of various types and calibers was manufactured at most of the same establishments. Fabrication of projectiles for smoothbores followed those patterns already in service with production of solid shot, case shot, common shell, and canister. The Mallet polygonal cavity shell was developed in an effort to achieve better fragment dispersion.

Confederate conical projectiles show considerable innovation. Various systems were developed that had no Federal counterpart, such as the Archer, Burton, Mullane, New Orleans, and Selma patterns found in various calibers, although the first three proved ineffective and were discontinued during the war. There were also adaptations of the Federal Hotchkiss, James, Parrott, and Schenkl projectiles. Most used a variation of the expansion cup or forcing cone principle to allow the projectile to "take" the rifling of the gun. Confederate conical projectiles exhibit characteristics such as lathe finishing of bearing surfaces known as bourrelets and copper fuze plugs never seen in Federal service. In the case of larger projectiles a number of heavy armor-punching or crunching bolts were developed along the Brooke, Reed-Parrott, and Selma patterns for naval use against ironclads at point-blank range.

A lack of reliable fuzes was a problem that was never resolved. The Girardy percussion fuze was developed, but it came too late and never received wide distribution. The McEvoy fuze ignitor was used to ignite the fuze in conical projectiles independently rather than relying on ignition from flame from the propellant charge. Because of this deficiency, Confederate artillery did not function effectively.

[See also Columbus Naval Iron Works; Selma, Alabama, article on Selma Naval Iron Works; Tredegar Iron Works.]

BIBLIOGRAPHY

Daniel, Larry J., and Riley W. Gunter. *Confederate Cannon Foundries.* Union City, Tenn., 1977.

Dew, Charles B. *Ironmaker to the Confederacy: Joseph R. Anderson and the Tredegar Iron Works.* New Haven, 1966.

Hazlett, James C., Edwin Olmstead, and M. Hume Parks. *Field Artillery Weapons of the Civil War*. Newark, Del., 1983.

Kerksis, Sydney C., and Thomas S. Dickey. *Field Artillery Projectiles of the Civil War, 1861–1865*. Atlanta, Ga., 1968.

Kerksis, Sydney C., and Thomas S. Dickey. *Heavy Artillery Projectiles of the Civil War, 1861–1865*. Kennesaw, Ga., 1972.

Mallet, J. W. "Work of the Ordnance Bureau." *Southern Historical Society Papers* 37 (1909):1–20. Reprint, Wilmington, N.C., 1991.

Ripley, Warren. *Artillery and Ammunition in the Civil War*. New York, 1985.

Wise, Jennings Cropper. *The Long Arm of Lee: The History of the Artillery of the Army of Northern Virginia*. 2 vols. Lynchburg, Va., 1915.

RUSS A. PRITCHARD

Captured U.S. Artillery

In the post–Civil War years, former president Jefferson Davis wrote that "the South had gone to war without counting the cost. Our chief difficulty was want of arms and munitions." That may not have been entirely the case, however.

Under the Militia Act of 1808, substantial numbers of all types of arms including artillery had been transferred to the states and were in the hands of their militias. Besides guns received in this manner, the Confederacy acquired artillery through the seizure of Federal installations in the South, early battlefield recoveries, imports from abroad, and manufacture within the Confederacy.

The guns available to the state militias and those stored at various military academies had been secured primarily through the 1808 act, although there were some private purchases such as Virginia's acquisition of thirteen modern Parrott 3-inch rifles from Northern foundries. The best of the guns transferred under the act were the model 1841 6-pound bronze smoothbore field gun and the model 1841 12-pound bronze howitzer, both veterans of the Mexican War but still in service.

Actually, the seizure of Federal installations in the South netted the Confederacy a wealth of artillery, primarily heavy seacoast models but also a few batteries of field artillery. The guns acquired were four basic types: field artillery consisting of iron and bronze 6- and 12-pound guns; siege and garrison models consisting of iron 12-, 18-, and 24-pound guns; seacoast artillery, big iron 32- and 42-pound guns; and iron navy 32- and 64-pound guns, all smoothbore. Seized installations from Virginia to Texas furnished critical munitions, but it was the capture of the Gosport Navy Yard that proved the most fortuitous.

FEDERAL NAPOLEON GUNS.   Model 1857, 6-pound bronze Napoleons in the captured Confederate fortifications at Atlanta, Georgia. The dirt caked on the wheels of the guns shows that they had been dragged through miles of muddy roads to reach these defensive works at the end of Peachtree Street. The standing figure is one of William Tecumseh Sherman's cavalrymen.   NATIONAL ARCHIVES

PARROTT RIFLE.   A 200-pound Federal rifle photographed by Samuel A. Cooley at Fort Gregg, Morris Island, South Carolina, 1865.
                                                                          NATIONAL ARCHIVES

On April 21, 1861, barely a week after the fall of Fort Sumter at Charleston, Virginia troops occupied the U.S. Navy Yard at Gosport near Portsmouth. There they secured for the South 1,202 gun barrels (tubes) of large caliber, which were either in storage or aboard ships anchored in the yard. The bulk of this lot, 959 tubes, were various models of iron 32-pound smoothbore guns, which became the backbone of Confederate heavy artillery throughout the war. Substantial numbers of 8- and 9-inch guns were also seized plus a variety of other armaments. Such was the impact of this windfall that the Confederate need for siege, garrison, and coastal artillery was temporarily satisfied, and initial efforts to manufacture artillery could focus on the fabrication of field guns.

Southern troops also seized 1,750 cannons to add to an estimated 400 guns of smaller caliber already in state hands, 296 of them in Virginia alone. The same seizures secured some 282,149 pounds of old but usable cannon powder at Gosport, another 50,000 pounds at other sites,

sufficient ammunition for 60 field guns at Baton Rouge, and literally tons of projectiles. It appears that the Confederate artillery began the war with over 2,000 guns, most of them not of current pattern but certainly serviceable and of the same type with which Northern forces were then armed.

Early battlefield recoveries proved to be the best source of current-pattern artillery for Confederate forces. Sites of the Seven Days' Battles around Richmond were carefully gleaned. Later, after the Battle of First Manassas, officers reported capturing twenty-seven guns—one Parrott 30-pound rifle with 300 rounds of ammunition, nine Parrott 10-pound rifles with 900 rounds, nine James brass rifles with 900 rounds, three brass howitzers with 300 rounds, two brass boat howitzers with 200 rounds, and three brass 6-pound guns with 600 rounds. Of five Federal batteries that crossed Bull Run Creek, not one gun escaped.

At Harpers Ferry in September 1862, Confederate forces captured all the guns of the garrison—forty-nine fieldpieces and twenty-four mountain howitzers, a total of seventy-

MODEL 1845–1847 32-POUNDER. A good example of Confederate adaptive repair of damaged Federal ordnance, this
U.S. Navy gun has its barrel cut back and its breech banded.   LIBRARY OF CONGRESS

three guns with accoutrements and ammunition. And in
June the next year at Winchester, the captured field
artillery enabled the whole Second Corps of the Army of
Northern Virginia to complete its equipment. Almost every
gun in its batteries had been captured from the Federals.

The workhorse of the early war was the model 1841
bronze 6-pound field gun. These guns used a variety of
ammunition of standard types—shot, shell, spherical case,
and canister. In an effort to upgrade their performance,
workers rifled many of them just before and during the war
with a system of rifling developed by Gen. Charles Tilling-
hast James. These guns are sometimes called James rifles,
which is a misnomer. Actually, the guns were rifled
6-pounders that used the conical James projectile, either
bolt, shell, or canister.

Of all the captured field artillery pieces, two guns were
especially favored. These were the model 1857 field gun, a
bronze 12-pound smoothbore nicknamed the "Napoleon,"
and the model 1861 Ordnance rifle, an iron gun with 3-inch
rifled bore sometimes called the Griffen or Rodman gun, the
last also a misnomer. (It should be noted that many sources
use the terms *brass* and *bronze* interchangeably when
referring to field guns. This has become an accepted practice
over the years, but the guns are actually bronze.)

The smoothbore Napoleon, probably the best-known gun
of the Civil War, had a range of some 1,600 yards and fired
shot, shell, spherical case, and canister. The tube weighed
about 1,200 pounds, but mounted on a wooden carriage
drawn by a six-horse team, it was very mobile. The

ammunition chest contained thirty-two rounds—twelve
shot, twelve case, four shell, and four canister—and
weighed about 485 pounds. The gun was sturdy and easy to
maintain. Loaded with canister, the Napoleon was deadly
against massed troops at a quarter of a mile or closer. It was
also a very safe gun for the crew. There are no known
instances of this type of gun bursting in action.

The Ordnance rifle had a range of some 3,900 yards and
weighed about 820 pounds. These rifled guns fired conical
projectiles—bolts (solid), shell, case, and canister—which
were carried in a similar ammunition chest drawn by the
same type of team as the Napoleon. The Parrott rifle,
developed by Robert Parker Parrott, was another iron gun
that saw extensive use in a variety of sizes. The most
common in Confederate service were 10-, 20-, and 30-
pounders, although larger guns were made. The 10-pounder
had the same bore diameter, 3 inches, as the ordnance rifle
and could accommodate the same type of ammunition, a
great convenience in the field.

Another gun seen in some numbers was the model 1841
24-pound bronze field howitzer, which had a bore of 5.82
inches. Again, it used the same ammunition as the 6- and
12-pound guns. Canister of this size was highly effective
against infantry or cavalry assaults on a fixed fortification.
Other rather common fieldpieces included the model 1841
mountain howitzer and the 12-pound Dahlgren boat howitzer. Both guns had the same bore of 4.62 inches and used
the same projectiles as the Napoleon.

In the category of heavy guns, the most common was the

iron 32-pounder found in models 1821, 1829, 1841, 1845, and 1846. Weights of these guns varied from model to model, some short versions weighing about 3,500 pounds and long ones as much as 6,500 pounds. These were the guns so important to Confederate coastal and inland fortification defense. During the war many of these pieces were upgraded by rifling the smoothbore barrel and banding (reinforcing) the breech with a wrought-iron band. So modified, these guns became 6.4-inch rifles, for which a great many Confederate-made projectiles were developed.

A large number of mortars and of other guns of various calibers, large and small, saw service. The Confederates used everything that was available.

There was also a considerable diversity of ammunition for all these guns. Federal ammunition, unquestionably the most reliable, was much preferred because of its fuzing. Confederate-manufactured fuzes were notoriously unreliable. They would detonate prematurely, which endangered the gun crew, or not detonate at all, which was very demoralizing and hampered the effectiveness of Confederate artillery all during the war. This technological problem was never overcome. But necessity forced Confederate Ordnance to try to develop its own ammunition and fuzing because the captured superior ammunition was not always available. A dud rate of over 20 percent was not unusual.

Ammunition for smoothbore guns was relatively uniform by caliber, but that available for rifled guns was not. Patent projectiles and patent fuzes for the 3-inch Ordnance rifle and 10-pound Parrott were produced by Absterdam, Hotchkiss, Parrott, and Schenkl in at least bolt and shell configurations. All were very different, with the Hotchkiss round utilizing a lead driving band and the Schenkl round using a papier-mâché sabot. To further complicate matters, Confederate batteries more often than not comprised mixed-caliber guns, even batteries with only four guns. The study of such projectiles is a field all its own.

There is no question that Confederate artillery was a patchwork amalgamation of widely differing guns. But innovative adaptation and effective, sometimes brilliant, leadership played major roles in overcoming the obstacles. It has often been noted that at the end of the war the roads from Petersburg to Appomattox were blocked by guns with no teams to pull them. It cannot be said that the army surrendered for lack of ordnance.

BIBLIOGRAPHY

Alexander, E. P. "Confederate Artillery Service." *Southern Historical Society Papers* 11 (1883): 98–113. Reprint, Wilmington, N.C., 1990.

Davis, Graham. "Artillery at Southern Arsenals." *Southern Historical Society Papers* 12 (1884): 360. Reprint, Wilmington, N.C., 1990.

Kerksis, Sydney C., and Thomas S. Dickey. *Field Artillery Projectiles of the Civil War, 1861–1865.* Atlanta, Ga., 1968.

Kerksis, Sydney C., and Thomas S. Dickey. *Heavy Artillery Projectiles of the Civil War, 1861–1865.* Kennesaw, Ga., 1972.

Ripley, Warren. *Artillery and Ammunition in the Civil War.* New York, 1985.

Steuart, Richard D. "The Long Arm of the Confederacy." *Confederate Veteran* 35 (1927): 250–253. Reprint, Wilmington, N.C., 1985.

Thomas, Dean. *Cannons: An Introduction to Civil War Artillery.* Gettysburg, Pa., 1985.

Wise, Jennings Cropper. *The Long Arm of Lee; or The History of the Artillery of the Army of Northern Virginia.* 2 vols. Lynchburg, Va., 1915.

RUSS A. PRITCHARD

Imported English Artillery

As armed hostilities erupted, the Confederacy was faced with acute shortages of military supplies, particularly small arms and artillery. This critical problem was compounded by the South's inability to manufacture adequate stores.

To augment limited quantities of field and heavy artillery captured at former U.S. arsenals and fortifications, the Confederacy turned to the European market. Throughout the war, Great Britain was a prime supplier of artillery and munitions, although some French and Austrian field pieces were also imported through the blockade.

In England, Confederate purchasing agents were able to secure the most modern types of artillery available at the time. Although the quantity may have been inadequate, the quality was superb. Southern artillerists especially prized the guns manufactured by Armstrong, Blakely, and Whitworth.

Perhaps the most famous of the English manufactured artillery were the Whitworth guns. The concept created by Joseph Whitworth initially involved a rifled musket with a hexagonal bore that fired a hexagonal bore-shaped projectile. Although his rifled musket was not accepted by the British government, in the late 1850s he continued to refine and apply the proven concept to artillery. The best known of his hexagonal-bore cannons was the 12-pounder with 2.75-inch bore, which could be fired as a muzzleloader or breechloader.

Other hexagonal-bore Whitworths ranged in caliber from the tiny 3-pounder (1.65-inch) and 6-pounder (2.15-inch) to siege and heavy cannons such as the 32-pounder (3.75-inch), 80-pounder (5.0-inch), and 120-pounder (6.4-inch). Reports concerning the deployment of Whitworth guns around Charleston, Fort Fisher, and Gettysburg, for example, are found in the *Official Records of the War of the Rebellion* (1880–1901).

The Whitworth cannon may have been the most famous, but more commonly imported and employed in larger numbers were the guns manufactured by Capt. Alexander Theophilis Blakely, especially 12-pounder muzzle-loading

WHITWORTH RIFLE. Breech-loading 2.75-inch (12-pound) rifle.   NATIONAL ARCHIVES

rifles (3.5- and 3.6-inch). Various dome-shaped projectiles with soft lead sabot cups to expand into the rifling grooves have been excavated at sites in the western theater, the Deep South, and areas associated with the Army of Northern Virginia. Larger Blakely guns used during the war included the siege and heavy calibers of 4-inch, 6.4-inch, 7-inch, 7.25-inch, 8-inch, and a huge 12.75-inch gun that protected Charleston's inner harbor. Projectiles excavated in Virginia reflect Confederate usage of a 2.5-inch Blakely rifle, and shells recovered at Helena, Arkansas, were fired from a 3-inch Blakely rifle, although which side used this rifle is uncertain.

A few Armstrong 3-inch rifled guns were known to have been imported. Like some Whitworth cannons, Armstrongs were manufactured in both breech-loading and muzzle-loading versions. The breech-loading model appears to have used a conical projectile with a wide lead compression sabot covering much of the shell body. A cache of these was excavated in Virginia in the early 1960s. A second type of 3-inch projectile, also used in most larger-caliber guns, had a series of protruding pegs or shunts on the projectile body that matched and engaged the grooves of the rifled bore. Armstrong also produced 70-pounder (6.4-inch) and 150-pounder (8.5-inch) rifled cannons that saw service during the war.

The British-produced cannons were comparable to any made in the United States and probably were more technologically advanced. While their superior accuracy was a distinct asset to the Confederacy, ammunitions shortages due to the blockade of Southern ports and substandard Confederate-produced projectiles and fuzes often handicapped the potential of the imported Whitworth, Blakely, and Armstrong guns.

BIBLIOGRAPHY

Bartleson, John D. *Civil War Explosive Ordnance, 1861–1865*. Washington, D.C., 1972.

Dickey, Thomas S., and Peter C. George. *Field Artillery Projectiles of the American Civil War*. Atlanta, 1980.

Kerksis, Sydney C., and Thomas S. Dickey. *Field Artillery Projectiles of the Civil War, 1861–1865*. Atlanta, 1968.

Kerksis, Sydney C., and Thomas S. Dickey. *Heavy Artillery Projectiles of the Civil War, 1861–1865*, Atlanta, 1972.

Ripley, Warren. *Artillery and Ammunition of the Civil War*. New York, 1970.

C. A. HUEY

ASHBY, TURNER (1828–1862), brigadier general. Born October 23, 1828, at Rose Bank, near Markham in upper Faquier County, Virginia, Ashby demonstrated his horsemanship talents at an early age by winning top prizes at jousting tournaments. While in his midtwenties, Ashby organized his friends into a cavalry company known as the Mountain Rangers to protect his neighborhood from ruffians accompanying the construction crews of the Manassas Gap Railroad. Following John Brown's raid at Harpers Ferry in mid-October 1859, Ashby's company mustered into

TURNER ASHBY.   LIBRARY OF CONGRESS

the Virginia militia to perform guard and picket duty at Charles Town during the Brown trial and execution.

When civil war erupted sixteen months after Brown's execution, Ashby figured prominently in the plot to capture the Harpers Ferry arms factory and weapons' warehouses. Certain of Virginia's secession vote, Ashby and his brother Richard, along with former governor Henry A. Wise and other conspirators, persuaded Governor John Letcher to order Virginia militia to Harpers Ferry. When the Old Dominion seceded on April 17, Ashby immediately led forces in that direction. Unfortunately for the Virginians, as they awaited reinforcements on Bolivar Heights two miles west of Harpers Ferry, vigilant U.S. regulars torched the arsenal at 10:00 P.M. on April 18, destroying fifteen thousand small arms. Ashby led his cavalry into town too late to save the arsenal, but his men did help extinguish fires in the armory buildings.

While serving at Harpers Ferry during the spring of 1861, Ashby came under the command of Col. Thomas J. ("Stonewall") Jackson. Jackson assigned Ashby to guard Potomac River fords and bridges from Harpers Ferry fifteen miles downstream to Point of Rocks, Maryland. While in this capacity, Ashby's command assisted Maryland men across the river to join the Confederacy and interrupted Baltimore and Ohio Railroad traffic and the passage of boats on the Chesapeake and Ohio Canal. In addition, Ashby convinced Jackson and Jackson's successor at Harpers

Ferry, Brig. Gen. Joseph E. Johnston, that he should be lieutenant colonel of the newly organized Seventh Virginia Cavalry. On July 23, 1861, Ashby received his official appointment as second in command of the Seventh Cavalry, but he soon exercised control over half the regiment, conducting independent operations away from the regiment's ailing commander, Col. Angus W. McDonald. When McDonald retired in February 1862, Ashby became the Seventh Cavalry's colonel on March 12.

During the summer and early fall of 1861, Ashby's mission was to protect the border counties of the lower Shenandoah Valley and to systematically destroy the Baltimore and Ohio Railroad between Harpers Ferry and Martinsburg. Meanwhile, the Confederate War Departmer.t had authorized Ashby to raise additional cavalry companies and to organize the first Confederate horse artillery (Chew's Battery). By March 1862, Ashby's Seventh Cavalry had ballooned into twenty-seven companies—nearly three times the size of a typical regiment. Such a large force proved impossible to organize and administer, and Ashby's ignorance of drill and discipline further reduced his cavalry's efficiency.

To correct this unpalatable situation, Jackson, in late April, stripped Ashby of his cavalry and ordered it to report to two infantry brigadiers. An indignant Ashby submitted his resignation and threatened to organize an independent command. Jackson quickly backed down, explaining in a letter to Gen. Robert E. Lee, "if I persisted in my attempt to increase the efficiency of the cavalry it would produce the contrary effect as Colonel Ashby's influence, [which] is very popular with his men, would be thrown against me." Jackson continued to object, however, to Ashby's promotion to brigadier general, once stating, "he has such bad discipline and attaches so little importance to drill, that I would regard it as a calamity to see him promoted." Despite Jackson's reservations, Ashby became a brigadier on May 23, 1862.

Although Ashby failed Jackson's discipline tests, the cavalry commander's incessant scouting and screening missions accounted for much of Stonewall's stealth and success during the cross-country movements of the Shenandoah Valley campaign. Yet on two occasions Ashby blundered. The first occurred at Kernstown, when Ashby misinformed Jackson, reporting that a retreating Union column consisted of only four companies of infantry. Jackson subsequently attacked on March 23, and when he encountered James Shields's entire division of nine thousand men, Stonewall was forced to retreat in his only defeat of the war. Ashby's second failure occurred following the defeat of Nathaniel P. Banks at Winchester on May 25. As the routed Federals fled north toward the Potomac, Ashby failed to cut off the Union retreat, primarily because his companies were scattered and many of his troopers were plundering captured wagons. As a disappointed Jackson noted in his official report, "had the cavalry played its part in this pursuit . . . but a small portion of Banks's army would have made its escape to the Potomac."

General Ashby's final role in the Valley campaign occurred as Jackson's army retreated south and east from Harrisonburg toward Port Republic. As the Confederates' rear guard, Ashby had frustrated and delayed Maj. Gen. John C. Frémont's advance in the main valley. On June 6, 1862, however, two miles south of Harrisonburg, the First New Jersey Cavalry, led by Sir Percy Wyndham, rashly attacked Ashby's position on Chestnut Ridge. Ashby annihilated Wyndham's cavalry, but the affair soon produced an infantry engagement. While Ashby was leading the Confederate infantry into action, a bullet from a Pennsylvania Bucktail pierced his heart, killing him instantly.

Though Ashby had lacked skills in military organization and ignored drill and discipline, his scouting abilities, equestrian skills, and reckless daring earned him the soubriquet "White Knight of the Valley," as well as much praise and respect. Stonewall Jackson's report of the Harrisonburg engagement provided an appropriate eulogy for him: "As a partisan officer I never knew his superior; his daring was proverbial; his powers of endurance almost incredible; his tone of character heroic, and his sagacity almost intuitive in divining the purposes and movements of the enemy."

Ashby, originally buried at the University of Virginia cemetery, was reinterred at the Stonewall Cemetery in Winchester in October 1866.

BIBLIOGRAPHY

Ashby, Thomas A. *Life of Turner Ashby.* New York, 1914. Reprint, New York, 1988.

Avirett, James B. *The Memoirs of Turner Ashby and His Compeers.* Baltimore, 1867.

Bushong, Millard K. *General Turner Ashby and Stonewall's Valley Campaign.* Verona, Va., 1980.

Dabney, R. L. *Life and Campaigns of Lt. Gen. Thomas J. Jackson.* New York, 1866. Reprint, Harrisonburg, Pa., 1988.

Neese, George M. *Three Years in the Confederate Horse Artillery.* New York, 1911. Reprint, Dayton, Ohio, 1988.

DENNIS E. FRYE

ASHE, THOMAS S. (1812–1887), congressman from North Carolina. Scion of a distinguished North Carolina family, Thomas Samuel Ashe was born in Orange County July 19, 1812. He was raised in New Hanover (present-day Pender) County, lived briefly in Alabama, and then returned to North Carolina to attend the prestigious Bingham School and the University of North Carolina, from which he graduated in 1832. After studying law, he began practicing in Wadesboro in 1836. A Whig in politics, he represented Anson County in the house of commons in 1842 and in the state senate in 1854. In 1848 he was elected district solicitor and served in that position until 1852. He supplemented his legal practice by engaging in cotton planting and in 1860 owned seventeen slaves and an estate valued at $17,500.

Like most North Carolina Whigs, Ashe condemned the doctrine of secession as both unconstitutional and impractical. He supported the Constitutional Union party in 1860 and continued to oppose disunion after the election. At a Union meeting in December, he spoke out against "the dangerous consequences of secession." The meeting subsequently adopted resolutions declaring Lincoln's election "just cause for serious apprehension and alarm, but not of revolution or disunion." In February 1861 he ran as a Unionist for the state convention and won easily, even though slaves comprised over half of Anson County's population. The delegates never assembled, however, since the voters rejected the convention by a small majority. Although it is sometimes asserted that Ashe was also a delegate to the convention that passed the ordinance of secession in May, he did not serve in that body. Indeed, he emphatically refused to become a candidate, "not wishing to have anything to do with the secession of my State."

Once disunion had become an accomplished fact, Ashe embraced the notion of Southern independence and in the fall of 1861 announced as a candidate for Congress. His district consisted of seven counties in the heavily Whig and Unionist southern Piedmont, and no Democrat entered the race. Instead, four Whigs, all of whom had previously served in the General Assembly, campaigned for the seat. Ashe won the election with only 36 percent of the vote, edging out his closest competitor, Samuel H. Christian, by 181 votes.

During the first session of the First Congress (February 18, 1862–April 21, 1862), Ashe frequently supported the policies of the Davis administration. With Richmond in imminent danger of attack, he joined the vast majority of his colleagues in authorizing the president to suspend the writ of habeas corpus. He also voted in favor of a law providing for the destruction of tobacco and cotton in threatened areas, and he supported the produce loan program. He agreed with the administration's policy of financing the war through the issuance of Treasury notes. In March he submitted a report on behalf of the Judiciary Committee affirming the constitutionality of the notes and the power of Congress to levy a war tax for their redemption.

On the other hand, Ashe was one of the earliest opponents of conscription, believing that it would inevitably lead to "a strong military government." Faced with the possible collapse of the Confederate army as the one-year enlistments began expiring during the spring of 1862, Congress passed a bill drafting all men between the ages of eighteen and thirty-five. Although unwilling to oppose the bill outright, Ashe registered his disapproval by abstaining from the final vote. Like other opponents of conscription, he subsequently favored a policy of liberal exemptions and voted against any further extension of the draft age. He also supported bills to allow conscripts to serve in regiments from their own states and to permit battalions and companies to elect their own officers. For the most part, his voting record on military issues resembled that of the other Whigs in the North Carolina delegation. He was, however, the only North Carolina Whig to endorse the exemption of overseers.

Ashe became more adamant in his opposition to the administration after the first session. Like many other Whigs, he viewed its policies as unconstitutional efforts to enlarge the powers of the central government, particularly the executive, at the expense of the states. In October 1862 he was one of three North Carolinians who voted against a bill reaffirming the president's power to suspend the writ of habeas corpus. He also opposed the tax-in-kind, the arbitrary impressment of private property for military purposes, and the 2.5 percent sales tax on land, slaves, and farm products.

In 1863 Ashe announced himself as a candidate for reelection. By that time, he was an acknowledged member of the Conservative party, which a year earlier had driven the secessionists from power in North Carolina and had elected Zebulon Vance to the governorship. Although united in opposition to the centralizing policies of the Davis administration, the Conservatives were bitterly divided in their attitude toward the war. Ashe was associated with Vance's faction, which supported peace negotiations with the North but believed that the initiative lay exclusively with the president and Congress. The other faction, led by William W. Holden, took a more activist position, sponsoring scores of grass-roots peace meetings during the summer of 1863 and calling for a convention of the Southern states to propose terms of settlement.

Because of the weakness of the pro-administration party within Ashe's district, the two Conservative factions enjoyed the luxury of presenting their case directly to the voters. Holdenites rallied behind Samuel H. Christian, who had been the congressman's chief opponent two years earlier. The original secessionists joined the Vance Conservatives in support of Ashe. During September and October, the two contenders engaged in a vigorous canvass of the district and participated in numerous debates, thereby making the campaign the most hotly contested, widely reported, and closely watched in the state.

Christian unabashedly appealed to the war-weariness of the electorate by emphasizing the carnage, the lack of significant military accomplishments, the deranged state of the currency, the inadequate pay given to soldiers, and the ill treatment that North Carolina had received at the hands of the Confederate government. He laid the blame for this unhappy state of affairs squarely on the shoulders of his opponent and accused Ashe of conspiring with the administration "to take away the rights of the people."

Ashe defended his record in Congress and did his best to distance himself from unpopular administration policies. He justified his early vote in favor of suspending the writ of habeas corpus on the ground of military necessity but averred that he "had long since made up his mind never to vote for its suspension again." He also pointed to his opposition to the tax-in-kind and claimed credit for introducing an amendment that would have exempted the first $1,000 worth of property for each civilian and the first $2,000 for each soldier. In addition, he called attention to his efforts to increase the soldiers' pay. On the other hand, he defended the issuance of Treasury notes and their compulsory funding, arguing that the only alternative was "heavy & burdensome taxes upon the people."

The main differences between the candidates, however, centered on the peace issue. Although Christian denied that a reconstruction of the Union was his ultimate goal, he openly acknowledged that he "preferred it on terms of equality, and with proper guarantees, to subjugation." Implicit in his position was the belief that Southern independence could never be won on the battlefield—that "blood cannot settle this family strife." Thus, he called for a convention of Southern states, which would request an armistice during which the Northern states could initiate a similar convention.

Ashe dismissed his opponent's plan as vague, impractical, and unconstitutional, expressing skepticism as to whether the other Southern states would consent to a convention or whether the North was ready to sue for peace. He also blamed the peace faction for prolonging the war by sponsoring meetings that demoralized the army and encouraged the enemy to believe that the South had lost the will to fight. Although not adverse to negotiations undertaken by proper authorities, he placed his primary faith in a military, rather than diplomatic, solution to the conflict and suggested that the president should wait until a major Southern victory before extending peace feelers.

Notwithstanding the support he received from Vance and other prominent Conservatives, Ashe lost the election, garnering only 37 percent of the vote. His defeat was less a result of voter antipathy to his record in Congress, which was generally anti-administration, than a product of the war-weariness that pervaded much of North Carolina during the fall of 1863. Nor was Ashe the only victim of this widespread disenchantment. Of the six other incumbents who sought reelection that year, three went down to defeat and a fourth came within a few votes of being unseated. Indeed, seven of the state's ten representatives to the First Congress were replaced by Conservatives who took more advanced positions in opposition to the war.

A lame duck during the final session of the First Congress

(December 7, 1863–February 17, 1864), Ashe did not play an active role in its proceedings. He was absent during most of January, when numerous important war measures came to a vote. He once again registered his disapproval of the suspension of habeas corpus in February and reversed his earlier support for the exemption of overseers.

In the bitter contest for the governorship in 1864, Ashe supported Vance over Holden, who by now was agitating for separate state action. Vance carried all but one county in Ashe's district, receiving an overwhelming 97 percent of the vote in Anson County. In December 1864 the Vance Conservatives nominated Ashe for a seat in the Senate to succeed administration supporter William T. Dortch, who did not seek reelection. He easily defeated Edwin G. Reade, the candidate of the Holdenites, but the war ended before his term began. Ashe later claimed that he had not sought the senatorship and that his election had come as a surprise to him.

Despite his opposition to the peace movement, Ashe quickly became reconciled to the outcome of the war. He cooperated with Federal authorities in establishing an effective police force in Anson County and in reconstituting its local court system, and he publicly urged his constituents to take the amnesty oath. Like most Vance Conservatives, however, he opposed Congressional Reconstruction, the enfranchisement of the freedmen, and the state constitution of 1868. That year he ran as the Conservative candidate for governor, even though he was prohibited by the Reconstruction acts from voting. He lost to Holden, the Republican nominee, by a vote of 92,235 to 73,600.

In 1872 he was elected to the U.S. House of Representatives, becoming one of only two Confederate congressmen to represent North Carolina in the national legislature after the war. He was reelected in 1874. As a member of the Judiciary Committee, he played a prominent role in framing the bill that established an electoral commission to resolve the disputed presidential election between Rutherford B. Hayes and Samuel Tilden. He also took an active part in exposing corruption in the Grant administration. He failed to win his party's nomination for a third term. In 1878 he was nominated by the Democrats for associate justice of the state supreme court and was elected without opposition. He was reelected in 1886 but, after a brief illness, died in Wadesboro on February 4, 1887.

BIBLIOGRAPHY

Alexander, Thomas B., and Richard E. Beringer. *The Anatomy of the Confederate Congress: A Study of the Influences of Member Characteristics on Legislative Voting Behavior, 1861–1865.* Nashville, Tenn., 1972.

Ashe, Samuel A. *Biographical History of North Carolina.* 8 vols. Greensboro, N.C., 1905–1917.

Powell, William S. *Dictionary of North Carolina Biography.* 4 vols. to date. Chapel Hill, N.C., 1979–.

Wakelyn, Jon L. *Biographical Dictionary of the Confederacy.* Edited by Frank E. Vandiver. Westport, Conn., 1977.

Warner, Ezra J., and W. Buck Yearns. *Biographical Register of the Confederate Congress.* Baton Rouge, La., 1975.

THOMAS E. JEFFREY

ATKINS, J. D. C. (1825–1908), lieutenant colonel and congressman from Tennessee. The leading member of the Confederate House from Tennessee, John DeWitt Clinton Atkins was a gifted orator and eminent debater with considerable prewar officeholding experience, having sat in both bodies of the state legislature and in the Federal Congress (1857–1859). Elected without solicitation in August 1861 to represent the Ninth District in the Provisional Congress, Atkins, who had served less than three months as lieutenant colonel of the Fifth Tennessee Infantry, was reelected without opposition to the First and Second Confederate Congresses.

While in Richmond, Atkins assumed a conspicuous role, chairing the committees on Post Offices and Post Roads, as well as Ordnance, and serving on the Commerce, and Military and Foreign Affairs committees. He took a nationalist position, often participating in debate and seldom missing sessions, from the day he was admitted as a delegate on August 13, 1861, until March 18, 1865, when the House adjourned sine die. Atkins strongly supported impressment, sought to protect the Confederate currency by prohibiting speculation in gold and silver, and consistently favored reducing the number and categories of draft exemptions, such as those for men over the age of fifty-five and farm owners overseeing fifteen or more workers. Although opposed to the principle of allowing slaves to fight in the Confederate army, Atkins, a slaveholding planter of substantial means prior to the war, reluctantly acquiesced in the proposal as a last resort in February 1865. Generally supportive of the administration's policies and voting on several occasions against the repeal of the February 1862 measure that had suspended the writ of habeas corpus, Atkins nevertheless criticized President Jefferson Davis's handling of fiscal and foreign policy matters. He joined his colleagues in calling for the resignation of Christopher G. Memminger as secretary of the treasury and introduced the resolution that led to the appointment of the Hampton Roads peace commissioners. Moreover, he grew impatient with Gen. Albert Sidney Johnston's efforts in defending Tennessee and preferred the popular Joseph E. Johnston to Braxton Bragg as commander of the Army of Tennessee.

After the war Atkins, his finances depleted and his family residing as refugees in Texas, returned to his farm near Paris, Tennessee, engaged in stock raising, and founded and edited a newspaper. He was elected to five consecutive terms in Congress (1873–1883), was appointed President Grover Cleveland's Indian commissioner (1885–1888), and failed in a bid for the Democratic nomination to the Senate. He was also active in Confederate veterans' activities and was a popular Lost Cause lecturer and reunion speaker.

BIBLIOGRAPHY

"Hon. J. D. C. Atkins." *Confederate Veteran* 17 (1909): 607. Reprint, Wilmington, N.C., 1985.

Journal of the Congress of the Confederate States of America, 1861–1865. Washington, D.C., 1904–1905.

Porter, James D. *Tennessee.* Vol. 8 of *Confederate Military History.* Edited by Clement A. Evans. Atlanta, 1899. Vol. 10 of extended ed. Wilmington, N.C., 1987.

Speer, William S., ed. *Sketches of Prominent Tennesseans.* Nashville, Tenn., 1988.

Warner, Ezra J., and W. Buck Yearns. *Biographical Register of the Confederate Congress.* Baton Rouge, La., 1975.

R. B. ROSENBURG

ATLANTA, GEORGIA. [*This entry is composed of two articles,* City of Atlanta, *which profiles the city during the Confederacy, and* Atlanta Campaign, *which discusses the military action there in 1864. For further discussion of battles mentioned in these articles, see* Andrews Raid; Dalton, Georgia; Kennesaw Mountain, Georgia; Tupelo, Mississippi; Wheeler's Raids.]

City of Atlanta

In 1860, Atlanta, Georgia, was the fastest growing city in the state; only Savannah and Augusta were larger. Four railroads converged in the city, making it the largest rail center south of Richmond-Petersburg. Peachtree, Marietta, Whitehall, and Decatur streets formed the commercial center. Its population included 7,800 whites, 1,900 slaves, and 23 free blacks. Slaves accounted for more than a third of the tax base.

Support industries for the railroads made the city a significant manufacturing center of the Southeast. Four large machine shops produced various kinds of steam engines, railway cars, and castings. The largest factory was the Scofield and Markham Rolling Mill, which specialized in the technologically demanding operations of rerolling iron rails and plates.

Two major newspapers served the city. The *Daily Intelligencer* and the *Gate City Guardian,* soon to be renamed the *Southern Confederacy,* staunchly supported John C. Breckinridge. Numerous other short-lived publications appeared throughout the war. Atlanta's religious life was overwhelmingly Protestant; of the city's thirteen congregations, only one was Roman Catholic. Most Atlantans were either Baptists or Methodists.

Primary and secondary educational opportunities were

PEACHTREE STREET, ATLANTA.   Photographed by George N. Barnard, 1864.

NATIONAL ARCHIVES

limited to family-hired tutors or private schools. The apprentice system served the majority of youths. The tiny Atlanta Medical College was the only institution of higher learning in the city.

In the presidential election of 1860, the city's moderate temperament was not stampeded. Compromise-minded John Bell carried the city with a plurality totaling 48 percent of the 2,230 votes cast, John C. Breckinridge came in second with 37 percent, and Stephen A. Douglas received only 15 percent.

Immediately following the news that Abraham Lincoln was the president-elect, Atlanta witnessed fevered recruiting activity by various militia groups, but on November 12, the mayor spoke to a large crowd at the courthouse, urging caution. Less than two weeks later the state legislature called for ten thousand troops to be raised and for a special state constitutional election to be held on January 2. Secessionists claimed that conditions had reached a point that precluded any compromise or debate. One of the most outspoken moderates, James M. Calhoun, a cousin of John C. Calhoun, was soon elected the city's wartime mayor, however.

The position of the moderates was destroyed when news of South Carolina's secession reached Atlanta in late December. A fifteen-gun salute at sunrise signaled the beginning of a day-long celebration. Similar activity marked Georgia's secession in mid-January.

The city council now actively promoted Atlanta as the perfect site for either the Confederate constitutional convention or the permanent capital of the Southern Confederacy. The "healthful" climate and Stone Mountain's granite failed to lure the Confederate Congress. Amid these unsuccessful attempts, the city welcomed newly elected President Jefferson Davis en route to Montgomery for his inauguration.

In mid-March, Alexander H. Stephens, the vice president of the Confederacy, visited the city, and Atlantans gave him a similar reception. At least fourteen volunteer units now drilled in the city. By August, Fulton County was the "banner county" of the state, having the largest number of volunteers in local units.

News of the firing on Fort Sumter sent Atlanta into another round of frenzied celebration. Citizens of a more realistic mind formed aid and relief associations to support the troops. One of the most prominent relief groups was the Saint Philip's Hospital and Aid Society, sponsored by the local Episcopal church. The city's twenty physicians agreed to treat families of volunteers free of charge. Several professional fund-raisers similarly supported the war effort. They usually contributed half of their gate receipts to the aid and relief associations. One of the most popular performers was the pianist slave "Blind Tom," who always played to packed houses.

Confederate contracts soon had the economy booming. Freight cars and railroad supplies were produced in record numbers. Bakeries turned out hardtack, the staple food of soldiers. Saddles, harnesses, and other cavalry necessities poured from many shops. Spirits of nitre, vinegar, alcohol, artillery fuses, uniforms, knapsacks, rifles, and revolvers were made by scores of firms.

The regional office of the Commissary Department relocated here early in the war, and the city served as headquarters of the state Commissary Department with a former mayor of Atlanta as its commander. The Confederate Quartermaster Department also had its headquarters in the city. Under military supervision, shoe and garment factories became the main source of supply for Braxton Bragg's army. The assistant medical director of the Western Department chose Atlanta for his office. By 1862, numerous hospitals operated in all sections of the city. Despite the heroic efforts of their staffs, however, these institutions were soon unable to care for the ever-increasing number of patients.

As the war continued, lawbreaking grew in direct proportion to the number of able-bodied men called to the front. Petty crime increased dramatically, though major felonies did not escalate nearly as rapidly. Both the municipal and state superior courts regularly had full dockets. Counterfeiting of paper currency constantly plagued the city. By 1862 the council felt the need to create a vigilance committee of twenty-five men to help the police force, constantly understaffed and ineffective, maintain law and order.

In 1862 Union strategy began to focus on Atlanta's railroads. With these lines destroyed, the city would be isolated and of no strategic use to the Confederates. Led by Capt. James J. Andrews, a small band of Federal soldiers disguised as civilians attempted to destroy the Western and Atlantic Railroad. When Andrews's raiders pirated the locomotive General at Big Shanty, Confederates pursued them on the engine Texas. "The Great Locomotive Chase" ended near Chattanooga where most of the Federals were captured and taken to Atlanta for trial as spies. Bragg's response was to declare martial law, but the order was ignored and the city continued about its business.

To provide additional protection for Atlanta, L. P. Grant commenced construction of fortifications around the city. The project was not fully implemented until the following summer when repeated defeat turned Confederate attention toward defensive operations.

Immediately, prices for even the most necessary and crudely made products soared. Flour rose to over twenty-two dollars a sack; shoes that normally sold for four dollars a pair cost over twelve dollars. By the summer of 1864, even these grossly inflated prices would be unimaginable bargains. Desperate women caused a food riot, and barter

ATLANTA FORTIFICATIONS.   Confederate line near the Chattanooga Railroad, looking south.   NATIONAL ARCHIVES

replaced the money economy. Grand juries repeatedly labeled inflation the city's most pressing economic problem.

Along with economic adversity, the city suffered through a series of epidemics. Smallpox, which made its first appearance at the end of 1862, reappeared throughout the war. A scarlet fever outbreak crippled the already weakened health of the populace, and all attempts at curtailing the disease met with failure. In December, fire destroyed the largest military hospital in Atlanta.

Confederate losses in eastern Tennessee and northwestern Georgia drained the morale of the city, whose population had swelled to more than twenty-two thousand. The approach of William Tecumseh Sherman's forces along the Western and Atlantic tracks in the spring of 1864 added to the anxiety. All able-bodied men and boys were ordered to fight under the Army of Tennessee, commanded by Joseph E. Johnston, and defend Atlanta behind Grant's elaborate earthworks. Outnumbered two to one (100,000 Federals; 50,000 Confederates), Johnston prepared for the assault.

The Confederate government ordered most of the machinery and stores of the arsenal removed to more secure locations. The Quartermaster Department and many of the military hospitals were similarly evacuated. President Davis, under great public pressure for a victory, became increasingly impatient with Johnston and replaced him with aggressive John Bell Hood.

On July 20 Hood attacked Sherman at Peachtree Creek but was repulsed easily by the Northerners; Confederate casualties were high. Two days later, he again ordered his troops out of the trenches at the Battle of Atlanta, meeting with his second defeat in three days. Within a week he attacked at the Battle of Ezra Church. So great were Confederate casualties that Hood withdrew into the city and waited for Sherman's next move.

Sherman now laid siege to a city in collapse. Refugees, who earlier had sought haven in Atlanta, fought for space on every Macon-bound train. By the end of August fewer than three thousand Atlantans remained. Nearly every building in the city was damaged by bombardment. Looters roamed at will as exploding shells ripped open stores and homes. Mayor Calhoun met with the city council for the last time on July 18 and municipal government formally ceased to function.

At the end of August, Sherman moved his troops to Atlanta's southside, hoping to cut the last rail line from the city and lure Hood out. For the first time in forty days, Union siege guns did not fire, and Hood ordered an attack at Jonesboro. This was easily repulsed on the last day of

August. Having lost four straight battles and 25 percent of his army in attacks, Hood evacuated Atlanta on September 1.

All Confederate ammunition and military stores that could not be evacuated were destroyed. Shortly after midnight, the city was rocked by a series of explosions as seven locomotives and eighty-one rail cars loaded with military supplies were blown up. At dawn Mayor Calhoun and a group of citizens surrendered the city, and by noon Federal troops occupied Atlanta. Within a few days, Sherman ordered civilians to evacuate, and about 1,700 left under a flag of truce.

Hoping to get Georgia completely out of the war, Sherman proposed negotiating with Governor Joseph E. Brown and Vice President Stephens. Both refused his overture and Atlanta remained an occupied city until mid-November, when Sherman ordered the city's destruction. On November 15 most of the business district, but not the entire city, was burned. A heroic effort by Father Thomas O'Reilly saved some churches, residences, and City Hall from the torch. Sherman began his march across Georgia as the city smoldered.

Despite the widespread destruction, former residents quickly returned. One businessman wrote that the city was only a "dirty, dusty ruin." The city treasury held $1.64 in worthless Confederate currency. In less than a year, however, over 150 stores were open and Atlanta's trade was estimated to be 30 percent greater than before the war. The city's remarkable recovery as part of the New South would earn it national respect.

BIBLIOGRAPHY

Bowlby, Elizabeth C. "The Role of Atlanta during the War between the States." *Atlanta Historical Bulletin* 5 (July 1940): 177–195.

Bryan, T. Conn. *Confederate Georgia.* Athens, Ga., 1953.

Garrett, Franklin M. *Atlanta and Environs: A Chronicle of Its People and Events.* 3 vols. New York, 1954.

Harwell, Richard Barksdale. "Civilian Life in Atlanta in 1862." *Atlanta Historical Bulletin* 7 (October 1944): 212–219.

Key, William. *The Battle of Atlanta and the Georgia Campaign.* Atlanta, 1981.

Knight, Lucian Lamar. *History of Fulton County, Georgia.* Atlanta, 1930.

Kurtz, Wilbur G. *Historic Atlanta: A Brief History of Its Landmarks.* Atlanta, 1929.

Russell, James Michael. *Atlanta, 1847–1890: City Building in the Old South and the New.* Baton Rouge, La., 1988.

RALPH B. SINGER, JR.

Atlanta Campaign

The industrial and railroad heart of the cotton belt South, Atlanta was the focus of the crucial western campaign from May through September 1864 between Federal Maj. Gen. William Tecumseh Sherman and Confederate Gen. Joseph E. Johnston (until July 17) and Gen. John Bell Hood.

The campaign, which opened in the first week of May 1864, was the result of plans laid in February and March. When Ulysses S. Grant was elevated to the rank of lieutenant general and placed in command of all Union armies in February, he pieced together an uncomplicated grand strategy that called for the Army of the Potomac to concentrate on Robert E. Lee's Army of Northern Virginia, while Sherman, with three western armies, concentrated on the Army of Tennessee, then headquartered at Dalton, Georgia, under the command of General Johnston. The simultaneous application of pressure in both theaters would prevent the outnumbered Confederates from shuttling reinforcements between East and West. Grant left the details of the western campaign to his lieutenant, telling him only that he should "move against Johnston's army, . . . break it up and get into the interior of the enemy's country as far as you can."

The largest of Sherman's three armies was the 60,000-man Army of the Cumberland commanded by Maj. Gen. George H. Thomas, the hero of both Chickamauga and Missionary Ridge. Next was the 25,000-man Army of the Tennessee (not to be confused with the Confederate Army of Tennessee) commanded by Maj. Gen. James B. McPherson. The smallest of the three was the 14,000-man Army of the Ohio under John A. Schofield. Altogether, Sherman's forces numbered nearly 100,000 men.

Opposing him at Dalton, Georgia, behind Rocky Face Ridge, was Johnston's Army of Tennessee consisting of 45,000 men organized into two corps—those of William J. Hardee and John Bell Hood. Leonidas Polk commanded a force of 14,000 men in Alabama and Mississippi, which could be called upon in a crisis.

In addition to his numerical inferiority, Johnston suffered from a lack of support in Richmond. Never popular with President Jefferson Davis, Johnston had made himself even more unpopular by declining to attempt an offensive into Tennessee over the winter of 1863–1864, claiming shortages in transport animals, bayonets, food, forage, and other necessities. Though many of Johnston's complaints were justified, his record was such that Davis and his military adviser, Braxton Bragg, were skeptical.

The campaign opened on May 5 when Federal skirmishers drove in Confederate pickets near Tunnel Hill and advanced against Rocky Face Ridge. The Confederate defenders at Mill Creek Gap west of Dalton had no trouble holding their positions, but six miles to the south at Dug Gap, the Twentieth Corps of Joseph ("Fighting Joe") Hooker threatened to push past two small Arkansas regiments. Johnston sent the crack division of Patrick Cleburne to the threatened point, and the Federals withdrew.

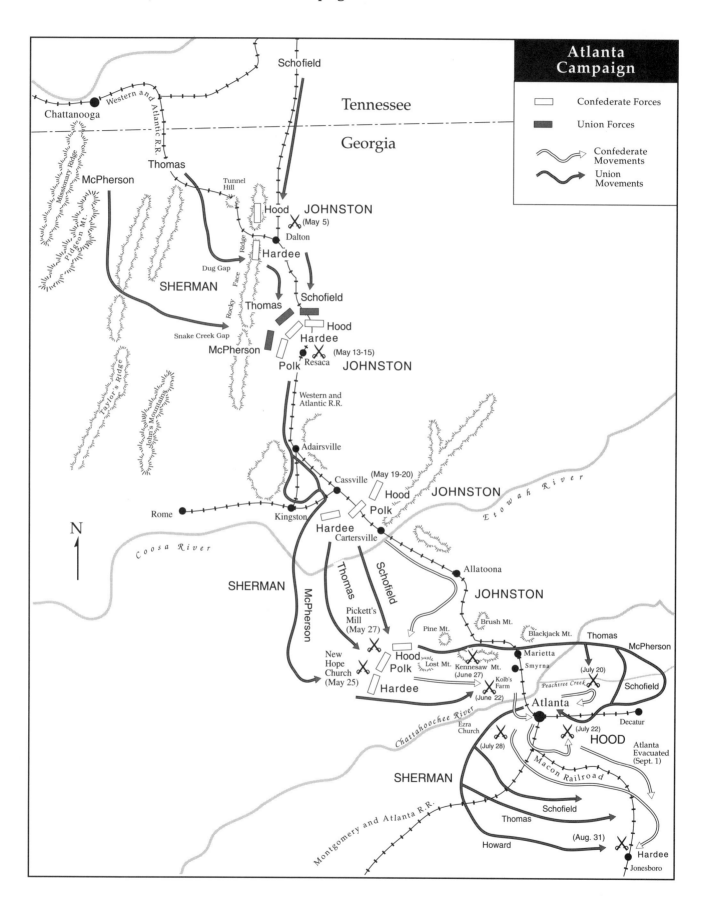

During the fighting near Dalton, McPherson's Army of the Tennessee embarked on a roundabout march to cut the Confederate army off from its line of transportation—the crucial Western and Atlantic Railroad. Johnston knew that there were Federal forces on the move behind the front, but he did not know in what numbers. This was mainly due to his inferiority in cavalry: his cavalry commander, Joseph Wheeler, was reluctant to expend his troopers in reconnaissance missions.

McPherson's troops passed through Snake Creek Gap eighteen miles south of Dalton on May 9 and advanced on the town of Resaca, defended by two Confederate brigades (about 1,400 men) under James Cantey. Though vastly superior in numbers, McPherson decided not to launch a direct assault and instead pulled back to await reinforcements. Johnston now faced threats from two directions. The main body of Federals continued to pound away at his lines on Rocky Face Ridge, and McPherson's army threatened his line of communications at Resaca. Uncertain which of these constituted the main Federal effort, Johnston waited until May 12 before taking the rest of the army south to join Cantey at Resaca. That day, he learned that Sherman was at Snake Creek Gap, and he decided that Resaca was the site of the principal Federal effort.

The Battle of Resaca (May 13–15) was a meeting engagement: as the Confederates moved into position behind Camp Creek, the Federal army was forming in front of them. The battle commenced in midafternoon on May 13 and lasted until nightfall with neither side gaining an advantage. The fight continued the next day, and that evening the divisions of Alexander P. Stewart and Carter Stevenson attacked the Federal left. Their attack drove the enemy several miles and was halted only by nightfall.

The arrival of Leonidas Polk's Army of Mississippi gave Johnston a third corps and raised his effective strength to 60,000. He planned to renew the attack the next day (May 15), but reports that the Federals had gained a toehold on the southern bank of the Oostanaula River convinced him that he would have to evacuate Resaca in order to protect his line of communication. That night his army conducted the first of several evacuations. Confederate losses at Resaca were 500 killed, 3,200 wounded, and 1,400 missing. Federal casualties were more than 900 killed and 5,600 wounded.

Sherman's move around Johnston's left flank at Dalton and Resaca set a pattern for the campaign. With his superiority of numbers, Sherman kept Johnston's army pinned within its defensive line by a frontal assault and then sent a column around the flank attempting to cut the Western and Atlantic Railroad. Each time Johnston fended off the attack and blocked the probe, but each time he had to surrender territory to do so.

From Resaca, Johnston retreated first to Calhoun and then to Adairsville, ten miles to the south. There, he hoped, the narrow valley would allow his army to use the hills to the east and west to secure his flanks while he confronted the Federals. But investigation revealed that the valley was too broad and the hills too low to make such a plan feasible. Instead Johnston determined to ambush part of the Federal army. South of Adairsville, the road forked with one branch heading due south to Kingston and another southeast to Cassville. By dividing his forces, Johnston anticipated that Sherman would do the same in pursuit. Johnston planned to unify his forces near Cassville and ambush whatever forces Sherman assigned to the Cassville road.

On May 19 all the Confederate forces were in position before first light, and Johnston issued a stirring call to battle to his troops. But at midmorning Hood, whose corps was assigned the principal role in the attack, reported that there were Federal forces on his flank and he was withdrawing. Johnston had no choice but to pull the army back to a ridge south of Cassville and invite the Federals to attack him. Even that strategy failed, for Hood and Polk argued that the position was vulnerable to Federal crossfire and urged Johnston to withdraw once again. On May 20 the Army of Tennessee conducted yet another evacuation, and the troops' morale fell.

The army halted at Allatoona three miles south of the Etowah River where it rested for three days. The peculiar geography of Allatoona made it a strong defensive site, and Sherman again looked to find a way around Johnston's position. Alerted by Wheeler's cavalry that Sherman had crossed the Etowah to the west, the Army of Tennessee moved westward in the predawn hours of May 24. The next day the armies clashed in the Battle of New Hope Church. The Federals launched five attacks, but each was beaten back. One Confederate soldier confided to his diary, "Such desperate fighting has never been witnessed in this army." The following day, May 27, the Federals tried to move around Johnston's right. At 4:30 in the afternoon Federal forces attacked Cleburne's division in the Battle of Pickett's Mill with similar results.

Calculating that since the Federals were moving to their left, their right might be vulnerable, Johnston asked Hardee to probe the Federal position, thus bringing on the Battle of Dallas (May 28). Hardee sent William Bate's division on a reconnaissance in force, but it was driven back as once again the attackers got the worst of it.

By June 4 it became evident that Sherman was returning to the line of the Western and Atlantic Railroad, and Johnston ordered the corresponding move eastward. The Army of Tennessee took up a position halfway between the Etowah River and Atlanta, anchored on a series of low hills. On one of those hills, Pine Mountain, Polk was killed by an artillery shell on June 14. His corps was given first to W. W. Loring and then to Alexander P. Stewart. When the

Confederate left was turned once again, Johnston withdrew the army about two miles to Kennesaw Mountain.

The Army of Tennessee now occupied a very strong position. Big Kennesaw rises some seven hundred feet above the surrounding countryside and so dominated the area that a Federal infantryman speculated that Providence must have placed it there as a barrier to invasion. Little Kennesaw to the south was less imposing, and farther south the ground gave way so that the Confederate left was again the weak spot. Accordingly, Johnston sent Hood's corps to guard the left and extend the Confederate line. Hood, however, overstepped his orders and ordered an attack against the Federal right in the Battle of Kolb's Farm (June 22). Though Hood reported a victory, he suffered 1,000 casualties while inflicting only 350.

Despite the strength of the Confederate position, Sherman was so frustrated by his inability to come to grips with Johnston, he decided to launch an all-out attack against the Confederate line. He planned a feint against the lines on Kennesaw Mountain and then a massive assault against Confederate forces on the left where the divisions of B. Franklin Cheatham and Cleburne were posted. The Battle of Kennesaw Mountain (June 27) resulted in 3,000 Federal casualties and Confederate losses of only 552.

Despite this victory, Johnston began to argue that the Confederates' only chance was to destroy Federal supply lines. Both armies entrenched daily, making frontal assaults unthinkable—as Kennesaw Mountain proved. Johnston therefore asked President Davis to order Nathan Bedford Forrest's cavalry to operate against Sherman's supply lines. But Davis and Bragg had become even more disenchanted with Johnston. His continuous retrograde movements proved to them that he did not need reinforcements as much as he needed a fighting spirit.

Sherman turned Johnston's left once again a week after the Battle of Kennesaw Mountain, and Johnston retreated to Smyrna (July 3) and then to the Chattahoochee River (July 6). On July 9 Johnston retreated south of the Chattahoochee. He had, in effect, given up the last ditch, and Davis's patience was exhausted. On July 17 he relieved Johnston and appointed Hood, temporarily promoted to the rank of general, to command.

Throughout the spring, Hood had advocated offensive action in a series of letters to Davis, Bragg, and Secretary of War James A. Seddon. Now given his opportunity, he wasted little time. Johnston had told Hood that he planned to attack the Federal army as it crossed Peachtree Creek north of Atlanta. Adopting the idea, Hood sent the corps of Hardee and Stewart to execute it. The Battle of Peachtree Creek (July 20) was disappointing to the Confederates' hopes. Though they attacked aggressively, the battle was not well coordinated, and the Federals fought stubbornly. The Federals lost 1,800 to the Confederates' 5,000.

Two days later Hood sent Hardee's corps to attack McPherson's army east of the city in the Battle of Atlanta (July 22). This time the Confederates inflicted 4,000 casualties on the Federals, including McPherson himself, but they suffered nearly 7,500 casualties of their own, and the battle did not drive the enemy from the gates of the city.

Sherman spent a week trying to cut the city off from its rail connections to the south by means of cavalry raids conducted by Maj. Gen. George Stoneman and Brig. Gen. Judson Kilpatrick. Not satisfied with their indifferent success, he sent McPherson's former army, now commanded by Oliver O. Howard, to threaten the Montgomery and Atlanta Railroad southwest of Atlanta. Hood dispatched Stewart's corps to intercept, and the result was the Battle of Ezra Church (July 28) where once again the Confederates were beaten back with losses more serious than they could afford—nearly 5,000 men as compared to Federal losses of only about 560.

Having lost 17,500 men in three battles, Hood had little choice but to fall back into the city defenses. For a month, Sherman worked his way around the city attempting to cut off its rail communications with the rest of the South. The last battle for Atlanta was fought on August 31 at Jonesboro, fifteen miles to the south, where Hood assailed the Federal right hoping to prevent encirclement of the city. With the failure of that attack, Hood determined to abandon Atlanta, which he evacuated on September 1.

BIBLIOGRAPHY

Castel, Albert. *Decision in the West: The Atlanta Campaign of 1864.* Lawrence, Kans., 1992.

Connelly, Thomas L. *Autumn of Glory: The Army of Tennessee, 1862–1865.* Baton Rouge, La., 1967.

Hoehling, Adolph A. *Last Train from Atlanta.* New York, 1958.

Hood, John B. *Advance and Retreat: Personal Experiences in the United States and Confederate States Armies.* New Orleans, 1880. Reprint, Bloomington, Ind., 1959.

Johnston, Joseph E. *Narrative of Military Operations.* New York, 1874. Reprint, Bloomington, Ind., 1959.

McDonough, James Lee, and James Pickett Jones. *War So Terrible: Sherman and Atlanta.* New York, 1987.

McMurry, Richard M. "Confederate Morale in the Atlanta Campaign of 1864." *Georgia Historical Quarterly* 54 (1970): 226–243.

McMurry, Richard M. *John Bell Hood and the War for Southern Independence.* Lexington, Ky., 1982.

Sherman, William T. *Memoirs of William T. Sherman.* New York, 1875. Reprint, New York, 1984.

Symonds, Craig L. *Joseph E. Johnston: A Civil War Biography.* New York, 1992.

CRAIG L. SYMONDS

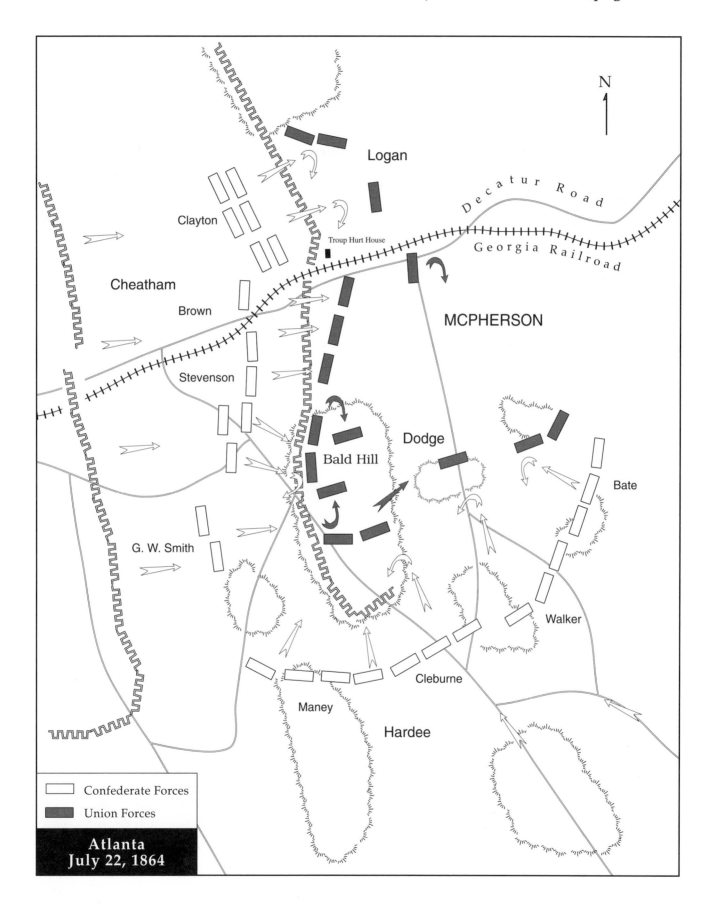

N

Logan

Clayton

Decatur Road

Troup Hurt House

Georgia Railroad

Cheatham

Brown

MCPHERSON

Stevenson

Dodge

Bald Hill

Bate

G. W. Smith

Walker

Cleburne

Maney

Hardee

Confederate Forces

Union Forces

**Atlanta
July 22, 1864**

ATLANTA. The sail–auxiliary propeller steamship *Fingal* was launched May 8, 1861, from the Scottish shipyard of James and George Thomson. The iron-hulled steamer measured 462 tons; 185 feet, 5 inches long; 25 feet, 4 inches wide; and 12 feet, 9 inches depth of hold. *Fingal* was powered by a direct-acting, inverted steam engine. Built for Scottish coastal trade, *Fingal* operated a short time before being purchased by James D. Bulloch and Edward C. Anderson, Confederate agents.

Fingal, with Bulloch and Anderson aboard, left the Clyde River loaded with 11,340 rifles, 12 tons of gunpowder, 2 large Blakely and 2 field artillery pieces, 500 sabers, 230 swords, and other supplies. After an adventurous voyage, the blockade runner entered Savannah, Georgia, on November 14, 1861.

Fingal was meant to be the first of a fleet of Confederate-owned blockade runners carrying arms and supplies from Great Britain to the South, but, trapped in Savannah by Northern blockaders, *Fingal* never ran back out. Instead, the steamer was sent to the shipyard of Nelson and Asa Tift, who converted it into *Atlanta* by building a massive antiramming knuckle around the hull, surmounted by a sloping armored casemate. A ram bow and two 7-inch and two 6.4-inch Brooke rifles made up the ship's armament. On June 17, 1863, Comdr. William A. Webb took *Atlanta* down the Wilmington River to attack the Federal monitors *Nahant* and *Weehawken*. *Atlanta* ran aground, and after firing only seven shots and receiving five in return, Webb was forced to surrender.

The ironclad was condemned by the prize court and bought by the U.S. Navy. After repairs, the ship served in blockading squadrons until the end of the war. *Atlanta* was sold in 1869 to the government of Haiti and renamed *Triumph*. While traveling south, it was lost without a trace off the North Carolina coast.

BIBLIOGRAPHY

Scharf, J. Thomas. *History of the Confederate States Navy from Its Organization to the Surrender of Its Last Vessel.* 2 vols. New York, 1887. Reprint, New York, 1977.

Silverstone, Paul H. *Warships of the Civil War Navies.* Annapolis, Md., 1989.

Still, William N., Jr. *Savannah Squadron.* Savannah, Ga., 1989.

Wise, Stephen R. *Lifeline of the Confederacy: Blockade Running during the Civil War.* Columbia, S.C., 1988.

KEVIN J. FOSTER

ATTORNEY GENERAL. *For discussion of the duties and functions of the Confederate attorney general, see* Cabinet; Judiciary. *For biographies of the Confederate attorneys general, see* Benjamin, Judah P.; Bragg, Thomas; Keyes, Wade; Watts, Thomas H.

AUSTIN, TEXAS. Founded in 1839 on a site on the Colorado River selected by a commission, Austin was the capital city of the Republic of Texas. When Texas joined the Union in 1845, Austin remained the seat of government, one of the two main props of the local economy. Agriculture and the businesses that served the surrounding farming country composed the other.

The city's population in 1860 totaled 3,494 people, of whom the census reported 2,505 were white, 977 were slaves (owned by about one-third of the white families), and 12 were free blacks.

During the secession winter, sentiment against disunion was stronger in Austin than in any other city in the state. "I am ashamed to say," a resident wrote in her diary, "that Austin is a scandalously Yankeefied Union-loving town." Unionists formed the Austin Association for Maintaining Our Rights in the Union, which held parades and circulated petitions. Opponents of secession included some of the city's most prominent and respected residents, such as Governor Sam Houston, Elisha Pease, a former Texas governor, and Thomas H. Duval, a Federal judge. When a referendum was held on secession, Travis County, of which Austin is the seat, opposed disunion by a vote of 704 to 450.

But it was the sentiment of the state as a whole, of course, that was reflected in the historic steps taken in Austin in early 1861. On February 1, a convention of the people of Texas meeting in the state capitol adopted an ordinance cutting the state's ties to the Union. After their action was ratified by the voters of the state, the convention reassembled in March to complete the work of joining the Confederacy.

The number of open Unionists in Austin dwindled once the war began, but they never disappeared entirely. Some, like Duval, left the state when conscription loomed. Others, like Pease, remained in the city during the war. They were required to carry passes but otherwise were seldom molested.

At the beginning of the war, the city temporarily "assumed a martial appearance," in the words of one resident, as enthusiastic volunteers formed themselves into such units as the Austin City Light Infantry Company, the Austin City Light Artillery, the Travis Rifles, the Tom Green Rifles, Terry's Texas Rangers, and the Quitman Rifles. They could be seen training in various parts of town for a few weeks, and then they marched away to make names for themselves in engagements that almost always occurred far from Texas.

In addition to manpower, Austin contributed ordnance to the war effort. A cartridge factory and a percussion cap factory began operating on the grounds of the capitol. A few blocks to the south, a cannon foundry produced light artillery. On Cypress Creek, eighteen miles northwest of town, Thomas Anderson manufactured gun powder at his mill.

No other Confederate state capital was as remote from the theaters of war as Austin. There was no telegraph, and railroads approached no nearer than Brenham, a hundred miles to the east. Most Austinites experienced the war as waiting for news that made its way to their city with excruciating slowness—it took ten days, for example, for the news of the surrender of Vicksburg to reach town. They then had to wonder whether the news was true. The local press continually presented misinformation as fact, such as reporting the death of Gen. William Tecumseh Sherman at Shiloh, the removal of the Confederate capital from Richmond to Charleston, and the destruction of Ulysses S. Grant's army at Vicksburg. During the peninsula campaign in Virginia in 1862, Austin got "drunk with excitement," a resident recorded, celebrating the false news that George B. McClellan had surrendered to Robert E. Lee. The Confederate capture of Cincinnati, Ohio, another event that never occurred, set off a cacophony of bells and cannon. Stories of overwhelming Confederate victories inflicting enormous casualties upon the enemy were regular journalistic fare. If the newspaper numbers were to be believed, an Austinite joked cynically at one point, the Union army had suffered more than 27 million casualties so far in the war.

A more subtle problem than outright errors was the misproportion of news. One could not have learned from the wartime Austin press that there had been a major battle at Sharpsburg in September 1862. In contrast, the Union's futile Red River campaign in 1864 received detailed attention because it was an important psychological watershed for Austinites. At least since the Union occupation of Galveston in late 1862, residents had lived in expectation of an imminent, full-scale invasion of the state and a move to occupy the capital city. Earthen fortifications were constructed on the outskirts of town. The repelling of the Federal initiative at Red River removed fears that Texas was marked for invasion and thus produced immense relief. The sense of delivery, however, was tempered by sadness. Killed leading a cavalry charge during the campaign was Brig. Gen. Thomas ("Tom") Green, an Austin lawyer whose extensive military service in the Texas Revolution, the Mexican War, and the first three years of the Civil War had made him a local hero. One resident said he had "never witness'd such gloom" as the news of Green's death cast over Austin.

The most chaotic chapter in the history of wartime Austin was the last—the lawless interval between the surrender of the various Confederate armies in the spring and the arrival of occupation forces in July. Governor Pendleton Murrah and other local authorities left town, many of them fleeing to Mexico. Observing their flight, a contractor replacing the capitol roof abandoned his job—with the roof off. The rains that never fail to arrive in such circumstances caused extensive damage to the building's contents, particularly official records. Defeated soldiers returning to town and others looted government supply storehouses, cotton warehouses, and stables, and broke into the state treasury looking for money. Other Confederate veterans organized themselves into a vigilance committee to restore order. Austin had almost returned to its accustomed rhythm by the time Union soldiers reached the city on July 25, 1865, and raised the U.S. flag over the still unrepaired capitol.

BIBLIOGRAPHY

Barkley, Mary Starr. *History of Travis County and Austin, 1839–1899*. Waco, Tex., 1963.

Gage, Larry Jay. "The City of Austin on the Eve of the Civil War." *Southwestern Historical Quarterly* 63 (1960): 428–438.

Humphrey, David C. *Austin: An Illustrated History*. Northridge, Calif., 1985.

Humphrey, David C. "A 'Very Muddy and Conflicting' View: The Civil War as Seen from Austin, Texas." *Southwestern Historical Quarterly* 94 (1991): 369–414.

Willoughby, Larry. *Austin: A Historical Portrait*. Norfolk, Va., 1981.

GEORGE B. FORGIE

AVERASBORO, NORTH CAROLINA.

Averasboro was the site of a battle fought on March 16, 1865. Although the fighting was heated, the battle had little significance beyond slowing the advance of Gen. William Tecumseh Sherman and thus paving the way for the Battle of Bentonville.

By March 1865 Sherman had moved his Union army north from Savannah, Georgia, through Columbia, South Carolina, and into North Carolina. His objective, in addition to the destruction of Southern resources and spirit, was the town of Goldsboro, which had important railway connections to the coast. Foraging as they went, the sixty thousand troops in Sherman's command traveled in two columns; Maj. Gen. O. O. Howard commanded the right wing, and Maj. Gen. Henry W. Slocum the left.

To oppose this formidable army, Confederate Gen. Joseph E. Johnston had troops from the Army of Tennessee, the Department of South Carolina, Georgia, and Florida, and all "the troops serving in North Carolina." These forces, if they could be brought together, amounted to no more than thirty thousand men, but Johnston had considerable artillery and strong cavalry forces under Gen. Wade Hampton. Johnston hoped to concentrate his forces and fall upon one of the two wings of Sherman's army.

As Sherman moved northeast from Fayetteville toward Goldsboro, he knew that Confederate forces were concentrating, and therefore he tried to keep his columns close together. Johnston positioned troops under Gen. Braxton Bragg at Smithfield. Gen. William J. Hardee's forces moved ahead of Sherman's army, falling back until they could see whether the Federals were moving on Raleigh or Goldsboro. Then either Bragg or Hardee would reinforce the other.

On March 15 the Federal cavalry under Brig. Gen. Judson Kilpatrick encountered Hardee's troops near the village of Averasboro. Although Hardee had less than six thousand men, he decided to fight in order to ascertain the strength of the Federal forces and their destination. After skirmishing on the first day, a sharp engagement took place on the sixteenth.

Initially the Eighth Indiana Cavalry drove Confederate skirmishers back into their works, but then Southerners of Brig. Gen. William Booth Taliaferro's division attacked in force. Timely reinforcements and effective artillery fire saved Kilpatrick's dismounted cavalrymen and drove the Confederates back to a second line of defense. Pressing forward, Federal troops of the Ninth Ohio tried to turn the Confederate left but were stymied by strong resistance from troops of Gen. Lafayette McLaws's division. Fighting continued all afternoon and into the evening, but the Federal troops were unable to take the Confederate works. That evening Hardee withdrew his forces toward Smithfield, as General Johnston had ordered.

Union commanders reported 682 casualties, of which 533 were wounded. All these wounded men had to be carried in ambulances, a noticeable burden for Sherman's moving army. Johnston stated that the Confederate casualties totaled 450, although scholars' estimates run as high as 845. Morale in the Southern ranks rose sharply despite these losses, because the men felt they had met and matched their foe. The battle, however, was in no way decisive. Its main significance lay in the fact that Hardee's resistance had slowed the advance of Sherman's left wing while his right wing continued toward Goldsboro. This fact gave Johnston hope of isolating and crushing one of the Federal columns.

BIBLIOGRAPHY

Barrett, John G. *The Civil War in North Carolina.* Chapel Hill, N.C., 1963.
Davis, Burke. *Sherman's March.* New York, 1980.
Glatthaar, Joseph T. *The March to the Sea and Beyond.* New York and London, 1985.

PAUL D. ESCOTT

AVERY, WILLIAM WAIGHTSTILL (1816–1864), congressman from North Carolina. Avery was born on his parents' Burke County, North Carolina, plantation May 25, 1816. A graduate of the University of North Carolina (1837), he studied law, was admitted to the bar (1839), and established his practice in Morganton, North Carolina.

Between 1842 and 1860 he served several terms in his state's legislature where he was recognized as a stout state rights Democrat. He headed his state's delegation to the Democratic National Conventions of 1856 and 1860. In the latter he was chairman of the Committee on Resolutions; but he and his colleagues did not join other Southern states in walking out when the convention adopted a popular sovereignty plank instead of a strongly proslavery minority report. Subsequently when the deadlocked convention reassembled in Baltimore, however, Avery and his delegation, along with other slave state delegations, withdrew and nominated John C. Breckinridge for president.

After the firing on Fort Sumter, North Carolina's secession convention took the state out of the Union on May 20, 1861, and selected Avery as one of the state's members of the lower house of the Confederacy's Provisional Congress. There he served until that body was succeeded, in February 1862, by the permanent Confederate legislature. In the temporary House he quickly distinguished himself as an impassioned Southern rights Democrat in the older tradition of John C. Calhoun, and he held the post of chairman of the chamber's Committee on Military Affairs.

He returned to private life upon failing to win a seat in the Confederate Senate. The North Carolina General Assembly had passed him over in favor of a less militant secessionist Democrat, William T. Dortch, who was chosen, after several ballots, as a compromise candidate upon whom a combination of the legislature's ex-Whigs and a minority of the Democrats could agree.

Although Avery raised a regiment for the Confederate Army in 1862, he did not accompany it to the field, in part because his sorely beleaguered family objected that its forty-six-year-old head was desperately needed at home. His life was cut short, however, on July 3, 1864, when, as an officer of the Burke County militia, he was fatally wounded leading his men in a skirmish with Tennessee Unionists who had invaded the county to capture a camp of conscripts near Morganton.

Avery was the oldest of five brothers, three of whom achieved the rank of colonel in the Confederate Army's service. Three of the five, including William, died in battle in the space of a single year, and a fourth died shortly thereafter of wounds sustained during the war.

BIBLIOGRAPHY

Watson, Elgiva D. "William Waightstill Avery." In *Dictionary of North Carolina Biography.* Edited by William S. Powell. Vol. 1. Chapel Hill, N.C., 1979.
Yearns, Wilfred B. *The Confederate Congress.* Athens, Ga., 1960.

RICHARD BARDOLPH

AYER, LEWIS MALONE (1821–1895), congressman from South Carolina. Born on November 12, 1821,

near Barnwell, South Carolina, Ayer attended South Carolina College and graduated from the University of Virginia in 1841. He attended Harvard Law School and was admitted to the bar in 1842. In 1846 Ayer began life as a planter and served in the state legislature (1848–1856). In 1856 he led a company of state militia to Kansas to support the proslavery forces.

Ayer was elected to the U.S. Congress in 1860, but the state seceded before he took his seat. He was a member of the secession convention, and in November 1861 he defeated David F. Jamison, president of the convention, for a seat in Congress. In 1863 he defeated Robert Barnwell Rhett, Sr.

In Congress Ayer was a strong advocate of state rights. He backed offensive warfare and opposed peace negotiations. His chief concern was finance. He was chairman of the Committee on the War Tax, proposing in December 1863 that the tax-in-kind be abolished and opposing the repudi-ation of redundant currency. Ayer also opposed giving the central government greater control over army personnel and organization as well as the power to suspend the writ of habeas corpus.

After the war, Ayer became a cotton merchant in Charleston, and in 1868 he returned to Barnwell to manage his 8,000-acre plantation. In 1872 he became a Baptist minister and served churches in Anderson, South Carolina, Texas, and Tennessee. In Anderson he also operated a girls' school (1879–1887) and taught in a military school from 1890 until his death.

BIBLIOGRAPHY

Cyclopedia of Eminent and Representative Men of the Carolinas of the Nineteenth Century. Vol. 1. Madison, Wis., 1892.

Warner, Ezra J., and W. Buck Yearns. *Biographical Register of the Confederate Congress.* Baton Rouge, La., 1975.

A. V. HUFF, JR.

BAGBY, ARTHUR P. (1833–1921), brigadier general and acting major general. Bagby was born on May 17, 1833, in Claybourne, Alabama. He graduated from the U.S. Military Academy in 1852 and served in various garrison assignments, ultimately in Texas. He resigned from the army to study law and was admitted to the bar in his native Alabama in 1855.

Bagby moved to Gonzales, Texas, in 1858, and with that state's secession, was elected major of the Seventh Texas Cavalry. While serving in this regiment, he participated in Gen. Henry Hopkins Sibley's New Mexico campaign, with all the trials and tribulations of that expedition. On January 1, 1863, as the newly promoted colonel of the regiment, Bagby distinguished himself in the March 1864 Confederate recapture of Galveston. His unit served on the frontier until called to Louisiana during the Red River campaign. In this campaign, Gen. Richard Taylor repeatedly referred to Bagby in complimentary terms, especially for action at Mansfield and Pleasant Hill, Louisiana. His character and abilities were so exemplary that Gen. E. Kirby Smith promoted him to major general on May 16, 1865, in recognition of his services.

After the surrender of the Trans-Mississippi Department, Bagby returned to his law practice. He died in Hallettsville, Texas, on February 21, 1921.

BIBLIOGRAPHY

Fitzhugh, Lester N., comp. *Texas Batteries, Battalions, Regiments, Commanders, and Field Officers, Confederate States Army, 1861–1865.* Midlothian, Tex., 1959.

Kerby, Robert Lee. *The Confederate Invasion of New Mexico and Arizona, 1861–1862.* Los Angeles, 1958.

Oates, Stephen B. *Confederate Cavalry West of the River.* Austin, Tex., 1961.

Roberts, O. M. *Texas.* Vol. 11 of *Confederate Military History.* Edited by Clement A. Evans. Atlanta, 1899. Vol. 15 of extended ed. Wilmington, N.C., 1989.

ROY R. STEPHENSON

BAKER, ALPHEUS (1825–1891), brigadier general. Baker was born May 23, 1825, in the Abbeville District, South Carolina. Educated in the law by his father, he was teaching school by the age of sixteen, in Abbeville, Lumpkin, Georgia, and Glenville, Alabama, where he settled. He also taught music and was admitted to the bar in Eufaula, Alabama, in 1849. In 1856, Baker, a Democrat, traveled to Kansas and returned home to arouse people to the importance of Kansas becoming a slave state.

In 1861, Baker was elected to the Alabama constitutional convention, representing Barbour County. He resigned his seat in the convention to enlist as a private in the Eufaula Rifles, subsequently a company in the First Alabama Infantry. Elected captain of the company, Baker led his men to Pensacola. In November 1861, he went to Tennessee and was elected colonel of the Fifty-fourth Alabama Regiment, which he led during the siege and Battle of New Madrid. He was captured at Island Number 10 on April 19, 1862, and imprisoned at Camp Chase and Johnson's Island.

After exchange he became commander of the reorganized Fifty-fourth Alabama and led the regiment during the Vicksburg campaign. Seriously wounded in the Battle of Champion's Hill, Mississippi, May 16, 1863, Baker recovered and was promoted to brigadier general to date from March 5, 1864. Taking command of the Alabama brigade, Baker participated in the Atlanta campaign where he was again wounded at the Battle of Ezra Church on July 28, 1864. After brief service in the Department of the Gulf, his brigade was rushed to North Carolina to participate in the

Carolinas campaign and the Battle of Bentonville March 19, 1865. He surrendered with his troops in North Carolina.

Baker, after the war, practiced law in Eufaula, Alabama. In 1878 he moved to Louisville, Kentucky, where he died October 2, 1891, and was buried.

BIBLIOGRAPHY

Faust, Patricia L., ed. *Historical Times Encyclopedia of the Civil War.* New York, 1986.

Owen, Thomas McAdory. *History of Alabama and Dictionary of Alabama Biography.* Vol. 2. Chicago, 1921.

Wakelyn, Jon L. *Biographical Dictionary of the Confederacy.* Edited by Frank E. Vandiver. Westport, Conn., 1977.

Warner, Ezra J. *Generals in Gray: Lives of the Confederate Commanders.* Baton Rouge, La., 1959.

JOHN R. WOODARD

BAKER, JAMES MCNAIR (1822–1892), congressman from Florida.

Baker, born in Robeson County, North Carolina, graduated from Davidson College in 1844 and practiced law in Lumberton, North Carolina, for the rest of the decade. After a severe bout with typhoid fever, he decided to move to Florida and arrived at Lake City around 1850. He soon became active in political affairs; he was state's attorney for Suwannee County in 1852 and served as judge for that circuit in 1859. A Whig, Baker tried unsuccessfully for a seat in the U.S. Congress in 1856 and supported John Bell for president in 1860. But he became a loyal Confederate after Florida seceded in January 1861.

Baker served for the duration of the war in the Confederate Senate and was an active and effective representative. He supported the Davis administration in the First Congress but opposed it in the Second. He was strongly against conscription and the suspension of the writ of habeas corpus. Baker served on numerous committees—Naval Affairs, Claims, Commerce, Public Lands, Post Office and Post Roads, Buildings, Engrossment and Enrollment—and was highly esteemed by his peers.

After Richmond fell, Baker returned to Florida and resumed the practice of law. He became a Bourbon or Conservative Democrat during Reconstruction and made his greatest professional reputation in land litigation cases. In 1881 he returned to public service as judge of the Fourth Circuit Court. He died in Jacksonville, Florida, on June 20, 1892.

BIBLIOGRAPHY

Rerick, Rowland H. *Memoirs of Florida.* 2 vols. Atlanta, Ga., 1902.

Sifakis, Stewart. *Who Was Who in the Civil War.* New York, 1988.

Wakelyn, Jon L. *Biographical Dictionary of the Confederacy.* Edited by Frank E. Vandiver. Westport, Conn., 1977.

ARCH FREDRIC BLAKEY

BAKER, LAURENCE SIMMONS (1830–1907), brigadier general.

The cavalry in the Army of Northern Virginia boasted some of the most legendary officers in the Confederacy. Its success in raids, reconnaissance, and combat for the first half of the war was due not only to J. E. B. Stuart but to his well-qualified brigade and regimental commanders as well, such as Laurence Simmons Baker.

Baker was born in Gates County, North Carolina, on May 15, 1830, and graduated from West Point in the class of 1851. He rose to the rank of captain in the Third U.S. Cavalry before his resignation in May 1861. Baker began his Confederate service as lieutenant colonel of the First North Carolina Cavalry and was promoted to colonel in March 1862. His regiment served in Stuart's and later Wade Hampton's brigade and participated in the cavalry's campaigns from the Seven Days' Battles through Gettysburg. Hampton and Robert E. Lee both recommended his promotion in the spring of 1863. After Hampton was wounded at Gettysburg, Baker commanded the brigade, was promoted to brigadier general to take rank from July 23, and was himself seriously wounded near Brandy Station in August.

When Baker recovered, he returned to service, though his wound prevented active duty with the cavalry. In June 1864 he was assigned to command a district in the Department of North Carolina and Southern Virginia, headquartered at Goldsboro, and helped organize the defense of eastern North Carolina. Baker, commanding a brigade of reserves, fought at Bentonville in March 1865 and surrendered at Raleigh in May.

He lived in North Carolina and Virginia after the war, was active in the United Confederate Veterans, and was an agent for the Seaboard Railroad for many years. Baker died in Suffolk, Virginia, on April 10, 1907.

BIBLIOGRAPHY

Compiled Military Service Records. Laurence S. Baker. Microcopy M331, Roll 13. Record Group 109. National Archives, Washington, D.C.

Hill, D. H., Jr. *North Carolina.* Vol. 4 of *Confederate Military History.* Edited by Clement A. Evans. Atlanta, 1899. Vol. 5 of extended ed. Wilmington, N.C., 1987.

J. TRACY POWER

BALDWIN, JOHN B. (1820–1873), congressman from Virginia.

John Brown Baldwin's involvement with the Confederacy, although not unimportant, was overshadowed by his experiences during the secession crisis and, subsequently, during Reconstruction.

A prominent lawyer, Baldwin lived his entire life in Staunton, Virginia, the seat of Augusta County, one of the

Whig citadels in a generally Democratic state. He served briefly in the legislature during the 1840s. He lost his seat, however, because he disagreed with the dominant public sentiment in the district, which favored legislative reapportionment on the basis of white population alone rather than on the traditional "mixed" basis that also gave weight to property, thereby favoring eastern Virginia. He campaigned in the 1860 presidential election for the Constitutional Union party, which won a narrow plurality in the state. Soon afterward he was elected to represent his home county in the Virginia convention of 1861.

There Baldwin and George W. Summers of Charleston led the nascent Union party, a coalition of conditional and unconditional Unionists, most of whom were former Whigs. He frequently participated in floor debate and also delivered a prodigious three-day Union oration. The most controversial and significant event in Baldwin's life occurred on April 4, 1861, when he met secretly with President Abraham Lincoln at the White House. Baldwin attempted without success to persuade Lincoln to preserve the peace and enable the upper South to remain in the Union. Never, he recalled, did he "make a speech on behalf of a client in jeopardy of his life, with such earnest solemnity and endeavor." That fateful interview impressed Baldwin as "a subject of more interest to me than anything that ever happened to me."

Baldwin's pro-Union stance was based on a belief that no irrepressible conflict divided North and South, and that few Northerners had any wish to interfere with slavery where it existed. He gave lip service to the idea that slavery as practiced in Virginia was "a right and a good thing," but he denied that the upper South and lower South had identical interests. Secession would, he warned, cut Virginia farmers off from their many Northern customers. Baldwin held out hope that the seceding states could be drawn back into the Union once it became apparent that the upper South would not join their bid for independence. For him, the Constitution contained more than adequate safeguards to protect the rights of slaveholders.

At no point during the critical six-week period between Lincoln's inauguration in early March and his proclamation for 75,000 troops in mid-April did a Southern Unionist in a position of authority have a comparably good opportunity to talk frankly with the new president. The Baldwin interview came about when Secretary of State William H. Seward urgently requested that Unionists in the Virginia convention send a spokesman to meet with Lincoln. Seward concealed from Baldwin the full circumstances that prompted the summons—that Lincoln had decided to risk a resupply mission to Fort Sumter, in the harbor of Charleston, South Carolina, and that peace hung by a thread.

The most plausible version of the discussion between Lincoln and Baldwin suggests that the president greeted the Virginian with the question: "Why do you not adjourn that Convention?"

Baldwin replied that Unionists controlled the convention and could not reasonably adjourn it until some resolution of the national crisis took place. The Virginian followed with a plea that Lincoln remove Federal troops both from Fort Sumter and from Fort Pickens, offshore from Pensacola, Florida, the one other point in the seceded states that remained in Federal hands. Were he then to call a national convention and "settle this thing . . . by consultation and votes rather than by an appeal to arms," Lincoln might hold the upper South in the Union and give antisecessionists there "a stand-point from which we can bring back the seceded states."

Lincoln instead expressed reservations and hinted obliquely that he intended to try to feed the troops at Sumter. "I told him that would not do," Baldwin recalled. Were fighting to occur, Virginia would be out of the Union "in forty-eight hours."

"Oh, sir," Lincoln responded, "that is impossible."

Baldwin retorted, "Mr. President, I did not come here to argue with you; I am here as a witness. I know the sentiments of the people of Virginia and you do not."

Lincoln thereupon told Baldwin, "I wish you had come sooner."

One of the inner circle of Virginia Unionists who debriefed Baldwin soon afterward vividly recalled his horror upon hearing that Lincoln wished Baldwin had come sooner. "I inferred from this remark of Mr. Lincoln, that he had taken a step, inconsistent with the view that you were urging upon him, that would result in war and bloodshed." Baldwin himself, who had gone to Washington "full of hope and confidence" about finding some basis for reaching "an understanding with Mr. Lincoln," returned to Richmond "much depressed and disappointed."

According to Baldwin, Lincoln never offered to evacuate Sumter in exchange for adjournment of the Virginia convention, nor did he make any "overture" or comment from which Baldwin "could infer it." Nevertheless, several days later Lincoln certainly did tell several visiting Virginians, among them the unconditional Unionist John Minor Botts, that Baldwin had summarily rejected an explicit offer to that effect. Botts concluded that Baldwin and his friends conspired to prevent Lincoln's offer from becoming known to the convention. The evidence suggests, however, either that Lincoln gave Botts a misleading version of his interview with Baldwin, or that Lincoln did not say to Baldwin what Baldwin thought he had said.

Virginia's secession and the start of the Civil War further depressed Baldwin. Deploring the "rabid" fever that seized many former Unionists, he voted against secession and predicted that "we are in danger of emerging from this revolution anything but a free people."

Baldwin nevertheless accepted appointment as inspector general of the state volunteers. Soon he was appointed colonel of the Fifty-second Virginia Infantry, raised at Staunton, which he commanded in the Allegheny campaigns in the fall of 1861. While still on duty in November 1861, Baldwin was elected over two opponents to the First Confederate Congress. He was reelected in May 1863, defeating the incumbent Virginia governor, John Letcher, an outcome that indicated popular discontent with the all-consuming war effort.

Baldwin's district encompassed parts of the fertile Shenandoah Valley. Not long after Congress convened in February 1862, the valley became the scene of intense fighting, as Thomas J. ("Stonewall") Jackson attempted to relieve growing Federal pressure on Richmond. For the duration of the war, or at least until Philip H. Sheridan's devastating campaign in the late summer and fall of 1864, Union and Confederate forces swept back and forth through the Shenandoah.

Baldwin, who served from the start of the First Congress in February 1862 until the final adjournment of the Second in March 1865, played an active role in the Confederate House. He held seats on the Committee of Ways and Means in both the First and Second Congresses, and in the latter he was selected to chair a Special Committee on Impressments. He attempted, as a congressman, to provide military and economic protection for his beleaguered constituents. More often than not, he voted to give President Jefferson Davis broad military authority to prosecute the war. At the same time, however, Baldwin sought to mitigate the impact of warfare on the civilian population and to maintain Southern food output, voting to exempt various classes of agricultural producers from military service.

Baldwin took pointed exception to impressment. Commanders in the field routinely impressed farm products to feed their armies. In so doing, they would strip bare an immediate locality rather than spread the burden over a wider area. Even if affected farmers were properly compensated—and often they complained that they were not—impressment caused local shortages and dislocations. In 1864 Baldwin sought to increase the tax-in-kind, which applied broadly to all producers, in order to lessen the inequalities that inevitably accompanied impressment. The shrinking perimeter of Confederate authority and the disintegration of transport doomed efforts to reform the impressment system, however.

Baldwin compiled an anti-administration record on some issues. Like other Union Whigs, he balked at proposals to suspend the writ of habeas corpus, and he opposed authorizing the enlistment of black soldiers. By the last months

of the war in early 1865, he was more ready than most to acknowledge the hopelessness of the war effort and to seek a negotiated surrender.

Baldwin's most conspicuous public role occurred in the years immediately following the war. Elected to the General Assembly of the restored state government in October 1865, he was selected two months later as Speaker of the House. The so-called Baldwin legislature, dominated by "Conservative" ex-Confederates, occupied a powerful position in 1866.

That February the Joint Committee on Reconstruction took testimony from a number of Virginians, among them Baldwin. There the erstwhile Unionist denied that he had concealed from the Virginia convention of 1861 a peace overture from Abraham Lincoln. Baldwin also insisted that defeated Virginians accepted the results of the war and were working to establish equal civil rights for blacks and whites. He strongly objected, however, to any extension of political rights to blacks.

With near unanimity, the Baldwin legislature spurned the proposed Fourteenth Amendment, which would have reduced the representation of former Confederate states that did not allow black voting and would also have disqualified from office many prominent ex-Confederates. Voters in the North, however, elected a decisive majority of Republicans to Congress in late 1866. Overcoming bitter-end obstruction from President Andrew Johnson, Congress soon moved to abolish the existing governments in the South and to require approval of the Fourteenth Amendment. By the winter of 1867–1868, a Republican-dominated constitutional convention met to lay the foundations for a new Virginia government.

The adroit Baldwin and his brother-in-law, Alexander H. H. Stuart, were among the principals on the so-called Committee of Nine, organized in December 1868, which enabled white Virginia to escape further Reconstruction. They agreed to accept universal suffrage so long as voters had the opportunity to strike the proscriptive test oath and disfranchisement clauses of the new Constitution. The Committee of Nine also masterminded the nomination for governor of conservative Republican Gilbert C. Walker. The adoption of the modified Constitution and the election of Walker in July 1869 made Virginia the first ex-Confederate state to fall into conservative hands.

John B. Baldwin vaulted to prominence during the great crisis of 1860–1861. Virginia still had a larger number of slaves than any other state, and it occupied a central position as the secession drama unfolded. Had he and the Union Whigs at the Virginia convention been able to arrange a modus vivendi with the Lincoln administration, Baldwin could well have become a power in national politics. It was not, of course, to be. The man who believed secession "an absurdity and humbug" performed creditably for Confederate Virginia and continued to demonstrate his political acumen in the turbulent postwar years.

BIBLIOGRAPHY

Alexander, Thomas B., and Richard E. Beringer. *The Anatomy of the Confederate Congress: A Study of the Influences of Member Characteristics on Legislative Voting Behavior, 1861–1865.* Nashville, Tenn., 1972.

Crofts, Daniel W. *Reluctant Confederates: Upper South Unionists in the Secession Crisis.* Chapel Hill, N.C., 1989.

Interview between President Lincoln and Col. John B. Baldwin, April 4th, 1861: Statements & Evidence. Staunton, Va., 1866.

Journal of the Congress of the Confederate States of America, 1861–1865. 7 vols. Washington, D.C., 1904–1905.

Lowe, Richard. *Republicans and Reconstruction in Virginia, 1856–70.* Charlottesville, Va., 1991.

Maddex, Jack P., Jr. *The Virginia Conservatives, 1867–1879: A Study in Reconstruction Politics.* Chapel Hill, N.C., 1970.

Reese, George H., ed. *Proceedings of the Virginia State Convention of 1861.* 4 vols. Richmond, Va., 1965.

Yearns, Wilfred B. *The Confederate Congress.* Athens, Ga., 1960.

DANIEL W. CROFTS

BALDWIN, WILLIAM EDWIN (1827–1864), brigadier general. Born at Statesburg, South Carolina, Baldwin spent most of his youth in Mississippi. He operated a bookstore in Columbus and for twelve years was a lieutenant in the Columbus Riflemen, a local militia company. On the eve of the war, he was elected captain of the company and served with it at Pensacola, where he was commissioned colonel of the Fourteenth Mississippi Infantry.

Baldwin's regiment was soon transferred to central Kentucky. At Fort Donelson Baldwin commanded the Second Brigade under Simon Bolivar Buckner, and he and his regiment were captured with the fall of the fort in February 1862. After his release from the Federal prison at Fort Warren, Baldwin was promoted to brigadier general on September 19, 1862. His brigade skirmished with Ulysses S. Grant's cavalry at Coffeyville, Mississippi, on December 5, 1862, and then saw its heaviest fighting during the Vicksburg campaign when Baldwin led it as part of Martin Luther Smith's command. It fought at Port Gibson, Champion's Hill, and Big Black River and was captured with the rest of John C. Pemberton's army when Vicksburg surrendered on July 4, 1863. After his exchange as a paroled prisoner, Baldwin served briefly with the Army of Tennessee. His final command was in the District of Mobile. On February 19, 1864, Baldwin died as the result of a fall from his horse when a stirrup broke.

BIBLIOGRAPHY

Rowland, Dunbar. *Military History of Mississippi, 1803–1898.* Jackson, Miss., 1908. Reprint, Spartanburg, S.C., 1978.

Warner, Ezra J. *Generals in Gray: Lives of the Confederate Commanders.* Baton Rouge, La., 1959.

WILLIAM L. BARNEY

BALLOON. Confederate experiments with balloons are not well known, unlike those of the Union's Thaddeus S. C. Lowe. An 1862 document on Union aeronautical activity during the Peninsular campaign contains the earliest mention of Confederate ballooning. Confusion exists about the balloon. Although two sites for balloon work are mentioned, the only documented use took place on the James River in 1862. Accounts of Confederate hot-air-filled cotton balloons and later coal-gas-filled silk balloons are unsupported. Another, undocumented, ballooning episode is suggested to have taken place at Charleston, South Carolina. [*See illustration on next page.*]

It is likely there was only a single Confederate balloon. This multicolored airship was constructed by Langdon Cheves and Charles Cevor in Savannah. They purchased silk, which was assembled and treated with gutta percha dissolved in naphtha to make it gas-proof.

The balloon was filled at the Richmond Gas Works and transported by rail. From about June 27, 1862, the balloon, tethered to either a boxcar or CSS *Teaser,* was used to observe Union troop movements. The Confederates, however, did not attempt to obtain an immediate tactical advantage by using a telegraph to direct artillery fire or troop movements according to the balloon's observations. Both balloon and tug were captured on July 4, 1862, when the tug ran aground.

It is unlikely Cevor and Cheves built a second balloon that was subsequently lost at Charleston; no evidence supports this speculation. Both men worked on the Charleston defenses, and accounts of their Virginia experiment may have been transposed to that city. The best source on Confederate ballooning uses Langdon Cheves's correspondence to show that one balloon was built in Savannah with multicolored silk bought for the purpose. The best descriptions of Civil War-era balloons can be found in the Union army's ballooning papers in the *Official Records.*

BIBLIOGRAPHY

Easterby, J. H. "Captain Langdon Cheves, Jr., and the Confederate Silk Dress Balloon." *South Carolina Historical Magazine* 44 (1943): 1–11, 99–110.

U.S. War Department. *War of the Rebellion: A Compilation of the Official Records of the Union and Confederate Armies.* Washington, D.C., 1880–1901. Ser. 3, vol. 3, pp. 252–319.

L. E. BABITS

THE BALLOON *INTREPID*.   One of several Federal balloons in use during the Civil War, *Intrepid* was employed to reconnoiter the Battles of Fair Oaks and Seven Pines, Virginia, May 3 to June 1, 1862.

BALL'S BLUFF, VIRGINIA. Fought October 21, 1861, some thirty-five miles upriver from Washington, this small battle on the Potomac River near Leesburg, Virginia, had great repercussions. Also called the Battle of Leesburg, it cost the Union force of 1,720 men 49 killed, 158 wounded, 553 taken prisoner, and 171 missing or drowned. Out of 1,709 Confederate men, 36 were killed, 117 wounded, and 2 taken prisoner.

The battle came about because George B. McClellan, commander of the Army of the Potomac, was heavily pressured by Radical Republican congressmen to advance against the Confederates in northern Virginia. McClellan, deciding to attack the isolated Confederate brigade at Leesburg, under Col. Nathan ("Shanks") Evans, telegraphed Gen. Charles Stone, commander of the Union division at Poolesville, Maryland, opposite Leesburg: "Perhaps a slight demonstration on your part would have the effect to move them." Stone was also informed by McClellan that George McCall's division of 12,000 would move upriver on the Virginia shoreline toward Leesburg via Dranesville.

Stone decided to cross the Potomac in a pincers movement. Willis Gorman's brigade would be the left pincer crossing at Edwards Ferry both to hold Evans in check and to link up with the advancing McCall. Meanwhile, a brigade commanded by the Radical Republican senator and colonel Edward D. Baker was to cross upriver at Smartt's Mill Ford to envelop Evans's extreme left flank. A small reconnaissance patrol was to scout between these two columns at Ball's Bluff. The patrol sent back an inaccurate report, which in turn led to its being ambushed by alert Confederate pickets of the Seventeenth Mississippi Infantry Regiment. This initial skirmish led to Union reinforcements moving across the Potomac to cross at Ball's Bluff instead of Smartt's Mill Ford, thus changing the entire axis of Stone's plan of assault.

At the same time, unknown to Stone—but not to Evans, who had captured a Union courier—McCall had turned around at Dranesville and marched back to his camps at Langley. These factors enabled Evans to first send Walter Jennifer's cavalry, William Duff's Mississippians, and the

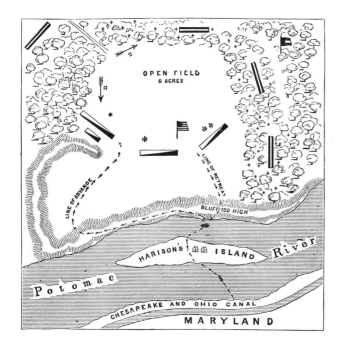

BATTLE OF BALL'S BLUFF.   *THE SOLDIER IN OUR CIVIL WAR*

Eighth Virginia Infantry Regiment under Col. Eppa Hunton to do battle around the Jackson house at 12:00 noon. Successful there, they then pushed the Union forces back to the edge of a cleared field of some eight to ten acres atop Ball's Bluff. Reinforcements on both sides now poured into the maelstrom, including Colonel Baker and three Union artillery pieces. Baker was killed just after 5:00 P.M. and his command was routed back across the Potomac into Maryland.

For his victory at Ball's Bluff, Colonel Evans was promoted to brigadier general to date from the day of the battle. On the Union side, this disaster three months to the day after First Manassas, combined with Baker's death, enabled the Radical Republicans in Congress to form the Joint Committee on the Conduct of the War. The committee met three times between December 1861 and March 1863 to investigate what had happened at Ball's Bluff. In February 1862 they illegally and falsely accused General Stone of treason and had him arrested without a writ of habeus corpus and thrown into the dungeon of Fort Lafayette and Fort Hamilton in New York Harbor for 189 days.

BIBLIOGRAPHY

Holien, Kim B. *Battle at Ball's Bluff*. Orange, Va., 1985.
Patch, Joseph D. *The Battle of Ball's Bluff*. Leesburg, Va., 1958.

KIM BERNARD HOLIEN

BALTIMORE RIOT. Baltimore in the spring of 1861 was a tinderbox. The secession crisis of the winter, complicated by depressed economic conditions, intensified sectional passions in Maryland. The bombardment of Fort Sumter and Abraham Lincoln's call for troops compounded the state's indecisiveness. Torn in their loyalties, Marylanders nevertheless opposed the coercion of the Southern states. Yet troops going by rail to the defense of Washington would have to pass through Baltimore.

On April 18 some Northern troops traveled through the city without incident. Police authorities, either unworried or merely neglectful, failed to make preparations for continued safe passages. On the following day, the public mood was more volatile. The legacy of the Know-Nothing riots in the 1850s, inflamed by the fiery rhetoric of Southern radicals and compounded by economic suffering, created a highly inflammatory atmosphere in Baltimore. News of the Sixth Massachusetts Regiment's arrival now provoked gathering mobs to obstruct its route. As the railway cars were drawn by horses through the city, crowds began to jeer and pelt the soldiers with stones and missiles. Disembarking from the coaches, the troops continued by marching to Camden Street Station. Despite police efforts to maintain order and Mayor George Brown's symbolic act of walking at the head of the troops, rioting ensued. In the exchange of fire and missiles, four soldiers and a number of citizens lay wounded and dead.

Hysteria gripped Baltimore. A mass meeting that evening evoked extreme state rights statements from Governor Thomas Hicks. Municipal authorities, fearing the possibility of additional arrivals, cut Northern rail links to the city. A delegation was sent to Washington for consultations with alarmed Federal authorities. Meanwhile, Baltimoreans prepared for a siege. Finally, by April 28 the crisis had passed, and Unionist sentiment reasserted itself in the city. Gen. Benjamin F. Butler sealed Federal control over the city with his occupation of Federal Hill on the night of May 13. Yet the rioting left its scar, as evident in the state song:

> Avenge the patriotic gore
> That flecked the street of Baltimore,
> And be the battle queen of yore,
> Maryland, my Maryland!

BIBLIOGRAPHY

Brown, George William. *Baltimore and the 19th of April, 1861*. Baltimore, 1887.
Brugger, Robert J. *Maryland: A Middle Temperament, 1634–1980*. Baltimore, 1988.
Clark, Charles B. "Baltimore and the Attack on the Sixth Massachusetts Regiment, April 19, 1861." *Maryland Historical Magazine* 56 (March 1961): 39–71.
Radcliffe, George L. P. *Governor Thomas H. Hicks of Maryland and the Civil War*. Baltimore, 1901.

RICHARD R. DUNCAN

BANKING. Prior to the secession crisis, several Southern states had banking systems as solid and sophisticated as those in the North. Northern attempts to coordinate the transmission of financial information and banks' responses to crises had yielded a range of structures and mechanisms from clearinghouses (where bankers met daily to clear their balances with each other) and safety funds (early forms of deposit insurance) to free banking laws that permitted anyone to start a bank.

Several Southern states, however, had developed a much more effective solution to those problems—namely, branch banking, in which a bank could open offices in other locations without separate acts of the state legislature. Branching, which the North ignored, allowed rapid transfer of resources among branches, treating the resources of each individual as part of the whole. Most important, branching allowed for more efficient transmission of information about financial conditions from one branch location to another. At the onset of the Civil War, the South's banking system had emerged virtually unscathed from the panic of 1857 and had seen the culmination of a decade of impressive growth.

Secession, however, changed things immediately. In states that seceded first, banks felt instant effects. South Carolina banks suspended (i.e., ceased paying gold and silver coin, or specie, for their notes) in late 1860; a number of New Orleans factorage houses with liabilities exceeding $30 million suspended during the first two weeks of December. But Mobile and New Orleans banks continued to redeem notes for specie until fall 1861. In order to do so, they dramatically cut their lending and circulation. Even in the states that did not secede, banks had to reduce circulation and increase reserves. Deposits in Louisiana and North Carolina remained high, and little evidence exists to show that throughout the South bankers gave much thought to the practical problems of a war that would separate them from their Northern correspondents (banks in other locations in which banks regularly kept balances). Some minor expansion of lending occurred to Southern borrowers—attempts to carry friends of business acquaintances—but no coherent policy appears to have emerged. Nevertheless, all major categories of bank statistics showed declines from 1860 to 1861; circulation fell by $12 million, deposits by $5 million, specie by $4.5 million, and loans by $22 million. The number of banks also shrank from 119 to 104.

In addition to the deleterious effects of the secession crisis itself, the Confederacy and the states themselves exacted a toll on Southern banks. Alabama banks had to provide a $2 million loan to the state of Alabama and had to accept Confederate Treasury notes at par. Each bank had to contribute an amount proportional to its capital. At the level of the Confederate government, banks had a twofold obligation. First, they had to support the Confederacy by a direct loan (April 1861) to the government. They accomplished that by redeeming in coin their own notes that the banks paid for the government bonds, which constituted the collateral for the loan. Even though the banks had suspended specie payments, their notes traded at only a slight discount and, at the beginning of the war, were "as good as gold." As a result, the Confederacy did not (and probably could not) insist on receiving specie directly for the bonds. In May 1861, Secretary of the Treasury Christopher G. Memminger contacted a number of banks to ask for further loans from each of them, paying for them with $1,000 and $500 Treasury notes. Banks were expected to pay out in specie at par on the Confederate notes, although some discounted the notes early. At that point, Memminger well knew, as he told Louisiana bankers in September 1861, the value of Confederate notes depended on the public's willingness to accept them as a circulating medium, not on the bankers' attitude.

A second obligation involved gaining the banks' participation in establishing the Confederate Treasury note currency. Achieving that meant convincing the New Orleans banks to participate in the program. But Louisiana's Constitution prohibited specie suspensions, and the New Orleans banks had remained absent from any of the banking conventions. Mobile's banks followed suit, continuing to pay specie. Thus the notion of a unified "national" currency never took hold.

Circulation of bank, local, private, and state issues rose 150 percent above the prewar average. The number of depreciated moneys rose dramatically, with the most discounted notes called shinplasters. Regardless of a bank's prewar position, that inflation would have undermined its notes' credibility even without the other problems brought on by the war. But three separate pressures combined to destroy the Southern banking system.

First, by offering their specie and notes for purchase of Confederate bonds, the banks assumed those bonds as collateral for their assets. When the Confederacy collapsed, the value of those bonds and hence those assets also collapsed.

Some assets would have remained, however, under other circumstances. Most Southern banks held large amounts of collateral in the form of Southern land (plantations) and property (chattel). The Union victories, combined with the perceived effects of the Emancipation Proclamation, eroded the value of those assets as well. That constituted the second process that destroyed the Southern banking system: even if a peace had been negotiated, if it came at the expense of slavery (as in some of the more desperate Southern ideas after 1864), the banks would have had virtually no assets left anyway.

Finally, Confederate and state policies during the war—independent of overall monetary policy and the one-third decline in money values—led to a staggering drain on a Southern bank's resources. One study has shown that a typical bank would have retained barely 36 percent of its assets by 1864, owing to taxation on stock, earnings, and various fees. What would the remainder of that bank's assets be worth if they consisted of slaves and Confederate bonds?

As if these pressures were not enough, banks in the Confederacy also had to deal with personnel problems and with the approach of enemy troops. Employees frequently moved in and out of civilian bank jobs, depending on the demands of the army or their families. Some bankers away at the front received instructions to return to their institutions. More disturbing were the problems associated with the impending arrival of Federal troops. Banks hid specie from the Union armies (as well as the Confederate government), and in one case a Tennessee banker escaped with his bank's specie to England and returned with it after the war to reopen his bank. Under other circumstances, banks saw Union troops issue counterfeit look-alike notes, which only further eroded the public's flagging confidence in paper money.

The collapse of the Southern banking system, although little appreciated by historians, constituted a dual tragedy. First, the dearth of financial institutions in the postbellum South led to major disruptions in commercial and agricultural lending. That, in turn, helped seal the fate of freedmen and whites alike by denying them access to credit under competitive circumstances. With virtually no banks in existence—and certainly no banks at all in direct, close competition—farmers and entrepreneurs either had to seek credit from furnishing merchants or other informal sources or, in the case of farmers, had to sharecrop. The record of black-owned insurance companies and savings and loans in the North suggests that at least *some* black-owned institutions would have appeared in a free market.

When combined with the undesirable and constrictive effects of the National Bank and Currency Acts, the ability of Southerners to start and grow banks almost vanished for decades. The second unappreciated aspects of Southern banking as it related to the Confederacy was that the Confederate experiment killed the extremely viable and healthy branch banking systems, almost unique to the South. Only in a few states—most notably California—did branching develop, and overall it remained absent from the political debates about banking that reformed the American system from the late 1800s to 1913. Thus, in addition to its other less than illustrious accomplishments, the Confederacy, through its failure, saddled much of the United States with an inferior unit banking system for years.

[*See also* Bonds; Counterfeiting; Currency; Shinplasters.]

BIBLIOGRAPHY

Ball, Douglas B. *Financial Failure and Confederate Defeat.* Urbana, Ill., 1991.

Calomiris, Charles W., and Larry Schweikart. "The Panic of 1857: Causes, Transmission, and Containment." *Journal of Economic History* 51 (December 1991): 807–834.

Morgan, James F. *Graybacks and Gold: Confederate Monetary Policy.* Pensacola, Fla., 1985.

Schweikart, Larry. *Banking in the American South from the Age of Jackson.* Baton Rouge, La., 1987.

Schweikart, Larry. "Southern Banks and Secession." *Civil War History* 31 (June 1985): 111–125.

LARRY SCHWEIKART

BANSHEE. The first steel vessel to cross the Atlantic, *Banshee* was also one of the first steam vessels built for blockade running. The light-weight hull was built of steel by Jones, Quiggin, and Company of Liverpool, and the engines by Laird Brothers of Birkenhead, England. John T. Lawrence ordered *Banshee* for the Anglo-Confederate Trading Company of Liverpool. Measuring 214 feet long and 20 feet wide and weighing 533 tons, *Banshee* was a sidewheeler driven by a 120-nominal-horsepower, two-cylinder oscillating engine and could attain speeds of about twelve knots. Steel boilers fore and aft of the paddlewheels and engines provided steam. A turtle-back deck forward allowed speed to be maintained in a seaway by driving through rather than over larger waves.

After initial problems in the design were corrected, *Banshee* enjoyed success as a blockade runner, passing through the blockade fourteen times under Capt. Jonathon Steele and supercargo Thomas Taylor. As the prototypical blockade runner, *Banshee* provided the pattern that most specially built runners would follow for the remainder of the war. *Running the Blockade,* Taylor's book about his experiences aboard *Banshee,* is the best contemporary account of the risky trade.

On November 21, 1863, USS *James Adger* captured the runner off the North Carolina coast. After being condemned by the prize court and sold to the U.S. Navy, it was strengthened, armed, and commissioned USS *Banshee.* While assigned to the North Atlantic Blockading Squadron in the navy, *Banshee* assisted at the first unsuccessful attack on Fort Fisher and was moved to the Potomac Squadron in January 1865. The navy sold the steamer in November to Samuel Ward, who sold it to Smallwood and Company. Renamed *J. L. Smallwood,* the ship was modified to carry cattle in the West Indies. Sold once again, in 1869, the ex-runner was renamed *Irene* and continued in Atlantic and Caribbean service until at least 1885.

BIBLIOGRAPHY

Spratt, H. Philip. *Transatlantic Paddle Steamers.* 2d ed. Glasgow, 1967.

Taylor, Thomas E. *Running the Blockade.* London, 1897.

Wise, Stephen R. *Lifeline of the Confederacy: Blockade Running during the Civil War.* Columbia, S.C., 1988.

KEVIN J. FOSTER

BAPTIST CHURCH. Practicing a pronounced belief in the autonomy of its individual congregations, the Baptist church was a perfect organizational analogue of the state rights orientation of many white Southerners. In 1860, nearly 650,000 white and black Southerners called themselves Baptist and had formed some 7,760 assemblies, scattered throughout the slaveholding states. Over 400,000 white Baptists were actively involved not only in evangelical enterprises but also in the major sectional questions of their day.

These folk contributed to Southern sectionalism in three ways. First, most Baptists believed and could justify through their reading of Scripture that slavery was a moral institution, as long as masters treated their slaves humanely. Second, Southern Baptists had divorced themselves from cooperative missionary enterprises with Northern Baptists during the 1840s and had established the Southern Baptist Convention, a fact that intensified their regional identification. Finally, during the critical decade of the 1850s, Baptist parsons and presses continually indicted Northern society as a source of sin, hypocrisy, and infidelity while upholding and, to some degree, attempting to transform Southern values and culture. In keeping with these ecclesiastical efforts, Baptist associations in all eleven seceding states passed resolutions that supported disunion, pledged support to the Confederacy, and offered intercession for the nascent nation. Basil Manly, a prominent Alabama Baptist clergyman, delivered the invocation at the inauguration ceremony for Jefferson Davis in February 1861.

During the secession winter, many Baptist writers and parsons proffered detailed advice concerning a proper course for Baptists and their political leaders to follow. In November 1860, James R. Graves, editor of the *Tennessee Baptist,* called for a convention of Southerners to demand ironclad protection of slavery in the territories through a federal slave code and in Southern states by means of a constitutional amendment and the rigid enforcement of the Fugitive Slave Law. If Northerners rejected these demands, then the South ought to secede as a unit. At the same time, the Alabama Baptist Convention argued that "the union of the states has failed" and pledged themselves to support the civil authorities who would protect the state's interest. Similarly, Mississippi Baptists urged immediate disunion as the best means to avert a civil war.

In contrast to Deep South Baptists, who came to support secession quickly, moderation characterized upper South Baptist responses to Abraham Lincoln's election and the secession crisis. For example, the *Biblical Recorder,* the Baptist paper in North Carolina, did not advocate secession until after Lincoln's call for troops following the shelling of Fort Sumter. But in both the upper and the lower South, Baptist leaders couched their cries for political action in evangelical terms. Secession would permit Southern Baptists to perform their religious duties unfettered by infidel notions of abolitionism and modernism.

Baptists supported the war effort in myriad ways. Approximately one hundred Baptist clergymen served as chaplains, and during 1862, the Southern Baptist Convention maintained an additional twenty-six missionaries in the field to work among the soldiers. Baptists supported interdenominational Bible societies and colportage efforts. Many Baptists, including clergymen, served as soldiers.

The vicissitudes of war brought subterranean stresses to the surface among Baptists, disrupting denominational schools and damaging church properties. Local associations lamented the loss of leadership, as parsons ministered at the front instead of in their prewar parishes. Some reform minded parsons, like Georgia's Nathaniel Macon Crawford, hoped to use secession as an opportunity to reform slavery. Recognizing slave marriages and making it legal to teach slaves to read typified these attempts. Evangelical enterprises among the slaves ultimately suffered, however, removing an important moral support for Southern separatism in the first place. Secession and slavery were good only if African Americans heard and responded to the true gospel. As a result, not a few Baptists interpreted Confederate defeat as a sign of divine displeasure. Baptists had not been faithful stewards of their holy message.

At the same time, Baptists could and did interpret their defeat not as Jehovah's rejection of their society but as a purifying process by which the "Lord chastens whom He loveth." Indeed, after the war, Baptists participated with other denominations in interfaith revivals that glorified the ideals that had prompted Southern secession. J. William Jones, a Virginia Baptist, became the best-known and one of the most influential of clerical exponents of Lost Cause religion. Gallant Confederates augmented biblical examples of righteous heroes in liturgical paeans to godly virtue. Jones led the attempt to rehabilitate the maligned image of Jefferson Davis and served as a longtime secretary-treasurer of the Southern Historical Society. He even utilized the failure of the Confederacy as a tool of religious conversion—mixing sacred and secular imagery into a hellfire and brimstone sermon. God could not have allowed the Confederacy to succeed with so many unconverted Southerners in its ranks. Along with many of his peers, Jones fought against what he perceived as immoral, modern tendencies in secular society, like skepticism, a threat he considered similar in nature to abolitionism. Prior, during, and after the war, Baptists looked to their scripture to defend their preindustrial world, including its racial mores, from what they considered infidelity.

[*See also* Bible Societies; Lost Cause, *overview article.*]

BIBLIOGRAPHY

Daniel, W. Harrison. *Southern Protestantism in the Confederacy.* Richmond, Va., 1989.

Goen, Clarence C. *Broken Churches, Broken Nation: Denominational Schisms and the Coming of the Civil War.* Macon, Ga., 1985.

Mathews, Donald G. *Religion in the Old South.* Chicago, 1977.

McBeth, Harry Leon. *The Baptist Heritage: Four Centuries of Baptist Witness.* Nashville, Tenn., 1987.

Wilson, Charles Reagan. *Baptized in Blood: The Religion of the Lost Cause, 1865–1920.* Athens, Ga., 1980.

EDWARD RILEY CROWTHER

BARKSDALE, ETHELBERT (1824–1893), congressman from Mississippi. Barksdale was born in Tennessee and moved to Mississippi as a teenager. At the age of twenty-one, he became a journalist, as had his brother, William Barksdale—later a Confederate general killed at Gettysburg. Barksdale edited the *Democrat,* a newspaper in Yazoo City, Mississippi, from 1845 to 1850. Afterward, he moved to Jackson to edit the *Mississippian,* the official journal of the state.

In his first experience as a politician, he became a delegate to the Democratic National Convention that met in Charleston in 1860. At this convention, a split developed between the Northern supporters of Stephen A. Douglas for president and Southerners who wanted a plank endorsing Federal protection of slave property in the territories. Barksdale delivered a strong speech advocating the Southern point of view. Nevertheless, the convention was controlled by a small Douglas majority, and when the Southerners' position was defeated, Barksdale, along with the other members of the Mississippi delegation and the delegations from other Southern states, walked out and agreed to meet later in Richmond.

At that meeting of Southern Democrats, Barksdale served on the platform committee, which advocated that the Federal government "protect, when necessary, the rights of persons and property in the Territories." The Southerners then nominated John C. Breckinridge for president. Barksdale vigorously supported Breckinridge despite the likelihood of Abraham Lincoln's election; he wrote that if Lincoln were elected, "99 out of every 100 men" who supported Breckinridge would be for secession. Although Barksdale had not always been a secessionist, the events in 1860 drove him to support separation.

In the fall of 1861, Barksdale was elected to the First Congress and was easily reelected in 1863. In this political role, Barksdale became an active Confederate, enjoying argument and defending controversial positions. He once said that, if necessary, he would be willing to "throw aside the Constitution." He introduced measures in the First Congress allowing President Jefferson Davis to suspend habeas corpus and to impose martial law. He favored the draft, draft exemptions, and an agricultural tax—positions also favored by Davis. Later, when the Confederacy was seriously threatened, he advocated increasing the number of soldiers and introduced a bill allowing the arming of slaves. He argued for his position by reading a statement from Robert E. Lee that also supported arming slaves.

After the war, he resumed newspaper editing; this time he edited the influential *Clarion.* During Reconstruction, Barksdale deplored the bitterness and resentment of many white Mississippians; he counseled acceptance of the results of the war and advised giving rights to the freed blacks. Otherwise, he said, white Mississippians would lose to Radical Republicans all power to control affairs. Barksdale's newspaper called for whites to register, vote, and aid in the process of Reconstruction.

His popular and influential columns advocating the interests of small farmers led to his election to the U.S. Congress in 1882 and 1884. He was defeated, however, in campaigns for Congress in 1886, 1890, and 1892. Until his death, he lived and farmed at Oak Valley, a plantation in Yazoo County.

BIBLIOGRAPHY

Peterson, Owen. "Ethelbert Barksdale in the Democratic Convention of 1860." *Journal of Mississippi History* 14 (October 1952): 274–276.

Warner, Ezra J., and W. Buck Yearns. *Biographical Register of the Confederate Congress.* Baton Rouge, La., 1975.

RAY SKATES

BARKSDALE, WILLIAM (1821–1863) U.S. congressman and Confederate brigadier general. Barksdale, born August 21, 1821, was a native of Tennessee who grew up an orphan in Mississippi. He served as a captain of commissary in the Mexican War, but saw no battle action. Barksdale won election to the U.S. House of Representatives in 1853 and was reelected every two years until the Civil War in campaigns marked by violent episodes that included a knife fight and a duel. In Washington the fiery Mississippian regularly engaged in vitriolic debate that led to baring of knives, a near duel, and a famous fistfight on the floor of the House in 1858. Despite the decade of noisy oratory, Barksdale was able to declare in 1860, "Never have I desired a dissolution of this union"—but the "sectional and hostile platform" of the Republicans in that year prompted him to insist that the South must not accept Abraham Lincoln's goverance.

WILLIAM BARKSDALE.

HARPER'S PICTORIAL HISTORY OF THE GREAT REBELLION

Barksdale served briefly in early 1861 as quartermaster general of the short-lived Army of Mississippi before becoming colonel of the Thirteenth Mississippi Infantry. He took the regiment to Virginia barely in time to take part in First Manassas, arriving on the Confederate far left near Chinn Ridge at the moment of decision. That fall Colonel Barksdale got into serious trouble for drunkenness. His superior, Gen. Nathan G. ("Shanks") Evans (himself notoriously intemperate), brought the colonel before a court-martial. Barksdale escaped the sentence of the court in part by giving "a solemn pledge" of temperance for the duration of the war and in part because he had meanwhile fought with distinction on the Edward's Ferry front during the Battle of Ball's Bluff.

Richard Griffith, a new brigade commander, recommended Barksdale for promotion in April 1862. The promotion came a few months later when Griffith fell mortally wounded during the Seven Days' Battles. As acting brigade commander, Colonel Barksdale won plaudits from both his division commander and Robert E. Lee. Promoted to brigadier general August 12, 1862, he led his command north with the army into Maryland after missing Second Manassas as part of the rear guard. He commanded it in a difficult and successful attack on Maryland Heights above Harpers Ferry and then participated in the brightest tactical moment for the Confederates at Sharpsburg, battering Sedgwick and Sumner in the West Woods.

General Barksdale's greatest day came on December 11, 1862, when he defended the riverfront in Fredericksburg against Federals attempting to cross. The next spring, on nearly the same ground, however, the general and his brigade came to grief when a vastly stronger Northern column forced them away from their rearguard post on Marye's Heights during the Chancellorsville campaign. At Gettysburg on July 2, 1863, William Barksdale led his seasoned veterans across the Emmitsburg Road in a successful assault on the Peach Orchard. As he rode at their head beyond the orchard toward Plum Run, the general fell from his horse struck by several projectiles. He died early the next day in enemy hands. In molding his Mississippi regiments into a potent force and leading them to distinction on several fields, Barksdale carved one of the best military records achieved by any of the antebellum political fire-eaters.

BIBLIOGRAPHY

Humphreys, Benjamin G. "Recollections of Fredericksburg." *Land We Love* 3 (1867): 443–460.
McKee, James W. "William Barksdale: The Intrepid Mississippian." Ph.D. diss., Mississippi State University, 1966.
Rand, Clayton. *Men of Spine in Mississippi*. Gulfport, Miss., 1940.

ROBERT K. KRICK

BARKSDALE'S MISSISSIPPI BRIGADE.

This brigade of four Mississippi infantry regiments won one of the highest reputations as a fighting unit earned by any organization in the Army of Northern Virginia. The Thirteenth Mississippi was made up of companies from the state's east-central counties. Its first and best-known commander was William Barksdale. The Seventeenth came from Mississippi's far northern tier of counties, the Eighteenth was raised in west-central Mississippi, and the Twenty-first included companies from several widely separated regions.

The regiments had separate baptisms of fire at First Manassas and Ball's Bluff before they were united as a brigade under Gen. Richard Griffith in December 1861. After Griffith was mortally wounded at Savage Station, Barksdale became brigadier.

The Mississippi Brigade impressed an admiring Virginia major as "the finest body of men I ever saw . . . almost giants in size and power . . . and . . . almost without exception fine shots." When they screeched the rebel yell, the major wrote, "the volume of sound was tremendous." The men of the brigade performed ably throughout the war as some of Lee's most reliable shock troops. They won special distinction under Barksdale defending the riverfront at Fredericksburg in December 1862 and attacking to and beyond the Peach Orchard at Gettysburg. The brigade's most difficult day came on May 3, 1863, when it was driven from Marye's Heights near Fredericksburg, but because of the circumstances no discredit was attached to the brigade.

Gen. B. G. Humphreys, who had been colonel of the Twenty-first, commanded the brigade after Barksdale's death at Gettysburg.

BIBLIOGRAPHY

Rietti, John C. *Military Annals of Mississippi.* [Jackson, Miss.?], 1895.
Rowland, Dunbar. *The Official and Statistical Register of the State of Mississippi.* Nashville, Tenn., 1908.
Stiles, Robert A. *Four Years under Marse Robert.* New York, 1903. Reprint, Dayton, Ohio, 1977.

ROBERT K. KRICK

BARNWELL, ROBERT W. (1801–1882), congressman from South Carolina. After a brief term in the U.S. Senate in 1850 and a stint as a delegate to the Southern rights convention in 1852, Barnwell retired to his plantation near Beaufort in St. Helena's Parish, South Carolina. He was considered a cooperationist, but took little part in the heated political scene of the 1850s. With the exception of attending the 1852 convention, his only public activity involved writing in defense of slavery.

Elected by his home parish to the South Carolina secession convention, Barnwell played an active role in the affairs of that body. He was named as one of the seven members of the committee to draw up the "Declaration of the Immediate Causes which Induce and Justify the Secession of South Carolina." This document did not shy away from slavery as the primary cause for South Carolina's leaving the Union. Barnwell was also elected one of three commissioners to treat with President James Buchanan on the issue of Federal property in South Carolina. The South Carolinians arrived in Washington at almost the same time as did news of Maj. Robert Anderson's removal of his troops from Fort Moultrie to Fort Sumter. The commissioners considered this to be a hostile act, and their last message to President Buchanan was so insulting he refused to receive it.

The South Carolina convention had also elected Barnwell as one of eight delegates, mostly cooperationists, to the Montgomery convention. There he was a key figure in persuading the radical Robert Barnwell Rhett, Sr., to support Jefferson Davis for president. Upon his election, Davis offered Barnwell the post of secretary of state. He refused, pleading that he was incapable, but he also knew that the state's delegation had already agreed to support Christopher G. Memminger for secretary of the treasury. The president had wanted Robert Toombs of Georgia for the Treasury, but he acquiesced to the South Carolinians' wishes. Back home, Rhett and Lawrence Keitt spoke against the new Confederate Constitution, but Barnwell led the successful effort to ratify it.

In the Provisional Congress, observers had already noted that the shy delegate from South Carolina was a loyal Davis supporter. Mary Boykin Chesnut described him as a Pickwickian character in his spectacles and commented that above all else, Carolinians revered his goodness. Such a person would hardly have seemed much of a politician. Nevertheless, when elections were held for South Carolina's senators to the First Congress, Barnwell and James L. Orr joined forces and defeated James Chesnut, a former U.S. senator and ambitious politician.

Although a staunch Davis loyalist, Barnwell, by May 1862, was having second thoughts about praising the president in the Charleston press. He did, however, loyally support Davis to the bitter end. He also stood behind Memminger and his various programs. In May 1864, he introduced a bill in support of one of the secretary's ill-advised financial schemes. It was ignored.

For eight years after the war, Barnwell served as chairman of the faculty of the University of South Carolina. When the Radical Reconstruction regime seized control of the university in 1873, he resigned and opened a school for girls in Columbia. Four years later, with the conservatives back in power, he returned to the university as librarian, a position he held until his death.

Robert Woodward Barnwell was, in many respects, more a product of the eighteenth century than the nineteenth. He was considered by most who knew him to be "one of the last of the old Carolina gentlemen."

BIBLIOGRAPHY

Bleser, Carol, ed. *Secret and Sacred: The Diaries of James Henry Hammond, a Southern Slaveholder.* New York, 1988.
The Correspondence between the Commissioners of the State of South Carolina to the Government at Washington and the President of the United States; Together with the Statement of Messrs. Miles and Keitt. Charleston, S.C., 1861.
Perry, Hext M. *Reminiscences of Public Men by Ex-Gov. B. F. Perry.* Philadelphia, 1883.
Woodward, C. Vann, ed. *Mary Chesnut's Civil War.* New Haven, 1981.
Yearns, Wilfred B. *The Confederate Congress.* Athens, Ga., 1960.

WALTER B. EDGAR

BARRINGER, RUFUS (1821–1895), brigadier general. The first—and possibly the only—Confederate general to meet Abraham Lincoln during the war was a lawyer prior to the attack on Fort Sumter. Barringer was born in Cabarrus County, North Carolina, on December 2, 1821. He graduated from the University of North Carolina in 1842, and after studying law, he opened his legal practice in Concord. As a Whig, Barringer served in the State Assembly in 1848 and 1850 and was a Bell and Everett elector in 1860.

He was a strong Unionist and was so outspoken in his convictions that he once was publicly ridiculed on the streets of Charlotte. When he discerned that secession was imminent and that war was inevitable, however, he urged the legislature to arm the state and prepare for the coming conflict.

In April 1861, Barringer raised a company that became Company F, First North Carolina Cavalry. He was commissioned a captain on May 16. Barringer fought well with the Army of Northern Virginia in the Peninsular campaign, at Second Manassas, Sharpsburg, Fredericksburg, and Chancellorsville. He was still a captain in June 1863 when, though severely wounded in the face at Brandy Station, he "bore himself with marked coolness and good conduct," according to Wade Hampton, his commanding officer.

Barringer's rise in rank was rapid thereafter. He was promoted to major in August 1863, lieutenant colonel three months later, and brigadier general in June 1864, commanding four North Carolina cavalry regiments. His troopers were assigned to the division of William Henry Fitzhugh ("Rooney") Lee and served in that capacity until near the end of the war. A subordinate officer described the general as "prudent, methodical and cautious" on the battlefield.

Barringer's last of seventy-six engagements was fought at Namozine Church on April 3, 1865. Attempting to extricate a regiment from a perilous situation, he was captured by Jesse scouts, Union soldiers in Confederate disguise. He was taken to City Point, arriving at Federal headquarters at a time when Lincoln was visiting Ulysses S. Grant.

Barringer was in a tent preparing to shave when he heard a voice inquire, "Mr. President, have you ever seen a live Rebel general in uniform?" Lincoln replied, "No," at which point the flap of the tent was withdrawn and the first voice answered, "Here is one now." Lincoln greeted Barringer warmly. In the cordial conversation that ensued, the president recalled that in his years as a congressman, he had shared a desk with a Carolinian named Barringer. "That was my brother [D. Moreau Barringer]," the general said. Before parting, Lincoln wrote a note that he handed to Barringer. It was addressed to Edwin M. Stanton, asking that the secretary of war show special consideration to the prisoner. As a result of the president's thoughtfulness, Barringer was sent to Fort Delaware rather than disreputable Old Capitol Prison in Washington.

By his marriage to Eugenia Morrison, Barringer was a brother-in-law of Thomas J. ("Stonewall") Jackson and D. H. Hill. In 1862 Jackson had offered Barringer the position of quartermaster on his staff. The kinsman declined the honor, saying he preferred to remain with his men.

Following his release from prison in August 1865, Barringer transferred his law practice to Charlotte where he was "a conspicuous figure in his military cape with his green bag in his hand." In a county that was strongly Democratic, Barringer joined the Republican party. He was a member of the constitutional convention in 1875 and an unsuccessful candidate for lieutenant governor in 1880. He retired in 1884 and devoted the remainder of his life to writing treatises on the war and advocating better education in the public schools. He died in Charlotte on February 3, 1895, and was buried there.

BIBLIOGRAPHY

Barringer, Paul B. *The Natural Bent.* Chapel Hill, N.C., 1949.
"Gen. Rufus Barringer." *Confederate Veteran* 9 (1901): 69–70. Reprint, Wilmington, N.C., 1985.
Hill, D. H., Jr. *North Carolina.* Vol. 4 of *Confederate Military History.* Edited by Clement A. Evans. Atlanta, 1899. Vol. 5 of extended ed. Wilmington, N.C., 1987.
Warner, Ezra J. *Generals in Gray: Lives of the Confederate Commanders.* Baton Rouge, La., 1959.

LOWELL REIDENBAUGH

BARRY, JOHN DECATUR (1839–1867), brigadier general. Barry was born June 21, 1839, in Wilmington, North Carolina. After graduating in 1860 from the University of North Carolina, he worked in a Wilmington bank until August 26, 1861, when he enlisted as a private in Company I, Eighteenth North Carolina. In the April 1862 reorganization of the regiment, Barry became captain of his company. The young North Carolinian fought in the Seven Days' Battles and received a wound at Frayser's Farm that incapacitated him until autumn. On November 11, Barry gained promotion to major. Following the deaths at Chancellorsville of his two superiors, Barry on May 29, 1863, became colonel of the Eighteenth North Carolina.

He led his men well in the Battles of Gettysburg, the Wilderness, and Spotsylvania. At Cold Harbor, Barry commanded his brigade in the absence of wounded Gen. James Lane. On August 3, 1864, Barry received appointment as brigadier general. A few days later, however, while reconnoitering along his lines, he was shot in the hand. By the time he returned to duty early in 1865, Lane had resumed command of the brigade. Barry's promotion was thereupon rescinded. "On account of his wounds and impaired health," the regimental historian wrote, Barry accepted departmental command in his native state during the last weeks of the war. In May, he was paroled at Raleigh.

Barry began editing a Wilmington newspaper, but his health soon failed. He died March 24, 1867, at the age of twenty-seven and was buried in Wilmington's Oakdale Cemetery. A lieutenant who served with Barry thought the commander "as gallant a soldier as ever buckled on a sword."

JOHN DECATUR BARRY.   Shown as a colonel in the North Carolina Infantry.   LIBRARY OF CONGRESS

BIBLIOGRAPHY

Clark, Walter, ed. *Histories of the Several Regiments and Battalions from North Carolina in the Great War, 1861–'65.* 5 vols. Raleigh, 1901. Reprint, Wilmington, N.C., 1991.

Warner, Ezra J. *Generals in Gray: Lives of the Confederate Commanders.* Baton Rouge, La., 1959.

JAMES I. ROBERTSON, JR.

BARRY, WILLIAM TAYLOR SULLIVAN

(1821–1868), president of Mississippi's secession convention, Confederate congressman from Mississippi, and colonel. Barry, a Mississippi lawyer, farmer, and politician, served in several state legislatures from 1850 to 1858 and briefly in the U.S. Congress. He was a staunch secessionist and called for immediate secession if a "Black Republican"

was elected in 1860. At the 1860 Democratic National Convention in Charleston, where he was a delegate, he walked out with others when the convention refused to accept a plank protecting slave property in the territories. R. D. Shropshire, a newspaper editor from Aberdeen, had written candidate Stephen A. Douglas earlier warning him of Barry's position; Barry, he said, was a member of a faction in Mississippi "known as 'fire-eaters' of the most rabid description—advocating a re-opening of the African Slave Trade, and a protective code for the Territories." Said Shropshire, "They, of course, will appear in the Charleston Convention, as your most violent and uncompromising enemies, and will, no doubt, refuse to entertain any condition, idea, or proposition that will present your name before the people for Presidential honors." Although all Mississippians did not support Barry's position, it eventually won out.

When Abraham Lincoln was elected in November 1860, the idea of secession gained momentum. Elections held on December 20, 1860, sent a large majority favoring immediate secession to the state convention. On January 7, 1861, Barry was elected president of the convention, and he appointed a committee to draw up an ordinance of secession, which passed 84–15 on January 9.

Barry represented Mississippi in the Provisional Congress, where he advocated such radical positions as reopening the slave trade and banning any Confederate state from abolishing slavery without the unanimous approval of the others. He resigned in 1862 and with the rank of colonel organized and led the Thirty-fifth Regiment of Mississippi infantry. His regiment fought against Ulysses S. Grant's army and surrendered after the siege of Vicksburg. Later, after a prisoner exchange, Barry moved to the Georgia campaign, and at Allatoona, while serving in the Army of Tennessee, he was wounded. He rejoined his regiment near Mobile and was captured at Blakeley, Alabama, April 9, 1865.

After the war, Barry became despondent, leading what he called a "negative existence." He wrote that he was trying to recover from "the wreck which the war made of all our fortunes." He died in 1868.

BIBLIOGRAPHY

Alexander, Thomas B., and Richard E. Beringer. *The Anatomy of the Confederate Congress: A Study of the Influences of Member Characteristics on Legislative Voting Behavior, 1861–1865.* Nashville, Tenn., 1972.

Warner, Ezra J., and W. Buck Yearns. *Biographical Register of the Confederate Congress.* Baton Rouge, La., 1975.

RAY SKATES

BARTON, SETH MAXWELL (1829–1900), brigadier general. One of four brothers to serve in the Confed-

SETH MAXWELL BARTON.   LIBRARY OF CONGRESS

erate army, Barton was born at Fredericksburg, Virginia, on September 8, 1829. He was two months shy of his sixteenth birthday when, on July 1, 1845, he was admitted to the U.S. Military Academy. Barton graduated in 1849, ranking twenty-eighth in a class of forty-three that was distinguished chiefly by the fact that one of its members was author Stephen Vincent Benét, who ranked third. As a cadet, Barton was said to be "fond of reading and gave more attention to the pursuit of general knowledge than to the specific requirements of the course."

Barton's first assignment as a second lieutenant of infantry was at Fort Columbus in New York Harbor. A year later he was transferred to New Mexico. During his years on the frontier Barton was promoted twice, to first lieutenant in 1853 and to captain in 1857. He served as adjutant of the First Infantry from 1853 to 1857 and saw action against the Comanches the latter year.

Resigning his commission in June 1861 while at Fort Leavenworth, Barton offered his services to the South. He was commissioned a captain of infantry initially and then lieutenant colonel of the Third Arkansas on July 8. In early August, Barton wrote to Samuel Cooper, apprising the adjutant general of conditions in his command. "The clothing is mostly furnished from private sources," he revealed. Barton added that the muster rolls, though correct, "are not as intelligible as they should be for want of proper clerks." Last, the colonel lamented, "The want of stationary here may be well understood, from the fact that I have to tie up the muster rolls . . . with the ravelling of a tent cord."

Barton took part in the operations at Cheat Mountain and Greenbrier River and was acting chief engineer for Thomas J. ("Stonewall") Jackson's Romney campaign in January 1862. Jackson thought so highly of Barton that he recommended him for a brigadier's commission. The nomination was submitted to the Senate, withdrawn by Jefferson Davis a few days later, and ultimately confirmed on March 11, 1862. Barton's brigade was with E. Kirby Smith in East Tennessee and joined the defenses of Vicksburg in December 1862. He was captured on July 4, 1863, when that river bastion surrendered to Ulysses S. Grant, but he was exchanged almost immediately.

On September 21, Barton joined George E. Pickett's division, taking over the brigade that had been led by Lewis A. Armistead prior to his fall at Gettysburg. In the operations around New Bern, Barton was charged with "want of cooperation." He was censured again in May 1864 for his handling of troops south of the James River. He was relieved of command and, despite the petitioning for reinstatement by his regimental colonels, remained idle until late in the year when he took charge of a brigade in the defenses of Richmond. He was in George Washington Custis Lee's division in the retreat from the capital and was captured at Sayler's Creek on April 6, 1865. Barton was imprisoned at Fort Warren until July 1865.

After the war Barton resided in Fredericksburg where, it was said, he was "one of the finest chemists in the country." He died on April 11, 1900, while visiting his son in Washington, D.C., and was buried in City Cemetery, Fredericksburg.

BIBLIOGRAPHY

Compiled Military Service Records. Seth Maxwell Barton. Microcopy M331, Roll 17. Record Group 109. National Archives, Washington, D.C.

Hotchkiss, Jed. *Virginia*. Vol. 3 of *Confederate Military History*. Edited by Clement A. Evans. Atlanta, 1899. Vol. 4 of extended ed. Wilmington, N.C., 1987.

Obituary. *Daily Star* (Fredericksburg, Virginia), April 11, 1900.

LOWELL REIDENBAUGH

BARTOW, FRANCIS S. (1816–1861), congressman from Georgia and colonel. Bartow was born into an affluent Savannah family on September 6, 1816. The son of an

FRANCIS S. BARTOW.   NATIONAL ARCHIVES

eminent physician, he was well educated at home before attending Franklin College (the University of Georgia), where he graduated with honors in 1835, and Yale Law School. He returned to Savannah in 1837 before completing his degree. He continued his study of law under Judge John McPherson Berrien and later married his daughter. Once admitted to the bar in 1839, he opened his own law practice and soon became active in state and local politics. He was elected as a Whig to two terms in the state house of representatives and one in the state senate in the 1840s, though he failed in his 1857 bid to represent Georgia's First District in Congress, when he ran on the Know-Nothing, or American party, ticket. Bartow was also active in local military endeavors, and from 1856 on, he served as captain of the Oglethorpe Light Infantry, an elite militia company made up of young men from Savannah's leading families. He had by then become a wealthy planter, and in 1860 he owned eighty-nine slaves.

Though once Unionist in sentiment, Bartow had by 1860 become both a Democrat and an ardent secessionist. Convinced that the Republican party and Abraham Lincoln were fanatics bent on the subjugation of the South, he campaigned actively for secession through the fall of 1860 in Georgia and other Southern states and supported the Southern Democratic candidate John C. Breckinridge in

that fateful presidential race. His powerful speeches, once referred to as "logic on fire," proved persuasive. On December 28, 1860, he was speaking in Atlanta when word arrived of the burning of Fort Moultrie in Charleston, and he used the news to whip the crowd into frenzied support of South Carolina's course of action. Fulton County's delegates to the state secession convention in Milledgeville credited their pro-secession votes cast two weeks later to that speech. Bartow himself played a prominent role at that convention and was on the seventeen-member committee that drew up Georgia's ordinance of secession.

He was soon thereafter elected to the new Confederacy's Provisional Congress, which met in Montgomery in February. As chairman of its Committee on Military Affairs, Bartow succeeded in his push for gray uniforms for Confederate troops but failed in his attempt to limit volunteer military service to sixty-day terms. Others more sure of the inevitability of war, including Jefferson Davis, persuaded him to accept instead a twelve-month term of enlistment. Bartow had remained active in his leadership of the Oglethorpe Light Infantry and participated with it in seizing Fort Pulaski and Fort McAllister on the Savannah River from Federal hands. While in the Provisional Congress, he offered the service of his Savannah company to President Davis, thus making it, according to tradition, the first such company tendered for the Confederate cause.

Under the provisions of the Confederacy's permanent Constitution, which took effect in April, officials of the central government could not hold military positions as well, which forced a number of congressmen, including Bartow, to choose their means of service to the Confederacy. He resigned from the Provisional Congress and on May 21, took his Oglethorpe Light Infantry to Virginia. This move led to strenuous objections from Governor Joseph E. Brown, who had planned to use such units to build a state army. Bitter words were exchanged through correspondence, as Bartow remained defiant in denying the governor the right to choose how he would serve his new country.

On June 21, Bartow was elected colonel of the Eighth Georgia Infantry and served under Gen. Joseph E. Johnston in the lower Shenandoah Valley. From there they proceeded to Manassas, where on July 21 he led his own and four other regiments into the first battle of the war. After being wounded in the leg and having his horse shot from under him, he rallied his men for an assault on a Union battery on the Henry House Hill. There he was shot in the chest and died almost instantly. His final words, often cited later, were "They have killed me, boys, but the day is ours. Never give up the field."

Bartow's death made him one of the first and most honored Confederate martyrs. Fellow Georgia congressman Robert Toombs was among several to eulogize him on the floor of the Confederate Congress, which then adjourned for the day in his honor. His body was brought to Richmond and lay in state in the capitol. Gen. Lucius Jeremiah Gartrell of Georgia made much of the fact that he had caught the dying Bartow as he fell from his horse and was responsible for publicizing his final words. By December 1861, Cass County in northwest Georgia had been renamed Bartow County, and its congressman, Warren Akin, wrote his wife that "if we ever have another boy, I now feel like I will call him Bartow."

BIBLIOGRAPHY

Coleman, Kenneth, and Charles Stephen Gurr, eds. *Dictionary of Georgia Biography.* Vol. 1. Athens, Ga., 1983.

Henderson, Lindsey B. *The Oglethorpe Light Infantry.* Athens, Ga., 1961.

Knight, Lucian Lamar. *Reminiscences of Famous Georgians.* Vol. 2. Atlanta, 1908.

Northen, William W., ed. *Men of Mark in Georgia.* Vol. 3. Atlanta, 1908. Reprint, Spartanburg, S.C., 1974.

Wiley, Bell Irvin, ed. *Letters of Warren Akin, Confederate Congressman.* Athens, Ga., 1959.

JOHN C. INSCOE

BASS, NATHAN (1808–1890), congressman from Georgia. Bass was born in Putnam County, Georgia, on October 8, 1808. He attended Mount Pleasant Academy and in 1840 moved to Floyd County in the northwest corner of the state. He acquired large tracts of land there and became a successful cotton planter and large slaveholder. In 1850 he moved to Macon, where he established an even larger plantation while retaining his Floyd County holdings. Those, plus absentee interest in plantations in Alabama, made Bass one of Georgia's wealthiest men on the eve of the Civil War. He played a prominent role in the Cotton Planters' Association, serving as vice president of its 1851 convention and president in 1860.

Bass was also active in politics. In 1856 he was chairman of the state's Kansas Aid Meeting, an organization formed to support the proslavery settlers of the beleaguered territory and to hamper abolitionist influence there. In 1860, he was a delegate at the Democratic convention, and his support of Stephen A. Douglas made him one of few Unionists in the Georgia delegation. After that convention dissolved without selecting a presidential nominee, Bass, along with Herschel V. Johnson and Eugenius Aristides Nisbet, toured Georgia in an effort to convince voters of the necessity of a united Democratic front and a compromise candidate to prevent a Republican presidential victory. He refused to attend the second convention in Baltimore.

After Abraham Lincoln's election, Bass reluctantly supported secession. Through much of 1861, he attempted to rally the Cotton Planters' Association to organize its support, financially and in kind, for the war effort. He was selected to serve as Nisbet's replacement in the Provisional Congress when Nisbet resigned late in 1861, though he served only a month in 1862. He refused to run for election to the First Congress and returned to Macon, where he served sporadically as an adviser to Governor Joseph E. Brown on the state's cotton production and on fluctuations in the market abroad.

The war took a heavy toll on Bass's fortune, and the loss of slaves and decline in cotton prices eventually forced him to give up his Macon holdings and return to Rome, in Floyd County, in the early 1870s. There he spent the rest of his life, never recouping his losses, and died on September 22, 1890.

BIBLIOGRAPHY

Battey, George. *A History of Rome and Floyd County.* Atlanta, 1922.

Wakelyn, Jon L. *Biographical Dictionary of the Confederacy.* Edited by Frank E. Vandiver. Westport, Conn., 1977.

Warner, Ezra J., and W. Buck Yearns. *Biographical Register of the Confederate Congress.* Baton Rouge, La., 1975.

JOHN C. INSCOE

BATE, WILLIAM BRIMAGE (1826–1905), major general, postwar governor of Tennessee, and U.S. senator. Bate was born on October 7, 1826, in what is now Castalian Springs, Tennessee. He received little formal education and left school soon after his father's death in 1842. For several years thereafter he worked as a clerk on a steamboat plying the rivers between Nashville and New Orleans.

Bate served in the Mexican War, becoming a lieutenant in the Third Tennessee Infantry Regiment. Upon returning to Tennessee, he edited a newspaper in Gallatin and served one term in the state legislature. After studying law at what is now Cumberland University, he established a practice in Nashville.

In 1854 Bate was elected attorney general of a district around Nashville. He was an ardent Democrat and in the late 1850s became a strong proponent of Southern rights. In 1860 he served as a Tennessee presidential elector for John C. Breckinridge, the Southern Democrats' presidential candidate.

In the spring of 1861 Bate—a staunch secessionist— played the key role in organizing the Walker Legion, a unit that evolved into the Second Tennessee Infantry Regiment. Bate joined the unit as a private, but he was soon elected captain of Company I and then colonel of the regiment. Mustered into Confederate service at Lynchburg, Virginia, the regiment spent an uneventful year there. Upon its reorganization in early 1862, it was transferred to the West to join what eventually became the Army of Tennessee.

WILLIAM BRIMAGE BATE.   NATIONAL ARCHIVES

At Shiloh on April 6, 1862, soon after he entered the battle, Bate was badly wounded in his left leg. The bullet broke two bones, and surgeons wanted to amputate the limb. Bate, however, held off the doctors with a pistol and had himself conveyed to a relative's home in Huntsville, Alabama, where he waited for the wound to heal.

Bate's wound kept him away from the army for ten months. His conduct at Shiloh, however, had won wide praise, and he was promoted to brigadier general on October 3, 1862. During his convalescence, he held minor administrative commands in northern Alabama and southeastern Tennessee. In February 1863 he returned to the Army of Tennessee where he was assigned to command a Tennessee-Alabama-Georgia brigade in the division of Maj. Gen. Alexander P. Stewart.

At Chickamauga, Bate, who still had to use crutches, had three horses shot from under him as he directed the Confederate attack. When the army was reorganized after Chickamauga, Bate's brigade was transferred to the division of Maj. Gen. John C. Breckinridge. Breckinridge soon took command of a corps, and Bate as the senior officer assumed command of the division.

Bate was one of the few Southern generals to give a creditable performance at Missionary Ridge in late November 1863. He and his men did not retreat from the battleground until advancing Federals chased off the units on both sides of his position and threatened to envelop the division.

Bate's army record in 1863 won widespread acclaim from both military figures and the Tennessee congressional delegation. On March 5, 1864, while the army was in its winter quarters at Dalton, Georgia, Bate was promoted to major general, to date from February 23. He was assigned to command a division in Lt. Gen. William J. Hardee's corps.

Bate turned in a mixed performance in the Atlanta campaign of 1864. On May 28, near New Hope Church, he did not keep tight control over his division. As a result, some of his officers, mistaking the sound of skirmishing for the signal to attack, threw their troops into an unsuccessful assault on a very strong enemy position. The Confederates lost some seven hundred men in the attack. At both Peachtree Creek (July 20) and Atlanta (July 22) Bate was hampered by difficult terrain and changing, sometimes unclear orders. As a result, he accomplished little in either battle. In early August, on the other hand, he caught the Northerners in a clever ambush southwest of Atlanta and inflicted several hundred casualties. In this affair, however, he was again wounded and spent six weeks recovering.

In the fall Bate returned to command his division in the Franklin and Nashville campaign. His men were engaged at Franklin on November 30 and at Murfreesboro on December 7. At Nashville on December 16 Bate's overextended division was posted to hold a poorly selected and incompetently fortified area on the Confederate left, which is now called Shy's Hill. The effort was hopeless, and a massive Federal assault overran the Southern position. The survivors from Bate's command joined the rest of the army in a mad flight southward.

The Confederates finally got south of the Tennessee River where they were safe from pursuit and made their way to Tupelo, Mississippi. From there, part of the army was sent to join the Confederates in North Carolina, where Bate commanded a small corps in some of the closing operations of the war. At the time of the army's surrender, he was back in command of his division. After the surrender, he was paroled at Greensboro, North Carolina, on April 28, 1865.

Returning to Tennessee, Bate resumed the practice of law, worked to end Reconstruction in the state, and reentered Democratic politics. He served as a presidential elector in 1876 and was elected governor in 1882 and 1884. In 1886 he was named to the U.S. Senate where he served until his death on March 9, 1905. While in the Senate, he sponsored an 1893 bill that, in effect, repealed Reconstruction by ending Federal supervision of elections in the Southern states. Bate is buried in Nashville's Mount Olivet Cemetery.

BIBLIOGRAPHY

Hewitt, Laurence J. "William Brimage Bate." In *The Confederate General.* Edited by William C. Davis. Vol. 1. Harrisburg, Pa., 1991.

Kelly, Dennis. "Back in the Saddle: The War Record of William Bate." *Civil War Times Illustrated* 27, no. 8 (1988): 26–33.

Marshall, Park. *William B. Bate.* Nashville, Tenn., 1908.

RICHARD M. MCMURRY

BATON ROUGE, LOUISIANA.

Located on the Mississippi River, Baton Rouge was the capital of Louisiana from 1850 to April 25, 1862, when Confederate authorities abandoned it a week before Union forces occupied New Orleans, eighty miles away. An unsuccessful Confederate attempt to recapture the town resulted in a battle against Union occupying forces on August 5, 1862. Briefly evacuated by the Federal army, Baton Rouge was reoccupied on December 17, 1862, and remained under Union control for the duration of the war.

In 1860 Baton Rouge had a population of 5,429, of whom 1,247 were slaves. In the presidential election that year, the town's voters cast 379 ballots for the Constitutional Union candidate, John Bell; 274 for the slavery expansionist, John C. Breckinridge; and 98 for the national Democrat, Stephen A. Douglas. Baton Rouge's livelihood was based on retail outlets serving the surrounding farms and plantations. Because these stores were supplied by riverboats, the economy could thrive only if peace prevailed and river traffic was undisturbed. With these economic facts in mind, a majority of Baton Rouge voters understandably supported the more moderate Bell and Douglas rather than the extremist Breckinridge.

As elsewhere in the Deep South, however, secessionists seized the initiative in Louisiana after Abraham Lincoln's election. On January 10, 1861 (sixteen days before Louisiana seceded from the Union), state military forces obtained the surrender of the Federal arsenal in Baton Rouge without firing a shot. In the euphoria that followed formation of the Confederacy, several units of troops were raised in the Baton Rouge area, of which the Fencibles, Delta Rifles and Chasseurs à Pied were among the earliest and more prominent. After Louisiana joined the Confederacy, most residents of the community supported the Southern cause—at least during the single year in which they were free to do so.

On May 9, 1862, Union naval forces arrived in Baton Rouge from New Orleans and received the town's surrender without resistance. On May 28, Confederate guerrillas fired on Union sailors attempting to come ashore at Baton Rouge. Adm. David Farragut in retaliation ordered that the town be shelled, which caused considerable destruction and civilian distress. On the next day, 2,600 Union infantry arrived in Baton Rouge under the command of Brig. Gen. Thomas Williams. General Williams soon left for the vicinity of Vicksburg, Mississippi, to assist in the futile assault on that Confederate stronghold. When he returned to Baton Rouge in late July, his men were sick and physically exhausted from digging a useless canal aimed at diverting the Mississippi River around Vicksburg, which did not surrender until a year later.

In the meantime, Maj. Gen. Earl Van Dorn, the Confederate district commander, had decided to retake Baton Rouge. With the town restored to Confederate control, Van Dorn believed he could break the Union blockade of the mouth of the Red River and perhaps recapture New Orleans. Van Dorn ordered John C. Breckinridge, now a major general, to proceed by rail from Vicksburg with 5,000 men to Camp Moore, seventy miles northeast of Baton Rouge. There he would secure another thousand troops for the attack on Baton Rouge. But sickness and exhaustion from the intense summer heat had reduced the number of Breckinridge's men to about 3,400 by the time he left Camp Moore.

BATON ROUGE, LOUISIANA, C. 1860.

HARPER'S PICTORIAL HISTORY OF THE GREAT REBELLION

Breckinridge arrived at the Comite River, ten miles east of Baton Rouge, on August 4. Disease, hunger, and exhaustion had further reduced his units to only 2,600 men. Breckinridge divided his weakened force into two divisions, which commenced their attack at sunrise on August 5. On the right was Brig. Gen. Charles Clark's First Division, consisting of eight regiments, plus supporting artillery. On the left, the Second Division of Brig. Gen. Daniel Ruggles comprised six regiments, a battalion, and supporting artillery. On the Union side, General Williams commanded seven regiments.

Success of the Confederate attack would depend on the timely arrival of the ram *Arkansas* from Vicksburg. The mission of this heavily armed Confederate vessel was to sink or damage Union gunboats anchored in the river so that they could not fire over the heads of the Union garrison into Breckinridge's advancing columns. But *Arkansas* developed engine trouble just north of Baton Rouge and was abandoned and destroyed by its crew. Consequently, Union gunboat fire raked the Confederate units with devastating effect. Breckinridge called off his attack and withdrew to Port Hudson. Confederate losses were 467 killed, wounded or missing; Union casualties were 383 killed (including General Williams), wounded, or missing.

Federal forces left Baton Rouge on August 21 for New Orleans. But on December 17, Brig. Gen. Cuvier Grover returned with 8,000 Union troops, and Baton Rouge remained in Federal hands for the remainder of the war. It served as a staging base for Union operations against Port Hudson and Confederate-held northern Louisiana.

Baton Rouge accepted the reality of Federal occupation, and most citizens adjusted calmly to the presence of many blue uniforms. (The town had been predominantly Unionist in sentiment on the eve of secession.) Quite probably, saloon keepers, hotel owners, and restauranteurs pocketed many Yankee dollars providing the creature comforts of the Federal garrison. On the other hand, Baton Rouge became the destination of a large black migration from plantations in the vicinity, creating immense problems in housing, employment and sanitation. The Gothic statehouse burned during the occupation, and the war damage remained evident for years. The town did not become the state capital again until 1882.

BIBLIOGRAPHY

Carleton, Mark T. *River Capital: An Illustrated History of Baton Rouge.* Woodland Hills, Calif., 1981.
Moneyhon, Carl, and Bobby Roberts. *Portraits of Conflict: A Photographic History of Louisiana in the Civil War.* Fayetteville, Ark., 1990.
Winters, John. *Louisiana in the Civil War.* Baton Rouge, La., 1963.

MARK T. CARLETON

BATSON, FELIX I. (1819–1871), congressman from Arkansas. Felix Ives Batson was born September 6, 1819, in Tennessee and moved to Clarksville, Johnson County, Arkansas sometime before the 1850s. There he became a prominent antebellum jurist, serving as a judge on the state supreme court from 1858 to 1860. He ran for the state secession convention of 1861 as a secessionist in a pro-Union district and was elected. In the convention's first session Batson unsuccessfully proposed a popular election on disunion when the Unionist majority blocked secession. He joined a military company at the outbreak of war but did not enter regular Confederate service.

Batson was elected to the House of Representatives of the First Congress in 1861 from the First Congressional District. In that session he was a strong supporter of President Jefferson Davis, although he tried to obtain enough support from the Confederate government to protect his state. In 1862, with other Arkansas congressmen he requested the removal from command of Gen. Thomas C. Hindman, who had declared martial law in Arkansas to defend the state against a Federal invasion force led by Gen. Samuel R. Curtis. They urged that President Davis place Gen. Sterling Price in command of troops in Arkansas and Missouri and that his army be reinforced. Batson was reelected to the Second Congress in 1863 but did not return to Richmond until November 1864, missing the first two sessions. As a Congressman, Batson generally supported measures advanced by the Davis administration. He particularly backed conscription and attempts to restrict exemptions. When he returned to Richmond in 1864, however, he became a strong opponent of attempts to enlist and arm slaves.

At the end of the war he returned to Clarksville and the practice of law. He died there on March 11, 1871.

BIBLIOGRAPHY

Hempstead, Fay. *A Pictorial History of Arkansas.* St. Louis, Mo., 1908.
Thomas, David Y. *Arkansas in War and Reconstruction, 1861–1875.* Little Rock, Ark., 1926.
Warner, Ezra J., and W. Buck Yearns. *Biographical Register of the Confederate Congress.* Baton Rouge, La., 1975.

CARL H. MONEYHON

BATTLE, CULLEN ANDREWS (1829–1905), brigadier general. Battle, born June 1, 1829, was a native of Georgia, but moved with his family to Alabama in 1836. He graduated from the University of Alabama in 1850 and earned a name for himself as a lawyer and a political orator of stridently secessionist bent. Battle's only prewar military experience was as captain of a volunteer company raised during the John Brown affair. Two years later Captain

Battle led the company into Confederate service as part of the Third Alabama Infantry. At the organization of the regiment, Battle won election as its major, and in July 1861 he was promoted to lieutenant colonel.

In the regiment's first battle, Seven Pines, its colonel was killed and Battle assumed command. He acted as colonel through the rest of 1862 and was wounded at the head of the regiment at both South Mountain and Sharpsburg, but his formal commission as colonel was not confirmed until March 26, 1863. Well before that date, Alabama politicians were pushing for Battle's promotion to brigadier general. As part of Rodes's Brigade, Battle led the Third at Chancellorsville, where he suffered two painful falls from horseback, and at Gettysburg. Battle was only Rodes's fourth choice as his replacement when promoted, but the Alabamian received his general's wreath August 20, 1863.

Despite two extended absences on sick leave, Battle commanded his brigade competently until a serious wound at Cedar Creek ended his war experience in October 1864. After the war Battle edited a newspaper in North Carolina. He died in Greensboro on April 8, 1905.

CULLEN ANDREWS BATTLE.   LIBRARY OF CONGRESS

BIBLIOGRAPHY

Brewer, Willis. *Alabama.* Montgomery, Ala., 1872. Reprint, Tuscaloosa, Ala., 1964.

Freeman, Douglas S. *Lee's Lieutenants: A Study in Command.* 3 vols. New York, 1942–1944. Reprint, New York, 1986.

Hawthorne, J. B. *Cullen Andrews Battle.* N.p., 1905?

ROBERT K. KRICK

BATTLES, NAMING OF. Confederates and Federals sometimes differed in their designations of a particular engagement. D. H. Hill, lieutenant general, C.S.A., afterward wrote:

So many battle-fields of the Civil War bear double names, that we cannot believe the duplication has been accidental. It is the unusual which impresses. The troops of the North came mainly from cities, towns, and villages, and were, therefore, impressed by some natural object near the scene of the conflict and named the battle from it. The soldiers from the South were chiefly from the country and were, therefore, impressed by some artificial object near the field of action. In one section the naming has been after the handiwork of God; in the other section it has been after the handiwork of man.

Whether or not Hill's explanation is correct, his observation itself is borne out by a number of examples. Confederates named battles after such man-made objects as towns or settlements (Manassas, Leesburg, Boonsboro, Sharpsburg, Perryville, Murfreesboro) and buildings (Elkhorn Tavern, Gaines' Mill, Shiloh Church). Federals used the names of watercourses (Bull Run, the Chickahominy, Antietam Creek, Stones River) and other natural

Battles with Dual Names

DATE OF BATTLE	CONFEDERATE NAME	FEDERAL NAME
July 21, 1861	First Manassas	Bull Run
Aug. 10, 1861	Oak Hills	Wilson's Creek
Oct. 21, 1861	Leesburg	Ball's Bluff
Jan. 19, 1862	Mill Springs	Logan's Cross Roads
Mar. 7–8, 1862	Elkhorn Tavern	Pea Ridge
Apr. 6–7, 1862	Shiloh	Pittsburg Landing
June 27, 1862	Gaines' Mill	Chickahominy
Aug. 29–30, 1862	Second Manassas	Second Bull Run
Sept. 1, 1862	Ox Hill	Chantilly
Sept. 14, 1862	Boonsboro	South Mountain
Sept. 17, 1862	Sharpsburg	Antietam
Oct. 8, 1862	Perryville	Chaplin Hills
Dec. 31, 1862– Jan. 2, 1863	Murfreesboro	Stones River
Apr. 1864	Mansfield	Sabine Cross Roads
Sept. 19, 1864	Winchester	Opequon Creek

features (Ball's Bluff, Pea Ridge, Pittsburg Landing, South Mountain, Chaplin Hills).

But this distinction did not always hold, nor was the same pattern consistently followed. Although some Federals used the term "Pittsburg Landing," others, including Ulysses S. Grant, called the battle "Shiloh," as Confederates did. Originally Union officers reported one engagement as "Chaplin Hills," but eventually the designation "Perryville" came to be standard North as well as South. Both Confederates and Federals referred to artificial rather than natural objects in the case of "Mansfield" and "Sabine Cross Roads." And the pattern was reversed when the Confederates were impressed by a natural feature, "Ox Hill," and the Federals by a man-made structure, a residence known as "Chantilly."

In quite a few instances multiple names were used indiscriminately by both sides. An extreme example is the June 30, 1862, clash in Virginia that bore the names of a great variety of objects, all of them manmade (Glendale, White Oak Swamp Bridge, Frazier's or Frayser's Farm, Nelson's Farm, Charles City Cross Roads, New Market Road, Willis Church). Still other battles always and everywhere were known by but a single name (Gettysburg, for example).

BIBLIOGRAPHY

Boatner, Mark M., III. *The Civil War Dictionary.* New York, 1959.
Davis, Burke. *Our Incredible Civil War.* New York, 1960.

RICHARD N. CURRENT

BATTLES AND BATTLEFIELDS. *The encyclopedia contains 114 entries on particular battles. For discussion of the strategic and tactical importance of these battles, see also* Civil War, *article on* Strategy and Tactics. *For discussion of the commemoration and preservation of Civil War battlefields, see* Monuments and Memorials, *article on* Battlefields.

BAXLEY, CATHERINE VIRGINIA (c. 1812–?), spy. Born in Winchester, Virginia, Baxley was a teacher in Baltimore before the war. In late December 1861, Baxley, a widow with one son in the Confederate service, was arrested by the provost marshal in her hometown, Baltimore, and sent to Greenhow Prison, the jail of renowned spy Rose O'Neal Greenhow, in Washington, D.C. Baxley was charged with having carried letters from President Jefferson Davis in Richmond to Baltimore; among the incriminating articles found on her at the time of her arrest was a surgeon's commission she had obtained from Davis for a friend.

In January, Baxley, along with Greenhow, was transferred to Old Capitol Prison in Washington. Greenhow despised Baxley; she complained of Baxley's rantings against her captors. Baxley was so ardent a secessionist that she even refused to sleep under blankets bearing the U.S. emblem. She appealed by letter to both Secretary of State William H. Seward and Secretary of War Edwin M. Stanton, begging her release on the ground that the papers she had carried were not state papers but private ones.

On June 2, 1862, Baxley, along with Greenhow and a third female spy, Augusta Hewitt Morris, was paroled and sent south to Richmond. Shortly thereafter she was paid a fee of five hundred dollars by the Confederate government in return for her services as a courier. Baxley was briefly incarcerated at Old Capitol again in April 1865 on unspecified charges. While in prison she penned a takeoff on the "Star-Spangled Banner" which lambasted Union officials for their ill-treatment of Southern women. Nothing is known of Baxley after the war.

BIBLIOGRAPHY

Ross, Ishbel. *Rebel Rose: Life of Rose O'Neal Greenhow, Confederate Spy.* New York, 1954.
Schultz, Jane Ellen. *Women at the Front: Gender and Genre in Literature of the American Civil War.* Ann Arbor, Mich.: University Microfilms, 1989.
Sigaud, Louis A. "Mrs. Greenhow and the Rebel Spy Ring." *Maryland Historical Magazine* 41 (1946): 173–198.

ELIZABETH R. VARON

BAYLOR, JOHN R. (1822–1894), colonel, territorial governor of Arizona, and congressman from Texas. John Robert Baylor was born at Paris, Kentucky, July 27, 1822. As a child, Baylor moved with his father to Fort Gibson in the Indian Territory. Sent to Cincinnati for an education, he left school to live with an uncle near Rocky Creek, Texas.

A man of vigor and magnetism, he was elected to the Texas legislature and in 1855 was appointed agent to the Comanches on the Clear Fork of the Brazos. Baylor, however, came to possess a burning hatred of the Comanches and was dismissed. While helping to edit an anti-Indian newspaper, *The White Man,* in Weatherford, Baylor led 350 frontiersmen who forced the expulsion of the Indians from Texas in 1859.

With the coming of the Civil War, Baylor was selected as a lieutenant colonel in the Second Texas Mounted Rifles and given the responsibility of garrisoning the forts along the Lower Military Road from San Antonio to Franklin (El Paso). In July 1861, with less than four hundred men, Baylor invaded the Mesilla Valley from his base at Fort Bliss, Texas. After occupying the town of Mesilla, he forced the evacuation of Fort Fillmore and the surrender of six companies of the Seventh Infantry and two of Mounted Rifles at San Agustin Pass in the Organ Mountains. After creating the Confederate Territory of Arizona and appointing himself governor, Baylor issued a controversial order for the extermination of a band of Apaches near Pinos Altos. Referring to the order as an "infamous crime," President Jefferson Davis revoked Baylor's commission in the Confederate army. After the New Mexico campaign and a feud with Brig. Gen. Henry Hopkins Sibley, Baylor fought as a private at the Battle of Galveston and was elected to the Second Confederate Congress. In Richmond, he served on the Patents and Indian Affairs committees and supported a number of war measures but was opposed to martial law.

Baylor, who was active in politics after the war, died at Montell, Texas, on February 6, 1894.

BIBLIOGRAPHY

Baylor, George W. *John Robert Baylor.* Tucson, Ariz., 1966.

Finch, L. Boyd. "Arizona's Governors without Portfolio: A Wonderfully Diverse Lot." *Arizona Historical Quarterly* 26 (Spring 1985): 81–87.

Hall, Martin H. "Planter vs. Frontiersman." In *Essays on the American Civil War.* Edited by William F. Holmes and Harold M. Hollingsworth. Austin, Tex., 1968.

Thompson, Jerry. *John Robert Baylor: Texas Indian Fighter and Confederate Soldier.* Hillsboro, Tex., 1971.

JERRY THOMPSON

BEALE, RICHARD LEE TURBERVILLE

(1819–1893), U.S. congressman and brigadier general. Beale, the descendant of seventeenth-century Virginia settlers, was born at Hickory Hill, Westmoreland County, May 22, 1819. He was educated at Dickinson College and the University of Virginia. He was admitted to the bar in 1839 and practiced law near his birthplace. Beale was a member of Congress from 1847 to 1849, a delegate to the state constitutional convention in 1851, and a state senator from 1858 to 1860.

In May 1861 Beale was mustered into Confederate service as a first lieutenant of "Lee's Legion" or "Lee's Light Horse." The legion was ordered to the aid of P. G. T. Beauregard on July 21, but arrived a day after the Battle of First Manassas. Beale was promoted to captain in July 1861 and to major in October. When the legion was merged with the Ninth Cavalry in the spring of 1862, he was appointed lieutenant colonel under William Henry Fitzhugh Lee. On the promotion of Lee to brigadier, Beale was appointed colonel of the regiment.

In December 1862, Beale led a bold expedition into Rappahannock County, capturing a Federal garrison without a single loss. Later Beale was cited by J. E. B. Stuart for repelling a threatened raid by Stoneman's cavalry.

Dissatisfaction over details made concerning his regiment without his permission led Beale to submit his resignation three times, on November 22, 1862, February 8, 1863, and August 25, 1863. In his third effort, Beale asserted he was "devoted as ever to Southern Independence" and asked to be allowed to raise a company of rangers or enlist as a private. His resignation was not accepted.

Beale played a prominent role in crushing Dahlgren's raid in January 1864 and assumed command of the brigade in August following the death of John Randolph Chambliss, Jr. Beale was recommended for brigadier by W. H. F. Lee in October. Wade Hampton and Robert E. Lee endorsed the recommendation, which was misplaced in the office of the adjutant general because an inordinate number of clerks had just been drafted for service in the field. The appointment was made on February 6, 1865.

Following the surrender Beale was paroled at Ashland, April 27, 1865. He resumed his legal practice and served a term in Congress from 1879 to 1881. He died on April 21, 1893, and was buried at Hickory Hill.

BIBLIOGRAPHY

Compiled Military Service Records. Richard L. T. Beale. Microcopy M331, Roll 19. Record Group 109. National Archives, Washington, D.C.

Hotchkiss, Jed. *Virginia.* Vol. 3 of *Confederate Military History.* Edited by Clement A. Evans. Atlanta, 1899. Vol. 4 of extended ed. Wilmington, N.C., 1987.

Warner, Ezra J. *Generals in Gray: Lives of the Confederate Commanders.* Baton Rouge, La., 1959.

LOWELL REIDENBAUGH

BEALL, JOHN Y.

(1835–1865), privateer and special agent. Beall was born January 1, 1835. His family, which pronounced the name "Bell," lived in Jefferson County, Virginia (present-day West Virginia). Beall attended the University of Virginia (1852–1853). Widely regarded as a young man of great promise, he had many friends and relatives prominent in the Confederate government.

His first military service was with a company formed in Jefferson at the time of the John Brown raid, called the Botts Grays. This unit became part of the Second Virginia Regiment, Stonewall Brigade. Beall, with Turner Ashby's cavalry at Harpers Ferry on October 16, 1861, was severely wounded, which forced an end to his regular service.

In February 1863 Beall was appointed acting master in the Confederate volunteer navy and was known forever afterward as "Captain Beall." From April to November 1863, Beall, assisted by a number of his neighbors, conducted active partisan warfare—privateering—on the Chesapeake Bay. On November 14, 1863, Beall was captured and subsequently imprisoned at Fort McHenry. He was exchanged in March 1864.

In September 1864 Beall was involved in operations

aimed at freeing the Confederate officers imprisoned on Johnson's Island in Lake Erie. He led a party of twenty in the capture of the steamers *Philo Parsons* and *Island Queen.* But needing still more hardware to attack the formidable guard-ship USS *Michigan,* the Confederates arranged to purchase a lake ship, *Georgian,* and ordered cannon made for it at Guelph, Ontario. Believing incorrectly that Beall was managing this enterprise, U.S. officials pressed the Canadians to arrest him. The Canadians apprehended the wrong man and Beall escaped.

Late in 1864 Beall was part of a group that tried to intercept and release seven imprisoned Confederate general officers being moved from Johnson's Island to Fort Lafayette in New York. On December 16, near Suspension Bridge, New York, Beall and one young companion were captured. Beall tried to conceal who he was, but the companion testified against him, and Beall was tried and convicted as a guerrilla and spy.

Beall was hanged at Governor's Island, New York, on February 24, 1865. After Abraham Lincoln's assassination, there was some allegation that John Wilkes Booth, a friend of Beall's, had been motivated to kill the president in retaliation for not preventing Beall's hanging. Lost Cause devotees later lionized Beall as a heroic martyr.

BIBLIOGRAPHY

Markens, Isaac. "Defense of John Yates Beall." *Confederate Veteran* 35 (1928): 59–62. Reprint, Wilmington, N.C., 1985.

McNeilly, Rev. James H. "John Yates Beall: Account of his Thrilling Career for the South." *Confederate Veteran* 7 (1900): 66–69. Reprint, Wilmington, N.C., 1985.

Tidwell, William A., with James O. Hall and David Winfred Gaddy. *Come Retribution: The Confederate Secret Service and the Assassination of Lincoln.* Jackson, Miss., 1988.

U.S. War Department. *War of the Rebellion: Official Records of the Union and Confederate Navies.* Washington, D.C., 1894–1927. Ser. 1, vol. 3, p. 716; ser. 1, vol. 9, pp. 305–307, 318.

"Why Booth Killed President Lincoln." *Confederate Veteran* 9 (1902): 3–4. Reprint, Wilmington, N.C., 1985.

HERMAN HATTAWAY

BEALL, WILLIAM N. R.

BEALL, WILLIAM N. R. (1825–1883), brigadier general. Born in Bardstown, Kentucky, March 20, 1825, Beall relocated to Arkansas as a child. Finishing thirtieth of thirty-eight at West Point in 1848, he became a brevet second lieutenant in the Fourth Infantry. Promoted to second lieutenant, Fifth Infantry, April 30, 1849, and to first lieutenant, First Cavalry, March 3, 1855, Beall became a captain twenty-four days later. He fought Indians on the Great Plains and pro- and antislavery forces in Kansas before resigning August 20, 1861.

WILLIAM N. R. BEALL.   LIBRARY OF CONGRESS

Commissioned a captain of cavalry in the Confederate army to date from March 16, 1861, Beall initially served in Arkansas. In early 1862, Maj. Gen. Earl Van Dorn appointed him his assistant adjutant general. Promoted to brigadier general April 11, he assumed command of the cavalry near Corinth, Mississippi.

When he was assigned to command the District of East Louisiana August 29, Port Hudson became his main responsibility. Relieved of district command by Brig. Gen. John B. Villepigue (October 14–November 9) and by Maj. Gen. Franklin Gardner on December 27, Beall commanded a brigade at Port Hudson in 1863. During the siege he supervised the center and significantly contributed to the garrison's holding out until July 9. He was captured when the garrison fell.

Imprisoned on Johnson's Island, Beall was released in 1864 to sell Confederate cotton in the North and to purchase supplies for Confederate prisoners. After his parole on August 2, 1865, Beall became a merchant in St. Louis. He died July 26, 1883, in McMinnville, Tennessee, and was buried in Nashville. His sister was Confederate Maj. Gen. James Fleming Fagan's first wife.

BIBLIOGRAPHY

Hewitt, Lawrence Lee. *Port Hudson, Confederate Bastion on the Mississippi.* Baton Rouge, La., 1987.

Harrell, John M. *Arkansas.* Vol. 10 of *Confederate Military History.* Edited by Clement A. Evans. Atlanta, 1899. Vol. 14 of extended ed. Wilmington, N.C., 1988.

LAWRENCE L. HEWITT

BEAUREGARD, P. G. T. (1818–1893), general. Destined for a military career marked by controversy and conflict with superiors and colleagues, Pierre Gustave Toutant Beauregard was born at Contreras Plantation in St. Bernard Parish, Louisiana, just south of New Orleans, on May 28, 1818. Much has been made of his French creole origins, leading some to ascribe his later difficulties to aristocratic haughtiness derived from a fiery Gallic inheritance, but such theorizing stems largely from romantic notions of creole society. One of only eight full generals in the Confederate forces, he would see action in almost every theater of the Civil War, from the firing on Fort Sumter to a final surrender in the Carolinas during the last days of the conflict.

Beauregard entered West Point at the age of sixteen after several years at the French School in New York City, already a committed disciple of Napoléon Bonaparte and the military theorist Henri de Jomini. Immersion in this new Anglo-Saxon milieu led to his abandonment of the hyphen from the Toutant-Beauregard family name, prelude to his eventual discarding of "Pierre" for his favored "G. T. Beauregard." Graduating second in the academy's class of 1838, he received a lieutenant's commission in the Corps of Engineers and quickly distinguished himself in building and repairing coastal fortifications at Pensacola, Florida, and near the mouth of the Mississippi in his native state.

Assigned to Winfield Scott's command at the outbreak of the Mexican War, he won that crusty soldier's praise for skillful reconnaissance missions in the campaign from Tampico to Mexico City, particularly impressing the general with the precision and acuity of his recommendations as to the best line of march against the enemy capital. Despite a brevet as major for bravery in the attack on Chapultepec, Beauregard came away from the war embittered against Scott, resentful that his contributions to victory had not won official commendation greater than that accorded fellow officers like Robert E. Lee and George B. McClellan. A comparable conceit as to his talents and accomplishments would continue to plague his relationships in the years ahead, and his scathing criticism of what he saw as the weaknesses in Scott's generalship revealed what would be an abiding tendency to accept conventional abstract theory rather than imaginative pragmatic execution as the measure of military performance.

From 1848 to 1860 Beauregard served as engineering officer in charge of "the Mississippi and Lake defences in Louisiana," and after 1853 as superintendent responsible for building the Federal Custom House at New Orleans, establishing in both assignments a reputation for superior engineering skills. After an unsuccessful try for the mayoralty of New Orleans in 1858, he enlisted the aid of Senator John Slidell, husband of his wife's sister, to win appointment in 1860 as superintendent of West Point. But his clear secessionist sympathies led to dismissal from the post on January 28, 1861, a mere five days after his installation.

Beauregard resigned his Federal commission effective February 20, 1861, and returned to Louisiana in expectation that he would be made commander of the state's now-independent military forces, an appointment that went instead to Braxton Bragg. In resentful pride, he refused any other commission in the state army, enlisting perversely as a private in the Orleans Guards. That unit saw little of him, for Slidell and other influential political leaders had already pressed his claim with Jefferson Davis for appointment in the Confederate army. Convinced that the Louisianan's vaunted gunnery expertise made him particularly suited to the task, Davis commissioned him as brigadier general on February 27, 1861, with command of the Confederate and South Carolina forces aligned against the Federal garrison at Fort Sumter in Charleston Harbor.

Assuming his post on March 6, Beauregard quickly rearranged gun implacements on the Charleston Battery and the islands to its left and right to mount a circle of fire around Fort Sumter in the center, confident that this concentration would keep at bay any Federal vessels attempting to reinforce the fortification and also allow for its destruction should that become necessary. His efforts proved highly effective. When negotiations with U.S. Maj. Robert Anderson, commander of the Federal garrison, failed to secure Union withdrawal from the island stronghold, Beauregard opened fire on Sumter during the early morning hours of April 12, and the fateful years of civil war had begun.

The events at Charleston made Beauregard an immediate Confederate hero, hailed as "Old Bory" and praised as one of the world's great soldiers. President Davis, the Confederate Congress, newspapers across the South, and smitten female admirers showered him with gratitude, while an equally responsive Northern editor placed a price on his head. If all this tended to reinforce an already prickly self-esteem, for the moment at least he gave no time to reveling in applause, but set about buttressing the defenses of Charleston by shifting the target of his batteries from Sumter to the harbor entrance.

Early in May 1861, he testily rejected a suggestion by Davis that he go to Pensacola to take Fort Pickens, thus crossing swords with his superiors for the first but not the

P. G. T. Beauregard.

last time. However much he might have offended the president, it did not keep Davis from appointing him in mid-May to command of the defenses of the Mississippi from Vicksburg to the Kentucky-Tennessee border. But by May 28 things looked dramatically different. Now the Confederate capital had been shifted to Virginia and new orders sped him on to Richmond.

Federal troops had crossed the Potomac to occupy Alexandria, pointing clearly to an impending attack upon the Confederate railroad junction at Manassas just north of the capital, and it was here that Davis and Robert E. Lee, his personal military adviser, wished Beauregard to take command. He did so on June 3, launching a dizzying round of activity centering on earthworks around Manassas, troop reorganization, and grandiose plans for a full-scale campaign into enemy territory across the Potomac, tactfully but resolutely rejected by his Richmond superiors. With a Federal attack obviously imminent, Davis and Lee ordered Gen. Joseph E. Johnston to move his army from the Shenandoah Valley to reinforce Beauregard. As the senior officer, Johnston had right of command of the joined forces, but recognizing Beauregard's longer presence on the scene and better knowledge of the terrain, he allowed his colleague to retain that prerogative, a courtesy Beauregard eventually repaid by asking Johnston to leave the field when actual fighting began.

Luckily for the Southern cause, Gen. Irvin McDowell's attack upon the Confederate positions just north of Manassas at Bull Run on July 21 preempted Beauregard's battle plan. As presented to a dismayed Johnston, that blueprint reflected many of the weaknesses of Beauregard's generalship. It abounded in a bewildering confusion of orders and lines of authority and gave little attention to possible responses of the adversary. Its implementation might well have spelled disaster for the Southern forces. But despite indescribable disarray and inefficiency in his headquarters, once the fighting began Beauregard revealed his essential strength as a commander, what historian Frank Vandiver has called a "soldier's greatest asset—battle sense." Skillfully countering McDowell's moves, he sent the Federal force reeling back toward Washington.

A grateful President Davis raised him to full generalship on the morning after the battle, confirmed when Congress dated his commission fifth in seniority behind only Adj. Gen. Samuel Cooper, Albert Sidney Johnston, Robert E. Lee and Joe Johnston. Once again he heard his praises sung in all quarters of the South, and for a brief moment he seemed indeed to be what one Richmond editor dubbed him, "Beauregard Felix," favorite of the gods. Mindful of the troubles experienced in distinguishing friend from foe during the fighting at Manassas because of the similarity between the Confederate and Union standards, he added to his honors by designing the famous Southern battle flag, replacing the Stars and Bars.

His universal acclaim proved short-lived. To an old feud with Commissary Gen. Lucius B. Northrop over supposed lack of supplies to his troops, he now added a blustery dispute with Secretary of War Judah P. Benjamin for what he perceived as meddling interference with his command prerogatives. Davis attempted to calm these imbroglios but began to grow more impatient with Beauregard when it became clear that his complaints to opposition members of Congress fed increasing attacks upon administration policy. Disaffection increased with reports that the general had wide backing to contest for the permanent presidency in the coming elections ending the provisional status of the government.

But it was Beauregard's report to Congress on the Battle of Manassas that caused the greatest uproar. Although denying opposition claims that Davis had prevented pursuit of retreating Federal troops, the general implied that the taking of Washington had been nonetheless sacrificed by Davis's rejection of his original invasion plan and by the president's slowness in ordering Johnston's army to join forces with his own. Furious, Davis shot back that no such strategy had ever been presented to him and charged Beauregard with attempting to exalt himself at his superior's expense. Unrepentant, Beauregard countered with a letter to the *Richmond Whig* in which he obliquely chastised Davis anew. His persistence struck many as sheer contumacy, and the heading of his communication— "Centreville, Va., Within hearing of the Enemy's Guns"— made him seem vainglorious and ridiculously pompous.

Whether on the initiative of his congressional friends or at the instigation of the president, late in January 1862, Beauregard was ordered west as second in command to Albert Sidney Johnston. As Johnston's position crumbled along the Tennessee-Kentucky border, he rejected Beauregard's pleas to mount a concentration of all available troops in defense of Fort Donelson against Ulysses S. Grant's certain attack, sending him instead to supervise the withdrawal of Gen. Leonidas Polk's army from Columbus, Kentucky.

Falling back all along their lines, Johnston and Beauregard gathered a force of some 35,000 men at Corinth, Mississippi. From there they moved on April 3 to attack Grant's army in camp at Pittsburg Landing on the west bank of the Tennessee River near a small church called Shiloh. Delay in the deployment of troops and careless noise in the undisciplined ranks convinced Beauregard that the element of surprise critical to his battle plan was now lost, and he urged postponement of the attack. Johnston demurred, and on April 6 the Confederates struck. From his position in the rear of the Confederate troops, Beauregard exercised more general command of the field than did Johnston, who threw himself into the thick of the fray like a corps leader until he fell fatally wounded. With Johnston's death Beauregard assumed full command and at day's end had almost forced Grant's army into the river. But the desperate weariness of his men led him to call a halt, and by next morning Don Carlos Buell's army had arrived to give Grant reinforcement sufficient to push back the exhausted Confederate foe.

Failure to clinch victory when it seemed in his grasp exposed Beauregard to renewed criticism by his enemies and even by one of his subordinates, Braxton Bragg. His own attempts to portray Shiloh as a misrepresented success only further diminished his reputation, an erosion heightened when Gen. Henry Halleck drove him from Corinth south to Tupelo. There, suffering from a chronic throat ailment from which he hoped to seek relief in Mobile, he turned temporary leadership of the Army of the West over to Bragg without authorization from Richmond, giving Davis the pleasure of ordering his immediate dismissal from command.

Determined to keep Beauregard out of the field, Davis next assigned him to head the Department of South Carolina and Georgia, headquartered at Charleston, where he arrived on September 15, 1862. Still convinced that the best way to protect the city lay in concentrating such firepower on the entrance to the harbor that Federal naval vessels would be unable to break through, he successfully hectored Richmond for increased matériel to strengthen his batteries and fortifications. In April 1863, he turned back a Union flotilla of nine ironclads and later that year withstood a siege by combined army and navy forces that inflicted heavy damage on Fort Sumter and surrounding island installations but failed to dislodge his hold on the city. In all, he had effectively managed what has been called "the war's longest and most skillful defense of a land point against attack from the sea."

During that extended standoff some additional opportunities had come his way. Lee wanted him to serve in northern Virginia while he led the campaign into Maryland and Pennsylvania, and Samuel Cooper invited him to aid Joe Johnston by guarding against Union incursions into Mississippi. But with his heart still set on an independent field command, Beauregard stubbornly rejected all such offers, until in April 1864, at Lee's instigation, he was given charge of the Department of North Carolina and Southern Virginia, responsible for holding the southern approaches to Richmond.

The advance of the Army of the Potomac against Confederate forces in northern Virginia made Beauregard's mission vitally important, for loss of the Southern supply lines would spell almost certain collapse of Lee's attempts to hold the capital. When Union Gen. Benjamin Butler in early May moved troops up the James River to Drewry's Bluff, midway between Petersburg and Richmond, Beauregard managed to drive him back into a position bottled up between the James and Appomattox rivers, despite frequent interference from Davis and Bragg, now chief of staff. Again

his critics charged that he had allowed an enemy force to escape destruction. His continuing reluctance to send reinforcements to Lee as Grant maneuvered to get his army between the Virginian and Richmond produced even more friction with his superiors.

Whatever his failings, he alone among the Confederate leaders anticipated Grant's move south of the James after the battle at Cold Harbor. While Lee for almost forty-eight hours remained ignorant of his opponent's whereabouts, Beauregard successfully blocked Grant's advance upon Petersburg until increasingly desperate communiqués convinced his skeptical colleague that it was indeed the full force of the Army of the Potomac pushing against his lines. Lee then moved quickly south and Petersburg was saved. It remains Beauregard's finest hour.

In the ensuing siege of Petersburg, he continued under Lee's direction, restive again in a subordinate position and frequently at odds with the high command. Bragg and Davis persisted in their long established animosity by charging him with various acts of malfeasance. He consequently welcomed assignment in October 1864 to head a new department called the Military Division of the West, with oversight of the armies of Gen. John Bell Hood in Georgia and Richard Taylor in Alabama.

Suggestive that the appointment represented primarily an attempt at political fence-mending by the administration, Davis severely limited Beauregard's authority in this new assignment, restricting him to basically advisory powers. Exploiting this opportunity, Hood won Beauregard's reluctant approval for a push into Tennessee but then proceeded to ignore the department commander in the campaign that led him to disaster at Nashville in December. Beauregard meanwhile proved incapable of divining William Tecumseh Sherman's objectives in his march east from Atlanta, failing to concentrate Confederate forces as the Federal juggernaut moved inexorably toward the sea. With his command widened to the Atlantic coast, he attempted to hold a line from Augusta to Charleston, where he expected the main Federal attack. But again Sherman confounded him, striking instead at Columbia in February 1865 and driving Beauregard's forces back into North Carolina before he could unite with those of Gen. William J. Hardee as they evacuated a now indefensible Charleston.

On the advice of Lee, a dismayed Davis dispatched Joe Johnston to take over Beauregard's command, leaving the Louisianan to direct rear-area troop movements and protect lines of communication. Apparently resigned to the war's inevitable conclusion, he declined appointment to small field commands in western Virginia and eastern Tennessee, preferring to remain under Johnston. When a gloomy April 13 conference with President Davis and Secretary of War John C. Breckinridge in Greensboro confirmed Lee's capitulation to Grant, Johnston surrendered his army to Sherman near Hillsboro, North Carolina, on April 26, 1865, and on May 1 Beauregard headed home to Louisiana.

Unlike most of his fellow Confederate generals, he found the postwar years generally prosperous and rewarding. Occasional moments of dejection in the Reconstruction period led to flirtation with various possibilities of foreign military service in Brazil, Romania, Egypt, Spain, and Argentina, none of which materialized, turning him to his old engineering skills. Appointed superintendent of the New Orleans, Jackson, and Great Northern Railroad late in 1865, he also served as president of the New Orleans and Carrollton street railway from 1866 until he was ousted as part owner of the company a decade later. Recovery from that setback came the next year, when he and Jubal Early began a long stint as supervisors of the drawings of the infamous Louisiana Lottery for reportedly handsome salaries. Some restoration of military status came with his appointment in 1879 as adjutant general and commander of the Louisiana militia, a position he held until 1888, when he was elected commissioner of public works for New Orleans.

Inevitably, passage of the years caught him up in a series of literary clashes with Joe Johnston over events at Manassas, with various promoters of Albert Sidney Johnston as the true hero of Shiloh, and with his old nemesis Jefferson Davis over just about everything, in a flurry of conflicting reminiscences. His chief contributions to the fray appeared in *The Military Operations of General Beauregard,* attributed to a friend, Alfred Roman, but essentially his own creation, and a *Century* magazine article, "The Battle of Bull Run," later expanded into *A Commentary on the Campaign and Battle of Manassas.*

After a brief illness he died in New Orleans on February 21, 1893. He was interred in that city's tomb of the Army of Tennessee in Metairie Cemetery, dominated, ironically, by the equestrian statue of Albert Sidney Johnston.

BIBLIOGRAPHY

Basso, Hamilton. *Beauregard, The Great Creole.* New York, 1933.

Beauregard, P. G. T. "The First Battle of Bull Run." *Century Illustrated Monthly Magazine* 19 (1884): 80–106.

Freeman, Douglas S. *Lee's Lieutenants: A Study in Command.* 3 vols. New York, 1942–1944. Reprint, New York, 1986.

Horn, Stanley F. *The Army of Tennessee.* Indianapolis, 1941.

Roman, Alfred. *The Military Operations of General Beauregard.* 2 vols. New York, 1884.

Vandiver, Frank E. *Their Tattered Flags: The Epic of the Confederacy.* New York, 1970. Reprint, Texas A & M University Military History Series, no. 5. College Station, Tex., 1987.

Williams, T. Harry. *P. G. T. Beauregard: Napoleon in Gray.* Baton Rouge, La., 1954.

JOSEPH G. TREGLE, JR.

BEAUVOIR. Developed in the late 1840s and early 1850s by Mississippi planter James Brown, this waterfront estate near Biloxi, Mississippi, was home to Jefferson Davis during the final twelve years of his life. The Beauvoir estate was dominated by a raised, single-story Greek Revival cottage and flanking pavilions. Having escaped the ravages of war, the property was purchased in 1873 by Davis family acquaintance and author Sarah Anne Ellis Dorsey, who gave her new home its French name because of the "beautiful view" of the Gulf of Mexico.

Responding to an offer from Mrs. Dorsey, Jefferson Davis decided to write at Beauvoir rather than develop and occupy his own property in the area. By February 1877, Davis was at work on *The Rise and Fall of the Confederate Government* in the east, or library, pavilion. He was assisted by personal secretary William T. Walthall and Mrs. Dorsey. Upon her arrival in 1878, Varina Howell Davis replaced Mrs. Dorsey, whom she disliked. Despite Sarah Dorsey's intention to bequeath Beauvoir to Davis, he purchased the estate in 1879 for $5,500. The Davises, later joined by daughter Varina Anne ("Winnie"), entertained a variety of notables while residing at Beauvoir.

Following the deaths of Jefferson in 1889 and Winnie in 1898, Varina Davis sold the property for $10,000 to the Mississippi Division, United Sons of Confederate Veterans. The organization, in accordance with her wishes, leased the property to the state of Mississippi for a Confederate soldiers' home. The Jefferson Davis Memorial Home, from 1903 to 1957, provided shelter and care for about two thousand residents, including veterans and their wives, widows, and servants. Museum operations at the site were initiated in 1941 with the opening of the main house for tours. Today, the entire eighty-four-acre estate operates as a historic landmark.

BIBLIOGRAPHY

Davis, Varina. *Jefferson Davis, Ex-President of the Confederate States of America: A Memoir by His Wife, Varina Davis.* New York, 1890. Reprint ed. Introduction by Craig L. Symonds. Baltimore, 1990.

Strode, Hudson. *Jefferson Davis: Tragic Hero.* Vol. 3 of *Jefferson Davis.* New York, 1964.

Thompson, James W. *Beauvoir: A Walk through History.* Edited by Keith A. Hardison. Biloxi, Miss., 1988.

KEITH ANDERSON HARDISON

BEAVER DAM CREEK, VIRGINIA. *See* Mechanicsville, Virginia.

BEE, BARNARD E. (1824–1861), brigadier general. Though a South Carolinian by birth, Bee spent his formative years in Texas. He entered West Point in 1841, graduating four years later with a class standing of

BARNARD E. BEE.   NATIONAL ARCHIVES

thirty-third. Bee served with distinction in the Mexican War and saw duty along the western frontier on the eve of the Civil War. He envisioned a terrible conflict if disunion became a reality. Not wishing to participate in such a struggle, he retired to his brother's ranch in Texas.

Bee's misgivings over secession disappeared when his native state pulled out of the Union. He resigned from the U.S. Army on March 3, 1861, before the firing on Fort Sumter. Bee began his Confederate service as a major, but on June 17, 1861, he received a brigadier-generalship and a brigade. At First Manassas on July 21, 1861, Bee tried to rally his troops as they retreated. He pointed to Thomas J. Jackson's stalwart brigade and exclaimed: "There stands Jackson like a stone wall! Rally around the Virginians!" The sobriquet "Stonewall," which attached itself to Jackson and his Virginia brigade for the rest of the war, is still used. Bee fell with a mortal wound shortly after he uttered these famous words, and he died the next day. He was buried in Pendleton, South Carolina.

BIBLIOGRAPHY

Capers, Ellison. *South Carolina*. Vol. 5 of *Confederate Military History*. Edited by Clement A. Evans. Atlanta, 1899. Vol. 6 of extended ed. Wilmington, N.C., 1987.

Hennessy, John. "Stonewall Jackson's Nickname: Was It Fact or Was It Fiction?" *Civil War* 7 (March–April 1990): 10–17.

PETER S. CARMICHAEL

BEE, HAMILTON P. (1822–1897), brigadier general. Born in Charleston, South Carolina, Bee, the older brother of Brig. Gen. Barnard E. Bee, moved to Texas in the 1830s where he was active in state politics. In 1861, Bee was elected brigadier general in the Texas militia and in March 1862 received the same rank in the Confederate army. He was assigned to command Texas coastal defenses, with the primary duty of circumventing the Union blockade by conducting business between Brownsville and Matamoros, Mexico. He proved very successful in importing munitions and supplies as well as exporting cotton.

In 1864 he was called upon to help halt Nathaniel P. Banks's drive up the Red River in Louisiana. During this campaign his brigade fought at Mansfield (April 8), Pleasant Hill (April 9), and Blair's Landing (Pleasant Hill Landing, April 12). Afterward Gen. Richard Taylor ordered Bee to move his small cavalry force around Banks's army and cut off the Union retreat while Taylor's remaining force pursued from the rear. At Cane River Crossing (Monett's Bluff, April 23) Bee's badly outnumbered force was knocked quickly out of the way and the Union retreat continued. Though not questioning Bee's gallantry, Taylor blamed him for Banks's escape and said he showed "no generalship." Bee claimed that Banks had gotten away "because success was impossible." Other officers, including Gen. E. Kirby Smith, defended Bee. Late in the war he served under Gen. John Austin Wharton and in Samuel Bell Maxey's division in Indian Territory. Bee surrendered with the Army of the Trans-Mississippi and was paroled as a major general. There is no official record of his promotion, and he appears to be one of a number of officers promoted by E. Kirby Smith after his command was cut off from the East.

At the end of the war, Bee, along with many other Texas civil and military officials who feared possible retribution from the U.S. government, led a number of former Confederate soldiers to Mexico to live in exile. He finally returned to Texas in 1876 and died in San Antonio in 1897.

BIBLIOGRAPHY

Kerby, Robert L. *Kirby Smith's Confederacy: The Trans-Mississippi South, 1863–1865*. New York, 1972.

Roberts, O. M. *Texas*. Vol. 11 of *Confederate Military History*. Edited by Clement A. Evans. Atlanta, 1899. Vol. 15 of extended ed. Wilmington, N.C., 1989.

Walker, John C. "Reconstruction in Texas." *Southern Historical Society Papers* 24 (1896): 41–57. Reprint, Wilmington, N.C., 1991.

THOMAS J. LEGG

BEEFSTEAK RAID. During the dark early morning hours of September 14, 1864, Confederate cavalry Maj. Gen. Wade Hampton led 4,000 horsemen on a circuitous route toward Coggins Point, Virginia, just below the Union's general headquarters at City Point. The object was some 2,500 head of cattle to feed Robert E. Lee's war-weary and starving Army of Northern Virginia. The Beefsteak Raid, also known as the Hampton-Rosser Cattle Raid, was an overwhelming success with Confederates capturing the herd with few losses in manpower and much material gain.

On September 5, 1864, a Confederate cavalry scout named George D. Shadbourne had brought information of the herd kept by the Union army at Coggins Point, Virginia. Hampton promptly requested permission from General Lee to lead an expedition into Union lines to capture the cattle. With the Federal army daily tightening its hold on Lee's supply lines at Petersburg, the Army of Northern Virginia was suffering a severe lack of food. Lee consented, and Hampton quickly made plans for his surprise raid to commence on September 14.

By the morning of September 16, 1864, Brig. Gen. Thomas L. Rosser's Laurel Brigade had reached the Federal outposts that protected the cattle grazing peacefully on lush grassy fields. Rosser's men swiftly charged into the quiet Union camp of the First D.C. Cavalry. The First D.C. was a specially trained crack unit of cavalrymen armed with Henry repeating rifles. But taken by surprise, the Federals offered feeble resistance to the raiding graycoats who managed to capture nearly all the First D.C.'s officers. Rosser's men next challenged members of the Thirteenth Pennsylvania Cavalry who guarded the prized animals. They refused Rosser's demand to surrender, and a hot fight ensued with Confederates driving the Union cavalrymen back. The hungry Southerners eagerly seized cases of champagne, sardines, cigars, peaches, and other luxuries from abandoned sutler wagons. They then forced several Union civilian herdsmen to help them drive 2,486 cattle into a seven-mile-long column and headed toward Confederate lines.

When reports of the raid reached the Union command, Federals were incredulous over the speed and skill with which the Confederates had captured the cattle a mere six miles from Union central headquarters. Union gunboats had arrived on the James River to shell an enemy long gone. A detachment of Union cavalrymen set out in an angry search for the stolen cattle and their captors.

At 4:00 P.M. Rosser's men turned to fight the pursuing Federals at Ebenezer's Church. For four hours they held off the enemy while the rest of Hampton's troopers led the steers toward Confederate lines. By 9:00 the next morning, the raid had ended. Although the Federal forces outnumbered the Confederates twenty to one, Southern losses numbered a mere sixty-one; the surprised Federals had incurred some four hundred casualties.

The Beefsteak Raid brought enough meat to feed Lee's army for forty days and no doubt helped the Confederates survive their fourth winter of war. It proved one of the South's last dramatic cavalry sweeps into enemy territory and marked one of the largest cattle-rustling expeditions in U.S. history.

BIBLIOGRAPHY

Boykin, Edward. *Beefsteak Raid.* New York, 1960.
Cardwell, D. "A Brilliant Coup. How Wade Hampton Captured Grant's Entire Beef Supply." *Southern Historical Society Papers* 22 (1894): 147–156. Reprint, Wilmington, N.C., 1990.
Lykes, Richard W. "The Great Civil War Beef Raid." *Civil War Times Illustrated* 5, no. 10 (February 1967): 4–12.
McDonald, W.N. "Hampton's Cattle Raid." *Confederate Veteran* 31 (1923): 94–96. Reprint, Wilmington, N.C., 1985.

LESLEY JILL GORDON-BURR

BEERS, FANNIE (1840?–?), hospital matron. Born in the North, probably in Connecticut, and well educated, Fannie married Augustus P. Beers, a Yale-educated Southerner, sometime in the 1850s. They resided in New Orleans where Fannie became an ardent Southern sympathizer. At the outbreak of the war she was visiting her mother while expecting a baby, but the infant died at birth. Fannie's known Confederate sympathies created much hostility in the community, so she and her small son, Georgie, fled to Virginia. Meanwhile, her husband had joined Dreaux's Battalion and was stationed in Virginia.

Fannie was obsessed with a desire to aid the Confederate cause, but at first her attempts to nurse the sick and wounded were discouraged because she was considered too young and delicate. At last she gained experience in a private hospital in Richmond called the Soldier's Rest, following which she became the matron of a hospital for Alabama soldiers where she worked for a few months until felled by illness.

Following a period of recuperation among her husband's relatives in Alabama, Fannie answered an advertisement during the summer of 1862 for a matron to help Dr. William T. McAllister organize the Buckner Hospital for Army of Tennessee troops at Gainesville, Alabama. During the course of the war, she moved with this hospital to Ringgold, Newnan, and finally, Fort Valley, all in Georgia. In her capacity as matron Beers supervised all aspects of hospital life that did not involve diagnosis, prescription, and surgery. She saw to it that the hospital was clean and the beds were properly supplied with linens. In addition she supervised the preparation and serving of food, personally cooking for and feeding the very ill. She helped care for and settle new patients and often sat with the dying during their last moments. While in Newnan her hospital contained a thousand beds.

Dissatisfied because so few patients were sent to Fort

Valley, and driven by a need to serve, Beers asked to be assigned to a hospital nearer the front. After a few weeks in Macon, Georgia, she spent the winter of 1864–1865 in a very primitive tent hospital at Lauderdale Springs, Mississippi, where she nursed a number of soldiers through a smallpox epidemic. Broken in health, in February 1865 Beers returned for the duration of the war to her husband's relatives in Alabama where she experienced the destruction caused by Wilson's raid.

Where the Beers family lived immediately after the war is not known. Eventually they returned to New Orleans where she promoted remembrance of the Lost Cause by participating in veterans' gatherings and writing articles for the *Southern Bivouac,* of which she was at one time assistant editor. In 1888 she published *Memories: A Record of Personal Experience and Adventure during Four Years of War,* in which she recounted some of her hospital experiences as well as other wartime stories she heard from friends. Because she lost her Civil War diary and memorabilia during a raid, her book includes few specifics about time and people. She also included little information about her personal life. Her date of death is unknown.

BIBLIOGRAPHY

Beers, Fannie A. *Memories: A Record of Personal Experience and Adventure during Four Years of War.* Philadelphia, 1888. Reprint, Alexandria, Va., 1985.
Sifakis, Stewart. *Who Was Who in the Confederacy.* New York, 1988.

GLENNA R. SCHROEDER-LEIN

BELL, CASPAR WISTAR

BELL, CASPAR WISTAR (1819–1898), congressman from Missouri. Bell was born in Welch's Tract, Prince Edward County, Virginia, on February 2, 1819. He graduated from William and Mary College in 1837 and then read law in Mississippi. He received an LL.B. degree from the University of Virginia in 1839 and settled in Brunswick, Missouri, in 1843, where he began practicing law. Originally a Whig, he became a Democrat in 1854, the same year he secured part ownership of the *Brunswick Brunswicker.*

Originally a Unionist, Bell eventually supported secession. At the commencement of the war he recruited volunteers for the Confederate army. In 1861 he served as adjutant general of Gen. John B. Clark's Missouri State Guard and saw action at Wilson's Creek, Dry Wood, and Lexington.

In late October 1861, Bell was unanimously elected by the rump Neosho legislature members of the General Assembly to serve in the Confederate Congress. Until 1864 he was the only anti-Davis representative from Missouri. Bell invariably wanted to limit Jefferson Davis's powers and opposed practically all of his vetoes. He sponsored and supported legislation to require Southern guerrillas to report to some department of the army. He further angered Davis by championing the appointment of Sterling Price as a major general in the Confederate army, and by his alliance with Tennessean Henry J. Foote, one of Davis's formidable legislative foes. Bell also found time to write a "Missouri Column" for the *Richmond Examiner.* He held office until May 1864.

After the war Bell practiced law first in Danville, Virginia, and then in Brunswick. He served as prosecuting attorney of Chariton County from 1874 until 1885, when he resigned to become an attorney for the U.S. Department of Interior in Washington. Bell returned to Missouri in 1889 and practiced law in Salisbury until his death.

BIBLIOGRAPHY

History of Howard and Chariton Counties, Missouri. St. Louis, 1883.
Portrait and Biographical Record of Clay, Ray, Carroll, Chariton and Linn Counties, Missouri. Chicago, 1893.
Wakelyn, Jon L. *Biographical Dictionary of the Confederacy.* Edited by Frank E. Vandiver. Westport, Conn., 1977.
Warner, Ezra J., and W. Buck Yearns. *Biographical Register of the Confederate Congress.* Baton Rouge, La., 1975.

JAMES W. GOODRICH

BELL, HIRAM PARKS

BELL, HIRAM PARKS (1827–1907), colonel and Confederate and U.S. congressman from Georgia. Bell was born to poor farmers in Jackson County, Georgia, and grew up in adjacent Forsyth County. His formal education consisted of only two years at a local academy in Cumming, but he went on to teach himself for two years at an academy in Ellijay in the north Georgia mountains. While there he studied law on his own, was admitted to the Georgia bar in 1849, and returned to Cumming, where he practiced law for the next decade. Bell was a Whig who in 1860 actively campaigned for the Constitutional Union party and its presidential candidate John Bell (no relation). He opposed Georgia's secession as a delegate to the state convention that met for that purpose in December.

Once Georgia left the Union, however, Bell became a loyal Confederate and even represented the state as part of a commission sent to Tennessee to urge it to follow the same course. He was elected to the state senate in October 1861 but resigned a year later when a company he raised and led as captain was mustered to Kentucky as part of the Forty-third Georgia Regiment. He fought at the Battle of Second Manassas and at Chickasaw Bayou near Vicksburg in December 1862. He was promoted to colonel after that battle, but because of serious wounds he had received, he resigned from the army in March 1863. In October he was elected to represent Georgia's Ninth District in the Second

Congress. Unlike other Georgia congressmen, he joined Governor Joseph E. Brown in opposing Jefferson Davis's administration. He was particularly outspoken in his opposition to Davis's taxation policy and joined a state movement to suspend taxes.

After the war, Bell resumed his law practice in Cumming. He became active in state Democratic politics and was elected to the U.S. House of Representatives in 1872 and 1876. He served in the state legislature at various intervals until 1900. His lengthy biographical memoir, *Men and Things,* published just before his death in 1907, is a useful commentary on Georgia politics during and after the Civil War.

BIBLIOGRAPHY

Bell, Hiram P. *Men and Things: Being Reminiscent, Biographical, and Historical.* Atlanta, 1907.

Northen, William W. *Men of Mark in Georgia.* Vol. 3. Atlanta, 1908. Reprint, Spartanburg, S.C., 1974.

Wakelyn, Jon L. *Biographical Dictionary of the Confederacy.* Edited by Frank E. Vandiver. Westport, Conn., 1977.

JOHN C. INSCOE

BELL, TYREE HARRIS

BELL, TYREE HARRIS (1815–1902), brigadier general. Bell was born in Covington, Kentucky, on September 5, 1815. As a child, he moved to Gallatin, Tennessee, where he was reared and educated, eventually becoming a planter. In early 1861, he raised one of the first companies of the Twelfth Tennessee. Elected as captain, Bell subsequently became lieutenant colonel of the regiment. Although the unit spent most of 1861 in drill, it saw action at Belmont, Missouri, and Shiloh. Promoted to colonel in July 1862, Bell participated in Gen. Braxton Bragg's Kentucky campaign and fought at the Battle of Richmond. Because of heavy casualties, his regiment had to be consolidated with another twice during 1862 to bring it up to strength.

Bell transferred to the cavalry and on January 25, 1864, Maj. Gen. Nathan Bedford Forrest placed him in charge of the Tennessee brigade. He fought with distinction at Brice's Cross Roads, Mississippi, in June 1864. Subsequently he participated in the bloody fighting at Tupelo, Forrest's raid on Johnsonville, and Gen. John Bell Hood's Tennessee campaign. On February 28, 1865, Bell received a much-deserved commission as brigadier general. He remained with Forrest until their surrender in May 1865.

After the war, Bell relocated to Fresno County, California. There he prospered as a farmer and was active in the local community. He died in New Orleans on September 1, 1902, while returning from a nostalgic visit to Gallatin and a Confederate reunion.

BIBLIOGRAPHY

Bearss, Edwin C. *Forrest at Brice's Cross Roads.* Dayton, Ohio, 1979.

Henry, Robert Selph. *"First with the Most" Forrest.* Indianapolis, 1944.

Wills, Brian Steel. *A Battle from the Start: The Life of Nathan Bedford Forrest.* New York, 1992.

Wyeth, John Allan. *Life of General Nathan Bedford Forrest.* New York, 1899. Reprint, Baton Rouge, La., 1989.

BRIAN S. WILLS

BELLE ISLE PRISON

BELLE ISLE PRISON. In the summer of 1862, the Confederate authorities at Richmond relieved the overcrowding in their warehouse prisons for Union enlisted men by opening a camp on Belle Isle (or Island), an eighty-acre tract in the James River on which was already located an ironworks and workers' housing. The lower fifteen acres, where the prison was located, were flat and sandy. The proximity of the river's rapids and the connection to the south bank by a single railroad bridge simplified security. By mid-July, the island camp held 5,000 men. Though conditions during the first summer were relatively pleasant, they soon would make the island's name seem ironic indeed.

The opening of the prisoner exchange under the cartel of July 22, 1862, resulted in a rapid reduction of the prison population, and by September 23, the camp had closed. In January 1863, Belle Isle reopened at first as a temporary camp and then, with the breakdown of exchange, as a more permanent facility. In the camp's final form, the Confederates partially surrounded four to five acres with a deadline three feet wide by eight feet deep and with earthworks outside where the guards stood. A fenced walkway led to the river bridge. During the daytime the prisoners used the walkway to reach the river to drink, bathe, and use the sinks (latrines). Outside the prison were guards' quarters and a small hospital. Within the prison camp was a central thoroughfare from which radiated some sixty streets.

During the greater part of its history, the prison's commandant was Lt. Virginius Bossieux, a Virginian of French origin. Under him the prisoners were organized into squads of a hundred, headed by sergeants who called the roll and distributed rations.

By early fall 1863, the prison intended to hold 3,000 had some 6,300 captives. In early 1864, there were 8,000 or more within the camp. The overcrowded prisoners suffered greatly. To reduce escape attempts, they were not allowed access to the sinks after dark, so the ground became filthy. Although the Confederates supplied some tents, there were never enough, and prisoners either improvised shelter with pup tents made of blankets or simply burrowed in the soil. A few fires provided the only heat. The rations consisted of cornbread, rice, and occasional meat. Some prisoners tried

BELLE ISLE PRISON, JAMES RIVER, VIRGINIA.   From a sketch by Joseph Becker.

FRANK LESLIE'S ILLUSTRATED FAMOUS LEADERS AND BATTLE SCENES OF THE CIVIL WAR

to improve their lot by trading with one another and with the guards, using a variety of goods including prison-made jewelry and other souvenirs. Other prisoners stole scarce clothing, blankets, or food from one another.

In the winter of 1863–1864, the United States sent some clothing and food to the prisoners. The captive Union officers who distributed the goods—which many hungry prisoners quickly traded to guards for extra food—reported to their fellows and their government on the sad situation of the enlisted men. Though most sick prisoners were removed to hospitals on the island or in the city, deaths in the prison itself were numerous—ten or more men died each day. Because the prison was in full view of the Confederate capitol building, Union critics charged that Confederate leaders had to be aware of its deplorable conditions. This, together with the physical appearance of occasionally exchanged prisoners, was played up in Union propaganda.

By the end of March 1864, the Confederates had removed all the Belle Isle prisoners to Andersonville, Georgia. During that summer, the temporary cessation of shipments to that equally congested pen caused a renewed accumulation of some 6,000 prisoners on Belle Isle. The worried Confederates supplemented their inadequate guards with two howitzers. In October, the Confederates transferred their new captives to Danville or (mostly) to Salisbury. Once

again the Belle Islanders had gone from the frying pan to the fire. On February 10, 1865, the Confederates returned the island to its owners.

In the postwar period parts of the island served industrial functions. By the 1990s the city of Richmond had received title to the island and was contemplating recreational and historical uses for the prison site.

BIBLIOGRAPHY

Darby, George W. *Incidents and Adventures in Rebeldom: Libby, Belle-Isle, Salisbury.* Pittsburgh, 1899.

Hesseltine, William B. *Civil War Prisons: A Study in War Psychology.* Columbus, Ohio, 1930. Reprint, New York, 1964.

Parker, Sandra V. *Richmond's Civil War Prisons.* Lynchburg, Va., 1990.

FRANK L. BYRNE

BELMONT, MISSOURI. On November 7, 1861, Union forces under Ulysses S. Grant struck Confederates across the Mississippi from the Southern stronghold of Columbus, Kentucky, occupied by a garrison under Maj. Gen. Leonidas Polk. The result of the attack was inconclusive.

Grant was under orders from Western Department commander John C. Frémont to make demonstrations against the Confederate forces on the Mississippi. He was also concerned that Polk might move into Missouri to snap up some of the counterguerrilla forces operating there. Grant targeted Belmont for the attack because it was an important junction for roads leading from the west bank of the Mississippi opposite Columbus into the interior of Missouri.

Although Polk had toyed with the idea of sending troops into Missouri some weeks before, he was, by this time, convinced that he could not spare a man from the defense of Columbus and its environs and ought rather to be reinforced by Confederate western commander Albert Sidney Johnston. He had approximately 14,200 men under his command, but of these, only a regiment of infantry, a squadron of cavalry, and a battery of artillery were customarily maintained at Belmont. Upon receiving reports of the disembarkation of Grant's force a few miles upstream from Belmont (at the extreme range of the Confederate heavy batteries on the bluffs above Columbus), Polk dispatched four more regiments of infantry under the command of Brig. Gen. Gideon Pillow. Taken in by feints Grant had ordered east of the river, Polk remained apprehensive about the safety of his positions on the Kentucky shore and for the time declined to send further reinforcements to Belmont.

Grant had brought three thousand men from his base at Cairo, Illinois, and detached a battalion (about three hundred men) to guard his transports. Thus, as the opposing forces came in contact around 10:30 A.M. their numbers were roughly equal. The determination of the Northern forces combined with Pillow's ineptness to make the first phase of the battle a Confederate defeat. Pillow positioned his infantry poorly, sited his battery in such a way that he reduced its effectiveness, and ordered an uncoordinated and ill-advised bayonet charge. He also left uncovered a road that led through the dense bottomland timber around the Confederate left flank and into the rear of his position. The route was taken by Grant's right-flanking regiment and a portion of his cavalry, but by the time this blow fell, Pillow's line was already disintegrating. Confederate forces fell back in disorder to the vicinity of their camp at Belmont, where some of the regiments attempted to rally and make another stand. After a sharp but short conflict this resistance also was broken, and the surviving Confederates fled to the shelter of the steep bank (twelve feet high—higher in some places) of the river itself.

An aggressive Northern pursuit at this point would probably have resulted in the surrender of most of the remaining Southern forces west of the river. Upon entering the Confederate camp, however, the inexperienced Northern soldiers lost all discipline. Thinking the battle was over, they began celebrating and scavenging the captured tents and equipment. Even some of their amateur officers could

find nothing better to do than lead cheers and make speeches. The efforts of Grant and the handful of other professionals to regain order proved unavailing, and despairing of holding Belmont, Grant ordered the camp put to the torch.

Meanwhile, fragments of the five beaten Confederate regiments had formed up again under the shelter of the high riverbanks and were working their way upstream, around a wide bend in the river and then inland under the cover of dense woods toward a position between the Union forces and their transports. They were joined around noon by three fresh regiments sent across the river by Polk, who had finally decided that no attack was coming on the Kentucky side. Simultaneously, Polk, seeing the Confederate tents and camp equipment in flames, ordered his heavy batteries on the bluffs east of the river to take the position under fire.

The heavy shelling and the appearance of an enemy force squarely across their line of retreat finally got the attention of the green Northern troops. Acting quickly to prevent an outbreak of panic among the men, Grant gave the order to cut through the Confederate lines and get back to the boats. The resulting second phase of the battle was just as deadly as the first and even more confused, as brigades, regiments, and even companies lost track of each other in dense forest. The result, strangely enough, was satisfactory to both sides. Grant succeeded in breaking through to his transports. The Confederates, some of them under Pillow and some under Brig. Gen. B. Franklin Cheatham who had crossed with the reinforcements, succeeded in driving the Northern forces to their boats and recapturing some of the guns and prisoners taken by the Federals in the morning's battle.

Another lull followed the desperate fight in the woods, as the Confederates regrouped and Grant strove to get his troops, including his wounded, on board the transports. Riding out alone to see how closely the Confederates were following, Grant came within fifty yards of Southern troops advancing through dense foliage.

Polk had by this time arrived on the field in person with two more fresh regiments, and these opened fire on the transports but were driven back from the landing by the heavy cannon of the two gunboats Grant had brought along as escort.

Grant lost 80 men killed, 322 wounded (of whom 125 had to be left behind and were captured), and 99 missing out of 3,000 engaged. Confederate losses were 105 troops killed, 409 wounded, and 117 missing (of whom 106 were prisoners of war) out of about 5,300 who reached the west bank before the end of the fighting. The battle had little impact upon the course of the war. Grant believed it had prevented the Confederates from moving troops into Missouri but was mistaken, as such a move had not been contemplated. He also maintained that the fight gave his troops valuable experience and a sense of confidence. Polk, for his part, claimed a resounding victory. This, like his day-after-the-battle report that Grant was among the slain, was an exaggeration.

BIBLIOGRAPHY

Catton, Bruce. *Grant Moves South*. Boston, 1960.
Hughes, Nathaniel C., Jr. *The Battle of Belmont: Grant Strikes South*. Chapel Hill, N.C., 1991.
McFeely, William S. *Grant: A Biography*. New York, 1982.
McFeely, Mary D., and William S. McFeely, eds. *Memoirs and Selected Letters: Ulysses S. Grant*. New York, 1990.
Woodworth, Steven E. *Jefferson Davis and His Generals: The Failure of Confederate Command in the West*. Lawrence, Kans., 1990.

STEVEN E. WOODWORTH

BENAVIDES, SANTOS (1823–1891), colonel.

Known properly as José de los Santos Benavides, Benavides was born at Laredo, Texas, November 1, 1823. As a young man he fought in the Federalist Wars and in the struggle to create the Republic of the Rio Grande. Benavides was appointed *procurador* of Laredo in 1843 and served as mayor of the town from 1856 to 1857 and as Webb County judge in 1859. He also gained a reputation as an adept Indian fighter and led several forays against hostile Comanches and Lipan Apaches.

At the outbreak of the Civil War, Benavides raised a company of cavalry at Laredo and helped suppress a revolt against the Confederacy in Zapata County, where he decisively defeated the notorious Juan N. Cortina at Carrizo (present-day Zapata) on May 22, 1861. Along with his brothers, Refugio and Cristobal, both captains in the Confederate army, Benavides exerted considerable effort in combating raiding bands of Mexican revolutionaries from the right bank of the Rio Grande. In retaliation for the shooting of one of his men, Benavides occupied Nuevo Laredo, Tamaulipas, Mexico, in March 1862, touching off a minor international incident.

Refusing the promise of a generalship in the Union army from one of his antebellum political allies, Edmund J. Davis, Benavides rose to the rank of colonel in command of Benavides's Regiment, thus becoming the highest-ranking Mexican American in the Confederate army. On March 19, 1864, Benavides drove off a Union force at Laredo that was intent on capturing or destroying a large quantity of cotton in the town.

From 1879 to 1884, Benavides served in the Texas House of Representatives. In 1884 he was appointed Texas commissioner to the World's Cotton Exposition. He served two terms as alderman in Laredo and was one of the founders of the reform-minded Guarache party in Webb County. He died at his home in Laredo on November 9, 1891.

BIBLIOGRAPHY

Riley, John Denny. "Santos Benavides: His Influence on the Lower Rio Grande, 1823–1891." Ph.D. diss., Texas Christian University, 1976.
Thompson, Jerry. "A Stand along the Border: Santos Benavides and the Battle for Laredo." *Civil War Times Illustrated* 19 (August 1980): 26–33.
Thompson, Jerry. *Vaqueros in Blue and Gray*. Austin, Tex., 1976.
Thompson, Jerry. *Warm Weather and Bad Whiskey*. El Paso, Tex., 1991.

JERRY THOMPSON

BENJAMIN, JUDAH P. (1811–1884), U.S. senator,

Confederate attorney general, secretary of war, and secretary of state. Born a British subject in the British West Indies on August 6, 1811, Benjamin was taken to the United States in his early youth. The child of Sephardic Jewish settlers, he was descended from families that could be traced back to fifteenth-century Spain.

Judah Benjamin's boyhood was much more steeped in Jewish culture and tradition than either Southern or Jewish historians have acknowledged. He was reared in Charleston, South Carolina, and grew to manhood in New Orleans, two of the largest Jewish communities in the United States in the early nineteenth century. His father was one of the twelve dissenters in Charleston who formed the first Reform Congregation of America. Although the records of Beth Elohim congregation were burned and we cannot know for certain, he probably was one of the first boys confirmed at the new reform temple, which was founded when he was thirteen years old. The character of a Jewish boy reared by a deeply involved Jewish family would be shaped by that experience the rest of his life.

He went to Yale Law School at fourteen, left under mysterious circumstances, and was admitted to the Louisiana bar in 1832. A strategic marriage to Natalie S. Martin, whose family belonged to the ruling creole aristocracy in New Orleans, propelled him into financial success and subsequently into a political career. He participated in the explosive growth of New Orleans between 1820 and 1840 as a commercial lawyer and political advocate for banking, finance, and railroad interests.

Benjamin prospered for a time as a sugar planter, helped organize the Illinois Central Railroad, and was elected to the Louisiana legislature in 1842. As a rising political star in the Whig Party, he was the first acknowledged Jew to be elected to the U.S. Senate (1852; reelected as a Democrat, 1858). In the Senate he was noted as an eloquent defender of Southern interests and has been ranked by some historians as one of the five great orators in Senate history, the equal of Daniel Webster and John C. Calhoun.

In Washington, he met Jefferson Davis (1853) and forged

a friendship in an unusual confrontation. They were both intense and ambitious senators—Davis of Mississippi and Benjamin of Louisiana. Varina Howell Davis, the future First Lady of the Confederacy, wrote years later of them during this period, "Sometimes when they did not agree on, a measure, hot words in glacial, polite phrases passed between them." Because of a suspected insult on the floor of the Senate, Benjamin challenged Davis to a duel. Davis quickly and publicly apologized, and the incident of honor defended and satisfied drew them together in a relationship of mutual respect.

His wife had taken his only daughter, Ninnette, and moved to Paris in 1842. She joined him briefly after his election to the Senate, but returned again to Paris because of scandalous rumors about her in Washington. Thereafter Benjamin saw her once a year on trips to Paris. Only a fragment of a letter remains between them: "Speak not to me of economy," she wrote. "It is so fatiguing."

In the Senate, Benjamin was embroiled in the political turmoil leading to the Civil War, and he was frequently attacked on the basis of his religious background. Once in a debate on slavery when Senator Ben Wade of Ohio accused Benjamin of being an "Israelite with Egyptian principles," Benjamin is reported to have replied, "It is true that I am a Jew, and when my ancestors were receiving their Ten Commandments from the immediate Deity, amidst the thunderings and lightnings of Mount Sinai, the ancestors of my opponent were herding swine in the forest of Great Britain." It was a rare reply. Usually, when newspapers, political enemies, and military leaders insulted him with stinging phrases of religious prejudice, he almost never answered, but simply retained what observers called "a perpetual smile."

After secession, President Jefferson Davis appointed Benjamin as his attorney general on February 21, 1861. The president chose him because, in Davis's own words, Benjamin "had a very high reputation as a lawyer, and my acquaintance with him in the Senate had impressed me with the lucidity of his intellect, his systematic habits, and capacity for labor." Since the office of attorney general was a civilian post, the leadership in the capital considered it of little consequence, but this did not deter Benjamin. He plunged into the cabinet policy debates on all aspects of the Confederacy and developed a reputation as one who loved details, complexity, and problem solving. He became the administrator to the president, called by observers "the Poo Bah" of the Confederate government. At his first cabinet meeting, Secretary of War Leroy P. Walker said, "there was only one man there who had any sense, and that man was Benjamin." During his tenure at the Justice Department, Benjamin became a strong advocate of cotton diplomacy (the policy of shipping cotton to Europe as barter for arms and supplies, and of denying cotton to countries that did not support the South).

Davis then appointed Benjamin acting secretary of war in September, making the appointment permanent on November 21. By appointing a brilliant administrator without military experience, Davis could thereby be his own secretary of war, a position he had held in the Franklin Pierce administration. But Benjamin was a failure because when the war went badly on the battlefield, the military turned on him as a scapegoat. Frustrated generals who could not attack the president publicly had a convenient target in his secretary of war. As the Union forces struck back, criticism of Benjamin mounted. He was not a military man, and his orders, though flowing from constant meetings with the president, were treated as originating from him and were resented in the field as interference and amateurism.

Benjamin had highly publicized quarrels with Gen. P. G. T. Beauregard and Gen. Thomas J. ("Stonewall") Jackson. Beauregard called Benjamin in a letter to Davis "that functionary at his desk, who deems it a fit time to write lectures on law while the enemy is mustering at our front." Jackson threatened to resign, writing Davis that "with such interference in my command, I cannot be expected to be of much service in the field." Davis defended his "right hand," as Varina described Benjamin, who was working twelve and fourteen hours a day with Davis and was being blamed by the military for carrying out the president's orders.

Benjamin was berated by Northern generals as well. When Benjamin Butler, who commanded the forces that conquered New Orleans, issued a statement about the city, he said "the most effective supporters of the Confederacy have been . . . mostly Jews . . . who all deserve at the hands of the government what is due the Jew Benjamin."

The anger against Benjamin came to a head after the fall of Roanoke Island in early February 1862. Benjamin had been under intense pressure from Gen. Henry A. Wise at Roanoke and Governor Henry T. Clark of North Carolina to send many more men and arms to the garrison there. He had resisted for reasons that would not be known until twenty-five years after the war, and he accepted the subsequent public condemnation in silence to protect his country. Roanoke was sacrificed because to have done otherwise would have revealed to the enemy just how desperate the South was.

At the dedication of the Robert E. Lee monument in Richmond in 1890, Col. Charles Marshall, an aide-de-camp on General Lee's staff, read part of a letter from Benjamin, which revealed that President Davis had agreed to allow Benjamin to be publicly censured:

> I consulted the President whether it was best for the country that I should submit to unmerited censure or reveal to a Congressional Committee our poverty and my utter inability to supply the requisitions of General Wise, and thus run the risk that the fact should become known to some of the spies of the enemy, of whose activity we were well assured. It was thought

best for the public service that I should suffer the blame in silence and a report of censure on me was accordingly made by the Committee of Congress.

When Benjamin resigned, Davis, as a reward for loyalty, promptly named him secretary of state.

On the subject of slavery, both Davis and Benjamin were "enlightened" Southerners whose attitudes were evolving. Most Jewish historians have understandably reacted with revulsion to the fact that Benjamin owned 140 slaves on a sugar plantation, and they have been unable to consider the question of his views on slavery with anything but embarrassed dismay. To comprehend Benjamin on this score, one must put him into context as a political figure against a backdrop of planter dogmatism and abolitionist fervor.

Such an exploration leads directly to an extraordinary episode of the war in which Benjamin played a central role: the effort to persuade Davis to issue a Confederate emancipation proclamation, which would promise slaves freedom in exchange for military service. That move, which began to take shape early in the war in the minds of military and political leaders but did not surface until 1864, is usually dismissed as a desperate gamble made at the end of the war to lure Britain into the fight. But as secretary of state, Benjamin's obsession all along had been to draw England into the war. Slavery, however, was a stumbling block because England had abolished slavery in 1833. As the clouds of defeat gathered, Benjamin spoke before ten thousand people in Richmond, delivering a remarkable speech in favor of a Confederate offer to free slaves who would fight for the South. Although the idea of arming slaves as soldiers was supported by Lee, who needed more men in the field, the public and political reaction was fierce. Howell Cobb, the former governor of Georgia, wrote that "if slaves will make good soldiers, our whole theory of slavery is wrong." Nevertheless, the Confederate Congress passed a partial version of the measure on March 13, but by then it was too late. Richmond fell less than a month later.

Benjamin's apparent change of personality after the war has puzzled historians. The utter secrecy and privacy of his later life is anomalous, given his earlier hunger for fame. No one can ever know, but certainly one key to understanding his silence after the war is his creation of a Confederate spy ring in Canada and the subsequent proclamation, conceived by the Union's secretary of war, Edwin Stanton, and issued by Lincoln's successor, President Andrew Johnson, for the arrest of Davis and seven Canadian Confederate spies after the Lincoln assassination. History, by means of the trials of the conspirators and by exhaustive investigations, has absolved both Benjamin and Davis from any responsibility. But the psychological and emotional impact on Benjamin of the long period of hysteria that followed the assassination must have taken its toll, especially since Lincoln's death fell on Good Friday and 2,500 sermons were given on Easter Sunday comparing Lincoln to a fallen Christ figure, as the nation acted out a passion play. There is no record of what Benjamin thought of the various published accusations against him.

If Benjamin's role in history has been misjudged by historians and was minimized even by participants, much of the responsibility for that lies with Benjamin himself. He chose obscurity early in the war with the unwavering decision that he could best serve the South by serving Davis and remaining in the presidential shadow. For reasons that have puzzled historians, Benjamin burned his personal papers—some as he escaped from Richmond in 1865 and almost all of the rest just before he died—and he left only six scraps of paper at his death. One historian has called him a "virtual incendiary."

Benjamin fled to England after the war and built a second career as a successful international lawyer. He was called to the bar (June 1866) after only five months' residence and achieved enormous financial success in his new home country. In 1868, he wrote a classic treatise on commercial law in England (Treatise on the Law of Sale of Personal Property) known even today to law students as "Benjamin on Sales." In 1872, he became a queen's counsel, practicing with wig and robes in the House of Lords and appearing in 136 major cases.

Although he had been known in the U.S. Senate as an outstanding orator, in England he gave no published speeches on the war. He left no articles, essays, or books about his role in the war or any other aspect of it. Indeed, he made only two public statements in nineteen years that concerned the war. The first was a three-paragraph letter to the Times of London in September 1865, just after he arrived in England, protesting the imprisonment of Jefferson Davis. The second was a short letter in 1883 contradicting the charge that millions of dollars in Confederate funds were left in European banks under his control. There were no letters defending strategy or admitting error; nor does history record any war-related conversations with students or scholars. He spent a few evenings at dinner with Davis when the ex-president visited London five times between 1868 and 1883. Otherwise, he avoided nostalgic encounters with friends from the South. It is one of the enduring mysteries that Benjamin chose to erase all ties to his previous life. In fact, he never even returned to the United States.

Late in life, he retired and moved to Paris to be with his family. Benjamin died on May 6, 1884, and was buried in Père Lachaise cemetery in Paris under the name of "Philippe Benjamin" in the family plot of the Boursignac family, the in-laws of his daughter. Three grandchildren died in childhood and no direct descendants survived. In 1938, the Paris chapter of the Daughters of the Confederacy finally provided an inscription to identify the man in the almost anonymous grave:

JUDAH PHILIP BENJAMIN
BORN ST. THOMAS WEST INDIES AUGUST 6, 1811
DIED IN PARIS MAY 6, 1884
UNITED STATES SENATOR FROM LOUISIANA
ATTORNEY GENERAL, SECRETARY OF WAR AND
SECRETARY OF STATE OF THE CONFEDERATE STATES
OF AMERICA, QUEEN'S COUNSEL, LONDON

In life, as in death, he was elusive, vanishing behind his agreeableness, his cordiality, his perpetual smile. To blend into the culture—whether Southern or English—was bred into him, a matter of the Jewish Southerner's instinct for survival. The public man celebrated on two continents sought a kind of invisibility, not unlike the private man nobody knew. Shunning his past, choosing an almost secret grave, with calculated concealment, he nearly succeeded in remaining hidden from history.

Since his death, Benjamin's life has remained relatively unchallenged in the images that have come down through history. Although historians have routinely called him "the brains of the Confederacy," they know relatively little about him. Many historians of the Civil War have referred to him as President Davis's most loyal confidant, but Davis himself in his 1881 memoir of the Confederacy, referred to Benjamin in the most perfunctory fashion, mentioning his name only twice in the 1,500-page, two-volume work. That is especially odd if, as Varina Davis testified in a letter written in 1889, Benjamin spent almost every day in the office with her husband and was a central figure in events.

Benjamin's image comes down through history as "the dark prince of the Confederacy," a Mephistophelian Jewish figure. Stephen Vincent Benét in *John Brown's Body* reflected the contemporary view of him:

Judah P. Benjamin, the dapper Jew,
Seal-Sleek, black-eyed, lawyer and epicure,
Able, well-hated, face alive with life,
Looked round the council-chamber with the slight
Perpetual smile he held before himself
Continually like a silk-ribbed fan.
Behind the fan, his quick, shrewd, fluid mind
Weighed Gentiles in an old balance. . . .

The mind behind the silk-ribbed fan
Was a dark-prince, clothed in an Eastern stuff,
Whole brown hands cupped about a crystal egg
That filmed with colored cloud. The eyes stared,
searching.

"I am a Jew, What am I doing here?"

Pierce Butler in 1907 and Robert Douthat Meade in 1943 wrote the two standard biographies of Benjamin in the first half of the twentieth century, pulling together the thou-

sands of Civil War orders and letters to friends and family in England, France, New Orleans, Charleston, and elsewhere that he was unable to destroy after the war. Butler interviewed Benjamin's contemporaries, including Varina Howell Davis. Meade spent twelve years traveling—researching diaries, memoirs, and papers and interviewing family members and friends. His book revealed Benjamin to have been a gifted tactician with a philosophical nature and an urbane manner, a gourmet, an inveterate gambler, and a man whom women adored. Still, it acknowledged a paucity of material.

Meade and Butler also drew from the research of the spare beginnings of an unfinished biography by Francis Lawley, the Richmond and Washington correspondent of the London *Times* during the war, who became, according to Meade, "devoted to Benjamin, who doubtless helped to color his vivid dispatches with a sympathetic attitude toward the Confederacy." Benjamin kept up a relationship with Lawley for the rest of his life, but only six pages survive of the biography Lawley planned, along with fewer than a dozen letters.

Meade and Butler were both Southern historians unfamiliar with American Jewish history. Judaism for them represented strange and unsteady territory that they, perhaps too deeply ingrained with the attitudes of their time, were not prepared to explore. Butler, in 1907, treated Jewishness as if it were an unpleasant component of his admiring portrait, one that he was reluctant but duty-bound to include briefly. He referred to Benjamin's father as "that *rara avis,* an unsuccessful Jew" and described Benjamin in England as "this wonderful little Jew from America." Meade, writing during that sensitive period of the rise of Nazi Germany just before World War II, was more circumspect, yet observed that "like so many of Jewish blood today, Benjamin tended to become cosmopolitan." In the late 1930s, no Southern historian could convey the harshness of the anti-Semitism surrounding Benjamin without seeming prejudiced himself. In a steady drumbeat of insults in Richmond, Confederate opponents would later refer to Benjamin as "Judas Iscariot Benjamin," and, according to Mary Boykin Chesnut's diary, "Mr. Davis's pet Jew." The Jewish aspect of Benjamin's life and career was not fully examined until it was taken up in an 1988 biography, almost fifty years after the publication of Meade's book.

Historians have pointed out ways in which Jews and Southerners were alike—stepchildren of an anguished history—and yet different. Whereas the Jewish search for a homeland contrasted with the Southerner's commitment to place, Southern defenders of the Confederacy often used Old Testament analogies in referring to themselves as "the chosen people" destined to survive and triumph against overwhelming odds. Benjamin is fascinating because of the extraordinary role he played in Southern history and the ways in which Jews and non-Jews reacted to him. He was the prototype of the contradictions in the Jewish Southerner and the stranger in the Confederate story, the Jew at the eye of the storm that was the Civil War.

Objectively, with so few Jews in the South at the time, it is astonishing that one should appear at the very center of Southern history. Benjamin himself avoided his Jewishness throughout his public career, though his enemies in the Southern press and in the halls of the Confederate Congress never let the South forget it. The virulence of the times required a symbolic figure as a catalyst for an ancient hostility and perhaps contributed to his intentional elusiveness. As Bertram Korn pointed out in *American Jewry and the Civil War,* the nation both North and South experienced "the greatest outpouring of Judeophobia in its history" during the Civil War, and Benjamin was a convenient target.

Benjamin achieved greater political power than any other Jew in the nineteenth century—perhaps even in all American history. Although he was a nonpracticing Jew, he never attempted to deny his faith and contemporary society treated him as Jewish. Benjamin thus must stand as a symbol of American democracy and its openness to religious minorities. In spite of the bigotry surrounding him, not only was he elected to the U.S. Senate and appointed to three high offices in the Confederacy, but he was also offered an appointment as the ambassador to Spain and a seat on the U.S. Supreme Court. The nineteenth-century emancipation of the Jews, which began in Europe after the French Revolution, was as great a shock to Jews as were the centuries of persecution that preceded it. Benjamin was the main beneficiary of that emancipation and its most visible symbol in America.

In the final years before the war, Benjamin was widely admired nationally in both Jewish and non-Jewish communities for his prestige as a Southern leader and his eloquence as an orator. His election to the U.S. Senate was a watershed for American Jews. Because of the war, he became the first Jewish political figure to be projected into the national consciousness. Jews in the South were especially proud of his achievement because he validated their legitimacy as Southerners. A pivotal figure in American Jewish history, Benjamin broke down the barriers of prejudice to achieve high office. After him, it was more acceptable for Jews to be elected to office and to aspire to service in the councils of national power.

BIBLIOGRAPHY

Benjamin, Judah P. *Treatise on the Law of Sale of Personal Property, with Reference to the American Decisions, to the French Code and Civil Code.* 1868.

Butler, Pierce. *Judah P. Benjamin.* Philadelphia, 1907. Reprint, New York and London, 1980.

Evans, Eli N. *Judah P. Benjamin: The Jewish Confederate.* New York, 1988.

Meade, Robert Douthat. *Judah P. Benjamin, Confederate Statesman.* New York, 1943. Reprint, New York, 1975.

ELI N. EVANS

BENNING, HENRY L. (1814–1875), brigadier general. Benning was born in Columbia County, Georgia, on April 2, 1814, and graduated with honors from the University of Georgia in 1834. He studied law at Talbottown, Georgia, in the office of George W. Towns, a lawyer who would rise to become a member of Congress and governor of Georgia. Benning was admitted to the bar in 1835 at Columbus, and there he began the practice of law. He became the chief prosecutor for his circuit in 1838. In 1839 Benning joined his father-in-law in a law partnership and in 1855 was elected a justice of the Supreme Court of Georgia.

As strong a Democrat as he was an advocate of state rights, Benning served as vice president of the Democratic convention in Baltimore that nominated Sen. Stephen A. Douglas for the presidency in 1860. With the election of Abraham Lincoln and the rise of the secession movement, Benning was named a delegate to the Charleston convention in 1860 and was elected a delegate to the convention that adopted the ordinance of secession for the state of Georgia. He also served as a commissioner to the Virginia secession convention.

With the outbreak of hostilities, Benning entered Confederate service as colonel of the Seventeenth Georgia Infantry. Part of Robert Toombs's brigade, Benning's Seventeenth Georgia fought gallantly on the Virginia Peninsula in the spring and early summer of 1862.

After little more than a year in the field, Henry Benning was elevated to the rank of brigadier general and placed in command of Toombs's old brigade, composed of four Georgia infantry regiments. Benning led these regiments, part of Gen. James Longstreet's First Corps of the Army of Northern Virginia, through the Battles of Second Manassas, Sharpsburg, Fredericksburg, and Gettysburg. Ordered to the western theater of war in the late summer of 1863, Benning and his men fought through the Battle of Chickamauga and the siege of Knoxville. Returning to the east, Benning led his regiments through the Battle of the Wilderness where he was severely wounded in the right shoulder. After recovering, he resumed command of his brigade in the fighting before Petersburg. Benning was with his old brigade when it surrendered with Gen. Robert E. Lee's Army of Northern Virginia on April 9, 1865.

Benning stood nearly six feet in height and was massive in frame. His commanding presence and deep voice made him a natural leader. Although not a professional soldier, he was an able and reliable commander. For his coolness under fire, courage, and steadfastness, his men gave him the sobriquet "Old Rock."

After the war, Benning returned to Columbus, Georgia, where he resumed the practice of law. He died while on his way to court on July 10, 1875, and was buried in Columbus.

BIBLIOGRAPHY

Cobb, James C. "The Making of a Secessionist: Henry L. Benning and the Coming of the Civil War." *The Georgia Historical Quarterly* 60, no. 4 (Winter 1976): 313–323.

Derry, Joseph T. *Georgia.* Vol. 6 of *Confederate Military History.* Edited by Clement A. Evans. Atlanta, 1899. Vol. 7 of extended ed. Wilmington, N.C., 1987.

Warner, Ezra J. *Generals in Gray: Lives of the Confederate Commanders.* Baton Rouge, La., 1959.

KENT MASTERSON BROWN

BENTON, SAMUEL (1820–1864), brigadier general.

A nephew of Senator Thomas Hart Benton, Samuel Benton was born in Williamson City, Tennessee, and after moving to Mississippi became a schoolmaster, attorney, and state legislator. Serving as a delegate from Marshall County to the state convention in 1861, he voted for secession.

He served briefly as a captain in the Ninth Mississippi Infantry before being appointed colonel of the Thirty-fourth Mississippi Infantry in April 1862. The regiment saw service in northern Mississippi before being assigned to the Army of Tennessee. It lost a third of its men at Chickamauga. Benton also temporarily commanded the Twenty-fourth and Twenty-seventh Mississippi (consolidated) before resuming command of his own regiment in the spring of 1864.

Benton and his Thirty-fourth Mississippi were frequently engaged in skirmishes and battle during the Atlanta campaign. He ascended to brigade command when Edward C. Walthall received a promotion to major general. Benton led the brigade in attacks at Kolb's Farm and Peachtree Creek. During the Battle of Atlanta a shell fragment penetrated his chest and part of one foot was blown off. Following an amputation, he died of his wounds in Griffin, Georgia, on July 28, 1864, shortly before his promotion to brigadier general arrived.

BIBLIOGRAPHY

Crute, Joseph H., Jr. *Units of the Confederate States Army.* Midlothian, Va., 1987.

Evans, Clement A., ed. *Confederate Military History.* 12 vols. Atlanta, 1899. Extended ed. in 19 vols. Wilmington, N.C., 1987–1989.

Warner, Ezra J. *Generals in Gray: Lives of the Confederate Commanders.* Baton Rouge, La., 1959.

DENNIS KELLY

BENTONVILLE, NORTH CAROLINA. On

March 19 through 21, 1865, the town of Bentonville, twenty-five miles southwest of Goldsboro, was the site of the Confederate's last major challenge to Gen. William Tecumseh Sherman's sweep through the Carolinas. Joseph E. Johnston's attempt to rout Sherman cost the Confederates 2,347 soldiers wounded, captured, or missing and the Federals 1,455 men.

By the early spring, Union troops had reached North Carolina in their ruinous push toward Richmond. Sherman's army headed north in two columns under the leadership of Generals John McAllister Schofield and Jacob Dolson Cox. Their ultimate objective was to reunite in Goldsboro, where they planned to resupply the troops with boots and clothing and establish a supply line to the coast.

From Petersburg and Raleigh, Robert E. Lee and Johnston speculated about Sherman's intentions and planned their strategy. Lee was intent on maintaining an unobstructed line of communication and supplies from Raleigh to Petersburg. Johnston did not have the manpower to attack Sherman's entire force: the Army of Tennessee had suffered greatly during the Tennessee campaign; most of the officers had fallen during the disasters at Franklin and Nashville. Hence, Johnston preferred to strike before Sherman could reunite his army. Although Lee agreed that Johnston should attack, he urged caution; by the spring of 1865 the Confederacy could not afford unnecessary losses.

At Bentonville Johnston saw his chance. On March 16 Union Gen. Henry Slocum's troops ran into Confederate troops at Averasboro, and on March 18 Slocum and his men skirmished with Wade Hampton's cavalry until dark. Both sides withdrew that night, but, at dawn, the Confederate troops renewed their attack.

Sherman had expected Johnston to hinder his movement; he assumed that the danger to his troops had passed after Slocum and Hampton's clash at Averasboro. Therefore he moved to the right and joined Schofield en route to Goldsboro.

During the afternoon of the nineteenth, however, Joseph E. Johnston attacked Slocum yet again. At first Slocum thought that he confronted only cavalry, but it became increasingly apparent that he faced a sizable infantry force. Hence he sent a dispatch asking for support. The Confederates continued to launch attacks on the Union line until sundown. As night fell, the Confederates had not gained any ground, but they had not lost any either.

On March 20, massive numbers of Union reinforcements began to arrive, and the Confederates assumed a defensive position. Johnston remained optimistic, but by 4:00 P.M. the Union army had reunited in front of him. The Southerners hoped to wear down the Federal troops and subsequently launch a crippling attack. Union forces, however, moved to flank the Confederate left and advance on its rear. The

Southerners held off the Federal troops until the following evening (March 21), when Johnston ordered his troops to withdraw.

As the Confederate army headed northwest in the direction of Smithfield, the Union army offered virtually no pursuit. Sherman felt confident that he had sufficiently eliminated the threat from Johnston's army, and he and his troops headed, uncontested, for Goldsboro.

Johnston had succeeded in delaying Sherman at Bentonville, but only temporarily. Sherman charged on, and a month later, Johnston followed General Lee's example at Appomattox and surrendered his forces.

BIBLIOGRAPHY

Barrett, John Gilchrist. *North Carolina as a Civil War Battleground, 1861–1865.* Raleigh, N.C., 1980.
Luvaas, Jay. *The Battle of Bentonville: March 19–20–21, 1865.* Smithfield, N.C., 1965.

JENNIFER LUND

BERRY, HARRISON (1816–1882?), writer. Berry is the only Georgia slave known to have written publicly about chattel servitude while still in bondage. Largely self-educated, he tried unsuccessfully to purchase his freedom and subsequently aligned himself with the American Colonization Society, an organization promoting black emigration from the United States to Liberia as a solution to the dual problems of slavery and racial prejudice.

The society's doctrines strongly influenced the content of Berry's first published essay, a forty-six-page pamphlet entitled *Slavery and Abolitionism as Viewed by a Georgia Slave.* Written during the racial tension of the secession crisis, *Slavery and Abolitionism* was partially a response to the campaign of violence and terrorism directed at black Georgians in the wake of John Brown's raid. Superficially a proslavery document, the pamphlet assured planters that most slaves were loyal and singled out elusive "abolition emissaries" as the proper targets for white suspicion. In castigating the antislavery movement, Berry repeated the familiar colonizationist argument that insurmountable white racial prejudice made domestic abolition both impractical and pointless. *Slavery and Abolitionism* stopped short of openly endorsing emigration, but, with intentional ambiguity, Berry voiced his conviction that there was "no such thing as a free negro in this country. . . . The colored man is a colored man anywhere."

Although discussed widely at the time of its publication, *Slavery and Abolitionism* received little attention after 1861 and played no direct role in Georgia's wartime legislative debates over legalizing slave literacy. Quite possibly the omission reflected skepticism over Berry's sincerity in the wake of massive black defections to Union lines. In any case Berry's postwar conduct brought his Confederate credentials into serious question. During Radical Reconstruction he turned to the Republican party and published an 1869 pamphlet stressing the common oppression of blacks and yeoman whites at the hands of a "diabolical aristocratic slave power."

BIBLIOGRAPHY

Mohr, Clarence L. "Harrison Berry: A Black Pamphleteer in Georgia during Slavery and Freedom." *Georgia Historical Quarterly* 67 (1983): 189–205.
Mohr, Clarence L. *On the Threshold of Freedom: Masters and Slaves in Civil War Georgia.* Athens, Ga., and London, 1986.

CLARENCE L. MOHR

BIBLE SOCIETIES. The principal function of Bible societies in the Confederacy was to provide Bibles, New Testaments, or portions of the scriptures to men in the army. It was believed that such literature would have a positive influence on the behavior and attitude of young men away from home and facing the dangers of war. Christian readings, it was assumed, would serve to assist the men to keep the faith and might also help to convert those who were not professing Christians. It was also assumed that Bibles and other Christian readings would boost morale and thereby make the men both better Christians and more effective soldiers. Agents of the different societies, called colporters, also distributed and sold some of this literature to civilians, principally in the rural areas of the South. Some of these agents were also active in organizing Sunday Schools and distributing tracts.

Bible societies were an integral part of the structure of evangelical Protestantism in the South. They were ecumenical in nature, were found throughout the South, and represented practically all the denominations in the region. In 1860 there were approximately a thousand Bible societies in the South. Most were local organizations, representing a municipality or a county, and were affiliated with their state's Bible society. Both the local and state organizations were auxiliaries of the American Bible Society, whose headquarters was in New York City. For example, the Rowan County Bible Society in North Carolina was affiliated with the North Carolina Bible Society, which was an auxiliary of the American Bible Society. The Bible societies usually had a president, a secretary-treasurer, and a board of managers or directors. The societies held annual meetings but during the year the operations or business of the society was conducted by the president, the secretary, and possibly a committee of the board of managers.

In addition to the societies, some denominations had their own agencies to promote Bible work. For example, the Sunday School and Bible Board of the Baptist General

Association of Virginia employed colporters to distribute religious literature—including Bibles—to the rural areas of the state. Collections for the board were taken periodically by individual Baptist congregations and at associational gatherings. During the war the board focused attention on work in the army.

Although there were many Bible societies in the South in 1860, no Bibles or New Testaments were printed there; all were printed in the North. Agents of the Southern societies obtained copies from headquarters and sold or distributed them to the people. With the outbreak of the Civil War in the spring of 1861, and President Abraham Lincoln's ban on trade with the seceding states and the blockade of the Confederacy, a Bible shortage soon developed. This shortage became more acute as Southerners sought to provide every man who entered the armed forces with a Bible.

In the summer of 1861 the Southwestern Publishing House and the Southern Methodist Publishing House, both in Nashville, Tennessee, were able to obtain plates from Philadelphia via Louisville for the publication of New Testaments and Bibles. Each firm printed some books before Nashville was occupied by Federal forces in February 1862. At that time the Bible plates of the Southwestern Publishing House were confiscated, but the New Testament plates of the Southern Methodist Publishing House were saved and soon removed from the city.

In the meantime, at the invitation of the Charleston, South Carolina, Bible Society, a group of people from throughout the South met at Augusta, Georgia, in March 1862 and formed the Bible Society of the Confederate States. Its members represented all the Protestant denominations in the South. After the formation of the society an invitation was issued to all local societies to affiliate with it. At its organizational meeting, the New Testament plates saved by the director of the Southern Methodist Publishing House were presented to the Bible Society of the Confederate States. A few weeks later the society contracted with a publisher in Atlanta to print 50,000 copies of the New Testament. Shortages of materials together with a disastrous fire at the publisher's paper mill delayed the completion of this order until spring 1863. In the summer of that year the Bible Society of the Confederate States provided the plates and entered into a contract with another publishing company, Evans and Cogswell of Columbia, South Carolina, for 100,000 copies of the New Testament. But again shortages of materials prolonged the completion of the project.

To alleviate the Bible shortage, some sought to obtain Bibles from outside the region and bring them through the blockade. In 1863 and again in 1864 agents of the Bible Society of the Confederate States imported 60,000 New Testaments from England. In 1863 an agent for the Virginia Bible Society also went to England to procure Bibles. He was warmly received by the British and Foreign Bible Society and was presented with a gift of 10,000 Bibles, 50,000 New Testaments, and 250,000 portions of Gospels and Psalms. Only an undetermined portion of this literature ever reached the Confederacy, however, as some of it was captured when blockade runners attempted to bring it from Nassau to Southern ports.

Although Lincoln's ban on trading with the South was never revoked, some Southern Bible societies were able to obtain Bibles and New Testaments from the North under a flag of truce. In 1862 and in 1863 the American Bible Society sent to the Virginia Bible Society two separate grants of Bibles. These books were allowed to pass from Fort Monroe, under a flag of truce, to agents of the Virginia society in the Confederacy. In the fall and winter of 1863–1864 the American Bible Society donated 25,000 Bibles to the Sunday School Board of the Southern Baptist Convention in Greenville, South Carolina, for distribution. These books, too, were allowed to pass through Federal lines. Other shipments from the American Bible Society were allowed to pass through the lines at Memphis to the Shelby County Bible Society and to the Soldiers' Bible Society of Mississippi. It is estimated that more than 300,000 copies of Bibles, New Testaments, and portions of Gospels and Psalms were permitted to pass through Federal lines during the war to representatives of various Bible societies in the Confederacy.

Despite the efforts to provide Bibles for the people of the South, it is claimed that there was never an adequate supply to meet the goal and aims of friends of the Bible in the South.

BIBLIOGRAPHY

Daniel, W. Harrison. "Bible Publication and Procurement in the Confederacy." *Journal of Southern History* 24 (1958): 191–201.

Dwight, Henry O. *The Centennial History of the American Bible Society.* New York, 1916.

Faust, Drew G. *The Creation of Confederate Nationalism: Ideology and Identity in the Civil War South.* Baton Rouge, La., 1988.

Hemphill, W. Edwin. "Bibles through the Blockade." *Commonwealth* 16 (1949): 9–12, 30–32.

W. Harrison Daniel

BIBLIOGRAPHY AND HISTORIOGRAPHY.

During the years since 1865 writings about the Confederate South have become an industry all their own. Collectors and dealers continue to multiply, and their collections rival research libraries in the number and quality of titles. For some appreciation of the enterprise involved in Confederate collections, see Douglas Southall Freeman, *The South to Posterity: An Introduction to the Writing of Confederate History* (New York, 1951); Richard

Harwell, *The Confederate Hundred: A Bibliophilic Selection of Confederate Books* (Urbana, Ill., 1964); and Richard Barksdale Harwell, *In Tall Cotton: The 200 Most Important Confederate Books for the Reader, Researcher and Collector* (Austin, Tex., 1978).

Major Themes of Historical Writing

Books about the Confederacy cover myriad subjects and themes. Although dividing them into broad categories risks oversimplification, three themes seem dominant in historical writings on the Confederate experience.

Apology. People who lose wars usually want urgently to explain or excuse their actions, attempting to vindicate themselves in print. Obvious examples are Jefferson Davis, *The Rise and Fall of the Confederate Government,* 2 vols. (New York, 1881), and Alexander H. Stephens, *A Constitutional View of the Late War between the States,* 2 vols. (Chicago, 1868–1870). Certainly Southerners of the Confederacy and after have poured forth prose and poetry in an effort to justify the Lost Cause. Edward A. Pollard, for example, in *The Lost Cause: A New Southern History of the War of the Confederates* (New York, 1867), concluded:

> It would be immeasurably the worst consequence of defeat in this war that the South should lose its moral and intellectual distinctiveness as a people, and cease to assert its well-known superiority in civilization, in political scholarship, and in all the standards of individual character over the people of the North.... That superiority the war has not conquered or lowered; and the South will do right to claim and cherish it.

Pollard, of course, wrote his history in the ashes of defeat, reflecting a persistent Southern nationalism that is, at the least, understandable. Confederate history as apology, however, did not die with the generation that lived the history. Even at this writing, subtle and not-at-all-subtle manifestations of neo-Confederate sentiment abound in popular culture and supposedly serious scholarship. Indeed, the uses and perversions of Confederate history are a fertile topic for analysis in and of itself.

Continuity or Discontinuity. To what extent did the Confederacy provoke or provide fundamental change in the American South? Among those historians who emphasize the Confederate experience as collective trauma for Southerners, some contend that the war for national survival produced social crisis among Southern whites. The demands of an extended war and the sacrifices imposed by the Richmond government, the argument goes, opened class divisions within the so-called Solid South. Plain folk resented the "rich man's war and poor man's fight" imposed upon them by a government dominated by planters or planter interests. So the Confederacy failed because of social issues latent in the antebellum South. This point of view is present in works as otherwise diverse as Frank L. Owsley, *State Rights in the Confederacy* (Chicago, 1925), and Paul D. Escott, *After Secession: Jefferson Davis and the Failure of Confederate Nationalism* (Baton Rouge, La., 1978).

Other historians have agreed that the Confederate era was crucial in Southern life, but they emphasize more positive aspects of the experience. Examples of some works that share this emphasis, if little else, include Nathaniel W. Stephenson, *The Day of the Confederacy* (New Haven, 1919); Frank E. Vandiver, *Their Tattered Flags: The Epic of the Confederacy* (New York, 1970); Raimondo Luraghi, *The Rise and Fall of the Plantation South* (New York, 1978); and Emory M. Thomas, *The Confederate Nation, 1861–1865* (New York, 1979).

However much the scholars cited above may differ about the substantive impact of the Confederate experience, they do agree that the Confederacy and the war were major watersheds in Southern life. Other scholars demur. Perhaps the most thoroughgoing among this group was W. J. Cash, whose *Mind of the South* (New York, 1941) contended that the Confederacy was an expression of continuity and consensus. More recently, the collaboration of Richard E. Beringer, Herman Hattaway, Archer Jones, and William N. Still, Jr., *Why the South Lost the Civil War* (Athens, Ga., 1986), suggests among other things that Confederate Southerners were less than committed secessionists. This point echoes the idea of Kenneth M. Stampp in "The Southern Road to Appomattox," an essay in Stampp's *The Imperial Union: Essays on the Background of the Civil War* (New York, 1980), that significant numbers of Confederates never really embraced the cause with much zeal from the outset.

In league with historians who question the importance of the Confederate period in Southern life are scholars who argue that nothing really consequential in the South changed from the inception of the slave plantation system until the triple trauma of Great Depression, New Deal, and World War II. An articulate example of this contention is Numan V. Bartley's *The Creation of Modern Georgia* (Athens, Ga., 1983).

Southern Distinctiveness. From Jamestown to Fort Sumter, a period of almost 154 years, Southerners had been Americans, and after Appomattox Southerners again became Americans with arguably greater zeal than most. However ironic, it is often true that descendants of those people who fought long and hard to leave the United States have been the strongest patriots, 110 percent Americans, ever since the Civil War. Such observations and others have led many historians to emphasize the *American* identity of Southern Americans and so consider the Confederate interlude an anomaly. This emphasis is perhaps best expressed in a collection of essays by Charles G. Sellers, Jr., *The Southerner as American* (Chapel Hill, N.C., 1960), and best analyzed and understood in David Potter's *The South* *and the Sectional Conflict* (Baton Rouge, La., 1968) and C. Vann Woodward's *American Counterpoint: Slavery and Racism in the North-South Dialogue* (Boston, 1971).

On the surface, at least, the issue seems simple enough. But like most matters that touch on human experience, this one is pregnant with subtle complexities. Consider, for example, the eloquent passage from Douglas S. Freeman's *R. E. Lee: A Biography,* 4 vols. (New York, 1934–1935) about the aftermath of the Battle of Malvern Hill. Freeman writes:

> Shattered bodies were everywhere and dead men in every contortion of their last agony. Weapons and the keepsakes of soldiers, caps and knapsacks, play-cards and pocket testaments, bloody heads with bulging eyes, booted legs, severed arms with hands gripped tight, torsos with the limbs blown away, gray coats dyed black with boys' blood—it was a nightmare of hell, set on a firm, green field of reality, under a workaday, leaden, summer sky, a scene to sicken the simple, home-loving soldiers who had to fight the war while the politicians responsible for bringing a nation to madness stood in the streets of safe cities and mouthed wrathful platitudes about constitutional rights.

The passage reflects Freeman's abhorrence of war, to be sure. But because he separates the "bloody heads with bulging eyes" from the "wrathful platitudes," Freeman encourages the notion that no connection existed between "the politicians" and "the simple, home-loving soldiers." Somehow, nice American boys found themselves killing each other for no good reason. They were all good Americans caught up in madness, Freeman implies, and the Southern soldiers were indistinct from their Northern adversaries. War is indeed madness. But to suggest that this war involved only "wrathful platitudes" trivializes the experience in which more than 600,000 men died.

Southerners had been and became again Americans. The Confederate experience, however, offers an opportunity to understand the Southern distinctiveness that seems to have sparked and sustained a terrible war.

A Selected Bibliography

Here follows a list of selected works arranged by topics touching on Confederate history. Because entries covering individual people and battles in this encyclopedia include pertinent bibliographies, this general bibliography omits biographies, battles, armies, ships, campaign studies, and personal narratives in all but a few cases. Also important is the fact that the list is of necessity only a sampling of a larger literature. In fact, the first category is a list of bibliographies.

Bibliographic Guides

These journals offer reviews and lists of published articles as well as articles that sometimes treat aspects of Confederate history.

Civil War History (Kent, Ohio).
Journal of American History (Bloomington, Ind.).
Journal of Southern History (Baton Rouge, La.).

Cole, Garold L. *Civil War Eyewitnesses: An Annotated Bibliography of Books and Articles, 1955–1986.* Columbia, S.C., 1988.
Coulter, E. Merton. *Travels in the Confederate States: A Bibliography.* Norman, Okla., 1948.
Dornbasch, C. E., comp. *Regimental Publications and Personal Narratives of the Civil War: A Checklist.* 2 vols. New York, 1961–1971.
Link, Arthur S., and Rembert W. Patrick, eds. *Writing Southern History: Essays in Historiography in Honor of Fletcher M. Green.* Baton Rouge, La., 1965.
Nevins, Allan, James I. Robertson, Jr., and Bell I. Wiley, eds. *Civil War Books: A Critical Bibliography.* 2 vols. Baton Rouge, La., 1965–1967.
Thomas, Emory M. *The Confederate Nation, 1861–1865.* New York, 1979 (pp. 323–372, bibliography).

Manuscript and Archival Materials

Beers, Henry Putney. *Guide to the Archives of the Government of the Confederate States of America.* Washington, D.C., 1968.
National Historical Publications Commission. *Guide to Archives and Manuscripts in the United States.* Edited by Philip M. Hamer. New Haven, Conn., 1961.
U.S. Library of Congress. *National Union Catalog of Manuscript Collections.* Washington, D.C., 1961–.

Printed Primary Sources

Confederate Veteran. Edited by S. A. Cunningham. 40 vols. Nashville, Tenn., 1893–1932. Reprint, Wilmington, N.C., 1985.
Confederate Veteran Index. Edited by Louis Manarin. 3 vols. Wilmington, N.C., 1987.
Evans, Clement A., ed. *Confederate Military History.* 12 vols. Atlanta, 1899. Extended ed. in 19 vols. Wilmington, N.C., 1987–1989.
Johnson, Robert U., and C. C. Buel, eds. *Battles and Leaders of the Civil War.* 4 vols. New York, 1887–1888. Reprint, Secaucus, N.J., 1982.
Journal of the Congress of the Confederate States of America, 1861–1865. 7 vols. Washington, D.C., 1904–1905.
Matthews, James M., ed. *Statutes at Large of the Confederate States of America.* Richmond, Va., 1862–1864.
Moore, Frank, ed. *The Rebellion Record.* 11 vols. and supp. New York, 1861–1871.
Parrish, T. Michael, and Robert M. Willingham, Jr. *Confederate Imprints: A Bibliography of Southern Publications from Secession to Surrender.* Austin, Tex., 1987.
"Proceedings of the Confederate Congress." *Southern Historical Society Papers* 45, n.s. 7 (1925). Reprint, Wilmington, N.C., 1992.
Ramsdell, Charles W., ed. *Laws and Joint Resolutions of the Last Session of the Confederate Congress. Together with the Secret Acts of the Previous Congress.* Durham, N.C., 1941.
Southern Historical Society Papers. 52 vols. Richmond, Va., 1876–1959. Reprinted with 2 vol. index. Wilmington, N.C., 1990–1992.

U.S. Naval War Records Office. *Official Records of the Union and Confederate Navies in the War of the Rebellion.* 30 vols. and index. Washington, D.C., 1894–1927.

U.S. War Department. *War of the Rebellion: A Compilation of the Official Records of the Union and Confederate Armies.* 70 vols. in 128 parts. Washington, D.C., 1880–1901.

Periodicals

Most of the following are available in microform at good research libraries.

The Countrymen.
De Bow's Review.
Magnolia: A Southern Home Journal.
Record of News, History, and Literature.
Richmond Age: A Southern Monthly Eclectic Magazine.
Southern Cultivator.
Southern Field and Fireside.
Southern Illustrated News.
Southern Literary Messenger.
Southern Punch.

Physical and Graphic Materials

Art and Photographs

The Civil War: A Centennial Exhibition of Eyewitness Drawings. Washington, D.C., 1961.

Davis, William C., ed. *The Image of War, 1861–1865.* 6 vols. Garden City, N.Y., 1981–1984.

Frassantino, William A. *Antietam: The Photographic Legacy of America's Bloodiest Day.* New York, 1978.

Frassantino, William A. *Gettysburg: A Journey in Time.* New York, 1975.

Frassantino, William A. *Grant and Lee: The Virginia Campaigns, 1864–1865.* New York, 1983.

Guernsey, Alfred H., and Henry M. Alden, eds. *Harper's Pictorial History of the Great Rebellion.* 2 vols. New York, 1866–1868.

Miller, Francis T., ed. *The Photographic History of the Civil War.* 10 vols. New York, 1912.

Neely, Mark E., Jr., Harold Holzer, and Gabor S. Boritt. *The Confederate Image: Prints of the Lost Cause.* Chapel Hill, N.C., 1987.

Simpson, Marc. *Winslow Homer: Paintings of the Civil War.* San Francisco, 1988.

Maps

Cowels, Calvin D., comp. *Atlas to Accompany the Official Records of the Union and Confederate Armies.* 2 vols. Washington, D.C., 1891–1895.

Esposito, Vincent J., ed. *The West Point Atlas of American Wars.* 2 vols. New York, 1959.

A Guide to Civil War Maps in the National Archives. Washington, D.C., 1986.

Symonds, Craig L. *Gettysburg: A Battlefield Atlas.* Baltimore, 1992.

Geographical Guides

Cromie, Alice Hamilton. *A Tour Guide to the Civil War.* Chicago, 1965.

Kennedy, Frances H. *The Civil War Battlefield Guide.* Boston, 1990.

Stevens, Joseph E. *America's National Battlefield Parks: A Guide.* Norman, Okla., 1990.

Thomas, Emory M. *Travels to Hallowed Ground: A Historian's Journey to the American Civil War.* Columbia, S.C., 1987.

General Histories of the Confederate Period

Barney, William L. *Battleground for the Union: The Era of the Civil War and Reconstruction, 1848–1877.* Englewood Cliffs, N.J., 1990.

Brock, W. R. *Conflict and Transformation: The United States, 1844–1877.* New York, 1973.

Foote, Shelby. *The Civil War: A Narrative.* 3 vols. New York, 1958–1975.

Luraghi, Raimondo. *Storia della guerra civile americana.* Turin, Italy, 1966.

McPherson, James M. *Battle Cry of Freedom.* New York, 1987.

McPherson, James M. *Ordeal by Fire.* New York, 1982.

Parish, Peter J. *The American Civil War.* New York, 1975.

Randall, James G., and David Donald. *The Civil War and Reconstruction.* Boston, 1969.

Roland, Charles P. *An American Iliad: The Story of the Civil War.* Lexington, Ky., 1991.

Vandiver, Frank E. *Blood Brothers: A Short History of the Civil War.* College Station, Tex., 1992.

General Histories of the Confederacy

Coulter, E. Merton. *The Confederate States of America.* A History of the South, vol. 7. Baton Rouge, La., 1950.

Eaton, Clement. *A History of the Southern Confederacy.* New York, 1954.

Roland, Charles P. *The Confederacy.* Chicago, 1960.

Thomas, Emory M. *The Confederate Nation, 1861–1865.* New York, 1979.

Vandiver, Frank E. *Their Tattered Flags: The Epic of the Confederacy.* New York, 1970. Reprint, College Station, Tex., 1987.

Collected Essays

Belohlavek, John M., and Lewis N. Wynne, eds. *Divided We Fall: Essays on Confederate Nation-Building.* Saint Leo, Fla., 1991.

Bleser, Carol, ed. *In Joy and in Sorrow: Women, Family, and Marriage in the Victorian South, 1830–1890.* New York, 1991.

Clinton, Catherine, and Nina Silber. *Divided Houses: Gender and the Civil War.* New York, 1992.

Crow, Jeffrey J., Paul D. Escott, and Charles L. Flynn, Jr. *Race, Class and Politics in Southern History: Essays in Honor of Robert F. Durden.* Baton Rouge, La., 1990.

Donald, David, ed. *Why the North Won the Civil War.* Baton Rouge, La., 1960.

Gallagher, Gary W., ed. *Antietam: Essays on the 1862 Maryland Campaign.* Kent, Ohio, 1989.

Gallagher, Gary W., ed. *The First Day at Gettysburg: Essays on Confederate and Union Leadership.* Kent, Ohio, 1992.

Gallagher, Gary W., ed. *Struggle for the Shenandoah: Essays on the 1864 Valley Campaign.* Kent, Ohio, 1991.

Owens, Harry P., and James J. Cooke, eds. *The Old South in the Crucible of Civil War.* Jackson, Miss., 1983.

Potter, David. *The South and the Sectional Conflict.* Baton Rouge, La., 1968.

Robertson, James I., Jr., and Richard M. McMurry, eds. *Rank and File: Civil War Essays in Honor of Bell Irwin Wiley.* San Rafael, Calif., 1976.

Stampp, Kenneth M. *The Imperiled Union: Essays on the Background of the Civil War.* New York, 1980.

Woodward, C. Vann. *American Counterpoint: Slavery and Racism in the North-South Dialogue.* Boston, 1971.

Woodward, C. Vann. *The Burden of Southern History.* Rev. ed. Baton Rouge, La., 1968.

Wyatt-Brown, Bertram. *Yankee Saints and Southern Sinners.* Baton Rouge, La., 1985.

Extended Essays and Interpretive Works

Beringer, Richard E., Herman Hattaway, Archer Jones, and William N. Still, Jr. *Why the South Lost the Civil War.* Athens, Ga., 1986.

Degler, Carl N. *The Other South: Southern Dissenters in the Nineteenth Century.* New York, 1974.

Escott, Paul D. *After Secession: Jefferson Davis and the Failure of Confederate Nationalism.* Baton Rouge, La., 1978.

Faust, Drew Gilpin. *The Creation of Southern Nationalism.* Baton Rouge, La., 1988.

Hill, Louise B. *State Socialism in the Confederate States of America.* Charlottesville, Va., 1936.

Luraghi, Raimondo. *The Rise and Fall of the Plantation South.* New York, 1978.

McMurry, Richard M. *Two Great Rebel Armies: An Essay in Confederate Military History.* Chapel Hill, N.C., 1989.

McWhiney, Grady, and Perry D. Jamieson. *Attack and Die: Civil War Military Tactics and the Southern Heritage.* University, Ala., 1982.

Owsley, Frank L. *State Rights in the Confederacy.* Chicago, 1925.

Ramsdell, Charles W. *Behind the Lines in the Southern Confederacy.* Baton Rouge, La., 1944.

Stephenson, Nathaniel W. *The Day of the Confederacy.* New Haven, 1919.

Thomas, Emory M. *The Confederacy as a Revolutionary Experience.* Englewood Cliffs, N.J., 1971. Reprint, Columbia, S.C., 1991.

Wiley, Bell I. *Road to Appomattox.* New York, 1968.

Wyatt-Brown, Bertram. *Southern Honor: Ethics and Behavior in the Old South.* New York, 1982.

Secession

Barney, William L. *The Road to Secession.* New York, 1972.

Barney, William L. *The Secessionist Impulse: Alabama and Mississippi in 1860.* Princeton, 1974.

Crofts, Daniel W. *Reluctant Confederates: Upper South Unionists in the Secession Crisis.* Chapel Hill, N.C., 1989.

Ford, Lacy K., Jr. *Origins of Southern Radicalism: The South Carolina Upcountry, 1800–1860.* New York, 1988.

Inscoe, John. *Mountain Masters: Slavery and Sectional Crisis in Western North Carolina.* Knoxville, Tenn., 1989.

Johnson, Michael P. *Toward a Patriarchal Republic: The Secession of Georgia.* Baton Rouge, La., 1977.

McCardell, John. *The Idea of a Southern Nation: Southern Nationalists and Southern Nationalism, 1800–1860.* New York, 1972.

Potter, David M. *The Impending Crisis, 1848–1861.* New York, 1976.

Politics and Government

Alexander, Thomas B., and Richard E. Beringer. *The Anatomy of the Confederate Congress: A Study of the Influence of Member Characteristics on Legislative Voting Behavior, 1861–1865.* Nashville, Tenn., 1972.

Ball, Douglas B. *Financial Failure and Confederate Defeat.* Urbana, Ill., 1991.

Lee, Charles R., Jr. *The Confederate Constitutions.* Chapel Hill, N.C., 1963.

Moore, Albert B. *Conscription and Conflict in the Confederacy.* New York, 1924.

Patrick, Rembert W. *Jefferson Davis and His Cabinet.* Baton Rouge, La., 1944.

Ringold, May Spencer. *The Role of State Legislatures in the Confederacy.* Athens, Ga., 1966.

Robbins, John Brawner. "Confederate Nationalism: Politics and Government in the Confederate South, 1861–65." Ph.D. diss., Rice University, 1964.

Tatum, Georgia L. *Disloyalty in the Confederacy.* Chapel Hill, N.C., 1934.

Todd, Richard C. *Confederate Finance.* Athens, Ga., 1954.

Yearns, Wilfred B. *The Confederate Congress.* Athens, Ga., 1960.

State and Local Studies

Ash, Stephen V. *Middle Tennessee Society Transformed, 1860–1870: War and Peace in the Upper South.* Baton Rouge, La., 1988.

Barrett, John G. *The Civil War in North Carolina.* Chapel Hill, N.C., 1963.

Bergeron, Arthur W., Jr. *Confederate Mobile.* Jackson, Miss., 1991.

Bryan, T. Conn. *Confederate Georgia.* Athens, Ga., 1953.

Burton, Orville Vernon. *In My Father's House Are Many Mansions: Family and Community in Edgefield, South Carolina.* Chapel Hill, N.C., 1985.

Durrill, Wayne K. *War of Another Kind: A Southern Community in the Great Rebellion.* New York, 1990.

Escott, Paul D. *Many Excellent People: Power and Privilege in North Carolina, 1850–1900.* Chapel Hill, N.C., 1985.

Hermann, Janet Sharp. *The Pursuit of a Dream.* New York, 1981.

Kenzer, Robert C. *Kinship and Neighborhood in a Southern Community: Orange County, North Carolina, 1849–1881.* Knoxville, Tenn., 1988.

Kruman, Marc W. *Parties and Politics in North Carolina, 1836–1865.* Baton Rouge, La., 1983.

Paludan, Phillip Shaw. *Victims: A True Story of the Civil War.* Knoxville, Tenn., 1981.

Robertson, James I., Jr. *Civil War Virginia: Battleground for a Nation*. Charlottesville, Va., 1991.

Thomas, Emory M. *The Confederate State of Richmond: A Biography of the Capital*. Austin, Tex., 1971.

Thornton, J. Mills, III. *Politics and Power in a Slave Society*. Baton Rouge, La., 1978.

Wallenstein, Peter. *From Slave South to New South: Public Policy in Nineteenth Century Georgia*. Chapel Hill, N.C., 1987.

Wiener, Jonathan M. *Social Origins of the New South: Alabama, 1860–1885*. Baton Rouge, La., 1978.

Yearns, Wilfred Buck, ed. *The Confederate Governors*. Athens, Ga., 1985.

African Americans in the South

Brewer, James H. *The Confederate Negro: Virginia's Craftsmen and Military Laborers, 1861–1865*. Durham, N.C., 1969.

Cornish, Dudley T. *The Sable Arm: Negro Troops in the Union Army, 1861–1865*. New York, 1956.

Duncan, Russell. *Blue-Eyed Child of Fortune: The Civil War Letters of Colonel Robert Gould Shaw*. Athens, Ga., 1992.

Durden, Robert F. *The Gray and the Black: The Confederate Debate on Emancipation*. Baton Rouge, La., 1972.

Fields, Barbara Jeanne. *Slavery and Freedom on the Middle Ground: Maryland during the Nineteenth Century*. New Haven, 1985.

Genovese, Eugene D. *Roll, Jordan, Roll: The World the Slaves Made*. New York, 1974.

Glatthaar, Joseph T. *Forged in Battle: The Civil War Alliance of Black Soldiers and White Officers*. New York, 1990.

Johnson, Michael P., and James L. Roark. *Black Masters: A Free Family of Color in the Old South*. New York, 1984.

Mohr, Clarence L. *On the Threshold of Freedom: Masters and Slaves in Civil War Georgia*. Athens, Ga., 1986.

Wiley, Bell I. *Southern Negroes, 1861–1865*. New Haven, 1938.

Confederate Women

Clinton, Catherine. *The Plantation Mistress: Woman's World in the Old South*. New York, 1982.

Fox-Genovese, Elizabeth. *Within the Plantation Household: Black and White Women of the Old South*. Chapel Hill, N.C., 1988.

Friedman, Jean E. *The Enclosed Garden: Women and Community in the Evangelical South, 1830–1900*. Chapel Hill, N.C., 1985.

Massey, Mary Elizabeth. *Bonnet Brigades: American Women and the Civil War*. New York, 1966.

Rable, George. *Civil Wars: Women and the Crisis of Southern Nationalism*. Urbana, Ill., 1989.

Scott, Anne Firor. *The Southern Lady: From Pedestal to Politics, 1830–1930*. Chicago, 1970.

Wiley, Bell I., *Confederate Women*. Westport, Conn., 1975.

Society and Culture

Aaron, Daniel. *The Unwritten War: American Writers and the Civil War*. New York, 1973.

Andrews, J. Cutler. *The South Reports the War*. Princeton, 1970.

Bailey, Fred Arthur. *Class and Tennessee's Confederate Generation*. Chapel Hill, N.C., 1987.

Cunningham, Horace H. *Doctors in Gray: The Confederate Medical Service*. Baton Rouge, La., 1960.

Dumond, Dwight L., ed. *Southern Editorials on Secession*. New York, 1931.

Eaton, Clement. *The Waning of the Old South Civilization*. Athens, Ga., 1968.

Harwell, Richard B. *The Brief Candle: The Confederate Theatre*. Worcester, Mass., 1971.

Harwell, Richard B. *Confederate Music*. Chapel Hill, N.C., 1950.

Hill, Samuel S., Jr. *Religion in the Southern States: A Historical Study*. Macon, Ga., 1983.

Hill, Samuel S., Jr. *The South and the North in American Religion*. Athens, Ga., 1980.

Jimmerson, Randall C. *The Private Civil War: Popular Thought during the Sectional Conflict*. Baton Rouge, La., 1988.

Massey, Mary Elizabeth. *Ersatz in the Confederacy*. Columbia, S.C., 1952.

Massey, Mary Elizabeth. *Refugee Life in the Confederacy*. Baton Rouge, La., 1964.

Powell, Lawrence N. *New Masters: Northern Planters during the Civil War and Reconstruction*. New Haven, 1980.

Silver, James W. *Confederate Morale and Church Propaganda*. Tuscaloosa, Ala., 1957.

Wiley, Bell I. *Plain People of the Confederacy*. Baton Rouge, La., 1943.

Wilson, Edmund. *Patriotic Gore: Studies in the Literature of the American Civil War*. New York, 1962.

Economic Studies

Black, Robert C., III. *The Railroads of the Confederacy*. Chapel Hill, N.C., 1952.

DeCredico, Mary A. *Patriotism for Profit: Georgia's Urban Entrepreneurs and the Confederate War Effort*. Chapel Hill, N.C., 1990.

Dew, Charles B. *Ironmaker to the Confederacy: Joseph P. Anderson and the Tredegar Iron Works*. New Haven, 1966.

Goff, Richard D. *Confederate Supply*. Durham, N.C., 1969.

Lonn, Ella. *Salt as a Factor in the Confederacy*. New York, 1933.

Roland, Charles P. *Louisiana Sugar Plantations during the American Civil War*. Leiden, Netherlands, 1957.

Still, William N., Jr. *Confederate Shipbuilding*. Athens, Ga., 1969.

Vandiver, Frank E. *Ploughshares into Swords: Josiah Gorgas and Confederate Ordnance*. Austin, Tex., 1952.

Wise, Stephen R. *Lifeline of the Confederacy: Blockade Running during the Civil War*. Columbia, S.C., 1988.

Foreign Relations

Bernath, Stuart L. *Squall across the Atlantic: American Civil War Prize Cases and Diplomacy*. Berkeley, Calif., 1970.

Case, Lynn M., and Warren F. Spencer. *The United States and France: Civil War Diplomacy*. Philadelphia, 1970.

Crook, D. P. *The North, the South, and the Powers, 1861–1865*. New York, 1974.

Cullop, Charles P. *Confederate Propaganda in Europe, 1861–1865*. Coral Gables, Fla., 1969.

Ellison, Mary. *Support for Secession: Lancashire and the American Civil War*. Chicago, 1972.

Ferris, Norman B. *The Trent Affair*. Knoxville, Tenn., 1975.

Jones, Howard. *Union in Peril: The Crisis over British Intervention in the Civil War*. Chapel Hill, N.C., 1992.

Lester, Richard I. *Confederate Finance and Purchasing in Great Britain.* Charlottesville, Va., 1975.

Merli, Frank J. *Great Britain and the Confederate Navy, 1861–1865.* Bloomington, Ind., 1970.

Owsley, Frank L. *King Cotton Diplomacy: Foreign Relations of the Confederate States of America.* Rev. ed. Chicago, 1959.

Spencer, Warren F. *The Confederate Navy in Europe.* University, Ala., 1983.

General Military Studies

Barton, Michael. *Goodmen: The Character of Civil War Soldiers.* University Park, Pa., 1981.

Connelly, Thomas L., and Archer Jones. *The Politics of Command: Factions and Ideas in Confederate Strategy.* Baton Rouge, La., 1973.

Glatthaar, Joseph T. *March to the Sea and Beyond: Sherman's Troops in the Savannah and Carolinas Campaign.* New York, 1985.

Griffith, Paddy. *Battle Tactics of the Civil War.* New Haven, 1989.

Jones, Archer. *Civil War Command and Strategy: The Process of Victory and Defeat.* New York, 1992.

Jones, Archer. *Confederate Strategy from Shiloh to Vicksburg.* Baton Rouge, La., 1961.

Jones, Virgil C. *The Civil War at Sea.* 3 vols. New York, 1960–1962.

Linderman, Gerald F. *Embattled Courage: The Experience of Combat in the American Civil War.* New York, 1987.

Luvaas, Jay. *The Military Legacy of the Civil War: The European Inheritance.* Chicago, 1959.

Merrill, James M. *Battle Flags South: The Story of the Civil War Navies on Western Waters.* Rutherford, N.J., 1970.

Mitchell, Reid. *Civil War Soldiers.* New York, 1988.

Perry, Milton F. *Infernal Machines: The Story of Confederate Submarine and Mine Warfare.* Baton Rouge, La., 1965.

Robertson, James I., Jr. *Soldiers Blue and Gray.* Columbia, S.C., 1988.

Robinson, William N. *Confederate Privateers.* New Haven, 1928.

Royster, Charles. *The Destructive War: William Tecumseh Sherman, Stonewall Jackson, and the Americans.* New York, 1991.

Scharf, J. Thomas. *History of the Confederate States Navy.* New York, 1887. Reprint, New York, 1977.

Still, William N., Jr. *Iron Afloat: The Story of the Confederate Armorclads.* Nashville, Tenn., 1971.

Vandiver, Frank E. *Rebel Brass: The Confederate Command System.* Baton Rouge, La., 1956.

Weigley, Russell F. *The American Way of War: A History of United States Military Strategy and Policy.* New York, 1973.

Wiley, Bell I. *The Life of Johnny Reb: The Common Soldier of the Confederacy.* Indianapolis, 1943.

Woodworth, Steven E. *Jefferson Davis and His Generals: The Failure of Confederate Command in the West.* Lawrence, Kans., 1990.

The Lost Cause

Connelly, Thomas L., and Barbara L. Bellows. *God and General Longstreet: The Lost Cause and the Southern Mind.* Baton Rouge, La., 1982.

Foster, Gaines M. *Ghosts of the Confederacy: Defeat, the Lost Cause, and the Emergence of the New South.* New York, 1987.

Sutherland, Daniel E. *The Confederate Carpetbaggers.* Baton Rouge, La., 1988.

Wilson, Charles Reagan. *Baptized in Blood: The Religion of the Lost Cause, 1865–1920.* Athens, Ga., 1983.

[*For further discussion of historiographic shifts in the interpretation of the causes and outcome of the Civil War, see* Civil War, *articles on* Causes of the War *and* Causes of Defeat. *See also* Discography; Museums and Archives; *the extensive bibliography for the entry* Diaries, Letters, and Memoirs; *and the bibliographies of particular entries on battles and campaigns, biographical figures, governmental branches and departments, military units, ships, and states.*]

EMORY M. THOMAS

BIG BETHEL, VIRGINIA.

The Civil War was less than two months old when this first significant military action in Virginia occurred. Even after the Old Dominion became the pivotal state in the Southern Confederacy, Federal troops continued to occupy Fort Monroe at the tip of the Virginia Peninsula. In command of that force was Maj. Gen. Benjamin F. Butler, a shrewd politician who owed his general's commission solely to his political power in Massachusetts. His second-in-command was Brig. Gen. Ebenezer W. Pierce, head of the Massachusetts Militia.

Early in June 1861, Butler learned that Confederates had constructed a battery emplacement at a bend in a branch of Black River at Big Bethel Church. The position was only eight miles northwest of Butler's outposts at Fort Monroe. The inexperienced Butler concluded that the 1,400 Southerners (mostly Col. D. H. Hill's First North Carolina and Maj. George Wythe Randolph's battery of howitzers) ought to be driven away. Butler thereupon organized an expedition of 4,400 men under General Pierce to do the job. Yet the grand strategy devised by Butler proved to be too sophisticated for the raw recruits under his command.

Butler's plan called for a march on the night of June 9–10, with a convergence of four separate regiments at the point of attack the next morning. Everything went wrong during the Federal movement. Nervous soldiers forgot the watchword; white badges issued for identification could not be seen in the darkness; some units were unable to find the roads they were supposed to take. The climax to the march came when two Federal regiments collided in the night and began shooting at each other. This brisk action alerted Confederates to the enemy's presence.

Late on Monday morning, June 10, with the temperature approaching ninety degrees, Federals lurched forward in an assault that quickly lost all semblance of order. Confederates squatting in the underbrush raked the Federals with

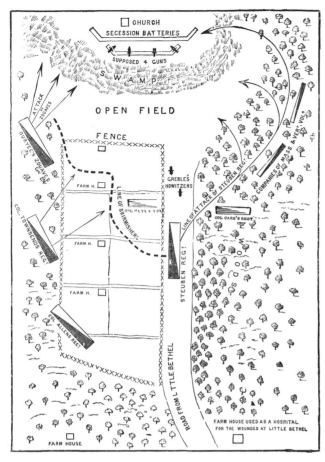

BATTLE OF BIG BETHEL.   *THE SOLDIER IN OUR CIVIL WAR*

musketry and cannon fire. Colonel Hill reported that his Southern troops "were in high glee, and seemed to enjoy it as much as boys do rabbit-shooting."

The one-sided contest lasted barely half an hour, after which Pierce's men fled back to their encampments in utter rout. Pierce had seemed bewildered throughout the contest. Instead of acknowledging defeat because of poor intelligence service and organizational breakdowns, Pierce blamed the outcome on the reluctance of New York colonels to obey a Massachusetts brigadier.

Union casualties were 18 killed, 53 wounded, and 5 missing. Among the dead was Maj. Theodore Winthrop, a globe-trotting journalist who was acting as Butler's military secretary. Southern losses were 1 killed and 7 wounded.

Later in the war, an action of such limited scope would have been termed a mere skirmish. Yet at this opening stage of hostilities, the steadfastness in battle of green Confederates sent encouragement through the South and gave credence to earlier boasts that "one Reb could lick ten Yankees any day." Richmond merchants proudly displayed

battlefield relics in the windows of their shops. Conversely, Big Bethel sent a shock wave of embarrassment through the North.

BIBLIOGRAPHY

Dinkins, James. *1861 to 1865, by an Old Johnnie.* Dayton, Ohio, 1975.

Freeman, Douglas Southall. *Lee's Lieutenants: A Study in Command.* Vol. 1. New York, 1942. Reprint, New York, 1986.

West, Richard S., Jr. *Lincoln's Scapegoat General.* Boston, 1965.

JAMES I. ROBERTSON, JR.

BLACK BELT. The black belt stretched from central Georgia westward through middle Alabama and Mississippi and north into Tennessee. The region was more than four hundred miles long and approximately thirty miles wide. Named originally for its fertile black soil, the area attracted low-country planters moving west during the early nineteenth century in search of appropriate land on which to grow short-staple cotton. After the cotton gin came into use in the 1790s, the demand for the fiber increased on the world market, and white Southerners considered the commodity the bastion of their economy. Along with the planters came African American slaves. In fact, blacks formed a majority of the population in many of the black belt counties during the nineteenth and twentieth centuries. For example, in 1860 slaves constituted 68.1 percent of the black belt population. Therefore, the name *black belt* signified both the color of its rich soil and the racial composition of its inhabitants.

The people who settled the region and supported and fought for the Confederacy created a rough frontier society. They crushed and removed the Native Americans of the four of the Five Civilized Tribes (Cherokee, Creek, Choctaw, and Chickasaw) who had originally inhabited the land. Establishing plantations, farms, and crossroad villages, black belt settlers promoted individualism, agrarianism, land speculation, and slave labor. The raucous spirit of antebellum black belt life was captured in Joseph G. Baldwin's *Flush Times in Alabama and Mississippi* and Augustus B. Longstreet's *Georgia Scenes.* The area supported few towns; Macon, Georgia, Montgomery, Alabama, and Jackson, Mississippi, were the largest. They served primarily as agricultural trading centers linked by rivers and railroads to the larger port cities on the Atlantic and Gulf coasts. In large part, railroads did not connect the interior black belt towns, resulting in inefficient movement of men and materials during the war.

The black belt harbored vast disparities in landownership. For example, according to historian Jonathan Wiener, in 1860, 5 percent of the landowners in black belt Alabama controlled 24 percent of the improved land. In addition, they owned 26 percent of the slaves and 30 percent of all farm value. Such maldistribution of wealth resulted in a crowding out of yeoman farming families and the perpetuation of a slaveholding plantation elite.

Fire-eating secessionists predominated in the region before and during the Civil War. Planters of the area (such as William Lowndes Yancey of Alabama, Isham G. Harris of Tennessee, and John Quitman of Mississippi) had long advocated disunion and perceived Southern independence as the only option for protecting the South's economic and political security. When the Confederacy declared its independence, the region's leaders originally placed the capital in Montgomery, the center of Alabama's black belt, although, as a reward to the Old Dominion for joining the Confederacy, political leaders moved it to Richmond, Virginia. Still, black belt planters certainly remained the most ardent of Southern nationalists.

While forming the bedrock of the secessionist movement, black belt planters also produced nearly two-thirds of the South's cotton between 1845 and 1861. Cotton yields in the region ranged from eight hundred to a thousand pounds per acre. Although well suited for food production, the black belt remained primarily a cotton-producing region during the war. When farmers and planters joined the Confederate army, they left the management of their plantations to family members and overseers who continued to grow the staple even though the Federal naval blockade excluded much of their product from the world market. As a result, unused cotton accumulated in Southern ports while the Confederacy's vital food needs went unmet. By 1863, the critical year of the war, Union troops had occupied the South's main food-producing areas in Virginia and Tennessee. The combined effects of continued cotton planting and inadequate food production seriously hobbled the Confederate war effort.

Much of the black belt remained in the Confederacy until the last year of the war. Gen. William Tecumseh Sherman's destruction of Atlanta and March to the Sea opened the eastern black belt to the Union in the summer of 1864. That fall Federal troops led by Gen. John Schofield smashed Confederate Gen. John Bell Hood's Army of Tennessee at Nashville, leaving the western black belt unprotected. In March 1865 Maj. Gen. James H. Wilson led over thirteen thousand Northern cavalrymen on a raid through the black belt regions of Mississippi, Alabama, and Georgia. Destroying virtually everything in their way, Wilson's troops captured the old capital, Montgomery, and the important industrial towns of Selma, Alabama, and Columbus, Georgia. In April 1865, the black belt submitted to Federal power.

In several ways the black belt demonstrated the inherent weaknesses of the Confederacy. Wedded to agrarianism and cotton production, the region, like the rest of the South, had failed to build an industrial and transportation infrastructure that could sustain manufacturing needs through a nineteenth-century war. With an inefficient internal railroad network and a planter class that valued cash crop production over growing food, the region collapsed in the final year of the war.

BIBLIOGRAPHY

Odum, Howard W. *Southern Regions of the United States.* Chapel Hill, N.C., 1936.

Thomas, Emory M. *The Confederate Nation: 1861–1865.* New York, 1979.

Wiener, Jonathan M. *Social Origins of the New South: Alabama 1860–1885.* Baton Rouge, La., 1978.

Wright, Gavin. *The Political Economy of the Cotton South: Households, Markets, and Wealth in the Nineteenth Century.* New York, 1978.

RIC A. KABAT

BLACKS. *For discussion of African Americans in the Confederacy and the Civil War era, see entries beginning* African American. *See also under* Army *and* Navy *for articles devoted specifically to African Americans in the Confederate army and navy.*

BLANCHARD, ALBERT GALLATIN (1810–1891), brigadier general. Born September 10, 1810, in Charlestown, Massachusetts, Blanchard graduated from West Point in 1829, twenty-sixth in a class of forty-six. After resigning from the army in 1840, he moved to New Orleans where he became a merchant and director of the state's public schools. When the Mexican War broke out, Blanchard rejoined the regular army in May 1847 and served as a major in the Twelfth Infantry only to resign again in July 1848.

When the Civil War began, Blanchard became colonel of the First Louisiana Volunteer Infantry and was sent to Norfolk, Virginia, where he served under Benjamin Huger. Blanchard, who was promoted to brigadier general on September 21, 1861, fought in the peninsular campaign but saw little active duty after 1862. He returned to Louisiana where he organized camps of instruction and oversaw conscript duty. He served in the field briefly in early 1863 when he was ordered to report to E. Kirby Smith, but he was back in a desk position by August. Gen. Richard Taylor considered Blanchard utterly incompetent, and he was heavily criticized for allowing Ulysses S. Grant's army to march down the Louisiana bank of the Mississippi River in the Vicksburg campaign. In 1865 he was transferred to South Carolina where he headed a brigade of reserves in the Carolina campaign.

Following the war Blanchard served as assistant city surveyor in New Orleans. He died there on June 21, 1891, and is buried in the city at St. Louis Cemetery No. 1.

BIBLIOGRAPHY

Warner, Ezra J. *Generals in Gray: Lives of the Confederate Commanders*. Baton Rouge, La., 1959.
Winters, John D. *The Civil War in Louisiana*. Baton Rouge, La., 1963.

ANNE J. BAILEY

BLANDFORD, MARK HARDIN (1826–1902),

captain and congressman from Georgia. Blandford was born to affluent planter parents in Warren County, Georgia, in 1826. He was educated at Mercer University, studied law, and was admitted to the bar in 1844 before he was eighteen years old, which required a special act of the Georgia legislature. He had practiced law for only two years—first in Hamilton, then in Tazewell, Georgia—when the Mexican War broke out. He immediately volunteered and served as a sergeant with the First Georgia Regiment for almost a year. He returned home in 1847 and opened a new law practice and store in Buena Vista, both of which thrived.

As soon as Georgia seceded from the Union in January 1861, Blandford raised a company and served as its captain in Georgia's "Bloody Twelfth" Regiment. It served under Thomas J. ("Stonewall") Jackson's command during the Shenandoah Valley campaign of 1862 and participated in the Battle of McDowell, Virginia, on May 8. It was during that engagement that Blandford was shot in the right arm, which had to be amputated at the shoulder. He returned home, and while his wound was still healing in April 1863, Jefferson Davis appointed him to a judgeship of the Confederate military court, with the rank of lieutenant colonel. He served in this capacity until October, when he ran for election to the Second Congress from Georgia's Third District and easily defeated the incumbent, Hines Holt, who had already resigned his seat.

As congressman, Blandford demonstrated a strong commitment to Confederate military strength. In November 1864, he proposed a law that would eliminate all class exemptions from military service; the use of troops thus raised would be the president's prerogative. This led to strong protest from state rights adherents in and out of Congress, and final passage of an exemption act came only in March 1865 in much amended form. Only on certain economic measures did Blandford protest too much central power on the part of the Davis administration. He urged Congress to repeal a ban on imported luxury items and to enact a law stipulating that only specifically appointed agents be authorized to carry out impressments. Neither proposal ever passed.

Blandford remained in Congress until the government in Richmond collapsed. He returned to his law practice and mercantile operation in Buena Vista until 1869, when he moved to Columbus. In 1872 when Martin J. Crawford died, Blandford was named by the legislature as his replacement on the Georgia Supreme Court. He followed that term with a full term of his own, serving on the bench until 1881. He then returned to Columbus and resumed his law practice, which he continued until his death on January 31, 1902.

BIBLIOGRAPHY

Northen, William J., ed. *Men of Mark in Georgia*. Vol. 3. Atlanta, Ga., 1908. Reprint, Spartanburg, S.C., 1974.
Warner, Ezra J., and W. Buck Yearns. *Biographical Register of the Confederate Congress*. Baton Rouge, La., 1975.
Yearns, Wilfred B. *The Confederate Congress*. Athens, Ga., 1960.

JOHN C. INSCOE

BLEDSOE, ALBERT T. (1809–1877), chief of the

Bureau of War, Confederate agent in England. A Kentucky classmate of Jefferson Davis and Robert E. Lee at West Point, Albert Taylor Bledsoe graduated from the U.S. Military Academy in 1830 and served in Indian wars until 1832. He read law at Richmond, Virginia, before becoming a tutor at Kenyon College, where he studied theology. Ordained an Episcopal priest, he resigned from the clergy because of his scruples against infant baptism. In 1836 he taught mathematics at Miami University in Ohio before he and his wife moved to Springfield, Illinois, where he practiced law from 1838 to 1848, next door to his fellow Union Whig Abraham Lincoln. He taught mathematics at the University of Mississippi from 1848 to 1854 and at the University of Virginia from 1854 to 1861. In spite of his academic and political background, he won dubious fame as a hater of Yankees, democracy, and Thomas Jefferson.

In 1861 Bledsoe was colonel of the Thirty-sixth Virginia Infantry before he entered the Confederate War Department as chief of the Bureau of War. At Maj. Josiah Gorgas's request, Governor John Letcher named Bledsoe to a commission to supervise the transfer of the Virginia State Armory and its contents to the Confederacy. Besides performing routine office tasks, Bledsoe reviewed courts-martial for Secretary of War Judah P. Benjamin. After Thomas Jefferson's grandson, George Wythe Randolph, replaced Benjamin as secretary of war, it was remarkable that Bledsoe was not transferred from the War Office. In 1864 President Davis sent him as an agent to England in the avowed hope that he could influence prominent Britons to support the Confederacy. Presumably, Bledsoe contributed propaganda to Henry Hotz's *Index*.

In 1866 Bledsoe moved to Baltimore, where he taught school and founded the *Southern Review*. In 1871 he became a Methodist minister. Besides two theological works, Bledsoe had published in 1856 his *Essay on Liberty and Slavery*. In 1866 he recapitulated the results of his legalistic research concerning the American Constitution, slavery, and state rights in his book *Is Davis a Traitor; or, Was Secession a Constitutional Right?* He showed himself the extreme unreconstructed Southerner, declaring that secession was a constitutional right, that slavery was sanctioned by the Bible, and that Thomas Jefferson and democracy were the sources of all the South's woes. Furthermore, Bledsoe condemned evolutionary theory, industrialism, predestination, and science. One can only speculate on the meaning of Lee's comment to Bledsoe: "We all look to you for our vindication."

BIBLIOGRAPHY

Herrick, Sophia Bledsoe. "Albert Taylor Bledsoe." In *Library of Southern Literature.* Edited by Edwin A. Alderman. Vol. 1. New Orleans, 1907.

Kean, R. H. Garlick. *Inside Confederate Government.* Edited by Edward Younger. New York, 1957.

Lincoln, Abraham. *Collected Works.* Edited by Roy P. Balser et al. Vol. 1. New Brunswick, N.J., 1953.

Shackelford, George Green. *George Wythe Randolph and the Confederate Elite.* Athens, Ga., 1988.

U.S. War Department. *War of the Rebellion: A Compilation of the Official Records of the Union and Confederate Armies.* Washington, D.C., 1880–1901. Ser. 1, vol. 51, pt. 2, pp. 123, 251; ser. 2, vol. 1, pp. 867–868; ser. 2, vol. 3, p. 712; ser. 4, vol. 1, pp. 534, 1176; ser. 4, vol. 2, p. 1074.

GEORGE GREEN SHACKELFORD

BLEEDING KANSAS. The term *Bleeding Kansas* arose from a series of events that followed the passage of the Kansas-Nebraska Act in 1854. The act invalidated the restrictions on the expansion of slavery in the Missouri Compromise of 1820, initiating the struggle to make Kansas a free or slave state under the doctrine of popular sovereignty advocated by Senator Stephen A. Douglas of Illinois.

The conflicts in territorial Kansas from 1854 to 1861 involved much more than the slavery question; also at work were the insatiable hunger for both public and Indian lands, the desire by political parties for patronage appointments, competition for town sites, selection of railroad routes, and at times outright banditry and personal plunder. Yet the struggle between free-state and proslavery elements was evident even in some of these contests, and it was this controversial question that attracted national attention, with newspaper editors and politicians often exaggerating its significance.

Competition between the North and South resulted in organized efforts to encourage migration to Kansas. The New England Emigrant Aid Company was formed in Massachusetts, and more limited efforts were made in the South with the encouragement of such leaders as Col. Jefferson Buford of Alabama. In the subsequent patterns of settlement, proslavery groups were concentrated in the towns of Atchison, Leavenworth, and Lecompton and free-state settlers in Lawrence, Topeka, Manhattan, and Osawatomie.

When the time came to organize a legislature, armed proslavery Missourians crossed the border on election day 1855 to cast some of the 4,968 illegal votes against 1,210 lawful ones. Consequently the legislature and the laws it passed were denounced as bogus. The free-state groups organized separately and held a constitutional convention in Topeka in October 1855, which proposed a constitution that would admit Kansas as a free state without benefit of an enabling act of Congress (usually required) but would provide for exclusion of free blacks and mulattoes from the state. Congress refused admission under this constitution.

A series of acts and threats of violence gave unhappy substance to the term *Bleeding Kansas*. Lawrence as the main seat of free-state activity became the locus of conflict in the so-called Wakarusa War in 1855, triggered when a proslavery settler killed his free-state neighbor over a boundary dispute. A military confrontation was prevented only by the intervention of the territorial governor, Wilson Shannon. A year later the city suffered an attack called the "sack of Lawrence" on May 21, led by the Douglas County proslavery sheriff Samuel J. Jones. Raiders destroyed two free-state presses and burned a hotel occupied by the New England Emigrant Aid Company and the home of the free-state leader Dr. Charles Robinson (later state governor). Upon receipt of this news John Brown, Sr., in the Osawatomie area set out to help protect Lawrence but turned back with his party of six men on May 24 to murder in especially brutal fashion five of his proslavery neighbors along Pottawatomie Creek. Two days before the sack of Lawrence, Senator Charles Sumner of Massachusetts had indicted the South in a speech, "The Crime against Kansas," which so provoked Congressman Preston Brooks of South Carolina that he beat Sumner with a cane on the floor of the Senate. The emerging Republican party thereupon coined the term "Bleeding Sumner."

The turmoil in Kansas had an impact upon the changing scene of political parties and the increased tension between the North and South. The declining Whig party sought to revive its fortunes by protesting the Kansas-Nebraska Act and its impact on the slavery issue. Its efforts between 1854 and 1856, however, were hampered by the increasing nativist opposition to Catholics and immigrants articulated by the Know-Nothing party. Attempts to fuse the interests of the two groups eventually failed. The new Republican party, which had tried to bring together one group of Whigs and Free-Soilers as early as the Jackson, Michigan, convention in 1854 , had succeeded by 1856 in becoming the major anti-Democratic party in the North. The Know-Nothings, then, can be viewed as a bridge or an intermediate phase between Whiggism and the expansion of Republicanism. The Republican party exploited in the North the proslavery sack of Lawrence and the attack on Sumner by distributing nearly a million copies of the "Crime against Kansas" speech.

National attention, both North and South, continued to focus on Kansas with the Lecompton convention meeting in the territorial capital in 1857. Delegates, elected primarily by proslavery voters (free-state electors abstained), crafted a proslavery constitution. Because it was not voted on by all the people in the territory, Senator Douglas was convinced that the principle of popular sovereignty had been violated. He broke with President James Buchanan in his opposition to the document, thereby losing much of the support once given him by fire-eaters in the South and contributing to the split in the Democratic party in the presidential election of 1860. Congress then passed the English bill, which provided for a popular vote on the Lecompton constitution. But even with the bill's provisions for generous public land grants for Kansas if the constitution were ratified, the document was rejected in the territory by a vote of 1,788 for and 11,300 against. Admission of the state into the Union was then delayed until 1861.

The violence that had flared intermittently in Kansas had caused an estimated fifty to over one hundred deaths. As late as 1858 five free-state men were killed in the Marais des Cygnes massacre by proslavery partisans.

Yet by the time Southern states were seriously debating secession, the Kansas question had become significantly muted. During the controversy over the Lecompton constitution, Governor H. R. Runnels of Texas had asserted that the rejection of Kansas as a slave state would further threaten the South, and he urged military preparations to protect the rights and honor of his state. Governor Joseph E. Brown of Georgia was equally concerned and threatened to call a convention to determine the status of Georgia if Kansas were rejected. But a Georgia citizen writing to Alexander H. Stephens expressed a more widespread view that there was little if any chance of Kansas becoming a slave state and that nothing more should be made of the issue. Many had come to realize that geographical and economic factors discouraged the expansion of slavery into Kansas and had contributed to the fact that there were only two slaves in the territory in 1860. Among the many newspaper editorials concerning secession, the *Charleston Mercury* in February 1860 was one of the very few, if not the only one, still arguing that the soil and climate of Kansas could sustain slavery. Other newspaper editors and political leaders turned their attention in 1860 and 1861 to different issues.

[*See also* Republican Party; Sumner, Caning of.]

BIBLIOGRAPHY

Craven, Avery O. *The Growth of Southern Nationalism, 1848–1861.* A History of the South, vol. 6. Baton Rouge, La., 1953.

Dumond, Dwight L., ed. *Southern Editorials on Secession.* New York and London, 1931.

Gienapp, William E. *The Origins of the Republican Party, 1852–1856.* New York and Oxford, 1987.

Malin, James C. *John Brown and the Legend of Fifty-Six.* Philadelphia, 1942.

Potter, David M. *The Impending Crisis, 1848–1861.* New York, Hagerstown, San Francisco, and London, 1976.

Rawley, James A. *Race and Politics: "Bleeding Kansas" and the Coming of the Civil War.* Philadelphia and New York, 1969.

Robinson, W. Stitt. "The Role of the Military in Territorial Kansas." In *Territorial Kansas: Studies Commemorating the Centennial.* Lawrence, Kans., 1954.

Stampp, Kenneth M. *America in 1857: A Nation on the Brink.* New York and Oxford, 1990.

W. STITT ROBINSON

BLOCKADE. [*This entry is composed of three articles describing the Union strategy to prevent shipping through Southern ports and the Confederate efforts to combat that strategy:* An Overview; Blockade Running; *and* Blockade Runners. *For further discussion of the blockade and responses to it, see* Anglo-Confederate Purchasing; Charleston, South Carolina; Commerce Raiders; Erlanger Loan; Fort Fisher, North Carolina; Fort Wagner, South Carolina; Hunley, H. L.; Mobile, Alabama; New Orleans, Louisiana; New Plan; Port Royal, South Carolina; Privateers; Trent Affair; Virginia; Wilmington, North Carolina.]

An Overview

The Union moved quickly to begin a blockade of the Confederacy. On April 19, 1861, Abraham Lincoln declared a blockade of the ports of South Carolina, Georgia, Alabama, Florida, Louisiana, and Texas, and eight days later extended it to Virginia and North Carolina. This was not intended to be a paper blockade. The object was to station enough ships to block entrance to or departure from Southern ports in order to prevent the South's obtaining essential war materials, to deny it the ability to export its cotton, and to deter Southern privateers and raiders from harassing Union shipping. But it also presented both diplomatic and physical problems for the North. Since the early years of the American Revolution, freedom of the seas and the defense of neutral rights had been an essential ingredient in American foreign policy. In pursuing its blockade of the Southern states, the North wished at the same time to avoid precedents that would hamper its own trade during future European wars. The attitude of Great Britain was helpful in achieving this objective, for the

British did not want to insist on a freedom to trade that might be used against them in the future.

To close some 3,500 miles of coastline, the North had fewer than fifty ships in commission at the beginning of the war. Although the temporary Confederate policy of withholding cotton exports in an attempt to influence the British worked to the advantage of the blockaders, the Union navy had too few vessels to mount an effective blockade. So the North bought or chartered civilian vessels to fill immediate needs until more ships could be built. By the latter part of the war, nearly five hundred vessels were taking part in the operation.

During the first months, blockade runners found it comparatively simple to slip into Southern ports, but the blockade quickly became more effective. As direct entry into Southern ports from Europe became more difficult, goods intended for the Confederacy were sent on neutral vessels to Nassau in the Bahamas, Bermuda, or Havana. There they were transferred to Southern blockade runners who brought in both essential war materials and luxuries.

Dramatizing the possibilities for evading the blockade was the South's announcement in the fall of 1861 that

James M. Mason and John Slidell, who were to represent the Confederacy in England and France, would proceed to Europe on a Confederate raider after running the blockade at Charleston. The Union strengthened its blockade off the port, but the two envoys were able to reach Havana on a chartered vessel. From there they attempted to travel to St. Thomas on the English ship *Trent*. *Trent* was stopped by a Union ship, and Mason and Slidell were taken to the North. For a few weeks there was fear of open conflict with England, but the crisis was defused. Neither side wanted war. American Secretary of State William H. Seward indicated that the action had not been authorized by the American government, the stern British protest stopped short of an ultimatum, and the North released the Southern emissaries.

The difficulty of blockading the numerous ports and inlets of the Confederacy and the necessity for better positioned Union bases persuaded the Union Navy Strategy Board that the blockade would have to be tightened by the use of amphibious operations to seize key inlets and provide new bases for Union vessels. The first of these operations was intended to make the blockade of Virginia more

"BLOCKADE ON THE 'CONNECTICUT PLAN.'"   Northern satire of early Federal blockading efforts under Secretary of the Navy Gideon Welles of Connecticut. The outdated U.S. blockading fleet is represented by two wooden washtubs, *Cambridge* and *Gemsbok*, firing miniature cannons in an attempt to stop the Confederate blockade runner *Nashville*. Lithograph on wove paper. Published by Currier and Ives, 1862.

LIBRARY OF CONGRESS

efficient. Union ships in the Chesapeake were being evaded by shallow draft vessels that connected Richmond and Norfolk by canal with the sounds of Virginia and North Carolina. Blockade runners made extensive use of this route in the early months of the war. But in late August 1861, a Union force attacked forts guarding Hatteras Inlet and captured Forts Clark and Hatteras. The latter was converted into a Union base.

An advantage for Confederate blockade runners was the distance of the Union bases at Hampton Roads and Key West from many of the ports and inlets that had to be blockaded. The Atlantic Blockading Squadron, based in Hampton Roads, found it difficult to police the whole area, and in the early fall of 1861 it was divided into northern and southern sections. Lincoln and his cabinet also accepted a proposal, presented by Secretary of the Navy Gideon Welles, for an attack on Port Royal. Situated between Charleston and Savannah, Port Royal possessed a fine natural harbor, capable of serving all the needs of the blockaders. In early November, a large Union force of some twelve thousand troops and numerous ships occupied Port Royal after the Confederates abandoned its defending forts. This led to the Union control of a whole string of sea islands and made possible further amphibious operations along the south Atlantic coast.

In the winter of 1861–1862, the Union tried again to make blockade evasion more difficult in the North Carolina–Virginia region. The North Carolina sounds continued to present great opportunities for blockade runners, and early in the new year the Union sent some 11,500 men to attack Roanoke Island. They hoped to capture the island and to move against the towns on Albemarle Sound to disrupt Confederate canal and rail communication. Not all the objects were attained, but Roanoke Island was taken and the noose around the South was drawn a little tighter.

In an effort to break the tightening cord, the Confederacy in March 1862 sent its ironclad CSS *Virginia* (previously the USS *Merrimack*) to try to break the Union blockade at Hampton Roads. *Merrimack* had been partially burned and scuttled by Union forces when Norfolk was taken by the Confederates early in the war. The Confederates had rebuilt it as an ironclad. The Union knew of this potential threat and had built its own ironclad—*Monitor*—to counter it. In trying to break the blockade, *Virginia* at first had some success, but *Monitor* fought it to a standoff, which left the blockade intact. The Confederacy experimented with ironclads and submarines throughout the war, but the North had the resources to counter all such efforts to break the blockade. The submarine CSS *H. L. Hunley* did succeed in sinking a blockading vessel off Charleston in February 1864 but did not return from the engagement.

In the first year of the war the Union had difficulty in mounting an effective blockade of the ports along the Confederate coastline in the Gulf of Mexico. Ultimately, the Union blockade in that region came to depend heavily on amphibious operations. Both New Orleans and Mobile provided great opportunities for Southern blockade runners. Of the two, New Orleans presented somewhat fewer problems for direct assault, and the Union determined to capture this vital Southern port. Preliminary footholds were gained in the fall of 1861, but the main attack was launched early the next year. In April, Flag Officer David G. Farragut combined forces with Commdr. David D. Porter and Gen. Benjamin Butler to capture the city, thereby delivering a powerful blow to Confederate trade. Mobile was too heavily defended to be taken, but Union forces put it under an increasingly stringent blockade. The North also launched a series of attacks against Texas ports.

In the early months of the war, Confederate privateers had caused considerable havoc to Union commerce, but as the blockade tightened in 1862 and 1863, and as neutrals refused to accept Confederate prizes in their ports, the main assault on Union merchant ships was launched by Confederate government raiders. From time to time these succeeded in slipping into Confederate ports. Also, blockade runners continued to bring in much needed supplies, usually sailing from neutral ports in the Caribbean.

A major problem experienced by the Confederacy was that of private owners of blockade runners seeking greater profits by importing scarce luxury goods rather than the necessities needed by Southern armies. The government first urged private blockade runners to carry military supplies, then made use of government-owned ships, and finally, in 1864 decreed that only necessary articles could be imported. Private owners were also ordered to provide half of the cargo space in their blockade runners for use by the Confederate government. Blockade runners continued to operate until the end of the war, but they never met all the needs of Southern armies.

In its efforts to prevent the activities of the blockade runners, the Union was prepared to interpret its maritime rights in ways that it had challenged in earlier years. The Union defended the doctrine of "continuous voyage," which had been used against the United States by Great Britain during the Napoleonic Wars. This doctrine allowed the seizure of ships trading between neutral ports if the cargo was ultimately destined for a blockaded port or, in the case of a ship carrying contraband, if it was destined for any port in enemy territory. American courts upheld the seizure of British ships destined for neutral ports when the cargo was ultimately intended for the Confederacy. In the *Peterhoff* case this doctrine was extended even to goods that were destined to come into the Confederacy overland from the Mexican port of Matamoros. (The Mexican-Texas border was used for widespread evasion of the blockade.).

The situation of both neutrals and Confederate blockade

runners became more precarious after September 1862 when the Union Navy Department created a West India Squadron, with the intention of both protecting Union ships from Confederate cruisers and reducing the activities of blockade runners.

In the last two years of the war, evasion of the Union blockade became much more difficult, although runners were still able to enter some of the major Southern ports. Charleston was a heavily used point of entry until September 1863 when Union forces captured Fort Wagner. The city, however, was able to resist attack from the sea and remained in Confederate hands until 1865.

Mobile was another port that presented major problems for Union blockaders; it possessed formidable defenses against amphibious operations. Not until August 1864 did Farragut have the strength necessary to take the Mobile Bay forts, when he pressed ahead relentlessly with his famous cry, "Damn the torpedoes." Mobile itself was not occupied until the very end of the war, but the capture of the forts effectively closed the port to Confederate vessels.

By 1864 Wilmington, North Carolina, offered the most opportunities for blockade runners. It was the vital supply port for Confederate armies in Virginia and was also a port through which the South continued to export cotton. Access to the port by way of the Cape Fear River was defended primarily by Forts Fisher and Caswell. Until these were taken the port could not be closed. A strong Union attack on Wilmington's defenses failed in December 1864, but in January 1865 a large fleet and some eight thousand troops took Fort Fisher and closed the last major gap in the Union blockade.

The Union, however, never completely sealed the coastline of the Confederacy. Even in the last year of the war, half of the blockade runners were getting through. The Union blockade nevertheless was a success. Southern imports and exports dropped dramatically during the war. This was at a time when the Confederacy desperately needed increased imports to supply its armies and maximum sales of cotton to finance its huge war effort. Largely because of the Union blockade, Southern armies were undersupplied and Southern finances became increasingly chaotic as the war progressed. The South's lack of naval power allowed the North to pursue a relentless war of attrition.

BIBLIOGRAPHY

Anderson, Bern. *By Sea and by River: The Naval History of the Civil War.* New York, 1962.

Bernath, Stuart L. *Squall across the Atlantic: American Civil War Prize Cases and Diplomacy.* Berkeley, Calif., 1970.

Jones, Virgil C. *The Civil War at Sea.* 3 vols. New York, 1960–1962.

Nash, Howard P., Jr. *A Naval History of the Civil War.* South Brunswick, 1972.

Owsley, Frank. *King Cotton Diplomacy: Foreign Relations of the Confederate States of America.* 2d ed. Chicago, 1959.

West, Richard S., Jr. *Mr. Lincoln's Navy.* London, 1957.

Wise, Stephen R. *Lifeline of the Confederacy: Blockade Running during the Civil War.* Columbia, S.C., 1988.

REGINALD HORSMAN

Blockade Running

Throughout the Civil War, munitions, uniform material, leather, food, and other essential military and civilian goods poured into the Confederacy on board vessels known as blockade runners. These vessels were a vital element in the Confederate supply system. Before the war ended, blockade running would be sustaining the Southern armies, but at the beginning of the conflict few realized the tremendous volume of trade that would eventually exist between the Confederacy and the outside world.

In early 1861, the head of the Confederate Ordnance Bureau, Col. Josiah Gorgas, had three sources of supplies for the Confederate armed forces: goods on hand, home production, and imports. By using the arms seized in Federal arsenals, Gorgas had enough weapons and supplies to outfit the 100,000 men called out by President Jefferson Davis. Unlike others in the South, Gorgas did not believe that the war would be a quick one, and he knew that his on-hand stocks of munitions would soon disappear. In time, he planned to establish munition plants that would make the new nation self-sustaining, but Gorgas realized that until the factories could be completed, certain "articles of prime necessity" would have to be imported from Europe. Imports were supposed to be only a stopgap measure, something to fill the void between the depletion of existing stocks and the beginning of home production. But the Confederates were never able to meet their needs with domestic industry, and the flow of imports grew until it eventually became the most important element in the Confederate supply system.

In April 1861, in order to gain foreign supplies, Gorgas dispatched Capt. Caleb Huse to Great Britain to serve as a purchasing agent. Huse was later joined by Maj. Edward C. Anderson, and together they began work with Comdr. James Dunwoody Bulloch, the purchasing agent for the Navy Department. To provide funds for their agents the Confederacy contracted with the Charleston firm of John Fraser and Company, who sent bills of exchange to its Liverpool office of Fraser, Trenholm, and Company, from which cash was provided to the War Department's European officials. But even with the funds, the agents still faced two problems: the Confederacy's determination to follow a foreign policy known as "King Cotton," and the Federal blockade.

King Cotton. The blockade of the Southern coast had been established shortly after the firing on Fort Sumter. Though in the beginning it was enforced by only a handful of vessels and its legality was questioned, it was recognized by the major European powers. At the same time, the British monarch, Queen Victoria, called upon her subjects to avoid giving assistance to either side.

Though disappointed by the European response, the Southerners were not worried because they believed that King Cotton would protect their new nation. King Cotton was an economic and political theory based on the coercive power of Southern cotton. The British textile industry imported 80 percent of the South's cotton. Without the cotton, the theory held, the industry would fail, and the entire economic fabric of Great Britain would collapse. In order to avoid that disaster, the British would have to intervene in the war on the South's side.

It was for this reason that during the summer of 1861, local politicians, merchants, newspapermen, and planters banded together to enforce an embargo keeping the South's cotton at home. Though never sanctioned by the government, the embargo was unofficially approved by Davis and his advisers, who felt it would bring Great Britain into the war. At the same time, in order to aid the financially disrupted planters, the Confederate government purchased over 400,000 bales of cotton. Initially viewed as a white elephant, this cotton eventually played an important role in the blockade-running system.

Though designed to bring the British into the war, the embargo also had the side effect of depriving Anderson, Huse, and Bulloch of a means to transport supplies. No vessels were coming from the South, and for the moment, British shippers were reluctant to go against the wishes of their queen or the guns of the Union navy. For the moment the purchasing agents were stymied, and for assistance they turned to the firm of Fraser, Trenholm, and Company, the Confederacy's European financial agents, for help in shipping their goods.

Fraser, Trenholm, and Company was a branch of the Charleston-based John Fraser and Company. Both were directed by George Alfred Trenholm. From his Charleston office Trenholm backed the cotton embargo, but at the same time allowed his partner in Liverpool, Charles K. Prioleau, to outfit a steamer to run the blockade. The vessel readied by Prioleau was the screw steamer *Bermuda*, organized as a private commercial venture. Prioleau agreed to sell cargo space to Anderson and Huse.

Though the agents felt the cost to be high, they also realized that this was their best opportunity to deliver their goods. They met Prioleau's price and on September 18, 1861, after an uneventful voyage, *Bermuda* successfully arrived at Savannah, Georgia, becoming the first steam blockade runner to reach the South. After landing its cargo,

Bermuda returned to Liverpool with over two thousand bales of cotton. Profits were tremendous, and this example soon caused other firms to organize blockade-running ventures. Any hesitation brought on by the blockade or Queen Victoria's proclamation soon disappeared in the quest for money.

Although *Bermuda*'s success inspired additional blockade-running companies, it did little to relieve the problems confronting the Confederate purchasing agents. They still had no government-owned vessels to carry their munitions, and private firms were escalating their rates on government cargoes. Anderson, the senior agent, decided that it was in the best interest of the Confederacy to cut out the middleman and purchase a steamer. With financial help from the Navy Department agents, the steamer *Fingal* was obtained and sent through the blockade, arriving at Savannah in mid-November 1861. Equipment from the vessel was enough to outfit ten regiments. As Bulloch stated, the ship carried "the greatest military cargo ever imported into the Confederacy."

Besides the armaments, *Fingal* also carried Anderson and Bulloch. Anderson went on to Richmond where he pushed the concept of government-owned-and-operated blockade runners, but he found no backers. Neither the War Department nor the Navy Department would consider any involvement with blockade running. Officials preferred to leave it in the hands of private shippers while waiting for British intervention. Disillusioned with the results of his visit, Anderson returned to Savannah, where he served out the war as an artillery officer.

While Anderson began working on Savannah's defenses, Huse continued to purchase supplies in Europe, and since there were still no Southern vessels arriving in Great Britain, he contracted with local firms to carry the goods into the Confederacy. Huse's supplies arrived by two methods. He contracted for direct delivery to the South by British shippers, or he sent cargoes to Havana, Cuba, or Nassau, Bahamas, where they were transferred to steamers for the final run through the blockade. The latter system of transshipping proved more popular, and, by early 1862, vessels owned by British blockade-running companies and Trenholm's firms were operating between Havana and Nassau and the Confederacy. For their services, the private shippers charged the government extremely high rates, which Huse and other Southern agents had to meet.

Assisting Huse were Confederate consuls Charles J. Helm in Havana and Louis Heyliger in Nassau. Besides serving as government representatives, the two consuls had the crucial responsibility of making sure that cargoes received from Huse were properly transshipped. Both performed admirably, but because of the early capture of New Orleans, Heyliger soon found himself overseeing the bulk of the supplies coming from Great Britain.

During the spring and summer of 1862, Heyliger worked with private shippers to deliver vital munitions. The task posed problems. Even though Heyliger paid extraordinary fees for cargo space, he found that many companies refused to work with him, preferring instead to carry more profitable civilian goods rather than the bulky and often dangerous munitions. The best deals were made with Trenholm's firms, who gave the government preferred rates, though their patriotism never cut too deeply into their profit margin.

Although Trenholm's firms were on occasion willing to offer special deals to the Confederacy, British manufacturers cautiously regulated their involvement with Huse, being careful not to overextend their credit. By the end of 1862, the Confederate purchasing agent was £900,000 in debt and his means of payment seemed at an end. The ever-increasing premiums on bills of exchange soon ended their use and Huse had nearly expended his supply of specie. Without some form of exchange, Huse's operations would collapse. Then the Confederacy discovered a new use for King Cotton.

Cotton Bonds. When the South's cotton embargo failed to bring Great Britain into the war, many thought that the hundreds of thousands of cotton bales purchased by the government at the start of the war would become the predicted white elephant, but this was not the case. Cotton, so long an instrument of foreign policy, was now converted to a medium of exchange.

Following the lead of the Navy Department, the government began to use cotton to finance its overseas ventures. Employing the cotton purchased early in the war, the Confederacy issued a variety of cotton bonds. There were two ways to make a profit off the bonds: one could receive interest and redeem the bond at face value after a set length of time, or the holder could bring the bond to the Confederacy and receive cotton.

It was the latter method that made the bonds so popular. Cotton could be obtained in the South at about ten cents a pound and then sold in Great Britain for forty-eight cents a pound, thus making a cotton bale purchased for $50 in Charleston worth nearly $250 on the Liverpool market. There was a wide variety of bonds, or as they were sometimes called, certificates. Even some of the Southern states, such as Georgia and North Carolina, issued them and used them to sponsor their own blockade-running ventures.

The use of the bonds allowed the Confederacy to pay off Huse's debt and provide him with new funds and credit for additional supplies. They were the basis for contracts between the South and its suppliers and were also used to finance the purchase and construction of blockade runners and warships. Private blockade-running ventures used them to guarantee outgoing cargoes for their steamers,

because with the bonds and the right type of vessels, blockade running could be an extremely profitable business.

Using the bonds, many War Department bureaus, such as the Subsistence, Quartermaster, and Medical bureaus, withdrew their business from Huse and entered into one-sided partnerships with blockade-running companies—and there was never any shortage of such companies. The largest and most successful were the two companies operated by George Trenholm. Together his firms operated over thirty blockade runners and cargo vessels and grossed millions of dollars, which were reinvested in ships, cargoes, real estate, and Confederate bonds.

Other important firms included the Importing and Exporting Company of South Carolina, the Chicora Importing and Exporting Company, and the Charleston Importing and Exporting Company. These Charleston-based companies paid handsome dividends to their investors. Among the prominent British companies were the highly successful Anglo-Confederate Trading Company and the less lucrative Collie and Company. All these firms delivered civilian and military goods to the Confederacy. The civilian goods were immensely profitable since they were sold at outrageous wartime prices that contributed to inflation throughout the South.

The delivery of military goods also gave a good return, as the firms made extremely favorable contracts with the various War Department bureaus. One bargain, struck between the Confederacy and Crenshaw and Collie and Company, had the government paying 75 percent of all expenses plus the commission fees for the purchasing of ships and supplies, while allowing its civilian partners to use one-quarter of the cargo space for privately owned goods. Though a lopsided venture, the contract was similar to many issued during the war. Because of the need for supplies, most government agencies felt that a bad contract was better than no contract.

The Ordnance Bureau. The one notable exception to this arrangement was Gorgas's Ordnance Bureau. Like Anderson, Gorgas realized the advantage in using government-owned-and-operated vessels. Instead of making contracts with blockade-running firms, Gorgas had his agents purchase steamers in Great Britain. A depot headed by Maj. Norman S. Walker was established in St. George, Bermuda; from there the goods purchased and shipped by Huse were transferred to Ordnance Bureau steamers and sent to Wilmington, North Carolina, where they were met by Capt. James Sexias.

The Ordnance Bureau's blockade-running operation was under the control of Gorgas's brother-in-law, Maj. Thomas L. Bayne. Bayne supervised not only the landing and distribution of incoming cargo but also the purchasing and loading of government cotton. Initially Bayne's section worked out of Wilmington, but before the war ended, his command was upgraded to bureau status with agents at Charleston, Mobile, and St. Marks, Florida.

The line established by Gorgas and operated by Bayne employed five vessels. The most successful were *Cornubia, Robert E. Lee,* and *Eugenie,* captained by the furloughed Confederate naval officers Richard N. Gayle, John Wilkinson, and Joseph Fry, respectively. A typical cargo consisted of cases of Enfield rifles, cartridges, leather, knapsacks, stationery, sewing thread, lead, saltpeter, and uniform cloth. Though in service only from November 1862 to November 1863, Gorgas's vessels made forty-seven runs through the blockade. They delivered, among other things, nearly 100,000 Enfield rifles, tens of thousands of cartridges, and thousands of pounds of lead and saltpeter, all basic military necessities needed to keep the Confederate army alive.

The vessels operated by Gorgas were products of an ongoing maritime revolution brought about by blockade running. Steam warships had ended the days of sailing ships, and to counter their pursuers, the blockade runners also turned to steam engines. By the time the war ended, blockade running had helped launch a new generation of steam vessels, including the first successful commercial use of twin-screw-propeller vessels. The class of steamer that started the revolution was that found in the United Kingdom's coastal and cross-channel passenger trade, known as Clyde steamers. These were later replaced by iron- and steel-hulled vessels built exclusively for blockade running. Designed to carry an immense amount of cargo, these ships could make a profit of $100,000 on a single voyage from the Confederacy.

Blockade-Running Routes. The new vessels were needed. By December 1864, all of Gorgas's ships had been lost. At first the Confederate government did not replace them, but instead increased their reliance on private vessels. Operating out of Havana, Nassau, and Bermuda, the steamers delivered their cargoes to Charleston and Wilmington on the east coast and Mobile and Galveston in the Gulf of Mexico.

In the Gulf, Mobile grew in importance as an importation site for government supplies. From there supplies were sent to Selma and other western depots for distribution or use in munition plants. Down the coast, Confederate cargoes delivered to Galveston rarely crossed the Mississippi River. Logistics coupled with political instability in Mexico kept Texas from ever becoming a major landing site. What did come in remained in the Trans-Mississippi Department for use by the local military.

The Confederacy directed the majority of its shipments to Charleston and Wilmington where the goods could be easily transported to depots, factories, and armies. The most popular routes were from Nassau to Charleston and Bermuda to Wilmington. After the attack on Charleston during the summer of 1863, the bulk of the Nassau trade shifted to Wilmington, making it the South's main port of entry and one of the most strategic points in the Confederacy.

The ships carrying supplies to the east coast had a very high success rate. During the war, runners were successful on over 75 percent of their runs, and most of the time the ships passed in and out unseen by the blockaders. The runners had the advantages of speed and surprise over their adversaries. Rarely would a cannon shell find its mark and even then the Union warships did not try to sink the blockade runners; when captured, most blockade vessels were taken north, condemned at prize courts, and sold with their cargoes at auction. The money was divided among the captors, thus making it far more advantageous for Northern crews to capture than to sink the runners.

Confederate Regulation of Blockade Running. Because of the high success rate and resulting profits,

ROBERT E. LEE. Watercolor by Erik Heyl, 1951.   NAVAL HISTORICAL CENTER, WASHINGTON, D.C.

private companies dominated the trade until August 1863, when the Confederate government was finally forced to take an active hand in blockade running. Defeats at Gettysburg and Vicksburg had resulted in an increased demand for supplies and had dealt a severe blow to the Southern bond market, shattering the Confederacy's overseas finances. In order to revive the South's credit and gain new supplies, Secretary of War James A. Seddon turned to an expanded use of cotton. He ordered his commanders at Wilmington, Charleston, and Mobile to requisition cargo space for the shipment of government cotton. The operators of the blockade runners were paid a fair rate for the space, and any refusal would result in their vessels being seized.

This was only the beginning of Seddon's plans. In March 1864 his initial instructions were tightened and, with presidential approval, passed into law. The stricter regulations allowed the Confederacy to take up to 50 percent of a vessel's outgoing and incoming cargo space. This guaranteed that the South would be able to export its cotton to pay for European goods and would have stowage space for incoming supplies. At the same time Gorgas's bureau was expanded to supervise all government overseas shipping. In Europe, operations were consolidated under Colin J. McRae, who, in effect, became the Confederacy's European secretary of the treasury.

The unheralded McRae did a remarkable job in establishing a centralized system in Europe. He also revived Anderson's and Gorgas's plan for a line of Confederate-owned blockade runners. He ordered fourteen vessels in Great Britain and planned eventually to remove all private operators from the business of carrying government supplies.

McRae was soon joined by another official who also realized the importance of government-sponsored blockade running. During the summer of 1864, the Confederacy called upon the director of the largest blockade-running operation, George Alfred Trenholm, to become secretary of the treasury. Trenholm accepted the position, resigned from his companies, and set to work running the government's overseas operations. He promulgated additional, stricter regulations and made plans for the government's fourteen blockade runners being built in Great Britain. Only two of these specialized vessels, however, saw Confederate service before the war ended.

Even without these super–blockade runners, the flow of supplies continued. Under Trenholm's and McRae's guidance the Confederacy received more munitions during their tenure than at any time earlier, but the men were fighting a losing battle. The South, battered by Northern armies and suffering massive desertions from its own ranks, was running out of men. Nor could it keep its vital ports open. In August 1864 Mobile was captured; Wilmington was closed in early January 1865; and a month later Charleston was evacuated. The fall of these harbors cut the Confederacy's lifeline.

Because of the determined work of a few relatively unknown individuals, the economic power of cotton, and specialized steamers, the Confederate military was never without the means to fight. By Confederate records the South imported during the war 60 percent of its arms, 30 percent of its lead for bullets, 75 percent of the army's saltpeter, and nearly all its paper for cartridges. The majority of cloth for uniforms and leather for shoes and accoutrements came through the blockade, as well as huge amounts of metals, chemicals, and medicine. During the last months of the war, the Army of Northern Virginia received the bulk of its food via blockade runners. Though the lifeline was fragile and tenuous, it worked until the ports were captured. Defeat did not come from lack of materials. In fact, by the end of the war, the South had more munitions and goods than men; manpower was the one thing the blockade runners could not supply.

BIBLIOGRAPHY

Bradlee, Francis B. C. *Blockade Running during the Civil War and the Effect of Land and Water Transportation on the Confederacy.* Salem, Mass., 1925.
Gorgas, Josiah. "Notes on the Ordnance Department of the Confederate Government." *Southern Historical Society Papers* 12 (1884): 68–75. Reprint, Wilmington, N.C., 1990.
Hobart-Hampden, Augustus C. *Never Caught.* London, 1867.
Soley, James R. *The Blockade and the Cruisers.* New York, 1883.
Taylor, Thomas E. *Running the Blockade.* London, 1897.
Vandiver, Frank, ed. *Confederate Blockade Running through Bermuda, 1861–1865: Letter and Cargo Manifests.* Austin, Tex., 1947.
Wise, Stephen R. *Lifeline of the Confederacy: Blockade Running during the Civil War.* Columbia, S.C., 1988.

STEPHEN R. WISE

Blockade Runners

A blockade runner was any vessel that challenged the U.S. Navy's blockade of the Confederate coastline. Though a few Confederate warships such as *Nashville, Sumter,* and *Florida* and some privateers ran the blockade, the vast majority were cargo vessels that carried civilian and military supplies into the South and transported cotton to neutral ports. The motivating factor behind these ships was the profit derived from the sale of their cargoes.

Men served as captains of blockade runners for a variety of reasons. Such Southerners as Thomas Lockwood, Robert Lockwood, James Carlin, Louis Coxetter, and Robert Smith were motivated by both patriotism and the desire for profits. Others such as naval officers John Wilkinson, John Newland Maffitt, Joseph Fry, and Richard N. Gayle oper-

Blockade Runners: A Cross Section

Name	Builder/Place of Construction	Hull and Propulsion/ Dimensions	Tonnage	Successful Runs/ Port of Entry	Fate
Annie	John and William Dudgeon London, 1863	iron, twin-screw 170′ × 23′4″ × 13′4″	687 gross tons	13 runs Wilmington	captured 11/1/64
Banshee	Jomes, Quiggin and Company Govan, Scotland, 1863	steel, paddlewheel 214′ × 20′ × 8′	325 gross tons	14 runs Wilmington	captured 4/27/63
Bermuda	Pearse and Lockwood Stockton-on-Tess, England, 1861	iron, single-screw 211′ × 21′4″ × 21′2″	897 gross tons	2 runs Savannah	captured 4/27/62
Colonel Lamb	Jones, Quigin and Company Liverpool, 1864	steel, paddlewheel 281′ × 36′ × 15′6″	1132 gross tons	2 runs Wilmington	survived the war
Denbigh	Laird and Sons Birkenhead, England	iron, paddlewheel 182′ × 22′ × 8.7′	250 gross tons	26 runs Mobile and Galveston	destroyed 5/23/65
Fingal	J. & G. Thomson Govan, Scotland, 1861	iron, single-screw 178′ × 25′ × 18′	462 registered tons	1 run Savannah	converted into ironclad *Atlanta*
Herald	John Reid and Company Port Glasgow, Scotland, 1860	iron, paddlewheel 221.6′ × 22′ × 10.4′	446 gross tons	24 runs Charleston and Wilmington	destroyed 12/19/63
Kate	Samuel Sneden Greenpoint, N.Y.	wood, paddlewheel 165′ × 29′10″ × 10′4″	477 burden tons	20 runs Charleston and Wilmington	destroyed 11/18/62
Margaret and Jessie	Robert Napier & Sons Glasgow, Scotland, 1858	wood, paddlewheel 205′ × 26′ × 14′	950 burden tons	18 runs Charleston and Wilmington	captured 11/5/63
Matagorda	Harlan and Hollingsworth Wilmington, Del., 1858	iron, paddlewheel 220′ × 30′ × 10.5′	1250 gross tons	18 runs Mobile and Galveston	captured 9/10/64
Robert E. Lee	J. & G. Thomson Govan, Scotland, 1860	iron, paddlewheel 268′ × 26′ × 12′	900 burden tons	14 runs Wilmington	captured 1/9/63
Syren	Builder not listed Greenwich, Kent, England, 1863	?, paddlewheel 169.5′ × 24′ × 15.5′	475 burden tons	33 runs Wilmington and Charleston	captured 2/18/65

ated blockade runners under orders from the Confederate government. British citizens Joannes Wyllie, Johnathon Steele, Augustus Charles Hobart-Hampden, and the Irishman William Ryan ran blockade runners for adventure and profit. Whatever their motive, their skills were an important factor in a vessel's success or failure.

At the start of the war, many shipowners attempted to use sailing vessels, but quickly realized that they would not do. Sailing ships large enough to carry a profitable amount of cargo were easy marks for steam warships, and the small brigs, schooners, and sloops that could slip in and out of harbors and sounds had insufficient cargo capacity. After June of 1862, sailing ship blockade runners virtually disappeared along the east coast. They were used somewhat more often in the Gulf of Mexico, where many operated

along the Texas coast; but supplies from east of the Mississippi River rarely crossed the river and imports coming into Texas had no impact on the war's major theaters.

To counter their steam-powered pursuers, the blockade runners turned to steam engines. Early in the war, before the blockade tightened, any steamer had a good chance of reaching a Southern port, and the first vessels to run the blockade were large, deeply laden ships such as the propeller-driven *Bermuda* and *Fingal*. Both were conventional merchantmen with large cargo capacities, but they had short careers because their deep drafts restricted them to main ship channels where eventual capture was inevitable. By the spring of 1862, the large steamers that had escaped capture were relegated to ferrying goods between

Great Britain and Nassau, Bermuda, and Havana. From these ports a more elusive style of blockade runner was employed in order to avoid the Federal warships.

The steamship type that first began transshipping cargoes to and from the Confederacy were American-built coastal packets. These paddlewheel vessels were built with a low freeboard which, coupled with a wide beam, gave the steamers a shallow draft. They were sturdy and well adapted to negotiating the shallow southern coastline. Once their staterooms were removed, the vessels could carry between two hundred and five hundred bales of cotton.

Along the east coast such ships as *Gordon, Cecile,* and *Kate* became prominent blockade runners. *Kate,* a 477-ton packet measuring 165 feet by 29 feet, 10 inches by 10 feet, 4 inches, was successfully guided through the blockade twenty times by Capt. Thomas Lockwood. In the Gulf the New Orleans–based vessels *Matagorda* and *William G. Hewes* also became renowned blockade runners under the names *Alice* and *Ella and Annie.* Before its capture in 1864 off Mobile, *Alice,* commanded by Robert Smith, made eighteen trips through the blockade.

Though many packets were successful blockade runners, investors continued to seek out ships that could turn an even greater profit, and by early 1862, operators began using a style of paddlewheel steamer that had been developed for the United Kingdom's coastal and cross-channel passenger trade. Since many were built in and around Glasgow on the Clyde River, the ships were called Clyde steamers. Usually built with an iron hull, they were rugged, fast, and maneuverable and had a shallow draft and large cargo capacity that allowed them to carry from five hundred to one thousand bales of cotton. In a short time they became the mainstay of blockade running.

The first Clyde steamer to begin blockade running was *Herald,* a 450-ton iron-hulled sidewheeler that made 24 trips through the blockade before being destroyed off Wilmington. In all, over 80 Clyde steamers were converted to blockade runners. Among their ranks were the war's top runners, including the most successful, *Syren,* which made 33 trips in and out of Wilmington and Charleston. It was followed by *Denbigh* with 26 runs from Havana to Mobile and Galveston. Other ships of this class included *Alice,* with 25 trips; *Fannie,* with 20 trips; and the Confederate Ordnance Bureau's *Cornubia,* with 18 trips. Another well-known ship was *Margaret and Jessie,* which also made 18 trips and was considered the war's fastest blockade runner.

Although these ships were very successful, business interests demanded still better, and soon British dockyards were turning out ships built specifically for running the blockade. The first was *Banshee,* a steel-hulled 533-ton sidewheeler that measured 214 feet by 20 feet by 8 feet. In May 1863, it became the first steel-hulled vessel to cross the Atlantic Ocean. Then, under the command of Johnathon Steele, it became a successful blockade runner operating primarily between Nassau and Wilmington.

At first these ships were designed simply to meet the trade's basic requirements, but soon, seeking to increase profits, builders began to experiment with design and construction techniques, resulting in a revolution in ship-building. Engines were placed so that they were surrounded by coal bunkers to protect them from enemy shot. Many of the new runners were built of steel and designed with rounded deck structures, underwater blow-off pipes, hinged masts, and telescoping smokestacks. Builders experimented with paint schemes to camouflage the runners from enemy warships and increased engine size as well as the size and number of boilers. For additional speed, vessels were made longer with extremely narrow beams. Because of their design, the runners contained more cargo space than contemporary merchant ships.

The first generation of these super–blockade runners often suffered from many engineering and mechanical problems. *Banshee,* with steel plates of only ⅛ inch and ³⁄₁₆ inch, leaked badly, and others like the *Flamingo* spent more time being repaired than running the blockade. But builders soon overcame these problems and by the end of the war were producing such vessels as *Chicora, Lucy,* and *Fox,* which between them made fifty-two trips through the blockade without being captured. The epitome of the final generation of runners was *Colonel Lamb,* which was partially designed by Capt. Thomas Lockwood, the war's most successful blockade-running captain and the acknowledged "father of the trade." The 1,788-ton *Colonel Lamb* was the finest vessel built for blockade running. It measured 281 feet by 36 feet by 15.5 feet and could carry 2,000 bales of cotton, which translated into a profit of $100,000 on a single voyage from the Confederacy.

Though most blockade runners were sidewheelers, the war also saw the first successful commercial use of twin-screw-propeller steamers. Some fourteen of these novel vessels attempted to run the blockade, the most successful being *Annie,* which made thirteen trips. The twin screws proved to be sturdy, reliable vessels that combined light draft, speed, and great carrying capacity.

The specialized vessels used for blockade running were, for the most part, owned by private companies. But the Confederate Ordnance Bureau operated a line of blockade runners, and the Treasury Department also owned a few. In 1864, the government ordered fourteen super–blockade runners, but most were unfinished at the war's end.

The Confederate navy made use of some of its outdated Southern-built warships as runners and used the British-built twin-screw *Coquette* to transport cotton and supplies. The navy also employed the British-built *Juno* as a picket vessel at Charleston and in 1864 purchased at Wilmington the twin-screws *Atalanta* and *Edith* for use as commerce raiders. In Great Britain, Comdr. James Dunwoody Bulloch ordered a number of twin-screw vessels that were designed to serve as both blockade runners and commerce raiders, but none was finished in time to see active duty.

In all just under 300 steamers tested the blockade. Out of approximately 1,300 attempts, over 1,000 were successful. The average lifetime of a blockade runner was just over four runs, or two round trips. Some 136 were captured and another 85 destroyed.

By war's end, the blockade runners had evolved into very specialized vessels that carried out their missions with a high success ratio. They were so successful that the Federal navy converted captured blockade runners into gunboats and used them as blockaders, but even this could not stop the blockade runners from delivering their cargoes. Throughout the war, the Confederate military was well served by the runners.

Besides their impact on the war, blockade runners greatly influenced subsequent ship design. They expanded maritime technology by advancing the development and use of steel, twin-screw propulsion, enclosed ship bridges, fast hull forms, and camouflage paint schemes, all innovations that are still used in ship construction today.

BIBLIOGRAPHY

Foster, Kevin. "Phantoms, Banshees, Will of the Wisps and the Dare; or, the Search for Speed under Steam: The Design of Blockade Running Steamships." M.A. thesis, East Carolina University, 1991.

Price, Marcus. "Masters and Pilots Who Tested the Blockade of the Confederate Ports, 1861–1865." *American Neptune* 8 (April 1961): 81–106.

Wise, Stephen R. *Lifeline of the Confederacy: Blockade Running during the Civil War.* Columbia, S.C., 1988.

STEPHEN R. WISE

BLUFFTON MOVEMENT. The Bluffton movement, led by Robert Barnwell Rhett, Sr., of South Carolina, aimed to sever connections with the Democratic party, to challenge the leadership of John C. Calhoun, and to advance the cause of disunion. Launched on July 31, 1844, at a dinner in Rhett's honor in the low-country town of Bluffton, South Carolina, the movement quickly spread to the neighboring Beaufort, Colleton, Orangeburg, and Barnwell districts, enlisting men in the cause of separate state action against a hostile national government.

The causes of the movement were the abolition by Congress of the gag rule—the ban on antislavery petitions presented to Congress—and the tabling of the McKay bill, which would have lowered tariff duties, in the spring of 1844. Suspicious of ties with a national party composed of Northern as well as Southern members, Rhett wanted to repudiate the Democratic party and its presidential nominee, James K. Polk. Unlike Calhoun, who believed that the Democrats would protect Southern interests, Rhett feared that the Northern majority threatened to destroy slavery. Moreover, he was concerned about Northern Democratic equivocation on the annexation of Texas. Though Polk favored annexation and the Democratic platform advocated territorial expansion, Rhett and the "Bluffton Boys" suspected that Northern Democrats could not be trusted to redeem those pledges after the election.

The movement revealed the beginning of a generational split in South Carolina politics. The Blufftonites were largely younger, inexperienced men drawn to the leadership of Rhett, who was twenty years younger than Calhoun. Hoping to secure the presidential nomination in 1848, Calhoun and his allies supported Polk, and their influence first weakened and then ended the Bluffton movement six weeks after it began. Rhett returned to the Calhoun fold. But a rising generation of leaders, too young to have experienced the nullification movement, had received their first schooling in Carolina radicalism. In time, they would be further emboldened to calculate the value of the Union.

BIBLIOGRAPHY

Boucher, Chauncey S. "The Annexation of Texas and the Bluffton Movement in South Carolina." *Mississippi Valley Historical Review* 6 (1919): 3–33.

Walther, Eric H. *The Fire-Eaters.* Baton Rouge, La., 1992.

White, Laura A. *Robert Barnwell Rhett: Father of Secession.* New York, 1931.

JOHN MCCARDELL

BOCOCK, THOMAS S. (1815–1891), congressman from Virginia and Speaker of the House of Representatives. Thomas Stanley Bocock was born in Buckingham County, Virginia, on May 18, 1815. He graduated from Hampden-Sydney College in 1837, earning a B.A. degree in two years. He served in the Virginia House of Delegates and as first commonwealth attorney for Appomattox County in the 1840s.

Thomas served in the U.S. House of Representatives as an old-line Union Democrat from 1847 until 1861 when Virginia seceded from the Union. In Congress he was a strong advocate of state rights and served as chairman of the Committee on Naval Affairs. He ran unsuccessfully for the speakership in 1859 to 1860.

On February 18, 1862, Bocock was elected to the Confederate Congress, having served in the Provisional Congress after July 23, 1861. A member of all three Confederate Congresses, he was unanimously elected Speaker of the First and Second Congresses. Because in

1862 and 1863 his district was heavily burdened by impressment, high taxes, and other economic hardships, he spoke out against many of these war measures. But later, as the war progressively worsened, he reconciled himself to the need for sacrifice and opposed only the arming of slaves for service in the Confederate army. In January 1865, Bocock led the Virginia delegation in a meeting with President Davis. He stated that they wished a change in the cabinet since the public had lost confidence in it. The House was also ready to confirm this by passing a resolution. Reacting to these feelings, Secretary of War James A. Seddon tendered his resignation, but Davis adamantly refused to accept it. While Seddon nevertheless left his post, the president declared this action would have no effect on the rest of his policy or administration. When Gen. Robert E. Lee approached Appomattox Court House in the retreat from Richmond and Petersburg on April 8, 1865, Bocock fled his nearby plantation, Wildway, to escape the pursuing Federal army.

After the war, Bocock worked as an attorney and served again in the Virginia House of Delegates where he was cosponsor of the Bocock-Fowler bill, which was "designed to relieve the financial troubles of Virginia after the Reconstruction period." Retiring to Wildway in 1880, he died there on August 5, 1891.

BIBLIOGRAPHY

Featherston, Nathaniel Ragland. *The History of Appomattox, Virginia.* Marceline, Mo., 1948.

Robinson, Calvin. "Life Story of Appomattox County's Famed Thomas S. Bocock." *Times-Virginian* (Appomattox, Va.), June 18, 1959.

Pollard, Edward A. *Life of Jefferson Davis with a Secret History of the Southern Confederacy.* Philadelphia, 1869.

The South in the Building of the Nation. Vol. 11. Richmond, Va., 1909, p. 95.

Warner, Ezra J., and W. Buck Yearns. *Biographical Register of the Confederate Congress.* Baton Rouge, La., 1975.

Yearns, Wilfred B. *The Confederate Congress.* Athens, Ga., 1960.

CHRIS CALKINS

BOGGS, WILLIAM ROBERTSON (1829–1911),

brigadier general. Boggs, who was born March 18, 1829, in Augusta, Georgia, attended Augusta Academy before entering West Point. He graduated in 1853, fourth in a class of fifty-two, and served in the army until 1861, resigning the day that Georgia seceded.

He offered his services to his home state and was first appointed to Governor Joseph E. Brown's staff before joining P. G. T. Beauregard at Charleston. From there he was transferred to Pensacola where he served as chief of engineers and artillery under Braxton Bragg. When he felt that Bragg unjustly failed to promote him, Boggs resigned

his Confederate commission on December 21, 1861, and became chief engineer for Georgia. He reentered Confederate service in 1862, however, and served on E. Kirby Smith's staff during the Kentucky campaign. Although Boggs was always on staff duty, never holding a field command, he was commissioned a brigadier general on November 4, 1862. When Smith took over the Department of the Trans-Mississippi in 1863, Boggs accompanied him and served as his chief of staff until Smith began to question his competence. As a result Boggs resigned in the spring of 1865. He briefly held command of the District of Louisiana but was replaced by Harry Thompson Hays. Boggs was paroled at Shreveport on June 9, 1865.

After the war Boggs lived in Georgia and St. Louis before joining the staff of the Virginia Polytechnic Institute, where he taught from 1875 until 1881. He died in Winston-Salem, North Carolina, on September 11, 1911, and is buried there in Salem Cemetery.

BIBLIOGRAPHY

Boggs, William Robertson. *Military Reminiscences of Gen. Wm. R. Boggs, C.S.A.* Durham, N.C., 1913.

Kerby, Robert L. *Kirby Smith's Confederacy: The Trans-Mississippi South, 1863–1865.* New York, 1972.

Parks, Joseph H. *General Kirby Smith, C.S.A.* Baton Rouge, La., 1954.

ANNE J. BAILEY

BONDS. Prior to 1861, Americans had financed their wars by three basic means: their government collected taxes, confiscated the property of alien enemies, and borrowed money from its citizens. Given the American distaste for heavy taxation and the inability of the Confederacy to seize and sell Unionist property by sequestration, the Confederate Congress had to depend heavily on loans to finance its war effort.

Loans came in several forms. The government issued Treasury notes, with or without interest, that could be used as money. Interest-bearing notes were intended to be closely held by investors. Circulating Treasury notes, if overused, would cause serious inflation. In addition, the Treasury needed to avoid selling securities that would fall due before the war was over; otherwise it would have to pay such debts at a time when it was hard-pressed to meet its current obligations. Therefore, government borrowing efforts had to be directed toward the sale of coupon and registered bonds, payable five or more years after their date of issue.

Confederate loans fell into several categories. The government could receive money on deposit and issue to the lender a certificate payable on demand, together with the accumulated interest. This kind of loan was styled a "call certificate."

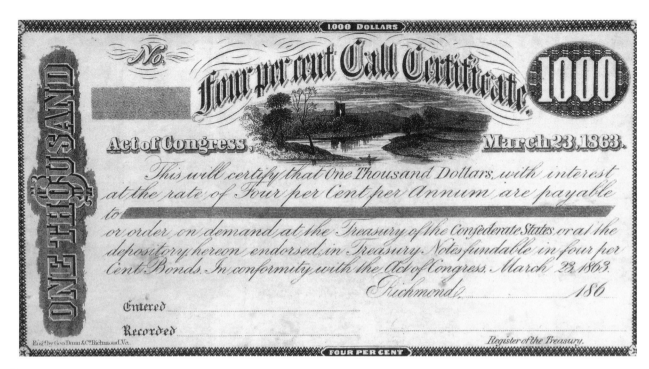

CONFEDERATE $1,000 CALL CERTIFICATE.   GORDON BLEULER

CONFEDERATE $10,000 BOND.   GORDON BLEULER

Confederate Bond Issues[a]

February 28, 1861, Specie Loan

AMOUNT: $15 million. DENOMINATIONS: $50 or higher in stocks or bonds. MATURITY: Ten years (September 1, 1871); callable after five years. INTEREST RATE: 8 percent, bonds to be sold at par in coin; coupons receivable for export dues. TOTAL ISSUED: $15 million.

August 19, 1861, Funding and Produce Loan

AMOUNT: $100 million. DENOMINATIONS: $50 and above in bonds (stock authorized August 27, 1861). MATURITY: Various dates; July 1, 1864–July 1, 1881. INTEREST RATE: 8 percent bonds in lieu of those authorized by the Act of May 16, 1861. TOTAL ISSUED: Coupon bonds totaling $74,422,700; stock totaling $25,147,850; grand total: $99,570,550.

April 12 (18), 1862

AMOUNT: $165 million in stocks or bonds. DENOMINATIONS: $100 and up. MATURITY: Ten years, but Congress could extend the loan up to thirty years on same terms. INTEREST RATE: 8 percent loan to be effected at home or abroad for specie, foreign exchange, or treasury notes. TOTAL ISSUED: bonds totaling $3,839,600; stock totaling $404,450; grand total: $4,244,050.

February 20, 1863, Funding Loan

AMOUNT: Unlimited. DENOMINATIONS: $100 and up in stocks or bonds. MATURITY: Five years, but Congress could defer payment up to thirty years at same rate of interest. INTEREST RATE: 8 percent bonds to be sold until April 21, 1863; 7 percent bonds to be sold until August 1, 1863. TOTAL ISSUED: 8 percent stock totaling $14,912,800; 8 percent bonds totaling $81,668,100; 7 percent stock $totaling $12,758,100; 7 percent bonds totaling $54,183,100; grand total: $76,941,200.

March 23, 1863, Funding Loan

AMOUNT: Unlimited. DENOMINATIONS: $100 and up. MATURITY: Thirty years, callable after five years. INTEREST RATE: 6 percent for those dated April 6, 1863; 4 percent for those dated December 2, 1862. TOTAL ISSUED: 6 percent stock totaling $4,278,100; 6 percent bonds totaling $16,740,300; 4 percent bonds totaling $22,300; grand total: $21,040,700.

April 30, 1863, Funding Loan

AMOUNT: $100 million. DENOMINATIONS: $1,000 in coupon bonds. MATURITY: Twenty years, not callable. INTEREST RATE: 6 percent payable in coin or one 500-pound bale of cotton (12¢ per pound). TOTAL YIELD: $8,393,000 issued; $4,285,000 in premiums paid; grand total: $12,678,000.

February 17, 1864 (Section 2), Funding Loan

AMOUNT: Unlimited. DENOMINATIONS: $100 to $5,000. MATURITY: Twenty years, not callable. INTEREST RATE: 4 percent. TOTAL ISSUED: Bonds totaling $10,183,900; certificates totaling $350,800,000; grand total: $360,983,900.

February 17, 1864 (Section 6), General Expenses

AMOUNT: $500 million. DENOMINATIONS: $100 to $10,000. MATURITY: Thirty years. INTEREST RATE: 6 percent. TOTAL ISSUED: $60,000,000 sold; $20,000,000 in premiums paid; grand total: $80,000,000.

February 17, 1864 (Section 12); amended June 19, 1864, to fund state-held notes

AMOUNT: Unlimited. DENOMINATIONS: None specified, but $100 to $10,000. MATURITY: Twenty years. INTEREST RATE: 4 percent and 6 percent. TOTAL ISSUED: 6 percent bonds totaling $6,000,000; 4 percent bonds totaling $4,000,000; grand total: $10,000,000.

February 17, 1864 (Section 14), General Loan

AMOUNT: Unlimited. DENOMINATIONS: None specified, but $100 to $10,000. MATURITY: Two years after peace. INTEREST RATE: 6 percent tax free. TOTAL ISSUED: $57,392,200 to March 29, 1865.[b]

March 17, 1865

AMOUNT: $3 million. DENOMINATIONS: None specified. MATURITY: Two years after peace. INTEREST RATE: 6 percent payable in coin. TOTAL ISSUED: No bonds issued, but $300,000 seized from banks on a pledge of bonds. TOTAL ISSUED: $835,000,000 (approximately).

---

[a]Figures based on Raphael P. Thian, *Register of the Confederate Debt*, Boston, 1972, and on numismatic collections examined by Douglas B. Ball.
[b]Real sales unknown; amount sent to depositories.
SOURCE: Douglas Ball, *Financial Failure and Confederate Defeat*, Urbana and Chicago, 1991.

Loans were secured by selling bonds, which were paid directly for goods and services or exchanged for money. To sustain the value of the bonds, tax revenues were needed. The Treasury also required a supply of gold and silver coins ("specie"), which would ensure that the interest on the public debt was paid with something of known and stable value. Without taking this step, the value of the bonds could not be maintained.

Since the amount of money needed to finance the war was far greater than the banks, savings associations, and insurance companies could provide, massive bond sales made directly to the general public were needed. This meant that the bankers had to act as government loan agents; the Treasury also promptly set up government agencies (depositories) in areas where there were no banks.

Unfortunately, the accumulation of a coin reserve was almost totally neglected, and not until 1863 was an adequate system of loan offices set up. These errors were compounded by the illiquid character of the South's commercial agricultural economy. Cut off from its Northern and European cotton markets by the blockade, the Confederacy's capacity to borrow was greatly restricted.

Nevertheless, the Confederate States did sell $577 million of bonds and $291 million of call certificates. The funds procured from these sources provided the means for slightly less than one-third of the Confederacy's cash expenditures.

The first loan act, that of February 28, 1861, was authorized to cover $15 million of congressional defense appropriations. The purchasers were offered an 8 percent bond, whose payable coupons were made receivable for customs dues and the cotton export duty. But instead of insisting that the subscribers pay for these bonds with coin, as required by law, Secretary of the Treasury Christopher G. Memminger agreed to receive bank notes. As a result, the Confederacy received very little coin and had to suspend specie interest payments after July 1, 1862.

A second loan, dated May 16, 1861, authorized up to $20 million of ten-year 8 percent securities that were a combination of a bond and a call certificate. Because the loan could either be held to maturity or be converted upon demand into Treasury notes, it remained an attractive investment until July 1863, when Congress unilaterally changed the terms, damaging the government's credit.

The third loan, that of August 19, 1861, was the first attempt by Congress to pass a comprehensive law sustaining the value of $100 million of Treasury notes by making them fundable into 8 percent bonds with serial maturities. The basic idea behind this loan was that the currency's value could be maintained by permitting the noteholder to purchase at face value in currency a bond whose interest was payable in coin. When specie payments were suspended, Confederate bonds became an unattractive investment because the interest was paid in rapidly depreciating Treasury notes that offered a very poor return to the investor. Bond sales languished, while nervous investors bought the $71 million of the 6 percent call certificates authorized by the act of December 24, 1861.

Efforts to sell general loans, such as that authorized on April 12, 1862, met with a poor response. Everyone preferred the 7.3 percent Treasury notes that were issued in lieu of the 8 percent bonds, simply because for only a modest reduction in interest, the holder could get a note usable as currency instead of a cumbersome bond. The act of October 17, 1862, authorizing a reduction in the interest paid on notes funded into bonds, resulted in the sale of almost $164 million of 8 percent and 7 percent bonds issued under the act of February 20, 1863.

Because of the large amount of bonds purchased under that act, the public bought only $21 million of the funding loan of March 23, 1863. Once again, the government was saved by the purchase of almost $74 million of call certificates. An attempt to sell bonds whose interest was payable in cotton (Act of April 30, 1863), resulted in only $12 million of sales, chiefly because the public correctly suspected that the government would refuse to pay the cotton or coin interest called for.

On February 17, 1864, Congress passed another act with a view to forcibly funding the entire outstanding currency into 4 percent bonds. About $361 million of these were sold and another $147 million of 6 percent nontaxable bonds and certificates of indebtedness were disposed of. Again, however, such revenues were nearly matched by the sales of 4 percent call certificates, which amounted to $135 million. By the end of 1864, even this inadequate source of funds dried up. The public, recognizing the inevitility of defeat, refused to advance any more money to a failing cause. As a result, a large number of prepared but unsold bonds were captured by the Federal forces at the end of the war.

[See also Erlanger Loan; Produce Loan.]

BIBLIOGRAPHY

Ball, Douglas B. *Financial Failure and Confederate Defeat.* Urbana, Ill., 1991.

Criswell, Grover C., Jr. *Confederate and Southern State Bonds.* Citrus, Fla., 1972.

Thian, Raphael P. *Register of the Confederate Debt.* Edited by Douglas B. Ball. Boston, 1972.

Todd, Richard C. *Confederate Finance.* Athens, Ga., 1954.

DOUGLAS B. BALL

BONHAM, MILLEDGE L.

BONHAM, MILLEDGE L. (1813–1890), brigadier general and South Carolina congressman and governor. Born in Edgefield District, December 25, 1813, Milledge Luke Bonham graduated from South Carolina College and practiced law in Edgefield. He served in the South Carolina General Assembly from 1840 to 1844 and in the U.S. House of Representatives from 1857 to 1860, filling the seat left vacant by the death of his cousin Preston S. Brooks. He had considerable military experience before the Civil War, commanding the South Carolina Brigade in the Seminole War and serving as lieutenant colonel with the Palmetto Regiment in the Mexican War.

Bonham anticipated the secession crisis as early as 1858, once remarking that Republican success "ought to be and will be the death signal of this Confederacy, come when it may." When the crisis broke in December 1860, he promptly resigned his seat in the House and went home. South Carolina sent him to Mississippi to help persuade that state to follow its action. At the outbreak of the war Bonham commanded the South Carolina militia with the rank of major general. He relinquished this position to accept a Confederate brigadier's commission under P. G. T. Beauregard. He commanded the South Carolina troops moving to the defense of Richmond and led his brigade throughout the First Manassas campaign. Mary Boykin Chesnut reported that an observer told her that " 'no general ever had more to learn than Bonham,' when he first saw him in command, and truly he believed no one ever learned more in a given time."

Although he served admirably, Bonham, when he was passed over for promotion, joined several other officers that

MILLEDGE L. BONHAM.   NATIONAL ARCHIVES

autumn in protesting Jefferson Davis's policy of ranking officers from the "old army" over militia officers. He resigned his commission on January 29, 1862, having secured election to the First (regular) Confederate Congress. There he questioned Davis's initial plan for conscription, preferring to rely on volunteers until their numbers proved inadequate. Later, however, Bonham supported the administration's bill authorizing the president to suspend the writ of habeas corpus whenever he believed it necessary to do so.

When Governor Francis W. Pickens's term expired in December 1862, Bonham was chosen by the state legislature to replace him. The new governor inherited two major problems from his predecessor: coastal defense and military conscription. In the minds of many South Carolinians the two were closely intertwined. The state had contributed liberally to the Confederate army. Yet most of the South Carolinians were serving on the Virginia front or in the West at a time when the state's coastal region lay threatened. The taking of Port Royal by the Union navy in November 1861 had been a particularly hard blow. Many in the state questioned whether their defense was being neglected. As enlistments fell off, South Carolina adopted conscription even before it passed the Confederate Congress.

For all his previous differences with the Davis administration, Bonham was determined that South Carolina "in every legitimate way should sustain the Confederate authorities." In spite of the continuing drain of Carolina troops to other fronts and the unrelenting shelling and raiding of the Sea Islands in the Charleston area including Fort Sumter, he made good his inaugural promise to cooperate with the Confederacy in contrast to his neighboring governors in Georgia and North Carolina. While they made wide use of their discretionary powers in granting exemptions from conscription for state officers, Bonham refused to follow that course.

In yet another matter of exemptions, which arose shortly after he took office, Bonham worked diligently for compromise. On May 1, 1863, the Confederate Congress repealed the section of the Conscription Act that exempted overseers on large plantations. This threatened to place an economic hardship on South Carolina and ran contrary to state law, which provided for such exemptions. Bonham felt obligated to uphold the state statute. Until he could secure its repeal, which he did in December 1863, he recommended that South Carolinians exempt under state law claim a similar exemption with Confederate enrolling officers. He induced the latter to agree to this arrangement until he could bring the state statute in line with the new Confederate regulations. South Carolina continued on the course of cooperation until the end of 1864, when it reversed its policy of claiming no exemptions because of increasing dissatisfaction with the Davis government's failure to provide adequately for the state's defense and the immediate threat of invasion from William Tecumseh Sherman's army.

Meanwhile Bonham worked closely with his former commander General Beauregard, who had been placed in charge of South Carolina's defenses. When the general ordered the evacuation of Charleston by all noncombatants in February 1863, Bonham reluctantly agreed. When he then called up all white males beyond draft age for the defense of the city, the question arose of alien residents' liability for service. His predecessor had excused them, but Bonham refused to do so. The legislature backed his position in September 1863, with a law requiring alien residents to serve when needed. President Davis agreed to accept these state troops for three months' service (half the regular time) on the condition that South Carolina arm and equip them. The governor agreed to arm them but reported that resources for their supply were thin because of prior commitments to the Confederacy. For all these difficulties, Union efforts to take Fort Sumter failed twice in 1863, although Charleston continued under intermittent bombardment.

By the fall of 1863 Bonham began receiving reports from enrolling officers in the northwestern corner of the state that they were meeting with widespread resistance to conscription as well as desertion by those who had already served. This could be attributed not only to the Confederate military reverses of that summer but to local conditions as well. This region, which backed up against the mountains of North Carolina where many deserters found refuge, was mostly populated by nonslaveholders who had never been enthusiastic about secession. Bonham dispatched state troops to the area, obtained the cooperation of Governor Zebulon Vance of North Carolina in suppressing the disturbances, and called the legislature into special session. It responded with strong legislation making sheriffs and others liable to fines and imprisonment for failure to cooperate in curtailing draft evasion and desertion. It even agreed to a Confederate proposal to raise a special force from those not liable to conscription for special service against deserters. There was some improvement; but as the military and economic situation deteriorated further by the summer of 1864, conditions in that corner of the state once again worsened. All of Bonham's further efforts to curtail disaffection met with little success.

Yet another manpower problem confronting Bonham in 1863 was the need for slave labor to build and maintain coastal fortifications. This was not a new concern. The impressment of slaves for this purpose had begun early in the war, affecting primarily slave owners in the coastal areas. It met with little opposition initially; but as more slaves were taken for varying lengths of time by both state and Confederate authorities, the mood of the planters changed. Part of the problem lay in the inadequacy of supporting legislation relative to the length of impressment and compensatory pay to the owners. The legislature sought to remedy this by passing a law in December 1862, just as Bonham took office, limiting requisitions for slaves to thirty days' service and providing owners eleven dollars a month compensation. The law was flawed in many respects, however, including one provision that allowed owners to pay a dollar a day instead of furnishing a slave, an option many of them took. Enforcement was difficult, and only a few hundred slaves were recruited by this means in spite of Bonham's efforts to make the process work. Finally, in August 1863, Beauregard announced that his agents would assume responsibility for impressment. Some 3,500 slaves were now secured through impressment and voluntary action by their owners, but this number soon dwindled as planters complained that their blacks were ill treated and not returned promptly and that their labor was needed at home. Enforcement became increasingly difficult, and Bonham was never able to solve the problem adequately.

Bonham was also confronted with popular dissatisfaction over the impressment of provisions and supplies for the Confederate army. This practice had been carried on informally since early in the war, arousing protest in South Carolina and elsewhere. When Congress formalized the procedure in the Confiscation Act of March 26, 1863, it became the new governor's specific problem. As complaints mounted, the governor brought the issue to the legislature's attention in its special session in September 1863. He indicated his displeasure at the frequently high-handed methods being used by Confederate commissioners and secured a legislative resolution supporting his position. While not specifically disavowing confiscation, both governor and legislature expressed concern that the law be administered evenly and fairly and only when absolute necessity dictated. Bonham conveyed these sentiments to Secretary of War James A. Seddon, who replied in a conciliatory fashion that he would investigate any complaints. As these continued to come in, Bonham brought the matter back to the legislature in November. It responded with resolutions asking the state's congressional delegation to work for change in Richmond. The governor was also requested to inform the state's citizens of their rights under the impressment law. Bonham continued to forward complaints to Seddon, but this problem, too, remained unresolved until war's end.

As Bonham's term came to an end in December 1864, it was evident that South Carolina faced imminent invasion. Over the governor's strong protest, the state had been ordered to give up most of its remaining cavalry for duty in Virginia the previous March. Now Bonham asked the legislature for authority to call up all males between sixteen and sixty for militia duty within the state with those between sixteen and fifty being allowed to go to Georgia in view of the menace in that direction. He also sought to have all militia forces and others deemed necessary for the state's defense declared exempt from Confederate service. The legislature promptly approved his request. This was a decided reversal of South Carolina's previous cooperation with the Confederacy, but the state's situation called for drastic action.

Following the completion of his term, Bonham again became a brigadier general of Confederate troops, commanding a cavalry brigade under Joseph E. Johnston until war's end. He then returned to his law practice in Edgefield. He served in the General Assembly during Presidential Reconstruction only to be sidelined during the Republican years. Active in the restoration of white rule, he was appointed state railroad commissioner in 1878 and continued in that position until his death on August 27, 1890.

BIBLIOGRAPHY

Bonham, Milledge Lipscomb. "Unpublished Biography of Milledge L. Bonham." Manuscript in South Caroliniana Library, University of South Carolina, Columbia.

Cauthen, Charles E. *South Carolina Goes to War, 1860–1865.* Chapel Hill, N.C., 1950.

Chesnut, Mary Boykin. *Mary Chesnut's Civil War.* Edited by C. Vann Woodward. New Haven, 1981.

Edmunds, John B., Jr. "South Carolina." In *The Confederate Governors.* Edited by W. Buck Yearns. Athens, Ga., 1985.

Freeman, Douglas S. *Lee's Lieutenants: A Study in Command.* Vol. 1. New York, 1942. Reprint, 1986.

WILLIAM E. PARRISH

BOOK PUBLISHING. Prior to 1861 Southern authors and readers had generally been content to publish with and to buy their books from firms in New York, Philadelphia, Boston, and England. Few Southern publishers, to be sure, had been sufficiently capitalized over a long enough period to compete successfully with Harper, Appleton, Putnam, or Scribner in New York, with Carey and Hart or Lippincott in Philadelphia, or with Ticknor and Fields in Boston. William Gilmore Simms, the leading Southern man of letters of the antebellum period, published, for example, many of his books with Harper, Putnam, and others in New York and with Carey and Lippincott in Philadelphia, but only occasionally with Southern publishers, usually firms in Charleston such as Walker, Richards, and Company, and John Russell.

It is not strange, then, that the establishment of the Confederate government and the beginning of hostilities in 1861 should have suddenly thrust a considerable burden upon the few relatively successful publishing houses in the new nation. Among these, West and Johnston in Richmond; Evans and Cogswell, and John Russell, in Charleston; Burke, Boykin, and Company in Macon; and S. H. Goetzel in Mobile were well known. Working under incredible difficulties, these houses and others in Richmond, Raleigh, Columbia, Atlanta, Augusta, and New Orleans supplied books, magazines, pamphlets, documents, and other printed materials despite eventual severe shortages of paper, personnel, and printing equipment. The established firms and many other short-lived ones responded to the demand and somehow provided the new nation with reading matter over its four-year life span.

As early as February 20, 1861, Simms urged William Porcher Miles, a friend and member of the Provisional Congress of the Confederacy, to be mindful of "the interests of Literature in the formation of the new Government," and he discoursed especially on "the privileges of Copyright." Subsequently a copyright act was passed by the Congress and signed by Jefferson Davis on May 21, 1861.

Such encouragement of writing led established publishers like West and Johnston, according to the *Southern Literary Messenger,* to pay royalties of "over $15,000" in 1862 and even to make arrangements for payments to foreign authors. The Richmond firm reprinted Wilkie Collins's *No Name* in 1863, for example, and S. H. Goetzel republished Bulwer-Lytton's *A Strange Story* in the same year, informing the author, as reported in the *Messenger,* that "ten thousand copies in two editions" had been issued and that "one thousand dollars" had been placed to his credit according to "an international copyright."

Fiction and other forms of belles lettres were, as usual, popular with the public and publishers, but they did not dominate publishing lists. Even so, two of the best-selling books of the period—Augusta Evans Wilson's *Macaria* (1864) and a translation of Victor Hugo's *Les Misérables* in five parts (1863–1864)—were novels; West and Johnston published both, in addition to short fiction, drama, and poetry by George W. Bagby, James Dabney McCabe, Jr., and John Hill Hewitt. Over 20,000 copies of *Macaria* were issued, for example. Works by Edward A. Pollard and others on history, biography, politics, and military science, however, ran through more printings than most volumes of belles lettres. Moreover, such titles as John Esten Cooke's *The Life of Stonewall Jackson* (1863) and William J. Hardee's *Rifle and Infantry Tactics* (1861), though not published by West and Johnston, were popular enough for Cooke's biography to be pirated in New York and for Hardee's book to be reprinted and abridged by many firms from Richmond to Houston, in addition to the nine editions and countless reprints issued by 1863 by S. H. Goetzel, holder of its copyright since 1861.

Goetzel, indeed, was one of the leading publishers of the Confederacy and, aside from Bulwer-Lytton's novel and Hardee's *Tactics,* issued reprints of Charles Dickens and George Eliot and translations from the German of Luise Mühlbach's (Klara Mundt's) novels, *Henry VIII and His Court* (1865) and *Joseph II and His Court* (1864). Goetzel also brought out Sally Rochester Ford's *Raids and Romance of Morgan and His Men* (1863, 1864) and Lt. Col. Arthur J. L. Fremantle's diary, *Three Months in the Southern States* (1864).

Second perhaps only to West and Johnston, Evans and Cogswell, a Charleston house that could trace its beginnings under other company titles to the 1820s, had in the 1850s momentarily provided Charleston with the essential elements of a literary center. During the war, Evans and Cogswell served as printers for the Confederate government and the South Carolina Tract Society and published Francis Peyre Porcher's *Resources of the Southern Fields and Forests* (1863)—one of the most valuable books brought out during the war because of its useful information on native products as substitutes for unobtainable items. The company also published W. W. Lester and W. J. Bromwell's compilation of *A Digest of the Military and Naval Laws of the Confederate States* (1864), a title issued after the firm moved to Columbia in 1864. In the same year, W. M. Thackeray's *The Adventures of Philip* and Paul Feval's *The Golden Daggers* were reprinted, but though the

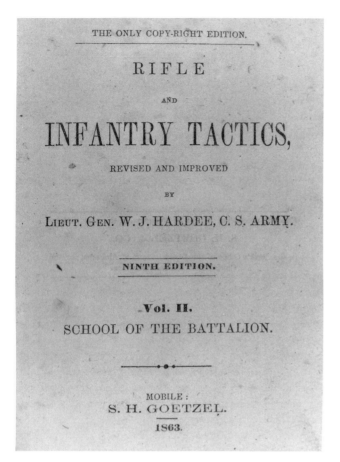

THE ONLY COPY-RIGHT EDITION.

RIFLE

AND

INFANTRY TACTICS,

REVISED AND IMPROVED

BY

LIEUT. GEN. W. J. HARDEE, C. S. ARMY.

NINTH EDITION.

Vol. II.

SCHOOL OF THE BATTALION.

MOBILE :
S. H. GOETZEL.
1863.

RIFLE AND LIGHT INFANTRY TACTICS. When this work by William J. Hardee was first published in 1855, it became the standard for infantry training and tactics, remaining so through the Civil War. With the outbreak of war, Northern publishers refused to ship copies to the South, forcing Southerners to begin producing and pirating their own editions. The firm of S. H. Goetzel of Mobile, Alabama, which held Hardee's official copyright, issued nine editions of his book by 1863, despite paper shortages and economic chaos. Pictured above is an 1863 edition with a wallpaper cover, an ingenious solution to the scarcity of conventional materials.

CIVIL WAR LIBRARY AND MUSEUM, PHILADELPHIA

company had published Simms's *The Golden Christmas* and *The Sword and the Distaff* (subsequently *Woodcraft*) in 1852, these works were never reprinted during the war; in fact, the firm published few books of belles lettres during the entire period.

Ultimately, of course, the Confederacy lacked the industries to provide the printing equipment and paper necessary to serve its publishing houses adequately. By the late spring of 1863, publishers were using paper made of raw cotton and other fibers, since rags for the manufacture of paper were in short supply, and books began to appear in wallpaper covers. The edition of *Les Misérables,* for example, brought out by West and Johnston in 1863–1864 was issued in five parts and printed on green paper manufactured from raw cotton. By 1865 few titles were being issued, though Bibles, tracts, and school textbooks continued to be printed until the end.

The publishing business had emerged to meet a need, and though it had not in the final analysis offered much of lasting literary merit, it had served the public and the government well for four years during which difficulties of all sorts had been met and often overcome under nearly impossible conditions. Despite these obstacles, as historian John Tebbel concludes, "the performance of the Confederate publishers was extraordinary," and accordingly, "remarkable things were accomplished."

[*See also* Bible Societies; Literature, *article on* Literature in the Confederacy; Textbooks.]

BIBLIOGRAPHY

Dzwonkoski, Peter, ed. *Dictionary of Literary Biography: American Literary Publishing Houses, 1638–1899.* Vol. 46. Detroit, 1986.

Hubbell, Jay B. *The South in American Literature, 1607–1900.* Durham, N.C., 1954.

London, Lawrence F. "Confederate Literature and Its Publishers." In *The James Sprunt Studies in History and Political Science.* Edited by J. C. Sitterson. Vol. 39. Chapel Hill, N.C., 1959.

Muhlenfeld, Elisabeth. "The Civil War and Authorship." In *The History of Southern Literature.* Edited by Louis D. Rubin, Jr., et al. Baton Rouge, La., 1985.

Oliphant, Mary C. Simms, et al., eds. *The Letters of William Gilmore Simms.* Vol. 4. Columbia, S.C., 1956.

Parrish, T. Michael, and Robert M. Willingham, Jr., comps. *Confederate Imprints: A Bibliography of Southern Publications from Secession to Surrender.* Austin, Tex., and Katonah, N.Y., 1987.

Tebbel, John. *A History of Book Publishing in the United States.* Vol. 1. New York, 1972.

RAYBURN S. MOORE

BOONSBORO, VIRGINIA. *See* South Mountain, Virginia.

BOOTH, JOHN WILKES (1838–1865), assassin of Abraham Lincoln. Born in Maryland, the son of a slave-owning actor of English birth, Booth followed in his father's footsteps with a successful stage career, but his youth in Maryland made him a slavocrat in lifestyle—riding horses, shooting guns, holding violent opinions in politics, and disdaining blacks. He seems to have thought of himself as a Northerner but wrote in 1864, "My love (as things stand today) is for the South alone."

Although he left few letters for historians, Booth did compose two long political statements, one in the winter of

BIBLIOGRAPHY

Hanchett, William. *The Lincoln Murder Conspiracies.* Urbana, Ill., 1983.
Tidwell, William A., with James O. Hall and David Winfred Gaddy. *Come Retribution: The Confederate Secret Service and the Assassination of Lincoln.* Jackson, Miss., 1988.

MARK E. NEELY, JR.

JOHN WILKES BOOTH.   NATIONAL ARCHIVES

1860–1861 and the other in November 1864. The first justified secession as constitutional and blamed abolitionists for the nation's crisis. "This country was formed for the *white,* not the black man," he wrote in the later statement, and slavery was "one of the greatest blessings (both for themselves and us)" bestowed by "God . . . upon a favored nation." Intense identification with the Confederate cause and fear that Lincoln's reelection in 1864 would make him a dictator led Booth to begin planning that summer to kidnap Lincoln, take him to Richmond, and exchange him for Confederate prisoners of war.

Booth recruited Southern-sympathizing idlers, ex-Confederate soldiers, and a spy in Maryland for his kidnapping scheme and visited Montreal late in 1864, where he may have contacted Confederate agents. He decided very late to murder Lincoln. Acting as a self-styled "Confederate . . . doing duty *upon his own responsibility,*" he shot the president at Ford's Theatre in Washington, afterward shouting the Virginia state motto, "Sic semper tyrannis" [thus always to tyrants]. Confederate sympathizers helped hide him from pursuing soldiers, but he died on Virginia soil twelve days later, shot by a Union cavalryman.

[*See also* Lincoln, Abraham, *article on* Assassination of Lincoln; Espionage, *article on* Confederate Military Spies.]

BORDER STATES. Composed of Delaware, Kentucky, Maryland, and Missouri, the border states were divided in their allegiance between the Union and the Confederacy. Geographically situated along a thousand-mile frontier dividing North from South, the border states in many ways resembled both sections.

In 1861 these four states possessed a total population of 2,137,000, of whom 430,000 were slaves. Although slavery was constitutionally legal in all, only in Kentucky did slaves represent a sizable portion of the population, reaching nearly 20 percent. Figures for Maryland, Missouri, and Delaware were substantially smaller, equaling only 13, 10, and 2 percent, respectively. At the same time, these states were similar to those in the North in that large numbers of immigrants, especially Germans and Irish, had settled in major port cities such as Baltimore, Louisville, and St. Louis. The major agricultural products of the region—corn, hemp, tobacco, horses, and mules—also reflected an interesting mixture of Northern and Southern farming.

Differences among the Border States. Although they occupied a position physically and demographically between the North and the South, the border states did not constitute a unit. Indeed, considerable geographic, social, political, and economic differences separated them along an east-west division. The Allegheny Mountains served as a barrier to trade and settlement and effectively partitioned Maryland and Delaware from Kentucky and Missouri. As a consequence, Kentucky and Missouri, settled largely by Virginians and Tennesseans, were economically oriented toward the Midwest and New Orleans, whereas Maryland and Delaware were linked more to the cities and markets of the Mid-Atlantic and New England states.

The border states also demonstrated little unity in the election of 1860, Maryland and Delaware voting for Southern Democrat John C. Breckinridge, Kentucky for Constitutional Unionist John Bell, and Missouri for Northern Democrat Stephen A. Douglas. Furthermore, Maryland and Delaware possessed large free black populations (the number of free blacks in Maryland nearly equaled the number of slaves), whereas in Kentucky and Missouri the number of free blacks in proportion to the overall population was negligible.

Attitudes toward Secession. As the secession crisis erupted, it was unclear which way the border states would go. Although their slave populations were considerably smaller than those of the eleven states that seceded, all but Delaware contained large, determined, and well-led secessionist minorities. In Maryland, where Southern rights Democrats controlled the legislature, secession activity centered in the southern tobacco-growing and eastern coastal counties and in the city of Baltimore. Only the refusal of Governor Thomas Hicks, a moderate Unionist, to convene the legislature prevented that body from forcing the state's secession. In Missouri, where the governor, lieutenant governor, Speaker of the house, and a majority of the Democratically controlled legislature supported disunion, secession found favor primarily among the farmers and planters of the rich Missouri River bottomlands. In Kentucky, a state noted for its long tradition of sectional compromise, secessionism tended to be concentrated in the planter-dominated Bluegrass region. Nevertheless, the vast majority of border state citizens overall sought to steer a middle course between Union and disunion. Efforts by secessionists to have conventions called to deliberate the question of separation were defeated in Maryland and Kentucky. And although a convention was held in Missouri, antisecession delegates quickly gained the upper hand and quashed any attempt to take their state out of the Union.

Indicative of their reluctance to choose sides, several politicians from the border states endeavored to mediate peace between the warring sections. In the U.S. Senate, John J. Crittenden offered a forlorn compromise that sought to restore the Union and preserve the institution of slavery. His fellow Kentuckian, Governor Beriah Magoffin, called on the governors of three midwestern states, as well as those of Missouri and Tennessee, to work together to avert civil war. All such attempts collapsed, however, in the wake of the firing on Fort Sumter and President Abraham Lincoln's call for volunteers. The governors of Missouri and Kentucky defiantly refused Lincoln's request, and those of Maryland and Delaware simply ignored the president.

Unwilling to face the difficult choice between Union and secession, two border states adopted a position of neutrality during the spring of 1861. When the Maryland legislature finally succeeded in pressuring Governor Hicks to call it into session, that body condemned the Federal government's war on the Confederacy but refused to consider an ordinance of secession. Instead, the legislators accepted the governor's recommendation that the state assume a position of neutrality. A desire to restore economic ties with the North and the continued Federal military buildup to protect Washington, D.C. (which was situated on the state's border with Virginia), however, made neutrality an impossibility. Similarly, in Kentucky, Governor Magoffin declared a policy of neutrality, all the while permitting Confederate recruiting agents to enter the state and supplies to travel southward. Eventually, Kentucky was forced to abandon its

fence-sitting when Confederate forces occupied the Mississippi River town of Columbus, triggering a Federal countermove into the state.

Only in Missouri did the state government make an overt attempt to join the Confederacy. There, Governor Claiborne F. Jackson mobilized the state militia and tried to seize the U.S. Arsenal in St. Louis. He was foiled by Union Capt. Nathaniel Lyon, who captured Jackson's entire force and drove secessionists from the state capital in Jefferson City. By the end of 1861, most of Missouri and Kentucky were firmly under Federal control. This, however, did not prevent their pro-secession governments from operating in exile. Indeed, Missouri and Kentucky enacted ordinances of secession, were admitted to the Confederacy as its twelfth and thirteenth states, and sent senators and representatives to the Congress in Richmond.

Effects on the Confederacy. In losing the border states, the Confederacy lost manpower and matériel that would have significantly increased its chances for success. The accession of Kentucky, Maryland, and Missouri would have added 45 percent to the white population of the seceded states, 80 percent to its manufacturing base, and almost 40 percent to its supply of mules and horses. The Confederacy also would have gained the highly defensible Ohio River, which traverses Kentucky's northern border for nearly five hundred miles, offering a shield to the South's vulnerable heartland.

Still, thousands of Missourians, Kentuckians, and Marylanders served in the Confederate army. Approximately one-fourth of the white men in Missouri, one-third of those in Maryland, and two-fifths of those in Kentucky who fought in the Civil War served in Southern units. Among them were some of the South's outstanding military leaders: Bradley Tyler Johnson and Isaac Trimble of Maryland; Sterling Price of Missouri; and Simon Bolivar Buckner, Albert Sidney Johnston, John Hunt Morgan, and John C. Breckinridge of Kentucky. In addition, border state politicians and military leaders known as the "western concentration bloc" influenced policy in Richmond by urging President Jefferson Davis to launch a campaign to reclaim Kentucky and plant the Southern banner on the banks of the Ohio.

The border states were the longest Federally occupied part of the South. Union troops entered Maryland in April, Missouri in June, and Kentucky in September of 1861. Only Robert E. Lee's campaign in Maryland in September 1862 and that of Braxton Bragg in Kentucky during the same period seriously threatened the Union stronghold in those states. Even then, Confederate authorities were bitterly disappointed by the failure of Marylanders and Kentuckians to rally to the Southern cause. Incursions during 1864 by Jubal Early into Maryland and Sterling Price into Missouri also failed to elicit public support.

Despite the fact that the Lincoln administration cracked down on Southern sympathizers in the border states, jailing many without charges and confiscating the property of others, little could be done to shake the Unionism of their populations. Even Lincoln's Emancipation Proclamation, which aroused the fears of many border state slaveholders, failed to produce widespread disaffection or pro-Confederate sympathy.

[*See also* Early's Washington Raid; Kentucky; Missouri; Population; Sharpsburg Campaign.]

BIBLIOGRAPHY

Coulter, E. Merton. *The Civil War and Readjustment in Kentucky.* Chapel Hill, N.C., 1926.

Fields, Barbara Jeanne. *Slavery and Freedom on the Middle Ground: Maryland during the Nineteenth Century.* New Haven, 1985.

Hancock, Harold Bell. *Delaware during the Civil War: A Political History.* Wilmington, Del., 1961.

Harrison, Lowell. *The Civil War in Kentucky.* Lexington, Ky., 1975.

Parrish, William E. *Turbulent Partnership: Missouri and the Union, 1861–1865.* Columbia, Mo., 1963.

Smith, Edward Conrad. *The Borderland in the Civil War.* New York, 1927.

W. TODD GROCE

ALEXANDER ROBINSON BOTELER.   LIBRARY OF CONGRESS

BOTELER, ALEXANDER ROBINSON

(1815–1892), congressman from Virginia and colonel. Boteler was a native of Shepherdstown, Virginia (now West Virginia), but because his mother died when he was four, he grew up in the Baltimore home of his maternal grandmother, a daughter of Charles Wilson Peale. After graduating from Princeton in 1835, he completed a master's degree and returned to live on his father's estate, Fountain Rock, in Shepherdstown.

A prominent Presbyterian member of his community, Boteler for a time concentrated on writing and experimental farming. He reluctantly stood for the state senate as a Whig in 1850 but was defeated by the overwhelmingly Democratic electorate in the district. He served as a Whig presidential elector, ran two unsuccessful campaigns for the House of Representatives, and won election in 1859 as an independent American party candidate. Because of a three-way contest for the speakership, Boteler, surprisingly for a freshman congressman, was nominated for the post.

He did not long enjoy his newfound prominence, however. When the secession crisis arose, he counseled against rash action and called for the creation of a special committee, to be composed of one representative from each state, that would work to avert disunion. In the House he gave a strong speech, much commented on for its eloquence, appealing for preservation of the Union. He invoked the image of Washington the Virginian coming to the aid of Massachu-

setts at the beginning of the Revolution. Despite this effort, and his support for the Crittenden Compromise, the actions of rasher men forced unpleasant choices on Boteler and other Southern Unionists. Like a number of Virginians facing this dilemma, Boteler let the action of his state determine his decision. When Virginia seceded, he chose to go with it rather than stay with the Union he had so passionately defended and resigned from the U.S. Congress.

Boteler won election to the Virginia state legislature, but before he could take office he accepted appointment to the Provisional Congress. He later barely won election to the First Congress. During his legislative term, he generally supported the Davis administration on a number of committees: Indian Affairs, Buildings, Flag and Seal (he submitted a design for the flag and had a hand in the seal that was adopted), Ordnance and Ordnance Stores, Printing, and Rules and Officers. Because his district was on the fringes of Confederate-controlled territory and most of it in fact became part of West Virginia when that state was created, Boteler had a special interest in supporting efforts to oust occupying Federal forces.

Unlike many of his colleagues who stayed in Richmond when Congress was not in session, Boteler alternated his legislative work with military service. With the rank of colonel, he was a volunteer aide on the staff of his friend, Thomas J. ("Stonewall") Jackson. He became a kind of public relations officer and served as a conduit for Jackson's appeals to Congress on several occasions. Right after the Battle of Winchester in 1862, in which Boteler's teenaged son was wounded twice, Jackson sent him to Richmond to plead for reinforcements. Boteler recalled that Jackson believed he could then "raise the siege of Richmond and transfer this campaign from the banks of the James to those of the Susquehanna." Boteler made two other similar trips to the capital, but Robert E. Lee and the administration officials to whom he spoke either could spare no more men or were not persuaded by Jackson's argument. After Jackson's death, Boteler served as an aide on the staff of J. E. B. Stuart.

The war was not without its personal danger for the congressman. As a member of the Provisional Congress, he was taken prisoner in his own house by Union troops on August 13, 1861, but was released the same day. Mary Boykin Chesnut noted his capture snidely in her diary, saying, "He was preaching Union & distracting us last year—when if we had been united all, this civil war might have been avoided." The homes of prominent members of the Confederate government often became targets in contested areas, but Boteler's limestone mansion remained untouched until it came to the attention of a Union raiding party on July 19, 1864. After the war, devotees of the Lost Cause liked to tell the story of how Boteler's daughter Helen defiantly sang "Dixie" while the Yankees put Fountain Rock to the torch. A neighbor who witnessed the event discounted this heroic scene: the daughter was too busy salvaging family valuables to stand around singing while the house burned.

After Boteler failed to gain reelection to the Second Congress, he served as adviser to Virginia governors William Smith and John Letcher. From November 1864 until the end of the war he was a member of the Military Court Department. He was with Lee's army at Appomattox.

After the war he returned to his farm, now in West Virginia. As during the decade before the war, he combined interests in agriculture and public affairs. He did not harbor the same unreconstructed opinion of the Republican party as most Confederates did, and he accepted several political appointments from the national administration, including membership on the U.S. Centennial Commission and Tariff Commission. He also served as a Republican assistant attorney in the Department of Justice and as a pardon clerk. Influenced by his great-grandfather's example, if not his genes, he took up painting and completed oils of the principal Confederate military heroes. Writing historical articles also occupied his later years. One of them described John Brown's raid, which took place near his home and part of which he had witnessed in person. The bespectacled, bearded former Confederate congressman became known after the war as one of the most colorful characters of Shepherdstown. He died there on May 8, 1892.

BIBLIOGRAPHY

"Alexander Robinson Boteler." *Magazine of the Jefferson County Historical Society* 20 (1954): 19–27.

Boteler, A. R. "Stonewall Jackson in Campaign of 1862." *Southern Historical Society Papers* 40 (1915): 162–182. Reprint, Wilmington, N.C., 1992.

Norris, J. E., ed. *History of the Lower Shenandoah Valley.* Chicago, 1890. Reprint, Berryville, Va., 1972.

Wakelyn, Jon L., ed. *Biographical Dictionary of the Confederacy.* Edited by Frank E. Vandiver. Westport, Conn., 1977.

Warner, Ezra J., and W. Buck Yearns, eds. *Biographical Register of the Confederate Congress.* Baton Rouge, La., 1975.

NELSON D. LANKFORD

BOUDINOT, ELIAS C. (1835–1890), lieutenant colonel and congressional delegate of the Cherokee tribe. Boudinot was born in Georgia of a Cherokee missionary and a woman from Connecticut. He was reared in New England after his father's death in 1839 and moved to Arkansas in 1856. When the Civil War began, he was a lawyer and newspaper editor, active in Democratic party politics. Although not a slave owner, he favored secession and was elected secretary of the Arkansas secession convention that voted to join the Confederacy.

Boudinot enlisted in the First Cherokee Mounted Rifle Regiment commanded by his uncle, Stand Watie. The regiment fought against U.S. forces at the Battle of Chustenahlah in Indian Territory, and Boudinot advanced to the rank of lieutenant colonel. Lame in one knee after the 1861–1862 winter campaign, he resigned his commission to campaign successfully for the office of Cherokee delegate to the Confederate House of Representatives. He took his seat in Congress at Richmond on October 2, 1862, serving until mid-March 1865, three weeks before the Confederate surrender at Appomattox. During his time in office, he repeatedly made horseback journeys between Richmond and Indian Territory to confer with his own people and others of the Five Civilized Tribes.

The young Cherokee legislator heard many complaints at home, most of them concerned with the Confederacy's inability to fulfill its treaty obligations with the Five Tribes. Most of Boudinot's labors as a delegate revolved around attempts to gain adequate supplies for the Cherokee and other Indian military units and relief aid for the growing numbers of tribal refugees fleeing into Texas after Federal forces invaded Indian Territory in 1863. He introduced a bill, signed into law by President Jefferson Davis on January 22, 1864, for the relief of the Cherokee Nation in the amount of $100,000. He also pushed for legislation to expedite the payment of claims against the Confederate government of widows and orphans of deceased Indian soldiers.

Boudinot wielded some influence outside the halls of Congress. He met with President Davis to discuss Confederate policy regarding Indian Territory and wrote letters to the chief executive calling for three Indian regiments to be formed as a brigade under his uncle Stand Watie's command and for the reorganization of the territorial military structure, making Indian Territory a department separate from the existing Trans-Mississippi Department. In February 1864, Davis constituted Indian Territory as a separate military district and appointed Stand Watie a brigadier general to command a new brigade.

During the waning months of the war, Boudinot teamed with Samuel B. Callahan, delegate of the Creeks and Seminoles, in successfully amending anti-inflationary legislation to favor their Indian constituents holding Confederate Treasury notes. Boudinot was a major figure in the Southern Cherokee delegation sent to Washington to negotiate a treaty after the collapse of the Confederacy and remained a force in tribal business and politics until his death.

BIBLIOGRAPHY

Abel, Annie. *The American Indian as Participant in the Civil War.* Cleveland, Ohio, 1919.
Colbert, Thomas Burnell. "Visionary or Rogue? The Life and Legacy of Elias Cornelius Boudinot." *Chronicles of Oklahoma* 65 (1987): 268–281.
Dale, Edward E., and Gaston Litton, eds. *Cherokee Cavaliers: Forty Years of Cherokee History as Told in the Correspondence of the Ridge-Watie-Boudinot Family.* Norman, Okla., 1939.
Wilson, Terry P. "Delegates of the Five Civilized Tribes to the Confederate Congress." *Chronicles of Oklahoma* 53 (1975): 353–366.

TERRY P. WILSON

BOWEN, JOHN STEVENS (1830–1863), major general. A native of Georgia, Bowen graduated from West Point in 1853. After garrison and frontier duty he resigned his commission and practiced as an architect in Savannah and St. Louis. At the outbreak of the war he was a captain in the pro-secession Missouri militia. In May 1861, he was captured while serving as chief of staff to Gen. Daniel Marsh Frost at Camp Jackson on the outskirts of St. Louis. Upon his release he joined the Confederate army and organized the First Missouri Infantry out of Memphis. As colonel of this regiment, his first command was under Gen. Leonidas Polk at Columbus, Kentucky.

After his promotion to brigadier general on March 14, 1862, Bowen was involved in all the major campaigns in the western theater against Ulysses S. Grant's advancing army. He was wounded at Shiloh, where his brigade was part of John C. Breckinridge's division. He fought at Iuka and Corinth in the fall of 1862 and then led the Confederate

resistance at Port Gibson on May 1, 1863, when Grant's army pushed eastward from its crossing at Bruinsburg, south of Vicksburg. His stand at Port Gibson, where his forces were outnumbered by about four to one, earned Bowen a promotion to major general on May 25, 1863. Bowen further distinguished himself in the series of battles that culminated in Grant's siege of Vicksburg. He contracted dysentery during the siege and survived his parole after the surrender at Vicksburg by only a few weeks. He died near Raymond, Mississippi, on July 13, 1863.

BIBLIOGRAPHY

Henry, Pat. "Maj. Gen. John S. Bowen, CSA." *Confederate Veteran* 22 (1914): 171–172. Reprint, Wilmington, N.C., 1985.
Wells, W. Calvin. "General John S. Bowen." *Confederate Veteran* 21 (1913): 564. Reprint, Wilmington, N.C., 1985.

WILLIAM L. BARNEY

BOYCE, W. W. (1818–1890), congressman from South Carolina. Boyce, unlike many of his fellow South Carolina politicians in the 1850s, was a reluctant secessionist. First elected to the U.S. Congress in 1852 as a state rights Democrat, he held relatively moderate views on secession, which linked him to the cooperationist camp. Fears of the Republican party led him to change his mind. In August 1860 he wrote that "negro equality, the only logical *finale* of which is emancipation," was the foundation upon which the party was built. Therefore, he cast his lot with those

W. W. BOYCE.   *HARPER'S PICTORIAL HISTORY OF THE GREAT REBELLION*

calling for secession if Abraham Lincoln was elected. When South Carolina adopted its ordinance of secession in December 1860, Boyce resigned his seat.

Although not a member of the secession convention, he was elected as one of the eight members of South Carolina's delegation to the Montgomery convention. There he supported a constitution that was virtually identical to that of the United States with one exception. He and James Chesnut proposed that the constitution guarantee the right of secession. Only the South Carolina delegation favored the idea and it died. Along with fellow ex-congressman Lawrence Keitt, he supported Howell Cobb for the presidency.

In the Provisional Congress, Boyce was a member of the Postal Affairs and Inauguration committees. He also served on the committee that established the executive department. By the time the Confederate government had moved to Richmond, Boyce and Keitt were rumored to be leaders of a "coalition against Jeff Davis." That fall the "coalition" was being called a "party" and Richmond gossips were naming Boyce its primary leader. Some historians have even referred to anti-Davis politicians as the "Boyce Party."

Although word of his opposition to Davis circulated in South Carolina, it did not damage Boyce's relations with his constituents. In elections for the First and Second Congresses, he ran unopposed in South Carolina's Sixth Congressional District. He made no secret of his dislike for the president. In a March 1862 letter to James H. Hammond, Boyce wrote that "Davis is puffed up with his own conceit, and looks upon an independent opinion as an attack on him." "Common sense," he added, "he considers treason." Hammond shared the congressman's contempt and thought that the only hope for the South lay in impeaching Davis and calling for a convention of the states.

Among Boyce's main complaints were the president's thin skin, "West Point red tape," interference in military matters, and lack of boldness. The Confederacy was a revolution that initially had had a chance to succeed, but Davis's caution, Boyce thought, had foreordained the South's failure. He was fearful that the Confederacy would be "Davis-ized into nothing." Several weeks later, in another letter, he lamented, "Jeff Davis has brought us to the brink of ruin."

In Congress, Boyce was a member of several key committees including Ways and Means, Naval Affairs, and Currency. He vehemently opposed conscription but had no compunction about supporting legislation to destroy private property in the face of the enemy's advance. He advocated a scorched-earth policy so that Federal forces would find only desolation. In 1864, he proposed redeeming Confederate currency at its real, not face, value (about five cents on the dollar). This move would eliminate the need for other measures to stabilize the Confederate money supply. This

proposal got nowhere. Although it was presented in opposition to legislation supported by the administration, there was not much reaction to it. The same could not be said for his espousing peace with the Union.

As early as February 1863, word leaked from secret House sessions that Boyce had suggested the South seek an accommodation with the states of the Old Northwest. Nothing happened, but obviously it was an idea that Boyce thought had merit. He simply bided his time. Following Confederate victories at Spotsylvania and the Wilderness, he met with a group that included Senators William A. Graham of North Carolina, Herschel V. Johnson of Georgia, James L. Orr of South Carolina, and John W. C. Watson of Mississippi. The men thought that the time was propitious to work for a negotiated peace based upon Southern independence. On June 2, 1864, resolutions were introduced into both houses of Congress calling for the Confederate government to dispatch peace commissioners. That did not occur, but there were two abortive meetings between representatives of both governments—one at Niagara Falls and the other in Richmond. The meetings failed because each side presented nonnegotiable stipulations. The Confederacy insisted upon independence and slavery and the Union on reunion and the abolition of slavery.

In private, Boyce continued to stew over the president's policies: "It looks to me like we are going under the Jeff Davis lead very fast over the precipice. His intermeddling with the armies is usually disastrous, and he has no diplomacy." The Confederacy was "a country dying from the incompetency of its presumptuous chief." In October 1864, he let some of these same frustrations boil over into public print.

In August 1864, the Democratic convention had adopted a platform that called for cessation of hostilities and a convention of the states to restore peace. Distressed at the devastation the Confederacy was suffering, Boyce independently decided it was time to make the issue public. On September 29, he wrote an open letter to Davis that was released to the press several weeks later. It created a sensation.

In reviewing forms of government, Boyce concluded that a republic, "especially [in] the form of a Confederacy of free States," was designed to be a government for peace. Such a form of government was ill suited to prosecuting a war. A military dictatorship was the most effective form for waging war. "A Republic forced to the wall by a powerful enemy must end in despotism." In case anyone missed his drift, he spelled it out. Hadn't the South become a dictatorship? Boyce then listed what he considered examples of the Confederacy's slide into despotism: conscription "carried to its last limits" of taking men ages seventeen to fifty; direct taxes in clear violation of the Constitution; the issuance and then repudiation of vast sums of paper currency; the seizure and construction of railroads; the establishment of a state monopoly to control the exportation of staples; the ban on importation of luxuries; the taking of food from farmers "at our prices"; the suspension of the writ of habeas corpus; the use of passports, which "we used to think belonged to the iron despotism of Europe." Rhetorically, he asked Davis what greater powers could he have as a military dictator than the ones he enjoyed in 1864?

Boyce urged Davis to declare that the Confederacy was willing to accept an armistice and to agree to the call for a council of the states. By so doing, he would strengthen the chances for a Democratic victory in November 1864. The only hope for the Confederacy lay in doing what it could to advance the cause of the Democratic party in the North. The Democrats wanted peace and reconciliation, and they were "rational on the subject of slavery." The president had to act, and act soon, because Congress would not return to Richmond before the election. If Davis acted, there would be a real chance for real peace—one that would restore harmony. "The question," wrote Boyce, "rests with you. The responsibility is with you; the consequences will be with your country."

The letter appeared in Southern newspapers the second week of October. On the thirteenth, it was printed on the front page of the *Charleston Daily Carolinian* with a favorable notice from the *Columbus* (Georgia) *Sun*. For the next several weeks there was heated debate in the pages of the Southern press. Among the newspapers that thought the congressman's letter had merit were the *Raleigh Standard, Montgomery Mail, Mobile Tribune,* and *Lynchburg Virginian*. The *Charlotte News* called it treason.

In Columbia, the capital of South Carolina, a large gathering of citizens elected a committee that denounced Boyce's argument and called upon him to resign. The congressman was in town and defended himself ably, but he failed to alter the mood of the assembled throng. He refused to resign and his fellow citizens of Winnsboro rallied to his side.

The vehemence of Boyce's letter had the opposite effect from what he had intended. Instead of weakening and exposing the president, it elicited an outpouring of support for the beleaguered chief executive. Davis, emboldened by expressions of support from across the South, attacked Boyce's proposals. He did nothing to give war-weary voters in the North any indication that there might be a prospect of peace. And, by so doing, he did exactly what the congressman had predicted he would do: "traverse the same bloody circles you have been moving in for the past four years."

The South Carolina congressman was not deterred. He returned to Richmond where Mary Boykin Chesnut reported that despite his letter he had not "lost caste." She also reported that there was open talk of a "Boyce party" in Congress. There was never any formally organized faction, but like-minded politicians continued to meet. Following the failure of the Hampton Roads peace conference on February 3, 1865, Boyce realized that the only hope for the Confederacy was continued armed resistance. He urged that Robert E. Lee continue the fight by falling back to defensive positions in the Tennessee mountains.

Traditional interpretations of the Boyce letter have been that he was finished in South Carolina because of it. Certainly, Davis in his *Rise and Fall of the Confederate Government* ignores Boyce and the congressional peace movement. That omission—in fact, the entire publication—simply confirms Boyce's description of Davis's exalted opinion of himself.

In 1866, Boyce moved to the nation's capital and opened a law practice. Because he left the state, some have assumed that he was persona non grata in the Palmetto State. That really wasn't the case. At the turn of the century, the congressman was defended by a Fairfield County historian who noted that William Waters Boyce was a man who "had convictions and courage enough to express and maintain them. Had he lived in a wiser age, he would have been more appreciated."

BIBLIOGRAPHY

Beringer, Richard E. "Political Factionalism in the Confederate Congress." Ph.D. diss., Northwestern University, 1966.

Cauthen, Charles Edward. *South Carolina Goes to War, 1860–1865*. Chapel Hill, N.C., 1950.

Channing, Steven A. *Crisis of Fear: Secession in South Carolina.* New York, 1970.

Daily Carolinian (Charleston, S.C.), October 13–31, 1864.

Edrington, William. *History of Fairfield County, South Carolina.* Edited by B. H. Rosson, Jr. Tuscaloosa, Ala., n.d.

Taylor, Rosser H. "Boyce-Hammond Correspondence." *Journal of Southern History* 3 (August 1937): 348–354.

Woodward, C. Vann. *Mary Chesnut's Civil War*. New Haven, 1981.

Yearns, Wilfred B. *The Confederate Congress*. Athens, Ga., 1960.

WALTER B. EDGAR

BOYD, BELLE (1844–1900), spy. The most famous of the Confederacy's female operatives, Boyd was born in or near Martinsburg, Virginia (present-day West Virginia). Although most scholars agree that Boyd made important contributions to the Shenandoah Valley campaigns, some of the dramatic details of her memoir, *Belle Boyd, in Camp and Prison,* are still controversial. When Martinsburg came under Union occupation in 1861, Boyd's exploits included shooting at a Federal trooper who broke into her family's home (July 4, 1861) and charming attentive Union officers into divulging military information that she transmitted through secret messengers to Confederate leaders. During the fall of 1861 Boyd served as a courier for Gens. Thomas

BELLE BOYD.   NATIONAL ARCHIVES

J. ("Stonewall") Jackson and P. G. T. Beauregard. Early in 1862 she was arrested by Union forces and detained for a week in Baltimore. In mid-May 1862, Boyd claims, she spied on a secret Union strategy session in Front Royal while crouched in a closet above the meeting room and then made a midnight ride of fifteen miles, through Federal sentries, to inform Col. Turner Ashby of her findings.

Boyd's most significant feat came on May 23, 1862, as General Jackson's forces approached Front Royal. Having obtained information on the status of Federal forces in the area, she dashed from Front Royal—on foot—to meet the advance guard of Jackson's troops. Caught in the crossfire of the opposing armies and waving her white bonnet to cheer on the Confederate troops, she reached Maj. Henry Kyd Douglas and reported that Jackson would have to hurry his attack in order to seize the town before retreating Federal forces burned its supply depots and bridges. Her message confirmed Jackson's own intelligence, and the Confederates were victorious.

Her deed sealed her status as a Confederate celebrity and resulted in her arrest on July 30, 1862, and imprisonment in Washington's Old Capitol Prison. She was released as part of a prisoner exchange a month later and sent to Richmond, Virginia, where she spent a few months among her admiring countrymen. Sometime in the winter of 1862–1863, she was appointed an honorary aide-de-camp, with the rank of captain, by General Jackson's headquarters.

In the summer of 1863 she returned to Martinsburg, only to be arrested again by Union forces. Her second incarceration at Old Capitol Prison lasted until December 1863, when she was released and banished South for the remainder of the war. In May 1864, she set sail for England, carrying Confederate dispatches. Her ship was captured by a Union vessel. She was sent to Canada and made her way to England, where, on August 25, 1864, she married Samuel Hardinge, Jr., the Union officer who had been put in charge of the captured blockade runner.

That winter, Hardinge was briefly incarcerated in America under suspicion of treason, and in order to support herself, Boyd wrote and published her memoirs in London. In 1866, after Hardinge's death, she took up acting. Later that year she returned to the United States, where she continued her acting career until 1869, when she married English businessman John Swainston Hammond. The couple was divorced in 1884, and in 1885 she married a young actor, Nathaniel Rue High, Jr., of Ohio. She toured the country giving recitals on her wartime experiences, earning the praise of Union and Confederate veterans alike. Boyd died of a heart attack in 1900 in Kilbourne City (Wisconsin Dells), Wisconsin, and was buried there.

BIBLIOGRAPHY

Boyd, Belle. *Belle Boyd, in Camp and Prison.* London, 1865. Reprint, New York, 1968.

Davis, Curtis Carroll. " 'The Pet of the Confederacy' Still? Fresh Findings about Belle Boyd." *Maryland Historical Magazine* 78 (1983): 35–53.

Scarborough, Ruth. *Belle Boyd: Siren of the South.* Macon, Ga., 1983.

Sigaud, Louis A. *Belle Boyd: Confederate Spy.* Richmond, Va., 1944.

ELIZABETH R. VARON

BRADFORD, ALEXANDER BLACKBURN

(1799–1873), congressman from Mississippi. Bradford, a lawyer, started his political career in his native state of Tennessee, serving in the state senate. He also began his association with the military; he served as a soldier under Andrew Jackson from 1812 to 1815 and commanded the Second Tennessee Regiment in the Seminole War of 1836.

In 1839 Bradford moved to Holly Springs, Mississippi, to practice law. He served in several state legislatures as a member of the Whig party. When the First Mississippi Infantry, the Mississippi Rifles, was organized to fight in the Mexican War, Bradford ran for the position of colonel against Jefferson Davis. Bradford got 350 votes, and Davis, 300; Bradford, however, withdrew and settled for the rank of major of the regiment. He fought under Davis at the Battles of Monterrey and Buena Vista. When he returned from the war, he was honored for his bravery and nominated by the Whig party as a gubernatorial candidate. He was defeated in 1847, however, by the Democratic candidate, Joseph W. Matthews—probably a reflection of the Whigs' diminishing importance in the state. In 1853, Bradford ran for the U.S. Congress but lost to Democrat William Barksdale.

While serving in the Mississippi House of Representatives, Bradford was elected in May 1861 to fill the last months of the term of Alexander M. Clayton, who had resigned from the Provisional Congress. Bradford served on the Committee on Public Lands from December 5, 1861, to February 17, 1862. During his brief stay he moderated his state rights views to support the Davis administration. He did not seek reelection and instead returned to the Mississippi legislature in 1863 and 1864. After the war, he practiced law until his death.

BIBLIOGRAPHY

Alexander, Thomas B., and Richard E. Beringer. *The Anatomy of the Confederate Congress: A Study of the Influences of Member Characteristics on Legislative Voting Behavior, 1861–1865.* Nashville, Tenn., 1972.
Warner, Ezra J., and W. Buck Yearns. *Biographical Register of the Confederate Congress.* Baton Rouge, La., 1975.

RAY SKATES

BRADLEY, BENJAMIN FRANKLIN (1825–1897), major and congressman from Kentucky.

Bradley was a most unlikely Confederate, and historians have uncovered few clues as to why he sided with the South in the Civil War. "If anyone allied himself to the Confederacy on principle," explains historians Ezra J. Warner and W. Buck Yearns, "it was Bradley. He owned no Negroes, was a native of a border state, and had lived for seven years in a northern city."

Born near Georgetown, Scott County, Kentucky, Bradley was educated at Georgetown College (Kentucky) and then studied law at Transylvania University. After practicing law, he recruited a regiment of Kentucky volunteers for service in the Mexican War. Bradley served as adjutant at both the regimental and the brigade levels. After returning to his Georgetown law firm, Bradley in 1854 moved to Chicago where he joined the bar and established a profitable practice.

Once the war broke out, however, Bradley returned to Kentucky to recruit troops for the Confederacy and served as assistant adjutant to Gen. Humphrey Marshall. In 1862 he was commissioned major of the First Battalion of Kentucky Mounted Rifles and fought in West Virginia. In 1863 Bradley resigned from the army because of ill health and, in February 1864, was elected to the Second House of Representatives from Kentucky's Eleventh District. He held memberships on the Ordnance and Ordnance Stores, and Post Office and Post Roads standing committees. A vigorous supporter of the Confederacy, Bradley voted to support the army at all costs and opposed a negotiated peace. He spoke in favor of humane treatment of Union prisoners of war.

After the war, Bradley practiced law in Georgetown, served as clerk of the Scott County Circuit Court, and was elected to the Kentucky Senate.

BIBLIOGRAPHY

Quisenberry, A. C. "The Alleged Secession of Kentucky." *Register of the Kentucky State Historical Society* 15 (1917): 15–32.
Wakelyn, Jon L. *Biographical Dictionary of the Confederacy.* Edited by Frank E. Vandiver. Westport, Conn., 1977.
Warner, Ezra J., and W. Buck Yearns. *Biographical Register of the Confederate Congress.* Baton Rouge, La., 1975.

JOHN DAVID SMITH

BRAGG, BRAXTON (1817–1876), general and military adviser to Jefferson Davis.

Bragg was born in Warrenton, North Carolina, on March 21, 1817. He attended West Point, graduating fifth in the 1837 class of fifty. He served in the Seminole Wars, where his health began its lifelong decline, and won two brevet promotions for gallantry during the Mexican War. In 1856, after marrying Eliza (Elise) Brooks Ellis, Bragg resigned from the army to become a successful sugar planter in Louisiana. When the state seceded in January 1861, the governor made Bragg a major general in command of the state's forces.

On March 7 President Jefferson Davis appointed Bragg brigadier general in the Confederate army. Ordered to Pensacola, Florida, Bragg quickly changed the volunteers he found there into drilled, disciplined soldiers. On September 12 Davis, pleased with Bragg's performance, promoted him to major general and on October 7 assigned him command of western Florida and all of Alabama.

In February 1862 Davis directed Bragg to proceed with his troops to Gen. Albert Sidney Johnston's army in northern Mississippi. Here Bragg shouldered two responsibilities—command of the Second Corps and chief of staff of the army—positions he held at the Battle of Shiloh. The Confederates attacked on April 6, slowly advancing throughout the day, despite the dispersal and tangling of corps, divisions, and brigades. Bragg commanded

BRAXTON BRAGG.   LIBRARY OF CONGRESS

the forces near the center of the battlefield for several hours before moving to the Confederate right where the advance had stalled at the Hornet's Nest. Here he spent five hours directing piecemeal assaults before the Nest fell about 5:00 P.M. As the troops pushed forward, P. G. T. Beauregard, in command of the army since Johnston's death earlier in the day, called off the advance, an action that Bragg believed cost them the victory. By 2:00 P.M. the next day the Confederate line had collapsed before the weight of the reinforced Union army.

Bragg became a full general on April 12, 1862, the fifth ranking officer in the Confederacy. This promotion allowed Davis to assign Bragg to permanent command of the Western Department when Beauregard took an unauthorized sick leave. For a number of reasons, Bragg decided in July that an invasion of Kentucky could reap many benefits for the South. In anticipation of this move, he began an unprecedented transfer of an army by rail on the twenty-third. The move from Tupelo to Chattanooga—776 miles via six railraods—went without a hitch and proved to be the most successful part of the entire enterprise.

Advancing from Chattanooga on August 28 with 27,000 soldiers, Bragg encountered the enemy at Munfordville, where the heavily outnumbered Federal garrison of 4,000 surrendered on September 17. In an attempt to unite forces, Bragg traveled to Lexington to confer with Gen. E. Kirby Smith, leaving the army under his second in command, Gen. Leonidas Polk. As Federal Gen. Don Carlos Buell advanced,

Polk disobeyed orders from Bragg, orders that might have enabled the Confederates to concentrate and defeat the Federals. Instead, Polk moved to Perryville where his deployment of the army for battle proved faulty. Bragg rejoined the army on October 8 and, despite Polk's mistakes, managed to push Buell's army back nearly two miles before the advance stalled. By midnight, however, Bragg began a retreat that ended in Tennessee. Despite the early promise of the Kentucky campaign, Bragg had achieved nothing of lasting value for the Confederacy.

Bragg next met the Federal army on December 31, 1862, about three miles northwest of Murfreesboro, in open farm country with small stands of thick cedar trees. Bragg ordered the Army of Tennessee, 35,000 strong, to pivot on its right, swinging northeast in an effort to force Gen. William S. Rosecrans back beyond the Nashville Pike and to cut the Federal line of retreat. The grand pivot proved unsuitable on the rough and broken terrain, and, although Bragg managed to surprise Rosecrans, within an hour the Federals rallied, took strong positions, and fought fiercely for ten hours. On January 2, following a day of desultory firing, Bragg ordered an assault on a Union division threatening Polk's position. Eighty minutes of bloody combat convinced Bragg that the Federals could not be dislodged, and at 11:00 P.M. his army retreated from Murfreesboro.

For the next six months Bragg dallied in the Tullahoma area, reorganizing his army, quarreling with his subordinates, and caring for his ailing wife. In late June, Rosecrans again advanced, forcing Bragg to retreat to Chattanooga where he remained for several weeks. By late August Rosecrans began a flanking movement around the city, compelling Bragg to scurry southward in order to cover his line of communications. The Union's three corps were widely separated as they maneuvered through the mountainous country, and twice Rosecrans presented Bragg with excellent opportunities to strike the Federal forces in detail. Each time, however, the cowardice or disobedience of Bragg's subordinate commanders allowed the Federals to escape.

Rosecrans, scenting the danger, hurriedly pulled his scattered corps together at Chickamauga Creek. On September 19 and 20 a mighty battle raged as Bragg attempted another grand pivot, hoping to force the Federals into McLemore's Cove and destroy them. The Army of Tennessee held its own through the nineteenth, and advanced at some points. That night the long-awaited Gen. James Longstreet arrived from Virginia, and Bragg reorganized the army into two wings, again hoping that a grand pivot would yield handsome results. Polk, however, attacked hours later than Bragg ordered and then allowed piecemeal assaults to exhaust his resources.

On the left, Longstreet formed his wing and waited for

Polk's attack to produce results. Bragg, active on the field all day (contrary to Longstreet's postwar assertions), ordered Longstreet's troops forward at the precise moment a gap inadvertently opened in the Union line, thus initiating the famous breakthrough long credited solely to Longstreet. The timing of the assault and Longstreet's judicious troop deployment proved highly successful. The Union line broke and fled. The last Federal stand took place at Snodgrass Hill where Gen. George Thomas held fast until nightfall, covering the wild retreat of Rosecrans and the Federal army.

Moving the army to the heights overlooking Chattanooga, where Rosecrans had ensconced the Union army, Bragg spent the next several weeks quarreling with his subordinates and frittering away the advantages he had gained over the Federals at the Battle of Chickamauga. While his attention was thus occupied, the Federals replaced Rosecrans with Gen. Ulysses S. Grant. On November 24 Grant's forces easily swept the few Confederate soldiers deployed on Bragg's left off of Lookout Mountain and the following day chased the entire Army of Tennessee down the far side of the seemingly impregnable Missionary Ridge. On November 29 Bragg asked to be relieved from command. To Bragg's chagrin, Davis accepted the resignation with unseemly haste.

In February 1864, however, Davis, ever loyal to his friends, summoned the general to Richmond to serve as his military adviser, an office that allowed Bragg to wield considerable power among his army cohorts. Bragg served Davis and the Confederacy well during the eight months he spent in the capital city. The efficiency of several military institutions improved under his supervision, primarily through changes in department heads. In an extreme case Bragg initiated the dismantling of the Bureau of Conscription after finding it riddled with corruption. Davis relied heavily upon Bragg's understanding of military affairs, often seeking Bragg's expertise or opinion on a variety of matters. Bragg, however, never became a sycophant to Davis; indeed, the two often disagreed. Approaching his responsibilities with a characteristic intensity and devotion to duty, Bragg willingly shouldered censures and criticisms that otherwise would have fallen on Davis or, in at least one instance, Gen. Robert E. Lee. Unfortunately, Bragg's appointment as military adviser came too late in the war for him to make a great impact. Had he been assigned the post earlier, the Confederacy could have profited more from his considerable administrative talents.

In October 1864, while still performing the duties of military adviser, Bragg returned to field command when Davis ordered him to Wilmington, North Carolina, the last Confederate port remaining open to blockade runners. Bragg's performance here was shameful. He failed to prepare properly for anticipated attacks, and when the Federals made a concerted assault against Fort Fisher in January 1865, the commanding general stood by several miles away, wringing his hands and refusing to give credence to desperate appeals for aid from inside the fort. Bragg's explanations for his conduct were pusillanimous and illogical.

Bragg spent the last weeks of the Confederacy's life as a subordinate to Gen. Joseph E. Johnston, who, with the remnants of the Army of Tennessee, unsuccessfully attempted to block Gen. William Tecumseh Sherman's advance through North Carolina. As the Confederate government fled Richmond, Bragg joined Davis just in time to use his influence in convincing the president that the Confederacy had indeed been defeated. On May 10, 1865, as Bragg and his wife wended their way home, Union cavalry caught up with them near Concord, Georgia. Bragg was granted a parole on the spot and received no further trouble from the Federals; he died in Galveston, Texas, on September 27, 1876. He is buried in Magnolia Cemetery, Mobile, Alabama.

Bragg held a greater range of responsibilities than any other Confederate during the Civil War. He began in command of the Gulf coast fortifications at the start of the war; served as corps commander and chief of staff under Albert Sidney Johnston; was promoted to command of the Army of Tennessee, a position he held longer than anyone else, leading the western army to its northern high tide and to its one great victory; was one of only two people (the other was Lee) to serve as military adviser to the president; and ended his Civil War career as a subordinate field commander once again.

As an army field commander Bragg left much to be desired. Many factors contributed to his poor generalship. He suffered from myriad illnesses—migraine headaches, boils, dyspepsia, and rheumatism, to name a few—which frequently were brought on by stress. The diseases alone were enough to debilitate anyone, but the remedies he used to relieve his pain and discomfort may have been as damaging. He failed to inspire loyalty, confidence, or obedience in his subordinates, and he lacked the steadiness, the resolution, and the good luck of a successful field commander. A West Point–trained career officer, Bragg had little patience with his volunteer soldiers, and his harsh efforts to discipline them seemed sometimes to go beyond the bounds of reason and necessity. Bragg also failed to learn from his mistakes, and to the end of the war he remained seemingly ignorant of the technological changes that required corresponding changes in tactics.

His personality may have been Bragg's greatest shortcoming. Although severely criticized and denigrated over the years, during his lifetime he had many staunch supporters, as evidenced by declarations of support and admiration even when he wielded little or no influence.

Bragg, however, saw people in either black or white. Those he considered friends received his unwavering support and praise; all others he went out of his way to criticize and annoy. This flaw in his character frequently led to and exacerbated embarrassing quarrels with his subordinates, some of whom on two extraordinary occasions conspired together in petitioning Davis to remove Bragg from command of the Army of Tennessee. While serving as military adviser, Bragg took every opportunity to denigrate or thwart those he disliked, and he carried much of the responsibility for the removal of Joseph E. Johnston, a friend and supporter, from command of the Army of Tennessee in July 1864.

Bragg remains a study in contrasts and illuminates the Confederacy's serious misuse of talent. An able administrator, he spent most of the Civil War as a mediocre (at best) army field commander; although he maintained many loyal friendships, he went out of his way to create lasting enmities; sincerely devoted to the Confederate cause, he contributed greatly to its demise.

BIBLIOGRAPHY

Connelly, Thomas L. *Army of the Heartland: The Army of Tennessee, 1861–1862.* Baton Rouge, La., 1967.

Connelly, Thomas L. *Autumn of Glory: The Army of Tennessee, 1862–1865.* Baton Rouge, La., 1971.

Hallock, Judith Lee. *Braxton Bragg and Confederate Defeat.* Vol. 2. Tuscaloosa, Ala., 1991.

McWhiney, Grady. *Braxton Bragg and Confederate Defeat.* Vol. 1. New York, 1969. Reprint, Tuscaloosa, Ala., 1991.

Woodworth, Steven E. *Jefferson Davis and His Generals: The Failure of Confederate Command in the West.* Lawrence, Kans., 1990.

JUDITH LEE HALLOCK

BRAGG, THOMAS (1810–1872), governor of North Carolina, U.S. senator, and Confederate attorney general. A successful attorney, former two-term governor of North Carolina, and former U.S. senator, Bragg served as attorney general in Jefferson Davis's cabinet from November 21, 1861, to March 18, 1862. He was a capable man whose sentiments represented well the feelings of many North Carolinians. Bragg had been unenthusiastic about secession and privately doubted the Confederacy's prospects, yet he served faithfully in his four months in office and afterward continued to support the Confederate government.

Bragg was born on November 9, 1810, in Warrenton, North Carolina, and was one of six sons. Braxton Bragg, the Confederate general, was one of his brothers, and an older sibling, John, was a successful lawyer. Thomas Bragg studied first at Warrenton Academy and then in Middletown, Connecticut, at Norwich Military Academy. Returning to North Carolina to read law, Thomas followed John's example by studying under the supervision of Judge John Hall of Warrenton, a member of the North Carolina Supreme Court. In 1832 he was admitted to the bar.

Bragg opened a law practice in the town of Jackson in neighboring Northampton County and became a diligent, respected lawyer. Success in politics proved more difficult, however, because he was a Democrat in a strongly Whig county. Winning elections for county attorney and a single term in the state legislature in 1842, Bragg then had to be content with an advisory role in the party's state conventions until he received the Democratic nomination for governor in 1854. Bragg prevailed in a tight race and won reelection in 1856. As governor he stressed one of his party's popular issues, a wider franchise, and worked for internal improvements, expansion of railroads, and a better banking system.

Thomas Bragg was a reserved, sober, and conservative man who expressed himself confidently when asked but did not push for attention. He carried these traits into the higher positions that he occupied, beginning with his election to the U.S. Senate in 1859. As the sectional crisis deepened, Bragg remained loyal to the South but was distinctly unenthusiastic about secession. Saying little publicly, he indicated privately that he felt secession was impractical and unwise, no matter how justified. He doubted that the South was united or determined enough to endure a severe contest, despite the fervor that surrounded national politics. Honor, he wrote in his diary, had led Southerners in Congress to resign quickly after Abraham Lincoln's election. He himself did not withdraw from the Senate until March 6, 1861.

Back in North Carolina, Bragg helped prepare the state's military forces for the approaching conflict until he received an invitation from Richmond. Judah P. Benjamin, the Confederacy's attorney general, had taken over the responsibilities of the War Department ad interim after Alabama's Leroy P. Walker resigned, and Benjamin performed the duties of that arduous post so satisfactorily that President Davis decided to keep him there. Thus Benjamin's old post needed to be filled. Bragg enjoyed a fine reputation as a lawyer, but more important was the fact that he came from North Carolina. Already that state was furnishing disproportionately large quantities of men and matériel for the Confederate war effort, but Tarheel newspaper editors and politicians complained that their state was neglected and unappreciated. North Carolina had no one in the cabinet, and Davis remedied that deficiency with Bragg's acceptance of the office of attorney general.

In the brief four months that he discharged his responsibilities, Thomas Bragg addressed few matters of importance. Although he worked smoothly with President Davis, Bragg felt that he was rarely asked for advice on matters of significance. Legally, he worked to organize his department and rendered careful, conservative opinions on the few questions referred to him. Bragg advised the War Department, for example, that the government remained responsible for property taken by impressment. He also held that the Treasury Department should honor requisitions approved by the War Department without investigating their legality, and he wrote opinions on smaller questions such as pardons, the distribution of prize money for capture of a ship, or a clerk's salary. Many citizens contacted Bragg's office seeking his opinion on various acts of the Congress or administration. Wisely Bragg refused to comment, explaining that his duty under the law was to advise the president or other department heads. In his one report to Congress, he urged the establishment of a supreme court.

More striking than his official actions were Bragg's private comments in his diary. These revealed a lack of confidence in the cause that, though rarely voiced, was fairly widespread in the South and quite strong in North Carolina. On February 17, 1862, as the Provisional Congress expired, Bragg asked, "Will the Gov't endure? Can we repel the enemy? . . . I am by no means confident as to the issue." He found it difficult to take seriously the phrase "permanent government" and on February 20 wrote: "I must confess that taking a survey of our whole field of operations it seems to me that our cause is hopeless—God grant that I may be mistaken."

A month later Bragg left the cabinet for reasons that remain difficult to ascertain precisely. A Petersburg, Virginia, newspaper commented on his ill health, but since Bragg was enamored with neither his role in the cabinet nor the prospects of the cause, it is possible that he chose to end his service with the conclusion of the provisional government. The desire of Union Whigs to have a representative in the cabinet may also have played a role in Bragg's replacement by Thomas H. Watts of Alabama.

However pessimistic Bragg may have been privately, he continued to give public support to the Confederacy in North Carolina. He advised the government on sentiment in his state and accepted an appointment in 1864 to examine arrests under suspension of the writ of habeas corpus. When William W. Holden's *Raleigh Standard* began to agitate for peace, Bragg reportedly headed an effort to buy a paper and present an opposing, pro-Confederate viewpoint. After the war Bragg resumed the practice of law and was active in the Democratic party.

BIBLIOGRAPHY

Bragg, Thomas. Diary. Manuscripts Department, University of North Carolina at Chapel Hill.
Patrick, Rembert W. *Jefferson Davis and His Cabinet.* Baton Rouge, La., 1944.
Powell, William S., ed. *Dictionary of North Carolina Biography.* Vol. 1. Chapel Hill, N.C., 1979.

PAUL D. ESCOTT

BRANCH, ANTHONY MARTIN (1823–1867),
captain and congressman from Texas. Born on July 16, 1823, in Buckingham County, Virginia, Branch received a degree in 1842 from Hampden-Sydney College. By 1847 he had become an attorney in Huntsville, Texas. Branch won election as district attorney during 1850, became a member of the state house of representatives in 1859, and favored the nomination of Sam Houston for president in 1860. Although he achieved a seat in the Texas senate during 1861, Branch resigned to join the Twenty-first Texas Cavalry as a company commander in the spring of 1862. The regiment under Col. George Washington Carter became an often detached part of William Henry Parsons's cavalry brigade in Arkansas and Missouri defending the Trans-Mississippi region.

East Texans opposed to exemptions of overseers from conscription elected Captain Branch to the Confederate House of Representatives in 1863. In Congress he served on the committees for elections, for military affairs, and for territories and public lands. He favored keeping western troops in the Trans-Mississippi Department, although he sought to limit the authority of its commander, E. Kirby Smith. Branch also voted against the exercise of some Confederate government controls over economic activities. Yet he voted with President Davis on several other issues.

In 1866 his East Texas district sent Branch to the U.S. House of Representatives, which rejected him since he would not take the required loyalty oath. He fell victim to yellow fever on October 3, 1867, at Huntsville.

BIBLIOGRAPHY

Bailey, Anne J. *Between the Enemy and Texas: Parsons' Texas Cavalry in the Civil War.* Fort Worth, Tex., 1989.
Friend, Llerena. *Sam Houston: The Great Designer.* Austin, Tex., 1954.
Warner, Ezra J., and W. Buck Yearns. *Biographical Register of the Confederate Congress.* Baton Rouge, La., 1975.

ALWYN BARR

BRANCH, LAWRENCE O'BRYAN (1820–1862), U.S. congressman and Confederate brigadier general. Branch, born November 28, 1820, was the scion of a wealthy North Carolina family. He graduated from Princeton in 1838, practiced law in three Southern states, and served as president of a North Carolina railroad. Branch's sole antebellum military experience came as an aide for a few weeks in 1841 during the Second Seminole War. He

LAWRENCE O'BRYAN BRANCH.   LIBRARY OF CONGRESS

represented his North Carolina district in the U.S. House of Representatives for three terms.

In 1861, Branch served for four months as quartermaster general of his home state. On September 20 he was commissioned colonel of the Thirty-third North Carolina Infantry and less than two months later was promoted to brigadier general—still without any real experience of war. In March 1862, Federals drove Branch out of New Berne. In Virginia two months later, Branch and his command were on the fringes of the Shenandoah Valley campaign, during which the new general exhibited considerable disdain for trained and professional military officers. On May 27, Branch commanded independently in another disaster, near Hanover Court House. The brigade then joined A. P. Hill's newly formed division and fought with it through the Seven Days' campaign.

Branch's Brigade performed solidly at Cedar Mountain, though not as well as he boasted in both public and private writings, and helped defend the army's left at Second Manassas. Hill's division arrived barely in time to save the day at Sharpsburg, and Branch led his troops into the confused fighting. Shortly after his climactic arrival, a

Federal bullet killed him. Branch is buried in Raleigh, North Carolina.

BIBLIOGRAPHY

Branch, Lawrence O'Bryan. Papers, including autobiography. University of Virginia, Charlottesville.
Davis, Archie K. *Boy Colonel of the Confederacy: The Life and Times of Henry King Burgwyn, Jr.* Chapel Hill, N.C., 1985.
Freeman, Douglas S. *Lee's Lieutenants: A Study in Command.* 3 vols. New York, 1942–1944. Reprint, New York, 1986.
Hughes, John. *Lawrence O'Brian* [sic] *Branch.* N.p., 1884.

ROBERT K. KRICK

BRANDON, WILLIAM LINDSAY

BRANDON, WILLIAM LINDSAY (1800 or 1802–1890), brigadier general and conscription officer for Mississippi. Because fire destroyed the family records, Brandon's year of birth in Adams County, Mississippi, is uncertain. When nearly sixty years old, the planter and former state legislator entered Confederate service as major on June 11, 1861, and quickly became lieutenant colonel of the Twenty-first Mississippi on July 17. He fought in the famous Barksdale Brigade, which saw service in a number of key battles with the Army of Northern Virginia. Brandon lost a leg during the assault on Malvern Hill (July 1, 1862), which disabled him for some months but did not prevent his return to the army.

When Benjamin Grubb Humphreys succeeded the slain William Barksdale as brigade commander after Gettysburg, Brandon became colonel in charge of the Twenty-first. The regiment went west with First Corps commander James Longstreet to Chickamauga and Knoxville, Tennessee, in the fall of 1863. On June 18, 1864, Brandon was promoted to brigadier general and accepted the frustrating duty of conscription officer for his state. He spent the remainder of the war battling with the governor over transferring home guards into the Confederate army.

After the war, Brandon returned to his plantation, Arcole, in Wilkinson County, passing away there on October 8, 1890, after years of comparative quiet outside the public arena.

BIBLIOGRAPHY

Evans, Clement A., ed. *Confederate Military History.* 12 vols. Atlanta, 1899. Extended ed. in 19 vols. Wilmington, N.C., 1987–1989.
Warner, Ezra J. *Generals in Gray: Lives of the Confederate Commanders.* Baton Rouge, La., 1959.

WILLIAM ALAN BLAIR

BRANDY STATION, VIRGINIA.

BRANDY STATION, VIRGINIA. This village, some seven miles northeast of Culpeper, Virginia, on the Orange and Alexandria Railroad, bordered the site of a June 9, 1863, battle that witnessed the largest clash of mounted

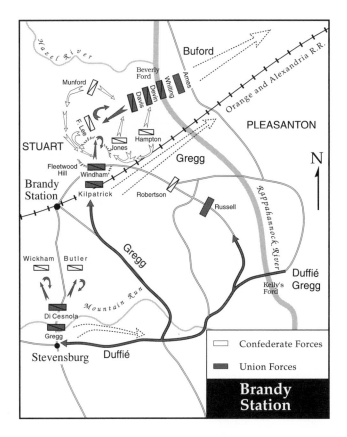

units during the Civil War. By the narrowest of margins, Maj. Gen. J. E. B. Stuart wrestled a tactical victory from the Union cavalry under Brig. Gen. Alfred Pleasonton. Although they were defeated, Federal troopers demonstrated for the first time that they could hold their own against Stuart's soldiers. Imbued with a new sense of confidence, Union cavalry in Virginia became a formidable opponent for the rest of the war. Never again would Gen. Robert E. Lee's horsemen enjoy the degree of success that had marked their earlier campaigns. Southern casualties at Brandy Station amounted to 51 killed, 250 wounded, and 132 missing; the Federals lost 1,651.

The Rappahannock River divided the two antagonists after the smashing Confederate victory at Chancellorsville (May 1–4, 1863). Planning to launch a second raid of the North on June 9, Lee instructed Lt. Gen. Richard S. Ewell's Second Corps and Lt. Gen. James Longstreet's First Corps to abandon their camps in Culpeper County for the Shenandoah Valley. Stuart's troopers were to cross the Rappahannock the same day and screen the infantry's movements. Six batteries of horse artillery and five brigades of cavalry, totaling just more than 9,500 troopers and gunners, made up the Army of Northern Virginia's cavalry division. Supremely confident, as always, Stuart commanded the largest force of his career.

The night before the scheduled advance, Stuart's brigades were widely scattered along the Rappahannock. He hoped they could cross the river with little delay at dawn. Brig. Gen. Fitzhugh Lee's regiments were seven miles northwest of Stuart's headquarters at Fleetwood Hill, and Brig. Gen. William Henry Fitzhugh ("Rooney") Lee's soldiers bivouacked two miles west of the Rappahannock River and along the banks of the Hazel River. Brig. Gen. William E. ("Grumble") Jones's troopers spent the night along the Beverly's Ford Road, two miles south of the Rappahannock and not far from Saint James Church. Brig. Gen. Beverly H. Robertson's men rested southwest of Brandy Station on John M. Bott's farm. Brig. Gen. Wade Hampton's command also spent the night southwest of Brandy Station at Stevensburg. Because Stuart had failed to send pickets to the northern banks of the Rappahannock, he had little idea of the enemy's intentions.

Before the Confederates had stirred from their camps on June 9, Maj. Gen. Joseph Hooker had determined that Lee intended to move his army northward. The Northern commander ordered Pleasonton to take 11,000 cavalrymen and 3,000 infantry across the Rappahannock and "disperse and destroy the rebel force assembled in the vicinity of Culpeper." Pleasonton divided his command into two columns: the right wing under Brig. Gen. John Buford would cross at Beverly's Ford while the left wing under Brig. Gen. David M. Gregg would cross at Kelly's Ford. Both commands would reunite at Brandy Station and then push toward Culpeper where Pleasonton mistakenly believed Stuart's cavalrymen were encamped. He hoped to catch his adversary off guard, as Stuart edged his men to the banks of the river during the night of June 8. The Union officer, however, did not confirm reports that placed Confederate cavalry within a few hundred yards of the Rappahannock. A surprise was in store for both Pleasonton and Stuart in the morning.

Under a thick fog, Buford's men stormed past the Confederate pickets at Beverly's Ford around five in the morning. As the Northerners pounded down the Beverly's Ford Road, "Grumble" Jones roused his sleepy troopers, sending the exposed batteries of Maj. Robert F. Beckham a mile behind the lines to Saint James Church. Jones slowed Buford's rushing horsemen, slashing at the sides of the Union column with his nearest units, while Beckham sent canister flying down the road with the one cannon he had left at the front.

Jones reluctantly pulled his advanced regiments back to the high ground around Saint James Church. The entire brigade positioned itself west of the building; the artillerists were east of the church, extending the line just across Beverly's Ford Road. When the Federals raced across the exposed plain that rested below the Confederates, a barrage of shells, followed by a series of mounted counterattacks, sent the Northern cavalrymen scurrying to the woods. Although Jones had stabilized the Southern line, Stuart could not have been pleased by the enemy's fording of the

Rappahannock. With his brigades widely dispersed, he frantically called on his subordinates for assistance.

From his camp at Stevensburg, Hampton hurried to the front at 6:00, leaving one regiment at Fleetwood Hill and placing his other three units to the right of Beckham. On the western end of the line, Rooney Lee's brigade connected with the left flank of Jones's brigade. Lee posted his soldiers along Yew Ridge, a hulking eminence near the western tip of Fleetwood Hill. Hampton and Lee extended the line into the shape of a "huge crescent" that overlapped the flanks of Buford's troopers. To relieve the pressure from Hampton's probing skirmishers, Buford sent the Sixth Pennsylvania Cavalry against the Confederate center at Saint James Church. The Union soldiers made a gallant charge, as they fought hand to hand among Beckham's guns, but without sufficient support they were forced to retire. The failed attack brought a period of relative calm over this portion of the field.

The fighting now shifted toward Rooney Lee's position atop Yew Ridge, as Buford realized that the route to Brandy Station, via the Beverly's Ford Road, had been sealed off by the Confederates. Since 8:30 that morning, Buford had tested the enemy's left flank. Lee's troopers stood firm behind a stone wall until noon, when Federal infantry slipped around the end of the Southern line at Dr. Daniel Green's farm. Obliged to withdraw to the northwest end of Fleetwood Hill, Lee's soldiers now faced to the north and west. They waited for Buford to renew his assaults, as gunfire echoed two miles to their southeast. It warned of Stuart's newest threat.

About the time Hampton's men reinforced Jones at Saint James Church, Stuart learned of Gregg's crossing at Kelly's Ford. He sent the First South Carolina to the scene with the promise that Robertson's brigade would relieve them shortly. Gregg discovered that Robertson's troopers were galloping down the same road that he had planned to use to arrive at Brandy Station. Turning his column down a different road just west of Paoli's Mill, Gregg picked a less direct route to the battlefield, but it offered little Confederate resistance along the way. It was close to 9:00 when Gregg's hard-riding troopers passed Mount Dumpling. Fleetwood Hill was only two miles away, and Gregg ordered his men to attack the prominent eminence immediately. Only one Confederate cannon stood in the way of the Northern onslaught—an attack aimed at the rear of the Confederate line around Saint James Church. Stuart had been surprised for the second time that day.

The Southern cavalry chieftain mistakenly believed that Robertson's regiments could handle whatever enemy force had crossed Kelly's Ford. When Jones reported Federal activity around Brandy Station, Stuart quickly dismissed his subordinate's claim, remarking, "Tell General Jones to attend to the Yankees in his front, and I'll watch the flanks." Oblivious to the danger that lurked behind him, Stuart even disregarded the messages of Maj. Henry B. McClellan, a member of his staff, who watched the leading elements of Gregg's division steadily push toward Fleetwood Hill from the direction of Brandy Station. The lone Confederate cannon initiated a duel with three Union field pieces. The banging guns finally convinced Stuart that a potential disaster brewed behind his lines.

Stuart immediately ordered two regiments from Jones's brigade to Fleetwood Hill. Unit formations disintegrated as the troopers made a hard ride from Saint James Church. When Jones's cavalrymen reached the crest of the hill, they launched a ferocious attack that blunted the Union advance. Both sides continued to send reinforcements to the southern end of Fleetwood. Charge and countercharge characterized the next phase of the battle. The clash of sabers, not the ringing shots of pistols, pierced the air. It was a dramatic moment, but one that has created the false impression that the Battle of Brandy Station was limited to the ground surrounding Stuart's headquarters.

Four of Hampton's regiments followed Jones into the cauldron. Just as his troopers surged across the top of the hill, a fresh Union brigade under Col. Judson Kilpatrick struck opposite the terminus of Fleetwood. A confusing melee ensued and most of Kilpatrick's regiments were repulsed. Desperate to salvage the day, he called on the First Maine to make a final charge. The Union cavalrymen swept forward, gaining a temporary hold on Fleetwood Hill, but the momentum of the assault carried the members of the First Maine a mile across the hill where they found themselves "cut off from all support." After their attack, Beckham placed all his available guns along the ridge, as the Confederates established permanent control of Fleetwood Hill.

Two hours of severe fighting had exhausted Gregg's division, and reinforcements were not at hand. His supporting division, under Col. Alfred N. Duffié, stumbled into Col. M. C. Butler's Second South Carolina at Stevensburg. Though Duffié could see Fleetwood, he made little attempt to break through the enemy's thin line. If Duffié had aggressively led his command, he could have aided Gregg at Brandy Station or marched to Culpeper to discover the disposition of Lee's infantry. With only two hundred men at hand, Butler's energetic defense saved Stuart from a potential fiasco.

After Gregg's battered command galloped off the field, heading toward the Rappahannock Railroad Bridge, Stuart consolidated his position along a two-mile front with Hampton on the right, stretched east across the Orange and Alexandria Railroad. Jones occupied the center of the line while Rooney Lee anchored the left flank, which bent around the northern rim of Fleetwood. Stuart wanted to pursue Gregg, but enemy activity on his left made this venture impossible, as Buford and Lee had been hotly engaged for most the afternoon.

Unlike Duffié, Buford tried to assist Gregg by concentrating his forces, mostly dismounted cavalry and infantry, against Lee's refused left flank. Just when Buford's men seized the northern crest of Fleetwood around 3:30, they received the order to retire to Beverly's Ford. Pleasonton had already decided on a general withdrawal. Reports of Confederate infantry, the failure of Gregg's attack, and Buford's slow progress against Rooney Lee convinced Pleasonton that little more could be achieved south of the river.

Although Stuart could claim a tactical victory at Brandy Station, he had been badly surprised by Pleasonton, an incident that tarnished his reputation. After the battle, one Southern cavalryman wrote, "Stuart was certainly surprised and but for the supreme gallantry of his subordinate officers and men in his command it would have been a day of disaster and disgrace." In his official report, Stuart refused to admit that he had not been prepared for Pleasonton's assault but conceded that his troops nearly lost the field to the enemy. Stuart criticized Robertson for failing to block Gregg's advance and chastised Col. Thomas T. Munford, the temporary commander of Fitzhugh Lee's brigade, for his tardy arrival on the battlefield.

Stuart's insatiable need for approbation was not satisfied by his commanding officer, who offered few words of praise after Brandy Station. Lee must have been pleased by Stuart's aggressive leadership on the battlefield, which prevented the Federals from unmasking the location of the Confederate infantry. Nevertheless, criticism came from all circles and wounded Stuart's sensitive pride. A North Carolina woman wrote that "the more we hear of the battle at Brandy Station, the more disgraceful is the surprise." Mindful of public reaction to Brandy Station, Stuart tried to redeem himself in the coming campaign by launching a raid in Pennsylvania that possessed little military value and virtually paralyzed the entire army.

BIBLIOGRAPHY

Blackford, William W. *War Years with Jeb Stuart.* New York, 1945.

Coddington, Edwin B. *The Gettysburg Campaign: A Study in Command.* New York, 1968.

Gallagher, Gary W. "Brandy Station: The Civil War's Bloodiest Arena of Mounted Combat." *Blue & Gray Magazine* 8 (October 1990): 8–22, 44–53.

McClellan, Henry B. *The Life and Campaigns of Major-General J. E. B. Stuart, Commander of the Cavalry of the Army of Northern Virginia.* Boston, 1885.

Thomas, Emory M. *Bold Dragoon: The Life of J. E. B. Stuart.* New York, 1986.

U.S. War Department. *The War of the Rebellion: A Compilation of the Official Records of the Union and Confederate Armies.* Ser. 1, vol. 27, pts. 1–2. Washington, D.C., 1893.

PETER S. CARMICHAEL

BRANTLY, WILLIAM FELIX

BRANTLY, WILLIAM FELIX (1830–1870), brigadier general. Born in Greene County, Alabama, March 12, 1830, Brantly (often spelled Brantley by historians) grew up in Mississippi. After reading law, he entered that profession in Greensboro. A Whig and then a Know-Nothing in the 1850s, he came to favor secession and represented Choctaw County in the 1861 convention that voted Mississippi out of the Union.

Brantly was elected captain of Company D, Fifteenth Mississippi Infantry Regiment. After suffering a serious wound at Shiloh where he commanded the Fifteenth, he was chosen lieutenant colonel of the newly organized Twenty-ninth Mississippi. He led that unit through the 1862 and 1863 campaigns of the Army of Tennessee. He was wounded at Murfreesboro (December 1862) and won a reputation as a fine officer. Meanwhile, he became known as "a firm friend" of Confederate President Jefferson Davis and of Gen. Braxton Bragg, controversial commander of the Army of Tennessee, who became Davis's chief military adviser early in 1864.

When Brig. Gen. Samuel Benton was mortally wounded at Atlanta on July 22, 1864, Brantly was promoted four days later to replace him. He commanded his brigade through the Franklin and Nashville campaign and the Carolinas campaign. He surrendered with the Army of Tennessee and was paroled at Greensboro, North Carolina, on May 1, 1865.

Brantly resumed his law practice after the war. On November 2, 1870, near Winona, Mississippi, he was murdered by an unknown assassin. He is buried three miles north of Tomnolen, Mississippi (site of the town of Greensboro).

BIBLIOGRAPHY

Bearss, Edwin C. "William Felix Brantly." In *The Confederate General.* Edited by William C. Davis. Vol. 1. Harrisburg, Pa., 1991.

Evans, Clement A., ed. *Confederate Military History.* 12 vols. Atlanta, 1899. Extended ed. in 19 vols. Wilmington, N.C., 1987–1989.

RICHARD M. McMURRY

BRATTON, JOHN

BRATTON, JOHN (1831–1898), brigadier general and U.S. congressman. Born March 7, 1831, at Winnsboro, South Carolina, Bratton attended Mount Zion Academy and graduated from South Carolina College in 1850. He earned a diploma from South Carolina Medical College three years later and opened a practice in his hometown.

When his state seceded, Bratton enlisted as a private in the Sixth South Carolina. Almost immediately he was promoted to captain. Twice thereafter, however, he reenlisted as a private when his regiment was reorganized at the expiration of enlistment periods. In 1862 he was elected colonel of the Sixth South Carolina, which became part of Micah Jenkins's brigade, James Longstreet's corps. Bratton was severely wounded in the shoulder and arm in the Battle of Seven Pines and was captured and imprisoned at Fortress Monroe for several months.

Testimony to Bratton's exceptional qualities as a soldier is found in endorsements by his superior officers. Richard Anderson lauded him for "skill and courage, coolness and good management" at Seven Pines. In January 1863, Micah Jenkins notified Secretary of War James A. Seddon that "in character and integrity, in gallant conduct on the field & judicious discipline in the camp this officer fully merits" promotion. In April five South Carolinians in Congress encouraged Seddon to promote their favorite son.

More than a year later Bratton received his promotion. It occurred on June 9, 1864, to rank from May 6, the date of Jenkins's death in the Battle of the Wilderness. On June 27, Bratton was assigned command of the brigade. At Appomattox he surrendered the largest brigade in the Army of Northern Virginia.

After the war, Bratton abandoned the medical profession and turned to farming in South Carolina. He took an active part in Reconstruction politics. He was a state senator (1865–1866) and a U.S. congressman (1884–1885). He served as chairman of the state delegation to the Democratic National Convention of 1876 and as state comptroller in 1881. He ran unsuccessfully for the governorship in 1890. Bratton died January 12, 1898, and was buried in Winnsboro, South Carolina.

BIBLIOGRAPHY

Bratton, John. "The Sixth Carolina at Seven Pines." *Southern Historical Society Papers* 13 (1886): 132–133. Reprint, Wilmington, N.C., 1990.

Capers, Ellison. *South Carolina.* Vol. 5 of *Confederate Military History.* Edited by Clement A. Evans. Atlanta, 1899. Vol. 6 of extended ed. Wilmington, N.C., 1987.

Compiled Military Service Records. John Bratton. Microcopy M331, Roll 31. Record Group 109. National Archives, Washington, D.C.

LOWELL REIDENBAUGH

BREAD RIOTS. There is no incident on the Confederate home front more misunderstood than the Richmond bread riot of April 2, 1863, and no civilian subject less studied than that of other food riots, mostly in the springs of 1863 and 1864, although New Orleans experienced a disturbance as early as July 1861. These events have been attributed to wartime inflation and a lack of adequate food supplies at fair prices.

A series of incidents that preceded the April 1863 disturbance in the Confederate capital helped cause it and explain why it occurred when it did. Specific local factors increased demand for shrinking supplies, exacerbating inflation that led to hoarding and speculation. Further irritants to a disgruntled population were the explosion of the Confederate ordnance laboratory on March 13, which killed more than sixty poor women, and a heavy snowfall the next week. The snow quickly melted, making roads nearly impassable and causing flooding of the James River, which shut down the waterworks and public hydrants.

Crime and vice were common in Richmond, especially at night. The bread riot was organized violence on a large scale conducted openly. It was also political protest, planned and led by women, a purposeful rather than a spontaneous event.

Its timing was related to a series of outbreaks elsewhere. Atlanta, Georgia, had a food riot on March 16, 1863, as did Macon, Columbus, and Augusta about the same time. On a main rail link between Virginia and the lower South, Salisbury, North Carolina, witnessed a flour riot on March 18, when soldiers' wives raided merchants. Raleigh, High Point, and Boon Hill in the same state all experienced food riots that month. Mobile, Alabama, had one on March 25 (and a more serious incident in mid-April, as well as disturbances in August and on September 4). In Petersburg, Virginia, there was a bread riot on April 1. Most of these events were reported in Richmond papers, often with favorable editorial comments about the alleged hoarders, speculators, or profiteers who were targeted.

There had been talk about a protest in Richmond for several weeks, but final plans were made at a meeting held in Belvidere Baptist Church the night of April 1. Women from all over the city, particularly poorer neighborhoods, attended, as did some from outlying counties. Their participation indicates prior knowledge that something was about to happen.

The riot began before nine in the morning when Mary Jackson, a painter's wife, left her butcher's stall in the Second Market. Followed by a growing crowd of women and boys she marched to the Governor's Mansion. It is unclear whether Governor John Letcher actually addressed the group. The crowd became a mob when it surged out of Capitol Square, down Ninth Street, and invaded the business district on Main and Cary streets, sacking about twenty stores.

Mayor Joseph Mayo tried to quell the women by reading the Riot Act, but he was ignored. Governor Letcher called out the Public Guard, a state security force for the Capitol and other buildings, under its acting commander, Lt. Edward Scott Gay. There is no reliable evidence for the story that President Jefferson Davis took command of the Guard, ordering the men to prepare to fire while confronting the looters and giving them a deadline to disperse.

Estimates of the mob's size have ranged from a few

hundred to twenty thousand, but careful scholars argue for about one thousand actual participants, as distinguished from spectators. Richmond's tiny police force was no match for the rioters. There are a few references in some accounts to bloodshed, shots fired, and injuries suffered, but none has been substantiated. The riot was over by eleven.

Forty-four women and twenty-nine men are known to have been arrested, but not all of them were charged or tried. Court records later burned, so the disposition of many cases is unknown. Only twelve women were convicted, one of a felony. A majority were probably poor women, but others were or had once been members of the middle class, including at least eight of those arrested; a few owned land and even slaves. Male rioters got stiffer penitentiary sentences, four for felonies and two for misdemeanors.

The Confederate government failed in its attempt to censor news of the riot. Telegrams reached Danville and Lynchburg within hours. Reports were carried throughout the South by railroad passengers leaving Richmond and to the North by Union prisoners exchanged soon after the event. Most of the city's editors initially honored a request not to print articles about the incident, but John Moncure Daniel, a bitter critic of the Davis administration, blasted the authorities in his *Examiner* for their lenient treatment of the rioters, calling for a dictator to suppress lawlessness. He also attacked the women with ethnic, sexist, and religious slurs. Ironically, his colorful but distorted accounts are the basis for most historians' descriptions.

Sullen crowds gathered again on April 3, but were promptly dispersed by the City Battalion. Troops under Maj. Gen. Arnold Elzey, commander of the Department of Richmond, who had already withheld reinforcements from Lt. Gen. James Longstreet because of the crisis, strengthened Provost Marshal John Winder's men. Cannon were placed at the edge of the business district amid rumors of another riot planned for the night of April 10. The city moved quickly to enlarge its parsimonious welfare program.

Another rash of incidents the next spring suggests that the pinch of hunger became painful enough to move women to desperate action as their winter food supplies were exhausted. Savannah had a riot on April 17, 1864, and one occurred in Bladenboro, North Carolina, the same month. There are sketchy details about incidents in the last year of the war at Abingdon, Virginia; Lafayette, Alabama; Forsyth, Thomasville, and Marietta, Georgia; and Sherman, Texas.

Of their importance there can be no doubt. Historian Emory M. Thomas has called the Richmond riot "the best case study of the results of Southern food supply problems." Three levels of government in the capital were shaken, and all took steps to prevent another incident. Morale plummeted throughout the Confederacy. The food riots were a sign of urban unrest, similar to the yeoman discontent

expressed in rural areas by women's raids on government storage depots, like that at Jonesville, North Carolina, in 1865. They were also disturbing evidence that the war had become a poor woman's fight, as well as a poor man's. Women who demonstrated in city streets and country crossroads and openly defied civil and military authorities hardly conformed to traditional Southern definitions of patriotism and female roles.

[*See also* Poor Relief; Poverty; Speculation.]

BIBLIOGRAPHY

Amos, Harriet E. "'All Absorbing Topics': Food and Clothing in Confederate Mobile." *Atlanta Historical Journal* 22 (1978): 17–28.
Chesson, Michael B. "Harlots or Heroines? A New Look at the Richmond Bread Riot." *Virginia Magazine of History and Biography* 92 (1984): 131–175.
Coulter, E. Merton. *The Confederate States of America, 1861–1865*. A History of the South, vol. 7. Baton Rouge, La., 1950.
Simkins, Francis Butler, and James Welch Patton. *The Women of the Confederacy*. Richmond, 1936.
Tice, Douglas O. "'Bread or Blood!': The Richmond Bread Riot." *Civil War Times Illustrated* 12 (1974): 12–19.

MICHAEL B. CHESSON

BRECKINRIDGE, JOHN C. (1821–1875), U.S. congressman, vice president, and presidential candidate, major general, and secretary of war. Breckinridge, who was born into one of Kentucky's most illustrious families, studied at Centre College, the College of New Jersey (Princeton), and Transylvania University. He practiced law briefly in Iowa and then in his home state. Major of the Third Regiment of Kentucky Volunteers, he arrived in Mexico too late for significant participation in the Mexican War. Breckinridge was elected to the Kentucky House of Representatives in 1849 as a Democrat and to the U.S. House in 1851 and 1853. In 1856 at age thirty-five he was elected vice president of the United States on the Democratic ticket with James Buchanan. In 1859, over a year before his term expired, the Kentucky legislature chose him for the Senate term beginning March 4, 1861. As the slavery controversy developed in the 1850s, Breckinridge had called for "perfect non-intervention" on the part of Congress on the issue of slavery in the territories.

When the Democrats split in 1860, Breckinridge became the candidate of the Southern party. Though he believed that a state had the right to secede, he denied that he was the secession candidate. Breckinridge lost his home state to Constitutional Unionist John Bell, but he carried eleven of the fifteen slave states and won 72 electoral votes to 39 for Bell and 12 for Stephen A. Douglas, the Northern Democratic candidate. But Republican Abraham Lincoln received 180 votes for a clear majority. As vice president, Breckin-

JOHN C. BRECKINRIDGE.   NATIONAL ARCHIVES

ridge announced the election of Lincoln on February 13, 1861, when the electoral votes were officially counted.

Breckinridge hoped that some compromise would save the Union, but in the Senate he defended the actions of the Southern states. After the war started, he served on a six-man committee that formulated Kentucky's unique neutrality policy. When that troubled status ended in September 1861, Breckinridge fled to Virginia to avoid arrest. The Senate expelled him on December 2.

Considered an important asset for the Confederacy, Breckinridge was commissioned brigadier general on November 2 and given the Kentucky Brigade in Gen. Simon Bolivar Buckner's Second Division in southern Kentucky. He helped organize the Confederate government of Kentucky, which was admitted into the Confederacy on December 10, 1861. One of the best of the "political generals," Breckinridge won the respect and admiration of most of his peers, with the conspicuous exception of irascible Braxton Bragg.

Breckinridge's first major engagement was at Shiloh where, in command of the Confederates' Reserve Corps, he performed well enough to merit promotion to major general as of April 14. After serving with Earl Van Dorn at Vicksburg, Breckinridge led an unsuccessful attempt to

take Baton Rouge. Rejoining the Army of Tennessee, he incurred heavy casualties in his division at Murfreesboro in a charge ordered by Bragg. Several Kentuckians urged Breckinridge to seek a duel with his caustic commander.

Breckinridge then returned to the Vicksburg area and participated in Joseph E. Johnston's vain efforts to relieve that city. After it fell, he was ordered to rejoin Bragg's army in eastern Tennessee. At Chickamauga on September 19–20, 1863, Breckinridge's division was in D. H. Hill's corps. His assaults on the Federal left flank helped break the Union line but failed to destroy the army. Breckinridge commanded a corps on Lookout Mountain and Missionary Ridge above Chattanooga on November 25, 1863, when the Confederates were overrun. Bragg charged Breckinridge with drunkenness and removed him from command. But Confederate leaders had learned to discount Bragg's frequent accusations, and in February 1864 the Kentuckian was given command of the Department of Southwest Virginia. He built his command from scratch, and on May 15, with the aid of cadets from the Virginia Military Institute, he defeated Gen. Franz Siegel's larger force at New Market. It was perhaps Breckinridge's finest performance of the war.

Soon transferred to the Army of Northern Virginia, Breckinridge helped check Ulysses S. Grant at Cold Harbor. Then, as commander of a small corps, he accompanied Jubal Early on his raid to the outskirts of Washington. When they returned to the Shenandoah Valley, the Confederates were under intense pressure from Gen. Philip Sheridan's much larger force. Gen. John B. Gordon penned a vivid picture of Breckinridge at this stage of the war:

> Tall, erect, and commanding in physique ... he exhibited in marked degree the characteristics of a great commander. He was fertile in resource, and enlisted and held the confidence and affection of his men, while he inspired them with enthusiasm and ardor. Under fire and in extreme peril he was strikingly courageous, alert, and self-poised.

Later, Gen. Basil W. Duke also praised his fellow Kentuckian but added, "His chief defect as a soldier—and, perhaps, as a civilian—was a strange indolence or apathy which at times assailed him. . . . When thoroughly aroused he acted with tremendous vigour, . . . but he needed to be spurred to action. . . . He was at his best when the occasion seemed desperate."

After John Hunt Morgan's death on September 4, 1864, Breckinridge was returned to command of the Department of Southwest Virginia. Despite inadequate resources, he was able to fend off Union attacks against the vital saltworks in that area.

Meanwhile, the Department of War had become one of the most troubled spots in the Confederate government, and in February 1865 President Jefferson Davis appointed Breckinridge secretary of war. In 1861 Breckinridge had doubted that the Confederacy could win the war, and as he viewed the situation from his new position, he soon concluded that the cause was hopeless. He worked to bring the struggle to an honorable conclusion, which, in his view, rejected guerrilla warfare. "This has been a magnificent epic," he declared. "In God's name let it not terminate in a farce." When Richmond fell he was instrumental in preserving many of the military records.

Briefly with Lee, then with Joseph E. Johnston, and finally accompanying President Davis on his flight, Breckinridge made a daring and dangerous escape through Florida to Cuba. He went on to Europe and Canada where he remained in exile until President Andrew Johnson extended a general amnesty on Christmas Day, 1868. Breckinridge returned to his Lexington home in March 1869 after an absence of over eight years. Comparing himself to "an extinct volcano," he practiced law, worked for economic development in the state, and urged national conciliation until his death on May 17, 1875. He was only fifty-four.

BIBLIOGRAPHY

Davis, William C. *Breckinridge: Statesman, Soldier, Symbol.* Baton Rouge, La., 1974.

Davis, William C. "John C. Breckinridge." *Register of the Kentucky Historical Society* 85 (Summer 1987): 197–212.

Harrison, Lowell H. "John C. Breckinridge: Nationalist, Confederate, Kentuckian." *The Filson Club History Quarterly* 47 (April 1973): 125–144.

Heck, Frank H. *Proud Kentuckian: John C. Breckinridge, 1821–1875.* Lexington, Ky., 1976.

Klotter, James C. *The Breckinridges of Kentucky, 1760–1981.* Lexington, Ky., 1986.

LOWELL H. HARRISON

BRECKINRIDGE, ROBERT J. (1800–1871),

minister, politician, educator, and Unionist. Breckinridge was born into one of Kentucky's most illustrious families at Cabell's Dale, outside Lexington, on March 8, 1800. His father, John Breckinridge, became a U.S. senator and then attorney general in President Thomas Jefferson's cabinet; his mother, Mary Hopkins (Polly) Cabell Breckinridge, was related to several prominent Virginia families. He graduated from Union College, Schenectady, New York, in July 1819. Robert's health was poor, and he spent two years traveling and reading before studying law and receiving a license in 1824. But he was more interested in developing his farm, Braedalbane, in Fayette County than in building up his practice. Elected to the state house of representatives in 1824, he supported the conservative Old Court in a savage controversy over relief legislation. Reelected annually, he represented Fayette County until 1829.

Breckinridge's continued illness and the deaths of two of his children changed his attitude toward religion. He made a profession of faith in 1829 and decided to become a

ROBERT J. BRECKINRIDGE.   LIBRARY OF CONGRESS

Presbyterian minister. He received his license to preach in April 1832 and then went to the Princeton Theological Seminary for further study. A few months later he accepted a call to Baltimore's Second Presbyterian Church. Robert's eloquence, persistence, and conviction that he was right soon made him a conspicuous but controversial figure in the denomination. He was largely responsible for the 1834 "Act and Testimony" that by 1837 had split the Presbyterians into New School–Old School factions. Breckinridge sided with the latter. During his stormy thirteen years in Baltimore he attracted national attention with his prolonged debates with Catholic spokesman (later Bishop) John Hughes and with Universalists.

Breckinridge and his wife spent a year abroad in 1836–1837 when he served as a church delegate. His fame as a controversialist was enhanced by an extended debate in Glasgow, Scotland, with George Thompson on the slavery question. By 1830 Breckinridge owned seventeen slaves, and the number continued to grow, although during his Maryland years he sent eleven freed blacks to Liberia. Breckinridge believed that slavery was wrong, but he insisted that it could be eliminated only through gradual, compensated emancipation, followed by colonization that would remove free blacks from the white community. His 1840 debates in Kentucky with Robert Wickliffe, the "Old Duke," resulted in other vitriolic exchanges. Breckinridge enraged both proslavery advocates and abolitionists, whom he denounced as extremists who endangered the nation.

When Kentucky's third constitutional convention met in 1849, emancipationists hoped to include in the new document a provision that would allow the legislature to consider emancipation whenever it wished. Breckinridge advanced a plan that would free at age twenty-five those slaves born after the adoption of Kentucky's new constitution but allow public authorities to hold them in service until they had earned enough to pay their way to Liberia. Although they polled over ten thousand votes collectively, all emancipationist candidates were defeated. Breckinridge attributed this defeat to the apathy of nonslaveholders.

In 1845 Breckinridge became president of Jefferson College in Pennsylvania. But his tenure there was unhappy, and in January 1847 he accepted an offer to become minister of the First Presbyterian Church in Lexington, Kentucky.

Breckinridge entered upon a new phase of his career in September when Governor William Owsley appointed him superintendent of public instruction. The office had been created in 1838, but six predecessors had done little to improve Kentucky's deplorable public schools. By the time of his resignation in 1853, Kentucky rivaled North Carolina for the best public school system among the slave states. Enrollments had soared and expenditures for education had increased dramatically. But his reforms also attracted opposition. He alarmed those who believed in the separation of church and state when he insisted that the Bible be adopted as the reading text in the elementary grades, and his advocacy of emancipation aroused protests. His presbytery finally ordered his pastoral relations dissolved and suggested strongly that he take a position at the new Danville Theological Seminary.

When the seminary opened on October 13, 1853, Breckinridge was named Professor of Exegetic, Polemic, and Didactic Theology. He remained at the seminary until 1869. Two of his best known books were published during his tenure there: *The Knowledge of God, Objectively Considered* (1858) and *The Knowledge of God, Subjectively Considered* (1859). He edited the *Danville Review* (1861–1865), which gave him an outlet for his political writings. His clashes with colleague Stuart Robinson, who referred to Breckinridge's "despotic and intolerant spirit," contributed to the schism between Northern and Southern factions of the Presbyterian church.

Despite poor health, Breckinridge was an imposing figure when he went to the seminary. Tall and slender, he had a full white beard and dark gray sideburns. Friends often referred to his kindness, his sense of humor, his capacity for affection and sympathy, his courage; opponents saw him as impulsive, combative, irritable, prejudiced, and vindictive. He was given to dogmatic opinions, which he seldom changed.

As the sectional crisis intensified, Breckinridge was a determined foe of secession. In an address in Lexington on January 4, 1861, he declared that if Kentucky did secede, it should form a confederation with Tennessee, Virginia, North Carolina, Maryland, and Missouri. If that approach failed, he preferred that Kentucky remain separate rather than be swallowed up in a confederacy of all the slave states in which Kentucky would be a mere tool of the cotton states. When Governor Beriah Magoffin proposed calling a convention to determine the state's future, Breckinridge, fearing that it might result in secession, advised his associates to delay and defeat it by every possible means. If a convention was held, he asserted that its decision should be submitted to the people for approval. He conceded that the will of the people must then be accepted.

In June 1861, during the state's period of troubled neutrality, Breckinridge warned that secession and rebellion would ultimately destroy slavery. That institution would be safe only in a sound Union. In order to save the old Union, he was willing to divide the territories between slave and free. Although he hoped to see slavery extinguished at some future date, he saw no practical way to deal with the large number of blacks in the cotton states except to continue slavery for the present.

Kentucky remained in the Union when its unique policy of neutrality ended in September 1861, and Breckinridge gave strong support to the war effort. Hailed as the "staunchest friend of the Union in the state," he was believed to have more influence with President Abraham Lincoln than any other Kentuckian. In his own family Breckinridge experienced the agonies of the divided country: two sons joined the Confederacy; two enlisted in Union forces. He supported the harsh measures of Gen. Stephen G. Burbridge and other Union officers who tried to suppress pro-Confederate sympathies and actions in the state. Because of his alleged influence with Lincoln, Breckinridge received numerous appeals for assistance, but he responded favorably to few of them. Instead, he declared that too few suspects were being arrested and that many of those who were arrested were being released too soon. "Treat them all alike," he demanded, "and if there are any among them who are not rebels at heart, God will take care of them and save them at least." Breckinridge insisted that violators of the law were not as entitled to its protection as those who obeyed. He did bend his principles occasionally, however, to help members of his family.

Yet Breckinridge disagreed upon occasion with Lincoln. He called the Emancipation Proclamation unnecessary, and he doubted its constitutionality. In 1849 he had declared that "emancipation is not the main thing—not even *a* main thing except as it may act on an object more important than itself, *Unity of race, and that the white race for Kentucky.*" Nevertheless, when Governor Thomas E. Bramlette's opposition to the enrollment of blacks for possible military service threatened to result in open warfare, Breckinridge was among those who persuaded the angered governor to accept the Federal policy.

In 1864 when most Kentuckians were opposed to the Lincoln administration, Breckinridge was a leader in organizing an Unconditional Union party in the state. When it failed to get the cooperation of the Union Democrats, the party held a convention and endorsed the crushing of the rebellion and restoration of the Union. Breckinridge went to Baltimore as a delegate to the national Union party and was elected temporary chairman. In his address he called for the end of slavery, rigorous prosecution of the war, restoration of the Union, and punishment of traitors. He campaigned hard for Lincoln's reelection. In one of his most controversial suggestions, he proposed that loyal Kentuckians not be paid for confiscated slaves until after the election and "let their votes be the test of their loyalty." Although military authorities blatantly interfered with the election in the state, George B. McClellan carried Kentucky by a wide margin over Lincoln.

Breckinridge was delighted by the collapse of the Confederacy, but he was disturbed by the postwar strength of the "Confederate Democrats" in Kentucky. He even feared for a time that war would begin again. Southern sentiment appeared dominant in his denomination, and in October 1865 he introduced a resolution that declared a majority of the Louisville presbytery was "in open rebellion against the Church, and in open contempt and defiance of her scriptural authority"; such members were "unqualified, unfit and incompetent" to participate in church affairs. His motion lost, 25 to 102, but the next year the Kentucky synod split into Northern and Southern branches. Critics of Breckinridge charged that he "would rule or ruin."

Breckinridge died in Danville on December 27, 1871, and was buried in Lexington. He had once remarked, "I am a wonder to myself." He was also a wonder to many of his contemporaries.

BIBLIOGRAPHY

Coulter, E. Merton. *The Civil War and Readjustment in Kentucky.* Chapel Hill, N.C., 1926. Reprint, Gloucester, Mass., 1966.

Gilliam, Will D., Jr. "Robert J. Breckinridge: Kentucky Unionist." *Register of the Kentucky Historical Society* 69 (October 1971): 362–385.

Gilliam, Will D., Jr. "Robert Jefferson Breckinridge, 1800–1871." *Register of the Kentucky Historical Society* 72 (July 1974): 207–223; (October 1974): 319–336.

Harrison, Lowell H. *The Antislavery Movement in Kentucky.* Lexington, Ky., 1978.

Howard, Victor B. "Robert J. Breckinridge and the Slavery Controversy in Kentucky in 1849." *Filson Club History Quarterly* 53 (October 1978): 328–343.

Klotter, James C. *The Breckinridges of Kentucky.* Lexington, Ky., 1986.

Tapp, Hambleton. "Robert Jefferson Breckinridge during the Civil War." *Filson Club History Quarterly* 11 (April 1937): 120–144.

Vaughan, William Hutchinson. *Robert Jefferson Breckinridge as an Educational Administrator.* Nashville, Tenn., 1937.

LOWELL H. HARRISON

BRECKINRIDGE, ROBERT J., JR.

(1834–1915), congressman from Kentucky and colonel. Breckinridge, son of a minister, was born in Baltimore on September 14, 1834. Because of a drinking problem, he was expelled from three schools before graduating from the University of Virginia in 1852. Cousin John C. Breckinridge found him a patronage job in the Coastal Survey, but Robert left in 1854 to study law. He opened a practice in Lexington, moved to Missouri, and then returned to become the Lexington city attorney.

Robert campaigned for John C. Breckinridge in his 1860 bid for the presidency. Despite his father's staunch Unionism and Kentucky's unique neutrality, Robert entered Confederate service and on July 5, 1861, was elected captain of Company B, Second Kentucky Infantry. Then, elected largely by the soldier vote, he served in the House of the First Congress. Usually a supporter of administration measures, Breckinridge sometimes differed when individual rights were concerned. He tried unsuccessfully to allow volunteers who were conscripted for additional service to enlist in any company, and he opposed some fiscal policies, such as the compulsory funding of Treasury notes.

Bored with legislative routine and often absent, in August 1864 Breckinridge asked President Jefferson Davis for a commission as cavalry colonel and permission to enter Kentucky to recruit and to form a secret society to hamper the Union war effort.

Captured in Woodford County on February 22, 1865, Breckinridge was sent to the Columbus, Ohio, state prison and was transferred in May to Johnson's Island. After his father's intercession, President Andrew Johnson authorized Robert's release when he took the oath of allegiance. In 1871 Congress removed an indictment for treason he had incurred in 1861.

Breckinridge's postwar career was devoted largely to the law and Kentucky politics. Usually a liberal Democrat, he served several years as a state judge and ran for attorney general on the William Goebel ticket in 1899. His election was contested, and he never occupied the position. Breckinridge died in Danville on March 13, 1915, and was buried in Lexington.

BIBLIOGRAPHY

Alexander, Thomas B., and Richard E. Beringer. *The Anatomy of the Confederate Congress: A Study of the Influences of Member Characteristics on Legislative Voting Behavior, 1861–1865.* Nashville, Tenn., 1972.

Breckinridge, Helen C. *Cabell's Dale: The Story of a Family.* N.p., 1980.

Klotter, James C. *The Breckinridges of Kentucky.* Lexington, Ky., 1986.

Levin, H. *Lawyers and Lawmakers of Kentucky.* Chicago, 1897.

Obituary. *Louisville Courier-Journal,* March 14, 1915.

LOWELL H. HARRISON

BREVARD, THEODORE WASHINGTON

(1835–1882), politician and brigadier general. Brevard was born on August 25, 1835, in Tuskegee, Alabama. Moving to Florida in 1847, he studied law at the University of Virginia and was admitted to the state bar in 1858. He was elected to the state assembly and was appointed adjutant and inspector general of the state in 1860. At the outbreak of war, he resigned his position and raised a battalion of four cavalry companies for the Department of Florida. In December 1863, Brevard's battalion, now the First Florida, was increased to five companies and he was promoted to lieutenant colonel. As part of Brig. Gen. Joseph Finegan's Brigade, the unit fought in the Battle of Olustee on February 20, 1864. Following this, Brevard was sent on an expedition to south Florida with Bonaud's battalion. Their purpose was to protect local inhabitants' property against plundering raiding parties and to collect cattle for the Commissary Department.

When the 1864 spring campaign opened in Virginia, Finegan's Brigade was sent to Richmond and participated in the Battle of Cold Harbor. In August 1864, Brevard was promoted to colonel of the Eleventh Florida Infantry. On March 28, 1865, he was commissioned a brigadier general, the last general officer appointed by President Jefferson Davis. Tradition has it that he was captured in the final days of the war near Saylor's Creek by Gen. George Armstrong Custer's command and imprisoned at Johnson's Island in Lake Erie.

After the war, he resumed his law practice in Florida where he died on June 20, 1882. He is buried in Tallahassee.

BIBLIOGRAPHY

Evans, Clement A., ed. *Confederate Military History.* 12 vols. Atlanta, 1899. Extended ed. in 19 vols. Wilmington, N.C., 1987–1989.

"Florida Heroes in War." *Confederate Veteran* 22 (1914): 157. Reprint, Wilmington, N.C., 1985.

Warner, Ezra J. *Generals in Gray: Lives of the Confederate Commanders.* Baton Rouge, La., 1959.

CHRIS CALKINS

BRICE'S CROSS ROADS, MISSISSIPPI.

Also known as Tishomingo Creek and Guntown, the June 10, 1864, Battle of Brice's Cross Roads, west of Baldwyn, Mississippi, was the scene of Confederate Maj.

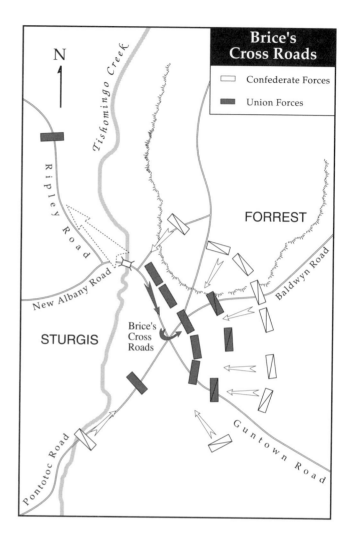

Gen. Nathan Bedford Forrest's most spectacular victory. Forrest's numerically inferior force routed Brig. Gen. Samuel D. Sturgis's Union command. Sturgis's advance was designed, in large part, to keep Confederate cavalry raiders, particularly Forrest, from threatening Union Maj. Gen. William Tecumseh Sherman's vulnerable supply lines as he drove toward Atlanta. Forrest had actually begun such a raid when the Union advance into northern Mississippi compelled him to return.

Sturgis's expedition started in Memphis, Tennessee, and consisted of a combined infantry and cavalry force of 8,300, with 22 pieces of artillery and 250 wagons. Heavy rains slowed the Union column and this pace concerned Sturgis. On the evening of June 8, he held a conference at which he contemplated turning back to Memphis. Meanwhile, Forrest dispersed his 4,800 men so as to react to any line of advance the Federals might take.

On June 9 Sturgis massed his army on the Stubbs plantation, ten miles from Brice's Cross Roads. Confederate department commander Stephen D. Lee planned for Forrest to engage the Federals near Okolona. Forrest, however, held a council of war and informed his commanders that he intended to attack the Federals as soon as possible. He anticipated that Sturgis would send his cavalry to seize Brice's Cross Roads and then hurry his infantry along the muddy roads to reinforce them once the battle had begun. In this fashion Forrest predicted he could "whip" the cavalry first and then defeat the exhausted infantry as they reached the battlefield.

Although Forrest had hoped to reach Brice's Cross Roads first, Sturgis's 3,300 cavalry, under Brig. Gen. Benjamin H. Grierson, had been up since 5:30 A.M. and got there ahead of him. Lead elements of Grierson's cavalry easily dispersed a small Confederate patrol; but, as the Union cavalrymen fanned out along the Baldwyn Road, they encountered more Southerners.

At the same time, Sturgis allowed the infantry to prepare for the day at a more leisurely pace. Finally, about 7:00 A.M., the infantry formed to follow their comrades. This delay gave Forrest the opportunity to defeat the Union cavalry as he had planned.

Meanwhile, the combat was becoming more intense as both commands dismounted to fight amid the thick stands of blackjack and dense undergrowth. Forrest arrived at the scene and assumed command. Although heavily outnumbered, he used a series of sharp attacks to mask his numerical weakness, keep his opponents off balance, and hold the initiative. He added regiments into the line as they reached the field, constantly maintaining pressure on the Union cavalry.

By 1:00 P.M. the rest of Forrest's men and his artillery had arrived. Brig. Gen. Abraham Buford paused on his way only long enough to dispatch Col. Clark S. Barteau and 250 men to move along the farm lanes in an attempt to get into the Federals' rear. Shortly thereafter, the first of Sturgis's infantry staggered onto the battlefield, exhausted from struggling through the mire, and feeling the effects of the heat and humidity. As the infantrymen arrived, they slowly began to replace the cavalry on the front lines.

Following a brief lull, Forrest unleashed his entire command against the Federals, including a small force on the Union right flank and Barteau's men on the Union left. The fighting continued relentlessly for more than two hours as the Federals slowly gave ground. Finally, with his own lines shortened and his firepower concentrated, Forrest ordered the assault he felt sure would win the day.

The Confederates surged forward along the entire line, and first the Union right and then the left gave way. The Southerners continued to press home their assaults with vigor. In the confusion of the battle, and under constant pressure from their opponents, any Union hopes for an organized retreat disappeared. Finally, between 4:00 and 5:00 P.M., the Federal line collapsed. To make matters worse, some of the supply wagons had crossed the bridge over Tishomingo Creek and parked on the east side. Thus, when the Union line folded, the panicked teamsters entangled the wagons and blocked the bridge, creating a bottleneck that added to the confusion.

The Confederates spent the next two days hounding the retreating Federals. Forrest personally led the pursuit, until, faint with fatigue, he eventually had to be helped from his saddle. Other Southerners maintained the pressure on their battered opponents until they were themselves thoroughly exhausted. Indeed, the Federals were so badly routed that at one point an exasperated Sturgis remarked to a subordinate, "For God's sake, if Mr. Forrest will let me alone, I will let him alone." By June 13, Sturgis had his wish, as his shattered army finally reached the safety of Memphis.

On the day following the battle, Gen. S. D. Lee called Brice's Cross Roads "one of the most signal victories of the war for the forces engaged." Forrest's loss of 96 killed and 396 wounded was proportionately heavier than Sturgis's, but he inflicted far worse overall losses on the Federals— 223 killed, 394 wounded, and 1,623 captured or missing. He also captured 16 artillery pieces, 176 wagons, 1,500 stand of small arms, and vast quantities of ammunition.

In the aftermath of the disastrous defeat, Sherman angrily observed to Secretary of War Edwin M. Stanton: "Forrest is the very devil, and I think he has some of our troops under cower." He vowed to send out two new commanders with orders to "follow Forrest to the death, if it cost 10,000 lives and breaks the Treasury." Nevertheless, Sherman's supply lines remained intact. Forrest had won his greatest victory, but it had proven to be of far greater tactical than strategic importance.

BIBLIOGRAPHY

Bearss, Edwin C. *Forrest at Brice's Cross Roads*. Dayton, Ohio, 1979.

Henry, Robert Selph. *"First with the Most" Forrest*. Indianapolis, 1944.

Wills, Brian Steel. *A Battle from the Start: The Life of Nathan Bedford Forrest*. New York, 1992.

Wyeth, John Allan. *Life of General Nathan Bedford Forrest*. New York, 1899. Reprint, Baton Rouge, La., 1989.

BRIAN S. WILLS

BRIDGERS, ROBERT R. (1819–1888), congressman from North Carolina. Born on November 28, 1819, in Edgecombe County, North Carolina, Robert Rufus Bridgers graduated from the University of North Carolina in 1841 and established a successful law practice. He also distinguished himself as a progressive planter, bank president, and railroad director. He served four terms as a Democrat in the House of Commons (1844–1845, 1856–1861).

Although frequently classified by historians as an original secessionist, Bridgers supported the Crittenden Compromise and did not become completely reconciled to Southern independence until after the firing on Fort Sumter. Elected without opposition to the First Congress, he was among its wealthiest members, owning over one hundred slaves and an estate valued at more than $200,000 in 1860. An expert in financial matters, he tried unsuccessfully to encourage cotton production as a basis for attaining a stable currency and establishing credit abroad. Although less supportive of Jefferson Davis's policies than the secessionists in the North Carolina delegation, he was generally friendly toward the administration, and he opposed the initiation of peace negotiations.

In 1863 he was reelected by a narrow majority over Edward C. Yellowley, the Conservative candidate, and was the only North Carolina Democrat to serve in the Second Congress. Although he frequently voted against administration measures during his second term and eventually came to favor a negotiated peace, he was considerably more pro-administration than most of the North Carolina delegation.

After the war Bridgers eschewed politics in favor of business, serving as president and general manager of the Wilmington and Weldon Railroad. He died in Columbia, South Carolina, on December 10, 1888.

BIBLIOGRAPHY

Alexander, Thomas B., and Richard E. Beringer. *The Anatomy of the Confederate Congress: A Study of the Influences of Member Characteristics on Legislative Voting Behavior, 1861–1865.* Nashville, Tenn., 1972.

Ashe, Samuel A. *Biographical History of North Carolina.* 8 vols. Greensboro, N.C., 1905–1917.

Powell, William S. *Dictionary of North Carolina Biography.* 4 vols. to date. Chapel Hill, N.C., 1979–.

Warner, Ezra J., and W. Buck Yearns. *Biographical Register of the Confederate Congress.* Baton Rouge, La., 1975.

THOMAS E. JEFFREY

BRIERFIELD PLANTATION. *See* Davis Bend.

BRISTOE STATION, VIRGINIA. This village,
eight miles south of Manassas on the Orange and Alexandria Railroad, was the site of an October 14, 1863, battle that was Confederate Gen. A. P. Hill's most stunning defeat of the Civil War.

By early autumn of that year, the opposing armies of Generals Robert E. Lee and George G. Meade faced each other again along the Rappahannock-Rapidan river line.

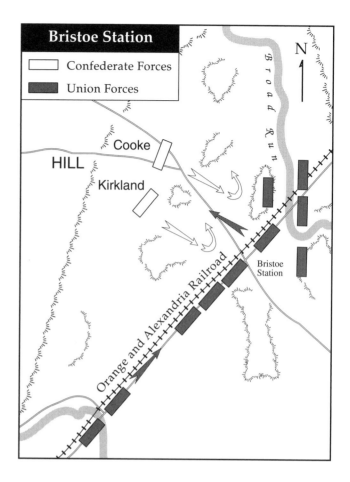

Lee received word that Meade had transferred two Federal corps from his army to duty in Tennessee. The Confederate commander decided to go on the offensive to exploit this weakness. Lee's plan was to draw Meade away from the vital road junction of Culpeper and sever the Federal lines of communication with Washington. As the Southern army began a circuitous march on Meade's flank, the Federals rapidly fell back to the north.

On October 14, Hill's corps from Lee's army arrived on high ground overlooking Bristoe Station. Below was a Federal corps, seemingly caught in a horrendous traffic jam as men, horses, and wagons were trying to get across a ford on rain-swollen Broad Run. Hill immediately ordered an attack on what appeared to be an isolated and disorganized Federal force.

The first mistake made by the still-new Southern corps leader was in not reconnoitering the area with proper care. Hill's second error, which reflected his inexperience at corps level, was in sending only two brigades into action against a Federal host several times larger in size.

The two Confederate units—North Carolina brigades under Generals John Rogers Cooke and William Whedbee Kirkland—rushed across eight hundred yards of open fields.

Too late Hill discovered that another Federal corps was also at Bristoe Station. It was posted along the railroad and squarely on the right flank of the attacking Southerners. Thus, massed Federals in a huge L-shaped line waited for two undersized brigades to charge into the angled line. It was one of the deadliest traps of the entire war.

The major fighting that afternoon lasted only forty minutes. Union musketry and artillery cut the attacking columns to pieces. A Tarheel soldier exclaimed that the Southern ranks "were mowed down like grain before a reaper." The Twenty-seventh North Carolina lost over half its men, including 33 of its 36 officers. Bristoe Station cost Hill almost 1,400 men killed, wounded, and missing, as well as five cannon seized in a brief Federal counterattack. Union casualties were fewer than 600 men.

Meade's army continued its withdrawal under cover of darkness. Rain was falling the next day when a shocked Lee rode with Hill over the battlefield. Southern bodies still lay scattered over the torn ground. Hill was trying to explain what happened when Lee uncharacteristically interrupted him: "Well, well, General, bury those poor men, and let us say no more about it."

Lack of supplies forced Lee to abandon his advance a few days later. The Confederates returned to the Rappahannock country and its rail connections with Richmond.

BIBLIOGRAPHY

Freeman, Douglas S. *Lee's Lieutenants: A Study in Command.* Vol. 3. New York, 1944. Reprint, New York, 1986.

Henderson, William D. *The Road to Bristoe Station.* Lynchburg, Va., 1987.

Humphries, Andrew A. *From Gettysburg to the Rapidan.* New York, 1883. Reprint, Baltimore, 1987.

Meade, G. G. *The Life and Letters of General George Gordon Meade.* Vol. 2. New York, 1913.

Robertson, James I., Jr. *General A. P. Hill.* New York, 1987.

JAMES I. ROBERTSON, JR.

BROADSIDES. Unfolded single sheets printed on one side, broadsides were a major means of popular communication in the Confederacy from its inception until its end. The dissolution of the Union was heralded in broadsides hastily printed in Charleston on December 20, 1860, immediately after passage of South Carolina's secession ordinance. From then on, the broadside was the medium of choice, and often necessity, for dissemination of the urgent, the occasional, and the ephemeral. In its final days, lacking both printing facilities and paper, the Confederacy almost certainly uttered its last printed words on a broadside.

Ranging in size from less than six square inches to a full newspaper sheet and, in the case of posters, even larger, the broadside was a convenient vehicle for news, proclamations,

"SOUTHERN RIGHTS."   Broadside with a facsimile of Jefferson Davis's autograph.   GORDON BLEULER

announcements, propaganda, advertisements, prayers, memorials, parodies, jests, songs, and poems. Readily produced on the simplest hand press and on any available paper, broadsides were turned out by even the smallest print shop. They often were struck from the form for a newspaper or magazine column, printed before or after the broadsides. Press runs varied from a few copies for friends of the printer to enough for statewide distribution. While announcements and advertisements were often posted, other broadsides were given away or sold (often for five cents or less) at print shops, newspaper offices, and bookstores and in the streets. In quality they ranged from fancy typography with elaborate borders and cuts in three colors on laid paper to the plainest type poorly printed on cheap newsprint or worse. In the later days of the war, they appeared on whatever paper might be found, including the backs of checks of failed banks.

Often the community's first source of war news, casualty lists, and government policies, broadsides also provided popular entertainment and literature. They were a common medium for ballads, satires, elegies, and other occasional verse and were the only printed outlet for more scurrilous or irreverent pieces deemed beneath the dignity of newspapers and periodicals. Aside from numerous song sheets, with musical notation, many of these broadside poems indicated the air to which they were to be sung. Early in the war, Henry Timrod's hymn to the new nation, "Ethnogenesis," appeared along with jaunty celebrations of victories and ridicule of Union politicians, generals, and soldiers; toward the end, defiant laments and elegies for fallen Confederates predominated.

Often unattributed, seldom mentioning place of publication, and almost never identifying its printer, the broadside was the ideal medium for surreptitious publication. In Union-controlled areas, it was the only relatively safe means of distribution for politically dangerous material. Maryland, where printing facilities and paper remained available but broadsides sympathetic to the Southern cause were expressly forbidden, was a major source of broadsides supporting the Confederacy, some of the most elegant produced anonymously by Baltimore printer Louis Bonsal, who openly published Union broadsides.

Although by nature ephemeral, Confederate broadsides have been gathered in numerous collections, offering a rich and largely untapped record of events and popular sentiments in the Confederacy.

BIBLIOGRAPHY

Hummel, Ray O., Jr. *Southeastern Broadsides before 1877: A Bibliography*. Richmond, Va., 1971.

Moss, William. *Confederate Broadside Poems*. Westport, Conn., 1988.

Parrish, T. Michael, and Robert M. Willingham, Jr. *Confederate Imprints: A Bibliography of Southern Publications from Secession to Surrender*. Austin, Tex., 1987.

Wolf, Edwin, II. *American Song Sheets Slip Ballads and Poetical Broadsides, 1850–1870*. Philadelphia, 1963.

WILLIAM MOSS

BROCK, SALLIE A. (1828–1911), nurse. Sallie Ann Brock (who became Sallie A. Putnam upon her marriage to Richard Putnam) was a volunteer nurse in Civil War Richmond and an ardent Confederate patriot. Immediately following the war, she wrote her memoirs, *Richmond during the War: Four Years of Personal Observations by a Richmond Lady*, published in 1867. In 1869 she edited a collection of poems written by various Southern writers, which she dedicated to the Confederate dead. In her memoirs, Brock described with sadness scenes of death and disease in Richmond hospitals, but expressed pride in women's ability to do men's work in this time of crisis. Brock wrote from the perspective of the planter class: she lamented the simpler diets dictated by war, the increasingly dilapidated appearance of Richmond, and the outrageous prices of French marino and mohair goods, balmoral shoes, and Irish linen. She did not blink at claiming that the pauper class suffered far less from the war than did the "salaried" classes because of food commodities provided them by the Common Council of Richmond.

Sallie Brock vividly described the "stony, calm despair" among Confederate Southerners that followed the surrender, and the general pandemonium that resulted from thousands of people evacuating the fallen Confederate capital. Like many stalwart Confederates, she remained convinced almost to the end that the Southern nation was built "upon a rock." After the war Brock moved north, where she continued to publish under the pen name of Virginia Madison, an inversion of Madison County, Virginia, where she was born.

BIBLIOGRAPHY

Brock, Sallie A. *Richmond during the War: Four Years of Personal Observations by a Richmond Lady*. New York, 1867. Reprint, Alexandria, Va., 1983.

Brock, Sallie A, ed. *The Southern Amaranth*. New York, 1869.

Jones, Katharine M. *Ladies of Richmond, Confederate Capital*. Indianapolis and New York, 1955.

Simkins, Frances Butler, and James Welch Patton. *The Women of the Confederacy*. Richmond and New York, 1936.

VICTORIA E. BYNUM

BROCKENBROUGH, JOHN MERCER

(1830–1892), brigade commander (1862–1863). Brockenbrough graduated from the Virginia Military Institute in 1850 and spent the prewar years as a prominent planter on Virginia's Northern Neck. The outbreak of war in 1861 prompted him to raise and equip a regiment from his neighborhood. Brockenbrough led this unit—which became the Fortieth Virginia Infantry—from 1861 until July 1863, at which time he resigned. Although he never rose above the rank of colonel, Brockenbrough commanded an entire brigade of Virginians through the desperate battles of 1862 and 1863 that forged the reputation of the Army of Northern Virginia as a peerless fighting force.

The pinnacle of Colonel Brockenbrough's career came with the performance of his troops at Chancellorsville in May 1863. But the resulting euphoria soon gave way to the despair of failure at Gettysburg in early July. Brockenbrough's Brigade was shredded on July 1, and the feeble remnants of that once-proud body of men were the first to collapse on July 3 in the famous Confederate assault. That misfortune was exceeded by the further disaster at Falling Waters, Maryland, on July 14, 1863. As the Confederate army withdrew across the Potomac River, Brockenbrough's handful of survivors found themselves encircled and eventually captured. The colonel was not present at the destruction of his brigade. A few weeks later Henry H.

Walker, one of Brockenbrough's subordinates, was promoted to brigadier general over the colonel's head. The implied rebuke prompted Brockenbrough's resignation, and he finished the war as an officer of reserves.

Brockenbrough divided his time after the war between the Northern Neck and Richmond, where he died in 1892.

BIBLIOGRAPHY

Compiled Military Service Records. John Mercer Brockenbrough. Microcopy M324, Roll 853. Record Group 109. National Archives, Washington, D.C.

Krick, Robert E. L. *40th Virginia Infantry*. Lynchburg, Va., 1985.

ROBERT E. L. KRICK

BROCKENBROUGH, JOHN WHITE (1806–1877), peace commissioner, congressman from Virginia, and judge.

Born in Hanover County, Virginia, Brockenbrough was educated at the College of William and Mary, the University of Virginia, and law school in Winchester, Virginia. Admitted to the bar in 1827, he served as commonwealth attorney in Hanover but soon moved to Lexington, Virginia. Brockenbrough was active in Democratic politics and accepted appointment by President James K. Polk as federal judge for the Western District of Virginia. Before the war he operated his own law school in Lexington and sat on the board of Washington College. He was defeated for the Democratic gubernatorial nomination in 1858 and, as an avowed secessionist, lost in his bid for election to the state convention in 1861.

In February 1861, however, he was one of five peace commissioners sent by the Virginia legislature to Washington to try to avert war. After hostilities began, he was elected to the Provisional Congress and sat on its Judiciary Committee. Brockenbrough endorsed the Davis administration's major programs for prosecuting the war. He chose not to seek election to the Regular Congress but instead became Confederate judge for the same district he had presided over before the war—that part of the state that became West Virginia in 1863. In that capacity, he worked vigorously to establish Confederate rule in an unwilling district that was soon overrun by Federal armies.

After Appomattox he reopened his law school in Lexington and, serving as rector of the trustees of Washington College, helped persuade Robert E. Lee to become its president. Brockenbrough died on February 20, 1877.

BIBLIOGRAPHY

Graves, C. A. "Judge John W. Brockenbrough." *Virginia Law Register* 2 (1896–1897): 157–160.

Laughlin, Charles V. "John White Brockenbrough." In *Legal Education in Virginia, 1779–1979: A Biographical Approach.* Edited by W. Hamilton Bryson. Charlottesville, Va., 1982.

Paxton, Matthew W., Jr. "A Judge's School: A Brief Biography of John White Brockenbrough." *Rockbridge Historical Society Proceedings* 8 (1970–1974): 85–104.

Wakelyn, Jon L. *Biographical Dictionary of the Confederacy.* Edited by Frank E. Vandiver. Westport, Conn., 1977.

Warner, Ezra J., and W. Buck Yearns. *Biographical Register of the Confederate Congress.* Baton Rouge, La., 1975.

NELSON D. LANKFORD

BROOKE, JOHN MERCER (1826–1906), naval officer.

Born at Fort Brooke (present-day Tampa), Florida, Brooke joined the U.S. Navy as a midshipman in 1841, graduated from the Naval Academy in 1847, and was promoted to lieutenant in 1855. As a young naval officer, he invented deep-sea sounding leads that eventually made possible the laying of an Atlantic cable.

In April 1861, Brooke resigned his commission when Virginia seceded. He joined the Confederate navy as a lieutenant, and a June meeting with Secretary of the Navy Stephen R. Mallory led to his appointment to supervise work on armor and guns for CSS *Virginia*. His achievements are surprising, given his youth and lack of experience in these areas. Brooke was responsible for *Virginia's* slanted armor casemate, copied in other Confederate ironclads, as well as the idea of extensions of bow and stern under water. Friction between Brooke and constructor John D. Porter, who claimed credit for the ironclad's design, contributed to his subsequent lack of interest in the ironclad program.

In September 1862, Brooke was promoted to commander. In March 1863, he was named chief of the Confederate Bureau of Ordnance and Hydrography, a post he held until the end of the war. He designed a variety of ordnance for the Confederacy, including 32-pounder and 10- and 11-inch smoothbore guns. He is, however, best known for his double- and triple-banded rifled guns, produced in 6.4-inch, 7-inch, and 8-inch sizes. They were probably the finest rifled navy guns on either side in the war.

After the war, Brooke served as professor of astronomy, meteorology, and geography at the Virginia Military Institute from 1865 until 1899.

BIBLIOGRAPHY

Brooke, George M., Jr. *John M. Brooke: Naval Scientist and Educator.* Charlottesville, Va., 1980.

Brooke, John Mercer. "The *Virginia* or *Merrimac:* Her Real Projector." *Southern Historical Society Papers* 19 (1891): 3–34. Reprint, Wilmington, N.C., 1990.

SPENCER C. TUCKER

BROOKE, WALKER (1813–1869), congressman from Mississippi and judge.

Brooke, a native of Virginia and

a graduate of the University of Virginia, moved to Lexington, Mississippi, to open a law office in 1838. A member of the Whig party, he served in the state house of representatives in 1848 and in the senate from 1850 to 1852. He also served in the U.S. Senate, filling a vacancy from 1852 to 1853. In 1857 he moved to Vicksburg. Brooke was a supporter of the Union, and in the years preceding secession he opposed the growing power of the fire-eaters, believing they would lead the South into revolution.

In 1861, Brooke was a delegate to Mississippi's secession convention. He argued for cooperating with the Federal government and working out sectional differences within the Union. Eventually, however, he voted for secession when it became apparent on test votes that the ordinance of secession would pass overwhelmingly. As a last resort, he sought to postpone action by offering an amendment that would require the ordinance to be submitted to a vote by the people. Brooke's amendment was defeated 70–29.

Brooke served one year in the Provisional Congress at Montgomery as chairman of the Committee on Patents. While in Congress, he supported a strong central government for the Confederacy and suggested a valuable produce loan program. After leaving Congress, Brooke was appointed to the permanent military court of the Confederate States.

BIBLIOGRAPHY

Alexander, Thomas B., and Richard E. Beringer. *The Anatomy of the Confederate Congress: A Study of the Influences of Member Characteristics on Legislative Voting Behavior, 1861–1865.* Nashville, Tenn., 1972.

Warner, Ezra J., and W. Buck Yearns. *Biographical Register of the Confederate Congress.* Baton Rouge, La., 1975.

RAY SKATES

BROTHERS OF WAR.

BROTHERS OF WAR. From a white population of 5.5 million people, the South sent about 1 million males—the very cream of its manhood—into Confederate service. Rare indeed was the family without some member in the armed forces. Owing to the always-urgent need for manpower at the front, many Southern families contributed a startling number of soldiers to the Confederate cause. As examples: ten sons and five sons-in-law of the Bledsoe family in Mississippi wore the gray; Mrs. Enoch Hooper Cook of Alabama saw her husband, ten sons, and two grandsons all enter military service.

Locally raised units were often termed a "cousinwealth" because of the presence in their ranks of so many kinsmen, and war's heavy hand struck hard at many households as a result.

Eighteen members of the same Bell family served in one infantry company. In the course of the war, six were killed and five died of disease. All six sons of David Barton of Winchester, Virginia, were soldiers in the Stonewall Brigade. Two were wounded and two were killed, one almost within sight of his home. Four Timberlake brothers were compatriots of the Bartons. All four were crippled by battle injuries. Four Carpenter brothers from Allegheny County, Virginia, were members of an artillery unit named for the oldest of the boys. He was killed in 1862 and succeeded in command by the next brother, who lost an arm in battle. The third sibling soon struggled home with a bullet wound in his lungs. The last of the brothers lost a leg in the closing weeks of the war.

Like all civil wars, the American struggle of the 1860s tore asunder many family loyalties. This was especially true in such border states as Virginia, Kentucky, and Tennessee, which, sandwiched between North and South with respect to geography, society, economics, and politics, caused family ties to snap traumatically. Three brothers-in-law of U.S. President Abraham Lincoln were Confederate officers. Two sons of Federal Adm. David D. Porter served in a Confederate artillery battery. John J. Crittenden, U.S. senator from Kentucky, also had two sons, one of whom, George, became a major general in the Confederate army, and the other, Thomas, a major general in the Federal forces. Both men survived the war.

Other brother-generals were not so fortunate. William Rufus Terrill and James Barbour Terrill were sons of a prominent Virginia legislator. The former graduated from West Point; the latter obtained his degree from the Virginia Military Institute. William Terrill served in the Union army, became a brigadier general in September 1862, and was killed a month later at Perryville, Kentucky. James Terrill joined the Confederate army and became a brigadier general on June 3, 1864, the day he was slain at Cold Harbor, Virginia. A brokenhearted father collected their bodies, took them home, and buried them in a single grave. The headstone read: "Here lie my two sons. Only God knows which was right."

BIBLIOGRAPHY

Eaton, Clement. *A History of the Southern Confederacy.* New York, 1954.

Robertson, James I., Jr. *The Stonewall Brigade.* Baton Rouge, La., 1963.

Wiley, Bell Irvin. *Confederate Women.* Westport, Conn., 1975.

JAMES I. ROBERTSON, JR.

BROWN, ALBERT GALLATIN

BROWN, ALBERT GALLATIN (1813–1880), Mississippi governor, captain, and congressman. Unlike many more privileged politicians of the period who were educated at prestigious schools, Brown was educated in the

ALBERT GALLATIN BROWN.   LIBRARY OF CONGRESS

frontier schools of Mississippi. His father, a poor farmer, had brought his family from South Carolina to Mississippi in 1823 when Brown was ten years old. His early life on the farm created sympathies that earned him the reputation in Mississippi as the "poor man's friend." After studying at Mississippi College and Jefferson College, he read law and was elected a brigadier general of militia when he was just twenty years old. Soon he was elected to the state legislature and gained prominence by opposing the Bank of the United States.

A combination of his opposition to the Bank and his personal attractiveness helped him win election to the U.S. Congress in 1839. After refusing renomination, he became a circuit judge. Two years later he ran for governor on a platform calling for the repudiation of Union Bank bonds on the ground that they were not a debt of the state. He was elected by a large majority and served two terms during which he strenuously promoted education and help for the disadvantaged; he called for "a general system of common

schools, which should be open to all and at which the poor should be educated gratis."

Brown returned to Congress as a senator in 1848. There he actively participated in the sectional debates. He usually allied himself with Jefferson Davis but was a stronger advocate of resistance to national authority than Davis was. He denied that the Federal government had the power to prohibit slavery in the territories. Agitated by the war with Mexico and the policy on slavery in acquired territory, Brown as governor had summarized in a message his position on state rights:

> The power to legislate in regard to slavery has not been delegated, and therefore does not belong to the federal government, but remains with the States respectively. The question in the Territories, it seems to me, must be left, as in the States, to be settled by the people who inhabit them.

He declared in 1858, "It is futile . . . to try to compromise the slavery question. The difference between the North and South is radical and irreconcilable." He also advocated the United States' taking Central America and converting it to slavery. Before the 1860 Democratic National Convention, Brown wrote to Stephen A. Douglas insisting that the platform at the convention must recognize both slavery in the territories and that slave property was equivalent to any other property.

The views of Mississippi's two senators, Brown and Jefferson Davis, now diverged. Brown spoke of the "radical and irreconcilable" split between the North and the South, whereas Davis, who traveled to New England for his health in 1858, delivered speeches supporting a strong Union. The newspapers at the time expressed some surprise at the contrasting positions. One wrote, "Jefferson used to be a ranting fire-eater, now he is a Union shrieking conservative. Albert Gallatin used to be a mild conservative, now he is a ranting fire-eater."

Brown's position on slavery was indeed radical. He enthusiastically justified the institution, declaring that a society with two classes—white and black—was superior to one divided along the lines of wealth, inheritance, occupation, or fate. During Brown's tenure in the Senate, Davis introduced a resolution calling for "protection of Constitutional rights in a Territory." Brown sought stronger wording, and he proposed an amendment to Davis's resolution, calling on Congress to pass laws that would "afford to slave property in the territories that protection which is given to other kinds of property." Davis's resolution passed overwhelmingly; Brown's amendment received only three votes.

Brown favored immediate secession when Abraham Lincoln was elected in 1860. He declared unequivocally, "The Union is dead and in process of mortification, and nothing remains to be done but to bury the rotten carcass."

But despite his fire-eater sentiments, on November 22, 1860, at a conference called by Governor J. J. Pettus on the subject of secession, Brown initially sided with Davis and L. Q. C. Lamar in opposing a resolution to call a state secession convention. The resolution passed nevertheless, and the three dissenters then sided with the majority.

After Mississippi passed its ordinance of secession on January 9, 1861, Davis delivered a farewell address to the U.S. Senate, and two days later, Brown also resigned, saying but a few words, which were uncharacteristically temperate. After his resignation, Brown was elected to the Confederate Senate, but before he took his seat, he entered the Confederate army as a captain of the Brown Rebels, a company he had recruited. Assigned to the Eighteenth Mississippi Regiment, the company was commanded by Col. E. B. Burt and was sent to Virginia early in the war. It participated in the Battles of Manassas and Leesburg, where Colonel Burt was killed.

In the Senate, Brown headed the Committee on Naval Affairs. To ensure the survival of the Confederacy, he argued that the South's priority ought to be to "save the country first, and settle constitutional constructions afterwards." He introduced bills to restrict the production of cotton, draft all white men fit to serve, and free and draft 200,000 slaves. His committee proposed a volunteer navy for privateering. Stressing the honor and necessity of military service, Brown strongly opposed draft-exemption laws, which, he said, "stunk in the nostrils of the people." He denounced those who sought the security of government jobs rather than serving on the battlefield:

> While the young men of the country were day after day enduring uncomplainingly the hardships of the camp, parching under the noonday sun or wet with the dews of night, eating the commonest of food, wearing the coarsest apparel, aye, traveling barefoot over the flinty hills in the pursuit of the enemy, and content with eleven dollars a month, these clerks were quartered in snug apartments and employing their time in drawing up petitions for an increase of pay, and a consequent increase of comforts and luxuries.

Immediately after the war Brown dropped completely out of politics. In a letter published in 1867 in the *Jackson Clarion,* he seemed dramatically changed from the fire-eater of his Senate days. His appropriate role, he felt, was to keep quiet and not interfere in government. He accepted defeat, viewing the Confederacy as a conquered nation that must submit to its conqueror "as gracefully as possible." He urged the people of the state to "meet Congress on its own platform and shake hands" and claimed to be willing to "make the best of it."

In 1868, a controversy developed over a Reconstruction constitution for Mississippi, and a proposed constitution framed by a Republican convention was rejected by the voters. The document would have proscribed from public office every man who had had any connection with the Confederacy and who refused to take an oath swearing belief in the political and civil equality of all men. Brown and other influential Mississippians journeyed to Washington to consult with President Ulysses S. Grant. The president suggested removing the proscriptive clauses and submitting the constitution to another vote. Brown agreed that Grant's plan was the quickest solution and the best way to avoid "discord and disorder."

After the revised constitution was ratified, Brown again retired from politics to ride out the Republican administrations of Governors James L. Alcorn and Adelbert Ames. When Brown did speak out, he took a moderate and conciliatory position, advocating public education for both races, opposing separate black and white political parties, and encouraging black political involvement. He continued to scorn politics and refused all efforts to persuade him to run for office.

BIBLIOGRAPHY

Alexander, Thomas B., and Richard E. Beringer. *The Anatomy of the Confederate Congress: A Study of the Influences of Member Characteristics on Legislative Voting Behavior, 1861–1865.* Nashville, Tenn., 1972.

Cluskey, Michael W., ed. *Speeches, Messages, and Other Writings of the Hon. Albert G. Brown, a Senator in Congress from the State of Mississippi.* Philadelphia, 1859.

Ranck, James B. *Albert Gallatin Brown, Radical Southern Nationalist.* New York, 1937.

RAY SKATES

BROWN, ISAAC NEWTON (1817–1889), naval officer. Born in Caldwell County, Kentucky, May 27, 1817, Brown entered the U.S. Navy as a midshipman in 1834. His twenty-seven-year career in the U.S. Navy included active service in the Seminole wars and the Mexican War; duty on various warships including *Falmouth, Susquehannah, Niagara,* and the famous frigate *Constellation;* cruises to all parts of the world; a stint with the U.S. Coast Survey; and a tour with Matthew Fontaine Maury at the U.S. Naval Observatory. He was at sea returning from Japan when secession occurred. Upon reaching Boston, he promptly resigned his commission.

Brown was appointed a lieutenant in the Confederate navy on June 6, 1861. He was first assigned to assist the commanding general of the Army of the West in establishing naval defenses on western rivers. Under his direction, crews installed river batteries, mine fields, and obstructions at Fort Pillow and Columbus, Kentucky. He also supervised the outfitting of gunboats on the Cumberland River and the construction of four ironclad warships at Algiers, opposite

New Orleans, Louisiana. The ironclads were still on the stocks when New Orleans fell in late April 1862. A month later Brown was ordered to complete the construction of the ironclad *Arkansas* at Yazoo City, Mississippi. He was to take command of the vessel when completed.

Arkansas had been laid down at Memphis, Tennessee, but upon the approach of Union forces, she was towed down the Mississippi and up the Yazoo River. Despite serious problems in securing labor and materials, the Confederates completed the ironclad, and on July 15, she steamed down the Yazoo River. After putting to flight two Union vessels, *Arkansas* entered the Mississippi. Anchored in two lines between the Yazoo's mouth and Vicksburg were the squadrons of Union flag officers Charles Davis and David Farragut. *Arkansas* steamed down between the lines, inflicting severe damage on several of the anchored Union warships. The Confederate ship was also damaged but made it to Vicksburg safely. There she withstood additional attacks by the Federal ships including one by Farragut's squadron as it headed back downstream. *Arkansas* was later destroyed by her crew when her machinery broke down as she approached Union warships near Baton Rouge, Louisiana. Brown was not in command at the time, having left the vessel at Vicksburg on sick leave.

On August 25, 1862, Brown was promoted to commander. In the months after the destruction of *Arkansas,* he directed the planting of mines and the establishment of batteries. He also commenced building new warships on the Yazoo. Gen. Ulysses S. Grant's army threatened the Yazoo River valley in the spring of 1863, and Brown took command of a small combined army and navy force to defend the area. His men engaged Union troops attacking Fort Pemberton near Vicksburg. When that town surrendered to Grant in July, Brown was ordered to take command of the ironclad *Charleston* in Charleston Harbor, South Carolina. That ship and the other vessels of the Charleston Squadron cooperated in the defense of the port until it surrendered in January 1865. The war ended before Brown could assume another position in the Confederate navy.

After the war, Brown farmed in Bolivar County, Mississippi, and in the early 1880s he migrated to Corsicana, Texas. He died there on September 1, 1889, at the age of seventy-two. Brown was recognized by his fellow naval officers as unusually energetic—"a pushing man," one officer recalled. Another wrote that Brown was "not afraid of responsibility and there is nothing of the Red Tape about him."

BIBLIOGRAPHY

Getchell, Charles Munro, Jr. "Defender of Inland Waters: The Military Career of Isaac Newton Brown, Commander, Confederate States Navy, 1861–1865." M.A. thesis, University of Mississippi, 1978.

Still, William N., Jr. *Iron Afloat: The Story of the Confederate Armorclads.* Columbia, S.C., 1986.

WILLIAM N. STILL, JR.

BROWN, JOHN CALVIN

BROWN, JOHN CALVIN (1827–1889), major general and postwar governor of Tennessee. Born in Giles County, Tennessee, January 26, 1827, Brown came from a prominent family; his brother was governor from 1847 to 1849. He graduated from Jackson College in Columbia in 1846, read law, and began practice in Pulaski. Brown was successful and soon became locally prominent. Originally a Whig, he became a Constitutional Unionist. In 1860 he campaigned for that party and served as a presidential elector on its ticket.

Brown opposed secession, but when the Civil War began he joined Company A, Third Tennessee Infantry Regiment (called Brown's or Clack's Third Tennessee). Brown was elected the company's captain, and when the regiment was formed he was named colonel. In September 1861 the regiment went to Bowling Green, Kentucky, and Brown soon found himself commanding a brigade.

Early in 1862 Brown's brigade was sent to Fort Donelson where it was captured with the garrison on February 16. Brown was incarcerated at Fort Warren, Massachusetts,

JOHN CALVIN BROWN.   NATIONAL ARCHIVES

until exchanged that summer. On September 30 he was promoted to brigadier general, to date from August 30. On October 8 at Perryville, Kentucky, he was severely wounded while commanding a brigade.

When Brown returned to duty early in 1863 he took command of a Tennessee brigade that was eventually assigned to Maj. Gen. Alexander P. Stewart's division. On September 19 at Chickamauga, Brown was slightly wounded. Back for the fighting around Chattanooga in November, he temporarily commanded the division of Maj. Gen. Carter Stevenson (to which his brigade had been transferred).

Brown directed his brigade through the first part of the Atlanta campaign of 1864. On July 7, when Stewart was promoted to corps command, Brown was assigned to temporary command of his division. For two months he was shifted about, serving temporarily as commander of other divisions while their commanders were absent. On many occasions Brown had won praise, and throughout 1864 his superiors recommended his promotion. Stevenson called him "a gentleman of extraordinary ability," and Lt. Gen. William J. Hardee declared, "He will make an excellent Division Commander." On August 4, Brown became major general.

On October 8 Brown took command of the division formerly under Maj. Gen. B. Franklin Cheatham. Severely wounded at Franklin on November 30, he did not rejoin the army until April 2, 1865. He surrendered with the rest of the army at Greensboro, North Carolina.

Brown was elected to the Tennessee legislature in 1867 and served as president of the 1868 state constitutional convention. He was elected Tennessee's first postwar Democratic governor in 1870 and reelected in 1872. His terms are noted for mostly successful efforts to establish public schools, encourage economic development, and stabilize Tennessee's political and economic environment by reducing the public debt.

Brown spent his last years building and managing railroads. He died August 17, 1899, and is buried in Maplewood Cemetery, Pulaski, Tennessee.

BIBLIOGRAPHY

Bearss, Edwin C. "John Calvin Brown." In *The Confederate General.* Edited by William C. Davis. Vol. 1. Harrisburg, Pa., 1991.

Losson, Christopher. *Tennessee's Forgotten Warriors.* Knoxville, Tenn., 1989.

RICHARD M. MCMURRY

BROWN, JOSEPH E. (1821–1894), Georgia governor and U.S. senator. Born in South Carolina to a middle-class farm family that soon moved into the hill

JOSEPH E. BROWN.   LIBRARY OF CONGRESS

country of North Georgia, Joseph Emerson Brown completed his education at Yale Law School and then prospered in law and land speculation. In 1849 he won election to the state senate. He quickly emerged as a leader of the Democrats and in 1857 was elected governor. A skillful politician who understood the white masses of Georgia, he won reelection in 1859, 1861, and 1863. Generally a domestic liberal, in national affairs he became an ardent secessionist.

Governor Brown directed a strengthening of the militia and other military preparations, and after the election of Abraham Lincoln he warned against abolition, racial equality, and intermarriage as he championed immediate secession. When a convention of delegates was called to consider the issue, he refused to reveal the close vote between secessionists and cooperationists—those who opposed immediate secession and favored cooperation with other Southern states to win redress of their grievances. He ordered the seizure of Federal installations even before the convention formally voted to secede.

Following that vote on January 19 the governor worked forcefully to organize Georgia's considerable resources. He mobilized troops and equipment, but he did not fully cooperate with the new Confederate government, which was trying to mobilize the resources of a whole new nation. First, last, and always Brown was a Georgian, and he consistently defended traditional state rights, individual freedoms, and strict legalism against the encroachments of the Confederacy, no matter how great the emergency.

On April 12 the war began, and six days later, Brown called for volunteers. Thousands of new troops rallied but equipment was scarce, and Brown tried to keep departing Georgia troops from carrying weapons out of the state. He also attempted to maintain control of military units that were being integrated into the Confederate armed forces. This was only the beginning of his clashes with Confederate authorities.

But within the state Brown was a brilliant politician who understood his constituents in all their differences and variations from poor whites on up through wealthy planters. Most of all he understood the yeoman masses who would have to do most of the fighting and sacrificing, and in that respect he had clearer vision than President Jefferson Davis and his principal aides.

Early in the war Governor Brown worked hard to obtain adequate clothing and equipment for Georgia troops, and later he dispatched state purchasing agents all over the South and even abroad in chartered steamships, which often carried out state-owned cotton and brought back blankets, clothing, and medicine. He acted with equal vigor to look after the masses at home. He directed the state penitentiary to produce cotton cards so that thread could be prepared for spinning, and he also organized an efficient system for obtaining and fairly distributing scarce salt so that meat could be preserved. The governor also organized relief for the needy families of soldiers; during the last two years of the war his administration's heaviest expenditures went into an extensive and effective welfare system that assisted the yeoman masses bearing the main burdens of the war. Brown greatly increased taxes during the war, but he made the system more progressive by exempting many of the poor and increasing the burden on the rich. Neither he nor anyone else in the Confederacy, however, could control the raging inflation that was undermining the whole Southern economy. Brown restricted cotton acreage, and the teetotaler Baptist governor further boosted food production by restricting distilling, which was a booming business in his own hill country of North Georgia. Within Georgia, Brown ran an efficient operation; indeed at that level he was very likely the most effective Southern governor, the state leader who got the most out of his beleaguered people.

But Governor Brown could not or would not see the larger picture, and all too often he ignored or rejected the need for Confederate unity, the obligation of the individual Southern states to close ranks behind the central government in Richmond if the rebellion was to have any real chance of success. From the beginning he had chafed at Confederate control, and in April 1862 he challenged the Confederates directly.

At that time the Confederate government, desperately short of troops, enacted the first national draft in American history. Immediately Brown challenged this dramatic but necessary expansion of Confederate power, denouncing it as "at war with all the principles for the support of which Georgia entered into this revolution." He tried to maintain control of all state military forces, but the legislature gave him only limited support, and the state supreme court backed the Confederates. Grudgingly Brown yielded, though he continued to protest as he rebuilt his state military forces with men too young or too old for conscription. Each time the embattled Confederates later expanded the age limits of the draft, the governor waged the same noisy struggle first to hold on to his army and then to rebuild it with older and younger recruits. Also he granted draft exemptions to thousands of state employees, including militia officers, setting a precedent that made it more and more difficult to enforce Confederate conscription throughout the crumbling Southland.

Brown also led his Georgians in opposition to impressment, especially the requisition of slave laborers by the Confederate army. He stopped the imposition of martial law in Atlanta in 1862 and frustrated Confederate efforts to seize the state-owned Western and Atlantic Railroad in 1863 and 1864. He frequently criticized Confederate tax and blockade-running policies. His opposition to the Davis administration reached a peak with his denunciations of arbitrary arrests and the suspension of the writ of habeas corpus, and early in 1864 the war-weary legislature backed him on this issue.

The governor did not always resist the Confederates, but his opposition grew steadily and led to an increasingly bitter correspondence with President Davis. Brown had the support of some powerful Georgians like Vice President Alexander H. Stephens and his brother Linton Stephens in the legislature and former secretary of state Robert Toombs and a growing number of planters and other influential people, but his main backing came from the yeoman masses. These were his people; he had sprung from this sturdy stock, and he, not the old planter elite, knew them best. And yet finally, whatever his intentions, he led them down the road to ruin with his state rights extremism.

Even the invasion of Gen. William Tecumseh Sherman's mighty army in 1864 did not dilute Brown's resistance to the fading Confederate government. Just at the time Atlanta fell to the invaders in September, Governor Brown furloughed the ten-thousand-man Georgia militia to keep it from coming under Confederate control. This left his state even more vulnerable to Sherman's devastating march to the sea, and though he rejected Sherman's peace feelers, Brown was soon calling for peace as morale plummeted all over the state.

The Confederates made one last desperate move late in the war by calling for the use of black troops—Southern slaves—in the Confederate army with the promise of freedom for honorable service, and Brown ran true to form. He denounced the plan as another dramatic departure from tradition. Once again, in the last days of the Confederacy, he showed himself unable or unwilling to make the adjustments necessary for victory in total war.

Inevitably defeat came in the spring of 1865 when Robert E. Lee surrendered in Virginia in April and the last scattered Confederates laid down their arms in May. Union troops arrested Governor Brown who was briefly imprisoned in Washington, D.C. Soon paroled, he returned to Georgia and supported the Reconstruction program of President Andrew Johnson who pardoned him in September. Opportunistically Brown supported Radical Reconstruction and served as chief justice of the state supreme court for two years, but when that regime collapsed in Georgia, he swung back to the Democrats. He prospered as a lawyer and businessman and served in the U.S. Senate from 1880 to 1890 when he resigned. Four years later one of Georgia's most successful and enduring politicians died at his home in Atlanta.

BIBLIOGRAPHY

Boney, F. N. "War and Defeat." In *A History of Georgia*. Edited by Kenneth Coleman. Athens, Ga., 1991.

Bragg, William Harris. *Joe Brown's Army: The Georgia State Line, 1862–1865*. Macon, Ga., 1987.

Bryan, T. Conn. *Confederate Georgia*. Athens, Ga., 1953.

Escott, Paul D. "Georgia." In *The Confederate Governors*. Edited by W. Buck Yearns. Athens, Ga., 1985.

Hill, Louise B. *Joseph E. Brown and the Confederacy*. Chapel Hill, N.C., 1939.

Parks, Joseph H. *Joseph E. Brown of Georgia*. Baton Rouge, La., 1977.

Thomas, Emory M. *The Confederate Nation: 1861–1865*. New York, 1979.

F. N. BONEY

BROWNE, WILLIAM M.

BROWNE, WILLIAM M. (1823–1883), colonel, commandant of conscripts for Georgia. Born in County Cork, Ireland, July 7, 1823, Browne came to the United States in the 1850s. In 1857 he became a naturalized citizen.

Not long after arriving in the United States, Browne began writing for the New York *Journal of Commerce*. In 1859 he moved to Washington, D.C., where he was associate editor and then owner of the *Constitution*. Meanwhile, he had become associated with several prominent Democrats and with the pro-South administration of President James Buchanan. He favored secession and left Washington early in 1861 to go South.

President Jefferson Davis appointed Browne assistant secretary of state. For a few weeks early in 1862 he was interim secretary of state. In April 1862 he resigned the assistant secretaryship and was appointed a colonel of calvary and aide-de-camp to the president. Browne undertook several assignments for the president, many of which involved efforts to secure the cooperation of Georgia authorities with the Confederate government. On occasion he also commanded local defense troops in Virginia and Georgia.

In December 1863 Davis appointed Browne brigadier general (to date from November 11), but in February 1865 the Confederate Senate refused to confirm the appointment. This action was probably a senatorial slap at Davis.

After the war Browne settled in Athens, Georgia, where he farmed, practiced law, resumed newspaper work, and from 1874 until his death on April 28, 1883, taught history and political science at the University of Georgia.

BIBLIOGRAPHY

Coulter, E. Merton. *William Montague Browne: Versatile, Anglo-Irish-American, 1823–1883*. Athens, Ga., 1967.

Warner, Ezra J. *Generals in Gray: Lives of the Confederate Commanders*. Baton Rouge, La., 1959.

RICHARD M. MCMURRY

BROWNLOW, WILLIAM G. (1805–1877), Unionist editor, Reconstruction governor of Tennessee, and U.S. senator. William G. "Parson" Brownlow relished the role of scourge of the Confederacy. The career of this native Virginian and adopted Tennessean was characterized by a series of vehement, and sometimes violent, controversies. During his years as a Methodist circuit rider in the Appalachians his main talent was vilifying spokesmen of other religious denominations. Obliged by marriage to find more remunerative employment, Brownlow turned to journalism, which provided a fresh and larger outlet for his contentiousness. By 1861 Brownlow's slashing brand of journalism had earned his *Knoxville Whig* a circulation that surpassed that of all his competitors combined. By then he had also penned an anti-Presbyterian book, three anti-Baptist volumes, an anti-Catholic and anti-immigrant book, and one implacably hostile to the Democratic party.

Brownlow described himself as a "Federal Whig of the Washington and Alexander Hamilton school," and he opposed the doctrines of nullification and secession after 1832. He believed that slavery was countenanced by scripture, and he took the proslavery stance in a series of 1858 debates with abolitionist Abraham Pryne. But when the crisis came he said, "I am for the Union though every other institution in the country perish."

Anticipating an unfavorable verdict in the June 8, 1861,

Tennessee referendum on disunion, he helped convene East Tennessee delegates who unsuccessfully petitioned for separate statehood for their Unionist region. His newspaper supported the Union even after Tennessee joined the Confederacy, and though he never overtly called for rebellion, his was the only newspaper in the Confederacy that opposed the existence of a Confederate government.

Under threat of indictment for treason, Brownlow left Knoxville for nearby Maryville. Soon afterward Unionists burned five important bridges. Brownlow denied complicity but was suspected. After a time, on receiving assurances from authorities in Richmond, he returned to Knoxville, only to be lodged in jail. Confederate Attorney General Judah P. Benjamin felt obliged to honor earlier assurances, so Brownlow was allowed to cross into Union lines near Nashville on March 15, 1862.

Within two weeks Brownlow had begun a speaking tour of Northern cities during which he recounted to his audiences the Confederate atrocities visited upon East Tennessee Unionists. That summer he penned *Sketches of the Rise, Progress, and Decline of Secession,* better known simply as *Parson Brownlow's Book.* Within a few months 100,000 copies were sold.

Brownlow returned to Knoxville with Ambrose Burnside's army in September 1863, and the first issue of the *Knoxville Whig and Rebel Ventilator* appeared on November 11. In January 1865, at a closely supervised wartime election, Brownlow was elected governor of Tennessee by 23,352 votes to 35 for his opponents. As Reconstruction governor he imposed a "damnesty oath" that excluded former Confederates from voting. By ratifying the Thirteenth, Fourteenth, and Fifteenth Amendments, Tennessee became the first Confederate state to be readmitted to the Union.

Brownlow's election to the U.S. Senate in 1869 roughly coincided with the enfranchisement of former Confederates and the end of Brownlowism in Tennessee. Two years after the expiration of his term in 1875, the "Fighting Parson" died in Knoxville.

BIBLIOGRAPHY

Coulter, E. Merton. *William G. Brownlow, Fighting Parson of the Southern Highlands.* Chapel Hill, N.C., 1937. Reprint, Knoxville, Tenn., 1971.

Humphrey, Stephen. *"That D—d Brownlow" Being a Saucy and Malicious Description of Fighting Parson William Gannaway Brownlow, Knoxville Editor and Stalwart Unionist . . . .* Boone, N.C., 1978.

Kelly, James C. "William Gannaway Brownlow, Part I." *Tennessee Historical Quarterly* 43 (Spring 1984): 25–43.

Kelly, James C. "William Gannaway Brownlow, Part II." *Tennessee Historical Quarterly* 43 (Summer 1984): 155–172.

JAMES C. KELLY

BROWNSVILLE, TEXAS. [*This entry includes two articles,* City of Brownsville, *which profiles the city during the Confederacy, and* Battles of Brownsville, *which discusses the military actions there.*]

City of Brownsville

The seat of Cameron County, Brownsville is located on the north bank of the Rio Grande, approximately twenty-five miles from the Gulf of Mexico. The city developed as a trading center in the late 1840s immediately upriver from a fort that had been constructed in 1846 by American troops across the Rio Grande from Matamoros, Mexico. The fort, and after it the city, were named for Maj. Jacob Brown, who was mortally wounded defending the post from bombardment across the river at the beginning of the Mexican War.

Brownsville's population in 1860 was 2,734, of whom approximately 75 percent were of Mexican origin or descent and 10 percent of European birth. Most of the rest of the population had come from elsewhere in the United States. Because labor was inexpensive, slavery never took root in the Rio Grande valley. According to the 1860 census, there were only seven slaves in Cameron County, all of whom lived in Brownsville.

The city's antebellum economy was based upon the cross-border trade and on the military garrison maintained by the U.S. Army. But before the Civil War, Brownsville was never more than an insignificant border town, its development retarded by its isolation from the rest of Texas and by the limited navigability of the Rio Grande. Bars at the mouth of the river restricted commerce to shallow-draft vessels. Major cargo had to be hauled from Brownsville overland to Point Isabel on the Gulf of Mexico.

When Texas seceded from the Union, U.S. forces peaceably abandoned all federal positions in the state, including their installation at Fort Brown, which was evacuated on March 20, 1861. Troops of the Texas Volunteers under Col. John S. ("Rip") Ford occupied Brownsville and other locations on the Rio Grande. Gen. Hamilton Prioleau Bee replaced Ford in command of Confederate troops at Brownsville in January 1863. The city was headquarters for the West Texas Sub-Military District, which stretched inland along the Rio Grande from the Gulf of Mexico to Eagle Pass and comprised about 1,200 troops.

Brownsville's significance in the Civil War resulted from the combined effects of the blockade imposed by the Union navy and the city's unique location on the border of a neutral nation with access to the ocean-borne commerce of the world. Like other Confederate port cities, Brownsville was blockaded—after a fashion. Beginning in early 1862, the Federals positioned themselves off Point Isabel. (The navy was prevented from effectively blockading the Rio Grande by its shallow depth and by a stipulation in the

Treaty of Guadalupe Hidalgo, the instrument that made the Rio Grande the boundary between the United States and Mexico.) Rather than strangling Brownsville, the Union presence merely rerouted commerce across the border to Mexico, where, of course, the blockade did not apply. A flourishing pattern of trade developed that sustained the Confederate war effort in the Trans-Mississippi region and created several private fortunes. Cotton, the only significant Texas export, was drawn by wagon from all over the southwestern corner of the Confederacy to Brownsville, ferried across the Rio Grande to Matamoros, carted to the wharves that sprang up at the fishing village of Bagdad on the Mexican coast, transferred by lighter to vessels anchored in the Gulf of Mexico, and then shipped to the textile mills of Europe and the northeastern United States. Specie, weapons and ammunition, medicine, and other supplies moved in the opposite direction and entered the Confederacy.

This traffic was facilitated by an agreement that Colonel Ford negotiated with Mexican authorities in Matamoros and was orchestrated by three masters of the carrying trade, who placed their riverboats under Mexican registry after the war began—Charles Stillman, Mifflin Kenedy, and Richard King, the founder of the King Ranch. (The fluid political situation of Mexico, torn by factional conflict and distracted by the encroachment of the empire-building French under the leadership of Maximilian, added flavor to wartime life in Brownsville, particularly when losers in the latest turn of fortune took refuge there, but it did not materially hinder the flow of goods.) Thousands of ambitious people were attracted to the opportunities provided by the lucrative cotton trade. At times during the war, the number of inhabitants in the city swelled to ten times the 1860 population. As in any number of frontier boomtowns, law and order were frequent casualties of the explosive but temporary growth. Arthur J. L. Fremantle, a British officer who visited the area at the peak of its fortunes, concluded that "Brownsville was about the rowdiest town in Texas, which was the most lawless state in the Confederacy."

Brownsville's commercial contribution to the Confederate effort was limited by the greed and ingenuity of thieves and other opportunists and by the remoteness of the city from the heart of the South and the major theaters of war. This distance could be negotiated only by wagon trails; no railroad reached the city until after the war. Even so, it is clear that the Brownsville trade significantly aided the Confederate cause in the Trans-Mississippi theater. In one notable instance, Confederate troops in Little Rock, Arkansas, received a shipment of four thousand Enfield rifles that had been transported from England by way of Brownsville.

The notoriety of what became known as the "backdoor to the Confederacy" and a desire to forestall possible French designs on Texas eventually prompted Federal action. After

Gen. Nathaniel P. Banks's defeat at Sabine Pass in 1863 dashed his plans to invade Texas from the east, he sent some seven thousand troops to the mouth of the Rio Grande. They landed on the Gulf coast on November 2, 1863, under the command of Napoleon J. T. Dana, and moved promptly inland toward Brownsville. Rather than defend the city, an outnumbered General Bee decided to abandon it. Before departing for Richard King's ranch, Confederate troops pushed their artillery into the Rio Grande and burned other military equipment as well as cotton awaiting export. The spreading fire, which set off an explosion in the magazine at Fort Brown, destroyed a significant portion of Brownsville. Federal troops moved into the city on November 6 and undertook repairs. They were soon followed by Abraham Lincoln's appointee as provisional governor of Texas, Andrew J. Hamilton, who was prepared to govern the state from any toehold he could establish on its edge.

His regime was premature. In 1864, Ford organized a company he named the Cavalry of the West, comprising about 1,500 conscription-exempt volunteers, to drive what he called "a mongrel force of Abolitionists, negroes, plundering Mexicans, and perfidious renegades" out of the Rio Grande valley. To defend the Union position, Gen. Francis J. Herron, who had succeeded Dana at Brownsville, requested cavalry support from his superiors in New Orleans. He was instead ordered to evacuate the city. Failure to halt the contraband trade (the occupation merely forced the border crossing point upriver), the difficulty in maintaining a secure supply line to the Gulf, and the need to use their troops elsewhere induced the Federals in July 1864 to abandon Brownsville for the second time. Under pressure from Ford, Herron's troops withdrew from South Texas, except for a detachment left behind on the Gulf coast. Confederate troops reentered Brownsville on July 30, 1864, and remained in control of the city until the end of the war.

An attempt by Union forces to retake Brownsville in the spring of 1865 led to the last land battle of the Civil War. A month after Appomattox, but before the surrender of Confederate forces in the Trans-Mississippi Department, Federal troops under the command of Theodore H. Barrett advanced toward the city. On May 13, they encountered Ford's Cavalry of the West at Palmito Ranch, on the Rio Grande midway between Brownsville and the Gulf. The Texans routed Barrett's troops and drove them back to their position on the coast. When U.S. troops again attempted to occupy Brownsville two weeks later, they faced no opposition. The city had been abandoned on May 29 by Ford's unit, many of whom crossed the river to seek sanctuary in Mexico.

BIBLIOGRAPHY

Ford, John Salmon. *Rip Ford's Texas*. Edited by Stephen B. Oates. Austin, Tex., 1963.

Irby, James A. *Backdoor at Bagdad: The Civil War on the Rio Grande.* El Paso, Tex., 1977.

Kearney, Milo, ed. *More Studies in Brownsville History.* Brownsville, Tex., 1989.

Lea, Tom. *The King Ranch.* 2 vols. Boston, 1957.

Pierce, Frank C. *A Brief History of the Lower Rio Grande Valley.* Menasha, Wis., 1917.

GEORGE B. FORGIE

Battles of Brownsville

The keys to Federal border defenses in the lower Rio Grande valley of Texas were Fort Brown and its coastal outlet at Brazos Santiago. In April 1861, after the bombardment of Fort Sumter in South Carolina, Texas state forces under Col. John S. ("Rip") Ford captured the small Union garrison at Brazos Santiago along with several pieces of heavy artillery, several hundred stand of small arms, and thousands of dollars worth of government property. The Confederates then transformed the border community into a thriving port for shipping Confederate cotton across the Rio Grande. Agents transported cotton to Matamoros, where English and European ships waited with munitions and medicine, thereby circumventing the Federal blockade.

Brownsville became the focus of Federal military atten-

tion in 1863. Gen. Nathaniel Banks, with six thousand men under Maj. Gen. Napoleon Dana, landed at Brazos Santiago on the Gulf of Mexico on November 2. Twenty-four miles away in Brownsville, the few hundred Texan cavalrymen under Brig. Gen. Hamilton P. Bee withdrew, setting vast stores of cotton, gunpowder, and supplies ablaze before retreating. Four days later, Union troops occupied the city, closing that route for Confederate blockade running and beginning several months of occupation. Federal troops then advanced up the Rio Grande, eventually occupying all border towns up to Laredo.

In March 1864, a Confederate army of four hundred irregular cavalrymen under Texas Ranger Colonel Ford drove the Union troops back down the valley. In July, Ford and his troopers reoccupied Brownsville, driving the Union garrison to the coast. The Confederates then reopened the cotton trade with Matamoros. In September the Federals made an advance toward the city, but turned back after light skirmishing.

Entrenched Union troops maintained a tenuous hold at Brazos Santiago throughout the rest of the year, sending occasional raiding parties and scouts inland to skirmish with Confederate cavalry. On May 13, 1865, a five-hundred-man Union brigade composed of the Thirty-fourth

CONFEDERATE EVACUATION OF BROWNSVILLE, NOVEMBER 2 TO 6, 1863.   HARPER'S PICTORIAL HISTORY OF THE GREAT REBELLION

Indiana Infantry, the Sixty-second U.S. Colored Infantry, and the Second Texas Cavalry (U.S.) under Col. Theodore Barrett marched inland to retake Brownsville.

On May 12, the Federals occupied a Confederate camp at Palmito Ranch east of the city. The following day, Colonel Ford and four hundred horsemen who called themselves the "Cavalry of the West," aided by a battery of Confederate artillery partially manned by French gunners from Mexico, attacked the Federal column. The Union troops, expecting a fairly easy advance since the principal Confederate armies had surrendered over a month earlier, fled back to Brazos Santiago. This Confederate victory marked the last land battle of the war. Two dozen Federals were killed or wounded while eighty-five were captured. Ten Texans were also wounded.

The Battle of Palmito Ranch had no impact on the war and served mainly as an ironic parting shot for the Southern cause. On May 26, 1865, Lt. Gen. E. Kirby Smith, commander of the Trans-Mississippi, began negotiations to surrender his command, which officially occurred on June 2.

BIBLIOGRAPHY

Evans, Clement A., ed. *Confederate Military History*. 12 vols. Atlanta, 1899. Extended ed. in 19 vols. Wilmington, N.C., 1987–1989.

Ford, John S. *Rip Ford's Texas*. Edited by Stephen B. Oates. Austin, Tex., 1963.

DONALD S. FRAZIER

BRUCE, ELI M.

BRUCE, ELI M. (1828–1866), congressman from Kentucky. Eli Metcalfe Bruce brought an unusual entrepreneurial background to his service in the Confederate government. This experience made him an influential legislator who helped supply the new republic but whose labors ultimately proved unsuccessful in keeping Confederate finances solvent.

Born in Flemingsburg, Kentucky, where he attended school, Bruce moved to Maysville, Kentucky, in 1846 and clerked in a dry goods store. This business experience inclined him to other ventures, including pork-packing in Cincinnati and pig-iron manufacture near Terre Haute, Indiana. In 1859 Bruce moved to St. Louis where he set up a chain of packing houses, distributing meat along the Wabash, Missouri, and Mississippi rivers.

When the war broke out, Bruce represented Nicholas County, Kentucky, in the November 1861 sovereignty convention that led Kentucky out of the Union. He served as a member of the Executive Council of the Provisional Government of Kentucky. But he soon relocated to Tennessee, Georgia, and other spots where he became a major supplier to the Confederacy. During the war Bruce carried on a broad range of business activities, including purchasing blockade runners and exporting cotton in exchange for war matériel. He contributed generously to the Kentucky soldiers' relief fund.

In 1862 Bruce was elected to the First House of Representatives from Kentucky's Ninth District. He was reelected in 1864. In Congress Bruce focused keenly on the Confederacy's overwhelming fiscal dilemmas, challenged Jefferson Davis's efforts at centralization, and opposed governmental intervention in the South's economy. He unsuccessfully advocated curbing Confederate inflation by lowering the amount of currency in circulation. At times Bruce's speculative ventures—for example, his involvement in the Erlanger loan—left him vulnerable to charges of conflict of interest. "He put some of his own money in the loan," explain historians Thomas B. Alexander and Richard E. Beringer, "and got his hands slapped, albeit lightly, by a slightly indignant Congress." A congressional investigation, initiated by Bruce himself, exonerated him from any serious wrongdoing, however.

After the war, Bruce received a pardon from President Andrew Johnson. He ran New York City's "Southern Hotel" on Broadway where, according to tradition, no ex-Confederate, no matter how destitute, ever was turned away as a guest.

BIBLIOGRAPHY

Quisenberry, A. C. "The Alleged Secession of Kentucky." *Register of the Kentucky State Historical Society* 15 (1917): 15–32.

Wakelyn, Jon L. *Biographical Dictionary of the Confederacy*. Edited by Frank E. Vandiver. Westport, Conn., 1977.

Warner, Ezra J., and W. Buck Yearns. *Biographical Register of the Confederate Congress*. Baton Rouge, La., 1975.

JOHN DAVID SMITH

BRUCE, HORATIO WASHINGTON

BRUCE, HORATIO WASHINGTON (1830–1903), congressman from Kentucky. "In all respects," write historians Ezra J. Warner and W. Buck Yearns, Bruce "was probably an exemplar of southern sentiment in his state."

Descended from Virginians, Bruce was born near Vanceburg, Kentucky, and attended private schools in Lewis County and Manchester, Ohio, before embarking on a varied career as bookkeeper, postmaster, and teacher in his hometown. In 1851 he was admitted to the Kentucky bar, practicing first in Lewis County and, for much of his career, in Jefferson County. Though originally a Whig, in 1855 and 1856 Bruce represented Fleming County in the Kentucky legislature as a Know-Nothing. From 1856 to 1859 he served as commonwealth attorney for the Tenth Judicial District and, in 1858, joined Benjamin Hardin Helm, who later became a Confederate general, in a law practice in Louisville.

In the election of 1860, Bruce supported Constitutional Union party candidate John Bell and in the following year was defeated as a state rights candidate in a special election for Congress. In October 1861, Bruce attended the southern conference at Russellville, Kentucky, and the following month represented the city of Louisville in the sovereignty convention that led Kentucky out of the Union. He served as a member of the Executive Council of the Provisional Government of Kentucky. In 1862 Bruce was elected to the First Congress to represent the Seventh District and was reelected in 1864. In Congress Bruce generally supported the Davis government and voiced "mortification and almost despair" because his fellow congressmen were so negligent in attending sessions of congress. He served on the Commerce, Enrolled Bills, Salt Mining, Foreign Affairs, and Patents committees. In April 1862, he coauthored a special report on the surrender of Fort Donelson. In December 1864, Bruce submitted a resolution against a negotiated peace. He accompanied President Jefferson Davis in his flight from Richmond.

After the war, Bruce became a Democrat and served as judge for the Ninth Judicial District. He was professor of law and chancellor of the University of Louisville and later was appointed general counsel for the Louisville and Nashville Railroad.

BIBLIOGRAPHY

Quisenberry, A. C. "The Alleged Secession of Kentucky." *Register of the Kentucky State Historical Society* 15 (1917): 15–32.
Wakelyn, Jon L. *Biographical Dictionary of the Confederacy.* Edited by Frank E. Vandiver. Westport, Conn., 1977.
Warner, Ezra J., and W. Buck Yearns. *Biographical Register of the Confederate Congress.* Baton Rouge, La., 1975.

JOHN DAVID SMITH

BRYAN, GOODE (1811–1885), brigadier general.

Bryan, born August 31, 1811, was a native of Georgia, who was educated at the U.S. Military Academy at West Point. After failing one year, Bryan graduated in the lower third of the class of 1834. Unlike most of his contemporaries from the academy, Bryan resigned from the U.S. Army soon after graduation. He participated in the Mexican War as a major in state service and held rank of captain in the Georgia militia, but for most of the two decades before the Civil War, Bryan occupied himself as a planter and engineer.

Bryan's Confederate career began in 1861 as lieutenant colonel of the Sixteenth Georgia Infantry. After being commissioned its colonel on February 15, 1862, Bryan led the regiment through all the battles of the Army of Northern Virginia in 1862 and at Chancellorsville and Gettysburg. On August 31, 1863, Bryan was promoted to brigadier general and took command of a Georgia brigade

that had been commanded by Paul J. Semmes (killed at Gettysburg). As part of McLaws's division, Bryan and his brigade fought well during the Knoxville campaign and in the May 1864 battles in Virginia. Then chronic illness, which had plagued him for much of the war, took him out of the army on a long furlough that eventually led to his resignation in September 1864.

Bryan's performance as a Confederate military leader was neither of epic proportions nor unsuccessful. He was one of dozens of brigadier generals who displayed competence but not brilliance. After the war Bryan worked for the city government of Augusta, Georgia. He died August 16, 1885, and is buried in Augusta.

BIBLIOGRAPHY

Compiled Military Service Records. Goode Bryan. Microcopy M331, Roll 38. Record Group 109. National Archives, Washington, D.C.
Northen, William J., ed. *Men of Mark in Georgia.* Atlanta, 1910–1912.
Obituary. *Augusta Chronicle,* August 18, 1885.

ROBERT K. KRICK

BUCHANAN, FRANKLIN (1800–1874), naval officer.

Buchanan was born in Baltimore, Maryland, on September 17, 1800. As the child of a prominent Maryland physician, he enjoyed a comfortable life while growing up. He received a commission in the U.S. Navy in January 1815 and served initially under Oliver Hazard Perry. Buchanan was promoted to the rank of lieutenant in 1825 and commander in 1841. Four years later, Secretary of the Navy George Bancroft chose him as the first superintendent of the newly created U.S. Naval Academy at Annapolis, Maryland. Buchanan served in the Mexican War as a sloop commander and later commanded Matthew C. Perry's flagship in the latter's expedition to Japan in 1852. Promoted to captain in 1855, Buchanan then commanded the Washington Navy Yard.

He resigned his commission in April 1861 and offered his services to the Confederacy the following August. Confederate Secretary of the Navy Stephen R. Mallory issued Buchanan a commission as captain on September 5. His first major assignment was as chief of the Office of Orders and Details in the Navy Department, where he made all assignments of personnel, helped to formulate naval policy, and acted as adviser to Secretary Mallory. On February 24, 1862, Buchanan became flag officer in command of the naval defenses on the James River. Moving to Gosport Navy Yard, Buchanan made the new ironclad ram CSS *Virginia* (formerly USS *Merrimack*) his flagship.

Buchanan took *Virginia* into Hampton Roads on March 8, 1862, to attack the Federal squadron there. His first target was the frigate *Cumberland.* After exchanging

FRANKLIN BUCHANAN. Photograph by Mathew Brady, taken some time between 1855 and 1861.

NAVAL HISTORICAL CENTER, WASHINGTON, D.C.

broadsides with this adversary, *Virginia* rammed it. *Cumberland* began sinking and threatened to take *Virginia* down with it because the ironclad's ram was stuck in its hull. Fortunately for the Confederates, the ram broke off, and the ship was freed to continue the attack. Buchanan turned *Virginia* toward the frigate *Congress,* whose captain ran the ship aground to avoid being rammed. An hour's pounding by *Virginia*'s cannons set *Congress* afire and killed and wounded dozens of its crew. The Federal captain then struck his colors and surrendered. Because fire from Federal shore batteries and sharpshooters prevented Buchanan from receiving the surrender, he ordered his gunners to destroy *Congress.* While supervising this destruction, Buchanan was wounded in the thigh by a rifle bullet. Subsequently, he yielded command of the operation to Lt. Catesby Jones.

Buchanan's wound prevented him from participating in the famous confrontation on the following day between *Virginia* and the Federal ironclad *Monitor.* He convalesced

first at Norfolk and later moved to Greensboro, North Carolina. The Confederate Congress confirmed Buchanan's appointment as admiral on August 21, 1862, making him the ranking officer in the Confederate navy. In September, Mallory assigned Buchanan to command the naval forces in Mobile Bay, Alabama, hoping he would be more active and aggressive than his predecessor, Capt. Victor M. Randolph, had been. At Mobile, Buchanan won the respect not only of his command but of the army officers as well. This resulted in a spirit of cooperation between the two branches not found in other areas of the Confederacy.

Under Buchanan's command, the Mobile squadron had as its primary goal the defense of Mobile Bay rather than the breaking of the Union blockade. Buchanan had under him at first *Baltic,* a weak ironclad, and three wooden gunboats, *Morgan, Gaines,* and *Selma.* Work on two ironclad floating batteries, *Huntsville* and *Tuscaloosa,* and an ironclad ram, *Tennessee,* had begun at Selma, Alabama, that fall. Construction of a second ironclad ram, the sidewheeler *Nashville,* had commenced at Montgomery, Alabama, at about the same time. Buchanan had *Tennessee, Huntsville,* and *Tuscaloosa,* all of which were launched in February 1863, brought to the Mobile Navy Yard to receive their machinery, armament, crews, and iron plating. In June, *Nashville* reached the city to go through the same process of completion. The admiral kept his gunboats in the lower bay near Fort Morgan, Fort Gaines, and Fort Powell to help guard the bay entrances while he pushed for completion of the ironclads.

Buchanan had to endure delays in getting the work done and problems in obtaining cannon, armor plating, and seamen. These difficulties meant that the two ironclads would not reach completion that summer as Buchanan had hoped. When *Tennessee* was finally commissioned February 16, 1864, Buchanan ordered it taken into Mobile Bay, but the ironclad's deep draft prevented it from passing over the Dog River bar. Workmen constructed camels (wooden caissons), which they used to raise the ship and float it over the bar on May 18. Four days later, Buchanan shifted his flag from *Baltic* to *Tennessee.* Later that month, he planned an attack on the Union blockading fleet. *Tennessee* ran aground near Fort Morgan, delaying the strike, and Buchanan soon canceled the offensive because he considered the Federals too strong for his little squadron.

On August 5, 1864, Union Adm. David Farragut led his fleet against the Confederate forts and warships in the Battle of Mobile Bay. The superior Federal vessels quickly dispersed or destroyed the Confederate wooden gunboats, leaving *Tennessee* to face Farragut's squadron alone. Almost all the Union ships joined in the fray. Three gunboats rammed *Tennessee* but caused little damage. Buchanan, however, suffered a broken leg when an enemy shell knocked loose a port cover and it struck him. The

Federal fire cut *Tennessee*'s steering chains, making it impossible for the crew to change its position. When the ram's smokestack was shot away, the ship filled with smoke, and the crew could not answer the increasing hail of enemy shells. Commander James D. Johnston received Buchanan's permission to surrender the ironclad after an hour-long engagement.

Buchanan was taken to Fort Lafayette, New York, where he was held prisoner until February 1865. After his exchange, he was reassigned to Mobile but did not reach the city before its surrender in mid-April. Buchanan participated in the surrender of the Department of Alabama, Mississippi, and East Louisiana on May 8, 1865.

After the war, Buchanan returned to his home in Maryland. He served as president of Maryland Agricultural College, which later became the University of Maryland, for one year. He then retired to his home at Easton, where he lived until his death on May 11, 1874.

BIBLIOGRAPHY

Bergeron, Arthur W., Jr. "Franklin Buchanan." In *Dictionary of American Military Biography*. Edited by Roger E. Spiller. Vol. 1. Westport, Conn., 1984.

Lewis, Charles L. *Admiral Franklin Buchanan: Fearless Man of Action*. Baltimore, 1929.

Still, William N., Jr. *Iron Afloat: The Story of the Confederate Armorclads*. Nashville, Tenn., 1971.

Todorich, Charles M. "Franklin Buchanan: Symbol for Two Navies." In *Captains of the Old Steam Navy: Makers of the American Naval Tradition, 1840–1880*. Edited by James C. Bradford. Annapolis, Md., 1986.

Wells, Tom H. *The Confederate Navy: A Study in Organization*. University, Ala., 1971.

ARTHUR W. BERGERON, JR.

BUCKLAND MILLS, VIRGINIA.

Eight miles east of Warrenton, Buckland Mills was the scene of a cavalry battle on October 19, 1863, between the divisions of J. E. B. Stuart and Hugh Judson Kilpatrick. Kilpatrick's Third Division was thoroughly routed by Wade Hampton's and Fitzhugh Lee's divisions, with the Union force suffering two hundred casualties to Stuart's thirty.

On October 17 Stuart, with Hampton's division, had moved as far east as the Little River Turnpike in Fairfax County. The next day, the Confederates began riding west along the Warrenton Pike when Stuart learned that Kilpatrick's division and six artillery pieces, with infantry, were on the move. Kilpatrick had been ordered to ascertain the Confederate positions, so he rode to Gainesville along the same pike. At Groveton the two forces met, and the Confederates slowly withdrew to Gainesville. At this point, Stuart and Fitz Lee, at Auburn (to the south), decided on a plan of attack for the nineteenth. Fitz Lee suggested that Stuart slowly retire before the Federals back to Warrenton, drawing Kilpatrick's division down the road. Fitz Lee would attack the Federal's left flank and rear once they had crossed Broad Run. Hampton was instructed to attack the Federal's front on the sound of Fitz Lee's guns. On October 19 Kilpatrick moved out at 8:00 A.M. toward Warrenton, driving Stuart's cavalry from Gainesville. At Buckland Mills, on Broad Run, the Confederates made a stand around 10:00 A.M. By noon Stuart had withdrawn farther up the Warrenton Pike to Chestnut Hill, about three miles west of Warrenton, and formed a line of battle, awaiting the Federal advance. Kilpatrick sent scouts forward at 1:00 P.M. to ascertain Stuart's position.

Kilpatrick then sent his Second Brigade, under George Armstrong Custer, to the front. Custer, in turn, put the Seventh Michigan Cavalry in the lead. This unit came within several hundred yards of Hampton's troopers, when Fitz Lee's Second Virginia, supported by the Confederate artillery, attacked Kilpatrick's left flank and rear. When Stuart heard the cannon, he ordered Hampton's First North Carolina to charge the Union horsemen. "I pressed them suddenly and vigorously in front," Stuart wrote. Initially the Federals resisted stubbornly, "but once broken the rout was complete," as the Seventh Michigan was driven back into the rest of Custer's Second Brigade. This caused Henry E. Davies's First Brigade, coming up the pike, to be driven in as well. The Confederates pursued Kilpatrick's troopers, "at full speed the whole distance" from Warrenton to Buckland. One Union trooper wrote, "The scene was one of great confusion and distress." In the rout, Custer's division recrossed Broad Run at Buckland Mills while Davies's remained on the western side of the stream. At this point Fitz Lee's division occupied the bridge at Broad Run, cutting Davies's men off and forcing them to leave the road in order to escape. "This they [the Federals] did pell-mell, in great disorder and confusion, to save themselves the best way they could; but a great many were captured, killed, and drowned, and a number of their wagons and ambulances were also captured in their flight," reported Col. Thomas Owen of Fitz Lee's brigade.

As Custer was pursued up the pike to Gainesville, Davies was chased cross-country to the Hay Market Road. Near Hay Market and Gainesville the Confederates encountered Federal infantry, which had come up to cover Kilpatrick's retreat. After initially engaging the infantry, Stuart's cavalry withdrew at nightfall and encamped near Buckland Mills. As Fitz Lee wrote in his report, Kilpatrick "was easily misled, . . . [and] his command was routed and pursued until after dark." Kilpatrick lost 150 men and eight wagons, and some 50 Federal infantrymen were captured. Stuart's force suffered 30 casualties in the "Buckland Races," as it came to be called by the Confederates.

BIBLIOGRAPHY

Blackford, William Willis. *War Years with J. E. B. Stuart.* New York, 1945.

McClellan, H. B. *The Life and Campaigns of Maj.-Gen. J. E. B. Stuart.* Richmond, 1885.

Thomas, Emory M. *Bold Dragon: The Life of J. E. B. Stuart.* New York, 1986.

Wells, Edward L. *Hampton and His Cavalry in '64.* Richmond, 1899.

KENNETH L. STILES

BUCKNER, SIMON BOLIVAR (1823–1914), brigadier general and postwar governor of Kentucky. Born in Hart County, Kentucky, on April 1, 1823, Buckner entered West Point at the age of seventeen. He won the saber championship there and graduated eleventh in his class of twenty-five in 1844. He was teaching at West Point when he transferred to Winfield Scott's army to fight in the Mexican War. He was slightly wounded and breveted first lieutenant and captain. He returned to teach at West Point but transferred in 1849 in protest of compulsory chapel attendance. In 1855 he resigned from the army and went to

SIMON BOLIVAR BUCKNER.   LIBRARY OF CONGRESS

Chicago to manage the estate inherited by his wife, Mary Jane Kingsbury. In 1858 he moved to Louisville, where he organized the Citizens' Guard company of militia and in 1860 took command of the state guard, the pro-Southern state militia.

At the outbreak of the Civil War, Buckner supported neutrality, and when the state legislature went Unionist, he resigned from the state guard. Turning down offers of a general's commission from Winfield Scott and Abraham Lincoln, he joined the Confederate army in September 1861. On the fourteenth, Albert Sidney Johnston appointed him brigadier general, and with 4,500 men he occupied Bowling Green, Kentucky.

When the Confederates withdrew from Kentucky, Buckner marched to Fort Donelson and commanded the right wing against Ulysses S. Grant's advancing army. Surrounded and outnumbered, Buckner agreed with Gideon Pillow and fort commander John B. Floyd that they should break through on Grant's left and escape. On the morning of February 15, 1862, the divisions commanded by Pillow and Buckner charged and drove back the enemy, opening the way to evacuate the fort or assault the Federal flank and rear. Pillow telegraphed Johnston that the battle was won. Then, apparently assuming that the Confederates could rest and finish the battle the next day, Pillow ordered the men back into their morning trenches. Buckner appealed the order to Floyd, but Floyd upheld Pillow. When Buckner's men returned to their former positions, they were overwhelmed by advancing Federal troops and had to retreat still farther. After dark, Buckner, demoralized by the retrograde movement, inspected his lines and realized that his men were too exhausted to dig new trenches. "It was not your fault, my brave boys, it was not your fault," he declared. That night Buckner insisted on surrendering. Pillow wanted to fight, but he and Floyd fled and Nathan Bedford Forrest broke out, leaving Buckner to surrender. At daylight on February 16, he proposed a truce and his prewar friend Grant demanded "unconditional and immediate surrender."

Imprisoned at Fort Warren until August 1862, Buckner was exchanged and promoted to major general. During the Kentucky invasion he commanded a division in William J. Hardee's corps. At Munfordville, he had the unusual experience of advising Union Col. John T. Wilder on whether Wilder should surrender his 4,000-man garrison to Braxton Bragg's surrounding army of 27,000 men. Satisfied with Buckner's professional counsel, Wilder surrendered. On October 8, in the Battle of Perryville, Buckner skillfully deployed his artillery in an attack on Union Gen. James S. Jackson's division on the Union left, an assault that killed Jackson and forced his men from their position.

From December 1862 to April 1863, Buckner commanded the Department of the Gulf. Then, on May 12, 1863, he assumed command of the Department of East Tennessee. In late August, Bragg ordered him to evacuate Knoxville before the advancing army of Ambrose Burnside, which outnumbered Buckner's force. In the Battle of Chickamauga, on September 20, 1863, he commanded a corps in James Longstreet's left wing. In the late afternoon Buckner led his men in a frontal assault on the log breastworks on Snodgrass Hill, a position that seemed almost impregnable. They drove the enemy from their trenches and into the ravines beyond, where large numbers were captured. Subsequently, when Bragg failed to capitalize on the advantage and lost golden opportunities in the Chattanooga campaign, Buckner signed the petition demanding Bragg's removal.

After convalescing from an illness, Buckner served in several temporary assignments and on March 8, 1864, once again took over the Department of East Tennessee. On April 28, he was ordered to the Trans-Mississippi Department, where E. Kirby Smith recommended him for promotion to lieutenant general, effective September 20. Smith appointed him commander of the District of West Louisiana.

When the war ended, the War Department restricted him to Louisiana. He engaged in business in New Orleans before finally going home in 1868. Wealthy and influential, he was elected Democratic governor of Kentucky in 1887 and served four years with honesty and efficiency. In 1896 he ran for vice president for the Gold Democrat party. He died January 8, 1914, near Munfordville and is buried in Frankfort, Kentucky.

BIBLIOGRAPHY

Harrison, Lowell. "Simon Bolivar Buckner: A Profile." *Civil War Times Illustrated* 16 (February 1978): 36–45.
Stickles, Arndt M. *Simon Bolivar Buckner: Borderland Knight.* Chapel Hill, N.C., 1940.

JAMES A. RAMAGE

BUFORD, ABRAHAM (1820–1884), brigadier general. Buford was born in Woodford County, Kentucky, on January 18, 1820. After attending Centre College in Kentucky, he enrolled in the U.S. Military Academy and graduated fifty-first in the class of 1841. After service in Kansas and Iowa, he fought in the Mexican War and was promoted to brevet captain for gallantry at the Battle of Buena Vista. He resigned his commission in 1854 and returned to Kentucky, where he raised cattle and thoroughbred horses.

Buford did not become involved in the war until Gen. Braxton Bragg's Kentucky campaign in 1862. Joining the Confederate army, he was appointed a brigadier general September 2, 1862, and fought in the Vicksburg campaign at Champion's Hill.

On March 2, 1864, Buford became part of Maj. Gen. Nathan Bedford Forrest's cavalry corps. During that year, he served with distinction at Brice's Cross Roads and Tupelo and participated in the Johnsonville raid in November. At Brice's Cross Roads, the 300-pound general continued the pursuit of the routed Union forces when Forrest was overcome with fatigue and had to be helped from his saddle. On December 24, 1864, during the rearguard fighting to protect Gen. John Bell Hood's retreating Army of Tennessee, Buford was badly wounded and relinquished his command.

Following the war, Buford returned to his farm and the stock raising for which he had achieved some fame. In 1879, he served a term in the Kentucky legislature and was for a time president of the Richmond and Danville Railroad. Grief-stricken by the loss of his wife and son, and suffering financial reverses that cost him his home, Buford committed suicide at Danville, Indiana, on June 9, 1884.

BIBLIOGRAPHY

Bearss, Edwin C. *Forrest at Brice's Cross Roads.* Dayton, Ohio, 1979.
Henry, Robert Selph. *"First with the Most" Forrest.* Indianapolis, 1944.
Johnson, Allen, and Dumas Malone, eds. *Dictionary of American Biography.* New York, 1937–1964.
Wills, Brian Steel. *A Battle from the Start: The Life of Nathan Bedford Forrest.* New York, 1992.
Wyeth, John Allan. *Life of General Nathan Bedford Forrest.* New York, 1899. Reprint, Baton Rouge, La., 1989.

BRIAN S. WILLS

BULLOCH, JAMES DUNWOODY (1823–1901), naval agent in Europe. Bulloch was born near Savannah, Georgia, of a distinguished Southern maritime family—his half-sister became the mother of Theodore Roosevelt. He went to sea at an early age, became a midshipman in the U.S. Navy in 1839, served briefly in California during the Mexican War, and then commanded naval and commercial mail steamers. After a naval career of some fourteen years he resigned his commission in 1854 for personal reasons. By the outbreak of war in 1861, he was an experienced and competent sea captain familiar with a wide range of nautical skills and "completely identified with the shipping interests of New York." Soon after the firing on Fort Sumter, however, he offered his services to the South. Secretary of the Navy Stephen R. Mallory sent him to Europe to buy and build a navy for the new nation.

Bulloch arrived in Liverpool, England, in June 1861 with a daring three-part plan designed to build a navy for an unrecognized country with almost no seafaring tradition and only minimal support services for maritime activities. First, he was to buy or build for the South a fleet of swift and world opinion were beginning to tell against the South, he dispatched yet another commerce destroyer, a worthy consort of the first two. These ships dealt a deadly blow to the American merchant marine, one from which it never fully recovered. The careers of *Florida, Alabama,* and *Shenandoah* remain a potent reminder of what a small-navy power might do to a more powerful large-navy adversary.

During the war, after some months of divided counsel and administrative inefficiency, Bulloch took command of the program to put the most advanced products of European naval technology in the hands of Jefferson Davis. Such ships, usually subsumed under the name of the "Laird Rams," might have given the Confederacy a weapon with which to redress the naval balance of power between the North and the South. It was widely thought that these ultimate weapons of the time might lift the Union blockade and take the war to Northern coastal cities.

But such ships posed a more blatant challenge to British neutrality than either blockade runners or wooden commerce raiders. Their fate, therefore, depended on how Her Majesty's Government defined the rules of proper neutral conduct and the limits of lawful commercial enterprise. It was one thing to say, as a British court did in the case of *Alexandra,* that a reinforced wooden ship did not transgress the law and quite another to argue that iron-plated ships with gun turrets and a ram posed no threat to the Foreign Enlistment Act of 1819. If two such ships might go to the South, how could the crown prevent the departure of two hundred similar ships? In cabinet discussions of such matters it soon became apparent to Lord John Russell that it would be necessary to go "above and beyond the law" to halt Confederate efforts to build or buy a navy in Great Britain.

But before the government arrived at that decision, Bulloch put on a virtuoso performance of naval procurement. To do so he had to outmaneuver his Union adversary, Thomas Haines Dudley, the American consul in Liverpool. The duel they waged in the dives and dockyards of Merseyside did much to determine the outcome of the war in America, although given the wide disparity of resources that each commanded, the result had elements of inevitability. Still, before he was overwhelmed by his enemy's resources (and a growing circumspection on the part of the British), Bulloch achieved great things in the realm of international naval procurement and diplomacy.

After the war, Bulloch settled in Liverpool and became prominent in that city's commercial and cotton trade. When he died there in 1901, he was buried in Toxeth Cemetery. His Merseyside grave remains a reminder of the international dimension of the American Civil War and of Bulloch's role in it.

JAMES DUNWOODY BULLOCH.

NAVAL HISTORICAL CENTER, WASHINGTON, D.C.

commerce raiders that would prey on the North's merchant marine and distract its blockade of Southern ports. Second, he was to exploit the naval revolution of the mid-nineteenth century and secure for the Confederacy a flotilla of the most advanced vessels of war that British shipyards could produce. Then, somewhat later in the war, he assumed responsibility for procuring a fleet of government-owned-and-operated blockade runners to establish and maintain a European lifeline to the South. Seldom in history has such an important part of the fate of a nation rested so completely on the shoulders of a single naval officer.

Few servants of the South did more than Bulloch did to advance the Confederate cause in Europe. In the early months of his mission, he purchased *Fingal* and ran it through the Union blockade with the largest cargo of military supplies ever to reach the Confederacy. In early 1862, he sent out two immensely successful commerce raiders. Later in the war, when the forces of military defeats

BIBLIOGRAPHY

Bulloch, James Dunwoody. *The Secret Service of the Confederate States in Europe; or, How the Confederate Cruisers Were Equipped.* 2 vols. New York, 1884. Reprint, New York, 1959.

Jones, Wilbur D. *The Confederate Rams at Birkenhead.* Tuscaloosa, Ala., 1961.

Merli, Frank J. "The Confederate Navy." In *In Peace and War: Interpretations of American Naval History, 1775–1984.* Edited by Kenneth J. Hagan. 2d ed. Westport, Conn., 1984.

Merli, Frank J. *Great Britain and the Confederate Navy, 1861–1865.* Bloomington, Ind., 1970.

Parkes, Oscar. *British Battleships, 1860–1950: A History of Design, Construction, and Armament.* Hamden, Conn., 1971.

Spencer, Warren. *The Confederate Navy in Europe.* University, Ala., 1983.

FRANK J. MERLI

BULLOCK, ROBERT

BULLOCK, ROBERT (1828–1905), brigadier general and U.S. congressman. Born in Greenville, North Carolina, December 8, 1828, Bullock moved to Florida in 1844. Settling near what is now Ocala, he was a schoolteacher and court clerk. In the 1850s he saw eighteen months of military service against the Seminole Indians.

In 1861 Bullock was elected captain of a volunteer company. In April 1862 the company became part of the Seventh Florida Infantry Regiment, and Bullock was chosen lieutenant colonel. Going with the regiment to Tennessee that summer, he took part in the Kentucky campaign.

After the retreat from Kentucky, the regiment garrisoned various points in eastern Tennessee. On June 3, 1863, Bullock was promoted to colonel. After playing a gallant role at Chickamauga, Bullock and his men were posted in the Confederate line at Missionary Ridge. On November 25, when the Federals overran that position, Bullock was captured.

Exchanged in 1864, Bullock returned to the army for the Atlanta campaign. When the brigade commander was wounded, Bullock took his place. In early August Bullock was severely wounded. Returning to duty in time for the Franklin and Nashville campaign, he was slightly wounded at Franklin. A third wound, received near Murfreesboro, Tennessee, December 4, disabled him from further duty. On January 17, 1865, he was promoted to brigadier general, with date of rank set at November 29, 1864.

Returning to Florida after the war, Bullock became a lawyer and served in judicial and political offices, including the U.S. House of Representatives (1889–1893). He died July 27, 1905, and is buried in Evergreen Cemetery in Ocala.

BIBLIOGRAPHY

Bergeron, Arthur L. "Robert Bullock." In *The Confederate General.* Edited by William C. Davis. Vol. 1. Harrisburg, Pa., 1991.

Connelly, Thomas L. *Army of the Heartland: The Army of Tennessee, 1861–1862.* Baton Rouge, La., 1967.

Connelly, Thomas L. *Autumn of Glory: The Army of Tennessee, 1862–1865.* Baton Rouge, La., 1971.

Evans, Clement A., ed. *Confederate Military History.* 12 vols. Atlanta, 1899. Extended ed. in 19 vols. Wilmington, N.C., 1987–1989.

RICHARD M. MCMURRY

BULL RUN, VIRGINIA. *For discussion of the two battles fought at Bull Run, see* Manassas, First; Manassas, Second.

BUMMERS. This term, probably from the German *bummler,* or "loafer," was applied, by Federals and Confederates alike, to the foragers of William Tecumseh Sherman's army on its March to the Sea from Atlanta and then northward through the Carolinas in the winter of 1864–1865. One veteran painted a verbal portrait of a bummer: "Fancy a ragged man . . . stealing his way through the pine forests far out on the flanks of a column. Keen on the scent of rebels, or bacon, or silver spoons, or corn, or anything valuable and you have him in your mind."

Initially, these foragers were selected from each regiment to do double duty as scouts and scavengers. Before dawn each day, they mounted horses (often taken from Southern plantations) and rode out on both flanks in advance of the army to secure supplies and to serve as a screen of mounted infantry that could provide advance notice of the approach of any Confederate force.

The foragers were ordered to avoid the destruction of private dwellings, the theft of personal property, and even the use of abusive language. But because they operated miles from their units, beyond effective command and control of their senior officers, they frequently ignored such orders. The term *bummer* was sometimes used to distinguish those who most frequently abused their authority, though within Sherman's army, anyone who served as a forager was a *bummer.* On the march through the Carolinas, the bummers made little pretense of attempting to protect private property, and they often burned whatever they could not steal. Plantation owners who tried to conceal their valuables discovered that the bummers were expert at discovering their hiding places.

So closely associated was Sherman's campaign with the activities of these foragers that they were given a place at the end of each brigade during the Grand March of the armies through Washington at the end of the war. They rode through the capital in their ragged field uniforms with chickens and hams thrown across their saddles and plundered booty covering the pack mules they led.

[*See also* Foraging.]

SHERMAN'S BUMMERS, 1865.

BIBLIOGRAPHY

Glatthaar, Joseph T. *The March to the Sea and Beyond: Sherman's Troops in the Savannah and Carolinas Campaigns.* New York, 1985.

Harwell, Richard, and Philip N. Racine, eds. *The Fiery Trail: A Union Officer's Account of Sherman's Last Campaigns.* Knoxville, Tenn., 1986.

CRAIG L. SYMONDS

BURIAL OF LATANÉ. An enduring icon of the Lost Cause, the history and genre painting *The Burial of Latané,* touched the hearts of generations of Southerners despite what may seem to modern eyes only stilted composition and crude rendering.

Its inspiration came on June 13, 1862, when Capt. William Latané became the sole Confederate casualty of J. E. B. Stuart's reconnaissance on the Virginia peninsula. Latane's body was taken to a nearby plantation for burial. When enemy forces barred a local clergyman from the scene, the resident women conducted a funeral service themselves.

The incident inspired a popular poem and then the canvas executed by Richmond portraitist William D. Washington (1834–1870). It showed a pious matron preaching the burial service in an Eden-like bower that suggested the sacred beauty of the Southern landscape. Women gathering about the coffin symbolized the enduring strength of Confederate womanhood. Blacks assisting with the burial gave visual prominence to the Lost Cause myth of slave loyalty. And a well-clothed child decorating Latané's bier contradicted reports of home front poverty. Most important, *The Burial of Latané* offered reassurance to anxious wives and parents that their loved ones in arms would be buried with dignity and respect wherever they fell.

Washington's "touching and impressive scene," in the words of one early critic, caused a sensation when first exhibited in Richmond. And an 1868 engraved adaptation, offered for $1.50 a copy by publisher William Smith of New York, became a huge best-seller in the postwar South, where it was advertised as a "beautiful and appropriate ornament for any parlor."

BIBLIOGRAPHY

Faust, Drew Gilpin. "Race, Gender, and Confederate Nationalism: William D. Washington's Burial of Latane." *Southern Review* 25 (April 1989): 197–307.

BURIAL OF LATANÉ.   An 1868 engraving by A. G. Campbell, after the painting by W. D. Washington. Photograph by Katherine Wetzel.

ELEANOR S. BROCKENBROUGH LIBRARY, THE MUSEUM OF THE CONFEDERACY, RICHMOND, VIRGINIA

Neely, Mark E., Harold Holzer, and Gabor S. Boritt. *The Confederate Image: Prints of the Lost Cause.* Chapel Hill, N.C., 1987.

Salmon, Emily J. "The Burial of Latane: Symbol of the Lost Cause." *Virginia Cavalcade* 29 (Winter 1979): 118–129.

HAROLD HOLZER

BURNETT, HENRY C. (1825–1866), colonel and congressman from Kentucky. Henry Cornelius Burnett ranked as one of the most vocal members of the Confederacy's "Kentucky bloc"—generals and politicians determined to recapture Kentucky as part of an overall concentration in the West.

Born in Virginia, Burnett came to Kentucky as a child and attended the local academy at Hopkinsville. He later studied law and was admitted to the bar in Cadiz, Kentucky, in 1847.

After practicing law and serving as clerk of the Trigg County Circuit Court, in 1855 Burnett was elected as a Democrat to the U.S. House of Representatives.

In October and November 1861, respectively, Burnett presided over both the southern conference and the sovereignty convention in Russellville, Kentucky. The November meeting established the Provisional Government of Kentucky which joined the Confederacy. Because of his active role in Kentucky's secession movement, Burnett was expelled from Congress on December 3, 1861. He was the only Kentucky representative ousted from office for his support of the South. The Provisional Government of Kentucky appointed Burnett a commissioner "with power to negotiate . . . the earliest practicable admission of Kentucky into . . . the Confederate States of America." He also served as a colonel in the Eighth Kentucky Infantry and fought at Fort Donelson.

In 1861 Burnett was elected to the Provisional Senate and served in the First and Second Congresses as well. A strong supporter of President Jefferson Davis, Burnett criticized Gen. Braxton Bragg's disastrous 1862 invasion of Kentucky and attempted to mobilize partisan raiders to liberate the commonwealth from Union control. One of the most active Confederate senators, Burnett served on the Commerce, Judiciary, Claims, Military Affairs, and other influential committees. Though he favored Confederate conscription policies, Burnett expressed concern over violations of state rights. In February 1865, Burnett endorsed the arming of the slaves as a military necessity.

Following the war, Burnett practiced law and worked to advance the Democratic cause in Kentucky.

BIBLIOGRAPHY

Quisenberry, A. C. "The Alleged Secession of Kentucky." *Register of the Kentucky State Historical Society* 15 (1917): 15–32.
Wakelyn, Jon L. *Biographical Dictionary of the Confederacy.* Edited by Frank E. Vandiver. Westport, Conn., 1977.
Warner, Ezra J., and W. Buck Yearns. *Biographical Register of the Confederate Congress.* Baton Rouge, La., 1975.

JOHN DAVID SMITH

BURNETT, THEODORE LEGRAND (1829–1917), major and congressman from Kentucky. Burnett followed the path of many Kentuckians in 1861. Though an old Whig and a Unionist, he nonetheless cast his lot with the Confederacy once President Abraham Lincoln sent troops into the commonwealth.

Born in Spencer County, Kentucky, Burnett graduated from Transylvania University and read law with judge Mark Houston. He joined the bar in 1846, served briefly with Kentucky volunteers in the Mexican War, and then practiced law in Taylorsville, Kentucky. In 1847 Burnett was elected attorney for Spencer County and then returned to private practice.

Once the Civil War broke out, Burnett joined the Confederate army, serving as a major on the staff of Gen. John Stuart Williams in the Army of Tennessee. In November 1861, he represented Spencer County in the sovereignty convention and declined the post of state treasurer in the newly established Provisional Government of Kentucky. He was elected from the Third District to the Confederacy's Provisional Congress and, in 1862 and again in 1864, from the Sixth District to the House of Representatives. Burnett served on the Claims, Pay and Mileage, and Commerce committees. In 1862 he urged an investigation into the Confederate debacle at Fort Donelson. Though Burnett generally supported President Jefferson Davis, late

in the war he began to doubt Davis's selection of high-ranking commanders. According to historians Ezra J. Warner and W. Buck Yearns, Burnett's unwillingness to invest the War Department with a broad range of emergency powers was "most unusual for a Kentucky congressman." (Generally they supported military measures that might result in the liberation of their state.)

After the war, Burnett practiced law first in Taylorsville and later in Louisville. In 1870 he was elected Louisville's city attorney and served many terms as a judge. His death in 1917 marked Burnett as one of the last surviving members of the Confederate Congress.

BIBLIOGRAPHY

Quisenberry, A. C. "The Alleged Secession of Kentucky." *Register of the Kentucky State Historical Society* 15 (1917): 15–32.
Wakelyn, Jon L. *Biographical Dictionary of the Confederacy.* Edited by Frank E. Vandiver. Westport, Conn., 1977.
Warner, Ezra J., and W. Buck Yearns. *Biographical Register of the Confederate Congress.* Baton Rouge, La., 1975.

JOHN DAVID SMITH

BURNSIDE'S EXPEDITION TO NORTH CAROLINA. This expedition began when Union Brig. Gen. Ambrose E. Burnside left Fort Monroe, Virginia, on January 11, 1862, with fifteen thousand men and eighty vessels of various descriptions. Subsequently, seventeen warships from the North Atlantic Blockading Squadron, commanded by Flag Officer Louis M. Goldsborough, joined Burnside's flotilla off the coast of North Carolina. The target of Burnside's expedition was Roanoke Island. Located behind the barrier islands of North Carolina's outer banks, the island provided access to the surrounding sounds and waterways of the state. Control of the island was vital to the success of any future operations against the ports and cities of eastern North Carolina.

Despite the size of the operation, Burnside and other Union military and political officials managed to keep the expedition's destination a secret. At one point, President Abraham Lincoln was supposed to have responded to a persistent questioner: "Now I will tell you in great confidence where they are going, if you will promise not to speak of it to any one . . . the expedition is going to sea!"

The Federals overcame repeated obstacles and endured numerous delays before they succeeded in clearing the sandbars at Hatteras Inlet and entering Pamlico Sound. During the considerable effort to coax the fleet into the sound, three of the ships and two of Burnside's officers were lost. Finally, on February 4, the entire Union armada was anchored safely in Pamlico Sound and prepared for action.

On the morning of February 5, the fleet proceeded toward Roanoke Island, with the warships escorting and protecting the packed troop transports. As the Federals neared the island, they were careful to conceal shipboard lights that might warn the defenders of their presence.

In actuality, the Southerners were already aware of the Union fleet's close proximity and had taken steps to upgrade the island's defenses. Three forts were located on the northwestern shore, but none of these was adequately placed to prevent or effectively resist any landing in force on the center or southern end of the island. To man these positions, the Confederates scratched together a force of some 1,500 troops under Col. Henry M. Shaw, augmented by a small fleet of seven vessels under Capt. William F. Lynch. Confederate Secretary of War Judah P. Benjamin dispatched Henry A. Wise, the fiery brigadier general and former governor of Virginia, to assume command at Roanoke Island.

The new commander spent much of the ensuing time in Virginia, attempting to procure additional men, arms, and equipment. But by the time Burnside's expedition came steaming into Croatan Sound on February 7, 1862, the Confederates still had barely 3,000 men, poorly armed and ill-trained to resist the Federals. To compound matters, Wise suffered from an attack of pleurisy, which confined him to his headquarters on nearby Nags Head.

Admiral Goldsborough's fleet opened the engagement at 11:30 A.M. on February 7 and endured a very ineffectual fire from the Confederates. The Union navy quickly sank one ship and disabled another, and Lynch retreated with his remaining gunboats. Obstructions placed by the Southerners at the northern end of Croatan Sound proved of little nuisance to the attacking Federals.

This activity cleared the way for Burnside to land his forces, sometime around 3:30 or 4:00 P.M., on the beach at Ashby's Harbor at the center of the island. These troops came ashore on large surf boats, towed close to the shore by light-draft vessels. The naval warships provided covering fire with artillery, although the Federals did not actually need it. The Confederate commander had assigned a small force of men to delay the Federal landing, but these men failed to offer any resistance, and by midnight, 10,000 Union troops were ashore at Ashby's Harbor.

At 8:00 the next morning the Federals moved out to challenge the main Confederate defense line on Roanoke Island. Waiting for them at the northern end of the low-lying, sandy island were 1,500 Confederates and a three-gun battery. Surprisingly, none of the Southerners on hand knew how to fire the artillery pieces, and an officer had to rush over from headquarters on Nags Head to teach them. The Federals appeared before the lesson could be completed.

Burnside divided his men into three sections for the final assault. Leaving a holding force at the center of his line, he dispatched two brigades to strike the Confederates on either flank. These flanking forces struggled through thick undergrowth and marshes before arriving in position to attack the Southern lines. The combined assault proved too much for the defenders, who broke and fled. Seriously outnumbered and without the benefit of their entrenchments or the means to escape, the Confederates had no choice but to surrender.

The victory netted Burnside approximately 2,500 prisoners and cost the Southerners 23 dead, among them O. Jennings Wise, the son of General Wise. The Federals lost 37 killed, 214 wounded, and 13 missing in the operation. The loss of Roanoke Island struck a blow at Southern morale and, at the same time, gave a boost to Union spirits, sagging since First Manassas. Capturing the island also opened the way for further Union advances along the eastern seaboard of North Carolina. A Confederate congressional committee investigated the debacle but provided little more than a platform for Wise's recriminations against the department commander, Benjamin Huger, Secretary of War Benjamin, and others whom he blamed for the disaster.

BIBLIOGRAPHY

Johnson, Robert U., and C. C. Buel, eds. *Battles and Leaders of the Civil War.* 4 vols. New York, 1887–1888. Reprint, Secaucus, N.J., 1982.

Marvel, William. *Burnside.* Chapel Hill, N.C., 1991.

Thomas, Emory M. *Travels to Hallowed Ground.* Columbia, S.C., 1987.

U.S. Naval War Records Office. *Official Records of the Union and Confederate Navies in the War of the Rebellion.* Washington, D.C., 1894–1927. Ser. 1, vol. 6, pp. 549–600, 581.

U.S. War Department. *War of the Rebellion: A Compilation of the Official Records of the Union and Confederate Armies.* Washington, D.C., 1880–1901. Ser. 1, vol. 9, pp. 73–191.

BRIAN S. WILLS

BUSINESS. *See* Economy.

BUTLER, MATTHEW CALBRAITH

BUTLER, MATTHEW CALBRAITH (1836–1909), major general and U.S. senator. Born in Greenville, South Carolina, Butler attended South Carolina College, but withdrew in 1856 after participating in a student riot. He studied law and was admitted to the South Carolina bar the following year. His marriage in 1858 to the daughter of Governor Francis W. Pickens led to a career in politics, and he was elected in 1860 to the South Carolina House of Representatives as a state rights advocate and Democratic secessionist.

Butler joined the call for a secession convention, and at the outbreak of hostilities, he resigned from the legislature to lead the Edgefield Hussars into Confederate service. An accomplished horseman, he joined Hampton's Legion in May 1861 and commanded a mounted unit at First Manassas. His actions there gained him recognition for his physical courage and tactical skill and earned him a promotion to the rank of major. During the Peninsular campaign, Butler displayed his mastery of cavalry tactics by successfully screening Confederate withdrawals and rapidly shifting to the offensive during the Battle of Williamsburg. He was promoted to colonel in August 1862, fought at Sharpsburg and Fredericksburg, and made a decisive contribution at Brandy Station in June 1863 by repulsing a Union flanking movement. He was wounded during this engagement by enemy artillery, resulting in the amputation of his right leg, but he was appointed brigadier general during his convalescence and returned to command in 1864 with no loss of enterprise or skill. Butler participated with distinction in numerous cavalry engagements including Hawes Shop and Trevillian Station and achieved the rank of major general in September 1864.

Butler returned to his law practice after the war and was again elected to the South Carolina legislature in 1866. Concluding that Republican rule was beyond reform, he joined forces with Martin Witherspoon Gary to return the Democratic party to power and restore the conservative regime. He assisted Gary in organizing the Red Shirt movement, Democratic gun clubs whose purpose was to intimidate and suppress the basic element of Republican power, the black voter. After the Democratic victory of 1876, Governor Wade Hampton appointed Butler to the U.S. Senate, where he served until 1894. Butler died in April 1909 in Washington, D.C.

BIBLIOGRAPHY

Brooks, U. R. *Butler and His Cavalry in the War of Secession, 1861–1865.* Columbia, S.C., 1909.
Williams, Alfred B. *Hampton and His Red Shirts: South Carolina's Deliverance in 1876.* New York, 1935.

ROBERT T. BARRETT

BUTLER'S WOMAN ORDER. Issued on May 15, 1862, from the headquarters of the Department of the Gulf in Union-occupied New Orleans, General Order No. 28 declared in part that "when any female shall, by word, gesture, or movement, insult or show contempt for any officer or soldier of the United States, she shall be regarded and held liable to be treated as a woman of the town plying her avocation." No other action during Gen. Benjamin F. Butler's controversial seven-month command of southern Louisiana raised more outcry than his eighty-two-word "woman order."

The directive was typical of the sternness with which Butler suppressed the disorder greeting his troops' arrival

BENJAMIN F. BUTLER.   NATIONAL ARCHIVES

in New Orleans. While white men rioted, women sporting secessionist insignia turned up their noses and drew aside their skirts when passing Federal soldiers on the street. Others left streetcars and church pews whenever blue-clad conquerors entered. One woman emptied her slop jar on Adm. David Farragut's head as he walked beneath her balcony. Butler's patience snapped when another woman spat in the face of two Federal officers. The woman order followed hard upon this incident. Its implied authorization to treat demonstrative women as though they were street-walkers struck a raw nerve in a community where harlotry had historically been widespread.

At home and abroad, the outcry against the woman order was loud and abusive. New Orleans's own creole general P. G. T. Beauregard was characteristic of Confederate commanders in using Butler's order to arouse his troops: "Men of the South! shall our mothers, our wives, our daughters and our sisters be thus outraged by the ruffianly soldiers of the North?" The Confederate state governor called on

Southern soldiers to avenge this "foul conduct." Later in the year President Jefferson Davis branded Butler a common felon and ordered his immediate execution should he ever fall into Confederate hands. Meanwhile, on the floor of the British House of Commons, the prime minister, Lord Palmerston, called Butler's proclamation "infamous."

Butler imprisoned Mayor John Monroe for assailing the directive as uncivilized and un-Christian, but neither the Massachusetts general nor his troops ever executed the woman order. Local women thereafter behaved more circumspectly toward occupying troops, except for the prostitutes who reportedly pasted Butler's likeness in "the bottom of their tinklepots."

BIBLIOGRAPHY

Bragg, Jefferson Davis. *Louisiana in the Confederacy.* Baton Rouge, La., 1941.
Capers, Gerald. *Occupied City: New Orleans under the Federals, 1862–1865.* Lexington, Ky., 1965.
Foote, Shelby. *The Civil War: A Narrative, Fort Sumter to Perryville.* New York, 1958.
Holzman, Robert S. *Stormy Ben Butler.* New York, 1954.
Parton, James. *General Butler in New Orleans.* New York, 1864.

LAWRENCE N. POWELL

BUTTERNUT. *See* Unionism.

C

CABELL, WILLIAM LEWIS (1827–1911), brigadier general. Born January 1, 1827, in Danville, Virginia, Cabell graduated from West Point in 1850, thirty-third out of forty-four. He served in the regular army in the Indian Territory and in 1856 married an Arkansas woman.

When the Civil War began, he headed for Richmond and entered the Confederate service after his resignation from the Federal army was accepted. Cabell, commissioned a major and appointed chief quartermaster and commissary officer in Virginia, participated in First Manassas. Following that battle he helped P. G. T. Beauregard and Joseph E. Johnston design the Confederate battle flag. In January 1862 he became chief quartermaster for Earl Van Dorn in the Trans-Mississippi District of Department No. 2, where his experience in logistics proved invaluable. He was wounded while taking part in the siege of Corinth, and the next day his horse fell on him, leaving his left leg paralyzed. After he returned to duty he was assigned to the Trans-Mississippi Department, where he became chief quartermaster. Cabell was promoted to brigadier general on April 23, 1863, to date from January 20, and returned to active service. He participated in the Camden campaign in the spring of 1864 and took part in Sterling Price's final raid into Missouri where he was captured on October 25, 1864.

After the war Cabell returned to Fort Smith and in 1872 moved to Dallas. He served four terms as mayor, was a U.S. marshal, and engaged in railroading. He died in Dallas on February 22, 1911, and is buried in Greenwood Cemetery.

BIBLIOGRAPHY

Harvey, Paul, Jr. *Old Tige: General William L. Cabell, CSA.* Hillsboro, Tex., 1970.
Kerby, Robert L. *Kirby Smith's Confederacy: The Trans-Mississippi South, 1863–1865.* New York, 1972.
Rea, Ralph R. *Sterling Price: The Lee of the West.* Little Rock, Ark., 1959.

ANNE J. BAILEY

CABINET. The Confederate cabinet consisted of President Jefferson Davis, Vice President Alexander H. Stephens, and the secretaries of the six departments that composed the executive branch of the Confederate government: State, War, Justice, the Treasury, the Navy, and the Post Office. With several important exceptions, each of these departments replicated its counterpart in the prewar Union.

In organizational terms, most of the exceptions involved the offices of the attorney general, which, for the first time in American history, were given departmental status in the new Department of Justice. At the same time, the Confederacy failed to create a Department of the Interior. Its functions, such as the Bureau of Printing, the Patent Office, and territorial affairs, were transferred to Justice, which, as a consequence, was a much larger and more important department than the small suite of offices that served the Union attorney general. Another factor that greatly enhanced the attorney general's office was the decision not to establish a Confederate supreme court. In the absence of a supreme tribunal, the attorney general served as final interpreter of the constitutionality of legislation, a task made easier by the fact that state and Confederate district courts generally upheld war measures. Even so, had the Confederacy survived, these written interpretations of statutory and constitutional law might have provided an enduring basis for administrative centralization.

Although the formal organizational missions of the other departments closely corresponded to those in the prewar Union, most departments found their administrative chal-

FIRST PRESIDENTIAL CABINET.   First of many permutations of the Confederate Cabinet. Standing in the back, from left to right, are Secretary of the Treasury Christopher G. Memminger and Secretary of War Leroy P. Walker. Seated at the table, from left to right, are Attorney General Judah P. Benjamin, Secretary of the Navy Stephen M. Mallory, Vice President Alexander H. Stephens, President Jefferson Davis, Postmaster General John R. Reagan, and Secretary of State Robert Toombs.   HARPER'S PICTORIAL HISTORY OF THE GREAT REBELLION

lenges dramatically altered by the Civil War. For example, the Department of the Navy, under Stephen R. Mallory, began the war without a major vessel and soon lost easy access to international sea-lanes from Southern ports. Improvisation and, at times, brilliant ingenuity introduced the ironclad to modern warfare, but the construction of a large, or even small, oceangoing fleet was well beyond the material capacity of the South.

The Treasury Department was similarly hamstrung by an underdeveloped banking system, a shortage of gold bullion, and the limited utility of a plantation economy based on the export of cotton as a source of revenue for wartime government operations. In all these respects, the challenge facing Confederate Treasury secretaries was very different from that faced by their prewar Union predecessors. Similar shortages of natural resources and productive capacity led the War Department to direct a wide program of confiscation, government-owned industry, and allocation of Southern manpower in order to mobilize men and matériel for the front. As was true of the other departments, these activities broke new ground in their innovative use of government authority and attempts at centrally directed economic coordination.

The two departments least changed by the war may also have been those least important to the Southern war effort. The Department of State had little to do beyond entertain-

ing foreign representatives and giving advice to largely autonomous commissioners pursuing diplomatic recognition of the Confederacy in European courts. More active but also more mundane was the Post Office, which attempted the most thorough reproduction of prewar Federal organization. Absorbing with little change the antebellum system for delivering the mails, the Confederate Post Office moved letters in that part of the South that remained outside Federal control throughout the war.

As his first cabinet, President Davis appointed Judah P. Benjamin of Louisiana, attorney general; Stephen R. Mallory of Florida, secretary of the navy; Christopher G. Memminger of South Carolina, secretary of the treasury; John H. Reagan of Texas, postmaster general; Robert Toombs of Georgia, secretary of state; and Leroy P. Walker of Alabama, secretary of war. In making these selections, Davis chose men who had been major rivals for the Confederate presidency or those his rivals recommended. He also gave geographical balance to his administration by allocating each of the states that seceded before the attack upon Fort Sumter at least one representative in the first cabinet. (Davis himself represented Mississippi.) As was also true in the Union, administrative ability and personal friendship played but minor roles in these early appointments. As a group, this cabinet lasted only from early March, when Reagan was appointed, until July 1861, when

The Confederate Cabinet

POSITION	NAME	DATES OF SERVICE[1]
Attorney General	Judah P. Benjamin	Mar. 5–Nov. 21, 1861[2]
	Thomas Bragg	Nov. 21, 1861–Mar. 18, 1862
	Thomas H. Watts	Mar. 18, 1862–Oct. 1, 1863
	Wade Keyes	ad interim, Oct. 1, 1863– Jan. 2, 1864
	George Davis	Jan. 2, 1864–Apr. 24, 1865[3]
Postmaster General[4]	John H. Reagan	Mar. 6, 1861–May 10, 1865[5]
President	Jefferson Davis	Feb. 18, 1861–May 10, 1865[6]
Secretary of the Navy	Stephen R. Mallory	Mar. 4, 1861–May 3, 1865[7]
Secretary of State	Robert Toombs	Feb. 21– July 24, 1861
	Robert M. T. Hunter	July 24, 1861–Feb. 22, 1862
	William M. Browne	ad interim, Mar. 7–Mar. 18, 1862[8]
	Judah P. Benjamin	Mar. 18, 1862–May 2, 1865[9]
Secretary of the Treasury	Christopher G. Memminger	Feb. 21, 1861– July 17, 1864
	George Trenholm	July 18, 1864–Apr. 27, 1865[10]
Secretary of War	Leroy Pope Walker	Feb. 21–Sept. 16, 1861
	Judah P. Benjamin	Nov. 21, 1861–Mar. 17, 1862[11]
	George Wythe Randolph	Mar. 18–Nov. 15, 1862
	Gustavus Woodson Smith	ad interim, Nov. 17–20, 1862
	James A. Seddon	Nov. 21, 1862–Feb. 5, 1865
	John C. Breckinridge	Feb. 6–May 3, 1865[12]
Vice President	Alexander H. Stephens	Feb. 11, 1861–May 11, 1865[13]

[1]Unless otherwise indicated, starting date is date of confirmation by the Senate; ending date is date on which resignation became effective.

[2]Benjamin was appointed acting secretary of war on September 17, but the position was not made permanent and confirmed by the Senate until November 21. During the interim, Assistant Attorney General Wade Keyes ran the Justice Department.

[3]Ending date is that of the last cabinet meeting Davis attended, in Charlotte, North Carolina, after which he resigned.

[4]On February 25, 1861, Jefferson Davis nominated and the Senate confirmed Henry T. Ellet as postmaster general, but Ellet declined the appointment.

[5]Ending date is that of Reagan's capture by Union troops near Irwinville, Georgia.

[6]Starting date is that of Davis's inauguration; ending date is that of his capture by Union troops near Irwinville, Georgia.

[7]Mallory composed and dated his letter of resignation on May 2, following the cabinet meeting at Abbeville, South Carolina, but he did not present it to the president until the following day at Washington, Georgia. Mallory left the cabinet immediately, but Jefferson Davis's letter officially accepting his resignation is dated May 4.

[8]Browne had been running the state department since, at latest, February 22, 1861, but Jefferson Davis did not officially designate him secretary of state ad interim until March 7.

[9]Ending date is that of the cabinet meeting at Abbeville, South Carolina, after which Benjamin left the cabinet and fled the country, reaching Bimini on July 10.

[10]Ending date is that on which Trenholm submitted his letter of resignation. Trenholm left the cabinet immediately, although Davis's letter officially accepting the resignation is dated April 28. Davis then appointed John H. Reagan as secretary of the treasury ad interim, a position Reagan held until his capture by Union troops near Irwinville, Georgia, on May 10.

[11]Benjamin was appointed acting secretary of war on September 17, 1861, and he continued to run the department unofficially until March 24, 1862.

[12]Ending date is that of the remaining cabinet members' arrival at Washington, Georgia. Afterward, Breckinridge and John H. Reagan separated from the president with the intent of rejoining him later, but Breckinridge was unable to do so. He eventually fled to Cuba.

[13]Starting date is that on which Stephens took the oath of office; ending date is that on which he was arrested by Union cavalry at his home in Crawfordville, Georgia.

SOURCE: All dates are taken from Rembert W. Patrick, *Jefferson Davis and His Cabinet*, Baton Rouge, La., 1944.

Toombs resigned in order to accept an appointment as brigadier general in the Confederate army.

Jefferson made in all sixteen appointments, aside from acting secretaries, to head the six Confederate departments. One man, Judah Benjamin, accounted for three of these as he was appointed, in succession, to Justice, War, and State. (He owed his survival to his close relationship with Davis; no other adviser so often or so influentially had the president's ear.) Benjamin, along with Mallory at Navy, Reagan at the Post Office, Davis as president, and Stephens as vice president, served in the cabinet throughout the life of the Confederacy. There was substantial turnover among the others. The War Department alone had five permanent secretaries, Justice had four, State had three, and the Treasury had two. The cabinet that sat between November 21, 1862, and September 8, 1863, had the longest tenure in terms of continuous membership. Along with Davis, Stephens, Mallory, and Reagan, that cabinet had James A. Seddon at War, Thomas H. Watts at Justice, Benjamin at State, and Memminger at Treasury. Even though these men served together for only ten months, they had the deepest influence upon the performance and development of their respective departments.

Under President Davis, the cabinet met frequently and, when it met, deliberated for hours. Though these meetings were often indecisive, Davis appears to have heeded what advice was given. For the most part, however, the cabinet served the president in other ways. One of these was as a structure for an immense delegation of authority over executive administration of the Southern war effort. With few exceptions, the secretaries, their assistant secretaries, and subordinate bureau chiefs were solely responsible for departmental operations within wide-ranging grants of statutory authority from the Confederate Congress. For the most part, Davis involved himself only in the detailed decision making of the War Department and, within its sphere, imposed his views only in military operations.

Another way that the cabinet served Davis was as a political lightning rod. Even though most departments were more or less autonomous of both legislative and executive direction, the deteriorating military position of the South and the ever-escalating demands that the war effort imposed upon civilians produced in the Congress repeated and bitter denunciations of executive performance. Although the president resisted many calls for the resignation of department secretaries, most of the turnover in his cabinet in fact reflected timely sacrifices to this congressional clamor.

[*See also* Judiciary; Navy Department; Post Office Department; Presidency; State Department; Treasury Department; Vice Presidency; War Department; *and biographies of numerous figures mentioned herein.*]

BIBLIOGRAPHY

Coulter, E. Merton. *The Confederate States of America, 1861–1865.* A History of the South, vol. 7. Baton Rouge, La., 1950.

Eaton, Clement. *A History of the Southern Confederacy.* New York, 1954.

Patrick, Rembert W. *Jefferson Davis and His Cabinet.* Baton Rouge, La., 1944.

Thomas, Emory M. *The Confederate Nation: 1861–1865.* New York, 1979.

Vandiver, Frank E. *Their Tattered Flags: The Epic of the Confederacy.* New York, 1970. Reprint, Texas A & M University Military History Series, no. 5. College Station, Tex., 1987.

RICHARD FRANKLIN BENSEL

CALHOUN, JOHN C. (1782–1850), author of the constitutional justification for secession. The son of a well-to-do slave owner who opposed ratification of the U.S. Constitution, John Caldwell Calhoun was born and raised in the up-country of South Carolina. He graduated from Yale College and then attended the Litchfield, Connecticut, law school of Tapping Reeve at a time when both institutions were under the control of extreme state-rights Federalists. Acquiring an up-country plantation and slaves, he looked upon himself as a kindly master, though he once

JOHN C. CALHOUN.

HARPER'S PICTORIAL HISTORY OF THE GREAT REBELLION

ordered "30 lashes well laid on" as punishment for a runaway. Between 1810 and 1850 he served as a congressman, secretary of war (one of the best), vice president, senator, and secretary of state, while continually aspiring to be president.

At first, Calhoun assumed that the Federal government possessed broad powers, and he advocated an "enlarged policy" of protective tariffs, internal improvements, and a national bank. By 1828, however, he had reversed himself on the tariff, which South Carolina cotton planters blamed for their economic troubles. Some talked of secession as a way out. Seeking a less radical alternative, Calhoun came up with the idea of nullification, which he presented anonymously in "The South Carolina Exposition" (1828) and later elaborated in various writings, especially in his posthumous *Discourse on the Constitution and Government of the United States* (1851).

His theory may be summarized as follows: Sovereignty, or the ultimate source of power within a body politic, resides in the people of each of the separate states. By ratifying the U.S. Constitution, these people delegated certain powers to the Federal government but gave up none of their sovereignty. The people of each state must therefore decide for themselves whether the Federal government, their agent, is at any time violating their instructions as given in the "constitutional compact." They can nullify any law they consider unconstitutional. The law then remains null and void within the state until three-fourths of all the states have ratified an amendment giving the Federal government the power in question. If this happens, the aggrieved state has a recourse: it can secede. To do so, it needs only to repeal its ratification of the U.S. Constitution.

According to Calhoun, the whole process was perfectly constitutional, but when South Carolina attempted to put his theory into practice by nullifying the tariff laws in 1832, President Andrew Jackson threatened to use force against the state, and Federal laws were never suspended within it. Realizing that one state alone could not effectively resist the Federal government, Calhoun thereafter devoted himself to uniting the South behind him and his principles. He did so by taking an extreme stand against antislavery activities of whatever kind. Slavery, he maintained, had a special place in the Constitution, for it was the only kind of property mentioned there (though not by name). Therefore, the Federal government, in the exercise of its legitimate powers, must always promote the interests of slave owners, and the free states must do nothing to interfere with its efforts.

Calhoun objected to the Compromise of 1850 primarily on the ground that it would increase the power of the North by admitting California as a free state. He now warned Northerners that the Southern states might leave the Union unless slavery was made absolutely secure. "If you are unwilling we should depart in peace, tell us so, and we shall know what to do, when you reduce the question to submission or resistance." Here was a hint that, unless secession was permitted, there would be war.

As Calhoun lay on his deathbed, his enemy Francis P. Blair wrote of him: " 'tis given out that having completed the ground work he does not look to live to enjoy it—poor old man, he resolved to die in giving birth to the Southern Confederacy." The formation of the Confederacy was delayed for eleven years, but Calhoun had indeed laid the groundwork for it. When South Carolina seceded, it followed exactly the procedure he had prescribed: an elected convention repealed the ratification of the U.S. Constitution. Other seceding states did the same. The Confederate Constitution embodied his principles in guaranteeing slavery and in acknowledging the sovereignty of the states, though it did not recognize the right of nullification or secession.

In 1860 Jefferson Davis had tried to incorporate a set of Calhoun's proslavery and state-rights resolutions in the Democratic party platform. As president of the Confederacy, however, he needed to exert the powers of his government in enforcing conscription and other war measures. Vice President Alexander H. Stephens accused him of abandoning the state-rights principles of Calhoun and adopting the consolidationist heresy of Andrew Jackson. After the war, Davis as well as Stephens nevertheless claimed to be a faithful disciple of Calhoun. When Stephens gave his apologia the title *A Constitutional View of the Late War between the States* (1868–1870), he originated the designation "War between the States," which continues to serve as a reminder that a particular "constitutional view" underlay the attempt of Southerners to gain their independence.

BIBLIOGRAPHY

Calhoun, John C. *A Disquisition on Government and a Discourse on the Constitution and Government of the United States.* Vol. 1 of *The Works of John C. Calhoun.* Edited by Richard K. Cralle. Charleston, S.C., 1851.

Current, Richard N. *John C. Calhoun.* The Great American Thinkers Series. New York, 1963.

Dodd, William E. *Statesmen of the Old South; or, From Radicalism to Conservative Revolt.* New York, 1911.

Niven, John. *John C. Calhoun and the Price of Union.* Baton Rouge, La., 1988.

Wiltse, Charles M. *John C. Calhoun.* 3 vols. Indianapolis and New York, 1944–1951.

RICHARD N. CURRENT

CALLAHAN, SAMUEL BENTON (1833–1911),

captain and congressional delegate of the Seminole and Creek tribes. A non-Indian, Callahan was born in Alabama, educated in Texas, and became a cattleman near Okmulgee,

Indian Territory, in 1858. In 1861 he enlisted in the Confederate army as a member of the First Creek Mounted Volunteers, which served in Arkansas and Indian Territory. His unit fought at the Battle of Poison Springs, Arkansas, April 18, 1864, and was involved in numerous raids and skirmishes. Callahan resigned his commission as captain on May 18, 1864, to serve as the nonvoting delegate representing the Creeks and Seminoles in the Confederate House of Representatives.

Callahan's tenure as a representative was brief: he took his seat on May 30, 1864, and left Richmond in mid-March 1865, three weeks before the Confederate surrender at Appomattox. He and the two other delegates from the Five Civilized Tribes were authorized to introduce legislation and speak on the floor of the House. On January 20, 1865, Callahan proposed a bill to pay in cotton the annuities due the Creek and Seminole nations from the Confederacy. The House Committee on Indian Affairs incorporated it into a broader act benefiting the Choctaw and Chickasaw tribes as well.

Callahan spoke against a bill concerning the redemption of old issue Confederate Treasury notes in favor of a new issue. He feared that his Indian constituents would lose about one-third the value of the old issue notes they held. His amendment to that effect was adopted, and the Creeks and Seminoles were exempted from the one-third discount. Callahan died in Muskogee, Oklahoma, on February 17, 1911, having lived long enough to become one of the last survivors among those who served in the Confederate Congress.

BIBLIOGRAPHY

Wilson, Terry P. "Delegates of the Five Civilized Tribes to the Confederate Congress." *Chronicles of Oklahoma* 53 (1975): 353–366.

Wright, Muriel H. "Samuel Benton Callahan." *Chronicles of Oklahoma* 33 (1955): 314–315.

TERRY P. WILSON

CAMILLA. The wooden schooner yacht *America* measured 100 tons, 111 feet long, and 25 feet wide, and drew 12 feet of water. It was built in 1851 by William H. Brown of New York. *America* crossed the Atlantic and raced the fastest yachts in Great Britain, capturing the Queen's Cup, known thereafter as the America's Cup. Sold to a succession of British owners, the yacht was renamed *Camilla* and rebuilt of teak in 1858.

Owner Capt. Henry Decie guided it through the blockade into Savannah, Georgia, in early 1861. Decie sold *Camilla* to the Confederate government and continued in command. The schooner ran back through the blockade to Ireland, carrying government purchasing agents Capt. James Hey-

ward North, CSN, and Maj. Edward C. Anderson. As cover for its operations, *Camilla* took part in a regatta at Queenstown and a race around the Isle of Wight before returning to the Confederacy. In August 1861 *Camilla* ran the blockade into the St. Johns River, Florida, carrying Confederate diplomatic dispatches. On the advance of a Union naval force up the river, *Camilla* was hidden and scuttled in a shallow tributary. A force led by USS *Ottawa* discovered and salvaged *Camilla*. The schooner was repaired, armed, and renamed USS *America*. After serving briefly in the blockade, *America* became a school ship at the U.S. Naval Academy. Sold in 1873, it was later owned by Gen. Benjamin Butler. *America* was given back to the Naval Academy in 1921 for preservation as a relic. It was scrapped in 1945.

BIBLIOGRAPHY

Anderson, Maj. Edward C. *Confederate Foreign Agent: The European Diary of Major Edward C. Anderson.* Edited by W. Stanley Hoole. University, Ala., 1976.

Bruzek, Joseph C. "The U.S. Schooner Yacht *America.*" *Naval Institute Proceedings* 43 (September 1967): 1159–1187.

Neblett, Thomas R. "The Yacht *America*: A New Account Pertaining to Her Confederate Operations." *American Neptune* 27, no. 4 (1967): 233–253.

Thompson, Winfield M., William P. Stephens, and William V. Swan. *The Yacht America.* Boston, 1925.

KEVIN J. FOSTER

CAMPBELL, ALEXANDER WILLIAM (1828–1893), brigadier general.

Born in Nashville, Tennessee, June 4, 1828, and educated at West Tennessee College and Lebanon Law School, Campbell was an attorney in his native city before the Civil War.

After Tennessee's secession, Campbell joined the Provisional Army being organized by the state. On May 9, 1861, he was named assistant inspector general on the staff of Maj. Gen. Gideon Pillow. When the state army entered Confederate service, Campbell became a member of Brig. Gen. B. Franklin Cheatham's staff. In December 1861 he was appointed colonel of the Thirty-third Tennessee Regiment.

Campbell won praise for his heroic conduct at Shiloh, where he was badly wounded, but when the regiment was reorganized in May 1862, he was not elected colonel. He remained on duty as a supernumerary officer by order of Maj. Gen. Leonidas Polk. On December 25, 1862, he was appointed as Polk's adjutant and inspector general. He was soon placed in charge of the conscript camp at Fayetteville, Tennessee.

Captured on July 29, 1863, while recruiting near Lexington, Tennessee, Campbell was exchanged in late 1864. He was then assigned to the staff of Lt. Gen. Nathan Bedford Forrest and on March 1, 1865, became commander of a cavalry brigade. Campbell was promoted to brigadier general March 1, 1865. On May 11, he surrendered with Forrest's command.

Campbell resumed the practice of law and in 1880 unsuccessfully sought the Democratic nomination for governor of Tennessee. He died June 13, 1893, and is buried in Riverview Cemetery, Jackson, Tennessee.

BIBLIOGRAPHY

Bearss, Edwin C. "Alexander William Campbell." In *The Confederate General*. Edited by William C. Davis. Vol. 1. Harrisburg, Pa., 1991.

Connelly, Thomas L. *Army of the Heartland: The Army of Tennessee, 1861–1862*. Baton Rouge, La., 1967.

Connelly, Thomas L. *Autumn of Glory: The Army of Tennessee, 1862–1865*. Baton Rouge, La., 1971.

RICHARD M. MCMURRY

CAMPBELL, JOHN A. (1811–1889), associate justice of the U.S. Supreme Court and Confederate assistant secretary of war. Born in Washington, Georgia, the son of a distinguished lawyer, Campbell was educated at Franklin College (now the University of Georgia) and at West Point. The sudden death of his parent curtailed his military career and he returned home. A precocious youth, after studying law privately, he was admitted to the bar at nineteen. The following year he moved to Montgomery (later to Mobile), Alabama, where he practiced law, married, and served as a Democrat in the legislature several times. His rise to prominence as a brilliant member of the Alabama bar, gifted with an unusual memory and wide knowledge of history, made him an attractive public figure as well.

In 1850 he was named delegate to the Nashville Convention, where he avoided the sectional stridency of Robert Barnwell Rhett, William Lowndes Yancey, and other firebrands to help draft the conciliatory resolutions adopted by that body. At forty, Campbell had achieved a national reputation as a lawyer, and in March 1853, he was appointed an associate justice of the U.S. Supreme Court by Franklin Pierce. His selection had been made at the request of jurists on the Court and was widely praised. He soon rose to equal the best on the bench and in the following years delivered many important opinions. In the controversial *Dred Scott* decision of 1854, he concurred with the majority ruling in holding that a slave was not a citizen and that the Missouri Compromise did not bestow citizenship upon him. At this time Campbell held no slaves, having earlier freed all he owned and thereafter employing as servants only free persons of color. A strict constructionist and state rights champion, he was also a strong Union man who repeatedly rose above his section on many sensitive national issues. In 1860, in briefs before the Federal court at New Orleans, he opposed William Walker's filibustering ventures in Latin America as violations of America's neutrality laws.

Campbell's fearful concern for peace drew him into the Fort Sumter crisis in early 1861. Although strongly opposed to secession (Alabama had left the Union on January 11), he remained in Washington and on the bench, as he worked ceaselessly to promote compromise between the two sections. These efforts made him unpopular in Alabama and were not entirely met with sincerity by Secretary of State William H. Seward, spokesman for the new Lincoln administration, with whom he was negotiating. After weeks of efforts to reach an accord and thus avoid war (which he believed would be long and disastrous for the South), he was finally compelled to admit defeat. Abraham Lincoln refused to receive the Confederate commissioners sent by Jefferson Davis and, despite Seward's assurances that force would not be used to hold the fort, Lincoln sent the *Star of the West* with arms and men to Charleston. Many Southerners charged the judge with betrayal, Seward with duplicity, and Lincoln with open hostility to the South. Feeling that he had been misused, Campbell resigned and returned to Alabama.

"A resigned judge of the Supreme Court of the United States!" Mary Boykin Chesnut exclaimed in her famous diary. "Resigned—and for a cause that he is hardly more than half in sympathy with. His is one of the hardest cases." Hard it was, and though his motives were suspicious to many, in time it would be seen that his conduct, in the supreme crisis of his life, was above reproach.

Not until the fall of 1862 did Campbell agree to serve the Confederate cause. He had earlier moved his family to Richmond, where he was offered several positions of importance. Though he differed from Jefferson Davis, the latter respected his gifts and his loyalty, and on October 22, acting upon the urgings of Secretary of War George Wythe Randolph, appointed Campbell assistant secretary. His assignment called for legal knowledge and administrative ability to help carry out the first military draft in America—which Randolph and the Confederate Congress had brought into being in April and September 1862.

In late November, Secretary Randolph suddenly quit his post (for personal reasons and differences with Davis), and Campbell found himself second in command in the War Office to another Virginian, James A. Seddon. A strong Southern nationalist, lawyer, and politician, Seddon threw the full force of his personality, class, and political connections into his stewardship. He was a man of independent thought and an able administrator. Campbell would work with him until the last weeks of the war, and between them developed a close and successful relationship. In time Seddon expanded the judge's purview and powers; the assistant secretary was charged with overseeing most of the routine of the department and its various bureaus, as well as drafting correspondence, especially with Southern governors over conscription and other matters.

Relations with other departments (Navy, Treasury) could at times be touchy, coordination with Adjutant and Inspector General Samuel Cooper not always harmonious, and orders to military leaders in the field difficult and unpleasant. But Campbell's customary detachment from personalities, evenhandedness, and steadfastness to duty strengthened the direction and effectiveness of the War Office—the busiest and most vital powerhouse of the Confederate government. To most, this tall, bald old gentleman, with deep penetrating eyes and sharp features, who dispatched orders with both alacrity and common sense, yet often with kindness, was the indispensable man in the Richmond bureaucracy. He ultimately emerged as the real power behind the scenes of the civilian war effort and, in the end, became what Gen. Josiah Gorgas observed: "the mainstay of the War Dept."

In the course of the war, Campbell differed with the Davis administration on major issues, and on several occasions he took issue with the president directly. He expressed his criticism respectfully to his superior or to his bureau chiefs. More a realist than most, he urged draconian measures when need warranted, as in matters of exemptions, martial law, taxes-in-kind, and impressment. He advocated control of the railroads, trading cotton with the enemy for food, and regulation of blockade runners. Eventually the War Department acquired a handful of runners to bring in munitions, medicine, and other essentials for the fighting forces. On larger issues, he was one with Seddon in urging a vigorous western theater strategic policy, early in 1863 stating bluntly that Davis was without any plan and seemed "to be drifting on the current of events." The next year, after the dual disasters of Gettysburg and Vicksburg, massive manpower shortages, and desertions, he urged that slaves be recruited as soldiers—knowing full well that freeing blacks for military service "would be the knell of slavery as it exists." By 1865 he realized that the war had been lost: "No money in the Treasury—no food to feed Gen. Lee's army— no troops to oppose Gen. Sherman—what does it all mean. Is [not] the cause really hopeless?"

It was, and yet Davis and the diehards held on. Campbell pleaded with the new secretary, John C. Breckinridge, to prepare for the inevitable collapse of the Confederacy. But first, and for the second time in his public life, he offered his talents as conciliator-mediator between the two governments in the special accords achieved by his old friend Francis P. Blair with the Lincoln administration—the Hampton Roads Conference.

For the better part of six hours, on February 3, 1865, Campbell, Robert M. T. Hunter, and Alexander H. Stephens

conversed and talked history distant and present, all to the end of bringing about a cessation of hostilities. But as the Confederate peace commissioners had been instructed by Davis to negotiate only on a basis of Southern independence and Lincoln was holding firm to a restoration of the Union, the prospects for an armistice were doomed. Campbell later submitted his report of the transactions to the Confederate president and awaited events.

The end came on April 2, when Richmond was evacuated by the government, and Davis and most of the cabinet fled south. At considerable risk to himself, Campbell remained in the capital. Later he was successful in meeting with Lincoln and discussed at length proposals for peace and reconstruction (of at least the state of Virginia). With Robert E. Lee's surrender a few days later and Lincoln's assassination, these efforts came to nothing. Much to his surprise, on May 23 he was arrested by Federal authorities and confined to Libby Prison. Soon after, he was dispatched with Seddon and Hunter on a ship to imprisonment at Fort Pulaski, Georgia. Here he remained with many old associates for six months. Much of the time was passed in talk and thought of recent events and in correspondence with his family.

When finally released, he returned to his family and relocated to New Orleans. His property in Mobile had been destroyed by the invaders, and his house in Washington had been seized and sold for taxes. At fifty-four he set about rebuilding his law practice. Cases before Federal courts with periodic appearances before the Supreme Court, several on important national issues (such as monopolies, the Slaughterhouse cases, and Reconstruction tax issues), filled these last decades. Toward the end he was drawn back to Washington, but soon found his old haunt uncongenial and moved on to Baltimore, where he died. Campbell wrote and published chapters of an autobiography, which he regrettably never completed—a poignant loss to history, for the judge was an interesting man, honest, highly intelligent, often original in his thought, and a witness to much that posterity would love to know.

BIBLIOGRAPHY

Campbell, John A. *Reminiscences and Documents Relating to the Civil War*. Baltimore, 1887.

Connor, Henry Graves. *John Archibald Campbell, Associate Justice, 1853–1861*. Boston, 1920.

Jones, J. B. *A Rebel War Clerk's Diary at the Confederate States Capital*. 2 vols. Philadelphia, 1866.

Patrick, Rembert W. *Jefferson Davis and His Cabinet*. Baton Rouge, La., 1944.

Vandiver, Frank E., ed. *The Civil War Diary of General Josiah Gorgas*. University, Ala., 1947.

Younger, Edward, ed. *Inside the Confederate Government: The Diary of Robert Garlick Hill Kean*. New York, 1957.

JOHN O'BRIEN

CAMPBELL, JOSIAH A. PATTERSON

(1830–1917), congressman from Mississippi and lieutenant colonel. Born in South Carolina and educated in Georgia and North Carolina, Campbell started a law practice in Kosciusko, Mississippi, when he was eighteen years old. Three years later, he was elected to the state legislature. In 1859 he was elected for a second time and became Speaker of the House.

In 1861 he was chosen to represent his county at Mississippi's secession convention, and that convention named him one of Mississippi's seven delegates to the Provisional Congress in Montgomery, Alabama. While serving, he was primarily interested in the way Confederate territories would be organized. He supported a strong central government but at the same time sought to establish effective state militias.

With the coming of the war, Campbell entered military service. He organized the Campbell Guards, which was renamed Company K and became part of the Fortieth Mississippi Infantry. Campbell rose from the rank of captain to lieutenant colonel, commanding his regiment at the Battles of Iuka and Corinth. At Corinth in October 1862, he was wounded but recovered enough to rejoin the regiment at Grenada. He saw action at Vicksburg, where President Jefferson Davis appointed him colonel of cavalry. He then served in the military court of Leonidas Polk's corps from 1863 to 1865.

At the end of the war, Campbell resumed his influential role in state affairs. He was named to an unexpired term on the circuit court in his district and was chosen for a full term in 1866. But he was forced to resign because he would not take the oath required by the Reconstruction Acts. On the issue of the status of the freedmen, Campbell, unlike some of his Democratic colleagues, counseled a course of compromise and moderation. He called the Black Codes "foolish" and supported the enfranchisement of the freedmen in 1867. White Southerners, he said, should "acquire ascendancy over them and become their teachers and controllers instead of allowing the Republicans to do so."

In 1876 with the return of the Democrats to power, Governor John M. Stone appointed Campbell to the state supreme court, where he served for the next eighteen years. Among his last formal services to the state was his work as a delegate to the constitutional convention of 1890.

BIBLIOGRAPHY

Alexander, Thomas B., and Richard E. Beringer. *The Anatomy of the Confederate Congress: A Study of the Influences of Member Characteristics on Legislative Voting Behavior, 1861–1865.* Nashville, Tenn., 1972.

Warner, Ezra J., and W. Buck Yearns. *Biographical Register of the Confederate Congress.* Baton Rouge, La., 1975.

RAY SKATES

JOSIAH A. PATTERSON CAMPBELL.   LIBRARY OF CONGRESS

CANADA. With the outbreak of the Civil War, Canada emerged as a potential battleground between North and South. The *Trent* affair (in which Confederate envoys en route to Europe were seized by U.S. officials) and the subsequent strain in U.S.-British relations in November and December 1861 raised the danger of war in Canada and unleashed animosities toward the inhabitants of the border states. Disaffected pro-Confederate elements in Canada merely increased the tensions. Much of Canadian opinion was outspokenly anti-Northern, some even pro-Southern. Conservative opinion, like that in Britain, claimed a dislike for American democratic institutions and "mob rule." Yet the North had its staunch supporters in the Canadian press; Canadian leaders hesitated to endorse the Confederate cause. Richmond reacted slowly to the possibilities of using Canada as a base for harassing the border states and encouraging anti-Union sentiment in the North. Southern leaders looked to Britain and France, not Canada, for effective intervention in the American conflict.

With the apparent Confederate failure to enlist support in Europe, the Richmond government in late 1863 prepared to use Canada as a second front in its war against the North. President Jefferson Davis absolved the Confederacy of any obligation to honor U.S. treaties. Pro-Southern forces in Canada could now ignore past barriers to offensive action, including the restraints imposed by Britain's official neutrality. Lord Charles Stanley Monck, governor general of Canada, informed Washington of Confederate plots, including one of November 1863 to release Southern prisoners being held at Johnson's Island in Lake Erie. Union officials alerted the area and forced the abandonment of the plot. In December Confederate conspirators succeeded in capturing the American-owned coastal steamer *Chesapeake* to convert it into a privateer. A U.S. naval vessel recaptured *Chesapeake* in Nova Scotian waters, and a boarding party apprehended a Nova Scotian raider, John Wade, who managed to escape. When a Confederate legal expert failed to establish Confederate citizenship for the plotters, a New Brunswick magistrate declared the attack on *Chesapeake* an act of piracy, not the capture of a prize. A Halifax vice admiralty court ordered the ship returned to its owners. Washington dropped the case, unwilling to press for extradition to try British subjects for piracy.

Following the *Chesapeake* affair, the Confederate government moved at last to exploit Canada's anti-Northern sentiment. In April 1864 President Jefferson Davis appointed a commission consisting of Jacob Thompson of Mississippi, Clement C. Clay of Louisiana, and University of Virginia professor J. P. Holcombe, already in Canada, "to crystallize anti-Northern feeling in Canada and mould it into some form of hostile expression." At the outset the commission was aided by the overwhelming Union victories at Gettysburg and Vicksburg. Never had Canada appeared so vulnerable to U.S. power. Operating out of Queen's Hotel in Toronto, the commissioners planned a variety of border assaults from Maine to Ohio. They fostered a peace movement in the North to diminish support for the Union war effort, stepping up their activity as the 1864 election approached. One Confederate agent boasted that the Southerners in Canada would "do such deeds . . . as shall make European civilization shudder." Still the Southern efforts to defeat President Abraham Lincoln and undermine morale in the United States were few and inept. The Confederate agents in Canada suffered from a pro-Southern bias that rendered them ineffective; they recognized no legitimate or practical limits to their anti-Union plots.

In September 1864 the Virginian John Y. Beall planned an attack on Johnson's Island by gaining possession of USS *Michigan*. The plot failed when crew members apprehended Beall's accomplice, who had been sent abroad to drug them. In October some twenty Kentuckians, led by Lt. Bennett H. Young, attacked the Vermont town of St. Albans, robbing three banks and setting off a melee that resulted in one death. Gen. John A. Dix, commander of the Military District of the East, ordered his troops to pursue the raiders into Canada and either destroy them or bring them back for trial. Vermonters captured Young and others and turned them over to Canadian authorities. Later a Montreal court freed them.

Secretary of State William H. Seward warned London that the United States, if the raids continued, would terminate the Rush-Bagot agreement of 1817 that demilitarized the U.S.-Canadian boundary and proceed to strengthen its border defenses. President Lincoln instituted a burdensome passport system to check movement across the border. Canadian opinion now became more contrite, troubled by the South's abuse of Canada's official neutrality. As peace returned to the border, Washington, in March 1865, terminated the passport system and reaffirmed the Rush-Bagot convention.

[*See also* Espionage, *articles on* Confederate Secret Service *and* Confederate Military Spies; Propaganda.]

BIBLIOGRAPHY

Crooks, David Paul. *The North, the South, and the Powers, 1861–1865.* New York, 1974.

Owsley, Frank Lawrence. *King Cotton Diplomacy: Foreign Relations of the Confederate States of America.* Revised by Harriet Chappell Owsley. Chicago, 1959.

Winks, Robin W. *Canada and the United States: The Civil War Years.* Baltimore, 1960.

NORMAN A. GRAEBNER

CANTEY, JAMES (1818–1874), brigadier general. South Carolinian James Cantey already possessed an intimate knowledge of war when he volunteered to fight for the Confederacy; he had been wounded during the Mexican War while serving as a captain in his home state's Palmetto Regiment. As a state politician in the years preceding 1861, Cantey had advocated secession, and so once again he eagerly enlisted, this time in the Confederate army to defend the South's separation from the Union.

During the first year of the war, the Fifteenth Alabama Regiment elected Cantey colonel. He served in this position in the Shenandoah Valley under Thomas J. ("Stonewall") Jackson. He saw action in the battles near Richmond during the summer of 1862, and his superiors credited him for the Confederate victory at Cross Keys, Virginia, on June 8. Later that year, he received a transfer to the West where he organized a brigade that established camp in Mobile to defend the city.

In the winter of 1864 Cantey's brigade underwent reorganization at Dalton, Georgia, and joined the recently restructured Army of Tennessee. Newly reinforced, the brigade moved southward in an attempt to defend Atlanta from the advancing line of Union troops.

During the last years of the war, poor health forced Cantey to spend long periods away from his command. He joined his brigade only intermittently as it served in Tennessee with John Bell Hood, and, finally, in the Carolina campaign with Joseph E. Johnston.

After the war Cantey returned to his plantation in

JAMES CANTEY.   Shown as a colonel in the First Alabama Infantry.
LIBRARY OF CONGRESS

Alabama, where he remained until his death, having never requested a pardon from the Union.

BIBLIOGRAPHY

Evans, Clement A., ed. *Confederate Military History*. 12 vols. Atlanta, 1899. Extended ed. in 19 vols. Wilmington, N.C., 1987–1989.

Wakelyn, Jon L. *Biographical Dictionary of the Confederacy*. Edited by Frank E. Vandiver. Westport, Conn., 1977.

Warner, Ezra J. *Generals in Gray: Lives of the Confederate Commanders*. Baton Rouge, La., 1959.

JENNIFER LUND

CAPERS, ELLISON (1837–1908), brigadier general.

Capers was born to a prominent Charleston family and graduated from the South Carolina Military Academy in 1857. He became a professor there, teaching mathematics and rhetoric.

With war rapidly approaching, Capers was elected major of the First South Carolina Regiment of Rifles and was present on Sullivan's Island during the bombardment of Fort Sumter. Afterward he helped Clement H. Stevens recruit the Twenty-fourth South Carolina Infantry and was elected its lieutenant colonel. The regiment served around the Charleston environs until mid-1863 and helped repel the Union assault at Secessionville, June 16, 1862, on James Island. Capers was wounded at Jackson when his regiment was dispatched to Mississippi to attempt relief of the siege of Vicksburg and four months later he was again wounded at Chickamauga. He also fought at Missionary Ridge. Promoted to colonel, Capers led the Twenty-fourth South Carolina through the Atlanta campaign and the invasion of Tennessee until he was wounded at Franklin. At times he commanded States Rights Gist's brigade but did not receive his promotion to brigadier general until March 1, 1865. He led the brigade briefly in the Carolinas.

With peace returned, Capers became secretary of state for South Carolina at thirty years of age. He then entered the Episcopal ministry and in 1884 served as bishop of the state. Active in veterans' affairs, Capers was chaplain general of the United Confederate Veterans. He died in Columbia, South Carolina, in 1908.

BIBLIOGRAPHY

Evans, Clement A., ed. *Confederate Military History*. 12 vols. Atlanta, 1899. Extended ed. in 19 vols. Wilmington, N.C., 1987–1989.

Warner, Ezra J. *Generals in Gray: Lives of the Confederate Commanders*. Baton Rouge, La., 1959.

DENNIS KELLY

CAPERTON, ALLEN T. (1810–1876), congressman from Virginia.

Scion of a wealthy planter family, Caperton was born at Elmwood, the family estate near Union, in Monroe County, Virginia (present-day West Virginia). He was educated at the University of Virginia and Yale University, where he finished seventh in the class of 1832. The next year he married Harriet Echols and studied law in Staunton, Virginia. After admission to the bar, he practiced in Monroe County for only a brief time before entering politics and business.

The economic interests of western Virginia form a theme throughout Caperton's life before, during, and after the war. Internal improvements were especially important to him as a way to tie the mountainous western portion of the state into the national market. Through his interests in the economic well-being of his region he did very well for himself. Caperton was a director of the largest engineering project in Virginia before the war, the James and Kanawha Canal, and by the end of the antebellum period his investments had made him a wealthy man.

A Whig, he represented Monroe County in the Virginia House of Delegates and Senate off and on during the 1840s and 1850s. He served as a delegate to the Virginia constitutional convention (1850–1851) where regional antagonisms predominated. Not surprisingly, he championed the western Virginia argument that voter representation should be based on the white population only rather than continuing to permit eastern Virginia slaveholders to inflate their influence by including their bondsmen in the calculation.

When the secession crisis arose, Caperton was elected as a Unionist to the Virginia convention in 1861. On the first vote, he cast his ballot with the majority against secession. Like many other members of the convention, however, his Unionism was conditional. When Abraham Lincoln called for volunteers to suppress the rebellious South, Caperton switched sides and voted for disunion.

When William B. Preston died in November 1862, five candidates sought his seat in the Confederate Senate. No front-runner emerged at first, and it took twenty ballots before the General Assembly elected Caperton to the post on January 26, 1863. He served in that capacity until the dissolution of the Confederate Senate in 1865. His committee assignments included Accounts, Conference, Engrossment and Enrollment, Foreign Relations, and Judiciary. His legislative service was influenced by his interest in maintaining a sound economy and by his championing of the interests of small farmers. These two goals reflected genuinely held opinions, but they also allowed him ample scope to express his personal animus toward Jefferson Davis.

Especially in his position as chairman of the Committee on Accounts he opposed the administration by insisting that efforts to foster a sound economy not be sacrificed to military necessity. He opposed Davis at nearly every point, in particular arguing against government authority in monetary policy, suspension of habeas corpus, conscription, and impressment. He opposed substitution, calling it class favoritism. He thought arming the slaves was tantamount to emancipation. Toward the end of the war, he tried to wrest foreign policy from Davis's hands. Though a wealthy man, Caperton represented the interests of yeomen farmers in tax policy: he wanted taxes based on financial assets rather than land.

After Appomattox he returned to his hometown in Monroe County, now part of the new state of West Virginia. When restrictions on his participation in public life lapsed in 1875, he was elected as a Democrat to the U.S. Senate. Still keen to promote the economic development of the region, he used his seat to that end, though he did not have time to make much of a mark in the Senate. He died in Washington, D.C., on July 26, 1876.

BIBLIOGRAPHY

Gaines, William H., Jr. *Biographical Register of Members, Virginia State Convention of 1861, First Session.* Richmond, Va., 1969.
Wakelyn, Jon L. *Biographical Dictionary of the Confederacy.* Edited by Frank E. Vandiver. Westport, Conn., 1977.
Warner, Ezra J., and W. Buck Yearns. *Biographical Register of the Confederate Congress.* Baton Rouge, La., 1975.

NELSON D. LANKFORD

CAROLINAS CAMPAIGN OF SHERMAN.

On December 22, 1864, Maj. Gen. William Tecumseh Sherman sent the following telegram to President Abraham Lincoln: "I beg to present you as a Christmas gift the city of Savannah." With this communication Sherman brought to a conclusion his dramatic March to the Sea. By all standard rules of strategy, his next move should have been the immediate transfer of his army by water to Virginia where Lt. Gen. Ulysses S. Grant had the Army of Northern Virginia bottled up behind fortifications at Petersburg. The Federal navy had the ships for this move, and both Lincoln and Grant supported the plan. Sherman, however, did not. He wanted instead to apply total war, as he had done in Georgia, to the Carolinas, especially the Palmetto State for its role in bringing on the conflict. He believed that by bringing the war to the Carolina home front his operations would have a direct bearing on the struggle in Virginia.

Sherman, a very persuasive individual, was granted permission for the Carolinas march, his position having been strengthened considerably by the news of Maj. Gen. George Thomas's near-annihilation of the Confederate Army of Tennessee at Nashville in mid-December 1864.

Sherman's plan of campaign called for feints on Charleston, South Carolina, and Augusta, Georgia, followed by a move on Columbia, South Carolina's capital city. From there he planned to march in a northeasterly direction first to Fayetteville on the Cape Fear River in North Carolina and then to Goldsboro, which was connected to the North Carolina coast by two railroads. By this circuit he could cripple the chief lines of communication in the Carolinas as well as destroy all public and industrial property in his line of march. Furthermore, by bringing war to the home front, he felt certain that a defeatist psychology would be instilled in civilians and soldiers alike.

Since Sherman planned to sever all connections with his base at Savannah, the men would have to forage liberally in the countryside to survive. Army wagons could transport only a limited quantity of provisions, and no government supplies could be expected until the army reached the Cape Fear River. In an attempt to regulate the foraging parties, Sherman issued very strict orders, but as had been the case on the March to the Sea, there was a wide discrepancy between the orders and the actions of some of the men. Most of the outrages committed in the Carolinas were the work of "bummers," self-constituted foragers who operated on their own and not under supervision.

By late January 1865, Sherman's sixty thousand veterans had begun crossing the Savannah River into South Caro-

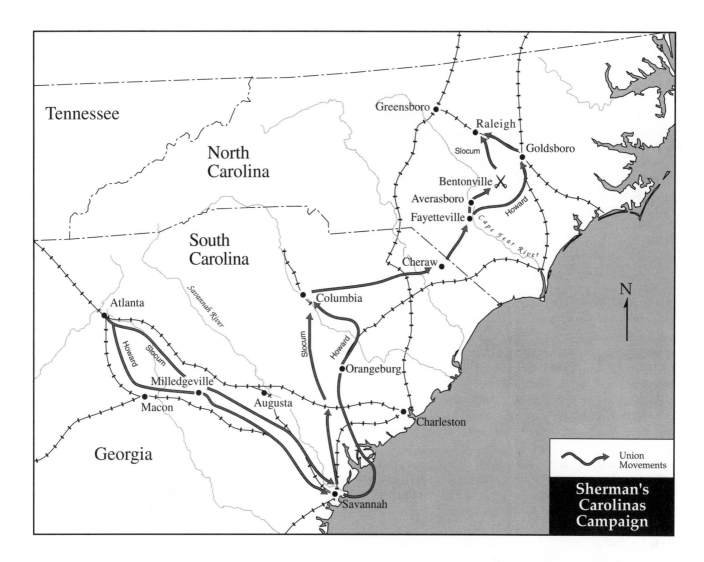

lina. The army was divided into two wings, the left commanded by Maj. Gen. Henry W. Slocum, the right by Maj. Gen. O. O. Howard. Each wing in turn comprised two corps, and each corps followed a different line of advance, forming a front over forty miles wide. Brig. Gen. Judson Kilpatrick was in charge of the cavalry.

When Sherman commenced his Carolinas campaign, the meager Confederate forces that might oppose him were scattered from Mississippi to Virginia, so by the second week in February the Federal army had penetrated well into South Carolina. On the twelfth, Orangeburg was occupied and five days later Columbia was in Sherman's hands. Much of South Carolina's capital city went up in flames on February 17. Burning cotton, high winds, and drunken Federal soldiers were to blame for this conflagration. "Though I never ordered it," Sherman said, "and never wished it, I have never shed any tears over the event, because I believe that it hastened what we all fought for, the end of the war." Lt. Charles A. Brown of the Twenty-first

Michigan commented: "South Carolina may have been the cause of the whole thing, but she has had an awful punishment."

At Cheraw, the army's last stop in South Carolina, Sherman learned that Gen. Joseph E. Johnston had replaced P. G. T. Beauregard as commander of Confederate forces in the Carolinas and Georgia. He now concluded that his antagonist of the Atlanta campaign would somehow manage to unite his forces and give battle at a place of his own choosing. This Sherman had hoped to avoid.

On March 8 North Carolina for the first time felt the full weight of the Federal army. Sherman, assuming a friendly reception from North Carolina's pro-Union element, issued orders for the gentler treatment of the local citizens, but he did nothing to stop the burning of the state's great pine forests. North Carolina's turpentine woods blazed in "splendor as bummers touched matches to congealed sap in notches on tree trunks."

The most formidable obstacle in Sherman's path lay in

the swirling waters of the Lumber River and the adjacent swamps. The region prompted him to remark, "It was the damnedest marching I ever saw." Fortunately for him, his engineers by now had become skilled at bridging streams and corduroying roads.

Federal cavalry crossed the Lumber on March 8. Upon learning that Confederate horsemen under Lt. Gen. Wade Hampton were nearby, Kilpatrick set a trap for him, only to have his own camp surprised by the enemy on the morning of the tenth. Kilpatrick escaped capture by hastily departing the bed of a female traveling companion. Eventually the Federals retook their camp. As a result there is some disagreement over who won the cavalry engagement at Monroe's Crossroads, contemptuously tagged by some as "Kilpatrick's Shirt-tail Skedaddle."

By engaging the Federals in battle, the horsemen in gray opened the road to Fayetteville. That night near the city, the Confederate cavalry under Hampton and Maj. Gen. Joseph Wheeler joined forces with Lt. Gen. William J. Hardee's small command, which had been moving north just ahead of Sherman. On the eleventh as the Federals entered the city from the south, the Confederates withdrew across the Cape Fear, burning the bridge behind them.

At Fayetteville Sherman ordered the arsenal destroyed along with other properties. He also took the opportunity to clear his columns of the vast numbers of white refugees and blacks following his army. He referred to them as "twenty to thirty thousand useless mouths."

From Savannah to Fayetteville, Sherman had managed his army in an almost flawless manner. From the Cape Fear to Goldsboro, however, it was a different story. He not only mistakenly placed little emphasis on Hardee's delaying action at Averasboro on March 16 but also allowed his own columns to become so strung out that Johnston came close to crushing one of the Federal corps near Bentonville. At this village, twenty miles west of Goldsboro, Johnston had skillfully managed on the nineteenth to concentrate his scattered forces, although a sparse group it was, totaling no more than 21,000 effectives. Seldom in history have so few been led in battle by so many officers of high rank. Present on the battlefield that day were two full generals of the Confederacy, three lieutenant generals, and numerous brigadier and major generals.

Completely ignorant of Johnston's bold move, Sherman allowed his Fourteenth Corps to be caught off guard. For a while it seemed the Confederates would carry the day, but Federal reinforcements in the afternoon blunted Johnston's offensive. More Federal troops reached Bentonville on the twentieth, and by the next day Sherman had his entire army on the field. That night Johnston withdrew to Smithfield, ten miles to the west.

Though Bentonville was the largest battle fought on North Carolina soil (Confederate casualties, 2,606; Federal,

1,527), it was not one of the war's decisive engagements. Nevertheless, it must rank as an important battle. It marked the successful conclusion of Sherman's Carolinas campaign, and it was large in scope; 81,000 men were locked in combat over a three-day period.

At Goldsboro, Sherman's victorious troops linked up with Maj. Gen. John M. Schofield's command, and on March 25 the first train from the coast arrived. This completed the task Sherman had set for himself upon leaving Savannah.

After the war, Sherman commented that he would be remembered for the March to the Sea but that that operation was child's play compared to the Carolinas campaign. He characterized it as "one of the longest and most important marches ever made by an organized army in a civilized country. The distance from Savannah to Goldsboro is four hundred and twenty-five miles and the route embraced five large navigable rivers. . . . The country generally was in a state of nature with innumerable swamps . . . mud roads, nearly every mile of which had to be corduroyed. . . . We had captured . . . important cities and depots of supplies. . . . We had in mid-winter accomplished the whole journey . . . in fifty days . . . and had reached Goldsboro with the army in superb order."

The Federal march was a remarkable logistical feat that brought home to the people of the Carolinas the realities of war. Still, this operation had little direct bearing on Gen. Robert E. Lee's decision to surrender. It was the decisive Confederate defeat at Nashville coupled with the collapse of the transportation system in Virginia that paved the way for Appomattox.

[See also Averasboro, North Carolina; Bentonville, North Carolina; Bummers; Fort Fisher, North Carolina.]

BIBLIOGRAPHY

Barrett, John G. Sherman's March through the Carolinas. Chapel Hill, N.C., 1956.

Glatthaar, Joseph T. The March to the Sea and Beyond: Sherman's Troops in the Savannah and Carolinas Campaigns. New York, 1985.

Lewis, Lloyd. Sherman, Fighting Prophet. New York, 1932.

Luvaas, J. "Johnston's Last Stand—Bentonville." North Carolina Historical Review 33 (1956): 332–358.

JOHN G. BARRETT

CARROLL, DAVID W. (1816–1905), colonel and congressman from Arkansas. David Williamson Carroll was born March 11, 1816, in Maryland and moved to Arkansas in 1836. He was a land agent, schoolteacher, attorney, and Democratic politician in Pine Bluff, Jefferson County. He supported secession in 1860 and 1861.

In February 1862, he organized a military company at Pine Bluff that became Company K, Eighteenth Arkansas

Infantry. He was elected colonel of the regiment the following April. Carroll's regiment was at Corinth in May 1862, and the colonel contracted a fever and began to suffer from chronic diarrhea. As a result of his medical problems he resigned from the army on August 4 and returned to Pine Bluff, where he used his connection with Senator Robert W. Johnson to obtain the position of commissary.

In the summer of 1864 Carroll was elected to the House of Representatives to replace Augustus H. Garland who had been chosen for the Senate. He reached Richmond in January 1865. In Congress he witnessed the collapse of the Confederacy and supported most of the measures introduced to prolong its survival. He opposed increased taxes and legislation to arm slaves, however. Along with Congressmen Batson and Hanley of Arkansas, Carroll remained at Richmond until its evacuation.

After the war he returned to Pine Bluff, where he served as probate and county judge, practiced law, and farmed until his death, June 24, 1905.

BIBLIOGRAPHY

Hallum, John. *Biographical and Pictorial History of Arkansas*. Albany, N.Y., 1887.
Obituary. *Arkansas Gazette* (Little Rock), June 24, 1905.
Warner, Ezra J., and W. Buck Yearns. *Biographical Register of the Confederate Congress*. Baton Rouge, La., 1975.

CARL H. MONEYHON

CARROLL, WILLIAM HENRY (1810–1868),

brigadier general. Born in Nashville, Tennessee, Carroll moved during his youth to Panola County, Mississippi, and returned to his native state in 1848 to serve as postmaster of Memphis. At the beginning of the war, Carroll received a commission as a brigadier general in the Tennessee Provisional Army and, once in the Confederacy, as colonel of the Thirty-seventh Tennessee Infantry. In September 1861, Maj. Gen. Leonidas Polk sent Carroll to eastern Tennessee to recruit at least one regiment into military service and to persuade inhabitants of Unionist counties to support the Confederate government.

After a promotion to brigadier general on October 26, Carroll went to Knoxville to become the commander of that post and "to guard the railroads and crush the tory combinations." Passing briefly through Chattanooga, Carroll was noticed by Col. S. A. M. Wood of the Seventh Alabama Volunteers, who wrote to Maj. Gen. Braxton Bragg that Carroll "has been drunk not less than five years. He is stupid, but easily controlled." Arriving at Knoxville in late November, Carroll and his force of five thousand poorly armed men attempted to maintain control over the area's disaffected population. Carroll proclaimed martial law in Knoxville and the surrounding county to the distance of one

mile from the corporate limits of the city. He also sent out troops to hunt down suspected bridge-burners, especially those insurgents who destroyed the Lick Creek Bridge on the East Tennessee and Virginia Railroad.

On December 10, Carroll received orders for his brigade to join Brig. Gen. Felix K. Zollicoffer north of the Cumberland River at Beach Grove, Kentucky. Hesitant to march his ill-equipped force through Unionist counties, Carroll did not arrive at his destination until January 15. The combined forces of Carroll and Zollicoffer, under the command of Brig. Gen. George B. Crittenden, engaged and were defeated by nearby Federal troops led by Maj. Gen. George Henry Thomas at the Battle of Mill Springs. For his part, Carroll blamed the defeat on "the inefficient and worthless character of [his] arms, being old flint-lock muskets and country rifles, nearly half of which would not fire at all."

The disastrous nature of the defeat at Mill Springs raised questions about the competency of Carroll and Crittenden (Zollicoffer was killed during the battle). On March 31, 1862, at Iuka, Mississippi, Maj. Gen. William J. Hardee "found sufficient evidence" against the two to require their arrest. Carroll was charged with "drunkenness, incompetency, and neglect of his command." After requesting a court of inquiry on his own behalf, Carroll held his rank for the remainder of the year, but saw little duty other than the "command" of seven hundred convalescents who left Knoxville in October to join their regiments in Kentucky. Having been labeled by Bragg as "unsuited" for responsibility and "not safe . . . to intrust with any command," Carroll resigned his commission on February 1, 1863, and joined his recently emigrated family in Canada. He died in Montreal five years later.

BIBLIOGRAPHY

Jones, Terry. "William Henry Carroll." In *The Confederate General*. Edited by William C. Davis. Vol. 1. Harrisburg, Pa., 1991.
Porter, James D. *Tennessee*. Vol. 8 of *Confederate Military History*. Edited by Clement A. Evans. Atlanta, 1899. Vol. 10 of extended ed. Wilmington, N.C., 1987.
Warner, Ezra J. *Generals in Gray: Lives of the Confederate Commanders*. Baton Rouge, La., 1959.

ALAN C. DOWNS

CARTER, JOHN CARPENTER (1837–1864),

brigadier general. Born in Waynesboro, Georgia, December 19, 1837, Carter was educated at the University of Virginia and Cumberland University. He studied law at the latter institution and taught there before moving to Memphis in 1860.

Carter helped organize a Memphis military unit that became Company L of the Thirty-eighth Tennessee Infantry Regiment. Carter became captain of the company in September 1861, replacing the original captain. When the regiment reorganized early in 1862, Carter became colonel. For more than two years he commanded either the regiment or—when the brigade commander was absent—the brigade.

Meanwhile, Carter and his command participated in most of the major battles of the Army of Tennessee, winning high praise for gallantry at Shiloh, Perryville, and Murfreesboro. Carter was commanding the brigade when the Atlanta campaign opened in May 1864. His fine conduct during the first part of that struggle led to his promotion to brigadier general, to date from July 7.

After the fall of Atlanta, Carter and his brigade participated in the Franklin and Nashville campaign. On November 30, 1864, while directing his men in the great assault on the Federal works at Franklin, Tennessee, Carter was mortally wounded. He was taken to a nearby house where he died on December 10. He was buried in Rose Hill Cemetery in Columbia, Tennessee.

BIBLIOGRAPHY

Bergeron, Arthur W., Jr. "John Carpenter Carter." In *The Confederate General*. Edited by William C. Davis. Vol. 1. Harrisburg, Pa., 1991.
Riley, Harris D. "A Gallant Adopted Son of Tennessee—General John C. Carter, C.S.A." *Tennessee Historical Quarterly* 48 (1989): 195–208.

RICHARD M. MCMURRY

CARTER, JONATHAN H. (1823 or 1824–1887), naval officer. Born in North Carolina, Carter graduated from the U.S. Naval Academy in 1846. Resigning his commission April 25, 1861, he joined the Confederate navy and was ordered to the Western Department. Maj. Gen. Leonidas Polk gave Lieutenant Carter *Ed Howard* and instructed him to proceed to New Orleans, strip the vessel to its shell, and convert it into a gunboat. In late September Carter was reassigned, but Polk's protest enabled Carter to finish *General Polk* in mid-October and become its commander.

After assisting in the evacuation of New Madrid, Missouri, on March 14, 1862, Carter engaged the enemy near Island Number 10. When USS *Carondelet* passed the island on April 4, Carter, under orders from Confederate Como. George N. Hollins, took *General Polk* up the Yazoo River, where it was burned June 26 to prevent its capture.

In October, Carter undertook the construction of ironclads on the Red River, and by early 1863 he was supervising similar work at Shreveport. Overcoming almost insurmountable obstacles, Carter on April 13 launched *Missouri*, which still lacked iron cladding and propulsion machinery.

Circumstances prevented the construction of additional vessels, so when the government accepted *Missouri* on September 12, Carter labored to secure cannon and crewmen for it. The ship was finally completed in early 1864, but low water prevented Carter from engaging the enemy during the Red River campaign that spring. He surrendered *Missouri* in Shreveport June 3, 1865, and was paroled.

After the war Carter operated a cotton plantation near Shreveport until financial difficulties forced him to abandon the project. He died in 1887 in Shirley, Virginia.

BIBLIOGRAPHY

Jeter, Katherine Brash. "Against All Odds: Lt. Jonathan H. Carter, CSN, and His Ironclad." *Louisiana History* 28 (1987): 263–288.
Still, William N., Jr. "The Confederate Ironclad *Missouri*." *Louisiana Studies* 4 (1965): 101–110.
Still, William N., Jr. *Iron Afloat: The Story of the Confederate Armorclads*. Nashville, Tenn., 1971.

LAWRENCE L. HEWITT

CARUTHERS, ROBERT LOONEY (1800–1882), congressman from Tennessee. Caruthers was born in Smith County, Tennessee, on July 31, 1800. Orphaned at the age of twelve, he lived his teenage years with his grandparents and attended Greeneville College briefly. In 1823 he was admitted to the bar and opened a law office in Carthage. In the same year he became principal clerk of the state house of representatives before moving to Lebanon, Tennessee, in 1826 and establishing a law practice there.

Caruthers in 1827 was appointed attorney general of the Sixth Circuit, a position he held for five years. He viewed politics as a means of getting ahead, and he soon became an active Whig and follower of John Bell. In 1835 he was elected to the state legislature, and six years later he replaced Bell as U.S. congressman from the Sixth District when Bell chose not to run for reelection. He became a founder and chairman of the Board of Trustees of Cumberland University in 1842 and of the law department of the university in 1847. By 1852, he had caught the eye of Whig governor William B. Campbell who appointed him to membership on the state supreme court. In the meantime he accumulated considerable wealth, owning in 1860 property estimated at $400,000 and holding more than a hundred slaves.

As civil war approached, Caruthers took the same position that other Whigs did in denouncing secession and urging a peaceful solution to the nation's crisis. He supported John Bell for the presidency in 1860, and early the following year joined John Tyler and others in Washington at the peace conference where delegates tried to find a way to avoid war. Finally, when Tennessee seceded, he was elected to the Confederate Congress as the representative of the Sixth District. A few months after his election to the House, legislators considered his candidacy for the Confederate Senate, but he was defeated on the thirty-second ballot. During the few months he served in Congress he strongly supported President Jefferson Davis and the administration, but he actually attended only a few of the congressional sessions.

In 1863, Caruthers was elected governor of Tennessee but was unable to serve because of the Federal occupation of Nashville and much of the rest of the state. Shortly after the election he returned to Lebanon and became a professor of law at Cumberland University, a position he held until his death on October 2, 1882. One of his colleagues on the law faculty described him as "tall and spare with . . . paucity of flesh, loose jointed and ungainly of limb . . . large mouth and thin lips, straight nose, grey eyes, heavy and capacious brow and head."

Caruthers was buried in the Cedar Grove Cemetery in Wilson County.

BIBLIOGRAPHY

Bone, Winstead P. *A History of Cumberland University, 1842–1935.* Lebanon, Tenn., 1935.

Martin, Andrew B. *Life and Character of Judge Robert L. Caruthers, an Address by Andrew B. Martin.* Pamphlet. Nashville, Tenn., 1883.

McBride, Robert, and Dan M. Robison. *Biographical Directory of the Tennessee General Assembly.* Vol. 1. Nashville, Tenn., 1975.

Roller, David C., and Robert W. Twyman. *The Encyclopedia of Southern History.* Baton Rouge, La., 1979.

Warner, Ezra J., and W. Buck Yearns. *Biographical Register of the Confederate Congress.* Baton Rouge, La., 1975.

ROBERT E. CORLEW

CARY, HETTY

CARY, HETTY (1836–1892), Confederate belle. Hetty Cary, a well-known belle of Baltimore and Richmond society, endeared herself to the Confederacy forever when she and her sister Jennie and cousin Constance sang "Maryland, My Maryland" to Southern troops, just after the First Battle of Manassas. On that same occasion, Gen. P. G. T. Beauregard reportedly feted the Cary women in a mock ceremony wherein Hetty was dubbed a lieutenant colonel, Jennie a first lieutenant, and Constance a captain general. The Confederacy displayed a buoyant optimism during this early stage of war, and the Cary women symbolized a confident, even playful, sense of invincibility.

Although all three Cary women were well-known patriots, and Jennie Cary set the lyrics of "My Maryland" to the tune of "Lauriger Horatius," it was Hetty Cary who most captured the imagination of Lost Cause chroniclers— perhaps because of her striking looks and flair for the dramatic. The Civil War memoirs of Mrs. D. Giraud Wright

described Hetty Cary as a "titian-haired" beauty with a "lilies and roses" complexion. Mrs. Wright reported that Hetty was once imprisoned at Fort McHenry for publicly wearing Confederate colors, and that on another occasion she had waved a Confederate flag from her Baltimore window as Federal troops passed by. Supposedly, the Union colonel below pronounced Hetty too beautiful to arrest.

Hetty Cary's 1865 wedding in Richmond, Virginia, to Confederate Col. John Pegram three weeks before his death on the Petersburg battlefield provided a final tragic flourish to her identification with the Confederacy. In 1879 Cary married Professor H. Newell Martin. She spent her remaining years teaching and touring Europe.

BIBLIOGRAPHY

Brock, Sallie A. *Richmond during the War: Four Years of Personal Observations by a Richmond Lady.* New York, 1867. Reprint, Alexandria, Va., 1983.

Harwell, Richard B., ed. *The Confederate Reader.* New York, 1957.

Simkins, Francis Butler, and James Welch Patton. *The Women of the Confederacy.* Richmond and New York, 1936.

Wright, Mrs. D. Giraud. *A Southern Girl in '61: The War-Time Memories of a Confederate Senator's Daughter.* New York, 1905.

VICTORIA E. BYNUM

CASTLE THUNDER PRISON

CASTLE THUNDER PRISON. In August 1862, the Confederates opened this facility for the provost marshal of their capital's Eastern District. Their largest prison of its type, it consisted of three impressed commercial buildings on Cary Street near Libby Prison. The largest of the brick structures, Gleanor's Tobacco Warehouse and Factory, three and a half stories high, was divided into several large rooms and a number of cells. Gas and water were piped in, but because many of the windows were boarded up, the air was foul. The prison confined Confederate deserters, civilians, and political enemies. On either side were Whitlock's Warehouse, used for blacks and women, and Palmer's Factory, which held Federal deserters and others. These winglike prisons were connected by a wall, thus creating an enclosed yard for exercise by some of the prisoners. Newspapers gave the complex its ominous name, pairing it with another warehouse prison they called "Castle Lightning."

The first inmates were several hundred men transferred from Castle Godwin, a "Negro Jail" that had been used earlier as a provost prison. The Confederates intended Castle Thunder to hold 1,400 people, but, as in other prisons, its capacity was often exceeded. In mid-1863, the buildings held more than 3,000 prisoners. Among those confined in Castle Thunder in the course of the war were about 100 women, including accused spies, women who had disguised themselves as men to enter the Confederate army, and captured Unionists. Among the latter, the most famous was the first female U.S. Army surgeon, Dr. Mary Walker. Another woman achieved notoriety by naming her child born in the prison "Castellina Thunder Lee."

The prison's best-known head was Capt. George W. Alexander. A Georgia native, he was a prewar veteran of the Navy who had joined the Confederates, been captured in Maryland, and escaped from prison. In Richmond, he became part of the circle of Marylanders around Gen. John H. Winder, who made him an assistant provost marshal in charge of Castle Thunder. Alexander was a flamboyant man who sang in a Richmond theatrical, dressed all in black, rode a black horse, and used an enormous black dog named Nero to intimidate his prisoners.

Like many supervisors of provost prisons, Alexander believed that it required stern discipline to deal with social outcasts who frequently robbed one another and tried to escape. He punished one group by forcing them to stand outdoors in a winter rain for several days. Others he had flogged, hung by the thumbs, bucked and gagged, dressed in a "barrel shirt," and shut up in a tiny "sweat room." Rumors about such abuses led to an investigation by a committee of the Confederate House of Representatives in April 1863.

In his defense Alexander cited orders from General Winder to use corporal punishment. He also pointed to his creation of a thirty-bed hospital run by his wife and to his provision of a physician's supervision for the occasional branding of prisoners. The majority of the committee praised Captain Alexander, but a minority denounced his treatment of prisoners as unjust. In December 1863, Alexander was arrested for trading in Federal money and taking bribes from prisoners. Though acquitted by a court-martial, he was subsequently transferred to the Salisbury Prison. His successor, Capt. Lucien W. Richardson, a Virginian, succeeded better in maintaining order and improving conditions enough to win the praise of Confederate inspectors.

On the night of the fall of Richmond, guards removed the remaining prisoners. Castle Thunder's front door key was taken to New York where it was auctioned for the benefit of orphans of Union soldiers. Like several other prison officials, Captain Alexander found it expedient to leave the country, returning to Baltimore when the political climate cooled. The prison buildings were returned to their previous owners. In 1879, the Castle burned, and the site today is a corporation parking lot.

[See also Provost Marshal.]

BIBLIOGRAPHY

Blakey, Arch Frederic. General John H. Winder, C.S.A. Gainesville, Fla., 1990.

Byrne, Frank L. "Prison Pens of Suffering." In Fighting for Time. Vol. 4 of The Image of War, 1861–1865. Edited by William C. Davis. Garden City, N.Y., 1983.

Parker, Sandra V. Richmond's Civil War Prisons. Lynchburg, Va., 1990.

Radley, Kenneth. Rebel Watchdog: The Confederate States Army Provost Guard. Baton Rouge, La., 1989.

FRANK L. BYRNE

CASUALTIES. *For discussion of the number of casualties in the Civil War, see* Civil War, *article on* Losses and Numbers, *and entries on particular battles. For discussion of the types of casualties, see* Health and Medicine, *article on* Battle Injuries.

CAVALRY. The Confederate cavalry reigned supreme for the first two years of the Civil War. Even Philip Sheridan, the cavalry commander for Ulysses S. Grant's Army of the Potomac, wrote in his memoirs, "From the very beginning of the war the enemy had shown more wisdom respecting his cavalry than we. Instead of wasting its strength by a policy of disintegration he, at an early day, had organized his mounted force into compact masses, and plainly made it a favorite."

Part of the Southern superiority was probably due to the caliber of such leaders as J. E. B. Stuart, Wade Hampton, Fitzhugh Lee, and Nathan Bedford Forrest. But there were other reasons. The Confederate cavalry, early in the war, was organized into one independent, autonomous unit and acted as such. The regiments never suffered from the piecemeal detachment to individual infantry units that plagued the Federal mounted arm until 1863 when it too was organized into one unit. Stuart was given command of the cavalry of the Confederate Army of the Potomac (the precursor to Robert E. Lee's Army of Northern Virginia) in October 1861. In the West, the Confederate Army of Tennessee brigaded its cavalry in November 1862. It consisted of four brigades under Joseph Wheeler, John Austin Wharton, Nathan Bedford Forrest, and John Hunt Morgan.

Given this structure, the Confederates were able to introduce new tactics into cavalry doctrine—making large-scale mounted raids and putting cavalry into the battle to fight dismounted. Stuart conceived of the raid as a viable operation and other Confederate commanders followed suit, as did the Federals later in the war. The Confederates also introduced the tactic of having the cavalry ride to the strategic point on the battlefield to fight dismounted on a regular basis. Both these innovations rested upon the first—the new, and superior, organization of the Confederate cavalry.

Organization

In the Virginia theater, Stuart, and later Hampton and Fitz Lee, commanded the Army of Northern Virginia's cavalry, and Wheeler commanded the horsemen in the Army of Tennessee. The Army of Northern Virginia's cavalry began with about 1,700 troopers in six regiments in late 1861. By mid-1862 Stuart's division had grown to six brigades under Fitz Lee, William Henry Fitzhugh Lee, Beverly Holcombe Robertson, William Edmondson ("Grumble") Jones, Wade Hampton, and Albert Gallatin Jenkins, and numbered some 4,000 present for duty out of an aggregate of some 7,000. By mid-1863 the cavalry had grown to 10,000 men in seven brigades—much too large a force for its organizational makeup. Because of this, Stuart's division was broken into two divisions under Fitz Lee and Hampton, each with three brigades of two to four regiments.

Stuart's cavalry corps soon numbered 20,000 present and absent. Though the rolls contained nearly 20,000 names, only about a third might be present at any one time because of the way the cavalry had been established. Each trooper provided his own mount and was paid sixty cents a day for its use. When a trooper lost his horse, because of disease or battle wounds, he had to secure another, which usually meant traveling home to get another horse from the farm. As the war dragged on, it became harder and harder to find serviceable mounts, and this added to the number of cavalrymen absent because of sickness, wounds, or desertion.

In May 1864 the Army of Northern Virginia's cavalry was further enlarged organizationally into three divisions, with William Henry Fitzhugh Lee becoming the new major general. After Stuart was killed at Yellow Tavern in May 1864, Hampton was given command of the cavalry corps and Matthew Calbraith Butler was promoted to take Hampton's place in command of one of the divisions. By mid-1864 the number of cavalry had begun to decline. Of an aggregate of 14,418 in November, only 6,051 were present for duty, and 1,224 were dismounted. By the time of the surrender at Appomattox in April 1865, the cavalry numbered 134 officers and 1,425 enlisted men. It must be remembered, though, that a large portion of the Army of Northern Virginia's cavalry escaped from Appomattox to Lynchburg, some disbanding and riding home, others traveling south to continue the war in the Carolinas with Joseph E. Johnston's Army of Tennessee.

In 1862, the Army of Tennessee's four brigades comprised sixteen regiments in all. By January the next year, Wheeler's division numbered 8,300 men present for duty. In March a true cavalry corps was created for the Army of Tennessee when Wheeler's force was divided into three divisions under Morgan, Wharton, and William Thompson Martin. Each division had at least two brigades (Morgan's had three), with each brigade composed of two to five regiments. The corps' total strength was 6,872 men present for duty from an aggregate of 13,820. Forrest's division had two brigades of four and five regiments. By late 1863 Wheeler's troopers numbered 11,700 present of 28,000 on the rolls. In March 1865 this tally had dropped to 5,105 cavalrymen present of 7,042 on the rolls. On April 26, 1865, 175 officers and 2,331 enlisted men were paroled at Greensborough, North Carolina, when the Army of Tennessee surrendered.

Tactics

In addition to its initial superior organization, the Confederate cavalry's early ascendency over its Federal opponent stemmed from the less dogmatic approach its commanders took to the employment of mounted forces. Prior to the war, many of the future commanders of both North and South had been trained at West Point and Jefferson, and later Carlisle, Barracks. Their cavalry training revolved around Napoleon's maxims of war and the theories expounded by Henri de Jomini. These two Europeans believed that cavalry served a specific purpose on the battlefield as a supporting arm to the infantry and that its role within the army was limited. Basically, they thought that the cavalry was best suited for scouting, covering the army's flanks and rear, and charging infantry formations (but only after the main infantry attack) to ensure victory and cause confusion during the enemy's retreat. It was believed that cavalry could not act alone, either offensively or defensively, and that when in action cavalry should rely on the saber. These theories were mirrored in the doctrine and tactics taught within the U.S. Army prior to the Civil War.

The tactics that evolved from these theories were used throughout the war by the Confederate cavalry. At Manassas, independent companies like the famed "Black Horse Troop" of Warrenton and regiments of cavalry were used to seal the Southern victory by pursuing the retreating Federals across Stone Bridge, down the Warrenton Pike, to Centreville, and beyond. Throughout the war the Army of Northern Virginia and the Army of Tennessee used cavalry to scout the enemy's position and determine the intentions of the Union armies, both prior to Southern offensives and during the campaigns. Stuart's cavalry did an excellent job in covering Lee's flanks when the Army of Northern Virginia was marching south to the Rappahannock line in October 1862 after the Sharpsburg campaign. Stuart screened Lee's movements again when the Confederate army marched north on its way to Gettysburg in June 1863.

The cavalry was also used to control the area between the armies and to keep the Southern generals informed about Federal movements, intentions, and positions. In early 1861, prior to First Manassas, Stuart's horsemen did an excellent job of keeping Robert Paterson's Union force in

CONFEDERATE CAVALRY.   Shown attacking a Federal supply train near Jasper, Tennessee.

FRANK LESLIE'S ILLUSTRATED FAMOUS LEADERS AND BATTLE SCENES OF THE CIVIL WAR

the Shenandoah Valley from knowing the exact where-abouts of Joseph E. Johnston's army until after it had reached Manassas. After Manassas Stuart set up a line of outposts along the Potomac River to keep Johnston informed of enemy movements before him.

In April and May 1862, the Southern cavalry on the peninsula did another good job of keeping tabs on the Federals around Yorktown and covering John B. Magruder's withdrawal to Williamsburg. Throughout the war, whether along the Potomac, Rappahannock, Rapidan, or elsewhere, the Southern cavalry was used to cover the army's front by keeping tabs on the enemy before it, countering any Federal scouting raids, and warning of any major buildups that might signal an attack.

Throughout the war both Stuart's cavalry in Virginia and Wheeler's cavalry in the West were used to obtain supplies for their respective armies. This included everything from wagons, horses, and mules to uniforms, tents, money, and arms—horses and arms probably being the most important.

The charging of infantry formations by cavalry, in the traditional mounted attack was exemplified by Jubal Ear-

ly's use of his cavalry at Fisher's Hill on October 18, 1864. As dawn broke, the Confederate cavalry, positioned prior to sunrise on the Federal right flank, stormed into Sheridan's encampment, driving the men out of their camp and back beyond Middletown. After Sheridan's successful counter-attack, Early's cavalry covered the army's retreat by holding the pursuing Federals at bay while the infantry moved up the road and past key road and river crossings. From mid-March 1865 until Lee surrendered at Appomattox, covering the Army of Northern Virginia's rear was a full-time job for the cavalry as Grant relentlessly pushed Lee westward. This last campaign saw the Confederate cavalry mix mounted fighting with dismounted rearguard action to protect Lee's wagon trains and infantry formations from being surrounded and cut off.

Cavalry Raids. The most notable change in the use of cavalry, inaugurated by Stuart, was the large-scale mounted raid. Prior to 1862 it would have been thought foolish, and potentially disastrous, to send an army's cavalry force into enemy territory alone. But Stuart's "Ride around McClellan" in June 1862 changed that perception. Taking 1,200 men, Stuart covered 150 miles behind George B. McClellan's army to reconnoiter the Federal right flank and rear. By destroying considerable amounts of stores and capturing prisoners (with very little Confederate loss), Stuart changed the role of cavalry in this American war and established Confederate preeminence, at least until the Federals learned from their mistakes. During 1862 Stuart undertook three more raids, Forrest went on two, and Morgan conducted three.

Other famous raids by Stuart included assaults on Catlett's Station (August 22–23, 1862), Chambersburg (October 9–12, 1862), and Dumfries (December 26–31, 1862). During the raid on Catlett's Station, Stuart took 1,500 men to capture John Pope's headquarters. Besides destroying Federal stores, Stuart seized a large amount of money as well as Pope's papers, which gave Lee the information he needed to undertake the Second Manassas campaign. For Chambersburg, Stuart led 1,800 men into Pennsylvania to destroy machine shops and stores in the city and to round up about a thousand horses badly needed by the Army of Northern Virginia. The Dumfries raid was the fourth of a series of excursions against Ambrose Burnside's rear during November and December 1862. Stuart and 1,800 troopers destroyed a large amount of property, capturing prisoners, horses, wagons, and arms. But in July 1863 Stuart undertook his disastrous Gettysburg raid. This time he went too far afield with his force, and instead of gaining intelligence for Lee or securing supplies in a quick strike, he got bogged down with his booty and effectively took himself out of the Gettysburg campaign.

Forrest led 1,000 men in July 1862 on his first raid and captured 1,000 Federals at Murfreesboro along with a million dollars worth of stores, destroying important railroad bridges along the way. This action delayed a planned Federal offensive and forced two Union divisions to be diverted from the front to guard the rail lines of the rear. Forrest's second raid, in December 1862, was aimed at the rail line connecting Grant's headquarters at Columbus, Kentucky, and Federal troops in northern Mississippi. Forrest's 2,500 men tore up the Mobile and Ohio Railroad during this foray.

In Morgan's first raid, in July 1862, 800 troopers captured 1,200 prisoners and a number of Federal depots while covering one thousand miles. This raid lowered Northern morale and delayed another planned Federal offensive. Morgan's October 1862 raid against Lexington, Kentucky, involved 1,800 men and resulted in the capture of a number of posts and the destruction of several key railroad bridges. In December 1862 he conducted a raid at the head of 4,000 men; they netted 1,800 prisoners and destroyed $2 million worth of Federal stores. But as had Stuart's raid at Gettysburg, Morgan's July 1863 Ohio raid ended in disaster. His force of 2,400 endured terrible fighting and covered a very long distance before surrender-

ing at New Lisbon (Beaver Creek) on July 26. This failure, too, was the result of a mounted force being gone too long and too far from its main army, thus encountering stronger opposition and critical delays.

The tactic had been proven time and again: an independent body of cavalry could cover long distances in the enemy's rear, capturing stores and prisoners, gathering intelligence, and destroying vital supplies and lines of communication—if it were done quickly and with a force large enough to counter any opposition it might meet. These operations also forced the enemy to dedicate front-line troops to guard the rear from other mounted raiders or guerrilla forces, thus making the cavalry a force multiplier. The success of these raids, then, rested on several factors: the raiders had to be heavily armed (to defeat any opposition encountered); they had to be familiar with the terrain to be traversed; the operation had to be kept secret; and the force had to keep moving at all times.

Raiding continued as a main operation of the Confederate cavalry into the middle years of the war. But after Gettysburg, its usefulness began to ebb. This was due, in part, to the fact that the Federal cavalry had begun to operate as the Confederates had all along—in large, independent bodies moving offensively and not just in reaction to Southern thrusts.

At the Battle of Brandy Station, the largest mounted clash of the war (involving some 10,000 cavalry), the Federal horsemen discovered they could ride and fight against Stuart as equals. On the morning of June 9, 1863, Alfred Pleasonton rode out of Fredericksburg and attacked Stuart's force as it guarded the Rappahannock River line. Under cover of a morning haze John Buford surprised William Edmondson ("Grumble") Jones's force and drove them to Brandy Station. At the same time David Gregg pushed Beverly Holcombe Robertson's men from Kelly's Ford. Just as Fleetwood Hill, the site of Stuart's headquarters, was about to be overrun by the Federals, Wade Hampton arrived and counterattacked, driving the Union force from the battlefield. Though Pleasonton retreated from the field, he had accomplished much. He had learned that Lee was moving north, he had surprised and humiliated the seemingly invincible Stuart, and he had shown his men that the Southern cavalry could be bested. As historian H. B. McClellan wrote, "It made the Federal cavalry. Up to that time confessedly inferior to the Southern horsemen, they gained . . . that confidence in themselves and in their commanders which enabled them to contest" the Southern cavalry from then on. By the time of the Gettysburg campaign, the Federal cavalry was gaining experience, its leaders were becoming bolder, its mounts were improving, and its equipment, superior to the Confederate arms, was at last plentiful. In addition, the numbers of Federal cavalry were growing.

Dismounted Fighting. The third important innovation that developed during the war was the large-scale use of dismounted cavalry in battle. By 1864, the Confederates were outnumbered and outgunned by the Federals. Confederate mounts were degenerating in both quality and quantity, and the cavalry could no longer attack en masse Federal cavalry formations—their numbers were too large. Nor could the Confederates ride with impunity around the Federal flanks and through the rear area, for the Southern horses were not up to such arduous tasks. As the Confederate army began to fight an almost exclusively defensive war, the chances to use the mounted arm in offensive charges or to follow up a victory with a mounted pursuit diminished—thus the turn to fighting as mounted *infantry*. Like brigading the cavalry and raiding, this innovation was eventually copied by the Federals.

One of the best examples of dismounted cavalry tactics was the role played by Stuart's cavalry in the Battle of the Wilderness in May 1864. The Federal army, under Grant, threw 127,000 troops, 21,000 of which were cavalry commanded by Sheridan, into this campaign. Lee's Army of Northern Virginia was composed of only 54,000 infantry and 9,000 cavalry, and the disadvantage in numbers had to be compensated for somehow. On May 5 Stuart's cavalry rode to Todd's Tavern, where they encountered Federal cavalry coming up a road. Here the Confederates dismounted and held the enemy in check until dark, fighting like infantry. The next day saw similar action near the intersection of the Catharpin and Brock roads. One Confederate diary entry reads, "Our regiment was moved to the front and dismounted to fight." Sheridan then moved his cavalry to Spotsylvania Court House, where Fitz Lee's men had ridden, dismounted, and erected barricades behind which to fight. This action allowed Lee to rush Anderson's corps to the crossroads and secure the Army of Northern Virginia's flank. The ability of Stuart's cavalry to move quickly to a strategic point, dismount, and hold the ground until reinforcements arrived gave Lee the time he needed to move up a heavier force. The fighting continued on May 8 with the cavalrymen felling trees and building barricades to block the road. As one trooper wrote, "We boys of the cavalry were not much on using spades and shovels, but could use axes very well. We . . . cut down a long line of trees . . . and these made a pretty good obstruction to fight behind." By midmorning Lee's infantry had arrived and replaced the cavalry in the rifle pits.

This was the first battle in which the Confederate cavalry fought almost exclusively as infantry, but it was not to be the last. During Early's 1864 Shenandoah Valley campaign, dismounted cavalry was used extensively to slow the pursuit of Sheridan's Federal horsemen. Early's cavalry would fall back to important gaps or crossroads, dismount, and build barricades from which they were able to delay the Union forces. Prominent use was made of dismounted cavalry at Front Royal on September 20, Milford on September 22, and Luray on September 24.

Though true cavalry clashes did occur throughout 1864, dismounted fighting began to occupy more and more of the cavalry's time in battle, and it was the Confederates who adopted the practice first. In late 1863, the colonel of the First Vermont Cavalry ordered his men to charge a dismounted Confederate force in a tree line. His report stated, "To charge into woods with the saber against . . . dismounted cavalry requires high courage, and is against immense odds." The Federals' adherence in the beginning to the traditional European manner of cavalry fighting—mounted with saber in hand—derived, in part, from the philosophical outlook of Union officers, particularly George B. McClellan who had studied and reported on European mounted training and tactics prior to the war. The Federals emphasized that the strength of the cavalry lay in its spurs and sabers and neglected to train its men in the tactics and weapons of dismounted combat. Their fondness for the saber caused them to be slow to adopt new tactics for fighting. Only after the Confederates used them to their advantage did the Federals follow suit. By war's end, though, after Union cavalrymen had learned to ride into battle, dismount, and fight on foot, the Federals again bested their Confederate adversary. They could put more men with greater firepower (because of their breech-loading repeating carbines) into the battle at a given time. Once again, the Federals had learned from the Confederates and gained the advantage.

Throughout the war, however, the Confederate cavalry was held in awe for its ability to strike quickly and deeply into enemy territory. After the fighting in the Wilderness, the infantry in the Army of Northern Virginia no longer joked about "never having seen a dead cavalryman." As one Southern artilleryman wrote, the Confederate cavalry "had shown itself signally possessed of the quality, that the infantry and artillery naturally admired most . . . obstinacy in fight." The Confederate cavalry became a major player in the army's campaigns. Its place in the history books was assured for the depth it added to the mounted arm.

[*See also* Beefsteak Raid; Brandy's Station, Virginia; Chambersburg, Pennsylvania; Early's Washington Raid; Fisher's Hill, Virginia; Forrest's Raids; Front Royal, Virginia; Gettysburg Campaign; Horses and Mules; Morgan's Raids; Price's Missouri Raid; Shenandoah Valley, *article on* Shenandoah Valley Campaign of Sheridan; Stoneman's Raids; Stuart's Raids; Wheeler's Raids; Wilderness Campaign; Wilson's Raid on Selma; *and biographies of numerous figures mentioned herein.*]

BIBLIOGRAPHY

Averell, William Woods. *Ten Years in the Saddle: The Memoirs of William Woods Averell.* San Rafael, Calif., 1978.

Longacre, Edward G. *The Cavalry at Gettysburg.* Rutherford, N.J., 1986.

Starr, Stephen Z. *The Union Cavalry in the Civil War.* 3 vols. Baton Rouge, 1979.

Stiles, Kenneth Lamarr. "The Evolving Tactics of the 4th Virginia Cavalry: A Study of the Adaptability of Stuart's Cavalry, 1861–1865." M.A. thesis, Old Dominion University, 1988.

Sheridan, P. H. *Personal Memoirs of P. H. Sheridan.* 2 vols. New York, 1888.

Thomas, Emory M. *Bold Dragoon: The Life of J. E. B. Stuart.* New York, 1988.

Wyeth, John Allan. *That Devil Forrest: Life of General Nathan Bedford Forrest.* New York, 1899. Reprint, New York, 1959.

Young, Bennett H. *Confederate Wizards of the Saddle.* Boston, 1914.

KENNETH L. STILES

CEDAR CREEK, VIRGINIA.

Ten miles south of Winchester, Virginia, Cedar Creek was the site of an October 19, 1864, battle that witnessed the destruction of Maj. Gen. Jubal Early's Army of the Valley. Never again would the Confederacy draw provisions from the Shenandoah Valley. Southern casualties amounted to around 2,900 men killed, wounded, or missing; the Federals lost 5,665.

Confederate debacles at Third Winchester (September 19) and Fisher's Hill (September 22) swept Early's troops from the lower Valley and allowed Maj. Gen. Philip Sheridan to lay waste to the region. When the Union army retreated, Early followed, arriving at Strasburg on October 13. A few miles to the north on the hills above Cedar Creek stood Sheridan's Army of the Shenandoah.

Early desired offensive action but realized that without reinforcements and supplies he had little hope of achieving a decisive victory. Gen. Robert E. Lee was not of the same mind. Discounting reports that had placed Sheridan's army at 35,000 to 40,000 men, Lee grossly underestimated the enemy's strength. He demanded that Early take his 10,000 rifles and "move against" Sheridan.

On October 17, Early sent Maj. Gen. John B. Gordon and Jedediah Hotchkiss, topographical engineer, to Massanutten Mountain. They discovered that the left flank of Sheridan's army was not prepared to resist a sudden assault. The Union Eighth Corps had encamped east of the Valley Turnpike while the Sixth and Ninth Corps had bivouacked west of the road and around the mansion Belle Grove.

Conferring with his subordinates the next day, Early approved one of the most audacious flanking maneuvers of the entire war. It called for Gordon to take three divisions—those of Brig. Gen. John Pegram, Maj. Gen. Dodson Ramseur, and Brig. Gen. Clement A. Evans—across the north fork of the Shenandoah at Fisher's Hill, skirt the end of Massanutten, cross the river again, and then form for an assault against the eastern flank of the camp of the Eighth Corps. Maj. Gen. Joseph B. Kershaw's division was ordered to move through Strasburg, cross Cedar Creek at Bowman's Mill, and coordinate his attack with Gordon. The remaining infantry division, commanded by Brig. Gen. Gabriel Colvin Wharton, would advance down the Valley Pike in a supporting role while Brig. Gen. Thomas Lafayette Rosser's horsemen were to protect Early's left flank.

Gordon's column moved out at 8:00 P.M. on October 18, stumbling across a mountain trail that resembled "a pig's path." Because victory depended on surprise, the soldiers removed equipment that might create noise and alert the enemy's pickets. After fording the Shenandoah for a second time, they went into position a half-mile east of the enemy's camp, just before 5:00 in the morning. Forty-five minutes later, concealed by a heavy fog, Gordon's troops and Kershaw's division stormed the Union camps. For the next three hours the Confederates drove the Eighth and Nineteenth Corps toward Middletown. Confident that he had attained a remarkable victory, Early told Gordon, "This is glory enough for one day." His soldiers had bagged eighteen pieces of artillery and 1,300 prisoners.

The Federals had formed a final defensive line three miles north of their camps. By 10:00 Early had edged his way toward the enemy, but the momentum of the Confederate assault had disappeared. Early believed that "it would not do to press my troops further." His men were exhausted and the famished soldiers abandoned the ranks to plunder Northern camps.

Away from his men when the fighting erupted, Sheridan had rushed to the scene where he massed his cavalry against Early's left flank. At 3:30 his troopers pounced on the exposed position. Up and down the line echoed the cry, "We are flanked," as the Confederates fell back in disorder. While trying to restore calm in his command, Ramseur, the youngest West Pointer to achieve the rank of major general in the Confederacy, received a mortal wound.

Early's army retreated to Fisher's Hill where the general bitterly remarked, "The Yankees got whipped and we got scared." Although his subordinates had flawlessly executed his plan, Early did not have sufficient numbers to compensate for surrendering the initiative to Sheridan. Defeat at Cedar Creek eliminated the Army of the Valley as an effective fighting force for the rest of the war. While Early headed south with his battered army, the morale of the Northern people soared. Together with the capture of Atlanta and Mobile Bay, Sheridan's triumphs in the Valley ensured Abraham Lincoln's victory in the presidential elections that November.

BIBLIOGRAPHY

Gallagher, Gary W., ed. *Struggle for the Shenandoah: Essays on the 1864 Valley Campaign.* Kent, Ohio, 1991.
Wert, Jeffry D. *From Winchester to Cedar Creek: The Shenandoah Campaign of 1864.* Carlisle, Pa., 1987.

PETER S. CARMICHAEL

CEDAR MOUNTAIN, VIRGINIA. This landmark in southern Culpeper County dominated the battlefield where Thomas J. ("Stonewall") Jackson fought a battle on August 9, 1862, that climaxed his last independent campaign. The fragmented Federal command in Virginia during August 1862 dictated Confederate strategy that led to the Battle of Cedar Mountain on the ninth and to Second Manassas at the end of the month. Robert E. Lee, recently victorious in the Seven Days' Battles, sent Jackson north to the vicinity of Gordonsville at the end of July to face the threat posed by a new Federal general, John Pope. Pope's strident anticivilian orders irritated Lee, who wrote to Jackson, "I want Pope to be suppressed." Lee referred to the Federal general with unaccustomed venom as "the miscreant Pope." While Gen. George B. McClellan's defeated army remained in the vicinity of Richmond, Jackson would head north alone against Pope. When McClellan's army abandoned the Richmond line and headed back to the environs of Washington, Lee would go to join Jackson. The Southern strategy worked: Jackson trounced Pope at Cedar Mountain, and then Lee and Jackson together defeated Pope's army at Second Manassas as it was drawing major reinforcements from McClellan's returning troops.

Jackson started his army north from Orange County on August 7, but it made negligible progress because of intense heat and dust, and as a result of the commanding general's stubborn unwillingness to discuss details with subordinates. Confusion over terse marching orders on this day led to a bitter controversy between Jackson and A. P. Hill that persisted while both lived. Jackson's highest-ranking subordinate insisted, "I do not know whether we will march north, south, east, or west, or whether we will march at all." The army moved somewhat more smoothly on August 8, pushing through a corner of Madison County into Culpeper County, but even so the next morning a disconsolate Jackson telegraphed to Lee, "I am not making much progress."

On August 9, near noon, the head of Jackson's column came upon a Federal advance guard in the valley of Cedar Run, beneath the imposing bulk of a steep-sided ridge known as Cedar Mountain or—ominously—as Slaughter Mountain. There, on the farms of the Crittenden and Slaughter families, Jackson fought a meeting engagement with Federals under Gen. Nathaniel P. Banks, who commanded the advance elements of Pope's army. The contending forces reached the field piecemeal, many arriving after darkness ended serious fighting, but by the time of the late-afternoon climax Jackson had about twenty thousand men at his disposal and the Federals had fewer than fifteen thousand. The battle unfolded in searing heat of about 100°, making August 9 the hottest day on which major combat occurred in the Virginia theater during the war.

Confederate infantry opened the battle by driving Northern cavalry away from a position near the Crittenden house. Southern artillery reached the shoulder of Cedar Mountain after tremendous exertion. From there they dominated a large part of the field and afforded Jackson an impregnable right anchor for his position. While their troops filed into a haphazard and misshapen line without adequate high-level supervision, Jackson and Gen. Charles S. Winder supervised the Confederate half of an artillery duel that raged for more than an hour. Winder fell mortally wounded by a shell. Soon thereafter a small Federal attack force surged across a wide wheat field near the Confederate left under orders to drive away the Southern cannon in that quarter. Although Banks had no idea of the strength or positions of his opponents and sent far too few troops for the circumstances, the attackers fell upon a seam in the Confederate line and tore it apart. The three and a half Northern regiments rolled southward through Jackson's position, wreaking havoc as they flanked one unit after another.

The Federal advance nearly captured Stonewall Jackson himself. The Confederate general desperately sought to rally the shattered ranks of his nearest units, shouting to them to support him and waving a battle flag in one hand and his sword and scabbard in the other. Jackson's wife later wrote that her husband considered Cedar Mountain "the most successful of his exploits." He must have based that feeling on his personal involvement, with adrenaline surging through his veins as bullets flew past from three directions, because August 9 did not develop tactically as a masterpiece.

Jackson's personal efforts rallied many of his soldiers, but the tide turned in his favor primarily on the basis of substantial reinforcements who arrived quickly from Hill's division. The first arrivals helped stitch together the tattered and broken line; then more brigades wrested the initiative from the Federals and charged back through the wheat field to win the day. A battalion of the First Pennsylvania Cavalry galloped into the teeth of the Southern position in a forlorn attempt to stem the onslaught, but as darkness descended, Jackson's troops were advancing on every corner of the field.

During the night Federals arrived in great strength opposite Jackson. When a Confederate battery that pushed well to the front took a dreadful beating from several enemy artillery units, Jackson halted and consolidated his gains on what had been the initial Union position before the battle.

He had lost about 1,400 casualties and inflicted about 2,600 on his foe.

On August 10 and 11 the two armies faced each other without renewing the serious fighting. The Confederates fell back into Orange County on the night of the eleventh. Jackson had achieved his purpose by blunting Pope's initiative in north-central Virginia, defeating an exposed portion of the Federal army, and buying time for Lee to break away from Richmond in order to head for a junction with him. When Lee arrived the following week, he and Jackson collaborated on one of their most dazzling tactical ventures in the Second Manassas campaign.

BIBLIOGRAPHY

Allan, William. *The Army of Northern Virginia in 1862.* Boston, 1892. Reprint, Dayton, Ohio, 1984.

Grimsley, Daniel A. *Battles in Culpeper County.* Culpeper, Va., 1900.

Krick, Robert K. *Stonewall Jackson at Cedar Mountain.* Chapel Hill, N.C., 1990.

ROBERT K. KRICK

CENSORSHIP. The Union needed no spies because Confederate newspapers told everything there was "to be told," according to Mary Boykin Chesnut. Her observation describes the surprising degree of freedom of the press under a fledgling government that permitted almost absolute freedom of editorial expression and made diligent but often ineffective attempts to suppress vital military news. Most Southern editors exercised extreme discretion in what they published and engaged in an informal and voluntary censorship. Others, however, insisted on their right to publish anything. This included scathing attacks on elected officials and military commanders, criticisms of military strategy and government policies, and even sensitive military information. Nevertheless, the Richmond government, unlike its Union counterpart, never shut down a newspaper.

In his inaugural address, President Jefferson Davis stressed his administration's support for the constitutional guarantee of freedom of the press. Secretary of War George Wythe Randolph echoed this sentiment in 1862 when he expressed his hope that the war could be won without the suppression of a single newspaper. Taking advantage of the virtual immunity from interference, some Confederate papers, led by the *Charleston Mercury* and *Richmond Examiner,* subjected Davis, his cabinet, congressmen, and various military leaders to an unrestrained chorus of criticism, invective, and abuse. In response to the *Examiner's* bitter denunciations, Judah P. Benjamin endeavored to have the newspaper closed down but failed to secure the support of the administration. Likewise, Speaker of the House Thomas S. Bocock, another victim of the *Examiner's* intemperate remarks, urged the paper's destruction, but to no avail. Nathaniel Morse's *Augusta Chronicle* and the Unionist William W. Holden's *Raleigh Standard* consistently took what many regarded as treasonous editorial lines, yet the government never intervened. When some irate Georgia soldiers passing through Raleigh attacked the offices of the *Standard,* North Carolina Governor Zebulon Vance acted quickly to prevent the complete destruction of the paper's equipment. A rare instance of actual newspaper suppression occurred when Tennessee authorities arrested William G. ("Parson") Brownlow for treason and suspended publication of his *Knoxville Whig.* The Davis administration, however, pressured state officials to release the outspoken editor on condition that he agree to leave the South.

In 1863 the Judiciary Committee introduced into the Senate a sedition bill that would have curtailed freedom of expression and of the press, but it failed to pass. It was not until January 29, 1864, that the House, provoked by the increased frequency of press attacks on the government, approved a bill creating a Department of Inspection and Censorship. In the same year, however, Davis failed to obtain legislation that would have provided greatly strengthened government control over the press.

While strongly advocating freedom of expression, the government attempted to restrict access to sensitive military information. Congress excluded reporters from its sessions dealing with military matters and in the spring of 1861 passed laws giving the administration authority to control information sent over the telegraph and through the mail. Although censorship of mail dispatches occurred infrequently, government agents in telegraph offices, War Department officials, and army commanders were more zealous in suppressing military news.

The War Department, which initially relied on the cooperation and discretion of correspondents and their editors, gradually tightened its restrictions. Early on, Secretary of War Leroy P. Walker permitted reporters in the army camps on condition that they not report on troop dispositions, movements, and strengths. But in January 1862, the Army of the Potomac banished all correspondents, and the Confederate Congress made the publication of any news about disposition, movements, or numbers of army and naval forces a crime. Subsequently, reporters had to submit telegraphic dispatches to military authorities who frequently suppressed material they considered damaging. Army leaders, exercising virtually complete control over correspondents in their commands, not only reserved the right to dictate what was reported by telegraph but went so far as to exclude correspondents from their camps.

Gen. Braxton Bragg became notorious for his antagonism toward the press. In April 1861, during operations against

Fort Pickens, Bragg had L. H. Mathews of the *Pensacola Observer* arrested for publishing information that supposedly jeopardized military security. Bragg frequently ordered censorship of telegraph reports; and when a Henry Watterson editorial critical of Bragg appeared in the *Chattanooga Rebel,* the general banned the newspaper from his lines. In September 1863, John Linebaugh of the *Memphis Appeal* was arrested for treason. The grounds for the charge, never clear and subsequently dropped, may have been that he had filed a report concerning troop movements, but the charge may have been provoked by Linebaugh's criticisms of Bragg.

Other Confederate generals hostile to correspondents were Earl Van Dorn, Joseph E. Johnston, P. G. T. Beauregard, John Bell Hood, the always secretive Thomas J. ("Stonewall") Jackson, and Robert E. Lee. In July 1862, Van Dorn ordered fines or imprisonment for correspondents who wrote anything about troop movements or that undermined public confidence in commanding officers. Public and congressional protests, however, prevented Van Dorn from strictly enforcing the order. A report filed by the *Richmond Dispatch*'s William Shepardson in December 1861 so incensed Johnston that he banned correspondents from his command. And in 1864 as Johnston retreated across Georgia, military authorities censored all press dispatches from his army.

Official battle reports required presidential approval before publication, and Beauregard became the center of a mild controversy when a synopsis of his report of First Manassas appeared in the *Richmond Dispatch* without President Davis's authorization. While near Corinth, Mississippi, in May 1862, Beauregard ordered that all correspondents be shipped out on the first available train. Hood had a correspondent with him in Alabama during the fall of 1864 but refused to allow him to send telegraphic reports. The plainspoken Jackson openly expressed his contempt for newsmen. Military censors tried to limit news reports during the Seven Days' Battles, and not until Fredericksburg were Richmond newspaper correspondents allowed to accompany the Army of Northern Virginia to a major battle—and then their presence resulted from a bureaucratic error. P. W. Alexander, the South's most reliable reporter, however, found himself excluded from Lee's army on the eve of the battle.

Nevertheless, carelessness, lax enforcement, different interpretations of censorship rules, and indiscretions on the part of some journalists resulted in frequent leaks. Many generals believed that the failure to control the press significantly undermined the Confederate war effort. Bragg's defenders charged that the 1863 battles around Chattanooga had been lost because of newspaper reports. Shortly after the Seven Days' Battles, Lee criticized the *Richmond Dispatch* for revealing the disposition of his forces at the very time the Union army was on his front. In October 1863, Lee wrote Secretary of War James A. Seddon to protest Richmond newspaper accounts about his troop movements, which he claimed added to his difficulties. Lee was convinced that the enemy, having learned of Bragg's movement to Georgia from Savannah newspapers, had launched an attack on Wilmington. And after the war he bristled upon recalling that when James Longstreet went south in the summer of 1863, the newspapers told everything despite his best efforts to keep the matter secret.

What seems clear is that the legal and institutional apparatus to censor military information worked better in theory than in practice. It functioned best when journalists, acutely aware of their patriotic duty and dedicated to the cause, voluntarily exercised restraint in reporting on vital military matters.

[*See also* Freedom of the Press; Habeas Corpus; Newspapers; War Correspondents.]

BIBLIOGRAPHY

Andrews, J. Cutler. *The South Reports the Civil War.* Princeton, N.J., 1970.

Mathis, Robert Neil. "Freedom of the Press in the Confederacy: A Reality." *Historian* 37 (1975): 633–648.

Randall, James G. "The Newspaper Problem in Its Bearing upon Military Secrecy during the Civil War." *American Historical Review* 33 (January 1918): 303–323.

Towery, Patricia. "Censorship of South Carolina Newspapers, 1861–1865." In *South Carolina Journals and Journalists.* Edited by James B. Meriwether. Spartanburg, S.C., 1975.

Wilson, Quintus Charles. "A Study and Evaluation of Military Censorship in the Civil War." Masters thesis, University of Minnesota, 1945.

CHARLES McARVER

CENTRALIA MASSACRE. On September 27, 1864, the village of Centralia, Missouri, 121 miles northwest of St. Louis, was the scene of one of the worst guerrilla atrocities committed in the state during the Civil War.

Prior to his invasion of Missouri from Arkansas in the fall of 1864, Confederate Gen. Sterling Price sent orders to leaders of Southern guerrillas to increase their activities north of the Missouri River. Price reasoned that marauding bands would lure Union troops from St. Louis and elsewhere to defend northern Missouri, thus drawing them away from his line of march from southern Missouri to St. Louis.

In response to Price's orders, William ("Bloody Bill") Anderson, George Todd, John Thrailkill, and other guerrillas created havoc in the state during August and September. Particularly in Clay, Ray, Lafayette, Howard, and Boone counties, they burned, looted, and murdered civilians and Union troops. The most notorious of these episodes occurred at Centralia, a railroad terminal in northeastern Boone County, on September 27.

The evening before, Anderson, Todd, Thrailkill, and some two hundred of their men had camped four miles south of the town. On the morning of the twenty-seventh, Anderson, wanting news of the war in Missouri, rode with thirty of his henchmen into the village to obtain St. Louis newspapers. The guerrillas, yelling and shooting, woke the villagers, who found themselves at the mercy of the band. For the next three hours the guerrillas plundered and burned the town, and when the morning stage from Columbia arrived, they robbed the passengers.

Shortly before noon the whistle of a passenger train from St. Louis sounded. Anderson's men piled railroad ties on the track of the Northern Missouri Railroad and then hid, awaiting the train's arrival at the smoking depot. As the train pulled in, the guerrillas sprang from hiding, yelling and shooting their pistols. As the terrified passengers disembarked, the guerrillas robbed them and then looted the train cars.

Among the passengers were twenty-five unarmed Union troops. Anderson's psychopathic lieutenant, Archie Clements, and fifteen guerrillas ordered the soldiers into line and marched them down the platform. Within minutes Anderson, astride his horse, questioned them and ordered them to strip off their uniforms. Anderson asked if there were any commissioned or noncommissioned officers among his captives. Thomas Goodman finally admitted that he was a sergeant in the Missouri Engineers and was told to get out of line. Anderson then gave Clements orders to "muster out" the remaining Union troops, and Clements and his guard shot them dead. The unattended passenger train was set on fire and sent down the track toward Sturgeon, five miles to the west. Their grisly work finished, Anderson and his guerrillas, with Goodman in tow, rode back to rejoin their fellows. (Goodman was later released.)

Late that afternoon, Maj. A.V.E. Johnson with 150 mounted troops of the Thirty-ninth Missouri Infantry arrived at Centralia. Thinking that Anderson had only thirty guerrillas with him, Johnson left half of his command in Centralia and set out in pursuit.

A mile from town Johnson encountered ten guerrillas who immediately retreated. Johnson rode after them into an ambush set by Anderson. Believing that his troops stood a better chance of survival on foot, the major ordered his men to dismount. Spurring their horses the guerrillas charged, and the Union infantry fired their single-shot muskets too high. The rebels, with pistols firing, swarmed their enemy. Within minutes Major Johnson and his men were dead.

The guerrillas then rode back to Centralia. They killed all the Union troops left there except for the captain in command and eighteen of his men who escaped to the blockhouse at Sturgeon. Anderson and his men had killed 116 members of the Thirty-ninth Missouri before leaving the area to go into hiding. Anderson himself died on October 16 during a skirmish with Union troops near Albany, Missouri.

BIBLIOGRAPHY

Brownlee, Richard S. *Gray Ghosts of the Confederacy: Guerrilla Warfare in the West, 1861–1865*. Baton Rouge, La., 1958.

Castel, Albert E. *General Sterling Price and the Civil War in the West*. Baton Rouge, La., 1968.

Fellman, Michael. *Inside War*. New York, 1989.

March, David D. *The History of Missouri*. Vol. 2. New York and West Palm Beach, Fla., 1967.

Parrish, William E. *A History of Missouri, Volume III: 1860 to 1875*. Columbia, Mo., 1973.

JAMES W. GOODRICH

CHALMERS, JAMES RONALD

CHALMERS, JAMES RONALD (1831–1898), brigadier general and U.S. congressman. Chalmers was born in Halifax, Virginia, on January 11, 1831, and as a young boy, moved with his family to Holly Springs, Mississippi. After graduating from South Carolina College, he returned to Holly Springs, where he passed the bar. He was a delegate to the Democratic National Convention in 1852 and later served as district attorney for Marshall County. He attended the convention that took Mississippi out of the Union on January 9, 1861.

Chalmers entered Confederate service as a captain in March 1861, becoming colonel of the Ninth Mississippi Infantry the next month. Promoted to brigadier general on February 13, 1862, Chalmers fought at Shiloh under Gen. Braxton Bragg. During the bitter fighting of the first day, he led his men in numerous advances, including a futile assault against the final Union line. He led his brigade in Bragg's Kentucky campaign and fought in the Battle of Murfreesboro, where he suffered a severe head wound in the fighting at the Round Forest.

Following his recovery, Chalmers took charge of the District of Mississippi and East Louisiana in April 1863. In January 1864, when Maj. Gen. Nathan Bedford Forrest assumed command of all mounted troops in western Tennessee and northern Mississippi, Chalmers became one of his division commanders. He served under Forrest briefly before being temporarily relieved.

Chalmers clashed with his volatile superior for a number of reasons. He had cooperated with Forrest in a raid into western Tennessee at the end of 1863 and probably believed he had as much reason to be Forrest's commander, or at least his equal, as to be his subordinate. For his part, Forrest reacted to what he felt was interference with the prerogatives of command, claiming to be "satisfied" that he would "not receive the co-operation of Brigadier-General Chalmers." The matter went to the two officers' superiors, who rescinded the dismissal and restored Chalmers to his command. To their credit, the men operated well together thereafter.

Chalmers was present at the controversial action at Fort Pillow in April 1864, during which some Confederates killed members of the black and Tennessee Unionist garrison who had already surrendered. In July, he engaged in the fighting at Tupelo and assumed temporary command when Forrest was wounded. In August, Chalmers held Union Gen. Andrew J. Smith in check while Forrest carried out a daring raid on Memphis. Later in the year, he participated in Gen. John Bell Hood's Tennessee campaign, serving as Hood's cavalry commander while Forrest undertook a detached operation against the Union garrison at Murfreesboro. During the subsequent retreat from Nashville, Chalmers performed admirably in Forrest's rearguard actions.

Following the war, Chalmers returned to Mississippi and became active in politics. He served in the Mississippi Senate (1876–1877) and represented his state in the U.S. House of Representatives (1877–1882, 1884–1885). Subsequently, Chalmers practiced law in Memphis, Tennessee, until his death on April 9, 1898.

BIBLIOGRAPHY

Bearss, Edwin C. *Forrest at Brice's Cross Roads.* Dayton, Ohio, 1979.

Cozzens, Peter. *No Better Place to Die: The Battle of Stones River.* Urbana, Ill., 1990.

McDonough, James Lee. *Shiloh: In Hell before Night.* Knoxville, Tenn., 1977.

U.S. War Department. *War of the Rebellion: A Compilation of the Official Records of the Union and Confederate Armies.* Washington, D.C., 1880–1901. Ser. 1. Vol. 10, pt. 1, pp. 547–553; vol. 32, pt. 1, pp. 361, 623; vol. 39, pt. 1, pp. 325–328.

Wills, Brian Steel. *A Battle from the Start: The Life of Nathan Bedford Forrest.* New York, 1992.

BRIAN S. WILLS

CHAMBERS, HENRY COUSINS (1823–1871), congressman from Mississippi. Born in Alabama and educated at what is now Princeton University, Chambers moved in 1843 to Mississippi, where he became a planter and politician. In 1850, Chambers was a delegate to the Nashville Convention, which sought to settle the question of slavery in the territories. In 1859, he was elected to the Mississippi legislature. In 1860, after the Democrats split—some supporting Stephen A. Douglas and others John C. Breckinridge—Chambers joined the Breckinridge camp and served as a presidential elector for him.

Chambers sought election as a delegate to the First Congress, which was to convene in Richmond in 1862. His opponent was William A. Lake, an outspoken Unionist. During the campaign, the two men engaged in an irreconcilable argument. No one knows the cause of the disagreement; a newspaper at the time simply referred to "its origin in a personal matter." The result was a duel in which the two fought at fifty paces with rifles. At the third firing, Lake was struck in the head and died. Chambers easily won the seat over Lake's replacement. In the election for the Second Congress, no opposition could be mounted against him since his northern district was at that time under Federal control.

In Congress, Chambers strongly supported the policies of Jefferson Davis. He preferred military strength to be centered in the national government rather than the individual states. Although he accepted the need for certain exemptions from military service, he wanted their number to be extremely limited, and he advocated imposing a fee of five hundred dollars per exemption. As the South grew more desperate, he backed impressment unsuccessfully, but he never sought to increase the military by arming slaves as did some others in Congress.

In the years before his death in 1871, Chambers gave up politics and returned to his Bolivar County plantation, which had suffered wartime destruction. Although pardoned by the Federal government for his role in the war, he never resolved his financial difficulties.

BIBLIOGRAPHY

Alexander, Thomas B., and Richard E. Beringer. *The Anatomy of the Confederate Congress: A Study of the Influences of Member Characteristics on Legislative Voting Behavior, 1861–1865.* Nashville, Tenn., 1972.

Warner, Ezra J., and W. Buck Yearns. *Biographical Register of the Confederate Congress.* Baton Rouge, La., 1975.

RAY SKATES

CHAMBERSBURG, PENNSYLVANIA.

Chambersburg was the target of two raids by the cavalry of the Army of Northern Virginia, the first in October 1862 and the second in July 1864. J. E. B. Stuart passed through Chambersburg on October 10 and 11 during his second "Ride around McClellan." The Confederates captured and paroled some 300 Federal soldiers and confiscated a large number of horses, muskets, pistols, sabers, and other arms before destroying the rail lines, depot, and shops of the city. This raid also provided Lee with vital information about the Army of the Potomac's disposition and intentions.

The second raid was conducted by a much less disciplined force bent on retribution. In late July 1864, Maj. Gen. Jubal Early ordered Brig. Gens. John McCausland and Bradley Tyler Johnson to cross the Potomac and ride to Chambersburg. Early wanted the Confederate raiders to take the town and demand a payment of $100,000 in gold or $500,000 in currency as retribution for Federal depredations committed in the Shenandoah Valley by Maj. Gen. John Hunter during the previous month. If the town did not pay the ransom, McCausland was to burn it to the ground.

Leaving their encampment at Martinsburg, McCausland's brigade of five regiments and Johnson's of two regiments and four battalions (a total of 4,000 men), accompanied by six pieces of artillery, crossed the Potomac River at McCoy's Ferry around daylight on July 29. The First and Second Maryland Cavalry units led the column and drove a small force of between 300 and 400 Federals from their front back to Hagerstown. After encountering light opposition throughout the day, the Confederates reached Mercersburg around 5:00 P.M. Here the Thirty-sixth Virginia Battalion drove the Federals out of the town, securing it so the Confederate column could close up and eat. After four hours of rest, McCausland led the men on to Chambersburg, skirmishing most of the way.

At 3:00 A.M. on July 30, the column was checked by Federal forces outside of Chambersburg. After two hours of fighting, the Federals withdrew and the Confederates occupied the fairgrounds outside the city. At 5:30 in the morning, the Twenty-first Virginia was sent into the town with the dismounted Thirty-sixth in support. McCausland entered Chambersburg, arrested the principal citizens and officials, and demanded that $100,000 in gold or $500,000 in currency be handed over under threat of torching the city. When the general was told that no more than $50,000 was available, the horsemen fired the city in fifty places. Some Confederates pillaged the shops and stores before burning the buildings, but others helped citizens evacuate prior to putting the torch to their structures. A number of the cavalrymen did not carry out the order to burn the town, including Col. W. E. Peters of the Twenty-first Virginia who was arrested when he refused to obey (he was later released). Some six thousand citizens lost their homes and the property damage totaled about $1.5 million. The Confederates left the town around noon. About two hours later, a Federal column under W. W. Averell, which had been chasing McCausland, rode into Chambersburg.

The Confederate raiders reached McConnelsburg around 5:00 P.M. and encamped. At sunrise on July 31, McCausland led his raiders to Hancock, which they reached a little after noon. Here the general demanded $30,000 and five thousand cooked rations for his troopers. During that night the men went on to Bevansville where they rested and fed their horses before starting out for Cumberland at sunrise. About 3:30 in the afternoon, the Southerners encountered a Federal force two and a half miles outside of Cumberland. McCausland, not knowing the size of the Union force or the surrounding countryside, withdrew. By August 2, the raiders had reached Old Town on the Potomac where they

captured a Union force after a brief artillery duel. Crossing the Potomac, the Southern raiders rode to Springfield and encamped. From there McCausland took his troopers to Oldfields, near Moorefield, where they rested.

Meanwhile Averell had crossed the Potomac, and he caught up with the Confederate raiders on August 6. The next day, the Union cavalry attacked McCausland's encampment at dawn, routing the entire force and capturing 27 officers (one of them being Johnson, who later escaped), 393 enlisted men, four artillery pieces, and four hundred horses. Disgusted with the undisciplined actions of the troopers throughout the raid—from stealing and looting to drunkenness and extorting money from the citizens of Chambersburg to spare their homes—Johnson reported, "Thus the grand spectacle of a national retaliation was reduced to a miserable hunkstering for greenbacks." He was also upset because McCausland had not informed him about the distribution of the troops in the encampment at Moorefield—which led to the routing of the brigades—and had not slept with his men, but stayed in town.

The action at Chambersburg was in marked contrast to the mounted raids undertaken earlier in the war. Where the raids of J. E. B. Stuart, Nathan Bedford Forrest, and John Hunt Morgan had tactical or strategic goals such as reconnaissance, disruption of the enemy's rear areas, or the capture of supplies, McCausland's raid was simply an act of revenge. Somewhere in 1863 the war had changed. It was no longer a duel between gentlemen, but rather it had become more like a street fight. The horrors of total war had become commonplace by 1864.

BIBLIOGRAPHY

Cooling, B. F. *Jubal Early's Raid on Washington, 1864.* Baltimore, 1989.

Corson, William Clark. *My Dear Jennie.* Edited by Blake W. Corson, Jr. Richmond, Va., 1982.

McClellan, H. B. *I Rode with Jeb Stuart: The Life and Campaigns of Major-General J. E. B. Stuart, Commander of the Cavalry of the Army of Northern Virginia.* Richmond, Va., 1885. Reprint, New York, 1968.

KENNETH L. STILES

CHAMBLISS, JOHN RANDOLPH, JR.

(1833–1864), brigadier general. This renowned cavalryman was born at Hicksford (now Emporia), Greensville County, Virginia, on January 23, 1833. He graduated from the U.S. Military Academy in 1853, ranking thirty-first in a class of fifty-two that included Philip H. Sheridan and John Bell Hood. After a year at the cavalry school at Carlisle, Pennsylvania, Chambliss resigned his commission and returned to Hicksford, where his father was a wealthy planter. For the next seven years he engaged in farming. His

JOHN RANDOLPH CHAMBLISS, JR.   LIBRARY OF CONGRESS

dier general in December 1863, Chambliss was operating in a heavily wooded area along the Charles City Road on August 16, 1864, when he was confronted by Federals. Lt. Samuel E. Cormany ordered Chambliss to surrender. When the Confederate attempted to escape, two rifle shots toppled him from his horse. Union Gen. David M. Gregg recognized Chambliss from their West Point days and sent the body through the lines. He also sent a note of condolence to Mrs. Chambliss, as well as her husband's West Point ring, his pocket testament, and other effects.

Learning of Chambliss's death, Robert E. Lee wrote that "the loss sustained by the cavalry . . . will be felt throughout the army in which, by his courage, energy, and skill he had won for himself an honorable name." Chambliss was buried at Hicksford.

BIBLIOGRAPHY

Balfour, Daniel T. *13th Virginia Cavalry.* Lynchburg, Va., 1986.
"General J. E. B. Stuart's Report of Operations after Gettysburg." *Southern Historical Society Papers* 2 (1876): 73. Reprint, Wilmington, N.C., 1990.
Hampton, Wade. "Engagement at Sappony Church." *Southern Historial Society Papers* 7 (1879): 170.
Hotchkiss, Jed. *Virginia.* Vol. 3 of *Confederate Military History.* Edited by Clement A. Evans. Atlanta, 1899. Vol. 4 of extended ed. Wilmington, N.C., 1987.
"Peace Pipe: Civil War Officers' Kin to Meet." *Richmond News Leader,* September 7, 1990.

LOWELL REIDENBAUGH

military training was not ignored during this period, however. He was aide-de-camp to the governor with the rank of major, commanded a regiment of militia with the rank of colonel, and served as brigade inspector for the state.

When war erupted, Chambliss was commissioned colonel of the Forty-first Virginia Infantry and in July 1861 became colonel of the Thirteenth Virginia Cavalry. The mounted regiment became part of William Henry Fitzhugh Lee's brigade in November 1862. When Lee was wounded at Brandy Station in June 1863, Chambliss succeeded to command of the brigade.

Accolades gravitated freely to Chambliss. J. E. B. Stuart cited him for the "spirit which has always distinguished him," and Wade Hampton spoke of "his gallantry, his zeal and his knowledge of the country [that] contributed largely to the success we gained" at Sappony Church.

Chambliss performed admirably at Middleburg and Aldie and during the Gettysburg campaign. Promoted to briga-

CHAMBLISS, JOHN RANDOLPH, SR.

(1809–1875), congressman from Virginia. Born into a family that had resided in Sussex County, Virginia, for several generations, Chambliss made his home as an adult in neighboring Greensville County on the North Carolina border. As a young man he taught school and then studied law in Winchester, Virginia, before attending the College of William and Mary for a year. Admitted to the bar in Greensville County, he took up residence in Hicksford (now Emporia). He combined legal work with farming and public affairs, including service as county clerk and member of numerous commissions for internal improvements aimed at the economic development of his region. An active Baptist layman, he also served as county superintendent of schools. In 1849 he was elected commonwealth attorney for the county and the following year sat in the Virginia constitutional convention.

A Whig before the war, he was elected to the 1861 Virginia convention as a Unionist. But like many other Virginians whose Unionist sentiments were conditional, by April he had turned in favor of secession. In the first year of the war he drew on his brief experience as a prewar colonel in the state militia to help equip the companies of Confederate troops raised in his county.

In November 1861 he defeated several other candidates for election to the Confederate House of Representatives. Though opposed to conscription on principle, he generally supported giving strong powers to the central government to prosecute the war. The Davis administration found Chambliss a supporter on measures for greater government control over prices and production. As a member of the Committee on Naval Affairs, he worked to build a fleet of gunboats to protect Virginia's shore. Although he approved of giving the War Department greater authority over the organization of the army, Chambliss did oppose extending the suspension of habeas corpus. In February 1864 he argued successfully against the exemption of overseers from conscription. He considered running for reelection on the basis of his opposition to conscription but dropped out of the race.

Despite his prominence in his community before the war, heavy debts plagued him much of the rest of his life. Nevertheless, after Appomattox he took the oath of allegiance and, as before, worked to build the local economy. He died near Hicksford on April 3, 1875, and was buried in the family cemetery beside his son (named for him), who had reached the rank of brigadier general when he was killed in action near Richmond in August 1864.

BIBLIOGRAPHY

Gaines, William H., Jr. *Biographical Register of Members, Virginia State Convention of 1861, First Session*. Richmond, Va., 1969.

Wakelyn, Jon L. *Biographical Dictionary of the Confederacy*. Edited by Frank E. Vandiver. Westport, Conn., 1977.

Warner, Ezra J., and W. Buck Yearns. *Biographical Register of the Confederate Congress*. Baton Rouge, La., 1975.

NELSON D. LANKFORD

CHAMELEON. *See entry on the ship* Tallahassee.

CHANCELLORSVILLE CAMPAIGN. This country intersection in Spotsylvania County, Virginia, became the focal point of a vast battlefield spread across some fifty square miles, on which Robert E. Lee and Thomas J. ("Stonewall") Jackson collaborated on April 29–May 6, 1863, for their greatest joint victory. Chancellorsville also was Jackson's last battle. His mortal wounding by the mistaken fire of his own men was one of the most important military events of the war.

After its resounding and easy victory in the Battle of Fredericksburg on December 13, 1862, Lee's Army of Northern Virginia spent the winter centered in that vicinity, but with flanks spread more than a dozen miles upstream

and twice that far downstream. The Rappahannock River served as the military frontier between the contending countries; the Federal Army of the Potomac remained opposite Lee on the river's left bank. In the aftermath of the aptly named "Mud March" in January, President Abraham Lincoln replaced Ambrose E. Burnside with brash and boastful—but politically well-connected—Joseph Hooker. Hooker revamped his army's support functions, inaugurated an efficient intelligence service, and greatly improved morale. As he planned for spring campaigning, Hooker also produced an outstanding scheme designed to force Lee from the heights behind Fredericksburg that had proved so daunting a few months earlier.

Hooker intended to send his revitalized cavalry arm on a raid deep into the Confederate rear and at the same time to move his army far upriver and surprise Lee by crossing well west of Fredericksburg. The cavalry excursion faltered in attempts to get underway during mid-April as a result of bad weather and the lack of energy of its chief. The raiders finally departed on April 29 and spent a week ricocheting through central Virginia, harassed and controlled by a small Southern mounted detachment while Lee's main cavalry force remained with the army to perform vital screening and reconnaissance duties. A few weeks later during the Gettysburg campaign the same situation prevailed, only in reverse; it was as though the Federals had learned from their experience while the Confederates ignored the lesson they had taught so skillfully at Chancellorsville.

Meanwhile General Hooker put into motion his plan to move upriver to get behind Lee. The march covered considerable distance and required heavy logistical support, but it succeeded remarkably well. By the end of April 30 Hooker had moved much of his army nearly thirty miles, crossed two rivers by various fords, and concentrated in the densely wooded Wilderness of Spotsylvania around Chancellorsville crossroads. "Chancellorsville" was not a town or even a hamlet, but rather a single building—a half-century-old inn at the intersection of the Orange Turnpike and Orange Plank Road. Hooker was unpopular with most of his high-ranking subordinates for various reasons, but his daring maneuver prompted Gen. George G. Meade to chortle, "Hurrah for old Joe! We're on Lee's flank and he doesn't know it." Hooker clearly was hoping that his coup would force the Confederate army to abandon its position and retire well to the south. He outnumbered Lee by more than two to one, having 130,000 men against 60,000, and could hardly imagine his opponent facing both those odds and the successful opening march by the Army of the Potomac.

By April 30 Lee did know where Hooker was and had boldly determined to gather his own army west of Fredericksburg to fight. The Federals had left a strong detachment feinting toward Fredericksburg, so Lee put Jubal Early in

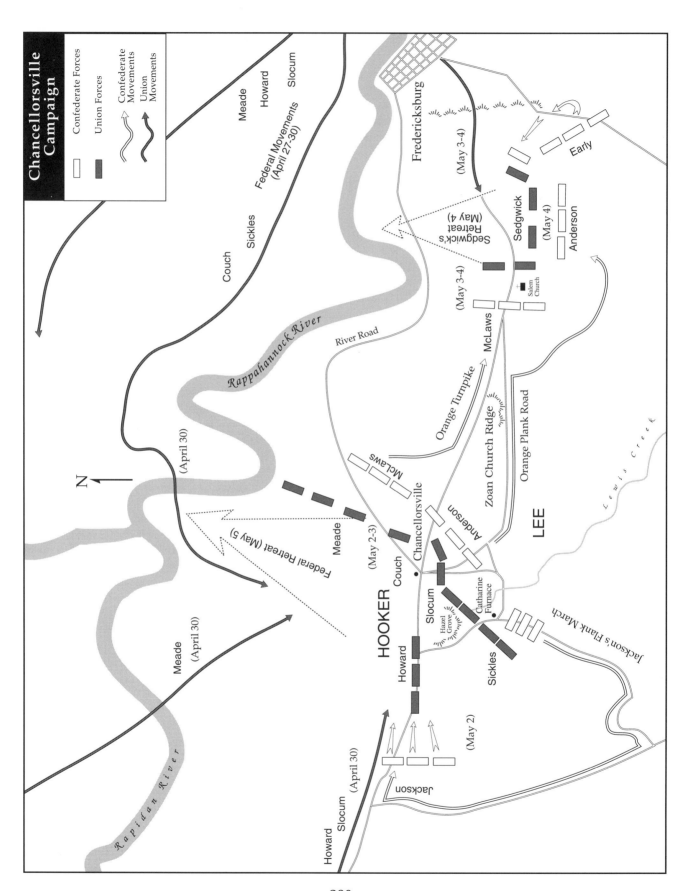

Chancellorsville Campaign

Confederate Forces
Union Forces
Confederate Movements
Union Movements

charge of a rear guard to face that threat. He hurried the rest of the Army of Northern Virginia in the direction of Chancellorsville. The few Confederates who had been retiring in the face of Hooker's host held a tenuous grip on the Zoan Church ridge east of Chancellorsville on the morning of May 1 when Lee and Jackson approached with the vanguard of the army. The Zoan ridge was not only strong high ground but also in the open, outside the seventy-square-mile morass known as the Wilderness. In the tangled Wilderness, Hooker would lose much of the advantage of his huge preponderance in numbers, so taking Zoan Church offered him a tremendous opportunity. The campaign turned in that moment when Stonewall Jackson arrived on the scene and ordered the corporal's guard of Confederates on hand to attack. The bravado that had sustained Hooker to this time evaporated in the face of a determined foe. During the rest of the campaign the Federal command story was one of steady spiritual deterioration. There was much talk at the time that Hooker was drunk, but the conventional wisdom soon emerged that he had given up his customary high alcoholic intake on assuming command and that the change had thrown his nervous system out of balance. Some reasonably strong contemporary evidence now available suggests that Hooker may indeed have been in liquor during the campaign.

From the Zoan Church ridge the Confederates pushed Hooker's troops steadily back toward Chancellorsville on May 1. Jackson orchestrated a tangled tactical combination of brigades, assigned in the order they arrived; ignoring divisional lines, they advanced westward on the roughly parallel Plank Road and Turnpike. The Confederates exploited an unfinished railroad grade as a third corridor through the Wilderness. Using that route, the Georgia brigade of Gen. Ambrose Ransom ("Rans") Wright slipped past the Federal right flank and forced it to swing northward nearly ninety degrees. The new configuration would be a central feature of the next day's operations.

At night on May 1 the Confederate high command gathered at a crossroads one mile from Chancellorsville to consider its options. Despite the enormous disparity in manpower that he faced, Lee was determined to assume the offensive. He had reconnoitered personally on his right during the day and found the ground there both heavily defended and nearly impassable. A small party of staff officers scouted through the brightly moonlit night directly toward Chancellorsville and came back to report that no opening offered in that direction. Through the night reports came in from a number of sources—a topographical engineer, a local furnace operator, a Presbyterian clergyman who knew the region, and cavalry officers—suggesting that a way might be found to turn the Federal right. For Lee to move a column across his enemy's front, leaving a very small force as a decoy, violated the basic principles of war.

To take such a risk when outnumbered more than two to one went beyond that to the verge of folly. Lee decided to go ahead.

When Jackson headed into the Wilderness early on May 2, he took some thirty thousand men with him, leaving Lee only about fifteen thousand with whom to face Hooker. For ten hours Lee feigned attacks and threw forward entire regiments as skirmishers responsible for scouting and screening the line. Tactical doctrine suggested that one or at most two of the ten companies in a regiment should provide a skirmish force in front of the main line of defense. At times Lee had no main line, just skirmishers. While Lee played his desperate game, Stonewall Jackson marched on a long looping route across Hooker's front and toward his right flank. Less than a mile into the march Jackson's men had to cross a high open spot that exposed them to Federal view. They double-timed through the ensuing artillery barrage and continued on their way. Aggressive Federal Gen. Daniel E. Sickles pushed infantry southward to interdict the Confederate movement. The Northern probe clashed with a rear guard near Catharine Furnace but did not deflect Jackson from his purpose.

Jackson rode near the head of his long column as it neared the point at which he and Lee had planned that the attackers should turn toward the enemy. He soon found that the Federal line stretched farther west than had been assumed; carrying through the original intention would not prove very effective. To meet this changed situation, Jackson marched farther north before turning east. Early in the afternoon his advance brigades arrived on a high wooded ridge that overlooked the unprotected right flank of the Union army. Hard marching and careful planning and daring had presented Jackson with one of the great opportunities of the war. As his brigades arrived, Jackson arranged them into a mighty attacking force two miles long, straddling the Orange Turnpike and overlapping the Federal line by a mile on each side. When two divisions had arrived, Jackson nodded to division commander Robert Rodes and said quietly, "You can go forward then."

The Confederates pouring out of the woods and screaming the rebel yell routed Federal Gen. O. O. Howard's Eleventh Corps and smashed two miles through the enemy positions. The bravest Northern defender could not stand long against a force that overlapped him on both sides as far as he could see. Flagrant disobedience of attack orders by Confederate Gen. Alfred H. Colquitt neutralized fully 40 percent of Jackson's line, but the rest surged irresistibly forward. The Federal position next beyond Howard's belonged to Sickles's troops, but most of them had marched south to investigate around Catharine Furnace, so Howard's retreat roared unchecked through the vacuum. For the rest of his life Hooker blamed Howard for the disaster (soon after the war he called Howard a "hypocrite . . . totally incompetent . . . a perfect old woman . . . a bad man"). In fact, no force of any sort could have faced successfully so massive a surprise attack in flank and rear.

Darkness and the confusion inherent in the wide-ranging advance stopped Jackson's momentum a mile short of Chancellorsville. As the general returned from a mounted reconnaissance beyond his amorphous front line at about 9:00 P.M., Confederates of the Eighteenth North Carolina Infantry fired in confusion on his party and wounded Jackson in three places. Early the next morning surgeons amputated his shattered left arm in a field hospital tent.

Cavalry Gen. J. E. B. Stuart assumed temporary command of Jackson's corps during the night of May 2–3 and prepared to drive the Federals from Chancellorsville. Southern artillerists identified an open knoll called Hazel Grove as the key to the battlefield, and Stuart prepared to seize it at dawn. Before Stuart could take Hazel Grove, Joe Hooker abandoned it. Confederate guns hurried to the hilltop and opened a steady fire that did much to win the day. Bitter and terribly confused woods fighting on May 3 between Hazel Grove and Chancellorsville exacted more casualties than had the dramatic actions of May 2, but in impenetrable obscurity. A knowledgeable Confederate officer who later wrote of the battle concluded resignedly, "It would be useless to follow in detail the desperate fighting which now ensued and was kept up for some hours." Its net result was gradual establishment of Confederate control around Chancellorsville. When Lee rode into the clearing around the house with his reunited army, the troops hailed him with a celebration so long and heartfelt that a staff officer wrote, "I thought that it must have been from such a scene that men in ancient days rose to the dignity of gods."

Lee's moment of triumph was interrupted when word arrived from near Fredericksburg that Early's rear guard had been penetrated by a Federal force under Gen. John Sedgwick. Lee suspended operations around Chancellorsville and sent reinforcements eastward under Gen. Lafayette McLaws. Near Salem Church, four miles west of Fredericksburg, part of the rear guard brought the Federals to a halt. McLaws handled his role poorly, and Lee went to the area in person on May 4 to arrange the attack that pushed Sedgwick back across the river during the night. The next night Hooker abandoned his position north of Chancellorsville and returned to the left bank of the Rappahannock, ending the campaign. Lee had suffered about thirteen thousand casualties; Hooker, eighteen thousand. The astonishing Confederate triumph under adverse circumstances is often, and aptly, called Lee's greatest victory, but its final act constituted a Southern disaster unequaled during the entire war. On May 10 Stonewall Jackson died at Guiney Station, south of Fredericksburg, removing what might have been the South's best hope for independence by military means.

The spectacular opening of the 1863 campaign at Chancellorsville presented Lee with an opportunity to raid north of the Potomac. He and his army, full of almost unlimited confidence in one another, carried their Chancellorsville momentum into Pennsylvania, but found a strikingly different set of circumstances at Gettysburg. There the ultimate consequence of Chancellorsville became apparent at a time "when every moment . . . could not be balanced with gold," in the words of a Confederate staff officer, who could only mutter sadly, "Jackson is not here."

BIBLIOGRAPHY

Alexander, Edward Porter. *Military Memoirs of a Confederate*. New York, 1907. Reprint, Dayton, Ohio, 1977.

Bigelow, John. *The Campaign of Chancellorsville*. New Haven, 1910. Reprint, Dayton, Ohio, 1983.

Ferguson, Ernest B. *The Souls of the Brave*. New York, 1993.

Hamlin, Augustus C. *The Battle of Chancellorsville*. Bangor, Me., 1896.

Hotchkiss, Jedediah, and William Allan. *The Battle-Fields of Virginia: Chancellorsville*. New York, 1867. Reprint, Baltimore, Md., 1985.

Krick, Robert K. "Lee's Greatest Victory." *American Heritage* 41 (March 1990): 66–79.

ROBERT K. KRICK

CHAPLAINS.

CHAPLAINS. Clergy from all the mainline denominations volunteered for service in the Confederate military throughout the Civil War. Many of them were selected as chaplains by officers or by the troops; others were recruited by general officers, church leaders, or the Confederate Chaplaincy Association. The largest numbers came from the Methodists and Baptists, although Episcopalians, Lutherans, Presbyterians, and Roman Catholics also served. Of the approximately 640 recorded chaplains, most held rank as first lieutenants in their regiments, although occasionally a chaplain served at the brigade level and held higher rank. They received low monthly wages and a bit of forage for their horses and generally lived the same hard lives as the ordinary soldiers.

Duties of chaplains were numerous and varied according to military location, the desires of the regimental commander, or their own views of their tasks. Along with the colporteurs (peddlers of religious works), chaplains distributed religious tracts, printed sermons, and special Bibles printed for the Confederate troops. They often wrote articles for the religious press and for their hometown newspapers. Chaplains also wrote letters to loved ones for sick, wounded, or illiterate soldiers. They encouraged local preachers and evangelists to join them in regimental religious services and even theaterwide revivals, several of which swept through the Confederate armies.

Their other religious duties consisted of leading prayer

meetings, baptizing soldiers, tending to moral order and abstinence in the camps, and conducting Sunday services for the troops. As spiritual leaders they delivered sermons on duty, loyalty, and bravery and used biblical stories to stress the righteousness of the Confederate cause. Chaplains went into the front lines during battle to comfort the wounded and perform last rites for the dying. Occasionally they were captured and treated as ordinary prisoners of war. During battle a few even rounded up stragglers and urged them to return to the front. At base hospitals they cared for the wounded, and at Confederate prisons they led religious services. A number of the chaplains actually fought in battle, and a few became famous as soldiers and military leaders.

Troops occasionally complained that a few chaplains used their offices to avoid the arduous duties of the war, but the majority ably served as moral and spiritual forces in the camps and for the civilians behind the lines, lightening the fears of the troops and urging patriotic sacrifices for the Confederate cause. Late in the war, some hardened troops rejected the chaplains' admonitions and the call to fight bravely. And, as the war progressed, many of those evangelical chaplain-preachers themselves depicted a lost cause and a God who had deserted the Confederacy, certainly contributing to diminished troop morale. On the whole, however, the chaplains well served the spiritual needs of the troops and the Confederate government.

[See also Sermons.]

BIBLIOGRAPHY

Faust, Drew Gilpin. "Christian Soldiers: The Meaning of Revivalism in the Confederate Army." *Journal of Southern History* 53 (February 1987): 63–90.

Pitts, Charles Frank. *Chaplains in Gray.* Nashville, Tenn., 1957.

Robertson, James I., Jr. "Chaplain William E. Wiatt: Soldier of the Cloth." In *Rank and File: Civil War Essays in Honor of Bell Irwin Wiley.* Edited by James I. Robertson and Richard M. McMurry. San Rafael, Calif., 1976.

Wiley, Bell Irwin. "'Holy Joes' of the Sixties: A Study of Civil War Chaplains." *Huntington Library Quarterly* 16 (1953): 287–304.

JON L. WAKELYN

CHAPLIN HILLS, KENTUCKY. *See* Perryville, Kentucky.

CHAPMAN, CONRAD WISE (1842–1910), artist.
Chapman was the most gifted artist to emerge in the Confederate period. The son of history painter John Gadsby Chapman (whose *Marriage of Pocahontas* is in the U.S. Capitol), Chapman was descended from a distinguished family. Born in Washington, D.C., on February 14, 1842, he trained under his father in Italy, where he absorbed something of the light of the Mediterranean and bright colors of the Italian masters that later characterized his best work.

Ardent in his feelings for Virginia, Chapman left Rome in 1861, determined to enlist in the Confederate army. Unable to reach Richmond, he entered the Confederacy through Texas and traveled to Kentucky in September. Here he painted his first notable work, *Confederate Camp, 3rd Kentucky Infantry, at Corinth, Miss.,* in the spring of 1862.

After being wounded at Shiloh, he was ordered to Virginia and assigned to the Forty-sixth Regular Virginia Volunteers, where he did numerous drawings and paintings in camp and beyond. In 1863, when his unit was transferred to Charleston, the artist-soldier was assigned by Gen. P. G. T. Beauregard to make a series of sketches of the city's defenses. These, drawn between September 1863 and March 1864, became the basis for his finest work, the series of thirty-one pictures painted in Rome (1864–1866), where he was on health leave. Early in 1865 he sought to return to the South, but Robert E. Lee's surrender ended the cause for him. He appeared briefly in Maximilian's Mexico before returning to Italy and his art. He died in Hampton, Virginia, December 10, 1910.

Recognition and fame never came to Chapman in his lifetime; only in the twentieth century would his true worth be rediscovered. His known works, over six hundred paintings, watercolors, and drawings, are today largely divided between the Valentine Museum and the Museum of the Confederacy, both in Richmond. Among his best-known images, frequently reproduced, are *Flag over Sumter; Evening Gun of Sumter* with the Charleston skyline in the distance; and the aesthetically and historically important *Submarine Boat H. L. Hunley.* Chapman had a predilection for shadowy, yet glowing landscapes, flat terrain with undulating water, trees under luminous skies, and scenes often peopled with figures—all in a romantic manner that paralleled the work of his best late-nineteenth-century contemporaries. His own best works, especially the Charleston series, are distinguished by compositional breadth and originality as well as by close attention to both color and light, resulting in extraordinary atmospheric effects, none of which would be lost on the young Winslow Homer.

[See illustration on next page.]

BIBLIOGRAPHY

"Conrad Wise Chapman." *Newsletter.* Museum of the Confederacy, Richmond, Va., 1982.

"Conrad Wise Chapman, 1842–1910." Exhibition catalogue. Valentine Museum, Richmond, Va., 1962.

Stern, Philip Van Doren. *They Were There: The Civil War in Action as Seen by Its Combat Artists.* New York, 1959.

JOHN O'BRIEN

CONFEDERATE FLAG OVER FORT SUMTER, OCTOBER 20, 1863. Painting by Conrad Wise Chapman. Photograph by Katherine Wetzel.

THE MUSEUM OF THE CONFEDERACY, RICHMOND, VIRGINIA

CHARLESTON, SOUTH CAROLINA. [*This entry is composed of two articles,* City of Charleston *and* Bombardment of Charleston. *See also* David; Fort Sumter, South Carolina; Hunley, H. L.; Port Royal, South Carolina.]

City of Charleston

Founded in 1670 as Charles Town, the settlement was moved from its original site to a nearby peninsula at the confluence of the Ashley and Cooper rivers, which flowed into the Atlantic. The economy flourished with the export of low-country rice and the import of African slaves. Approximately 40 percent of all Africans involuntarily shipped to America entered across Charles Town's wharves. It became the principal city of the South and the capital of South Carolina. After the Revolutionary War, the city's name was changed to Charleston, and Columbia became the capital of the new state.

Postwar booms in the export of rice and the new staple of cotton sputtered during the 1820s, and Charleston's economy stagnated. The city's poor rail connections westward, its shallow harbor, and the lack of a variety of exports and

of a pool of free, educated workers especially hurt small retailers and skilled laborers. The wealthy planter-merchant elite, however, prospered since the price of rice and luxury Sea Island cotton declined only slightly less than the cost of living.

The city was the economic, social, and cultural capital for the great planters of the low country. Here they built summer homes to escape the isolation and the sickly season on the plantations. They preempted the choice residential sites on the lower peninsula or its flanks where they could enjoy salubrious sea breezes and proximity to social institutions. They also brought their families to Charleston from January through March to enjoy the annual social season, which featured horse races, balls, concerts, and the theater. The planters' emphasis on family connections, sociability, and conspicuous leisure activities strongly influenced the city's character.

William Gilmore Simms was antebellum Charleston's most famous literary figure, but he was discontented with the city's intellectual life. The few citizens who were interested in ideas met periodically at Russell's Book Store and during the 1850s founded *Russell's Magazine,* the last of the Old South's literary publications. In the same decade the South Carolina Historical Society and the Carolina Art Association were founded. Physicians and naturalists made the greatest contributions to the city's intellectual life. Recognized nationally, Dr. Lewis R. Gibbes of the College of Charleston helped make the city the center of scientific activity in the Southeast.

During the late antebellum period local businessmen used their influence on City Council to invest municipal money in improving the city's rail connections. They revived its merchant marine and obtained funds to dredge the harbor, helping stimulate an economic boom. By the early 1850s Charleston had become the manufacturing center of the state, but its economy was soon in trouble again. Competing railroads siphoned off traffic, and the city's hinterland dependencies remained too few and too small to promote Charleston's growth. The city remained a colonial outlier of the northeastern regional system.

The faltering economy coupled with a steady stream of immigrants, sailors, and vagrants straggling into the port city seeking work caused growing unemployment. Prostitution flourished. With a population of 40,522 in 1859—it had declined about 2,500 since the beginning of the decade—the city of Charleston ranked twenty-second in the nation. It was the most populous of the South Atlantic ports and the major distribution center for the state. The out-migration of slaves and the immigration of Irish and Germans transformed Charleston from a city that was 53 percent black to 58 percent white, from a city dominated by a skilled black labor force to one in which two-fifths of the working class were white and 60 percent were foreign-born.

The inequality in the distribution of wealth was enormous in comparison to Northern cities: just over 3 percent of the 4,644 free white heads of households owned approximately half of the wealth in Charleston. Most Charlestonians owned neither land nor slaves, and class divisions were as obvious as racial divisions. Economically most whites living in the city had more in common with African Americans than with the white elite.

An increase in thefts and homicides, and rising Northern antislavery rhetoric, which Charlestonians feared would encourage slave insurrections, alarmed the propertied classes. Faced with these problems of social instability, they embarked on a program of reforms. They inaugurated a public school system, built a larger poorhouse, established a professional police force, and remodeled the jail. Charleston's problems were compounded by its large slave population for which there existed several separate agencies of social control.

In April 1860 the Democratic National Convention met in Charleston only to split quickly into Northern and Southern wings and arrange to reconvene elsewhere. When the national Republican party nominated Abraham Lincoln for

president, Charleston became the South's leading publisher of secession pamphlets.

As the crisis worsened, the city's authorities harassed Charleston's 3,237 free blacks, including 122 of the city's mulatto aristocracy, themselves slaveholders. The police began a systematic door-to-door search and interrogation of the African American community. Poor free blacks unable to produce absolute proof of their emancipated status were reenslaved. The mulatto aristocracy was terrified. They faced the same fate. Previously, they had escaped police harassment because of their relationships with the white elite, but as the calls for secession grew louder, their white guardians fell silent. Many of Charleston's mulatto elite considered emigrating from the city but felt that they could not leave successful careers, take enormous losses through sale of their real estate, or even get safe passage out of South Carolina. But hundreds of less prosperous free blacks sold what they could, packed what they could carry, and fled. Some sold their property at huge losses and felt cheated by whites who took advantage of their predicament.

Following Lincoln's election, delegates from across South Carolina convened in Charleston where on December 20 they adopted the ordinance of secession from the Union. Bells rang throughout the city, cannons were fired, and volunteers jammed the streets.

On December 26 Maj. Robert Anderson commanding the U.S. garrison on Sullivan's Island moved his troops to Fort Sumter in Charleston Harbor. A few days later, in the first military encounter of the war, South Carolina troops seized three local sites occupied by Federal troops. In January the vessel *Star of the West* attempted to reinforce Fort Sumter, but it was fired on by batteries on Morris Island and turned back.

Following the formation of the Confederate States of America, Gen. P. G. T. Beauregard took command at Charleston. He redeployed the troops and rearranged the ring of batteries around Fort Sumter. When Major Anderson refused to surrender the fort, Beauregard ordered its bombardment on April 12, 1861. After Anderson surrendered the following day, his troops embarked for the North and Confederate soldiers occupied the fort. President Lincoln called for 75,000 volunteers and a blockade of Southern ports.

Gen. Robert E. Lee arrived in Charleston on November 6 to take command of the Military Department of South Carolina, Georgia, and Florida. The following day Hilton Head Island, Port Royal, and Beaufort fell to Union forces. Charlestonians panicked. In December a devastating fire swept across the city, and some suspected slave arsonists.

Union strategists were determined to seize Charleston, "the cradle of secession," to stop the daily manufacture of cartridges there and the building of ironclad vessels. The steam-powered workshops of the former U.S. arsenal

CHARLESTON AND ENVIRONS, JULY 1863. Numbers on the illustration indicate: (1) Charleston and Savannah Railroad, (2) Ashley River, (3) city of Charleston, (4) Cooper River, (5) Wando River, (6) Castle Pinckney, (7) Fort Ripley, (8) Fort Johnson (James Island), (9) Stono River, (10) Fort Sumter, (11) Fort Moultrie, (12) Battery Gregg (Cummings's Point), (13) Fort Wagner, (14) General Gilmore's advanced batteries, (15) captured works (Morris's Island), (16) Lighthouse Inlet, (17) Union battery (Folly Island), (18) Ironclad and wooden ships, (19) hotel, (20) Sullivan's Island and Confederate batteries, (21) Moultrieville, (22) Mount Pleasant, (23) Breach Inlet, (24) Confederate batteries on James Island.

HARPER'S PICTORIAL HISTORY OF THE GREAT REBELLION

located on the western edge of the city produced artillery shells and thousands of cartridges daily for the Confederacy. Construction was nearing completion on the 150-foot *Palmetto State,* commissioned by the Confederate government for harbor defense, and *Chicora,* a vessel protected by 500 tons of iron armor and mounting six guns, the cost of which was funded by the state of South Carolina. The third ironclad built in the city during the war was named *Charleston.* The Federal high command also wanted to stem the flow of vast amounts of military supplies and luxury goods brought in by blockade runners. The first attack came in June 1862 when six thousand Federal troops landed southeast of the city and a fierce firefight erupted on James Island. Casualties were heavy on both sides and the Union forces retreated. In April 1863 nine Federal ironclads attacked Fort Sumter, but were forced to withdraw owing to Confederate fire and the threat of mines or submarine torpedoes, a weapon developed by the Confederate Torpedo Bureau that inaugurated a new era in naval warfare. The third attack, jointly planned by the army and navy, began in July when a large Union force occupied most of Morris Island. When the last Confederate redoubt could not be taken after heroic but costly attacks by black troops, Union forces began a bombardment of the city to force its surrender. The siege lasted for 587 days. Although the harbor defenses remained too formidable for the Union navy, its increased surveillance and the occupation of Morris Island severely curtailed blockade running at Charleston.

Occasionally, daring military exploits boosted briefly the spirits of Charlestonians. In October the Confederate ship *David,* the first combat submarine, disabled a Union blockader off Charleston; in early 1864, *H. L. Hunley* became the first submarine to sink an enemy vessel.

By this time the city was deserted below Market Street where the Union shells could reach; above this point, the life and business of the city went on. In December Gen. William J. Hardee redeployed the demoralized troops around Charleston to meet an anticipated attack by Gen. William Tecumseh Sherman. But Sherman's destination was the state capital. In mid-February 1865 General Hardee decided that Charleston was no longer defensible, and it was evacuated. Union troops immediately seized the city. The following September a Northern reporter in Charleston described it as "a city of ruins, of desolation, of vacant homes, of widowed women . . . of deserted warehouses, of weed-wild gardens, of miles of grass-grown streets."

For nearly two centuries Charleston had been the most important city in the vast territory of the Carolinas and Georgia. From about 1837 to 1862 Southern policies had been largely determined by South Carolina, and South Carolina had been largely controlled by Charlestonians. But in three years the city lost forever both its wealth and its influence.

BIBLIOGRAPHY

Burton, E. Milby. *The Siege of Charleston, 1861–1865.* Columbia, S.C., 1970.

Cauthen, Charles Edward. *South Carolina Goes to War, 1860–1865.* Chapel Hill, N.C., 1950.

Fraser, Walter J., Jr. *Charleston! Charleston!: The History of a Southern City.* Columbia, S.C., 1989.

Greb, Gregory Allen. "Charleston, South Carolina, Merchants, 1815–1860: Urban Leadership in the Antebellum South." Ph.D. diss., University of California, Riverside, 1978.

Johnson, Michael P., and James L. Roark, eds. *No Chariot Down: Charleston's Free People of Color on the Eve of the Civil War.* Chapel Hill, N.C., 1984.

Longton, William Henry. "Some Aspects of Intellectual Activity in Ante-Bellum South Carolina, 1830–1860: An Introductory Study." Ph. D. diss., University of North Carolina, Chapel Hill, 1969.

Marszalek, John F., ed. *The Diary of Miss Emma Holmes, 1861–1866.* Baton Rouge, La., 1979.

WALTER J. FRASER, JR.

Bombardment of Charleston

Early in the war Union military strategists determined to seize Charleston, the hated symbol of rebellion, to stop the daily manufacture of thousands of cartridges, the building of ironclads, and the flow of military supplies brought in by blockade runners. Following two unsuccessful attempts to take the city in June 1862 and April 1863, the Federals planned a joint army-navy operation. Following the capture of Morris Island and the reduction of nearby Fort Sumter by the army, Union vessels were to steam into the harbor and demand the surrender of the city.

In July a force of 6,000 Federal troops under Gen. Quincy A. Gillmore quickly occupied most of Morris Island. A heroic and costly attack by African American troops failed to overrun Fort Wagner, the Confederate strong point. This prevented the navy from executing its role in the operation since the harbor defenses remained formidable. General Gillmore dug in on Morris Island, constructed batteries, and trained his rifled long-range guns on Fort Sumter. One 200-pounder Parrott rifled gun was aimed at Charleston some four miles away.

On August 21, 1863, Gillmore sent a message to the commanding officer of Charleston, Gen. P. G. T. Beauregard, demanding the evacuation of Fort Sumter and Morris Island within four hours or bombardment of the city would commence. Beauregard dashed off a reply charging that by not giving "timely notice," Gillmore was committing "an act of . . . barbarity." But in the early morning hours of August 22, Gillmore ordered the bombardment to begin. It would continue for 587 days.

Charlestonians were angry and frightened. Those who could afford to took trains or carriages out of the city to

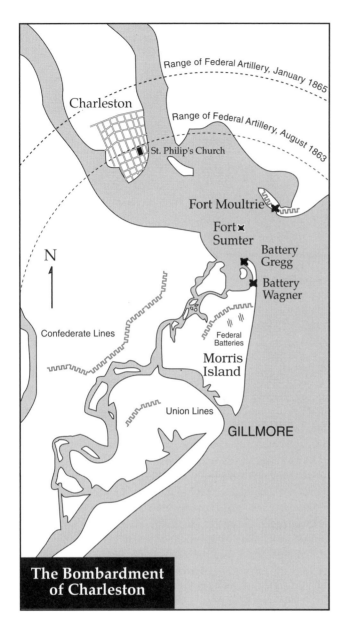

Range of Federal Artillery, January 1865

Charleston

Range of Federal Artillery, August 1863

St. Philip's Church

N

Fort Moultrie

Fort Sumter

Battery Gregg

Battery Wagner

Confederate Lines

Federal Batteries

Morris Island

Union Lines

GILLMORE

The Bombardment of Charleston

City Hall and the guard house were punctured with shell fragments. But because the city below Market Street was deserted, few people were killed during the bombardment.

With many of the city's firemen and police doing soldier duty, city services began to break down. Robberies increased dramatically. The bombardment, coupled with declines in student enrollments, severely impaired classroom instruction in the public schools.

General Beauregard was ordered to North Carolina in mid-April 1864 and Maj. Gen. Samuel Jones assumed command of the defenses of Charleston. By this time thousands of Union troops had occupied all of Morris Island, and their artillery was pounding Fort Sumter into rubble. During the summer fierce skirmishes broke out on islands around the city, and the Union artillery increased its shelling. Two of the worst days of the bombardment were September 30 and October 10 when 110 and 165 shells, respectively, fell into the city. During the fall several civilians were killed.

In October Lt. Gen. William J. Hardee arrived in Charleston to replace General Jones and take command of the remnants of the Department of South Carolina, Georgia, and Florida. About 12,500 soldiers—poorly trained, armed, clad, and fed—were concentrated around the city and Savannah. During mid-November Hardee turned over the defense of Charleston to Maj. Gen. Robert Ransom, Jr., and took hundreds of troops with him to defend Savannah against William Tecumseh Sherman, who was marching toward the city with 60,000 battle-hardened troops.

General Hardee evacuated Savannah in December and retreated toward Charleston where he redeployed 16,000 soldiers around the city. By January 1865 amphibious assaults on the city's defenses were increasing and Union shells were falling onto the Neck north of Calhoun Street. In mid-February Hardee concluded that it was no longer feasible to defend Charleston. During the night of February 17–18, the soldiers and most of the few remaining well-to-do evacuated the city and its defenses. Some 10,000 Confederate troops retreated northward up the peninsula.

On February 18 the Federals took possession of the city. The Union flag was raised over all public buildings and fortifications, and martial law was declared. One Union officer remarked that Charleston had fallen "after a siege which will rank among the most famous in history."

safer communities. The poorer people remained. Authorities moved the post office, banks, and hospitals north of Calhoun Street, beyond the range of the Union artillery, and evacuated the city's orphans to Orangeburg.

The Union occupation of Morris Island and the increased surveillance by the Union navy severely curtailed blockade running while Federal land forces inched closer to the city. Confederate money depreciated and the costs of goods and services soared in Charleston. A few speculators in foodstuffs made huge profits, but destitution was widespread.

The bombardment of the city was sporadic until late 1863 when the shelling began with regularity. During nine days in January 1864, some 1,500 shells were fired into Charleston; occasionally they started fires. St. Philip's Church was hit repeatedly and its interior wrecked, and

BIBLIOGRAPHY

Burton, E. Milby. *The Siege of Charleston, 1861–1865.* Columbia, S.C., 1970.

Fraser, Walter J., Jr. *Charleston! Charleston!: The History of a Southern City.* Columbia, S.C., 1989.

Sutor, Jack. "Charleston, South Carolina, during the Civil War Era, 1858–1865." M.A. thesis, Duke University, 1942.

WALTER J. FRASER, JR.

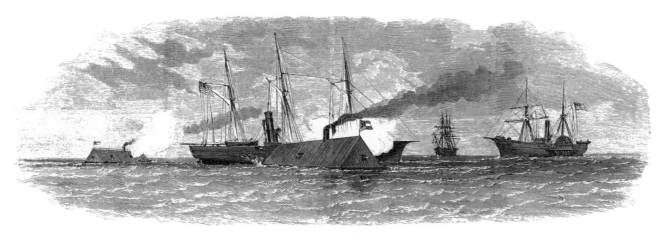

CHARLESTON SQUADRON.   CSS *Chicora* (at left) and CSS *Palmetto State* engaging the blockading USS *Mercedita* (second from left) and USS *Keystone State* on January 31, 1863. The ship in the distance is unknown.   *HARPER'S PICTORIAL HISTORY OF THE GREAT REBELLION*

CHARLESTON SQUADRON. South Carolina's state navy was absorbed into Confederate service in April 1861 under Commdr. H. J. Hartstene. In November Capt. Duncan N. Ingraham assumed command, and in 1862 the Charleston Squadron acquired strength with the addition of the ironclads *Chicora* and *Palmetto State.*

On January 31, 1863, the squadron struck the Union blockade, seeking to open the city to outside commerce. The Charleston command declared the blockade broken, but little damage had been done and the city remained sealed. Soon after, Captain Ingraham was replaced as commander afloat by Capt. John Randolph Tucker of *Chicora.*

While the naval command concentrated on ironclads, Charleston was becoming a center for experimentation with mines and torpedoes. A cadre of young officers in the squadron pushed their superiors for action, and expeditions to attack Union monitors were organized. On October 5, 1863, Lt. William T. Glassell attacked USS *New Ironsides* with the torpedo boat *David.* The damage inflicted kept *New Ironsides* out of action for more than a year.

In late 1863 the ironclad *Charleston* was added to the squadron and became Tucker's flagship. Torpedo expeditions against the blockade continued (the submarine *H. L. Hunley's* successful attack was under army command), but the ships and gunboats engaged in purely defensive operations for the rest of the war, bombarding the Union troops and batteries besieging the city. When Charleston was evacuated, the squadron was destroyed.

BIBLIOGRAPHY

Melton, Maurice. *The Confederate Ironclads.* South Brunswick, N.J., 1968.

Parker, William H. *Recollections of a Naval Life.* New York, 1883. Reprint, Annapolis, Md., 1985.

Rochelle, James H. *Life of Rear Admiral John Randolph Tucker.* Washington, D.C., 1903.

Scharf, J. Thomas. *History of the Confederate States Navy.* New York, 1887. Reprint, New York, 1977.

Still, William N. *Iron Afloat.* Nashville, Tenn., 1971.

MAURICE K. MELTON

CHARLOTTE AND MECKLENBURG COUNTY, NORTH CAROLINA. Charlotte, the permanent courthouse town of Mecklenburg County, North Carolina, since 1774, was strategically important during the Civil War: it had acquired excellent railroad connections in the early and mid-1850s, and it was far removed from the fields of battle, hence secure, until the final stages of the war. Although Mecklenburg County furnished 2,713 men to the Confederate military, including the troops of the Charlotte Greys and the Hornet's Nest Rifles and, most notably, D. H. Hill, head of the North Carolina Military Institute, which had opened in Charlotte in 1859, Charlotte's greatest contribution to the Confederate cause was logistical.

The Confederacy established several important military support facilities in Charlotte and Mecklenburg County. The largest and most significant was the Naval Ordnance Works, which was moved from Norfolk, Virginia, to Charlotte in 1862. Superintended by Harry Ashton Ramsay, who had been chief engineer on *Virginia,* the naval yard employed some three hundred workers to manufacture such items as propellor shafting, crankshafts for gunboats, crank axles for locomotives, and gun carriages, and also to repair equipment for cotton and woolen mills.

Also situated in Charlotte was the site of the Confederate States Acid Works. Sulfuric and nitric acids were needed to produce fulminate of mercury, which was used in percussion caps for muskets and rifles. Sulfuric acid was indispensable in the making of wet cell batteries, an essential source of electric power for the Confederacy's telegraph system. Headed by Charles Henry Wilson, the acid works operated from 1862 until 1864 in the buildings formerly used by the Rudisell Gold Mine. Charlotte served, too, as a major storage depot for the Confederate quartermaster's warehouses. Cotton and food supplies, as well as soldiers' clothing and blankets, were deposited in warehouses that stood beside the track of the North Carolina Central and the South Carolina railroads near the center of town.

Private industries in Charlotte and Mecklenburg County made crucial contributions to the Confederate military. The North Carolina Powder Manufacturing Company, operated by its president, S. W. Davis, stood near the Tuckaseegee Ford on the Catawba River. It suffered massive accidental explosions, once on May 23, 1863, and again on August 4, 1864. The Mountain Island Woolen Mills, also on the Catawba, employed about three hundred women in the production of "soldiers' round jackets." The New Manufacturing Company of Charlotte, located on East Trade Street, produced wooden canteens for the army, and an enterprise owned by J. M. Howie produced belt buckles and wire.

In 1860, the population of Mecklenburg County was 17,374, of whom 2,265 lived in Charlotte. There were 2,500 to 3,000 slaves and an unknown number of free blacks. Not surprisingly, the great majority of the rank-and-file white population of Charlotte and Mecklenburg County labored mightily throughout the Civil War to assist North Carolina and the Confederate States of America. The women carded, spun, and wove cloth for the troops. The Ladies Hospital Association of Mecklenburg County, one of the first of its kind in the South, gathered worn garments, bedding, bandages, and other hospital supplies to help the wounded. In October 1861, the citizens of Charlotte held a benefit concert to raise money for North Carolina soldiers. The local Methodist, Episcopal, Baptist, and Lutheran churches donated their bells in April 1862 to be melted down for use in manufacturing Confederate cannons.

Mecklenburg slaves were donated to the Confederate cause on at least three occasions, primarily to erect fortifications and to repair railroads. In March 1865, Gen. P. G. T. Beauregard issued an appeal from his headquarters in Charlotte for owners to furnish slaves to assist in blocking roads and fords leading to South Carolina, where Gen. William Tecumseh Sherman's Federal army was fast approaching. In two days over three hundred slaves were ready for service.

The most dramatic moments in the Civil War history of Charlotte and Mecklenburg County occurred in April and May 1865. Churches overflowed with wounded soldiers who had been transferred from Raleigh and other cities that seemed more threatened by Sherman's relentless push northward. Maj. Gen. George H. Stoneman, commander of a Federal force sent over the North Carolina mountains to capture a Confederate prison at Salisbury, dispatched to the Catawba River a contingent of troops who skirmished with Confederate cavalry at Tuckaseegee Ford, ten miles west of Charlotte. On April 18, 1865, President Jefferson Davis, members of his cabinet, and a thousand cavalrymen arrived in Charlotte. During his stay, which lasted until April 26, Davis learned that President Abraham Lincoln had been assassinated. The Ninth New Jersey Volunteers, commanded by Capt. Morris C. Runyan, were the first Federal troops to arrive in Charlotte. They occupied the town without a fight on May 7, 1865.

BIBLIOGRAPHY

Alexander, J. B. *History of Mecklenburg County, 1840–1902.* Charlotte, N.C., 1902.
Blythe, Legette, and Charles R. Brockman. *Hornet's Nest: The Story of Charlotte and Mecklenburg County.* Charlotte, N.C., 1961.
Kratt, Mary Norton. *Charlotte: Spirit of the New South.* Tulsa, Okla., 1980.

DAN L. MORRILL

CHARLOTTE NAVY YARD. The impending evacuation of the Gosport Navy Yard at Norfolk, Virginia, in May 1862 caused Navy Secretary Stephen R. Mallory to order the relocation of the facility's heavy machinery and ordnance stores. Officials chose the southern North Carolina city of Charlotte for the new yard because of its inland location and excellent rail connections with coastal ports. The government acquired a site bordered by two rail lines, and workers erected new structures. By year's end the Charlotte Navy Yard was producing gun carriages, projectiles, and other ordnance equipment. The addition of a large steam hammer permitted the forging of heavy propeller shafts, large anchors, and wrought-iron armor-piercing bolts unobtainable elsewhere in the Confederacy. The navy yard also produced torpedoes and wooden blocks and repaired locomotives. Many of the establishment's employees came with the machinery from Gosport. They were joined by local workmen and, in 1864, by skilled mechanics recruited in England.

Capt. Samuel Barron apparently was the installation's first commander but was replaced in October 1862 by Commdr. Richard L. Page. Page was followed in rapid succession by Capt. George N. Hollins and Commdr. Catesby Jones before again assuming command in May 1863. Chief Engineer Henry Ashton Ramsay superintended the works from the spring of 1864 until the end of the war.

With the rapid disintegration of the Confederacy in April 1865, the Charlotte Navy Yard was abandoned. Symbolic of that end was the destruction at the yard of the records of the Navy Department after their removal from Richmond.

BIBLIOGRAPHY

Alexander, Violet G. "The Confederate States Navy Yard at Charlotte, N.C., 1862–1865." *Southern Historical Society Papers* 40 (1915): 184–192. Reprint, Wilmington, N.C., 1991.

Donnelly, Ralph W. "The Charlotte, North Carolina, Navy Yard, C.S.N." *Civil War History* 5 (March 1959): 72–79.

Still, William N. *Confederate Shipbuilding.* 2d ed. Columbia, S.C., 1987.

A. ROBERT HOLCOMBE, JR.

CHATTAHOOCHEE. A wooden, twin-screw-propeller sail- and steam-powered gunboat measuring 130 feet in length, 30 feet in width, and 10 feet in depth of hold, *Chattahoochee* was built on the river for which it was named by David S. Johnston of Saffold, Early County, Georgia, pursuant to an October 19, 1861, contract with the Navy Department. Its armament consisted of a rifled and banded 32-pounder forward, a 9-inch Dahlgren smoothbore aft, and four 32-pounder smoothbores in broadside.

Under the command of Lt. Catesby Jones, *Chattahoochee* was commissioned January 1, 1863, and immediately began the monotonous task of defending the Apalachicola-Chattahoochee-Flint river system against anticipated Federal naval excursions from the Gulf of Mexico. The following May 27, while commanded by Lt. John J. Guthrie, *Chattahoochee* suffered a boiler explosion near Blountstown, Florida, which killed nineteen of its crew and resulted in its sinking. The vessel was raised several months later and taken to Columbus, Georgia, for repairs. Although lacking replacement boilers, *Chattahoochee* was placed into service for a brief time in the spring of 1864 when its crew, led by Lt. George W. Gift, participated in an abortive small-boat attack against Union blockaders off Apalachicola, Florida.

Still without operative steam machinery, *Chattahoochee* was scuttled to prevent capture twelve miles below Columbus soon after the April 16, 1865, fall of that city. In 1964 thirty feet of *Chattahoochee*'s stern was recovered and placed at the Confederate Naval Museum in Columbus.

BIBLIOGRAPHY

Castlen, Harriet Gift. *Hope Bids Me Onward.* Savannah, Ga., 1945.

Turner, Maxine. *Navy Gray: A Story of the Confederate Navy on the Chattahoochee and Apalachicola Rivers.* Tuscaloosa, Ala., 1988.

A. ROBERT HOLCOMBE, JR.

CHATTANOOGA, TENNESSEE. [*This entry includes two articles,* City of Chattanooga, *which profiles the city during the Confederacy, and* Chattanooga Campaign, *which discusses the military action there in 1863. See also* Wheeler's Raids.]

City of Chattanooga

At the beginning of the Civil War, Chattanooga was a little-known commercial and manufacturing town of 2,500 people, about a fourth of whom were African American slaves. Another 10 percent were free blacks. Despite its small size and relative obscurity, it was a community of great strategic importance because of its role as a transportation hub. The only rail route that provided an unbroken connection between Virginia and the West and another important line connecting the Deep South with the upper South converged in the little town that had been established only twenty-three years earlier as a river port. Before the war more than 45,000 bales of cotton were shipped by rail through Chattanooga annually to points north and to the Southern ports of Savannah and Charleston. The railroad was only one aspect of Chattanooga's importance as a transportation center. The town's key location on the Tennessee River linked it with the other important water transportation routes of the Southeast, and until the advent of the railroad in the 1850s, Chattanooga was almost totally dependent on the river for its livelihood.

During the secession crisis, Chattanoogans were a deeply divided people. Reflecting the town's location on the edge of Unionist eastern Tennessee, up to a third of its population openly opposed secession and voted to keep Tennessee in the Union. After the firing on Fort Sumter, however, Tennessee joined the Confederacy, and for the next two years Southern sympathies and authority prevailed in the town. Divided sympathies aside, Chattanooga was important for the contending armies because of its location. Its geographic importance became evident early in the war when Confederate troops garrisoned the area and converted the town into a major supply depot. Indeed, by early 1862, Chattanooga was a military community in almost every respect. Warehouses, barracks, hospitals, fortifications, and men in uniform everywhere became as much a part of the town as all of its civilian vestiges. With large armies present, the town's prewar population mushroomed as much as fivefold.

In the late summer of 1863, when Gen. William S. Rosecrans forced Braxton Bragg's Confederate army out of Tennessee, Union troops occupied Chattanooga. After a decisive victory at Chickamauga, Confederate forces moved north to try to recapture Chattanooga. For the next two months, Bragg's army besieged the town, cutting Federal supply lines and reducing Union troops and civilians to starvation rations. A large army under Ulysses S. Grant, however, broke the siege and dealt the Confederates a crushing defeat at Missionary Ridge on November 25. Chattanooga remained firmly under Union control until the end of the war and served as a key supply center for William

Tecumseh Sherman's army as it moved into Georgia in the spring of 1864.

For the people of Chattanooga, the war years meant great social unrest and disruption, problems only exacerbated by the town's divided loyalties. During the first two years, the strong core of Unionists suffered persecution at the hands of their fellow citizens with Confederate leanings. Many Unionists were jailed, and scores of others fled to Federal-occupied areas. Confederate sympathizers, however, experienced the reverse when Chattanooga fell under Union control. Federal authorities confiscated the property of Southern sympathizers, jailed or expatriated others, and enforced strict martial law. In addition to maintaining control of the town's normal civilian population, Federal military authorities faced another major challenge. A large influx of former slaves added to the turmoil of the town in the summer of 1864.

Freed from the fetters of slavery, thousands of men, women, and children from Georgia, Alabama, and Tennessee flocked into Chattanooga seeking refuge and sustenance. With them came massive problems of hunger, disease, and civil unrest. For Union military authorities, dealing with social chaos in Chattanooga became almost as challenging as fighting the Confederate army. Even stricter martial law was established, and little by little, segregated tent cities for black refugees were set up, ringing the town. By the end of 1864, nearly four thousand black refugees lived in the makeshift tents and huts. At war's end, the Freedmen's Bureau assumed the administration of the refugee camps, instituting active educational and job placement programs for the former slaves.

With the return of peace in 1865, military authorities turned over to civilian authorities a town with serious problems. The strains of war had imposed a heavy financial burden on the municipal government, and most of the town's public buildings had been destroyed or rendered useless. A scourge of smallpox in the wake of the war lasted until the great flood of 1867 that washed away homes, industries, and a military bridge, keeping the town isolated for days.

Nevertheless, Chattanooga experienced a speedy recovery in the postwar years. The abundance of raw materials, its advantage as a transportation center, and cheap labor were successfully touted by local authorities to attract manufacturing enterprises. The development of business and industry by Northern investors immediately after the war spurred the local economy and helped city revenues rise to above prewar levels by 1870. The iron industry, in particular, boomed in the early 1870s, and the city's importance as a rail hub increased accordingly. Only twenty years after the war, the town was entered by nine trunk lines. Despite the many travails it had brought, the war served as a stimulus for the town's development. With its natural assets, its key geographic location, and large infusions of Northern capital in the immediate postwar years, Chattanooga changed from a simple crossroads town into a major industrial and commercial center.

BIBLIOGRAPHY

Bryan, Charles F., Jr. "The Civil War in East Tennessee: A Social, Political, and Economic Study." Ph.D. diss., University of Tennessee, 1978.

Govan, Gilbert E., and James W. Livingood. *The Chattanooga Country, 1540–1951: From Tomahawk to TVA*. New York, 1952.

Wilson, John. *Chattanooga's Story*. Chattanooga, Tenn., 1980.

CHARLES F. BRYAN, JR.

Chattanooga Campaign

A series of battles fought around Chattanooga, Tennessee, during October and November 1863, the campaign had ruinous consequences for the South. It cost the Confederacy some 6,700 killed, wounded, missing, or captured; the North suffered 5,800 casualties.

Following the defeat of the Federal Army of the Cumberland at Chickamauga on September 20, 1863, the routed Union troops had raced north through Rossville Gap to the safe haven of Chattanooga, Tennessee. On September 24, Gen. William Rosecrans, commander of the Northern soldiers in Chattanooga, withdrew from Lookout Mountain one of his brigades, which had originally been posted there to guard supply routes coming into the city from the west. Upon learning of this withdrawal, Gen. Braxton Bragg, commander of the Confederate Army of Tennessee, occupied this strategic mountain. He also fortified Missionary

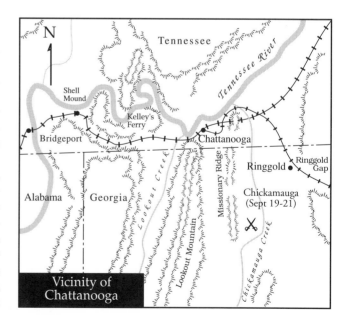

Vicinity of Chattanooga

Ridge, which ran northeast to southeast on the east side of the city, and Lookout valley and Raccoon Mountain to the west.

In such a commanding position, Bragg, with about 46,000 effective troops, felt that Rosecrans had no choice but to abandon Chattanooga or face the destruction of his 35,000-man army. But Rosecrans, fearing to leave the comparative safety of the city with the Tennessee River guarding his rear, instead heavily fortified his front and awaited reinforcements. These troops consisted of two corps of about 16,000 men from the Army of the Potomac under Gen. Joseph Hooker, which began to arrive at Bridgeport, Alabama, twenty-seven miles west of Chattanooga, in the first part of October. There, the corps were assigned to guard the railroad that led back to Federal supply depots in Nashville.

At about the time that Hooker was beginning to arrive in Bridgeport, Bragg was despairing of Rosecrans abandoning Chattanooga voluntarily. He decided to starve the army out and ordered all river and rail traffic to the city stopped. In addition, Gen. Joseph Wheeler, who commanded the cavalry of the Army of Tennessee, took his troopers on a successful raid during the first week of October, destroying Federal wagon trains hauling supplies from the railhead in Bridgeport. (The Confederates had previously burned the railroad bridge that crossed the Tennessee River at Bridgeport, and consequently wagon trains had to negotiate a tortuous system of barely passable roads to reach Chattanooga, the trips sometimes taking up to twenty days as compared to about an hour by rail.) As a result of Wheeler's raiding parties, Rosecrans had no choice but to put his soldiers on reduced rations.

When Gen. Ulysses S. Grant was appointed commander of the newly created Federal Military Division of Mississippi in mid-October, he relieved Rosecrans and assigned Gen. George H. Thomas as the new commander of the Army of the Cumberland. On October 23, Grant arrived in Chattanooga to talk over the situation with Thomas and Gen. William F. Smith, chief engineer of the Department of the Cumberland. Smith proposed an innovative plan that was to become known to history as the "Cracker Line." West of the city was a bend in the river called Moccasin Point. Smith's idea was to send 3,500 infantrymen under Gen. John B. Turchin, supported by three batteries of artillery, over an existing pontoon bridge to this neck of land and from there move them overland to a point on the east bank of the river opposite Brown's Ferry. At the same time, 1,500 more infantry under Gen. William B. Hazen were to drift downstream in fifty pontoon boats and drive in Confederate pickets guarding Brown's Ferry on the west bank. With that accomplished, the Federals on both sides would span the river with another pontoon bridge, allowing those soldiers on Moccasin Point to cross the Tennessee in force. The whole operation was to be supported by three divisions from Hooker's command, which would cross the Tennessee at Bridgeport and move to an area just west of Lookout Mountain. From Brown's Ferry, a road—entirely out of range of Southern artillery—led to another ferry on the river known as Kelley's. With Kelley's Ferry in Federal hands, it would be but a short steamboat run from Bridgeport to that point and a relatively safe eight-mile overland trip to Chattanooga.

The operation commenced well before dawn on October 27. Upon landing at Brown's Ferry and driving in the pickets, Hazen's men ran into about 400 of Gen. James Longstreet's troops, commanded by Col. William C. Oates, who temporarily held off the Federals, but could not do so for long. The pontoon bridge from Moccasin Point was in place that afternoon, and the Union plan went almost without a hitch. Only thirty-eight Federals and an undetermined but small number of Confederates were lost.

Advance elements from Hooker's command reached the vicinity of the village of Wauhatchie and Lookout valley not far from Brown's Ferry on the evening of the twenty-eighth. There, they were attacked in a night fight by Longstreet's troops. After a sharp battle, however, the Confederates ceased firing about 3:30 the next morning, and the Cracker Line was secure. The besieged Union garrison in Chattanooga was soon receiving food and ammunition: the first steamboat arrived at Kelley's Ferry on the first of November.

As a result of Longstreet's withdrawal from Lookout Mountain, Grant was able to garrison the south side of the Tennessee River with about 20,000 troops, and Bragg then was forced to end his siege of Chattanooga.

On November 5, Longstreet and his 12,000 troops were ordered to leave the Chattanooga area and move to Knoxville to confront the Union army's Ninth Corps under Gen. Ambrose E. Burnside. Under the circumstances, Bragg could ill afford to lose that many men while Grant was gaining strength every day. Longstreet was incredulous at the order, but felt that he might be able to beat Burnside quickly and return to the Confederate lines at Chattanooga in time for the impending battle. Grant, for his part, when he learned of Longstreet's departure, immediately began formulating plans to smash Bragg's lines on Missionary Ridge. The stage was set for Confederate disaster.

On November 13, 17,000 Federal troops of the Army of the Tennessee arrived at Bridgeport; these soldiers were mostly veterans of the Vicksburg campaign under the command of Gen. William Tecumseh Sherman. Gen. Henry W. Halleck, general-in-chief of the Union armies, had ordered Sherman to relieve Chattanooga, but to repair rail lines as the soldiers came forward. Impatient for Sherman to come to his aid, however, Grant had canceled Halleck's order on October 27. Sherman arrived in Chattanooga on

November 14, and Grant ordered him to reconnoiter the northern end of Missionary Ridge. Following a discussion with Grant of a plan of battle to defeat the Confederates on the ridge, Sherman returned to Bridgeport and brought his troops up through Lookout valley to Brown's Ferry to reinforce the Federal army and prepare for the coming action.

Before a full attack could take place on Missionary Ridge, a strategic foothill to the east of Chattanooga, called Orchard Knob, had to be secured. On the morning of November 23, two divisions under Gen. Philip Sheridan and Gen. Thomas Wood were sent out of Chattanooga in the direction of Orchard Knob as if on a grand parade, though the movement was, in fact, a reconnaissance in force of the foothill. The Confederates, observing from Missionary Ridge, were taken in, and before they could respond appropriately, the Union divisions rushed the Southern defenses on Orchard Knob and won a quick, decisive victory. The Federal army then moved out of Chattanooga and forward to new positions facing the Confederate lines on Missionary Ridge.

To assault Bragg's army, Sherman was to attack the Confederate right on the northern end of the Ridge, while Hooker, after moving his men into position across Chattanooga valley, attacked Bragg's left. In the meantime, Thomas's Army of the Cumberland would hold the center

of the Federal line in reserve, merely threatening the Confederate center or, if necessary, coming to the aid of either flank attack. The Union assault was set for November 25.

While Sherman was moving his troops across the Tennessee River at Brown's Ferry and into position on the left of the Army of the Cumberland during the foggy, rainy day of November 24, Hooker's Federals, too, were on the move. At about 8 o'clock that morning, Hooker ordered one of his divisions, Gen. John W. Geary's, to cross Lookout Creek and assault the southern position on the side of Lookout Mountain. Later in the day the divisions of Gen. Charles Cruft and Gen. Peter J. Osterhaus, about 10,000 men, were to follow. These Federals faced about 2,700 Confederates under the command of Gen. John Jackman, who had dug in a strong line around the Craven home on the slopes of the mountain. In addition, scattered over the mountain were another 4,000 Southerners.

Taking Lookout Mountain, however, was not Hooker's main objective. Rather, by crossing Chattanooga valley between Lookout Mountain and Missionary Ridge, he planned to clear that area of Confederate troops, take the town of Rossville, and bring himself up into position on the right of the Federal lines to attack Bragg's left flank and possibly move to his rear. Nevertheless, if he saw an opportunity to clear the Southerners from the heights of

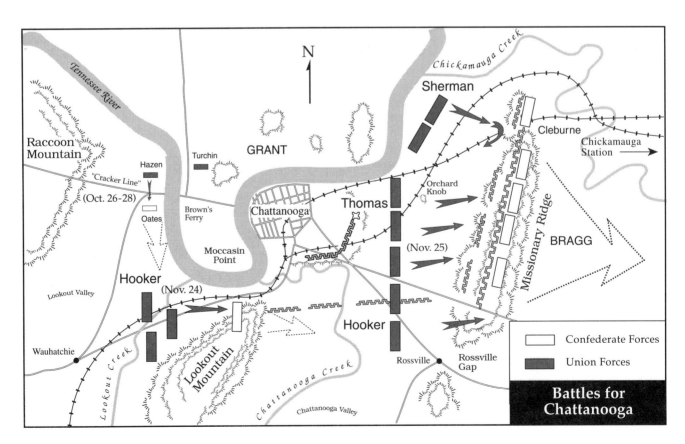

Battles for Chattanooga

Lookout Mountain, he planned to exercise that option. He did see an opportunity that day and took advantage of it.

After crossing Lookout Creek, the advancing Federals climbed up the steep western slope of the mountain in fog so thick the men could barely see in front of them. Working their way around to the northern side, they continued their arduous climb up the nearly vertical walls of the mountain. After battling the Federals all day, the Southerners withdrew to Missionary Ridge that night, and the Stars and Stripes were planted atop Lookout Mountain for all to see on the bright morning of November 25. The Battle of Lookout Mountain—known to history as "The Battle above the Clouds"—was, in truth, not much of a battle by Civil War standards. Because of the dense fog and rain, neither side could see the other very clearly, and Union artillery, firing on the mountain from Moccasin Point, was ineffective. With Hooker's capture of Lookout Mountain, however, Grant had in effect a relatively straight line of battle on Missionary Ridge, with little danger now on his flanks.

The Battle of Missionary Ridge began on the morning of the twenty-fifth. By the previous evening, Sherman had gained an advanced position on Bragg's right in the foothills below the ridge, and Hooker was moving steadily in the direction of Bragg's left. At 11:00 A.M., Sherman assaulted the Confederate right, but made little progress. Under the nominal command of Gen. William J. Hardee, Bragg's right had just been reinforced by Gen. Patrick Cleburne's division. Cleburne, considered one of the finest fighting generals of the Confederacy, had been sent on November 23 to help Longstreet in his efforts against Burnside. But as Bragg finally came to realize Grant's intentions, Cleburne had been hurriedly recalled from Chickamauga Station and had arrived in time to fortify the northern end of Missionary Ridge, blunting Sherman's assault.

Off toward the southern end of the ridge, Hooker had stalled at Chattanooga Creek waiting for a pontoon bridge to be built so he could cross his command.

Meanwhile, in the center, after being stripped of a corps and then a division to aid Sherman, the Army of the Cumberland, with three divisions remaining, sensed disaster on the Union left and right. At 3:00 P.M., Thomas, who had been given a halfhearted order by Grant to advance his troops, decided to take matters into his own hands. Forming Sheridan's and Wood's divisions of Granger's Corps, along with Gen. Richard Johnson's and Gen. Absolam Baird's divisions as support, he attacked through Orchard Knob. At first the Union soldiers were bogged down in the Confederate trenches they had captured at the foot of the ridge, but the unrelenting Southern artillery fire aimed at them elicited an amazing response. With orders from no one, the soldiers of the Army of the Cumberland rose and, in a brilliant, unstoppable assault, charged up the six hundred feet to the Confederate center on the crest of Missionary Ridge. The attack broke and routed the Confederate center, and soon all the Southern units from left and right followed the retreat down the opposite side of Missionary Ridge, across Chickamauga Creek, and, by early morning on November 26, through Ringgold Gap. This retreat in effect ended the Chattanooga campaign.

The battles around Chattanooga had significant results for the North. The city and its railroads were now under permanent Federal control, and in the spring of 1864, Sherman would use Chattanooga as a staging area for his Atlanta campaign. The railroads would, in turn, supply his successful assault on the Deep South. Grant would become commander-in-chief of all the Federal armies and lead the Union to victory in April 1865.

BIBLIOGRAPHY

Connelly, Thomas L. *Autumn of Glory: The Army of Tennessee, 1862–1865.* Baton Rouge, La., 1971.

Downey, Fairfax D. *Storming of the Gateway: Chattanooga, 1863.* New York, 1960.

Horn, Stanley F. *Tennessee's War, 1861–1865.* Nashville, Tenn., 1965.

Taylor, Benjamin F. *Missionary Ridge and Lookout Mountain.* Chicago, 1872.

Tucker, Glenn. "Chattanooga!" *Civil War Times Illustrated,* August 1971.

WARREN WILKINSON

CHEATHAM, B. FRANKLIN

CHEATHAM, B. FRANKLIN (1820–1886), major general. Born on a plantation near Nashville, Benjamin Franklin Cheatham served in the Mexican War as a captain in the First Tennessee and later as colonel of the Third Tennessee, a unit he helped raise. He traveled to California in the gold rush of 1849 and returned to his native state in 1853. Before the Civil War he farmed, was a major general in the Tennessee militia, and participated in local political affairs as a Democrat.

Governor Isham G. Harris appointed Cheatham a brigadier general in the Provisional Army of Tennessee on May 9, 1861. When the army entered Confederate service, Cheatham was commissioned a brigadier on July 9. His actions at Belmont helped him win a promotion to major general as of March 10, 1862.

Cheatham's division experienced heavy fighting at Shiloh, Perryville, Murfreesboro, Chickamauga, and Missionary Ridge, and in the Atlanta and Nashville campaigns. The division earned a reputation among both Confederate and Union observers as one of the hardest-hitting units in the western theater. The strong bond between Cheatham and his men contributed to the division's élan and to their battlefield success.

B. Franklin Cheatham.   Library of Congress

Yet Cheatham also sparked controversy. His relationship with Braxton Bragg, commander of the Army of Tennessee from June 1862 to December 1863, was marked by discord. Bragg resented Cheatham's close ties to Leonidas Polk, regarded Cheatham as an incompetent political appointee, and sought in vain to remove Cheatham from command. Hostility flared between the two men after Bragg accused Cheatham of drunkenness at Murfreesboro. After Chickamauga, Bragg's army reorganization broke up the division and sent most of Cheatham's Tennesseans to other units. Cheatham, now a prominent member of the anti-Bragg faction, asked to be relieved from duty on October 31, 1863. Richmond authorities rejected the request.

Joseph E. Johnston, taking charge of the army, restored Cheatham's former division, and the reunited command fought in the Georgia campaign of 1864. Cheatham and his men distinguished themselves at Kennesaw Mountain, where they defended a salient in the Confederate line against a massive Union assault on June 27. After John Bell Hood replaced Johnston, Cheatham led Hood's old corps at Peachtree Creek and the Battle of Atlanta. When William J. Hardee left the army in September 1864, Cheatham assumed command of Hardee's corps and guided it throughout Hood's invasion of Tennessee.

Cheatham led the Confederate advance to Spring Hill on November 29, 1864, but he failed to either launch an attack on Spring Hill or block the turnpike between Columbia and Franklin. As a result, John M. Schofield's troops stole along the turnpike after nightfall virtually unimpeded. The Union escape ignited an acrimonious debate between Cheatham and Hood that extended into the postwar period. At Franklin the next day Cheatham's corps bore the brunt of the fighting and suffered heavy casualties. Cheatham fought at Nashville two weeks later and retreated with the remnants of the army after that disaster. He surrendered with Johnston in North Carolina.

After the war Cheatham returned to Tennessee, where he farmed, lost an 1872 congressional race, and served as superintendent of the state prison system for four years. He was postmaster of Nashville at the time of his death on September 4, 1886.

BIBLIOGRAPHY

Lindsley, John Berrien, ed. *The Military Annals of Tennessee: Confederate.* Nashville, Tenn., 1886.

Losson, Christopher. *Tennessee's Forgotten Warriors: Frank Cheatham and His Confederate Division.* Knoxville, Tenn., 1989.

Porter, James D. *Tennessee.* Vol. 8 of *Confederate Military History.* Edited by Clement A. Evans. Atlanta, 1899. Vol. 10 of extended ed. Wilmington, N.C., 1987.

CHRISTOPHER LOSSON

CHEROKEES. By 1860, the Cherokees had split into two distinct tribes. In the 1830s, the United States had forced the majority of Cherokees from their homeland in Georgia, Alabama, Tennessee, and North Carolina to what is today Oklahoma. These people formed the Cherokee Nation. Another group of Cherokees, the Eastern Band, remained in North Carolina. In 1860, the Cherokee Nation's population was 17,000 (13,800 Indian, 700 white, 2,500 black), and the Eastern Band numbered about 2,000. The Eastern Band was more culturally conservative and homogeneous than the Cherokee Nation. Deep cultural divisions in the West manifested themselves during the Civil War and produced an internecine struggle within the Cherokee Nation.

Before their removal to the West, a number of Cherokees had adopted racial slavery. The slaveholding population lived primarily in the broad river valleys of northern Georgia and Alabama; few slaveholders lived in the mountains of western North Carolina. Consequently, slavery was never important to the Eastern Band. When the Cherokee Nation moved, slaveholders took their bondsmen with them. They recognized slaves as property, denied them political rights, and limited their freedom through written laws. In the West, slaves helped the economic elite retain their dominance through their labor in agriculture, livestock herding, and salt making. By the beginning of the Civil War, slavery was well established in the Cherokee Nation, but almost unknown among the Eastern Band.

Not all Cherokees in the Nation supported the institution, however, and during the 1850s they became more active in their opposition. Culturally conservative Cherokees regarded slavery as an alien institution that had enabled a highly acculturated elite to assume inordinate political and economic power. These conservatives found unlikely allies in Protestant missionaries, particularly the Baptists John and Evan Jones, who openly espoused abolitionist sentiments. The antislavery stance of many missionaries created a crisis among the elite, who recognized the crucial role of Northern philanthropy, now largely directed toward abolition, in their Nation's history.

In an address to the National Council, Principal Chief John Ross pointed out the dilemma facing the Cherokees: "Our locality and situation ally us to the South, while to the North we are indebted for a defense of our rights in the past and that enlarged benevolence to which we owe our progress in civilization." Ross's solution was neutrality, which meant that treaties with the United States remained in effect. The treaties provided for annuities, annual Federal payments for land previously ceded, on which the Cherokees depended for the operation of their schools, printing press, and government.

Most Cherokees, however, had already taken sides in the conflict. Although the division had roots in removal factionalism, it also stemmed from disparate acculturation of which slaveholding was an indicator. Stand Watie, the brother of a slain pro-removal leader, organized the Knights of the Golden Circle, or as they later became known, the Southern Rights party. These men sought to bring the Cherokees into the Confederate fold. In opposition to the Knights were the Keetowahs, or Pins (for their insignia of two crossed pins worn under the lapel), who favored Union alliance based on previous treaties. In the summer of 1861, the two groups clashed briefly at Webbers Falls when the Pins prevented the Knights from raising a Confederate flag.

By the end of the summer, Ross was under intense pressure to ally with the Confederacy. The Southerners had commissioned Albert Pike to offer the Cherokees very favorable treaty terms that included continuation of their annuities, Confederate purchase of the Cherokees' neutral lands on the Kansas border at the price they wanted, and representation in the Confederate Congress. The other Southern Indians had joined the Confederacy, Federal forces had withdrawn from the forts protecting Indian Territory, and a Confederate invasion seemed imminent. Furthermore, Watie had raised a company of Cherokees for the Confederacy and seemed ready to establish a separate Confederate Cherokee government. In August, Ross authorized John Drew to organize a Cherokee regiment and opened negotiations with Pike. In October, he signed a Confederate alliance.

Dissatisfaction with the Confederate treaty soon became apparent. In December 1861, many men in John Drew's regiment, which never merged with Watie's command, deserted when Col. Douglas Hancock Cooper ordered them to attack the Creek chief Opothleyahola who was fleeing to Kansas with women and children. They shared Opothleyahola's opposition to a Confederate alliance and seized the opportunity to escape. Some of these men went on to Kansas to join the Union army, but others returned to their homes and waged a local war against Confederate Cherokees. Watie's command, however, continued in Confederate service and participated in the Battle of Elkhorn Tavern, Arkansas, on March 7, 1862.

In the summer of 1862, Federal troops invaded the Cherokee Nation and escorted John Ross back to Kansas. The principal chief claimed that he had no choice in the Confederate alliance and hurried to Washington to make amends. Watie promptly declared the office of principal chief vacant and assumed the position himself. The Cherokee Nation, therefore, was effectively divided. Federal troops invaded again in 1863, and many slaveholding Cherokees fled to the Red River where they remained for the rest of the war. Although Drew's regiment had dissolved, Watie's men continued to serve as a home guard, and Watie rose to the rank of brigadier general. He surrendered on June 23, 1865.

The Eastern Band in North Carolina experienced less dissension at the beginning of the war than their fellow Cherokees in the West. The white man who served as their leader and agent, William Holland Thomas, was an ardent Confederate who enlisted about four hundred Cherokees in the Confederate army. They originally served as home guards. In the first year of the war, about a dozen were captured near Bryson City and imprisoned in Knoxville. Most of these ultimately enlisted in the Union army. One or two of Thomas's Confederate companies ultimately transferred to Virginia in 1864, and several Cherokees were present at the fall of Richmond. The main body of Eastern Band Confederates surrendered at Waynesville, North Carolina, in May 1865.

[*See also* Watie, Stand.]

BIBLIOGRAPHY

Abel, Annie Heloise. *Slaveholding Indians*. 3 vols. Cleveland, Ohio, 1915–1925.

Franks, Kenny A. *Stand Watie and the Agony of the Cherokee Nation*. Memphis, Tenn., 1979.

Gaines, W. Craig. *The Confederate Cherokees: John Drew's Regiment of Mounted Rifles*. Baton Rouge, La., 1989.

Godbold, E. Stanly, Jr., and Mattie U. Russell. *Confederate Colonel and Cherokee Chief: The Life of William Holland Thomas.* Knoxville, Tenn., 1990.

Perdue, Theda. *Slavery and the Evolution of Cherokee Society.* Knoxville, Tenn., 1979.

THEDA PERDUE

CHESNUT, JAMES (1815–1885), brigadier general and congressman from South Carolina. Although Chesnut was a member of President Jefferson Davis's inner circle, his military and political accomplishments have been eclipsed by the writings of his wife, Mary Boykin Chesnut, whose perceptive diary of Southern society during the war has become a major source of knowledge about life in the Confederacy.

Chesnut was a South Carolinian of distinguished lineage who broke with the family's planter tradition and sought a career in public service. His Princeton training was followed in 1835 by the study of law under the famous Charlestonian James Louis Petigru, who was considered the undisputed leader of the South Carolina bar. It doubtless was Petigru's competence in the practice of law and not his politics that was attractive to the young Chesnut. Petigru frequently represented slaves and spoke out against disunion at every opportunity. Chesnut, considered a political moderate by his contemporaries, did not dispute Petigru's antisecession philosophy, but he was firmly convinced that "commerce, culture, and Christianity derived their 'chief earthly impulse' from slavery." This principle guided Chesnut as he entered public office in 1840, the same year he wed Mary Boykin Miller.

Between 1840 and 1858 Chesnut served several terms in both the state legislature and senate. In 1858 he was unanimously elected to the U.S. Senate, where his oratorical skills immediately made him conspicuous among fellow Southerners. During the tumultuous months following John Brown's raid, Chesnut assailed the abolitionists, and after Abraham Lincoln's election he had the distinction of being the first senator from the South to resign his seat in protest.

As a member of South Carolina's secession convention, Chesnut helped draft the document that dissolved the Union, and in February 1861, he traveled to Montgomery, Alabama, to represent the Palmetto State in the Provisional Confederate Congress. Here Chesnut nurtured a friendly relationship with Jefferson Davis, which paid tremendous dividends during his Confederate career.

Chesnut was in Charleston as the crisis over the Federal occupation of Fort Sumter worsened. Without prior military experience, Chesnut's role in this affair was relegated to that of a volunteer aide to the commander of the Confederate forces, Brig. Gen. P. G. T. Beauregard, but his contribution was arguably his greatest of the war.

On April 11, 1861, Beauregard sent Chesnut and two fellow aides, Capt. Stephen D. Lee and Col. Alexander Chisolm, to Fort Sumter to demand the evacuation of the fort. Federal commander Maj. Robert Anderson handed Chesnut a written refusal and remarked in passing that the garrison had food enough to last only a few more days. This news Chesnut relayed to Beauregard and a telegram was sent to the Confederate capital requesting further instructions. In reply, Beauregard was directed to avoid needless bloodshed and not injure the fort unnecessarily, if Anderson would state the time he would evacuate the fort. Chesnut returned to Fort Sumter to negotiate the evacuation details, provided he found Anderson's departure schedule acceptable. Otherwise Chesnut had full authority to order the bombardment to commence. Anderson's response contained numerous provisos that Chesnut found unsatisfactory, so he drafted a reply stating that in one hour the Southern guns would open fire. At 4:30 A.M., April 12, 1861, the Civil War began.

For the next thirty-four hours Chesnut witnessed the bombardment from his assigned post on Morris Island. About 1:00 in the afternoon of April 13, with fires blazing

JAMES CHESNUT.   NATIONAL ARCHIVES

out of control inside Fort Sumter, the Union garrison surrendered. Chesnut carried this news to the Confederate commander in Charleston, but he had little opportunity to savor the hero's welcome he received. Beauregard sent him for the third time in as many days to Fort Sumter, accompanied this time with a fire engine and a surgeon.

Early June found Chesnut leaving his beloved South Carolina. While retaining his seat in the Confederate Congress, Chesnut followed Beauregard to northern Virginia, where the Southern army took up a defensive position around Manassas Junction. Many hours were spent on horseback as the general and his aide studied the topography of the Bull Run valley. When not escorting the general, Chesnut served as judge advocate and carried correspondence to Davis detailing Beauregard's never-to-be-attempted plan for a grand but impractical offensive that later was the subject of considerable controversy. At the First Battle of Manassas, Chesnut relayed orders to the regimental commanders, led the legion of South Carolinians in their final charge after their leader Wade Hampton was wounded, and joined in the pursuit of the fleeing Federals in the company of Capt. John Lay's Virginia cavalry squadron.

For his early military contributions and as a special favorite of Davis, Chesnut could have requested and received a commission, as he did for others. But his aristocratic code was "too high South Carolina" to have anyone intercede on his behalf. He remained in Congress through the fall of 1861 despite some speculation that he might not win reelection in December. When the votes were tallied, Chesnut indeed lost his seat, which his wife attributed to political maneuvering and his aversion to "electioneering for such a place as Senator." The loss was diminished somewhat when Chesnut agreed to serve on the South Carolina Executive Council, which was designed to circumvent the powers of an ineffective governor. The council, described by Mary Chesnut as "trouble-bringing—and no glory-giving," was charged with controlling all aspects of the military affairs of the state. Council business periodically took Chesnut to Richmond, where he found pleasurable company with the president and Robert E. Lee.

In the fall of 1862 an official aideship on the staff of President Davis was offered to Chesnut, a position he eagerly accepted. As the president's representative, Chesnut examined the lengthy lines of fortifications constructed around Richmond and traveled throughout the Confederacy on inspection trips. On April 30, 1864, Chesnut was commissioned brigadier general of reserves and returned to South Carolina to finish out the war. As commander of the state reserve forces, Chesnut organized local opposition to William Tecumseh Sherman's advance through Georgia and South Carolina.

James Chesnut returned to his plantation, Mulberry,

after the war, dabbled in politics, and died at age seventy from the effects of a stroke. He was buried in the family cemetery near Camden, South Carolina.

BIBLIOGRAPHY

Chesnut, Mary Boykin. *Mary Chesnut's Civil War.* Edited by C. Vann Woodward. New Haven, 1981.
Doubleday, Abner. *Reminiscences of Forts Sumter and Moultrie in 1860–61.* New York, 1876. Reprint, Spartanburg, S.C., 1976.
Nevins, Allen. *The War for the Union.* New York, 1959.
U.S. War Department. *The War of the Rebellion: A Compilation of the Official Records of the Union and Confederate Armies.* Washington, D.C., 1880–1901. Ser. 1, vol. 1, pp. 59–62.

DAVID R. RUTH

CHESNUT, MARY BOYKIN (1823–1886), diarist. The author of the finest firsthand account of the social world of the Confederacy, published as *Mary Chesnut's Civil War,* Chesnut was born on March 31, 1823, in Statesburg, South Carolina, first child of Mary Boykin and Stephen Decatur Miller, state senator and former U.S. congressman. Miller, a proponent of nullification, was elected governor when Mary was five and in 1830 won a U.S. Senate seat.

Mary's formal education in Camden and Charleston ended in 1838 with her father's death. At seventeen, she married James Chesnut, Jr., only surviving son of one of the largest land and slaveholders in the state, and went to live at Mulberry Plantation south of Camden. The Chesnuts were childless, and during the next two decades Mary found few emotional or intellectual outlets other than the voracious reading that would later inform her famous record of the war years. James was elected in 1858 to the U.S. Senate and took Mary to Washington where she formed friendships with many prominent Southern legislators and their wives.

After Abraham Lincoln's election, Chesnut resigned his Senate seat and went to Montgomery as delegate to the Confederate Provisional Congress. In Montgomery, Mary's hotel quarters served as the first of her remarkable wartime salons, to which the men and women who were creating a new nation came to socialize, exchange information, and—eventually—to grieve. Mary began a private diary in February 1861, candidly recording what she saw and heard, conscious of the magnitude of the events into which she had been drawn and attuned to the ironies and jealousies around her. (Seven volumes of her wartime journals survive, covering most of 1861 and three months in 1865.) A close friend of Varina Davis and an ardent supporter of the president, she observed and recorded as early as February 1861, "these men have brought old hatreds & grudges & spites from the old Union. Already we see they will willingly injure our cause to hurt Jeff Davis."

Mary Chesnut found herself in an excellent position to

view the upheavals of her world. In March 1861, James, as aide to P. G. T. Beauregard, participated in the negotiations over Fort Sumter, and Mary recorded the attack from her vantage point on a rooftop. In Richmond, she waited with Varina Davis for news of Manassas, visited the first wounded of the war, heard over and over the dreaded "dead march," and at times expressed anguish in her journal over what she regarded as the foolishness of most men. "Jeff Davis ill & shut up," she wrote in August, "& none but *noodles* have the world in charge."

Frustrated at her woman's role as mere observer, she was troubled by her husband's lack of ambition for the spotlight. By the close of 1862, she had convinced James to accept a colonelcy and return to Richmond where he served for the next fifteen months as personal aide to Davis. Mary found lodgings near the White House of the Confederacy, and the Chesnut home was constantly filled with people seeking patronage, support, respite, or recuperation from the chaos of war. In her journal, Mary recorded everything: wartime romances, quarrels, parties, funerals, constant rumors, and firsthand reports of battles—both military and political.

In April 1864, General and Mrs. Chesnut returned to Columbia, where Mary worked at Louisa McCord's hospital and again kept open house, entertaining Davis himself in October. In early 1865 she fled to Lincolnton, North Carolina, and following Robert E. Lee's surrender, to Chester, South Carolina. There, as always, governors, generals, and friends flowed through her tiny rented rooms— among the last of them, Varina Davis and her children.

Chesnut ceased keeping her journal in June 1865, uncertain of the future. Mulberry had been ravaged; the Chesnut fortune was gone and the lands tangled in debt. Mary took over running the household, made a home for less fortunate family members, operated a small dairy business that brought in the family's only cash, and experimented with literary projects. In the next twenty years, she tried her hand at fiction, but her most compelling task was the preparation of her journals for publication.

After a first attempt in the mid-1870s, she began a full-scale expansion and revision in 1881, retaining the diary format and allowing no anachronisms or hindsight to intrude. The book was still unfinished when she put the more than 2,500-page manuscript aside in late 1884 to struggle with the last illness and death of both James and her mother. Embroiled in legal entanglements and herself suffering from a recurring heart condition, Chesnut could not return to her book before her own death on November 22, 1886.

Prior to her death, Chesnut had asked a much younger friend to take responsibility for her journals: Isabella Martin (the "irrepressible Isabella" of the revised journal), who, following the war, had become a schoolteacher in Columbia. Martin made little effort to find a publisher until, in 1904, she met a New York writer and journalist, Myrta

Lockett Avary, who read the journals and insisted they be published. The firm of D. Appleton agreed and arranged for several long excerpts to appear in the *Saturday Evening Post* under the title "A Diary From Dixie." The Appleton edition appeared in 1905 as *A Diary from Dixie, as Written by Mary Boykin Chesnut, Wife of James Chesnut, Jr., United States Senator from South Carolina, 1859–1861, and afterward an Aide to Jefferson Davis and a Brigadier-General in the Confederate Army*. Edited by Martin and Avary with a heavy hand, it contained only about half the manuscript (most of the material dealing with Camden and Columbia, for example, was cut). In 1947, a second edition entitled *A Diary from Dixie* was published, edited by novelist Ben Ames Williams, who again cut out much material and "smoothed up" Chesnut's writing. Neither edition made clear that the manuscript was in fact a much expanded, changed, and thoroughly restructured version of the original journal. Not until the 1981 publication of *Mary Chesnut's Civil War*, edited by C. Vann Woodward, was the full revised journal as Chesnut wrote it made available to the public. Woodward's edition, which clarified the precise nature of Chesnut's work, was awarded the Pulitzer Prize.

Chesnut's panorama of her times ranges from the plantation to the corridors of the capitol. A veritable "Who's Who" of the Confederacy, it provides particularly vivid portraits of the Davises, the Lees, the Louis T. Wigfalls, C. Clement Clays, John Smith Preston and his family, Stephen R. Mallory, John Bell Hood, Wade Hampton, Robert M. T. Hunter, and Joseph E. Johnston, as well as her own family members and hundreds of ordinary people from spies and shopkeepers to slaves. The book reveals a surprising range of interests and viewpoints among the members of Chesnut's circle. Strongly partisan, she was conscious of historical context from the first, and within her kaleidoscopic picture of the effects of war on everyday lives, she discerned pattern and meaning.

Chesnut offers a richly textured view of the concerns of women; indeed she was herself a complex and paradoxical woman. Private, intellectual, and often lonely, she was magnetic, charming, sought after. She loathed slavery from girlhood and asserted in March 1861, "[Senator Charles] Sumner said not one word of this hated institution which is not true," but she viewed blacks through the racist lens of her time and place. Admiring the Southern woman as noble, she nevertheless linked the plight of women to that of slaves. Gifted with wit, an ironic eye, a passionate intellect and heart, and objectivity about her own shortcomings and those of her world, Chesnut provides us a stunning eyewitness account of the society that was the Confederacy.

BIBLIOGRAPHY

Chesnut, Mary Boykin. *Mary Chesnut's Civil War*. Edited by C. Vann Woodward. New Haven, 1981.
Chesnut, Mary Boykin. *The Private Mary Chesnut: The Unpub-*

lished Civil War Diaries. Edited by C. Vann Woodward and Elisabeth Muhlenfeld. New York, 1984.

Fox-Genovese, Elizabeth. *Within the Plantation Household: Black and White Women of the Old South.* Chapel Hill, N.C., 1988.

Muhlenfeld, Elisabeth. *Mary Boykin Chesnut: A Biography.* Baton Rouge, La., 1981.

Wiley, Bell Irvin. *Confederate Women.* Westport, Conn., 1975.

Wilson, Edmund. *Patriotic Gore: Studies in the Literature of the American Civil War.* New York, 1962.

ELISABETH MUHLENFELD

CHICKAHOMINY, VIRGINIA. *See* Gaines' Mill, Virginia.

CHICKAMAUGA. The iron-hulled, schooner-rigged, twin-screw-propeller steamship *Edith* was built by John & William Dudgeon of Millwall, London, in 1864. It measured 370 gross tons, 174.1 feet long, 25.1 feet in beam, and 14.2 feet in depth of hold. *Edith* was jointly owned by the Confederate government (three-quarters) and by Crenshaw & Collie, a private company. It made nine successful runs through the blockade, carrying mixed government and private freight.

The Confederate navy bought *Edith* at Wilmington, North Carolina, for use as a commerce raiding cruiser in September 1864. Commissioned CSS *Chickamauga* by 1st Lt. John Wilkinson, it was armed with a 12-pounder rifle forward, a 32-pounder rifle aft, and a 64-pounder rifle amidships. *Chickamauga,* with a complement of approximately 120 men, left Wilmington October 29, 1864, cruised off New York approaches, called at Bermuda (November 7–15), and returned to Wilmington on November 18. It captured seven vessels: two barks, two schooners, and the clipper ship *Shooting Star* were destroyed; two barks were bonded and set free.

An anticipated second cruise was canceled to help defend Wilmington. A detachment from *Chickamauga*'s crew manned a two-gun naval battery in defense of Fort Fisher during the first attack (December 20–27, 1864). Of thirty-two men working the guns, nineteen were killed or wounded. During the second attack (January 12–15, 1865), the gunboat carried reinforcements and shelled attacking troops. It escaped capture at the fort and harried the Union advance up the Cape Fear River until scuttled on January 25 near Indian Wells, North Carolina, to block the river. The wreck was subsequently raised, removed, and converted to a fast fruit carrier.

BIBLIOGRAPHY

Scharf, J. Thomas. *History of the Confederate States Navy.* New York, 1887. Reprint, New York, 1977.

Wilkinson, John. *The Narrative of a Blockade Runner.* New York, 1877. Reprint, Alexandria, Va., 1984.

CSS *CHICKAMAUGA.* Wash drawing by Clary Ray, 1897.   NAVAL HISTORICAL CENTER, WASHINGTON, D.C.

Wise, Stephen R. *Lifeline of the Confederacy: Blockade Running during the Civil War.* Columbia, S.C., 1988.

KEVIN J. FOSTER

CHICKAMAUGA CAMPAIGN. The Battle of Chickamauga on September 19 and 20, 1863, was a decisive Confederate victory after three defeats—at Gettysburg, Vicksburg, and Knoxville. Although the Confederates did not retake Chattanooga, their objective, the victory brought new life to their cause. Chickamauga was one of the few Civil War battles fought with Southern troops (66,000) outnumbering Union troops (58,000). The victory came at a high price, however, with the Confederacy reporting nearly 18,000 casualties, and the Union, nearly 16,000. Known for its ferocity, the battle was often described by the men who fought it as a soldiers' fight. In many areas, the underbrush would not allow the use of artillery, leaving small units of infantry to do the fighting on their own, and the thick woods and smoke from battle made it difficult for officers to control their commands. But because both armies were composed of veterans by this time, officer control was not as important as it might have been.

The Chickamauga campaign began in early summer when the Union Army of the Cumberland moved from Murfreesboro toward Confederate defensive positions around Tullahoma, Tennessee. The Army of Tennessee, commanded by Gen. Braxton Bragg, fell back into the shelter of Chattanooga after the Union army, under Maj. Gen. William S. Rosecrans, carried out a series of skillful maneuvers that threatened the Confederate supply lines.

The Union military objective then became the important railroad hub of Chattanooga. Bragg fully expected to be overwhelmed by a Union force of over 100,000 men as he prepared to defend this vital Confederate position. In addition, the Confederate high command felt Chattanooga, because of the geography, was the last position strong enough to stop the invading Northern army. (The ridges surrounding the city only opened up to possible Union attack at one point, Lookout Valley, west of the town.)

Confederate commanders were slow in establishing a strategy, allowing the Union plan to take shape. From the end of July until September 9, the Union Army of the Cumberland set off on a maneuver that took Bragg by surprise. Rosecrans divided his army, sending two corps south to cross the Tennessee River in Alabama and one corps north. Bragg believed that the corps moving north of Chattanooga was the primary force. The Union plan worked. On September 9, the Confederates abandoned Chattanooga and moved south to block the Union advance into North Georgia by way of LaFayette.

Bragg had trouble determining where the various Union corps were located. Between September 11 and 17, he tried several probing movements in an effort to isolate and destroy the corps one by one in the mountain coves of North Georgia. He was unsuccessful, so on September 17, he decided on a plan that would place the now-reinforced Army of Tennessee between Chattanooga and the widely separated corps of the Union army. Bragg selected two crossings over the West Chickamauga Creek—Reed's Bridge and Alexander's Bridge—which he assumed would put him well north of the Union left flank at Lee and Gordon's Mill, about ten miles south of Chattanooga. Once the Confederates were across the Chickamauga, they could use the creek as an anchor on the left, push the Union corps back into the narrow mountain coves west of LaFayette, and destroy them.

With his army still widely scattered, Rosecrans now realized he had to concentrate his forces before the Confederates severed his supply lines with Chattanooga. He ordered his two southernmost corps—those of Maj. Gen. George H. Thomas and Maj. Gen. Alexander McCook—to move north as quickly as possible and concentrate at the little town of Crawfish Spring. This maneuver was carried out by the eighteenth. That evening, the Union left was extended three miles north of Lee and Gordon's Mill along the LaFayette Road and north of Bragg's crossing points on the Chickamauga Creek. Union cavalry had attempted to keep the Confederates east of the creek on the eighteenth, but the cavalry was outnumbered and the Southerners were able to cross at both locations late in the afternoon.

Early on the morning of Saturday, September 19, George Thomas sent Brig. Gen. John Brannan's division east of the LaFayette Road toward Reed's Bridge in order to capture an isolated Confederate brigade reported to be on the west side of the Chickamauga Creek. Brannan met Brig. Gen. Nathan Bedford Forrest's cavalry corps at the edge of the Jay field, just west of Jay's Mill. As Forrest was drawn into battle, he realized he was facing infantry, and he quickly searched out Confederate infantry for help. Soon there was fighting along a mile-long front extending from the Reed's Bridge Road south into the Winfrey fields. As both sides committed additional units to the battle, the woods and fields south of Reed's Bridge Road erupted with fierce fighting that spread south for almost four miles.

Meanwhile Rosecrans moved his headquarters from Crawfish Spring to a local farmstead, which brought him closer to the center of the fighting.

As the battle on the north end of the field began to subside, assaults intensified on the Union center and right. In the early afternoon, an attack against the Union center by Confederate Maj. Gen. Alexander P. Stewart's division broke through the Union line at the Poe house. Stewart's division pushed that of Brig. Gen. H. P. Van Cleve across the LaFayette Road, west through the Poe fields, and into the North Dyer fields and the Tan yard. Stewart, being

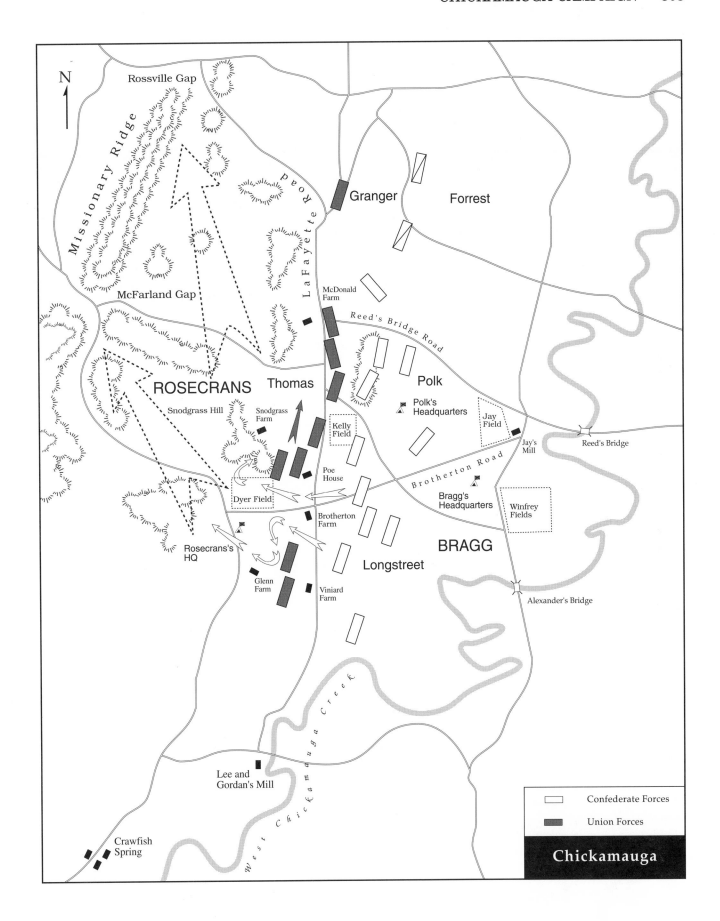

N

Rossville Gap

Missionary Ridge

McFarland Gap

LaFayette Road

Granger

Forrest

McDonald Farm

Reed's Bridge Road

Polk

Polk's Headquarters

Jay Field

Jay's Mill

Reed's Bridge

ROSECRANS

Thomas

Snodgrass Hill

Snodgrass Farm

Kelly Field

Poe House

Brotherton Road

Bragg's Headquarters

Winfrey Fields

Dyer Field

Brotherton Farm

Rosecrans's HQ

BRAGG

Longstreet

Glenn Farm

Viniard Farm

Alexander's Bridge

West Chickamauga Creek

Lee and Gordan's Mill

Crawfish Spring

☐ Confederate Forces

▉ Union Forces

Chickamauga

unsupported, was forced to retire after heavy losses when he was hit on both flanks.

Around 2:00 P.M., a fierce contest occurred around the Viniard farm less than a mile east of Rosecran's headquarters and still farther south from where the fighting had begun. Rosecrans ordered Brig. Gen. Jefferson C. Davis forward to seek the Confederate line, and he was soon hotly engaged with Brig. Gen. Bushrod Rust Johnson's division and Col. Robert Trigg's brigade. Davis was forced back across the LaFayette Road into the fields west of the Viniard house, but he was soon reinforced by two brigades. Facing withering fire from Col. John Wilder's artillery, Johnson and Trigg were forced to retire to the woods east of the LaFayette Road.

As darkness covered the battlefield, fighting broke out in the center of the Confederate line. Maj. Gen. Patrick Cleburne's division, moving west from Jay's Mill along Brotherton Road, struck at the Union line confronting two Southern divisions. Two brigades from B. Franklin Cheatham's division supported Cleburne's men. After an hour of confused fighting, both sides retired with heavy losses. Confederate Brig. Gen. Preston Smith and Union Col. Philemon Baldwin were both killed.

That evening, Braxton Bragg reorganized his army, dividing it into two wings, the right commanded by Lt. Gen. Leonidas Polk and the left by Lt. Gen. James Longstreet. Longstreet, who arrived about midnight, had no time to scout the field and was not familiar with the terrain.

Rosecrans, at his headquarters, held a council of war with his corps commanders and staff. He was advised to withdraw and take defensive positions along Missionary Ridge to protect Chattanooga. But thinking he had won the day, he decided to stay and force Bragg from the field.

Bragg had ordered Polk to strike the Union left at daylight on the twentieth, but the battle did not get underway until midmorning. This so infuriated Bragg, he later ordered Polk's arrest. The delay, however, did give Longstreet an opportunity to look over his wing formations.

When the battle began, the Confederates met with success on their right near the McDonald farm. Two brigades of Maj. Gen. John C. Breckinridge's division enveloped the Union left and gained the rear of the northernmost Union position. Being unsupported in the attack, however, Breckinridge had to retire when faced with a flank attack from the last of the Union reserves. The Confederates, along the center of their line, had three divisions poised in the thick woods east of the Brotherton farm.

Just before noon as the battle moved south all along the line, about 11,000 Confederates crossed the LaFayette Road on a mile-long front. They caught the Union troops in Wood's division in an administrative marching formation, as they moved from their position in the Brotherton fields north to close up with another division. This unsupported

movement of troops (in response to an unverified order by Rosecrans to Wood) and the timing of the Confederate's attack, led to the defeat of the Union army at Chickamauga. Longstreet's troops poured through the gap in the Union lines, causing a general rout of the Union center and right.

Brief but effective countercharges by isolated Union regiments and brigades gave George H. Thomas time to gather retreating units to form a new line facing south around the Snodgrass farm. Thomas's part of the original line east of the LaFayette Road continued to hold through the afternoon of the twentieth. The new line on Snodgrass Hill was in serious trouble when reinforcements under Maj. Gen. Gordon Granger arrived. Because Rosecrans and two of his corps commanders left the field when the Confederate breakthrough occurred, Thomas, a Southerner by birth, was now the ranking Union officer. All afternoon, the Confederates assaulted the Federals on Snodgrass Hill. There were minor successes, but it was not until dark that the Union regiments, under Thomas's orders, began to fall back north through Rossville and McFarland gaps in Missionary Ridge toward Chattanooga.

The Confederates had won an important tactical victory, but they failed to follow up their success with quick pursuit. Instead, Bragg, feeling he had failed to destroy the Union army according to his plan, decided to lay siege to the defeated Union army in Chattanooga. Over the next two months, the Confederates tried to starve the Union army into submission. But the Federals received supplies and reinforcements until they were strong enough to break the siege in late November 1863 in the Battles of Orchard Knob, Lookout Mountain, and Missionary Ridge.

Twenty-seven years after the Battle of Chickamauga, Union and Confederate veterans returned to create the Chickamauga and Chattanooga National Military Park, the first such park. It was to be used as a place for military and historical study. It was also a place of healing for old bitter feelings between the two sides.

BIBLIOGRAPHY

Boynton, Henry V. *The Chickamauga National Military Park.* Cincinnati, Ohio, 1895.

Connelly, Thomas L. *Autumn of Glory: The Army of Tennessee, 1862–1865.* Baton Rouge, La., 1971.

Davis, William C. *The Orphan Brigade.* Baton Rouge, La., 1983.

Tower, R. Lockwood, ed. *A Carolinian Goes to War: The Civil War Narrative of Arthur Middleton Manigault.* Columbia, S.C., 1983.

Tucker, Glenn. *Chickamauga—Bloody Battle in the West.* Dayton, Ohio, 1961.

JOHN F. CISSELL

CHICKASAWS. Nearly all the five thousand members of the Chickasaw Indian Nation fervently supported the new Confederate States of America. In spite of their earlier forced removal from Mississippi to southern Indian Territory, or what is now Oklahoma, ties to the South proved compelling in 1861. Economic links with the South influenced Chickasaw attitudes, as did mixed-blood leaders who owned slaves and advocated secession, geographical connection to Southern states, Federal abandonment of the Indians as war neared, and the regional presence of Confederate armed forces. The vast majority of Chickasaws officially allied with the Confederacy through a joint Choctaw treaty signed with Albert Pike on July 12, 1861. To the Southern cause, the Chickasaw Nation contributed matériel, foodstuffs, and a haven for war refugees.

The Chickasaw Nation also provided four military units to the Confederate war effort. The most famous of these was the joint Choctaw and Chickasaw First Regiment Mounted Rifles under the direct leadership of Col. Tandy Walker and later Maj. Mitchell LaFlore, and under the broader command of Mississippi secessionist and former Choctaw-Chickasaw Indian agent Douglas Hancock Cooper. Early in the war in Indian Territory, Cooper used the regiment to attack fleeing Union sympathizers of Creek Chief Opothleyahola at the Battles of Round Mountain (November 16) and Chusto-Talasah (Caving Banks, December 9). The badly mauled Northerners escaped into Kansas refugee camps, only to return to the territory as part of the Union Indian expedition the following year, seeking revenge.

A fearless Indian-regiment cavalry charge on September 30, 1862, repulsed a Federal thrust at Newtonia, Missouri. Federal Brig. Gen. James Blunt, however, forced Cooper's Indian troops to retreat from the field a month later on the Arkansas border at Fort Wayne (October 22), halting Confederate plans for an invasion of Kansas.

Blunt's artillery dominance again overwhelmed Cooper's larger command in the climactic battle at Honey Springs on July 17, 1863. Located southwest of Fort Gibson, the Honey Springs clash opened the Union pathway the following September for seizure of Fort Smith, Arkansas, and Federal control of Indian Territory. Combined with the loss at Elkhorn Tavern the previous year, the Confederate defeat at Honey Springs doomed Southern attempts to regain supremacy over Indian Territory.

In 1864, Choctaw and Chickasaw success in Arkansas stymied the Union threat to Texas. In the April 18 battle of Poison Spring, near Camden, the Second Indian Cavalry Brigade under Walker seized a cannon battery and a supply train in spite of devastating Federal fire from one of the first black units to serve in the Union army. As early as 1863, however, Chickasaw soldiers turned increasingly to guerrilla resistance in the region as Union control tightened. Chickasaws participated in the daring month-long cavalry raid behind Federal lines in April 1864 under Col. William Penn Adair, as well as in the battle at Iron Bridge near

Keota, Oklahoma, in June under the command of Lt. Col. Thomas C. Reynolds.

Armed opposition from Chickasaw soldiers finally ended July 14, 1865, when the governor of the Chickasaw Nation, Winchester Colbert, surrendered with his Chickasaw and Caddo troops. He was the last Confederate leader in Indian Territory to surrender (a full three months after Gen. Robert E. Lee had surrendered at Appomattox). Colbert formally announced the Chickasaw proclamation of peace on July 16. The growing numbers of non-Indians in the Chickasaw Nation who had seen the lush region during the war and returned to it after the conflict ended presented the Chickasaw Nation with its greatest threat, as pressure steadily grew to end tribalism in the postwar era.

BIBLIOGRAPHY

Gibson, Arrell M. *The Chickasaws*. Norman, Okla., 1971.
Moore, Jessie. "The Five Great Indian Nations." *Chronicles of Oklahoma* 29 (Autumn 1951): 324–336.

BLUE CLARK

CHILDHOOD. [*This entry is composed of two articles that discuss the experiences of children in the Confederacy:* Free Children *and* Slave Children. *See also* Education, *article on* Primary and Secondary Schools; Family Life; Slavery, *article on* Slave Life.]

Free Children

Children in the Confederacy shared virtually every one of their parents' experiences. From a demographic standpoint, the war seemed not to have affected Southern children; their percentage of the total population of the South continued a gradual decline that had begun in the 1830s with no dramatic change during the 1860s. Qualitatively, however, the war had a deep impact on the youngest Confederates. Thousands of young boys served in Southern armies, and even on the home front, the children of the South endured the hardships that plagued most inhabitants of the Confederacy. J. B. Jones, the government clerk who kept a famous wartime diary of life in Richmond, recorded the fairly representative details of his large family's declining standard of living. They survived on a monotonous diet of rice, eggs, and, by war's end, an ounce of meat or less per day. Yet for their four children's sake, Jones and his wife continued to function as a normal family, celebrating Christmas and keeping a small menagerie of pets in spite of dwindling resources.

Of course, differences in socioeconomic status caused the degree of privation to vary. Children of well-to-do planter families continued their relatively comfortable lives, with enough food—if not a great variety of it—and more or less

STATE OF *Virginia*   TOWN OF *Richmond,*

I, *Dudley Marvin Stone* born in *Richmond* in *Virginia* aged *Thirteen and a half* years, and by occupation a _____ Do HEREBY ACKNOWLEDGE to have voluntarily enlisted this ____ day of *February* 18*64*, as a ~~Soldier~~ *musician* in the Marine Corps of the Confederate States of America, to serve for the period of ~~four~~ *3* years, unless sooner discharged by proper authority: Do also agree to accept such bounty, pay, rations, and clothing, as are, or may be, established by law. And I, *D. M. Stone* , do solemnly swear, that I will bear true faith and allegiance to the Confederate States of America, and that I will serve them honestly and faithfully against all their enemies or opposers whomsoever; and that I will observe and obey the orders of the President of the Confederate States, and the orders of the officers appointed over me, according to the Rules and Articles of War.

Sworn and subscribed to, at *Richmond City Va* this *23* day of *February* 18*64* *D M Stone*
BEFORE *me John G Hedgman & co* *Notary Public for the City aforesaid*
John G Hedgman
Notary Public

I CERTIFY, ON HONOR, That I have carefully examined the above named Recruit, agreeably to the General Regulations of the Marine Corps, and that in my opinion he is free from all bodily defects and mental infirmity, which would, in any way, disqualify him from performing the duties of a soldier.

M P Christian
EXAMINING SURGEON.

I CERTIFY, ON HONOR, That I have minutely inspected the Recruit, previously to his enlistment, and that he was entirely sober when enlisted; that, to the best of my judgment and belief, he is of lawful age; and that, in accepting him as duly qualified to perform the duties of an able-bodied soldier, I have strictly observed the Regulations which govern the recruiting service. This soldier has *gray* eyes, *light* hair, *light* complexion, is *4* feet *11* inches high.

Nat Venable
1st Lt. RECRUITING OFFICER. *C.S.M.C.*

1864 ENLISTMENT FORM. On this form Dudley Marvin Stone, age "thirteen and a half," enlisted for three years of service as a musician in the Confederate Marine Corps.
GORDON BLEULER

regular attendance at private schools. Yeoman and poor white families endured near-subsistence levels of basic necessities and could rarely count on their public schools to remain open, as teachers enlisted in the army and many county governments diverted funds from education to war-related matters. For students who were able to remain in class, patriotic Confederate authors produced pro-Southern textbooks like *A Confederate Spelling Book,* the *First Dixie Reader,* and the *Southern Confederacy Arithmetic.*

The war spawned dangers and new responsibilities for Southern children, even as it exposed them to unprecedented adventures and freedom from adult supervision. Life as refugees, to which thousands of Southern children had to submit, provided both kinds of experiences. Kate Stone's published diary describes the adjustments she and her adolescent brothers made to frontier life and unfriendly neighbors in their new home in Texas after the fighting around Vicksburg forced their family from their plantation. Children fleeing with their mothers from Baton Rouge in 1862 had to run a gauntlet of shells thrown into the city by Federal forces. At least some children worked in war industries; an 1863 explosion hurt or killed dozens of young girls employed at a Richmond munitions factory. Teenaged boys took on their fathers' responsibilities and girls helped their mothers administer plantations, nurse the wounded, and make clothing and bandages for soldiers. At the very least, the war forced many children to grow up very quickly.

The war also affected Southern children and their families on an emotional level. Southerners shared the concept of the child-centered family and the sentimental attitudes about children that had developed in Western society since the seventeenth century. As a result, the absence of hundreds of thousands of fathers created a wave of guilt and longing that was reflected in a rich literature of correspondence among family members; mothers attempted to mediate between lonely fathers and confused children by providing elaborate details of life at home in general and of their growing sons' and daughters' exploits in particular.

Finally, white Southern children became, in many ways, the most ardent "unreconstructed rebels" through their enthusiastic membership in postwar organizations like the United Daughters of the Confederacy, the Sons of Confederate Veterans, and Children of the Confederacy. Southern children did not escape the scars left by the Civil War on the former Confederacy.

BIBLIOGRAPHY

Anderson, John Q., ed. *Brokenburn: The Journal of Kate Stone, 1861–1868.* Baton Rouge, La., 1955.

Censer, Jane Turner. *North Carolina Planters and Their Children, 1800–1860.* Baton Rouge, La., 1984.

Rable, George C. *Civil Wars: Women and the Crisis of Southern Nationalism.* Urbana, Ill., 1989.

Rozier, John, ed. *The Granite Farm Letters: The Civil War Correspondence of Edgeworth & Sallie Bird.* Athens, Ga., 1988.

JAMES MARTEN

Slave Children

In 1860, there were 1,565,608 slaves fifteen years of age and under in the Confederacy. Many performed domestic chores or worked in the fields or in industry as they always had, but the jobs of some were directly related to the war. Young body servants, for example, sometimes accompanied their owners to war. Thomas ("Blind Tom") Bethune, a twelve-year-old pianist, was featured in an 1861 concert for the benefit of sick and wounded Confederate soldiers.

Leisure activities often reflected the times. Children enacted skirmishes, sat around the fire to imitate the soldiers on picket, or played "Harpers Ferry," a game based upon John Brown's 1859 raid of the Federal arsenal. Enslaved children in Mississippi chanted:

> Jeff Davis, long and slim
> whipped old Abe with a hickory limb.
> Jeff Davis is a wise man, Lincoln is a fool
> Jeff Davis rides a gray and Lincoln rides a mule.

A less innocuous verse subjected them to reprisals from owners:

> Old Gen'l Pope had a shotgun,
> filled it full o' gum,
> killed 'em as dey come.
> Called a Union band,
> Make de Rebels understand
> To leave de land,
> Submit to Abraham.

Taking advantage of loosened controls over slaves' activities during wartime, many children learned to read and write. The free woman Mary Peake reported that scores of them attended her school near Fortress Monroe, Virginia.

Once fighting came close to their home, slaves fled by the thousands on foot, in wagons, and in boats. The Northern teacher Elizabeth Botume observed that a "half-grown boy had his blind daddy [upon his back] toting him along 'to freedom.'" But children left behind by fathers joining the Union army faced sale, whippings, or eviction. Homeless and reduced to begging, many fled to Union lines where those too small to care for themselves or to work were unwelcome encumbrances. Housed in contraband camps, they struggled to survive by assisting cooks and washerwomen.

Hundreds of thousands of slave children were not affected by the January 1, 1863, Emancipation Proclamation, which applied only to certain designated areas. But the fourteen-year-old Georgian Susie King Taylor said it was a glorious day when she heard it read. The imminence of freedom prompted a superannuated slave to say, "I'se berry ol massa, but de little one—dey'l see it; dey'l see it yit."

BIBLIOGRAPHY

Botume, Elizabeth Hyde. *The First Days amongst the Contrabands.* New York, 1968.

Howard, Victor B. "The Civil War in Kentucky: The Slave Claims His Freedom." *Journal of Negro History* 67 (Fall 1982): 245–256.

Litwack, Leon F. *Been in the Storm So Long: The Aftermath of Slavery.* New York, 1980.

Ripley, C. Peter. "The Black Family in Transition: Louisiana, 1860–1865." *Journal of Southern History* 41 (August 1975): 369–380.

Wiley, Bell Irvin. *Southern Negroes, 1861–1865.* New Haven, 1965.

WILMA KING

CHILTON, ROBERT HALL

CHILTON, ROBERT HALL (1815–1879), brigadier general. Chilton, born February 25, 1815, was a native Virginian who graduated third from the bottom in the West Point class of 1837. For nearly a quarter-century Chilton served in the U.S. Army in postings from Detroit to Texas, reaching the rank of major and winning a brevet at the 1847 Battle of Buena Vista.

Chilton in April 1861 entered Confederate service as a lieutenant colonel. For over a year he held down a post in the Richmond bureaucracy. When his antebellum acquaintance Robert E. Lee took command of the Army of Northern Virginia in June 1862, Chilton joined him as chief of staff. The next month, Chilton wrote some negative but accurate remarks about John B. Magruder's performance. Magruder bristled about the comments, and his supporters in Congress denied promotion to Chilton by way of retribution. When the Senate rejected his nomination as brigadier general, Chilton accepted a commission as colonel to date from October 1862. He finally was made brigadier general December 21, 1863.

Meanwhile Chilton had performed poorly in a critical task at Chancellorsville and eventually returned to duty in Richmond. Knowing that his high rank had been intended for the chief of Lee's staff, he resigned his commission in April 1864 and finished the war in charge of the Bureau of Inspection. Although Lee admired Chilton's "fidelity, honesty and intelligence" and wrote that he had been "zealous and active," it seems apparent that the commanding general was not entirely satisfied with his chief of staff. Chilton did not perform as skillfully as others on Lee's staff, and he does not have their reputation.

He died February 18, 1879, and is buried in Richmond.

BIBLIOGRAPHY

Compiled Military Service Records. Robert Hall Chilton. Microcopy M331, Roll 54. Record Group 109. National Archives, Washington, D.C.

Evans, Clement A., ed. *Confederate Military History.* 12 vols. Atlanta, 1899. Extended ed. in 19 vols. Wilmington, N.C., 1987–1989.

Freeman, Douglas S. *Lee's Lieutenants: A Study In Command.* 3 vols. New York, 1942–1944. Reprint, New York, 1986.

ROBERT K. KRICK

CHILTON, WILLIAM P.

CHILTON, WILLIAM P. (1810–1871), congressman from Alabama. Born April 10, 1810, near Elizabethtown in Adair County, Kentucky, Chilton never attended college. He was tutored at home by family members and was of such high intellectual ability that he taught school at age seventeen. Chilton read law under a judge in Athens, Tennessee, and in 1834 moved to Talladega, Alabama, where he entered the legal profession.

A Whig in politics, he represented Talladega County in the state legislature in 1839 but was defeated in a race for the U.S. House of Representatives. Steadfast in the party's ranks, Chilton campaigned for every Whig presidential candidate from William Henry Harrison in 1840 to Millard Fillmore in 1856. One year after moving to Tuskegee (Macon County) in 1846, he won election from a Democratic legislature to the Alabama State Supreme Court. While in Tuskegee, Chilton established a private law school that drew students from Alabama and surrounding states. He became chief justice in 1852 and held the position until 1856. In 1859 he was elected to the state senate from Macon County, but soon afterward moved to the capital at Montgomery. There he and two sons joined with William Lowndes Yancey, Alabama's leading advocate of secession, and his son to form the law practice of Chilton and Yancey, with offices at Montgomery and Tuskegee.

Over six feet tall and physically impressive (the *Charleston Courier* described him at the secession convention in 1861 as "a delegate of striking and prepossessing appearance"), Chilton was a powerful debater, devout Baptist, and dedicated Mason. He carved an exemplary record as a judge, an achievement that later gave him wide influence as a politician. Reacting to the deepening sectional crisis, and perhaps influenced by Yancey's fire-eating convictions, Senator Chilton was the author of an act by the state legislature organizing a military corps of eight thousand men and appropriating funds to equip them. Although Chilton's reputation was that of a Unionist, he began appearing at public meetings with Democrats who were ardent advocates of Southern rights. Averring that he had always been a Union man and still was, Chilton added that patriots of the South should boldly defend their region within the Union, but if that was not possible, then defend it outside the Union.

He was appointed by Alabama's secession convention to represent the Montgomery district in the unicameral Provisional Congress when the Confederacy was formed. At the opening session on February 4, Chilton was the first person to speak: he nominated Robert W. Barnwell of South Carolina as temporary chairman. During the inauguration of Jefferson Davis, Chilton was a member of the Committee on Ceremonies and rode in the ceremonial parade. At the state capitol he and Robert Barnwell Rhett, Sr., of South Carolina escorted the president-elect across the grounds and into the hall of Congress.

Chilton was elected a representative to the First Congress and was reelected in 1863. Of the 267 men who sat in the Congress, Chilton was one of 27 who served continuously. He was an influential member, participating in floor debates and committee work. He advocated strong war measures but introduced proposals to exempt mechanics and farmers from military service and opposed sections of the draft and currency laws that he considered unconstitutional violations of contracts with individuals. The Confederate government never had a committee comparable to the U.S. Congress's Committee on the Conduct of the War, and late in the conflict (January 1865) Chilton failed to get adopted a proposal to create such a committee (made up of one member from each state) for the Confederacy.

Chilton was chairman of the Post Office Committee in all three Congresses, of the Quartermaster's and Commissary committees in the First, and of the Flag and Seal Committee in the Second. He also served on the Buildings and Printing committees in the Provisional Congress, on the Patents Committee in the First and Second Congresses, and on the Rules and Officers Committee in the Second.

In the absence of presiding officers, the respected Chilton was frequently asked to substitute. He was a talented orator. Epigrammatic and anecdotal, Chilton also exhibited a wry sense of humor, and the combination made him a formidable debater. He once accused an opponent of "reaching an extreme medium." His colleague Jabez L. M. Curry said of Chilton's contribution to the legislative branch (the overall achievement of which cannot be evaluated as an unqualified success), "It was a common remark that he was the most laborious member of the body."

After the war Chilton returned to the practice of law in Montgomery and was associated with Jack Thorington. His death on January 20, 1871, came as the result of internal injuries sustained after an accidental fall. Governor Robert B. Lindsay sent a message of sympathy to the general assembly then in session, as Alabamians mourned a favorite son. In every sense a self-made man, Chilton epitomized an era. His passing touched off statements of respect and admiration, and, fittingly, a fellow judge best summed up his career: "He was a learned and conscientious jurist, a steadfast friend, a placable enemy, a useful citizen and a pure judge."

BIBLIOGRAPHY

Brewer, Willis. *Alabama: Her History, Resources, War Record and Public Men from 1540 to 1872.* Montgomery, Ala., 1872.
Chilton, Claudius Lysias. *Centenary Sketch of William P. Chilton.* Montgomery, Ala., 1910.
Obituary. *Montgomery Advertiser,* January 22, 1871.
Owen, Thomas McAdory. *History of Alabama and Dictionary of Alabama Biography.* 4 vols. Chicago, 1921.
Warner, Ezra J., and W. Buck Yearns. *Biographical Register of the Confederate Congress.* Baton Rouge, La., 1976.

WILLIAM WARREN ROGERS

CHOCTAWS. In 1860 the Choctaw Nation occupied the southeastern part of present-day Oklahoma. In the 1830s the U.S. government had displaced the Choctaws from their homeland in Mississippi and from the spiritual center of their universe, the sacred mound of Nanih Waiya. After removal they regrouped and developed a government based on male suffrage and representative democracy. By the terms of the 1860 Doaksville Constitution, the Nation was divided into three districts and operated under an executive branch, a bicameral legislature, and national and county courts. The Constitution legalized slavery, and a law of January 1860 forbade abolitionism. The Choctaws had a system of public education consisting of neighborhood schools and national seminaries, and the Nation provided financial support for young men and women to attend colleges in the United States.

According to the 1860 Federal census the Choctaw Nation had a population of 13,666 Choctaws, 804 whites, 67 free African Americans, and 2,349 slaves held by 385 owners. Some of the Choctaws were artisans and merchants in such towns as Doaksville, Skullyville, and Boggy Depot, but most practiced subsistence agriculture. A few possessed large plantations and ranches and exported large amounts of cotton, lumber, and cattle. The Nation's wealthiest citizen was Robert M. Jones, who managed 27 trading stores and owned 6 plantations, 2 steamboats, and at least 227 slaves. Approximately 2,000 Choctaws still lived in Mississippi and 200 in Louisiana, deprived of treaty rights and eking out an existence on marginal lands.

Because of their support of slavery and proximity to Texas and Arkansas, the Choctaws wholeheartedly supported an alliance with the Confederacy. Only 212 Choctaws were later identified as being loyal to the Union, and 12 fought with the Union Indian Brigade organized in Kansas. On February 6, 1861, the Choctaw Council authorized its delegates at Washington to withdraw the Nation's trust funds, if necessary, and deposit them in Southern banks. The council also instructed Chief George Hudson to send delegates to any intertribal convention that would determine relations with the United States. Hudson was also required to communicate with the governors of Southern states, expressing the nation's regrets over the "present unhappy political disagreement" and its "natural affection" for the South.

On February 18, the council instructed Hudson to confer with the Chickasaws, and on March 11 the two tribes agreed to prepare jointly for military duty. On June 14 Hudson ordered all male citizens and residents between the ages of eighteen and forty-five to ready themselves "for the defense of the nation at a minute's warning." By this time, Confederate troops from Texas had seized Federal posts in the Choctaw Nation. On July 12, at North Fork Village in the Creek Nation, Choctaw delegates signed a treaty with the Confederacy. The Choctaws and Chickasaws were to organize ten companies, whose service would be restricted to Indian Territory. The Confederacy recognized absolute, perpetual Choctaw title to their lands, assumed all financial obligations of the United States, and agreed to provision and pay Choctaw troops.

By July 31, the First Choctaw and Chickasaw Mounted Rifles, under Col. Douglas H. Cooper, was organized. Other Choctaw units followed: the Second Regiment of Choctaw Cavalry, under Col. Simpson N. Folsom; the Third Regiment of Choctaw Cavalry, under Col. Jackson McCurtain; the First Choctaw Mounted Rifles, under Col. Sampson Folsom; Deneale's Regiment of Choctaw Warriors, under Col. George Deneale; and Captain Williams's Company of Choctaw Infantry, under Capt. John Williams.

These Choctaw units served primarily as home guards, but they did see combat in eight major battles. Their first action was to pursue Union Indian sympathizers under Opothleyahola, who were trying to reach safety in Kansas. Confederate forces, including the First Choctaw and Chickasaw, engaged this retreating party in battles at Round Mountain on November 19, at Chusto-Talasah or Caving Banks on December 9, and at Chustenahlah on December 26. The next year, despite treaty provisions, the Choctaws fought in two campaigns outside Indian Territory. On March 8, the First Choctaw and Chickasaw joined the battle at Elkhorn Tavern, Arkansas, protecting the Confederate retreat and escorting a supply wagon to Elm Springs. In September Confederate forces invaded southwestern Missouri. Union troops counterattacked at Newtonia on September 30. Choctaw reinforcements, led by Lt. Col. Tandy Walker, charged the village at full gallop and routed the Union infantry. Later that day Col. Simpson N. Folsom and his Choctaws

repulsed Union soldiers attempting to flank the Southern position.

The year 1863 was a dreary one for the Choctaws. On July 17, they took part in the Confederate defeat at Honey Springs in the Creek Nation. On August 25, Confederate forces were again defeated at the Battle of Perryville in the Choctaw Nation. These defeats assured Union control of the territory north of the Arkansas River and opened the Choctaw country to invasion and constant raiding. Refugees became a major concern. By August 1864, over 10,000 Confederate Indians, including 1,400 Choctaws, were receiving aid from camps located near the Red River. By war's end, this number rose to nearly 16,000. The Choctaw government also provided its own Treasury warrants to indigent Choctaws, to be exchanged for food and other provisions.

In 1864 the Choctaws were again asked to serve outside Indian Territory. On April 18 the First Choctaw and Chickasaw saw action in the Battle of Poison Springs, ten miles west of Camden, Arkansas. The Choctaws helped take a Union supply train, capturing 170 wagons and burning 30 more. Gen. Samuel B. Maxey commended the Choctaws for participating voluntarily and for performing their duty "nobly, gallantly, and gloriously."

Mississippi Choctaws were also mustered into service. Late in 1862, 180 were organized as the First Mississippi Choctaw Infantry, under the command of Maj. J. W. Pearce. This entire unit was captured at Camp Moore, Louisiana, in March 1863. An exception to the general fate of Mississippi Choctaws was former chief Greenwood Leflore. The owner of fifteen thousand acres, four hundred slaves, and a fifteen-room mansion, Leflore remained loyal to the Union, for which he suffered the opprobrium of his neighbors and the loss of much of his property.

In February 1864, a Union force under Col. William A. Phillips struck deep into the Choctaw Nation, systematically wasting the countryside. Phillips sent a message to the Choctaw Council, urging it to "choose between peace and mercy and destruction." The Choctaws refused to surrender, but by the spring of 1865, they realized that defeat was inevitable. On June 10, the council asserted its right to surrender independently of the Confederacy. Nine days later, Chief Peter P. Pitchlynn surrendered the nation's military forces to Lt. Col. Asa C. Matthews and agreed to an armistice. On September 6, the council appointed twenty-one delegates to treat with U.S. representatives at Fort Smith, Arkansas. On September 16, the Choctaws began negotiations and ably defended their alliance with the Confederacy. A treaty was not signed, however, until April 29, 1866, in Washington, D.C. For the Choctaws the war had finally ended with the abolition of slavery, the loss of the western third of their country, and a new relationship with the United States.

BIBLIOGRAPHY

Abel, Annie H. *The Civil War in the Indian Territory.* Cleveland, Ohio, 1919.

Fisher, LeRoy, ed. *The Civil War in Indian Territory.* Los Angeles, 1972.

Fisher, LeRoy, and Jerry Gill. "Confederate Indian Forces outside of Indian Territory." *Chronicles of Oklahoma* 46 (1968): 249–284.

Rampp, Lary C., and Donald L. Rampp. *The Civil War in the Indian Territory.* Austin, Tex., 1975.

Rowland, Dunbar. *Military History of Mississippi, 1803–1898; Taken from the Official and Statistical Register of the State, 1908.* Jackson, Miss., 1908. Reprint, Spartanburg, S.C., 1978.

CHARLES ROBERTS

CHRISMAN, JAMES STONE (1818–1881), congressman from Kentucky.

No Confederate congressman professed more loyalty to the Confederacy and to President Jefferson Davis than Chrisman. According to historians Ezra J. Warner and W. Buck Yearns, "Few members demonstrated a greater willingness to sacrifice local and personal interests to the central government, even allowing for the fact that Kentucky members were more often than not of this persuasion."

Born in Monticello, Wayne County, Kentucky, he attended local schools, read law, and was admitted to the bar in 1849. He practiced law in Wayne County. A Democrat, Chrisman represented Kentucky in the U.S. House of Representatives from 1853 to 1855, but generally he had an unsuccessful political career. Warner and Yearns describe "Chrisman's track record as a politician" as "largely that of a loser."

Nevertheless, in November 1861, Chrisman served as a delegate from Wayne County to the sovereignty convention in Russellville, Kentucky, where he was elected to the Executive Council of the Provisional Government of Kentucky that joined the Confederacy. In 1862 he was elected to the Confederate House of Representatives from the Fifth District and was reelected in 1864. Chrisman served on the Medical Department, Elections, Territories and Public Lands, War Tax, and Indian Affairs committees. With only one major exception—his adamant opposition to the arming of the slaves—Chrisman supported the full range of Davis's economic and political programs, including conscription. He repeatedly urged the Davis administration to invade the commonwealth both to damage the Union cause and to rally troops for the South.

Following Appomattox, Chrisman returned to his home and served in the state house of representatives.

BIBLIOGRAPHY

Quisenberry, A. C. "The Alleged Secession of Kentucky." *Register of the Kentucky State Historical Society* 15 (1917): 15–32.

Wakelyn, Jon L. *Biographical Dictionary of the Confederacy.* Edited by Frank E. Vandiver. Westport, Conn., 1977.

Warner, Ezra J., and W. Buck Yearns. *Biographical Register of the Confederate Congress.* Baton Rouge, La., 1975.

JOHN DAVID SMITH

CHURCHILL, THOMAS JAMES (1824–1905), major general.

Born March 10, 1824, near Louisville, Kentucky, Churchill attended St. Mary's College at Bardstown and Transylvania University in Lexington. He fought in the Mexican War with the First Kentucky Mounted Riflemen and after the war moved to Arkansas.

Churchill, who was the Little Rock postmaster when the Civil War began, raised a regiment, joined Ben McCulloch at Fort Smith, and fought at Oak Hills, Missouri, and Elkhorn Tavern, Arkansas. On March 4, 1862, he was promoted to brigadier general and crossed the Mississippi River with Earl Van Dorn. He joined E. Kirby Smith in the Kentucky campaign and fought with distinction at Richmond. On December 10, 1862, Churchill was sent to the Trans-Mississippi Department where he took command of Fort Hindman at Arkansas Post. On January 11, 1863, he surrendered the fort when a white flag mysteriously appeared in the ranks. He and his men were sent to Northern prison camps and after being exchanged were assigned to the Army of Tennessee. But the men from the fort blamed him for their capture and resented being ordered to serve under him. He was therefore reassigned to the Trans-Mississippi in December 1863. There he was given command of Texan troops, but they too protested because of his reputation. He then commanded troops from Arkansas in the Red River and Camden campaigns. Although he did not distinguish himself in Louisiana, he did well in Arkansas and was promoted to major general to date from April 30.

After the war Churchill became active in Arkansas politics and was elected governor in 1880. He died on May 14, 1905, at Little Rock and is buried in Mt. Holly Cemetery.

BIBLIOGRAPHY

Bailey, Anne J. *Between the Enemy and Texas.* Fort Worth, Tex., 1989.

Donovan, Timothy P., and Willard B. Gatewood, Jr., eds. *The Governors of Arkansas: Essays in Political Biography.* Fayetteville, Ark., 1981.

McCaffrey, James M. *This Band of Heroes: Granbury's Texas Brigade, C.S.A.* Austin, Tex., 1985.

ANNE J. BAILEY

CITADEL, THE.

The Citadel originated out of the fears of the white population of antebellum South Carolina. In 1822, the discovery of free black Denmark Vesey's slave insurrection conspiracy in Charleston prompted the state's legislature to authorize the construction of a fortified armory, or citadel, to defend the city from similar disturbances in the future. Funding lagged, however, until the nullification crisis of the early 1830s when state leaders, facing possible conflict with Federal troops, hastily appropriated over $200,000 to complete The Citadel in Charleston and The Arsenal in the capital city of Columbia.

In 1842, the legislature combined the two facilities into an institution of higher education, the South Carolina Military Academy. Students spent one year at The Arsenal and their final three years at The Citadel. The cadets guarded the weapons at the two sites while receiving "a broad and practical education" in military and academic disciplines. Graduates were not required, and most did not elect, to pursue a career in the armed forces, but their four years of military training gave them the skills to function as a sort of informal reserve officer corps in case of a large mobilization.

South Carolina began such a mobilization after it seceded from the Union in December 1860. Cadets from The Citadel played an important role in setting up defensive implacements around Charleston Harbor. On the morning of January 9, 1861, cadets stationed at an artillery battery on nearby Morris Island spotted and fired three shots at *Star of the West,* a merchant vessel that had been dispatched by President James Buchanan to resupply the federal garrison at Fort Sumter. The ship survived what was the first hostile fire of the secession crisis but was forced to abandon its mission. Three months later, Citadel cadets were also present at, and may have participated in, the more famous bombardment of Fort Sumter.

Over the next four years, a large percentage of The Citadel community participated in the conflict. Discounting 14 alumni who died before the spring of 1861, 226 men graduated from The Citadel between 1846 and 1864. Of them, 209 entered the armies of the Confederacy. Twenty-nine served as noncommissioned soldiers, 2 as chaplains, 11 as surgeons, and 167 as officers. The highest rank was achieved by Johnson Hagood (class of 1847), Micah Jenkins (1854), Evander McIvor Law (1856), and Ellison Capers (1857), all of whom rose to brigadier general. Forty-nine of the graduates died in the Confederate armies, 94 suffered nonfatal wounds, and 16 became prisoners of war. Citadel alumni took part in the great majority of the major engagements of the war.

In a separate category were 36 cadets who left the academy in 1862 to form their own cavalry company, the Cadet Rangers. Incorporated into the Sixth South Carolina Cavalry, they performed routine duties until March 1864 when their unit was sent to reinforce a division of the Army of Northern Virginia under Maj. Gen. Wade Hampton. The Cadet Rangers skirmished against Federals in Virginia and engaged elements of William Tecumseh Sherman's advancing Union army on the routes leading into Columbia.

The Citadel continued to operate for all but the last four months of the war. The legislature exempted students from the draft and placed them in a special branch of the state militia subject to mobilization only by order of the governor. Perhaps as a result, enrollment at the academy increased from 125 cadets in late 1861 to 325 in late 1864.

Throughout the war, the governor ordered the cadets out of class periodically to provide support services for the Confederacy. Cadets drilled recruits, mounted defensive fortifications, manufactured ammunition, protected arms depots, guarded Union prisoners, and performed picket duty along Charleston's southern defensive perimeter. On one occasion, in December 1864, the battalion of state cadets suffered eight casualties in a skirmish with Union forces at Tulifinny Creek. Afterward, the cadets marched to Spartanburg in the western part of the state where the governor had moved the seat of his collapsing administration. Four months later, in the wake of Robert E. Lee's surrender, the governor placed the cadets on what turned out to be an indefinite furlough.

The Civil War took a significant toll on the South Carolina Military Academy. The Arsenal was burned when Sherman's army passed through Columbia in February 1865. That same month, Union forces spearheaded by black troops entered Charleston, occupied The Citadel, and closed it as an academic institution.

The Citadel reopened as a state-owned military college for men in 1882. Soon thereafter, it resumed paying homage to the Confederacy. Indeed, very late into the twentieth century, "Dixie" was regularly played by the school's band at Friday afternoon parades, the Confederate battle flag was a common sight at athletic contests, and the most prestigious academic scholarship awarded by the college was named "The Star of the West."

BIBLIOGRAPHY

Baker, Gary R. *Cadets in Gray: The Story of the Cadets of the South Carolina Military Academy and the Cadet Rangers in the Civil War.* Columbia, S.C., 1989.

Bond, Oliver J. *The Story of The Citadel.* Richmond, 1936. Reprint, Greenville, S.C., 1989.

Thomas, John Peyre. *History of the South Carolina Military Academy.* Charleston, S.C., 1893.

WINFRED B. MOORE, JR.

CITIZENSHIP. The American Constitution recognized dual American citizenship—that of the nation and that of the state. Early Supreme Court decisions gave the state the claim to precedence. It was not until the adoption of the Fourteenth Amendment in 1868 that U.S. citizenship became primary and that of the state derivative. The permanent Constitution of the Confederacy made one significant change in the matter of citizenship. As a concession to state rights, federal jurisdiction was removed from controversies between citizens of different states, leaving such matters entirely to state courts. The Confederacy inherited the remaining U.S. laws and rulings on citizenship when Congress ordered the continuation of all U.S. laws not inconsistent with the Confederate Constitution.

The only subsequent change was a law of August 22, 1861, conferring all the rights of citizenship upon noncitizens in the army and promising them full citizenship after the war in any state of their choice if they would renounce all other allegiance and swear to uphold the Confederate Constitution and its laws.

The naturalization laws inherited from the United States required five years of continued residence in a Confederate state, a declaration of intent at least two years before admission to citizenship, a renunciation of past allegiance, and an oath to support the Confederate Constitution and that of the state in which the person resided. Thus Congress implied that allegiance to the state was as important as that to the Confederacy.

Several efforts were made to give the states a stronger role in the process. In January 1862 Congress passed a bill repealing all existing laws of naturalization and putting the process entirely in the states' hands. President Jefferson Davis vetoed it on the grounds that it did not protect the right of foreigners living in the Confederacy and that it violated a constitutional provision that Congress set the rules for naturalization. Several efforts to pass a similar bill were made, but all failed.

Alien enemies residing in the Confederacy suffered the tribulations of wartime. A law of August 8, 1861, required all alien enemies to leave the Confederacy within forty days. Under the sequestration laws, the courts issued thousands of writs of garnishment against their property. Both Confederate and state courts refused to hear cases when the plaintiff was an alien enemy. Those Union sympathizers who kept their sympathies secret and did not resort to treasonable activities, however, seem to have escaped with both life and property intact.

The possibility that Confederates who fell into enemy hands might be treated as rebels never materialized. Though the United States never recognized the Confederacy, it regarded the Southern nation as a belligerency, and captured Confederate soldiers and alien enemies were treated as legitimate prisoners of war. Confederates abroad suffered no discrimination, though Confederate agents could never confer officially with foreign governments.

[See also Confiscation; article on Confederate Sequestration; Foreigners; Northerners.]

BIBLIOGRAPHY

Kettner, James H. *The Development of American Citizenship, 1608–1870.* Chapel Hill, N.C., 1978.

Moore, Albert B. *Conscription and Conflict in the Confederacy.* New York, 1924.

Robinson, William M., Jr. *Justice in Grey: A History of the Judicial System of the Confederate States of America.* Cambridge, Mass., 1941.

Yearns, Wilfred B. *The Confederate Congress.* Athens, Ga., 1960.

W. BUCK YEARNS

CIVIL LIBERTIES. On February 22, 1862, the president of the Confederate States of America proclaimed in his inaugural address that his administration would continue to cherish and preserve the personal liberties of citizens. Protecting individual rights was a paramount reason for secession, and the Confederate Constitution (Article I, Section 9) incorporated all of the guarantees of civil liberties found in the amended U.S. Constitution. Jefferson Davis boasted that, in contrast to the United States of America, which continued to exercise "tyrannical" authority as it had in suppressing civil liberties in Maryland, "there has been no act on our part to impair personal liberty or the freedom of speech, of thought, or of the press."

Events in the next few months demonstrated the great difficulty of maintaining such a position while fighting an unlimited modern war for the Confederacy's survival. This war forced the mobilization of most human and material resources and the centralization of authority, processes that inevitably challenged individual liberties as well as state rights. If the Confederate government assiduously protected civil liberties, its war effort could be undermined by spoken and written criticism, unfettered movement of people and information, and severe shortages of troops. If, however, it restricted the spoken and written word and the activities of its citizens or suspended civil government and the writ of habeas corpus, it risked alienating the public whose support was essential for military success.

Faced with this dilemma and hard-pressed on the battlefield, Confederate leaders at both the national and the state levels heatedly debated civil libertarian issues. Military necessity ultimately dictated the three areas in which they reluctantly, but legally, restricted civil liberties: declaring martial law, conscripting men into military service, and suspending the privilege of the writ of habeas corpus. In each case, unlike President Abraham Lincoln, President Davis adhered to strict constructionist principles and persuaded Congress to pass appropriate enabling legislation before he approved restrictions on civil liberties.

On February 27, 1862, Congress authorized the president to suspend the privilege of the writ of habeas corpus and to declare martial law in areas threatened by the enemy. Davis immediately placed Norfolk and Portsmouth under martial law so that the military could arrest and detain disloyal individuals. Then on March 1, in a controversial and perhaps excessive attempt to curtail spying and criminal activity in the vulnerable capital, Davis appointed Gen. John H. Winder the military governor of Richmond. Within a year, Congress permitted generals to declare martial law so they could enforce conscription and maintain public order near the front. This was especially detested in Unionist strongholds, such as eastern Tennessee, and in locales with burgeoning peace societies, such as Alabama, northeastern Mississippi, and southwestern Virginia. Within his own administration Davis faced a harsh and outspoken critic, Vice President Alexander H. Stephens, who repeatedly denounced martial law, conscription, and the suspension of habeas corpus as unnecessary violations of civil rights that undermined the integrity of the Southern republic. These issues further polarized Confederate politics into pro- and anti-Davis factions.

In the spring of 1862, with casualties mounting and one-year volunteers heading home, the Confederacy resorted to conscription. This infringement upon personal liberty incensed many Southerners, including several outspoken generals. Critics recalled the denunciation of forced service in the Declaration of Independence and, ironically, noted its similarity to slavery. Governor Joseph E. Brown of Georgia called Davis an "emperor" and began a lengthy debate on the unconstitutionality of conscription. Citing state rights, Governor Zebulon B. Vance exempted North Carolina officials from the despised draft. Some judges even issued writs of habeas corpus to free draftees.

The widespread opposition to conscription convinced Congress to permit President Davis to suspend the privilege of the writ of habeas corpus three separate times for a total of sixteen months. They justified these suspensions and the repeated use of martial law as necessary for apprehending thousands of draft evaders and keeping them in the ranks. Yet such measures inevitably produced further dissent among Southerners. Georgia's legislature unanimously condemned the third suspension, and state legislators in Mississippi and Louisiana passed hostile resolutions.

Southern newspapers took Davis to task, violently attacking him, his administration, and his generals for interfering with habeas corpus, imposing conscription, and abusively enforcing the Impressment Act. The fiercely independent press undermined morale on the home front and ignored the censorship restrictions intended to protect the military. Congress passed a law in January 1862 making it a crime to publish news about Confederate land and naval forces. Yet neither national nor state authorities ever suppressed such outspoken journals as the *Richmond Examiner,* the *Charleston Mercury,* or the *Raleigh Standard.* Eventually, several prominent generals closed their camps to reporters, and irate troops and vigilantes destroyed a few presses.

Early in 1863 the Confederate Senate considered a sedition bill that would have curtailed freedom of the press and of speech. The measure died because most Southern legislators were avid proponents of free speech. Among the most vociferous was Henry S. Foote of Tennessee, who compiled a "shocking catalogue" of his government's questionable arrests following the suspension of habeas corpus. For example, General Winder jailed John Minor Botts, a former U.S. congressman, for declaring his neutrality, and the Reverend Alden Bosserman for openly praying for the defeat of "this unholy rebellion." Most preachers and teachers accepted the restrictions on free speech in the South's closed society. But some who merely questioned the course of events lost jobs, and staunch Unionists fled northward. Others secretly supported peace societies, and angry mobs and zealous soldiers forcibly expelled a few. In lieu of specific legislation, the public pressures that had long stifled discussion about slavery now tried to impose loyalty to the Confederacy through intimidation and book burning.

As death and deprivation intensified public disaffection, tighter restrictions upon Southerners proved counterproductive. Disloyal words and deeds became too widespread to curtail. By early 1865, despite presidential pleas, Congress refused to sanction further suspensions of the writ of habeas corpus. De jure and de facto proscriptions of civil liberties repeatedly generated profound controversies, but ultimately they had only marginal impact on the demise of the war-torn Confederacy.

[*See also* Conscription; Freedom of the Press; Habeas Corpus; Military Justice.]

BIBLIOGRAPHY

Beals, Carleton. *War within a War: The Confederacy against Itself.* Philadelphia, 1965.

Eaton, Clement. *A History of the Southern Confederacy.* New York, 1954.

Ramsdell, Charles. *Behind the Lines in the Southern Confederacy.* Baton Rouge, La., 1944.

Robbins, John B. "The Confederacy and the Writ of Habeas Corpus." *Georgia Historical Quarterly* 55 (1971): 83–101.

Tatum, Georgia Lee. *Disloyalty in the Confederacy.* Chapel Hill, N.C., 1934.

BLAKE TOUCHSTONE

CIVIL SERVICE. The Confederate government had more than 70,000 civilian employees at its peak, compared to 100,000 for the Union. The administration was organized into six departments: a staff of 29 in the State Department; 125 in the Department of Justice; 1,016 in the Navy

Department; 2,780 at the Treasury; 9,183 in the Post Office; and 57,124 civilians in the War Department.

Some efforts were made at formalizing procedures. The Ordnance Bureau used competitive science examinations for its skilled positions. The postal service organized a formal training school for clerks and officers. The Treasury Department established written work regulations. The standard workday in the State Department and the Treasury was 9:00 A.M. to 3:00 P.M., in contrast to the eleven-hour average in industry in that era. But senior officials were expected to put in whatever hours were necessary.

Cabinet secretaries received $6,000 per year; clerks' salaries generally ranged from $700 to $1,500 and did not keep pace with inflation. Bureau chief Robert Kean complained in 1863 that his $3,000 salary went only as far as $300 "in ordinary times." In at least three instances, government workers went on strike for higher pay: postal clerks at Richmond and women at the Brown's Island arsenal (twice).

Civil servants were exempted from military service. But 2,000 clerks from all departments were organized into a military home guard, which was called out periodically to defend the Richmond capital.

The postal service was the first department organized. This was accomplished largely because Postmaster General John H. Reagan had persuaded five high-ranking Southern officials of the U.S. Post Office to join the Confederacy, bringing with them organizational documents, and because he absorbed nearly intact the U.S. postal service of the Southern states, as personnel shifted their allegiance. The Union maintained U.S. mail service throughout the South (and collected receipts from Confederate postmasters) until June 1, 1861.

At peak strength, the postal service employed 9,183: 72 at the central office; 7,009 postmasters and 93 clerks; 1,950 mail contractors; and 59 telegraph workers. Clerks in the Richmond Post Office earned $700 to $800 per year. They went on strike from August 21 through 23, 1863, until the postmaster general agreed to press Congress for a pay increase. The service showed a financial surplus every year, and Reagan boasted that he had needed proportionately only half the personnel that the U.S. Post Office had used.

The Department of State, usually the most prestigious in a government, was the smallest of the Confederacy's departments and was described as a "backwater office." It had only 29 staff members: the secretary ($6,000), four clerks ($1,000 to $1,500), a messenger ($500), and a porter ($360) in the central office, and 22 commissioners and agents in the diplomatic service. Secretary Robert Toombs remarked that there was so little to do that he "carried the State department in his hat."

The Department of Justice had a roster of 126: 14 in its central office; 16 district judges throughout the Confeder-

acy, each with a district attorney and marshal, plus a total of 54 clerks; and 10 in other offices. The Constitution provided for a supreme court, but it was never established. The attorney general appointed judges (whose salaries ranged from $5,000 in Louisiana to $2,500 in Florida), issued patents (75 in 1862), and provided legal opinions for the other departments (217 in all).

Military officers headed the five bureaus of the Navy Department, but a civilian staff of 16 was employed at its Richmond headquarters and approximately 1,000 civilian laborers at its more than a dozen shipyards, laboratories, cannon foundry, and powder mill. Clerks earned salaries of $1,000 to $2,100, messengers $500, and laborers an estimated $800 per year. The department was noteworthy for its developments in ironclad ships, the submarine, and torpedo mines, all of which transformed naval warfare.

Next to the military, finance was the gravest issue for the Confederacy. The Treasury Department had some 2,780 civilian employees: 562 clerks and messengers and 14 officials in its central office; 400 customs collectors (a declining number as the Union blockade intensified); and 1,789 appraisers, tax collectors, and other staff.

Secretary Christopher G. Memminger promulgated a written set of work regulations providing for a six-month probationary period for new employees before "permanent commission," a six-hour workday, and standards of conduct. The rules drew some criticism, and one man was fired for "communication to a Richmond newspaper." Chief clerk Henry Capers attributed the dissent to the disposition of Southerners: "To command was so much the nature of our people that it was, of all things, most repugnant to their natures to be commanded."

The department employed a large number of women as "note clippers" and "note signers." The currency was lithographed, but, unlike modern procedure, the signatures of officials were added by hand. The so-called Treasury girls faced a quota of 3,200 notes to sign per day and had their pay docked ten cents for each note spoiled. Women clerks were paid $65 per month in 1863. Although this rate matched that of male postal clerks, it was barely half the standard $125 per month for men in comparable Treasury positions.

The War Department was by far the largest office, with an estimated 57,124 civilian employees. There were 277 clerks and other staff at Richmond headquarters. Wartime constraints forced even small economies: envelopes from correspondents were turned inside out and reused.

The Ordnance Bureau operated 17 arsenals, foundries, and powder mills employing by 1865 some 3,691 white men and 2,245 black men, plus a number of women. In addition, 13,228 government miners dug for gunpowder ores and 11,500 constructed railroads and fortifications: 1,500 whites and 10,000 slaves and freedmen. The Conscription

Bureau had 2,443 agents, the Tax Collection Bureau 2,965, and the Supply Service 12,533. The Medical Corps operated dozens of hospitals with a civilian staff of 8,250.

Women were employed in great numbers in the War Department: 3,300 as nurses, matrons, and laundresses in the hospitals, and at least 5,000 making clothing in the quartermaster factories. An 1863 explosion in a Brown's Island "condemned cartridge" refitting shop killed 45 women and 2 men. Later that year, a wage strike there raised government pay from $2.50 to $3.00 per day. By 1864, married women were earning $7.00 per day and single women $5.00. Another strike by 100 women, seeking to eliminate the differential, was unsuccessful. In their wartime work, women proved themselves as capable as men.

The Confederate government generally attracted effective civil servants. Governmental operations were reasonably efficient despite the lack of resources. But the Confederacy did not match the levels of centralization and administrative coordination among departments that marked the U.S. government under Abraham Lincoln.

[*See also* African American Forgeworkers; Conscription; Judiciary; Medical Department; Navy Department; Ordnance Bureau; Patent Office; Post Office Department; State Department; Niter and Mining Bureau; Taxation; Treasury Department; War Department.]

BIBLIOGRAPHY

Capers, Henry D. *Recollections of the Civil Service of the Confederate Government.* Atlanta, 1887.

Jones, John B. *A Rebel War Clerk's Diary.* Edited by Earl S. Miers. New York, 1961.

Kaufman, Janet E. "Treasury Girls." *Civil War Times Illustrated* 25 (May 1986): 32–38.

Kean, Robert G. H. *Inside the Confederate Government.* Edited by Edward Younger. New York, 1957.

Van Riper, Paul P., and Harry N. Scheiber. "The Confederate Civil Service." *Journal of Southern History* 25 (1959): 448–470.

JAMES J. HORGAN

CIVIL WAR. [*This entry is composed of five articles that discuss the war and its relation to Confederate history:*
>   Names of the War
>   Causes of the War
>   Strategy and Tactics
>   Causes of Defeat
>   Losses and Numbers
For discussion of the course of the war itself, see entries on particular battles and states.]

Names of the War

With the echo of the first shot in April 1861, Americans began arguing over a name for the conflict. The debate has waned with the passing decades, but it still has not ended. By far the most popular of the titles is "The Civil War." Both sides used the term throughout the four-year struggle. In the South, generals such as Lee, Longstreet, and Gordon, as well as wartime Richmond newspapers, referred to the war by that name. The term's opponents, concentrated in the South, argue that "The Civil War" suggests a rebellion against lawful authority. It also implies that two different sections of the nation were fighting for control of a single government, when in fact the Confederacy was seeking to exist independently. Justifications for the name are that the struggle came within the definition of civil war expounded by many philosophers of that day, that the conflict was indeed a civil war in areas like Missouri, Tennessee, and Kentucky, and that the term is short, convenient, and less controversial than any of the other names.

"War between the States" has been a favorite Southern appellation since the conflict ended. Not used during the war itself, the term came into use with the publication in 1868 of Alexander H. Stephen's *A Constitutional View of the Late War between the States.* It enjoyed its highest boost in popularity during the Spanish-American War, when Americans of North and South joined together in a common cause. Southern congressmen once sought to make the term the official title, but a resolution to that effect was tabled. An objection to this name is that it is long and cumbersome. Further, the Southern nation was a confederation of eleven sovereignties, with much more involved than merely state rights. This title is thus misleading.

The Union counterpart in titles is "War of the Rebellion." Northerners at the time considered the South to be in rebellion, and many Confederates seemed to take pride in being called "Rebels." This name is too long, however, and it is also erroneous because it was a full-scale war, with two organized governments respecting the rules of war. Yet "War of the Rebellion" continues to live as the title of the 128 huge volumes containing the official records of the Union and Confederate armies.

Two names, "Second American Revolution" and "War for Southern Independence," were outgrowths of Confederate beliefs that their struggle paralleled the colonists' fight in the 1770s to break away from British control. Foreign writers often referred to the North-South contest as "The Confederate War," and a Maryland writer proposed "War of Secession." Both terms, however, suggest that secession was the primary cause of the war, which then puts the blame for hostilities solely on the South.

In many parts of the old Confederacy today, "The War" is a phrase that needs no explanation. Other titles with short-lived appearances have included "War of Sections," "The War for Nationality," "Conflict of the Sixties," "The War against Slavery," "The Uncivil War," "The Brothers' War," "War against the States," and "The Lost Cause."

Among the somewhat facetious names given by Southerners are "The Yankee War," "The Southern Defense against Northern Aggression," and "Mr. Lincoln's War." By far the most diplomatic of all the titles for the American struggle is "The Late Unpleasantness."

[See also Battles, Naming of.]

BIBLIOGRAPHY

Fish, Carl Russell. The American Civil War. New York, 1937.
Roller, David C., and Robert W. Twyman, eds. The Encyclopedia of Southern History. Baton Rouge, La., 1979.

JAMES I. ROBERTSON, JR.

Causes of the War

During the Civil War, few people on either side would have dissented from Abraham Lincoln's statement in his second inaugural address that slavery "was, somehow, the cause of the war." After all, had not Jefferson Davis, a large slaveholder, justified secession in 1861 as an act of self-defense against the Lincoln administration, whose policy of excluding slavery from the territories would make "property in slaves so insecure as to be comparatively worthless . . . thereby annihilating in effect property worth thousands of millions of dollars"? And had not the new vice president of the Confederate States of America, Alexander H. Stephens, said in a speech at Savannah on March 21, 1861, that slavery was "the immediate cause of the late rupture and the present revolution" of Southern independence? The old confederation known as the United States, said Stephens, had been founded on the false idea that all men are created equal. The Confederacy, by contrast, "is founded upon exactly the opposite idea; its foundations are laid, its cornerstone rests, upon the great truth that the negro is not equal to the white man; that slavery, subordination to the superior race, is his natural and moral condition. This, our new Government, is the first, in the history of the world, based on this great physical, philosophical, and moral truth."

Historical Views of the Causes of the War

For at least a half century after the war, this remained the predominant interpretation of its causes. In 1913 the foremost Civil War historian of his day, James Ford Rhodes, declared definitively that "of the American Civil War it may safely be asserted that there was a single cause, slavery." Although no historian today would put it quite so baldly, most of them would agree with the basic point. But during the century and a quarter since the guns ceased firing, dissenters from this viewpoint have provoked many rhetorical battles over the causes of the war.

Early Dissension. Two of the earliest dissenters were none other than Jefferson Davis and Alexander Stephens. After 1865 slavery was a dead and discredited institution. It

no longer seemed appropriate, as it had in 1861, to emphasize it proudly as the reason for secession. To salvage honor and assert a sound constitutional basis for their lost cause, Stephens and Davis now insisted that Southern states had seceded and gone to war not to protect slavery but to vindicate state sovereignty. In A Constitutional View of the War between the States, which invented the favorite Southern name for the conflict three years after it was over, Stephens maintained that "the War had its origin in opposing principles" concerning not slavery and freedom but rather "the organic Structure of the Government of the States. . . . It was a strife between the principles of Federation, on the one side, and Centralism, or Consolidation, on the other." And Davis, writing his book The Rise and Fall of the Confederate Government in the 1870s, insisted that the Confederates, like their forefathers of 1776, had fought solely "for the defense of an inherent, unalienable right . . . to withdraw from a Union into which they had, as sovereign communities, voluntarily entered. . . . The existence of African servitude was in no wise the cause of the conflict, but only an incident."

The Progressive Theory. This virgin-birth theory of secession became widely accepted among Southern whites: the Confederacy had been conceived by no worldly cause but by constitutional principle. Thus the Civil War was a war of Northern aggression against Southern rights, not a war to preserve the American nation and, ultimately, to abolish slavery. By the 1920s, though, the notion that a people would go to war over principles had become suspect among historians. Human behavior, most of them thought, is rooted in materialism. The "Progressive school" dominated American historiography from the 1920s to the 1940s. This school posited a clash between interest groups and classes as the central theme of American history: industry versus agriculture, capital versus labor, railroads versus farmers, manufacturers versus consumers, and so on. The real issues of American politics, in this interpretation, revolved around the economic interests of these contesting groups: tariffs, taxes, land policies, industrial and labor policies, subsidies to business or agriculture, and the like.

The Progressive school explained the causes of the Civil War within this interpretive framework. The war transferred to the battlefield a long-running contest between plantation agriculture and industrializing capitalism, and the industrialists emerged triumphant. It was not primarily a conflict between North and South: "Merely by the accidents of climate, soil, and geography," wrote the foremost Progressive historian Charles A. Beard, "was it a sectional struggle"—the accidental fact that plantation agriculture was located in the South and industry mainly in the North. Nor was it a contest between slavery and freedom. Slavery just happened to be the labor system of plantation agriculture, as wage labor was the system of Northern industry. For some Progressive historians, neither system was significantly worse or better than the other—"wage slavery" was as exploitative as chattel bondage. In any case, they said, slavery was not a moral issue for anybody except a tiny handful of abolitionists; its abolition was a mere incident of the destruction of the plantation order by the war. The *real* issues between the North and the South in antebellum politics were the tariff, government subsidies to transportation and manufacturing, public land sales, and related questions on which manufacturing and planting interests had clashing viewpoints.

This interpretive synthesis proved a godsend for a generation of mostly Southern-born historians who seized upon it as proof that slavery had little to do with the origins of the Confederacy. The Nashville Fugitives, an influential group of historians, novelists, and poets who gathered at Vanderbilt University and published in 1930 a famous manifesto, *I'll Take My Stand,* set the tone for the new Southern interpretation of the Civil War's causes. It was a blend of the old Confederate apologia voiced by Jefferson Davis and the new Progressive synthesis created by Charles Beard. The Confederacy fought not only for the constitutional principle of state rights and self-government but also for the preservation of a stable, pastoral, agrarian civilization in the face of the overweening, acquisitive, imperialistic ambitions of an urban-industrial Leviathan. The real issue that brought on the war was not slavery—this institution, wrote one of the Nashville Fugitives, "was part of the agrarian system, but only one element and not an essential one"—but rather such matters as the tariff, banks, subsidies to railroads, and similar questions in which the grasping businessmen of the North sought to advance their interests at the expense of Southern farmers and planters. Lincoln was not elected in 1860 in the name of freedom over slavery; rather, his election represented the ascendancy of tariffs and railroads and factories over agriculture and the graces of a rural society. The result was the triumph of acquisitive, power-hungry robber barons over the highest type of civilization America had ever known—the Old South. It was no coincidence that this interpretation emerged during the same period that the novel and movie *Gone with the Wind* became one of the most popular literary and cinematic successes of all time; history and popular culture on this occasion marched hand in hand.

Revisionism. An offshoot of this interpretation of the Civil War's causes dominated the work of academic historians during the 1940s. This offshoot came to be called revisionism. The revisionists denied that sectional conflicts between North and South—whether over slavery, state rights, or industry versus agriculture—were genuinely divisive. The differences between North and South, wrote one of the leading revisionists, Avery Craven, were "no greater than those existing at different times between East

and West." The other giant of revisionism, James G. Randall, suggested that they were no greater than the differences between Chicago and downstate Illinois.

Such disparities did not have to lead to war; they could and should have been accommodated peacefully within the political system. The Civil War was therefore not an irrepressible conflict, as earlier generations had called it, but *The Repressible Conflict,* as Craven titled one of his books. The war was brought on not by genuine issues but by extremists on both sides—rabble-rousing abolitionists and Southern fire-eaters—who whipped up emotions and hatreds in North and South for their own partisan purposes. The passions they aroused got out of hand in 1861 and erupted into a tragic, unnecessary war that accomplished nothing that could not have been achieved by negotiation and compromise.

Of course, any such compromise in 1861 would have left slavery in place. But the revisionists, like the Progressives and the Vanderbilt agrarians, considered slavery unimportant; as Craven put it, the institution of bondage "played a rather minor part in the life of the South and the Negro." Slavery would have died peacefully of natural causes in another generation or two had not fanatics forced the issue to armed conflict. This hints at another feature of revisionism: while blaming extremists on both sides, revisionists focused most of their criticism on antislavery radicals, even antislavery moderates like Lincoln, who harped on the evils of slavery and expressed a determination to rein in what they called "the Slave Power." This had goaded the South into a defensive response that finally caused Southern states to secede to free themselves from the incessant pressure of these self-righteous Yankee zealots. Revisionism thus tended to portray Southern whites, even the fire-eaters, as victims reacting to Northern attacks; it truly was a war of Northern aggression.

Slavery

Since the 1950s, however, historiography has come full circle to Lincoln's assertion that "slavery was, somehow, the cause of the war." The state rights, Progressive, agrarian, and revisionist schools seem moribund if not actually dead. To be sure, echoes of some of these interpretations can still be heard. Economic conflicts of interest, for example, did occur between the agricultural South and the industrializing North. These conflicts emerged in debates over tariffs, banks, land grants, and similar issues. But these matters divided parties and interest groups more than North and South. The South in the 1840s and 1850s had its advocates of industrialization and protective tariffs and a national bank, just as the North had its millions of farmers and its low-tariff, anti-bank Democratic majority in many states. The Civil War was not fought over issues of the tariff or banks or agrarianism versus industrialism. These and similar kinds of questions have been bread-and-butter issues of American politics throughout the nation's history, often generating a great deal more friction and heat than they did in the 1850s. But they have not caused any great shooting wars. Nor was the Civil War a consequence of false issues trumped up by demagogues or fanatics. It was fought over real, profound, intractable problems that Americans on both sides believed went to the heart of their society and its future.

In 1858 two prominent political leaders, one of whom expected to be elected president in 1860 and the other of whom *was* elected president, voiced the stark nature of the problem. The social systems of slave labor and free labor "are more than incongruous—they are incompatible," said Senator William H. Seward of New York. The friction between them "is an irreconcilable conflict between opposing and enduring forces, and it means that the United States must and will, sooner or later, become either entirely a slaveholding nation, or entirely a free-labor nation." In Illinois, senatorial candidate Abraham Lincoln launched his campaign with a theme taken from the Bible: "A house divided against itself cannot stand." The United States, he said, "cannot endure, permanently, half *slave* and half free.... It will become *all* one thing, or *all* the other." The policy of Lincoln's party—and Seward's—was to "arrest the further spread of [slavery], and place it where the public mind shall rest in the belief that it is in the course of ultimate extinction."

Sectionalism. When Seward and Lincoln uttered these words, the free and slave states had coexisted peacefully under the same Constitution for seventy years. They shared the same language, legal system, political culture, social mores, religious values, and a common heritage of struggle to form the nation. Yet by the late 1850s, Southern spokesmen agreed with Lincoln and Seward that an irreconcilable conflict within a house divided into free and slave states had split the country into two antagonistic cultures. "In this country have arisen two races," said a Savannah lawyer—and he meant not black and white but Northern and Southern —"two races which, although claiming a common parentage, have been so entirely separated by climate, by morals, by religion, and by estimates so totally opposite to all that constitutes honor, truth, and manliness, that they cannot longer exist under the same government."

What lay at the root of this antagonism? Slavery. It was the sole institution not shared by North and South. Both had cities, farms, railroads, ports, factories, colleges, literary societies, poets, poverty, wealth, slums, mansions, capitalists, workers, riverboats, gamblers, thieves, racial segregation, immigrants, Protestants, Catholics, Jews, ethnic and class conflict, and almost anything else one might name— but only one had slavery. That "peculiar institution" defined the South. The *Charleston Mercury* stated in an editorial in 1858 that "on the subject of slavery the North and South ... are not only two Peoples, but they are rival, hostile Peoples." When the members of a South Carolina planter family who contributed four brothers to the Confederate army learned of Lincoln's election as president, they agreed that "now a stand must be made for African slavery or it is forever lost." In going out of a Union ruled by Yankee fanatics, "we ... are contending for all that we hold dear—our Property—our Institutions—our Honor.... I hope it will end in establishing a Southern Confederacy who will have among themselves slavery a bond a union stronger than any which holds the north together."

Slaves were the principal form of wealth in the South. The market value of the 4 million slaves in 1860 was $3 billion—more than the value of land, or cotton, or anything else in the slave states. It was slave labor that made it possible for the American South to grow three-quarters of the world's cotton, which in turn constituted half of all American exports. But slavery was much more than an economic system. It was a means of maintaining racial control and white supremacy. Northern whites were also committed to white supremacy. But with 95 percent of the nation's black population in the South, the region's scale of concern with this matter was so much greater as to constitute a different order of magnitude and create a radically different set of social priorities.

The economic, social, and racial centrality of slavery to "the Southern way of life" focused the region's politics overwhelmingly on defense of the institution. Many Southern leaders in the age of Thomas Jefferson had considered slavery a "necessary evil" that would eventually disappear from this land of liberty. But with the rise of the cotton kingdom, slavery had become in the eyes of Southern whites by the 1830s a "positive good" for black and white alike. Proslavery pamphlets and books became a cottage industry. Their main themes were summed up in the title of a pamphlet by a clergyman published in 1850: *A Defense of the South against the Reproaches and Encroachments of the North: In which Slavery Is Shown to Be an Institution of God Intended to Form the Basis of the Best Social State and the Only Safeguard and Permanence of a Republican Government.* The foremost defender of slavery until his death in 1850 was John C. Calhoun, who noted proudly that "many in the South once believed that slavery was a moral and political evil. That folly and delusion are gone. We see it now in its true light, and regard it as the most safe and stable basis for free institutions in the world" and "essential to the peace, safety, and prosperity" of the South.

The defensive tone of much of the proslavery argument was provoked by the rise of militant abolitionism in the North after 1830. William Lloyd Garrison, Theodore Weld,

Wendell Phillips, Frederick Douglass, and a host of other eloquent crusaders branded slavery as a sin, a defiance of God's law and of Christian ethics, immoral, inhumane, a violation of the republican principle of liberty on which the nation had been founded. Although the radical abolitionists did not get far in the North with their message of racial equality, the belief that slavery was an unjust, obsolete, and unrepublican institution—a "relic of barbarism" as the new Republican party described slavery in its 1856 platform—entered mainstream northern politics in the 1850s. "The monstrous injustice of slavery," said Abraham Lincoln in 1854, "deprives our republican example of its just influence in the world—enables the enemies of free institutions, with plausibility, to taunt us as hypocrites."

Expansion of Slavery. But it was not the *existence* of slavery that polarized the nation to the point of breaking apart. It was the issue of the *expansion* of slave territory. Most of the crises that threatened the bonds of union arose over this matter. The first one, in 1820, was settled by the Missouri Compromise, which balanced the admission of Missouri as a slave state with the simultaneous admission of Maine as a free state and banned slavery in the rest of the Louisiana Purchase territory north of 36° 30′ while permitting it south of that line. Paired admission of slave and free states during the next quarter century kept their numbers equal. But the annexation of Texas as a huge new slave state—with the potential of carving out several more within its boundaries—provoked new tensions. It also provoked war with Mexico in 1846, which resulted in American acquisition of three-quarters of a million square miles of new territory in the Southwest. This opened a Pandora's box of troubles that could not be closed.

Convinced that the "slave power" in Washington had engineered the annexation of Texas and the Mexican War, the "antislavery power" in Congress determined to flex its muscles. In 1846 David Wilmot of Pennsylvania introduced in the House of Representatives a resolution banning slavery in all territory that might be conquered from Mexico. By an almost unanimous vote of all Northern congressmen against the virtually unanimous vote of all Southern representatives, the resolution passed—because the larger Northern population gave the free states a majority in the House. Equal representation in the Senate enabled Southerners to block the Wilmot Proviso there. But this issue framed national politics for the next fifteen years.

The most ominous feature of the Wilmot Proviso was its wrenching of the normal pattern of party divisions into a sectional pattern. On most issues before 1846, Northern and Southern Whigs had voted together and Northern and Southern Democrats had done likewise. But on the Wilmot Proviso, Northern Whigs and Democrats had voted together against a solid alliance of Southern Whigs and Democrats. This became the norm for all votes on any issue concerning

slavery—and most of the important national political issues in the 1850s did concern slavery. This sectional alignment reflected a similar pattern in social and cultural matters. In the 1840s the two largest religious denominations, the Methodists and Baptists, had split into separate Northern and Southern churches over whether a slave owner could be appointed as a bishop or missionary of the denomination.

In addition to a growing conviction in the North that slavery was contrary to the teachings of Christ, a secular free-labor ideology had become the dominant Northern worldview. It held up the ideals of equal opportunity, equal rights, the dignity of labor, and social mobility. Slavery represented the opposite. It denied equal opportunity and rights, degraded the concept of labor, and blocked social mobility. Most important, it afflicted poor but aspiring white men as well as slaves. "Slavery withers and blights all it touches," wrote a free-labor advocate. "It is a curse upon the poor, free, laboring white men. . . . They are depressed, poor, impoverished, degraded in caste, because labor is disgraceful." Wherever slavery goes, said a New York congressman in 1849, "there is in substance no middle class. Great wealth or hopeless poverty is the settled condition."

The national political controversy focused on slavery in the territories because though the Constitution protected the institution in the states where it existed, Congress could presumably legislate the status of territories. And equally important, the territories represented the future. In 1850 they constituted more than half of the landmass of the United States. From 1790 to 1850 the territories that became states accounted for more than half of the nation's increase in population. As that process continued, the new territories would shape the future. To ensure a free-labor destiny, Northerners wanted to keep slavery out of these territories. In 1848 a new political party, the Free-Soil party, was founded on this platform. "We are opposed to the extension of slavery," declared a Free-Soil newspaper, because if slavery goes into a new territory "the free labor of the states will not. . . . If the free labor of the states goes there, the slave labor of the southern states will not, and in a few years the country will teem with an active and energetic population." And eventually, the expansion of free territory and the containment of slavery would make freedom the wave of the future, placing slavery "in the course of ultimate extinction," as Lincoln phrased it.

That was just what Southerners feared. The North already had a majority in the House; new free states would give them a majority in the Senate as well as an unchallengeable domination of the electoral college. "Long before the North gets this vast accession of strength," warned a South Carolinian, "she will ride over us rough shod, proclaim freedom or something equivalent to it to our

Slaves and reduce us to the condition of Haiti. . . . If we do not act now, we deliberately consign our children, not our posterity, but *our children* to the flames."

This argument swayed white nonslaveholders in the South as much as it did slaveholders. Whites of both classes considered the bondage of blacks to be the basis of liberty for whites. Slavery, they declared, elevated all whites to an equality of status and dignity by confining menial labor and caste subordination to blacks. "If slaves are freed," maintained proslavery spokesmen, whites "will become menials. We will lose every right and liberty which belongs to the name of freemen." The Northern threat to slavery thus menaced all whites. Nonslaveholders also agreed with slaveholders that the institution must be allowed to go into the territories. Such expansion might increase their own chances of becoming slave owners. The attempt by Northern Free-Soilers to exclude slavery from the territories united Southern whites in a conviction that Northerners were trying to place a stigma on the South of "degrading inequality . . . which says to the Southern man, Avaunt! you are not my equal, and hence are to be excluded as carrying a moral taint." The South could not tolerate such an insult. "Death is preferable to acknowledged inferiority."

The controversy over slavery in the region conquered from Mexico led to a crisis that almost provoked secession in 1850. In the end, the complex Compromise of 1850 narrowly averted this outcome. The essential features of the Compromise admitted California as a free state and divided the remainder of the Mexican Cession into two large territories, New Mexico and Utah, whose residents were given the right to decide for themselves whether or not they wanted slavery. (Both territories subsequently legalized slavery, but few slaves were taken there.)

State Rights and Slavery. The Compromise of 1850 also included a concession to the South in the form of the Fugitive Slave Law that gave unprecedented powers to the Federal government. This raises an important point about the state rights theory. State rights, or sovereignty, was a means rather than an end, an instrument more than a principle. Its purpose was to protect slavery from the potential hostility of a national majority. Southern political leaders from the 1820s to the 1840s jealously opposed the exercise of national power for a variety of purposes. "If Congress can make banks, roads, and canals under the Constitution," said Nathanial Macon of North Carolina, "they can free any slave in the United States." Calhoun, the South's leading political philosopher, formulated an elaborate constitutional structure of state rights theory to halt any use of Federal power that might conceivably be construed at some future time as a precedent with negative consequences for slavery.

At the same time, though, Southerners were not averse to using national power in defense of slavery. Indeed, this was a more reliable instrument than state rights. And the South had the power to wield. During forty-nine of the seventy-two years from 1789 to 1861 a Southerner—and slaveholder—was president of the United States. Twenty-four of the thirty-six Speakers of the House and presidents pro tem of the Senate were from the South. At all times during those years a majority of Supreme Court justices were Southerners. This happened because, though the South had only a minority of the national population, it usually controlled the Jeffersonian Republican party and, after 1828, the Democratic party, which in turn usually controlled the government. Southern domination of the Democratic party increased during the 1850s, so that even though both Democratic presidents in that decade—Franklin Pierce and James Buchanan—were Northerners, they were beholden to Southerners and did their bidding.

The usefulness of this national power had been demonstrated in the 1830s when Congress imposed a gag rule to stifle antislavery petitions and the post office banned antislavery literature from the mail in Southern states. But the Fugitive Slave Law of 1850 provided an even more striking example. It was the strongest manifestation of national power thus far in American history. It overrode the laws and officials of Northern states and extended the long arm of Federal law, enforced by the army and navy, into Northern states to recover escaped slaves and return them to their owners. Senator Jefferson Davis, who later insisted that the Confederacy fought for the principle of state sovereignty, voted with enthusiasm for the Fugitive Slave Law. When Northern state legislatures and courts invoked state rights and individual liberties against this Federal law, the U.S. Supreme Court with its majority of Southern justices reaffirmed the supremacy of national law to protect slavery.

Calhoun died in 1850, and during the following decade the South moved further away from his principles of state sovereignty and used its leverage in the Democratic party to wield greater national power than ever. Jefferson Davis was one of the principal architects of this process. As secretary of war in President Franklin Pierce's cabinet, he helped persuade a reluctant Pierce to cave in to Southern demands for repeal of the Missouri Compromise restriction on slavery in the territories north of 36° 30'. Pierce endorsed repeal as a party measure; so did Senator Stephen A. Douglas of Illinois, who knew that he would need Southern votes if he expected to win the presidency. Patronage and pressure induced just enough Northern Democrats to vote for the Kansas-Nebraska Act in 1854 to obtain its passage.

But this turned out to be the first of several Pyrrhic victories for the South. It drove tens of thousands of angry Northern Democratic voters out of the party and gave birth to the Republican party, which by 1856 had become the second major party in the North. Running on the Wilmot

Proviso platform of excluding slavery from the territories, the Republicans carried most Northern states in the presidential election of 1856. James Buchanan won the election only because of Southern support. Open warfare between proslavery and antislavery settlers in Kansas spilled over into the halls of Congress, where fistfights broke out between Northern and Southern representatives, members came armed to the floor of Congress, and South Carolinian Preston Brooks caned Senator Charles Sumner of Massachusetts into unconsciousness at his seat in the Senate. Presidents Pierce's and Buchanan's actions—and nonactions—favored the proslavery side in Kansas. Under heavy Southern pressure, Buchanan in 1858 even went so far as to endorse the fraudulently ratified Lecompton constitution to bring Kansas into the Union as a slave state. Kansas "is at this moment," the president told Congress, "as much a slave state as Georgia or South Carolina." This was too much for most remaining Northern Democrats, who followed Douglas's leadership and broke with the president to defeat the Lecompton constitution.

Each incident in the Kansas controversy propelled more Northern voters into the Republican party. So did the Supreme Court's *Dred Scott* decision in 1857 in which five Southern and one Northern Democratic justice overturned precedents to rule that Congress had no power to prohibit slavery in the territories. This made slavery legal not only in Kansas but in every other territory as well. But this would remain a barren right unless the territorial legislatures enacted and enforced a slave code. In Kansas, where antislavery settlers were in a clear majority by 1858, there was faint chance of that. So Southern politicians, led by Jefferson Davis, made their boldest bid yet to use national power in the interest of slavery. They introduced in Congress a Federal slave code for the territories and demanded its endorsement by the Democratic National Convention in 1860.

Meanwhile the abolitionist John Brown, who had gained experience as an antislavery guerrilla fighter in Kansas, led a quixotic but violent raid to seize the Federal armory at Harpers Ferry in Virginia. He planned to arm the slaves and foment a chain reaction of slave uprisings throughout the South. The raid was a total failure: Brown and most of his followers were captured or killed; Brown was hanged. This affair sent shock waves of fear and outrage through the South. It also confirmed Southern convictions that loss of control of the national government would be fatal. U.S. Marines commanded by Robert E. Lee had captured Brown. But what if the Federal government had been in Republican hands? Southerners equated John Brown with all abolitionists, and abolitionists with the "Black Republicans."

The Brown raid formed the backdrop of a bitter contest for Speaker of the House in the 1859–1860 session of Congress. The Republican candidate gained a plurality but not the necessary majority of votes. For eight weeks the donnybrook went on. Congressmen hurled bitter insults at one another, and one observer reported with perhaps some exaggeration that on the floor of the House "the only persons who do not have a revolver and a knife are those who have two revolvers." A Southerner wrote that a good many slave-state congressmen wanted a shoot-out in the House; they "are willing to fight the question out, and settle it right there. . . . I can't help wishing the Union dissolved and we had a Southern confederacy." At one point during the contest, the governor of South Carolina wrote to one of his state's representatives: "If you upon consultation decide to make the issue of force in Washington, write or telegraph me, and I will have a regiment in Washington in the shortest possible time."

The Speakership fight was finally settled by election of a nonentity. A few weeks later, Southern delegates walked out of the 1860 Democratic National Convention when Northerners refused to accept a platform endorsing a Federal slave code for the territories. All efforts to reunite the severed party failed, and the bolters nominated a "Southern rights" candidate. This ensured the election of Abraham Lincoln, who carried every Northern state and therefore the election. For the South, this was the handwriting on the wall. They had lost control of the government, probably permanently. It was not state rights they had contended for in this contest. It was national power, power that they had held and had used to secure the Fugitive Slave Law, the Kansas-Nebraska Act, the *Dred Scott* decision, and other measures to protect slavery. But every such victory had driven more Northern voters into the anti–slave power camp, which finally elected a president who believed slavery a "monstrous injustice" that should be "placed in the course of ultimate extinction." So seven slave states left the Union and formed the Confederate States of America.

Secession. But that did not necessarily mean war. The government could have acquiesced in the division of the United States into two nations. Some Northerners did propose to "let the erring sisters depart in peace." But most were not willing to accept the dismemberment of the United States. They feared that toleration of disunion in 1861 would create a fatal precedent to be invoked by disaffected minorities in the future, perhaps by the losing side in another presidential election, until the United States dissolved into a dozen petty, squabbling, hostile autocracies. The great experiment in republican self-government launched in 1776 would collapse, proving the contention of European monarchists and conservatives that this upstart republic across the Atlantic could not last. "The doctrine of secession is anarchy," declared a Cincinnati newspaper in an editorial similar to hundreds in other newspapers. "If the minority have the right to break up the Government at pleasure, because they have not had their way, there is an end of all government." Even the lame-duck President

CHARLES SUMNER.   After he was attacked with a cane on the floor of the Senate by South Carolina representative Preston Brooks on May 22, 1865, Sumner became for the Republican party a symbol of Southern arrogance.   HARPER'S PICTORIAL HISTORY OF THE GREAT REBELLION

Buchanan, in his last message to Congress in December 1860, said that the Union was not "a mere voluntary association of States, to be dissolved at pleasure." The founders of the nation "never intended to implant in its bosom the seeds of its own destruction, nor were they guilty of the absurdity of providing for its own dissolution." If secession was legitimate, said Buchanan, the Union became "a rope of sand" and "our thirty-three States may resolve themselves into as many petty, jarring, and hostile republics. . . . The hopes of the friends of freedom throughout the world would be destroyed. . . . Our example for more than eighty years would not only be lost, but it would be quoted as conclusive proof that man is unfit for self-government."

No one held these convictions more strongly than Abraham Lincoln. "Perpetuity . . . is the fundamental law of all national governments," he declared in his inaugural address on March 4, 1861. "No State, upon its own mere motion, can lawfully get out of the Union." Later in the year, Lincoln told his private secretary that

> the central idea pervading this struggle is the necessity that is upon us, of proving that popular government is not an absurdity. We must settle this question now, whether in a free government the minority have the right to break up the government whenever they choose. If we fail it will go far to prove the incapability of the people to govern themselves.

But even this refusal to countenance the legitimacy of secession did not make war inevitable. Moderates on both sides sought a compromise formula. Nothing availed to stay the course of secession in the seven lower South states. Delegates from these states formed the Confederate States of America in February 1861, elected Jefferson Davis president, and proceeded to establish a new nation with the appearance of permanence. But the other eight slave states were still part of the United States when Lincoln took the oath of office. He hoped to keep them there by assurances that he had no intention or right to interfere with slavery in the states and by refraining from hostile action against the Confederate states, even though they had seized all Federal property and arms within their borders—except Fort Sumter and three other less important forts. By a policy of watchful waiting, of maintaining the status quo, Lincoln hoped to allow passions to cool and enable Unionists to regain influence in the lower South. But this hope was doomed. Genuine Unionists had all but disappeared in the lower South, and Fort Sumter became a flash point of contention.

A large brick fortress on an artificial granite island in the middle of Charleston Bay, Fort Sumter could not be seized by the Confederates as easily as other Federal property had been, even though it was defended by only some eighty-odd soldiers. Lincoln came under great pressure from conservatives and upper South Unionists to yield the fort as a gesture of peace and goodwill that might strengthen Southern Unionism. After leaning in this direction for a time, Lincoln concluded that to give up Sumter would do the opposite; it would demoralize Unionists and strengthen the Confederacy. Fort Sumter had become a master symbol of sovereignty. To yield it would constitute de facto recognition of Confederate sovereignty. It would surely encourage European nations to grant diplomatic recognition to the Confederate nation. It would make a mockery of the national government's profession of constitutional authority over its own property.

So Lincoln devised an ingenious plan to put the burden of decision for war or peace on Jefferson Davis's shoulders. The garrison at Fort Sumter was about to run out of provisions in April 1861. Giving advance notice of his intentions, Lincoln sent a fleet toward Charleston with supplies and reinforcements. If the Confederates allowed unarmed boats to bring in "food for hungry men," the warships would stand off and the reinforcements would return north. But if they fired on the fleet, the ships and the fort would fire back. In effect, Lincoln flipped a coin and told Davis: "Heads I win; tails you lose." If the Confederate guns fired first, the South would stand convicted of starting a war. If they let the supplies go in, the American flag would continue to fly over Fort Sumter. The Confederacy would lose face; Unionists would take courage.

Davis did not hesitate. He considered it vital to assert the Confederacy's sovereignty. He also hoped that the outbreak of a shooting war would force the states of the upper South to join their fellow slave states. Davis ordered Gen. P. G. T. Beauregard, commander of Confederate troops at Charleston, to open fire on Fort Sumter before the supply ships got there. At 4:30 A.M. on April 12, Confederate artillery started the Civil War by firing on Fort Sumter. After a thirty-three-hour bombardment in which the Confederates fired four thousand rounds and the skeleton crew in the fort replied with a thousand—killing no one on either side in the first clash of this bloodiest of wars—the burning fort lowered the American flag in surrender. As Lincoln put it four years later in his second inaugural address: "Both [sides] deprecated war; but one of them would *make* war rather than let the nation survive; and the other would *accept* war rather than let it perish. And the war came."

[*See also* Compromise of 1850; Cornerstone Speech; Declaration of Immediate Causes; Dred Scott Decision; Election of 1860; Expansionism; Fort Sumter, South Carolina; Fugitive Slave Law; Harpers Ferry, West Virginia, *article on John Brown's Raid;* Kansas-Nebraska Act; Missouri Compromise; Nullification Controversy; Secession; State Rights; Sumner, Caning of; Wilmot Proviso; *and biographies of numerous figures mentioned herein.*]

BIBLIOGRAPHY

Barney, William L. *The Road to Secession: A New Perspective on the Old South.* New York, 1972.

Cooper, William J., Jr. *The South and the Politics of Slavery, 1828–1856.* Baton Rouge, La., 1978.

Craven, Avery. *The Coming of the Civil War.* 2d ed., rev. Chicago, 1957.

Current, Richard. *Lincoln and the First Shot.* Philadelphia, 1963.

Fehrenbacher, Don E. *The Dred Scott Case: Its Significance in American Law and Politics.* New York, 1978.

Foner, Eric. *Free Soil, Free Labor, Free Men: The Ideology of the Republican Party before the Civil War.* New York, 1970.

Freehling, William W. *The Road to Disunion: Secessionists at Bay, 1776–1854.* New York, 1990.

McCardell, John *The Idea of a Southern Nation: Southern Nationalists and Southern Nationalism, 1830–1860.* New York, 1979.

Nevins, Allan. *The Emergence of Lincoln.* 2 vols. New York, 1950.

Nevins, Allan. *Ordeal of the Union.* 2 vols. New York, 1947.

Potter, David M. *The Impending Crisis, 1848–1861.* New York, 1976.

Potter, David M. *Lincoln and His Party in the Secession Crisis.* 2d ed. with new preface. New Haven, 1962.

Pressly, Thomas J. *Americans Interpret Their Civil War.* 2d ed., with new introduction. Princeton, 1962.

Stampp, Kenneth M. *America in 1857: A Nation on the Brink.* New York, 1990.

Stampp, Kenneth M. *And the War Came: The North and the Secession Crisis, 1860–61.* Baton Rouge, La., 1950.

JAMES M. MCPHERSON

Strategy and Tactics

The strategy and tactics of the Civil War reflected the influence of the Napoleonic Era, with its appealing popular belief that wars could be won in climactic battles. They also reflected the engineering curriculum at West Point, which helped American officers adapt the products of the Industrial Revolution to local conditions. The curriculum at West Point, which supplied most of the leading officers on both sides, spent little time on European warfare, although Dennis Hart Mahan had organized the Napoleon Club at the academy in order to encourage extracurricular study of the subject. Nevertheless, only a few officers had read any of the work of Antoine Henri de Jomini, the principal interpreter of Napoleon's campaigns. Jomini's allegedly rigid prescriptions for warfare conducted along geometric lines and his emphasis on limited war were not generally accepted doctrine. Technology, training, and the practical engineering education received by the leading Civil War generals, not Jominian influence, determined the limits of thought that would decide wartime strategy (planning the allocation of resources to achieve the military goals of a war or campaign) and tactics (the utilization of those resources when an engagement was pending or actually under way).

Tactics

The tactics employed by the Union and Confederate armies were much the same. During the early months of the war formations were generally quite irregular, as green officers and their equally green troops were just learning tactics, and outmoded tactics at that. Later, the armies frequently relied mainly on one or two lines of two ranks each, in close order, perhaps a thousand men long, and sometimes followed skirmishers (soldiers who precede the main body to discover or delay the enemy). These lines might attack similar lines in close formation, much as in the days of the inaccurate smoothbore musket. Or they might shoot at or charge lines in entrenchments or behind breastworks.

In either event, the rifle-musket, developed in the 1850s, made such tactics quite obsolete. The invention of the minié ball—a bullet with a hollow base that would expand upon firing so as to catch the rifling grooves in the gun barrel—so improved the accuracy and range of the musket that battles were more deadly than in the past. Properly used, the Civil War rifle-musket made it extremely difficult to destroy an opponent who was comparably equipped and manned. Armies could be defeated and badly crippled, but they would survive to fight another day.

The combination of new weapons technology, frontal assaults, and commonsense use of the ax and spade made the Civil War the bloodiest of American wars. Under such conditions it did not take men in the ranks long to learn to dig in with amazing speed when their safety required it (Union troops approaching Atlanta could entrench for the night in less than an hour). Thus, judicious use of trenches or breastworks gave the defense a significant advantage, sometimes estimated at three to one, over an offense of equal size. The resulting carnage, especially to the attacker, appalled many officers. Union Gen. William Tecumseh Sherman, for example, attempted with some success to employ skirmishers instead of the customary two-rank line as a way to avoid the extraordinary casualties usually suffered by troops attacking a well-protected adversary equipped with rifle-muskets.

Although Civil War officers welcomed new technology, they did not always grasp its significance when applied to the fate of their soldiers. Close-order frontal assaults had become foolish, so tactical turning movements, in which part of one's force was stealthily moved to the flank or rear of the enemy, were often attempted in order to avoid bloody frontal encounters. The commander on the tactical defensive, however, knowing the dangers of frontal assault to the tactical offensive, preferred to receive his enemy from the front. Therefore, the defender either changed front, retreated, or kept his flanks so well guarded by troops or features of the terrain that effective tactical turning movements were frequently impossible. Frontal assaults sometimes became inevitable if there were to be any battle at all. Under the circumstances, by the middle of the war, generals on the defensive put much thought into field fortifications and entrenchments and sometimes discovered that the men had thought out the problem for themselves and prepared trenches on their own initiative.

Professional officers on both sides were also receptive to other new technology, notably the steam engine and the telegraph. Steamboats played a vital role, making river supply and combat practical, and one cannot underestimate the role of the rickety Southern rail network in supporting Confederate strategy. Rail movement between main armies in Virginia, Tennessee, and Mississippi facilitated redeployment of small detachments from all over the Confederacy in order to hit the Union army at its perceived weak spots.

Clearly, speedy steam transportation gave new meaning to the Jominian concept of interior lines, which supposed an advantage to a force that was closer to separated enemy contingents than they were to each other, and therefore permitted that force to concentrate first against one enemy contingent and then the other before they would be able to concentrate in response. Steam could provide an advantage equivalent to interior lines to the side that had the most conveniently located railroads. In theory, possession of interior lines could be countered by simultaneous advances of two or more forces of the adversary. The most notable examples of simultaneous advances are the campaigns of Ulysses S. Grant and Sherman during the last year of the war, although Abraham Lincoln and H. W. Halleck had ordered such advances in late 1862. But such movements required swift relay of information and orders. Thus, the telegraph was an essential partner with the steamboat and railroad in permitting coordinated advances or rapid concentrations.

Strategy

The technology of transportation, information, and rifle-muskets, plus extensive use of entrenchments, created the stalemate that marked the Civil War. The major goal of strategy on both sides was to break that stalemate. American generals had learned about the defensive power of entrenchments at West Point and saw the offensive potential of the turning movement in the Mexican War. Indeed, the turning movement was the motif of most Civil War campaigns, because it was a potentially effective means of breaking the impasse by avoiding bloody frontal offensives against entrenchments. Yet armies moved over great distances and still fought bloody battles without decisive result.

Opening Strategies. Initially the Union considered a logistic strategy, as typified by the proposals of Winfield Scott, the general in chief of the Union army, who had demonstrated the utility of the turning movement in the Mexican War. Scott sought to avoid bloody battles caused by attacking large armies. Instead, he sought to deprive the Confederacy of military resources. A naval blockade would be established along the Confederacy's coastline, and an army of eighty thousand men and another naval force would operate on the Mississippi River to turn Southern positions and bisect the Confederacy. Labeled the "Anaconda Plan" because it was aimed at squeezing the Confederacy to death, Scott's plan was not adopted because of the impatience of Union politicians who expected quick victory.

Nevertheless, progress along the Mississippi was satisfactory, and the Union had substantial control of the river after July 1863. On the other hand, the Union blockade of the Atlantic and Gulf coasts was not particularly effective. Many blockade runners got through the blockade successfully. At the port of Wilmington alone, for example, over 80 percent of Confederate attempts to run the blockade were successful. This result was replicated elsewhere, as the Confederacy purchased vessels with high speeds and low profiles that made it relatively easy to evade the blockade. Moreover, ships of the blockading squadrons were limited by the amount of coal they could carry. Rapid consumption of fuel and frequent breakdowns meant much time spent off-station either recoaling or repairing.

President Jefferson Davis initially attempted a comprehensive defense of the entire Confederacy, as illustrated in 1861 when Albert Sidney Johnston did not concentrate his troops pending possible enemy threats in Kentucky, but rather established what historian Archer Jones has characterized as a "system of strong points with troops attached to them," called a cordon defense. Davis admitted this decision to be wrong after setbacks at Fort Henry, Fort Donelson, and Roanoke Island, because it dispersed Confederate forces rather than concentrated them. The early emphasis on territorial defense, however, not only met the political need to sustain morale but also served the military need to protect Confederate resources. For example, with the only important ironworks in the Confederacy in 1861 located in Richmond—the Tredegar company—that city's defense became vital.

The New Confederate Strategy. Davis soon rejected passive defense and pursued instead an "offensive-defensive" strategy that frequently employed raids. Davis's strategy was also politically motivated: by going on the offensive, he might influence Northern elections and increase the chance of foreign recognition. In this effort time was on the Confederates' side; the longer they could keep armies in the field, the greater the political impact of their offensive victories.

Offensive-Defensive. Davis's strategy called for a defensive posture that would emphasize the strategic turning movement for both offensive and defensive purposes. In the strategic (as opposed to tactical) turning movement, one placed one's own army at a favorable point on the adversary's line of communication, forcing him to recover his communications by attacking on ground of one's choice. In this way, one could seize the advantage of the tactical defensive when on the strategic offensive. Although relying on defense, stressed historian Frank E. Vandiver, Confederates would exploit opportunities for counterattacks. The offensive-defensive enabled the South to take maximum advantage of its vast geography and the supremacy of the defense. Confederates were forced to trade space for time. A retreating force moved faster than its pursuer, for it could hinder pursuit by destroying bridges, blocking roads, or taking up rails, and while it moved toward its base it gathered more troops as it relieved itself of the obligation to guard bridges, junctions, and population centers. Some historians have been critical of the offensive-defensive; E. Merton Coulter, for example, thought that the defensive was a disaster for the Confederacy, and T. Harry Williams believed that a defensive war meant a long war, a disadvantage to the side with inferior resources. Yet it seems difficult to imagine a better strategy, taking all Southern circumstances into account.

The shift to the offensive-defensive was illustrated by the way in which Confederates met the 1862 threat to Richmond posed by the approach of the Army of the Potomac under George B. McClellan. In order to avoid frontal conflict, McClellan himself planned a strategic turning movement. He went around Joseph E. Johnston by moving his troops south on Chesapeake Bay to Union-held Fortress Monroe, at the tip of the peninsula formed by the York and James rivers. By moving up the peninsula and threatening Richmond, McClellan hoped to force Johnston onto the tactical offensive, thereby giving McClellan the defensive advantage. Typically, turning movements failed to trap defending armies, except at Vicksburg and Appomattox, but they frequently forced retreats. They also provoked counteroffensives to regain lost territory or prevent losing more. Thus the threat to Richmond posed by McClellan's turning movement caused Confederates to attack at Fair Oaks and the Seven Days' Battles, where the South lost a larger percentage of forces engaged than the Federals. The affair was a tactical victory for the Union, but Confederates won a significant strategic and political battle when they forced McClellan back, a move that led to his evacuation of the peninsula. The results were not decisive, however, and McClellan's withdrawal only set the stage for future bloody battles.

Southerners also used the railroad, steamboat, and telegraph for counteroffensive concentrations that embraced almost the entire Confederacy, as in the Shiloh and Chickamauga campaigns. Prior to the Shiloh campaign, Halleck, Grant, and Flag Officer Andrew Foote had conducted a grand turning movement in the West, capturing

Forts Henry and Donelson in February 1862, turning the Confederates out of Columbus and Nashville, and forcing them to abandon their cordon defense. Under the influence of P. G. T. Beauregard, however, Confederates used the railroad, steamboat, and telegraph to prepare a counteroffensive to win back western Tennessee in spring 1862 by concentrating in northern Mississippi troops from all over the middle and western South. This plan was in accord with Davis's offensive-defensive strategy; the goal was to drive back Grant, who was on the Tennessee River, before the army of Gen. Don Carlos Buell could join him. Surprise at Shiloh was complete, and Grant was driven back to the protection of his gunboats. Maneuverable armies with rifle-muskets proved virtually indestructible, however, and when Buell reached Grant the tables were turned. Confederates lost their gains on the second day and withdrew to Corinth, Mississippi, evacuating it a month later when menaced by Halleck's leisurely advance. Since the South lost a greater percent of forces engaged than the North, the campaign proved to be a military defeat, and the loss of territory produced serious political attrition in the Confederacy.

The Confederate counteroffensive concentration at Chickamauga came in response to Gen. Braxton Bragg's retreat from Tennessee to northern Georgia in the summer of 1863. After threatening to turn Buell and forcing the Union general to retreat to the Ohio River, Bragg was himself forced back by Buell's successor, William S. Rosecrans, who conducted a series of turning movements against him. Bragg's retreat, however, provided the Confederates the occasion to implement a long-contemplated offensive plan—to make another concentration by rail. Part of a corps from the Army of Northern Virginia under the command of James Longstreet, plus other troops from eastern Tennessee, Mississippi, and northern Georgia, were sent to Bragg. Longstreet arrived in time to take an important part in the September 1863 Battle of Chickamauga, driving the Union forces into Chattanooga, where they remained under siege for over a month. Although the two most important Confederate concentrations in space, Shiloh and Chickamauga, did not lead to ultimate Confederate victory, they nonetheless bought time and caused Union planners to prepare their future course of action more carefully than they had before.

Politics and Raids. As the war progressed, Davis added a political element to his strategy. Tentatively in 1862, but definitely in 1864, he sought to influence Union politics, with some limited success, as the peace Democrats illustrated in their 1864 platform. Understanding the political overtones of Davis's thinking helps to understand some otherwise inexplicable Confederate actions, notably the 1862 movements north by Robert E. Lee and Bragg, and the 1864 replacement with the aggressive John Bell Hood of

Joseph E. Johnston. Both actions were attempts to undermine Northern morale by inflicting defeats upon the Union Army and thus affect Federal elections.

Davis's plans to influence the Union elections of 1864 depended upon clear Confederate victories, and Johnston's retreats, however skillful, did not contribute to a political strategy because they were perceived as defeats by Confederate civilians. Johnston was therefore replaced by Hood, who attacked Sherman, failed to drive him back, and retreated into the defenses around Atlanta. Once more Sherman employed a turning movement, forcing Hood's withdrawal from Atlanta on September 2, 1864. Because of Atlanta's symbolic significance, Confederate morale was significantly weakened.

Throughout the war, the Confederate leadership had relied on raids to supplement major offensive and defensive movements. Raids maintained the offensive initiative and involved a minimum of bloody contact with the enemy. They were part of a logistic strategy aimed at crippling the Federals by undermining their supply. For example, in late 1862 Grant, using Memphis as his base, had advanced south along the railroad in an attempt to turn Vicksburg from favorable ground to the east. The Confederates stopped him at Oxford, Mississippi, when Earl Van Dorn raided Grant's supplies at Holly Springs and Nathan Bedford Forrest simultaneously raided Grant's railroad in Tennessee. These raids, involving a minimum of contact with the Federals, temporarily stopped the advance of a 40,000-man Union army. The Confederate raids forced Grant to cope with attacks on his railroads and supply depots by basing his army on the river, keeping limited communications, using interior lines, and living off the land. Grant persisted, until in April 1863 he crossed his troops over to the west bank of the Mississippi, marched south of Vicksburg, and ferried back to the east bank. Grant turned Vicksburg and forced the surrender of the city and 29,000 men on July 4, 1863.

Raids also had political effect. The cavalry raids that defeated Grant's December 1862 march on Vicksburg, frustrated the summer 1863 advance of Buell on Chattanooga, and delayed for months offensive action by Rosecrans against Bragg all raised Southern morale. Although such small raids were very helpful to the Confederate cause, major moves north, such as Lee's raid into Maryland in 1862, Bragg's invasion of Kentucky in 1862, and Lee's raid into Pennsylvania in 1863, proved to be less valuable owing to heavy casualties and the political attrition created by civilians' perceptions of defeat when the Confederate armies withdrew, as raiders inevitably had to do. Although it seemed so to those on the home front, Sharpsburg was not part of an invasion, for Lee aimed not to occupy territory, but only to supply his troops on Northern soil, gather recruits, encourage foreign recognition, influence the Union's fall elections, and encourage Northern peace movements.

Lee's hopes were largely in vain, for although he won a tactical victory at Sharpsburg, Confederates suffered twice the percentage of casualties than the Union and then retreated. Confederate civilians, untutored in the subtleties of military strategy, looked upon the battle as a defeat, perceiving that Confederates had gained territory and then lost it.

Events proceeded no better for Lee in 1863. He planned a second raid across the Potomac into Pennsylvania to secure supplies from Union territory, leaving the resources of the Shenandoah Valley available for the following fall. As in 1862, however, the Confederacy ran a risk. If Lee returned to Virginia too soon after major battle, the public on both sides would assume that he had been defeated. Nevertheless, Lee attacked in a three-day battle at Gettysburg, was twice repulsed, and withdrew. Even if Lee had won a tactical victory, withdrawal, and the consequent drop in civilian morale, would have been inevitable: his foragers were unable to fan out widely in the face of the enemy. Some scholars have seen in Lee's operations an effort to win the war by destroying the enemy army in battle. But his use of raids for supply makes this thesis doubtful. Like so many other Confederates, Lee hoped for victory by political means, expecting the Republican party to be displaced by Democratic peace advocates in the 1864 elections.

The New Federal Strategy. Even with the fall of Atlanta in 1864, the war was still in a strategic stalemate. After three years, Tennessee was the only Confederate state to be substantially restored to the Union. The problem of continued stalemate has caused historians such as Archer Jones and Russell F. Weigley to reinterpret Grant's later strategy. Grant understood the importance of river transport, and if he appeared to rely on a strategy of attrition, it was not by choice. Once Grant became general in chief, writes Weigley, he sought "the utter destruction of the Confederacy's capacity to wage war," although he preferred enemy destruction that was due to "capture, not . . . attrition and ultimate annihilation." In the spring of 1864 now General in Chief Grant recognized the difficulties of weakening the Confederates by conquering enough of the South to deprive them of supplies and recruits. Progress was too slow and garrisons in occupied territory absorbed too many men.

Instead Grant planned to use simultaneous advances to counter Confederate interior lines. The telegraph naturally played a vital role in Grant's plans, which called for raids to isolate Confederate soldiers from their supplies by destruction of the railroads and other facilities that provided them. But none of the raids took place until November 1864, when Sherman began his march from Atlanta through Georgia to Savannah. Facing token opposition, Sherman took only a month to devastate an area of Georgia about 50 miles wide and 250 miles long. By February 1865 he had turned north to raid the Carolinas. Sherman saw clearly the tremendous nine months, and the Southern army was well on its way to exhaustion. Steady attrition destroyed Southern morale, will, and psychological capacity to resist. Events had forced the Union to adopt a raiding logistic strategy, and in the end, as Archer Jones remarks, "political attrition had won the war before the military attrition of Grant's logistic strategy could bring military victory." But Davis's offensive-defensive strategy, supplementing a defensive posture with raids, turning movements, and offensive concentrations, had enabled the Confederacy to fight much longer than anyone could have predicted from a simple comparison of Union and Confederate resources.

[*For further discussion of specific technological advances in weaponry, see* Arms, Weapons, and Ammunition. *See also entries on the numerous biographical figures and campaigns and battles mentioned herein.*]

BIBLIOGRAPHY

Beringer, Richard E., Herman Hattaway, Archer Jones, and William N. Still, Jr. *Why the South Lost the Civil War.* Athens, Ga., 1986.

Hattaway, Herman, and Archer Jones. *How the North Won: A Military History of the Civil War.* Urbana, Ill., 1983.

Jones, Archer. *Civil War Command and Strategy: The Process of Victory and Defeat.* New York, 1992.

Mahon, John K. "Civil War Infantry Assault Tactics." *Military Affairs* 25 (Summer 1961): 57–68.

Nelson, Larry E. *Bullets, Ballots, and Rhetoric: Confederate Policy for the United States Presidential Contest of 1864.* University, Ala., 1980.

Vandiver, Frank E. "Jefferson Davis and Confederate Strategy." In *The American Tragedy: The Civil War in Retrospect.* Edited by Bernard Mayo. Hampden-Sydney, 1959.

Vandiver, Frank E. *Rebel Brass: The Confederate Command System.* Baton Rouge, La., 1956.

Vandiver, Frank E. *Their Tattered Flags: The Epic of the Confederacy.* New York, 1970.

Weigley, Russell F. "American Strategy from Its Beginnings through the First World War." In *Makers of Modern Strategy: From Machiavelli to the Nuclear Age.* Edited by Peter Paret, with Gordon A. Craig and Felix Gilbert. Princeton, 1986.

RICHARD E. BERINGER

Causes of Defeat

Efforts to explain the causes of Confederate defeat in the Civil War have generated a great deal of controversy over the past century and a quarter. The debate began with the publication in 1866 of *The Lost Cause* by Richmond journalist Edward Pollard, who blamed Jefferson Davis, and it continues today. Yet despite all the efforts to determine "Why the North Won" or "Why the South Lost"—the difference in phraseology is sometimes significant—there is no consensus among students of the

ULYSSES S. GRANT.   NATIONAL ARCHIVES

political and military impact such raids would have on Confederate morale and desire to continue the war.

While Sherman was making his way to Atlanta, Grant kept Lee so busy in Virginia that he could not again send Longstreet west, but Grant's efforts to gain decisive victories only forced Lee into the trenches around Petersburg and Richmond and began a siege. This dubious achievement cost Grant so many casualties that Northern morale was seriously compromised. Confederate civilians took heart from Grant's difficulties, but by April 1865 he had finally stretched Confederate defenses so thin that Lee was forced to evacuate Richmond and Petersburg and flee west, hoping to turn south into North Carolina and join Joseph E. Johnston. Lee got as far as Appomattox Courthouse, where he was turned by Union troops and surrendered to Grant on April 9, 1865. The Confederate attempt to unite Lee and Johnston failed.

The military, social, and political will of the Confederacy was drained. The South was not defeated by a strategy of annihilation, for 326,000 men were still available at the end of 1864, but desertion had almost doubled in the previous war. The best way to approach the problem is to review the principal explanations for Confederate defeat with an eye to the defects and virtues of each.

Major Explanations

Most interpretations fall into one of two categories: internal or external. Internal explanations focus mainly or entirely on the Confederacy and usually phrase the question as "Why did the South lose?" External interpretations look at both the Union and the Confederacy and often phrase it as "Why did the North win?" No matter which approach they take, most analyses assume, at least implicitly, that Union victory was inevitable. But this is a fallacy. The Confederacy had several opportunities to win the war and came close to doing so more than once.

Overwhelming Numbers and Resources. The earliest and perhaps most durable explanation of Confederate defeat is an external one. It was advanced by Robert E. Lee himself in his farewell address to his soldiers at Appomattox: "The Army of Northern Virginia has been compelled to yield to overwhelming numbers and resources." This explanation enabled Southerners to preserve their pride in the courage and skill of Confederate soldiers, to reconcile defeat with their sense of honor, even to maintain faith in the righteousness of their cause while admitting that it had been lost. The Confederacy, in other words, lost the war not because it fought badly, or because its soldiers lacked courage, or because its cause was wrong, but simply because the enemy had more men and guns.

This thesis remains alive and well today. In a symposium at Gettysburg College in 1958 on "Why the North Won the Civil War," historian Richard N. Current reviewed the statistics of Northern demographic and economic preponderance—two and one-half times the South's population,

WILMER MCLEAN'S HOUSE. This house in Appomattox, Virginia, was the site of Robert E. Lee's surrender to Ulysses S. Grant on April 9, 1865.

NATIONAL ARCHIVES

three times its railroad capacity, nine times its industrial production, and so on—and concluded that "surely in view of the disparity of resources, it would have taken a miracle . . . to enable the South to win. As usual, God was on the side of the heaviest battalions." And in 1990, Civil War historian Shelby Foote declared that "the North fought that war with one hand behind its back." If necessary, "the North simply would have brought that other arm from behind its back. I don't think the South ever had a chance to win that war."

Many Southerners, however, began to question this overwhelming-numbers-and-resources thesis soon after the war, and by the twentieth century many of them had rejected it. This explanation did credit to Confederate skill and courage in holding out for so long against such great odds, but it seemed to do little credit to their intelligence. After all, Southerners in 1861 were well aware of their disadvantages in numbers and resources. Yet they went to war confident of victory. Were they naive? Irrational? Inexcusably arrogant?

As they pondered this matter, numerous Southerners—and non-Southerners—concluded that overwhelming numbers and resources were not the cause of Northern victory after all. History offered many examples of a society winning a war against greater odds than the Confederacy faced. The outstanding example in the minds of everyone in 1861 was the United States in its War of Independence against the most powerful nation in the world. In our own post-Vietnam generation we too are familiar with the truth that victory does not always ride with the heaviest battalions.

To win the Civil War, Union armies had to invade, conquer, and occupy the South and to destroy the capacity of Confederate armies to wage war and of the Southern economy to sustain it. But victory for the Confederacy did not require anything like such a huge effort. Confederate armies did not have to invade and conquer the North in order to win the war; they needed only to hold out long enough to force the North to the conclusion that the price of conquering the South and crushing its capacity to wage war was too high, as Britain had concluded in 1781 and as the United States concluded with respect to Vietnam in 1972. Most Southerners thought in 1861 that their resources were more than sufficient to win on these terms. And even after losing the war, many of them continued to insist they could have won. Former Confederate Gen. Joseph E. Johnston wrote in the 1870s that the Southern people had not been "guilty of the high crime of undertaking a war without the means of waging it successfully." And former Gen. P. G. T. Beauregard wrote in 1884: "No people ever warred for independence with more relative advantages than the Confederacy."

Although Johnston's and Beauregard's memoirs had a self-serving quality—they too blamed Jefferson Davis, partly in order to deflect blame from themselves—their assertions find plenty of echoes in modern studies. Most historians in the twentieth century have rejected the overwhelming-numbers-and-resources thesis as a sufficient explanation for Confederate defeat. Instead, they have advanced a variety of *internal* explanations.

Internal Conflicts. One such approach focused on what might be termed the internal-conflict thesis. Several variations on this theme have emerged. One of the earliest and most persistent was spelled out by Frank Owsley in his book *State Rights in the Confederacy*, published in 1925. Owsley maintained that the centrifugal force of state rights fatally crippled the central government's efforts to prosecute the war. Owsley singled out Governors Joseph E. Brown of Georgia and Zebulon Vance of North Carolina as guilty of obstructive policies, of withholding men and arms from the Confederate army to build up their state militias, and of petty political warfare against the Davis administration. On the tombstone of the Confederacy, wrote Owsley, should be carved the epitaph: "Died of State Rights."

A variant on the state rights thesis focuses on the resistance by many Southerners, including Vice President Alexander H. Stephens, to such war measures as conscription, certain kinds of taxes, suspension of the writ of habeas corpus, and martial law. Opponents based their denunciations of these "despotic" measures on grounds of civil liberty, or state rights, or democratic individualism, or all three combined. This opposition crippled the army's ability to fill its ranks, obtain food and supplies, and stem desertions. It hindered the government's ability to curb antiwar activists who divided the Southern people and sapped their will to win. The persistence during the war of the democratic practices of individualism, dissent, and carping criticism of the government caused historian David Donald in 1958 to amend that inscription on the Confederacy's tombstone to: "Died of Democracy."

Three flaws mar the power of the internal-conflict thesis to explain Confederate defeat. First, recent scholarship has demonstrated that the negative effects of state rights sentiment have been much exaggerated. State leaders like Brown and Vance did indeed feud with the Davis administration. But at the same time these governors as well as others took the initiative in many areas of mobilization: raising and equipping regiments, providing help for the families of soldiers, organizing war production and supply, building coastal defenses, and so on. Rather than hindering the efforts of the government in Richmond, the activities of states augmented them. "On balance," concludes a recent study, "state contributions to the war effort far outweighed any unnecessary diversions of resources to local defense."

As for the died-of-democracy thesis, it appears that, on the contrary, the Confederate government enforced the draft, suppressed dissent, and suspended civil liberties at least as thoroughly as did the Union government. The

Confederacy enacted conscription a year before the Union and raised a larger proportion of its troops by drafting than did the North. And though Abraham Lincoln used his power to suspend the writ of habeas corpus and to arrest antiwar activists more vigorously than did Jefferson Davis, the Confederate army suppressed Unionists with as much ruthlessness, especially in eastern Tennessee and western North Carolina, as Union forces wielded against Copperheads in the North or Confederate sympathizers in the border states.

This points to a second flaw in the internal-conflict thesis: we might term it "the fallacy of reversibility." If the North had lost the war—which came close to happening on more than one occasion—the same thesis of internal conflict could be advanced to explain *Northern* defeat. Bitter divisions existed in the North over conscription, taxes, suspension of habeas corpus, martial law—and significantly, in the case of the North, over emancipation as a war aim. If anything, the opposition was more powerful in the North than in the South. Lincoln endured greater vilification than Davis during much of the war. And Lincoln had to face a campaign for reelection in the midst of the most crucial military operations of the war—an election that for a time it appeared he would lose, an outcome that might well have led to peace negotiations with an independent Confederacy. This did not happen, but its narrow avoidance illustrates the intense conflict within the Northern polity that neutralized the similar but perhaps less divisive conflicts within the South as an explanation for Confederate defeat.

Third, one might ask whether the internal conflicts between state and central governments or among different factions and leaders were greater in the Confederacy than they had been in the United States during the Revolution. Americans in the war of 1776 were more divided than Southerners in the war of 1861, yet the United States won its independence and the Confederacy did not. This suggests that we must look elsewhere for an explanation of Confederate defeat.

Internal Alienation. Similar problems taint another interpretation that overlaps the internal-conflict thesis. This one might be termed the internal-alienation argument. Much scholarship recently has focused on two large groups in the South that were or became alienated from the Confederate war effort: nonslaveholding whites, and slaves.

The nonslaveholders were two-thirds of the Confederacy's white population. Many of them, especially in mountainous and up-country regions of small farms and few slaves, opposed secession in 1861. They formed significant enclaves of Unionism in western Virginia where they created a new Union state, in eastern Tennessee where they carried out guerrilla operations against the Confederacy and contributed many soldiers to the Union army, and

elsewhere in the upland South. Other nonslaveholders who supported the Confederacy and fought for it became alienated over time because of ruinous inflation, shortages of food and salt, high taxes, and a growing suspicion that they were risking their lives and property to defend slavery. Clauses in the conscription law that allowed a drafted man to buy a substitute and exempted from the draft one white man on every plantation with twenty or more slaves gave rise to a bitter cry that it was a rich man's war but a poor man's fight. Many families of soldiers suffered malnutrition as food shortages and inflation worsened. Bread riots occurred in parts of the South during 1863—most notably in Richmond itself. Numerous soldiers deserted from the army to return home and support their families. Several historians have argued that this seriously weakened the Confederate war effort and brought eventual defeat.

The alienation of many Southern whites was matched by the alienation of a large portion of that two-fifths of the Southern population that was black and slave. Slaves were essential to the Confederate war effort. As the South's principal labor force, they enabled the Confederacy to mobilize three-quarters of its white men of military age into the army—compared with about half in the North. Slavery was therefore a source of strength to the Confederacy, but it was also a source of weakness. Most slaves who reflected on their stake in the war believed that a Northern victory would bring freedom. Tens of thousands voted with their feet for the Union by escaping to Federal lines, where the North converted their labor power and eventually their military manpower into a Union asset. This leakage of labor from the Confederacy and the unrest of slaves who remained behind retarded Southern economic efficiency and output.

The alienation of these two large blocs of the Southern people seems a plausible explanation of Confederate defeat. But some caveats are necessary. The alienated elements of the American population in the Revolution were larger than those in the South during the Civil War. Many slaves ran away to the British, and the Loyalists undoubtedly weakened the American cause more than disaffected nonslaveholders weakened the Confederate cause. It is easy to exaggerate the amount of nonslaveholder alienation in the South; some historians have done precisely that. And though large numbers of slaves ran off to Union lines, this happened only where Union military and naval forces invaded and controlled Confederate territory—an external factor—and the great majority of slaves remained at home.

But perhaps the most important weakness of the internal-alienation thesis is that same fallacy of reversibility mentioned earlier. Large numbers of the Northern people were bitterly alienated from the Lincoln administration's war policies. Their opposition weakened and at times threatened to cripple the Union war effort. About one-third of the border-state whites actively supported the Confederacy, and many of the remainder were at best lukewarm Unionists. Guerrilla warfare behind Union lines occurred in these regions on a larger scale than in Unionist areas behind Confederate lines. The Democratic party in the free states denounced conscription, emancipation, certain war taxes, the suspension of habeas corpus, and other measures. Democrats exploited these issues in an aggressive attempt to paralyze the Lincoln administration. The peace wing of the party—Copperheads—opposed the war itself.

If the South had its class conflict over the theme of a rich man's war and poor man's fight, so did the North. If the Confederacy had its bread riots, the Union had its more dangerous and threatening draft riots. If many soldiers deserted from Confederate armies, a similarly large percentage deserted from Union armies until late in the war. If the South had its slaves who wanted Yankee victory and freedom, the North had its Democrats and border-state whites who strongly opposed emancipation and withheld support from the war because of it. Internal alienation, therefore, provides no more of a sufficient explanation for Confederate defeat than internal conflict, because the similar—perhaps greater—alienation within the North neutralized this factor, too.

Lack of Will. Another explanation for Confederate defeat overlaps the internal-conflict and internal-alienation theses. This one can be termed the lack-of-will thesis. It holds that the Confederacy could have won if the Southern people had possessed the will to make the sacrifices necessary for victory. In his book *The Confederate States of America,* the North Carolina–born E. Merton Coulter declared flatly that the Confederacy lost because its "people did not will hard enough and long enough to win." And in 1986 the four authors of *Why the South Lost the Civil War* echoed this conclusion: "We contend that lack of will constituted the decisive deficiency in the Confederate arsenal."

The lack-of-will thesis has three main facets. First is an argument that the Confederacy did not have a strong sense of nationalism. The Confederate States of America, it is said, did not exist long enough to give their people that mystical faith called nationalism or patriotism. Southerners did not have as firm a conviction of fighting for a country, a flag, a deep-rooted political and cultural tradition, as Northerners did. Southerners had been Americans before they became Confederates, and many of them—especially former Whigs—had opposed secession. So when the going got tough, their residual Americanism reemerged and triumphed over their newly minted, glossy Confederate nationalism.

This is a dubious argument. If the rhetoric of Confederate nationalism did not contain as many references to abstract symbols or concepts like flag, country, Constitution, and democracy as did Union rhetoric, Southerners felt a much stronger and more visceral commitment to defending land, home, and family from invasion by "Yankee vandals." In this sense, Confederate nationalism was if anything stronger than its Union counterpart. In their letters and diaries, Southerners expressed a greater determination to "die in the last ditch" than Northerners did. As the Confederate War Department clerk John Beauchamp Jones expressed it in his diary in 1863, the Southern people had far more at stake in the war than did Northerners: "Our men *must* prevail in combat, or lose their property, country, freedom, everything. . . . On the other hand, the enemy, in yielding the contest, may retire into their own country, and possess everything they enjoyed before the war began."

A Union officer who was captured in the Battle of Atlanta on July 22, 1864, and spent the rest of the war in Southern prisons, wrote in his diary on October 4 that from what he had seen in the South "the End of the War . . . is some time hence as the Idea of the Rebs giving up until they are completely subdued is all Moonshine they submit to privations that would not be believed unless seen." The Southern people persisted through far greater hardships and suffering than Northern people experienced. Northerners almost threw in the towel in the summer of 1864 because of casualty rates that Southerners had endured for more than two years. Thus it seems difficult to accept the thesis of lack of will stemming from weak nationalism as a cause of Confederate defeat.

A second facet of the lack-of-will interpretation is what might be termed the guilt theme—the suggestion that many Southern whites felt moral qualms about slavery, which undermined their will to fight a war to preserve it. The South, wrote historian Kenneth M. Stampp, suffered from a "weakness of morale" caused by "widespread doubts and apprehensions about the validity of the Confederate cause." Defeat rewarded these guilt-ridden Southerners with "a way to rid themselves of the moral burden of slavery," so a good many of them, "perhaps subconsciously, welcomed . . . defeat." Other historians with a bent for social science concepts agree that the Confederates' morale was undermined by the "cognitive dissonance" of fighting a war to establish their own liberty but at the same time to keep 4 million black people in slavery.

This also seems doubtful. To be sure, one can turn up quotations from Southern whites expressing reservations about slavery, and one can find statements by Southerners after the war expressing relief that it was gone. But the latter are suspect in their sincerity. And in any event one can find far more quotations on the other side—assertions that slavery was a positive good, the best labor system and the best system of social relations between what were deemed a superior and an inferior race. As one study of former slave owners after emancipation expressed it, "nothing in the postwar behavior and attitudes of these people suggested that the ownership of slaves had necessarily compromised their values or tortured their consciences."

In any case, most Confederates thought of themselves as fighting not for slavery but for independence. If slavery weakened Southern morale to the point of causing defeat, it should have weakened American morale in the Revolution of 1776 even more, for Americans of that generation felt more guilt about slavery than did Southerners of 1861. That sentiment helped produce the abolition of slavery in Northern states and the large number of manumissions in the upper South in the generation after 1776. And it is hard to see that Robert E. Lee, for example, who did have reservations about slavery—and about secession for that matter—made a lesser contribution to Confederate success than, say, Braxton Bragg, who believed firmly in both slavery and secession.

A third facet of the lack-of-will interpretation focuses on religion. At the outset, Southern clergymen preached that God was on the side of the Confederacy. But as the war went on and the South suffered so much death, disaster, and destruction, some Southerners began to wonder if God was on their side after all. Perhaps, on the contrary, he was punishing them for their sins. "Can we believe in the justice of Providence," asked one prominent Confederate, "or must we conclude that we are after all wrong?" Several historians have pointed to these religious doubts as a source of defeatism and loss of will that corroded Confederate morale and contributed to Southern defeat.

But note the phrase *loss of will* in the preceding sentence: not *lack,* but *loss.* There is a difference—a significant difference. A people whose armies are destroyed or captured, railroads wrecked, factories and cities burned, ports seized, countryside occupied, and crops laid waste quite naturally lose their will to continue the fight because they have lost the means to do so. That is what happened to the Confederacy. If one analyzes carefully the lack-of-will thesis as it is spelled out in several studies, it becomes clear that the real topic is *loss* of the will to carry on, not an initial *lack* of will. The book *Why the South Lost the Civil War,* which builds its interpretation around the *lack*-of-will thesis, abounds with *loss*-of-will phraseology: Union military victories "contributed to the *dissolution* of Confederate power and will . . . *created* war weariness and *destroyed* morale. . . . The loss of Atlanta and Sherman's march, combined with Lincoln's reelection, severely *crippled* Confederate will to win. . . . By 1865 the Confederacy had *lost* its will for sacrifice" (italics added).

This is the right way to put it. The cause-effect relationship is in the correct order: military defeat caused loss of will, not vice versa. It introduces external agency as a crucial explanatory factor—the agency of Northern military success, especially in the eight months after August 1864. The main defect of the lack-of-will thesis and of the internal-conflict and internal-alienation theses discussed earlier is that they attribute Confederate defeat to factors intrinsic to the South and tend to ignore that outside force battering away at the Confederacy. Thus the authors of *Why the South Lost the Civil War* conclude flatly, in the face of much of their own evidence, that "the Confederacy succumbed to internal rather than external causes." The overwhelming-numbers-and-resources interpretation at least had the merit of recognizing the external aspects of Confederate defeat, although the weaknesses of that interpretation remain.

Inferior Leadership. Another category of interpretation with an external dimension might seem to resolve the dilemma of explanation. This one focuses on leadership. Numerous historians of both Northern and Southern nativity have argued that the North developed superior leadership that became the main factor in ultimate Union victory. This literature deals mainly with three levels of leadership.

First, generalship: The Confederacy benefited from better generalship in the first half of the war, particularly in the eastern theater and at the tactical level. But by 1864 a group of generals, including Ulysses S. Grant, William Tecumseh Sherman, and Philip Sheridan, had emerged to top commands in the North with a grasp of the need for coordinated offensives in all theaters, a concept of the total-war strategy necessary to win this conflict, the skill to carry out the strategy, and the relentless determination to keep pressing it despite a high cost in casualties. In this interpretation the Confederacy had brilliant tactical leaders like Lee, Stonewall Jackson, Nathan Bedford Forrest, and others who also showed strategic talent in limited theaters. But the South had no generals who rose to the level of overall strategic ability demonstrated by Grant and Sherman. Lee's strategic vision was limited to the Virginia theater, where his influence concentrated Confederate resources at the expense of the western theaters in which the Confederacy suffered from poor generalship and where it really lost the war.

The second level where numerous historians have identified superior Northern leadership is in management of military supply and logistics. In Secretary of War Edwin M. Stanton, Quartermaster General Montgomery Meigs, Assistant Secretary of the Navy Gustavus Fox, Chief of U.S. Military Railroads Herman Haupt, and many other officials the North developed by 1862 a group of top- and middle-level managers who organized the Northern economy and the flow of supplies to Union armies with unprecedented efficiency and abundance. The Confederacy could not match Northern skill in organization and administration. In this interpretation, it was not the North's greater resources but

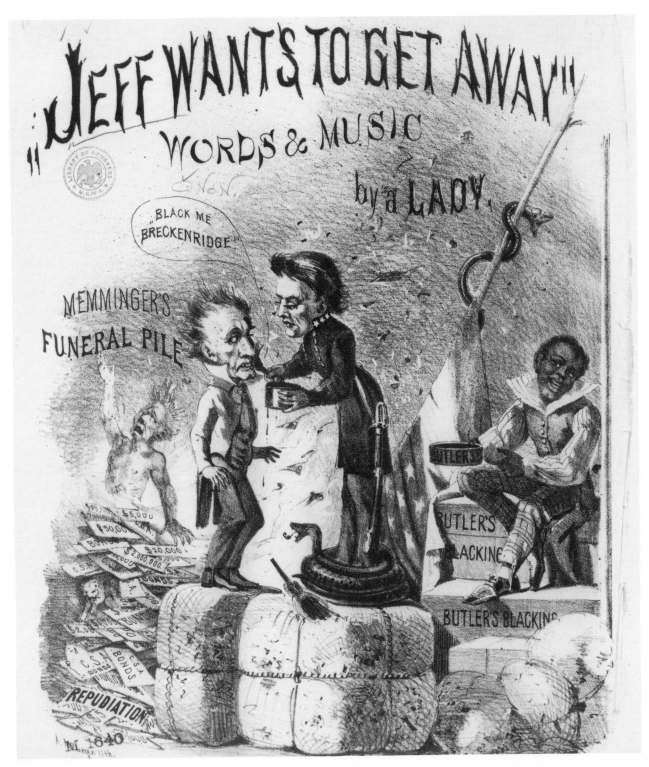

"JEFF WANTS TO GET AWAY."   Illustrated sheet music cover for a Northern song lampooning the imminent collapse of the Confederacy. Jefferson Davis, standing on a bale of cotton, demands that John C. Breckinridge "black me" (presumably to facilitate his escape). At left, Secretary of the Treasury Christopher G. Memminger drowns in worthless Confederate bonds. "Butler's Blacking" at right probably refers to the Union general Benjamin F. Butler, who had forced the Confederacy to recognize the status of African American troops. A copperhead, symbol used by Republicans to vilify Peace Democrats, curls around Breckinridge's feet. Another coils around the broken staff of a Union flag. Lithograph by Alexander McLean on wove paper. Published in St. Louis, Missouri, 1864.

its better management of those resources that won the war.

Third, presidential leadership: Lincoln proved to be a better commander in chief than Davis. A surprising number of Southern-born historians join Northerners in this conclusion. Two quotations to illustrate the point: Northerner James Ford Rhodes wrote at the beginning of the twentieth century that "the preponderating asset of the North proved to be Lincoln." And in 1960 the Southern-born historian David Potter put it even more strongly: "If the Union and Confederacy had exchanged presidents with one another, the Confederacy might have won its independence."

This may overstate the case. In any event, a broad consensus exists that Lincoln was more eloquent than Davis in expressing war aims, more successful in communicating with the people, more skillful as a political leader in keeping factions working together for a common goal, better able to endure criticism and work with his critics. Lincoln was flexible and pragmatic, and possessed a sense of humor that helped him survive the stress of his job; Davis was austere, rigid, humorless, with the type of personality that readily made enemies. Lincoln had a strong physical constitution; Davis was frequently prostrated by illness. Lincoln picked good administrative subordinates (with some exceptions) and knew how to delegate authority; Davis went through six secretaries of war in four years and spent a great amount of time on petty administrative details that he should have left to subordinates. A disputatious man, Davis sometimes seemed to prefer winning an argument to winning the war; Lincoln was happy to lose an argument if it would help win the war. Davis's well-known feuds with two of the Confederacy's top generals, Beauregard and Joseph E. Johnston, undoubtedly hurt the South's war effort.

The thesis of superior Northern leadership seems more convincing than other explanations for Union victory. But once again, caveats are in order. With respect to generalship, even if the North did enjoy an advantage in this respect during the last year or two of the war, the Union army had its faint-hearts and blunderers, its McClellan and Pope and Burnside and Hooker who nearly lost the war to superior Confederate leadership in the East despite what was happening in the West. On more than one occasion the outcome seemed to hang in the balance because of *incompetent* Northern military leadership.

As for Union superiority in the management of production and logistics, this was probably true in most respects. The Northern war effort could draw on a wider field of entrepreneurial skills to mobilize men, resources, technology, industry, and transportation than could the South. Yet the Confederacy could boast some brilliant successes in this area of leadership. Ordnance Chief Josiah Gorgas almost literally turned plowshares into swords, building from scratch an arms and ammunition industry that kept Confederate armies better supplied than had seemed possible at the outset. The Rains brothers, George and Gabriel, accomplished miracles in the establishment of nitrate works, the manufacture of gunpowder, and the development of the explosive mines (then called torpedoes) that were the Confederacy's most potent naval weapon. Secretary of the Navy Stephen R. Mallory's boldness and resourcefulness turned out to be a pleasant surprise. What seems most significant about Confederate logistics is not the obvious deficiencies in railroads and the commissariat—to cite two notorious examples—but rather the ability of some Southern officials to do so much with so little. Instead of losing the war, their efforts went far toward keeping the Confederacy fighting for so long.

Finally, what about Lincoln's superiority to Davis as commander in chief? This might seem self-evident. Yet Lincoln did make mistakes. He went through a half-dozen failures as commanders in the eastern theater before he found the right general. Some of his other military appointments and strategic decisions could justly be criticized. And as late as the summer of 1864, when the war seemed to be going badly, when Grant's forces had suffered enormous casualties to achieve a stalemate at Petersburg and Sherman seemed equally stymied before Atlanta, Lincoln came under great pressure to negotiate peace with the Confederacy. To have done so would have been to admit Northern defeat. Lincoln resisted the pressure, but at what appeared to be the cost of his reelection. If the presidential election had been held in August 1864 instead of November, Lincoln would have lost. He would thus have gone down in history as an also-ran, a loser unequal to the challenge of the greatest crisis in the American experience. And Jefferson Davis might have gone down in history as the great leader of a war of independence, the George Washington of the Southern Confederacy.

That this did not happen was owing to events on the battlefield—principally Sherman's capture of Atlanta and Sheridan's striking victories over Jubal Early in the Shenandoah Valley. These turned Northern opinion from deepest despair in the summer to confident determination by November. This transformation of the Northern will illustrates the point made earlier that the will of either the Northern or the Southern people was primarily the result of military victory rather than a cause of it. Events on the battlefield might have gone the other way on these and other occasions during the war. If they had, the course of the war might have been quite different.

The Factor of Contingency

It is this element of contingency that is missing from generalizations about the cause of Confederate defeat, whether such generalizations focus on external or internal factors. There was nothing inevitable about Northern victory in the war. Nor was Sherman's capture of Atlanta any more inevitable than, say, McClellan's capture of Richmond in June 1862 had been. There were several major turning points, points of contingency when events moved in one direction but could well have moved in another. Two have just been mentioned: McClellan's failure to capture Richmond and Sherman's success in capturing Atlanta. The latter, coupled with Sheridan's victories in the Shenandoah Valley, proved to be the final and decisive turning point toward Union triumph. Two earlier moments of contingency that turned in favor of the North were of equal importance, however.

The first occurred in the fall of 1862. Confederate offensives during the summer had taken Southern armies from their backs to the wall in Mississippi and Virginia almost to the Ohio River and across the Potomac River by September. This was the most ambitious Confederate effort to win European recognition and a victorious peace on Union soil. But in September and October Union armies stopped the invaders at Sharpsburg and at Perryville, Kentucky. This forestalled European intervention, dissuaded Northern voters from repudiating the Lincoln administration by electing a Democratic House of Representatives in the fall of 1862, and gave Lincoln the occasion to issue the Emancipation Proclamation, which enlarged the scope and purpose of the war.

The other major turning point came in the summer of 1863. Before then, during the months between Union defeats at Fredericksburg and Chancellorsville, a time that also witnessed Union failures in the western theater, Northern morale and especially army morale dropped to its lowest point in the war. The usually indomitable Capt. Oliver Wendell Holmes, Jr., recovering from the second of three wounds he received in the war, wrote during the winter of 1862–1863 that "the army is tired with its hard and terrible experience. . . . I've pretty much made up my mind that the South have achieved their independence."

But then came the Battle of Gettysburg and the capture of Vicksburg. This crucial turning point produced Southern cries of despair. At the end of July 1863 Ordnance Chief Gorgas wrote:

One brief month ago we were apparently at the point of success. Lee was in Pennsylvania. . . . Vicksburgh seemed to laugh all Grant's efforts to scorn. . . . Now the picture is just as sombre as it was bright then. . . . It seems incredible that human power could effect such a change in so brief a space. Yesterday we rode on the pinnacle of success—today absolute ruin seems to be our portion. The Confederacy totters to its destruction.

Predictions in July 1863 of the Confederacy's imminent collapse turned out to be premature. More twists and turns marked the road to the end of the war. This only accentuates the importance of contingency. All the factors discussed in this essay—numbers and resources, leadership, will, internal conflicts and alienation—formed the context of the specific events of the war. Separately or collectively, in complex and indirect ways, they influenced the direction that events took at crucial points of contingency. To understand why the Confederacy lost, in the end, we must turn from large generalizations that imply inevitability and study instead the contingency that hung over each military campaign, each battle, each election, each decision during the war. The chain of cause and effect from each of these events to the next will enable us, as with the piece-by-piece completion of a jigsaw puzzle, to get the big picture into some kind of focus.

[See also African Americans in the Union Army; Civil Liberties; Class Conflict; Conscription; Desertion; Morale; Nationalism; Slavery, article on Slavery during the Civil War; State Rights; Taxation.]

BIBLIOGRAPHY

Beringer, Richard E., Herman Hattaway, Archer Jones, and William N. Still, Jr. Why the South Lost the Civil War. Athens, Ga., 1986.

Boritt, Gabor S., ed. Why the Confederacy Lost. New York, 1992.

Coulter, E. Merton. The Confederate States of America, 1861–1865. A History of the South, vol. 7. Baton Rouge, La., 1950.

Donald, David, ed. Why the North Won the Civil War. Baton Rouge, La., 1960.

Escott, Paul D. After Secession: Jefferson Davis and the Failure of Confederate Nationalism. Baton Rouge, La., 1978.

Faust, Drew Gilpin. "Altars of Sacrifice: Confederate Women and the Narratives of War." Journal of American History 76 (1990): 1200–1228.

Faust, Drew Gilpin. The Creation of Confederate Nationalism: Ideology and Identity in the Civil War South. Baton Rouge, La., 1988.

Hattaway, Herman, and Archer Jones. How the North Won: A Military History of the Civil War. Urbana, Ill., 1983.

Owsley, Frank L. State Rights in the Confederacy. Chicago, 1925.

Scarboro, David D. "North Carolina and the Confederacy: The Weakness of States' Rights during the Civil War." North Carolina Historical Review 56 (1979): 133–149.

Tatum, Georgia Lee. Disloyalty in the Confederacy. Chapel Hill, N.C., 1934.

Thomas, Emory. The Confederate Nation, 1861–1865. New York, 1979.

Wesley, Charles H. The Collapse of the Confederacy. Washington, D.C., 1922.

Wiley, Bell Irvin. The Road to Appomattox. Memphis, Tenn., 1956.

Woodworth, Steven E. Jefferson Davis and His Generals: The Failure of Confederate Command in the West. Lawrence, Kans., 1990.

JAMES M. McPHERSON

Losses and Numbers

The Civil War was the bloodiest war in the history of the United States. An estimated 1,166,850 American soldiers became casualties in this conflict, 665,850 of whom died. Disease killed almost twice as many men as bullets and shot. Inadequate medical facilities and a lack of understanding of

TABLE 1. *Civil War Casualties*

CASUALTIES	UNION	CONFEDERATE	TOTAL
Died of Disease	224,000	140,000[a]	364,000[a]
Died in Prison	30,200	26,000[a]	56,200[a]
Missing, Presumed Dead	6,750	not available	
Other Nonbattlefield Deaths	34,800	not available	
Total Nonbattlefield Deaths	**295,750**	**166,000[a]**	**461,750[a]**
Killed in Action	67,100	54,000	121,100
Died of Wounds	43,000	40,000	83,000
Total Battlefield Deaths	**110,100**	**94,000**	**204,100**
Total War-Related Deaths[b]	**405,850**	**260,000[a]**	**665,850[a]**
Nonmortally Wounded	275,000	226,000	501,000
Total Battlefield Casualties[c]	**385,100**	**320,000**	**705,100**
Total Casualties[d]	**680,850**	**486,000[a]**	**1,166,850[a]**

[a]Approximate figure.
[b]Total nonbattlefield deaths plus total battlefield deaths.
[c]Total battlefield deaths plus nonmortally wounded.
[d]Total war-related deaths plus nonmortally wounded.
SOURCE: Data taken from Thomas L. Livermore, *Numbers and Losses in the Civil War in America, 1861–1865*, Boston, 1901, and from E. B. Long and Barbara Long, *The Civil War Day by Day: An Almanac, 1861–1865*, Garden City, N.Y., 1971.

TABLE 2. *Ten Battles with the Highest Casualties*

Battle	Date	CASUALTIES		
		Union	Confederate	Total
Gettysburg	July 1–3, 1863	17,684	22,638	40,322
Seven Days	June 25–July 1, 1862	9,796	19,739	29,535
Chickamauga	Sept. 19–20, 1863	11,413	16,986	28,399
Spotsylvania	May 8–19, 1864	17,500	10,000[a]	27,500[a]
Wilderness	May 5–6, 1864	17,666	7,500[a]	25,166[a]
Shiloh	Apr. 6–7, 1862	13,047	10,694	23,741
Sharpsburg	Sept. 17, 1862	11,657	11,724	23,381
Chancellorsville	May 1–4, 1863	11,116	10,746	21,862
Second Manassas	Aug. 29–30, 1862	10,096	9,108	19,204
Murfreesboro	Dec. 31,1862–Jan. 2, 1863	9,220	9,239	18,459

[a]Approximate figure.
SOURCE: Data taken from Thomas L. Livermore, *Numbers and Losses in the Civil War in America, 1861–1865*, Boston, 1901, and from E. B. Long and Barbara Long, *The Civil War Day by Day: An Almanac, 1861–1865*, Garden City, N.Y., 1971.

the germ theory caused many wounded to perish from infection long after the fighting had ended. Table 1 illustrates the distribution of casualties in both Union and Confederate armies.

Battlefield casualties resulted from a variety of innovations in technology compounded by a profound lack of updated tactics. This gap between technology and tactics— sometimes referred to as the "Tec-Tac Disjoint"—killed many men needlessly. Both armies continued to employ linear tactics even in the face of the withering fire of newly perfected rifled weapons, dooming many of their troops. The

Confederate propensity to attack also led to enormous losses that the South could ill afford. Later in the war, however, both Union and Confederate armies increasingly relied on entrenchments. Table 2 lists the war's ten bloodiest battles, which accounted for 38 percent of all battlefield casualties.

The staggering losses were more damaging to the South, since the North had a sizable advantage in population. In part, the war was decided by attrition. Napoleonic tactics, still in use by most Civil War leaders, advocated moving masses of troops into one cataclysmic battle that would

TABLE 3. *Population and Military Manpower in 1860*

	North[a]	South[b]	Border States[c]
Total Population[d]	19,086,250	9,101,450	3,211,897
Total Males Age 10 to 49[e]	6,128,138	2,837,819	1,019,340
White Males Age 10 to 49	6,057,644	1,712,064	850,552
Black Males Age 10 to 49	70,494	1,125,755[f]	168,788[g]

[a]Includes California, Connecticut, Illinois, Indiana, Iowa, Maine, Massachusetts, Michigan, Minnesota, New Hampshire, New Jersey, New York, Ohio, Pennsylvania, Oregon, Rhode Island, Vermont, and Wisconsin. Population of U.S. territories not included.
[b]Includes the eleven states that had seceded by May 20, 1861: Alabama, Arkansas, Florida, Georgia, Louisiana, Mississippi, North Carolina, South Carolina, Tennessee, Texas, and Virginia.
[c]Includes Delaware, Kentucky, Maryland, Missouri and the District of Columbia.
[d]Includes males and females of all races and ages.
[e]Includes males of all races. Although the age group fifteen to thirty-nine is commonly regarded as the appropriate pool of military manpower, this table lists ten years of age as the lower limit to reflect the fact that, as the war went on, youths age ten to fifteen became eligible for duty. The Union did not draw heavily on the youngest cadre of would-be soldiers, but the Confederates did enlist substantial numbers of fourteen- and fifteen-year-old boys toward the end of the war. Similarly, this table lists forty-nine as the upper age limit because, as the war continued, increasingly older men were called upon to serve, particularly in the Confederacy. At the outbreak of the conflict, the most common age of those enlisting was eighteen years.
[f]Includes 1,088,464 slaves and 37,291 free blacks.
[g]Includes 131,708 slaves and 37,080 free blacks.
SOURCE: Roger L. Ransom, *Conflict and Compromise: The Political Economy of Slavery, Emancipation, and the American Civil War*, Cambridge, Mass., 1989, pp. 90–91. Computed from figures in U.S. Census Office, Eighth Census [1860], Population, Washington, D.C., 1864. Total population of the South is listed as 360 persons higher than reported in the census, reflecting an upward adjustment of 360 slaves for the original purposes of the table.

TABLE 4. *Military Strength[a]*

	Union			Confederate		
	Present	Absent	Total	Present[b]	Absent	Total
Army Strength, July 1861	183,588	3,163	186,751	—	—	112,040[c]
Army Strength, Jan. 1862	527,204	48,713	575,917	258,680	68,088	326,768
Army Strength, Jan. 1863	698,802	219,389	918,191	304,015	145,424	449,439
Army Strength, Jan. 1864	611,250	249,487	860,737	277,970	186,676	464,646
Army Strength, Jan. 1865	620,924	338,536	959,460	196,016	204,771	400,787
Total Manpower, 1861–1865			2,213,000[d]			900,000[e]

[a]Unless otherwise noted, all figures from E. B. Long and Barbara Long, *The Civil War Day by Day: An Almanac, 1861–1865*, Garden City, N.Y., 1971. Because of the inaccurate procedures used during the war to record troop strength and the difficulty after the war of collecting those records and assessing their validity, these figures are at best approximations. Union figures for January 1862 and following were calculated for January 1 of each year listed. Corresponding Confederate figures were actually calculated for December 31 of the previous year.
[b]For Confederates this table lists as present only those figures Long and Long in *Civil War Day by Day* classify as "aggregate present," not those classified as "present for duty," which tend to be 40,000 to 50,000 men lower at each point.
[c]Separate present and absent figures not available. Total figure taken from Thomas L. Livermore, *Numbers and Losses in the Civil War in America, 1861–1865*, Boston, 1901.
[d]Includes both army and navy. Army alone totals 2,129,000 men. Figures taken from U.S. Census Bureau, *Historical Statistics of the United States, Colonial Times to 1970*, Washington, D.C., 1975, pt. 2, ser. Y856–Y857, p. 1140.
[e]Includes both army and navy. This figure, taken from Roger L. Ransom, *Conflict and Compromise: The Political Economy of Slavery, Emancipation, and the American Civil War*, Cambridge, Mass., 1989, is an approximation of the greatest number of men likely to have fought for the South. Livermore in *Numbers and Losses* has calculated that 1,003,600 men served, but this number is probably inflated. On the low end of the spectrum is the figure of 750,000 men, calculated by Long and Long in *Civil War Day by Day*. James M. McPherson in *Battle Cry of Freedom: The Civil War Era*, New York, 1988, calculates a more likely figure of 882,000 men by extrapolating from records of surviving Confederate veterans in 1890. According to Ransom, McPherson's method of calculation may slightly overestimate the number of deaths between 1865 and 1890.

decide the war. In the Civil War, however, huge armies constantly bludgeoned each other, but very few decisive battles occurred. In the end, the North's ability to replace losses in the field was a decisive factor in victory.

Not to be discounted was the role of immigrants, African Americans, and whites from the border states. An estimated 178,892 free blacks and former slaves—93,346 from the seceded states—served in the Union army, a manpower resource the South did not have. Nearly 500,000 foreign-born troops also served in the armies of the North. Furthermore, the majority of white men from the slaveholding border states of Delaware, Kentucky, Maryland, and Missouri fought for the North; only approximately 185,000 served in the Confederate army. But even discounting these blacks, immigrants, and border state whites, the North still enjoyed a tremendous advantage in its reserve of military-age men. In all, two and a quarter million men served in the Union army and approximately 900,000 served the Confederacy. Tables 3 and 4 show the distribution of Union and Confederate populations and military strength during the conflict.

All of these statistics translate into a Civil War soldier's grim reality. The chances of death or dismemberment were very high, with nearly 30 percent of all Union troops and 48 percent of Confederate troops becoming casualties. As an illustration, consider a typical company of one hundred men. In Federal armies, six would be killed on the battlefield or from wounds, eight would die of disease, and fifteen others would be wounded. In a Confederate company, ten would die as a result of combat, sixteen would fall to disease, and twenty-two would be wounded.

[See also Health and Medicine, articles on Sickness and Disease and Battle Injuries.]

BIBLIOGRAPHY

Livermore, Thomas L. Numbers and Losses in the Civil War in America, 1861–65. Boston, 1900. Reprint, Dayton, Ohio, 1986.

Long, E. B. The Civil War Day by Day: An Almanac, 1861–1865. Garden City, N.Y., 1971.

McWhiney, Grady, and Perry Jamieson. Attack and Die: Civil War Military Tactics and the Southern Heritage. Tuscaloosa, Ala., 1982.

Ransom, Roger L. Conflict and Compromise: The Political Economy of Slavery, Emancipation, and the American Civil War. Cambridge, Mass., 1989.

DONALD S. FRAZIER

CLANTON, JAMES HOLT (1827–1871), brigadier general.

Born in Columbia County, Georgia, on January 8, 1827, Clanton moved to Macon County, Alabama, in 1835. He attended Alabama University before enlisting for service in the Mexican War. Returning home, he studied law and opened a practice in Montgomery. Clanton was elected to the Alabama legislature in 1855 and as a presidential elector for the Constitutional Union party in 1860.

Although Clanton originally opposed secession, he was elected captain of Company K of what became the First Alabama Cavalry in 1861 and served in Florida. He was commissioned a colonel on March 18, 1862, with a date of rank of December 3, 1861. Clanton led his troops into Tennessee and fought at Shiloh, Corinth, Farmington, and Booneville. After serving as an aide-de-camp to Braxton Bragg, Clanton raised the Sixth, Seventh, and Ninth Alabama Cavalry in 1863 and on November 13 of that year was promoted to brigadier general in command of the Second Brigade of the Department of the Gulf.

At Ten Islands on the Coosa River, Clanton's entire staff was either killed or wounded. He also fought at Resaca, Adairsville, and Cassville and served as Leonidas Polk's aide-de-camp before being transferred to the Department of

Alabama, Mississippi, and East Louisiana. In March 1865, Clanton was wounded and captured at the Battle of Bluff Spring in Florida and remained a prisoner until the war's end.

Clanton resumed his law practice until he was murdered in Knoxville, Tennessee, after being provoked into a quarrel by a former Union officer who was the son of a former pro-Northern congressman from eastern Tennessee. Clanton is buried in Montgomery, Alabama.

BIBLIOGRAPHY

Evans, Clement, A., ed. Confederate Military History. 12 vols. Atlanta, 1899. Extended ed. in 19 vols. Wilmington, N.C., 1987–1989.

Johnson, Robert U., and C. C. Buel, eds. Battles and Leaders of the Civil War. 4 vols. New York, 1887–1888. Reprint, Secaucus, N.J., 1982.

KENNY A. FRANKS

CLARK, CHARLES (1810–1877), brigadier general and governor of Mississippi.

Clark, a native of Ohio, moved to Mississippi when he was twenty-one. A Whig and a successful lawyer, Clark represented Jefferson County in the legislatures of 1838, 1839, 1842, and 1843. During the Mexican War, he formed a company that became part of the Second Mississippi Regiment led by Col. Reuben Davis; Clark became colonel when Davis resigned. As a civilian, Clark moved to Bolivar County and represented it in the legislatures of 1856, 1859, 1860, and 1861. At the Democratic National Convention of 1860, Clark and others from the Mississippi delegation walked out when the convention refused a plank guaranteeing slavery in the territories. He sought a seat in the state's secession convention in 1861, but was defeated by a more moderate candidate.

Clark, early in the Civil War, became a brigadier general of state troops and was later promoted to major general. On May 22, 1861, he became a brigadier general in the Confederate army and was assigned to command a brigade under Gen. Albert Sidney Johnston in Kentucky. After retreating with the army from Kentucky, Clark was named to command a division of Gen. Leonidas Polk's corps, which was ordered to proceed toward Corinth, Mississippi, to prepare for a surprise attack on Ulysses S. Grant's army at Shiloh. In the Battle of Shiloh, Clark suffered a serious shoulder wound but was soon back in command of his division. He then reported for duty with Maj. Gen. Earl Van Dorn at Vicksburg, who ordered an attack on Baton Rouge, which had recently fallen to Federal forces. In the attack, a minié ball shattered Clark's hip and inflicted what appeared to be a mortal wound. He was captured and sent to New Orleans. During treatment, Clark's wife was allowed to cross enemy lines and assist in his recovery. After his release, Clark returned to Mississippi an invalid, and he never again could stand erect or walk without crutches or a cane.

With his military service ended, Clark turned again to politics and in 1863 was elected governor of Mississippi. The next year he was especially concerned with the state's chaotic finances. Its treasury contained only about $800,000 in Confederate treasury notes. He was also alarmed by the deteriorating conditions in the Confederacy. He and other Southern governors called for Confederate officers to arrest deserters and impress black males for public service. In November 1864, there were so many deserters Clark was forced to offer amnesty to all who would return to duty. Anarchy was threatening, and the legislature authorized Clark to use the militia to restore order.

When surrender became inevitable, Clark sent the legislature a message that all should cooperate and return without rancor to the Union. Realistically, he called for citizens to "assist the returning soldiers to obtain civil employment, condemn all twelfth-hour vaporers, and meet facts with fortitude and common sense." Evidently, he felt that Reconstruction would be the duty of the state authorities.

Governor Clark expressed regret over Abraham Lincoln's assassination in 1865, calling the act "repugnant to the instincts of our heart" and expressing "the profoundest sentiments of detestation." Nonetheless, Gen. E. D. Osband, who commanded a brigade of black troops, disbanded the legislature and threatened arrest of anyone who sought to govern. Clark, who was ordered to surrender custody of all elements of government, did so "under protest, but without asking to have force employed." To General Osband, the governor strongly protested the usurpation of Mississippi's sovereignty, insisting, "I am the duly and constitutionally elected governor of the State of Mississippi, and would resist, if in my power, to the last extremity, the enforcement of your order. I only yield obedience, as I have no power to resist."

After a few days Federal authorities arrested and imprisoned him at Fort Pulaski, Georgia. He was soon released, but wrote the legislature that he could not address the body because he was "still a prisoner of state and on parole." Mississippi was without a government for a time, until President Andrew Johnson appointed Judge William L. Sharkey provisional governor. Clark returned home to his law practice. He served as chancellor of his district from 1876 until his death in 1877.

BIBLIOGRAPHY

Bettersworth, John K. *Confederate Mississippi*. Baton Rouge, La., 1943.
Dobbins, Austin C. *Grandfather's Journal*. Dayton, Ohio, 1988.
Hooker, Charles E. *Mississippi*. Vol. 7 of *Confederate Military History*. Edited by Clement A. Evans. Atlanta, 1899. Vol. 9 of extended ed. Wilmington, N.C., 1987.

RAY SKATES

CLARK, EDWARD

CLARK, EDWARD (1815–1880), governor of Texas. Born in Louisiana, Clark migrated first to Alabama and then to Texas in 1842, opening a law practice in Marshall. He served in the state constitutional convention in 1845 and later volunteered for the Mexican War, being cited for bravery at Monterrey. During the 1850s he served in several state offices before being elected lieutenant governor as an Independent Democrat in 1859.

Clark assumed the governorship when Governor Sam Houston refused to support secession and was removed from office by the legislature in March 1861. He worked diligently to shore up the state's defenses along the Rio Grande and the northwestern frontier against Indian depredations. He wrote his gubernatorial counterparts in northern Mexico, seeking friendly relations and cooperation against marauders. Clark worked hard to meet Confederate troop quotas and established a network of local committees to collect clothing and supplies. He wrote Secretary of State Leroy P. Walker that wool was available in Texas for conversion into cloth by state penitentiary prisoners, which led to contracts by Confederate quartermasters for woolen cloth throughout the war. In the fall state elections a divided Democratic party could not agree on an endorsement for governor. In a spirited election Francis R. Lubbock outdistanced Clark by 124 votes. Clark accepted the verdict in spite of allegations of fraud. He accepted a commission as colonel of the Fourteenth Texas Infantry Regiment and saw service in Louisiana during 1863 and 1864. He fled to Mexico at war's end, but later resumed his law practice in Marshall.

BIBLIOGRAPHY

Larison, Tinsie. "Edward Clark." In *Ten Texans in Gray*. Edited by W. C. Nunn. Hillsboro, Tex., 1968.
Nichols, James L. *The Confederate Quartermaster in the Trans-Mississippi*. Austin, Tex., 1964.
Wooster, Ralph A. "Texas." In *The Confederate Governors*. Edited by W. Buck Yearns. Athens, Ga., 1985.

WILLIAM E. PARRISH

CLARK, HENRY T.

CLARK, HENRY T. (1808–1874), governor of North Carolina. Born into a prominent planter family, Henry Toole Clark was raised on a plantation near Tarboro, North Carolina. He graduated from the University of North Carolina in 1826. Although he read law and was admitted to the bar, Clark spent most of his adult life supervising his family's extensive holdings. He served as a state senator from Edgecombe County from 1850 to 1861, and in 1858, as a secession Democrat, was elected Speaker of the Senate, then the second most powerful post in North Carolina government. When Governor John W. Ellis died in July 1861, Clark was appointed by the legislature to serve as governor until his term as senator ended in August 1862.

Although intelligent and a hard worker, Clark was politically unambitious and uninspiring as a leader. His greatest contribution as governor was his successful mobilization of North Carolina troops for the war effort and his outfitting of some fifty regiments for the cause. When he asked the War Department to furnish North Carolina troops with supplies, his request was denied on the ground that the blockade made it impossible for the central government to help. The legislature then passed a law requiring the state to equip its own troops. In a deal made with the Confederate Quartermaster Department, North Carolina agreed to furnish its troops with clothes, shoes, and blankets in return for commutation money. No other Confederate state made such an agreement.

Under Clark's leadership, North Carolina also proved resourceful in providing arms and ammunition to its troops. In September 1861, the state established a powder mill for munitions production in Raleigh. In October, the governor sent an agent to Europe to purchase arms and ammunition for state troops (North Carolina was the only state to buy arms directly from Europe). He had his adjutant general let out contracts with firms across the state to produce weapons. And in April 1862, he sent agents into every county to buy, borrow, or impress firearms in the hands of citizens. In all, he obtained about 51,000 stand of arms for state troops during his administration.

Federal forces in August 1861 captured Forts Hatteras and Clark and in February 1862 took Roanoke Island. By May, Federal forces had control of all of coastal North Carolina except for Wilmington and the lower Cape Fear region. Clark received blame from across the state for the loss of the sound region. The governor in turn accused Richmond of neglecting the defense of coastal North Carolina.

Clark was keen to repress any sign of disloyalty in the state. In an effort to raise a state force quickly to help defend the coastal region, in March 1862 he had ordered a draft of one-third of the state militia. In reaction, militant Unionists in the central counties of Randolph and Davidson held meetings in which leaders demanded peace and reunion. Clark sent in 300 troops to quell the insurrection. Earlier in July 1861, he had sent 160 troops into the same region to put down a "rebellious disturbance" by an underground band of reunionists who drilled under the U.S. flag and pledged themselves to fight for the Union.

Governor Clark played a key role in establishing the Salisbury Prison, the first prisoner-of-war camp in the Confederacy. He suggested the Salisbury site because the town was an important railroad terminus and grain-producing center. It also contained an abandoned three-story cotton mill near the railroad that could house up to 2,000 prisoners. Clark offered to furnish state troops to serve as prison guards. By March 1862, there were about 1,500 prisoners at Salisbury.

Clark chose not to run for election in 1862, and fellow party members did not urge him to do so. Clark was not a viable candidate: besides blaming him for the Federal occupation of the coastal region, citizens resented his enforcement of the conscription laws. Zebulon Vance, candidate of the new Conservative party (mostly prewar Unionists and old-line Whigs) won the contest.

Clark was a man of unblemished character, but the times called for a forceful leader, and that he was not. After the inauguration of Vance, Clark returned to his plantation at Tarboro, where he remained until his death in 1874.

BIBLIOGRAPHY

Barrett, John G. *The Civil War in North Carolina.* Chapel Hill, N.C., 1963.

Crabtree, Beth G. *North Carolina Governors, 1585–1975.* Rev. ed. Raleigh, N.C., 1974.

Iobst, Richard W. "Henry Toole Clark." In *Dictionary of North Carolina Biography.* Vol. 1. Edited by William S. Powell. Chapel Hill, N.C., 1979.

Mercer, Gary Garnall. "The Administration of Governor Henry Toole Clark, 1861–1862." Master's thesis, East Carolina College, 1965.

WILLIAM THOMAS AUMAN

CLARK, JOHN B. (1802–1885), congressman from Missouri. Born in Madison County, Kentucky, on April 17, 1802, Clark moved with his family to Howard County, Missouri, in 1818. After studying law in Boonville, Clark in 1823 settled in Fayette, where he was appointed clerk of the county court, an office he held until 1842. He was admitted to the bar in 1824. Appointed a militia captain in 1823, Clark became a veteran Indian fighter, being wounded twice during the Black Hawk War. A major general by 1836, he commanded the militia during the Mormon War of 1838.

Originally a Whig, Clark campaigned as a state rights Democrat in 1850 and was elected to the Missouri General Assembly (1850–1851). He served in the U.S. Congress from 1857 until he was expelled on July 13, 1861, because of his avid pro-Southern beliefs.

A brigadier general in the Missouri State Guard, Clark was appointed by the rump Neosho legislature to the Provisional Congress. During the First Congress he served as chairman of the Senate Committee on Public Lands.

Clark consistently supported Missouri and western interests. He wanted the military draft excluded in areas in peril from Union guerrillas and advocated giving free rein to Confederate partisans. Clark favored promotion by seniority, supported martial law, and opposed the extension of presidential appointive powers.

Clark's impudence, bad manners, propensity to drink, and anti-administration biases prompted Missouri's governor to refuse to appoint him to a second term. But he won election to the House and continued his anti-administration activities.

In 1866 Clark returned to Fayette to practice law. He died October 29, 1885.

BIBLIOGRAPHY

History of Howard and Chariton Counties, Missouri. St. Louis, 1883.

Kirkpatrick, Arthur R. "Missouri's Delegation in the Confederate Congress." Civil War History 5 (1959): 188–198.

Matthews, J. A. Illustrated Atlas Map of Howard County Mo. St. Louis, 1876.

Wakelyn, Jon L. Biographical Dictionary of the Confederacy. Westport, Conn., 1977.

Warner, Ezra J., and W. Buck Yearns. Biographical Register of the Confederate Congress. Baton Rouge, La., 1975.

JAMES W. GOODRICH

CLARK, JOHN B., JR. (1831–1903), brigadier general and U.S. congressman. Born in Fayette, Missouri, John Bullock Clark, Jr., was named for his father, a prewar congressman who served briefly as a brigadier general in the Missouri State Guard and later as a Confederate senator. The son studied at the Fayette Academy and Missouri University (the University of Missouri) before spending two years in California. He then attended Harvard Law School, graduating in 1854. When the Civil War began he was a lawyer in his hometown of Fayette.

Like his father, Clark joined the Missouri State Guard, first as a lieutenant and then as captain of a company in the Sixth Missouri Infantry. Promoted to major, Clark fought under his father in the Battle of Carthage in July 1861 and was at Wilson's Creek in August. The elder Clark, in charge of the Third Division, Missouri State Guard, wrote to Maj. Gen. Sterling Price that during the Battle of Wilson's Creek command of the First Regiment fell on his son after Col. John Q. Burbridge was wounded. General Clark commented on the "efficient and intrepid manner in which he led his forces in every engagement," noting that he "seemed providentially to escape with but a slight wound to himself and his horse."

After this battle, the elder Clark left the military to pursue a political career, and the son was promoted to colonel in command of the Third Division, Missouri State Guard (divisions in the State Guard did not imply size of a command, but rather origin in one of the nine state military districts). Clark fought in March 1862 under Price at Elkhorn Tavern, Arkansas, where his division included six skeleton regiments.

Clark's Missourians officially joined the Confederate army on November 16, 1862; on January 31, 1863, his regiment formed part of Daniel Frost's brigade, Thomas C. Hindman's division, Army of the Trans-Mississippi. In May, Clark commanded the First Brigade consisting of two regiments, a battalion, and a battery (Defenses of Lower Arkansas). In the summer he was operating against Federal shipping on the Mississippi, and his regiment took part in the battle for Little Rock in August and September. After the fall of the state capital, Clark's command took a position at the rear of the army as the Confederates retreated toward Arkadelphia.

Although Clark's politician father proved to be controversial, his political connections must have benefited his son. On April 13, 1864, Gen. E. Kirby Smith appointed young Clark a brigadier general to date from January 1, but this appointment did not receive Senate approval. Submitted again, the promotion, dating from March 6, was eventually approved.

Clark took part in the Red River expedition in 1864 where Brig. Gen. Mosby Monroe Parsons commented on April 13 that Clark's "skillful maneuvering" had repulsed a Federal assault at Pleasant Hill, Louisiana. After the Missourians headed north to halt the advance of Frederick Steele's Federal army toward Shreveport, Clark received more praise for his actions in the Battle of Jenkins's Ferry, Arkansas.

Clark took part in Price's Missouri expedition in 1864, commanding Brig. Gen. John S. Marmaduke's old brigade. After Marmaduke was captured at Mine Creek, Kansas, on October 25, Clark assumed command of the division. When Price was driven from Missouri, he headed for Texas, accompanied only by Clark's brigade.

After the war Clark went into politics and served in Congress from 1873 until 1883 when he became clerk of the House of Representatives. He made Washington, D.C., his permanent home and practiced law there until his death on September 7, 1903. He is buried in Washington.

BIBLIOGRAPHY

Castel, Albert. General Sterling Price and the Civil War in the West. Baton Rouge, La., 1968.

Johnson, Ludwell H. Red River Campaign: Politics and Cotton in the Civil War. Baltimore, Md., 1958.

Kerby, Robert L. Kirby Smith's Confederacy: The Trans-Mississippi South, 1863–1865. New York, 1972.

ANNE J. BAILEY

CLARK, WILLIAM W.

CLARK, WILLIAM W. (1819–1883), congressman from Georgia. William White Clark was born on September 23, 1819, near Augusta, Georgia. He was educated at the Covington Manual Labor School (later Oxford College) and read law independently. Despite a lack of formal legal training, Clark passed the bar in 1841, established a practice in Covington, and soon earned a reputation as one of the state's most skilled trial lawyers. When the Manual Labor School moved to Oxford, Clark used his considerable earnings to buy the school's old property and convert it into a plantation he named Clark Grove. He speculated in other real estate ventures both in the area and in Texas.

Clark's only antebellum venture into politics was a single term in the state legislature at the time when he was establishing himself in Covington in 1841. He played no conspicuous role in Georgia's secession crisis, but he was elected in October 1861 to represent its Sixth District in the First Congress. Like many of his fellow Georgians in Congress, he was more supportive of the Jefferson Davis administration policy than of Governor Joseph E. Brown's strong opposition to the Richmond government. Clark supported most of Davis's wartime policies except conscription, which he felt placed far too much power in the hands of the government.

Clark was active on the Committee on Quartermaster and Commissary Departments and fought to preserve the productive capacity of the home front. He proposed military exemptions for mechanics and artisans and opposed the conscription of overseers. Though he failed to win approval for these measures, he was successful in securing an exemption of certain perishable goods from the Confederacy's tax-in-kind, owing to the impracticality of utilizing such goods before they spoiled.

Clark also served on the Medical Department Committee and was among those congressmen who made an inspection tour of army hospitals in and around Richmond early in 1862. The tour uncovered a number of complaints regarding the conduct of the doctors in these hospitals. Their worst offense was the failure to allow patients a hearing regarding their fitness for further service until they had been hospitalized for at least three months. Clark spoke out against the inflexibility and impracticality of such a system. He was defeated in his bid for reelection in October 1863 by Joseph Hubbard Echols, who ran on a far more aggressive state rights platform.

Clark returned to Covington, where he spent the Confederacy's final days. He resumed his law practice after the war, and though active in a variety of state and local civic affairs, he never again held political office. From 1873 to 1878 he served as a director of the Georgia Railroad and Banking Company. Poor health led him to seek treatment in Baltimore in the summer of 1883, and he died there on August 6.

BIBLIOGRAPHY

Warner, Ezra J., and W. Buck Yearns. *Biographical Register of the Confederate Congress.* Baton Rouge, La., 1975.
Yearns, Wilfred B. *The Confederate Congress.* Athens, Ga., 1960.

JOHN C. INSCOE

CLASS CONFLICTS.

CLASS CONFLICTS. In recent decades, the social history of the Confederacy has received substantial scrutiny, especially the role that class divisions among whites played in the South's eventual defeat. Much of this research has involved nonslaveholding men and women, significant numbers of whom became restive under Confederate rule. The areas of the Confederacy least dominated by plantation slavery were most disaffected, although debate continues as to the degree to which this class-based resistance undermined the Confederacy.

Personal ownership of slaves represented one measure of wealth and social standing, a critical benchmark in view of the importance of slavery in the sectional crisis. In 1860, three-quarters of Southern families owned no slaves; these families were concentrated in areas not suited to plantation agriculture, most notably the Appalachian and Ozark mountains. The social geography of the South thus dictated that regional differences would take on class overtones. These social cleavages had political ramifications as well. Before the war, farmers in the mountains and upper Piedmont generally backed the Democratic party, particularly in the lower South. Distrustful of centralized authority and Whiggish planters' social pretensions, they preferred the limited government espoused by the Democrats. The demands of the Confederate state would challenge their preference for small, locally based government.

After the election of Abraham Lincoln, nonslaveholder-dominated areas hesitated over the calls for secession. Opposition to immediate secession correlated with nonslaveholding, with the poorest mountain areas rejecting disunion decisively. In the upper South, nonslaveholding majorities prevented secession prior to the firing on Fort Sumter. After Lincoln's call for troops in April 1861, many rallied to the Confederacy in the face of invasion, especially in the lower South. Others lapsed into a passive acquiescence, but in eastern Tennessee and western Virginia, majorities opposed secession even after hostilities began.

Most white Southerners strongly supported the new republic for the first year of the war, but the demands of mobilization placed increasing pressures on the home front. Even wealthy slaveholders felt the impact, for the institution of slavery was vulnerable. Secession unsettled the plantations, since the slaves understood their status hinged on the outcome of the conflict. Furthermore, the Confederate practice of requisitioning slaves for fortification labor had a disruptive effect. The laborers were frequently ill-treated, and they always returned home with increased knowledge of the location of the nearest Federal army. The overriding issue was security; the departure of thousands of young white males for the front left the discipline of the slaves to untried hands. Young boys, old men, and women tried to overawe the slaves, and many expressed worry about the outcome. One man feared in May 1861 that "our entire white population will volunteer" and the "slaves will become our masters, if they can."

The planters' concerns carried substantial weight, for slaveholders were overrepresented in Confederate government. Several Southern governors retained rifles in state armories, while the central government had hundreds of thousands of volunteers it could not arm. Similarly, local officials demanded that troops and militia remain near home, where they could assist in the case of raid or insurrection.

When Confederate authorities resorted to conscription in 1862, they took measures to maintain security and production on the plantation. The law allowed draftees to hire substitutes, which encouraged wealthier potential conscripts to buy their way out. One South Carolina woman complained to President Jefferson Davis about these "big men about towns," adding that they were "no serviz to us at home." Several Confederate generals wrote in 1864 that "more than 150,000" men employed substitutes, adding that the soldiers thus furnished were of poor quality and frequently deserted. The conscription laws also exempted various classes from service, including one overseer or supervisor on plantations with more than twenty slaves. The stated goal was "to secure the proper police of the country," and some three to four thousand individuals reportedly utilized the provision.

One of the more striking instances of planter influence occurred late in the war. Strong planter opposition long prevented the Davis administration from considering the use of black troops, and even after Davis endorsed the policy, the Confederate Congress blocked their use until only days before Appomattox.

The solicitude accorded planters heightened the disaffection among others. With reason, nonslaveholder-dominated regions felt they bore a disproportionate burden. Military service removed a major portion of their labor force. The women and children left behind found it difficult to raise enough food, and it was hard for authorities to find and transport enough to aid them. The blockade cut off consumer goods, while catastrophic depreciation overcame the Confederate currency, amounting to some 9,000 percent inflation overall by the last days of the war. This severely hurt those poorer families primarily dependent on soldiers' pay, which remained eleven dollars per month for privates. And even this sum was often late; for example, in the Trans-Mississippi Department soldiers were months be-

hind in receiving their pay, which was depreciating all the while.

The fiscal policies of the Confederate government augmented such hardships. The Confederate Congress avoided most levies against plantations or slaves, and Treasury Secretary Christopher G. Memminger opposed direct taxation on constitutional grounds. Thus the government adopted other means of raising funds, with dire social effects. The tax-in-kind seized 10 percent of the agricultural surplus of all farms. Requisition agents roamed across the South, seizing food at government prices, which were well below the market price. For example, by July 1864 the agents were paying only 20 percent of the prevailing price of corn to farmers. The secretary of war himself described this as a "harsh, unequal, and odious mode of supply."

The conscription issue became the focal point for class resentment, especially the twenty-slave exemption. That provision achieved "universal odium," one Confederate congressman observed, but despite modifications it was not repealed until the closing days of the war. The various exemptions inspired complaints of a "rich man's war and a poor man's fight." As several North Carolinians observed, "the common people is drove of[f] in the ware to fight for the big mans negro," while the slaveholder himself was making money at home. Rich speculators provided a scapegoat for rampant inflation and shortages. The *Richmond Examiner* commented that the "disposition to speculate upon the yeomanry of the country . . . is the most mortifying feature of the war."

One manifestation of spreading class resentment was the difficulty of maintaining order behind Confederate lines. With implementation of the draft, lukewarm Confederates now faced a choice of military service or overt opposition. Resistance was less onerous for those with few possessions to sacrifice. Draft evaders gravitated toward the mountains and frontier areas, where it was easier to escape detection. This process concentrated disaffection in the very areas that had opposed secession, as did the departure of Confederate supporters for the army. When Confederate authorities tried to apprehend fugitives, the latter banded together to resist. Deserters and draft evaders dominated large areas.

Bitter conflict in northern Alabama illustrates these larger trends. Many small farmers initially tried to sit out the war. As one mountaineer wrote, the Confederates wanted "to git you pumpt up to go to fight for their infurnal negroes," and afterward "you may kiss there hine parts for o they care." With conscription, those trying to avoid the draft found it increasingly difficult to cultivate their farms without being captured. By 1862, thousands of guerrillas were roaming through the region, subsisting on food seized from Confederate sympathizers. As Confederate reprisals increased, the Federal occupation of the Tennessee valley provided escape, and nearly three thousand Alabama whites joined the First Alabama Cavalry and other Union regiments. The North's army recruited disproportionately from the poorest and most isolated hill counties. A study of one loyalist stronghold, Winston County, has revealed that Union enlistees substantially outnumbered Confederates and that the Union soldiers owned less land and were drastically poorer than their Confederate neighbors. This pattern was evident in nonplantation areas throughout the South, and Union recruitment attained substantial proportions as Northern troops penetrated the region. Some 100,000 whites from the Confederate states joined the Union army, including 30,000 from Tennessee and a roughly equal number from what would become West Virginia. This number is dwarfed by the 850,000 to 900,000 who served the Confederacy; nevertheless it represented a substantial drain on Southern manpower.

Although most overt resistance to the Confederacy occurred in the mountains or other inhospitable terrain, support eroded elsewhere, too. In eastern North Carolina, the arrival of Union troops in 1862 prompted something approaching class war in Washington County. Bands of Unionist irregulars appropriated the property of Southern sympathizers, culminating in a major Confederate massacre of Union collaborators and blacks. In the cities, swollen with refugees, rampant inflation and food shortages prompted repeated unrest. Food riots occurred in Mobile, Atlanta, and Macon. Even in Richmond, crowds of women chanting "bread or blood" broke into stores in April 1863. While cities remained securely under Confederate control, overt Unionist displays were suicidal, but as Federal troops entered one city after another, they were frequently welcomed by the urban poor and foreign-born. In occupied New Orleans, for example, large numbers of workingmen collaborated with the Union administration in efforts to reconstruct the state.

The Richmond government faced increasing political difficulties, and by 1863 several states had elected anti-administration governors and congressmen. The anti-Davis faction defies easy categorization, being composed in part of state rights proponents from the plantation areas who continued to support the Confederacy. Anti-administration men from the up-country were more willing to consider a negotiated peace, but both groups collaborated to protect their states from the demands of the Confederate government.

To some extent, the state rights controversies that bedeviled the Confederate government can be seen as a response by local officeholders to the growing disaffection. Governor Joseph E. Brown of Georgia, for example, was considered the spokesman of the small farmers of northern Georgia. Governor Brown had denounced conscription as unconstitutional, and he exempted thousands of local officials and militia officers from the draft. In North

Carolina, William W. Holden actually ran for governor in 1864 on a peace platform, and though he lost, he ran strongly in the mountainous western portion of the state. Covert "reconstructionist" sentiment became increasingly common among state and local officials. In Alabama, for example, a clandestine "peace society" was reportedly widespread in the Confederate army, and some army officials were surreptitiously exploring surrender terms before Richmond fell.

The growing incidence of desertion provided an obvious index of spreading disaffection. The first wave of desertion coincided with the draft legislation of 1862, which involuntarily extended the enlistments of many volunteers. As one Mississippi private observed, many of his comrades had left and added that "a heap says if their familys get to suffering they will go." As defeat followed defeat these numbers grew. After the Battle of Nashville in December 1864, the Southern army largely evaporated in the course of retreat. Robert E. Lee himself wrote during the siege of Petersburg that "hundreds of men are deserting nightly and I cannot keep the army together unless examples are made of such cases." In the spring of 1865 some 40 percent of Confederate troops east of the Mississippi were absent without leave, totaling some 100,000 Southern soldiers by war's end. Although desertions occurred among all social classes, it seems clear that the privations of the nonslaveholding families were a major cause. Without official censorship, soldiers were well aware of the hunger and violence their families faced at home. As one desperate wife wrote, "before God, Edward, unless you come home we must die." Many such men decided that their families came before an increasingly hopeless cause.

With the Confederate surrender at Appomattox, class tensions contributed to postwar disorder, especially as reflected in continuing conflict between Unionists and their late Confederate adversaries. Returning soldiers from both armies set out to avenge personal or family feuds, and violence remained pervasive. These conflicts took on political overtones, as individuals tried to use the judicial process to punish wartime misdeeds. Wartime Unionists saw themselves as victims of persecution, as Presidential Reconstruction returned Confederate sympathizers to local office. The continuing polarization was the major source of scalawag sentiment during Military Reconstruction. White Republican votes were concentrated in the poorer mountain and hill areas that had been most opposed to secession, and in which wartime Unionist sentiments had been most pronounced. In later years, these areas would be supportive of independent and populist insurgencies, too.

It is possible to exaggerate the significance of class differences within the Confederacy. Nonslaveholders did comprise the bulk of the Southern army, and most soldiers remained committed to independence until the war's final days. Still, substantial disaffection existed behind Confederate lines. Class resentment was not the only relevant variable, but it was a major one, given the widespread perception that nonslaveholders bore an excessive share of the war's privations. In order to prevail, Southerners probably needed more unity than their stronger adversary. They failed to achieve it, and class conflict represented one salient cause.

[*See also* Bread Riots; Conscription; Desertion; Impressment; Inflation; Morale; Peace Movements; Planters; Poverty; Society; Speculation; Tax-in-Kind; Unionism.]

BIBLIOGRAPHY

Crofts, Daniel. *Reluctant Confederates: Upper South Unionists in the Secession Crisis.* Chapel Hill, N.C., 1989.

Current, Richard Nelson. *Lincoln's Loyalists: Union Soldiers from the Confederacy.* Boston, 1992.

Durrill, Wayne K. *War of Another Kind: A Southern Community in the Great Rebellion.* New York, 1990.

Escott, Paul D. *After Secession: Jefferson Davis and the Failure of Confederate Nationalism.* Baton Rouge, La., 1978.

Hahn, Steven. *The Roots of Southern Populism: Yeoman Farmers and the Transformation of the Southern Upcountry, 1850–1890.* New York, 1983.

Rable, George C. *Civil Wars: Women and the Crisis of Southern Nationalism.* Urbana, Ill., 1989.

Thomas, Emory. *The Confederate Nation, 1861–1865.* New York, 1979.

MICHAEL W. FITZGERALD

CLAY, CLEMENT C. (1816–1882), congressman from Alabama and Confederate representative in Canada. Clement Claiborn Clay was born December 13, 1816, at Huntsville, Alabama. He was the son of Clement Comer Clay, an Alabama politician who served as governor in 1836 and 1837 and was named to the U.S. Senate shortly before the expiration of his term. As a result of his outspoken support of the secession movement, Clement Comer Clay was arrested by Federal troops after they occupied northern Alabama and was kept under military arrest for some time. Because of the similarity of the two men's names, Clement Claiborn Clay added Junior to his name and is often referred to as Clement C. Clay, Jr.

Young Clay graduated from the University of Alabama, receiving a bachelor's degree in 1834 and a master's degree in 1837. During his father's term as governor, he served as his private secretary and then studied law at the University of Virginia. He was admitted to the bar in 1840 and joined his father's law practice in Huntsville. Clay also operated a plantation called Wildwood in Jackson County and was the editor of the *Huntsville Democrat* from 1840 until 1842.

A member of the Democratic party, Clay was elected to

CLEMENT C. CLAY.   NATIONAL ARCHIVES

the Alabama General Assembly in 1842 and was reelected in 1844 and 1845. While completing his last term, Clay was elected by the legislators as judge of the Madison County Court in 1846, serving until 1848 when he resigned. In 1853 Clay ran for the U.S. House of Representatives but was defeated. That winter, the Alabama legislature elected him to the U.S. Senate, and he was unanimously reelected in 1859.

While in the Senate, Clay championed the cause of state rights and supported John C. Calhoun's interpretation of the U.S. Constitution, arguing that Congress had no power over slavery in the states, that the territories were joint property of the states, that Congress had no right to make any law discriminating between the states or depriving them of their full and equal rights in any territory, and that any law interfering with slavery was a violation of the Constitution.

Clay was especially outspoken in his opposition to Justin S. Morrill's land grant act to aid colleges. Morrill's proposal that the Federal government donate public land to support higher education in each state in proportion to its population passed the House of Representatives in April 1858, but was opposed by Clay in the Senate. Basing his arguments on state rights, he declared that the legislation "treats the States as agents instead of principals, as the creatures, instead of the creators of the Federal government." Because of his opposition and that of other Southern senators, it was not until February 1859 that the Morrill Act passed the Senate, and then it was vetoed by President James Buchanan.

Clay also supported the admission of Kansas into the Union under the provisions of the Lecompton constitution enacted by the proslavery Kansas legislature. The Lecompton constitution called for a vote on slavery by the citizens of Kansas. One article guaranteed the right of property in slaves and specified that should it be rejected by the voters, a constitution without slavery would be enforced but the right of property in slaves who were already in Kansas would not be abolished. The Lecompton constitution first was approved by the voters of Kansas when antislavery forces boycotted the election. Ultimately, however, Kansas was not admitted under the Lecompton constitution, which was later repudiated by a majority of the settlers.

Clay remained in the Senate until Alabama adopted its ordinance of secession on January 11, 1861. He was one of five Southern senators who made dramatic speeches on the floor before walking out of the chamber.

With the formation of the Confederate States of America, Clay was offered the position of secretary of war by President Jefferson Davis, but he declined the post in favor of Leroy P. Walker. Shortly afterward, in November 1861, the Alabama General Assembly elected Clay to the first regular session of the Confederate Senate on the tenth ballot by a vote of sixty-six for Clay, fifty-three for Thomas H. Watts, and five for George P. Beirne. Clay drew a two-year term and took his seat in February 1862. He was appointed to the Commerce, Conference, and Military Affairs committees. During his career in the Senate, Clay was a strong supporter of Secretary of Navy Stephen R. Mallory and was named chairman of a special joint committee to investigate the administration of the Navy Department. Clay apparently used his influence to exonerate Mallory.

Clay also supported the passage of legislation that would restrict a Confederate supreme court from having appellate jurisdiction over state courts in what was one of the strongest debates on state rights in the Confederate Congress. (A supreme court was never established.) He also authored legislation to conscript foreign nationals into the Confederate army. Clay's state rights stance also was evident when he joined with Alabama's other senator, William Lowndes Yancy, to protest to President Jefferson Davis that they were "mortified" because Alabama troops were being placed under the command of officers from other states.

Much of Clay's work in the Senate was devoted to mobilizing the Confederacy for total war. He became disheartened by what he perceived to be a lack of total support for the war effort on the part of many Southern officials, once writing that he was "sick of the selfishness, demagogism and bigotry that characterize a large portion of those in office." When Clay learned "how many are growing rich in the Commissary and Qr. Masters Departs. by defrauding the Government and the people and yet are unchecked," he said he could hardly stand to continue in public service.

Throughout his term of office, Clay was a staunch supporter of President Davis and often a confidante of Varina Howell Davis, the president's wife. She once wrote to Clay to express her concern over the toll the task of governing the Confederacy was taking on her husband's health, telling him that the "President hardly takes time to eat his meals and works late at night." Clay became one of Davis's closest advisers on foreign policy. In fact, he, along with Benjamin H. Hill, Howell Cobb, and Robert M. T. Hunter, became the chief administration leaders in the Senate.

Clay, however, privately blamed much of Davis's problems with Congress on the Confederate president's personality, which Clay described as being that of a complex and inscrutable man who would not ask for or receive counsel. Davis, said Clay, seemed bound to go exactly the way his friends advised him not to go. Clay lamented that he had difficulty being friends with Davis and regretted that Davis "will be in a minority." Although Clay nevertheless was one of Davis's strongest supporters, he was honest and open in his dealings with other Southern leaders, even the anti-Davis faction, and as such maintained their respect throughout his term of office.

His loyalty to Davis, however, cost him the support of many of his constituents, for Davis's policies were not well received by many Alabamians. When Clay stood for reelection in 1863, he was defeated by Richard W. Walker. Clay then joined his wife in Petersburg, Virginia, where he attempted to negotiate a deal to purchase 100,000 bales of cotton to be sold overseas by the Confederate government. The scheme was never completed.

In late April 1864, Clay and Jacob Thompson were appointed Confederate representatives to Canada, to join James P. Holcombe who was already there. It was to be a secret assignment that Clay commented he could not enjoy;

he accepted it only "with extreme reluctance, thro' a sense of duty to my country, & will do my best to serve her faithfully & efficiently." He left Petersburg on April 30 and traveled to Wilmington, North Carolina, where on May 6, he, Thompson, and their secretary, William W. Cleary, boarded a blockade runner for the trip to Canada via Bermuda. They reached Halifax, Nova Scotia, on May 19 and were joined by Holcombe.

Clay was entrusted with about $100,000 to finance his Canadian operations. One of his primary duties was to disrupt the North's war-making potential by sending secret agents south into the United States to contact copperheads, pro-Southern sympathizers, and members of the Knights of the Golden Circle and the Sons of Liberty. Two of Clay's most successful agents were Thomas H. Hines and John B. Castleman, who tried to persuade Illinois, Indiana, and Ohio to withdraw from the Union, form a northwestern confederacy, and enter into an alliance with the South. In addition they hoped to purchase several Northern newspapers and to disrupt the North's financial base through the spread of disinformation on the gold market.

Clay and his agents also had been given $25,000 with which to help Confederate prisoners held on Johnson's Island in Lake Erie escape to Canada. From there, they were to be shipped South through the blockade to rejoin their units, or they could remain in Canada to aid the Southern movement. Clay and the others recruited almost a hundred of the escapees who were willing to continue their service to the South.

Neither Clay nor Thompson, however, had the temperament to encourage a revolution. Eventually, they clashed over their objectives, and Thompson moved his base of operations to Toronto, Holcombe settled at Niagara Falls, and Clay moved to St. Catherines, Ontario.

Of more importance were Clay's secret contacts with Northern copperheads to seek a negotiated end to the fighting. Clay's counterpart in the North was Horace Greeley, who, although an abolitionist, hoped to end the slaughter on the battlefield through negotiations. When Greeley learned that Clay and Charles Francis Adams, whom he referred to as "two ambassadors of Davis & Co.," were in Canada with what he believed to be "full and complete powers for a peace," he pressured President Abraham Lincoln to meet with them. In arguing with Lincoln, Greeley pointed out that "our bleeding, bankrupt, almost dying country also longs for peace; shudders at the prospect of fresh conscriptions, or further wholesale devastations and of new rivers of human blood." Greeley's arguments reflected the growing pacifism and defeatism that by the summer of 1864 had added to the increased demand for a negotiated settlement of the war in the North. Faced with a Democratic call for an immediate cessation of hostilities, Lincoln's prospects for the 1864 election were

dimming. Although he had little faith in the success of Greeley's proposal, in reply to his request Lincoln agreed to talk "with any person anywhere professing to have any proposition of Jefferson Davis in writing, for peace, embracing the restoration of the Union and the abandonment of slavery."

Greeley was named the intermediary between Clay and Lincoln and was empowered to inform the Confederate commissioner of the North's intention to enter into talks with responsible negotiators. On July 15, 1864, Lincoln informed Greeley that "I not only intend a sincere effort for peace, but I intend that you shall be a personal witness that it is made," and he extended to Clay, Thompson, Holcombe, and G. N. Sanders, whom he called Confederate "commissioners," a formal letter of safe conduct to the national capital. Armed with Lincoln's letter, Greeley traveled to Niagara Falls on July 17 to talk with Clay and the others, but he was disappointed when he learned that they were not duly accredited representatives of the Confederate government. The men explained that their presence was unofficial and could not be acknowledged by Southern authorities. They promised, however, that if they were guaranteed safe conduct to Washington, D.C., and from there to Richmond, they could secure the necessary approval. Afterward Lincoln was convinced that Clay and the others were present not to negotiate a peace between the Union and the Confederacy but to incite peace activists in the North to obstruct the war effort. As a result, he declared that he would negotiate only with certified representatives of the South who were willing to restore the peace, preserve the Union, and abolish slavery.

Clay and his colleagues also wanted to influence the Democratic National Convention held in Chicago in August 1864, in the hopes of electing a Democratic president and negotiating an end to the war. The Democrats were badly divided between copperheads and those supporting the North's war effort, and many Northerners feared that Clay would be able to influence and perhaps even control the Democratic nomination. This rumor was so widespread that some newspapers reported that Clay had prepared a platform to be adopted by the Democratic delegates. It was said to call for the war to be continued only to restore the Union as it was before the fighting started, with "no further detriment to slave property" and permanent slave status for all blacks "not having enjoyed actual freedom during the war."

Seventy Confederate supporters led by Hines and Castleman did infiltrate Chicago during the Democratic convention, but they had to flee the city when the delegates adjourned. Splitting up, a third headed South and a third returned to Canada; the twenty-two remaining Confederates joined Hines and Castleman and traveled to south-central Illinois where they planned to destroy military supplies and disrupt railroad traffic in the St. Louis, Missouri, area. The plan failed, and in late October and early November, Hines's and Castleman's men returned to Chicago where they hoped to lead an armed uprising in conjunction with the presidential election; they were discovered, however, and most were arrested. This ended the Northwest Conspiracy.

Another major effort to encourage pro-Southern sentiment in the North took place on November 25, 1864, when eight Confederates led by Col. Robert M. Martin succeeded in setting fire to ten hotels, three theaters, and some vessels in the harbor of New York City. Although this caused much excitement, little actual damage was done and no uprising occurred because ten thousand Federal reinforcements had been sent to the city to discourage copperhead activities.

In October 1864, Clay gave $2,462 to Lt. Bennett H. Young to underwrite a Confederate raid on St. Albans, Vermont. Planned by Clay and Young, this was one of the most spectacular Confederate raids of the war. Young and twenty men quietly infiltrated St. Albans on October 18 and spent the day reconnoitering its defenses. The following day at 3:00 P.M. the Confederates robbed St. Albans's banks of $200,000 and herded its citizens onto the village green. The Southerners then tried to set fire to several hotels and other buildings, seized horses from the streets and livery stables, and shot up the town, wounding three civilians, one of whom later died. After occupying the village for about forty-five minutes (during which time Young claimed they were Confederate soldiers despite the fact that they were not uniformed or carrying a flag), the Southerners mounted the horses they had seized and rode for the Canadian border fourteen miles away.

Word quickly spread of the attack, and troops were rushed to the region. When the Confederates crossed the border into Canada, they abandoned their weapons and horses and separated. Pursuing Northerners crossed into Canada and captured seven of the troopers as well as Young. Canadian authorities then arrived and took charge of the prisoners. Eventually fourteen of the raiders were captured, and on November 7, 1864, they were brought to trial in Montreal Police Court. Clay paid $6,000 to hire three well-known attorneys to defend Young and the others. The Confederates asked for a delay to secure copies of their commissions from Richmond, and eventually the case was dismissed because the court had no jurisdiction; the arrests had not been made with warrants signed by the governor-general. Five of the raiders were rearrested, released again, and arrested a third time before they were finally released on bail and fled to Europe.

In seven months, Clay and the other Confederate representatives in Canada had spent more than $500,000, but had failed to instigate a northwestern revolution, negotiate a peace, nominate a peace candidate on the Democratic ticket, or seriously disrupt the North's war effort. They did cause much hysteria with their raids and terrorist activities. Realizing he could accomplish nothing more, Clay sailed from Halifax for Bermuda on January 13, 1865. In Bermuda he boarded a blockade runner and sailed to Charleston, arriving on February 2. On the tenth, he rejoined his wife in Macon, Georgia.

After the Confederate surrender, Clay decided to abandon his homeland and started on horseback for Texas. During the journey he learned that President Lincoln had been assassinated and that he had been implicated as one of the conspirators. When he discovered that a reward had been offered for his capture, Clay abandoned his plan to go to Texas and rode 150 miles to surrender to Federal authorities back in Macon. He was arrested and taken to Augusta, Georgia, where he was shipped, along with Davis, to Fortress Monroe, Virginia, and imprisoned.

Although never brought to trial, Clay was not released until May 1866 after his wife pleaded with President Andrew Johnson for his freedom. He returned to Wildwood and resumed his law practice. His health had deteriorated during the war, and he declined to reenter politics. Clay died on January 3, 1882, in Madison County. His papers, which are preserved at Duke University Library in Durham, North Carolina, offer some of the best insights into the inner workings of the Confederate government during the war and shed light on the various personalities involved.

BIBLIOGRAPHY

Brewer, W. *Alabama: Her History, Resources, War Record, and Public Men from 1540 to 1872.* Montgomery, Ala., 1872.

Fleming, Walter L. *Civil War and Reconstruction in Alabama.* New York, 1905.

Nuermberger, Ruth K. *The Clays of Alabama: A Planter-Lawyer-Politician Family.* Lexington, Ky., 1958.

Owen, Thomas M. *History of Alabama and Dictionary of Alabama Biography.* Chicago, 1921.

Pickett, Albert J. *History of Alabama and Incidentally of Georgia and Mississippi from the Earliest Period.* Birmingham, Ala., 1900.

Saunders, James E. *Early Settlers of Alabama.* New Orleans, La., 1899.

Wood, Gray. *The Hidden Civil War: The Story of the Copperheads.* New York, 1942.

KENNY A. FRANKS

CLAY-CLOPTON, VIRGINIA (1825–1915), society leader and suffragist. Virginia Tunstall was born in Nash County, North Carolina, the daughter of Dr. Peyton Randolph Tunstall and Ann (Arrington) Tunstall. Her mother died when she was a young child, and she was raised by relatives in Tuscaloosa, Alabama, who were politically prominent members of the planter and merchant class. She graduated in 1840 from the Nashville (Tennessee) Female Academy. On February 1, 1843, she married Clement Claiborne Clay of Huntsville, Alabama, who in 1853 was elected to the U.S. Senate. Childless and without household responsibilities, Virginia Clay was able to direct her considerable social talents to cultivating the political elite of the nation's capital.

In January of 1861, the Clays left Washington with the general withdrawal of the Southern senators. During the war, Clement Clay served in the Confederate Congress and as an adviser to Jefferson Davis. Despite the occupation of her family home in Huntsville in 1862 by Northern troops, Virginia Clay was buffered from much of the hardships of the war by her wealth and social position. In 1865, her husband was accused of complicity in the assassination of Abraham Lincoln and was imprisoned in Fort Monroe with Jefferson Davis. Virginia Clay played a leading role in securing his release eleven months later by writing letters to influential political figures and personally appealing to President Andrew Johnson.

Reduced financially by the war, the Clays took up farming in Huntsville. Clement Clay never recovered from the defeat of the Confederacy and died in 1882. Virginia Clay was remarried on November 29, 1887, to David Clopton, a justice on the Alabama Supreme Court. Upon his death in 1892, she took the name Clay-Clopton. She became an early and key figure in the Southern women's suffrage movement, serving as president of the Alabama Equal Rights Association from 1896 to 1900. In 1905 she published a volume of memoirs, *A Belle of the Fifties,* which focused upon her years as a Washington social figure and on her experiences during the Civil War.

BIBLIOGRAPHY

Bleser, Carol, and Frederick Heath. "The Clays of Alabama: The Impact of the Civil War on a Southern Marriage." In *In Joy and in Sorrow: Women, Family and Marriage in the Victorian South.* Edited by Carol Bleser. New York, 1991.

Nuermberger, Ruth. *The Clays of Alabama: A Planter-Lawyer-Politician Family.* Lexington, Ky., 1958.

Sterling, Ada. *A Belle of the Fifties: Memoirs of Mrs. Clay of Alabama, Covering Social and Political Life in Washington and the South, 1853–1866. Put into Narrative Form by Ada Sterling.* New York, 1905.

Wiley, Bell I. *Confederate Women.* Westport, Conn., 1975.

LEEANN WHITES

CLAYTON, ALEXANDER M. (1801–1889), congressman from Mississippi and judge. Alexander M. Clayton, born in Virginia, became a lawyer in 1823. He moved to Tennessee and in 1832 was appointed territorial judge in Arkansas. Weakened by an attack of cholera, he returned to

Tennessee after only one year. In 1837 he migrated to northern Mississippi and settled in Marshall County, where he started a law practice. In 1842 Clayton was named to the High Court of Errors and Appeals to fill a vacant seat. In 1844 he was elected to a full term and served until his defeat in 1851. Judge Clayton was an ardent advocate of state rights and a secessionist, and his defeat may have been caused by his support of disunion in the secession crisis of 1851. Clayton then returned to Marshall County and practiced law until 1853 when Franklin Pierce appointed him consul general to Havana. He served in that post only a few months because of a yellow fever epidemic.

Clayton was a delegate in 1860 to the Democratic National Convention, and in 1861, to Mississippi's secession convention. There he wrote a speech setting forth "the causes which induce and justify the secession of Mississippi from the Federal Union." In the same year he was a delegate to the Provisional Congress, where he served as chairman of the Judiciary Committee. He was responsible for including in the Confederate Constitution the same guarantees to the states found in the U.S. Constitution.

In 1861 Jefferson Davis named him district judge for Mississippi. During his tenure his court had to be moved several times in search of safety from Federal troops. In Clayton's only decision concerning the laws of war, he maintained that a government with no power to protect had no power to punish. He served as judge until removed by the Reconstruction government at the end of the war.

In 1866 Clayton was named to a circuit judgeship but was removed from office by military authorities because he would not take the oath required by the Reconstruction Acts. He returned to Marshall County and among other activities devoted himself to promoting the construction of the Mississippi Central Railroad.

BIBLIOGRAPHY

Alexander, Thomas B., and Richard E. Beringer. *The Anatomy of the Confederate Congress: A Study of the Influences of Member Characteristics on Legislative Voting Behavior, 1861–1865.* Nashville, Tenn., 1972.

Warner, Ezra J., and W. Buck Yearns. *Biographical Register of the Confederate Congress.* Baton Rouge, La., 1975.

RAY SKATES

CLAYTON, HENRY DeLAMAR (1827–1889), major general. Clayton was born March 7, 1827, in Pulaski County, Georgia. Not long afterward his family migrated to Lee County, Alabama. In 1848 he graduated from Virginia's Emory and Henry College. He then read law in Eufaula, Alabama, and in 1849 began practice in the nearby town of Clayton.

Soon Clayton drifted into politics and into the Southern

HENRY DELAMAR CLAYTON.   LIBRARY OF CONGRESS

rights camp. In 1857 he was among the Southerners who went to Kansas to "protect" their section's interest in that disputed area. From 1857 to 1861 he represented Barbour County in the lower house of the Alabama legislature, serving as chairman of the military committee. By 1860 he was a spokesman for secession. Active also in military affairs, he organized and was elected captain of a militia company. In August 1860 the governor appointed him colonel of the Third Regiment, Alabama Volunteer Corps.

Clayton's unit was not activated at the beginning of the Civil War, but he was named to the governor's staff and sent to Pensacola, Florida, to help administer the Alabama troops in that area. On March 28, 1861, he was elected colonel of the First Alabama Regiment. Desiring more active service, he resigned and helped organize the Thirty-ninth Alabama Regiment. When that unit was mustered into active service on May 15, 1862, Clayton was its commander.

Clayton's regiment was assigned to the Army of Tennessee. At the Battle of Murfreesboro, Clayton was severely wounded. His performance won praise. He was promoted to brigadier general, to date from April 22, 1863, and given

command of a brigade in Maj. Gen. Alexander P. Stewart's division.

At Chickamauga Clayton was knocked from his horse by grapeshot. The injury kept him from the fighting around Chattanooga in November, but he was with his brigade when the Atlanta campaign began in May 1864. He was promoted to major general to date from July 7 and assigned as permanent commander of what had been Stewart's division.

Clayton fought at the head of his division until early April 1865. In the Battle of Jonesboro, Georgia, in 1864, he had three horses killed under him. In late October his men secured the Tennessee River at Florence, Alabama, so that the army could cross on its way to middle Tennessee. After the defeat at Nashville in December, Clayton was with the rear guard and received high praise for covering the army's retreat. Upon reaching North Carolina in April 1865, Clayton withdrew from active service because of deteriorating health.

Clayton resumed his law practice after the war. He was elected circuit judge (1866, 1874, 1880), ran unsuccessfully for governor of Alabama (1886), and served as president of the state university from 1886 until his death in Tuscaloosa on October 3, 1889. He is buried in the Eufaula city cemetery.

BIBLIOGRAPHY

Bergeron, Arthur W., Jr. "Henry DeLamar Clayton." In *The Confederate General.* Edited by William C. Davis. Vol. 1. Harrisburg, Pa., 1991.

Jordan, Holman D. "The Military Career of Henry D. Clayton." *Alabama Review* 13 (1960): 127–134.

RICHARD M. MCMURRY

CLEBURNE, PATRICK

CLEBURNE, PATRICK (1828–1864), major general. Born in County Cork, Ireland, March 16, 1828, Patrick Ronayne Cleburne was the son of a fairly well-to-do doctor. In 1846 he failed a medical school entrance examination and, believing he had disgraced his family, enlisted in the British army. In September 1849 he purchased his discharge from the army and three months later arrived in New Orleans.

After clerking for a few months in Cincinnati, Cleburne was hired to manage a drugstore in Helena, Arkansas. The Irishman fit well into the small frontier community, joining the Masons, the Episcopal church, the Sons of Temperance, and (until 1856 when he became a Democrat) the Whig party. He also studied law. In 1855 he became a naturalized citizen, and in the next year he was admitted to the bar.

In 1860 citizens in the Helena area organized a military company called the "Yell Rifles." Cleburne enlisted as a

PATRICK CLEBURNE.   LIBRARY OF CONGRESS

private. He was soon elected captain to command the company. After Arkansas's secession, the company entered state service as part of the First Arkansas Infantry Regiment. On May 14, 1861, Cleburne was elected colonel of the regiment. He was an excellent officer and put his British army experience to good use.

That summer the regiment joined Brig. Gen. William J. Hardee's force at Pittmans Ferry, near Pocahontas, in northeastern Arkansas. There, on July 23, Cleburne and his command transferred from Arkansas to Confederate service.

Assignment to Hardee's command was, in many ways, the key event in Cleburne's Civil War career. A strong friendship developed between the two officers, and Cleburne's Confederate service—for better and worse—became tied inextricably to Hardee's.

That fall Hardee's command joined Gen. Albert Sidney Johnston's army at Bowling Green, Kentucky. Hardee was named major general to command a division, and Cleburne became commander of one of his brigades consisting of the First and Fifth Arkansas regiments, the Sixth Mississippi, and the Fifth Tennessee. The same skills and knowledge that made Cleburne a fine regimental commander enabled him to turn his brigade into one of the Confederate army's finest units.

Johnston was forced to evacuate Bowling Green in February 1862. He retreated to Corinth, Mississippi, where he organized troops collected from all over the Old Southwest into what eventually became the Army of Tennessee. Cleburne was promoted to brigadier general (to date from March 4, 1862) to command his brigade in Hardee's Third Corps of that army. At Shiloh Cleburne's brigade lost 1,013 of its 2,700 men—the heaviest loss of any Southern brigade in the battle. Cleburne himself received high praise for his conduct.

After Shiloh the Confederates were forced back into Mississippi, and the army's new commander, Gen. Braxton Bragg, determined to transfer the army to Tennessee. Along with the troops of Maj. Gen. E. Kirby Smith, he then marched into Kentucky. Bragg created a two-brigade provisional division under Cleburne and sent it to reinforce Smith's column advancing from eastern Tennessee. At the Battle of Richmond, Kentucky, on August 30, Cleburne was wounded in the jaw and was absent from his command about three weeks.

Cleburne was back with his brigade at the Battle of Perryville on October 8 and was twice wounded. In December, after the army had withdrawn to middle Tennessee, he was promoted to major general with date of rank set at November 23. He thus became the highest-ranking military officer of foreign birth in the Confederate army. He was assigned to command a division in Hardee's corps.

With his new command, Cleburne fought at Murfreesboro and was with the army on the retreat to North Georgia in the late summer of 1863. He participated in the great Confederate victory at Chickamauga in September and especially distinguished himself at Missionary Ridge and at Ringgold Gap in November where he covered the Confederate retreat to Dalton, Georgia.

Meanwhile, a civil war had erupted among the generals of the Army of Tennessee, and Cleburne had followed Hardee into the group that opposed Bragg. Most historians of the army believe that membership in the anti-Bragg faction hurt Cleburne's chances for further promotion. In January 1864 Cleburne proposed that the Confederacy free slaves and incorporate them into its armies. This proposal was rejected, and it too damaged Cleburne's chances for higher command.

Cleburne led his division through the Atlanta campaign of 1864 with his accustomed skill. He especially distinguished himself at Pickett's Mill and Atlanta. At Jonesboro, Hardee commanded a two-corps force, and Cleburne commanded Hardee's corps.

After the fall of Atlanta Hardee was sent away from the army. Maj. Gen. B. Franklin Cheatham took command of the corps, and Cleburne returned to his division. At

Franklin, Tennessee, on November 30, Cleburne went with his division into the desperate assault on the Federal works. His troops overran an advanced Northern position and swept on toward the main line. Two horses were killed under Cleburne as he moved forward with his men. Then Cleburne, on foot and with his hat in one hand and his sword in the other, disappeared into the holocaust. A few seconds later a bullet struck just below his heart; he died instantly. Buried first in Rose Hill Cemetery, Columbia, Tennessee, his body was soon taken to St. John's Churchyard at nearby Ashwood. In 1870 the body was moved to what is now Magnolia Cemetery in Helena, Arkansas.

Cleburne's career illustrates very well the problems the Confederates faced in the West. The internal politics of the Army of Tennessee that helped block his well-earned promotion also did much to bring about the Southern defeat in the all-important western theater.

BIBLIOGRAPHY

Buck, Irving A. *Cleburne and His Command.* Jackson, Tenn., 1959.
Durden, Robert F. *The Gray and the Black: The Confederate Debate on Emancipation.* Baton Rouge, La., 1972.
Nash, Charles Edward. *Biographical Sketches of Gen. Pat Cleburne and Gen. T. C. Hindman.* Little Rock, Ark., 1898. Reprint, Dayton, Ohio, 1977.
Perdue, Howell, and Elizabeth Perdue. *Pat Cleburne: Confederate General.* Hillsboro, Tex., 1973.
Woodworth, Steven E. *Jefferson Davis and His Generals: The Failure of Confederate Command in the West.* Lawrence, Kans., 1990.

RICHARD M. MCMURRY

CLEMENS, SAMUEL LANGHORNE (1835–1910), writer and humorist (pseudonym Mark Twain). A Mississippi steamboat pilot until war ended commercial river traffic, Clemens served briefly in the summer of 1861 in the Marion Rangers, a small Confederate militia company from his boyhood home of Hannibal, Marion County, Missouri, which disbanded without seeing combat.

Shortly afterward, Clemens left for Nevada with his brother Orion, who, having campaigned for Abraham Lincoln, was appointed secretary of the territory. Clemens remained in the West for the duration of the war, mining and prospecting for silver before becoming a reporter for the *Virginia City Territorial Enterprise,* where he first adopted the name Mark Twain, and later for the *San Francisco Call.* His connection with the war was limited to support for the U.S. Sanitary Commission fund for sick and wounded soldiers; newspaper reports of Gen. Irvin McDowell's inspection of the harbor defenses at San Francisco, of the reconstruction of the ironclad *Camanche,* and of activities of Confederate guerrillas; and derisive accounts of California Copperheads and secessionists. "Jim Smiley and His Jumping Frog," in the *New York Saturday Press,* November 18, 1865, first brought him national attention. At the close of the war he was in the Sandwich Islands (Hawaii) as correspondent for the *Sacramento Union.*

Twain's account of these years appeared in *Roughing It* (1872). In *Life on the Mississippi* (1883) he blamed Walter Scott and his "jejune romanticism of a dead past" for the Civil War. "The Private History of a Campaign that Failed," a humorous account of his militia service, appeared in the *Century Magazine* (December 1885). He became an ardent admirer of Ulysses S. Grant, whose *Personal Memoirs* Clemens's company published in 1885 and 1886.

BIBLIOGRAPHY

Benson, Ivan. *Mark Twain's Western Years.* Palo Alto, Calif., 1938.
Fatout, Paul. *Mark Twain in Virginia City.* Bloomington, Ind., 1964.
Lennon, Nigey. *Mark Twain in California.* San Francisco, 1982.
Mack, Effie Mona. *Mark Twain in Nevada.* New York, 1947.
Sanborn, Margaret. *Mark Twain: The Bachelor Years.* New York, 1990.

WILLIAM MOSS

CLINGMAN, THOMAS LANIER (1812–1897), U.S. congressman and brigadier general. Clingman was born in Huntsville, North Carolina, on July 27, 1812. He was educated at the University of North Carolina, where he graduated in 1832 at the head of his class. He then studied law and returned home to open a law practice in 1834. He was elected to the state legislature the next year, but his defeat in the following election and his less than successful practice led him to move to Asheville. In 1843, Clingman was elected to Congress as a Whig, but lost his seat in 1845. After another victory in 1847, he served in Congress until 1858, when he was appointed to the U.S. Senate. No other North Carolina congressman during the antebellum period served as long.

In Congress, Clingman became an increasingly zealous pro-Southern and proslavery spokesman, although he never owned a slave and represented a mountain constituency with one of the smallest slave populations in the South. His devotion to the Southern cause led him to abandon the Whig party, but he continued to win reelection as an independent until 1855 when he openly aligned himself with the Democratic party. He spoke out in Congress against the Wilmot Proviso in 1847 and opposed the compromise proposals of 1850 with one of the earliest and most blatantly secessionist speeches yet heard before Congress. He was widely perceived by then as "the most ultra-Southern of the North Carolina delegation in Congress," a reputation that he affirmed repeatedly in his strong stand on sectional issues throughout the 1850s.

Clingman's activities extended beyond politics. His interest in the geology of the Appalachians led to a rivalry with Elisha Mitchell over which peak was the range's highest and who deserved credit for its discovery. He was also interested in astronomy, physics, botany, and meteorology and was one of his region's most avid commercial boosters.

On May 6, 1858, Clingman was appointed to fill out the Senate term of Asa Biggs. He was returned to the Senate in 1860 but resigned on March 28, 1861, to campaign for North Carolina's secession, which came about on May 20.

Clingman was then named a commissioner to its provisional government at Montgomery. He served only a few weeks before winning a commission, despite no previous military experience, as colonel and head of the Twenty-fifth North Carolina Regiment in September 1861. He served with his regiment in eastern North Carolina and Virginia until he was promoted to brigadier general in May 1862 and took command of a brigade at Wilmington.

Clingman spent most of the next two years engaged in the coastal defense of the Carolinas and confronted Union troops in defending Goldsboro, Charleston, and New Bern in late 1863 and early 1864. He then moved with his brigade to Virginia, where he served with Gen. Robert Frederick Hoke's division in the Wilderness and saw action at Drewry's Bluff in May 1864. Clingman was wounded at Cold Harbor but recovered to participate in the early stages of the siege of Petersburg. A more severe wound received at the Weldon Railroad on August 19 incapacitated him until April 1865, when he rejoined his brigade, then serving under Joseph E. Johnston, only days before his surrender at Greensboro, North Carolina.

Clingman returned to Asheville after the war. Barred from seeking elective office, he resumed his law career, but channeled his energies into his scientific activities and regional boosterism. His geological studies of the Great Smoky Mountains resulted in its highest peak being named Clingman's Dome (though the Appalachians' tallest, Mount Mitchell, was named for his former rival). Clingman remained active in the Democratic party and served as a delegate to the state's constitutional convention in 1875 and the Democratic National Convention in St. Louis in 1876. He lectured widely and spent his later years compiling and editing his papers. He died in Morganton, North Carolina, on November 3, 1897.

BIBLIOGRAPHY

Bassett, John S. *The Congressional Career of Thomas L. Clingman.* Durham, N.C., 1900.

Clingman, Thomas L. *Selections from the Speeches and Writings of Hon. Thomas L. Clingman of North Carolina.* Raleigh, N.C., 1877.

Inscoe, John C. "Thomas Clingman, Mountain Whiggery, and the Southern Cause." *Civil War History* 32 (March 1987): 42–62.

Jeffrey, Thomas E. " 'Thunder from the Mountains': Thomas Lanier Clingman and the End of Whig Supremacy in North Carolina." *North Carolina Historical Review* 56 (October 1979): 366–395.

Kruman, Marc W. "Thomas L. Clingman and the Whig Party: A Reconsideration." *North Carolina Historical Review* 64 (January 1987): 1–18.

JOHN C. INSCOE

CLOPTON, DAVID (1820–1892), congressman from Alabama. Born on September 29, 1820, in Putnam County, Georgia, Clopton graduated from Randolph-Macon College in Virginia in 1840. He was admitted to the bar in 1841 and practiced law first in Griffin, Georgia, and then in Tuskegee, Alabama. In 1859 Clopton was elected as a Democrat to the U.S. House of Representatives.

When Alabama passed the secession ordinance in January 1861, Clopton, an ardent secessionist, returned to the state. In 1861 he enlisted as a private in the Twelfth Alabama Infantry and was promoted to assistant quartermaster with the rank of captain. Clopton was elected as a representative to the First and Second Confederate Congresses and served on the Claims, Naval Affairs, Illegal Seizures, and Medical Department committees. Although not an obstructionist, he was reluctant to grant expansive powers to the Confederate central government. He supported the arming of slaves, drafting of speculators, and Confederate control of commerce. He introduced proposals to moderate such existing programs as conscription and taxation.

DAVID CLOPTON.   *HARPER'S PICTORIAL HISTORY OF THE GREAT REBELLION*

In March 1866 Clopton opened a successful law practice in Montgomery and returned to politics in 1874 when the Democratic party was restored to power in Alabama. In 1878 he was elected to the Alabama legislature and in 1884 was appointed an associate justice on the Alabama Supreme Court, where he remained until his death in Montgomery on February 5, 1892.

BIBLIOGRAPHY

McMillan, Malcolm C. *The Alabama Confederate Reader.* University, Ala., 1963.

Owen, Thomas McAdory. *History of Alabama and Dictionary of Alabama Biography.* 4 vols. Chicago, 1921.

Thornton, J. Mills, III. *Politics and Power in a Slave Society: Alabama, 1800–1860.* Baton Rouge, La., 1978.

Wakelyn, Jon L. *Biographical Directory of the Confederacy.* Edited by Frank E. Vandiver. Westport, Conn., 1977.

Warner, Ezra J., and W. Buck Yearns. *Biographical Register of the Confederate Congress.* Baton Rouge, La., 1975.

SARAH WOOLFOLK WIGGINS

CLOTHING. Shortages of clothing in the Confederacy affected both soldiers and civilians but were less severe and occurred later than the widespread shortages of food. At the opening of war, an optimistic Confederate government issued specifications for soldiers' and officers' uniforms, envisioning a well-dressed army and navy. These orders detailed placement of ornamental braid, overcoat design, and the proper hat and insignia for each military position. Yet, initially, the government was ill prepared to provide such outfits. Instead Confederate regiments exhibited multicolored and varied clothing in the earliest battles, including U.S. Army regalia. Until official uniforms were available in the fall of 1862, the government issued soldiers money to purchase their own outfits or depended on states or individual families to provide clothing.

Women on the home front produced a variety of items of military clothing. Many stitched at home and carried their knitting and sewing wherever they went. Others joined ladies' and soldiers' aid societies, which received cloth and distributed it to be sewn at home or in women's groups that met periodically. Eventually the Confederate government purchased cloth from textile mills in North and South Carolina, Georgia, and Europe; established shops; and contracted with existing factories that paid women to sew uniforms. During the last year of the war, uniforms and thousands of yards of wool and cotton purchased by an overseas Confederate agent came through the blockade and helped clothe bedraggled soldiers.

As of June 1861, Confederate gray was the official color of the new army. But gray gave way to off-white and butternut when available dyes came only from fields and forests. Standardized uniforms purchased by the military often proved ill fitting and were never as popular with soldiers as homemade or tailor-made outfits. Still, many men had no choice but to wear what little they received. Generous clothing allowances at the beginning of the war had become Spartan by the end, and capes, hats, gloves, and coats were seldom seen luxuries by 1864.

Soldiers learned not to depend solely on the government for clothing. Uniforms wore out, and items might be lost in battle or stolen. Many men wrote home for essential items, specifying size and type of cloth, and sometimes requesting a plaid or stripe fashionable in their regiment. Some Confederates traded clothing with the enemy. Southerners also stole clothing from dead or wounded Federal troops, though all recognized the risk of wearing Yankee blue during battle.

It took only a few months of marching and fighting for soldiers to scale down their military wardrobe. Carrying extra changes of clothing on long marches proved burdensome, and most found that they needed only essentials. Although cold was the soldiers' main complaint, they found long coats and capes cumbersome. Gradually, bodies became hardened through constant exposure. A single uniform might be worn for weeks or months before patching and washing, and several pairs of socks and another pair of drawers were the only additional items worth carrying. By the war's end, most soldiers and officers were in tatters.

The greatest clothing shortages for both soldiers and civilians were boots and shoes. Before 1861, the South had depended on the North and Europe to shod its black and white populations. The blockade impeded such imports, and the South never was able to produce enough shoes for everyone. Leather was in short supply, and few Southerners were skilled at tanning hides and fashioning shoes, although a few individuals learned the skill quickly and capitalized on the trade. The government established a few tanning and shoemaking centers and exempted employees from military service. Thousands of pairs of boots came through the blockade during the final year of war and provided some relief.

Many soldiers preferred a simple, low shoe, much like the brogans that slaves wore, for heavy, high boots proved uncomfortable. A marching army's boots and shoes wore out quickly and had to be replaced, patched, or discarded. Even repairing shoes was difficult. Since most metal was designated for military use, tacks for reattaching soles of shoes were scarce. By 1863, many soldiers had neither shoes nor boots, and barefoot men marching hundreds of miles left bloody trails. In some battles, such as Sharpsburg, soldiers were unable to pursue the enemy because sore feet prevented further marching.

Civilians faced exorbitant prices and shortages of cloth, buttons, shoes, and hats. Most Southerners scaled down and donned a simpler wardrobe than they had worn prior to the war. Despite the war, however, a few privileged individuals insisted on remaining fashionable. The wealthy purchased expensive new suits, hats, and dresses that arrived through the blockade, notwithstanding prices that were ten- or even fiftyfold higher by the war's end. Visitors to Southern cities occasionally commented on residents who, at least at a distance, appeared well dressed. Women expressed a yearning for silk, poplin, demaine, and calico dresses, and men, for silk hats. Clothing denoted status and respectability, and for wealthy Southerners, it was important to maintain one's status in public. As the war progressed, however, the fashionably dressed often elicited jealous comments.

Few could afford such extravagant clothing, and most Southerners depended on their resourcefulness and skill to clothe themselves and their families. Those who had grown accustomed to factory-produced clothing now had to rely on home industry, for factories devoted most of their efforts to military needs. Instead of buying new outfits, women learned to turn dress hems, replace pant seats, add new flounces and buttons of bone or persimmon seeds to dresses, and create hoops for skirts and stays for corsets from grapevines and strips of wood. A wardrobe that had once contained a dozen outfits might be reduced to two or three. Slaves who had received two changes of clothing annually now were lucky to have a single new shirt or chemise. Thread was a precious commodity, and a single sewing needle often had to last the entire war. Women wove hats of palmetto or straw, adorned them with old pieces of ribbon and flowers, and knit or wove hats for their husbands. Others unraveled old silk gloves, rewove the thread, and fashioned a new pair.

Homespun became the most common material for clothing during the four years. This cloth had been worn only by slaves and the poor before 1861, and thus its popularity during the war leveled appearances among the middle and lower classes. For some, wearing homespun became a sign of patriotism. One of the most popular Civil War songs, entitled "The Homespun Dress," celebrated Southern girls who wore homespun and supported the cause. Women learned to weave pretty patterns of stripes and checks from homespun. Most individuals preferred the material for outer garments; they found it too scratchy for drawers and petticoats, which they usually made from cotton or linen.

Women learned or relearned the art of carding, spinning, and weaving, sometimes combining cotton or wool threads with squirrel, raccoon, or rabbit fur. They pulled cotton or wool stuffing from mattresses and spun it into thread. Women cut up adult clothing no longer fit to wear and from it fashioned children's outfits. Others made underclothes from bed linens and elegant dresses from draperies.

Shoes also were in short supply among the civilian population. Pairs wore thin and had to be patched with makeshift materials such as paper or felt. Children outgrew their shoes, and observers noted impoverished youngsters coming to church shoeless or, during winter, with their feet wrapped in cloth. Since prices ran as high as $50 to $125 a pair for leather shoes, Southerners learned to create makeshift shoes from the skins of deer, goats, squirrels, pigs, or alligators. Others reused old leather stripped from trunks, furniture, or saddles. Shoes sometimes were created from light woods, much like the Dutch wore, or from old carpet, felt, canvas, or knitted material.

Nearly all Southerners learned to do with less clothing and to lower expectations about their wardrobes. Soldiers managed to survive on few items, and women on the home front proved resourceful and frugal when clothing their families.

[*See also* Substitutes; Textile Industry; Uniforms.]

BIBLIOGRAPHY

Confederate States of America. War Department. *Uniform and Dress of the Army and Navy of the Confederate States of America.* Introduction by Richard Harwell. Richmond, Va., 1861. Reprint, New York, 1960.

Massey, Mary Elizabeth. *Ersatz in the Confederacy.* Columbia, S.C., 1952.

Rable, George C. *Civil Wars: Women and the Crisis of Southern Nationalism.* Urbana, Ill., 1989.

Ramsdell, Charles W. "The Control of Manufacturing by the Confederate Government." *Mississippi Valley Historical Review* 8 (1921): 231–249.

Wiley, Bell I. *The Life of Johnny Reb: The Common Soldier of the Confederacy.* Baton Rouge, La., 1971.

SALLY G. McMILLEN

CLOYDS MOUNTAIN, VIRGINIA. A forgotten part of Gen. Ulysses S. Grant's 1864 grand offensive in Virginia was an isolated raid described by one writer as "unprecedented in daring and execution." Late in April, Brig. Gen. George Crook led 6,500 Federal troops and twelve cannon through one hundred miles of mountain wilderness into southwestern Virginia. His target was the Virginia and Tennessee Railroad, the only line connecting the Southern capital at Richmond with the western theater. As Crook's force advanced slowly toward the railhead at Dublin, small and scattered Confederate units hastened a few miles north of the village to contest the Federals. In command of this hodgepodge army was Brig. Gen. Albert Gallatin Jenkins, a brave but controversial cavalryman still recovering from a wound received at Gettysburg.

Jenkins placed his 2,400 men and ten guns along a half-mile front on heights overlooking an open valley. At the far end of the flatland loomed Cloyds Mountain, large and solid save for the one pass through which the Federals were snaking. Crook surveyed the open land up to the Southern position and ruled out a frontal assault. Shortly after sunrise on May 9, Union soldiers launched a heavy surprise attack against the Confederate right. Southern musketry, which a Billy Yank likened to "one living, flashing sheet of flame," ripped through the blue ranks and ground the advance to a halt. A thick carpet of dead leaves soon burned out of control and eventually cremated an unknown number of wounded men.

At that critical moment, Brig. Gen. (and future president) Rutherford B. Hayes brought his Ohio brigade on the field and slammed into the Confederate right-center. Hand-to-hand combat erupted as both sides shifted troops to the new danger spot. For a quarter-hour the outcome of the contest hung in the balance. The thin Confederate line slowly began to crack. Simultaneous with fresh Union regiments moving into action, Confederate General Jenkins went down with a shattered arm. Gen. John McCausland took command and managed to maintain his lines long enough to consolidate the units. He then directed a spirited rearguard action as the Southerners abandoned the field.

The battle lasted about an hour. Casualties were disproportionate to the briefness of the fight. Union losses were 688 men, while Confederates suffered 538 troops killed, wounded, and missing. Federals captured the injured Jenkins, who died in a Union hospital following amputation of his arm.

Crook did some wreckage to the railroad and skirmished with Southern detachments on either side of the New River. The fact that he was 150 miles from Union lines soon caused the Federal general to lead his columns back into the mountains. Local work crews put the damaged railroad back into working order. Yet things were never the same in the region. Cloyds Mountain brought the full force of war to southwestern Virginia. Although other engagements would be fought later for control of the railroad, the salt fields, and the lead mines of that area, Cloyds Mountain remains the largest battle ever fought in that quadrant of the Old Dominion.

BIBLIOGRAPHY

McManus, Howard R. *The Battle of Cloyds Mountain.* Lynchburg, Va., 1989.
Walker, Gary G. *The War in Southwest Virginia, 1861–65.* Roanoke, Va., 1985.

JAMES I. ROBERTSON, JR.

CLUSKEY, M. W. (1832–1873), major and congressman from Tennessee. A secessionist from the start, Michael Walsh Cluskey, an officer in the Second (Robison's) Tennessee Regiment, spent much of the war on the staff of Gen. Preston Smith, receiving commendations for gallantry at

Shiloh and Murfreesboro, and sustaining a debilitating wound during the Atlanta campaign. At a special election held in August 1864 near Atlanta, Major Cluskey received all eighty-four votes cast by the surviving members of his regiment, entitling him to Tennessee's Eleventh District seat in the House in place of the recently deceased David Maney Currin. Admitted on November 7, 1864, the opening day of the last session of the Second Congress, Cluskey remained at his post until the final adjournment on March 18, 1865.

During his brief tenure in Richmond, Cluskey seemed ill-prepared for membership on the Conference and Naval Affairs committees. Before the war he had been postmaster of the U.S. House of Representatives and editor of the *Memphis Avalanche,* but had gained recognition during James Buchanan's presidency for editing a popular 640-page Democratic treatise, *The Political Text-book, or Encyclopedia* (1856), which went through fourteen editions by 1860. He generally supported Jefferson Davis, favoring practically any measure that would prolong the war, including the government's seizure of railroads, the establishment of an invalid corps, and the arming of slaves as soldiers. With his army constituents never far from his thoughts, he introduced legislation authorizing the issuance of tobacco rations to military personnel and the reorganization and improvement of Confederate hospitals.

After the war he resumed editorship of the *Avalanche* before relocating in Louisville, where he edited another Democratic paper until his death. He was also a founding member of the Southern Historical Society, based in New Orleans.

BIBLIOGRAPHY

Biographical Encyclopaedia of Kentucky. Cincinnati, Ohio, 1878.
Confederate Veteran 16 (1908): 78–79. Reprint, Wilmington, N.C., 1985.
Journal of the Congress of the Confederate States of America, 1861–1865. 7 vols. Washington, D.C., 1904–1905.
Warner, Ezra J., and W. Buck Yearns. *Biographical Register of the Confederate Congress.* Baton Rouge, La., 1975.

R. B. ROSENBURG

COBB, HOWELL (1815–1868), congressman from Georgia and major general. Howell Cobb was born at Cherry Hill, Jefferson County, Georgia, on September 7, 1815. He was the oldest of seven children and brother of Thomas R. R. Cobb, who would be the chief designer of the Confederate Constitution. In 1819 the Cobb family moved to Athens, home of Franklin College (the University of Georgia), where Howell acquired a Jacksonian Democratic bias against nullification before graduating in 1834. About a year later he married Mary Ann Lamar, daughter of a wealthy middle

HOWELL COBB.   LIBRARY OF CONGRESS

Georgia merchant-planter. They settled in Athens.

Admitted to the bar in 1836, Howell's political career began the following year with his appointment as solicitor general of the state's western district. He was elected to Congress in 1842 from the Sixth Georgia District and repeatedly reelected as a Democrat for the rest of the decade. Chosen Speaker of the 31st Congress, he helped steer through that body the Compromise of 1850. The next year his Georgia friends organized the Union party and elected him governor. Meanwhile his leadership in the state Democratic party had gone to others, while his support of Democratic presidential candidate Franklin Pierce in 1852 infuriated the Unionists. A politician without a party, he resumed his law practice after leaving the governorship in 1853. Two years later, running as a Democrat, he easily recaptured his old congressional seat. Back in Washington,

Cobb was soon hobnobbing with Democratic leaders. It paid off with his appointment in 1857 as secretary of the treasury by President James Buchanan. His conflict with the Georgia Democrats had taught Howell that to resonate with folks back home he had to move resolutely toward separatism.

On December 7, 1860, U.S. Secretary of the Treasury Cobb resigned from President James Buchanan's cabinet. A few days later he set out for his home in Athens, Georgia. He had scarcely settled when he headed for northern Georgia to turn the sentiment among old Unionist friends into passion for secession. But despite the best efforts of this born-again state rights advocate, many Unionist delegates were chosen on January 2, 1861, to attend the mid-January convention in Milledgeville, the state capital.

On the eve of the convention Cobb took his message to a gathering of friends and delegates at the Macon home of his brother-in-law, John B. Lamar. He implored his listeners to mute Unionism, a tactic he believed would permit the convention to take Georgia out of the Union with a minimum of bickering. Although not a delegate, Cobb accompanied Lamar and his guests to nearby Milledgeville and was honored with a chair on the convention floor. On January 19 he wired his son that the ordinance of secession had been adopted. The convention completed its work by naming ten delegates to a convention of seceded states to meet in Montgomery, Alabama, on February 4. Cobb and Robert Toombs were chosen delegates-at-large along with eight district delegates. One of the latter was Cobb's younger brother Thomas. The Cobbs had fared well, thanks to Howell's prominence and zeal.

Georgia's delegates to the Montgomery convention assembled with those from South Carolina, Florida, Alabama, Mississippi, and Louisiana. The convention unanimously chose Cobb as its presiding officer. In a short acceptance speech, the incipient Confederacy's first leader announced that separation from the United States was "perfect, complete, and perpetual." He continued by urging a cordial welcome be extended to those Southern states not yet in the fold, adding emphatically that peace must be maintained not only with the late sister states of the North but with the world at large as well. He concluded by predicting for the Confederacy an "era of peace, security, and prosperity."

That Cobb was accorded the distinction of being chosen the Confederacy's first leader was an acknowledgment of his skill as a negotiator. Whether he was being rewarded or punished is not altogether clear. Impassioned secessionists may have been playing a clever game. His plea for peace recalled his dexterity during the drafting of the Compromise of 1850 when, according to his critics, he had given away too much. By electing him president of the Montgomery convention they were withholding the bigger prize, president of the Confederacy. Although Cobb denied he had been the victim of such intrigue, some of his friends believed otherwise.

With the drafting of the Constitution of the Confederate States of America, the Montgomery convention became the Provisional Congress. Cobb was convinced that its crowning achievement was the unanimous adoption on March 11 of the Constitution. None had labored more diligently than his brother in framing the document that Howell proclaimed was the "ablest ever prepared . . . for a free people." Perhaps next in importance to the adoption of the Constitution was Cobb's administration of the oath of office to President Jefferson Davis on February 18. Although pleased with the selection of Davis by the Congress, Cobb was distressed by the choice of Alexander H. Stephens as vice president. Surmounting almost two decades of political rivalry between the two was Cobb's conviction that his fellow Georgian's Unionism had survived the birth of the Confederacy.

Having met twice in Montgomery, Congress moved the capital of the Confederacy to Richmond in late May. It would hold three meetings there. Until it adjourned sine die on February 17, 1862, Cobb was its presiding officer. Meanwhile he began a second career. Assisted by relatives and friends, during the summer of 1861 he recruited the Sixteenth Georgia Infantry Regiment. Congress rewarded him on August 28 by approving his nomination for a colonelcy.

Recruitment received a mighty boost on July 21 from the defeat of Union forces at First Manassas. Cobb agreed with his brother, also a colonel, that it "has secured our independence." Howell predicted the blockade would soon be lifted and peace would follow quickly. His boundless optimism was contagious, and nine hundred Georgians joined the Sixteenth Regiment to celebrate the imminent independence of the Confederacy.

By mid-August Howell's troops were quartered at Camp Cobb, located about a mile from the state house, which was the new headquarters of the Provisional Congress. Cobb's life of political leadership and soldiery continued for eight months. Soldiery promptly presented a litany of woes. Early in September the regiment was ravaged with mumps and measles, about thirty cases proving fatal in five weeks. Meanwhile a special agent dispatched to Savannah to pick up a shipment of Enfield rifles discovered that Governor Joseph E. Brown had confiscated them. When Cobb learned what had happened, he lost his self-control, excoriated Confederate authorities, and demanded such interference cease. His demand produced a thousand rusty rifles. Cleaned and polished, they moved an official of the State Department to congratulate the Georgian on having the best guns in the Confederate army. In mid-October his son boasted that the colonel had progressed enough to shout drill orders from horseback.

On October 18 and 19 Cobb moved his troops to the Yorktown area, where they joined Gen. John B. Magruder's Army of the Peninsula. Cobb quickly developed a liking for "Prince John." Both Cobb and his brother, whose Georgia Legion was encamped nearby, believed the general was competent, though somewhat excitable, and that he was unfairly charged with a weakness for strong drink. The clammy atmosphere of the lower peninsula defied Cobb's morale-boosting improvisations. He felt unappreciated as he prepared to depart for the final session of the Provisional Congress. His brother, likewise beset with gloom, joined him in addressing a letter to the War Department requesting transfer of their commands to Georgia. The request unheeded, Cobb set out for Richmond on October 18. He arrived amid excitement over the seizure by USS *San Jacinto* of two Confederate envoys aboard the British merchantman *Trent*. Cobb believed this act was a violation of international rights.

Once invited by presidents to confer on important matters of state, Cobb was to be granted no such courtesy by President Davis. Rather, Davis dismissed the *Trent* affair with a single reference before the opening of the final session of the Provisional Congress. As the prospect of England's entering the war faded, Secretary of the Treasury Christopher G. Memminger, lamenting to Cobb that the *Trent* affair had ended as it did, trusted that further complications "between them and England" would yet end the blockade. Cobb was to cling to the hope that England would go after the "cowardly Yankee" government.

The final session of the Provisional Congress lasted about three months. This was a difficult time for Cobb. When he was in Richmond, Magruder urged him to return to Yorktown; when he was with his troops, politicians wanted him in Richmond. Magruder's continual alarms over a likely attack may have been aimed at keeping Cobb on the lower peninsula. They became a routine of camp life, Cobb conceding that without "this amusement" soldiers would forget the war and become unfit. That many of them wished to return home with their arms at the end of their twelve months' enlistment was far more upsetting to Cobb than the general's monotonous alerts. The Georgian expressed his concern to Memminger, urging that Davis instruct all generals to see that discipline was tempered with kindness. Memminger responded that Davis had promised to do all he could to soften the "old habits" of the professionals, concluding on the considerate note that Cobb would soon be "up here" to help legislate on his concern.

When Cobb returned to Richmond in mid-January 1862, the Provisional Congress was entering its final weeks. Its leader was approaching the end of a political career that had spanned over a quarter century. For the first time he was dejected over the Confederacy's prospects. This was partly due to his presumption that Gen. George B. McClellan was about to deliver a crushing blow. Helping to push him closer to defeatism was a rumor that Savannah was about to be attacked. In desperation Cobb joined three fellow Georgians in urging a scorched-earth reception. Although his fears proved groundless and his call for destruction went unheeded, Confederate reverses in February convinced him of the necessity of putting the torch to homes and fields.

As he arose before the Provisional Congress on February 17 to deliver his valedictory, Cobb lacked his earlier optimism. After excoriating the enemy and extolling the Confederacy as true to the "conservative principles" of the Founding Fathers, he pronounced Congress adjourned. Five days later, on Washington's birthday, he called into session the House of Representatives of the newly elected bicameral Congress of the Confederate States of America, administered the oath of office to Speaker Thomas S. Bocock, and summarily became a warrior statesman without portfolio.

On March 8, 1862, Cobb took charge of the newly formed Second Brigade. Recently promoted to brigadier general, he now commanded over five thousand troops consisting of four regiments, including the Sixteenth Georgia and that of his brother. While conducting a chase after Federals in North Carolina, he was ordered to join Magruder on the peninsula in accordance with a plan prescribed by Gen. Robert E. Lee to concentrate forces near Richmond. His brigade took a position across the Warwick River from the Northerners. There was little action until April 16. Then a short but hot fight took place around Lee's Mill. In this, his first test under fire, Cobb was satisfied he had handled his men well. By late June Confederate forces had withdrawn to within a few miles of Richmond. On the twenty-fifth the Seven Days' Battles began, with Magruder putting on a show of force in front of the capital. Two days later McClellan began his retreat to Harrison's Landing with Southern forces in vigorous pursuit. After losing an artillery duel and failing to overrun a rear guard at Malvern Hill on July 1, the Confederates spent the next day burying their dead. Of Cobb's men engaged in this action, one-third had been killed or wounded.

Cobb needed a rest, but having attended two fruitless parleys with Union officers on the subject of prisoner exchanges, he was asked by General Lee to try again. He refused and went home instead. Within a month he was back with the Second Brigade, now assigned to Gen. Lafayette McLaws's division of the Army of Northern Virginia. Maryland was about to be invaded and Cobb's destination was Crampton's Gap in South Mountain. On September 14 McLaws ordered Cobb to hold the Gap "if it costs the life of every man." A disaster ensued. The Second Brigade was badly mauled and its commander blistered by the staccato expletives of McLaws. Because other passes could not be sealed either, the Battle of Sharpsburg

(September 17) was indecisive. Although the invasion failed, the Army of Northern Virginia survived. The hapless Cobb was sent to the Gulf coast.

Acting on instructions from Lee, the War Department ordered Cobb to report to Gen. P. G. T. Beauregard in Charleston. Early in November the Georgian conferred with the general about his assignment to the newly created Military District of Middle Florida, one of seven in Beauregard's department. With headquarters in Quincy, middle Florida was a rich agricultural area fronting on the Gulf of Mexico between the Suwannee and Choctawhatchee rivers. It was formed to defend vital rivers, particularly the Apalachicola and its tributaries, against Federal gunboats, to protect plantations and saltworks from raids, and to discourage collusion between Federal blockaders and Unionist Southerners.

Cobb planned to secure the coast with troops and seal the important river by filling its channel with obstacles. These operations required more than the thousand troops on duty when Cobb arrived. Warning the War Department in early March against the "delusion of an early peace," he requested five thousand men. Although denied his request, he was permitted to woo volunteers by suspending conscription. When Cobb left for another duty station in September, he had raised about half the number of troops he had requested.

In August 1863, Cobb was in Atlanta conferring with Gen. Braxton Bragg, commander of the Army of Tennessee, planning the defense of Georgia. As he was preparing to return to Quincy, he received orders to tidy up the assorted recruits Governor Brown had assembled in Atlanta. Thus was born the short-lived Georgia State Guard. Until its demise in February 1864, the State Guard supplied a few troops for Bragg and for defense units in North Georgia and Savannah as well. Cobb used it to track down deserters, stragglers, and profiteers. His new assignment made him a participant in the disaster that was unfolding in Georgia, and it enabled him to renew contacts with Richmond. He met with Davis twice in Atlanta, and when he learned that the controversial Bragg was to be replaced, he headed for Richmond to plead for his choice as successor. He was pleased with the appointment of Gen. Joseph E. Johnston.

Having been promoted on December 3, Cobb arrived in Richmond as a major general. He promptly expressed concern over the absence of a comprehensive military plan, conferred with the president, and submitted to the leaders of Congress a plan that would authorize him to recruit from the State Guard a new command. Because immediate action was not taken on his proposal, he conveyed to Vice President Stephens his conviction that Congress was lack-brained.

Cobb was relieved to be back in Georgia. He promptly visited the Army of Tennessee and predicted "Old Joe"

Johnston would drive the Federals out of the state. In an unofficial letter to the president, he explained that this could be done by means of a strong drive into Tennessee. Meanwhile enlistments in the State Guard were expiring and with them Cobb's command.

For over a month Cobb was without a unit. Finally Congress acted and on April 5 the War Department braced itself for the Confederacy's last effort in the Southeast by ordering Cobb to Macon to establish headquarters for the Georgia Reserve Force. With the heaviest concentration in Macon, fewer than five thousand troops, many of them part-time soldiers, were strung between Savannah and Columbus to repel hostile forays against railroads south of Atlanta. On July 30 Cobb repulsed Gen. George Stoneman's raiders in a sharp clash east of Macon, thereby setting the stage for the capture of some six hundred raiders and their commander.

With the fall of Atlanta on September 2, 1864, matters had become critical enough to oblige Davis to visit Georgia. Arriving in Macon on the twenty-fourth, he joined Cobb in paying a visit to the Army of Tennessee encamped about twenty-five miles south of Atlanta. When the two returned to Macon, Cobb was greeted with an additional assignment. Richmond had finally put together an overall military plan, a part of which was a new command known as the District of Georgia. It embraced Macon, Columbus, and Augusta and was responsible to the Army of Tennessee. On the twenty-eighth Cobb received orders to serve as its commander. He now had two commands, but few troops. (Yet, despite this lack of manpower, he opposed recruiting slaves. He would write the secretary of war in January 1865 that "if slaves will make good soldiers our whole theory of slavery is wrong.")

From Macon, Cobb and Davis went to Augusta where on October 2 they conferred with Beauregard, newly appointed commander of the Military District of the West. Cobb returned to Macon hoping to contribute his troops to a general confrontation with the enemy. This hope was destroyed on November 15, when Gen. William Tecumseh Sherman left Atlanta in flames and began his slash-and-burn March to the Sea. Although one of Cobb's plantations became a victim of Sherman's raiders, Cobb believed that they were less devastating than the reverses suffered by the Army of Tennessee. Early in January he confessed to Davis that his despair over Sherman's outrages paled beside his unease over southwestern Georgia, where his family had gone to escape the raiders. He believed that this food basket of the Confederacy was sitting on a potential slave insurrection that could easily be ignited by the inflammable Sumter Prison at Andersonville.

With over twelve thousand "splendidly equipped" troops under Maj. Gen. James H. Wilson rampaging eastward across Alabama, southwestern Georgia suddenly acquired importance. Cobb was ordered to turn Wilson back. He had half as many men, poorly equipped. Before undertaking his final military assignment, he made a fruitless appeal to Davis for more troops.

On April 11 the sinking Confederacy's birthplace caught a glimpse of its first leader, whose devotion and faith were vanishing. In conference with the governor of Alabama it was decided that Cobb would not try to defend Montgomery; rather, he would make a stand at Columbus. Six days later Columbus fell. Cobb escaped with six hundred men under cover of darkness. Upon reaching Macon he was handed a dispatch from Beauregard dated April 20 announcing an armistice. Two days later Cobb surrendered to Wilson, was arrested, and while on the way to prison was paroled by President Andrew Johnson.

After the war Cobb practiced law in Macon, was pardoned on July 4, 1868, and on October 9 dropped dead in the lobby of New York's Fifth Avenue Hotel. He was buried in Athens.

BIBLIOGRAPHY

Coulter, E. Merton. *The Confederate States of America, 1861–1865.* A History of the South, vol. 7. Baton Rouge, La., 1950.

Foote, Shelby. *The Civil War: A Narrative.* 3 vols. New York, 1958–1974.

Franklin, John Hope. *The Emancipation Proclamation.* Garden City, N.Y., 1963.

McFeely, William S. *Frederick Douglass.* New York, 1991.

McPherson, James M. *Ordeal by Fire: The Civil War and Reconstruction.* New York, 1982.

Montgomery, Horace. *Howell Cobb's Confederate Career.* Tuscaloosa, Ala., 1959.

Simpson, John Eddins. *Howell Cobb: The Politics of Ambition.* Chicago, 1973.

Thomas, Emory M. *The Confederate Nation, 1861–1865.* New York, 1979.

HORACE MONTGOMERY

COBB, THOMAS R. R. (1823–1862), constitutional authority, secessionist, congressman from Georgia, and brigadier general. Thomas Reade Rootes Cobb was born in Jefferson County, Georgia, on April 10, 1823, reportedly weighing an incredible twenty-one and a half pounds. He was named for his mother's father, Thomas Reade Rootes of Fredericksburg, Virginia, at whose home, Federal Hill, his parents had been married.

The brilliant Georgian finished atop his graduating class at Franklin College (later the University of Georgia) and passed the state bar while only eighteen years of age. His prodigious intellect and an immense capacity for hard work yielded legal and literary accomplishments of significance during his twenties and then placed him at the forefront of Georgia secessionists. Cobb published *The Supreme Court Manual* (Athens, 1849) when he was twenty-six. Two years

THOMAS R. R. COBB.   NATIONAL ARCHIVES

later his *Digest of the Statute Laws of the State of Georgia* (Athens, 1851) won for him an enviable reputation because of its importance, thoroughness, and skillful presentation.

As controversy over slavery intensified, Cobb undertook a scholarly study of legal and historical precedents on the subject. The resulting book remains an important exposition of Southern arguments, including justification of the status quo on the basis of biblical tenets. *An Inquiry into the Law of Negro Slavery in the United States of America to which is Prefixed an Historical Sketch of Slavery* (Philadelphia, 1858) offered elaborate scientific, sociological, economic, and philosophical grounds as support for the South's peculiar institution. Predictably, *An Inquiry* attracted wide support in the South and generated bitter invective in the North. Cobb himself owned twenty-three slaves in 1860.

In addition to his legal and scholarly endeavors, Cobb expended considerable energy on education and religious activities. His steady involvement in Georgia politics grew to overwhelm all other considerations as the secession crisis intensified. After Abraham Lincoln's election Cobb delivered a fiery address to the state legislature that, in the words of Alexander H. Stephens (whom Cobb loathed), "did more . . . in carrying the State out, than all the arguments and eloquence of all others combined." When the legislature called for a convention to consider secession, Cobb campaigned feverishly, attending rallies, writing articles and

letters, and orating across the state. Cobb carried on his crusade with such ardor that he reminded his sister-in-law of "the Methodist Circuit Riders I used to know in my childhood—so thoroughly infused with the Spirit and the righteousness of the cause—that no physical discomfort dampens his zeal."

Cobb's efforts reached fruition when the convention, in which he sat after winning election by a tiny margin, adopted the ordinance of secession. Cobb served as chairman of the working committee to revise the state constitution and was one of ten Georgia delegates to the convention of seceding states that met on February 4, 1861, in Montgomery. That body, with Tom's elder brother Howell presiding, approved a provisional constitution and became the Provisional Congress of the Confederate States. The younger Cobb worked on various projects with his accustomed zeal, stalking out of meetings and engaging in bitter verbal jousts when events went against his precepts. Among the legislation he introduced were bills banning importation of slaves, protecting international copyrights, controlling Sunday mail carriage, and protecting Southern cotton. Cobb wore homespun clothes to the sessions in ostentatious token of his resistance to Northern imports. He thought many of his colleagues guilty of "selfishness, intrigue, low cunning and meanness," writing in April that the "atmosphere of this place is positively tainted with selfish ambitious schemes for personal aggrandizement." Almost every Confederate leader fell short in Cobb's eyes.

The proud and sensitive Georgian inevitably clashed with an equally prickly Jefferson Davis. The new president "is chatty and tries to be agreeable," Cobb told his wife, but "is not great in any sense of the term." In February, while differing with Davis over some relatively unimportant legislation, Cobb wrote, "I shall strive hard to pass it over his head, it will do my soul good to *rebuke* him at the outset of his vetoing." He and Davis remained on uneasy terms for the rest of Cobb's life, with the result that Cobb's military service in the field was haunted by real or imagined episodes of negative influence from the executive mansion.

By the late spring of 1861 Cobb had determined to raise a unit for military service. His sole military experience to date had been unwarranted interference with the Confederacy's civil authorities on behalf of hometown troops. Cobb's temperance enthusiasm, religious ardor, and political quarrels had colored such military dealings as had come his way. He considered a Confederate setback early in the war to be "attributable entirely to a drunken, Godless general" willing to fight on a Sunday morning. The defeat might even be blamed on the president who, "obstinate as a mule," insisted on appointing such infidels. In the throes of enthusiasm for a local company headed for war, townspeople called on Cobb one Sunday for a patriotic speech, but he substituted "a lecture of five minutes length on Sabbath-breaking.'' In that stern spirit Tom Cobb undertook the task of raising a unit of civilians and turning them into soldiers, in an arena of which he knew precisely nothing.

Cobb fell upon the notion of organizing a legion—a military establishment that encompassed artillery, cavalry, and infantry in a single unit. The idea had popular appeal but no utility whatsoever in mid-nineteenth-century warfare. The novice soldier, however, had political power at his disposal adequate to smother the opposition of professional military men, and on August 28, 1861, Congressman Cobb became Colonel Cobb of Cobb's Georgia Legion. Companies of the legion had been reaching Richmond during the summer and going into a camp of instruction nearby.

The new colonel split his time between legislative duties in the Congress and attempts to put his troops into shape. Richard B. Garnett, a veteran soldier destined for Confederate prominence, contributed substantially to the latter effort from his post as second in command of the legion. The cavalry major, Pierce Manning Butler Young, was a brilliant military leader, but Cobb disliked his personality. In fact, the mercurial Cobb waxed wrathful against almost every one of his officers at one time or another. No doubt numbers of them suffered terribly under the circumstances. They had company in their misery in the form of Cobb's superiors in the War Department, whose efforts to integrate the colonel's misbegotten legion into the country's armed forces ran afoul of Congressman Cobb's political clout. His immediate superior for an extended period was his brother Howell, a spectacularly maladroit political general but, of course, an easy man for Tom to please.

Although most of the men in the ranks had less occasion to experience Cobb's mood swings, some of them thought poorly of him. Elijah H. Sutton of one of the Georgia regiments in Cobb's Brigade wrote that both Cobb brothers were failures in the eyes of their men. Howell was a "whipped cur" in battle and full of "incompetency." After Howell's resignation and Tom's death, a new brigadier "soon gained the love of the men, something the Cobbs failed to do." Sutton hinted that Tom Cobb bled to death at Fredericksburg when stretcher-bearers refused to brave a dangerous stretch of road to hurry their general to the rear. Another enlisted man later bluntly claimed that a Confederate comrade mistreated by the general inflicted the wound that killed him. Both stories were almost certainly inaccurate, but their very existence suggests some broad dissension among the soldiery.

Other observers, however, thought that Cobb met his military obligations well. Benjamin L. Mobley of the legion thought Cobb "the best Colonel in the Confederate States" because "he dont let his men stand garde when it is raining or when it is cold." Mobley also liked his colonel's fighting spirit when Cobb said in a speech excoriating Northerners "that he wanted to hate them so bad that he would feel just

as well with a stold sheep on his back as [with a] piece of yankee goods." Henry D. McDaniel, a bright young man who later became governor of Georgia, wrote soon after Cobb's death, "I admired him more, perhaps, than any other son of my state."

Cobb's Legion, the happy and the grumbling alike, received orders on September 11, 1861, to move to Virginia's peninsula. There the men spent nearly eight months of only occasionally lively duty, much of the time under the command of the excitable Gen. John B. Magruder. Colonel Cobb quickly discovered to his dismay that the legion would not be—could not be—used en masse. The military verities that had made the legion concept obsolete dictated that Cobb's cavalry and artillery and infantry must serve where needed at various points of the compass. With a paranoia that oozed from many of his letters, Cobb insisted that such pragmatic use of the South's military resources constituted "malignant persecution" by "Davis and his minions." He threatened to resign unless his superiors ceased using his cavalry as they thought best. Cobb identified, perhaps unconsciously, the basic issue when he wrote that spreading out his troops "is most mortifying to my pride."

By the time Robert E. Lee assumed command of the army near Richmond, Cobb had been in the field for nine months, but had not yet seen any intense combat. Lee irritated Cobb as much as other professional officers had. The general was "haughty and boorish and supercilious in his bearing and is particularly so to me," Cobb wrote. In fact he loathed all West Point graduates as a group, since "self-sufficiency and self-aggrandizement are their great controlling characteristics." But by the fall of 1862, Lee's calm poise had accomplished the remarkable feat of muting Cobb's antipathy, even as the Georgian remained steadily hostile toward some of the army's command and intermittently unhappy with most of the rest.

Colonel Cobb saw limited action with his legion's cavalry during the Seven Days' Battles, and his units arrived too late to take part in the Second Battle of Manassas. The components of the legion met their baptism of fire in sustained battle action during the Maryland campaign, during which Howell Cobb failed badly at Crampton's Gap; but Tom Cobb missed this action, having gone home on leave. When he returned to the army that fall, Cobb worked energetically in political circles to effect the transfer of his legion to another theater in hopes that a change of environment might bring him the satisfaction that so persistently eluded him. Although he had sought promotion to general officer's rank for months, Cobb now loudly announced he would refuse to accept such a commission. Nevertheless, when the promotion came, on November 1, 1862, Cobb received it gladly and assumed command of the brigade that had belonged to his brother.

General Cobb's brigade held the most famous Confeder-

COCKE, PHILIP ST. GEORGE 365

ate position on the battlefield at Fredericksburg, the Sunken Road and Stone Wall at the foot of Marye's Heights. In that stronghold Cobb moved among his men on December 13, 1862, as the initial Federal attacks built up on the broad killing plain stretching below the heights. A member of his brigade wrote four days later, "Our brave and beloved Genl Cobb . . . pulled off his hat & waving it over his head exclaimed 'Get ready Boys here they come' & they did come *sure*." Cobb's Georgians readily repulsed the attacks against them all through the afternoon, but they did so without their general's leadership after the first phase of the action. A piece of Federal iron "just grazed . . . the right thigh" of the general "and struck the left where it lodged, breaking the bone & lacerating the femoral artery." The stricken general died just after 2:00 P.M. at a nearby field hospital. Ironically, he had taken his mortal wound within clear view of Federal Hill, his mother's family home at the edge of Fredericksburg, only a few hundred yards from the Sunken Road. According to a contemporary, Lee said on December 14 in an informal eulogy, "If we gain our independence we will need such a man as General Cobb was to give our country tone and character abroad."

BIBLIOGRAPHY

Cobb, Thomas R. R. "Extracts from Letters to His Wife, February 3, 1861–December 10, 1862." *Southern Historical Society Papers* 28 (1900): 280–301.

Cobb, Thomas R. R. *An Inquiry into the Law of Negro Slavery in the United States of America to which is prefixed an Historical Sketch of Slavery.* Philadelphia, 1858.

Cobb, Thomas R. R. Papers. University of Georgia, Athens; Duke University, Durham, N.C.; Georgia State Archives, Atlanta.

McCash, William B. *Thomas R. R. Cobb.* Macon, Ga., 1983.

Porter, Rufus K. "Sketch of General T. R. R. Cobb." *Land We Love* 3 (1867): 183–197.

ROBERT K. KRICK

COCKE, PHILIP ST. GEORGE (1809–1861),
brigadier general. A graduate of West Point in 1832, Cocke served two years with the artillery stationed in Charleston. In April 1834 he resigned, and for the next twenty-seven years lived the life of a planter, managing his seven plantations in Virginia and Mississippi.

On April 21, 1861, Cocke was commissioned a brigadier general of Virginia troops and ordered to defend the military district astride the Potomac River. He entered Confederate service as a colonel on May 10, 1861, and on June 20 Gen. P. G. T. Beauregard appointed him commander of the Fifth Brigade of the Army of the Potomac, comprising the Eighth, Eighteenth, Nineteenth, Twenty-eighth, and Forty-ninth Virginia regiments. During First Manassas, Cocke com-

PHILIP ST. GEORGE COCKE.   LIBRARY OF CONGRESS

manded his own brigade and Col. Nathan Evans's partial brigade, stationed between Ball's Ford and the Stone Bridge. When Federal troops attempted to flank the Confederate left, he directed reinforcements to counteract the enemy's movements. Then, when the fighting shifted to another sector, he pulled his brigade out of the line to aid in the pursuit of the retreating Federal army.

Cocke's leadership in combat merited him high praise from his superiors, but Manassas was his last battle. After being promoted to brigadier general on October 21, 1861, he returned home a broken man. The rigors of active field service shattered him both physically and spiritually, and he killed himself on December 26, 1861.

BIBLIOGRAPHY

Freeman, Douglas S. *Lee's Lieutenants: A Study in Command.* 3 vols. New York, 1942–1944. Reprint, New York, 1986.

Hotchkiss, Jed. *Virginia.* Vol. 3 of *Confederate Military History.* Edited by Clement A. Evans. Atlanta, 1899. Vol. 4 of extended ed. Wilmington, N.C., 1987.

U.S. War Department. *War of the Rebellion: A Compilation of the Official Records of the Union and Confederate Armies.* Washington, D.C., 1880–1901. Ser. 1, vol. 2, pp. 473, 477, 823, 836–837.

MICHAEL G. MAHON

COCKRELL, FRANCIS MARION

COCKRELL, FRANCIS MARION (1834–1915), brigadier general and U.S. senator. A former teacher and lawyer, Cockrell joined the Missouri State Guard in May 1861 to resist Federal troops attempting to keep Missouri in the Union. Cockrell enlisted as a private, but rose through the ranks to earn the star of a brigadier general by war's end. While his native state remained bitterly split by the war, Cockrell sided with Confederate Missourians to fight through the battles of Carthage, Wilson's Creek, Elkhorn Tavern, Corinth, the siege of Vicksburg, Port Gibson, Lost Mountain, Jonesboro, Franklin, and Mobile.

Cockrell possessed no previous military training but proved a stern disciplinarian and competent officer. Soon after his enlistment as a private in the Missouri State Guard in May 1861, Cockrell was appointed first lieutenant and shortly thereafter captain. In May 1862, he became lieutenant colonel in the newly organized Company H of the Second Missouri Infantry. Six weeks later, he was promoted to colonel of the regiment. In July 1863, Cockrell's performance at Vicksburg merited his promotion to brigadier general. In March 1864 all Missourians in the eastern theater not already in Confederate service were placed under his command.

His unswerving devotion to the Southern cause and his bravery on the field gained him official thanks from the Confederate Congress on May 23, 1864. Five times wounded and three times captured, Cockrell never gave up the struggle. He remained a stalwart supporter of Southern independence until the Confederate surrender.

On April 9, 1865, while Robert E. Lee met with Ulysses S. Grant at Appomattox to discuss peace terms, Federal soldiers captured Cockrell for the last time. Paroled on May 14, 1865, he returned home to resume his law practice. In 1875 he began a thirty-year-long career as a U.S. senator, showing the same exuberance and longevity he had had as a Confederate soldier.

BIBLIOGRAPHY

"General Francis Marion Cockrell." *Confederate Veteran* 24, no. 3 (1916): 101.

Moore, John C. *Missouri.* Vol. 9 of *Confederate Military History.* Edited by Clement A. Evans. Atlanta, 1899. Vol. 12 of extended ed. Wilmington, N.C., 1988.

Warner, Ezra J. *Generals in Gray: Lives of the Confederate Commanders.* Baton Rouge, La., 1959.

LESLEY JILL GORDON-BURR

COINS. *See* Currency, *article on* Numismatics.

COLD HARBOR, VIRGINIA

COLD HARBOR, VIRGINIA. This crossroad tavern, some ten miles northeast of Richmond, was the site of a battle during the 1864 campaign waged by Federal forces under Lt. Gen. Ulysses S. Grant against Richmond and the Army of Northern Virginia commanded by Gen. Robert E. Lee.

After the Battles of the Wilderness and Spotsylvania and the maneuvering along the North Anna River in May 1864, Grant moved his Army of the Potomac southeast across the Pamunkey River to Cold Harbor. (In effect, Grant was moving along the circumference of a circle from north of Richmond to a point east of the city.) On May 31 Grant's cavalry drove back a small force of Confederates and seized the road junction at Cold Harbor.

On June 1 Lee made an effort to regain the road junction, but the attempt failed. Both sides continued to feed troops into the area and to entrench, so that soon there were two six-mile-long parallel lines of earthen fortifications running roughly from northwest to southeast.

The Federal line from right to left consisted of the Ninth Corps, the Fifth Corps, the Eighteenth Corps, the Sixth Corps, and the Second Corps. The Confederate line from left to right was made up of the Second Corps under Maj. Gen. Jubal Early, the First Corps under Lt. Gen. Richard Heron Anderson, and the Third Corps of Lt. Gen. A. P. Hill. The southeastern ends of both lines were very close to the Chickahominy River. The weather was hot and humid.

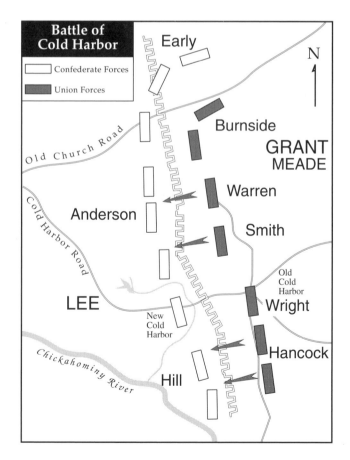

Battle of Cold Harbor
Confederate Forces
Union Forces

Skirmishing flared along the lines on June 1 and 2, although there was no significant change in the armies' positions.

Grant had planned to make a general attack on Lee's position on the morning of the second. He postponed it, however, first until 5:00 P.M. that day and then until 4:30 A.M. on the third. Grant's main effort was to be made by the Second, Sixth, and Eighteenth Corps (the left and center of his line) against Hill and Anderson (the right and center of Lee's position). The other Northern corps were to demonstrate against the Confederates in their fronts to draw attention from the real points of attack.

The Federal commander seems to have believed that the heavy fighting of the previous month had demoralized and weakened Lee's men. If the Northerners could break through the Cold Harbor line, they could destroy Lee's army, capture Richmond, and for all practical purposes end the war.

The Union soldiers knew better. Unlike Grant who had spent the war's first three years in the West, they had fought the Army of Northern Virginia for three years and Lee for two. Tradition has it that many Federal soldiers, realizing the strength of the Southern fortifications, wrote their names on slips of paper and pinned them to their uniforms so that their bodies could be identified after the battle.

The engagement itself was a short, fairly simple affair. Each of Grant's three attacking corps moved against the Confederate works in its front. The terrain and the opposing lines were such that the attacking Union columns diverged as they advanced. Each assaulting force was therefore exposed to fire from the defenders in its front as well as to that from Southerners on its flanks.

Bravery and numbers could not overcome such handicaps. The Northerners overran a few advanced Confederate outposts, but Lee's main line was far too strong to be carried. Several Federals got to within fifty yards of the main Southern works; a few to within thirty. Col. James P. McMahan carried the flag of the 164th New York regiment to the top of the Confederates' main fortification before he was shot down. Within fifteen minutes the battle, for all practical purposes, was over, and the Federal generals soon canceled plans for follow-up attacks.

Grant's army had numbered about 108,000 men in early June; Lee's about 59,000. The Federal attack at Cold Harbor cost Grant about 7,000 men. Lee lost perhaps 1,500. Grant's much heavier losses were made worse by his stubbornness. After the battle he refused to ask for a truce to bury his dead and retrieve his wounded because to do so would be to admit defeat. Not until June 7 did Grant request permission to send out parties to aid any surviving wounded soldiers and to bury those who had been killed or died from their wounds.

Soon after Cold Harbor, Grant decided on his next move.

He would make no more direct attacks on the Army of Northern Virginia. He would break away from Lee's front, cross the James River, and strike for Petersburg, some twenty-three miles south of Richmond. Early on June 13 Lee's scouts brought him word that Grant's army had disappeared.

BIBLIOGRAPHY

Dowdey, Clifford. *Lee's Last Campaign: The Story of Lee and His Men Against Grant, 1864.* Boston, 1960.

Humphreys, A. A. *The Virginia Campaign of 1864 and 1865.* New York, 1883.

Trudeau, Noah André. *Bloody Roads South: The Wilderness to Cold Harbor, May–June 1864.* Boston, 1989.

Wheeler, Richard. *On Fields of Fury: From the Wilderness to the Crater: An Eyewitness History.* New York, 1991.

RICHARD M. MCMURRY

COLLIER, CHARLES FENTON (1817–1899), congressman from Virginia. Born in Petersburg, Virginia, Collier was a leading public figure in his hometown for half a century. An Episcopalian, he attended Washington College, the University of Virginia, and Harvard. By 1860 he had become a prosperous, slave-owning planter and lawyer, with a farm in neighboring Prince George County and legal practice in town. A Unionist Democrat, Collier served in the Virginia House of Delegates from 1852 to 1854 and from 1859 to 1862.

Initially opposed to secession, he later changed his opinion and supported the Confederacy. In 1862 he replaced Roger Pryor in the Congress and served on the Commerce, War Tax, and Naval Affairs committees. His initial strong support for Jefferson Davis waned as he strove increasingly to assert congressional authority. On taxes, conscription, and impressment he diverged from the administration position. Though he generally supported conscription, by 1863 he argued for increased exemptions to cover those employed in vital civilian work. Collier belatedly favored Congress's prerogative to determine the suspension of habeas corpus but conceded authority to the president when it did not interfere with local interests. In 1863 Collier lost his bid for reelection to Judge Thomas S. Gholson.

During the remainder of the war he served on the Petersburg Common Council and earned a footnote in the history of the war as part of the delegation that formally surrendered control of the city on Monday, April 3, 1865. Under a makeshift flag of truce—a white handkerchief attached to a walking stick—he and the mayor crossed the breastworks at dawn and in a confusing scene accompanied the victorious Union troops back into the city.

The year after Appomattox, Collier was elected mayor of Petersburg, but in 1868 he was thrown out of office under

Reconstruction. Twenty years later he was again elected mayor. After a long illness, he committed suicide on June 29, 1899, and was buried in the cemetery of Blandford Church.

BIBLIOGRAPHY

Collier, Charles. "War Recollections." *Southern Historical Society Papers* 22 (1894): 69–73. Reprint, Wilmington, N.C., 1990.
Wakelyn, Jon L. *Biographical Dictionary of the Confederacy.* Edited by Frank E. Vandiver. Westport, Conn., 1977.
Warner, Ezra J., and W. Buck Yearns. *Biographical Register of the Confederate Congress.* Baton Rouge, La., 1975.

NELSON D. LANKFORD

COLONEL LAMB. The sidewheel blockade runner *Colonel Lamb,* named for William Lamb, the commander of Fort Fisher, and its sister ship *Hope,* were the largest of the blockade runners ordered by James D. Bulloch for the Confederacy through Fraser, Trenholm, and Company. Indeed, they were the largest built during the war.

Colonel Lamb, launched in May 1864, reached 16 ¾ knots on its trial trip. Designed carefully, the two ships were built of steel by Jones, Quiggin, and Company and engined by James Jack and Company, both of Liverpool, England. The steamer measured 281 feet long, 34.6 feet in breadth, 16.7 feet depth of hold, 1,132 tons gross, and 1,790 tons displacement. When loaded with 2,500 bales of cotton, *Colonel Lamb* drew eleven feet of water, or nine feet when loaded with 1,500 bales. The 350-nominal-horsepower inclined oscillating engines drove *Colonel Lamb* at fourteen knots with a full cargo.

The ship made two successful trips through the blockade into Wilmington, North Carolina, carrying provisions and munitions under Capt. Thomas Lockwood, an experienced blockade runner. When Wilmington fell, Lockwood headed for Havana, Cuba, to join other ships headed for ports on the Gulf of Mexico. When he discovered that Galveston was too shallow for the big runner, Lockwood repaired his ship at Havana and returned to Liverpool, surviving the war uncaptured.

After the Civil War ended, the blockade-running vessels were turned to other uses. Many became involved in blockade running in other conflicts. *Colonel Lamb* worked as the merchant ship *Ariel* until 1867, when the Greek government bought it for use as a military transport. Renamed *Boubalina,* the steamer suffered an explosion in its coal bunker that same year.

BIBLIOGRAPHY

Bulloch, James Dunwoody. *The Confederate Secret Service in Europe: or, How the Cruisers Were Equipped.* London, 1883.
"A Fast Blockade Runner," *Artizan* (London), October 1, 1864, p. 237.
Spratt, H. Philip. *Transatlantic Paddle Steamers.* 2d ed. Glasgow, Scotland, 1967.
Wise, Stephen. *Lifeline of the Confederacy: Blockade Running during the Civil War.* Columbia, S.C., 1988.

KEVIN J. FOSTER

COLQUITT, ALFRED H. (1824–1894), brigadier general, and postwar Georgia governor and senator. The son of a minister, Alfred Holt Colquitt was born at Monroe, Georgia, April 20, 1824. After graduating from Princeton and earning his law degree, Colquitt served as a staff officer in the war with Mexico, attaining the rank of major. A skilled orator, Colquitt was only twenty-nine when he won a seat in Congress in 1853. Because of his wife's fragile health he did not seek reelection. By 1859 Colquitt was in the political arena again, as a member of the state legislature. He was a Breckinridge elector in 1860 and helped vote the state out of the Union at the secession convention the same year.

As colonel of the Sixth Georgia, Colquitt was with the Army of Northern Virginia from the Peninsula campaign to Chancellorsville. In March 1862 John B. Magruder recommended him for promotion. Another superior lauded him as "a gallant man & skillful & experienced officer." Colquitt received his promotion September 1, 1862. Although he was criticized for his dilatory performance at Chancellorsville and for his "precipitate retreat" at Fort Fisher, he was praised by P. G. T. Beauregard for "much judgment and gallantry" at the Battle of Olustee, Florida.

Paroled at Greensboro, North Carolina, May 1, 1865, Colquitt plunged into Democratic politics again. He was twice elected governor and in 1883 was named to fill the unexpired term of U.S. Senator Benjamin H. Hill, who died in office. He served until March 26, 1894, when he, too, died in office. Colquitt was buried in Rose Hill Cemetery in Macon, Georgia.

BIBLIOGRAPHY

Compiled Military Service Records. Alfred Holt Colquitt. Microcopy M331, Roll 54. Record Group 109. National Archives, Washington, D.C.
Finnegan, Joseph. "Report of Joseph Finnegan." *Southern Historical Society Papers* 9 (1881): 18. Reprint, Wilmington, N.C., 1990.
Lamb, William. "Address by William Lamb." *Southern Historical Society Papers* 21 (1883): 289. Reprint, Wilmington, N.C., 1990.
Warner, Ezra J. *Generals in Gray: Lives of the Confederate Commanders.* Baton Rouge, La., 1959.

LOWELL REIDENBAUGH

COLSTON, RALEIGH EDWARD (1825–1896), brigadier general. Of Virginia lineage, Colston was born

RALEIGH EDWARD COLSTON.   NATIONAL ARCHIVES

October 31, 1825, in Paris, France. His father was a wealthy physician living abroad. Colston graduated in 1846 from the Virginia Military Institute and then joined the faculty as a professor of French, history, and military strategy. Thomas J. ("Stonewall") Jackson and Robert Rodes were academic colleagues.

In 1861 Colston was appointed colonel of the Sixteenth Virginia. His prewar standing brought him promotion on December 14, 1861, to brigadier general. Colston saw action at Williamsburg and had a controversial role at Seven Pines—in the confusion, he never got his brigade into the battle. For the remainder of 1862 he was disabled by illness. Colston was in command of Petersburg when, in April 1863, Stonewall Jackson chose him to head a brigade in the Second Corps. Less than a month later, Colston was leading a division into battle at Chancellorsville. The responsibilities were beyond his limited combat experience. Colston lost control of his troops on May 3; much of his division, A. P. Hill reported, was "somewhat broken and disordered" throughout that day. Transferred thereafter from the Army of Northern Virginia, Colston successively commanded garrisons at Savannah, Petersburg, and Lynchburg.

After the war he established a military school at Wil-

mington, North Carolina, but soon accepted a colonelcy in the Egyptian army. Prolonged desert service shattered his health. Impoverished and crippled, he returned to the United States in 1879 and accomplished little of note. He spent his last two years at the Confederate Soldiers' Home in Richmond, where he died July 19, 1896. Colston is buried in Richmond's Hollywood Cemetery.

BIBLIOGRAPHY

Couper, William. *One Hundred Years at V. M. I.* 4 vols. Richmond, Va., 1939.

Lewis, R. B. "General Raleigh E. Colston, C. S. Army." *Southern Historical Society Papers* 25 (1897): 346–351. Reprint, Wilmington, N.C., 1991.

JAMES I. ROBERTSON, JR.

COLUMBIA, SOUTH CAROLINA. The capital of South Carolina, Columbia is located in the geographical center of the state on a bluff overlooking the Congaree River. It played a significant role in the Confederacy from the meeting of the South Carolina secession convention on December 17, 1860, to the burning of the town during the occupation by William Tecumseh Sherman's army on February 17 and 18, 1865. Established as the state capital in 1786, Columbia had grown by 1860 to a population of 8,052. More than 3,500 of the residents were African Americans, only 250 of whom were free. The visual center of the town was the new State House, whose cornerstone had been laid in 1851 but which was still under construction. South Carolina College, founded in 1801, was located south of the State House, and the business district was clustered closely around Richardson (later Main) Street to the north. Businesses were interspersed with private dwellings. There was a market–town hall, four hotels, ten churches, and fourteen schools. Columbia was a large cotton marketing center, with warehouses and brokers located in Cotton Town on Upper Boundary (later Elmwood) Street on the town's northern border.

Intense excitement gripped Columbia when the state legislature met on November 5, 1860, and chose presidential electors, calling on the twelfth for a state convention to assemble on December 17. The streets filled with crowds as prominent leaders spoke from hotel balconies. At the annual meeting of the state agriculture society, the president denounced the Republican party as "vulgar, coarse, and insolent." It was, he said, "restricted by no Constitution, and only impelled by hatred to the slaveholder and his slave." South Carolina College professor Joseph LeConte said that secession was in the air "like a spiritual contagion."

The state convention met in the Baptist church and declared the state's intention to secede, but it adjourned to

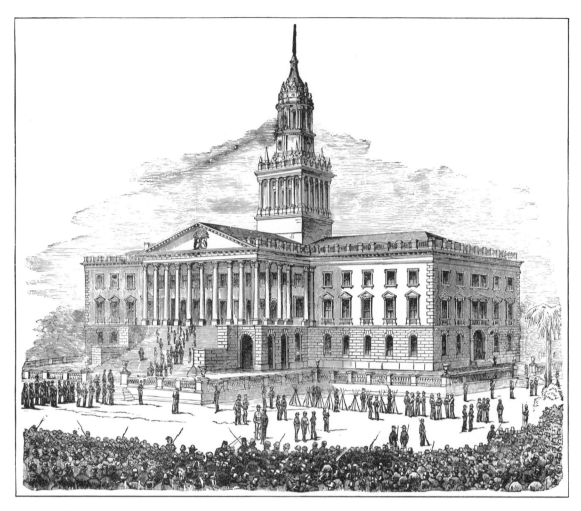

New State House at Columbia, South Carolina.

The Soldier in Our Civil War

Charleston when local cases of smallpox were reported. When news of secession reached Columbia from Charleston, it was greeted with bonfires, cannons, bell-ringing, and parades. P. F. Frazee, an abolitionist carriage maker, was whipped, tarred and feathered, and exiled to the North because of his views.

Local militia companies volunteered for Confederate service, and a training camp was established first at the fairgrounds and later at Lightwood Knot Springs. A prisoner of war camp for Union officers, called Camp Sorghum by inmates because of the poor rations, was located on the west bank of the Congaree River. State offices for Confederate bureaus in Columbia included the Conscription, Medical, Commissary, Quartermaster, and Paymaster departments.

In 1862 Confederate printing operations were moved to Columbia from Richmond. "Government girls" were employed to print currency and bonds. A military hospital opened at the fairgrounds, and in 1862 it moved to the South Carolina College campus. Professor Joseph LeConte

supervised the largest Confederate medical manufacturing facility at the fairgrounds, and a niter works for the making of gunpowder opened at the state hospital.

Local businesses also aided the war effort. The Saluda Factory on the west bank of the Congaree produced woolen cloth, and others made socks, buttons, shoes, uniforms, and hats for the army. On the Columbia Canal a mill produced gunpowder, and local foundries manufactured bayonets, swords, and cannonballs.

Persons engaged in these activities and refugees from the low country swelled the population to some 25,000 by 1865. Many people could not afford food at inflated prices, and a Corn Association was formed in April 1863 to distribute food. By September, 2,000 people were receiving relief. In 1864 the Board of Relief listed 1,100 names. Citizens used locally made soap, sea salt, and sorghum in place of manufactured products. No coffee was available, so they brewed beverages from parched sweet potatoes, okra seed, peanuts, and other substitutes.

As prices increased, there was public criticism of speculators and "extortioners." Increased supplies of paper money further depreciated its value. The cost of cloth produced by a local factory was attacked so fiercely that the owners sold out at half price. Flannel cloth soon cost forty dollars a yard. By January 1865, local merchants refused to accept Confederate currency for provisions.

The women of Columbia opened a soldiers' rest home in the Charlotte Railroad depot in late 1861. After it was moved to the South Carolina Railroad depot, it was enlarged and renamed the Wayside Hospital. Some 75,000 wounded soldiers are said to have been given aid. In 1862 the Ladies' Hospital opened near the Charlotte depot.

To raise funds for relief and hospital work the women of the town held concerts, dances, fairs, and suppers. The most elaborate event was the Great Bazaar held in the State House in January 1865. Booths represented every Southern state, and almost all items produced in the Confederacy were on sale. The remarkable amount of $350,000 was raised.

As the war continued, Columbia was used as a place of safe storage by low-country residents for silver plate, bank funds, and valuable possessions. The bells of St. Michael's Church in Charleston were sent to Columbia, as was the library of the College of Charleston. But by 1865 town law enforcement was breaking down. The gaslights went unlighted, and burglary was common.

In January 1865 General Sherman left Savannah and marched into South Carolina. At the request of the citizens of Columbia, Gen. Robert E. Lee ordered 2,000 cavalry under the command of Wade Hampton to defend Hampton's home. On February 16 Sherman's army arrived before Columbia and from a hill west of the Congaree River began to shell the South Carolina Railroad depot, troop concentrations, and other strategic points.

Sherman issued Special Field Order Number 26, instructing Gen. O. O. Howard to cross the river, occupy the town, and destroy public buildings, transportation, and manufacturing. They were to spare libraries, asylums, and private homes, however. Meanwhile, Confederate officials began an evacuation of the town. Sizable amounts of Confederate and state property were lost. Hampton ordered the cotton warehouses emptied and the cotton burned outside of town. For lack of transport facilities, the cotton was rolled into the streets. Before he left Columbia, however, Hampton canceled the order to burn the cotton.

During the night of February 16-17, Confederate troops withdrew, and stragglers and town residents plundered the warehouses and depots. Cotton was ignited and powder exploded at the South Carolina Railroad depot. The Charlotte depot was set on fire by the departing troops. On the morning of February 17, Mayor Thomas J. Goodwyn surrendered Columbia to the advancing Union army. As the troops entered the town, local citizens plied them with the ample stores of wine and whiskey.

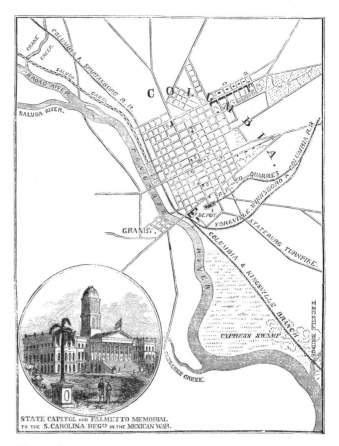

MAP OF COLUMBIA.

HARPER'S PICTORIAL HISTORY OF THE GREAT REBELLION

After nightfall on February 17 more fires broke out. Local fire companies were overwhelmed, and Union troops were ordered to extinguish the fires. A powerful wind came out of the northwest, fanning the flames. Accounts tell of sparks filling the air and blazing shingles blowing from one building to another. Roving bands of civilians and soldiers—both black and white—destroyed property, threatened citizens, and spread fires. Finally, between 1:00 and 2:00 in the morning troops were called in to restore order. The wind subsided about 3:00, and by 5:00 the streets were clear. Two soldiers had been killed, thirty persons wounded, and 370 arrested. Among them were officers, soldiers, and civilians.

On the morning of February 18 General Howard began locating shelters for the homeless. He established tight security in the city and turned over all food and supplies not needed by the army for distribution to citizens. He gave rifles and ammunition to the mayor to use for protection once the army left. Meanwhile Sherman ordered the destruction of railroads, bridges, and war matériel stored in the area. On February 20 the Union army marched northward out of Columbia.

For three months seven thousand to eight thousand persons were issued daily rations. Towns as far away as

Augusta and Charlotte sent supplies by wagon. After the surrender of the Confederate armies in the East in April, local and state government passed into the hands of the military. On May 25 troops of the Twenty-fifth Ohio Regiment arrived in Columbia, and the era of Reconstruction began.

Two major questions remained about the burning of Columbia—the extent of the fire and who was responsible. A few days after the fire Southern author William Gilmore Simms made a survey of Columbia and listed 1,386 buildings destroyed. A recent study by historian Marion B. Lucas, however, indicates the loss of 458 structures, including 193 public buildings. The major destruction was limited to the central business district—about one-third of the city.

Another lasting dispute was who was to blame for the destruction. Ten days after the fire Wade Hampton accused Sherman: "You laid the whole city in ashes, leaving in its ruins thousands of old men and helpless women and children." In his official report Sherman claimed to have saved what remained of the city and blamed Hampton for "filling it with lint, cotton, and tinder." In a series of newspaper articles in March and April 1865, Simms concluded that Sherman was responsible, and a local committee of citizens laid the blame on the Union soldiers. In 1873 the Mixed Commission on British and American Claims concluded that blame "was not to be ascribed to either the intention or default of either the Federal or confederate officers." A collection of data made by Senator Coleman L. Blease in 1929 and 1930 contained no new evidence. Marion Lucas concluded in his 1976 study that "the fire was an accident of war." Confederate confusion over whether the cotton was to be burned was reckless. Citizens giving whiskey to Union soldiers was inexcusable. Failure of Union officers to end the rioting in the city was careless. Only when the wind subsided was the fire controlled.

BIBLIOGRAPHY

Cauthen, Charles E. "Confederacy and Reconstruction." In *Columbia, Capital City of South Carolina, 1786–1936.* Edited by Helen K. Hennig. Columbia, S.C., 1936.

Edgar, Walter B., and Deborah K. Woolley. *Columbia, Portrait of a City.* Norfolk, Va., 1986.

Lucas, Marion B. *Sherman and the Burning of Columbia.* College Station, Tex., 1976.

A. V. HUFF, JR.

COLUMBUS NAVAL IRON WORKS. Estab-

lished in Columbus, Georgia, in 1853 on the Chattahoochee River as the Columbus Iron Works Company, this foundry and machine shop during the antebellum years engaged in the manufacture of a variety of iron and brass products, including steam engines and boilers. With the coming of the war, the company initially produced ordnance for the Confederate military, but the Navy Department leased the works on September 1, 1862, and converted it to the manufacture of marine steam machinery. Under the command of Chief Engineer James H. Warner and renamed the C.S. Naval Iron Works, the plant underwent expansion, ultimately acquiring as subsidiary works William Penny & Co. of Prattville, Alabama, and J. W. Young & Co. of Eufaula, Alabama. Workers started the construction of a large rolling mill capable of producing two-inch armor plate but never finished it. The Columbus unit employed nearly three hundred hands, about half of whom were black. Operations ceased April 16, 1865, when Federal troops under Gen. James H. Wilson captured Columbus and systematically destroyed all of the city's industries, including the Naval Iron Works.

As many as fourteen sets of engines and boilers were either manufactured or converted for use in Southern warships, making the Naval Iron Works the most important source of naval powerplants in the Confederacy. The ironclads *Columbia, Savannah,* and *Tennessee* were among those vessels supplied with Columbus machinery.

BIBLIOGRAPHY

Still, William N. *Confederate Shipbuilding.* 2d ed. Columbia, S.C., 1987.

Still, William N. *Iron Afloat: The Story of the Confederate Armorclads.* 2d ed. Columbia, S.C., 1985.

Turner, Maxine. *Navy Gray: A Story of the Confederate Navy on the Chattahoochee and Apalachicola Rivers.* Tuscaloosa, Ala., 1988.

A. ROBERT HOLCOMBE, JR.

COLYAR, A. S. (1818–1907), congressman from

Tennessee. Scion of an early Tennessee pioneer who had fought against British Loyalists at King's Mountain, North Carolina, Arthur Colyar, one of thirteen children, was born near Jonesboro, Washington County, Tennessee. When still a young boy, he moved west with his family to Franklin County, where he obtained a common school education and later commenced work as a schoolteacher. He also read law under Micah Tall, a former congressman from Kentucky, and was admitted to the bar at Winchester (1846). An ardent Whig in a traditionally Democratic stronghold, Colyar, who on the eve of the war owned more than two dozen slaves, was also a staunch Unionist and a member of the Constitutional Union party, which nominated John Bell of Tennessee for president. He opposed secession until his state declared its independence in June 1861, after, as he later recalled, "almost the entire people of his part of the state had taken ground against the United States Government."

In October 1861, while a candidate for the First Confederate Congress, Colyar contracted pneumonia and retired from the race, which was eventually won by William H. Tibbs. During the next two years, Colyar appears to have practiced law in Winchester (at one point risking his life to defend a Union man who had been unlawfully arrested) until he was forced to leave his home when William S. Rosecrans's Federals overran the town. Colyar was in Tullahoma, Tennessee, on the night of June 30, 1863, when he sent a message warning of the advancing army to the already-nervous Gen. Braxton Bragg, prompting the Confederate commander to order the full withdrawal of his troops below the Tennessee River.

Although he had not sought the office, Colyar was elected in November 1863 to represent Tennessee's Third District in Richmond in place of Tibbs. He finally took his seat on May 2, 1864, the first day of the opening session, and served continually until Congress adjourned sine die on March 18, 1865. A member of the House Ways and Means Committee, Colyar introduced eighteen bills, most having to do with fiscal matters. He disliked economic controls but supported direct taxation, the tax-in-kind on agriculture, and the levy on corporate profits. Colyar stood alone among the Tennessee delegation against a December 1864 measure that increased congressmen's salaries by 50 percent. He also opposed the sequestration of property belonging to persons fleeing the Confederacy to avoid the draft as well as the suspension of the writ of habeas corpus, and he steadfastly resisted the idea of permitting slaves to serve as support personnel in the Confederate army. In addition, he favored discussions with the North in December 1864 for "an early and honourable peace," and he voted against expelling fellow Tennessean Senator Henry S. Foote for undertaking such negotiations.

"No man has been in the Southern Congress who is more deserving of pardon than Mr. Collier [sic]," remarked Governor William G. Brownlow of Tennessee, whose unusually kind endorsement led to Colyar's receiving a presidential amnesty fairly early, on September 22, 1865. Afterward he resided in Nashville, practicing law and engaging in a variety of business and political activities. He was on several occasions throughout the 1870s a third-party candidate for governor and was elected as an independent to represent Davidson County in the general assembly (1877–1879). Colyar also owned and edited for several years the *Nashville American,* a newspaper that advocated the building of a New South by encouraging agricultural diversification, industrial development, Northern capital, and foreign immigration. It was during these postwar years that Colyar achieved his greatest renown and fortune, investing heavily in the coal and iron furnace industries. He was also largely responsible for locating the University of the South at Sewanee.

BIBLIOGRAPHY

Amnesty File. A. S. Colyar. Microcopy M1003, Roll 48. Record Group 94. National Archives, Washington, D.C.
Ball, Clyde. "The Public Career of Colonel A. S. Colyar: 1870–77." Master's thesis, Vanderbilt University, 1949.
Davis, Thomas W. "Arthur S. Colyar and the New South: 1860–1905." Ph.D. diss., University of Missouri, 1962.
Journal of the Congress of the Confederate States of America, 1861–1865. 7 vols. Washington, D.C., 1904–1905.
Warner, Ezra J., and W. Buck Yearns. *Biographical Register of the Confederate Congress.* Baton Rouge, La., 1975.

R. B. ROSENBURG

COMMERCE. *See* Economy.

COMMERCE RAIDERS. Raiders were naval warships that preyed upon the merchant ships of enemy nations. Commerce raiding, or *guerre de course,* was a strategy employed by weaker naval powers against nations with a large merchant marine. Raiders drove up insurance rates on the enemy's merchant shipping and caused many ships to flee to the protection of other countries' flags. They could be a powerful tool in economic warfare. Successful commerce raiders often forced the enemy to pursue them rather than participate in military actions against home shores. They generally sought to avoid contact with enemy warships because of their light armament.

The Confederacy employed both public (naval) and private (privateer) forms of commerce raiding. Commissioned naval vessels were sent to distant sea lanes to hunt, capture, or destroy traders. Privately owned, government-licensed warships, called privateers, generally sought to capture merchant vessels for profit in waters closer to home. Privateers had nearly become obsolete with the advent of steam propulsion. The Treaty of Paris of 1856 outlawed privateering and regulated government commerce raiding. The United States and Spain, alone among the major maritime nations, refused to sign. Thus neither the United States nor the Confederate States had renounced privateering when the Civil War began.

One of President Jefferson Davis's first actions in office was his April 17, 1861, call for privateers to be licensed. Letters of marque, the government commission papers of privateers, were issued quickly; within two months over a dozen prizes had been brought into Southern ports. Privateering vessels required speed, minimal armament, and a relatively small crew. Most were small, fast schooners and brigs, although some were steamships. Most privateers operated in the waters around weakly blockaded ports, dashing beyond the safety of friendly coastal defenses to snatch a prize sailing near shore. A few privateers made cruises off the New England coast and in the Caribbean.

Confederate Government Commerce Raiders

Cruiser Name	Dimensions[1]	Guns	Prizes
Alabama	L. 220', b. 31'6.7" dph. 17'8"	8	69 (58 sunk, 9 bonded, 2 ransomed)
Archer[2]	90 tons	1	1 (sunk)
Chickamauga	L. 174'1.2", b. 25'.8" dph. 14.2	3	4 (sunk)
Clarence[2]	L. 114', b. 24' dr. 11'	1	7 (6 sunk, 1 bonded)
Florida	L. 171', b. 29'11" dph. 9'6"	8	37 (33 sunk, 4 bonded)
Georgia	L. 212', b. 27' dph. 13'9"	5	9 (5 sunk, 4 bonded)
Nashville	L. 271', b. 62' dph. 13'	2	2 (sunk)
Shenandoah	L. 230', b. 32' dph. 20'6	8	37 (32 sunk, 3 bonded, 2 ransomed)
Sumter	L. 184', b. 30'	5	17 (7 sunk, 2 bonded, 8 released)
Tacony[2]	296 tons	1	14 (9 sunk, 4 bonded, 1 recaptured)
Tallahassee	L. 220', b. 24' dph. 14'	3	35 (sunk)
Tuscaloosa[3]	500 tons	3	2 (1 sunk, 1 bonded)

[1]Length (L.), beam (b.), drafts (dr.), and depth of hold (dph.) in feet; tons.
[2]Captured, commissioned, and armed at sea by *Florida*.
[3]Captured, commissioned, and armed at sea by *Alabama*.

Several ships were quite successful, but economic considerations led to the demise of privateering. By mid-1863 larger numbers of blockaders patrolling the coast decreased the chance to earn a profit in privateering while the potential profit from blockade running increased.

The naval vessels best suited for commerce raiding could make long cruises, had speed sufficient to run from more powerful ships, and an armament to match any adversary that could catch them. Generally, these vessels had full sailing rigs to minimize coal consumption, and steam engines driving a propeller to add speed for chasing and running. Government cruisers generally operated in areas far removed from Southern shores; indeed only five of the twelve most successful commerce raiders were ever in a Confederate port.

Commerce raiders, both naval and private, caused many problems for neutral nations. Foreign governments trod a narrow path to avoid favoring one side or the other in the struggle. Early in the war, as a result of President Abraham Lincoln's proclamation of blockade, Great Britain and France recognized the Confederacy as a belligerent. The recognition of belligerency allowed the infant nation to purchase stores and weapons. Both Great Britain and France, however, forbade the belligerents to recruit or fit out expeditions in their territory. Thus, vessels and their armament could be purchased in Europe, but ordnance could not be fitted, nor the crew engaged, at the time of sailing. This prevented several Confederate raiders from sailing after being purchased in Great Britain and France. Warships of both the Confederacy and the Union were allowed to replenish coal occasionally in neutral ports but could not recruit or engage the enemy while in neutral waters. Violations of the duties of neutrals and of their sovereignty caused a number of diplomatic incidents and led, after the war, to the international arbitration of the *Alabama* Claims.

Neutrality restrictions also prevented Confederate privateers and government warships from bringing prizes into foreign waters. This prohibition led to the slow death of privateering for economic reasons: prizes had to be brought into port and sold for profit. It also led to the destruction, rather than the appropriation, of prizes taken by government cruisers. After seven prizes captured by the raider *Sumter* were allowed to go free from Cienfuegos, Cuba, in 1861, Confederate cruisers destroyed prizes rather than attempting to send them to the South by way of neutral ports.

The first Confederate government commerce raider to prey on Northern shipping was the small steam-auxiliary *Sumter,* which sailed on June 30, 1861. The steamer was converted in New Orleans from a passenger-cargo vessel into an ocean cruiser. Under its talented captain, Raphael Semmes, *Sumter* captured eighteen Union vessels in a seven-month cruise through the Gulf of Mexico and the North Atlantic. Suffering from worn-out engines and boilers, *Sumter* was laid up and later sold at Gibraltar.

The next Confederate raider to sail was the former passenger steamer *Nashville*. It was seized at Charleston, armed with two small 12-pounder cannons, and commissioned CSS *Nashville*. Under Lt. Robert Pegram it made a voyage in 1861 from Charleston to Southampton, England. *Nashville* destroyed the U.S. clipper ship *Harvey Birch* in the English Channel on the outward voyage; on the return trip it burned another Union vessel. The Confederate navy sold it as unsuitable for its use, and the next owner converted *Nashville* into a blockade runner.

Several exceptional groups of Confederate commerce raiders used whaleboats and small schooners to hunt prizes.

Acting as maritime guerrillas, these men employed impudence, stealth, local knowledge, and careful planning to strike at unarmed Union merchant vessels, and occasionally warships, in waters throughout the Confederacy. Three maritime guerrillas were particularly successful: John Taylor Wood, John Y. Beall, and John Clibbon Braine.

Commander John Taylor Wood, CSN, captured seven Union vessels between October 1862 and February 1864. He conducted raids in whaleboats that had been carried to various river landings atop wagons. Wood became President Davis's naval aide and eventually commanded *Tallahassee,* a more capable vessel. At the war's end, Wood and several other prominent Confederates escaped to Cuba through Florida waters in a stolen small boat.

Master John Y. Beall, CSN, of Matthews County, Virginia, became the "Mosby of the Chesapeake," capturing small Union vessels on the bay. Beall and a party of watermen destroyed four Federal schooners on September 19, 1863. Beall was captured and imprisoned in November 1863, but was paroled in March 1864. He then organized a breakout attempt from Point Lookout Prison, Virginia, that failed. Leading another raiding party, he seized the steamers *Philo Parsons* and *Island Queen* on September 19, 1864. On December 16 of that year, while trying to free seven Confederate prisoners being moved to Fort LaFayette in New York, Beall was captured by Union forces. They hanged him as a spy at Governor's Island, New York Harbor, on February 24, 1865, although he was a warrant officer operating under orders.

Another Confederate commerce raider, John Clibbon Braine, sailed with clandestine parties of Confederates on board passenger steamers. Braine and his companions captured the steamer *Chesapeake* in December 1863, the steamer *Roanoke* in September 1864, and the schooners *St. Mary's* and *Spafford* in March 1865.

The largest Confederate commerce raiding program was based on the work of James Dunwoody Bulloch and other naval officers in Europe. They ordered vessels built for government service in foreign shipyards and arranged delivery of the armament and crew at some remote point. The first of Bulloch's ships completed was the cruiser *Florida.* Built on the plans of a British Royal Navy cruiser at Birkenhead, England, it sailed on March 22, 1862. *Florida* met the steamer *Bahama* in the Bahama Islands and received guns and crew. The raider was partially armed and commissioned August 10, 1862, but the men discovered that crucial parts of its guns had been left behind. *Florida* had to run the blockade in and out of Mobile, Alabama, for additional crewmen and ordnance parts. Operating under three captains, *Florida* captured thirty-seven Union merchant vessels. The Confederates converted one of its prizes, the bark *Clarence,* into a lightly armed cruiser. *Clarence* and a succession of armed prizes, the barks *Tacony* and

Archer, captured twenty-three further vessels. *Florida* was captured and towed from the harbor of Bahia, Brazil, by USS *Wachusetts* in violation of Brazilian neutrality. The United States promised to return *Florida* to Brazil, but the ship "accidentally sank" before the promise could be kept.

The most successful Confederate raider was CSS *Alabama.* It sailed on July 29, 1862, from Liverpool and met two ships carrying its officers, crew, and armament at Terceira in the Azores. On August 24, Raphael Semmes commissioned the ship CSS *Alabama.* It cruised the North Atlantic and sailed into the Gulf of Mexico where it sank the blockader USS *Hatteras* off Galveston, Texas. *Alabama* captured sixty-nine vessels, sinking fifty-eight of them. In the South Atlantic, Semmes commissioned the captured bark *Conrad* as the subsidiary cruiser CSS *Tuscaloosa.* It in turn captured two vessels. After a cruise through the Indian and Atlantic oceans, *Alabama* met and was sunk by the Union cruiser USS *Kearsarge* in battle off the coast of Cherbourg, France, in the English Channel.

Another purchasing agent, Capt. Matthew Fontaine Maury, CSN, bought the new iron, sail-auxiliary screw steamship *Japan* at Dumbarton, Scotland, for conversion into a cruiser. The ship left Scotland on April 1, 1863, and met the steamer *Alar* off Ushant, France, to receive arms and supplies. Its commander, William L. Maury, commissioned the vessel CSS *Georgia* on April 9, 1863. Maury burned five of the nine ships that he captured during a seven-month cruise in the Atlantic. When the iron hull proved unsuitable for a cruiser, *Georgia* was decommissioned at Liverpool and sold.

Another of Matthew Maury's purchases was not as successful. On November 24, 1863, the former Royal Navy cruiser *Victor* left Sheerness, England, under suspicion of violating British neutrality laws. Outside of British territorial waters it was commissioned CSS *Rappahannock.* The ship was to meet *Georgia* off the French coast to receive armament, but severe machinery problems forced it to put in at Calais, France, for repairs. The ship was found unsuitable for service as a cruiser and sat out the remainder of the war as a station ship at Calais.

American protests to the British government following the successes of *Florida, Alabama,* and *Georgia* led to the seizure of several vessels on suspicion of their violating British neutrality. The first was a small cruiser, *Alexandra,* being built as a gift for the Confederate government. A second, more substantial cruiser, similar to *Alabama,* was seized in Glasgow for similar reasons. This steam-auxiliary sailing ship, named *Canton* or *Pampero,* might have been a formidable commerce raider had it been commissioned.

When highly suitable vessels could not be found for commerce raiding, the Confederacy pressed other ships into service. In the summer and fall of 1864, two blockade runners were converted into commerce raiders while in

Confederate ports. The runner *Atalanta* became the raider CSS *Tallahassee* and later CSS *Olustee;* the runner *Edith* became CSS *Chickamauga.* Navy Secretary Stephen R. Mallory chose John Taylor Wood, who had done well in guerrilla raids on Chesapeake Bay, as *Tallahassee's* first commander. *Tallahassee-Olustee* captured and destroyed thirty-five vessels during two cruises. *Chickamauga* sank four during a single short cruise.

The last Confederate commerce raider to operate was the full-rigged clipper steam-auxiliary ship *Shenandoah.* Formerly the merchant vessel *Sea King, Shenandoah* cruised against the New England whaling fleets in the Pacific and Arctic. It captured thirty-seven vessels and burned thirty-two. Its commander, James Waddell, did not learn that the war had ended until August 2, 1865. *Shenandoah* sailed for the United Kingdom, arriving November 6, 1865, the last Confederate military unit to fly the national ensign.

A number of vessels intended for commerce raiding were nearing completion when the war ended. Four enlarged and improved *Alabama*-type corvettes built in France and six fast twin-screw steamers built in Great Britain were never delivered to the Confederacy. The French government prevented the corvettes from sailing, and the Confederacy sold the ships to raise money for other projects. The six guerrilla raiders built on the *Tallahassee* model were fast twin-screw steamers with a small sailing rig. They were designed to pay for themselves first by running the blockade and then by making dashes against coastal commerce, fishing fleets, and Northern seacoast cities. These ten ships were ultimately dispersed to the Prussian, Brazilian, and Peruvian navies.

Following the end of the war, the United States brought suit against Great Britain, holding that that country was liable for not exercising "due diligence" to prevent the depredations of the commerce raiders purchased there. An international tribunal of arbitration was established in Geneva, Switzerland, to decide the case. Great Britain, found liable for the acts of *Florida, Alabama, Shenandoah,* and their tenders, settled the case in 1873 by paying the United States $15.5 million in gold.

Confederate raiding of Northern merchant fleets was among the most successful programs of the government. The commerce raiders did great damage to the Northern economy. Over three hundred vessels were destroyed and many hundreds more were sold to foreigners to prevent financial ruin if captured by a raider. It took the U.S. merchant fleet over forty years to recover from the depredations of the Confederate commerce raiders.

[*See also Alabama* Claims; Anglo-Confederate Purchasing; Enchantress Affair; Privateers; *and entries on the ships* Alabama, Alexandra, Chickamauga, Florida, Georgia, Jefferson Davis, Nashville, Rappahannock, Savannah, Shenandoah, Sumter, Tallahassee, *and* Tuscaloosa.]

BIBLIOGRAPHY

Bulloch, James D. *The Secret Service of the Confederate States in Europe; or, How the Confederate Cruisers Were Equipped.* 2 Vols. New York, 1884. Reprint, New York, 1959.

Dalzell, George W. *The Flight from the Flag: The Continuing Effect of the Civil War upon the American Carrying Trade.* Chapel Hill, N.C., 1940.

Forrest, Douglas French. *Odyssey in Gray: A Diary of Confederate Service, 1863–1865.* Edited by William N. Still. Richmond, Va., 1979.

Lester, Richard I. *Confederate Finance and Purchasing in Great Britain.* Charlottesville, Va., 1975.

Merli, Frank J. *Great Britain and the Confederate Navy, 1861–1865.* Bloomington, Ind., 1970.

Robinson, William Morrison, Jr. *The Confederate Privateers.* New Haven, 1928.

Semmes, Raphael. *Memoirs of Service Afloat during the War between the States.* Baltimore, 1869. Reprint, Secaucus, N.J., 1987.

KEVIN J. FOSTER

COMMISSARY BUREAU.

On February 26, 1861, President Jefferson Davis signed a bill creating the Commissary Bureau (or Subsistence Department) whose function was to provide rations for the Confederate States army. The bureau was headed first by Col. Lucius B. Northrop of South Carolina (March 27, 1861–February 16, 1865) and then by Brig. Gen. Isaac M. St. John of Georgia (February 16, 1865, to the end of the war).

The bureau was originally designed to operate with one colonel who was to serve as commissary general, four captains called commissaries, and as many lieutenants (subalterans) of the line, called assistant commissaries, as were necessary to accomplish the bureau's mission. On March 14 and May 16, 1861, acts of Congress slightly altered the rank structure and added two more officers. Civilians were hired as clerks, and by 1863 the bureau employed thirty-six in Richmond.

Following the precedent established in the prewar U.S. Army, the commissary general was supposed to run a simple senior office with a minimum of personnel. His subordinates in the office would handle functional areas, such as the procurement of bacon or beans, and ensure that the right number of rations reached the right group of soldiers. Each of the major armies had a staff officer assigned as commissary. This relieved the commanding general of the onerous details of ordering the correct amount of bread or beans for subordinate units and ensuring that food got to where it was supposed to go. Often the officer was an experienced commissary with direct ties to the bureau and strong loyalty to the commissary general. This practice occasionally led to divided allegiance between the unit commander and the commissary general.

Custom dictated that each commander of a division, brigade, or regiment assign quartermaster duties to one of his officers. These men were usually not professional commissaries or experienced in supply matters. They rarely wanted this unglamorous job and often treated it as a curse or a sign of the commander's displeasure. Thus, commissary problems, because of divided loyalties and lack of attention by commanders, multiplied. These problems proved to be a major impediment to the combat efficiency of the Confederate army from its inception and were accentuated as the size of the army grew.

The problem of feeding the Confederate armies was exacerbated by Davis's choice of Lucius B. Northrop as the commissary general. Northrop, a West Point graduate in the class of 1833, had been dropped from army rolls in 1848 because of a string of sick furloughs. Davis, then U.S. secretary of war, had reinstated him eight months later, but Northrop's ill health kept him in South Carolina where he became a doctor. Northrop resigned his U.S. Army commission January 8, 1861, and on March 13, Davis offered him a captain's billet in the Commissary Bureau. Apparently because he was unable to find anyone else who would take the job as commissary general, Davis named Northrop to the post. Thus, the Confederacy had to make do with an inexperienced individual of dubious health in a vital position.

Northrop rapidly had subsistence matters in a shambles. Legislation passed on March 6, 1861, had provided that enlisted men, both regular and provisional, were to receive one ration a day. That ration, like so much else in the Confederacy, was based on prewar U.S. Army standards: ¾ pound of pork or bacon or 1¼ pounds of fresh or salt beef, and 18 ounces of bread or flour, or 12 ounces of hard bread, or 1¼ pounds of corn meal. In addition, units were to receive ample supplies of peas, beans, or rice; coffee; sugar; vinegar; tallow; soap; and salt. But in the agriculturally rich Confederacy, Northrop and his department failed miserably to provide even this simple staple diet to the South's common soldiers.

Not content with the process of procuring foodstuffs and distributing them to the army, Northrop soon attempted to control all food production in the Confederacy, and his bureaucratic nature added to the distribution problems. He maintained that the bureau could mass-purchase vital raw materials where they were cheapest, transport them to be processed, and then stockpile or distribute the product to the hungry armies. But he soon ran afoul of currency shortages, wartime inflation, transportation difficulties, and spoilage of perishables.

The plight of the Confederate army at Manassas, Virginia, in the spring and summer of 1862 illustrates the damage that Northrop did and foreshadowed the failure of the bureau throughout the war. As soon as the army started gathering at Manassas, Northrop ordered commissaries not to purchase local wheat because it cost more than wheat in south-central Virginia. Wheat would be shipped by railroad to Richmond to be milled into flour and subsequently shipped to the army farther north. Each stage added to the flour's cost and tied up limited rail assets. Thus officers at Manassas watched flour, raised and milled locally, being loaded onto trains going to Richmond, while government flour was being off-loaded from the same train. Northrop's policy of mass purchase was good in theory, but when applied it overburdened the limited Confederate railroad system. It also often left, as in the case of Manassas, vital assets of the Confederacy within easy reach of the enemy.

In addition to Northrop's inexperience and unrealistic economic ideas, other factors combined to ensure the Commissary Bureau's failure. Spiraling inflation caused prices for goods to escalate rapidly out of the purchase range of the commissaries. They were forced to resort to impressment to provide foodstuffs to satisfy the ever-increasing appetite of the army. Impressment, an emergency power granted under the Constitution, allowed government agents to commandeer private property as long as the owner was justly compensated. But the issue of just compensation was regulated by the commissary general and did not reflect local market prices. Commissaries often impressed goods at prices far below their true market value.

Impressment combined with the South's degrading transportation system, both rail and horse, detrimentally effected those Southerners living nearest the railroads. Unable to transport goods great distances, commissaries overburdened areas that were convenient to lines of communication. Thus, a farm owner near a railroad could be "impressed to death" by having his crops and horses taken while his peers in hard-to-reach rural areas would be unaffected. This practice led to numerous complaints and charges of corruption by the Confederate Congress.

As early as March 1862, commissaries in Tennessee were under investigation, and after the summer of 1862, the bureau was the target of a continual string of congressional investigations and special committees. In its attempt to control the bureau, Congress on December 31, 1864, debated an Act to Protect the Confederate States against Frauds. Senator George N. Lester of Georgia voiced the feelings of most of the Confederacy. He gave his support to the act and stated:

> From one end to the other of the Confederacy loud voices of complaint come up [that] . . . the quartermasters and commissaries . . . are growing vastly rich by fraud, corruption, mismanagement, and illegitimate use of public property and money entrusted to their custody and disbursement.

By 1865 charges of corruption were so strong that Congress attempted to legislate the Commissary Bureau almost out of existence and send the majority of the over two thousand civilians and soldiers controlled by the department to duty with the army. President Davis vetoed the bill because it would have been detrimental to the army.

Complaints by Robert E. Lee and other Confederate commanders led to the far more competent Brig. Gen. Isaac M. St. John replacing Northrop on February 16, 1865. St. John was a Yale graduate and had been an engineer and in the railroad business before the war. His skillful handling of the Niter and Mining Bureau led to his position as commissary general. But even St. John's skill could not overcome the problems created by Northrop and inflation, limited assets, and degraded railroads in the short life left to the Confederacy.

Civil War scholar James I. Robertson, Jr., has said that the Army of Northern Virginia did not lose any battles because of a lack of ammunition. The same cannot be said for a lack of rations. The Confederate soldier faced two enemies, the Federals and hunger. In the end both of these enemies won.

[*See also* Impressment; Northrop, Lucius B.; St. John, Isaac M.]

BIBLIOGRAPHY

Coulter, Merton E. *The Confederate States of America, 1861–1865.* A History of the South, vol. 7. Baton Rouge, La., 1950.

Davis, Jefferson. *Jefferson Davis, Constitutionalist: His Letters, Papers and Speeches.* Jackson, Miss., 1923.

Eaton, Clement. *A History of the Southern Confederacy.* New York, 1954.

Goff, Richard D. *Confederate Supply.* Durham, N.C., 1969.

U.S. War Department. *War of the Rebellion: A Compilation of the Official Records of the Union and Confederate Armies.* Washington, 1880–1901. Ser. 4, vol. 1, pp. 869–879.

Vandiver, Frank E. *Rebel Brass: The Confederate Command System.* Baton Rouge, La., 1956.

Weinert, Richard P. *The Confederate Regular Army.* Shippensburg, Pa., 1991.

P. NEAL MEIER

COMMUNITY LIFE. The degree to which community life in the South was altered during the years of the Confederacy is one of the central topics of Southern history. A primary difficulty is defining exactly what composed a Southern community before the war. For the vast majority of Southerners, both free and slave, antebellum community life encompassed a rural existence. Although substantial urban centers such as Richmond, Charleston, and New Orleans existed and exhibited distinctive characteristics, for most Southerners community life centered on their rural county of residence. These counties did contain some market towns and county seats, but population centers rarely numbered more than a thousand inhabitants.

Although their county was the fundamental administrative unit that governed their public lives, on a day-to-day basis the private lives of most Southerners centered on their rural neighborhood, an area of about fifty to a hundred square miles in which they and their relatives and friends were born, married, and died. These self-contained rural neighborhoods, which usually were named after the predominant river or creek in the area, were focused on a general store, post office, and church. In some areas of the South the rural neighborhood even defined the political party identification of most of its residents.

The events at the outset of the Civil War reflected the degree to which these rural neighborhoods had been the center of antebellum Southern community life. For years before 1861 they had formed the basis of the local militia. Hence, when the Southern states seceded and joined the Confederacy, the antebellum militia units could be rapidly transformed into state military companies that formed the basis of the Confederate army. For example, the militia unit in the northeastern rural neighborhood of Flat River in Orange County, North Carolina, produced the Flat River Guards under the command of the officers who had directed the antebellum volunteer company of the same name.

The fact that the military units consisted of men who resided in the same rural neighborhood and county was very important in the early years of the war. This link between community life and military structure probably eased the difficult transition many Southern soldiers must have experienced when for the first time in their lives they traveled far outside their community of birth. To share this experience with neighbors not only made the transition easier but also gave a community-based meaning to the cause for which these men were fighting. Since most Southern white men did not own slaves, they clearly could not have been motivated to risk their lives solely to protect other men's property. But once the public accolades and excitement that accompanied enlisting ended and these men found themselves on the battlefield, the fact that their companies were composed of relatives and neighbors provided them with a sense that they were fighting the war to defend their communities. But, in turn, as the war progressed and the first companies suffered casualties, soldiers who were not residents of the same rural neighborhood or even the same county had to be recruited to fill the ranks. The traditional sense of camaraderie must have severely declined, resulting in diminished morale.

The rural neighborhood basis of community life was also important for civilians during the Confederacy. During the initial mobilization in 1861 most Southern states, which were unprepared for war, relied on the counties and especially the rural neighborhoods to supply the troops with basic necessities. Much of this activity was led by the women's aid societies that were formed in nearly every town and neighborhood in Southern counties. The first task of the societies was to clothe the soldiers in the local companies. To do this, they raised money by holding concerts and other public events. The money was then used to buy material from which the societies sewed the company uniforms and blankets. The pace of the activity of the aid societies usually began to slacken within a year of mobilization, as the states acquired the resources to supply their troops and the civilian population began to experience shortages.

On the home front the war had a distinct impact on community life. Although the impact was most obvious in communities that became battlefields or were invaded by the enemy, life in other communities, too, was altered. For example, all Southern communities witnessed the departure of men between the ages of eighteen and forty-five. It was not unusual for at least 70 percent of the men of that age group to be absent from their community for some period during the war.

The departure of these men had a profound social and economic impact on community life. As they went off to war, the marriage and birth rates in most communities declined sharply. The impact of this development was not confined to the years of the Confederacy. With as many as one-fourth to one-third of all Confederate soldiers having died, many Southern women were never able to marry. Further, the departure of so many men also caused a severe decline in the labor force since the vast majority of families did not own slaves. As a result, by 1862 and increasingly in 1863 crop production in the South stood far below prewar levels and every community experienced the resulting inflation.

The loss of so many men also forced Southern county governments to assume far greater responsibilities for the welfare of their residents than before. County courts began to appropriate what had before the war been unheard of sums to provide relief for the wives and children of soldiers who could not care for themselves. Often the money was raised by taxing masters for their slaves at rates that would never have been possible before the conflict.

Although initially the county courts provided direct grants of money to the needy, it became apparent that this method was insufficient, as inflation caused Southern farmers to increase the prices they charged for their products. Hence, the counties found it necessary to send agents to other communities and even other states to purchase corn and other foodstuffs for distribution directly to the needy. In some communities the local government used the tax-in-kind law passed by the Confederate Congress in April 1863 to collect one-tenth of all farm products. Finally, many local governments began to attempt to fix prices to restrain the ravages inflicted by inflation. Hence, where before 1861 Southern rural neighborhoods had been

largely self-sufficient, during the last two years of the war they were forced to provide for the basic needs of a substantial share of their population and to intervene in the economy in ways never before considered legitimate for local government.

Besides the growing need to provide for the welfare of many of their residents, the economy of Southern communities was influenced by the tremendous civilian relocation that accompanied Union invasions of outlying regions of the Confederacy. For example, when the Union army invaded the Albemarle Sound of North Carolina in 1862, large numbers of planters and their slaves in the region rapidly relocated up-country. These refugees not only bid up the cost of supplies in the communities where they resettled, thereby worsening the problem of inflation; their decision to relocate their slaves caused other disruptions. Many of these low-country slaves were leased out to Piedmont masters who had little concern about their well-being. Further, the influx of slaves who had heard of and sometimes witnessed a Union invasion, combined with the shortage of white men, held the potential for significant conflict. In an extreme example, within a two-week period in 1863 two masters in Orange County, North Carolina, were murdered by their slaves.

The threat to traditional community norms not only came from changes in the slave community. Although scholars disagree over the extent of social unity among Southern whites before the war, there is general agreement that during the years of the Confederacy the degree of social tension increased. The change in social relations among whites can be observed in three communities in different regions of North Carolina. In Washington County, a low-country community that experienced invasion very early in the war, social unity declined rapidly when the property interests of yeoman farmers and planters clashed, as yeomen disagreed with the way planters led recruitment efforts and supported the draft. In turn, the yeoman challenge caused planters to tighten their control over local courts and the militia. By June 1862 yeomen with Unionist sympathies, combined with tenant farmers and white laborers, had begun to confiscate the property of planters who had moved up-country to avoid the Union invasion of the region. When planters tried to reassert their antebellum level of control, guerrilla warfare ensued.

Guerrilla warfare also characterized the decline in unity at the other end of North Carolina in the mountain community of Shelton Laurel in Madison County. Here the nature of class tension was far more complex than in Washington County, for Confederate supporters in this community tended to be both the wealthiest and the poorest residents, whereas the sympathies of Unionists were shaped by their physical distance from the slave population. When by the fall of 1862 the deprivations of war as well as the threat of conscription had led local Unionists to raid a village in their community, locally based Confederate forces responded in January 1863 by attacking civilians whom they believed to be Unionists. After capturing a number of men, most of whom had not participated in the raid, the Confederates murdered thirteen of them ranging in age from thirteen to sixty.

Although most Confederate communities did not experience the violence that shattered the traditional order of Washington County and Shelton Laurel, few could avoid the growth of dissension against the war effort. Even in Orange County, a Piedmont North Carolina county that did not face Union invasion until after Robert E. Lee's surrender to Ulysses S. Grant, after two years of war a marked decline in morale created political dissension. As early as August 1863 at meetings in the community there were calls for convening a peace convention. By the fall of 1864 some community leaders advocated peace even at the price of emancipation.

Although the Civil War clearly altered Southern community life during the years of the Confederacy, the long-term impact is less evident. Despite leaving their own communities for the first time as a result of the war and experiencing life in other communities where they served, once the war ended and they returned home the common goal of most Confederate soldiers was to reestablish as closely as possible their prewar lives. With the major exception of the effects of emancipation, white Southerners largely succeeded in re-creating a community life similar to that which had existed before the Confederacy.

[*See also* Class Conflict; Conscription; Crime and Punishment; Marriage and Divorce; Morale; Religion; Slavery, *article on* Slave Life; Society; Soldiers' Aid Societies; State Socialism.]

BIBLIOGRAPHY

Burton, Orville Vernon. *In My Father's House Are Many Mansions: Family and Community in Edgefield, South Carolina.* Chapel Hill, N.C., 1985.

Campbell, Randolph B. *A Southern Community in Crisis: Harrison County, Texas, 1850–1880.* Austin, Tex., 1983.

Durrill, Wayne K. *War of Another Kind: A Southern Community in the Great Rebellion.* New York, 1990.

Escott, Paul D. *After Secession: Jefferson Davis and the Failure of Confederate Nationalism.* Baton Rouge, La., 1978.

Harris, J. William. *Plain Folk and Gentry in a Slave Society: White Liberty and Black Slavery in Augusta's Hinterlands.* Middletown, Conn., 1985.

Kenzer, Robert C. *Kinship and Neighborhood in a Southern Community: Orange County, North Carolina, 1849–1881.* Knoxville, Tenn., 1987.

Paludan, Phillip Shaw. *Victims: A True Story of the Civil War.* Knoxville, Tenn., 1981.

ROBERT C. KENZER

COMPROMISE OF 1850.

In the 1840s Americans' enthusiasm for expansion collided with growing antislavery sentiments, and the resulting controversy spurred a search for some formula to resolve the issue of slavery in the territories. The Compromise of 1850 was the most comprehensive effort by Congress to solve territorial and slavery-related problems. For a few years it was applauded and sometimes revered, but by 1854 its flaws and new territorial disputes had revealed the failure of this legislation to remove the causes of conflict.

President James K. Polk entered the White House in 1845 determined to add territory to the United States, and the war with Mexico expanded the nation's borders to the Pacific Ocean. The Wilmot Proviso, however, offered in 1846 by David Wilmot, a representative from Pennsylvania who belonged to Polk's own Democratic party, exposed the internal dangers of such continental visions. Wilmot proposed that slavery be prohibited from any lands gained from Mexico. Though his idea never became law, it polarized Congress and aroused state legislatures, North and South.

In the 1848 presidential campaign, Democrat Lewis Cass advanced an idea that became known as "popular sovereignty." Although Congress at some point would have to approve statehood for a new territory, Cass suggested that it should "in the meantime" stay out of territorial questions, allowing the people living there "to regulate their own concerns in their own way." This was an attractive formula to many, but it raised doubts among Southern leaders, who insisted that slaveholders had a right to carry slaves into any territory during the territorial stage. Many Northerners, on the other hand, wanted and expected settlers to prohibit slavery before statehood. For political benefit Democrats interpreted Cass's idea differently to Northerners and Southerners, but distrust of Cass in the South helped elect his Whig opponent, slave-owning Zachary Taylor.

The gold rush of 1849 forced these divisive issues onto Congress's agenda as more than eighty thousand people streamed into California. President Taylor urged them to apply for admission into the Union, and they did so, proposing a state constitution that barred slavery. California's application threatened to end for the foreseeable future the balance between free and slave states in the Senate. Immediately some Southerners objected that California should be a slave state or that the Missouri Compromise line should at least be extended westward to the Pacific. Nine Southern states sent representatives to the Nashville Convention, which asserted slaveholders' rights and endorsed extension of the Missouri Compromise line. President Taylor remained adamant for California's admission, but his sudden death in July 1850 left the decision to Congress.

In these circumstances the venerable and respected

LEGISLATORS OF THE COMPROMISE OF 1850.   A commemoration of efforts to preserve the Union, the print may also refer to the presidential campaign of 1852, in which the Compromise became a key piece of rhetoric for both the Whig and the Democratic parties. In the front row, from left to right, are Winfield Scott (seated, holding a portfolio containing documents and maps of the Mexican War), Lewis Cass (with document "Protest Treaty"), Henry Clay (seated), John Calhoun (who actually opposed the compromise), Daniel Webster, and Millard Fillmore (with shield). Between Calhoun and Webster is a copy of the Constitution and a bust of George Washington. In the background at left are Howell Cobb, James McDowell, Thomas Hart Benton, and John M. Clayton. At far right, top row, are Willie P. Magnum, W. R. King, Daniel S. Dickinson, John McLean, John Bell, and John C. Frémont. Beneath them in the middle row are Thomas Corwin, James Buchanan, Stephen A. Douglas, John J. Crittenden, Sam Houston, and Henry Foote. In the distance is a temple with colonnade surmounted by a large ball, a figure with a liberty cap, and a phoenix. Engraving with etching and mezzotint on wove paper. Painted by Thomas H. Matteson, engraved by Henry S. Sadd, New York, 1852.   LIBRARY OF CONGRESS

Henry Clay, who had played a prominent part in the compromises of 1820 and 1833, assumed a central role. In January 1850 the Whig leader proposed an overall settlement packaged as one piece of legislation, the "omnibus bill." Stephen A. Douglas of Illinois, a rising star in the Democratic party, assisted Clay. The senators' proposals encompassed five major areas. First, California would enter the Union as a free state. Second, new territories called New Mexico and Utah would be organized in the Southwest with governments empowered to legislate on "all rightful subjects . . . consistent with the Constitution." This ambiguous

phrase, interpreted differently by Southerners and Northerners, continued the confusion inherent in Cass's original proposal. In fact, the legislation anticipated disagreement and provided for appeal of a territorial legislature's action directly to the U.S. Supreme Court. Third, Texas would give up its claims to a more extensive western boundary, and in exchange the United States would assume the state's public debt. Fourth, the slave trade in the District of Columbia would be ended. And fifth, a stronger fugitive slave law for the nation would be enacted.

For six months Clay and Douglas worked to arrange

support for the omnibus bill, but when it finally came to a vote, it was defeated. The prospect of an overall adjustment had not been attractive enough to overcome sectional objections. With Clay sick and absent from Washington, Douglas devised another strategy. He proposed the five elements of the compromise as five separate bills, hoping to piece together different majorities for each part of the compromise. The strategy worked, and by September 17 the Compromise of 1850 had become law. Each bill had gained a majority, although the bulk of Northern and Southern congressmen voted against each other in every instance but one.

Crowds in the capital celebrated the passage of the compromise, and initially political leaders hailed it as a settlement of the issues that threatened to divide the nation. In 1852 Franklin Pierce, who pledged to support the compromise, won a smashing victory in the presidential election. The views of his Whig opponent, Winfield Scott, were unknown, and Free Soil candidate John P. Hale openly repudiated the compromise. Thus, this legislation seemed to have won broad acceptance and growing prestige. By 1854, however, the peacemaking properties of the legislation had vanished.

What caused this great reversal? First, the Compromise of 1850 had skirted, rather than settled, the controversy over what rights proslavery and antislavery settlers had in the territories. The ambiguous language of the bill provided no formula to guide the future. Northerners continued to believe that slavery could and should be prohibited from the territories, whereas Southerners insisted that they had the right to carry slaves into any territory before it became a state. In 1850 one witty observer had remarked that Congress was passing a lawsuit rather than a law, and truly the compromise did nothing to settle the status of slavery in the territories. Thus, in 1854, when territorial organization for Kansas and Nebraska was considered, bitter disputes broke out anew. Second, the Fugitive Slave Law contained questionable features that soon fueled controversy. African Americans who were alleged to be escaped slaves had no opportunity in legal proceedings under the law to challenge that claim, and Federal commissioners received ten dollars for each fugitive they returned to slavery but only five dollars for alleged fugitives they set free. These provisions violated the beliefs many held about fair play and the right to a trial by jury. Moreover, under the Fugitive Slave Law, gripping human dramas began to occur in Northern towns and cities as freedom-loving men and women, some of whom had lived in the North for decades, were arrested and remanded to slavery. The Compromise of 1850 had proved, in the words of historian David Potter, to be only an "armistice," not "a true compromise."

[See also Georgia Platform; Bleeding Kansas; Dred Scott Decision; Fugitive Slave Law; Missouri Compromise; Wilmot Proviso.]

BIBLIOGRAPHY

Campbell, Stanley W. *The Slave Catchers: Enforcement of the Fugitive Slave Law, 1850–1860*. Chapel Hill, N.C., 1961.
Hamilton, Holman. *Prologue to Conflict: The Crisis and Compromise of 1850*. Lexington, Ky., 1964.
Potter, David M. *The Impending Crisis, 1848–1861*. New York, 1976.

PAUL D. ESCOTT

CONFEDERATE STATES OF AMERICA.

[*This entry serves as a general introduction to the history of the Confederacy. For further discussion of the origin of the Confederacy, see* Civil War, *article on* Causes of the War; Nationalism; Secession; State Rights. *For further discussion of Confederate government and politics, see* Cabinet; Congress; Constitution; Diplomacy; Judiciary; Politics; Presidency; Public Finance; *and articles on particular states. For further discussion of Confederate society, economy, and culture, see* Community Life; Economy; Nationalism; Slavery; Society. *For further discussion of the Civil War and its effects on the Confederacy, see* Army; Civil War; Morale; Navy; Prisoners of War. *See also* Bibliography and Historiography *as well as biographies of numerous figures mentioned herein.*]

Some Southerners came to believe that the South possessed a character quite distinct from that of the North, distinct enough to qualify the region for separate nationhood. They looked upon themselves as constituting a suppressed nationality comparable to the Irish or the Polish, though they could hardly claim a distinctive language, religion, or tribal history.

There were, of course, real differences between the North and the South. The most important consisted of the relatively rapid industrialization of the one section and the persistence of a slavery-based agricultural economy in the other. Cotton and slavery might have provided an adequate basis for Southern nationality and independence—if American nationalism and the spirit of Union had been less strong than they proved to be. Southern nationalists did not want war, but war came, and as a result their experiment with independence was brief, lasting only from 1861 to 1865.

Sectionalism and Secession. Ever since the founding of the American republic, sectionalism had erupted in a Union-threatening crisis from time to time. At the constitutional convention of 1787, the project for a "more perfect Union" was endangered when Northern and Southern delegates disagreed on such questions as the prohibition of slave imports. The Union seemed at risk in 1819 when a controversy arose over the admission of Missouri as a slave state, and again in 1832 when South Carolina nullified Federal tariff laws. An even more serious crisis occurred in 1850; it resulted from a number of sectional disputes, the most serious of which concerned the status of slavery in the territories. Compromises enabled the Union to survive each of these crises.

So long as political parties remained national in membership, partisanship offset sectionalism and made compromise possible. Then, in the 1850s, partisanship gave way to sectionalism as the Whig party disappeared, the Democratic party split, and the new Republican party gained strength. President George Washington had warned in his Farewell Address (1796) that the Union would be imperiled if a time should ever come when parties were organized on a geographical basis, with a party of the North and another of the South. By 1860, that time had arrived. The party of the North, the Republicans, now elected their presidential candidate, Abraham Lincoln, though they failed to win a majority in either house of Congress.

South Carolinians made Lincoln's election the occasion for adopting an ordinance of secession and declaring South Carolina an independent state on December 20, 1860. In doing so, they followed a theory and a procedure that John C. Calhoun had formulated years earlier. According to Calhoun's doctrine of state sovereignty and state rights, secession was a perfectly legal and constitutional process. By February 1, 1861, the other six states of the lower South—Mississippi, Florida, Alabama, Georgia, Louisiana, and Texas—had followed South Carolina's example, though some secessionists justified their action on the basis of a revolutionary rather than a constitutional right, citing the precedent of July 4, 1776.

In the slave states of the upper South and the border, leaders hoped for a compromise that would preserve the Union, and with that object in view Virginia invited the rest of the states, North and South, to a peace convention, which met in Washington, D.C., but accomplished nothing. Meanwhile another convention sat in Montgomery, Alabama, and organized a provisional government for the Confederate States of America.

The seceded states had taken over most of the Federal property within their borders. A few forts remained under Federal control, most conspicuously Fort Sumter in Charleston Harbor. Confederate policy, as set in a resolution of the Provisional Congress, looked to the acquisition of these forts by negotiation if possible and by force if necessary. Lincoln, however, announced his intention to "hold, occupy, and possess" all the forts and other Federal property, and he refused to deal with commissioners from the Confederacy. When a Federal relief expedition approached Charleston Harbor, the Confederates opened fire on Fort Sumter, April 12, 1861, and compelled its surrender on April 14. The next day Lincoln called upon the states remaining in the Union for troops to enforce Federal laws in the states that had withdrawn from it.

The governors of Virginia, Tennessee, Arkansas, North Carolina, Missouri, Kentucky, and Delaware rejected Lincoln's call. Virginia and Tennessee began at once to give military support to the Confederacy, without waiting for the referenda that eventually showed majorities in both states in favor of secession. Conventions in Arkansas and North Carolina soon voted to secede. Extralegal bodies later proclaimed the secession of Missouri and Kentucky, and the Confederacy claimed both of these states also. Both were represented in the Confederate Congress, but their legitimate governments and a majority of their people remained loyal to the Union.

Constitution and Government. Montgomery remained the Confederate capital until July 1862, when the government moved to Richmond, Virginia. Meanwhile the Montgomery convention performed three functions: it chose a provisional president and vice president, served as a Provisional Congress, and drew up a constitution for the Confederacy.

For president, the convention selected Jefferson Davis, recently a U.S. senator from Mississippi and formerly a secretary of war and a professional soldier. For vice president, the choice was Alexander H. Stephens, long a congressman from Georgia. Both men had been moderates rather than fire-eaters, or extreme secessionists. Both were later elected, without opposition, to regular terms in office.

The Provisional Congress reenacted all U.S. laws not inconsistent with the Confederate Constitution, and this document was an exact copy of the U.S. Constitution except for certain significant changes. For instance, the president was given an item veto, and he and the vice president were limited to a single six-year term. Protective tariffs were prohibited. So were slave importations, but the institution of slavery itself was guaranteed. As Stephens declared, the "cornerstone" of the Confederacy was the same as that of slavery—the principle of the inequality of the white and black races.

After the unicameral Provisional Congress (1861–1862), there were two regular Congresses (1862–1864, 1864–1865). Each of these, like the U.S. model, consisted of a House and a Senate. Of the 267 men who, during the life of the Confederacy, served as senators or representatives, almost a third had been members of the U.S. Congress at one time or another, and one had been a U.S. president—John Tyler.

The Confederate Congress established six departments: State, Treasury, War, Navy, Justice, and Post Office. These duplicated the U.S. departments except for Justice, which the United States had not yet created, and Interior, which the Confederacy omitted. The new postal service succeeded the old without a break, the Southern employees of the U.S. government becoming employees of the Confederate government overnight.

Heads of departments changed frequently, so that Davis's cabinet had much less stability than Lincoln's. The most influential of Davis's cabinet advisers was Judah P. Ben-

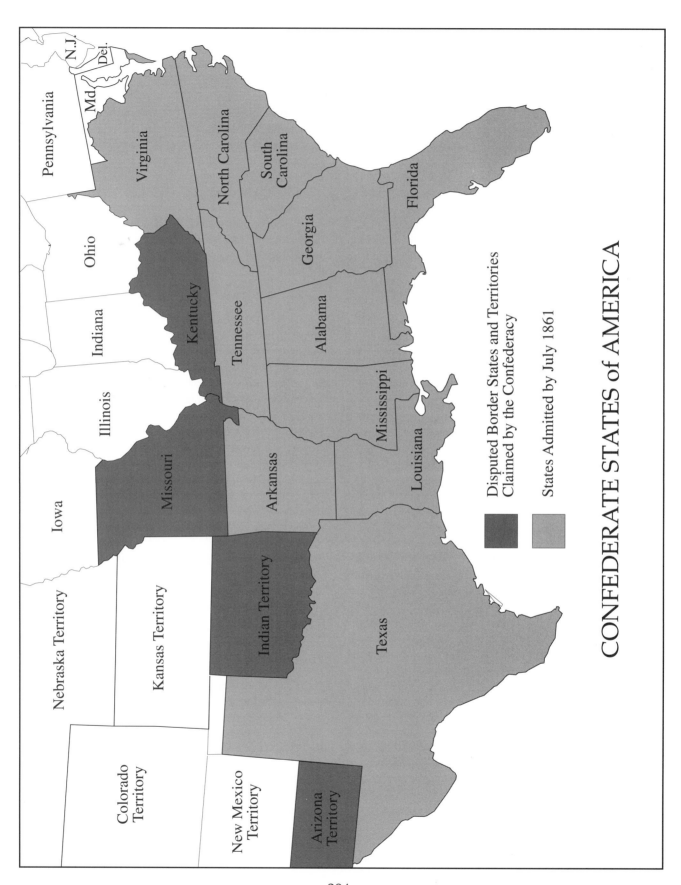

CONFEDERATE STATES of AMERICA

Disputed Border States and Territories Claimed by the Confederacy

States Admitted by July 1861

jamin, successively attorney general, secretary of war, and secretary of state.

The Confederate Constitution provided for a judiciary with a supreme court, but Congress included no such high tribunal when setting up a court system.

Diplomacy. At first, the Confederates looked confidently to Europe for assistance that would enable them to establish their independence. They were encouraged by the example of the Revolutionary War, in which France had intervened to help the rebellious English colonies succeed. They were further encouraged by the doctrine of King Cotton: they thought Great Britain and France were so dependent on Southern cotton that the two powers, to maintain their supply, would step in and end the war, with the Confederacy intact.

The Confederates promptly sent missions to Britain, France, Russia, and other countries to seek recognition and aid. It looked for a time as if Britain would go to war with the United States after a U.S. warship seized two of the Confederate emissaries, James M. Mason and John Slidell, from the British steamer *Trent* while they were on their way abroad (November 1861). But neither the British nor any other government ever officially received a diplomat from the Confederacy or recognized it as a member of the family of nations.

Britain did recognize the belligerency, though not the independence, of the Confederacy when Queen Victoria issued her proclamation of neutrality (May 13, 1861). Other countries did the same. This meant that they would extend to the Confederacy the rights of a nation at war under international law.

The British government violated its neutrality to the extent of allowing British shipbuilders to sell *Alabama* and other warships to the Confederacy. These, constituting the main force of the Confederate navy, engaged in commerce raiding on the high seas. They had access to foreign ports but not to their own, which were shut off by the Union blockade. Arguing that the blockade was ineffective and hence illegal, the Confederates tried unsuccessfully to persuade the British to break it.

When Emperor Napoleon III of France set up a puppet government in Mexico, the Confederates were willing to give it recognition (thus disregarding the Monroe Doctrine) in return for French recognition of their own government, but nothing came of this idea.

In the end, Confederate diplomacy failed partly because the European interest in Southern cotton was offset by other economic interests. More important, the European powers were divided, and Russia was conspicuously friendly to the United States. Neither Britain nor France dared risk intervention so long as the Confederacy had not clearly demonstrated its ability to survive with very little outside help.

The Army. The president of the Confederate States, like the president of the United States, was commander in chief of the army and navy. Except for what coordination President Davis could provide, the Confederacy had no unified command until near the end of the war, when Robert E. Lee became general in chief. Originally, both a Regular Army and a Provisional Army were contemplated, but the Regular Army never developed, and the Provisional Army fought the war.

Troops were recruited for this army directly as individuals and indirectly as members of state militias, which the governors furnished. From the outset men were impressed, or drafted, into state militias, but the Confederacy in its direct recruiting relied on volunteers until April 16, 1862, when its Congress passed the first national conscription act in American history. This act applied at first to able-bodied men from eighteen to thirty-five and eventually to those from seventeen to fifty. It exempted state officeholders, workers in a variety of presumably indispensable occupations, and one owner or overseer for every twenty slaves. It also exempted men who could provide substitutes. All these provisions were unpopular, and most were modified before the end of the war.

Volunteers continued to enlist and did so in about the same numbers as were conscripted. How many men, all together, served in the Confederate army can only be guessed at. The most reliable estimate is 850,000 to 900,000, or somewhat less than half as many as served in the Union army, but a much higher proportion of the white population. At any given time the effective strength of the armed forces was considerably less than the numbers on the rolls. Many were absent without leave—as many as two-thirds in late 1864 according to Davis himself. Some deserters joined the enemy, and so did some draft evaders. More than 100,000 such "tories" fought on the Union side.

The Confederacy also lost considerable numbers as prisoners of war. In 1862 the Federal and Confederate authorities agreed to a cartel providing for a regular and large-scale exchange of prisoners. The arrangement soon broke down because Davis refused to exchange black prisoners or their white officers and declared Benjamin F. Butler and his subordinates "outlaws" to be executed if captured. As Union prisoners accumulated, the Confederates were unable to provide suitable facilities for all of them, and terrible suffering resulted at Andersonville and other Southern prisons. Still, Union General in Chief Ulysses S. Grant was unwilling to renew the cartel, since the return of prisoners would benefit the Confederacy more than the Union, the Confederacy being more desperately in need of additional troops.

So desperate were Confederate leaders by 1865 that they finally decided to recruit slaves, but the war ended before any blacks actually served as Confederate soldiers.

Strategy. To maintain their independence, the Confederates needed not to win the war but only to keep the Federals from winning it. The Confederacy did not possess sufficient human and material resources to overwhelm the North in any case. Hence Davis adopted an essentially defensive though by no means entirely passive strategy. It was offensive-defensive. Throughout the war, while undertaking to repel Federal advances, the Confederates also made extensive counterthrusts from time to time.

Thus in 1862 Thomas J. ("Stonewall") Jackson sped northward down the Shenandoah Valley to threaten Washington and draw Federals away from beleaguered Richmond. Robert E. Lee and Braxton Bragg made simultaneous movements into Maryland and Kentucky, movements that culminated in the Confederate recapture of Harpers Ferry and in Confederate retreats from Sharpsburg, Perryville, and Murfreesboro.

In 1863 Lee invaded Pennsylvania with the twofold objective of intensifying the war-weariness of the North and relieving the pressure on Vicksburg, which was under siege. He retreated from Gettysburg and the Confederates surrendered Vicksburg on the same day, July 4, 1863.

Again in 1864, when Federals were hemming in Richmond and Petersburg, Jubal Early attempted to divert them by raiding the outskirts of Washington. And finally, after the fall of Atlanta, John Bell Hood attacked the Federals at Nashville, only to be routed.

Meanwhile John Hunt Morgan, Nathan Bedford Forrest, and Joseph Wheeler made cavalry raids into Union-held areas of the South and even into Kentucky, Indiana, and Ohio.

The Confederate strategy did not prevent the steady loss of territory to the Federals. After only a little more than a year of war, the Confederacy had lost control of northeastern Virginia, stretches of the coast from North Carolina to Florida, and a large part of both Tennessee and Louisiana, including the state capitals, Nashville and New Orleans. By the end of 1863 more than half of the original Confederacy had been isolated from the Richmond government because of Federal penetration, and by the end of 1864 no more than three states—most of Virginia and North and South Carolina—remained under the government's control.

This does not necessarily mean that the Davis policy was ill-advised. "If it did not win the war," as historian Frank Vandiver has written, "the offensive-defensive did enable the Confederates to outlast their resources—ample proof of the soundness of the strategy and the strategist."

The Economy. Far inferior to the Union in both human and material resources, the Confederacy at the start could claim only about two-fifths as many people (a third of them slaves), one-fourth as much bank capital, and one-tenth as great a manufacturing capacity. The Confederacy did produce more corn and livestock per capita, and it had a large potential asset in its cotton crop.

The Confederates failed to make timely and adequate use of the cotton as a basis for foreign credit. Hence financing the war proved difficult. Bullion and coin were relatively scarce, and the Confederates had to rely much more on the issue of paper money and much less on taxation and borrowing than the Union did.

The consequence was extreme inflation. This was made worse by a scarcity of many commodities, a scarcity that was due to the blockade and to extensive hoarding, which in turn was exacerbated by the government's policy of impressment, that is, the seizure of goods at arbitrary prices. Inflation was also intensified by the shrinkage of Confederate-held territory and the resulting increase in the ratio of currency to commerce as people in the occupied areas sent their Confederate money to what was left of the Confederacy, where the paper retained at least a little of its nominal value.

Transportation suffered from the inadequacy of the railroads, which had serious gaps to begin with. True, the Confederates were the first to reinforce an army by rail in the midst of battle, and their railroads gave the presumed advantage of "interior lines" some reality. Still, the government failed to take effective control of the railroad system until late in the war. By then, the tracks and rolling stock had deteriorated badly, and the gaps had grown worse with the loss of key junctions such as Chattanooga and Atlanta. River and coastal shipping similarly was obstructed by enemy occupation.

Horses and mules, together with horse-drawn and mule-drawn vehicles, played a larger role in Confederate life, both military and civilian, than did railroad trains or riverboats. In the beginning the Confederacy was well supplied with horses and mules, but these were rapidly used up, and replacements were hard to get. By 1863 there was a serious shortage.

The Confederates acquired some munitions and other war matériel by seizures of U.S. arsenals, purchases abroad, and captures on the battlefield. But they had to depend mainly on expanding their few existing facilities, such as the Tredegar Iron Works in Richmond, and on developing new ones. The government tried to stimulate war-related manufactures by various means, among them the granting of draft exemptions to needed laborers. There were remarkable achievements in the production of salt, nitrates, and other necessities, but not enough to meet all the military and civilian requirements. Even when a surplus of commodities, such as foodstuffs, existed in one place, there were often shortages in other places because of the transportation difficulties.

Economic exhaustion eventually set in. As Charles W. Ramsdell has said, "The Confederacy had begun to break down *within,* long before the military situation appeared to be desperate."

Society. The war brought significant, if not all of them permanent, changes in Southern society, especially in the role of women, the relationship of classes, and the position of blacks.

Women took up responsibilities that formerly had belonged to men. They assisted the war effort directly by encouraging men to enlist, by sewing for soldiers and nursing them, and by serving as spies, among whom the most famous were Belle Boyd and Rose O'Neal Greenhow. They ran farms and plantations and worked at factory and government jobs. As diarists and memoirists, most notably Mary Boykin Chesnut and Catherine Ann Edmondston, they left the best literature embodying the wartime experience.

At least for the duration, women were liberated from the romantic antebellum stereotype of the lady on the pedestal, though certainly not from family obligations and the necessity of work. The hardships of the farm eventually caused many wives to call their soldier husbands home, thus depriving the army of men instead of inducing them, as earlier, to enlist.

Planters could no longer base their prestige solely on the land and slaves they owned. A heroic war record also counted, and men of no previous high standing, such as Stonewall Jackson, rose to positions of leadership and fame. At the same time, class consciousness grew among small farmers and day laborers, who expressed their feelings in the common saying that it was "a rich man's war and a poor man's fight." Mobs of women occasionally engaged in bread riots, demanding price reductions and looting stores of groceries and other merchandise.

Black men and women, as slaves, kept the plantations going and thus enabled an unusually high proportion of white men to be absent in the army. Blacks also gave direct assistance to the military as construction gangs, teamsters, cooks, and the like. Afterward, members of planter families liked to tell of retainers who had remained loyal to them throughout the war.

Yet the slaves constituted at least as much of a liability as an asset to the Confederacy. They did not revolt, as whites had feared they would, but—especially after Lincoln's Emancipation Proclamation (January 1, 1863)—they flocked to the camps of oncoming Federals and assisted them as spies, guides, and laborers. About 100,000 blacks from the South (and others from the border states and the North) joined the Union army. In short, the slaves themselves contributed mightily to the final defeat of the Confederacy and the destruction of slavery—the institution upon which the Confederacy was based.

Politics. Political parties did not emerge in the Confederacy, though there remained in many cases a distinction between old Democrats and former Whigs. Politics, often virulent, nevertheless persisted in the form of rivalries for power and disagreements over governmental methods and even aims. These dissensions seriously weakened the Confederacy.

Politics pitted President Davis, always a Democrat, and his faithful followers against a growing number of opponents, the foremost of whom was Vice President Stephens, once a Whig. Davis, burdened with responsibility as he was, took a fairly broad view of the powers of the central government. Stephens became increasingly extreme in his devotion to state rights. He and other critics of Davis blamed him for practically everything that went wrong in the Confederacy.

Some of the severest critics were state governors. Davis had to contend with especially troublesome resistance from Joseph E. Brown of Georgia and Zebulon Vance of North Carolina. These governors wanted to keep control of their own state militias, and they objected both to Confederate conscription and to its enforcement by suspension of the writ of habeas corpus. Brown kept many Georgia soldiers inside the state, and Vance accumulated stocks of war matériel for the exclusive use of North Carolina troops.

Confederate nationalism had to compete not only with state rights but also with persisting Unionism. This was most pervasive in the Appalachian Mountains and in the adjoining hill country, where slaves were few. Fifty-two counties of northwestern Virginia rejoined the Union as the state of West Virginia in 1863. A third of the counties of Tennessee, those in the eastern part of the state, would probably have rejoined the Union as East Tennessee if Federal armies had established control there as early as they did in northwestern Virginia. From the outset Confederate leaders had worried about popular tendencies toward "reconstruction," and these tendencies increased with military reverses, multiplying casualties, economic hardships, and a consequent lowering of public morale.

Peace movements gained ground, particularly in North Carolina and Georgia. In North Carolina a secret society known as the Red Strings (or Heroes of America) cultivated defeatism, and William W. Holden ran for governor as a peace candidate in 1864. (He was easily defeated by Vance, who called for keeping up the war effort.) In Georgia, Stephens and Brown advocated negotiating with the enemy. Stephens was willing to settle for guarantees of state rights in a reunited nation, but Davis refused to consider anything short of peace with independence. Davis insisted on this as his minimum terms when he authorized Stephens and other envoys to meet with Lincoln and his secretary of state, William H. Seward, in the Hampton Roads conference of February 1865. Lincoln took the position that the war would end only when the Confederates laid down their arms, and before long they had no real choice except to do so.

BIBLIOGRAPHY

Beringer, Richard E., Herman Hattaway, Archer Jones, and William N. Still, Jr. *Why the South Lost the Civil War.* Athens, Ga., 1986.

Coulter, E. Merton. *The Confederate States of America, 1861–1865.* A History of the South, vol. 7. Baton Rouge, La., 1950.

Eaton, Clement. *A History of the Southern Confederacy.* New York, 1954.

Roland, Charles P. *The Confederacy.* Chicago, 1960.

Thomas, Emory M. *The Confederate Nation, 1861–1865.* New York, 1979.

RICHARD N. CURRENT

CONFEDERATE VETERAN. Published in Nashville, Tennessee, from 1893 until 1932, the *Confederate Veteran* became the most popular Southern magazine of its time because it marketed the myth of the Lost Cause, a romantic and emotional defense of the fallen Confederacy. Sumner Archibald Cunningham, the founder, typified his readers, a coterie of unreconstructed Southerners. Initially printed as a leaflet to report donations for the Jefferson Davis Memorial at Richmond, Virginia, the maiden issue of *Veteran* contained reminiscences, personal recollections of battles, accounts of United Confederate Veteran activities, and the defeatist poetry of Chaplain Abram Ryan interspersed with the listing of funds.

Reader response encouraged Cunningham to launch his leaflet as a regular monthly. Averaging thirty pages in length with distinctively Confederate covers, *Veteran* included personal anecdotes, nostalgia masquerading as Civil War history, Ku Klux Klan testimonials, and flowery obituaries submitted by a growing readership. With this blend of vindication, censorship, racism, and death, Cunningham created a golden past for white Southerners to remember: the Lost Cause. Accordingly, *Veteran* became the official organ of the United Confederate Veterans, the United Daughters of the Confederacy, the Sons of Confederate Veterans, and the Confederate Southern Memorial Society.

Veteran's popularity peaked in 1906 with 21,000 subscribers, but gradually the relentless march of time decimated readership and created serious funding problems for Cunningham. After his death at age seventy in 1913, the magazine struggled on until 1932 when time and economic depression ended publication.

BIBLIOGRAPHY

Connelly, Thomas L. *The Marble Man, Robert E. Lee.* New York, 1977.

Cresap, Bernarr. "The Confederate Veteran." *Alabama Review* 12, no. 4 (1959): 243–257.

Evans, Josephine King. "Nostalgia for a Nickel: The Confederate Veteran." *Tennessee Historical Quarterly* 48, no. 4 (1989): 238–244.

Foster, Gaines M. *Ghosts of the Confederacy: Defeat, the Lost Cause, and the Emergence of the New South.* New York, 1987.

Goff, Reda C. "The Confederate Veteran Magazine." *Tennessee Historical Quarterly* 331, no. 1 (1972): 45–60.

White, William. *The Confederate Veteran.* Tuscaloosa, Ala., 1962.

JOSEPHINE S. KING

CONFISCATION. [*This entry is composed of two articles,* Confederate Sequestration *and* Federal Confiscation, *which discuss the seizure of enemy property by the Confederate and U.S. governments.*]

Confederate Sequestration

Since the earliest conflicts between nations, belligerents have exercised the right to confiscate enemy property. The Civil War was no exception to this rule. Indeed, both the Confederate Congress and the U.S. Congress passed laws relating to the capture and disposition of enemy property.

After Abraham Lincoln's March 4, 1861, inauguration, Confederate Secretary of the Treasury Christopher G. Memminger sent a circular to all U.S. civil authorities still residing in the South. In this letter, Memminger ordered that they pay all outstanding debts due the United States to the Confederate Treasury. Just two months later, in May, the Confederate Congress passed a law that required all debts due to individuals or businesses in the North be paid to the Confederate Treasury. Congress followed up on these initiatives in an attempt to ensure the moneys owed to the Federal government would be deposited in the very limited Confederate Treasury.

The Confederates did not rely only upon the collection of these debts. In response to—and retaliation against—the U.S. Confiscation Act of August 6, 1861, the Confederate Congress passed the Sequestration Act on August 30, 1861. Although the Sequestration Act was modeled after the Union statute, it was in actuality much harsher. Whereas the Union's August 1861 act called for the seizure of all property, including slaves, used to "aid the rebellion," the Confederacy's Sequestration Act authorized agents to seize *all* property belonging to alien enemies still residing in the Confederate States as of May 21, 1861—three months before the passage of the act. Congress also directed that agents be appointed to enforce the provisions of the law: they were to hunt out alien enemy property, confiscate it, and sell it. The law was amended on February 15, 1862, to allow those Southerners whose property had been seized by the Federals to be compensated for their losses.

The district courts and the Board of Sequestration Commissioners provided the machinery used to enforce the Sequestration Act. As the judges appointed to hear the cases well knew, the act had to be administered with discretion to ensure that innocent citizens were not unduly punished—and impoverished.

Some Southern jurists questioned the constitutionality of the act. South Carolina's Confederate District Court judge, former U.S. Circuit Court judge A. G. Magrath, declared the act legal and constitutional on the grounds that the right to wage war included the right to seize property. Many in the Palmetto State, and the Confederacy as a whole, disputed this definition of war powers, maintaining that the Confederate Congress had no specific power that enabled them to seize enemy property. Citing precedents from 1794, these judges and attorneys argued that the United States had dispensed with the policy of confiscating enemy property and had signed a treaty with England guaranteeing that the practice would be abolished. They also argued that the Confederate Sequestration Act did not correspond to the Federal Confiscation Act because that statute limited the Union to confiscating only those articles defined as contraband of war, be they confiscated Confederate exports or other goods seized and deemed necessary for the war effort.

Defenders of the law, including the Confederate attorney general, maintained that independent, sovereign nations were definitely granted the power to confiscate enemy property. Since the Confederate States was as much an independent country as any European nation, these attorneys argued, the Confederacy was fully justified in adopting the policy of sequestration. In building this defense, the Confederacy's attorneys were forced to adopt a broad view of constitutional powers: they implied that they accepted the notion of a strong central government, equipped with the authority to enact sweeping war powers. In adopting this view, they belied the very foundation of the Confederate nation: state rights.

The Confederate Congress amended the Sequestration Act several times. On October 15, 1861, an assemblage of planters and merchants in Macon, Georgia, urged that the confiscation of alien property date from the date of the bill's passage, not three months retroactively. Toward the end of the war, Congress broadened the act still further: that body directed that anyone who fled the Confederacy without the permission of President Jefferson Davis or the commanding officer in charge of the Trans-Mississippi would be treated as an enemy alien and hence would have his property seized.

The individual Confederate states also enacted state-level versions of the Sequestration Act. In these instances, Confederate agents seized everything from tobacco and cotton to pianos, city property, and ship cargo. Some accounts note that Confederates confiscated three thousand acres of land in Florida; agents netted $500,000 from aliens residing in the capital city of Richmond; and even Thomas Jefferson's Monticello went on the auction block because its owner was a New Yorker serving in the Union navy.

Despite all the litigation and the operation of the sequestration commissioners, the Confederacy realized very little tangible gain from the enforcement of the act. Unfortunately, information on the amount of money and property seized remains scant; many figures are deemed unreliable. Still, historians have documented that between January 1 and September 30, 1863, and January 1 and September 30, 1864, $6,102,070.39 was deposited in the Confederate Treasury. In gold, this figure amounted to $380,000.

In spite of the active enforcement program, the Sequestration Acts proved to be unsuccessful. Secretary Memminger and others within the Confederate government expected to garner large sums from the confiscation of Northern property. The reality—less than a million dollars in gold—belied that expectation. Indeed, any hope that the seizure of enemy property would help make the Confederacy rich must have been dashed after only two years when it became evident that the money was just not there. Still, the Confederates saw fit to broaden their view of war powers and saw nothing constitutionally wrong with seizing the property of an enemy power. This shows that Southerners were fully cognizant of the changes that could occur to ideological conceptions when confronted by the realities of a modern war.

[See also Northerners.]

BIBLIOGRAPHY

Coulter, E. Merton. *The Confederate States of America, 1861–1865.* A History of the South, vol. 7. Baton Rouge, La., 1950.

Klingberg, Frank W. *The Southern Claims Commission.* Berkeley, Calif., 1955.

Randolph, Nowlin. "Judge William Pinckney Hill Aids the Confederate War Effort." *Southwestern Historical Quarterly* 68 (1964): 14–28.

Schwab, John Christopher. *The Confederate States of America, 1861–1865: A Financial and Industrial History of the South during the Civil War.* New York, 1901. Reprint, New York, 1968.

Turner, Martha L. "The Cause of the Union in East Tennessee." *Tennessee Historical Quarterly* 4 (1981): 366–380.

MARY A. DECREDICO

Federal Confiscation

The Union government's Confiscation Acts of 1861 and 1862 had their origins in the North's desire to facilitate the war effort, to punish the Southerners, to do something about slavery, and to lay the groundwork for a meaningful Reconstruction. As early as July 4, 1861, Secretary of the Treasury Salmon P. Chase suggested that the confiscated property of "insurgents" could help pay for a Union victory. Shortly thereafter, Republican Lyman Trumbull introduced a confiscation bill in the Senate that, with some modification, became law on August 6, 1861.

Some Democrats, especially those from slaveholding border states, expressed concern over the bill's potential disruptive impact on slavery and on the prospects of an early reconciliation with the seceded states. The law, however, was technically limited in its scope, especially since it had real force only where Federal authority existed. It gave the president the authority to confiscate property used "in aiding, abetting, or promoting" the Confederate cause, but it specifically limited the Federal government's grasp over slave property to those slaves actively employed in the Confederate war effort. The Federal government was to pursue confiscation through the courts and could do so without having the owner of the property present at the proceedings.

This Confiscation Act remained in effect throughout the war, but a second more comprehensive law addressed some of its inadequacies. In December 1861 Lyman Trumbull introduced in the Senate the new confiscation bill that finally became law on July 17, 1862. The bill became Congress's primary legislative attack on slavery. Unlike the first Confiscation Act, which had passed quickly in the rush of early wartime legislation, this one served as a catalyst for prolonged debate on more expansive issues, including the role of Congress in the conduct of the war, the nature of secession, and the role of confiscation and land redistribution in reconstructing the South. After it passed along partisan lines, Senator Orville Browning, who had broken with his fellow Republicans on this measure, petitioned Abraham Lincoln to veto the bill. He argued that because the bill would permanently confiscate an individual's property it violated the Constitution's attainder clause. Lincoln was ready to oblige him because of his own constitutional reservations but signed the bill after Congress passed a joint resolution explaining that the law would not be retroactive, nor would confiscation extend beyond the lifetime of the individual who fell under its provisions. (The Supreme Court eventually upheld the constitutionality of both Confiscation Acts in 1870 in *Miller v. U.S.*)

In its final form the Confiscation Act of 1862 gave the courts the option to punish treason with death or fine and imprisonment. As with the earlier act, proceedings could be conducted without the presence of the accused. Individuals found to be aiding the rebellion could be fined and imprisoned. Both classes were disqualified from holding political office. Furthermore, the president was empowered to confiscate immediately the property of Confederate government officials and military officers, former officials of the United States, and individuals who owned property in loyal territory. Individuals involved in the rebellion outside

these classes had sixty days from a presidential proclamation to abandon the rebellion or suffer confiscation of all their property.

Although confiscation remained a judicial proceeding, the new law gave the military a significant role in the way in which it dealt with the slavery issue. Slaves "shall be deemed captives of war, and shall be forever free of their servitude and not again held as slaves" if they escaped from disloyal masters to Union lines, were captured by Union forces, or were deserted by their owners and came under Union control. The law also gave the president the authority to employ slaves "for the suppression of this rebellion, and for this purpose he may organize and use them in such manner as he may judge best for the public welfare." It also rendered inoperative the Fugitive Slave Law except for loyal slave owners and gave the president the authority to initiate colonization of slaves freed by the law.

Ultimately, enforcement of both Confiscation Acts depended on the president and, particularly, his attorney general, Edward Bates, a Missouri Republican. Both lacked enthusiasm for confiscation, and Lincoln would use it only when it would help him achieve his primary goal: the restoration of the Union. In New Orleans in late 1863 and early 1864, for example, presidential pardons removed most of the individuals who would have been subjected to the provisions of the law. And President Andrew Johnson's liberal pardon policy after the war's end had a similar effect throughout the South. Ultimately, a relatively inconsequential amount of Confederate property in the North and the South was confiscated. The Captured Property Act of March 3, 1863, actually produced much more revenue for the government; captured property, almost 95 percent of which was cotton, netted about $25 million by May 1868. The government reaped about $300,000 from the Confiscation Acts.

The message contained in the laws, however, suggested an importance that went beyond anything measured in dollars and cents. The Confiscation Act of 1861 signaled the beginning of the North's move toward total war, and it indicated a willingness on the part of Congress to violate the sanctity of private property to make war on the South's aristocracy. Furthermore, the Confiscation Acts identified slaveholding with disloyalty. With the passage of the Confiscation Act of 1862, the safety of slave property in the loyal border states was threatened, and it could no longer be assumed that a black man or woman was a slave. The Confiscation Acts along with the Emancipation Proclamation and other wartime measures had a disruptive effect on the institution of slavery. Slaves learned of the measures through masters' reactions and the grapevine, picked up ideas about property redistribution, deserted their masters, and gave every indication that they knew the provisions of the second law well enough to defend their freedom by claiming to have belonged to disloyal masters. Ultimately, confiscation gave the army de facto power to free slaves. In the fall of 1862, for example, Gen. William Tecumseh Sherman ordered his men to treat the slaves who came within their lines as free until courts could give a final ruling.

Southerners reacted to these laws with anger and fear. In 1861 the Confederate Congress passed the Alien Enemies Act on August 8 and the Sequestration Act on August 30 probably in retaliation for the first Confiscation Act. The former gave aliens the options of becoming Confederate citizens, leaving the South, or being treated as enemies; the latter authorized the confiscation of their property. The Federal threat of confiscation gave Confederate propagandists ammunition to stir up hatred of the enemy by reminding Southerners that the loss of wealth was the price of defeat. Fear of confiscation prompted Confederate commanders and slaveholders near Union lines to remove able-bodied slaves. The Confiscation Acts combined with Reconstruction measures caused a lingering fear of confiscation into the 1870s, despite the fact that the issue was last brought up in Congress in March 1867.

[See also Contraband.]

BIBLIOGRAPHY

Berlin, Ira, et al., eds. *The Destruction of Slavery*. Ser. 1, vol. 1 of *Freedom: A Documentary History of Emancipation, 1861–1867*. Cambridge, Mass., 1985.

Lucie, Patricia M. L. "Confiscation: Constitutional Crossroads." *Civil War History* 23 (December 1977): 307–321.

Randall, James G. *Constitutional Problems under Lincoln*. 2d ed., rev. Urbana, Ill., 1951.

Shapiro, Henry D. *Confiscation of Confederate Property in the North*. Ithaca, N.Y., 1962.

Syrett, John. "The Confiscation Acts: Efforts at Reconstruction during the Civil War." Ph.D. diss., University of Wisconsin, 1971.

PAUL A. CIMBALA

CONGRESS. Upon voting to secede from the United States, the conventions of the seven original Confederate states sent delegations equal to their 1860 congressional representation to Montgomery, Alabama, to form a new nation. Fearful of delay, they adopted with only one day's discussion a one-year Provisional Constitution, which converted the Montgomery convention into the new government's legislative body. Congressmen from states that later seceded were elected by their convention or legislature. Thus, there were no popularly elected Provisional congressmen. In all, the Confederate Congresses had representatives from eleven seceded states and the extralegal Confederate governments of Kentucky and Missouri, plus nonvoting representatives from Arizona Territory and the Cherokee, Chickasaw, Choctaw, Creek, and Seminole Indian nations.

The average Confederate congressman was well off financially, with a median estate worth $47,000. Sixty-four percent had served in state legislatures and 32 percent in the U.S. Congress. Only 10 percent had had no previous political experience. Professionally they ranged from horse breeder to financier. At least 92 had been Whigs and most of these had been conservative on secession. At least 138 had been Democrats and most of them had been early secessionists. Political experience and wealth were greatest in the Provisional Congress, somewhat less in the First, and even less in the Second, though this decline was relatively slight.

The Provisional Congress. The Provisional Congress met until February 17, 1862. The Provisional Constitution permitted plural officeholding, so a number of members served both in Congress and in the army, a privilege denied by the Permanent Constitution. Voting was by state, as it had been in the Philadelphia Convention, and a tied vote in a delegation left that state's vote uncounted.

The business of nation building occupied the first months. Congress acquired a body of laws by adopting all U.S. laws consistent with the Confederate Constitution. It elected Jefferson Davis president and Alexander H. Stephens vice president, and then established executive departments much like those of the United States. Other aspects of government, such as a postal system, the judiciary, and citizenship and naturalization systems, were also carried over with little change. Congress contracted for the regular publication of its laws and had the major laws published in a newspaper in each state. The Senate and House rules were adopted almost bodily from the U.S. Congress, but recording of debates was left to newspaper reporters, with frequent secret sessions making adequate reporting impossible.

The delegates to Montgomery had hoped for a government without political parties, and to a large extent they succeeded. Old habits, however, could not be so easily abandoned. In private correspondence the erstwhile secessionists, Unionists, Democrats, and Whigs expressed distrust of their former political opponents. These feelings were of some importance in determining how people voted in elections, but there is no evidence of any significant voting alignment within Congress based on past politics until the Second Congress. Without specific party lines to guide them, therefore, each congressman had to decide for himself how he would vote.

This political vacuum worked in President Davis's favor. He was never without his congressional critics, but during the first year the war was going well and people were confident of victory. Demands upon them were relatively light. Criticism of the president was therefore mainly personal or doctrinal and did little to affect the course of legislation. Whigs and Unionists argued that Davis denied them patronage. Some secessionists felt that he was secretly a reconstructionist. Scattered armchair experts disliked his military policies. Extreme state rights advocates disliked his frequent vetoes. Meanwhile administration measures went through Congress almost intact, and the newspapers jeered at the legislature as being a "register of Executive decrees." Underneath all this, another factor operated in Davis's favor: during wartime people generally assume that their political and military leaders know best what to do, and that overt opposition borders on treason. Nothing but the firmest conviction would allow the Provisional Congress to tamper with administration requests.

Confederate leaders originally hoped to finance the government on a low tariff income, but as an interim device Congress authorized an issue of $1 million in Treasury notes guaranteed by a tax of $\frac{1}{8}$¢ per pound on cotton exported. It also provided for a Provisional Army of 100,000 militia volunteers, ordered the president to arm and equip them as he wished, and established a general staff.

The Fort Sumter affair necessitated a called session of Congress, but there seemed to be no alarm. On May 16 Congress authorized the issue of $20 million in fiat Treasury notes and $50 million in 8 percent bonds for general investment and for money pledged from the sale of agricultural produce—the first produce loan. This quick and easy financing set Congress on the road to a monetary policy based on Treasury notes and bond issues to absorb surplus currency. Congress now removed all restrictions on the number of volunteers who might be accepted in the army and bypassed the states by letting the president receive independent companies. The president was also given the right to control all telegraphic operations. On May 21 Congress finally established a tariff system that was to last for the duration. The leading rate was 15 percent on most commonplace items, with raw materials paying somewhat less and luxuries somewhat more.

Congress now removed itself from diplomatic strategy and accepted the administration's policy of cotton diplomacy. It prohibited the export of cotton and other staples except through Confederate ports or into Mexico, trying to cut off all supplies going to the United States and to force Europe to break the blockade and come get what it wanted. Some congressmen wished to buttress the policy with a promise of a lower tariff to any nation recognizing the Confederacy, but this movement floundered and was dropped.

The victory at First Manassas did little to influence the next sessions of Congress. It authorized a call for 400,000 volunteers and let the president accept units of specialists and local defense. During the winter it enacted several feeble acts to induce volunteering and reenlistments, none

of them very successful. Finally the Provisional Congress ordered a war tax of fifty cents on each one hundred dollars of goods named by the Treasury Department.

The Provisional Congress had spent much of its first month in writing a constitution for the permanent government of the Confederacy. The new Constitution provided for a Congress identical to that of the United States, and elections for representatives were held on the first Wednesday in November 1861. Each state had its former Federal representation and used old election procedures. Most states allowed absentee voting by soldiers and refugees at army camps and other designated places. Traditional politicking would have seemed divisive; candidates usually announced themselves briefly in newspapers and did little personal campaigning. A few districts engaged in vigorous battles over local issues, but national policy was seldom a subject of debate. Voters tended to support men whom they had favored before the war. Democrats and secessionists were popular at this time, and the election returns gave them about a three-to-two majority in the First Congress. Five state legislatures chose one former Whig and one former Democrat, and eight legislatures chose two former Democrats. The overall pattern of those elected seemed basically like that of the Provisional Congress.

The First Congress. When the First Congress convened on February 18, 1862, it was evident that the one-year volunteers were weary of military service. There was the possibility that more than half of them would not reenlist, and President Davis was compelled to ask for the conscription of all able-bodied men between the ages of eighteen and thirty-five. On April 16 Congress, over the objections of the Atlantic seaboard states above Florida, enacted such a law. It then conferred blanket exemptions on a long list of occupations whose personnel was deemed more important to the home front than to the army. That fall Congress extended the conscription age to forty-five but refused to reduce the number of class exemptions. By the end of 1863 the need for troops was becoming desperate, and on February 17, 1864, Congress set the conscription age from seventeen to fifty and pared the exemption list drastically.

Demands for changes in these laws occupied much of Congress's time. The first law had let eligible men offer substitutes. This obviously favored the wealthy, and Congress finally drafted both the substitutes and those who had hired them. Planters had been allowed one exempt overseer for every twenty slaves they owned, but this elitist practice had severe critics. In the end, Congress exempted only those overseers so employed before February 16, 1862. After a bitter debate, state rights advocates secured the exemption of all state officers certified by their governor as necessary for proper government.

Wedded to conservative financing, Secretary Christopher G. Memminger continued asking for more Treasury notes, backed by faith in the government and payable in specie after the war. He also requested great amounts of bonds into which currency could be invested and which would be exchangeable directly for agricultural products. Congress gave him most of what he requested, but people preferred to spend their rapidly inflating currency quickly rather than buy bonds. Near the end of the First Congress Memminger reported that funding was going badly, and at his suggestion Congress enacted a forced funding law, which set up a schedule by which currency would gradually decline to worthlessness unless funded into bonds. In January 1863, it levied its first significant tax on property, income, licenses, and businesses, plus a 10 percent tithe on slaughtered hogs and agricultural products.

The First Congress dealt with other matters of only slightly less importance. In their need for supplies, army agents often ruthlessly seized them from producers and wholesalers. The Impressment Act of March 26, 1863, permitted the seizure of agricultural products and military supplies at a "fair" price and established a system of arbitration whereby a former owner might negotiate a better price. Congress also permitted the destruction of property if it were in danger of being captured. On February 6, 1864, the legislature ordered that no major staple crop or military stores could be exported except under regulations established by the president, and it outlawed the importation of luxuries. Despite almost violent debate on the subject, Congress on three occasions gave the president authority to suspend the right of habeas corpus when deemed necessary.

Congress was noticeably reluctant to take any initiative in two areas. It left to the president all decisions about what manufactories were needed for the war effort, but when asked by the War Department it quickly encouraged private individuals to manufacture guns, ammunition, clothing, and other army accoutrements. It also flirted with the idea of price control to stem inflation, but never managed more than a vestige of such regulation.

By 1864 an important new alignment had appeared in the legislature. The Confederacy was now divided into what historians Alexander and Beringer term "exterior" and "interior" districts. Exterior districts were those occupied by the enemy and therefore little affected by the legislation of Congress. Their voters naturally preferred congressmen who would support any measure that might help redeem their homes. Interior districts were those still within Confederate jurisdiction and in which its laws could be enforced. They supported congressmen who would heed local grievances as well as tend to issues of national survival.

The Second Congress. Politics reverted to type during elections for the Second Congress during mid-1863. Louisiana, Missouri, Tennessee, and Kentucky—now almost entirely exterior areas—held elections by general ticket,

CONGRESSIONAL BILL. The bill amends procedures for purchasing rations and clothing from the Quartermaster's Department. Approved by the Confederate House of Representatives on February 17, 1864, and printed on May 3, 1864.

with each voter casting his ballot for one congressman from each district; other states continued to vote as before. The major issue now was the Davis administration and critics were in full cry. Usually they attacked the one or two programs that most closely affected their districts, but in the southeastern seaboard states they arraigned the government on almost everything. Past politics became openly important, and the general aura of discontent and war weariness helped candidates who had urged caution in 1860. In the Second Congress two-thirds f the new men were former Unionists and three-fifths were Whig. These men, however, were no less loyal Confederates than the two-term congressmen and remained so to the end of the war. They simply did not want a war that demanded further sacrifices.

In the Second Congress, which met on May 2, 1864, a congressman's former party, his secession stand, and the exterior or interior status of his district became ever more important in determining his vote. The First Congress had carried legislation about as far as it could go, and now the administration could ask only for refinements in the laws. The voting alignments, however, too often took precedence over national survival and made constructive legislation almost impossible. Meanwhile a peace movement was gaining momentum. But the president insisted that the North already knew the conditions on which the Confederacy would make peace and that further negotiations would signal irresolution. The result was that no significant law was enacted during the first session.

The last session of Congress, which began on November 9, 1864, was marked by a legislative stalemate. A majority of congressmen were now from exterior districts, but enough of them were willing to ally with interior-district men on certain issues to block new administrative programs. Until the last week, the administration won only two victories. There was talk in and out of Congress of depriving Davis of his constitutional prerogative as commander in chief and persuading Gen. Robert E. Lee to take full military command. Davis scotched this plan on February 6, 1865, by naming Lee general in chief, knowing that Lee would not exercise a broader command. Davis also virtually ended the peace agitation in Congress at about the same time by sending a commission to meet with Northern representatives, but he instructed them to accept peace only with independence. After the inevitable failure, Congress officially vowed to continue the war until victorious.

Meanwhile other matters were at a standstill. Congress refused all requests for financial reform and on December 28, 1864, merely extended the funding deadline to July 1, 1865. A few days before Congress ended, so many men had left Richmond that there was barely a quorum in the House and some compromise was absolutely essential. On March 13 Congress let the president call upon the states for as many slaves as he wished to serve as soldiers, but left it to the individual state to decide whether such men should be freed. There were 125,000 men still exempt or detailed. Davis wanted all exemptions ended and the men subject to detail to the army or the home front as the president wished; on March 16, 1865, Congress kept a few exemptions and let the president detail the rest. On March 18 Congress ordered that goods impressed must be paid for at market prices. On the same day the legislature gave the president his only outright defeat; it refused to pass a new habeas corpus suspension. All these desperation laws of Congress's last week were of course too late to be of any value.

Confederates generally had a low opinion of their Congress. Those approving President Davis's leadership chided Congress for tampering with administration requests; those critical of the administration considered Congress too submissive. Pragmatically, Congress had little alternative to such submissiveness. Survival of the Confederacy was uppermost in the minds of everyone, even congressmen, and legislative chaos would have been ruinous. As Alexander and Beringer so well demonstrate, past politics, position on secession, economic factors, and local conditions often influenced voting, but until late 1864 there is little evidence of bloc voting. In the Second Congress a definite Whig-Unionist versus Democrat-secessionist alignment began to emerge, as well as the important interior versus exterior district alignment. It was now obvious that the new congressmen were not decisively committed to Southern independence at the expense of their districts. By then, however, the limits of legislation had been reached and no obstructionist alignment had any measurable effect on the conduct of the war.

[*See also* Conscription; Economy; Habeas Corpus; Impressment; Montgomery Convention; New Plan; Poor Relief; Public Finance; State Rights; State Socialism; *entries on particular states; and biographies of numerous figures mentioned herein.*]

BIBLIOGRAPHY

Alexander, Thomas B., and Richard E. Beringer. *The Anatomy of the Confederate Congress: A Study of the Influences of Member Characteristics on Legislative Voting Behavior, 1861–1865.* Nashville, Tenn., 1972.

Beringer, Richard E. "A Profile of the Members of the Confederate Congress." *Journal of Southern History* 33 (1967): 518–544.

Curry, J. L. M. *Civil History of the Government of the Confederate States with Some Personal Reminiscences.* Richmond, Va., 1901.

Davis, Jefferson. *The Rise and Fall of the Confederate Government.* 2 vols. New York, 1881. Reprint, New York, 1958.

Journal of the Congress of the Confederate States of America, 1861–1865. 7 vols. Washington, D.C., 1904–1905.

Yearns, Wilfred B. *The Confederate Congress.* Athens, Ga., 1960.

W. BUCK YEARNS

CONNER, JAMES (1829–1883), brigadier general. Born in Charleston, South Carolina, Conner graduated from South Carolina College in 1849 and was admitted to the bar in 1852. In 1856 he was appointed U.S. district attorney for South Carolina and prosecuted the captain of *Wanderer* for trying illegally to import slaves into the state. Conner resigned as district attorney in December 1860 and joined a committee urging the state legislature to convene a secession convention.

Although Conner was named district attorney for his district after the Confederacy was formed, he preferred military service and enlisted as captain of the Montgomery Guards in the spring of 1861. In May, after participating in the capture of Fort Sumter, he was elected captain of the

JAMES CONNER. Portrait as a colonel in the Twenty-second North Carolina Infantry. LIBRARY OF CONGRESS

Washington Light Infantry of Hampton's Legion. During First Manassas, as the senior officer, he took over for the wounded Hampton and led the legion in a charge that captured Ricketts's battery. Soon after, Conner was promoted to major and served with the legion until elected colonel of the Twenty-second North Carolina in the spring of 1862.

Severely wounded at Mechanicsville, Conner recuperated until the spring of 1863, when he was appointed a judge advocate on Gen. Richard S. Ewell's staff. In June 1864 he was commissioned brigadier general and placed temporarily in command of Samuel McGowan's brigade. When McGowan returned to duty, Conner became commander of Joseph B. Kershaw's old brigade. But in October he was wounded again at Cedar Creek, and his leg was amputated.

After the war, Conner returned to his law practice. He assisted in the 1876 election that returned white rule to the Palmetto State. During his last years he was director and general counsel of the Greenville and Columbia Railroad. He is buried in Charleston at Magnolia Cemetery.

BIBLIOGRAPHY

Capers, Ellison. *South Carolina.* Vol. 5 of *Confederate Military History.* Edited by Clement A. Evans. Atlanta, 1899. Vol. 6 of extended ed. Wilmington, N.C., 1987.

Dickert, D. Augustus. *History of Kershaw's Brigade.* Newberry, S.C., 1899. Reprint, Dayton, Ohio, 1973.

Moffet, Mary Conner, ed. *Letters of General James Conner, CSA.* Columbia, S.C., 1950.

FRITZ P. HAMER

CONRAD, CHARLES M. (1804–1878), U.S. secretary of war and congressman from Louisiana. Conrad was born on December 24, 1804, in Winchester, Virginia, and his family moved to Louisiana while he was still young. Conrad studied law in New Orleans and joined the firm of Slidell, Conrad, and Benjamin in 1828. A passionate man, he killed a man in a duel. Conrad was married to Angela Lewis, the grandniece of George Washington.

Conrad developed an early interest in politics. He supported the Jacksonian Democrats but split with the party over the bank issue and joined the Whigs. He served several terms in the Louisiana legislature. In 1844 Conrad was named a delegate to the Louisiana constitutional convention and attended the Whig National Convention. He was elected to Congress in 1848, and in 1850, President Millard Fillmore appointed him secretary of war. A cooperationist, Conrad supported John Bell for president in 1860.

Conrad was elected to the Provisional Congress as well as to the First and Second Congresses. As chairman of the Committee on Naval Affairs, Conrad waged a bitter personal feud with Secretary of the Navy Stephen R. Mallory. Conrad held Mallory and the navy responsible for his loss of personal property following the fall of New Orleans and the Union occupation of the North Carolina coast. Conrad proposed abolishing the Navy Department as a means of removing Mallory from power.

Conrad was a strong supporter of Jefferson Davis, arguing that the war should be conducted by the president and his generals. He also sat on the Currency, Ways and Means, and Public Buildings committees. He opposed a bill requiring military officials to destroy cotton and foodstuffs that might fall into enemy hands. In early 1862 Conrad and other congressmen met with French minister Robert Mercier. They succeeded in convincing Mercier that the Confederacy was invincible, but no formal French recognition followed. After returning to private life, Conrad went to Richmond to testify before a commission investigating Mallory's competency. Conrad held the rank of brigadier general in the Louisiana state militia.

Following the war, Conrad fled to Mexico City. He returned in 1872 and waged a successful fight to regain his confiscated property. He practiced law in New Orleans until his death on February 11, 1878. He is buried in New Orleans.

BIBLIOGRAPHY

Durkin, Joseph T. *Stephen R. Mallory.* Chapel Hill, N.C., 1954.
Honeycutt, B. "The Early Political Career of Charles Magill Conrad." Master's thesis, Louisiana State University, 1939.
Warner, Ezra J., and W. Buck Yearns. *Biographical Register of the Confederate Congress.* Baton Rouge, La., 1975.
Yearns, Wilfred B. *The Confederate Congress.* Athens, Ga., 1960.

KEVIN S. FONTENOT

CONROW, AARON H. (1824–1865), congressman from Missouri. Born on June 19, 1824, near Cincinnati, Ohio, Conrow moved with his parents around 1840 to Ray County, Missouri. He taught school part-time before becoming a lawyer. He was appointed judge of the first Ray County probate court and served as a circuit attorney for the Fifth Judicial Circuit of Missouri from 1857 to 1861.

In 1860 Conrow had been elected to the Missouri legislature as a Democrat, and when war came, he aligned with the South. He became a colonel in the Missouri State Guard, having played a prominent part after a special session of the legislature in recruiting and equipping the first company organized in Ray County.

Conrow was elected to the Provisional, First, and Second Congresses. He proved to be one of the Davis administration's most loyal supporters. A diligent congressman, Conrow served on the Currency, War Tax, Finance, Naval Affairs, Public Buildings, Ordnance, and Ordnance Stores committees. Conrow pressed for total war. He favored extending the draft age and decreasing the list of exemptions. He championed and was instrumental in the passage of a modification of the Currency Act of 1864.

After the war, Conrow joined Joseph O. Shelby's brigade, which went into exile in Mexico. After Shelby's men disbanded, Conrow, along with Gen. Mosby Monroe Parsons and other Confederates, proceeded toward Monterey. On August 25, 1865, the party was captured by Mexican irregulars and all but Conrow's black servant were murdered.

BIBLIOGRAPHY

History of Ray County, Missouri. St. Louis, 1881.
Wakelyn, Jon L. *Biographical Dictionary of the Confederacy.* Edited by Frank E. Vandiver. Westport, Conn., 1977.
Warner, Ezra J., and W. Buck Yearns. *Biographical Register of the Confederate Congress.* Baton Rouge, La., 1975.
Williams, Walter, ed. *History of Northwest Missouri.* 5 vols. New York, 1915.

JAMES W. GOODRICH

CONSCRIPTION. The survival of the Confederacy depended on its ability to outlive the Civil War, and endurance required a proficient military force. When the Southern states went to war in April 1861, eager volunteers swelled the ranks of the army to defend their homeland and earn glory and fame. But by the end of the year, Southern soldiers were eager to return home. They had learned the reality of war: long hours of boredom, exhausting marches, and the ever-present threat of death. Self-preservation demanded that the Confederate government assume the liability of equipping the army with soldiers.

The Confederate government ultimately passed three conscription acts. These three measures were the most controversial pieces of legislation passed by the Confederate Congress. Conscription initiated heated debates between the states and the central government, sparked class conflict among Southerners, and created hostility between volunteers and conscripts in the army. Southerners had founded the Confederate States of America on the premise of the sovereignty of each state, and a national conscription law threatened the supremacy of state governments. Yet the need to fight a successful war dictated that the central government appropriate a great deal more power than Southerners had anticipated.

By December 1861, the war promised to be long and costly. Amassing a stable and effective army became a priority for Confederate leaders. The twelve-month volunteers, who had joined the army during the first flush of excitement, were now older and wiser and looking forward to returning to their homes before the end of winter. Confederate President Jefferson Davis and Secretary of War George Wythe Randolph began discussing the problem of keeping the veterans in the army and adding to their ranks as well. They turned to the idea of a national draft as a means of recruiting manpower and coordinating the war effort among the states.

First Conscription Act

The first Conscription Act became law April 16, 1862. It drafted for military service all white males between the ages of eighteen and thirty-five for a period of three years unless the war ended sooner. The law required that soldiers who had already enlisted serve three years from their original date of enlistment. To honor their patriotism, the government offered the twelve-month men sixty-day furloughs and allowed them the privilege of reorganizing and electing their officers. For newcomers, the act included a grace period that granted them the option of volunteering before conscription forced them into the army. Volunteers could elect their officers, or they could volunteer for an existing unit, permitting them to fight alongside friends or relatives.

The government also recognized the need to ensure that an adequate labor force remained at home to foster the nation's industrial and agricultural resources. Five days after passing the Conscription Act, Congress amended the bill by exempting from the draft individuals employed in occupations germane to the war effort and the maintenance of the country. Those exempted included Confederate and state officials; laborers employed for the war effort, such as factory hands, miners, and foundry workers; mail carriers and telegraph operators; railroad employees; teachers who had at least twenty pupils; ministers; druggists; hospital attendants; and the physically and mentally disabled. The secretary of war reserved the power to exempt specific superintendents and laborers in the cotton and wool industries. Six months later, the government added journalists, postmasters, physicians, and conscientious objectors to the list. Conscientious objectors reserved the option to provide a substitute or pay five hundred dollars into the Confederate Treasury.

To Southerners, the most antagonistic element of the act was the overseer clause, or the Twenty-Slave Law. This clause exempted one white male for every plantation with twenty slaves. In part, planters wanted assurance that they could maintain control over their slaves in the wake of Lincoln's Emancipation Proclamation. But most Southerners viewed the overseer clause as a means for the slaveholding class to avoid the draft.

The clause evoked such criticism that seven months later the legislature revised the law. Following May 1, 1863, the clause pertained only to plantations belonging to minors, women, or disabled planters. To prevent men from suddenly becoming overseers merely to evade the draft, the exempted person had to have been employed as an overseer prior to April 16, 1862. In addition, the law required the owner of the plantation to pay five hundred dollars to the Confederate Treasury. When even this failed to curtail abuse of the clause, the War Department began enrolling overseers and then detailing them to the plantations during harvesting season.

The overseer clause, even in its mitigated form, still aroused a great deal of class conflict among Southerners, as did the equally egregious substitution clause. This provision allowed an individual, referred to as a principal, to hire a substitute to fulfill his obligations as a conscript. The government expected that wealthy industrialists would use this clause to continue their work to the benefit of the Confederacy. In reality, it became a way for the wealthy to avoid a war that the less fortunate could not escape.

Southerners subject to the draft regarded substitution as blatant class favoritism, and they deplored exemption on the ground that so many men used it as a means of evading conscription. Employers sold positions that granted exemption to those who could afford it. Similarly, money could persuade certain physicians to sign a disability voucher. Despite its deleterious effect on national morale, the exemption clause remained law for the duration of the war, and Congress did not abolish substitution until December 1863.

Substitution not only heightened class conflict among Southerners but also placed unqualified men in the army and lowered morale among the soldiers. Many resourceful individuals made a career of posing as substitutes during the war. They would accept payment from a principal, enlist in the army, desert, and then repeat the cycle, thus making a living from the bounties. Those substitutes who did not desert at the first chance were often men who did not meet the physical qualifications for soldiering. The substitute market employed a large number of underage boys and overage men who did not have the physical stamina to fight at the front.

The Conscription Act engendered a great deal of opposition from state officials. Many felt the act was unconstitutional and that it conflicted with state rights ideology. Yet eventually, most state governors, whether they believed in the constitutionality of a national draft or not, recognized the need for conscription and agreed to work with the central government. They did, however, share a resentment toward the Confederate conscription officers who usurped the positions of state officials.

Governor Joseph E. Brown of Georgia was the most infamous exception to this attitude among the governors. Brown believed in state rights at all costs and fought to retain the sovereignty of state governments. He argued against the necessity of the draft, asserting that Georgia had always produced more than its quota of men for the army. He hindered the recruiting process by issuing large numbers of exemptions to Georgians called by conscription and resisted the enrollment of the state militia, declaring that he needed the men in Georgia for local protection. Though other governors would balk at the increasing power of the central government, Brown remained the most vehemently opposed to any challenge to state authority.

Second Conscription Act

Five months after the inauguration of the first act, the army continued to want for soldiers. Southerners had displayed enormous ingenuity in eluding the enrollment officers by finding work that qualified them for exemption, by spending a fortune in substitutes, and by outright deception. On the heels of the horror at Sharpsburg, where both armies suffered thousands of casualties, the Confederate Congress issued a second Conscription Act on September 27, 1862. With it, they hoped to create a more stringent law that would eliminate the instances of misuse and put more men on the battlefields.

The second Conscription Act enabled the president to enlist white males between the ages of eighteen and forty-five. At the time, Davis recruited only men eighteen to forty, but the Confederate losses at Vicksburg and Gettysburg forced him to call on forty-to-forty-five-year-old males as well.

Despite the discord it had engendered, the substitution clause remained intact in September 1862. In addition, the government extended the list of exemptions once again. Davis and his administration hoped that, by conscripting men between thirty-five and forty-five years old, they could eliminate the number of men available to serve as substitutes and hence reduce exploitation of the system. By extending the number of exemptions, they attempted to ensure that enough men remained in industrial and agricultural occupations to keep the nation functioning. The abuses continued, however, and the second Conscription Act did little to appeal to latent patriotism.

Southerners received the second act in much the same way they had reacted to the first—with anger and resentment. By conscripting men as old as forty-five, Congress depleted the number of men remaining at home to plant crops and serve in local defense. Poorer families, whose survival depended on an ample number of bodies to plant and harvest and who could not afford to buy a substitute, suffered the greatest hardships under the extended draft.

Southern outrage regarding the conscription acts manifested itself most intensely in the mountain regions. In these areas, a large percentage of the population did not share the viewpoints of their state politicians, who frequently favored the wealthier constituencies living in the lowlands. In fact, many nonslaveholding mountain inhabitants espoused Union sentiment and felt no obligation to fight for the Confederacy. Most important, the majority of these people barely subsisted on the food they grew each year; they could not spare an able-bodied man.

As the war ground on, organized resistance to the draft intensified, particularly in the mountain regions of eastern Tennessee, North Carolina, Alabama, and Mississippi. Armed men joined together to aid one another in eluding the enrollment officers and to fight them off when necessary. By the end of the war, a number of enrollment officers had lost their lives to men who were desperate to avoid conscription.

Desertion became more common as the war progressed. As the South's resources diminished, so did the soldiers' rations. Deteriorating conditions in the camps and disintegrating morale, caused by the Confederate defeats during the summer of 1863 and despondent letters from their families, compelled men by the thousands to turn homeward.

In a vain attempt to recover his troops, Jefferson Davis issued a Proclamation of Amnesty to all deserters in August 1863. He revoked the usual punishments of incarceration or death for anyone who would return to the army during the stated grace period. When that failed, he suspended the writ of habeas corpus in the areas where draft evasion was most successful.

Difficulties with enforcement and coordination of conscription plagued authorities; the enterprise needed organization. When conscription first became law, its administration and execution had fallen to the Adjutant and General Inspector's Office. Under the guidance of this office, individual states recruited and organized units. In December 1862, the Confederacy established a Bureau of Conscription, which took responsibility for enrolling all troops east of the Mississippi River. This act further empowered the central government to allocate manpower to the indigent areas.

From its inception, the Bureau of Conscription clashed with military officers who desired a more efficient and less bureaucratic method of raising soldiers. Braxton Bragg took direct action and authorized Brig. Gen. Gideon Pillow to establish a recruiting bureau of his own, which operated in direct competition with the Bureau of Conscription in Richmond. Pillow and his men engaged in field recruiting in Alabama, Mississippi, and Tennessee. Pillow experienced a great deal of success with military conscription, but the legality of his methods came into question, and the government subsequently abolished his independent bureau. Within a short time, however, he was recruiting once again in Joseph E. Johnston's department. While employed under Johnston, however, Pillow was not able to wield the power he had enjoyed under Bragg; from Richmond, the Bureau on Conscription closely audited his work. When John S. Preston became superintendent of the Bureau of Conscription in August 1863, he set out to reorganize its structure and increase its efficiency. Under his direction, the bureau eventually abolished military conscription altogether.

During 1863, the Confederacy suffered severe setbacks, including, in the last months of the year, Bragg's defeat at Chattanooga. The Bureau of Conscription could not recruit soldiers fast enough to replace the casualties, and once again, the government modified the conscription laws.

Third Conscription Act

The Conscription Act of February 17, 1864, revealed the desperation that would soon pervade the Confederate government. Extending the draft to include males seventeen to fifty, the bureau planned to detail older conscripts, or to assign them to local reserve units, thus freeing younger men to fight on the front. Authorities received instructions to reserve Confederate and state civil service positions for those unable to fight. In addition, to keep the men in the ranks, the government offered one-hundred-dollar government bonds, at 6 percent interest, to any noncommissioned officers or privates who did not desert.

Congress also used this Conscription Act to amend once again the overseer clause. Reflecting the decline in the worth of Confederate money, plantation owners would no longer pay five hundred dollars to the public treasury for each overseer; instead they had to produce a bond guaranteeing one hundred pounds of bacon or of beef and pork for every physically sound slave on their plantations. In addition, any surplus goods grown on the plantations had to be sold to the government at a fixed price.

The third act also eliminated almost half of the authorized exemptions. In an attempt to curtail the abuses generated by the exemption system, the Conscription Bureau now filled positions formerly held by laborers immune to the draft by detailing enlisted men. This provision gave the central government virtual dominion over the Confederate labor force.

The most astonishing provision of the new Conscription Act was that which authorized the government to employ up to twenty thousand free blacks and slaves. Although they did not propose to arm the slaves in early 1864, Southerners prepared to use them and free blacks for special detail, such as building fortifications and working in munitions factories.

The Conscription Act of 1864 and the heavy losses on the field further exacerbated conflict between the Confederate government and the state governments. The war was going badly. It had seriously depleted state resources, and even civilians faced severe deprivations. Individual states turned on the central government and blamed the president and Congress for their woes.

By the end of 1864, military commanders, desperate for soldiers, had turned against the Bureau of Conscription. The third act had not placed an adequate number of men at the front, and commanders cited the inefficiency of the Conscription Bureau as the reason. They had a point; during the early months of 1864, the bureau had issued more exemptions than it had received conscripts. Bragg, in particular, began pushing to reinstate military conscription.

President Davis and the secretary of war despaired of adding any more white Southerners to the ranks. They had already called out all men between seventeen and fifty; those who had not presented themselves for duty to this point were not likely to do so now. So, in desperation, Davis made the shocking proposal to arm slaves.

In March 1865, Congress made provisions to "recruit" slaves for field service. It carefully stipulated that the master must assent to the use of his slave for military service, that recruitment would not drain any state of more than 25 percent of its slave population and, especially important, that the slave would retain his slave status.

In March Congress also conceded to the abolishment of the Bureau of Conscription. Generals of state reserve forces, who reported directly to the War Department, received orders to take charge of enforcing the Conscription Acts. But by 1865, Southerners were no more eager to join the army than they had been in 1862.

A national conscription law was an extreme act for a confederation founded on the principle of the sovereignty of its individual states. It was bound to create conflict and unrest. Yet winning the war necessitated a degree of coordination, and with the Conscription Acts, Congress did attempt to lend organization to the war effort. It also strove to place unwilling soldiers at the front.

The number of soldiers the Conscription Acts added to the military ranks remains uncertain—perhaps ninety thousand conscripts reached the front. The Conscription Acts did encourage volunteerism and, in 1862, prevented the twelve-month veterans from leaving the army.

Ironically, although the Conscription Acts were intended to save the Confederacy, they no doubt promoted disunity within the nation. The substitution clause and the Twenty-Slave Law aggravated class tensions between Southerners, and the states rebelled against the power the Bureau of Conscription imparted to the national government. Yet the enactment of a national conscription law demonstrated how far some Southerners were willing to go to realize their dream of an independent South.

[*See also* Army, *articles on* African Americans in the Confederate Army *and* Manpower; Class Conflict; Desertion; Habeas Corpus; Morale; State Rights.]

BIBLIOGRAPHY

Brooks, Robert Preston. *Conscription in the Confederate States of America, 1862–1865.* Cambridge, Mass., 1917.

Escott, Paul D. *After Secession: Jefferson Davis and the Failure of Confederate Nationalism.* Baton Rouge, La., 1978.

Mitchell, Memory F. *Legal Aspects of Conscription and Exemption in North Carolina, 1861–1865.* Chapel Hill, N.C., 1965.

Moore, Albert Burton. *Conscription and Conflict in the Confederacy.* New York, 1924.

Thomas, Emory M. *The Confederate Nation, 1861–1865.* New York, 1979.

JENNIFER LUND

CONSTITUTION. The states that left the American Union in 1860 and 1861 brought with them a rich tradition of constitutionalism. Many Southern leaders explained their support for secession in terms of the failure of the federal compact. Most blamed Northerners for failing to live up to their obligations, although some thought it was structural flaws in the U.S. Constitution that made secession necessary.

The Provisional Constitution of the Confederate States of America signed on February 8, 1861, created a compact among six Deep South states. The Permanent Confederate Constitution, signed on March 11, 1861, created a political structure for what became the eleven-state Confederate nation. Both documents were similar to the U.S. Constitution. The differences between the two reflected the political struggles that had led to secession.

The Montgomery Convention and the Provisional Constitution. On February 4, 1861, forty-three delegates from South Carolina, Alabama, Mississippi, Georgia, Florida, and Louisiana assembled in Montgomery, Alabama, to write a provisional constitution for the Confederate States of America. The convention finished its work four days later. Such speed was possible because of the "mania for unanimity" among the delegates and because the Provisional Constitution was something of a cross between the Articles of Confederation and the U.S. Constitution and borrowed heavily, in language and concepts, from both documents. Like the Articles of Confederation, the Provisional Constitution created a unicameral Congress in which each state had a single vote. Borrowing from the British system, the Provisional Constitution allowed cabinet members to serve in Congress and stipulated that Congress choose the president. Like the Constitution of 1787, it provided for a president with a veto power and enumerated powers for the Confederate Congress similar to those given to the U.S. Congress. There were also a number of substantive differences between the Provisional Confederate Constitution and the Constitution of 1787.

Under this document Jefferson Davis became president of the fledgling nation and formed a government. By its own terms the Constitution was to last no more than a year, but it was in operation for only thirty-one days before the delegates wrote and signed a permanent constitution. The preamble of the Provisional Constitution reflected the state rights philosophy and Protestant culture of its framers: "We, the Deputies of the Sovereign and Independent States of South Carolina, Georgia, Florida, Alabama, Mississippi, and Louisiana, invoking the favor of Almighty God . . . ."

The Permanent Constitution. Under the terms of the Provisional Constitution, the Montgomery convention reconstituted itself as the Provisional Congress of the Confederate States of America until such time as a permanent constitution could be adopted and a permanent congress elected. There was no serious debate over the name of the new nation—the "Confederate States of America" reflected what the founders thought they were creating.

The delegates who gathered in Montgomery reflected, in their occupations, their interest in politics, and their stake in slavery, the elite of the society they represented. In early March when the Texas delegation arrived, their numbers rose to fifty. Of these, forty-two were lawyers and thirty-three described themselves as planters (including twenty-seven of the lawyers). Forty-eight were native Southerners, forty-nine were slaveowners. Twenty-one owned at least 20 slaves and one owned 473. Thirty-eight were college graduates. Almost all had extensive political experience: twenty-three had served in the U.S. Congress; sixteen were former or sitting judges, including two state chief justices; two had been in national cabinets, and a third had been in the cabinet of the Republic of Texas. Oddly, one of the most influential members of the convention had no political experience per se. Thomas R. R. Cobb, the "James Madi-

son" of the Confederate Constitution, had never held an elective office, although he had been the first reporter of the Georgia Supreme Court. He was also one of the South's foremost legal scholars and the author of the influential *An Inquiry into the Law of Negro Slavery* (1858).

On February 9, the day after the signing of the Provisional Constitution, members of the Provisional Confederate Congress appointed a twelve-man committee, chaired by South Carolina's secessionist leader Robert Barnwell Rhett, Sr., to draft a permanent constitution. Other important members of the committee included Thomas R. R. Cobb and Robert Toombs of Georgia; James Chesnut, Jr., of South Carolina; and Wiley Harris, a skilled Mississippi lawyer. On February 28 Rhett presented the Congress with a draft of a permanent Constitution. For the next ten days the Montgomery delegates functioned as a Congress during the morning and as a constitutional convention during the afternoon and evening. On March 11, 1861, the Montgomery convention adopted this document and sent it on to the seceded states for ratification.

Structurally the U.S. and Confederate Constitutions are nearly identical. Both have a preamble and seven articles, and both create a national president, a bicameral legislature, and a court system. The only major structural difference is that the first twelve amendments to the U.S. Constitution were incorporated, almost word for word, into the main body of the Confederate Constitution.

The Confederate Constitution is often seen as a document for a nation based on state rights and limited government. To a great extent this is true, but the document also vested the national government with some centralizing powers. Like the U.S. Constitution, the Confederate document had a necessary and proper clause, a supremacy clause, and a clause requiring all state officials to swear allegiance to the national government. Article I, Section 9 of the Confederate Constitution had a habeas corpus suspension provision that was identical to that of the U.S. Constitution. These certainly gave the national government power to act.

In addition, innovations in the Confederate Constitution gave the new government more power in some respects than the U.S. government had. The president was limited to one term, but that term was for six years. Thus he may have had more opportunity to implement his policies than his counterpart in Washington. The Confederate president had a line-item veto and the right to dismiss at will all cabinet members. Incorporating aspects of a parliamentary system, the document stipulated that Congress could grant cabinet officers "a seat upon the floor of either House, with the privilege of discussing any measures appertaining to his department." This gave the administration an advantage in getting its programs through Congress that the U.S. president lacked. Robert Toombs thought these provisions strengthening the executive branch were the most important differences between the two constitutions.

The most significant differences between the two, however, lay in the Confederate provisions limiting the power of the national government, protecting state rights and, most important, protecting slavery.

A limited government. A persistent complaint of antebellum Southerners had concerned the national government's assumption of increased power after 1789. Reflecting the divergent views of state rights advocates and nationalists were the fights over the establishment of a national bank, the 1828 "Tariff of Abominations," the doctrine of nullification, and the constitutionality of the federal government's funding internal improvements. Thus, the Confederate preamble differed significantly from that of the U.S. Constitution in order to cure what were seen as defects allowing centralization. Unlike its federal counterpart, the preamble did not state that the central government was to "provide for the common defense" or "promote the general welfare." It also contained an explicit reference to state sovereignty (discussed below) and a direct appeal for the "favor and guidance of Almighty God."

Article I granted the Confederate Congress the legislative powers "delegated" in the Constitution. This was a major limitation on the power of the Confederate government. The enumerated powers clauses (Art. I, Sec. 8) limited taxes to those providing "revenue necessary to pay the debts, provide for the common defence, and carry on the Government of the Confederate States." This clause specifically forbade any "bounties" or taxes "to promote or foster any branch of industry." Section 8 absolutely prohibited the Congress from appropriating money for "internal improvements intended to facilitate commerce" except for those directly connected to navigation, harbors, and rivers. Under this Constitution there would be no support for national roads, railroads, or other such improvements.

It also provided that the executive branch could propose appropriations and needed only a simple majority in Congress to have them adopted, whereas appropriations originating with Congress needed a two-thirds majority to pass. This particular provision strengthened the president vis-à-vis Congress but generally it made the national government less flexible than that of the United States. The Constitution also required that all appropriations be for exact amounts and declared that there could not be "extra compensation to any public contractor, officer, agent or servant." The absolute prohibition on "impa[i]ring the right of property in negro slaves" limited the use of slaves for war activities. These provisions, combined with the lack of a common defense clause in the preamble, were significant departures from the U.S. Constitution and at least potentially hampered the operations of a government that was about to fight a major war with a far richer and more powerful adversary.

Finally, in a move to eliminate patronage (which could have undermined the president's power to run the government), the Constitution prohibited the president from removing civil servants except for "dishonesty, incapacity, inefficiency, misconduct, or neglect of duty." The president, however, retained the explicit power to fire cabinet members and diplomats without cause.

During the war itself the Davis government was able to overcome some, but not all, of the constitutional obstacles to a strong government. President Davis amassed considerable power, but at great cost to his political capital. During the war the Davis administration often suppressed civil liberties to a greater extent than its counterpart in Washington. Only five days after Davis took office the Confederate Congress adopted legislation allowing the suspension of habeas corpus. Davis sporadically imposed martial law on Richmond and other major cities. In some areas of the Confederacy, like eastern Tennessee, martial law led to the summary executions of a few civilians and the mass incarceration of others. By the end of the war, Vice President Alexander Stephens and other leading politicians no longer supported the administration, in part because of Davis's "betrayal" of Southern Constitutional principles. "Our liberties, once lost," he declared, "may be lost forever."

State rights. Directly tied to the limitations on the national government was a respect for state rights. Some scholars have argued that the Confederate Constitution was so extreme on this issue that the Confederacy was doomed to lose the war. Others dispute this point. In any event, even a cursory glance at the document shows that in respecting state rights—and simultaneously limiting the power of the central government—the Confederate Constitution created a government that was quite different from that in place in the Union.

The state rights tone was set in the preamble, which added to "We, the people of the Confederate States," the significant phrase, "each State acting in its sovereign and independent character." Article I allowed the states to impeach "any judicial or other Federal officer, resident and acting solely within the limits of any state." Such an officer would then be tried by the Confederate Senate. This provision was never implemented during the life of the Confederacy. Nevertheless, the threat of impeachment may have undermined the ability of Confederate officials to enforce unpopular laws and policies in their state. Article I, Section 10, also allowed states to impose their own import and export duties, something prohibited to the states remaining in the Union.

Southern distrust for the national judiciary was apparent in the drafting of Article III of the Confederate document. A key provision of the U.S. Constitution is the clause creating diversity jurisdiction by giving the federal courts the power to hear cases "between Citizens of different States." The Confederate Constitution lacked such a provision, which in practice meant that civil suits between citizens of different states would have to be litigated in state courts. This undermined the nationalization of law and jurisprudence, and had the Confederacy survived, it probably would have led to unnecessary complications in litigation and complaints about the failure of litigants to get a fair trial in a neutral forum. Moreover, in a nation that was predicated on state rights and local interests, the abolition of diversity jurisdiction could have led to a judicial and business climate that would have hampered economic development. The Confederate Constitution also failed to include the phrase "law and equity" in granting jurisdiction to the national courts. This is generally seen as a concession to the civil law system in Louisiana and its vestiges in Texas. A final bow to state rights, and one that could have led to enormous instability, was a provision allowing a constitutional convention to be called on the demand of just three states.

During the war, state judges issued writs of habeas corpus directed against military officers trying to impose Confederate conscription. Without a functioning court system, which the Constitution would have allowed but did not mandate, the Davis administration and the Confederate military could only respond to these manifestations of state rights with suspensions of martial law.

Slavery. Far from a "peculiar institution," slavery was, as Confederate Vice President Alexander Stephens declared, "the cornerstone" of the Confederacy. As such, it was protected even more in the Confederate Constitution than it had been in the proslavery U.S. Constitution of 1787.

The most obvious difference between the two documents lay in their use of the term *slavery*. In deference in 1787 to some of the Northern delegates who thought their constituents might oppose the Constitution if the word appeared, the framers of the U.S. Constitution substituted such phrases as *other persons, such persons,* and *persons owing service* for the word *slaves*. No such problems arose in the framing of the Confederate document. The blatantly proslavery Confederate Constitution contains the words *slave* or *slavery* ten times in seven separate clauses.

As their predecessors had in the Philadelphia Convention of 1787, the South Carolina delegates in Montgomery wanted to count slaves fully for representation. South Carolina had a larger percentage of slaves than any other state and would have gained by their full representation. The delegates in Montgomery, however, must have understood that a full counting of slaves would have discouraged the other Southern states, with smaller percentages of slaves, from joining the Confederacy. Thus, the convention chose to continue the Federal compromise by maintaining the three-fifths clause for determining congressional apportionment.

The frequent refusal of Northern states to cooperate in the rendition of fugitive slaves had been a major irritant in the antebellum period. The Montgomery delegates did not, however, substantially alter the fugitive slave clause in their Constitution. There were probably two reasons for this. First, they were writing a constitution for a slaveholders' republic, and it was unlikely that any Confederate state would ever adopt legislation similar to the Northern personal liberty laws. Second, a substantial change in the wording of the clause would have undermined the Southern argument that the meaning of the clause in the U.S. Constitution was clear and that secession was justified by the North's refusal to fulfill its constitutional obligations.

The Confederate Constitution also mirrored, but surpassed, the federal Constitution on the issue of the slave trade by absolutely forbidding the operation of the African slave trade. This was done over protestations of South Carolinians, who wanted the matter left to Congress. Prohibiting the trade was not an indication of antislavery sentiment but the result of the distaste for the African trade by some slave owners, fear of Africans themselves, and the fear that Europe would not recognize the Confederacy if it did not unequivocally prohibit the trade. Permitting the trade also might have discouraged Virginia and Maryland from entering the Confederacy because of the excess of slaves in those states. Those states might not have wanted foreign competition with their interstate slave trade.

On all other issues the Constitution created a thoroughly proslavery republic. The Constitution authorized Congress to *limit* the importation of slaves from other nations and states but did not prohibit it altogether as current federal law did. The Constitution absolutely prohibited any law "impa[i]ring the right of property in negro slaves." Reflecting Southern states' rejection of Northern states' decisions that had freed the slaves of visitors, Article IV guaranteed that the citizens of each Confederate state "shall have the right of transit and sojourn in any State of this Confederacy, with their slaves and other property; and the right of property in said slaves shall not be thereby impaired." The Constitution's fugitive slave clause reiterated this right. Finally, the Constitution affirmed the proslavery holding of Chief Justice Roger B. Taney in the U.S. Supreme Court *Dred Scott* decision, by declaring that slavery could never be prohibited from any Confederate territory. At the same time, however, the Confederate authors jettisoned Taney's implausible argument that the national government could not regulate the territories. Thus, their territory clause accomplished two proslavery goals. It guaranteed both slavery in the territories and the ability of Congress to counter any antislavery movement that might arise in the Confederate hinterlands.

Ratification. On March 11 the Montgomery convention unanimously adopted the new Constitution. The next day Howell Cobb, president of the convention, sent the Constitution to the states for their approval. The ratification of five states would complete the process. On March 12 the Alabama secession convention debated and ratified the document by a vote of 87 to 5; on March 16 the Georgia convention read and ratified the Constitution by a unanimous vote of 260 to 0; on March 21, after some political maneuvering, Louisiana ratified 94 to 10; on March 23 the Texas Secession Convention approved the Constitution 126 to 2 after almost no debate; and on March 26 Mississippi ratified it by a vote of 78 to 7. The Confederate Constitution was now in force.

Radicals delayed ratification in South Carolina. Robert Barnwell Rhett, Sr., wanted to amend the document to prohibit any free state from entering the Confederacy. But finally, on April 3, South Carolina ratified by a vote of 138 to 21. The negative votes represented not latent Unionist sentiment but the proslavery extremism in the Palmetto State. After ratification the South Carolina convention proposed amendments to eliminate the three-fifths provision and count all slaves for representation; to prohibit free states from joining the Confederacy; to repeal the constitutional prohibition on the slave trade; and to prohibit the government from going into debt, except in the event of war.

Finally, on April 22, Florida ratified the Constitution with a vote of 50 to 0. By this time fighting between the Union and the Confederacy had begun. By the end of June, North Carolina, Arkansas, and Virginia had joined the Confederacy. Tennessee adopted an ordinance of secession in May and placed the Confederate Constitution before the voters, who endorsed it in August by a vote of 85,753 to 30,863. Rump governments in Kentucky and Missouri also eventually endorsed the Confederate Constitution, but those states remained firmly in the Union throughout the war.

[*See also* Congress; Conscription; Dred Scott Decision; Fugitive Slave Law; Habeas Corpus; Judiciary; Montgomery Convention; Presidency; State Rights; Vice Presidency; *and the Appendix for the text of the Constitution.*]

BIBLIOGRAPHY

Beringer, Richard E., Herman Hataway, Archer Jones, and William N. Still, Jr. *Why the South Lost the Civil War*. Athens, Ga. 1986.

Carpenter, Jesse T. *The South as a Conscious Minority: A Study in Political Thought*. New York, 1930.

Fehrebacher, Don. E. *Constitutions and Constitutionalism in the Slaveholding South*. Athens, Ga., 1989.

Finkelman, Paul. "Slavery and the Constitutional Convention of 1787: Making a Covenant with Death." In *Beyond Confederation*. Edited by Richard Beeman, Stephen Botein, and Edward C. Carter II. Chapel Hill, N.C., 1987.

Lee, Charles Robert, Jr. *The Confederate Constitutions*. Chapel Hill, N.C., 1963.

McCash, William B. *Thomas R. R. Cobb: The Making of a Southern Nationalist*. Macon, Ga., 1983.

Nieman, Donald. "Republicanism, the Confederate Constitution, and the American Constitutional Tradition." In *An Uncertain Tradition: Constitutionalism and the History of the South*. Edited by Kermit L. Hall and James W. Ely, Jr. Athens, Ga., 1989.

Owsley, Frank. *States Rights and the Confederacy*. Chicago, 1925. Reprint, Gloucester, Ma., 1961.

Thomas, Emory. *The Confederate Nation, 1861–1865*. New York, 1979.

PAUL FINKELMAN

CONSTITUTIONAL UNION PARTY. Comprising members of the old Whig and American parties, the Constitutional Union party organized for the presidential election of 1860. The party proposed to remove the slavery question from the political arena and adopted an ambiguous platform that supported the Constitution, the Union, and the enforcement of the laws of the United States.

In February 1860, thirty prominent leaders from among the old Whigs and Americans—including John J. Crittenden, William C. Rives, and Washington Hunt—issued an appeal to the American people, denouncing both the Democratic and the Republican parties and calling for the organization of a new party. Believing that the public was tired of slavery agitation, organizers of the Constitutional Union party felt they could relieve sectional strife by remaining silent on the slavery issue.

The first Constitutional Union National Convention was held at Baltimore in May 1860. Here party members nominated John Bell of Tennessee for president and Edward Everett of Massachusetts for vice president. Bell's conservatism on the slavery issue and his large slaveholdings made him an appealing candidate both to Northern moderates and to upper South Unionists. Also at the Baltimore convention, Constitutional Unionists declared all party issues secondary to preservation of the Union, and they denounced Breckinridge Democrats as disunionist conspirators.

As the November election approached, party members hoped that moderate Republicans, sensing defeat for their candidate, would vote for the Constitutional Union ticket to prevent a Democratic victory. Constitutional Unionists also thought that the division within the Democratic party between Stephen A. Douglas and John C. Breckinridge might convince Democrats that neither nominee would win and thus they would support John Bell in order to defeat Abraham Lincoln. Bell, however, received only 12.6 percent of the popular vote, carrying the three upper South states of Virginia, Kentucky, and Tennessee.

Throughout the secession winter of 1860–1861, Bell and other Constitutional Union party leaders urged Lincoln to adopt conciliatory measures toward the South. The outbreak of the Civil War ended all hopes of a peaceful reconciliation and signaled the demise of the Constitutional Union party.

[*See also* Whig Party.]

"GRAND NATIONAL UNION BANNER FOR 1860." Campaign banner for Constitutional Union party presidential candidate John Bell and vice presidential candidate Edward Everett. Lithograph on wove paper, published by Currier and Ives, 1860.

BIBLIOGRAPHY

Crofts, Daniel W. *Reluctant Confederates: Upper South Unionists in the Secession Crisis*. Chapel Hill, N.C., 1989.

Dumond, Dwight Lowell. *The Secession Movement, 1860–1861*. New York, 1931.

Parks, Joseph Howard. *John Bell of Tennessee*. Baton Rouge, La., 1950.

BRUCE W. EELMAN

CONTRABAND. From early modern times, the Western nations have elaborated increasingly detailed conventions of warfare governing persons and property. During the eighteenth century, the term *contraband of war* came into vogue to designate forbidden articles of commerce—chiefly arms and ammunition—that neutral nations might not furnish to belligerents in time of war. By the nineteenth century the term also applied to such articles captured from one belligerent by another. The Civil War stretched the meaning of the term in new and unforeseen directions.

The process began with the war scarcely a month old, when four escaped slaves forced the issue. The men had been impressed into service to build Confederate fortifications on Virginia's lower peninsula. They sought refuge at Fortress Monroe, the Union-held position at the tip of the peninsula, commanded by Gen. Benjamin F. Butler, a shrewd Massachusetts politician.

Prevailing Federal policy steadfastly supported the property rights of slaveholders, but Butler viewed that principle through the prism of his circumstances. Facing an array of slave-built earthworks, he had no doubt of the military usefulness of impressed slaves. If their masters considered them property, why could not the United States do the same, to deny the Confederacy the benefit of their labor and to turn it to the Union's advantage? On such a basis, he offered protection to the fugitives. Although at first he did not invoke the words *contraband of war*, the designation "contrabands" rapidly gained currency both in his command and throughout the North. In August 1861, Congress ratified the notion into law with the Confiscation Act, which authorized the seizure of all property (slaves included) used for belligerent purposes and freed the affected slaves.

Union soldiers lost no time putting the contrabands to work performing mundane camp chores. But during the spring and summer of 1862, as Union forces advanced into the Confederacy, the army required military laborers more

"THE (FORT) MONROE DOCTRINE." This crude caricature responds to Benjamin Butler's declaration of May 27, 1861. A slave and his master stand before the Union fort. The planter cracks his whip crying, "Come back you black rascal." The slave responds, "Can't come back nohow massa. Dis chile's contraban." In the background, other slaves leave the fields for the fort. Lithograph on wove paper, 1861.

LIBRARY OF CONGRESS

CONTRABAND CAMP, MANCHESTER, VIRGINIA.

than servants. Congress obliged first by prohibiting members of the armed forces from returning runaway slaves to their masters and second by passing a strengthened Confiscation Act and a new Militia Act, which freed the slaves of all disloyal persons and authorized the wholesale employment of former slaves in the Union war effort.

After President Abraham Lincoln issued the Emancipation Proclamation, the size of the contraband population soared. Concentrated mostly in the plantation regions of the Union-occupied South, it numbered several hundred thousand by the end of the war. Able-bodied men served as soldiers and military laborers; women were put to work as farm laborers under the direction of plantation lessees or army-appointed "superintendents of contrabands." Those incapable of labor took refuge at "contraband camps," where the army and Northern benevolent societies provided food, shelter, clothing, and other amenities. Such assistance provoked a wide-ranging debate over its economic and social implications, strains of which echoed into the twentieth century.

The North's designation of escaped and captured slaves as contraband of war caught the South on the horns of a dilemma. Neither politicians nor ideologues could find a means to undercut the contraband logic, except by continuing to sing the antebellum refrain that slaves loved their masters and had no desire to seek refuge with the Northerners. Although Confederate planners understood the importance of slave labor to their cause, they struggled in vain to halt the transformation of slaves into contrabands.

The popularity of the designation "contraband" arose largely from its wry play upon the contradictory nature of slaves as persons and property. Ironically, it also helped perpetuate an association of other-than-human attributes to the former slaves that lingered in the North as well as the South long after the dust of war had settled.

[*See also* African Americans in the Union Army; Confiscation, *article on* Federal Confiscation Acts.]

BIBLIOGRAPHY

Berlin, Ira, et al., eds. *Freedom: A Documentary History of Emancipation, 1861–1867.* 4 vols. to date. Cambridge, England, 1982–.

Butler, Benjamin F. *Private and Official Correspondence of Gen. Benjamin F. Butler during the Period of the Civil War.* Vol. 1. Norwood, Mass., 1917.

Gerteis, Louis S. *From Contraband to Freedman: Federal Policy toward Southern Blacks, 1861–1865.* Westport, Conn., 1973.

Quarles, Benjamin. *Lincoln and the Negro.* New York, 1962.

JOSEPH P. REIDY

COOK, PHILIP (1817–1894), politician and brigadier general. Cook was born in Twigg County, Georgia, on July 30, 1817. He attended Oglethorpe University near Milledgeville and graduated from the University of Virginia Law School in 1841. A state senator when war broke out, he enlisted as a private in the Macon County Volunteers, which became the Fourth Georgia Infantry. Initially the unit was assigned to Portsmouth, Virginia, where Cook was made adjutant. After the Seven Days' Battles near Richmond, during which he was wounded at Malvern Hill, he was commissioned a lieutenant colonel, and on November 1, 1862, following the Battle of Sharpsburg, he was commissioned colonel of the regiment. At Chancellorsville he was again wounded and took three months to recover. During this period he was elected to the Georgia state senate and served for forty days before rejoining the army for a short time. He returned to Georgia to serve out his senate term during the 1864 session.

Upon the death of Gen. George Pierce Doles at Bethesda Church, Colonel Cook was promoted to brigadier general, his commission bearing the date August 5, 1864. He participated in Gen. Jubal Early's Valley campaign and then joined Gen. Robert E. Lee's army at Petersburg. During the Battle of Fort Stedman on March 25, 1865, he was again wounded and taken to a hospital in Petersburg. Cook was captured when the city fell, and he was not paroled until July 30, 1865.

He returned to Americus, Georgia, where he practiced law until 1880. He served as a member of the constitutional convention of 1865, in Congress from 1873 to 1883, and as secretary of state of Georgia in 1890. He died in Atlanta on May 21, 1894, and is buried in Macon, Georgia.

BIBLIOGRAPHY

Derry, Joseph T. *Georgia*. Vol. 6 of *Confederate Military History*. Edited by Clement A. Evans. Atlanta, Ga., 1899. Vol. 7 of extended ed. Wilmington, N.C., 1987.

Johnson, Allen, ed. *Dictionary of American Biography*. Vol. 2. New York, 1964.

Warner, Ezra J. *Generals in Gray: Lives of the Confederate Commanders*. Baton Rouge, La., 1970.

CHRIS CALKINS

COOKE, JAMES W. (?–1869), naval officer.

Born in North Carolina and raised in Portsmouth, Virginia, James Wallace Cooke entered the U.S. Navy in April 1828 and rose to the rank of lieutenant. He resigned his commission on May 1, 1861, joining Virginia's state navy three days later and accepting a commission in the new Confederate navy in June. Shortly after the Battle of First Manassas, he gained command of a small armed steamer, CSS *Ellis,* one of a Confederate flotilla operating in Albemarle Sound. In an engagement off Roanoke Island, Cooke was wounded and captured. Held briefly, he was soon paroled to his home until he was exchanged in September 1862. Shortly afterward he was promoted to the rank of commander.

Along with his promotion, Cooke received orders to oversee the construction of the ironclad CSS *Albemarle* on the Roanoke River. Hampered by the lack of skilled shipwrights and shortages of vital equipment, Cooke especially had trouble obtaining iron for his vessel's armor. His constant demands for iron from the Tredegar Iron Works at Richmond, Virginia, and the Clarendon Foundry at Wilmington, North Carolina, led officials at those plants to call him the "Ironmonger Captain."

Cooke took his recently launched ironclad into action on March 19, 1864, ramming and sinking the Federal gunboat *Southfield* and driving off a second gunboat, *Miami,* with heavy casualties. Aided by *Albemarle,* the Confederates recaptured Plymouth, North Carolina. Cooke fought the entire Federal flotilla in Albemarle Sound on May 5, 1864, disabling USS *Sassacus* but suffering damage in return. After returning to Plymouth for repairs, Cooke's health broke, and he was relieved as commander of *Albemarle* by Lt. Alexander F. Warley. When he recovered, Cooke was promoted to command all Confederate naval forces in the Roanoke River region and was still on duty in Halifax, North Carolina, when the Confederates abandoned the city in April 1865. After the war, Cooke returned to Portsmouth, Virginia, where he died in 1869.

BIBLIOGRAPHY

Gibbons, Tony. *Warships and Naval Battles of the Civil War*. New York, 1989.

Scharf, J. Thomas. *History of the Confederate States Navy*. New York, 1887. Reprint, New York, 1977.

Still, William N., Jr. *Iron Afloat: The Story of the Confederate Armorclads*. Nashville, Tenn., 1971.

ROBERT S. BROWNING III

COOKE, JOHN ESTEN (1830–1886), novelist,

historian, and captain. Born in Winchester, Virginia, Cooke moved with his family in 1839 to Richmond, where he studied law and was admitted to the bar. Cooke's success in having his works published led him to a literary career in which he soon gained wide recognition.

In November 1859, he enlisted as a private in the Richmond Howitzers and, in 1861, was mustered into active service with the company, which was expanded into a battalion. He became a sergeant in the First Company, which was attached to Bonham's brigade at First Manassas. He was discharged in January 1862, but in May he was appointed a first lieutenant and assigned to J. E. B. Stuart's staff. Although he greatly admired Stuart, his close associate and relative by marriage, the cavalry chief once referred to Cooke as an "enormous bore." Cooke was promoted to captain and chief of ordnance, Stuart's cavalry division, and became inspector general of horse artillery, Army of Northern Virginia.

After the Civil War, Cooke returned to the Shenandoah Valley, where he spent the postwar years as a planter and writer at The Briars in Clarke County. He is buried at Old Chapel near Millwood. Cooke's *Life of Stonewall Jackson* was first published in 1863. His wartime contributions to the *Southern Illustrated News* have been published as *Outlines from the Outpost* (1961). His postwar writings included *Surry of Eagle's Nest* (1866) and its sequel *Mohun* (1869), *Wearing of the Gray* (1867), and *A Life of General Robert E. Lee* (1871).

BIBLIOGRAPHY

Beaty, John W. *John Esten Cooke.* New York, 1922.

Compiled Military Service Records. John Esten Cooke. Microcopy M331. Record Group 109. National Archives, Washington, D.C.

Cooke, John Esten. *Outlines from the Outpost.* Edited by Richard Harwell. Chicago, 1961.

LEE A. WALLACE, JR.

COOKE, JOHN ROGERS

COOKE, JOHN ROGERS (1833–1891), brigadier general. Unquestionably one of the most courageous brigadiers in the Confederate army, Cooke came from a family bitterly split by the Civil War. His father, Virginia-born Philip St. George Cooke, was an army officer stationed at Jefferson Barracks, Missouri, where John Cooke was born June 9, 1833. Cooke graduated from Harvard as a civil engineer. Painfully conscious of his shortcomings in that profession, he became an apprentice in the locomotive works at St. Louis. In 1855 Cooke entered the army as a lieutenant in the Eighth Infantry.

When civil war exploded, Cooke and his Virginia brother-in-law, J. E. B. Stuart, left duty posts in the Southwest and hastened to Richmond to join Confederate forces. Cooke's father became a Union major general. The family breach was not healed until years after the contest. For the first year of the war Cooke served successively as quartermaster and chief of artillery on Gen. Theophilus H. Holmes's staff. He entered the field in April 1862 as colonel of the Twenty-seventh North Carolina, and had he not been wounded seven times in the course of the war, "the gallant Cooke" undoubtedly would have achieved high-command rank.

He was a major participant in almost every important battle involving Robert E. Lee's army—and conspicuous in most. At Sharpsburg Cooke held his position in the Confederate center against Union assaults for two hours. He directed fire from behind a small, bullet-riddled hickory tree fifteen yards in advance of his lines. At the height of the fighting he sent an aide to headquarters with the message "I have not a cartridge in my command, but will hold my position at the point of the bayonet." Cooke proved true to his word.

Promoted to brigadier general on November 1, 1862, he assumed command of a brigade whose members thereafter proudly called themselves "Cooke's North Carolinians." A wound above the left eye at Fredericksburg incapacitated Cooke for a period, but he was at the head of his troops in the Pickett-Pettigrew charge at Gettysburg.

In October 1863 at Bristoe Station, Cooke received orders to make an assault that he felt strongly was suicidal. "Well, I will advance," he said, "and if they flank me, I will face my men about and cut my way out." That calamity occurred. Cooke lost half of his 1,400 men in the thirty-minute fight. He suffered a broken leg from a bullet and could not rejoin his troops until the following spring. He surrendered at Appomattox with the remnant of his brigade.

In the postwar years Cooke became a Richmond merchant and was active in veterans' affairs. He was instrumental in establishing that city's Confederate Soldiers' Home. Cooke died April 10, 1891, and was buried in Richmond's Hollywood Cemetery.

One of Cooke's soldiers praised the brigadier by stating: "He never pushed his command forward. He always *led* it." A staff officer wrote of Cooke: "He was always firm in the enforcement of his orders, yet not a martinet. . . . Off duty, he was as kind and pleasant a companion as I ever met."

BIBLIOGRAPHY

Brock, R. A. "General John Rogers Cooke." *Southern Historical Society Papers* 18 (1890): 322–327.

Clark, Walter, ed. *Histories of the Several Regiments and Battalions from North Carolina in the Great War, 1861–'65.* 5 vols. Raleigh, 1901. Reprint, Wilmington, N.C., 1991.

Hill, D. H., Jr. *North Carolina.* Vol. 4 of *Confederate Military History.* Edited by Clement A. Evans. Atlanta, 1899. Vol. 5 of extended ed. Wilmington, N.C., 1987.

JAMES I. ROBERTSON, JR.

COOKE, WILLIAM MORDECAI

COOKE, WILLIAM MORDECAI (1823–1863), congressman from Missouri. Born in Portsmouth, Virginia, on December 11, 1823, Cooke enjoyed a prosperous upbringing. A private tutor prepared him for his entry in the University of Virginia where he obtained a law degree. In 1843 Cooke decided to move to St. Louis. Six years later he left St. Louis to settle in Hannibal, Missouri, where he won election as judge of the Court of Common Pleas. He returned to St. Louis in 1854.

In March 1861, Missouri's pro-Southern governor, Claiborne F. Jackson, sent Cooke as a commissioner to the president of the Confederate States. Upon his return to Missouri he joined the Missouri State Guard and served as an aide to Governor Jackson. Cooke saw action during the Battles of Boonville and Carthage, and at the Battle of Wilson's Creek he served as aide-de-camp to Gen. Sterling Price. Afterward Governor Jackson sent Cooke and Gen. John B. Clark to the Confederate capital as special commissioners to President Davis. Soon after, Cooke was elected to the Provisional Congress.

During the First Congress, Cooke, who was ill for a time, usually supported Davis's administration. One source states that he was a trusted adviser to Davis. He served as a member of the Inauguration, Accounts, Commerce, Naval Affairs, Ordnance, and Ordnance Stores committees.

Cooke declined to stand for reelection to the Second Congress. He died April 14, 1863, at Petersburg, Virginia.

BIBLIOGRAPHY

Bay, W. V. N. *Reminiscences of the Bench and Bar of Missouri*. St. Louis, 1878.
Hyde, William, and Howard L. Conard. *Encyclopedia of the History of St. Louis*. 5 vols. New York, 1899.
Stevens, Walter B. *St. Louis: The Fourth City, 1764–1909*. 3 vols. St. Louis, 1909.
Wakelyn, Jon L. *Biographical Dictionary of the Confederacy*. Edited by Frank E. Vandiver. Westport, Conn., 1977.
Warner, Ezra J., and W. Buck Yearns. *Biographical Register of the Confederate Congress*. Baton Rouge, La., 1975.

JAMES W. GOODRICH

COOPER, DOUGLAS HANCOCK (1815–1879),

brigadier general. Born November 1, 1815, in Mississippi, Cooper attended the University of Virginia but did not graduate and returned home to become a planter. He fought in the Mexican War with Jefferson Davis's First Mississippi Rifles. In 1853 he was appointed Indian agent to the Choctaw Nation, and when the Civil War began, the Confederate government sent him to secure alliances with the five southern tribes.

Cooper became colonel of the First Choctaw and Chickasaw Mounted Rifles, seeing action at Chustenahlah in December 1861. When Brig. Gen. Albert Pike, commander of the Indian Territory, tried to persuade the Indians that the government lacked interest in the region, Cooper complained that Pike was either "insane or a traitor." In August 1862 he ordered Pike's arrest. Pike eventually resigned, and Cooper was nominated commander of the Indian Territory and superintendent of Indian affairs. But with Cooper's enemies working against him, the Confederate Senate refused to confirm the joint position. Nevertheless, Cooper had important connections in Richmond and was appointed a brigadier general on May 2, 1863. He fought at Honey Springs on July 17, 1863, and the next year on January 9, he was made commander of the Indian troops. After much political maneuvering and in spite of E. Kirby Smith's objections, Cooper assumed command of the District of Indian Territory and the superintendency early in 1865.

Following the war Cooper helped the Indians sue the U.S. government for claims dating back as far as the 1830s. He died in the Chickasaw Nation on April 29, 1879, and is buried in the Old Fort Washita cemetery in an unmarked grave.

BIBLIOGRAPHY

Gaines, W. Craig. *The Confederate Cherokees: John Drew's Regiment of Mounted Rifles*. Baton Rouge, La., 1989.
Rampp, Larry C., and Donald L. Rampp. *The Civil War in the Indian Territory*. Austin, Tex., 1975.

ANNE J. BAILEY

COOPER, SAMUEL (1798–1876), general. Born in Hackensack, New Jersey, on June 12, 1798, Cooper graduated from the U.S. Military Academy in 1815 and spent several decades with the artillery before being transferred to staff duty. In 1841 and 1842 he saw action against the Seminoles, before moving to Washington to join the War Department. In 1852, partly in recognition of his service during the Mexican War, where he was made a brevet colonel, Cooper was promoted to adjutant general of the United States. This position brought him immediately under the authority of the new secretary of war, Jefferson Davis, with whom he formed a warm friendship. Briefly in

SAMUEL COOPER.

HARPER'S PICTORIAL HISTORY OF THE GREAT REBELLION

1861, he was secretary of war ad interim under President James Buchanan.

In 1827 Cooper had married Sarah Maria Mason, a granddaughter of George Mason of Virginia, the Revolutionary era statesman. He soon became an adopted Southerner with this union; he was also a Democrat and a member of the Episcopal church. In 1836 Cooper wrote a military manual, *The Concise History of Instruction and Regulation for the Militia and Volunteers of the United States.* Living in Washington, D.C., he spent his spare moments with his family at Cameron, their estate near Alexandria. He and his family were friends of Robert E. Lee at nearby Arlington in the decade before the war.

On March 7, 1861, a few weeks after the establishment of the Confederacy, Cooper resigned his commission to cast his lot with the South. He arrived in Montgomery, where his old friend Davis appointed him adjutant general of the Confederate army. Too old for field command at age sixty-three, he was pleased with the assignment. Clean-shaven, with snow-white hair, clear penetrating eyes, and a healthy complexion, he appeared younger than his years. In May, with the removal of the government to Richmond, Cooper took up official residence with the War Department in an old brick building that once had housed the Mechanics Institute.

Cooper's duties were to issue orders and regulations, assign officers and men to their commands, maintain communications with generals in the field, inspect all army personnel, and oversee record keeping. Hundreds of officers (and politicians) paraded through his office in the opening weeks of the war. His were the tasks of providing order and system in a seemingly chaotic situation and of reviewing, and recommending or disapproving, the wishes of the commander in chief, the secretary of war, and others of influence in such matters. His judgment of personnel in the early stage of the war was invaluable. A seasoned military man who probably knew directly all the senior Southern officers in 1861, this cultivated, courtly gentleman was a resource and power to be reckoned with.

Of almost equal value to the cause by the summer of 1861 were Cooper's frequent consultations with the president, his military adviser Lee, and the cabinet regarding strategy. Virginia was soon to become a battlefield, as news arrived daily of large Union forces forming near Washington. As the conflict lengthened into years, his office, working with the various bureaus of the department, was an integral part of the nerve center of the overall war effort.

He seems to have gotten on well with his superiors—from Leroy P. Walker to Judah P. Benjamin and George Wyth Randolph. Especially noteworthy was his support for and contribution to Secretary James A. Seddon's major western strategy in November and December 1862. Together with Davis and Seddon, he helped establish the new Department of the West and to encourage its commander,

Joseph E. Johnston, to energize and make the most of it. He seems to have shared the high estimate of this officer held by the others. When Johnston later failed and was removed from command in July 1864, Cooper acted as a buffer against the barbs directed at the president by the general's numerous political friends.

In many ways Cooper was seen as a rubber stamp of the president or merely a figurehead. In a sense he was: it was in the nature of his position. To Garlick Kean, head of the War Bureau, Cooper was "uniformly courteous and uniformly non-committal," self-effacing, something of a mystery. This he had to be, at least publicly—always one in appearance and voice with the administration. Opinion is divided as to the quality of his work and its importance. Lee, Davis, Seddon, and Assistant Secretary of War John A. Campbell (who tapped his knowledge of military matters) valued him highly. To many others he was "clearheaded and without prejudice," the organizational genius who was most responsible for controlling the uncoordinated maneuvers of the early troops in 1861. Much of the success of First Manassas was justifiably credited to him. In 1862 he worked closely and effectively with Lee through the high summer of Confederate victories. Indeed, the old general, with his calm, friendly manner, was the indispensable bureaucrat at the top of the chain of command at Richmond. He usually was tolerant with the ambitious, conciliatory with the quarrelsome, diplomatic with factions and egos—and respected by most who sought his aid or counsel. His name on military orders and communiqués was the most familiar signature to officers and men in the Confederate army.

Cooper left Richmond in April 1865 with the fleeing government. Later, following the flight from Danville, he was released by Davis from his duties and subsequently surrendered to the enemy. With his parole, he turned over to the Union authorities all his records, the veritable archives of the Confederacy, intact. That he did so has won him the gratitude of historians and all who toil in the Confederate War Records today in the National Archives in Washington. Afterward, Cooper quietly returned to his home near Alexandria, impoverished by the war and too old to rebuild his fortunes. Lee and others soon helped with financial assistance to relieve his harsh circumstances. Cooper died, forgotten by most, on December 3, 1876, and was buried in Christ Church Cemetery, Alexandria.

BIBLIOGRAPHY

DeLeon, Thomas Cooper. *Belles, Beaux and Brains of the 60's.* New York, 1909.

Hattaway, Herman, and Archer Jones. *How the North Won: A Military History of the Civil War.* Urbana, Ill., 1983.

Jones, J. B. *A Rebel War Clerk's Diary at the Confederate States Capital.* 2 vols. Philadelphia, 1866.

O'Brien, G. F. J. "James A. Seddon: Statesman of the Old South." Ph.D. diss., University of Maryland, 1963.

Snow, William Parker. *Lee and His Generals.* New York, 1865. Reprint, New York, 1982.

Younger, Edward, ed. *Inside the Confederate Government: The Diary of Robert Garlick Hill Kean.* New York, 1957.

JOHN O'BRIEN

COOPERATIONISTS.

COOPERATIONISTS. Those politicians in the Deep South who opposed separate state action during the secession crisis of 1860 to 1861 were called cooperationists. Among their leaders were James H. Hammond of South Carolina, James L. Alcorn of Mississippi, Jeremiah Clemens and Benjamin Fitzpatrick of Alabama, and Herschel V. Johnson and Alexander H. Stephens of Georgia.

Despite their predominantly Democratic leadership, cooperationists were strongest in counties that had voted for the Constitutional Union party in 1860 and areas with few slaves, such as the mountains of northern Alabama and Georgia and the pine barrens of south central Georgia. Lacking a centralized organization, a coherent philosophy, or a coordinated strategy, cooperationists included genuine secessionists who believed that independence could best be achieved through cooperative action, conditional Unionists who opposed secession until a last effort at compromise had been made, and others who supported the cooperationist position primarily as a means of fending off radical action.

Demoralized by the secession of South Carolina in December 1860, the cooperationists nonetheless made strong showings in convention elections elsewhere in the Deep South, particularly in Alabama, Georgia, and Louisiana. Within the conventions they attempted to delay secession by sponsoring resolutions calling for a Southern convention and for a popular referendum on any secession ordinance. Ultimately, the cooperationists were unable to mount an effective challenge to the immediate secessionists. Indeed, as one state after another seceded from the Union, the secessionists turned the cooperative argument on its head by asserting that the only practical means of attaining a unified South was for the remaining slave states to join them in forming an independent Confederacy.

BIBLIOGRAPHY

Barney, William L. *The Secessionist Impulse: Alabama and Mississippi in 1860.* Princeton, 1974.

Johnson, Michael P. *Toward a Patriarchal Republic: The Secession of Georgia.* Baton Rouge, La., 1977.

Potter, David. *The Impending Crisis, 1848–1861.* New York, 1976.

Thornton, J. Mills, III. *Politics and Power in a Slave Society: Alabama, 1800–1860.* Baton Rouge, La., 1978.

Wooster, Ralph A. *The Secession Conventions of the South.* Princeton, 1962.

THOMAS E. JEFFREY

COPPERHEADS. The label was a smear term applied to Democratic critics of the Lincoln administration. Although many dictionaries still define "Copperhead" as "a Northern sympathizer with the South during the Civil War," some recent historians have characterized Democratic dissenters in the North more realistically, discrediting Radical Republican rhetoric and presenting the Copperheads simply as conservative and partisan critics.

Radical Republicans, led by Whitelaw Reid, the editor of the *Cincinnati Gazette,* sought to discredit Democratic dissenters in the upper Midwest by equating them with a poisonous snake that had a brown-blotched body and copper-colored head. After Democratic victories in the fall 1862 election, the Republicans intensified their smear campaign, invariably referring to the Democratic party as the Copperhead party and to its candidates as Copperheads. Some even referred to the conservative members of President Abraham Lincoln's cabinet as Copperheads.

Democratic dissent reached high tide during the first six months of 1863: in Indiana and Illinois the so-called Copperhead state legislatures feuded with their Republican governors; union military failures fostered a sense of defeat; many opposed Lincoln's emancipation measures; and widespread violations of civil rights (including the arbitrary arrest of Clement L. Vallandigham for alleged disloyalty on May 5, 1863) aroused resentment. Moreover, Federal conscription was highly unpopular in many quarters.

But Copperheadism, linked to the peace movement throughout the war, faded during the second half of the year as Union military victories at Gettysburg and Vicksburg lessened criticism of the Lincoln administration. Propeace Democratic gubernatorial candidates lost several election contests: Vallandigham in Ohio, George W. Woodward in Pennsylvania, and Thomas Seymour in Connecticut. The smear campaign was also instrumental in these defeats inasmuch as it discredited the Copperheads as pro-Southern and traitorous in their outlook.

Besides Vallandigham, Woodward, and Seymour, other well-known Copperheads included Samuel Medary (editor of the *Crisis* in Ohio), Wilbur F. Storey (editor of the *Chicago Times*), Dennis A. Mahony (editor of the *Dubuque Herald*), Daniel W. Voorhees (congressman from Indiana), Horatio Seymour (governor of New York), and Benjamin Wood (congressman and editor of the *New York Daily News*).

Radical Republicans, claiming that the Copperheads belonged to subversive secret societies, transformed three organizations into bogeymen in order to discredit the Democrats, influence elections, and serve as an excuse to organize Union Leagues (Republican-controlled secret patriotic societies). The three were Knights of the Golden Circle, Order of American Knights, and Sons of Liberty.

George W. L. Bickley, while residing in Cincinnati in

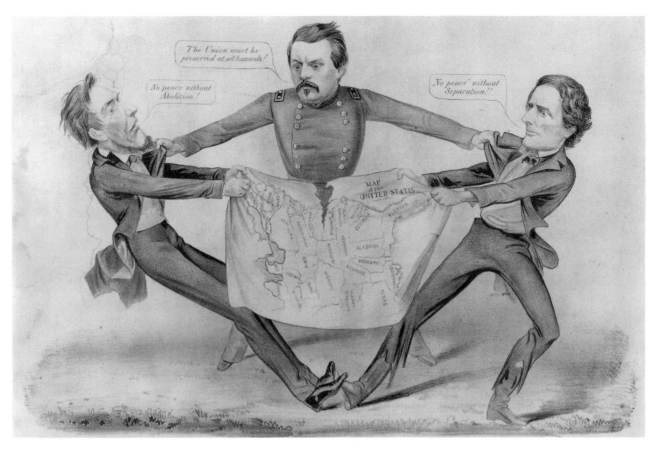

"THE TRUE ISSUE; OR, THATS WHATS THE MATTER."   Democratic presidential candidate George B. McClellan, affirming that "The Union must be preserved at all costs!" attempts to stop a tug-of-war between Abraham Lincoln and Jefferson Davis over the map of the United States. Lincoln, holding the northern half of the map, cries, "No peace without abolition!" while Davis, pulling the southern half, yells, "No peace without separation!" Lithograph on wove paper, published by Currier and Ives, New York, 1864.   LIBRARY OF CONGRESS

1859, had founded the Golden Circle as an agency to convert a part of northern Mexico into a personal fief and perhaps annex it to the United States. Early in the war he lived in Knoxville, Tennessee, where he tried to re-create the Golden Circle and work for the secession of Kentucky. Despite Republican contentions, not a single castle of the Knights of the Golden Circle existed north of the Ohio River during the war years.

The Order of American Knights, founded by Phineas C. Wright (a former resident of New Orleans) in St. Louis in early 1863, received considerable publicity in the Northern press during the last two years of the war. An "Occasional Address of the Supreme Commander" expressed an abhorrence of President Lincoln's "unconstitutional acts," including emancipation, and glorified state rights. Wright's incompetence and shabby reputation spelled failure for the largely paper-based organization. Col. John P. Sanderson, stationed in St. Louis, wrote "a grand exposé" of the O.A.K. in 1864. Sanderson imagined that the "traitorous organization" had half a million members in the upper Midwest,

with Vallandigham as head of the Northern branch and Confederate General Sterling Price commanding the Southern branch. Sanderson's suppositions found their way into Judge Advocate General Joseph Holt's report on subversive societies, printed as political propaganda preceding the 1864 presidential election.

The Sons of Liberty, based in Indianapolis, was founded by Harrison H. Dodd in early 1864. "Its objective and purposes, " a Dodd-printed booklet stated, "are the maintenance of constitutional freedom and State's rights, as recognized and established by the founders of our republic." No known chapters existed outside of Indianapolis, yet Dodd convinced Vallandigham, at the time an exile in Canada, to accept the nominal headship of the Sons of Liberty. Dodd's actions regarding a New York–to–Indianapolis arms shipment and suggestion of "a revolution" gave Republican leaders the chance to devise a devastating exposé and make arrests that led to two Indianapolis-based treason trials and much adverse publicity for the Sons of Liberty. Some detectives manufactured suppositions that

MASSACHUSETTS MOB WITH CONFEDERATE SYMPATHIZER. The victim is a publisher who apparently printed material supporting the Confederate cause.

THE SOLDIER IN OUR CIVIL WAR

also linked the S.L. to the Camp Douglas conspiracy.

Some Confederate agents in Canada and officials in Richmond accepted the Republican political propaganda at face value and supposed that a northwestern Confederacy was a possibility. Gen. P. G. T. Beauregard, for example, wanted Southern governors to issue a joint statement urging the upper Midwest to set up its own confederacy, promising friendship and free use of the Mississippi River.

[*See also* Northwestern Conspiracy; Peace Movements.]

BIBLIOGRAPHY

Gray, Wood. *The Hidden Civil War: The Story of the Copperheads.* New York, 1942.

Klement, Frank L. *The Copperheads in the Middle West.* Chicago, 1960.

Klement, Frank L. *Dark Lanterns: Secret Political Societies, Conspiracies, and Treason Trials in the Civil War.* Baton Rouge, La., 1984.

Klement, Frank L. "Economic Aspects of Middle Western Copperheadism." *Historian* 14 (1951): 27–44.

FRANK L. KLEMENT

CORINTH, MISSISSIPPI. The battle fought on October 3 and 4, 1862, in Corinth was one of three engagements (Perryville and Sharpsburg were the others) that had as their result the blunting of the Confederates' great fall 1862 offensive. In the summer of 1862 Gen. Braxton Bragg, commanding the Army of Tennessee, shifted his army from northeastern Mississippi—the scene of its recent operations—to eastern Tennessee and Kentucky. When Bragg departed for his new field of activity, he left behind in Mississippi two independent Southern forces. One, commanded by Maj. Gen. Earl Van Dorn, consisted of some cavalry and a division of infantry under Maj. Gen. Mansfield Lovell. Its strength was about 7,000 men. The other force (some 17,000 men) was commanded by Maj. Gen. Sterling Price. It was made up of two divisions—one under Brig. Gen. Dabney H. Maury and the other under Brig. Gen. Louis Hébert.

Van Dorn was the senior general, but he had no authority over Price unless their forces were united. Price, who loathed Van Dorn for personal reasons, had orders from Bragg to try to keep the Federals from sending troops from Mississippi to oppose Bragg in Tennessee. Van Dorn

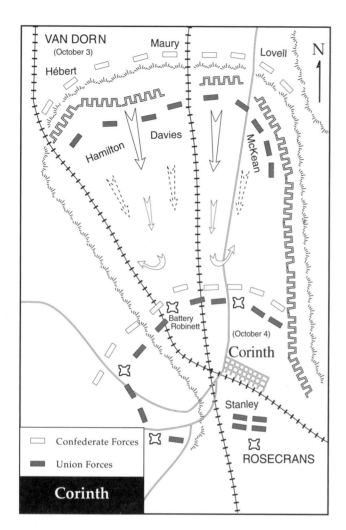

VAN DORN
(October 3)
Maury
Lovell
Hébert
N
Davies
Hamilton
McKean
Battery
Robinett
(October 4)
Corinth
Stanley
ROSECRANS

☐ Confederate Forces
■ Union Forces

Corinth

Believing that Rosecrans's defenses on the northwest side of Corinth were the weak point in the Union position, Van Dorn struck there on the morning of October 3. Had he been on the face of a clock, his army would have been deployed on a line curving around from 10 to 1. Lovell's division was on his right, Maury's in his center, and Hébert's on his left. Rosecrans had three of his divisions formed on a corresponding line—McKean facing Lovell, Davies in front of Maury, and Hamilton opposing Hébert. Stanley was in reserve.

Lovell led off the Confederate attack at 9:00 A.M. Van Dorn hoped that his onslaught would compel Rosecrans to shift troops from the right and center of the Union line. Then Maury and Hébert would strike. Soon all of the Southern divisions were pushing forward. Throughout that "terrible hot day" the Confederates slowly drove Rosecrans's men two miles back toward the center of the line. Four separate times the Federals tried unsuccessfully to stay the Confederate advance. By 5:00 P.M. Rosecrans was pushed back to in the heavily fortified inner line of defenses.

Van Dorn was convinced that one more effort would bring complete victory. He soon found, however, that the Northerners were still full of fight, and his officers came to him with reports of heavy casualties, low supplies of ammunition, and exhausted, hungry, and thirsty men who could fight no more that day. Van Dorn suspended the attack. He would finish Rosecrans on the fourth.

During the night medical personnel sought to help those wounded in the day's battle. Supply officers distributed what ammunition they had. The men sought water, food, and what rest they could get. Meanwhile, the generals pondered what they should do to prepare for the renewed battle.

Rosecrans brought Stanley's division into his line between Davies and McKean. The new Federal position, curving around the center of the clock, was anchored on five small forts (called "batteries"), the most important of which was Battery Robinett, near the center of the Union line.

Van Dorn planned to attack early on October 4. At 7:00 A.M., several hours after the assault was to get underway, Hébert, who was to lead off the effort, reported that he was too sick to exercise command. Brig. Gen. Martin E. Green was quickly assigned to his place, but it took him until 10:00 A.M. to get the division launched into its advance. Lovell, meanwhile, did almost nothing. The bulk of fighting fell on Maury and Green.

Once the attack got underway it did not last long. Some of Green's men broke through the Federal line, but they ran short of ammunition and were driven back. Parts of Maury's division fought their way into the streets of Corinth itself and battled the Federals house to house. Meanwhile, the rest of Maury's charge shattered on the

wanted to operate against the Northerners in western Tennessee.

At first ignoring Van Dorn, Price seized Iuka, Mississippi, on September 13. Several days of operations there forced him to withdraw to Ripley, where on the twenty-eighth he united with Van Dorn. Losses had reduced Southern strength to about 22,000, but Van Dorn decided to strike for Corinth—an important rail center that the Confederates had to capture if they were to advance farther northward.

Corinth was defended by 23,000 Federals commanded by Maj. Gen. William S. Rosecrans. The force consisted of four divisions under Maj. Gen. Charles Hamilton and Brig. Gens. David Stanley, Thomas Davies, and Thomas McKean. Other Federal forces were not far off and could quickly be rushed to Rosecrans's aid. Speed, therefore, was the key to Confederate success. The Southerners had to overrun Corinth before even more Federals could be brought in to reinforce the defenders. As he advanced, Van Dorn feinted at several towns, hoping to prevent the Federals from learning his objective and to keep them divided as long as possible.

fortifications of Battery Robinett where, in fierce fighting, the Federals held. The Confederates who had gotten into the town fled or were killed or captured. Van Dorn, realizing that Union reinforcements were approaching and that continued efforts to take the town would result in the complete destruction of his army, decided to withdraw.

For several days the Northerners attempted a pursuit, but they too were nearing exhaustion. By October 11 the Confederates had reached the relative safety of Holly Springs. Within a few weeks both sides in Mississippi had shifted their attention to Vicksburg and the struggle for control of the Mississippi River.

Van Dorn reported his losses at Corinth and on the retreat at 594 men killed, 2,162 wounded, and 2,102 missing (many captured, some deserted). Rosecrans listed 315 killed, 1,812 wounded, and 232 captured or missing.

For the Confederates, Corinth, like so many of the war's western battles, featured inept generals leading a courageous rank and file. The combination of brave soldiers and weak command could not overcome the great courage of the Federal troops who were backed by superior resources and commanded by better generals.

BIBLIOGRAPHY

Castel, Albert. *General Sterling Price and the Civil War in the West.* Baton Rouge, La., 1968.

Cockrell, Monroe F., ed. *The Lost Account of the Battle of Corinth and the Court Martial of Gen. Van Dorn.* Jackson, Tenn., 1955.

Hartje, Robert G. *Van Dorn: The Life and Times of a Confederate General.* Nashville, Tenn., 1967.

Lamers, William M. *The Edge of Glory: A Biography of General William S. Rosecrans.* New York, 1961.

RICHARD M. MCMURRY

CORNERSTONE SPEECH. Delivered by Confederate vice president Alexander H. Stephens on the night of March 21, 1861, at the Athenaeum in Savannah, Georgia, this speech became notorious for its declaration that the Confederate government's "cornerstone" rested on the inequality of the races and the institution of black slavery.

Delivered extemporaneously, the speech began with praise for the "improvements" the Confederate Constitution had made on the older one, such as the banning of a protective tariff and federal financing of internal improvements. The Constitution also set the slavery question to rest forever, Stephens said, and during the long justification of the institution that followed he uttered the phrase that gave the speech its name. He went on to commend the breadth and wealth of the Confederacy and its wise and conservative Congress and expressed the belief that the new nation would soon be enlarged by the border states. The prospect of war had diminished, but the South, though

desirous of peace with all, had to be ready to fight. He warned against factionalism in the South and praised its policy of free trade. If true to itself and its destiny, he concluded, the South would not fail.

The speech was widely reported. Thoughtful Southerners, including Jefferson Davis, deplored Stephens's emphasis on slavery rather than the politically advantageous theme of state versus national sovereignty. Northern reaction was uniformly hostile. The abolitionist press used the speech to demand harsh measures from Abraham Lincoln. The speech's value to the Union cause, one Northern paper later judged, was "incalculable."

[*See also* Confederate Constitution; Montgomery Convention; *and the Appendix for the text of the Cornerstone Speech.*]

BIBLIOGRAPHY

Avary, Myrta Lockett, ed. *Recollections of Alexander H. Stephens: His Diary Kept When a Prisoner at Fort Warren, Boston Harbor, 1865; Giving Incidents and Reflections of His Prison Life and Some Letters and Reminiscences.* New York, 1910.

Cleveland, Henry. *Alexander H. Stephens in Public and Private: With Letters and Speeches, Before, During, and Since the War.* Philadelphia, 1886.

Schott, Thomas E. *Alexander H. Stephens of Georgia: A Biography.* Baton Rouge, La., 1988.

THOMAS E. SCHOTT

CORSE, MONTGOMERY DENT (1816–1895), brigadier general. Born in Alexandria, Virginia, Corse attended a local military school and during the Mexican War was captain of an Alexandria company in the First Regiment of Virginia Volunteers. After his return from Mexico he went to California and mined gold before settling in Sacramento, where he was a steamboat agent, customs officer, and captain of the Sutter Rifles.

Corse returned to Alexandria in 1856 and became a banker. He was elected lieutenant colonel of the city's 175th Regiment of militia and, in January 1861, was elected major, commanding the Sixth Battalion of Virginia Volunteers, composed of Alexandria's uniformed militia companies. He was mustered into service with the battalion, and served as assistant adjutant general of the forces posted in Alexandria under Maj. George H. Terrett. On June 10, 1861, Corse was elected colonel of the Seventeenth Regiment of Virginia Infantry, which was with Longstreet's brigade at First Manassas. He was wounded at Second Manassas, South Mountain, and Sharpsburg. He was held in high esteem by Robert E. Lee, who said, "This regiment and its gallant colonel challenge the respect and admiration of their countrymen." On November 1, 1862, he was promoted to brigadier general and assigned to Pickett's

MONTGOMERY DENT CORSE.   NATIONAL ARCHIVES

division. His brigade remained in Virginia, however, and was not with the division at Gettysburg. Subsequently, he served in Tennessee, North Carolina, and in the battles around Richmond and Petersburg. On April 6, 1865, he was captured at Sayler's Creek and imprisoned at Fort Warren.

After his release he again became a banker. In 1870, Corse was seriously injured in the collapse of an overcrowded floor in the state capitol building, and was almost totally blind in his last years. He died in 1895 and was buried in St. Paul's Cemetery, Alexandria.

BIBLIOGRAPHY

Corse, Montgomery Dent. "Biography of General Montgomery D. Corse By His Son Montgomery D. Corse." Manuscript, Alexandria Library, Va.
Evans, Clement A., ed. *Confederate Military History.* 12 vols. Atlanta, 1899. Extended ed. in 19 vols. Wilmington, N.C., 1987–1989.
Wallace, Lee A., Jr. *Seventeenth Virginia Infantry.* Lynchburg, Va., 1990.

LEE A. WALLACE, JR.

COSBY, GEORGE BLAKE

COSBY, GEORGE BLAKE (1830–1909), brigadier general. Born January 19, 1830, in Louisville, Kentucky, Cosby graduated from West Point in 1852. He served with the cavalry on the frontier and was wounded in Indian fighting. An instructor of cavalry tactics at West Point when the war began, he resigned from the Federal army in May 1861 to become a captain in the Confederate cavalry.

Promoted to major in September 1861, Cosby saw his first service under Simon Bolivar Buckner in central Kentucky. As Buckner's chief of staff at Fort Donelson, Cosby sent the note to Ulysses S. Grant that resulted in the surrender of the fort in February 1862. After his capture and exchange, he was promoted to colonel in the cavalry and then, at the request of Gen. Joseph E. Johnston, to brigadier general in January 1863. As part of Gen. Earl Van Dorn's command, Cosby led a cavalry brigade at Thompson's Station, Tennessee, on March 4 and 5, 1863, a heavy engagement that blocked a Federal move from Franklin. In the spring and summer of 1863 Cosby served under Johnston during the Jackson campaign, an unsuccessful effort by Johnston to relieve Union pressure on the Confederate army at Vicksburg. Active thereafter in the Department of Alabama, Mississippi, and Eastern Louisiana, Cosby also saw heavy fighting in the Meridian campaign in February 1864.

Cosby moved after the war to California where he became a farmer and held several public positions. He took his own life in 1909, reportedly because of pain from his old war wounds.

BIBLIOGRAPHY

Obituary. *Confederate Veteran* 17 (1909): 425. Reprint, Wilmington, N.C., 1985.
Warner, Ezra, J. *Generals in Gray: Lives of the Confederate Commanders.* Baton Rouge, La., 1959.

WILLIAM L. BARNEY

COTTON

COTTON. In 1858 Senator James Henry Hammond of South Carolina replied to Senator William H. Seward of New York:

> Without the firing of a gun, without drawing a sword, should they [Northerners] make war upon us [Southerners], we could bring the whole world to our feet. What would happen if no cotton was furnished for three years? . . . England would topple headlong and carry the whole civilized world with her. No, you dare not make war on cotton! No power on earth dares make war upon it. Cotton is King.

Hammond, like most white Southerners, believed that cotton ruled not just in the South but in the United States and the world. Many economists agreed. In 1855, David Christy entitled his influential book *Cotton Is King.* Cotton indeed drove the economy of the South, affected its social structure, and, during the Civil War, dominated international relations of the Confederacy through "cotton diplomacy."

Cotton in the Antebellum Period

In the early eighteenth century, long-staple cotton was grown in Georgia and on the Sea Islands of South Carolina, but it depleted the soil and proved unprofitable to market. The intensive and laborious hand method of picking out cotton seeds severely restricted the amount of cotton that could be prepared for making into cloth. Cotton could not compete with rice and indigo for commercialization, and Southern colonialists experimented with the crop primarily for domestic use. Despite some increased cotton production during a tobacco depression between 1702 and 1706, few attempted to produce cotton commercially before the Revolutionary War.

Extensive production of cotton awaited the advent of Eli Whitney's cotton gin in the spring of 1793. To separate the seed from the cotton, gins first used spikes placed on rollers and then saws. The influence of the gin was instantaneous; soon Southern mechanics set up gins as far west as Mississippi. By 1804 the cotton crop was eight times greater than it had been the previous decade. The cotton gin made practical the use of the heavily seeded short-staple cotton, which could be grown in upland areas more readily than long-staple cotton. An increase in market demand growing out of England's textile industry ensured favorable prices and spurred the ascension of the short-staple cotton industry.

Cultivation of cotton, on both small and large farms, utilized relatively simple methods. Hoe ridge cultivation was developed after 1800 with ridges set apart about three to six feet, depending on the fertility of the land. After 1830 farmers used V-shaped harrows, which were converted into cultivators, side harrows, and double shovels. (Harrows raked soil with metal teeth to remove debris and smoothed out and leveled the soil once broken; cultivators turned the soil under; shovels were used as more traditional plows and also turned the soil over while digging deep furrows.) Cultivation procedures changed little throughout the nineteenth century. A bed for the cotton had to be prepared by clearing out the old stalks from the previous crop. Sometimes these stalks were beaten down with clubs, but if they were large (four to five feet), they had to be pulled by hand. Manure or commercial fertilizer was placed as deeply as possible in the furrow. Usually the cotton bed was built up in February and March. The actual planting of the cotton seed in most areas was in April: early planters risked frost; late planters risked dry spells. Planting was done by hand. In about a month, the plants were thinned. The crop was cultivated with a sweep plowed between the rows four or five times and hoed by hand three or four times. In the middle of June, when they were anywhere from six inches to a foot high, the cotton plants bloomed. Around the last of July or first of August, forty-two to forty-five days after they had blossomed, the cotton bolls opened. Picking usually began about August 20. Most of the crop was ginned immediately after picking.

Cotton prices fluctuated wildly over the years. Prices were high until 1819, then down, up, and down again. In 1837 they hit a crisis low and remained rather low until 1848. Prices rose sharply in 1849 and 1850 but dropped in 1851, though not as low as previously. Throughout the remainder of the 1850s prices rose.

The average amount of seed cotton used to make a 400-pound bale of lint ranged from about 1,200 to 1,400 pounds. The bales had to be transported from the gins to a local market and then on to larger markets. Cotton was shipped to market continually from September through January. Wagons loaded with bales of cotton often lined roads. The moving of cotton demanded better roadbeds, sometimes even plank roads, near market towns. River transportation to seaports was common from market towns located on rivers or canals. Major cities grew up at railroad stations as rail lines began to link the hinterland to ports and then to the Northeast and Midwest.

Improvements in the production and transportation of cotton and the new demand for the fiber led to a scramble for greater profits. To reap the most profits and to provide the labor needed for cotton picking, a large number of slaves were imported into South Carolina and Georgia, and slave labor became a valuable market throughout the South. The way into the Southern aristocracy was through the ownership of land and slaves, and the way to get land and slaves was to grow cotton: the crop provided the cash and credit to buy both. At this time, too, the cotton kingdom pushed ever westward with planters searching for new and richer soils to grow more white cotton with the labor of more black slaves. Ironically, just as abolitionist sentiment was increasing in the United States, the invention of the cotton gin instigated a deeper entrenchment of slavery into the Southern economy and society.

The Southern aristocracy, which slavery created, dominated Southern society and inhibited the development of efficient methods for soil use. In the face of soil exhaustion, Southern planters needed to extend control into the fresh lands of the western territories. Hence, territorial expansion became a sectional issue as both North and South realized that western lands were essential for the survival of Southern slave culture.

Most discussions of cotton dwell on the short period when cotton did rule as king. This "mature" period of cotton and slavery was not necessarily typical of or relevant to the earlier periods of plantation agriculture that accompanied the emergence of cotton monoculture. Discussions also tend to treat the South as one unit rather than the large and varied region it was. The cotton kingdom extended west through Texas and north about six hundred miles up the Mississippi River valley.

Antebellum history often seems dominated by scenes of plantations worked by slaves. Although thousands of large plantations employed slave labor and produced most of the

South's cotton, numerically there were more small farmers, mostly whites, who cultivated the upland areas. Many of these yeomen were subsistence farmers and produced only a surplus of cotton for market. Southern farmers who did not grow cotton sold some of their foodstuff to the planters. Cotton could bring prosperity or depression, according to changes in the market, and these fluctuations meant very differing experiences for whites, slaves, and antebellum free blacks of each different region of the South.

When at its peak, the demanding cultivation and transportation of cotton required the labor of the majority of men, women, and children in the rural South. Most Southern life was regulated by the agricultural economy, and more and more over time, this came to mean the cotton economy. Although free workers and slaves pursued a diversity of agricultural and industrial occupations in the antebellum South, by 1850 the routine of taking care of the white-blossomed, white-bolled short-staple cotton plants increasingly typified rural Southern existence.

By 1860, cotton ruled the South, which annually exported two-thirds of the world supply of the "white gold." Cotton ruled the West and Midwest because each year these sections sold $30 million worth of food supplies to Southern cotton producers. Cotton ruled the Northeast because the domestic textile industry there produced $100 million worth of cloth each year. In addition, the North sold to the cotton-growing South more than $150 million worth of manufactured goods every year, and Northern ships transported cotton and cotton products worldwide.

Cotton in the Confederacy

As the U.S. cotton industry developed, other countries became more dependent on cotton produced in the American South. The power of cotton allowed the Confederacy to employ cotton diplomacy as its foundation for foreign relations during the Civil War; Southerners attempted to use cotton to pressure countries such as England and France into the war on behalf of the Confederacy. Southern leaders were convinced that the key to their success lay in gaining international recognition and help from European powers in breaking the blockade that the Union had thrown up around coastal areas and ports and that was increasingly effective as the war went on. (Although the Union blockade never thoroughly sealed the Confederate coastline, it was successful in causing Southern imports and exports to drop drastically at a time when the Confederacy needed to fund its huge war efforts.)

Southerners saw cotton as the great leverage in this effort, and at the time this made sense. More than three-fourths of the cotton used in the textile industries of England and France came from the American South. Between a fifth and a fourth of the English population depended in some way on the textile industry, and half of the export trade of England was in cotton textiles. About a tenth of the nation's wealth was also invested in the cotton business. The English Board of Trade said in 1859 that India was completely inadequate as a source of raw cotton; England apparently was dependent on the American South for cotton. This concept of King Cotton led many Southerners to believe that England and France would have to intervene in the Civil War in order to save their own economies. The Confederacy began applying pressure on the neutral powers through a voluntary embargo of cotton. Although Congress never formally established the embargo, local "committees of public safety" prevented the shipping of cotton from Southern ports.

To exploit their leverage, the Confederate States sent William Lowndes Yancey, Pierre A. Rost, and A. Dudley Mann to England in the spring of 1861 to confer with Lord Russell, the British foreign secretary. As a result, the British and French granted the Confederacy belligerency status. It was a small victory, probably not very effective in helping the Confederacy. The cotton diplomats failed to arrange with England a denunciation of the blockade or the negotiation of a commercial agreement, let alone diplomatic recognition of the Confederacy.

Regardless of wishful beliefs and England's real economic dependence on cotton, at the time of the outbreak of the Civil War an overabundance of cotton existed in Europe. Furthermore, British hostility to slavery decreased the likelihood of intervention. Moreover, it was not in the vested interests of the neutral powers, particularly Great Britain, to denounce the blockade. The Confederate government attempted to convince the Europeans that the Federal blockade was ineffective and thus illegal under the terms of the 1856 Treaty of Paris. The Confederacy failed to acknowledge that Great Britain, as the world's foremost naval power, would desire to let stand any blockade, regardless of its legality or actual effectiveness. And to make matters even worse, the South's voluntary embargo undercut its own argument that the Federal blockade was porous.

Although the South never succeeded in convincing foreign powers to intervene against the North, cotton diplomacy was successful in obtaining financial help from abroad. This came in the form of loans and bonds, which Confederate Treasurer Christopher G. Memminger guaranteed with cotton. The Confederate Treasury Department issued $1.5 million in cotton certificates during the war for acquisitions abroad. One such loan backed by cotton was the Erlanger loan, signed on October 28, 1862, and modified on January 3, 1863. This loan, amounting to $15 million, was secured by cotton. At the time cotton was worth twenty-four pence a pound, and the Erlanger loan made cotton available to holders at six pence per pound.

This reliance on cotton for the security of loans, bonds, and certificates placed a great deal of responsibility on the

Produce Loan Office, whose agents had to ensure that planters would fulfill government subscriptions of cotton at a time when many planters were unwilling to sell to the government. Ultimately, however, cotton enabled the Confederacy to realize $7,678,591.25 in foreign exchange.

The Confederacy also hoped to raise tax revenue on the sale of cotton abroad. On February 28, 1861, Congress passed an act levying an export duty of ⅛ of a cent per pound on all cotton shipped after August 1 of that year. The government hoped to raise $20 million through the export tax in order to pay a $15 million loan funded by an issue of 8 percent bonds. But because of the tightening blockade and the South's own voluntary cotton embargo, the measure raised only $30,000. When the secretary of the treasury lobbied to have this minuscule tax raised, opposition from the planter class kept Congress from increasing it, even when the Confederacy's finances were desperate.

To a degree, planter opposition also undercut Southern efforts to shift from cotton production to the planting of foodstuffs. The Confederacy was convinced it could become self-sufficient. It would produce all the food and cotton it needed, and revenue from cotton could buy weapons, blankets, and other manufactured goods until the Confederacy started manufacturing its own. Planters believed that the yeomen and poor would fight in the army and that slaves would continue to produce food and the South's greatest weapon, cotton.

By the spring of 1862, however, there was already an abundance of cotton and a shortage of foodstuffs. In April 1862 yeomen soldiers could not go home to plant spring crops, and their families would again have no food. To encourage the growth of foodstuffs, every Southern cotton-producing state attempted to limit the amount of cotton that could be grown. State governors issued proclamations urging planters to reduce their cotton acreage by as much as four-fifths and encouraging them to plant enough wheat, corn, and beans to feed themselves, their slaves, the armies in the field. The planters responded, cutting their usual acreage of cotton to about half and devoting the rest to food crops. Many planters even had enough surplus foodstuffs to sell to the families of the yeoman poor whose husbands and sons were away in the war. Still, the planters did not reduce their cotton production as much as the state and Confederate governments wanted. Some scholars argue that this is an example of how the Confederacy contributed to its own defeat by refusing to disturb the interests of the planter class.

But even with resistance by the planters, the shift to the production of foodstuffs combined with the drain in manpower and the eventual Union occupation created a drastic drop in cotton production as the war dragged on: 4.5 million bales were grown in 1861; 1.5 million in 1862; 500,000 in 1863; and only 300,000 in 1864. As production

dropped, the price of cotton skyrocketed on the world market, and blockade runners decided the risks were worth taking; cotton-exporting corporations formed throughout the cotton kingdom. In addition, Mexico traded cotton directly across the Texas border.

In an attempt to control the flow of cotton to Europe and rectify the declining economy, Southern politicians in late 1863 introduced an approach called the "New Plan." Through this series of administrative actions and congressional laws, the Confederate government became directly involved in blockade running. Rather than making contracts for supplies payable in cotton, the government itself began selling the cotton abroad and buying supplies with the proceeds, thereby cutting out the middlemen. The plan's supervisor, Colin J. McRae, gained direct control over cargo space on blockade runners. Those who refused to accept a fair rate to transport cotton for sale by the government would have their vessels confiscated. The War Department increasingly turned to the sale of cotton to purchase needed supplies, and by the end of 1863 it had reserved fully one-third of all cargo space on blockade runners.

As a result of these measures and other financial consolidations under the plan, Confederate foreign financing was greatly improved and 27,229 bales of cotton were exported for $5.3 million in sales. But because of the Confederacy's early confidence in the diplomatic leverage of King Cotton, it did not institute measures such as the New Plan soon enough to make a considerable impact on the war effort. The South could not keep its vital ports open or continue to endure Northern attacks on the battlefield.

If the Confederate government was able, albeit partially and belatedly, to gain control over the cotton trade with Europe, it had much less success in curtailing the cotton trade with the Union. On May 21, 1861, the Confederate Congress prohibited the sale of cotton to the North. Yet an illicit trade across military lines flourished between Southern cotton farmers and Northern traders. President Abraham Lincoln gave licenses to traders, who followed the Union army into the South. On March 17, 1862, the Confederacy gave state governments the right to destroy any cotton that might fall into the hands of the Union army. Some devoted Confederates burned their own cotton to keep it out of enemy hands. Other Southerners, however, discovered that Union agents were willing to pay the highest prices in over half a century for cotton or offered badly needed supplies as barter. Ironically, valuable currency for cotton from the North saved some small Southern farmers from starvation. But this selling of cotton to the North undermined Confederate nationalism, as did the official Confederate trading of cotton with the North conducted in the last years of the war.

As the price of foodstuffs reached astronomical heights

and Confederate currency became worthless with inflation, the smuggling of cotton out of the South to the North increased. Women whose husbands had been killed or were away at the battlefield or in prison were heavily involved in forming these caravans. Rich planters and factors also made large deals with Federal officials. The situation became totally absurd when cotton was sold to Federal troops to get supplies for the Confederate army. Even President Lincoln approved an arrangement to send food for Robert E. Lee's troops at Petersburg in exchange for cotton for New York. Ulysses S. Grant stopped this exchange because he was attempting to cut off Lee's supplies, but other such exchanges occurred throughout the Civil War.

Some scholars have written with hindsight that the Confederacy might have been more successful, had it pursued a different strategy with its cotton. If Confederate leaders had confiscated all the cotton in the South and stored it, they could have used it as a basis to obtain credit from European nations. With credit, some scholars believe, the Confederacy could have bought a navy strong enough to break the Union blockade. Others argue that the Confederate government would have been better served if it had made cotton, not gold, the basis of its currency.

Although the Civil War ended the slave plantation system, it did not end the South's legacy of cotton. Cultivation of the crop had worn out much of the land. Many planted up and down on slopes, which then eroded. The concentration on cotton production meant complete reliance on a one-crop system; crop rotation was uncommon and farmers did not plow under clover or peas to restore humus to the soil. Diminishing fertility of cotton lands was a major problem farmers continued to face after the Civil War.

[*See also* Blockade, *overview article;* Diplomacy; Erlanger Loan; Expansionism in the Antebellum South; Farming; New Plan; Plantation; Produce Loan; Slavery; Urbanization.]

BIBLIOGRAPHY

Ball, Douglas. *Financial Failure and Confederate Defeat.* Urbana, Ill., 1991.
Burton, Orville Vernon. *In My Father's House Are Many Mansions: Family and Community in Edgefield, South Carolina.* Chapel Hill, N.C., 1985.
Gates, Paul. *The Farmer's Age: Agriculture, 1815–1860.* New York, 1960.
Gray, Lewis Cecil. *History of Agriculture in the United States to 1860.* 2 vols. Washington, D.C., 1932.
Hilliard, Sam Bowers. *Atlas of Antebellum Southern Agriculture.* Baton Rouge, La., 1984.
Owsley, Frank L. *King Cotton Diplomacy.* 2d ed. Chicago, 1959.
Powell, Lawrence, and Michael Wayne. "Self-Interest and the Decline of Confederate Nationalism." In *The Old South in the Crucible of War.* Edited by Harry P. Owens and James J. Cook. University, Miss., 1983.
Ramsdell, Charles W. *Behind the Lines in the Southern Confederacy.* Baton Rouge, La., 1944.
Todd, Richard Cecil. *Confederate Finance.* Athens, Ga., 1954.
Woodman, Harold D. *King Cotton and His Retainers.* Lexington, Ky., 1968.

ORVILLE VERNON BURTON and
PATRICIA DORA BONNIN

COTTONCLADS.

The term *cottonclads* is not an officially designated class of vessels; rather, it refers to vessels of any class that were clad with cotton, instead of iron or additional wood, as a protection against enemy fire. Of the twenty-eight such vessels in Confederate service, approximately half used cotton bales as bulwarks and half had cotton compressed between the original and a subsequently added wooden bulkhead. In half of the cottonclads, both of these construction methods were coupled with the addition of iron plates at least one inch thick on the bow. Despite cotton's combustibility, cotton cladding effectively shielded against fire from small arms and field pieces, and it significantly reduced the interior damage resulting from penetration by heavier projectiles fired from siege guns.

These vessels varied tremendously in regard to tonnage, length, draft, and performance. Their armament usually consisted of a single cannon, although CSS *Baltic* had six guns. Most of the seventeen cottonclads that were equipped as rams had been used as tugboats before the war and were side-wheelers, although at least one was a stern-wheeler, and two had single screw propellers. Side-wheelers predominated among the six transports and eleven miscellaneous gunboats.

Cottonclads saw action in every theater of the war. Six of the seven cottonclads lost in the defense of New Orleans in April and the seven lost near Memphis on June 6, 1862, were manned by army personnel as part of the River Defense Fleet. Five served in the Texas Marine Department of the Confederate army, being employed extensively at Galveston. Others saw action at Plymouth, Charleston, and Mobile. Probably the best known of the cottonclads was *Queen of the West.* Sunk off Fort De Russy, Louisiana, by the Confederates on February 14, 1863, it was salvaged and protected with cotton and iron; the vessel participated in the capture of USS *Indianola* on February 24. The Federals also constructed cottonclads, such as the captured CSS *Era No. 5.*

BIBLIOGRAPHY

Dictionary of American Naval Fighting Ships. Vol. 2. Washington, D.C., 1963.
Scharf, J. Thomas. *History of the Confederate States Navy from Its Organization to the Surrender of Its Last Vessel.* New York, 1887. Reprint, New York, 1977.

LAWRENCE L. HEWITT

COUNTERFEITING. Economic warfare is new in name; however, Confederate authorities feared that the United States engaged in such acts. While the Northern government did not pursue this strategy overtly (no counterfeits came from government presses), the United States authorities tacitly allowed civilian, nongovernmental presses to operate.

Confederate stamps and notes, state currency, and private change issues rolled off civilian presses. Even new fantasy notes were passed in the Confederacy. Two major counterfeiting firms were alleged to have existed during the war. Samuel C. Upham of Philadelphia printed over twenty-eight varieties of Confederate, state, and private notes, and fifteen varieties of Confederate postage stamps, with a face value of $15 million. Upham, calling them "souvenirs," printed that word on an easily removed border and operated from March 12, 1862, to August 1, 1863. He seemed alarmed by Confederate reaction and later made unsubstantiated claims that the Confederacy had offered a reward for his capture.

Winthrop E. Hilton of New York began printing in 1863. Detectives arrested him in 1864, however, claiming that he worked *with* the Confederates. (Hilton may not have confined his talents to Confederate issues.)

Counterfeiters and forgers fell under Confederate jurisdiction when they crossed Confederate lines or operated in the Confederacy. After Union Maj. Gen. John Pope encouraged the circulation of counterfeits, the Confederate Congress passed laws imposing death for counterfeiting and forging, but only one man ever paid with his life. John Richardson, alias Louis Napoleon, was hanged on August 22, 1862.

Confederate detectives confined anticounterfeiting efforts to paper money; stamps, when used for postage, and small change saw few counterfeits in circulation. But cases dragged out in the courts, and many offenders were pardoned or had their sentences commuted. The damage bogus currency did to the Confederates was undoubtedly real, but how damaging cannot be calculated today.

[*See also* Currency; Shinplasters.]

BIBLIOGRAPHY

Benner, Judith Ann. *Fraudulent Finance: Counterfeiting and the Confederate States, 1861–1865.* Waco, Tex., 1970.

Morgan, James F. *Graybacks and Gold: Confederate Monetary Policy.* Pensacola, Fla., 1985.

Robinson, William M., Jr. *Justice in Grey: A History of the Judicial System of the Confederate States of America.* Cambridge, Mass., 1941.

JAMES F. MORGAN

COURTSHIP. During the Civil War, like all other wars, matters of life and death spurred couples into accelerated romances and abbreviated courtships. The Confederacy was a new nation under siege and required the ultimate allegiance from its young men and women. Patriotism pushed couples into linking love with loyalty. In the heady early months of war, hasty marriages were common and brides bravely waved new husbands off to battle. But over time it became less easy to ignore the carnage and widowhood many feared.

Most couples survived their separations by pouring out their fears and affection in love letters. Martha Ready Morgan wrote to her husband of three weeks in January 1863: "I can bear anything Darling when you are with me, and so long as I have your love—but when separated from you and I know that you are surrounded by so many dangers and hardships as you have been on your last expedition I become a weak nervous child. . . . Good night, my *Hero*. My dreams are all of you." Her concerns were common, and her fears were justified: Morgan was captured and imprisoned later in the year.

Upon rare occasion, women resisted the enforced separations and followed loved ones. An intrepid few accompanied sweethearts and husbands to the front disguised as soldiers. Amy Clark even continued to serve after her husband was killed at Shiloh, until Union captors discovered her ruse.

Military enlistment, however, was not what the Southern nation expected of its women. Editors and statesmen advocated staunch support for their cause, illustrated by a tale that appeared in slightly varying forms in Southern newspapers throughout the war. In September 1863, the *Raleigh Register* related:

> A young lady was engaged to be married to a soldier in the army. The soldier suddenly returned home. "Why have you left the army?" she inquired of him. "I have found a substitute," he replied. "Well, sir, I can follow your example, and find a substitute, too. Good morning." And she left him in the middle of the room, a disgraced soldier.

The Confederacy counted on its women to reinforce patriotic sacrifice—to provide a moral anchor.

Although this kind of Confederate fervor was welcomed, it was not always the rule. Certainly men and women on the western frontier of the Confederacy were much more estranged from the cause of their wealthier coastal brethren. Starvation, guerrilla warfare, and other forces influenced men's decisions to remain nearer loved ones—the desertion rate escalated as the Union racked up victories and Southern soldiers fell in droves.

The press rallied women to the cause and many responded with public as well as private pledges. One young woman wrote to a newspaper:

> I had rather take to my heart the private soldier who had returned from the war maimed and penniless than the cold-blooded speculator who had grown rich, or the perfumed fop of

hereditary wealth who had nursed his moustache at home, while their betters were bleeding in my defence, and in defence of all that is worth living for—my country and her independence.

This kind of female passion, especially common among younger women, fired many courtships. A handful of Southern diarists, however, reveal that these girls may have wished to follow a fiancé to the front as much for the adventure of fighting for their beloved country as for the solace of being close to their loved one.

But for all too many the romance of war died quickly, although the rebel spirit lingered long past surrender. With over a quarter of a million young men dead, a generation of young Southern women faced futures without beaux or husbands. The impact of war and the consequences of loss nearly robbed the South of romance, but women's strenuous efforts allowed this postwar generation to redeem its defeat by fashioning a cult of the Lost Cause. And courtship took its place at center stage once the former Confederates felt able to throw off the shackles of Reconstruction. Belles were courted by a postwar generation marked not by wealth and success but by honor and loss. Indeed the male carpetbaggers who might try to woo the daughters of former Confederates were often scorned. And, as in the case of Winnie Davis, Jefferson Davis's beloved youngest daughter who became a symbol of the Confederacy, matches with Northerners were forbidden by parents still embittered over defeat. During and after the war patriotic affiliation often helped to determine romantic affection and the outcome of courtships, especially in the war-torn South.

[See also Marriage and Divorce.]

BIBLIOGRAPHY

Robertson, Mary D. *Lucy Breckenridge of Grove Hill.* Kent, Ohio, 1979.

Rothman, Ellen. *Hands and Hearts: A History of Courtship in America.* New York, 1985.

Stowe, Steven. *Intimacy and Power in the Old South.* Baltimore, 1987.

CATHERINE CLINTON

COURTS-MARTIAL. *See* Habeas Corpus; Military Justice; Provost Martial.

COX, WILLIAM RUFFIN (1832–1919), brigadier general and U.S. congressman. Cox was born at Scotland Neck, Halifax County, North Carolina, on March 11, 1832. He graduated from Franklin College in Tennessee and obtained a law degree at Lebanon College in the same state in 1852. He then returned to North Carolina and practiced law in Raleigh. As the sectional crisis deepened, Cox equipped a light battery at his own expense and later recruited a company of infantry.

In 1861 Cox was commissioned a major in the Second North Carolina Infantry Regiment. The regiment was the first to cross Meadow Bridge at the start of the Seven Days' campaign. Cox was severely wounded at Malvern Hill and was out of action until mid-September 1862. He was promoted to lieutenant colonel after Sharpsburg and to colonel after Fredericksburg.

After Chancellorsville, Stephen Dodson Ramseur cited Cox as "the Chivalrous Cox, the accomplished gentleman, the splendid soldier . . . who fought in spite of five bleeding wounds, till he sank exhausted." Ramseur and Robert Rodes recommended Cox for a brigadiership after Spotsylvania, a recommendation that was endorsed by Robert E. Lee. Cox received his promotion on June 2, 1864.

Cox participated in Jubal Early's Valley campaign of 1864. His brigade had the honor of firing the final volley at Appomattox.

Returning to Raleigh and his law practice after the war, Cox embarked on a career of public service. A leading Democrat, he was elected to three terms in Congress and in 1893 became secretary of the Senate, a post he held until 1900. He also served as grand master of Masonic lodges in North Carolina and was a trustee of the University of the South. On December 26, 1919, he died in Richmond, Virginia, where he spent his final years, and was buried in Oakwood Cemetery, Raleigh.

BIBLIOGRAPHY

"Appomattox Echo: The Last Volley on that Memorable Field. Statement of General Grimes." *Southern Historical Society Papers* 27 (1899): 92–96. Reprint, Wilmington, N.C., 1991.

Compiled Military Service Records. William Ruffin Cox. Microcopy M331, Roll 64. Record Group 109. National Archives, Washington, D.C.

Warner, Ezra J. *Generals in Gray: Lives of the Confederate Commanders.* Baton Rouge, La., 1959.

LOWELL REIDENBAUGH

CRAIGE, FRANCIS BURTON (1811–1875), congressman from North Carolina. Born in Rowan County, North Carolina, Burton Craige was educated in a private school in nearby Salisbury before entering the University of North Carolina. After receiving his B.A. degree in 1829, he studied law while working as an editor for the Salisbury *Western Carolinian.* In this latter capacity, Craige supported nullification and endorsed South Carolina's challenge to Federal authority in 1832. Despite being admitted to the bar that same year, Craige chose to enter state politics and was elected to the General Assembly. After an unsuccessful bid for Congress in 1835, Craige returned to the legal profession and raised a family.

The political crises of the 1850s drove Burton Craige to try once again to win national office. This time he was successful. Elected in 1853 as a Democrat to the House of Representatives, Craige joined the defenders of state rights and opposed the advocates of compromise. He remained in Congress until 1861, when he left Washington for Raleigh to participate as a delegate to North Carolina's secession convention. There Craige introduced the version of the ordinance of secession that was eventually unanimously adopted.

Elected by the secession convention to represent North Carolina in the Provisional Congress, Craige traveled to Richmond and assumed his new duties on July 23, 1861. His voting record includes support both for higher taxes to aid military preparedness and for limitations upon the central government's control over state militias. Craige chose not to seek election to the First Congress and returned to North Carolina to resume his law practice. He died while attending a session of the Cabarrus County Superior Court.

BIBLIOGRAPHY

Ashe, Samuel, et al., eds. *Biographical History of North Carolina: From Colonial Times to the Present.* 8 vols. Greensboro, N.C., 1905–1917.

Harris, William C. *North Carolina and the Coming of the Civil War.* Raleigh, N.C., 1988.

Journal of the Congress of the Confederate States of America, 1861–1865. 7 vols. Washington, D.C., 1904–1905.

Powell, William S. *Dictionary of North Carolina Biography.* 4 vols. to date. Chapel Hill, N.C., 1979–.

Warner, Ezra J., and W. Buck Yearns. *Biographical Register of the Confederate Congress.* Baton Rouge, La., 1975.

ALAN C. DOWNS

CRAWFORD, MARTIN J. (1820–1883), peace commissioner, congressman from Georgia, and colonel. Crawford was born into a prominent middle Georgia planter family in Jasper County on March 17, 1820. He was a cousin of both William H. Crawford, presidential candidate in 1824, and George W. Crawford, Georgia's only Whig governor (1843–1847). He was educated at the Brownwood Institute in LaGrange and attended Mercer University. Crawford was admitted to the bar in 1839, which, because he was only nineteen years old, required authorization by a special act of the legislature. He established a law practice in Hamilton and managed his family's plantation for several years after his father's death. From 1845 to 1847, Crawford represented the county in the legislature. In 1849, he moved to Columbus, formed a successful law partnership, and was appointed superior court judge in 1854. A year later, he was elected by a sizeable majority to Congress, representing Georgia's Second District. He continued to serve in the House of Representatives until he resigned on January 23, 1861, four days after Georgia seceded from the Union.

Long a committed state rights Democrat, Crawford had

MARTIN J. CRAWFORD.   *THE SOLDIER IN OUR CIVIL WAR*

been a delegate to the southern convention in Nashville in the summer of 1850, where representatives from nine slave states met in response to the threat posed by the Free-Soil issue. Though secession was discussed as a viable reaction, Crawford and most of the Georgia delegation made up a moderate faction that ultimately prevailed over the disunionist sentiments of William Lowndes Yancey, Robert Barnwell Rhett, Sr., and other fire-eaters. As the sectional crisis came to a head, Crawford in Congress continued to be a voice of reason while defending the Southern position regarding the territorial expansion of slavery and ultimately the right of states to secede from the Union.

When Crawford returned to Georgia from Washington in 1861, he was elected as one of nine delegates from the state to attend the Montgomery convention in February at which the Confederate States of America was formally established. There, along with fellow Georgian Thomas R. R. Cobb, he served on the committee to draft the Confederate Constitution. He actively supported Thomas's brother, Howell Cobb, who chaired the convention, in his bid for the Confederate presidency. On February 13, the Provisional Congress resolved to send a peace commission to Washington to secure from the Lincoln administration, not yet in office, formal recognition of the Confederacy and to work out problems of public debts and property, including the status of military property that lay within Confederate bounds. On February 25, President Jefferson Davis appointed Crawford to that commission, along with John Forsyth, Jr., of Alabama, and A. B. Roman, former governor of Louisiana. Throughout March and into April, the three commissioners sought an audience with Lincoln or Secretary of State William H. Seward, but with no success. Lincoln refused to acknowledge the Confederate representatives and divulged no information on his intentions regarding Forts Sumter and Pickens. Seward, though, communicated with them through intermediaries and continued to offer assurances of Federal plans to evacuate both forts, even as late as April 7, the day on which the fateful reinforcements set sail for Sumter.

Having failed to gain recognition, much less negotiation, from the new administration, Crawford and his fellow commissioners returned home. Crawford spent the rest of 1861 and early 1862 as a member of the Provisional Congress in Richmond, where he served on the Accounts and Commercial Affairs committees and again supported Howell Cobb's bid for the Confederate presidency. He declined to run for reelection after his term ended in February 1862 and instead returned to Georgia where in May he was appointed colonel in the newly organized Third Georgia Cavalry.

This military venture turned out badly. In early 1863, while stationed on outpost duty near Louisville, Kentucky, Crawford and most of his regiment were caught off guard by Union cavalry, who captured them all without firing a shot. Though paroled shortly thereafter, Crawford was found guilty by a general court-martial, given a formal reprimand, and sentenced to three months' suspension from rank and pay.

Crawford resigned his command in March 1863 before his suspension expired. He returned to Georgia and joined the staff of his friend and former political ally, Maj. Gen. Howell Cobb. He served as unofficial aide to Cobb, who commanded the Georgia Guard in the fall of 1863 and the Georgia Reserve Force, which comprised a variety of home guard units stationed at Macon, Augusta, Savannah, and Andersonville Prison, through most of 1864.

Wilson's raid destroyed most of Crawford's plantation in April 1865, and he returned home to Columbus, impoverished at age forty-five. He resumed his law practice and in 1875 was again appointed superior court judge of the Chattahoochee Circuit. In 1880, Crawford was appointed an associate justice of the Georgia Supreme Court by Governor Alfred H. Colquitt and served on the court until his death on July 22, 1883.

BIBLIOGRAPHY

Coleman, Kenneth, and Charles Stephen Gurr, eds. *Dictionary of Georgia Biography.* Vol. 1. Athens, Ga., 1983.

Knight, Lucian Lamar. *A Standard History of Georgia and Georgians.* Vol. 4. Chicago, 1917.

Montgomery, Horace. *Howell Cobb's Military Career.* Tuscaloosa, Ala., 1959.

Worseley, Etta Blanchard. *Columbus on the Chattahoochee.* Columbus, Ga., 1951.

JOHN C. INSCOE

CREEKS. Living in eastern Indian Territory (present-day Oklahoma), these Native Americans split in their allegiances during the Civil War, with about half of the tribe embracing the Confederacy. Originally an agricultural and hunting people, they were living in the southeastern United States in what is now Georgia and Alabama in the sixteenth century. By the early eighteenth century, the Creeks, most of whom spoke a Muskhogean language, had created the most powerful Indian confederacy in the South.

The Nation was divided into the Upper Creeks and the Lower Creeks, with a principal chief and council for each group. During the early eighteenth century English and Scottish fur traders established trading posts, primarily among the Lower Creeks, and took Creek wives. Consequently, these British traders helped to create a mixed-ancestry leadership with names like McGillivray and McIntosh. This leadership sharpened the division between Lower Creeks and Upper Creeks, who, for want of better terms, could be described as "progressives" and "traditionalists," respectively. By the turn of the century, however, leaders of mixed ancestry were present among the traditionalists as well.

Division became a schism in the 1820s because of the Federal government's Indian removal policy. Many of the Lower Creeks voluntarily followed their mixed-ancestry leaders to their new home in Indian Territory. The Upper Creeks viewed those who signed the land cession treaties as traitors. The conflict burst into violence when traditionalists led by Menawa assassinated William McIntosh, the principal chief of the Lower Creeks, and others of the so-called treaty party. In the final removal of the tribe, the Federal government forcibly uprooted the Upper Creeks, as well as the last remnants of the Lower Creeks, and brutally conducted them to Indian Territory in the 1830s.

The two factions remained geographically separated in the new land. The Upper Creeks settled along the banks of the Deep Fork, Canadian, and North Canadian rivers while the Lower Creeks established farms, plantations, and towns in the northern area along the Arkansas and Verdigris rivers. In spite of their antagonism toward each other, both groups cooperated in pragmatic fashion from time to time in many ways. They established a seat of government, created a phonetic written language, welcomed missionaries to build schools, wrote a slave code, and fashioned a short constitution.

The deep chasm between the two factions burst into a bloody fratricidal conflict when the Civil War erupted in

1861. The Lower Creeks, led by Principal Chief Motey Canard and the sons of William McIntosh, Chilly and Daniel N., signed a treaty of alliance with the Confederacy negotiated by Albert Pike at North Fork Town on July 10, 1861. Opothleyahola, an aged leader who had fought against removal, and Oktarharsars Harjo (called "Sands"), principal chief of the Upper Creeks, proclaimed their loyalty to the United States and announced that their people would remain neutral.

Opothleyahola acted as a magnet in drawing thousands of neutral Creeks, including entire families, as well as some Seminoles, Kickapoos, Shawnees, Wichitas, Delawares, and Comanches, to his camp on the Deep Fork River. Many of the refugees hurriedly left their homes with little more than the clothes on their backs, some baggage and food, a gun, and a horse or wagon.

The old Creek leader began to organize the group for a march. The people stored surplus food and buried their valuables. When Confederate soldiers from the neighboring states of Arkansas and Texas moved into Indian Territory to occupy recently abandoned Federal forts, the neutrals, fearful for their safety, broke camp on November 5, 1861, and began a long march to the safety of Kansas. Unfortunately, they were ill equipped either for the winter march or for military action.

On November 19, 1861, Confederate troops consisting of Southern whites, Creeks, and Seminoles under the command of Col. Douglas Cooper and Col. Daniel N. McIntosh attacked the group at Round Mountain, near the junction of the Cimarron and Arkansas rivers. When the Confederates failed to dislodge them, Opothleyahola quietly led his people under cover of darkness across the Arkansas River to resume their northward trek.

On December 9, the Cooper-McIntosh forces launched a second attack, this time at Chusto Talasah (Caving Banks) on Bird Creek. The neutrals, uniformed only with corn-shuck "badges" pinned to their coats, forced the Confederates to retreat. Once more the loyalists resumed their march. This time Cooper and McIntosh waited for reinforcements to arrive before continuing the pursuit.

In the Osage Hills the opposing forces fought their final battle when the Confederates, with a much enlarged force, attacked the neutrals on the bitterly cold day of December 26 at a place called Chustenahlah. In the midst of battle, the loyal Creeks ran out of ammunition. They fled the field in a rout, scattering in the wake of a freezing north wind and blowing snow. Some said that the survivors could be tracked by following their bloody footprints in the snow.

Some 5,600 Creeks made it to Kansas, along with about 1,000 other loyal Indians, all determined to have their revenge against the Confederate Creeks under McIntosh as well as the white troops of Douglas Cooper. In June 1862, an all-Indian force of Union soldiers, including two regiments of Creeks, marched into Indian Territory, engaged in

a few skirmishes, and captured the Cherokee capital of Tahlequah. Soon after, the white commander of the expedition turned his men back to Kansas.

In 1862 and 1863, Confederate Creeks under Colonels Daniel McIntosh and Canard were fighting Union regulars in Arkansas in a number of engagements including the Battle of Elkhorn Tavern. Aside from that one, the greatest battle to occupy Creek Confederates broke out on July 17, 1863, at a place on the Texas Road called Honey Springs. Two Creek Confederate regiments under Daniel McIntosh and his brother Chilly, along with Choctaw, Chickasaw, Cherokee, and Texas troops, were defeated in the engagement.

For the Creeks the cataclysmic effect of the war was second only to their forced removal from their ancient homeland. Those not engaged as soldiers found themselves engaged in a bloody guerrilla war at home in which scavenging bands often shot down those identified as members of the opposing faction, destroyed crops, burned homes, and butchered livestock.

After the war the loyalists returned from Kansas to a nation in ruin. The factions and hatred within the Creek Nation exacerbated by the fratricide would smolder into the twentieth century.

[*See also* Elkhorn Tavern, Arkansas.]

BIBLIOGRAPHY

Bearss, Edwin C. "The Civil War Comes to Indian Territory, 1861: The Flight of Opothleyahola." *Journal of the West* 11 (January 1972): 9–42.

Clark, Carter Blue. "Opothleyahola and the Creeks during the Civil War." In *Indian Leaders: Oklahoma's First Statesmen*. Edited by H. Glenn Jordan and Thomas M. Holm. Oklahoma City, 1979, pp. 49–63.

Clifford, Roy A. "Indian Regiments in the Battle of Pea Ridge." *Chronicles of Oklahoma* 25 (1947–1948): 314–322.

Debo, Angie. *The Road to Disappearance: A History of the Creek Indians*. Norman, Okla., 1941.

Josephy, Alvin M., Jr. *The Civil War in the American West*. New York, 1991.

DONALD E. GREEN

CREOLES. [*This entry discusses creoles of European descent living in Louisiana. For discussion of creoles of African and European descent living in Alabama, Florida, and Louisiana, see* Free People of Color, *article on* Free Creoles of Color.] The most common present-day usage defines a *creole* as a white descendant of the original French or Spanish inhabitants of Louisiana, but until the end of the Civil War era the term applied to any person born in the state, regardless of ethnic, racial, or legal status. Primarily because among whites only those of Latin ancestry clung to creole identity in post–Louisiana Purchase years and because black creoles were not considered to be central to public concerns, by the 1860s the phrase "*the* creoles" (plural) had come to be understood among whites as referring to white Latin natives of the state, unless context indicated otherwise.

The creole community of 1803 welcomed admission into the Union, fully aware that partnership in the Republic promised advantages, both political and economic, that it had never enjoyed as a colony of either France or Spain. Despite profound difficulties in accommodating their cultural and political interests to those of the Anglo-Americans who flooded into Louisiana after the Purchase, Latin creoles remained staunchly loyal to the new relationship. When, for example, Aaron Burr in 1806 set in motion what has come to be known as the Burr Conspiracy, looking to a probable invasion of Mexico and possibly a separation of western states from the Union, he seemingly expected creoles unreconciled to the Purchase to flock to his banner. But the records of his eventual trial for treason reveal not a single native Louisianian among his supporters.

Loyalty to their new identity could not, however, protect the Latin creoles from the consequences of their long colonial exploitation by France and Spain. Although the antebellum period saw a continuous erosion of their political and economic influence in the state, they remained a distinctive and important factor in its affairs. Identification with those southern portions of the state devoted to a sugar cane industry dependent upon a high protective tariff made them a principal constituency of Whig nationalism, a tradition maintained in their vigorous support of the pro-Unionists John Bell and Stephen A. Douglas in the presidential election of 1860.

This lack of enthusiasm for Southern radicalism surfaced again in the January 1861 election of delegates to the convention to decide Louisiana's relationship to the United States, when cooperationist candidates, generally considered to be opposed to immediate secession, carried a majority of the vote in thirteen black belt parishes comprising the heart of the creole southwestern quarter of the state. That not all creoles shared this cautionary position became clear, however, when one of their number, ex-governor Alexandre Mouton, presided over the convention's final decision in favor of secession and independence.

General creole acceptance of that determination was quick and resolute. A vigorous opponent of separation at the 1861 convention, ex-governor A. B. Roman reluctantly but firmly cast his lot with the new Confederate state, and yet another creole ex-governor, Paul O. Hébert, soon took the field as a Confederate brigadier general. Anti-Union sentiment surged especially among young creoles, expressed in an exuberant revitalization of Latin ethnic nationalism in the New Orleans publication *La Renaissance Louisianaise,* which first appeared in July 1861. Its protagonists, like the already famous historian Charles Gayarré and the eventually renowned Columbus expert Henri Vignaud, saw the Confederacy as a last beguiling opportunity to reestablish in Louisiana a state freed from puritanical Yankee hegemony and possessed once again of a true Gallic soul. This already anachronistic ethnic romanticism, largely propagated by creole intellectuals, soon yielded to the greater immediacy of an implacable negrophobia, which would continue to dominate general creole sensibilities into the postwar years.

For all these reasons, creoles gave unstintingly of their young men to the Confederate cause in a variety of colorful military units like the Orleans Guards and the Creole Regiment of Col. Leopold Armant attached to the brigade of Gen. Alfred Mouton, son of the ex-governor and himself no less a creole for his cajun origins. Both Armant and Mouton lost their lives leading Southern forces under the command of Gen. Richard Taylor at the Battle of Mansfield in 1864, the most decisive Confederate victory west of the Mississippi River. And no Louisiana Confederate won greater distinction, rank, and acclaim than the "Great Creole," Gen. P. G. T. Beauregard, hailed by many as the "Napoleon in Gray" after his successes in the taking of Fort Sumter and at First Manassas. His effectiveness as a commander, however, failed to fulfill its early promise as he became enmeshed in enduring conflict with President Jefferson Davis.

Collapse of the Confederacy ended all hopes for reestablishment of Gallic supremacy in Louisiana and committed creoles to a Lost Cause mentality even more expansive than that to be found elsewhere in the South. But the racial dislocations attendant upon Radical Reconstruction shifted their concerns from traditional fear of Anglo-American ascendancy to a dread that long established ambiguity as to creole definition might result in their being confused with the hated black minority. Desperate determination not to be excluded from the ranks of white supremacy led to the emergence of the late nineteenth century "creole myth" that has continued to insist, despite the clear historical record, upon exclusively European ancestry as the indispensable requisite of creole identity.

[*See also* Free People of Color, *article on* Creoles; Louisiana; Louisiana Tigers; *and biographies of numerous figures mentioned herein.*]

BIBLIOGRAPHY

Cable, George Washington. *Old Creole Days.* New York, 1879.
Tregle, Joseph G., Jr. "Creoles and Americans." In *Creole New Orleans.* Edited by Arnold Hirsch and Joseph Logsdon. Baton Rouge, La., 1992.
Winters, John D. *The Civil War in Louisiana.* Baton Rouge, La., 1963.

JOSEPH G. TREGLE, JR.

CRIME AND PUNISHMENT. The patterns of crime and punishment that emerged during the years of the Confederacy were unique partly because of the South's distinctive past and partly because of the inevitable disruptions of a wartime society. Before the Civil War, whites were most frequently prosecuted for crimes of violence, a pattern grounded in the belief that white crime was motivated not by evil but by passion. Assault, dueling, and carrying a concealed weapon were all common offenses during the antebellum years. So too were horse theft and counterfeiting, two offenses that clearly threatened the economic order and that most likely resulted from greed rather than need.

During wartime many of the customary rules of order ceased to apply, a fact that had a major impact on the nature and extent of unlawful behavior. As the relatively orderly society of the antebellum era began to disintegrate, so did traditional legal processes. Lacking any systematic record of crime statistics, historians must piece together information from contemporary accounts and from legislation enacted by Confederate states to deal with criminal activity. Taken together, this evidence leaves the impression that criminal behavior was on the rise as Confederate fortunes declined. Beginning in 1862, as the Confederacy experienced greater casualties and military defeats, particularly in the West, more sacrifice was demanded at home. At first the rural areas paid the heavy price of war, but by 1863 urban areas were facing serious food shortages. These developments, coupled with high inflation, heavier taxation, conscription laws, and poor transportation, created a fertile atmosphere for increased crime.

There is no better evidence for intensified unlawful behavior than Confederate legislation and various local ordinances that imposed martial law and authorized the government to suspend fundamental civil rights. Such efforts, however, proved ineffective as the war advanced. When local courts charged with enforcing the criminal law were disrupted, law enforcement became impossible. In areas where invasion seemed imminent, state legislatures authorized the courts to move to safer locations. But these moves did not solve the problem of court personnel—clerks, attorneys, witnesses, defendants—being absent because of wartime responsibilities. Some states tried to keep the courts in business by allowing men over the age of sixty to serve as jurors and clerks to serve as attorneys. States such as Alabama and Mississippi authorized the continuance of cases when key participants were away at war. Such efforts, however, were apparently insufficient.

During the last years of the Confederacy, governments resorted to the military to maintain law and order, but the military itself could do little. In fact, contemporary observers in states such as Virginia, North Carolina, and Louisiana complained about defense units in local communities themselves engaging in crime.

Early in the war the Confederacy turned its attention to slave resistance. To be sure, the presence of slavery posed special problems for white wartime society. Although black labor aided the war effort, at the same time the Confederacy witnessed an increase in theft, malingering, resistance, and running away among slaves. The fragile mechanisms of law enforcement during the war led to a much greater incidence, in particular, of theft. In Savannah near the end of the war, for example, more than half the arrests made by police were of slaves, whereas the prewar figure had been less than 20 percent. Since police power by this time was so diminished, the actual incidence of slave crime was probably much greater. In wartime Tennessee, theft by slaves grew as the institution itself began to fall apart. African Americans especially sought horses and mules for easy sale.

Confederate states responded by strengthening slave codes. In 1861, Florida put the militia on patrol duty, requiring weekly rounds. In other states, special slave patrols were created by county courts or justices of the peace, authorized to act more often and to impose stiffer penalties for neglect of duty. As slave crime became an increasing concern of the Confederacy, punishments were made more severe. Regulations were tightened on the sale of whiskey to slaves, and some states made arson, larceny, and burglary subject to much harsher penalties.

Although the data is scarce, unlawful behavior among whites was probably greater than among slaves. One Arkansas observer noted in 1861 that there are "more dangers from bad white men among us than from the poor slaves." Offenses committed by whites included property crimes (such as theft, arson, animal stealing, and counterfeiting), crimes of violence (assault, riot, rape, murder, poisoning), and crimes against morality (gambling, drinking, breaking the Sabbath).

One of the most vexing offenses of the Confederate years was theft, clearly on the rise because of wartime shortages. Planter complaints in the records blamed the "lower classes," but the poor were severely deprived and believed that the wealthy were not suffering at all. In one western Georgia county, more than one hundred people were prosecuted for theft from 1861 to 1865, whereas very few suspected thieves had been brought to court before the war. Suspects were also prosecuted in groups, a fact that reflects the unlawful activity of gangs of deserters or draft evaders. Banditry was very rare in the antebellum years, but common in the Confederacy. These dangerous groups of men, sometimes teenagers, had only one objective—plunder—which they might commit murder to achieve. There was little lawful response to their actions, especially in areas where conscription had depleted the male population, except for defensive efforts by communities themselves.

Other crimes on the rise during the Confederacy were counterfeiting, made a capital crime; prostitution, particularly at winter encampments; murder, often associated with matters of loyalty; and carrying concealed weapons. Confronted by alarming food shortages and by increased efforts to distill grain into more profitable alcohol, state legislatures enacted stiff penalties for distillers, but such laws could not be effectively enforced.

Records from individual states all point to increases in crime and the inability to control it. Georgia, for example, experienced a substantial rise in property and misdemeanor offenses during the war years. In North Carolina, slave owner Jonathan Worth noted with dismay that "theft, robbery, and almost every other crime are common in almost all the rural districts." By 1865, anarchy seemed to prevail in two Piedmont counties as judges refused to hold court. Rural areas of Tennessee were populated by gangs that apparently operated without restraint. Newspapers from the state leave the impression that property crime was widespread. Evidence from Virginia reveals many cases of gambling, theft, and robbery-related murders. In 1862, the Richmond city council must have been responding to increased crime when it made a request for more jails, although studies show that lawbreakers faced few penalties. The Confederacy generally prescribed harsh punishments to deter rising crime. In South Carolina, for example, arson was made a capital offense. A horse thief in Alabama faced the gallows. In Arkansas, the death penalty was meted out to those convicted of such offenses as slave stealing, forgery, perjury, incest, and kidnapping.

Clearly, the disruption and deprivation of war, particularly as 1865 approached, led to increased criminal activity across the South. As the records show, however, with their attention and resources focused on the war, there was little that Confederate governments could do to enforce laws or to capture and punish offenders.

[*See also* Bread Riots; Civil Liberties; Counterfeiting; Desertion; Dueling; Habeas Corpus; Military Justice; Prostitution.]

BIBLIOGRAPHY

Ash, Stephen V. *Middle Tennessee Society Transformed, 1860–1870.* Baton Rouge, La., 1988.

Ayers, Edward L. *Vengeance and Justice: Crime and Punishment in the 19th-Century American South.* New York, 1984.

Escott, Paul D. *Many Excellent People: Power and Privilege in North Carolina, 1850–1900.* Chapel Hill, N.C., 1985.

Ramsdell W., Charles. *Behind the Lines in the Confederacy.* Baton Rouge, La., 1944.

Ringold, May Spencer. *The Role of the State Legislatures in the Confederacy.* Athens, Ga., 1966.

DONNA J. SPINDEL

CRITTENDEN, GEORGE B. (1812–1880), major general. Crittenden, eldest son of Senator John J. Crittenden of Kentucky and brother of Union Gen. Thomas L. Crittenden, graduated from West Point in 1832. After a year in the U.S. Army he went to Texas to serve in its army. Reenlisting for the Mexican War, he continued in the regular army, rising to lieutenant colonel.

When the Civil War broke out, Crittenden joined the Confederacy. In October 1861 Jefferson Davis appointed him a major general and sent him to lead an army of invasion into his native Kentucky. In early 1862 he took command of the brigades of Gen. Felix K. Zollicoffer and Gen. William Henry Carroll at Beech Grove, Kentucky.

On January 19 Crittenden's army ran into Union pickets near Logans Crossroads, Kentucky, in what proved to be his first and last major battle. He attempted to defeat one of two Union armies before they could unite into one force. By late morning the Union commander, Gen. George Thomas, had outflanked and defeated Crittenden's army. Many claimed Crittenden was drunk at the time of the battle and demanded that he be replaced. But Albert Sidney Johnston, Confederate commander in the West, gave him command of the reserve corps in the army he was building in northern Mississippi. Crittenden lost his chance to restore his reputation on April 1, 1862, when Gen. William J. Hardee came into Iuka, Mississippi, and found Generals Crittenden

GEORGE B. CRITTENDEN.   LIBRARY OF CONGRESS

and Carroll drunk and their commands in a "wretched state of discipline." Crittenden was arrested and court-martialed. He resigned on October 23, 1862, but continued to serve in a subordinate role under various commanders in western Virginia.

After the war, Crittenden lived in Kentucky where he served as state librarian. He is buried in the state cemetery at Frankfort, Kentucky.

BIBLIOGRAPHY

Myers, Raymond Edward Marion. *The Zollie Tree*. Louisville, Ky., 1964.

The National Cyclopaedia of American Biography. Vol. 4. New York, 1897.

CHARLES M. SPEARMAN

CRITTENDEN COMPROMISE.

In December 1860, Kentucky senator John J. Crittenden proposed a comprehensive set of resolutions designed to avert secession and war. These resolutions became known as the Crittenden Compromise following their December 18 referral to the Senate Committee of Thirteen, a special committee set up to review methods for diffusing the sectional crisis.

Crittenden, nationally known for his past compromising efforts, offered the South protection by giving slavery in the slave states a permanent constitutional status while simultaneously allaying Northern fears of unchecked slave expansion. The Crittenden Compromise comprised six unamendable constitutional amendments: the first and most important restored and extended the old Missouri Compromise line by protecting slavery south of 36°30′ but prohibiting the institution north of the line, and citizens in territories were to decide for themselves whether new states would enter the Union free or slave; the second amendment prohibited Congress from abolishing slavery on government property in slave states; the third forbade

"A CURE FOR REPUBLICAN LOCK-JAW." Portrayal of Congress's effort to pass the Crittenden Compromise over Republican opposition. A sick man in a dressing gown, holding a paper inscribed "Republican Platform No Compromise," resists swallowing an enormous pill labeled "Crittenden Compromise." Three men, most likely members of Congress, force the pill down his throat with a "Petition of 63,000." More pills lie in a box labeled "Constitutional Remedies." The print was signed by Benjamin H. Day, Jr., and published by Benjamin Day, New York, 1861.

LIBRARY OF CONGRESS

the abolition of slavery in the District of Columbia unless it was abolished in both Maryland and Virginia, and not then without consent of the inhabitants or compensation to the owners; the fourth protected interstate transportation of slaves; the fifth compensated claimants of fugitive slaves rescued by mobs; and the sixth prohibited future constitutional amendments that would overturn these guarantees.

Initially, it appeared as if these resolutions had a real chance for passage. Upper South Unionists embraced the Crittenden Compromise as the only hope of avoiding secessionist victory in their states. Many in the Republican ranks were also sympathetic to conciliatory measures. President-elect Abraham Lincoln, however, made it clear that he would not waver on his commitment to contain slavery where it already existed. Although Lincoln was agreeable to some of the resolutions, his opposition to the restoration of the 36°30′ line made passage of the compromise impossible.

Following its failure in the Committee of Thirteen, Crittenden brought his compromise directly before the Senate on January 3, 1861, and called for a national plebiscite on the resolutions, arguing that the American people supported the compromise. On January 16, however, the Senate voted down Crittenden's appeal 25–23. The failure of the Crittenden Compromise ended any hope of halting the secession movement by congressional action. Lincoln's opposition to the compromise was a major setback to Southern Unionism.

BIBLIOGRAPHY

Crofts, Daniel W. *Reluctant Confederates: Upper South Unionists in the Secession Crisis.* Chapel Hill, N.C., 1989.

Kirwan, Albert D. *John J. Crittenden: The Struggle for the Union.* Lexington, Ky., 1962.

Potter, David M. *Lincoln and His Party in the Secession Crisis.* New Haven, Conn., 1942.

BRUCE W. EELMAN

CROCKETT, JOHN WATKINS (1818–1874),

congressman from Kentucky. Crockett's career underscores the frustrations experienced by Kentucky's Confederate congressmen. Virtually self-exiled from the commonwealth, they labored in Richmond with little hope of liberating Kentucky from its loyal state government and Union occupation troops.

Crockett, descended from Virginians (his grandfather led a regiment during the Revolution and played an influential role in establishing Kentucky's state government), was born in Jessamine County, Kentucky. He was educated in local schools there as well as in Hancock County, Illinois. Crockett began studying law in Hopkinsville, Kentucky, in

1839 and practiced law in Paducah until shortly before the outbreak of the war, when he relocated in Henderson, Kentucky.

Though originally a Whig and a Unionist, Crockett after the firing on Fort Sumter favored secession. In November 1861, he was a delegate from Henderson County to the sovereignty convention in Russellville, Kentucky, that led the commonwealth out of the Union. Crockett served as a member of the Executive Council of the Provisional Government of Kentucky. In 1862 he was elected to the Confederate House of Representatives from the Second District. He played a minimal role in the First Congress, serving only on the Elections Committee. On September 24, 1862, Crockett was granted a leave of absence until the commencement of the third session on January 12, 1863. Though Crockett opposed making Treasury notes legal tender, he generally supported the Davis administration and concluded that Congress was more often than not a hindrance to the prosecution of the war. He urged an aggressive military policy and led the move in the House to extend the draft age to forty-five.

Crockett did not stand for reelection in 1864, probably putting into practice his assertion that he could serve the South more profitably back in the commonwealth than in the Confederate capital. Following his congressional term, he returned to Henderson where he practiced law and continued this profession after the close of hostilities. Crockett eschewed any further involvement in politics.

BIBLIOGRAPHY

Quisenberry, A. C. "The Alleged Secession of Kentucky." *Register of the Kentucky State Historical Society* 15 (1917): 15–32.

Wakelyn, Jon L. *Biographical Dictionary of the Confederacy.* Edited by Frank E. Vandiver. Westport, Conn., 1977.

Warner, Ezra J., and W. Buck Yearns. *Biographical Register of the Confederate Congress.* Baton Rouge, La., 1975.

JOHN DAVID SMITH

CROSS KEYS AND PORT REPUBLIC, VIRGINIA.

These tiny villages in the central Shenandoah Valley were the scene of consecutive victories by Thomas J. ("Stonewall") Jackson's army on June 8 and 9, 1862, which climaxed his Valley campaign. During the first week of June, Jackson retreated steadily southward up the valley on the west side of fifty-mile-long Massanutten Mountain. Federals under Gen. John C. Frémont followed on his heels, while another enemy force under Gen. James Shields hurried southward on a parallel route east of the Massanutten. By June 4 Jackson had focused his intentions on the vicinity of Port Republic, south of the southern tip of the mountain and at the confluence of two rivers that formed the south fork of the Shenandoah River. There the ground would offer him the chance to face first one and then the other of his pursuers.

When Jackson turned southeast off the Valley Pike toward Port Republic, Northern cavalry assailed his rear guard near Harrisonburg on June 6. The Confederates repulsed the thrust, but the army's cavalry chieftain, Turner Ashby, was killed in the skirmish. At dawn on Sunday, June 8, Jackson had part of his army encamped on high ground across the river from Port Republic. Gen. Richard S. Ewell commanded a Confederate force that remained about four miles north of Port Republic on the Harrisonburg Road, around the Cross Keys settlement. Early on the eighth a small Union cavalry detachment burst into Port Republic and nearly cornered Jackson in his headquarters on the southern edge of town. Three of his staff members fell into enemy hands. A handful of Confederates stalled the cavalry raiders long enough for friendly infantry to hurry to the rescue.

Meanwhile Frémont approached Ewell's position and began a series of attacks that accomplished nothing. Ewell had spread four brigades across the crest of a long curving ridge rising from the south bank of Mill Creek. Strong artillery clusters guarded his line, especially on its left and center. Hours of artillery exchanges punctuated by an occasional brief Union infantry assault produced no results of consequence except casualties. The hottest fighting at Cross Keys developed on the Confederate right, where Ewell's feisty subordinate, Brig. Gen. Isaac Trimble, took the initiative. When the Eighth New York approached to point-blank range, Trimble unleashed the deadly fire of about a thousand muskets. The Eighth New York suffered in a few minutes about one-third of the total loss among the more than two dozen regiments in Frémont's army. Trimble then surged forward onto Frémont's left flank and curled it up. Acting under Jackson's general orders, Ewell rejected repeated pleas by Trimble for a further advance. When darkness closed the fighting, the Federals had lost nearly 700 men from a strength of 12,000, and Ewell had lost about 300 from his 5,000.

During the night of June 8–9, Jackson hurriedly cobbled together an awkward bridge over one of the rivers at Port Republic. He moved his army across it and northeast of the village early on the ninth in the overly ambitious hope that he could defeat Shields's advance guard there and then turn and go after Frémont again. The Federals waiting on the river plain below Port Republic numbered no more than 4,000, but they enjoyed the cover of a farm lane perpendicular to Jackson's line of advance. More important, they had the use of a clearing atop a finger of the Blue Ridge that reached down toward the main road. Artillery atop that ridge at the Lewis family's "coaling," or charcoal manufactory, dominated the plain and decimated Jackson's troops. For a time Jackson pushed forward just two regiments of his old brigade, together with some badly outmatched guns. His first attempts to get above the dominant Federal artillery pieces and drive them away failed miserably. As some of Ewell's troops began to arrive from Cross Keys in time to stabilize the bad situation near the river, Gen. Richard Taylor's Louisiana brigade scrambled through the densely thicketed mountainside toward the guns. The crisis of the battle came when the Louisiana men stormed into the coaling for a hand-to-hand fight over the artillery. After seemingly endless minutes of intensely violent personal encounters, the Federals regained the ground. Taylor finally secured the coaling and assured Jackson of victory. The much smaller Federal force broke and ran northward, having stood up stoutly to three times their numbers. Jackson lost more than eight hundred men. During the rout that followed Taylor's success atop the coaling, the Confederates gathered up hundreds of prisoners, who brought the otherwise moderate Federal loss to slightly more than one thousand casualties.

Stonewall Jackson's double victory at Cross Keys and Port Republic put the crowning touch on his spectacular three-month Shenandoah Valley campaign. The two battles forced the pursuing Federals to retire out of range, giving Jackson the opportunity to succor his weary army unhindered in the bountiful valley for a week. Then, free from the threat posed earlier by Frémont and Shields, Jackson and his army headed across the mountains toward Richmond. There they joined with Gen. Robert E. Lee and the Army of Northern Virginia to drive away the Federal army besieging the Confederate capital.

BIBLIOGRAPHY

Allan, William. *History of the Campaign of Gen. T. J. (Stonewall) Jackson in the Shenandoah Valley of Virginia.* Philadelphia, 1880.
Kelly, Henry Brooke. *Port Republic.* Philadelphia, 1886.
Tanner, Robert G. *Stonewall in the Valley.* Garden City, N.Y., 1976.
Taylor, Richard. *Destruction and Reconstruction.* New York, 1879.

ROBERT K. KRICK

CRUIKSHANK, MARCUS H. (1826–1881), congressman from Alabama. Born December 12, 1826, in Autauga County, Alabama, Marcus Henderson Cruikshank read law in Talladega and began his practice there in 1847. During the 1850s he served as register in chancery, mayor of Talladega, and editor of the Whig newspaper, the *Talladega Alabama Reporter.* He supported the Bell-Everett ticket in 1860 and warned against secession after Lincoln's election.

He continued as mayor during the early years of the Civil War and also directed a salt works for the Confederate government. A Unionist, he won election in 1863 to the

Second Confederate Congress along with other Alabama candidates who opposed the war, defeating Alabama's most able congressman, Jabez L. M. Curry. He served on the Enrolled Bills, Printing, and Ordnance Stores committees. He favored repeal of the act suspending the writ of habeas corpus and voted for every peace proposal introduced. He particularly objected to asking the public for any additional sacrifices.

After the war he was a major organizer of relief efforts for the destitute in Alabama. In 1873 he became owner and editor of the *Talladega Reporter and Watchtower*, which he edited until his death on October 10, 1881, in Talladega.

BIBLIOGRAPHY

McMillan, Malcolm C. *The Alabama Confederate Reader*. University, Ala., 1963.
Owen, Thomas McAdory. *History of Alabama and Dictionary of Alabama Biography*. 4 vols. Chicago, 1921.
Wakelyn, Jon L. *Biographical Directory of the Confederacy*. Edited by Frank E. Vandiver. Westport, Conn., 1977.
Warner, Ezra J., and W. Buck Yearns. *Biographical Register of the Confederate Congress*. Baton Rouge, La., 1975.

SARAH WOOLFOLK WIGGINS

CUBA. The jewel of Spain's remaining colonial empire, Cuba was of great interest to the Confederacy as a market for its cotton in exchange for durable goods. With a population of 1,396,530 (1,015,977 free, the majority of whom were white, of Spanish origin; 370,553 slave), Cuba was also of concern to the Union, which saw it as a source of support for the Southerners.

Spain maintained an official policy of neutrality during the Civil War but did not honor the Union blockade of the South until 1863 when it proved effective. In the first eighteen months of the war the South traded cotton in Havana for clothing, food, shoes, medicine, and other durable goods. Cuba was also the point of departure for Southern diplomats bound for Europe.

The Union seized dozens of blockade runners in Cuban waters, which created diplomatic tensions between Spain and the United States. The Cuban colonial government tolerated some economic relations with the South until it became obvious that the Confederacy would lose the war. In the early months of the war it was not uncommon to see dozens of Confederate ships in Havana Harbor. By the fall of 1863 that no longer was the case.

The Civil War led to an increase in abolitionism on the island following the end of hostilities on the North American continent. The threat of annexation to the United States, a long-standing source of tension between the United States and Cuba, declined during the early 1860s. Cuba, however, had little effect on the Civil War.

BIBLIOGRAPHY

Cortada, James W. *Spain and the American Civil War: Relations at Mid-Century, 1855–1868*. Philadelphia, 1980.
Thomas, Hugh. *Cuba: The Pursuit of Freedom*. New York, 1971.

JAMES W. CORTADA

CUMMING, ALFRED (1829–1910), brigadier general. Born to a wealthy cotton magnate in Augusta, Georgia, Alfred Cumming attended West Point, graduating in the 1849 class. He was posted on the western frontier, served two years as aide-de-camp to Brig. Gen. David E. Twiggs, escorted the Mexican Boundary Commission, and participated in the Mormon expedition in Utah Territory. He resigned his captaincy in the Tenth U.S. Infantry the same day Georgia seceded, January 19, 1861.

Cumming became successively lieutenant colonel of the Augusta Volunteer Battalion, major of the First Georgia Infantry, and lieutenant colonel and then colonel of the Tenth Georgia. At first assigned in Virginia, he led this regiment in the Peninsular campaign on the Yorktown line and fought with distinction in the Seven Days' Battles of Savage's Station and Malvern Hill, where he was wounded. Colonel Cumming gained further recognition for his stands at Crampton's Gap and Sharpsburg, where he was again wounded. During his recovery in Augusta he received promotion on October 29, 1862, to brigadier general. Thereafter he served in the western theater.

Cumming commanded a brigade of Georgians in the Battle of Champion's Hill, Mississippi, and the doomed siege of Vicksburg. Following his brigade's capture and parole, he reorganized it to fight again at Missionary Ridge. Noted as a skillful tactician, General Cumming in the Atlanta Campaign won praise for his role in the fighting at Rocky Face Ridge, Resaca, Kolb's Farm, and Atlanta. A disabling wound at Jonesboro rendered him unfit for further field service, though he was present on crutches at the final surrender.

Following the war Cumming became a farmer in Floyd County, Georgia, and then moved to Rome and finally to Augusta. As part of his public career he served on the American Military Commission to Korea in 1888.

BIBLIOGRAPHY

Evans, Clement A., ed. *Confederate Military History*. 12 vols. Atlanta, 1899. Extended ed. in 19 vols. Wilmington, N.C., 1987–1989.
Faust, Patricia L., ed. *Historical Times Illustrated Encyclopedia of the Civil War*. New York, 1986.
Warner, Ezra J. *Generals in Gray: Lives of the Confederate Commanders*. Baton Rouge, La., 1959.

DENNIS KELLY

CURRENCY. [*This entry is composed of three articles that discuss Confederate monetary policy, legislation to enact this policy, and the notes and coins that were issued in the Confederacy:* An Overview; Congressional Money Bills; *and* Numismatics. *For further discussion of the Confederate monetary system, see* Bonds; Counterfeiting; Inflation; Shinplasters; Treasury Department.]

An Overview

On November 1, 1860, just before the election of Abraham Lincoln, the currency of the eleven states that formed the Confederacy consisted of approximately $63 million of gold, silver, and copper coins together with about $85 million of notes put out by 144 state-chartered banks (some with branches) that existed in eight states. Three states—Arkansas, Mississippi, and Texas—had no banks.

The election of Lincoln caused a run on the banks, which, with the exception of those in Louisiana and a few in Alabama, promptly suspended the payment of coin on their notes and deposits. Gold and silver coins were immediately hoarded, and although the Confederacy took possession of three U.S. mints, for all practical purposes it never issued any coins of its own.

Since the banks were, for the most part, prohibited by state law from issuing notes under the denomination of $5, there was no means of effecting small transactions. Various state governments required that the banks issue low-denomination notes, including notes under a dollar. State bank note issues increased to approximately $125 million by 1865.

The state governments were prohibited by the Provisional Constitution from issuing their own notes, although the Permanent Constitution discarded this provision. As a result, most state legislatures avoided the issue of any but high-denomination, interest-bearing notes until February 18, 1862, when the new Constitution went into effect. Thereafter, there was a flood of notes ranging in denomination from 5 cents up to $500. Total outstanding state issues in 1865 came to about $65 million.

Cities and counties also issued a large amount of currency. In Virginia, Louisiana, and Texas such emissions were especially numerous and were motivated by the need to furnish the public with change, to raise funds for war mobilization, and to cover general expenses. Creditworthy private individuals and corporations (such as railroads and manufacturers) printed and circulated their own notes as a means of raising funds and making change. Such notes were usually repayable in goods and services or were made redeemable in Confederate Treasury notes in multiples of $5, $10, or $20. Local government and private issues are thought to have exceeded $25 million.

The major element in the Southern currency from 1861 through 1865 was undoubtedly the Treasury notes put out

Confederate Treasury Notes

INTEREST-BEARING NOTES

March 9, 1861; amended August 3, 1861

AMOUNT: $2 million. DENOMINATIONS: $50 to $1000. MATURITY: One year from date, interest runs for additional sixty days. PAYABLE: To order and transferable by endorsement only. INTEREST RATE: 3.65 percent payable with principal. TOTAL ISSUED: $2,021,100.

April 17, 1862

AMOUNT: Up to $165 million in lieu of the April 12 (18), 1862, bonds. DENOMINATIONS: $100 or higher. MATURITY: Six months after peace. INTEREST RATE: 2 cents per day per $100. TOTAL ISSUED: $128,241,400.

GENERAL CURRENCY

May 16, 1861

AMOUNT: $20 million. DENOMINATIONS: $5 to $100. MATURITY: Two years after date (July 25, 1861). PAYABLE: To bearer. FUNDABLE: In ten-year coupon bonds on stock of $100 denomination or higher, convertible back into treasury notes. TOTAL ISSUED: $17,347,955.

August 19, 1861; amended December 24, 1861, April 17, 1862, and September 23, 1862

AMOUNT: $78 million, plus additions of $50 million, $60 million, and finally an unlimited issue privilege. DENOMINATIONS: $5 to $100. MATURITY: Six months after ratification of a peace treaty. PAYABLE: To bearer. FUNDABLE: In 8 percent bonds payable from January 1, 1864, to July 1, 1881. TOTAL ISSUED: $291,961,830.

April 17, 1862, amended September 23, 1862

AMOUNT: $5 million, later raised to $10 million. DENOMINATIONS: $1 and $2. TOTAL ISSUED: $5,600,000.

October 13, 1862

AMOUNT: Unlimited. EXCHANGEABLE: Notes dated December 2, 1862, exchangeable for 7 percent bonds until August 1, 1863; afterward, for 4 percent bonds. AMOUNT ISSUED: $1 and $2 notes totaling $2,344,800; $5 to $100 notes totaling $138,056,000.

March 23, 1863

AMOUNT: $50 million per month (April 1863–February 1864); $1 and $2 notes then extended to $15 million. PAYABLE: Two years after peace. FUNDABLE: In 6 percent bonds until one year after stamped date; afterward, in 4 percent bonds. New $1 and $2 notes not fundable. EXCHANGEABLE: For 5 percent call certificates. TOTAL ISSUED: $50 to $500 notes totaling $514,032,000.00; $1 and $2 notes totaling $3,023,520.00; 50-cent notes totaling $915,758.50; grand total: $517,971,278.50[a]

February 17, 1864

AMOUNT: None specified, but issue limited to $250 million. DENOMINATION: $500. MATURITY: Two years after a ratification of peace. FUNDABLE: No fixed provisions, but a variety of bonds and certificates were available for investment. TOTAL ISSUED: $460,000,000 (est.)

[a]Figures based on James M. Matthews, ed., *Statutes at Large of the Provisional Government of the Confederate States of America*, Richmond, Va., on Raphael P. Thian, *Register of the Confederate Debt*, Boston, 1972, and on numismatic collections examined by Douglas Ball.

SOURCE: Douglas B. Ball, *Financial Failure and Confederate Defeat*, Urbana and Chicago, 1991.

by the Richmond government. Starting in 1861 with a mere authorization of $1 million, this currency reached $800 million in early 1864. Despite the reform act of February 17, 1864, it was once again at that level by early 1865.

As the territory under Confederate rule shrank, Federal legal tender notes and fractional currency steadily infiltrated into the South. By the end of the war, distrust of the local money had reached the point where even the Confederate troops insisted upon being paid in Union currency. This desire for something of real value proved well founded after the war when the entire Southern money stock became practically worthless. Nearly all the banks failed, paying only a few cents on the dollar. Payment on the government issues was prohibited by the fifth section of the Fourteenth Amendment.

BIBLIOGRAPHY

Ball, Douglas B. *Financial Failure and Confederate Defeat.* Urbana, Ill., 1991.

Criswell, Grover C., Jr. *Confederate and Southern State Currency.* Citrus, Fla., 1976.

Lerner, Eugene. *Money, Prices and Wages in the Confederacy, 1861–1865.* Chicago, 1954.

Schwab, John C. *The Confederate States of America, 1861–1865: A Financial and Industrial History of the South during the Civil War.* New York, 1901.

DOUGLAS B. BALL

Congressional Money Bills

Operating at first with a $500,000 loan from Alabama, Congress quickly established its monetary policy. On March 9, 1861, it authorized the issue of $1 million in interest-bearing Treasury notes. This proved hopelessly inadequate, and on May 16 Congress authorized $20 million notes and $50 million in 8 percent bonds. Secretary Christopher G. Memminger denied any danger of inflation, and on August 19 Congress authorized $100 million more notes, followed on December 24 by another $50 million new bond issues accompanying all note issues. Memminger had asked for more interest-bearing notes that could be held as investments, but the last three issues were non-interest-bearing notes more likely to be circulated than held for investment or retired into bonds.

The same pattern continued in 1862, with Congress authorizing three more issues of fiat Treasury notes and more bonds into which they might be funded. Funding, however, went slowly, and by 1863 $410 million in notes were circulating.

In 1863 Congress tried to stem inflation by forced funding. On March 23 it ordered a gradual reduction of the interest rate of bonds into which notes could be funded; after a certain date they would be acceptable only for government dues. In the same act, however, Congress authorized Memminger to issue $50 million of notes a month. Meanwhile the rapid inflation made bonds an increasingly poor investment.

On February 17, 1864, Congress boldly ordered that notes should be funded at a gradual reduction of their face value; on January 1, 1865, they would be abolished by a 100 percent tax. But most notes continued circulating at declining value, and on December 29 Congress extended the funding deadline to July 1, 1865.

There is little doubt that this flood of fiat money and the resulting inflation and speculation were major factors in demoralizing the Confederate home front.

BIBLIOGRAPHY

Ball, Douglas B. *Financial Failure and Confederate Defeat.* Urbana, Ill., 1991.

Lerner, Eugene M. "Monetary and Fiscal Programs of the Confederate Government, 1861–1865." *Journal of Political Economy* 62 (1955): 20–24.

Matthews, James M., comp. *Statutes at Large of the Confederate States of America.* Richmond, Va., 1861–1864.

Todd, Richard C. *Confederate Finance.* Athens, Ga., 1954.

Yearns, Wilfred B. *The Confederate Congress.* Athens, Ga., 1960.

W. BUCK YEARNS

Numismatics

In February 1861, when the Confederacy was established, the Treasury took over the mints in New Orleans, Dahlonega, and Charlotte. Acting on the public demand for a new coinage, the Treasury ordered the New Orleans mint to provide new designs and dies. A fifty-cent piece was prepared, but after only four pieces were struck, the collar for the edge reeding broke. The four coins were distributed

SOUTHERN CURRENCY *(facing page)*. *Top:* Confederate $2 note. Issued at Richmond, Virginia, June 2, 1862. In upper left is a portrait of Judah P. Benjamin, secretary of state at the time the note was issued. At center an allegorical figure representing the South strikes down an eagle and another figure representing the North. Engraved and printed by Blanton Duncan, Columbia, South Carolina. *Middle:* 25 cents note. Issued by the town of Staunton, Virginia, July 6, 1861. In lower left are laborers in a cotton field. At center is a pastoral harvest scene. Engraved by Hoyer and Ludwig, Richmond, Virginia. *Bottom:* Confederate $50 note. Issued at Montgomery, Alabama, May 1861. The front of the note depicts African American laborers hoeing a cotton field; the back is plain. Printed in green and black on bank note paper. Written date on the front is May 16, 1861. Endorsement on the reverse reads, "Issued May 23, 1861, John T. Shaaf, Capt. Subs. Dept., C.S.A." Part of the first Confederate currency order, this note was engraved by the National Bank Note Company of New York.

GORDON BLEULER

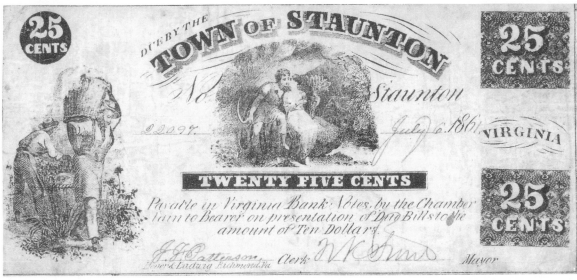

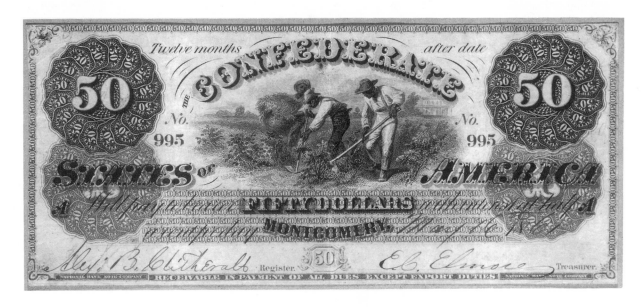

CONFEDERATE CURRENCY *(above)*. Confederate $500 note. Issued in Richmond, Virginia, February 17, 1864. Depicted at left are a Confederate battle flag, the seal of the Confederate States of America, and military accoutrements. In lower right is a portrait of Lt. Gen. Thomas J. ("Stonewall") Jackson. Engraved by Keatinge and Ball, Columbia, South Carolina.   GORDON BLEULER

to various officials. Three are now in museums and the fourth, the piece captured with President Jefferson Davis's baggage in 1865, is now worth approximately $500,000.

Without a coinage, the Confederate currency was practically confined to paper money. Yet the South had so shunned the mechanical arts that there were only eight security engravers in the whole country. Only three of these engravers had any experience with steel plate work; the rest were stationers or lithographers. Thus the first currency order was placed in New York on March 13, 1861, with the National Bank Note Company. The four type notes that were made (known as "Montgomeries" because they were issued from that city) are the most beautiful produced for the Confederacy. But when war broke out, the Treasury had to fall back on the Southern firms.

An agreement was signed May 13, 1861, with the New Orleans branch of the American Bank Note Company. Although the six designs printed were excellent, that firm's three workmen could not produce enough currency to pay for a war. Accordingly, other contracts, calling for lithographic work, were signed with Hoyer and Ludwig in Richmond. This firm took until November 1861 to finish

only $17 million of notes. Moreover, the designs were merely crude copies of Northern security work. As such, they were vulnerable to counterfeiting.

To overcome this problem, Thomas Bell was sent by Treasury Secretary Christopher G. Memminger in August 1861 to New York, where he hired, with the assistance of the American Bank Note Company, two of its steel plate engravers, William Leggett and Edward Keating. Together they established a Confederate security printing establishment. At the same time, agents in Europe hired Scottish lithographers, while the banks lent their note plates, three of which were converted into plates for Treasury notes. Thanks to these measures and the seizure of the American Bank Note Company branch in New Orleans, note production increased. But the continued use of poor lithographs and the failure to standardize denomination designs paved the way for a wave of counterfeiting in September 1862.

To meet this crisis, the Treasury Department organized a contest. Every printing firm submitted new designs for the Confederate currency utilizing original work. The new designs, it was hoped, would check counterfeiting and speed production. All the winning entries were provided by

CONFEDERATE CURRENCY *(facing page)*. *Top:* Confederate 50 cents note. Issued at Richmond, Virginia, February 17, 1864. The note features a portrait of President Jefferson Davis. Engraved by Acher and Halpin, Richmond, Virginia. *Middle:* Confederate $100 note, front. Issued at Richmond, Virginia, April 6, 1863. In lower left are figures representing the infantry and the artillery. At center is a portrait of Lucy Holcombe Pickens, wife of Francis W. Pickens, governor of South Carolina. In lower right is a portrait of George Wythe Randolph, who served as secretary of war in 1862. Printed in black. Engraved by Keatinge and Ball, Columbia, South Carolina. *Bottom:* Confederate $100 note, back. Printed in green.   GORDON BLEULER

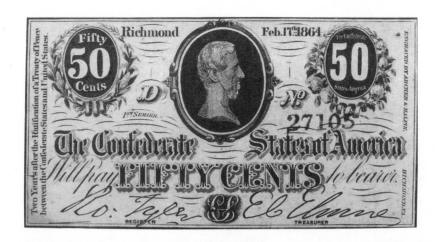

Edward Keatinge and George Dunn, a Scottish lithographer. Starting with the issue dated "December 2, 1862," the high-denomination notes were printed from copper plates and had green backs. The $20 and lower notes were all lithographed; the $20, $10 and $5 note backs were blue—hence the "blue back" nickname given Confederate currency. The $2 and $1 notes had no backs because they were not worth copying.

The accepted designs included portraits of Mrs. Lucy H. Pickens, the wife of South Carolina's governor, and George Wythe Randolph, secretary of war, on the $100 note; President Davis on the $50 note; Vice President Alexander H. Stephens on the $20 note, and Robert M. T. Hunter, former secretary of state, on the $10 note. In addition, the $5 bill honored Treasury Secretary Christopher G. Memminger and the Richmond capitol building, the $2 note had a portrait of Secretary of State Judah P. Benjamin, and the $1 note bore a picture of Alabama Senator Clement C. Clay.

Under an act of March 23, 1863, the engraved dates were altered from "December 2, 1862," to "April 6, 1863." A fifty-cent note was added with an image of President Davis copied from a Confederate stamp.

Finally, by an act of February 17, 1864, the Treasury ordered design changes to differentiate the new issues from the old. Accordingly, new backs were ordered in Europe and a red tint was added to the faces of every note. In addition, a battle scene was substituted for the Columbia capitol building on the $10 bill, and a $500 note honoring Gen. Thomas J. ("Stonewall") Jackson was added. The European-made backs were intercepted by the Union fleet, and Keatinge hurriedly prepared crude new blue backs for the $5 to $100 notes.

In 1865, the Confederate bills became war souvenirs or play money. Ten years later, there were a sufficient number of collectors to result in the publication of the first comprehensive catalogs. Prices were low, ranging from five cents or less for common 1862 to 1864 notes up to $5 to $10 for better items. Even in 1945, common Confederate notes could be bought for ten cents and the $1,000 and $500 "Montgomery" notes were priced at only $60.

With the Civil War Centennial of 1961 through 1964, prices rose rapidly. By the end of 1991, an uncirculated $1,000 "Montgomery" was worth over $18,000, and even the commonest Confederate notes in new condition commanded $15. Fascination with the Civil War in Europe drove up demand and prices. Despite the large quantities issued, the price of Confederate money seems destined to continue its rise in the future.

BIBLIOGRAPHY

Ball, Douglas B. "Confederate Currency Derived from Banknote Plates." *Numismatist* 85, no. 3 (March 1972): 339–352.

Ball, Douglas B. "The Confederate Currency Reform of 1862." In *America's Currency 1789–1866*. New York, 1985.

Ball, Douglas B. *Financial Failure and Confederate Defeat.* Urbana, Ill., and Chicago, 1991.

Slabaugh, Arlie R. *Confederate States Paper Money.* Iola, Wis., 1991.

DOUGLAS B. BALL

CURRIN, DAVID M. (1819–1864), congressman from Tennessee. Contrary to what has been written, it appears that Currin was a native of Fluvanna County, Virginia, who at an early age relocated with his family to Murfreesboro, Tennessee. A graduate of Nashville University, he read law and ran for the legislature but lost, though he was a presidential elector for James K. Polk and three other canvasses in 1848, 1852, and 1856. Moving in 1849 to Memphis, where he practiced law with Howell E. Jackson, Currin later served in the state house as a Democrat (1851–1853) and was an unsuccessful candidate for Congress in 1855.

A slave owner and a secessionist, Currin was elected as a delegate to represent the Eleventh District of Tennessee in the Provisional Confederate Congress. Taking his seat on August 16, 1861, in the midst of the third session, Currin served for the next several months on the Commerce and Naval Affairs committees, which provided natural conduits for the protection of his constituents. For example, one bill he introduced called for the appropriation of $160,000 to pay for the construction of two ironclads to defend Memphis. The boats, however, were probably not among the makeshift Confederate flotilla that was overwhelmed and outgunned when Memphis fell in June 1862. During this same period Currin also introduced a resolution of thanks to Generals Leonidas Polk, Gideon Pillow, and B. Franklin Cheatham for their actions in repulsing the Federal advance under Ulysses S. Grant at Belmont, Missouri. And in the controversy between Polk and Pillow that effectively hampered the western army's performance early in the war, Currin evidently sided with Pillow, judging from Currin's correspondence with Jefferson Davis.

Currin remained interested in military matters after his November 1861 election to the First Regular Congress. His March 1862 proposal for an investigation of the abandonment of army stores by the Confederate quartermaster's departments at Fort Donelson and Nashville was triggered by a loss of confidence in Gen. Albert Sidney Johnston for having surrendered the Tennessee capital. But Currin, while still a member of the Naval Affairs Committee, refused to sanction the resolution of his Tennessee colleague Senator Henry S. Foote, who called for the dismissal of Stephen R. Mallory. Moreover, he praised then-colonel Nathan Bedford Forrest for his capture of Murfreesboro in

August 1862. He actively sought the release of civilian prisoners of war and favored governmental compensation for persons whose cotton or tobacco had been burned in order to keep it from falling into enemy hands. On major legislation involving conscription and levying and collecting the direct tax, Currin voted in the affirmative and sided with the minority in April 1863 in recognizing the right of the president to declare martial law.

On January 11, 1864, in the midst of the fourth session, Currin was granted a leave of absence, owing to "shattered health" and an undisclosed "indisposition." Chances are he never returned to his seat, despite having been reelected several months earlier. He died on March 25, 1864, at the home of a relative in Virginia, and his body was later brought back to Memphis for burial.

BIBLIOGRAPHY

Elmwood: Charter, Rules, Regulations and By-laws. Memphis, Tenn., 1874.

Journal of the Congress of the Confederate States of America, 1861–1865. 7 vols. Washington, D.C., 1904–1905.

U.S. War Department. *War of the Rebellion: A Compilation of the Official Records of the Union and Confederate Armies.* Washington, D.C., 1880–1901. Ser. 1, vol. 4, pp. 364, 395; ser. 1, vol. 52, pt. 2, p. 369.

Vandiver, Frank E., ed. "Proceedings of the Second Confederate Congress." *Southern Historical Society Papers* 51 (1958): 127–128. Reprint, Wilmington, N.C., 1992.

Warner, Ezra J., and W. Buck Yearns. *Biographical Register of the Confederate Congress.* Baton Rouge, La., 1975.

R. B. ROSENBURG

CURRY, JABEZ L. M.

CURRY, JABEZ L. M. (1825–1903), congressman from Alabama, lieutenant colonel, and U.S. minister to Spain. Best known for his postwar educational activities, Curry was most notable in the Confederacy for his advocacy of a vigorous Southern war effort.

Born in Georgia, Curry moved to Alabama in his youth and became the owner of large land and slaveholdings in Talladega County. He graduated from Franklin College (University of Georgia) and earned a law degree from Harvard University. Returning south, Curry became a political disciple of John C. Calhoun and denounced both Northern abolitionism and government by majoritarian rule.

As a member of the Alabama legislature (1847–1848, 1853–1857) and the U.S. House of Representatives (1857–1861), Curry was a staunch defender of slavery and state rights. He considered the election of Abraham Lincoln to be "*the* overt act" against the South and advised Alabama in November 1860 "to act for herself and seek the simultaneous cooperation of her neighboring States, who will join her . . . in a Southern Confederacy."

JABEZ L. M. CURRY.   LIBRARY OF CONGRESS

Upon Alabama's secession on January 10, 1861, Curry resigned his seat in the U.S. Congress and was elected delegate to the convention of seceded states, which became the Provisional Congress. Elected subsequently to the First Confederate Congress, Curry served on the Rules and Commerce committees in both of those Congresses. Curry earned a reputation in Congress as a supporter of the administration of Jefferson Davis. Even more strongly, he advocated war measures that mobilized all the South's resources. He favored conscription and opposed draft exemptions for plantation owners, agents, overseers, and such groups as harness makers and saddlers.

What one Alabama newspaper described as his "ultra position with regard to the war effort and its future prosecution" cost Curry his job in 1863. Representing a district largely of nonslaveholders who had been hurt by the war, Curry lost his seat to peace candidate Marcus H. Cruikshank. A movement to give Curry the vacated Senate seat of William Lowndes Yancey proved short-lived, so Curry's political career ended with the expiration of the First Congress in February 1864.

Curry's influence in Congress was manifested most

clearly in the Address of Congress to the People of the Confederate States, which Curry wrote and Congress adopted in December 1863. The Address was an impassioned vindication of the Southern cause and an exhortation to Southerners to lay aside their differences, support their government, and endure all sacrifices in order to win the war. Curry warned those who—like the people who voted him out of office—had tired of war and advocated compromise with the North that pursuing such a course would bring subjugation and dishonor to the South.

From politics Curry turned to the army. A friend and chief patron of Lt. Gen. James Longstreet, Curry had shown an interest in army affairs since the beginning of the war and repeatedly visited Confederate armies in the field. From March through July 1864 Curry served on the staff of Gen. Joseph E. Johnston as habeas corpus commissioner (legal counsel in cases arising from the temporary suspension of the writ). For two months afterward he was special aide to Maj. Gen. Joseph Wheeler.

Although he had no military experience, Curry was appointed lieutenant colonel and commander of the Fifth Alabama Cavalry in October 1864. The regiment was part of Brig. Gen. Philip Dale Roddey's brigade defending northern Alabama and in the spring of 1865 operated with Lt. Gen. Nathan Bedford Forrest's forces in the defense of Selma. Curry narrowly avoided being wounded in a skirmish at Plantersville on April 1, 1865, and escaped with his command from Selma before its capture days later. Curry left the army on April 17 upon learning of his wife's death.

Out of the war's disruption Curry forged a new life. He moved from Alabama to Richmond, Virginia, remarried, and became a prominent Baptist minister and professor of history and English at Richmond College. Curry served as U.S. minister to Spain during Grover Cleveland's first administration, but his most important work was as general agent of the George Peabody Fund for education in the South (1881–1885, 1888–1903) and a trustee of the John F. Slater Fund for education of freedmen in the South (1890–1903). Those positions gave Curry an opportunity to realize his vision of a new South rising from emancipation and the ashes of war. Curry died on February 12, 1903, and was buried in Richmond's Hollywood Cemetery.

BIBLIOGRAPHY

Alderman, Edwin Anderson, and Armistead Churchill Gordon. *J. L. M. Curry: A Biography*. New York, 1911.

Curry, J. L. M. *Civil History of the Government of the Confederate States with Some Personal Reminiscences*. Richmond, Va., 1900.

Journal of the Congress of the Confederate States of America, 1861–1865. 7 vols. Washington, D.C., 1904–1905.

Rice, Jessie Pearl. *J. L. M. Curry: Southerner, Statesman and Educator*. New York, 1949.

JOHN M. COSKI